Essentials of Services Marketing

2nd Edition

Jochen Wirtz
Patricia Chew
Christopher Lovelock

Singapore London New York Toronto Sydney Tokyo Madrid
Mexico City Munich Paris Cape Town Hong Kong Montreal

Published in 2012 by

Pearson Education South Asia Pte Ltd
23/25 First Lok Yang Road, Jurong
Singapore 629733

Publishing Director: *Mark Cohen*
Project Editor: *Chelsea Cheh*
Prepress Executive: *Kimberly Yap*

Pearson Asia Pacific offices: *Bangkok, Beijing, Ho Chi Minh City, Hong Kong, Jakarta, Kuala Lumpur, Manila, Seoul, Singapore, Taipei, Tokyo*

Printed in Singapore

4 3 2 1
15 14 13 12

ISBN 978-981-06-8618-5

The authors, editor, and publisher gratefully acknowledged the permissions granted to reproduce the copyright materials in this book. Every effort has been made to trace copyright holders and to obtain their permissions for the use of copyright materials. The publisher apologizes for any errors or omissions in the credit list and would be grateful if notified of any corrections that should be incorporated in future reprints or editions of this book.

www.pearsoned-asia.com

Brief Contents

To Jeannette, the light of my life and wonderful mother of our three children,
Lorraine, Stefanie and Alexander, with love.

Jochen Wirtz

To my mentor, for your wisdom, strength and encouragement, and to
Ryan and Cherilyn, for the joy you bring to me.

Patricia Chew

About the Authors

This photo was taken on January, 25 2008 when the authors met to work on the 1st edition of Essentials of Services Marketing.

As a team, Christopher Lovelock, Jochen Wirtz, and Patricia Chew provide a blend of skills and experience that is ideally suitable for writing an authoritative, yet engaging and reader-friendly services marketing text. This book marks Christopher's and Jochen's third collaboration on a Services Marketing textbook, and is Patricia's first project as a coauthor with them.

Jochen Wirtz is Professor of Marketing at the National University of Singapore (NUS), the founding director of the dual-degree UCLA – NUS Executive MBA Program (which was ranked top 10 globally in its inaugural Financial Times EMBA ranking in 2011), and a member of the executive committee of the prestigious NUS Teaching Academy which is the university's think-tank in education matters. Furthermore, Dr. Wirtz is Associate Fellow at the Saïd Business School, the University of Oxford, and an International Fellow of Service Research Center at Karlstad University, Sweden. He holds a Ph.D. in services marketing from the London Business School.

Dr. Wirtz has published widely on services marketing in over 80 academic articles (incl. in *Harvard Business Review*), 100 conference papers, 50 book chapters and 10 books, including jointly with Dr. Lovelock one of the world's leading services marketing text books, *Services Marketing: People, Technology, Strategy*, 7th edition (Prentice Hall, 2011) and *Flying High in a Competitive Industry: Secrets of the World's Leading Airline* (co-authored with Heracleous and Pangarkar, McGraw Hill, 2009).

Dr. Wirtz serves on the editorial review boards of 11 academic journals, including the *Journal of Service Management*, *Journal of Service Research*, and *Cornell Hospitality Quarterly*, and he is also an ad hoc reviewer for the *Journal of Consumer Research*, *Journal of Marketing* and *Journal of the Academy of Marketing Science*. Dr. Wirtz chaired the American Marketing Association's biennial Service Research Conference in Singapore. In recognition of his excellence in teaching and research, Professor Wirtz has received over 30 awards. These include the "2012 Academy of Marketing Science (AMS) Outstanding Marketing Teacher Award," which is the highest recognition of teaching excellence of AMS globally, and the prestigious, top university-level Outstanding Educator Award at NUS. He also was the winner of the inaugural "Outstanding Service Researcher Award 2010" and the "Best Practical Implications Award 2009", both by Emerald Group Publications.

Dr. Wirtz has been an active management consultant, working with international consulting firms, including Accenture, Arthur D, Little, and KPMG, and major service firms in the areas of strategy, business development and customer feedback systems. Originally from Germany, Dr. Wirtz spent seven years in London before moving to Asia. For further information see www.JochenWirtz.com.

Patricia Chew holds a Ph.D. in services marketing from the National University of Singapore. She is a Senior Lecturer and Deputy Head of Business at SIM University in Singapore, where she oversees faculty appointment and maintains quality standards for the programme. Dr. Chew teaches Marketing at SIM University and has taught Services Marketing at the National University of Singapore in MBA and BBA programs, as well as for RMIT University.

Dr. Chew's research focuses on services marketing, where she has published several articles and conference papers, particularly on incentivized referrals and word of mouth. One of her articles on incentivized word of mouth won the "Emerald Literati Club Award for Excellence" for the "Most Outstanding Paper" of the year in the *International Journal of Service Industry Management.* She has served as an ad-hoc reviewer for the Journal of Business Research.

Dr. Chew is a consultant on services marketing-related project for companies like LG Capital, the National Library Board in Singapore, SK Telecoms, and Singapore Pools.

The late **Christopher Lovelock** was one of the pioneers of services marketing. He consulted and gave seminars and workshops for managers around the world, with a particular focus on strategic planning in services and managing the customer experience.

Professor Lovelock's distinguished academic career included 11 years on the faculty of Harvard Business School and two years as a visiting professor at IMD in Switzerland. He had also held faculty appointments at Berkeley, Stanford, and the Sloan School at MIT, as well as visiting professorships at INSEAD in France and The University of Queensland in Australia.

Author or coauthor of over 60 articles, more than 100 teaching cases, and 26 books, Dr. Lovelock had seen his work translated into 12 languages. He served on the editorial review boards of the *Journal of Service Management*, *Journal of Service Research*, *Service Industries Journal*, *Cornell Hospitality Administration Quarterly*, and *Marketing Management*, and was also an ad hoc reviewer for the *Journal of Marketing*.

Widely acknowledged as a thought leader in services, Professor Lovelock had been honored by the American Marketing Association's prestigious Award for Career Contributions in the Services Discipline. In 2005, his article with Evert Gummesson, "Whither Services Marketing? In Search of a New Paradigm and Fresh Perspectives," won the American Marketing Association's Best Services Article Award and was a finalist for the IBM award for the best article in the *Journal of Service Research*. Earlier, he received a best article award from the *Journal of Marketing*. Recognized many times for excellence in case writing, he had twice won top honors in the *BusinessWeek* "European Case of the Year" Award.

About the Contributors of the Cases

T. F. Cawsey is Professor Emeritus (Marketing) at the School of Business & Economics, Wilfrid Laurier University, Canada.

Mark Colgate is Associate Professor at the Peter B. Gustavson School of Business, University of Victoria.

John Deighton is Harold M. Brierley Professor of Business Administration at Harvard Business School.

Benjamin G. Edelman is Assistant Professor of Business Administration at Harvard Business School.

Lorelle Frazer is Professor at Griffith University, Australia.

Roger Hallowell is Affiliated Professor of Strategy at HEC Paris and former Professor at Harvard Business School.

Christopher W. Hart was former faculty at Harvard Business School.

Loizos Heracleous is Professor of Strategy and Organization at University of Warwick, UK.

James L. Heskett is Baker Foundation Professor, Emeritus at the Graduate School of Business Administration, Harvard University.

Sheryl E. Kimes is Professor at the School of Hotel Administration, Cornell University.

Suzanne Lowe is President of Expertise Marketing LLC.

Gordon H. G. McDougall is Professor at the School of Business & Economics, Wilfrid Laurier University, Canada.

Youngme Moon is Donald K. David Professor of Business Administration at Harvard Business School.

John A. Quelch is Senior Associate Dean and Lincoln Filene Professor of Business Administration at Harvard Business School.

Indranil Sen was a Research & Planning Manager at DHL Asia Pacific.

Stowe Shoemaker is Associate Dean of Research and Donald Hubbs Distinguished Professor at Conrad N. Hilton College of Hotel and Restaurant Management, University of Houston.

Sanjay Singh was an MBA student at NUS Business School, National University of Singapore, Singapore.

Sven Tuzovic is Assistant Professor of Marketing at Pacific Lutheran University in Tacoma, WA.

Rohit Verma is Professor of Service Operations Management at the School of Hotel Administration, Cornell University.

Lauren K. Wright is Professor of Marketing, California State College, Chico, USA.

Contents

Part V: Striving for Service Excellence 428

Part VI: Cases 502

The following cases are available for free download and class distribution on the Instructor's Resource Website for courses that adopt Essentials of Services.

Preface

Services dominate the expanding world economy as never before, and technology continues to evolve in dramatic ways. Established industries and their often famous and old companies decline and may even disappear as new business models and industries emerge. Competitive activity is fierce, with firms often using new strategies and tactics to respond to changing customer needs, expectations, and behaviors. This book has been written in response to the global transformation of our economies to services. Clearly, the skills in marketing and managing services have never been more important!

As the field of services marketing has evolved, so has this book. This new edition has been revised significantly since the first edition. It captures the reality of today's world, incorporates recent academic and managerial thinking, and illustrates cutting-edge service concepts.

What's New in This Edition?

The second edition of *ESM* retains some of the key features that have made it successful, and improves on other aspects of the textbook to help students understand services marketing more effectively. These features include the following:

1. **An Improved Framework**
   This new edition uses a clear and improved ESM framework that is tightly integrated with all chapters. At the beginning of each part, students can refer to the visual ESM framework to better understand how the subsequent chapters fit into the ESM framework. Each chapter has its own integrative framework that provides a visual representation of the chapter in the overall framework of the book, so as to communicate key chapter concepts and ideas quickly.

2. **Updated Content: Technology and Industry Developments**
   We have updated this edition with the most recent developments and trends in services marketing, including technological developments (e.g., social media) and industry advancements (e.g., emerging best practices in service management and service science).

3. **Global Outlook: A Balanced Mix of American, European, and Asian Cases**
   Students are better able to relate and recall what they are taught when they recognize examples of international brands and companies. We have taken great care to maintain the uniquely global outlook from the first edition by including cases and examples from around the world: 40% from an American context, 30% from a European context, and 30% from an Asian context. Also, the cases and examples in this book make use of highly recognizable brands and services companies.

4. **Simplified Language and Visual Pedagogy**
   This book delivers a concise and reader-friendly experience to students by using straightforward and direct language to teach concepts and cases. We have also included several visual learning aids that illustrate key concepts in figures and diagrams so that students will find it easier to understand and are motivated to learn visually with less text and more full-color learning cues.

5. **Easy-to-Relate-to Cases and Examples**
   Students will find the service examples and cases in the book easy to relate to. The new edition features familiar situations that students will probably have encountered before, as well as interesting and humorous ads from the USA Europe, and Asia. We have deliberately kept the cases short and focus on using data from the cases to analyze the situations presented. In this manner, students can apply theory in practice.

6. **Best-in-Class Features Retained from *ESM* 1st Edition**
   - Strong managerial focus supported by the latest academic research.
   - Systematic learning approach—Each chapter is organized in a way that is clear and easy to follow.
   - Teaching aids within the text:
     i. An opening vignette highlights key issues to be discussed in the chapter.
     ii. Learning objectives and milestone markers help to flag chapter milestones where content related to learning objectives is discussed.
     iii. Boxed inserts throughout each chapter lend themselves to in-class discussions.
     iv. Interesting graphics, photographs, and reproductions of advertisements help enhance student learning, provide opportunities for discussion, and add visual appeal.

refund as the sound of the traffic kept me awake all night. They gave me a
refund, no questions asked. These companies can be so stupid they need to
be more alert."

I've complained that service was too slow, too quick, too hot, too cold, too
bright, too dark, too friendly, too impersonal, too public, too private ... it
doesn't matter really, as long as you enclose a receipt with your letter, you just
get back a standard letter and gift coupon."

Firms cannot easily check whether a customer is faking dissatisfaction or truly is
unhappy. At the end of this section, we will discuss how to deal with this type of
consumer fraud.

The Thief

The thief jaycustomer has no intention of paying and sets out to steal goods and
services (or to pay less than full price by switching price tickets). Shoplifting is a
major problem in retail stores. For those with technical skills, it's sometimes possible
to bypass electricity meters, access telephone lines free of charge, or bypass normal
cable TV feeds. Riding free on public transportation, sneaking into movie theaters,
or not paying for restaurant meals are also popular. Finding out how people steal a
service is the first step in preventing theft or catching thieves and, charging them in
court where necessary. However, firms must take into account that there are some
honest but absentminded customers who forget to pay.

The Rulebreaker

Many service businesses need rules of behavior for employees and customers to guide
them safely through the various steps of the service encounter. Some of these rules
are set down by government agencies for health and safety reasons. Air travel provides
one of the best of examples of rules designed to ensure safety.

Rules set by service providers are meant to help smooth operations, avoid unreasonable
demands on employees, prevent misuse of products and facilities, protect themselves

Figure 13.11 Dangerous skiers are rule breakers who pose a danger to others and need to be policed.

412 Chapter 13 • Complaint Handling and Service Recovery

v. Important terms are tagged as key words to assist students in internalizing the language of services marketing. At the close of each chapter, students are invited to test their grasp of these key terms in a questionnaire.

vi. End-of-chapter summaries that review the learning objectives for each chapter.

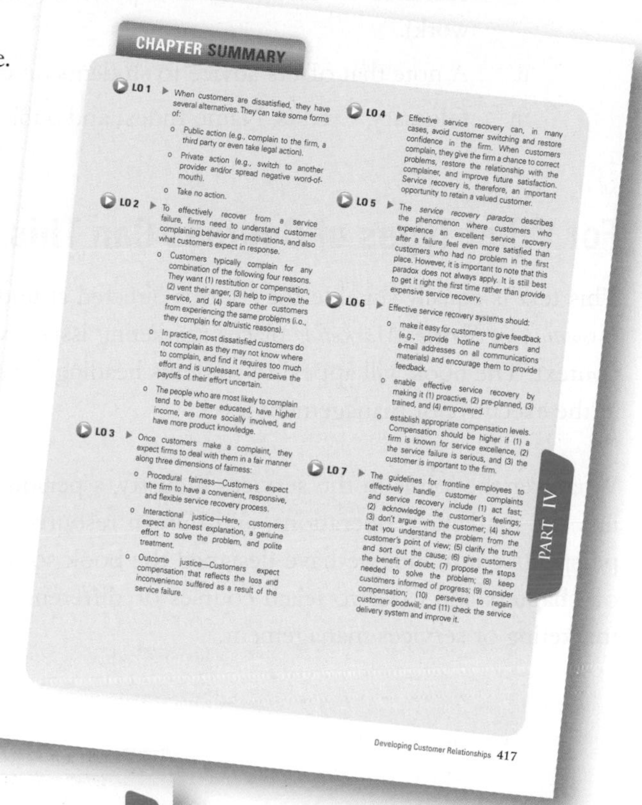

CHAPTER SUMMARY

LO 1 ▶ When customers are dissatisfied, they have several alternatives. They can take some forms of:

- Public action (e.g., complain to the firm, a third party or even take legal action).
- Private action (e.g., switch to another provider and/or spread negative word-of-mouth).
- Take no action.

LO 2 ▶ To effectively recover from a service failure, firms need to understand customer complaining behavior and motivations, and also what customers expect in response.

- Customers typically complain for any combination of the following four reasons. They want (1) restitution or compensation, (2) vent their anger, (3) help to improve the service, and (4) spare other customers from experiencing the same problems (i.e., they complain for altruistic reasons).
- In practice, most dissatisfied customers do not complain as they may not know where to complain, and find it requires too much effort and is unpleasant, and perceive the payoffs of their effort uncertain.
- The people who are most likely to complain tend to be better educated, have higher income, are more socially involved, and have more product knowledge.

LO 3 ▶ Once customers make a complaint, they expect firms to deal with them in a fair manner along three dimensions of fairness:

- Procedural fairness—Customers expect the firm to have a convenient, responsive, and flexible service recovery process.
- Interactional justice—Here, customers expect an honest explanation, a genuine effort to solve the problem, and polite treatment.
- Outcome justice—Customers expect compensation that reflects the loss and inconvenience suffered as a result of the service failure.

LO 4 ▶ Effective service recovery can, in many cases, avoid customer switching and restore confidence in the firm. When customers complain, they give the firm a chance to correct problems, restore the relationship with the complainer, and improve future satisfaction. Service recovery is, therefore, an important opportunity to retain a valued customer.

LO 5 ▶ The *service recovery paradox* describes the phenomenon where customers who experience an excellent service recovery after a failure feel even more satisfied than customers who had no problem in the first place. However, it is important to note that this paradox does not always apply. It is still best to get it right the first time rather than provide expensive service recovery.

LO 6 ▶ Effective service recovery systems should:

- make it easy for customers to give feedback (e.g., provide hotline numbers and e-mail addresses on all communications materials) and encourage them to provide feedback.
- enable effective service recovery by making it (1) proactive, (2) pre-planned, (3) trained, and (4) empowered.
- establish appropriate compensation levels. Compensation should be higher if (1) a firm is known for service excellence, (2) the service failure is serious, and (3) the customer is important to the firm.

LO 7 ▶ The guidelines for frontline employees to effectively handle customer complaints and service recovery include (1) act fast; (2) acknowledge the customer's feelings; (3) don't argue with the customer; (4) show that you understand the problem from the customer's point of view; (5) clarify the truth and sort out the cause; (6) give customers the benefit of doubt; (7) propose the stops needed to solve the problem; (8) keep customers informed of progress; (9) consider compensation; (10) persevere to regain customer goodwill; and (11) check the service delivery system and improve it.

PART IV

Developing Customer Relationships 417

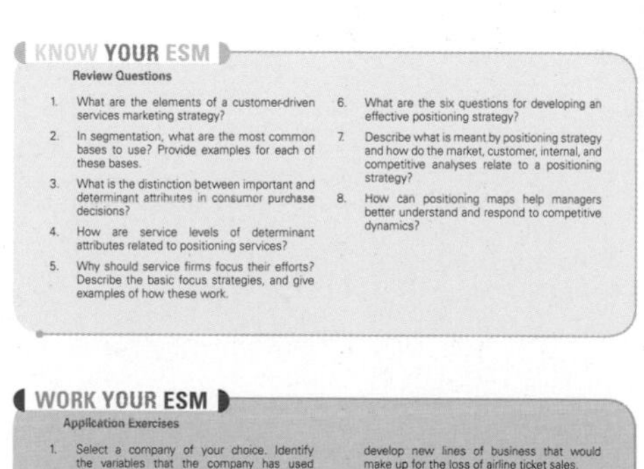

KNOW YOUR ESM

Review Questions

1. What are the elements of a customer-driven services marketing strategy?
2. In segmentation, what are the most common bases to use? Provide examples for each of these bases.
3. What is the distinction between important and determinant attributes in consumer purchase decisions?
4. How are service levels of determinant attributes related to positioning services?
5. Why should service firms focus their efforts? Describe the basic focus strategies, and give examples of how these work.
6. What are the six questions for developing an effective positioning strategy?
7. Describe what is meant by positioning strategy and how do the market, customer, internal, and competitive analyses relate to a positioning strategy?
8. How can positioning maps help managers better understand and respond to competitive dynamics?

PART I

WORK YOUR ESM

Application Exercises

1. Select a company of your choice. Identify the variables that the company has used to segment their customers. Support your answers with examples from the company.
2. Provide two examples of service firms that use service levels (other than airlines, hotels, and car rentals) to differentiate their products. Explain the determinant attributes and service levels used to differentiate the positioning of one service from another?
3. Find examples of companies that illustrate each of the four focus strategies discussed in this chapter.
4. Travel agencies are losing business to passengers booking their flights directly on airline websites. Identify some possible focus options open to travel agencies wishing to develop new lines of business that would make up for the loss of airline ticket sales.
5. Choose an industry you are familiar with (such as cell phone service, credit cards, or online music stores), and create a perceptual map showing the competitive positions of different service providers in that industry. Use attributes you believe are determinant attributes. Identify gaps in the market, and generate ideas for a potential "blue ocean" strategy.
6. Imagine that you have been hired as a consultant to give advice to the Palace Hotel. Consider the options facing the hotel based on the four attributes in the positioning charts (Figures 3.10 and 3.11). What actions do you recommend the Palace to take? Explain your recommendations.

Understanding Service Products, Consumers, and Markets 91

vii. *Know Your ESM* (review questions) asks pointed questions designed to consolidate the understanding of key concepts through discussion and study.

viii. *Work Your ESM* (application exercises) extends understanding beyond the question-and-answer format through to scenarios that apply the concepts learned.

- Additional pedagogical materials
    i. Around 20 case studies found in the appendix that can be used as student exercises or comprehensive projects (designed for either individual or team work).
    ii. A note that offers advice to students on case preparation and written analysis.
    iii. Glossary, Credits, Name Index, and Subject Index.

For What Types of Courses Can This Book Be Used?

This text is equally suitable for courses directed at undergraduate and polytechnic students. *Essentials in Services Marketing* places marketing issues within a broader general management context. The book will appeal to students heading for a career in the service sector, whether at the executive or management level.

Whatever the job is in the services industry, a person has to understand the close ties that link the marketing, operations, and human resources functions in service firms. With that perspective in mind, we have designed the book so that instructors can make selective use of chapters and cases to teach courses of different lengths and formats in either services marketing or services management.

The following table links the cases to the chapters in the book.

CASES		PRIMAR CHAPTEF
1	Sullivan Ford Auto World	1
2	Dr. Beckett's Dental Office	All chapte
3	Bouleau & Huntley: Cross-Selling Professional Services	2, 3
4	Banyan Tree: Branding the Intangible	3, 4
5	Giordano: Positioning for International Expansion	3, 5
6	Kiwi Experience	4, 5, 7
7	Distribution at American Airlines	5
8	Managing Word-of-Mouth: The Referral Incentive Program That Backfired	5
9	The Accra Beach Hotel: Block Booking of Capacity during a Peak Period	6
10	Revenue Management of Gondolas: Maintaining the Balance between Tradition and Revenue	6
11	Aussie Pooch Mobile: Expansion by Franchising	7
12	Shouldice Hospital Limited (Abridged)	8, 9, 10
13	Red Lobster	11
14	Singapore Airlines: Managing Human Resources for Cost-Effective Service Excellence	11, 15
15	Customer Asset Management at DHL in Asia	12
16	Dr. Mahalee Goes to London: Global Client Management	12
17	Hilton HHonors Worldwide: Loyalty Wars	12
18	The Royal Dining Membership Program Dilemma	12
19	The Complaint Letter	13
20	The Broadstripe Service Guarantee	13
21	Starbucks: Delivering Customer Service	12, 14, 15

CONDARY APTERS	CONTINENT	COUNTRY	INDUSTRY
2, 10	Americas	United States	Automobile Servicing
	Americas	United States	Medical
3	Asia/Americas	Philippines/United States	Management Consulting/ Auditing
5, 11	Asia/Global		Resort
11	Asia/Global		Clothing Retailing
3, 11	Oceania	New Zealand	Tourism
6	Americas	United States	Airline
	Asia	Vietnam	Insurance
9	Americas	Barbados	Resort
	Europe	Italy	Tourism
5	Australia	Australia	Pet Grooming
11, 14	Americas	Canada/United States	Medical
	Americas	United States	Food & Beverage
3, 4, 8	Global		Airline
	Asia		Logistics
8	Europe	United Kingdom	Private Banking
	Global		Hotel
6	Asia	Hong Kong	Food & Beverage
	Europe	United Kingdom	Hotel/Hospitality
	Americas	United States	Cable Service
5, 8, 9, 10, 11	Global		Food & Beverage

CASES		PRIMARY CHAPTER
Cases to Be Made Available on the Instructor's Resource Website (IRW)		
22	Susan Munro, Service Consumer	2
23	Four Customers in Search of Solutions – Cases A, B and C	2
24	Jollibee Foods Corporation	3, 4
25	Hotel Imperial	3, 4
26	Primula Parkroyal Hotel: Marketing a Business and Resort Hotel in Malaysia	3, 5, 6
27	Ginger: Smart Basics	4
28	Using Technology to Revolutionalize the Library Experience of Singaporean Readers	4, 8
29	TLContact: Care Pages Service (A + B)	4
30	Revenue Management at Prego Italian Restaurant	6, 8, 9
31	Massachusetts Audubon Society	7
32	Menton Bank	11
33	Bossard Asia Pacific: Can It Make Its CRM Strategy Work?	12
34	Accellion Service Guarantee	13

[SE]CONDARY [CH]APTERS	CONTINENT	COUNTRY	INDUSTRY
	Americas	United States	Range of B2C Services
13	Europe	Germany	Telecommunication
	Asia	Philippines	Fast Food
	Europe	Eastern Europe	Hotel/Hospitality
8, 11	Asia	Malaysia	Hotel
7, 8, 11, 14	Asia	India	Hotel
10	Asia	Singapore	Library
	Global		Online Service
	Asia	Singapore	Food and Beverage
3	Americas	United States	Nature Conservation
	Americas	United States	Banking
	Asia	Singapore	Industrial Supplies
	Global		IT Service

What Are the Book's Distinguishing Features?

The key features of this highly readable book includes:

- Strong managerial focus supported by the latest academic research. It not only helps service marketers to understand customer needs and behavior but also uses these insights to develop strategies for competing effectively in the marketplace.

- Full-color learning aids. This is at the time of printing the only full-color Services Marketing textbook. The well-designed graphics engage students with lively illustrations to make salient points come alive.

- The text is organized around an integrated framework students immediately can relate to. It allows students to progressively follow topics in a sequenced manner.

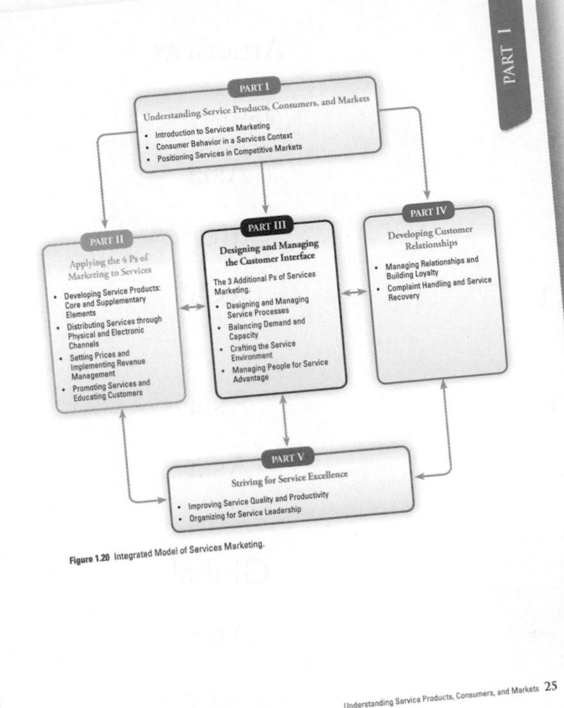

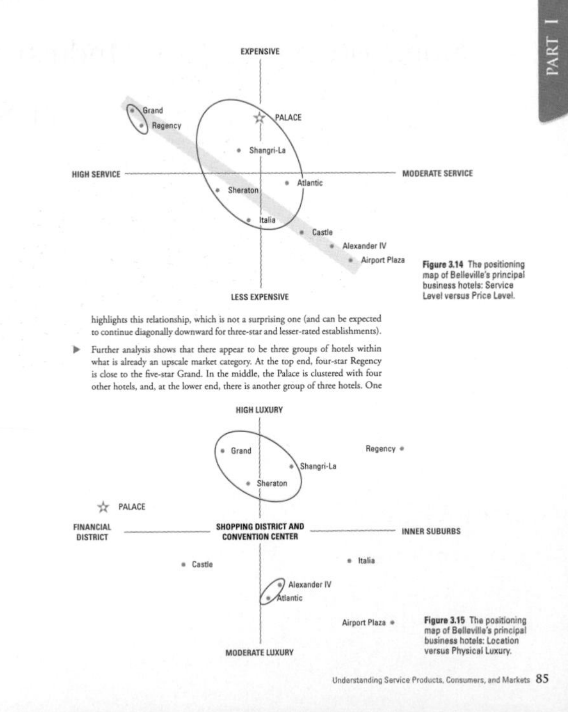

- An easy-to-read text that works hand in hand with visuals that make important concepts accessible.

- Systematic learning approach. Each chapter is organized in a way that is clear and easy to follow. Each chapter has:
  - an opening vignette, which introduces the concepts taught in the chapter;
  - learning markers that flag chapter milestones where contents related to learning objectives are discussed;
  - important terms, which are highlighted as key words to assist students in internalizing the language of services marketing;

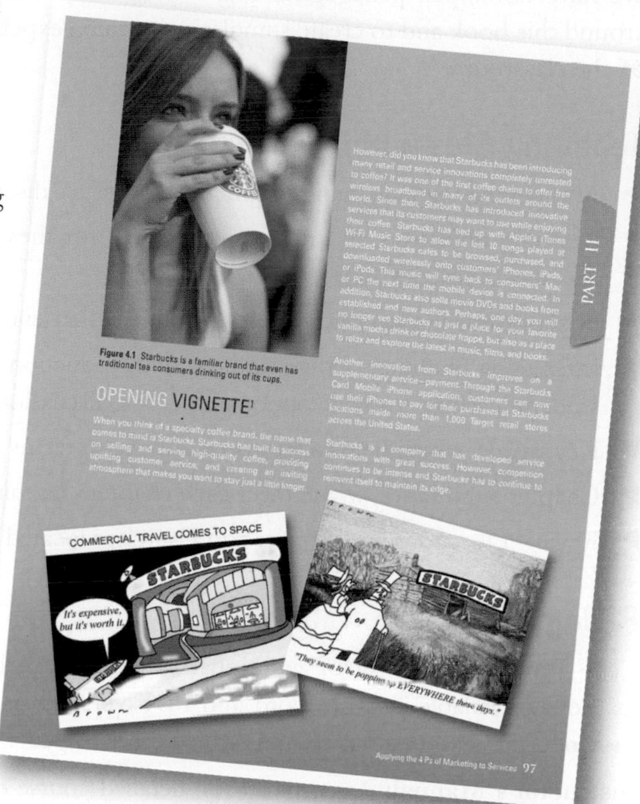

Figure 4.1 Starbucks is a familiar brand that even has traditional tea consumers drinking out of its cups.

OPENING VIGNETTE[1]

When you think of a specialty coffee brand, the name that comes to mind is Starbucks. Starbucks has built its success on selling and serving high-quality coffee, providing uplifting customer service, and creating an inviting atmosphere that makes you want to stay just a little longer.

However, did you know that Starbucks has been introducing many retail and service innovations completely unrelated to coffee? It was one of the first coffee chains to offer free wireless broadband in many of its outlets around the world. Since then, Starbucks has introduced innovative services that its customers may want to use while enjoying their coffee. Starbucks has tied up with Apple's iTunes Wi-Fi Music Store to allow the last 10 songs played at selected Starbucks cafes to be browsed, purchased, and downloaded wirelessly onto customers' iPhones, iPads, or iPods. This music will sync back to consumers' Mac or PC the next time the mobile device is connected. In addition, Starbucks also sells movie DVDs and books from established and new authors. Perhaps, one day, you will no longer see Starbucks as just a place for your favorite vanilla mocha drink or chocolate frappe, but also as a place to relax and explore the latest in music, films, and books.

Another innovation from Starbucks improves on a supplementary service—payment. Through the Starbucks Card Mobile iPhone application, customers can now use their iPhones to pay for their purchases at Starbucks locations inside more than 1,000 Target retail stores across the United States.

Starbucks is a company that has developed service innovations with great success. However, competition continues to be intense and Starbucks has to continue to reinvent itself to maintain its edge.

Applying the 4 Ps of Marketing to Services 97

  - use of interesting examples to link theory to practice; and
  - inclusion of carefully selected American, European, and Asian cases to accompany the text chapters, giving this book an international perspective;

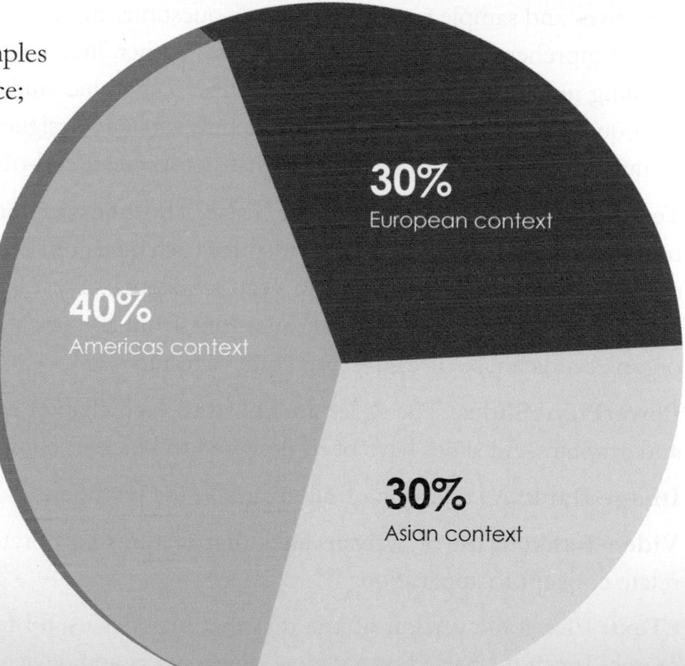

What Aids Are Available for Instructors?

We have developed pedagogical aids to help instructors develop and teach courses built around this book and to create stimulating learning experiences for students both in and out of the classroom.

Teaching Aids within the Text

- An opening vignette, which highlights key issues discussed in the chapter
- Learning objectives and milestone markers for these when a section provides material that meet these learning objectives
- Boxed inserts throughout the chapters, which often lend themselves well to in-class discussion
- Interesting graphics, photographs, and reproductions of advertisements, which enhance student learning, provide opportunities for discussion, and add a visual appeal
- Key words, which help to reinforce important terms and concepts
- Chapter summaries, which meet each chapter's learning objectives
- Review Questions and Application Exercises located at the end of each chapter

Pedagogical Materials Available from the Publisher

Case Bank: A large set of additional cases that can be used in courses that adopt this textbook. Available in both Word and PDF versions as a resource for instructors. A table shown in the textbook will suggest which cases to pair with which chapters.

Instructor's Manual: A repository of detailed course design and teaching hints, including sample course outlines; chapter-by-chapter teaching suggestions, plus discussion of learning objectives and sample responses to study questions and exercises; suggested student exercises and comprehensive projects (designed for either individual or team work); detailed case teaching notes, including teaching objectives, suggested study questions, in-depth analysis of each question, and helpful hints on teaching strategy designed to aid student learning, create stimulating class discussions, and help instructors create end-of-class wrap-ups and "takeaways."

Test Bank: Multiple choice True/False, short-answer, and essay questions, with page references and difficulty level provided for each question. Contents are classified into general and application. This is available in TestGen format, a test-generating program, which allows instructors to add, edit, or delete questions from the test item file; analyze test results; and organize a database of exams and student results.

PowerPoint Slides: The slides are linked to each chapter and featuring both "word" slides and graphics. All slides have been designed to be clear, comprehensible, and easily readable.

Image Bank: A collection of all images in the textbook.

Video Bank: A list of website links that features corporate videos and advertisements to relate concept to application.

eText: Electronic version of the text that includes useful features such as highlighting and search. It can be viewed on a variety of browsers and devices.

Please visit http://www.pearsoned-asia.com/wirtz for more details.

Acknowledgments

Over the years, many colleagues in both the academic and business worlds have provided us with valued insights into the management and marketing of services through their publications, in conference or seminar discussions, and stimulating individual conversations. In addition, both of us have benefited enormously from in-class and after-class discussions with our students and executive program participants.

We're much indebted to those researchers and teachers who helped to pioneer the study of services marketing and management, and from whose work we continue to draw inspiration. Among them are John Bateson of Granada Learning, Leonard Berry of Texas A&M University, Mary Jo Bitner and Stephen Brown of Arizona State University, Richard Chase of the University of Southern California, Pierre Eiglier of Université d'Aix-Marseille III, Raymond Fisk of the Texas State University, Christian Grönroos of the Hanken School of Economics in Finland, Stephen Grove of Clemson University, Evert Gummesson of Stockholm University, James Heskett and Earl Sasser of Harvard University, and Benjamin Schneider formerly of the University of Maryland. We salute, too, the contributions of the late Eric Langeard and Daryl Wyckoff.

A special acknowledgment is due to five individuals who have made exceptional contributions to the field not only in their role as researchers and teachers but also as journal editors, in which capacity they facilitated publication of many of the important articles cited in this book. They are Bo Edvardsson, University of Karlstad and former editor of *Journal of Service Research* (*JOSM*); Robert Johnston of the University of Warwick and the founding editor of *JOSM*; Jos Lemmink of Maastricht University and the former editor, *JOSM*; A. "Parsu" Parasuraman of the University of Miami and the former editor, *Journal of Service Research* (*JSR*); and Roland Rust of the University of Maryland and the editor of the *Journal of Marketing* and the founding editor of *JSR*.

Although it's impossible to mention everyone who has influenced our thinking, we particularly want to express our appreciation to the following: Tor Andreassen, of the Norwegian School of Management; David Bowen of Thunderbird Graduate School of Management; John Deighton, Jay Kandampully of Ohio State University, Theodore Levitt, and Leonard Schlesinger, all currently or formerly of Harvard Business School; Loizos Heracleous of the University of Warwick; Douglas Hoffmann of Colorado State University; Sheryl Kimes of Cornell University; Jean-Claude Larréché of INSEAD; David Maister of Maister Associates; Anna Mattila of Pennsylvania State University; Lia Patricio of University of Porto; Anat Rafaeli of Technion-Israeli Institute of Technology; Frederick Reichheld of Bain & Co; Bernd Stauss formerly of Katholische Universität Eichstät; Charles Weinberg of the University of British Columbia; Lauren Wright of California State University, Chico; George Yip of China Europe International Business School; and Valarie Zeithaml of the University of North Carolina.

We've also gained important insights from our co-authors on international adaptations of *Services Marketing* and are grateful for the friendship and collaboration of Guillermo D'Andrea of Universidad Austral, Argentina; Harvir S. Bansal of Wilfrid Laurier University, Canada; Fan Xiucheng of Fudan University, China; Keh Hean Tat of the University of Queensland, Australia; Luis Huete of IESE, Spain; Laura Iacovone of the University of Milan and Bocconi University, Italy; Jayanta Chatterjee of the Indian Institute of Technology at Kanpur, India, Miguel Angelo Hemzo, Universidade de São Paulo, Brazil; Denis Lapert of Telecom École de Management, France; Barbara Lewis of the Manchester School of Management, UK; Lu Xiongwen of Fudan University, China; Annie Munos, Euromed Marseille École de Management, France; Javier Reynoso of Tec de Monterrey, Mexico; Paul Patterson of the University of New South Wales, Australia; Sandra Vandermerwe of Imperial College, London, UK; and Yoshio Shirai of Takasaki City University of Economics, Japan.

It's a pleasure to acknowledge the insightful and helpful comments of reviewers of this edition: Leung Lai-cheung Leo of Lingnan University, Hong Kong; and Bernardette Jacynta Henry of Universiti Teknologi MARA (UiTM), Sabah, Malaysia. They challenged our thinking and encouraged us to include many substantial changes.

It takes more than authors to create a book and its supplements. Warm thanks are due to the editing and production team who worked hard to transform our manuscript into a handsome published text. They include Gloria Seow, Acquisitions Editor; Kimberly Yap, Pre-press Executive; Chelsea Cheh, Project Editor; Lo Hwei Shan, Copy Editor; and Ang Poh Tin and her team at Superskill Graphics Pte Ltd, Singapore.

Finally, we'd like to thank you, our reader, for your interest in this exciting and fast-evolving field of services marketing. If you have interesting research, cases or other materials such as advertisements, photos, cartoons, and anecdotes that would look good in the next edition of this book, or any other feedback, please contact us via www.JochenWirtz.com. We'd love to hear from you!

JOCHEN WIRTZ
PATRICIA CHEW

PART I

THE *ESM* FRAMEWORK

PART I

Understanding Service Products, Consumers, and Markets

- Introduction to Services Marketing
- Consumer Behavior in a Services Context
- Positioning Services in Competitive Markets

PART II

Applying the 4 Ps of Marketing to Services

- Developing Service Products: Core and Supplementary Elements
- Distributing Services through Physical and Electronic Channels
- Setting Prices and Implementing Revenue Management
- Promoting Services and Educating Customers

PART III

Designing and Managing the Customer Interface

The 3 Additional Ps of Services Marketing.

- Designing and Managing Service Processes
- Balancing Demand and Capacity
- Crafting the Service Environment
- Managing People for Service Advantage

PART IV

Developing Customer Relationships

- Managing Relationships and Building Loyalty
- Complaint Handling and Service Recovery

PART V

Striving for Service Excellence

- Improving Service Quality and Productivity
- Organizing for Service Leadership

PART I

Understanding Service Products, Consumers, and Markets

PART I of this book lays the building blocks for studying services and learning how one can become an effective service marketer. It consists of the following three chapters:

Chapter 1 Introduction to Services Marketing

This chapter highlights the importance of services in our economies. We also define the nature of services and how they create value for customers without transfer of ownership. The chapter highlights some distinctive challenges involved in services marketing and introduces the 7 Ps of services marketing. These are woven into an integrated model of services marketing that forms the basis for each of the five parts in this book. The framework is shown in the figure on the facing page, and it will accompany us through the book.

Chapter 2 Customer Behavior in a Services Context

This chapter provides a foundation for understanding consumer needs and behavior in both high-contact and low-contact services. The chapter is organized around the three-stage model of service consumption that explores how customers search for and evaluate alternative services, make purchase decisions, experience and respond to service encounters, and finally, evaluate service performance.

Chapter 3 Positioning Services in Competitive Markets

This chapter discusses how to develop a customer-driven services marketing strategy and how a value proposition should be positioned in a way that creates competitive advantage for the firm. This chapter first links the ***c***ustomer, ***c***ompetitor, and ***c***ompany (commonly referred to as 3 Cs) analysis links to a firm's positioning strategy. The core of the chapter is then organized around the three key elements of positioning—***s***egmentation, ***t***argeting, and ***p***ositioning (commonly referred to as "STP")—and shows how firms can segment a service market, position their value proposition, and finally focus on attracting their target segment.

CHAPTER 1

introduction to SERVICES MARKETING

LEARNING OBJECTIVES

By the end of this chapter, the reader should be able to:

- **LO 1** Understand how services contribute to a country's economy.
- **LO 2** Identify the powerful forces that are transforming service markets.
- **LO 3** Define services using the non-ownership service framework.
- **LO 4** Identify the four broad "processing" categories of services.
- **LO 5** Be familiar with the characteristics of services and the distinctive marketing challenges they pose.
- **LO 6** Understand the components of the traditional marketing mix applied to services.
- **LO 7** Describe the components of the extended marketing mix for managing the customer interface.
- **LO 8** Know the framework for developing effective services marketing strategies.

Figure 1.1 Tertiary education may be one of the biggest service purchases in life.

OPENING VIGNETTE

Introduction to the World of Services Marketing

Like every reader of this book, you are an experienced service consumer. You use a variety of services every day. You talk on the phone, use a credit card, ride a bus, or withdraw money from an ATM. Some of these services are so routine that you hardly notice them unless something goes wrong. Other service purchases may involve more planning and be more memorable. Examples of these include booking a cruise vacation, getting financial advice, and having a medical examination.

Enrolling in college or graduate school may be one of the biggest service purchases you will ever make. The typical university is a complex service organization that offers not only educational services but also libraries, student accommodation, health care, athletic facilities, museums, security, counseling, and career services. On campus, you may find a bookstore, a post office, photocopying services, Internet access, a bank, food, entertainment, and more.

Unfortunately, consumers are not always happy with the quality and value of the services they receive. Both individual and corporate customers complain about broken promises, poor value for money, lack of understanding of their needs, rude or incompetent personnel, inconvenient service hours, bureaucratic procedures, wasted time, malfunctioning self-service machines, complicated websites, and a host of other problems.

You probably have a few favorite service firms you like to patronize. Have you ever stopped to think about the way they succeed in delivering services that meet and sometimes even exceed your expectations? This book will show you how service businesses can be managed to achieve customer satisfaction and profitability. In addition to studying key concepts, organizing frameworks, and tools of services marketing, you will also be introduced to many examples from firms across the United States and around the world. From the experiences of other firms, you can draw important lessons on how to succeed in increasingly competitive service markets.

In this opening chapter, we provide an overview of today's ever-changing service economy, define the nature of services, and highlight some challenges involved in marketing services. We conclude the chapter by presenting a framework for developing and implementing services marketing strategies. This framework provides the structure for this book.

Figure 1.2 Happy people on a cruise vacation.

LO 1

Understand how services contribute to a country's economy.

WHY STUDY SERVICES?

Here's a paradox: While we live in a service-driven economy, most business schools still teach marketing from a manufacturing perspective. If you have taken a marketing course before, you most likely learned more about marketing manufactured products, especially consumer goods, than about services marketing. Fortunately, a growing and enthusiastic group of scholars, consultants, and educators—including the authors of this text—has chosen to focus on services marketing. Together, they build on the extensive research conducted in this field over the past three decades. We trust that this book will provide you with the knowledge and skills that are highly relevant in tomorrow's business environment.

Services Dominate the Economy in Most Nations

The size of the service sector is increasing in virtually all countries around the world—a trend that applies to both developed and emerging economies. Figure 1.3 shows the contribution of the service sector to the Gross Domestic Product (GDP) globally.

Figure 1.4 breaks this down further into a selection of countries. It shows the relative size of the service sector in a variety of both large and small economies. For most of the highly developed nations, services account for 67–75% of the GDP. One exception is South Korea, which is a manufacturing-oriented country with the service sector contributing only 58% to GDP. Which are the world's most service-dominated economies? One is the Cayman Islands (95%), a group of small, British-administered islands in the western Caribbean, known for both tourism and offshore financial and insurance services. Jersey, the Bahamas, and Bermuda—all small islands with a similar economic mix—are equally service dominated. Luxembourg (86%) has the most service-dominated economy in the European Union. Panama's strong showing (76%) reflects the fact that the Panama Canal is widely used by cruise ships as well as freight vessels. These ships are supported by related services such as container ports, flagship registry, and a free port zone, as well as financial services, insurance, and tourism (Figure 1.5).

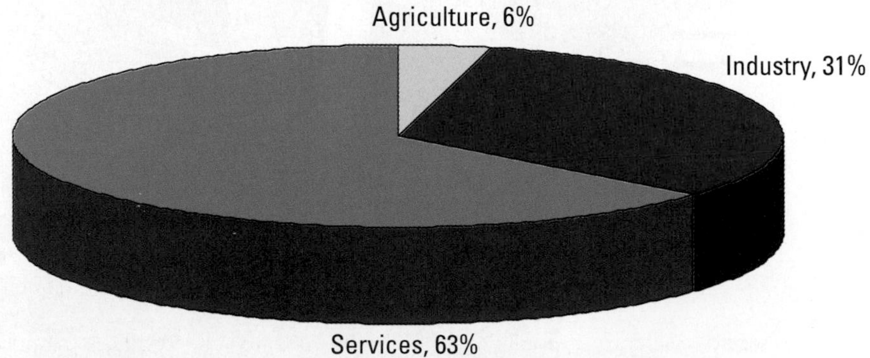

Figure 1.3 Contribution of services industries to GDP globally.

SOURCE

The World Factbook 2009, Central Intelligence Agency, https://www.cia.gov/library/publications/the-world-factbook/fields/2012.html, accessed March 12, 2012.

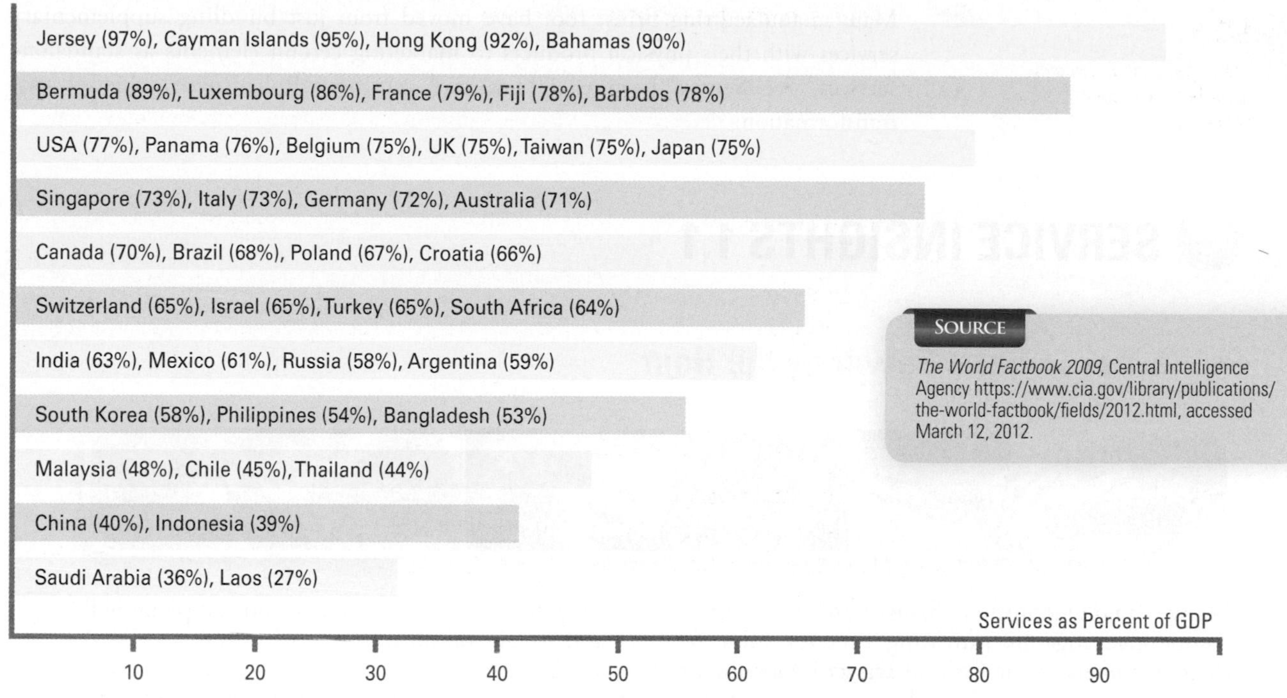

SOURCE

The World Factbook 2009, Central Intelligence Agency https://www.cia.gov/library/publications/the-world-factbook/fields/2012.html, accessed March 12, 2012.

Figure 1.4 Estimated size of service sector in selected countries as a percentage of GDP.

Near the opposite end of the scale is China (41%), whose emerging economy is dominated by a substantial agricultural sector and booming manufacturing and construction industries. However, China's economic growth is now leading to increased demand for business and consumer services. China's government is investing heavily in service infrastructure, including shipping facilities and new airport terminals. Last among relatively affluent countries is Saudi Arabia, with its oil-dominated economy to which services contribute only 36% of its GDP.

Figure 1.5 The Panama Canal forms the backbone of Panama's service economy.

Most New Jobs Are Generated by Services

Since the service sector is growing so rapidly in virtually all countries around the world, new job creation comes mainly from services. New services are being introduced all the time. Service jobs do not just refer to relatively lowly paid frontline jobs such as in restaurants or call centers. Rather, some of the fastest economic growth is in knowledge-based industries, such as professional and business services, education, and health care.[1] These jobs tend to be well paid, require good educational qualifications, and offer attractive careers.

Many manufacturing firms, too, have moved from just bundling supplementary services with their physical products to marketing certain elements as standalone services. See Service Insights 1.1 to find out how Rolls-Royce achieved that transformation.

SERVICE INSIGHTS 1.1

Rolls-Royce Sells Power by the Hour

Many manufacturing firms enhance their competitive edge by providing superior value to their customers in the form of service. Rolls-Royce is one such example. Rolls-Royce is a successful company because it focuses on technical innovation and makes world-class aircraft engines. Rolls-Royce engines power about half of the latest wide-bodied passenger jets and a quarter of all single-aisle aircrafts in the world today. A very important factor for its success has been its move from manufacturing to selling "power by the hour"—a bundle of goods and services that keeps the customers' engines running smoothly.

Imagine this: high above the Pacific, passengers doze on a long haul flight from Tokyo to Los Angeles. Suddenly, a bolt of lightning strikes the jet. Passengers may not think much of it, but on the other side of the world, in Derby, England, engineers at Rolls-Royce get busy. Lightning strikes on jets are common and usually harmless, but this one has caused some problems in one of the engines. The aircraft will still be able to land safely and could do so even with the affected engine shut down. The question is whether it will need a full engine inspection in Los Angeles, which would be normal practice but would also inconvenience hundreds of passengers waiting in the departure lounge.

A stream of data is beamed from the plane to Derby. Numbers dance across screens, graphs are plotted and drawn, and engineers scratch their heads. Before the aircraft lands, word comes that the engine is running smoothly and the plane will be able to take off on time.

Industry experts estimate that manufacturers of jet engines can make about seven times the revenue from servicing and selling spare parts than they do from just selling the engines. Since it is so profitable, many independent servicing firms compete with companies like Rolls-Royce and offer spare parts for as low as one-third of the price charged by the original manufacturers. To fend off these independent firms, Rolls-Royce has used a combination of technology and service to make it more difficult for competitors to steal its clients. Instead of selling engines first and then parts and service later, Rolls-Royce has created an attractive bundle, which it branded "TotalCare®". Its website advertises it as a solution ensuring "peace of mind" for the lifetime of an engine. Customers are charged for every hour that an engine runs. Rolls-Royce promises to maintain the engine and replace it if it breaks down. The operations room in Derby continuously monitors the performance of some 3,500 engines, enabling it to predict when engines are likely to fail and let airlines schedule engine changes efficiently and reduce repairs and unhappy passengers. Today, about 80% of engines shipped to its customers are covered by such contracts! Although Rolls-Royce had some troubles on its A380 engines, they were able to fix the problem quickly and bounced back from the incident with many more orders for their engines.

SOURCES

The Economist, "Briefing Rolls-Royce. Britain's Lonely High Flyer" January 10, 2009, pp. 58–60; www.rolls-royce.com, March 12, 2012. *The Economist*, "Per Ardua," February 5, 2011, p. 68. Source of photo: www.roll-royce.com, accessed March 12, 2012.

Just like Rolls-Royce, IBM was also previously known mainly as a manufacturer. The company also made the transformation to a service provider and today offers four main groups of services as part of IBM Global Services. They are strategic outsourcing, business consulting, integrated technology services, and maintenance.[2] Not only has IBM moved into delivering services, but it is also at the forefront of the movement to ensure that it trains workers for the service economy. Reflecting the ever tighter integration of value creation in the service economy, IBM came up with the term Service Science, Management and Engineering (SSME), often called Service Science for short, which integrates key disciplines required to design, improve, and scale service systems. A recent article in *Harvard Business Review* suggests that Service Science be a field of study in itself.[3] IBM believes that, to be effective in today's service-driven economies, future graduates should be "T" shaped. That is, they need a deep understanding of their own discipline such as business, engineering, or computer science (the vertical part of the T), as well as a basic understanding of service-related topics in other disciplines (the horizontal part of the T).[4]

POWERFUL FORCES ARE TRANSFORMING SERVICE MARKETS

LO 2

Identify the powerful forces that are transforming service markets.

What are the factors causing this rapid growth of the service sector? Government policies, social changes, business trends, advances in information technology, and globalization are among the powerful forces transforming today's service markets (Figure 1.6). The Internet, for example, transfers power from suppliers to customers, especially in consumer markets. In the travel industry, travelers can now easily check for alternatives and make their own bookings. Electronic distribution is changing relationships and roles between suppliers, intermediaries, and customers as traditional intermediaries (such as local travel agencies) are being replaced by innovative newcomers such as Expedia, Travelocity, and Priceline.[5] The Internet also helps to create additional outsourcing opportunities. Many professors now outsource their grading to companies like EduMetry Inc. The graders there are trained to provide good-quality grading and feedback that are very beneficial to helping students to improve on their weaknesses.[6] Table 1.1 shows specific examples of each of these forces and their impact on the service economy. Collectively, they influence the competitive landscape and the way customers buy and use services.

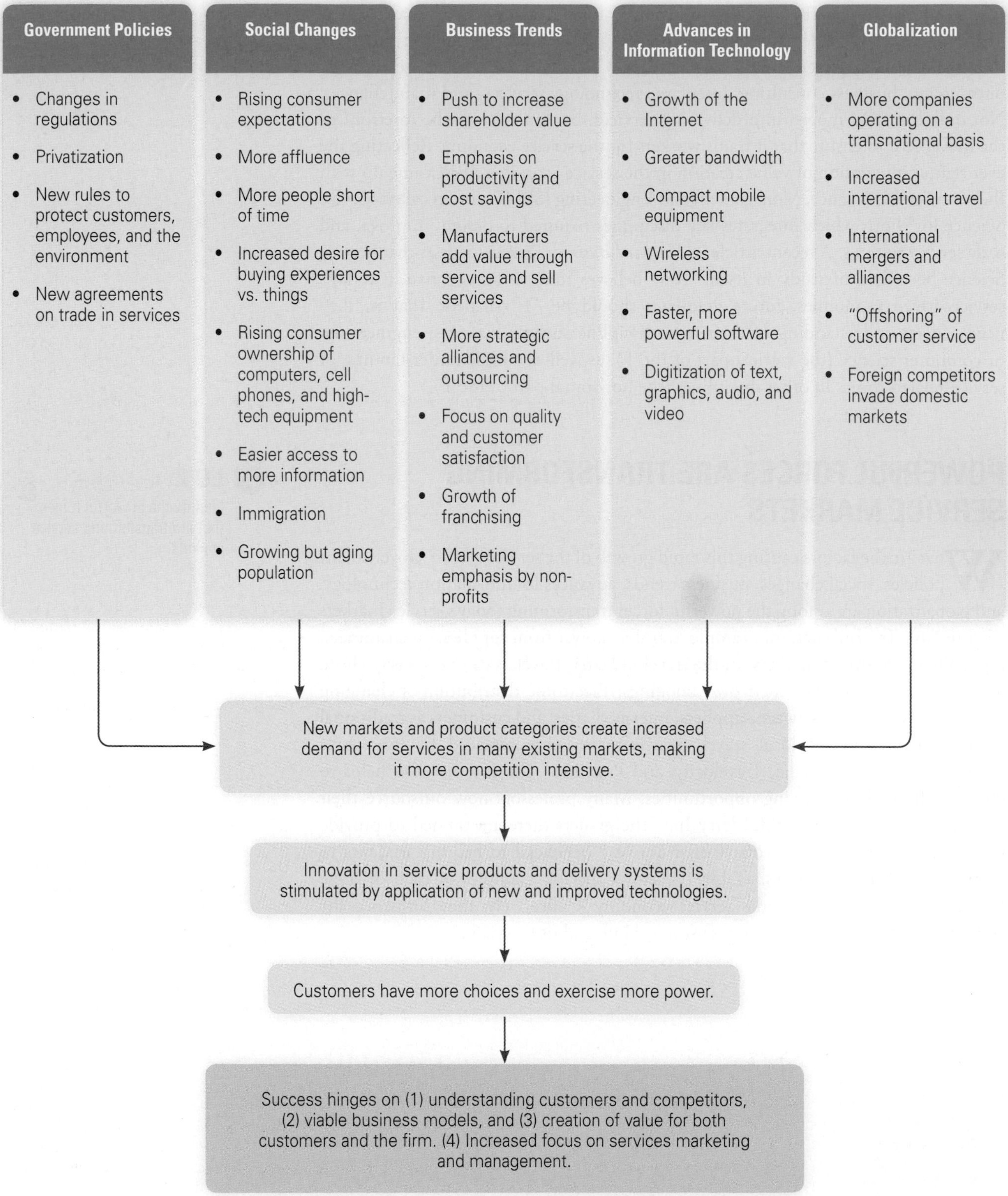

Government Policies

- Changes in regulations
- Privatization
- New rules to protect customers, employees, and the environment
- New agreements on trade in services

Social Changes

- Rising consumer expectations
- More affluence
- More people short of time
- Increased desire for buying experiences vs. things
- Rising consumer ownership of computers, cell phones, and high-tech equipment
- Easier access to more information
- Immigration
- Growing but aging population

Business Trends

- Push to increase shareholder value
- Emphasis on productivity and cost savings
- Manufacturers add value through service and sell services
- More strategic alliances and outsourcing
- Focus on quality and customer satisfaction
- Growth of franchising
- Marketing emphasis by non-profits

Advances in Information Technology

- Growth of the Internet
- Greater bandwidth
- Compact mobile equipment
- Wireless networking
- Faster, more powerful software
- Digitization of text, graphics, audio, and video

Globalization

- More companies operating on a transnational basis
- Increased international travel
- International mergers and alliances
- "Offshoring" of customer service
- Foreign competitors invade domestic markets

New markets and product categories create increased demand for services in many existing markets, making it more competition intensive.

Innovation in service products and delivery systems is stimulated by application of new and improved technologies.

Customers have more choices and exercise more power.

Success hinges on (1) understanding customers and competitors, (2) viable business models, and (3) creation of value for both customers and the firm. (4) Increased focus on services marketing and management.

Figure 1.6 Factors stimulating the transformation of the service economy.

Table 1.1 Examples of forces that transform and impact the service economy

Government Policies	Example	Impact on Service Economy
• **Changes in regulations**	• Ban on smoking in restaurants, and limitation of transfats in food preparation	• Improved customer comfort and health in restaurants will encourage people to dine out more often.
• **Privatization**	• Privatization of infrastructure services like utilities and transportation	• Existing suppliers may be retrenched in a more competitive environment, but there will also be job creation and investments by new players entering the market.
• **New regulations to protect customers, employees, and the environment**	• Increase in taxes to aviation industry for harmful gas emission	• Increased costs of air travel may dampen demand. Policy stimulates development of jet engines that are more fuel-efficient and less polluting.
• **New agreements on trade in services**	• Companies from foreign countries can take over basic services like water, health, transportation and education .	• Transfer of expertise across borders may take place. New investments result in improved infrastructure and better quality.
Social Changes	**Example**	**Impact on Service Economy**
• **Rising consumer expectations**	• Higher expectations of service quality and convenience	• Service staff are trained to deliver good service. Extended hours offer more part-time job opportunities.
• **Greater affluence**	• Higher spending on tourism	• A wider variety of offerings is created. Development of new services in new locations boosts local economies.
• **Personal outsourcing**	• Home cleaning services, baby and childcare services	• New service providers include both local firms and national/regional chains.
• **Increased desire for buying experiences vs. things**	• Higher spending on luxury services like spa treatments	• New players emerge; existing health clubs and resort hotels add spas to their offerings.
• **Rising consumer ownership of computers, cell phones, and high-tech equipment**	• Higher demand for laptops and smart phones	• There is a greater need for designers, engineers, and marketers for these types of equipment.
• **Easier access to more information**	• Internet and podcasting	• These allow firms to build closer, more focused relationships with customers and create new opportunities to reach them on the move in real time.
• **Migration**	• Many Indian nationals who have migrated to the USA now move back to their home country	• This transfers talent to their home country but may create a vacuum in the employment market of developed economies.
• **Growing but aging population**	• Matured European countries and China	• More services catering to the needs of elderly are required, including health care and construction of retirement communities.

Business Trends	Example	Impact on Service Economy
• **Push to increase shareholder value**	• Shareholders pressure company boards to deliver higher returns	• Companies search for new revenue sources such as additional fees and higher prices. They may adopt revenue management strategies, plus cuts in customer service, to reduce costs
• **Emphasis on productivity and cost savings**	• Move toward self-service technologies	• Companies rethink their service delivery system, and invest in new technologies that replace employees.
• **Manufacturers add value through service and sell services**	• German elevator manufacturers now move into maintenance service	• Manufacturers now compete against repair service companies.
• **More strategic alliances**	• Airlines form alliances such as Star Alliance and Oneworld	• Routes are rationalized to avoid duplications. Schedules and ticketing are coordinated. Marketing is leveraged and operating efficiency improved.
• **Focus on quality and customer satisfaction**	• Hotels and motels at all levels define standards more tightly and seek to meet them consistently	• Training programs are developed to equip service staff with necessary skills. There is investment in modernization of existing facilities and construction of new ones offering better amenities.
• **Growth of franchising**	• Fast-food chains expand around the world	• These chains face the challenge of maintaining consistent service standards worldwide while adapting to local food preferences and cultures.
• **Marketing emphasis by nonprofits**	• Museums seek to expand audiences and generate more frequent repeat visits	• They may carry out fund-raising for improved facilities, or add new revenue-generating services such as restaurants and facilities rental.

Advances in Information Technology	Example	Impact on Service Economy
• **Growth of the Internet**	• Information at the fingertips of the customers, making them more knowledgeable and informed	• New services are created to gather various sources of information and repackage them to provide value to customers.
• **Greater bandwidth**	• Allows for delivery of sophisticated and interactive educational content	• Service delivery processes need to be redesigned.
• **Compact mobile equipment**	• Smart phones that integrate many high-tech functions	• Advanced marketing and maintenance services are needed.
• **Wireless networking**	• Public libraries, cafes, and hotels provide this service (free or at a price) to attract customers	• More brick-and-mortar service firms are expected to provide similar benefits in order to stay competitive.
• **Faster, more powerful software**	• Customized software development by software consulting firms like Infosys	• There will be an increase in training software engineers to develop packaged services instead of piecemeal services.
• **Digitization of text, graphics, audio, and video**	• Online download services	• Service providers need to invest in maintaining a secure and credible website and guarantee virus-free files for download.

Globalization	Example	Impact on Service Economy
• **More companies operating on transnational basis**	• MNCs such as banks and the "Big Four" accounting firms have numerous operations around the world	• Companies increase the scope of services that can be provided. Staff in local markets are trained to upgrade their skills, capabilities, and service standards.
• **Increased international travel**	• More services offered to more places; new travel options for business and pleasure	• More services are provided by airlines, ferries and cruise ships, coach tours and international trains, leading to greater competition.
• **International mergers and alliances**	• Merger between international airlines (e.g., KLM and Air France), banks, insurance companies, etc.	• There is greater market leverage and operational efficiency, but consolidation may lead to job losses.
• **"Offshoring" of customer service (Figure 1.7)**	• Call center operations relocated to India, Philippines, etc.	• Investment in technology and infrastructure stimulates local economies, raises living standards, and attracts related industries.
• **Foreign competitors invade domestic markets**	• International banks such as HSBC and ING do business in the USA	• Build branch network by purchasing one or more regional banks; invest heavily in new and improved branches and in electronic delivery channels.

WHAT ARE SERVICES?

Thus far, our discussion of services has focused on different types of service industries. But now, it's time to ask the question: What exactly is a *service*?

Benefits without Ownership

Services cover a huge variety of different and often very complex activities, making them difficult to define.[7] Early marketing definitions of services described services as "acts, deeds, performances, or efforts" and contrasted them against goods by arguing that they had different characteristics from goods—defined as "articles, devices, materials, objects, or things."[8] This thinking has since advanced further and now focuses on the lack of transfer of ownership when buying a service. Suppose you stayed at a hotel last weekend or went to a physical therapist who worked on your injured knee or attended a concert. None of these purchases resulted in actual ownership of something. If you didn't receive a transfer of ownership the last time you purchased a service, then what did you buy? The distinction between ownership and *nonownership* is a one that has been emphasized by several leading services marketing scholars.[9]

Christopher Lovelock and Evert Gummesson argue that services involve a form of *rental* through which customers can obtain benefits.[10] What customers value and are willing to pay for are desired experiences and solutions. We use the term *rent* as a general term to describe payment made for use of something or access to skills and expertise, facilities, or networks (usually for a defined period of time) instead of buying it outright (which is not even possible in many instances).

Copyright 2005 by Randy Glasbergen.
www.glasbergen.com

GLASBERGEN

"We found someone overseas who can drink coffee and talk about sports all day for a fraction of what we're paying you."

Figure 1.7 Services today can be outsourced to cheaper destinations at the drop of a hat—so keep your job (and hat on) by remaining productive.

LO 3

Define services using the non-ownership service framework.

We can identify five broad categories within the nonownership framework that focus on (1) use of labor, skills, and expertise, (2 to 4) various degrees of use of goods and facilities (exclusive, defined, or shared), and (5) access and use of networks and systems:

1) **Labor, skills and expertise rentals.** Here, other people are hired to perform work that customers either cannot or choose not to do themselves. Some of these include:
   - Car repair
   - Medical checkup
   - Management consulting

2) **Rented goods services.** These services allow customers to obtain the exclusive temporary right to use a physical object that they prefer not to own. Examples of these include:
   - Boats
   - Fancy dress costumes
   - Construction and excavation equipment

Figure 1.8 Customers rent the right to use toll roads.

3) **Defined space and facility rentals.** This is when customers obtain the use of a certain portion of a larger facility such as a building, vehicle, or area. They usually share this facility with other customers. Examples of this kind of rental include:
   - A seat in an aircraft
   - A suite in an office building
   - A storage container in a warehouse

4) **Access to shared facilities.** Customers rent the right to share the use of the facility. The facilities may be a combination of indoors, outdoors, and virtual. Examples include:
   - Theme parks
   - *World of Warcraft* community site
   - Toll roads (Figure 1.8)

5) **Access and use of networks and systems.** Customers rent the right to participate in a specified network. Service providers offer a variety of terms for access and use, depending on customer needs. Examples of these include:
   - Telecommunications
   - Utilities
   - Banking

The difference between ownership and nonownership affects the nature of marketing tasks and strategies. For example, the criteria for a customer's choice of service will differ when something is being rented instead of owned. If you are looking for a rental car to be used on vacation, you are likely to focus on the ease of making reservations, the rental location and hours, the attitudes and performance of service personnel, the cleanliness and maintenance of vehicles, etc. If you are looking to own the car, then you are more likely to consider factors such as price, brand image, ease of maintenance, running costs, design, color, upholstery, etc.

Defining Services

Based on the nonownership perspective of services, we offer the following comprehensive definition of services:

DEFINITION OF SERVICES

Services are economic activities offered by one party to another. Often time based, these activities bring about desired results to recipients, objects, or other assets.

In exchange for money, time, and effort, service customers expect value from access to labor, skills, expertise, goods, facilities, networks, and systems. However, they do not normally take ownership of the physical elements involved.[11]

FOUR BROAD CATEGORIES OF SERVICES—A PROCESS PERSPECTIVE

LO 4

Identify the four broad "processing" categories of services.

Did you notice that the definition of services emphasizes not only value creation through rental and access but also the desired results that can be brought to recipients of the service, objects, and other assets? There are major differences among services depending on what is being processed. In services, people, physical objects, data, and information can be processed. The nature of the processing can be tangible or intangible. Tangible actions are performed on people's bodies or to their physical possessions. Intangible actions are performed on people's minds or to their intangible assets. This gives rise to the classification of services into four broad categories. They are *people processing, possession processing, mental stimulus processing*, and *information processing* (Figure 1.9).[12]

	Who or What Is the Direct Recipient of the Service?	
Nature of the Service Act	**People**	**Possessions**
Tangible Actions	**People processing** (services directed at people's bodies): • Hairstylist • Passenger Transportation • Health Care	**Possession processing** (services directed at physical possessions): • Freight Transportation • Laundry and Dry Cleaning • Repair and Maintenance
Intangible Actions	**Mental stimulus processing** (services directed at people's mind): • Education • Advertising PR • Psychotherapy	**Information processing** (services directed at intangible assets): • Accounting • Banking • Legal Services

Figure 1.9 Four broad categories of services.

Information Processing

Information can be processed by machines or by professionals who use their brains to perform information processing and packaging. Information is the most intangible form of service output. However, it can be transformed into more permanent and tangible forms like letters, reports, books, CD-ROMs, or DVDs. Some services that are highly dependent on the effective collection and processing of information are financial and professional services such as accounting (Figure 1.13), law, marketing research, management consulting, and medical diagnosis.

It is sometimes difficult to tell the difference between information processing and mental stimulus processing services. For example, if a stockbroker performs an analysis of a client's brokerage transactions, it seems like information processing. However, when the results of the analysis are used to make a recommendation about the most suitable type of investment strategy for the future, it would seem like mental stimulus processing. Therefore, for simplicity, mental stimulus processing services and information-processing services are sometimes combined and simply called *information-based services*.

LO 5

Be familiar with the characteristics of services and the distinctive marketing challenges they pose.

SERVICES POSE DISTINCT MARKETING CHALLENGES

Can the marketing concepts and practices developed in manufacturing companies be directly transferred to service organizations where no transfer of ownership takes place? The answer is often "no." Services tend to have different features from goods, including the frequently cited four characteristics of ***i***ntangibility, ***h***eterogeneity (variability), ***i***nseparability of production and consumption, and ***p***erishability of output,[13] or IHIP for short.[14] Table 1.2 explains these characteristics, and other common differences between services and goods. Together, these differences cause the marketing of services to differ from that of manufactured goods.

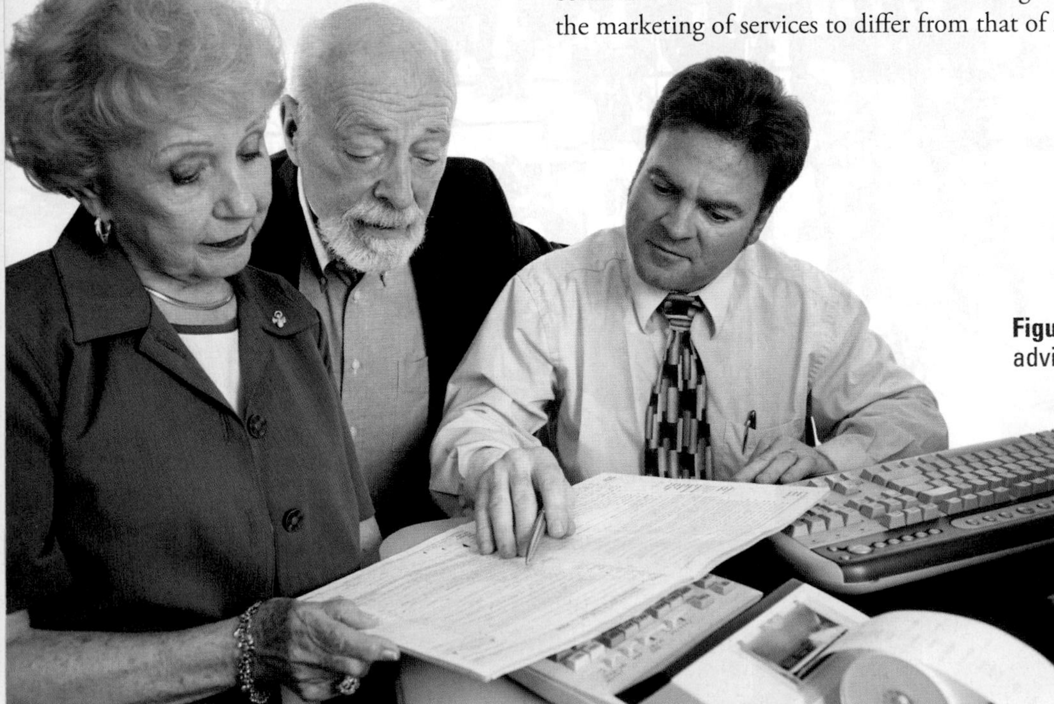

Figure 1.13 A couple getting financial advice on their pension.

Table 1.2: Managerial implications of eight common features of service

Difference	Implications	Marketing-related Topics
Most service products cannot be inventoried (i.e., output is perishable)	• Customers may be turned away or have to wait	• Smooth demand through promotions, dynamic pricing, and reservations • Work with operations to adjust capacity
Intangible elements usually dominate value creation (i.e., service is physically intangible)	• Customers cannot taste, smell, or touch these elements and may not be able to see or hear them • Harder to evaluate service and distinguish from competitors	• Make services tangible through emphasis on physical clues • Employ concrete metaphors and vivid images in advertising, branding
Services are often difficult to visualize and understand (i.e., service is mentally intangible)	• Customers perceive greater risk and uncertainty	• Educate customers to make good choices, explain what to look for, document performance, offer guarantees
Customers may be involved in co-production (i.e., if people processing is involved, the service is inseparable)	• Customers interact with providers' equipment, facilities, and systems • Poor task execution by customers may hurt productivity, spoil service experience, and curtail benefits	• Develop user-friendly equipment, facilities, and systems • Train customers to perform effectively; provide customer support
People may be part of the service experience	• Appearance, attitude and behavior of service personnel and other customers can shape the experience and affect satisfaction	• Recruit, train, and reward employees to reinforce the planned service concept • Target the right customers at the right times; shape their behavior
Operational inputs and outputs tend to vary more widely (i.e., services are heterogeneous)	• Harder to maintain consistency, reliability, and service quality or to lower costs through higher productivity • Difficult to shield customers from results of service failures	• Set quality standards based on customer expectations; redesign product elements for simplicity and failure-proofing • Institute good service recovery procedures • Automate customer-provider interactions; perform work while customers are absent
The time factor often assumes great importance	• Customers see time as a scarce resource to be spent wisely, dislike wasting time waiting, want service at times that are convenient	• Find ways to compete on speed of delivery, minimize burden of waiting, offer extended service hours
Distribution may take place through nonphysical channels	• Information-based services can be delivered through electronic channels such as the Internet or voice telecommunications, but core products involving physical activities or products cannot	• Seek to create user-friendly, secure websites and free access by telephone • Ensure that all information-based service elements can be downloaded from site

It's important to recognize that these differences, while useful generalizations, *do not apply equally to all services*. Intangibility, for example, ranges from tangible-dominant to intangible-dominant (see Figure 1.14 for a scale that presents a variety of examples).[15] Large differences also exist between the four categories of services we discussed in the previous section. For example, people tend to be part of the service experience only if the customer has direct contact with service employees. This is usually the case for people-processing services, but not for many information-processing service transactions such as online banking. You will recognize these

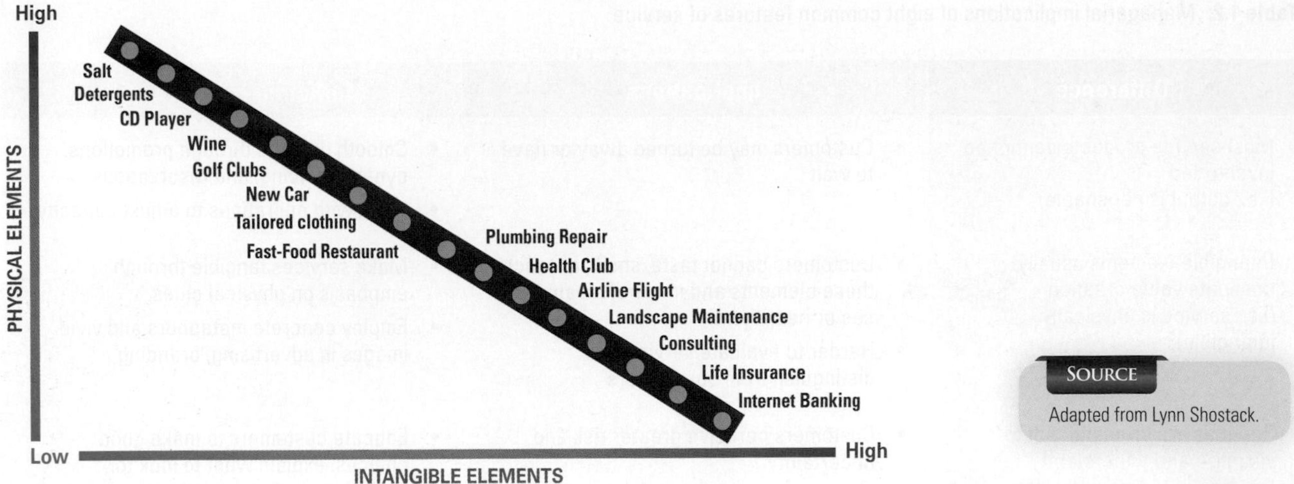

Figure 1.14 Relative value added by physical versus intangible elements in goods and services.

differences as we discuss the marketing mix for services later in this chapter and throughout this text.

THE 7 Ps OF SERVICES MARKETING

When developing ways to market manufactured goods, marketers usually focus on ***p****roduct*, ***p****rice*, ***p****lace* (or distribution), and ***p****romotion* (or communication). As a group, these are usually called the "4 Ps" of the marketing mix.[16] However, as shown in Table 1.2, the nature of services poses distinct marketing challenges. Hence, the 4 Ps of goods marketing are unable to deal with the issues arising from marketing services and have to be adapted and extended. We will therefore revisit the traditional 4 Ps of the marketing mix in this book and focus on applying them to service-specific issues.

Furthermore, the traditional marketing mix does not cover managing the customer interface. We therefore need to extend the marketing mix by adding three Ps associated with service delivery—*process, physical environment*, and *people*.[17] Together, we refer to them as the "7 Ps" of services marketing. Let us look briefly at each of the 7 Ps.

LO 6

Understand the components of the traditional marketing mix applied to services.

The Traditional Marketing Mix Applied to Services

Product Elements

Service products lie at the heart of a firm's marketing strategy. If a product is poorly designed, it won't create meaningful value for customers, even if the rest of the 7 Ps are well executed. Planning the marketing mix begins with creating a service concept that will offer value to target customers and satisfy their needs better than competing alternatives. Service products consist of a core product that meets the customers' primary need and a variety of supplementary service elements that are mutually reinforcing and add value to help customers to use the core product more effectively. Supplementary service elements include providing information, consultation, order taking, hospitality and handling exceptions.

Place and Time

Service distribution may take place through physical or electronic channels (or both), depending on the nature of the service (see Table 1.2). For example, today's banks offer customers a wide range of distribution channels, including visiting a bank branch, using a network of ATMs, doing business by telephone, and conducting banking transactions over the Internet. In particular, many information-based services can be delivered through the Internet. Firms may also deliver service directly to customers or through intermediary organizations such as retail outlets that receive a fee or commission in return. In order to deliver service elements to customers, companies need to decide where and when these services are delivered, as well as the methods and channels used.[18]

Distribution of Core versus Supplementary Services. The Internet is reshaping distribution strategy for a number of industries. We need to differentiate between delivering information-based core products (those that respond to customers' primary requirements) and providing supplementary services that facilitate the purchase and use of physical goods. Examples of information-based core products include online educational programs offered by the University of Phoenix and automobile insurance coverage from Progressive Casualty Co.

Importance of the Time Factor (see Table 1.2). Many services are delivered in real time while customers are physically present. Therefore, speed and convenience of place and time have become important determinants of effective distribution and delivery of services. Many customers today avoid wasting time. (You probably do, too.) They may be willing to pay extra to save time, such as taking a taxi when a city bus serves the same route (Figure 1.15). Many busy customers expect service when it suits them, rather than when it suits the supplier. If one firm responds by offering extended hours, its competitors often feel the need to do the same. Nowadays, a growing number of services are available 24/7.

Figure 1.15 Time is the essence—service providers must be swift and smart in their customer interactions.

Price and Other User Outlays

Like product value, payment is very important in allowing a value exchange to take place between the firm and its customers. For firms, the pricing strategy affects how much income is generated. This is used to cover the costs of providing service and to create profits. A firms pricing strategy often is highly dynamic, with price levels adjusted over time according to factors such as type of customer, time and place of delivery, level of demand, and available capacity.

For customers, price is a key part of the costs they must incur to obtain desired benefits. To calculate whether a particular service is "worth it," they may go beyond just money and assess how much time and effort are involved (Figure 1.16). Service marketers, therefore, must not set only prices that target customers are willing and able to pay. They must also understand and try to minimize other customer outlays. These outlays may include additional monetary costs (such as travel expenses to a service location), time spent, in the process of purchasing the service (such as the time taken to travel to a service location).

Most Service Products Cannot Be Inventoried. Since services involve actions or performances, they are temporary and perishable. Therefore, they usually cannot be stocked as inventory for future use (see Table 1.2). Although facilities, equipment, and labor can be prepared to create the service, each represents productive capacity, not the product itself. If there is no demand, unused capacity is wasted and the firm loses the chance to create value from these assets. During periods when demand exceeds capacity, customers may be sent away disappointed or asked to wait until later. A key task for service marketers, therefore, is to find ways of smoothing demand levels to match the firm's available capacity using dynamic pricing strategies.

Promotion and Education

What should we tell customers and prospects about our services? Few marketing programs can succeed without effective communications. This component plays three vital roles: (1) providing needed information and advice; (2) persuading target customers to buy the brand or service product; and (3) encouraging them to take action at specific times. In services marketing, most communication is educational in nature, especially for new customers. Suppliers need to teach their customers about the benefits of the service, where and when to obtain it, and how to participate in service processes to get the best results.

Services are Often Difficult to Visualize and Understand as Intangible Elements Usually Dominate Value Creation. Intangibility can consist of both mental and physical dimensions. Mental intangibility means it is not easily visualized and understood, while physical intangibility is that which cannot be touched or experienced by the five senses.[19] Intangible elements like processes, Internet-based transactions, and the expertise and attitudes of service personnel often create the most value in service performances. When services are physically intangible, it is harder for customers to evaluate important service features before purchase, or evaluate the quality of the performance itself (see Table 1.2).

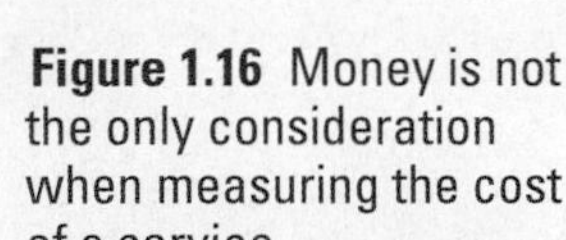

Figure 1.16 Money is not the only consideration when measuring the cost of a service.

Firms can use physical images and metaphors to promote service benefits and demonstrate the firm's competencies (see Figure 1.17). In addition, for many services, it is difficult for customers to visualize the experience prior to a purchase and to understand what they will be getting. This situation can make service purchases seem risky. Therefore, an important role of a service firm's communications is to create confidence in the firm's experience, credentials, and expertise of its employees. Well-trained service employees can help potential customers to make good choices by educating them on what to expect during and after service delivery and by helping them move smoothly through the service process.

Generally, service firms have much to gain from helping customers become more competent and productive.[20] After all, if you know how to use a service well, not only will you have a better service experience and outcome, but your greater efficiency may also eventually boost the firm's productivity, lower its costs, and perhaps even enable it to reduce the price you pay.

Figure 1.17 Insurance services are intangible, but Nationwide shows their reliability with a dash of creative advertising.

Customer-Customer Interactions Affect the Service Experience. When you encounter other customers at a service facility, they, too, can affect your satisfaction. How they're dressed, who they are, and how they behave can all enhance or negate the image a firm is trying to project and the experience it is trying to create. The implications are clear: We need to use marketing communications to attract the right segment of customers to the service facility, and also to educate them on the proper behavior.

PART I

The Extended Services Marketing Mix for Managing the Customer Interface

LO 7

Describe the components of the extended marketing mix for managing the customer interface.

Process

Smart managers know that where services are concerned, *how* a firm does things is just as important as *what* it does. Therefore, creating and delivering product elements require the design and implementation of effective processes. If service processes are badly designed, it could lead to slow and ineffective service delivery for staff. For customers, it could mean wasted time and a disappointing experience.

Operational Inputs and Outputs Can Vary Widely. Operational inputs and outputs tend to vary more widely for services and make customer service process management a challenge (see Table 1.2). When a service is delivered face-to-face and consumed as it is produced, final "assembly" must take place in real time. However, operations are often distributed across thousands of sites or branches. When operations are distributed (rather than centralized in a factory), it is difficult for service organizations to ensure reliable delivery, to control quality, and to maintain, if not improve, productivity. As a former packaged-goods marketer once observed after moving to a new position at Holiday Inn:

> We can't control the quality of our product as well as a Procter and Gamble control engineer on a production line can…When you buy a box of Tide, you can reasonably be 99 and 44/100ths percent sure that it will work to get your clothes clean. When you reserve a Holiday Inn room, you're sure at some lesser percentage that it will work to give you a good night's sleep without any hassle, or people banging on the walls and all the bad things that can happen in a hotel.[21]

Nevertheless, the best service firms have made significant progress in reducing variability by carefully designing customer service processes, adopting standardized procedures, implementing rigorous management of service quality, training employees more carefully, and automating tasks previously performed by humans.

Customers Are Often Involved in Co-production. Some services require customers to participate actively in co-producing the service product (see Table 1.2). For example, you're expected to help the investment banker understand what your needs are, how much you want to invest financially, the kind of risks you are willing to take, and the expected returns. This will enable the banker to give you advice on what to invest in. In fact, service scholars argue that customers often function as *partial employees*.[22] Increasingly, your involvement takes the form of self-service, often using self-service technologies (SSTs) facilitated by smart machines, telecommunications, and the Internet.[23] Whether customers co-produce or use SSTs, well-designed customer service processes are needed to facilitate service delivery.

Figure 1.18 Professional service is the key to customer satisfaction in the hospitality industry.

Demand and Capacity Need to Be Balanced. Manufacturing can ensure a smooth process flow by having an inventory of materials or parts ready for use. However, for services, the same thing would mean making customers wait in the service process! Therefore, effective service process management is closely related to the balancing of demand and capacity, the design of waiting systems and queues configurations, and the management of the customer's psychology of waiting.

Physical Environment

If your job is in a service business that requires customers to enter the service factory, you'll also have to spend time thinking about the design of the physical environment or "servicescape."[24] The appearance of buildings, landscaping, vehicles, interior furnishings, equipment, staff members' uniforms, signs, printed materials, and other visible cues provide tangible evidence of a firm's service quality. The servicescape also facilitates service delivery and guides customers through the service process. Service firms need to manage their servicescapes carefully, since they can have a profound impact on customer satisfaction[25] and service productivity.

Figure 1.19 Hospitality is shown through employees wearing smart outfits and a ready smile.

People

Despite advances in technology, many services will always need direct interaction between customers and service employees (see Table 1.2). You must have noticed many times how the difference between one service supplier and another lies in the attitudes and skills of their employees. Service firms need to work closely with their human resources (HR) departments and devote special care in selecting, training, and motivating their service employees (see Figure 1.19). In addition to possessing the technical skills required by the job, these individuals also need good interpersonal skills and positive attitudes. Having loyal, skilled, and motivated employees who can work well independently or together in teams represents a key competitive advantage for service firms.

 **LO 8**

Know the framework for developing effective services marketing strategies.

A FRAMEWORK FOR DEVELOPING EFFECTIVE SERVICES MARKETING STRATEGIES

The 7 Ps are integrated into the wider organizing framework of this book. It shows how each of the chapters fits together with the others as they address related topics and issues. Figure 1.20 presents the organizing framework for this book, which is divided into five parts: (1) *understanding service products, consumers, and markets*; (2) *applying the 4 Ps of marketing to services*; (3) *designing and managing the customer interface (i.e., the additional 3 Ps of services marketing)*; (4) *developing customer relationships*; and (5) *striving for service excellence*. Note that the arrows link the different boxes in the model—they stress the interdependences between the different parts. Decisions made in one area must be consistent with those taken in another, so that each strategic element will mutually reinforce the other elements.

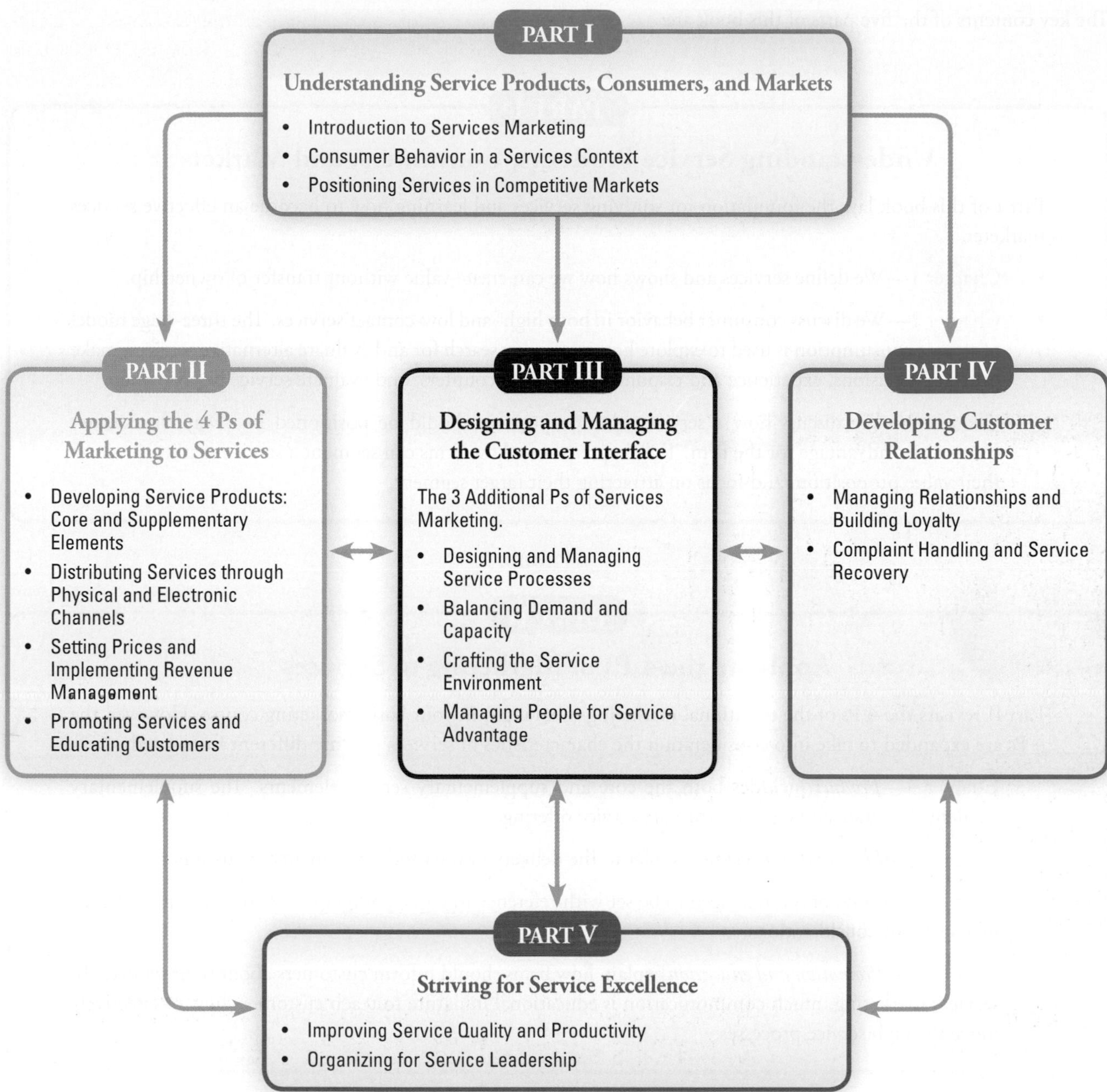

Figure 1.20 Integrated Model of Services Marketing.

The key contents of the five parts of this book are:

PART I

Understanding Service Products, Consumers, and Markets

Part I of this book lays the foundation for studying services and learning how to become an effective services marketer.

- Chapter 1—We define services and shows how we can create value without transfer of ownership.
- Chapter 2—We discuss consumer behavior in both high- and low-contact services. The three-stage model of service consumption is used to explore how customers search for and evaluate alternative services, make purchase decisions, experience and respond to service encounters, and evaluate service performance.
- Chapter 3—We discuss how a service value proposition should be positioned in a way that creates competitive advantage for the firm. The chapter shows how firms can segment a service market, position their value proposition, and focus on attracting their target segment.

PART II

Applying the 4 Ps of Marketing to Services

Part II revisits the 4 Ps of the traditional marketing mix taught in your basic marketing course. However, the 4 Ps are expanded to take into consideration the characteristics of services that are different from goods.

- Chapter 4—*Product* includes both the core and supplementary service elements. The supplementary elements facilitate and enhance the core service offering.
- Chapter 5—*Place and time* elements refer to the delivery of the product elements to customers.
- Chapter 6—*Prices* of services need to be set with reference to costs, competition and value, and revenue management considerations.
- Chapter 7—*Promotion and education* explain how firms should inform customers about their services. In services marketing, much communication is educational in nature to teach customers how to effectively move through service processes.

PART III

Designing and Managing the Customer Interface

Part III of the book focuses on managing the interface between customers and the service firm. It covers the additional 3 Ps that are unique to services marketing and not found in goods marketing.

- Chapter 8—*Processes* create and deliver the product elements. The chapter begins with the design of effective delivery processes, specifying how the operating and delivery systems link together to create the value proposition. Very often, customers are involved in these processes as co-producers, and well-designed processes should account for that.

- Chapter 9—This chapter also relates to process management and focuses on balancing fluctuating demand and productive capacity for each step of a customer service process. Marketing strategies for managing demand involve smoothing demand fluctuations, inventorying demand through reservation systems, and formalized queuing. Managing customer waiting is also explored in this chapter.
- Chapter 10—The *physical environment*, also known as the *servicescape*, needs to be designed and engineered to create the right impression and facilitate effective service process delivery. The servicescape provides tangible evidence of a firm's image and service quality.
- Chapter 11—*People* play a very important role in services marketing. Many services require direct interaction between customers and service personnel. The nature of these interactions strongly influences how customers perceive service quality. Hence, service firms devote a significant amount of effort to recruiting, training, and motivating employees. How to get all this right is explained using the Service Talent Cycle as an integrative framework.

PART IV

Developing Customer Relationships

Part IV focuses on how to develop customer relationships and build loyalty.

- Chapter 12—Achieving profitability requires creating relationships with customers from the right segments and then finding ways to build and reinforce their loyalty. This chapter introduces the Wheel of Loyalty, which shows three systematic steps in building customer loyalty. The chapter closes with a discussion of customer relationship management (CRM) systems.
- Chapter 13—A loyal customer base often is built from effective complaint handling and service recovery, which are discussed in this chapter. Service guarantees are explored as a powerful way of institutionalizing effective service recovery and as an effective marketing tool to signal high quality service.

PART V

Striving for Service Excellence

Part V focuses on how to develop and transform a firm to achieve service excellence.

- Chapter 14—Productivity and quality are both necessary and are strongly related to financial success in services. This chapter focuses on service quality, diagnosing quality shortfalls using the Gaps Model, and strategies to close quality gaps. Customer feedback systems are discussed as an effective tool for systematically listening to and learning from customers. Productivity is introduced as being closely related to quality, and it is emphasized that in today's competitive markets, firms need to simultaneously improve both quality and productivity—not one at the expense of the other.
- Chapter 15—The Service Profit Chain is used as an integrative model to demonstrate the strategic linkages involved in running a successful service organization. Implementing the service profit chain requires the integration of the three key functions of marketing, operations, and human resources. This chapter discusses how to move a service organization to higher levels of performance in each functional area, and closes with a discussion about the role of leadership in creating and maintaining a climate for service.

CHAPTER SUMMARY

LO 1 ▶ Services represent an important and growing contribution to most economies in the world. As economies develop, services form the largest part of the GDP of those economies. Globally, most new jobs are generated in the service sector.

LO 2 ▶ Many forces are transforming our economies, making them more *services-oriented*. They include government policies, social changes, business trends, advances in information technology, and globalization.

LO 3 ▶ What exactly is a service? The key distinguishing feature of a service is that it is a form of rental rather than ownership. Service customers obtain the rights to hire the labor, skills, and expertise of personnel; to use a physical object or space; or to access shared facilities, networks, and systems. Services are performances that bring about the desired results or experience for the customer.

LO 4 ▶ Services vary widely and can be categorized according to the nature of the underlying process: Is the service directed at customers or their possessions? Are service actions tangible or intangible in nature? These distinctions have important marketing implications and lead to four broad categories of services:

- o People processing
- o Possession processing
- o Mental stimulus processing
- o Information processing

Mental stimulus and information processing can be combined into what is called information-based services.

LO 5 ▶ Services have unique characteristics that make them different from products:

- o Most service products cannot be inventoried (i.e., are perishable).
- o Intangible elements usually dominate value creation (i.e., are physically intangible).
- o Services often are difficult to visualize and understand (i.e., are mentally intangible).
- o Customers may be involved in co-production (i.e., if people processing is involved, the service is inseparable).
- o People may be part of the service experience.
- o Operational inputs and outputs tend to vary widely (i.e., are heterogeneous).
- o The time factor often assumes great importance.
- o Distribution may take place through non-physical channels.

LO 6 ▶ Due to the unique characteristics of services, the traditional marketing mix of the 4 Ps needs to be amended. Some important amendments include:

- o *Product elements* include more than just the core elements. They also include supplementary service elements such as the provision of consultation, hospitality, or handling of exceptions.
- o *Place and time* elements refer to the delivery of the product elements to the customer; many information-processing elements are delivered electronically.
- o *Pricing* includes nonmonetary costs to the consumer and revenue management considerations.
- o *Promotion* is also viewed as a form of communication and education that guides customers through service processes, rather than focusing mainly on advertising and promotions.

LO 7 ▶ Services marketing requires three additional Ps that cover the management of the customer interface:

- o *Process* refers to the design and management of customer service processes, including managing demand and capacity and related customer waiting.
- o *Physical environment*, also known as the *servicescape*, facilitates process delivery and provides tangible evidence of a firm's image and service quality.
- o *People* covers the recruiting, training, and motivating of service employees to deliver service quality and productivity.

LO 8 ▶ A framework for services marketing strategy forms the underlying structure of this book. The framework consists of the following five interlinked parts:

- o Part I begins with the need for service firms to understand their markets, customers, and competition.
- o Part II shows us how to apply the traditional 4 Ps to services marketing.
- o Part III covers the 3 Ps of the extended services marketing mix and shows how to manage the customer interface.
- o Part IV illustrates how to develop lasting customer relationships through a variety of tools, ranging from the Wheel of Loyalty and CRM to effective complaint management and service guarantees.
- o Part V discusses how to improve service quality and productivity and closes with a discussion on how change management and leadership can propel a firm to become a service leader.

UNLOCK YOUR LEARNING

These keywords are found within the sections of each Learning Objective (LO). They are integral to understanding the services marketing concepts taught in each section. Having a firm grasp of these keywords and how they are used is essential to helping you do well on your course, and in the real and very competitive marketing scene out there.

LO 1
1 Knowledge-based industries
2 Service science
3 Service sector
4 Service-driven economy
5 Supplementary services

LO 2
6 Advances in information technology
7 Business trends
8 Globalization
9 Government policies
10 Social change

LO 3
11 Acts
12 Deeds
13 Economic activities
14 Efforts
15 Nonownership
16 Performances
17 Rental

LO 4
18 "Inventoried"
19 Information processing
20 Information-based services
21 Intangible actions
22 Mental stimulus processing
23 People processing
24 Possession processing
25 Tangible actions

LO 5
26 4 Ps
27 Heterogeneity
28 Inseparability
29 Intangibility
30 Intangible-dominant
31 Perishability
32 Tangible-dominant

LO 6
33 7 Ps
34 Core products
35 Place and time
36 Price
37 Product elements
38 Promotion and education
39 Service products
40 User outlays

LO 7
41 "Servicescape"
42 Capacity
43 Co-production
44 Demand
45 Operational inputs
46 People
47 Physical environment
48 Process

LO 8
49 Complaint handling
50 Customer feedback systems
51 Customer interface
52 Customer relationship management (CRM) systems
53 Customer relationships
54 Delivery processes
55 Gaps model
56 High-contact services
57 Human resources
58 Low-contact services
59 Marketing
60 Motivating
61 Operations
62 Productive capacity
63 Productivity
64 Quality
65 Recruiting
66 Service excellence
67 Service profit chain
68 Service recovery
69 Tangible evidence
70 Target segment
71 Training
72 Value proposition
73 Wheel of Loyalty

How well do you know the language of services marketing? Quiz yourself!

Not for the academically faint-of-heart

For each keyword you are able to recall without referring to earlier pages, give yourself a point (and a pat on the back). Tally your score at the end and see if you earned the right to be called—a *services marketeer.*

SCORE

01 – 12 Services Marketing is done a great disservice.
13 – 24 The midnight oil needs to be lit, pronto.
25 – 36 I know what you *didn't* do all semester.
37 – 48 By George! You're getting there.
49 – 60 Now, go forth and market.
61 – 73 There should be a marketing concept named after you.

KNOW YOUR ESM

Review Questions

1. What are the main reasons for the growing share of the service sector in all major economies of the world?
2. What are the five powerful forces transforming the service landscape, and what impact do they have on the service economy?
3. "A service is rented rather than owned." Explain what this statement means, and use examples to support your explanation.
4. Describe the four broad "processing" categories of services, and provide examples for each category.
5. What is so special about services marketing that it needs a special approach?
6. "The 4 Ps are all a marketing manager needs to create a marketing strategy for a service business." Prepare a response that argues against this, and support it with examples.
7. What types of services do you think are (a) the most affected and (b) the least affected by the problem of variable inputs and outputs? Why?
8. Why is time so important in services?
9. What are the elements in the framework for developing effective service marketing strategies?

WORK YOUR ESM

Application Exercises

1. Visit the websites of the following national statistical bureaus: US Bureau of Economic Analysis (www.bea.gov); Statistics Canada (www.statcan.ca); National Bureau of Statistics of China (www. stats.gov.cn/english/); Eurostat (http://europa.eu.int/en/comm/eurostat/); Japanese Statistics Bureau (www.stat.go.jp); Central Bureau of Statistics (Indonesia) (www.bps.go.id); Statistics South Africa (www.statssa.gov.za); and the respective websites for your country if it is not covered here. In each instance, obtain data on the latest trends in services as (a) a percentage of the GDP; (b) the percentage of employment accounted for by services; (c) breakdowns of these two statistics by type of industry; and (d) service exports and imports. Looking at these trends, what are your conclusions for the main sectors of these economies, and within services, for specific service sectors?
2. Legal and accounting firms now advertise their services in many countries. Search for a few advertisements and review the following: What do these firms do to cope with the intangibility of their services? What could they do better? How do they deal with consumer quality and risk perceptions, and how could they improve this aspect of their marketing?
3. Give examples of how Internet and telecommunications technologies (e.g., Interactive Voice Response Systems (IVRs) and mobile commerce (m-commerce) have changed some of the services you use).
4. Choose a service company you are familiar with, and show how each of the 7 Ps of services marketing applies to one of its specific service products.

PART I

ENDNOTES

1 Marion Weissenberger-Eibl and Daniel Jeffrey Koch, "Importance of Industrial Services and Service Innovations," *Journal of Management and Organization*, no. 13 (2007): 88–101; Jochen Wirtz and Michael Ehret, "Creative Restruction – How Business Services Drive Economic Evolution," *European Business Review*, 21, no. 4 (2009), 380–394.

2 http://www.ibm.com/us/en/, accessed March 12, 2012.

3 Henry Chesbrough, "Towards a New Science for Services," *Harvard Business Review*, February 2005, 43–44.

4 For more information on SSME, see IFM and IBM, *Succeeding through Service Innovation: A Discussion Paper*. Cambridge, UK: University of Cambridge Institute for Manufacturing, 2007; Paul P. Maglio and Jim Spohrer. "Fundamentals of Service Science," *Journal of the Academy of Marketing Science*, 36, no. 1 (2008): 18–20; R. C. Larson, "Service Science: At the Intersection of Management, Social, and Engineering Sciences," *IBM Systems Journal*, 47, no. 1 (2008); R. J. Glushko, "Designing a Service Science Discipline with Discipline," *IBM Systems Journal*, 47, no. 1 (2008): 15–27; Roberta S. Russell. "Collaborative Research in Service Science: Quality and Innovation," *Journal of Service Science*, 2, no. 2 (2009): 1–7.

5 Bill Carroll and Judy Siguaw, "The Evolution of Electronic Distribution: Effects on Hotels and Intermediaries," *Cornell Hotel and Restaurant Administration Quarterly* 44, (August 2003): 38–51.

6 Audrey Williams June, "Some Papers are Uploaded to Bangalore to Be Graded," *The Chronicle at Higher Education*, April 4, 2010; http://edumetry.com/, accessed March 12, 2012.

7 Robin G. Qiu, "Service Science: Scientific Study of Service Systems," *Service Science*. Retrieved at http://www.sersci.com/ServiceScience/paper_details.php?id=1, published on November 22, 2008.

8 John M. Rathmell, "What Is Meant by Services?" *Journal of Marketing* 30 (October 1966): 32–36.

9 Robert C. Judd, "The Case for Redefining Services," *Journal of Marketing* 28 (January 1964): 59; John M. Rathmell, *Marketing in the Service Sector*. Cambridge, MA: Winthrop, 1974; Christopher H. Lovelock and Evert Gummesson, "Whither Services Marketing? In Search of a New Paradigm and Fresh Perspectives," *Journal of Service Research* 7 (August 2004): 20–41.

10 Christopher H. Lovelock and Evert Gummesson, "Whither Services Marketing? In Search of a New Paradigm and Fresh Perspectives," *Journal of Service Research* 7 (August 2004): 20–41.

11 Adapted from a definition by Christopher Lovelock (identified anonymously as Expert 6, Table II, p. 112) in Bo Edvardsson, Anders Gustafsson, and Inger Roos, "Service Portraits in Service Research: A Critical Review," *International Journal of Service Industry Management* 16, no. 1 (2005): 107–121.

12 These classifications are derived from Christopher H. Lovelock, "Classifying Services to Gain Strategic Marketing Insights," *Journal of Marketing* 47, (Summer 1983): 9–20.

13 Valarie A. Zeithaml, A. Parasuraman, Leonard L. Berry, "Problems and Strategies in Services Marketing." *Journal of Marketing* 49, (Spring 1985): 33–46.

14 Christopher H. Lovelock and Evert Gummesson, "Whither Services Marketing? In Search of a New Paradigm and Fresh Perspectives," *Journal of Service Research* 7 (August 2004): 20–41.

15 G. Lynn Shostack, "Breaking Free from Product Marketing," *Journal of Marketing* 41 (April 1977): 73–80.

16 The 4 Ps classification of marketing decision variables was created by E. Jerome McCarthy, *Basic Marketing: A Managerial Approach* (Homewood, IL: Richard D. Irwin, Inc., 1960). It was a refinement of the long list of ingredients included in the marketing mix concept created by Professor Neil Borden at Harvard in the 1950s. Borden got the idea from a colleague who described the marketing manager's job as being a "mixer of ingredients."

17 An expanded 7 Ps marketing mix was first proposed by Bernard H. Booms and Mary J. Bitner, "Marketing Strategies and Organization Structures for Service Firms," in J. H. Donnelly and W.R. George, eds. *Marketing of Services* (Chicago: American Marketing Association, 1981, 47–51).

18 Philip J. Coelho and Chris Easingwood, "Multiple Channel Systems in Services: Pros, Cons, and Issues," *The Service Industries Journal* 24 (September 2004): 1–30.

19 John E. G. Bateson, "Why We Need Service Marketing" in *Conceptual and Theoretical Developments in Marketing*, ed. O. C. Ferrell, S. W. Brown and C. W. Lamb Jr. (Chicago: American Marketing Association, 1979), 131–146.

20 Bonnie Farber Canziani, "Leveraging Customer Competency in Service Firms," *International Journal of Service Industry Management* 8, no. 1 (1997): 5–25.

21 Gary Knisely, "Greater Marketing Emphasis by Holiday Inns Breaks Mold," *Advertising Age*, January 15, 1979.

22 The term "partial employee" was coined by P. K. Mills and D. J. Moberg, "Perspectives on the Technology of Service Operations," *Academy of Management Review* 7, no. 3: 467–478. For further research on this topic, see: Karthik Namasivayam, "The Consumer as Transient Employee: Consumer Satisfaction through the Lens of Job-performance Models, *International Journal of Service Industry Management* 14, no. 4 (2004): 420–435. An-Tien Hsieh, Chang-Hua Yen, and Ko-Chien Chin, "Participative customers as partial employees and service provider workload," *International Journal of Service Industry Management* 15, no. 2 (2004): 187–200.

23 For research on SST, see Matthew L. Meuter, Mary Jo Bitner, Amy L. Ostrom, and Stephen W. Brown, "Choosing Among Alternative Delivery Modes: An Investigation of Customer Trial of Self Service Technologies," *Journal of Marketing* 69, (April 2005): 61–84. A. Parasuraman, Valarie A. Zeithaml, and Arvind Malhotra, "E-S-QUAL: A Multiple Item Scale for Assessing Electronic Service Quality," *Journal of Service Research* 7, (February 2005): 213–233. Devashish Pujari, "Self-service with a Smile: Self-service Technology (SST) Encounters among Canadian Business-to-business," *International Journal of Service Industry Management* 15, no. 2 (2004): 200–219. Angus Laing, Gillian Hogg, and Dan Winkelman, "The Impact of the Internet on Professional Relationships: The Case of Health Care," *The Service Industries Journal* 25, (July 2005): 675–688.

24 The term "servicescape" was coined by Mary Jo Bitner, "Servicescapes: The Impact of Physical Surroundings on Customers and Employees," *Journal of Marketing* 56, (April 1992): 57–71.

25 Hei-Lim Michael Lio and Raymond Rody, "The Emotional Impact of Casino Servicescape," *UNLV Gaming Research and Review Journal* 13, no. 2 (October 2009): 17–25.

CHAPTER 2

consumer behavior in a SERVICES CONTEXT

LEARNING OBJECTIVES

By the end of this chapter, the reader should be able to:

- **LO 1** Understand the three-stage model of service consumption.
- **LO 2** Use the multi-attribute model to understand how consumers evaluate and choose among alternative service offerings.
- **LO 3** Learn why consumers often have difficulties evaluating services, especially those with many experience and credence attributes.
- **LO 4** Know the perceived risks customers face in purchasing services and the strategies firms can use to reduce consumer risk perceptions.
- **LO 5** Understand how customers form service expectations and identify the components of these expectations.
- **LO 6** Contrast how customers experience and evaluate high- versus low-contact services.
- **LO 7** Be familiar with the servuction model and understand the interactions that together create the service experience.
- **LO 8** Obtain insights from viewing the service encounter as a form of theater.
- **LO 9** Know how role and script theories contribute to a better understanding of service encounters.
- **LO 10** Describe how customers evaluate services and what determines their satisfaction.

Figure 2.1 New York University is the gateway to bigger and better things for students like Susan Munro.

OPENING VIGNETTE

Susan Munro, Service Customer

One morning, Susan Munro, a final-year business student, had her breakfast and then checked the local weather forecast on the Internet. It predicted rain, so she made sure to take an umbrella with her before leaving the apartment. On the way to the bus stop, she dropped a letter in a mailbox. The bus arrived on schedule. It was the usual driver, who recognized her and greeted her cheerfully as she showed her commuter pass.

Upon arriving at her destination, Susan walked to the College of Business. Joining a crowd of other students, she found a seat in the large lecture theater where her marketing class was held. The professor was a very dynamic individual who believed in engaging students in active dialog. Susan made several contributions to the discussion and felt that she had learned a lot from listening to others' analyses and opinions.

After class, Susan and her friends ate lunch at the recently renovated Student Union. It was a well-lit and colorfully decorated new food court that featured a variety of small stores. These included both local suppliers and brand-name fast-food chains, which offered different types of cuisine. There were stores selling sandwiches, crepes, health foods, a variety of Asian cuisine, and desserts. Although she had wanted a sandwich, there was a long queue of customers at the sandwich shop. Thus, Susan joined her friends at Burger King and then splurged on a café latte from the Have-a-Java coffee stand. The food court was unusually crowded that day perhaps because of the rain pouring down outside. When they finally found a table, they had to clear away the dirty trays. "Lazy slobs!" commented her friend Mark, referring to the previous customers.

After lunch, Susan stopped at the cash machine, inserted her bank card, and withdrew some money. When she remembered that she had a job interview at the end of the week, she telephoned her hairdresser and counted herself lucky to be able to make an appointment for later. This was because of a cancellation by another client. When she left the Student Union, it was still raining.

Susan looked forward to her visit to the hairdresser. The salon, which had a bright, trendy décor, was staffed by friendly hairdressers. Unfortunately, her hairdresser was running late and Susan had to wait for 20 minutes. She used that time to review material for her human resources course. Some of the other waiting customers were reading magazines provided by the salon. Eventually, it was time for a shampoo, after which her hairdresser proposed a slightly different haircut. Susan agreed, although she drew the line at the suggestion to lighten her hair color as she had never done it before and was unsure how it would look. She did not want to take the risk, especially just before her job interview. She sat still, watching the process in the mirror and turning her head when asked. She was very pleased with the result and complimented the hairdresser on her work. She left a tip for the hairdresser and paid at the reception desk.

When Susan left the store, the rain had stopped and the sun was shining. On the way home, she stopped by the dry cleaners to pick up some clothes she had left there previously. The store was rather gloomy and smelled of cleaning solution, and the walls badly needed repainting. She was annoyed to find that, although her silk blouse was ready as promised, the suit that she needed for the interview was not. The assistant, who had dirty fingernails, mumbled an apology in an insincere tone. Although the store was conveniently located and the quality of work was quite good, Susan considered the employees unfriendly and not very helpful, and was unhappy with their service. However, she had no choice but to use them, as there were no other dry cleaners close by.

Back at her apartment building, she opened the mailbox in the lobby. Her mail included a bill from her insurance company. However, it required no action since payment was deducted automatically from her bank account. She was about to throw away the junk mail when she noticed a flyer promoting a new dry cleaner nearby, which included a discount coupon. She decided to try the new store and kept the coupon.

Since it was her turn to cook dinner, she looked around in the kitchen to see what food was available. Susan sighed when she realized that there was nothing much. Maybe she would make a salad and call for delivery of a large pizza.

This story of Susan's day as a service consumer will follow us throughout this chapter to illustrate service-related consumer behavior concepts and theories.

Figure 2.2 Susan is just another customer facing a large selection of services out there.

LO 1

Understand the three-stage model of service consumption.

THE THREE-STAGE MODEL OF SERVICE CONSUMPTION

The story of Susan Munro shows consumer behavior in a variety of situations and stages. In marketing, it is very important to understand why customers behave the way they do. How do they make decisions about buying and using a service? What determines their satisfaction with it after consumption? Without this understanding, no firm can hope to create and deliver services that will result in satisfied customers.

Service consumption can be divided into three main stages. They are the pre-purchase, service encounter, and post-purchase stages. Figure 2.3 shows that each stage consists

High-Contact Services	Low-Contact Services	Stages of Service Consumption	Key Concepts
Can visit physical sites; observe (+ low-contact options)	Surf the web, view yellow pages, make calls	**1. Pre-purchase Stage** Awareness of need • Information search • Clarify needs • Explore solutions • Identify alternative service products and suppliers	*Need arousal* *Evoked set*
Can visit in person and observe (possibly test) facilities equipment, and operation in action; meet personnel; see customers (+ remote options)	Primarily remote contact (websites, blogs, phone, e-mail, publications, etc.)	Evaluation of alternatives (solutions and suppliers) • Review supplier information (e.g. advertising, brochures, websites) • Review information from third parties (e.g. published reviews, ratings, comments on web, blogs, complaints to public agencies, satisfaction ratings, awards) • Discuss options with service personnel • Get advice and feedback from third-party advisors and other customers	*Consideration set* *Multi-attribute model* *Search, experience, and credence attributes* *Perceived risk* *Formation of expectations* *- desired service level* *- predicted service level* *- adequate service level* *- zone of tolerance*
At physical site (or remote reservation)	Remote	Make decisions on service purchase and often make reservations	
At physical site *only*	Remote	**2. Service Encounter Stage** Request service from a chosen supplier or initiate self-service (payment may be upfront or billed later) Service delivery by personnel or self-service	*Moments of truth* *Service encounters* *Servuction system* *Role and script theories* *Theater as a metaphor*
		3. Post-purchase Stage Evalution of service performance	*Confirmation/ Disconfirmation of expectations* *Dissatisfaction, satisfaction and delight*
		Future intentions	*Repurchase* *Word-of-mouth*

Figure 2.3 The three-stage model of service consumption.

PART I

of several steps. The pre-purchase stage includes need awareness, information search, evaluation of alternatives, and making a purchase decision. During the service encounter stage, the customer initiates, experiences, and consumes the service. The post-purchase stage includes evaluation of the service performance, which determines future intentions such as wanting to buy again from the same firm and recommending it to friends.

As shown on the left-hand side of Figure 2.3, the nature of these steps varies, depending on whether the service is high-contact (a great degree of interaction between service employees and customers, usually in people-processing services) or low-contact (little to no face-to-face contact between service employees and customers, common for many information-processing services that can be delivered at arm's length). On the right-hand side of Figure 2.3 are the key concepts discussed in this chapter. The rest of this chapter is organized around the three stages and key concepts of service consumption.

PRE-PURCHASE STAGE

The pre-purchase stage begins with *need awareness* and continues through information search and evaluation of alternatives to deciding whether or not to buy a particular service.

Need Awareness

When a person or organization decides to buy or use a service, it is triggered by an underlying need or *need arousal.* The awareness of a need will lead to an information search and an evaluation of alternatives before a decision is reached. Needs may be triggered by the following:

- Unconscious minds (e.g., personal identity and aspirations)
- Physical conditions (e.g., Susan Munro's hunger drove her to Burger King.)
- External sources (e.g., a service firm's marketing activities) (See Figure 2.4.)

Figure 2.4 Hertz targets the environmentally conscious consumer who is more likely to recognize the need for an eco-friendly car.

When a need is recognized, people are likely to be motivated to take action to resolve it. In the story of Susan Munro, her need for hairstyling was triggered by her recollection that she had a job interview to attend at the end of the week, and her desire to look her best for the interview. In developed economies, consumers have a growing need to spend on vacations, entertainment, and increasingly novel and innovative service experiences. This shift in consumer behavior and attitudes provides opportunities for service providers that understand and meet consumers' changing needs. For example, some service providers have taken advantage of the increased interest in extreme sports by offering guided mountain climbs, paragliding, white-water rafting trips, and mountain biking adventures (see Figure 2.5).

Information Search

Once a need or a problem has been recognized, customers are motivated to search for solutions to satisfy that need. Several alternatives may come to mind, and these form the *evoked set*. The evoked set can be derived from past experiences or external sources such as advertising, retail displays, news stories, online searches, and recommendations from service personnel, friends, and family.[1] However, a consumer is unlikely to use all the alternatives in the evoked set for decision making. Instead, the consumer is likely to narrow it down to a few alternatives to seriously consider, and these alternatives then form the *consideration set*. For Susan, her consideration set for a quick lunch included the sandwich store and Burger King. During the search process, consumers also learn about service attributes they should consider, and form expectations of how firms in the consideration set perform on those attributes.

Evaluation of Alternative Services

Once the consideration set and key attributes are understood, the consumer typically makes a purchase decision. In marketing, we often use multi-attribute models to simulate consumer decision making.

LO 2

Use the multi-attribute model to understand how consumers evaluate and choose among alternative service offerings.

Multi-attribute Model

This model holds that consumers use product attributes that are important to them, to evaluate and compare alternative offerings of firms in their consideration set. Each attribute has an importance weight. A higher weight means that the attribute is more important. For example, let's assume that Susan has three alternative dry cleaners in her consideration set. Table 2.1 shows the alternatives, as well as the attributes she would use to compare them. The table shows that the quality of the dry cleaning

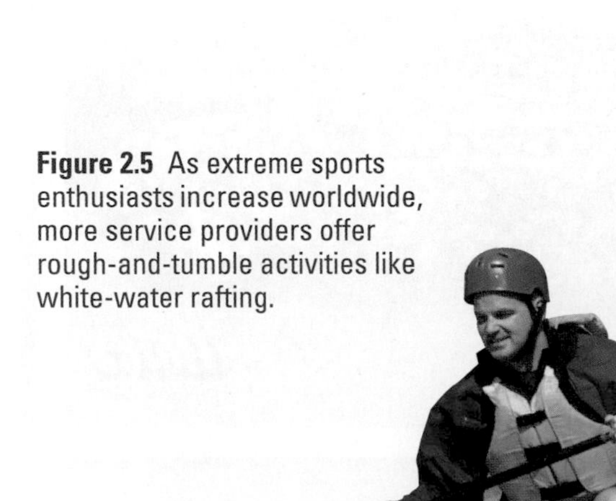

Figure 2.5 As extreme sports enthusiasts increase worldwide, more service providers offer rough-and-tumble activities like white-water rafting.

Table 2.1 Modeling consumer choice—Susan Munro's Multi-attribute Model for choosing a dry cleaner

	Current Dry Cleaner	Campus Dry Cleaner	New Dry Cleaner	Importance Weight
Quality of Dry Cleaning	9	10	10	30%
Convenience of Location	10	8	9	25%
Price	8	10	8	20%
Opening Hours	6	10	9	10%
Reliability of On-time Delivery	2	9	9	5%
Friendliness of Staff	2	8	8	5%
Design of Shop	2	7	8	5%
Total Score	7.7	9.2	9.0	100%

is most important to her, followed by convenience of location, and then price (see Table 2.1). Susan can use two common decision rules to come to a decision. They are the very simple linear compensatory rule, and the more complex but also more realistic conjunctive rule. Using the same information, Susan can end up choosing different alternatives if she uses different decision rules. It is therefore important for firms to understand through careful market research which rule their target customers are using!

Using the linear compensatory rule, Susan mentally computes a global score for each dry cleaner. This is done by multiplying the score of the dry cleaner for each attribute by the importance weight. The scores are then added up. For example, the current dry cleaner would score 9 × 30% for quality of dry cleaning, plus 10 × 20% for convenience of location, plus 8 × 15% for price, etc. If you do this computation for all three alternatives, you will get a total score for the current dry cleaner of 7.7, the campus dry cleaner of 9.2, and 9.0 for the new dry cleaner. Therefore, the choice would be the on-campus dry cleaner.

In the conjunctive rule, the consumer will make the decision based on the total overall score in conjunction with minimum performance levels on one or several attributes. For example, Susan may only consider a dry cleaner that scores a minimum of 9 for convenience of location, as she does not want to carry her dry cleaning over longer distances. In that case, she is left with a choice between the current and new dry cleaner in her neighborhood. Of the two, she will pick the new dry cleaner because it has the higher overall score. If none of the brands meets all the cutoffs in a conjunctive model, then Susan may delay making a choice, change the decision rule, or modify the cutoffs.

Service providers who understand how their target customers make decisions can try and influence that decision-making process in a number of ways to enhance their chance of being the chosen provider:

- First, firms need to ensure that their service is in the consideration set, since a firm cannot be chosen without first being considered! This can be done through advertising or viral marketing (see Chapter 7).
- Next, firms can change and correct consumer perceptions (e.g., if a clinic has truly superior performance on personalized and special care from their doctors but customers do not see this, it can focus its communications on correcting customer perceptions).
- They can also shift importance weights (e.g., communicate messages that increase weights of attributes the firm excels in, and de-emphasize those the firm is not so strong at).
- Firms can even introduce new attributes such as car rental company Hertz did when advertising the environmentally friendly car. Consumers who are eco-conscious would then consider the environmental aspect when deciding which car rental company to use.

The objective is to shape the firm's target customers' decision making so that they make the "right" choice, that is, to choose the firm's service offering.

LO 3

Learn why consumers often have difficulties evaluating services, especially those with many experience and credence attributes.

Service Attributes

The multi-attribute model assumes that consumers can evaluate all important attributes before purchase. However, this is often not the case, as some attributes are harder to evaluate than others. There are three types of attributes.[2] They are as follows:

- ***Search attributes*** are tangible characteristics customers can evaluate before purchase. Search attributes are found in many services. For example, search attributes for a restaurant include type of food, location, type of restaurant (e.g., fine dining, casual or family friendly), and price. You can also ask to view different rooms in a hotel or take a tour of a health club and try out one or two pieces of equipment before making a buying decision. These tangible search attributes help customers to better understand and evaluate a service and therefore reduce the sense of uncertainty or risk associated with the purchase.
- ***Experience attributes*** are those that cannot be evaluated before purchase. Customers must "experience" the service before they can assess attributes like reliability, ease of use, and customer support. Returning to our restaurant example, you won't know how much you actually like the food, the service provided by your waiter, and the atmosphere in the restaurant until you actually use the service.

Figure 2.6 Holiday-makers experiencing first hand the grandeur and beauty of Niagara Falls.

Vacations (Figure 2.6) and live entertainment performances all have high experience attributes. Although people can scroll through websites describing a specific holiday destination, view travel films, read reviews by travel experts, or hear about the experiences from family and friends, they cannot really evaluate or feel the beauty of hiking in the Canadian Rockies or snorkeling in the Caribbean, for example, until they experience these activities themselves.

- *Credence attributes* are characteristics that customers find hard to evaluate even after consumption. Here, the customer is forced to believe or trust that certain tasks have been performed at the promised level of quality. In the restaurant example earlier, credence attributes include the hygiene conditions in the kitchen and the healthiness of the cooking ingredients.

  It is not easy for a customer to determine the quality of repair and maintenance work performed on a car. Patients usually can't evaluate how well their dentists have performed complex dental procedures. How can one really be sure that the best possible job was done? Sometimes, it comes down to a matter of having confidence in the service provider's skills and professionalism.

All products can be placed on a continuum ranging from "easy to evaluate" to "difficult to evaluate," depending on whether they are high in search, experience, or credence attributes. As shown in Figure 2.7, most physical goods are located somewhere toward the left of the continuum because they are high in search attributes. Most services tend to be located from the center to the right of the continuum as they tend to be high in experience and credence attributes.

The harder it is to evaluate a service, the higher is the perceived risk associated with that decision. We will discuss perceived risk next.

Perceived Risk

LO 4

Know the perceived risks customers face in purchasing services and the strategies firms can use to reduce consumer risk perceptions.

If you buy physical goods that are unsatisfactory, you can usually return or replace them. With services, this option may not be possible. Susan Munro had not tried coloring her hair before and was uncertain how it would turn out. Hence, when

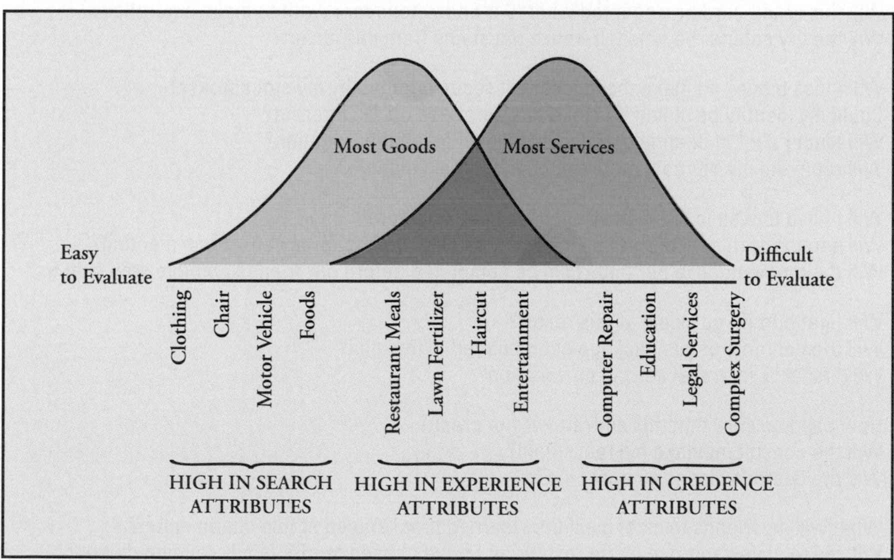

Figure 2.7 How product characteristics affect ease of evaluation.

SOURCE

Adapted from Valarie A. Zeithaml, "How Consumer Evaluation Processes Differ Between Goods and Services," in J. H. Donnelly and W. R. George, Marketing of Services (Chicago: American Marketing Association, 1981).

the hairdresser suggested she lighten her hair color, Susan was worried and therefore declined. Her uncertainty increased her *perceived risk*. Perceived risk is usually greater for services that are high in experience and credence attributes, and first-time users are likely to face greater uncertainty. Think about how you felt the first time you had to make a decision about an unfamiliar service, especially one with important consequences, such as choosing a college. It is likely that you were worried about the possibility of a negative outcome. The worse the possible outcome and the more likely it is to occur, the higher the perception of risk. Table 2.2 shows seven categories of perceived risks.

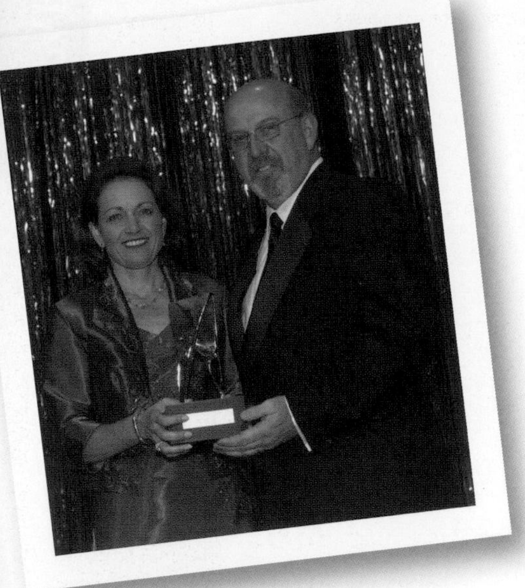

Figure 2.8 Winning awards is a tangible cue for service excellence.

How might consumers handle perceived risk? People usually feel uncomfortable with perceived risks and use a variety of methods to reduce them, including the following:

- Seeking information from trusted and respected personal sources such as family, friends, and peers
- Using the Internet to compare service offerings and to search for independent reviews and ratings
- Relying on a firm with a good reputation
- Looking for guarantees and warranties
- Visiting service facilities or trying aspects of the service before purchasing, and examining tangible cues or other physical evidence such as the feel and look of the service setting or awards won by the firm (see Figures 2.8 and 2.9)

Table 2.2 Perceived risks in purchasing and using services

Type of Risk	Examples of Customer Concerns
Functional (unsatisfactory performance outcomes)	• Will this training course give me the skills I need to get a better job? • Will this credit card be accepted wherever and whenever I want to make a purchase? • Will the dry cleaner be able to remove the stains from this jacket?
Financial (monetary loss, unexpected costs)	• Will I lose money if I make the investment recommended by my stockbroker? • Could my identity be stolen if I make this purchase on the Internet? • Will I incur a lot of unanticipated expenses if I go on this vacation? • Will repairing my car cost more than the original estimate?
Temporal (wasting time, consequences of delays)	• Will I have to wait in line before entering the exhibition? • Will service at this restaurant be so slow that I will be late for my afternoon meeting? • Will the renovations to our bathroom be completed before our friends come to stay with us?
Physical (personal injury or damage to possessions)	• Will I get hurt if I go skiing at this resort? • Will the contents of this package get damaged in the mail? • Will I fall sick if I travel abroad on vacation?
Psychological (personal fears and emotions)	• How can I be sure that this aircraft will not crash? • Will the consultant make me feel stupid? • Will the doctor's diagnosis upset me?
Social (how others think and react)	• What will my friends think of me if they learned that I stayed at this cheap motel? • Will my relatives approve of the restaurant I have chosen for the family reunion dinner? • Will my business colleagues disapprove of my selection of an unknown law firm?
Sensory (unwanted effects on any of the five senses)	• Will I get a view of the parking lot rather than the beach from my restaurant table? • Will the hotel bed be uncomfortable? • Will I be kept awake by noise from the guests in the room next door? • Will my room smell of stale cigarette smoke? • Will the coffee at breakfast taste disgusting?

- Asking knowledgeable employees about competing services

Customers are risk averse and—everything else equal—will choose the service with the lower perceived risk. Therefore, firms need to proactively work on reducing customer risk perceptions. Suitable strategies vary according to the nature of the service and may include all or some of the following:

- Encourage prospective customers to preview the service through brochures, websites, and videos.
- Encourage prospective customers to visit the service facilities before purchase.
- Offer free trials that are suitable for services with high experience attributes. Many caterers and Chinese restaurants allow potential wedding customers to have a free food tasting before making a booking for their wedding banquet (Figure 2.10).
- Advertise. This provides consumers with an idea of what the service is, as well as its value. For services with high credence qualities and high customer involvement, advertising helps to communicate the benefits, usage, and how consumers can enjoy the tangible product. For example, Zurich, an insurance company, helps customers to understand what they do in a very interesting advertisement (Figure 2.11).

IEP WINS AUSTRALIAN BUSINESS AWARD FOR EXCELLENCE

International Exchange Programs (IEP) is thrilled to have been honoured with an Australian Business Award (ABA) in the category of Service Excellence.

The non-profit organisation specialises in sending young Australians on working holidays overseas while also helping working holiday makers from overseas settle in Australia. With a small team of young, well travelled professionals, IEP prides itself on providing personal and friendly assistance to enquirers and participants alike.

IEP's Australian Business Award application highlighted their efforts to stay on top of advancements in communication technology in order to reach their targeted customers, Generation Y.

The IEP team are trained to provide prompt, friendly and upfront responses to their customers' queries via traditional methods such as phone, email and face to face but increasingly via social networking sites such as Facebook and Twitter, mediums which insist on transparency and honesty.

With the staff at IEP being a part of Gen Y themselves, they are able to communicate on the same level as their customers with a true understanding of the concerns and questions their enquirers have.

IEP's Company Director Brad Holland is thrilled with the award but admits he never had any doubt about the high level of customer service his team provided.

"IEP regularly receives positive feedback from customers who are satisfied with the assistance and personal service we provide so it's fantastic to be recognised with this award," Mr Holland said, "Gen Y expect nothing less than prompt, straight forward and friendly assistance, they are used to having many choices and don't hesitate to spread the word if they are unsatisfied, this encourages us to interact with our customers in a way that suits their lifestyle-which is proving to be successful."

IEP works closely with their international partners around the world to assist working holiday makers with all facets of their travel planning from visas, travel insurance and flights through to helping them find a job, a place to live, set up bank accounts and tax-file numbers as well as providing ongoing assistance throughout their entire stay.

This year's award for Service Excellence is IEP's second Australian Business Award in three years, their first was an award for Innovation in 2006 recognising their Work Canada program.

About the Awards

Established in 2003, the Australian Business Awards is an independent organisation incorporated in Australia as a proprietary limited company. Specialising in Quality Management, the Australian Business Awards administer and coordinate The Australian Business Awards™ program. As a private sector initiative, the Australian Business Awards is not affiliated with any larger or controlling entity to avoid any potential conflict of interest and does not rely on the financial support of government or other organisations.

The Awards are a national, all-encompassing awards program honouring organisations that demonstrate the core values of business excellence, product excellence, sustainability and commercial success in their respective industries. Entries are judged on specific criteria underpinned by the program's values of success, innovation and

Figure 2.9 International Exchange Programs (IEP), a work and travel organisation in Australia, won the Australian Business Award for Excellence in 2009.

Figure 2.10 A hotel in New Jersey organizes an annual free food tasting for couples who have not booked the wedding reception.

Figure 2.11 Zurich shows customers what the company can do for them.

- Display credentials. Professionals such as doctors, architects, and lawyers often display their degrees and other certifications because they want customers to "see" that they are qualified to provide expert services (see Figure 2.12). Many professional firms' websites take great care to inform prospective clients of their services, highlight their expertise, and even showcase their past successes.
- Use *evidence management.* This involves an organized approach in the use of the appearance of furnishings, equipment, and facilities as well as employees' dress and behavior to project the firm's target image and value proposition.[3] For example, the bright and trendy décor at the hairdressing salon may have helped Susan Munro choose the salon on her first visit. Now, it probably contributes to her feelings of satisfaction in the end, even though her hairdresser kept her waiting for 20 minutes.
- Have visible safety procedures that build confidence and trust.
- Give customers access to online information about the status of an order or procedure. Many courier service providers use this (e.g., FedEx, DHL, and UPS).
- Offer service guarantees such as money-back guarantees and performance warranties.

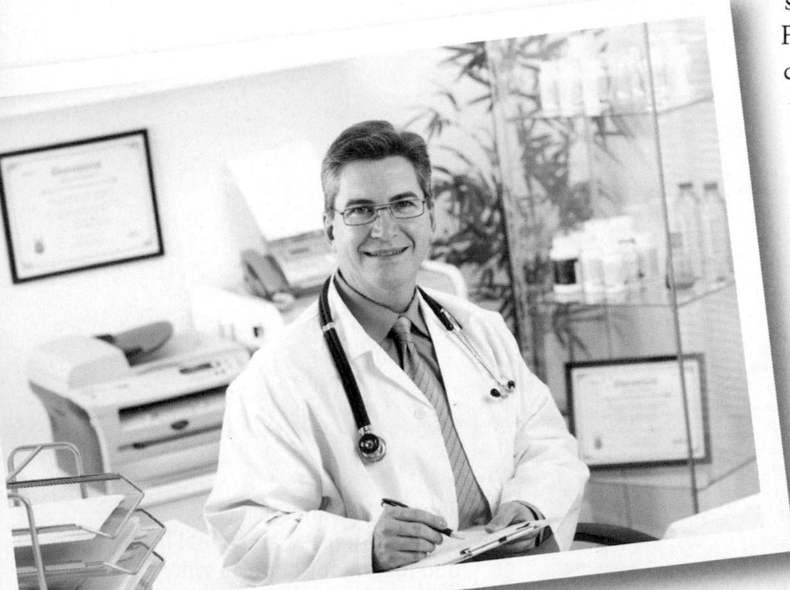

Figure 2.12 This doctor displays his accreditations to communicate his credentials.

When a company does a good job of managing potential customers' risk perceptions, uncertainty is reduced. This then increases the chance that it will be chosen as the customer's preferred service provider. Another important contributing factor to consumer choice (and later, satisfaction) is expectations, which we will discuss below.

Service Expectations

LO 5
Understand how customers form service expectations and the components of these expectations.

Customers assess attributes and risks related to a service offering. In the process, they develop expectations of how the service they have will perform. Expectations can be very firm if they are related to attributes that were important in the choice process. For example, if a customer paid a premium of $350 for an intercontinental direct flight, rather than one that has a stopover, to save four hours on a journey, then the customer will not take it lightly if there is a six-hour flight delay. A customer will also have high expectations if he paid a premium for high-quality service and will be deeply disappointed when the service fails to deliver (see Figure 2.13). We will discuss expectations again later on as part of the post-purchase satisfaction process. Here, we will focus on the formation and types of expectations.

Expectations are formed during the search and decision making processes, and they are heavily shaped by information searches and evaluations of alternatives. If you do not have any previous experience with a service, you may base your pre-purchase expectations on information obtained from word-of-mouth comments, news stories, or a firm's own marketing efforts. Expectations can even be situation-specific. For example, during a peak period, expectations of service delivery timing will be lower than during a nonpeak period. Expectations can change over time, too, as we discussed in the section on multi-attribute models. Firms try to shape consumers' expectations through advertising, pricing, new technologies, or service innovations. Increased access to information through the media and the Internet can also change expectations. For example, today's health care consumer is well informed and often wants to participate in decisions relating to medical treatment. Service Insights 2.1 describes a new assertiveness among parents of children with serious illnesses.

Figure 2.13 A frustrated customer waits for the late plane.

SERVICE INSIGHTS 2.1

Parents Seek Involvement in Medical Decisions Affecting Their Children

Many parents want to participate actively in decisions relating to their children's medical treatment. Thanks partly to in-depth media coverage of medical advances and health-related issues, as well as the educational efforts of consumer groups, parents today are better informed and more assertive than in previous generations. They are no longer willing to simply accept the recommendations of medical specialists. In particular, parents whose child is born with congenital defects or has developed a life-threatening illness are often willing to invest a lot of time and energy to learn everything they can about their child's condition. Some have even founded nonprofit organizations focused on a specific disease to bring together other families facing the same problems and to help raise money for research and treatment.

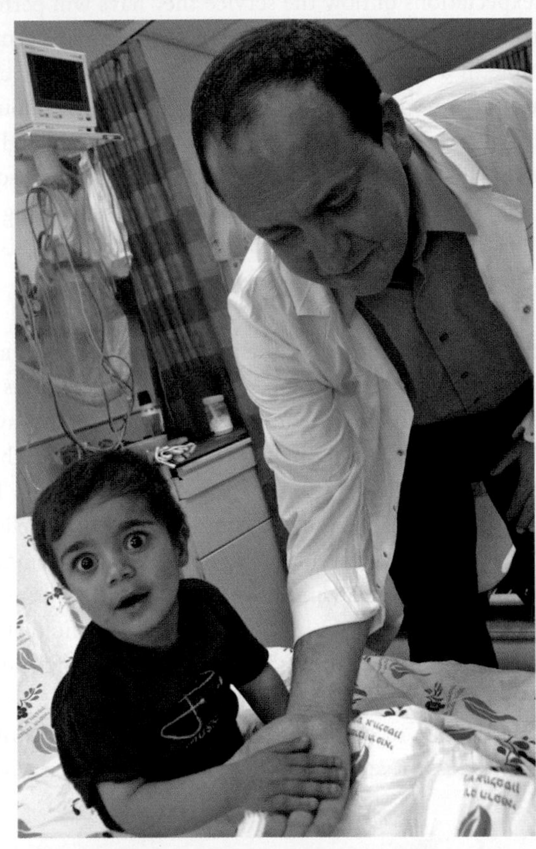

The Internet has made it much easier to access health-care information and research findings. A study by the Texas-based Heart Center of 160 parents who had children with cardiac problems found that 58% of these parents actively obtained information related to their child's diagnosis from the Internet. Four out of five users searching for cardiology-related information stated that locating the information was easy. Of those, half could name a favorite cardiology website. Almost all felt that the information was helpful in further understanding their child's condition. The study reported that six parents even created interactive personal websites specifically related to their child's congenital heart defect.[4]

Commenting on the phenomenon of highly informed parents, Norman J. Siegel, MD, former chair of pediatrics at Yale New Haven Children's Hospital, observed:

> It's a different practice today. The old days of "trust me, I'm going to take care of this" are completely gone. I see many patients who come in carrying a folder with printouts from the Internet and they want to know why Dr. So-and-So wrote this. They go to chat rooms, too. They want to know about the disease process, if it's chronic. Some parents are almost as well informed as a young medical student or house officer.

Dr. Siegel said he welcomed the trend and enjoyed the discussions but admitted that some physicians found it hard to adapt.

SOURCE

Christopher Lovelock and Jeff Gregory, "Yale New Haven Children's Hospital," New Haven, CT: Yale School of Management, 2003 (case).

What are the components of customer expectations? Expectations have several elements, including desired, adequate, and predicted service, and a zone of tolerance that falls between the desired and adequate service levels.[5] The model in Figure 2.14 shows the factors that influence the different levels of customer expectations. These factors are:

- **Desired service.** The type of service customers hope to receive is called desired service. It's a "wished for" level of service, which is a combination of what customers believe can and should be delivered based on personal needs. Desired service could also be influenced by explicit and implicit promises made by service providers, word-of-mouth, and past experience.[6] However, most customers are realistic. They recognize that a firm can't always deliver their desired level of service. Therefore, they also have a minimum level of expectations, called *adequate service*, as well as a predicted service level.
- **Adequate service.** The minimum level of service customers will accept without being dissatisfied.
- **Predicted service.** This is the level of service customers actually anticipate receiving. Predicted service can also be affected by service provider promises (Figure 2.15), word-of-mouth, and past experiences. The predicted service level directly affects how customers define "adequate service" on that occasion. If good service is predicted, the adequate level will be higher than if poorer service is predicted.

  Customer predictions of service are often situation-specific. From past experience, for example, customers visiting a museum on a summer day may expect to see larger crowds if the weather is poor than if the sun is shining. So, a 10-minute wait to buy tickets on a cool, rainy day in summer might not fall below their adequate service level. Another factor that may set this expectation is the service level anticipated from alternative service providers.

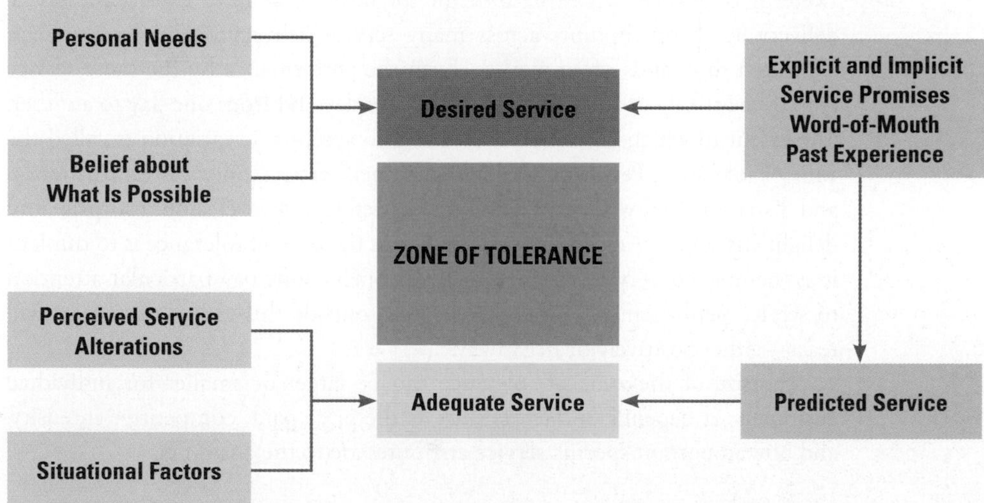

Figure 2.14 Factors influencing customer expectations of service.

SOURCE

Adapted from Valarie A. Zeithaml, Leonard A. Berry, and A. Parasuraman, "The Nature and Determinants of Customer Expectations of Service," *Journal of the Academy of Marketing Science*, 21, 1, 1993, 1–12.

Figure 2.15 This advertisement creates high expectations for Singapore Airlines Suites on its A380 Airbus aircraft.

- **Zone of tolerance.** It can be difficult for firms to achieve consistent service delivery at all touchpoints across many service delivery channels, branches, and often thousands of employees. Even the performance by the same service employee is likely to vary over the course of a day and from one day to another. The extent to which customers are willing to accept this variation is called the zone of tolerance. Performing below customers' expectations causes frustration and dissatisfaction, while exceeding the desired service level should surprise and delight customers. Another way of looking at the zone of tolerance is to think of it as the range of service within which customers don't pay particular attention to service performance.[7] When service falls outside this range, customers will react—either positively or negatively.

  The size of the zone of tolerance can be larger or smaller for individual customers. It depends on factors such as the price paid, competitive intensity, and how important specific service attributes are to the customer.

Each of these factors can influence the level of adequate service levels. By contrast, desired service levels tend to move up very slowly based on accumulated customer experiences. Consider a small business owner who needs some advice from her accountant. Her ideal level of professional service may be receiving a thoughtful response by the next day. However, if she makes her request at the time of year when all accountants are busy preparing corporate and individual tax returns, she will probably know from experience not to expect a fast reply. Although her ideal service level probably won't change, her zone of tolerance for response time may be broader because she has a lower adequate service level during busy times of the year.

The predicted service level is probably the most important level that affects a consumer's purchase decision, and we will discuss purchase decisions in the next section. Desired and adequate service levels and the zone of tolerance are more important in determining customer satisfaction, a topic we will cover when discussing the post-purchase stage.

Purchase Decision

In order to reach a purchase decision, consumers will evaluate possible alternatives. For example, they might compare the performance of important attributes of competing service offerings, assess the perceived risk associated with each offering, and develop their desired, adequate, and predicted service level expectations. After they have done these, they will be ready to select the option they like best.

Many purchase decisions for frequently purchased services are quite simple and can be made quickly without too much thought if the perceived risks are low, the alternatives are clear, and the service has been used before. In many instances, however, purchase decisions involve trade-offs and thus require further consideration. Price is often a key influencing factor. For example, is it worth paying more for a better seat in a theater performance (Figure 2.16)?

Figure 2.16 Consumers have to evaluate whether paying top dollar for better seats is worth the price.

For more complex decisions, trade-offs can involve multiple attributes, as we have seen previously based on the multi-attribute model. In choosing an airline, consumers will consider that convenience of schedules, reliability, seat comfort, attentiveness of the cabin crew, and availability and quality of meals may vary greatly among different carriers, even at the same fares.

Once a decision is made, the consumer is ready to move to the service encounter stage. This next step may take place immediately, like when deciding to enter a fast-food restaurant. At other times, it may first involve an advance reservation. This usually happens with taking a flight or attending a live theater performance.

SERVICE ENCOUNTER STAGE

After making a purchase decision, customers move on to the core of the service experience. The service encounter stage is when the customer interacts directly with the service firm. There are a number of models and frameworks that we use to better understand consumers' behavior and experience during the service encounter. First, the "moments of truth" metaphor shows the importance of effectively managing touchpoints. The second framework, the high-/low-contact service model, helps us to better understand the extent and nature of points of contact. The third concept, the servuction model, focuses on the various types of interactions that together create the customer's service experience. Finally, the theater metaphor, together with the script and role theories, communicates effectively how one can look at "staging" service performances to create the experience customers desire.

Service Encounters Are "Moments of Truth"

Richard Normann borrowed the "moment of truth" metaphor from bullfighting to show the importance of contact points with customers (Figure 2.17):

> [W]e could say that the perceived quality is realized at the moment of truth, when the service provider and the service customer confront one another in the arena. At that moment, they are very much on their own .... It is the skill, the motivation, and the tools employed by the firm's representative and the expectations and behavior of the client which together will create the service delivery process.[8]

In bullfighting, the life of either the bull or the matador (or possibly both) is at stake. The message in a service context is that at the "moment of truth", the relationship between the customer and the firm is at stake.

Figure 2.17 The service provider is the matador who skillfully manages the service encounter.

Jan Carlzon, a former chief executive of Scandinavian Airlines System (SAS), used the "moment of truth" metaphor as a reference point for transforming SAS from an operations-driven business into a customer-driven airline. Carlzon made the following comments about his airline:

> Last year, each of our 10 million customers came into contact with approximately five SAS employees, and this contact lasted an average of 15 seconds each time. Thus, SAS is "created" 50 million times a year, 15 seconds at a time. These 50 million "moments of truth" are the moments that ultimately determine whether SAS will succeed or fail as a company. They are the moments when we must prove to our customers that SAS is their best alternative.[9]

LO 6

Contrast how customers experience and evaluate high- versus low-contact services.

Each service business faces similar challenges in defining and managing the "moments of truth" its customers will encounter (Figure 2.18).

Figure 2.18 Discussing the house blueprints with the contractor is a moment of truth.

Service Encounters Range from High Contact to Low Contact

Services involve different levels of contact with the service operation. Some of these encounters can be very brief and may consist of a few steps, such as when a customer calls a customer contact center. Others may extend over a longer time frame and involve multiple interactions of varying degrees of complexity. For example, a visit to a theme park might last all day. In Figure 2.19, we group services into three levels of customer contact. These represent how much customers interact with service personnel, physical service elements, or both. Although we recognize that the level of customer contact covers a spectrum, it's useful to examine the differences between services at the high and low ends, respectively. For example, you'll notice that traditional retail banking, person-to-person phone banking, and Internet banking may deliver the same basic banking transactions such as funds transfer, but they are located in very different parts of the chart.

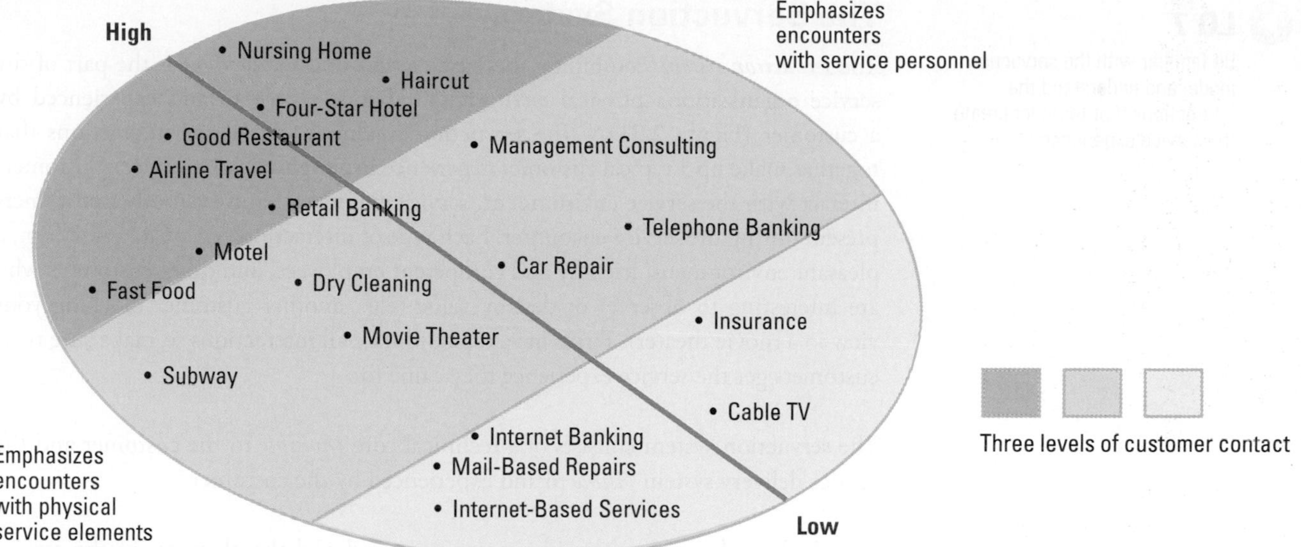

Figure 2.19 Levels of customer contact with service firms.

- **High-contact services.** Using a high-contact service means that there is a direct contact between customers and the firm throughout the service delivery. When customers visit the facility where service is delivered, they enter a service "factory." This is something that rarely happens in a manufacturing environment. When viewed this way, a motel is a lodging factory, a hospital is a health treatment factory, an airplane is a flying transportation factory, and a restaurant is a food service factory. Since each of these industries focuses on "processing" people rather than inanimate objects, the marketing challenge is to make the experience appealing to customers in terms of both the physical environment and their interactions with service personnel. During the service delivery process, customers usually are exposed to many physical clues about the firm. These include the exterior and interior of its buildings, equipment and furnishings, appearance and behavior of service personnel, and even other customers. Even the pace of service encounters can affect customer satisfaction.[10] For Susan Munro, the clues at the dry cleaners, such as the gloomy interior, the walls that needed repainting, all contributed to her experience of bad service.

- **Low-contact services.** At the opposite end of the spectrum, low-contact services involve little, if any, physical contact between customers and service providers. Instead, contact takes place at arm's length through electronic or physical distribution channels (see Figure 2.20). For example, customers conduct their insurance and banking transactions by mail, telephone, and the Internet. They may also buy a variety of information-based services online (e.g., buy songs from iTunes or download e-books to their Kindle) rather than from brick-and-mortar stores. In fact, many high and medium-contact services are changing into low-contact services as part of a fast-growing trend wherein convenience is increasingly important in affecting consumer choice.

Figure 2.20 Today's technology means that services can be conducted at arm's length through electronic or physical distribution channels.

LO 7

Be familiar with the servuction model and understand the interactions that together create the service experience.

The Servuction System

The *servuction system* (combining the terms *service* and *production*) is the part of the service organization's physical environment that is visible to and experienced by a customer (Figure 2.21).[11] The servuction system shows all the interactions that together make up a typical customer experience in a high-contact service. Customers interact with the service environment, service employees, and even other customers present during the service encounter. Each type of interaction can create value (e.g., a pleasant environment, friendly and competent employees, and other customers who are interesting to observe) or destroy value (e.g., another customer blocking your view in a movie theater). Firms have to coordinate all interactions to make sure their customers get the service experience they came for.

The servuction system consists of a technical core *invisible* to the customer and the service delivery system *visible* to and experienced by the customer.

- **Technical core**—where inputs are processed and the elements of the service product are created. The technical core is typically backstage and invisible to the customer (e.g., the kitchen in a restaurant). Like in the theater, the visible components can be termed "front-stage," or "front office," while the invisible components can be termed "backstage," or "back office".[13] What goes on backstage usually is not of interest to customers. However, if what goes on backstage affects the quality of front-stage activities, customers will notice. For example, if a kitchen reads orders wrongly, diners will be upset.
- **Service delivery system**—where the final "assembly" takes place and the product is delivered to the customer. This subsystem includes the visible part of the service operations system—buildings, equipment, and personnel—and possibly

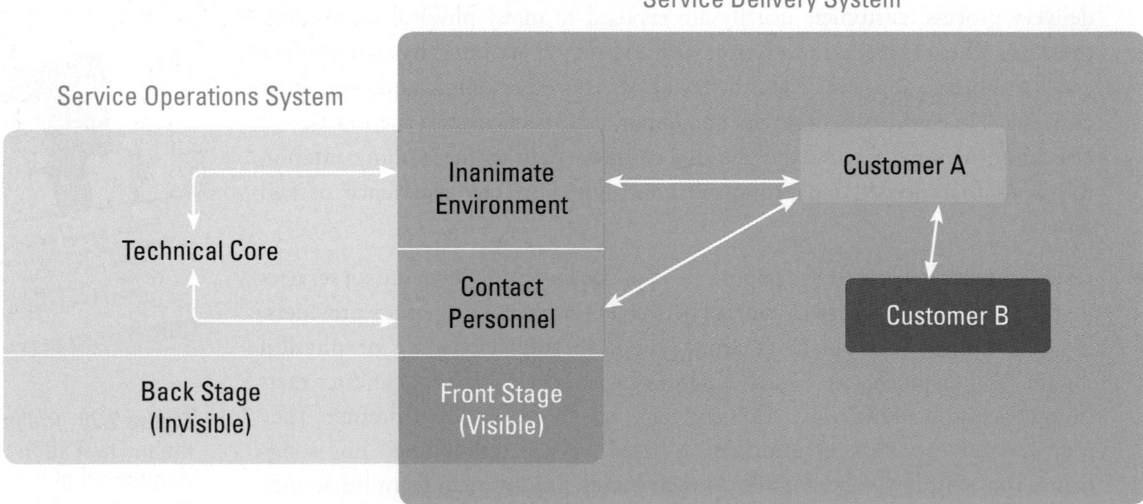

Figure 2.21 The servuction system.

SOURCE

Adapted and expanded from an original concept by Eric Langeard and Pierre Eiglier [12] other customers. Using the theater analogy, the visible front office is like a live theater where we stage the service experience for our customers.

The proportion of the overall service operation visible to customers depends on the level of customer contact. In high-contact services, the service operations tend to be substantial with many interactions—or moments of truth—that have to be managed. In contrast, low-contact services usually have most of the service operations system backstage with front-stage elements limited to mail and telecommunications contacts. Here, customers normally do not see the "factory" where the work is performed, making the design and management of such facilities much easier (Figure 2.22).

Figure 2.22 Back office operations are typically not seen by the customer.

Theater as a Metaphor for Service Delivery: an Integrative Perspective

LO 8

Obtain insights from viewing the service encounter as a form of theater.

The theater is an apt metaphor for understanding the creation of service experiences through the servuction system. This is because service delivery consists of a series of events that customers experience as a *performance*[14] (see Figure 2.23). This metaphor is a particularly useful approach for high-contact services such as hotels, hospitals, and entertainment. Let us discuss the stage (i.e., service facilities) and the members of the cast (i.e., frontline personnel):

- **Service facilities.** Imagine service facilities as containing the *stage* on which the drama unfolds. Sometimes, the setting changes from one act to another (e.g., when airline passengers move from the entrance to the terminal to the check-in counters and then on to the boarding gate, and finally inside the aircraft). Some stages have very few "props," like a taxi for instance. In contrast, other stages have more elaborate "props," such as resort hotels that have elaborate architecture, interior design, and landscaping.
- **Personnel.** The front-stage personnel are like the members of a cast, playing roles as *actors* in a drama, and supported by a backstage production team. In some instances, service personnel are expected to wear special costumes when on stage (such as the fanciful uniforms often worn by hotel doormen, or the more basic brown ones worn by UPS drivers) (Figure 2.24).

Figure 2.23 When service facilities and personnel are all in place, the stage is set for a memorable service performance for the customer.

The theater metaphor also includes the roles of the players on stage and the scripts they have to follow, which we will discuss next.

LO 9

Know how role and script theories contribute to a better understanding of service encounters.

The actors in a theater need to know what roles they are playing and need to be familiar with the script. Similarly, in service encounters, knowledge of role and script theories can help organizations to better understand, design, and manage both employee and customer behaviors during service encounters.

- **Role theory.** Stephen Grove and Ray Fisk define a role as "a set of behavior patterns learned through experience and communication, to be performed by an individual in a certain social interaction in order to attain maximum effectiveness in goal accomplishment."[15] Roles have also been defined as expectations of the society that guide behavior in a specific setting or context.[16] In service encounters, employees and customers each have roles to play. If either party is uncomfortable in the role or if they do not act according to their roles, it will affect the satisfaction and productivity of both parties.
- **Script theory.** Like a movie script, a service script specifies the sequences of behaviors that employees and customers are expected to learn and follow during service delivery. Employees receive formal training in the service script. Customers learn scripts through experience, communication with others, and designed communications and education.[17] The more experience a customer has with a service company, the more familiar that particular script becomes. A customer's unwillingness to learn a new script may be a reason not to switch to a competing organization. Any deviation from this known script may frustrate both customers and employees, and can lead to dissatisfaction. If a company decides to change a service script (e.g., by using technology to transform a high-contact service into a low-contact one), service personnel and customers need to be educated about the new approach and the benefits it provides.

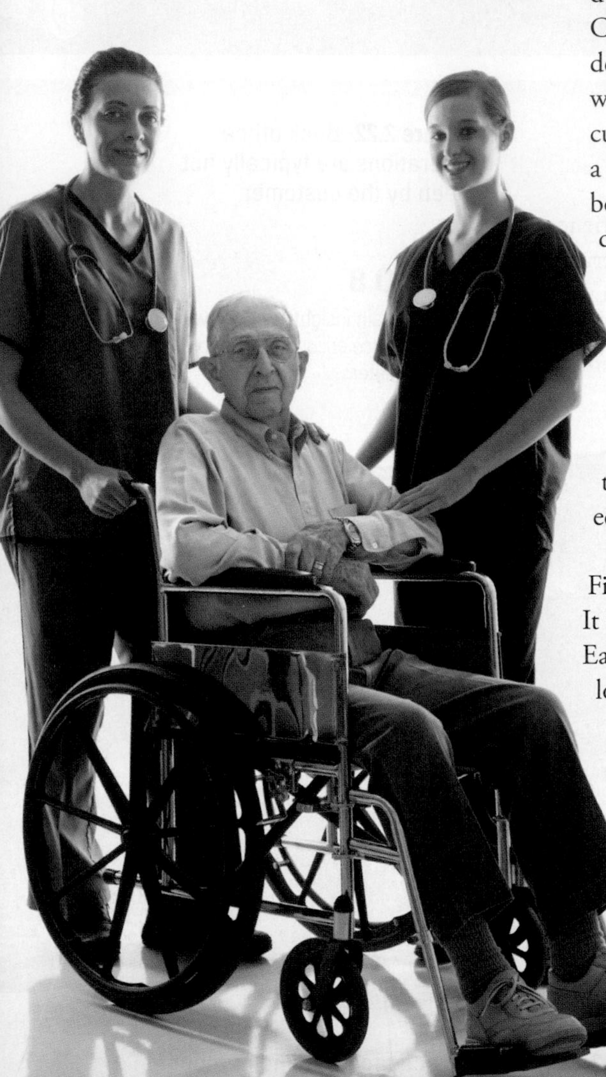

Figure 2.24 Health-care providers are easily recognizable in their nursing gowns.

Many service dramas are tightly scripted (like flight attendants' scripts for economy class). This reduces variability and ensures uniform quality. However, not all services involve tightly scripted performances. Scripts tend to be more flexible for providers of highly customized services—designers, educators, consultants—and may vary by situation and by customer.

Figure 2.25 shows a script for teeth cleaning and a simple dental examination. It involves three players—the patient, the receptionist, and the dental hygienist. Each has a specific role to play. The role of the customer (who is probably not looking forward to this encounter) is different from that of the two service providers. The receptionist's role differs from the hygienist's, as their jobs are different. This script is driven partly by the need to run an efficient dental office. More importantly, there is a need to perform a technical task proficiently and safely (note the mask and gloves). The core service of examining and cleaning teeth can only be accomplished satisfactorily if the patient cooperates in the delivery of the service.

Role theory and script theory complement each other in how we can understand both consumer and employee behavior during a service encounter. For example, think of professor and student *roles* in the classes that you've attended. What is the role of the professor? Typically, it's to deliver a well-structured lecture, focusing on the key topics assigned for that day, making them interesting, and engaging the students in discussion. What are the roles of a student? Basically, there are to come to class prepared and on time, listen attentively, participate in discussions, and not disrupt the class. In contrast, the opening portion of the *script* for a lecture describes specific actions to be taken by each party. For instance, students should arrive at the lecture hall before the class starts,

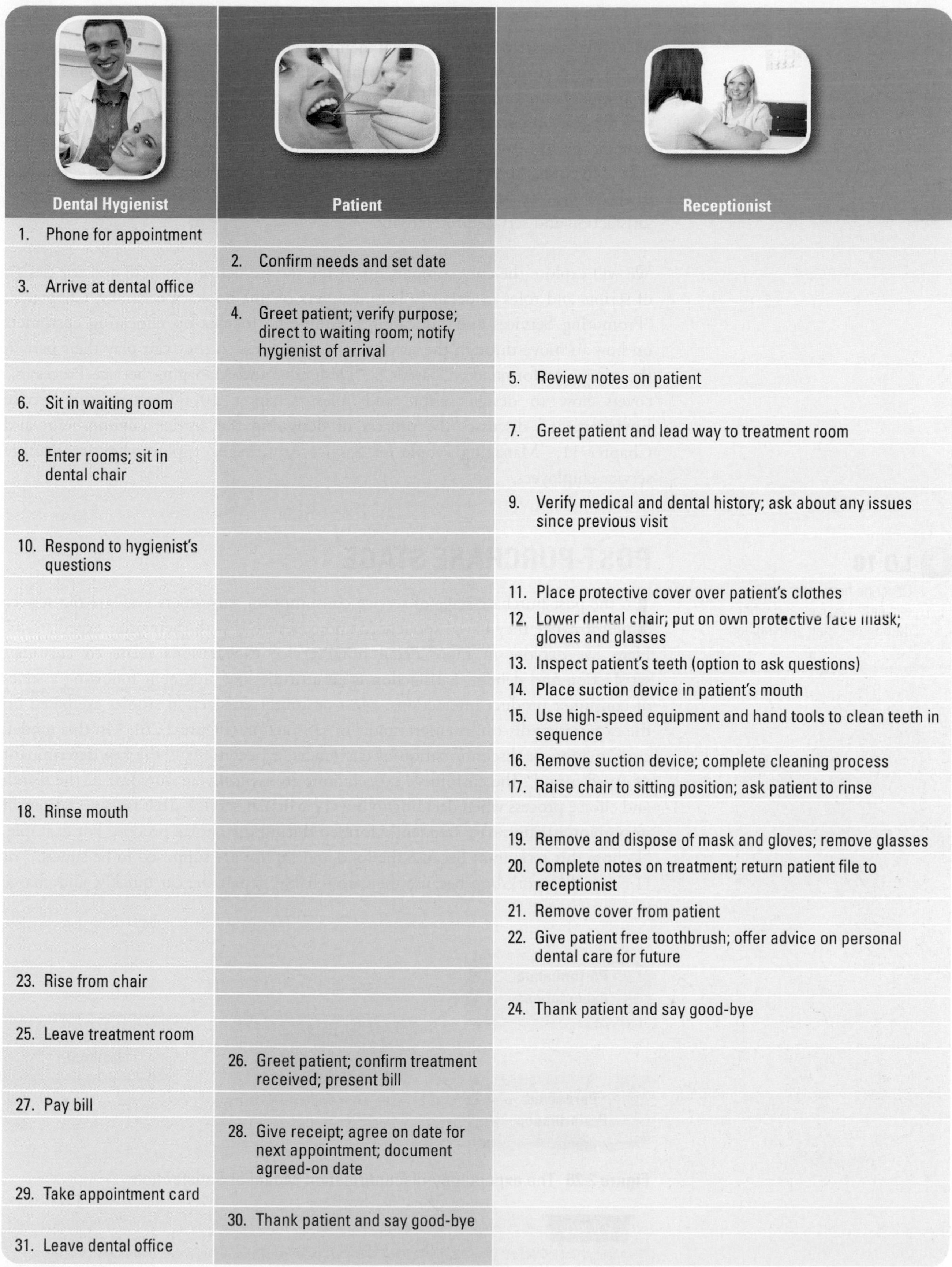

Dental Hygienist	Patient	Receptionist
1. Phone for appointment		
	2. Confirm needs and set date	
3. Arrive at dental office		
	4. Greet patient; verify purpose; direct to waiting room; notify hygienist of arrival	
		5. Review notes on patient
6. Sit in waiting room		
		7. Greet patient and lead way to treatment room
8. Enter rooms; sit in dental chair		
		9. Verify medical and dental history; ask about any issues since previous visit
10. Respond to hygienist's questions		
		11. Place protective cover over patient's clothes
		12. Lower dental chair; put on own protective face mask; gloves and glasses
		13. Inspect patient's teeth (option to ask questions)
		14. Place suction device in patient's mouth
		15. Use high-speed equipment and hand tools to clean teeth in sequence
		16. Remove suction device; complete cleaning process
		17. Raise chair to sitting position; ask patient to rinse
18. Rinse mouth		
		19. Remove and dispose of mask and gloves; remove glasses
		20. Complete notes on treatment; return patient file to receptionist
		21. Remove cover from patient
		22. Give patient free toothbrush; offer advice on personal dental care for future
23. Rise from chair		
		24. Thank patient and say good-bye
25. Leave treatment room		
	26. Greet patient; confirm treatment received; present bill	
27. Pay bill		
	28. Give receipt; agree on date for next appointment; document agreed-on date	
29. Take appointment card		
	30. Thank patient and say good-bye	
31. Leave dental office		

Figure 2.25 Script for teeth cleaning and simple dental examination.

select their seats, sit down, and open their notebooks. The professor enters, puts notes on the table, turns on the notebook and LCD projector, greets the class, makes any preliminary announcements that are needed, and starts the class on time. As you can see, the role and script theories describe behavior during the encounter from two different perspectives. Excellent service marketers understand both perspectives and take active steps to define, communicate, and train their employees and customers in their roles and service script to achieve a performance that yields high customer satisfaction and service productivity.

We will explore the core components of the service delivery system and the design of scripts and roles in detail in later chapters of this book. Specifically, Chapter 7, "Promoting Services and Educating Customers," focuses on educating customers on how to move through the service delivery process so they can play their part in the service performance; Chapter 8, "Designing and Managing Service Processes," covers how to design scripts and roles; Chapter 10, "Crafting the Service Environment," discusses the process of designing the service environment; and Chapter 11, "Managing People for Service Advantage," explores how to manage service employees.

LO 10

Describe how customers evaluate services and what determines their satisfaction.

POST-PURCHASE STAGE

In the post-purchase stage of service consumption, customers evaluate the service performance they have experienced and compare it with their prior expectations. Here, we explore in more detail how service expectations relate to customer satisfaction and delight. Satisfaction is an attitude-like judgment following a series of consumer product interactions. Most customer satisfaction studies are based on the expectancy-disconfirmation model of satisfaction (Figure 2.26).[18] In this model, confirmation or disconfirmation of customers' expectations is the key determinant of satisfaction.[19] The customer's expectations are typically an outcome of the search and choice process when deciding to buy a particular service. That is, expectations of important attributes are frequently formed during the choice process. For example, "I chose this restaurant because the food and service are supposed to be superb," or "I chose this workshop because they are reliable, repair the car quickly, and charge

Figure 2.26 The expectancy-disconfirmation Model of Satisfaction.

SOURCE

Adapted from Richard L. Oliver, *Satisfaction: A Behavioral Perspective on the Consumer*, 1997, New York: McGraw-Hill, p. 110.

a reasonable price." During and after consumption, consumers experience the service performance and compare it to their expectations. Satisfaction judgments are then formed based on this comparison. If performance perceptions are worse than expected, it is called *negative disconfirmation*. Susan Munro's expectations were negatively disconfirmed when her suit was not ready for pickup at the dry cleaner, leading to her dissatisfaction and her intention to give another dry cleaner a try in the future. If the performance is perceived to be better than expected, it is called *positive disconfirmation*, and if it is as expected, then it is simply called *confirmation* of expectations.

Customers will be reasonably satisfied as long as the perceived performance falls within the zone of tolerance, that is, above the adequate service level. As performance perceptions approach or exceed desired levels, customers will be very pleased. These customers are more likely to make repeat purchases, remain loyal to that supplier, and spread positive word-of-mouth.[20] However, if the service experience does not meet their expectations, customers may complain about poor service quality, suffer in silence, or switch providers in the future.[21] In highly competitive service markets, customers may expect service providers to even anticipate their unexpressed needs and deliver on them.[22]

The disconfirmation-of-expectations model works very well for search and experience attributes (e.g., "I know whether you kept your promise and delivered by 1 p.m."), but less so for credence attributes. Here, customers cannot assess these attributes directly, and rely on tangible cues (e.g., eye contact and clear explanations of a surgeon) and expectations (e.g., "I expected to receive the best surgery money can buy") to form their satisfaction. If no tangible evidence contradicts their expectations, customers tend to evaluate credence attributes as meeting expectations and will be satisfied.

Customer delight is a function of three components: (1) unexpectedly high levels of performance, (2) arousal (e.g., surprise, excitement), and (3) positive affect (e.g., pleasure, joy, or happiness).[23] A few innovative and customer-centric firms seem to delight customers even in seemingly mundane fields like insurance (see Service Insights 2.2). One thing to note, though, is that once customers have been delighted, their expectations are raised. They may be dissatisfied if service levels return to the previous levels, and it probably will take more effort to "delight" them in future.[24]

SERVICE INSIGHTS 2.2

Progressive Insurance Delights Its Customers

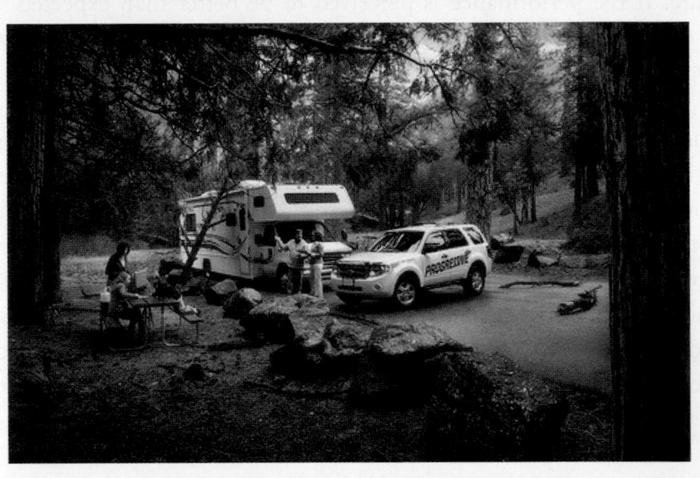

Progressive Insurance Corp. prides itself on providing extraordinary customer service—and its accomplishments in the area of claims processing are particularly impressive. To lower its costs and simultaneously improve customer satisfaction and retention, the company introduced its Immediate Response service, offering customers 24/7 access to claims handling. Adjusters work out of mobile claims vans rather than offices, and Progressive has a target of nine hours for an adjuster to inspect a damaged vehicle. In many instances, claims representatives actually arrive at the scene of an accident while the evidence is still fresh.

Consider the following scenario. The crash site in Tampa, Florida, is chaotic and tense. Two cars are damaged and, although the passengers aren't bleeding, they are shaken up and scared. Lance Edgy, a senior claim representative for Progressive, arrives on the scene just minutes after the collision. He calms the victims and advises them on medical care, repair shops, police reports, and legal procedures. Edgy invites William McAllister, Progressive's policyholder, into an air-conditioned van equipped with comfortable chairs, a desk, and two cell phones. Even before the tow trucks have cleared away the wreckage, Edgy is able to offer his client a settlement for the market value of his totaled Mercury. McAllister, who did not appear to have been at fault in this accident, later stated in amazement: "This is great—someone coming right out here and taking charge. I didn't expect it at all."

The shortened time cycle has advantages for Progressive, too. Costs are reduced, there's less likelihood that lawyers will become involved when settlement offers are made promptly, and it's easier to prevent fraud.

Still, Progressive continues to find new ways to delight its customers. Its website, www.progressive.com, has been consistently be rated as the top overall among Internet-based insurance carriers by Gómez.com (an Internet quality-measurement firm), which places a priority on a site's educational, purchasing, and servicing capabilities. Progressive has also been cited for pleasantly surprising its customers with consumer-friendly innovations and extraordinary customer service.

SOURCE

R. Henkoff, "Service is Everybody's Business," *Fortune*, June 27 1994, p. 50; M. Hammer, "Deep Change: How Operational Innovation can Transform Your Company," *Harvard Business Review*, 82 (April 2004), 84–95; www.progressive.com, accessed March 12, 2012.

CHAPTER SUMMARY

LO 1 ▶ Service consumption can be divided into the following three stages: (1) pre-purchase stage, (2) service encounter stage, and (3) post-purchase stage.

- The *pre-purchase stage* consists of the following four steps: (1) need awareness, (2) information search, (3) evaluation of alternative services, and (4) purchase decision. The following theories help us to better understand consumer behavior in this stage.

LO 2 ▶

- Recognizing a need motivates customers to search for solutions to satisfy that need. Several alternatives may come to mind, and these form the evoked set, which is further narrowed down to a few alternatives to seriously consider, that is, the consideration set.
- During the search process, consumers also learn about service attributes they should consider and form expectations of how firms in the consideration set perform on those attributes.
- *Multi-attribute model.* Many decisions involve complex trade-offs between several attributes. The multi-attribute model simulates this decision making by combining customers' attribute performance expectations of each firm in the consideration set and the importance weights of each attribute.
- Two common consumer decision rules in the multi-attribute model are the linear compensatory rule and the conjunctive rule. Given the same attribute ratings, consumers can arrive at different decisions when different decision rules are applied.
- Firms should actively manage key variables in the multi-attribute model to increase the chances of their service being the one chosen. This includes ensuring that the firm's services are in the consideration set and shaping their target customers' attribute performance perceptions, attribute weights, and even decision rules toward the firm's strengths.

LO 3 ▶

- *Service attributes.* People often have difficulty in evaluating services because services tend to have a low proportion of search attributes and a high proportion of experience and credence attributes that make it difficult for consumers to evaluate services before purchase. Tangible cues become important, and firms need to manage them carefully to shape customers' expectations and perceptions of experience and credence attributes.

LO 4 ▶

- *Perceived risk.* Because many services are hard to evaluate, consumers perceive higher risk when buying services. As customers do not like to take risks, successful firms employ risk reduction strategies such as offering free trials and guarantees.

LO 5 ▶

- *Service expectations.* These are shaped by the information search and evaluation of service attributes. The components of expectations include desired, adequate, and predicted service levels. Between the desired and adequate service levels is the zone of tolerance, within which customers are willing to accept variation in service levels.
- *Purchase decision.* The outcome of the pre-purchase stage is a purchase decision based largely on expectations of the likely performance of a service on important attributes and associated risk perceptions.
- In the *service encounter stage*, the customer initiates, experiences, and consumes the service. A number of concepts and models help us to better understand customer behavior in this stage.
- The *moment-of-truth metaphor* refers to customer touchpoints that can make or break a customer relationship.

LO 6 ▶

- We distinguish between *high-* and *low-contact services.* High-contact services are challenging as they have many points of contact and "moments of truth" that have to be managed. In contrast, low-contact services are mostly delivered via websites, equipment (e.g., ATMs), or call centers with relatively few customer interfaces.

LO 7 ▶

- The *servuction model* encompasses a technical core and a service delivery system.
- The *technical core* is backstage and *invisible* to the customers, but what happens backstage can affect the quality of front-stage activities. Therefore, backstage activities have to be coordinated with front-stage activities.
- The *service delivery system* is front-stage and visible to the customer. It includes all the interactions that together create the service experience. In a high-contact service, it includes customer interactions with the service environment, service employees, and with other customers. Each type of interaction can create or destroy value. Firms have to manage all these interactions to create a satisfying service experience.

LO 8 ▶

- Theater can be used as a metaphor for service delivery, and firms can view their service as "staging" a performance with props and actors, and manage them accordingly. The props are the service facilities and equipment. The actors are the service employees and customers.

LO 9 ▶

- Each of the actors needs to understand their roles and scripts in order to perform their parts of the service well. Firms can make use of the *role* and *script theories* to better design, train, communicate, and manage both employee and customer behaviors.

LO 10 ▶ In the *post-purchase stage*, customers evaluate the service performance and compare it with their prior expectations.

- The *expectancy-disconfirmation model of satisfaction* holds that satisfaction judgments are formed based on a comparison of expectations with performance perceptions. Customers will be reasonably satisfied as long as perceived performance falls within the zone of tolerance, that is, above the adequate service level. Performance below the adequate service level will result in dissatisfaction. Customers will be delighted at unexpectedly high levels of performance.

UNLOCK YOUR LEARNING

These keywords are found within the sections of each Learning Objective (LO). They are integral to understanding the services marketing concepts taught in each section. Having a firm grasp of these keywords and how they are used is essential to helping you do well on your course, and in the real and very competitive marketing scene out there.

LO 1
1 Consideration set
2 Evaluation of alternatives
3 Evoked set
4 Information search
5 Need arousal
6 Need awareness
7 Post-purchase
8 Pre-purchase
9 Purchase decision
10 Service consumption
11 Service encounter

LO 2
12 Conjunctive rule
13 Linear compensatory rule
14 Multi-attribute Model

LO 3
15 Credence attributes
16 Experience attributes
17 Search attributes

LO 4
18 Evidence management
19 Financial risk
20 Functional risk
21 Perceived risk
22 Physical risk
23 Psychological risk
24 Sensory risk
25 Social risk
26 Temporal risk

LO 5
27 "Moments of Truth"
28 Adequate service
29 Desired service
30 Predicted service
31 Purchase decision
32 Service encounters
33 Service expectations
34 Zone of tolerance

LO 6
35 High-contact services
36 Low-contact services

LO 7
37 Backstage
38 Front-stage
39 Service delivery system
40 Servuction system
41 Technical core

LO 8
42 Performance
43 Personnel
44 Service facilities
45 Theater as a metaphor

LO 9
46 Role theory
47 Script theory

LO 10
48 Confirmation
49 Delight
50 Expectancy-disconfirmation model of satisfaction
51 Negative disconfirmation
52 Positive disconfirmation
53 Satisfaction

How well do you know the language of services marketing? Quiz yourself!

Not for the academically faint-of-heart

For each keyword you are able to recall without referring to earlier pages, give yourself a point (and a pat on the back). Tally your score at the end and see if you earned the right to be called—a *services marketeer.*

SCORE

0 – 10	Services Marketing is done a great disservice.
11 – 20	The midnight oil needs to be lit, pronto.
21 – 30	I know what you *didn't* do all semester.
31 – 40	A close shave with success.
41 – 50	Now, go forth and market.
51 – 53	There should be a marketing concept named after you.

KNOW YOUR ESM

Review Questions

1. Explain the three-stage model of service consumption.
2. How can customer choice between services in their consideration set be modeled?
3. What is the difference between the linear compensatory rule and the conjunctive rule?
4. Describe search, experience, and credence attributes, and give examples of each.
5. Explain why services tend to be harder for customers to evaluate than goods.
6. Why do consumers' perceptions of risk play an important role in choosing between alternative service offers? How can firms reduce consumer risk perceptions?
7. How are customers' expectations formed? Explain the difference between desired service and adequate service with reference to a service experience you've had recently.
8. What are "moments of truth"?
9. Describe the difference between high-contact and low-contact services, and explain how the nature of a customer's experience may differ between the two.
10. Choose a service you are familiar with, and create a diagram that represents the servuction system. Define "front-stage" and "backstage" activities.
11. How do the concepts of the theater, role theory, and script theory help to provide insights into consumer behavior during the service encounter?
12. Describe the relationship between customer expectations and customer satisfaction.

WORK YOUR ESM

Application Exercises

1. Construct a multi-attribute model to compare three different restaurants for an important celebration in your family. Apply the two different decision rules and determine the choices that arise from that.
2. Select three services: one high in search attributes, one high in experience attributes, and one high in credence attributes. Specify what product characteristics make them easy or difficult for consumers to evaluate, and suggest specific strategies that marketers can adopt in each case to facilitate evaluation and reduce perceived risk.
3. Develop a simple questionnaire designed to measure the key components of customer expectations (i.e., desired, adequate, and predicted services and the zone of tolerance). Conduct 10 interviews with key target customers of a service of your choice to understand the structure of their expectations. Based on your findings, develop recommendations for firms offering this service.
4. What are the backstage elements of (a) a car repair facility, (b) an airline, (c) a university, and (d) a consulting firm? Under what circumstances would it be appropriate or even desirable to allow customers to see some of these backstage elements, and how would you do it?
5. What roles are played by front-stage service employees in low-contact organizations? Are these roles more or less important to customer satisfaction than in high-contact services?
6. Visit the facilities of two competing service firms in the same industry (e.g., banks, restaurants, or gas stations) that you believe have different approaches to service. Compare and contrast their approaches using suitable frameworks from this chapter.
7. Apply the script and role theories to a service of your choice. What insights can you gain that would be useful for management?
8. Describe a low-contact service encounter each via e-mail and via phone, and a high-contact, face-to-face encounter that you have had recently. How satisfied were you with each of the encounters? What were the key drivers of your overall satisfaction with these encounters? In each instance, what could the service provider have done to improve the service?
9. Describe an unsatisfactory encounter you experienced recently with (a) a low-contact service provider via e-mail, mail, or phone and (b) a high-contact, face-to-face service provider. What were the key drivers of your dissatisfaction with these encounters? In each instance, what could the service provider have done to improve the service?

ENDNOTES

1 Information search behavior is influenced by a variety of factors. For more information on information search behavior, see Linda Osti, Lindsay W. Turner, and Brian King, "Cultural Differences in Travel Guidebooks Information Search," *Journal of Vacation Marketing* 15, no. 1 (January 2009): 63–78; Cazilia Loibl, Soo Hyun Cho, Florian Diekmann, and Marvin T. Batte, "Consumer Self-Confidence in Searching for Information," *The Journal of Consumer Affairs* 3, no. 1 (Spring 2009): 26–55; Robin S. Poston, Katie J. Suda and Colin Onita, "Information Sources Consulted and Found Useful in Answering Drug-Related Questions," *e-Service Journal* 6, no. 3 (Winter 2009): 3–73.

2 Valarie A. Zeithaml, "How Consumer Evaluation Processes Differ between Goods and Services," in J. A. Donnelly and W. R. George, eds. *Marketing of Services* (Chicago: American Marketing Association, 1981, 186–190).

3 Leonard L. Berry and Neeli Bendapudi, "Clueing in Customers," *Harvard Business Review* 81, (February 2003): 100–107.

4 C. M. Ikemba *et al.*, "Internet Use in Families with Children Requiring Cardiac Surgery for Congenital Heart Disease," *Pediatrics* 109, no. 3 (2002): 419–422.

5 Valarie A. Zeithaml, Leonard L. Berry, and A. Parasuraman, "The Behavioral Consequences of Service Quality," *Journal of Marketing* 60, (April 1996): 31–46; R. Kenneth Teas and Thomas E. DeCarlo, "An Examination and Extension of the Zone-of-Tolerance Model: Comparison of Performance-Based Models on Perceived Quality," *Journal of Service Research* 6, no. 3 (2004): 272–286.

6 Cathy Johnson and Brian P. Mathews, "The Influence of Experience on Service Expectations," *International Journal of Service Industry Management* 8, no. 4 (1997): 46–61.

7 Robert Johnston, "The Zone of Tolerance: Exploring the Relationship between Service Transactions and Satisfaction with the Overall Service," *International Journal of Service Industry Management* 6, no. 5 (1995): 46–61.

8 Normann first used the term "moments of truth" in a Swedish study in 1978. Subsequently, it appeared in English in Richard Normann, *Service Management: Strategy and Leadership in Service Businesses*, 2nd ed. Chichester, UK: John Wiley & Sons, 1991, 16–17.

9 Jan Carlzon, *Moments of Truth*, Cambridge, MA: Ballinger Publishing Co., 1987, 3.

10 Breffni M. Noone, Sheryl E. Kimes, Anna S. Mattila, and Jochen Wirtz, "Perceived Service Encounter Pace and Customer Satisfaction," *Journal of Service Management* 20, no. 4 (2009): 380–403.

11 Pierre Eiglier and Eric Langeard, "Services as Systems: Marketing Implications," in Pierre Eiglier, Eric Langeard, Christopher H. Lovelock, John E. G. Bateson, and Robert F. Young, eds. *Marketing Consumer Services: New Insights.* (Cambridge, MA: Marketing Science Institute), Report # 77-115, November 1977, 83–103; Eric Langeard, John E. Bateson, Christopher H. Lovelock, and Pierre Eiglier, *Services Marketing: New Insights from Consumers and Managers*, Marketing Science Institute, Report # 81-104, August 1981.

12 Adapted from Pierre Eiglier and Eric Langeard, "Services as Systems: Marketing Implications," in Pierre Eiglier, Eric Langeard, Christopher H. Lovelock, John E. G. Bateson, and Robert F. Young, eds. *Marketing Consumer Services: New Insights.* (Cambridge, MA: Marketing Science Institute), Report # 77-115, November 1977, 83–103; Eric Langeard, John E. Bateson, Christopher H. Lovelock, and Pierre Eiglier, *Services Marketing: New Insights from Consumers and Managers*, Marketing Science Institute, Report # 81-104, August 1981.

13 Richard B. Chase, "Where Does the Customer Fit in a Service Organization?" *Harvard Business Review*, 56, (November–December 1978): 137–142. Stephen J. Grove, Raymond P. Fisk, and Joby John, "Services as Theater: Guidelines and Implications," in Teresa A. Schwartz and Dawn Iacobucci, eds. *Handbook of Services Marketing and Management* (Thousand Oaks, CA: Sage, 2000, 21–36).

14 Stephen J. Grove, Raymond P. Fisk, and Joby John, "Services as Theater: Guidelines and Implications," in Teresa A. Schwartz and Dawn Iacobucci, eds. *Handbook of Services Marketing and Management* (Thousand Oaks, CA: Sage, 2000, 21–36); Steve Baron, Kim Harris, and Richard Harris, "Retail Theater: the 'Intended Effect' of the Performance," *Journal of Service Research* 4, (May 2003): 316–332; Richard Harris, Kim Harris, and Steve Baron, "Theatrical Service Experiences: Dramatic Script Development with Employees," *International Journal of Service Industry Management* 14, no. 2 (2003): 184–199.

15 Stephen J. Grove and Raymond P. Fisk, "The Dramaturgy of Services Exchange: an Analytical Framework for Services Marketing," in L. L. Berry, G. L. Shostack, and G. D. Upah, eds. *Emerging Perspectives on Services Marketing* (Chicago, IL: The American Marketing Association, 1983, 45–49).

16 Michael R. Solomon, Carol Suprenant, John A. Czepiel, and Evelyn G. Gutman, "A Role Theory Perspective on Dyadic Interactions: the Service Encounter," *Journal of Marketing* 49, (Winter 1985): 99–111.

17 See R. P. Abelson, "Script Processing in Attitude Formation and Decision-Making," in J. S. Carrol and J. W. Payne, eds. *Cognitive and Social Behavior* (Hillsdale, NJ: Erlbaum, 1976, 33–45); Richard Harris, Kim Harris, and Steve Baron, "Theatrical Service Experiences: Dramatic Script Development with Employees," *International Journal of Service Industry Management* 14, no. 2 (2003): 184–199; John Bateson, "Consumer Performance and Quality in Services," *Managing Service Quality* 12, no. 4 (2003): 206–209.

18 Richard L. Oliver, "A Cognitive Model of the Antecedents and Consequences of Satisfaction Decisions," *Journal of Marketing Research* 17 (November 1980), 460–469; Richard L. Oliver and John E. Swan, "Consumer Perceptions of Interpersonal Equity and Satisfaction in Transactions: a Field Survey Approach," *Journal of Marketing* 53 (April 1989): 21–35; Eugene W. Anderson and Mary W. Sullivan, "The Antecedents and Consequences of Customer Satisfaction for Firms," *Marketing Science* 12, (Spring, 1993): 125–143.

19 Richard L. Oliver, "A Cognitive Model of the Antecedents and Consequences of Satisfaction Decisions," *Journal of Marketing Research* 17 (November 1980): 460–469; Richard L. Oliver, "Customer Satisfaction with Service," in Teresa A. Schwartz and Dawn Iacobucci, *Handbook of Service Marketing and Management* (Thousand Oaks, CA: Sage Publications, 2000, 247–254); Jochen Wirtz and Anna S. Mattila, "Exploring the Role of Alternative Perceived Performance Measures and Needs-Congruency in the Consumer Satisfaction Process," *Journal of Consumer Psychology* 11, no. 3 (2001): 181–192.

20 Gour C. Saha and Theingi, "Service Quality, Satisfaction and Behavioral Intentions," *Managing Service Quality* 19, no.3 (2009): 350–372; Jochen Wirtz and Patricia Chew, "The Effects of Incentives, Deal Proneness, Satisfaction and Tie Strength on Word-of-Mouth Behavior," *International Journal of Service Industry Management* 13, no, 2 (2002): 141–162; Chiung-Ju Liang, Wen-Hung Wang and Jillian Dawes Farquhar, "The Influence of Customer Perceptions on Financial Performance in Financial Services," *International Journal of Bank Marketing* 27, no. 2 (2009): 129–149.

21 Jaishankar Ganesh, Mark J. Arnold, and Kristy E. Reynolds, "Understanding the Customer Base of Service Providers: an Examination of the Differences between Switchers and Slayers," *Journal of Marketing* 64, no. 3 (2000): 65–87.

22 Uday Karmarkar, "Will You Survive the Service Revolution?" *Harvard Business Review* (June 2004): 101–108.

23 Richard L. Oliver, Roland T. Rust, and Sajeev Varki, "Customer Delight: Foundations, Findings, and Managerial Insight," *Journal of Retailing* 73, (Fall 1997): 311–336.

24 Roland T. Rust and Richard L. Oliver, "Should We Delight the Customer?," *Journal of the Academy of Marketing Science* 28, no. 1 (2000): 86–94.

CHAPTER 3

positioning SERVICES in COMPETITIVE MARKETS

LEARNING OBJECTIVES

By the end of this chapter, the reader should be able to:

- **LO 1** Understand how the _c_ustomer, _c_ompetitor and _c_ompany analysis (i.e., the ***3 Cs***) helps to develop a customer-driven services marketing strategy.
- **LO 2** Know the key elements of a positioning strategy (i.e., ***STP***), and explain why these elements are so crucial for service firms to apply.
- **LO 3** ***S***egment customers by needs first before using other common bases to further identify and profile the segments.
- **LO 4** Distinguish between important and determinant attributes for segmenting services.
- **LO 5** Use different service levels for segmenting services.
- **LO 6** ***T***arget service customers using the four focus strategies for competitive advantage.
- **LO 7** ***P***osition a service to distinguish it from its competitors.
- **LO 8** Develop an effective positioning strategy.
- **LO 9** Demonstrate how positioning maps help to analyze and develop a competitive strategy.

OPENING VIGNETTE

Positioning a Chain of Childcare Centers Away from the Competition

Roger Brown and Linda Mason met at business school, following previous experience as management consultants. After graduation, they operated programs for refugee children in Cambodia and then ran a "Save the Children" relief program in East Africa. When they returned to the US, they saw a need for childcare centers that would provide caring, educational environments and give parents confidence in their children's well-being.

Through research, they discovered that the childcare industry had many weaknesses. There were no barriers to entry; profit margins were low, the industry was labor intensive, there were low economies of scale, there was no clear brand differentiation, and there was a lack of regulation. Brown and Mason developed a service concept that would allow them to turn these industry weaknesses into strengths for their own company, Bright Horizons. Instead of marketing their services directly to parents, a one-customer-at-a-time sale, Bright Horizons formed partnerships with companies seeking to offer an on-site day-care center for employees with small children. The advantages included the following:

- A powerful, low-cost marketing channel.
- A partner/customer who supplied the funds to build and equip the center and would therefore want to help Bright Horizons to achieve its goal of delivering high-quality care.
- Benefits for parents, who would be attracted to a Bright Horizons center (rather than competing alternatives) because of its nearness to their own workplace, thus reducing travel time and offering greater peace of mind.

Bright Horizons offered a high pay and benefits package to attract the best staff so that they could provide quality service; this was one aspect that was lacking in the other providers. Since traditional approaches to childcare either did not have a proper teaching plan, or had highly structured, rigidly enforced lesson plans, Bright Horizons developed a flexible teaching plan instead. It was called "World at Their Fingertips," and had a course outline, but gave teachers control over daily lesson plans.

The company sought accreditation for its centers from the National Association for the Education of Young Children (NAEYC) and actively promoted this. Bright Horizons' emphasis on quality meant that it could meet or exceed the highest local/state government licensing standards. As a result, the lack of regulation became an opportunity, not a threat for Bright Horizons and gave it a source of competitive advantage.

With support and help from its clients, which included many technology firms, Bright Horizons developed innovative technologies such as streaming video of its classrooms to parents' desktop computers; digitally scanned or photographed artwork; electronic posting of menus, calendars, and student assessments; as well as online student assessment capabilities. All of these serve to differentiate Bright Horizons and help it to stay ahead of the competition.

Bright Horizons sees labor as a competitive advantage. It seeks to recruit and retain the best people. In 2011, it was been listed for the 12th time as one of the "100 Best Companies to Work for in America" by *Fortune* magazine. By then, Bright Horizons had some 20,000 employees globally, and was operating for more than 700 client organizations in the US, Canada, and Europe. These clients are the world's leading employers, including corporations, hospitals, universities, and government offices. Clients want to hire Bright Horizons as a partner because they know they can trust the staff.

CUSTOMER-DRIVEN SERVICES MARKETING STRATEGY

In an industry with low barriers of entry and a lot of competition, Bright Horizons managed to find a niche position and differentiate itself from the competition. They linked up with employers instead of individual parents, emphasized service quality, and used accreditation as a unique selling point. As competition intensifies in the service sector, it is becoming ever more important for service organizations to differentiate their products in ways that are meaningful to customers. This is especially so for many mature service industries (e.g., banking, insurance, hospitality, and education), where for a firm to grow, it has to take share from its competitors or expand into new markets. However, ask a group of managers from different service businesses how they compete, and the chances are high that many will say simply, "on service." Press them a little further, and they may add words and phrases such as "value for money," "service quality," "our people," or "convenience." None of this is very helpful to a marketing specialist who is trying to develop a meaningful value proposition and a viable business model for a service product that will enable it to compete profitably in the marketplace.

What makes consumers or institutional buyers select and remain loyal to one supplier over another? Terms such as "service" typically have a variety of specific characteristics. It ranges from the speed with which a service is delivered to the quality of interactions between customers and service personnel; and from avoiding errors to providing desirable "extras" to supplement the core service. Likewise, "convenience" could refer to a service that's delivered at a convenient location, available at convenient times, or easy to use. Without knowing which product features are of specific interest to customers, it's hard for managers to develop an appropriate strategy. In a highly competitive environment, there's a risk that customers will perceive little real difference between competing alternatives and so they make their choices based on who offers the lowest price.

This means that managers need to think systematically about all aspects of the service offering and emphasize competitive advantage on those attributes that will be valued by customers in their target segment(s). A systematic way to do this typically starts with an analysis of ***c***ustomers, ***c***ompetitors and the ***c***ompany, collectively often referred to as the 3 Cs. This analysis then helps a firm to determine the key elements of its services positioning strategy, which are ***s***egmentation, ***t***argeting and ***p***ositioning, frequently simply called *STP* by marketing experts. The basic steps involved in identifying a suitable market position are shown in Figure 3.1. The desired positioning has wide-reaching implications on the firm's services marketing strategy, including the development of its 7 Ps of services marketing (discussed in Parts II and III of this book), its customer relationship strategy (discussed in Part IV), and its service quality and productivity strategies (discussed in Part V).

LO 1

Understand how the *c*ustomer, *c*ompetitor and *c*ompany analysis (i.e., the ***3 Cs***) helps to develop a customer-driven services marketing strategy.

Customer, Competitor, and Company Analysis (3 Cs)

Customer Analysis

The *customer analysis* is typically done first and includes an examination of the overall market characteristics, followed by an in-depth exploration of customer needs and related customer characteristics and behaviors.

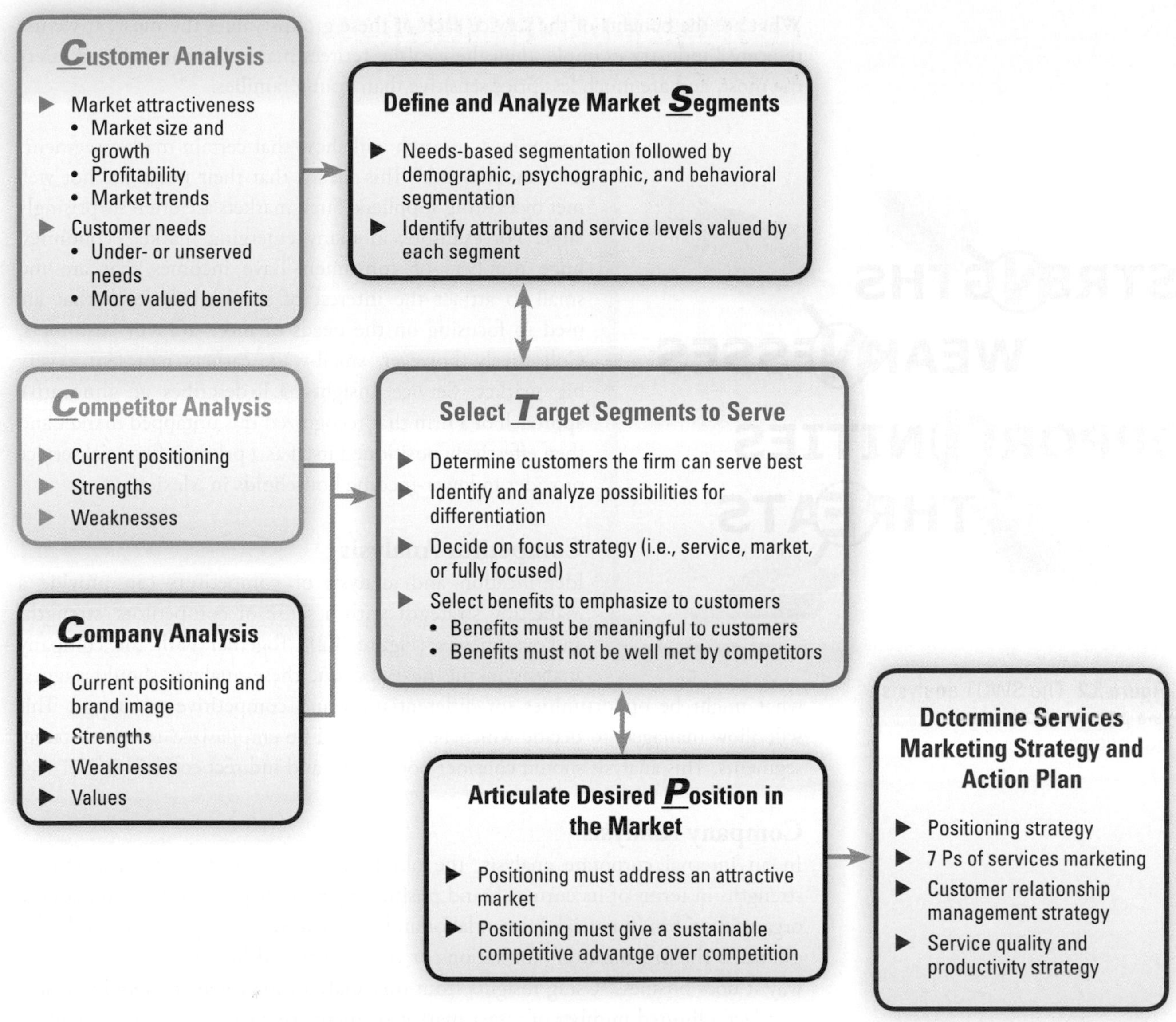

Figure 3.1 Developing a services marketing positioning strategy.

The *market analysis* tries to establish the attractiveness of the overall market and potential segments within. Specifically, it looks at the overall size and growth of the market, the margins and profit potential, and demand levels and trends affecting the market. Is demand increasing or decreasing for the benefits offered by this type of service? Are certain segments of the market growing faster than others? For example, if we look at the travel industry, perhaps there is a growing segment of wealthy retirees who are interested in traveling but want customized tours with personal guides and itineraries that are not too taxing. Firms should consider alternative ways of segmenting the market and make an assessment of the size and potential of different market segments.

The *customer needs analysis* involves answering a few questions. Who are the customers in that market in terms of demographics and psychographics? What needs or problems do they have? Are there potentially different groups of customers with differing needs and who therefore require different service products, or different levels of service?

What are the benefits of the service each of these groups values the most? If we use the travel industry example, then the wealthy retirees may value comfort and safety the most, and are much less price sensitive than young families.

Figure 3.2 The SWOT analysis is a popular method in businesses.

Sometimes, research will show that certain market segments are "underserved." This means that their needs are not well met by existing suppliers. Such markets are often surprisingly large. For example, in many emerging market economies, huge numbers of consumers have incomes that are too small to attract the interest of service businesses that are used to focusing on the needs of more affluent customers. Collectively, however, small-wage earners represent a very big market. Service Insights 3.1 describes an innovative approach of a firm that recognized this untapped market and then effectively positioned itself as a primary financial service provider to lower-income households in Mexico.

Competitor Analysis

Identification and analysis of competitors can provide a marketing strategist with a sense of competitors' strengths and weaknesses (Figure 3.2). Together with the company analysis in the next section, these analyses should suggest what might be opportunities for differentiation and competitive advantage. This will allow managers to decide which benefits could be emphasized to which target segments. This analysis should consider both direct and indirect competition.

Company Analysis

In an internal corporate analysis, the objective is to identify the organization's strengths in terms of its current brand positioning and image, and the resources the organization has (financial, human labor and know-how, and physical assets). It also examines the organization's limitations or constraints and how its values shape the way it does business. Using insights from this analysis, management should be able to select a limited number of target market segments that can be served with either existing or new services. The core question is: How well can our company and our services address the needs and problems faced by each customer segment?

LO 2

Know the key elements of a positioning strategy (i.e., *STP*), and explain why these elements are so crucial for service firms to apply.

Segmentation, Targeting, and Positioning (STP)

Linking customer and competitor analysis to company analysis allows the service organization to develop an effective positioning strategy. Here, the basic steps involved in identifying a suitable market position and developing a strategy to reach it are:

- Segmentation—This involves dividing the population of possible customers into groups. Those customers within the same segment share common service-related needs, for example, convenience. Once customers with similar needs are grouped together, demographic, geographic, psychographic, and behavioral variables can be used to describe them. Customers in the same segment should have as similar needs as possible, and between segments, their needs should be as different as possible.

SERVICE INSIGHTS 3.1

Banco Azteca Caters to the Little Guy

Banco Azteca, which opened in 2002, was Mexico's first new bank in nearly a decade. It initially targeted the 16 million households in the nation who earned the equivalent of $250–$1,300 a month working as taxi drivers, factory workers, and teachers among others. Despite their combined annual income of $120 billion, these individuals were of little interest to most banks, which considered small accounts a nuisance. Not surprisingly, only one in 12 of these households had a savings account.

Banco Azteca is the brainchild of Ricardo Salinas Pliego, head of a retail-media-telecommunications empire that includes Grupo Elektra, Mexico's largest appliance retailer. Its branches, located within the more than 900 Elektra stores, are decorated in the green, white, and red colors of the Mexican flag. They seek to create a welcoming atmosphere and feature posters with the Azteca slogan, which translates as "A bank that's friendly and treats you well."

Azteca's relationship with Elektra seeks to take advantage of the retailer's 50-year track record in consumer finance and the fact that some 70% of its merchandise is sold on credit. Elektra has an excellent record in credit sales, with a 97% repayment rate, and a rich database of customers' credit histories. So its top management felt it made sense to convert Elektra credit departments in each store into Azteca branches with an expanded line of services.

The new bank has invested heavily in information technology, including high tech fingerprint readers that eliminate the need for customers to present printed identification or passbooks. It also takes its services to the people through a 3,000-strong force of loan agents on motorcycles. The bank offers personal loans and time deposits and is rolling out used-car loans, low-income mortgages and debit cards. Loans may often use customers' previously purchased possessions as collateral.

In 2003, Grupo Elektra purchased a private insurance company, which it renamed Seguros Azteca. This firm offers basic insurance products at very low prices to a population segment that has historically been ignored by the Mexican insurance industry. Policies are distributed through Banco Azteca's branch network. The following year, the bank expanded its activities to finance individuals who wished to start or expand small businesses.

More recently, however, Banco Azteca has been criticized for profiteering from the poor through charging high effective annual percentage rates (APR) of 50–120% interest and of using high-pressure employee quotas and incentives to persuade customers to take loans, ideally with the longest possible period of 104 weeks. Has the bank been gouging its customers? Do a search online to find out the latest updates on this company.

SOURCES

Geri Smith, "Buy a Toaster, Open a Banking Account," *Business Week*, January 13, 2003, p. 54; Keith Epstein and Geri Smith, "The Ugly Side of Microlending: How Big Mexican Banks Profit as Many Poor Borrowers Get Trapped in a Maze of Debt," *Business Week*, December 12, 2007, http://www.businessweek.com/magazine/content/07_52/b4064038915009.htm, accessed March 12, 2012. https://www.gruposalinas.com, accessed March 12, 2012.

- Targeting—Once a firm's customers have been segmented, the firm has to assess the attractiveness of each segment, decide which segment(s) would most likely be interested in its service and focus on how to serve them well.
- Positioning—The unique place that the firm and/or its service offerings occupy in the minds of its consumers. Before a firm can create a unique position for its service, it must first differentiate its services from these of its competitors. Hence, differentiation is the first step towards creating a unique positioning for a service.

Table 3.1 shows the key elements of a service positioning strategy on the left-hand side and their related concepts on the right-hand side. We will discuss each concept in the remainder of this chapter.

Table 3.1 Elements and key concepts of a services positioning strategy

Elements of a Positioning Strategy	Key Concepts
Segmentation	• Segmenting service markets • Service attributes and service levels relevant for segmentation – Important versus determinant attributes – Establishing service levels
Targeting	• Targeting service markets through four focus strategies: – Fully focused – Market focused – Service focused – Unfocused
Positioning	• Positioning services in competitive markets • Developing an effective positioning strategy • Using positioning maps to plot a competitive strategy

LO 3

Segment customers by needs first before using other common bases to further identify and profile the segments.

SEGMENTING SERVICE MARKETS

Segmentation is one of the most important concepts in marketing. Service firms vary widely in their abilities to serve different types of customers. Hence, rather than trying to compete in an entire market, firms should segment the market. Through the process of market segmentation, firms will identify those parts or segments of the market that they can serve best. In order to segment the market, firms need to do a market analysis.

There are many ways to segment a market. Traditionally, demographic segmentation (e.g., based on age, gender, and income) has frequently been used. However, this often does not result in meaningful segmentation, as two people with the exact same demographics can exhibit very different buying behaviors (e.g., not all 20-year-old middle-class males feel and behave in the same way). As a result, psychographic segmentation has become more popular as it reflects people's lifestyles, attitudes, and aspirations. Psychographic segmentation can be very useful in strengthening brand identity and creating an emotional connection with the brand, but may not necessarily map on behaviors and sales. Behavioral segmentation addresses this shortcoming as it focuses on observable behaviors, such as people being nonusers, light users or heavy users. Needs-based segmentation focuses on what customers truly want in a service and maps closely on the multi-attribute decision models we discussed in Chapter 2 (e.g., a time- and quality-sensitive segment versus a price-sensitive segment).

You need to recognize that, often, people have different needs and decision making criteria according to:

- The purpose of using the service
- Who makes the decision
- The timing of use (time of day/week/season)
- Whether the individual is using the service alone or with a group, and if the latter, the composition of that group

Think about what determines your decision when choosing a restaurant for lunch (1) on vacation with friends or family, (2) for a meeting with a prospective business client, and (3) while going for a quick meal with a coworker . Given a reasonable selection of alternatives, it's unlikely that you would choose the same type of restaurant in each instance, let alone the same one. It's possible, too, that if you left the decision to another person in the party, he or she would end up with a different choice. It is therefore important to be quite specific about the occasion and context a service is purchased for and explicitly include that in one's segmentation.

For companies to effectively segment a market, it is often best to start with a deep understanding of customers' needs. Marketers can then combine this understanding with demographic, psychographic, behavioral, and consumption context variables to further define and describe key segments in a market.[1]

Contiki Holiday is an example of a company that uses needs-based segmentation as a foundation, and then fine-tunes it with other types of segmentation. It found that some single people do not want to join tours where there are families. They prefer a holiday where they can meet people with similar preferences (needs-based segmentation). Hence, Contiki serves this special group of people. In fact, it is a worldwide leader in vacation for those in the 18–35 age group (demographic segmentation) (Figure 3.3). Its holiday packages are aimed at fun-loving youths.

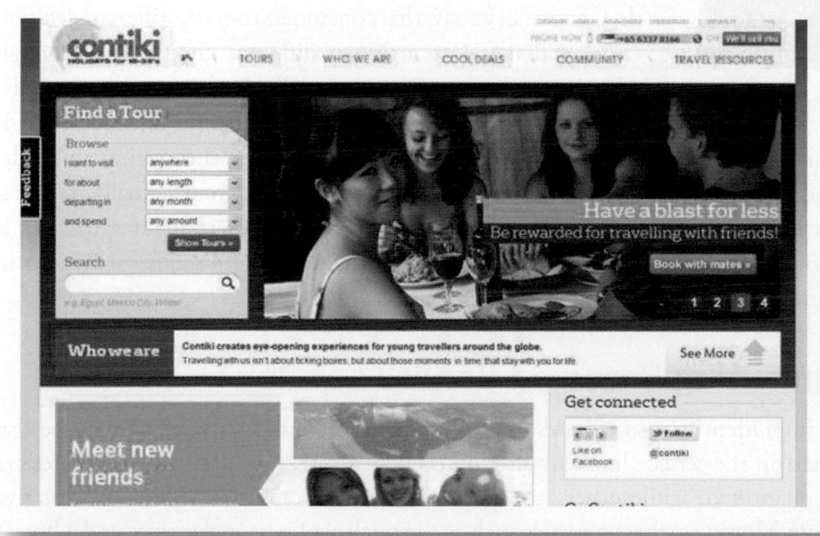

Figure 3.3 Contiki targets young and fun-loving travelers.

Contiki further segmented its packages and now caters to different lifestyles and budgets (psychographic segmentation). For example, those going to Europe can choose between "Camping" (for travelers who are very outgoing and do not mind roughing it out), "Concept/Budget" (for those who want more for their time and money, in backpacker-style accommodation) or "Time out/Superior" (for those who prefer lots of sightseeing, free time, extra excursions, and stays in superior-class tourist hotels).

LO 4

Distinguish between important and determinant attributes for segmenting services.

Important versus Determinant Service Attributes

It is important to select the right needs and their corresponding service attributes for segmentation. Firms need to know the attributes that will help to differentiate their offerings from competing offerings. However, the attribute that determines a consumer's final choice may not necessarily be the *most important attribute*. For example, many travelers rank "safety" as a very important attribute in their choice of airline. They may avoid traveling on airlines with a poor safety reputation. However, after eliminating such alternatives, a traveler is likely to have several choices of airlines perceived as equally safe. Therefore, safety usually is not an attribute that influences the customer's choice at this point.

Figure 3.4 Convenient departure times are determinant attributes for business travelers.

Determinant attributes (i.e., those that actually determine buyers' choices between competing alternatives) are often way down on the list of service characteristics that are important to purchasers. However, they are the attributes where customers see significant differences among competing alternatives. For example, convenience of departure and arrival times (Figure 3.4), availability of frequent flyer miles and related loyalty privileges, quality of inflight service, and ease of making reservations might be determinant characteristics for business travelers when selecting an airline. For budget-conscious vacation travelers, however, price might be the determinant characteristic.

In Chapter 2, we saw that consumers may use different decision rules and therefore arrive at different choices even though the important attributes are all the same. For example, in Table 2.1 on page 39 the most important attribute is the quality of dry cleaning. However, if the consumer uses the conjunctive rule, depending on what the cutoffs are, the determinant attribute may actually be price, which is the third most important variable. Identifying determinant attributes is therefore crucial to effective positioning, which makes a firm's service stand out in the minds of its target customers.

LO 5

Use different service levels for segmenting services.

Segmenting Based on Service Levels

Aside from identifying attributes to be used for segmentation, decisions must be also be made on the service levels to offer on each attribute.[2] Some service attributes are easily quantified, while others are qualitative. Price, for instance, is a quantitative attribute. However, characteristics such as the quality of personal service and a hotel's degree of luxury are more qualitative. Customers often can be segmented according to their willingness to give up some level of service for a lower price. Price-insensitive customers are willing to pay a relatively high price to obtain higher levels of service on each of the attributes important to them. In contrast, price-sensitive customers will look for an inexpensive service that offers a relatively low level of performance on many key attributes (see Service Insights 3.2).

Segmentation helps to identify potential attributes and service levels that have different degrees of relevance for key market segments. Once the segment structure of a market is understood, the firm can then move on to determining which of those segments could be targeted.

SERVICE INSIGHTS 3.2

Capsule Hotels

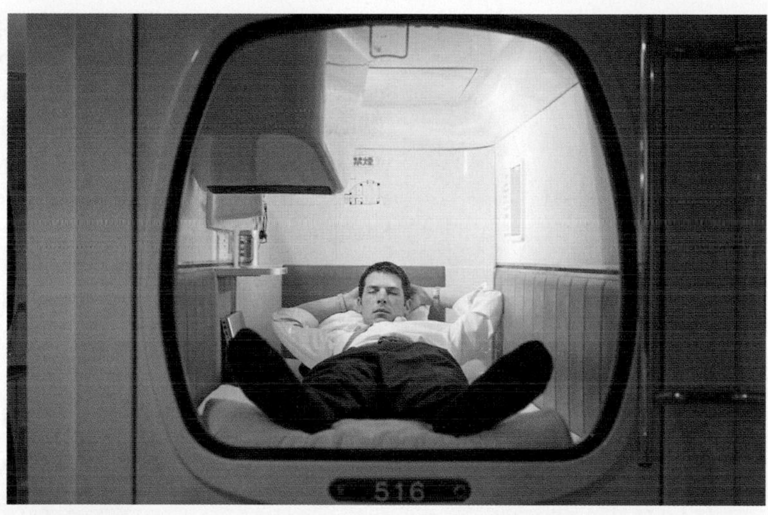

Capsule hotels consist of small rooms almost the size of large cupboards. Some of these capsule-like rooms cost only about $18 a night. The main benefits of these hotels are convenience and price. They started in space-constrained Japan in the 1980s but did not take off in other parts of the world until recently. Now, capsule hotel chains have been launched in many countries and include Pod Hotel in New York, Yotel in London, Citizen M and Qbic in Amsterdam, and StayOrange.com Hotel in Kuala Lumpur, Malaysia. Shanghai has also joined the trend; its first capsule hotel, called the Xitai Capsule Hotel, opened in January 2011.

These new chains have also modified their service offerings to differentiate themselves from the earlier generation of capsule hotels in Japan. For example, the Yotel group offers different classes of rooms which they call cabins. This concept came from the capsule hotels of Japan and the first-class cabins in British Airways airplanes. The premium Yotel cabin includes a double bed that can be changed into a couch at the touch of a button. It has tables that accommodate hand luggage, a luxury bathroom, and a study desk that unfolds. Yotel also offers free Internet access, a flat-screen TV, and 24-hour in-cabin service. The cost of the premium room at London's Heathrow Airport starts from £40 for four hours, and £6.50 per hour after that.

Both Yotel and Qbic have aggressive growth plans, and we can expect capsule hotels to become a mainstream choice for budget-conscious travelers in the future.

SOURCES

http://www.stayorange.com/; www.yotel.com; http://en.wikipedia.org/wiki/Capsule_hotel, accessed on March 12, 2012; *The Economist*, "Capsule Hotel: Thinking Small," November 17, 2007.

LO 6

***T**arget service customers using the four focus strategies for competitive advantage.*

TARGETING SERVICE MARKETS

Service firms vary widely in their abilities to serve different types of customers well. Hence, achieving competitive advantage usually requires a firm to be more focused,[3] which is what we will discuss next. Rather than trying to compete in an entire market, each company ideally focuses its efforts on those customers it can serve best—its *target segment*. Nearly all successful service firms apply this concept.

Achieve Competitive Advantage through Focus

In marketing terms, *focus* means providing a relatively narrow product mix for a particular target segment. The extent of a company's focus can be described in two dimensions: market focus and service focus.[4] *Market focus* is the extent to which a firm serves a few or many markets, while *service focus* describes the extent to which a firm offers few or many services. These two dimensions define the four basic focus strategies shown in Figure 3.5. The four focus strategies are the following:

- **Fully focused.** A fully focused organization provides a limited range of services (perhaps just a single core product) to a narrow and specific market segment. For example, private jet charter services may focus on high-net-worth individuals or corporations (Figure 3.6). Developing recognized expertise in a well-defined niche may provide protection against would-be competitors and allows a firm to charge premium prices. An example of a fully focused firm is Shouldice Hospital, featured in Case 12. The hospital performs only a single surgery (hernia) on otherwise healthy patients (mostly men in their 40s to 60s). Because of their focus, their surgery and service quality are superb.

NUMBERS OF MARKETS SERVED \ BREADTH OF SERVICE OFFERINGS	Wide	Narrow
Few	Market Focused	Fully Focused (Service and market focused)
Many	Unfocused (Everything for everyone)	Service Focused

Figure 3.5 Basic focus strategies for services.

SOURCE

Achieving Focus in Service Organization, Johnson, R. *The Service Industries Journal* 16 (January): 10–20. January 1, 1996, reprinted by permission of Taylor & Francis Ltd, http://www.tandf.co.uk/journals

There are key risks associated with pursuing the fully focused strategy. The market may be too small to get the volume of business needed for financial success, and the firm is vulnerable to decreasing demand because of new alternative products or new technologies.

- **Market focused.** In a market-focused strategy, a company offers a wide range of services to a narrowly defined target segment. Service Insights 3.3 features the example of Rentokil Initial, a provider of business-to-business (B2B) services. Rentokil has profited from the growing trend in outsourcing of services related to facility maintenance, which has enabled it to develop a large range of services for its clients.

  Following a market-focused strategy often looks attractive because the firm can sell multiple services to a single buyer. However, before choosing a market-focused strategy, managers need to be sure that their firms are capable of doing an excellent job of delivering each of the different services selected. They also need to understand customers' purchasing practices and preferences. In a B2B context, when trying to cross-sell additional services to the same client, many firms have been disappointed to find that decisions on purchasing the new service are made by an entirely different group within the client company.

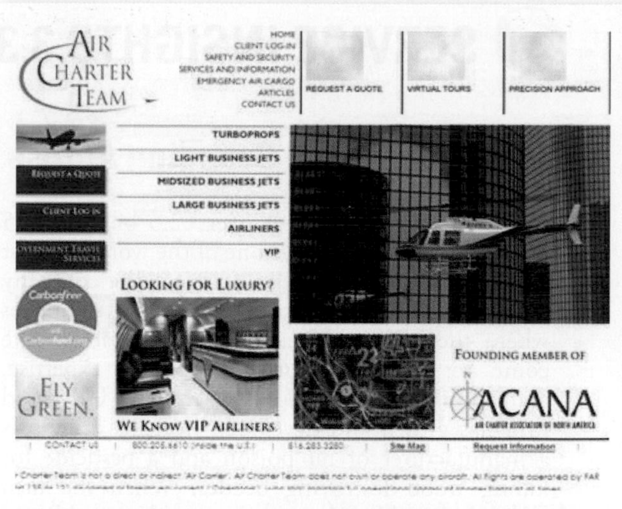

Figure 3.6 Private air charter services for VIPs.

- **Service focused.** Service-focused firms offer a narrow range of services to a fairly broad market (Figure 3.7). Lasik eye surgery clinics and Starbucks coffee shops follow this strategy, serving a broad customer base with a largely standardized product. However, as new segments are added, firms need to develop expertise in serving each segment. In addition, this strategy is likely to require a broader sales effort and greater investment in marketing communication, particularly in B2B markets.
- **Unfocused.** Finally, many service providers fall into the unfocused category because they try to serve broad markets and provide a wide range of services. The danger with this strategy is that unfocused firms are often "jacks of all trades and masters of none," and are unable to excel in providing any single service. In general, that's not a good idea, although public utilities and government agencies may feel the need to do so. A few department stores followed this strategy and, as a result, have been struggling against more focused competitors (e.g., hypermarkets and specialty stores).

Figure 3.7 Warehousing service firms provide logistics solutions for broad markets.

It is recommended that firms have some sort of focus, whether on market segments or on services. How then should a firm select which of the three alternative "focused" strategies to pursue? This decision relates back to the 3 Cs, segmentation, and targeting analyses. For example, a market-focused strategy may be appropriate if (a) customers value the convenience of one-stop shopping, (b) the firm is able to deliver these multiple services better than its

SERVICE INSIGHTS 3.3

Market-Focused Branding Across Multiple Services at Rentokil Initial

With revenue for 2010 at over £2.5 billion ($3.5 billion), Rentokil Initial is one of the world's largest business support service companies. The company has about 68,000 employees in over 50 countries where the "Rentokil" and "Initial" brands have come to represent innovation, deep expertise, and consistent quality of service. The UK-based firm has grown and developed from its origins as a manufacturer of rat poison and a pesticide for killing wood-destroying beetles. When the firm realized it could make more money by providing a service to kill rodents than by selling products that customers would have to use themselves, it shifted to pest control and extermination services.

Through organic growth and acquisitions, Rentokil Initial has developed a product range that includes testing and safety services, security, package delivery, interior plants landscaping (including the sale or rental of tropical plants), specialized cleaning services, pest control, uniform rental and cleaning, clinical waste collection and disposal, personnel services, and a washroom attendant service that supplies and maintains a full array of equipment, dispensers, and consumables.

Promoting the use of additional services to existing customers is an important aspect of the firm's strategy. Initial Integrated Services offers clients the opportunity to move beyond the established concept of "bundling" services—bringing together several free-standing support services contracts from one provider—to full integration of services. Clients purchase sector-specific solutions that deliver multiple services, but feature just "one invoice, one account manager, one help desk, one contract, and one motivated service team."

According to former chief executive, Sir Clive Thomson: "Our objective has been to create a virtuous circle. We provide a quality service in industrial and commercial activities under the same brand-name, so that a customer satisfied with one Rentokil Initial Service is potentially a satisfied customer for another. ... Although it was considered somewhat odd at the time, one of the reasons we moved into [providing and maintaining]

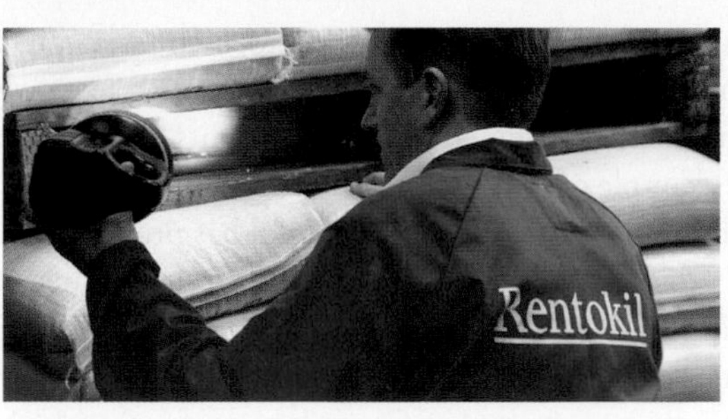

tropical plants [for building interiors] was in fact to put the brand in front of decision makers. Our service people maintaining the plants go in through the front door and are visible to the customer. This contrasts with pest control where no one really notices unless we fail. ... The brand stands for honesty, reliability, consistency, integrity and technical leadership."

Investment in R&D ensures constant improvement in its many service lines. For example, the company has built the RADAR intelligent rodent trap. RADAR attracts rats and mice into a sealable chamber and kills them humanely by injecting carbon dioxide. Using Rentokil's unique "pestconnect" technology, the trap, when triggered, sends e-mails to the customer and the local branch when a rodent is caught. In addition, a Rentokil technician receives a text message identifying which unit has been activated at which customer's premises, and its precise location. Pestconnect checks each individual RADAR unit every 10 minutes, 24/7. Getting information in real time enables technicians to remove dead rodents promptly and to control future infestation better.

Rentokil Initial's success, thus far, lies in its ability to position each of its many business services in terms of the company's core brand values, which include providing superior standards of customer care and using the most technologically advanced services and products. The brand image is strengthened through physical evidence in terms of distinctive uniforms, vehicle color schemes, and use of the corporate logo.

SOURCE

Clive Thompson, "Rentokil Initial: Building a Strong Corporate Brand for Growth and Diversity," in F. Gilmore (ed.) *Brand Warriors* (London: HarperCollinsBusiness, 1997), 123–124; TXT Technology 4 Pest Control, press release, December 6, 2005, www.rentokil-initial.com, accessed March 12, 2012.

competitors are, and/or (c) there are significant synergies in selling multiple services to the same customer (as is often the case in B2B services; see Rentokil Initial in Service Insights 3.3), which then enables the firm to either lower the price or provide better services.

A service-focused strategy can work best if the firm has a unique set of capabilities and resources to deliver a particular service exceptionally well or cost-effectively. The firm may then want to ride on its advantage to deliver the service to a broad market (i.e., many customer segments at the same time).

Finally, a fully focused strategy may work well if a particular segment has very specific needs and requires a unique service environment, service processes, and interaction with the firm's frontline employees. Here, a fully focused strategy can deliver superb quality and at low costs because of its focus and experience. The Shouldice Hospital is a good example. The entire hospital is designed around the needs of hernia patients who are otherwise well and do not have to stay in bed. Patients get their perfect hospital experience and outstanding surgery quality all at a low price. This makes Shouldice Hospital the perfect hospital for people who have hernia but are otherwise healthy. However, this hospital cannot deal with any other type of patients.

The decision on focus is very important for service firms, as they have distributed operations (each Starbucks café is like a mini-factory), and any additional service offered increases the complexity of processes and the costs of the operation significantly. Likewise, even if a firm wants to sell the same basic service to different segments, it will often find that each additional segment may require some changes to the facility and processes to cater to their different needs and requirements.

POSITIONING SERVICES

 **LO 7**
Position a service to distinguish it from its competitors.

Positioning strategy is concerned with creating, communicating, and maintaining distinctive differences that will be noticed and valued by customers with whom the firm would most like to develop a long-term relationship. Successful positioning requires managers to understand their target customers' preferences, their conception of value, and the characteristics of their competitors' offerings. Price and product attributes are two of the four Ps of marketing that are most commonly used in a positioning strategy. For services, however, positioning often relates also to other Ps of the services marketing mix, including service personnel, service processes (e.g., their convenience, ease of use), service schedules, locations, and the service environment.

Jack Trout distilled the essence of positioning into the following four principles[5]:

1. A company must establish a position in the minds of its targeted customers.
2. The position should be singular, providing one simple and consistent message (Figure 3.8).
3. The position must set a company apart from its competitors (Figure 3.9).
4. A company cannot be all things to all people—it must focus its efforts.

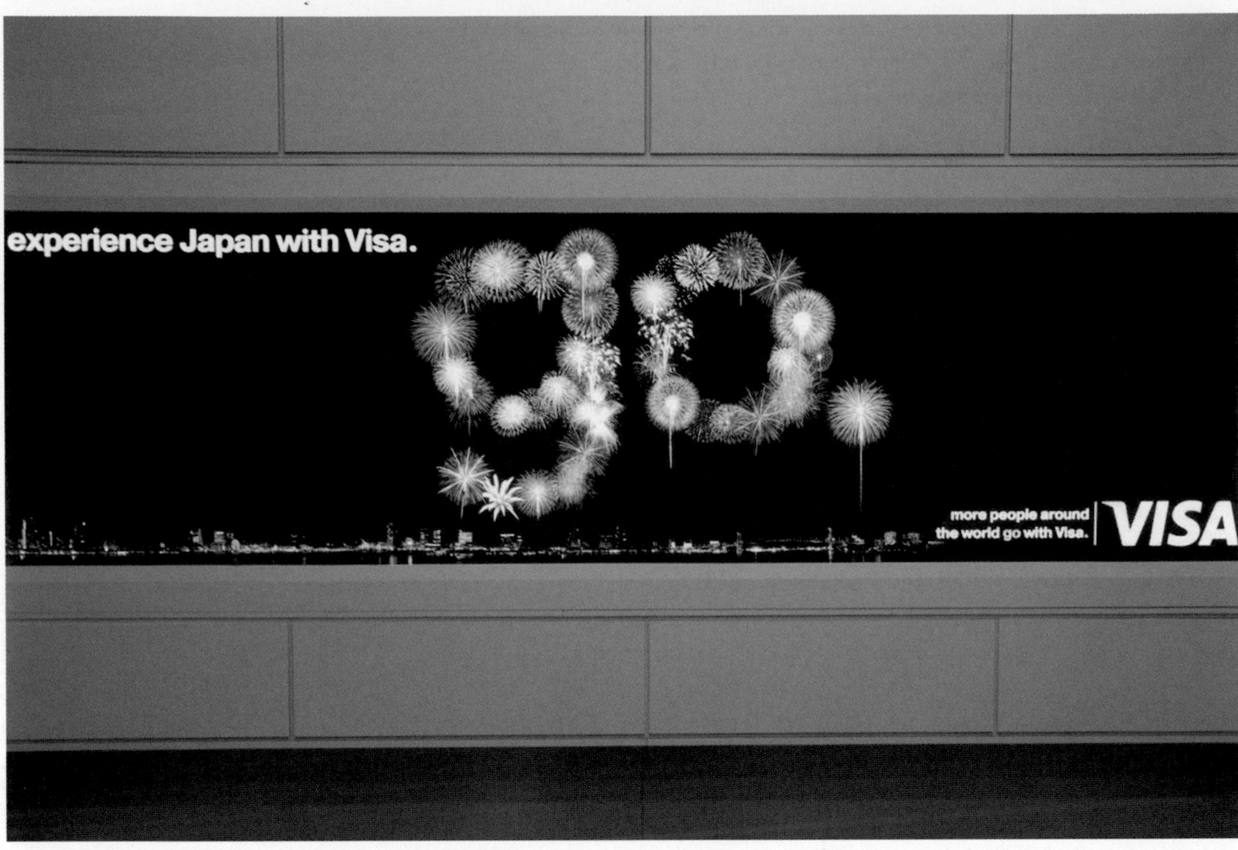

Figure 3.8 Visa has one simple message globally.

Figure 3.9 For powerful positioning, a firm needs to set itself apart from its competitors.

These principles apply to any type of organization that competes for customers. Firms must understand the principles of positioning in order to develop an effective competitive position. The concept of positioning offers valuable insights by forcing service managers to analyze their firms' existing offerings and to provide specific answers to the following six questions:

1. What does our firm currently stand for in the minds of current and potential customers?
2. What types of customers do we serve now, and which ones would we like to target in the future?
3. What is the value proposition of each of our current service offerings and what market segments does each one target?
4. How does each of our service products differ from those of our competitors?
5. How well do customers in the chosen target segments perceive our service offerings as meeting their needs?
6. What changes do we need to make to our service offerings in order to strengthen our competitive position within our target segment(s)?

One of the challenges in developing a viable positioning strategy is avoiding the trap of investing too much in points of difference that can easily be copied. As researchers Kevin Keller, Brian Sternthal, and Alice Tybout note: "Positioning needs to keep competitors out, not draw them in."[6] When Roger Brown and Linda Mason, founders of the Bright Horizons chain of childcare centers featured in the opening vignette of this chapter, were developing their service concept and business model, they took a long, hard look at the industry.[7] Discovering that for-profit childcare companies had adopted low-cost strategies, Brown and Mason selected a different approach that competitors would find very difficult to copy.

Similarly, it used to be that when large companies were looking for auditing services, they typically turned to one of the Big Four accounting firms (Figure 3.10). Now, a growing number of clients are switching to so-called "Tier Two" accounting firms in search of better service, a lower bill, or both.[8] Grant Thornton, the fifth-largest firm in the industry, has successfully positioned itself as offering easy access to partners and having "a passion for the business of accounting." Its advertising promotes an award from J. D. Powers ranking it as achieving "Highest Performance among Audit Firms Serving Companies with up to $12 billion in Annual Revenue".

Figure 3.10 The Big Four accounting firms refer to PricewaterhouseCoopers, Deloitte Touche Tohmatsu, Ernst & Young, and KPMG.

LO 8
Develop an effective positioning strategy.

Developing an Effective Positioning Strategy

Since we now understand the principles of positioning, let us discuss how to develop an effective positioning strategy. As shown in Figure 3.1 at the beginning of this chapter, *STP* links the *3 Cs* (i.e., customer, competitor, and company) analysis to the services marketing strategy and action plan. From what is found, a position statement can be developed that enables the service organization to answer the questions: "What is our product (or service concept)? Who are our customers? What do we want it to become? What actions must we take to get there?"

Figure 3.11 The rapid growth of the silver industry prompts companies to come up with products and services suitable for them.

There are four basic elements to writing a good positioning statement[9]. They are:

- Target audience—the specific group(s) of people that the brand wants to sell to and serve (e.g., wealthy retirees who desire a hassle-free holiday experience) see Figure 3.11.
- Frame of reference—the category that the brand is competing in (e.g., travel agency).
- Point of difference—the most compelling benefit offered by the brand that stands out from its competition (e.g., customized tour packages that come along with personal guides and designed for a relaxing experience just for you and your spouse) see Figure 3.12.
- Reason to believe—proof that the brand can deliver the benefits that are promised. (e.g., we are retirees who know what retirees want in a holiday).

The outcome of integrating the *3 Cs* and the *STP* analyses is the positioning statement that defines the desired position of the organization in the marketplace. With this understanding, marketers can now develop a specific plan of action that includes its positioning strategy along the *7 Ps* of services marketing, its customer relationship management and loyalty strategies, and its service quality and productivity strategies.

LO 9
Demonstrate how positioning maps help to analyze and develop a competitive strategy.

USING POSITIONING MAPS TO PLOT A COMPETITIVE STRATEGY

Positioning maps are great tools to visualize competitive positioning along key aspects of its services marketing strategy, to map developments over time, and to develop scenarios of potential competitor responses. Developing a positioning map, a task sometimes referred to as perceptual mapping—is a useful way of graphically representing consumers' perceptions of alternative products. A map usually has two attributes, although three-dimensional models can be used to show three of these attributes. When more than three dimensions are needed to describe product performance in a given market, then a series of separate charts needs to be drawn.

Figure 3.12 Executives conducting competitive analysis.

Information about a product (or a company's position relative to any one attribute) can be inferred from market data, derived from ratings by representative consumers, or both. If consumer perceptions of service characteristics differ sharply from "reality" as defined by management, then communications efforts may be needed to change these perceptions, which we will discuss in Chapter 7.

An Example of Applying Positioning Maps to the Hotel Industry

The hotel business is highly competitive, especially during seasons when the supply of rooms exceeds demand. Within each class of hotels, customers visiting a large city may find several options to choose from. Some customers may prefer a higher degree of luxury and comfort; others may focus on attributes like location, safety, cleanliness, or special reward programs for frequent guests (Figure 3.13).

Let's look at an example, based on a real-world situation, of how to apply positioning maps. Managers of the Palace, a successful four-star hotel, developed a positioning map showing their own and competing hotels to get a better understanding of future threats to their established market position in a large city that we will call Belleville.

Located on the edge of the booming financial district in Belleville, the Palace was an elegant old hotel that had been thoroughly renovated and modernized a few years earlier. Its competitors included eight four-star establishments, and the Grand, one of the city's oldest hotels, which had a five-star rating. The Palace had been very profitable in recent years and has had an above-average occupancy rate. For many months of the year, it was sold out on weekdays. This was because it attracted business travelers who were willing to pay higher room rates than tourists or conference delegates. However, the general manager and his staff saw problems ahead. Planning permissions had recently been granted for four large new hotels in the city, and the Grand had just started a major renovation and expansion project, which included construction of a new wing. There was a risk that customers might see the Palace as falling behind in the market.

To better understand the nature of the competitive threat, the hotel's management team worked with a consultant to prepare charts that displayed the Palace's position in the business traveler market both before and after the entrance of new competition. Four attributes were selected for study: room price, level of personal service, level of physical luxury, and location.

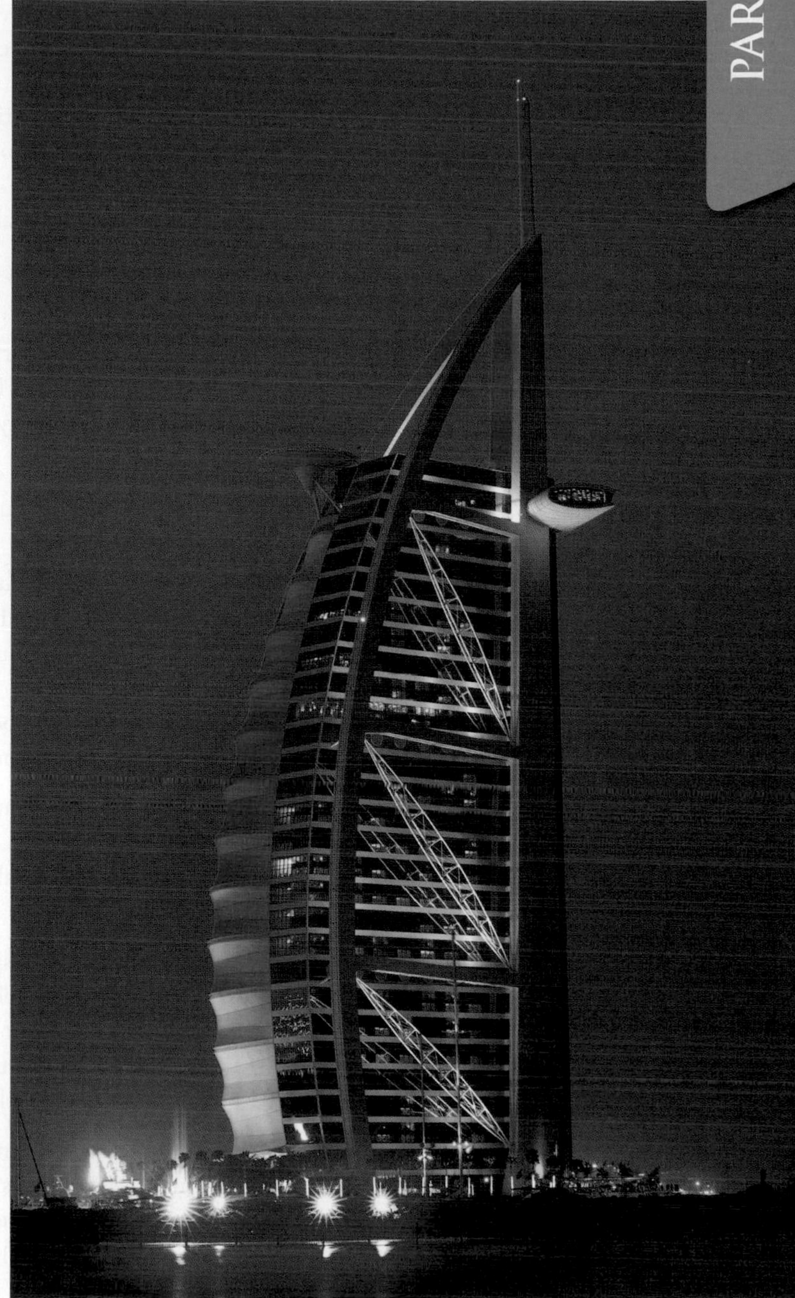

Figure 3.13 Dubai's Burj Al Arab is favorably positioned along many determinant attributes like personal service, level of physical extravagance, and location.

Data Sources

In this instance, the Palace's management did not conduct new consumer research. Instead, they obtained their customer perceptions data from various sources:

- Published information.
- Data from past surveys done by the hotel.

- Reports from travel agents and knowledgeable hotel staff members who frequently interacted with guests.

Information on competing hotels was not difficult to obtain, because the locations were known. Information was obtained through:

- Visiting and evaluating the physical structures.
- Having sales staff who kept themselves informed on pricing policies and discounts.
- To evaluate the service level, they used the ratio of rooms per employee. This is easily calculated from the published number of rooms and employment data provided to the city authorities.
- Data from surveys of travel agents conducted by the Palace provided additional insights into the quality of personal service of each competitor.

Scales and Hotel Ratings

Scales were then created for each attribute, and each hotel was rated for each of the attributes so the positioning maps could be drawn:

- Price was simple because the average price charged to business travelers for a standard single room at each hotel was already quantified.
- The rooms-per-employee ratio formed the basis for a service level scale, with low ratios equated to high service. This rating was then fine-tuned because of what was known about the quality of service actually delivered by each major competitor.
- The level of physical luxury was more subjective. The management team identified the hotel that members agreed was the most luxurious (the Grand) and then the four-star hotel that they viewed as having the least luxurious physical facilities (the Airport Plaza). All other four-star hotels were then rated on this attribute relative to these two benchmarks.
- Location was defined using the stock exchange building in the heart of the financial district as a reference point. Past research had shown that a majority of the Palace's business guests were visiting destinations in this area. The competitive set of 10 hotels lay within a four-mile, fan-shaped radius, extending from the exchange through the city's principal retail area (where the convention center was also located) to the inner suburbs and the nearby airport.

Two positioning maps were created to portray the existing competitive situation. The first (Figure 3.14) showed the 10 hotels on the dimensions of price and service level; the second (Figure 3.15) displayed them on location and degree of physical luxury.

Findings

Some findings were intuitive, but others provided valuable insights:

- A quick glance at Figure 3.14 shows a clear correlation between the attributes of price and service. Hotels that offer higher levels of service are relatively more expensive. The shaded bar running from the upper left to the lower right

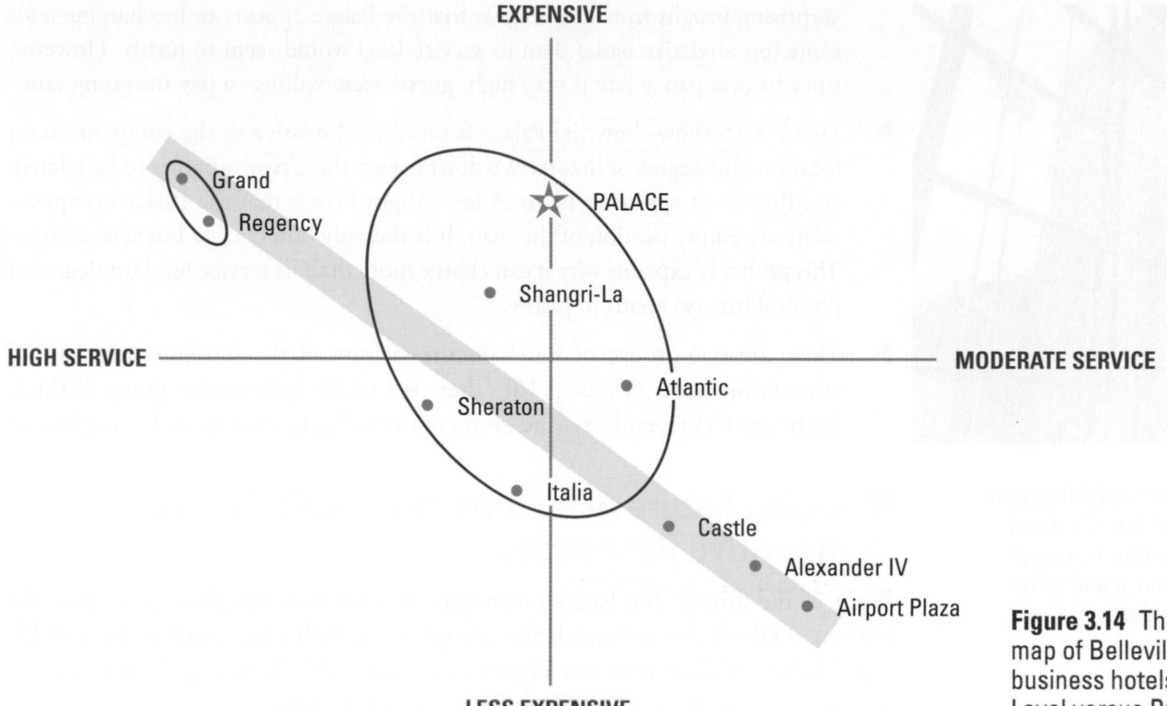

Figure 3.14 The positioning map of Belleville's principal business hotels: Service Level versus Price Level.

highlights this relationship, which is not a surprising one (and can be expected to continue diagonally downward for three-star and lesser-rated establishments).

- Further analysis shows that there appear to be three groups of hotels within what is already an upscale market category. At the top end, four-star Regency is close to the five-star Grand. In the middle, the Palace is clustered with four other hotels, and, at the lower end, there is another group of three hotels. One

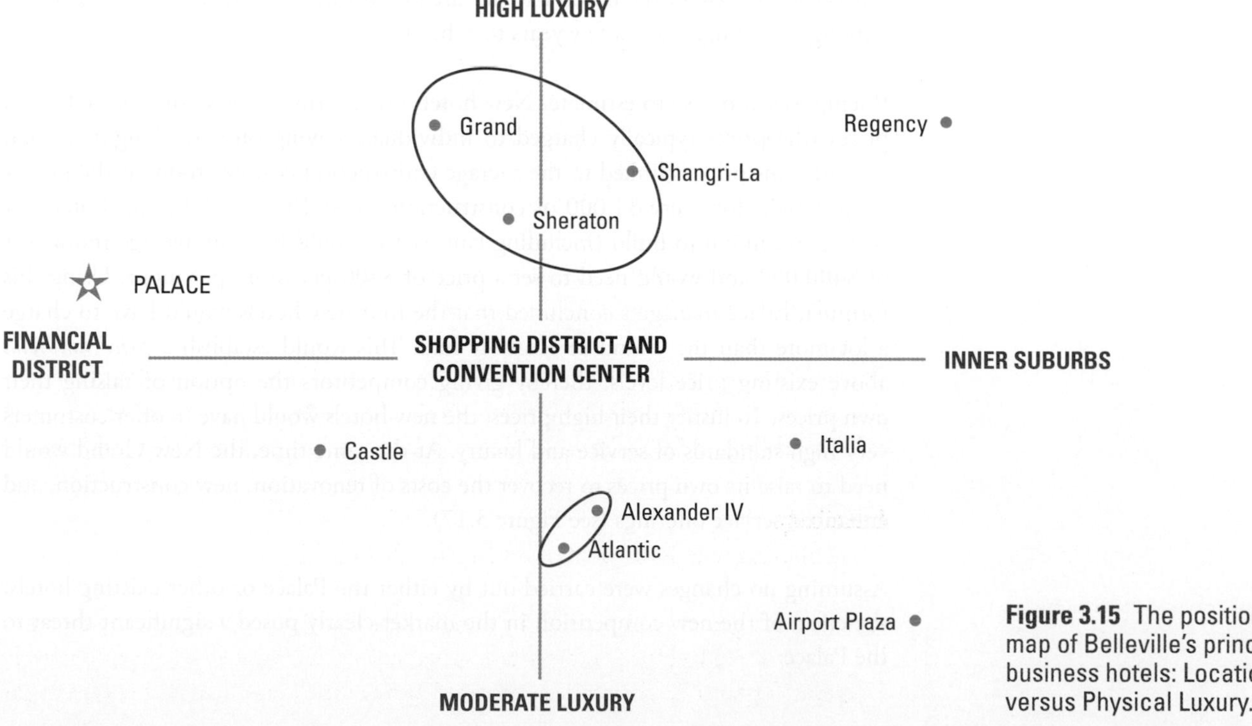

Figure 3.15 The positioning map of Belleville's principal business hotels: Location versus Physical Luxury.

Figure 3.16 The kaleidoscopic glass panes of the Montreal Convention Center is a huge draw for hoteliers and other services providers.

surprising insight from this map is that the Palace appears to be charging a lot more (on a relative basis) than its service level would seem to justify. However, since its occupancy rate is very high, guests seem willing to pay the going rate.

- Figure 3.15 shows how the Palace is positioned relative to the competition on location and degree of luxury. We don't expect these two variables to be related, and they don't appear to be so. A key insight here is that the Palace occupies a relatively empty portion of the map. It is the only hotel in the financial district. This probably explains why it can charge more than its service level (or degree of physical luxury) seems to justify.
- There are two groups of hotels in the vicinity of the shopping district and convention center (Figure 3.16). There is a relatively luxurious group of three, led by the Grand, and a second group of two offering a moderate level of luxury.

Mapping Future Scenarios to Identify Potential Competitive Responses

What of the future? The Palace's management team next sought to anticipate the positions of the four new hotels being constructed in Belleville, as well as the probable repositioning of the Grand (see Figures 3.17 and 3.18). Predicting the positions of the four new hotels was not difficult for experts in the field.

The construction sites were already known. Two would be in the financial district and two in the vicinity of the convention center, under expansion. Press releases distributed by the Grand had already declared its management's intentions: Not only would the "New" Grand be larger, the renovations would be designed to make it even more luxurious, and there were plans to add new service features. Three of the newcomers would be linked to international chains and their strategies could be guessed by examining recent hotels opened in other cities by these same chains. The owners of two of the hotels had declared their intentions to seek five-star status, although this might take a few years to achieve.

Pricing was also easy to estimate. New hotels use a formula for setting posted room prices (the prices typically charged to individuals staying on a weeknight in high season). This price is linked to the average construction cost per room at the rate of $1 per night for every $1,000 of construction costs. Thus, a 200-room hotel that costs $80 million to build (including land costs) would have an average room cost of $400,000 and would need to set a price of $400 per room per night. Using this formula, Palace managers concluded that the four new hotels would have to charge a lot more than the Grand or Regency had. This would establish a *price umbrella* above existing price levels, thereby giving competitors the option of raising their own prices. To justify their high prices, the new hotels would have to offer customers very high standards of service and luxury. At the same time, the New Grand would need to raise its own prices to recover the costs of renovation, new construction, and enhanced service offerings (see Figure 3.17).

Assuming no changes were carried out by either the Palace or other existing hotels, the effect of the new competition in the market clearly posed a significant threat to the Palace:

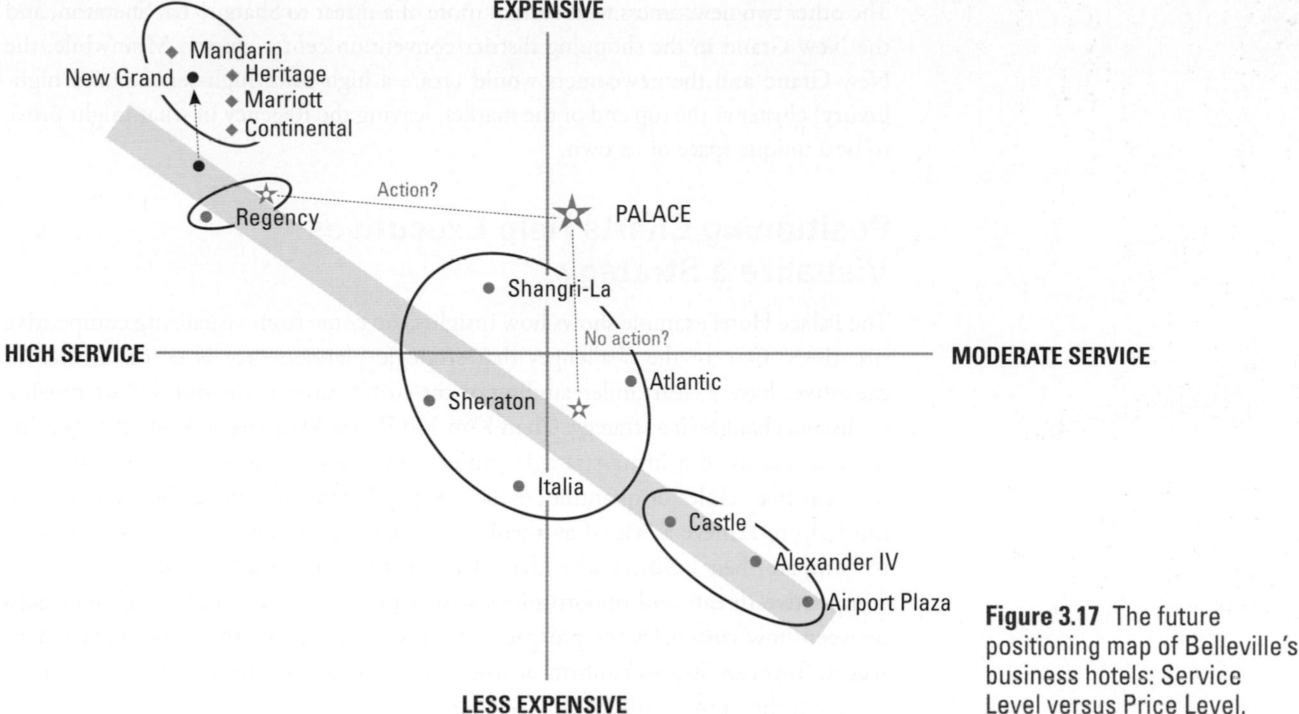

Figure 3.17 The future positioning map of Belleville's business hotels: Service Level versus Price Level.

It would lose its unique location advantage and, in the future, be one of the three hotels in the immediate vicinity of the financial district (Figure 3.18).

The sales staff believed that many of the Palace's existing business customers would be attracted to the Continental and the Mandarin and would be willing to pay higher rates to obtain the superior benefits offered.

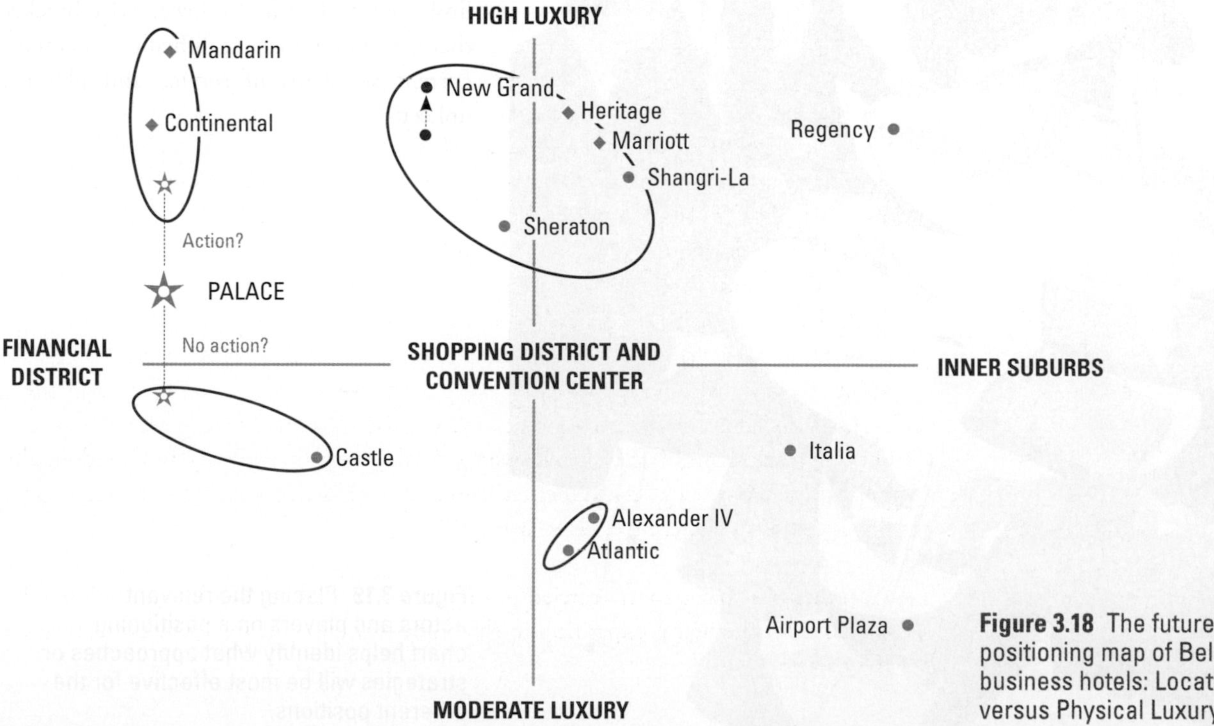

Figure 3.18 The future positioning map of Belleville's business hotels: Location versus Physical Luxury.

The other two newcomers were seen as more of a threat to Shangri-La, Sheraton, and the New Grand in the shopping district/convention center cluster. Meanwhile, the New Grand and the newcomers would create a high-price/high-service (and high-luxury) cluster at the top end of the market, leaving the Regency in what might prove to be a unique space of its own.

Positioning Charts Help Executives Visualize a Strategy

The Palace Hotel example shows how insights can come from visualizing competitive situations. One of the challenges that strategic planners face is ensuring that all executives have a clear understanding of the firm's current situation before moving to discuss changes in a strategy. Chan Kim and Renée Mauborgne argue that graphic representations of a firm's strategic profile and product positions are much easier to grasp than tables of quantitative data or paragraphs of words. Charts and maps can help to achieve a "visual awakening." In addition to allowing senior managers to compare their business with that of competitors and understand the nature of competitive threats and opportunities, visual presentations can also highlight gaps between how customers (or prospects) see the organization and how management sees it. This can help to confirm or dispel beliefs that a service or a firm occupies a unique niche in the marketplace[10] (Figure 3.19).

By examining how anticipated changes in the competitive environment would literally redraw the current positioning map, the management team at the Palace could see that the hotel could not hope to remain in its current market position once it has lost its location advantage. Unless it moved to improve its level of service and physical luxury, the Palace was likely to find itself pushed into a lower price bracket that might even make it difficult to maintain current standards of service and physical upkeep.

Figure 3.19 Placing the relevant actors and players on a positioning chart helps identify what approaches or strategies will be most effective for the different positions.

CHAPTER SUMMARY

LO 1 ▶ Developing an effective positioning strategy links *customer*, *competitor*, and *company analysis*, often called the *3 Cs*.

- o *Market analysis* looks at the market attractiveness (e.g., market size, growth, and trends) and customer needs (e.g., desired service levels, level of contact, delivery channel, time of consumption, and price sensitivity).
- o *Competitor analysis* examines competitors' current positioning, strengths, and weaknesses to spot opportunities for the firm.
- o *Company analysis* focuses on a firm's brand positioning and image, the firm's strengths and weaknesses (e.g., its resources and constraints), and how its values shape the way it does business.

LO 2 ▶ The key elements of developing a customer-driven services marketing strategy are *segmentation*, *targeting*, and *positioning*, commonly referred to as *STP*.

LO 3 ▶ *Segmentation* is the division of a market into groups. Customers within the same segment share common service-related needs. Segmentation is often based on customer needs first, to focus the firm on what customers truly want and on what drives their purchase decisions. Subsequently, demographic, psychographic, and behavioral variables can be used to further define and describe key segments.

LO 4 ▶ It is crucial for segmenting customers to understand the difference between important and determinant attributes for consumer choice.

- o *Important attributes* are important to the consumer but that may not be important for the buying decisions (e.g., safety is important, but all airlines a traveler considers are seen as safe). If that is the case, such an attribute should not be used as a basis for segmentation.
- o *Determinant attributes* often are way down on the list of service characteristics important to customers. However, they are attributes on which customers see significant differences between competing alternatives (e.g., convenience of departure times or quality of inflight service) and will determine the final purchase. Differences between customers regarding determinant attributes are therefore crucial for segmentation.

LO 5 ▶ Once the important and determinant attributes are understood, management needs to decide which *service level* different customers prefer on each of the attributes. Service levels often are used to differentiate customer segments according to their willingness to trade off price and service level.

LO 6 ▶ Next, each company needs to focus its efforts on those customers it can serve best—its *target segment*. Firms must have a competitive advantage on attributes valued by the target segment. To achieve competitive advantage, firms need to be focused. There are three focused strategies that firms can follow to achieve competitive advantage. They are:

- o *Fully focused*: A firm provides a limited range of services (perhaps only one) to a narrow target segment (e.g., Shouldice Hospital).
- o *Market focused*: A firm concentrates on a narrow market segment but offers a wide range of services to address the many diverse needs that segment (e.g., Rentokil).
- o *Service focused*: A firm offers a narrow range of services to a fairly broad market (e.g., Lasik eye surgery clinics or Starbucks cafés).
- o *Unfocused strategy*: It generally is not advisable for firms to choose an unfocused strategy, as this will mean that they spread themselves too thin to remain competitive (e.g., some department stores).

LO 7 ▶ Once we have understood determinant attributes and related service levels, we can decide how to best position our services in the market. *Positioning* is based on establishing and maintaining a distinctive place in the market for a firm's offerings. The essence of positioning is:

- o A company must establish a position in the minds of its targeted customers.
- o The position should be singular, providing one simple and consistent message.
- o The position must set a company apart from its competitors.
- o A company cannot be all things to all people—it must focus its efforts.

LO 8 ▶ The outcome of these analyses is the position statement that articulates the desired position of the firm's offerings in the marketplace. With this understanding, marketers can then develop a specific plan of action that includes its positioning strategy along the *7 Ps* of services marketing, its customer relationship management and loyalty strategies, and its service quality and productivity strategies.

LO 9 ▶ *Positioning maps* are an important tool to help firms develop their positioning strategies. They provide a visual way of summarizing customer perceptions of how different services are performing on determinant attributes. They can help firms to see where they might reposition and also to anticipate their competitors' actions.

UNLOCK YOUR LEARNING

These keywords are found within the sections of each Learning Objective (LO). They are integral to understanding the services marketing concepts taught in each section. Having a firm grasp of these keywords and how they are used is essential to helping you do well on your course, and in the real and very competitive marketing scene out there.

LO 1
1 Company analysis
2 Competitor analysis
3 Customer analysis
4 Customer needs analysis
5 Internal corporate analysis
6 Market analysis

LO 2
7 Market position
8 Positioning
9 Positioning strategy
10 Segmentation
11 Targeting

LO 3
12 Behavioral segmentation
13 Demographic segmentation
14 Needs-based segmentation
15 Psychographic segmentation

LO 4
16 Competing alternatives
17 Decision rules
18 Determinant attribute
19 Important attribute
20 Service attribute

LO 5
21 Qualitative attribute
22 Quantitative attribute
23 Segment structure
24 Service levels

LO 6
25 Competitive advantage
26 Focus
27 Focus strategies
28 Fully focused strategy
29 Market-focused strategy
30 Service-focused strategy
31 Target segment
32 Unfocused strategy

LO 7
33 Distinctive differences
34 Positioning services

LO 8
35 Effective positioning strategy
36 Frame of reference
37 Point of difference
38 Position statement
39 Reason to believe
40 Target audience

LO 9
41 Competitive responses
42 Future scenarios
43 Perceptual mapping
44 Positioning charts
45 Positioning maps
46 Visualize strategy

How well do you know the language of services marketing? Quiz yourself!

Not for the academically faint-of-heart

For each keyword you are able to recall without referring to earlier pages, give yourself a point (and a pat on the back). Tally your score at the end and see if you earned the right to be called—*a services marketeer.*

SCORE

0 – 8 Services Marketing is done a great disservice.
9 – 16 The midnight oil needs to be lit, pronto.
17 – 24 I know what you *didn't* do all semester.
25 – 32 A close shave with success.
33 – 41 Now, go forth and market.
42 – 45 There should be a marketing concept named after you.

KNOW YOUR ESM

Review Questions

1. What are the elements of a customer-driven services marketing strategy?
2. In segmentation, what are the most common bases to use? Provide examples for each of these bases.
3. What is the distinction between important and determinant attributes in consumer purchase decisions?
4. How are service levels of determinant attributes related to positioning services?
5. Why should service firms focus their efforts? Describe the basic focus strategies, and give examples of how these work.
6. What are the six questions for developing an effective positioning strategy?
7. Describe what is meant by positioning strategy and how do the market, customer, internal, and competitive analyses relate to a positioning strategy?
8. How can positioning maps help managers better understand and respond to competitive dynamics?

WORK YOUR ESM

Application Exercises

1. Select a company of your choice. Identify the variables that the company has used to segment their customers. Support your answers with examples from the company.
2. Provide two examples of service firms that use service levels (other than airlines, hotels, and car rentals) to differentiate their products. Explain the determinant attributes and service levels used to differentiate the positioning of one service from another?
3. Find examples of companies that illustrate each of the four focus strategies discussed in this chapter.
4. Travel agencies are losing business to passengers booking their flights directly on airline websites. Identify some possible focus options open to travel agencies wishing to develop new lines of business that would make up for the loss of airline ticket sales.
5. Choose an industry you are familiar with (such as cell phone service, credit cards, or online music stores), and create a perceptual map showing the competitive positions of different service providers in that industry. Use attributes you believe are determinant attributes. Identify gaps in the market, and generate ideas for a potential "blue ocean" strategy.
6. Imagine that you have been hired as a consultant to give advice to the Palace Hotel. Consider the options facing the hotel based on the four attributes in the positioning charts (Figures 3.10 and 3.11). What actions do you recommend the Palace to take? Explain your recommendations.

THE *ESM* FRAMEWORK

PART I

Understanding Service Products, Consumers, and Markets

- Introduction to Services Marketing
- Consumer Behavior in a Services Context
- Positioning Services in Competitive Markets

PART II

Applying the 4 Ps of Marketing to Services

- Developing Service Products: Core and Supplementary Elements
- Distributing Services through Physical and Electronic Channels
- Setting Prices and Implementing Revenue Management
- Promoting Services and Educating Customers

PART III

Designing and Managing the Customer Interface

The 3 Additional Ps of Services Marketing.

- Designing and Managing Service Processes
- Balancing Demand and Capacity
- Crafting the Service Environment
- Managing People for Service Advantage

PART IV

Developing Customer Relationships

- Managing Relationships and Building Loyalty
- Complaint Handling and Service Recovery

PART V

Striving for Service Excellence

- Improving Service Quality and Productivity
- Organizing for Service Leadership

PART II

Applying the 4 Ps of Marketing to Services

PART II of this book revisits the 4 Ps of the traditional marketing mix (*P*roduct, *P*lace, *P*rice, and *P*romotions). However, the 4 Ps are expanded to take into account the specific characteristics of services that make them different from goods marketing. It consists of the following four chapters:

Chapter 4 Developing Service Products: Core and Supplementary Elements

This chapter discusses the service concept that includes both the core and supplementary elements. The supplementary elements both facilitate and enhance the core service offering.

Chapter 5 Distributing Services Through Physical and Electronic Channels

This chapter examines the time and place elements. Manufacturers usually require physical distribution channels to move their products. Some service businesses, however, are able to use electronic channels to deliver all (or at least some) of their service elements. For the services delivered in real time with customers physically present, speed and convenience of place and time have become important factors in delivering service effectively.

Chapter 6 Setting Prices and Implementing Revenue Management

This chapter provides an understanding of pricing from both the firm's and customer's point of view. For firms, the pricing strategy determines income generation. Service firms need to implement revenue management to maximize the revenue that can be generated from available capacity at any given time. From the customers' perspective, price is a key part of the costs they must incur to obtain the desired benefits. However, the cost to the customer also often includes significant nonmonetary costs.

Chapter 7 Promoting Services and Educating Customers

This chapter deals with how firms should communicate with their customers about their services through promotion and education. Since customers are co-producers and contribute to how others experience service performances, a significant portion of communication in services marketing is meant to teach customers how to effectively move through a service process.

CHAPTER 4

developing service products: CORE and SUPPLEMENTARY ELEMENTS

LEARNING OBJECTIVES

By the end of this chapter, the reader should be able to:

- **LO 1** Describe the two components of the *Flower of Service*.
- **LO 2** Know how facilitating supplementary services relate to the core product.
- **LO 3** Know how enhancing supplementary services relate to the core product.
- **LO 4** Examine how service firms use different branding strategies.
- **LO 5** Understand how branding can be used to tier service products.
- **LO 6** Discuss how firms can build brand equity and offer a branded experience.
- **LO 7** List the categories of new service development, ranging from simple style changes to major innovations.
- **LO 8** Describe how firms can achieve success in new service development.

Figure 4.1 Starbucks is a familiar brand that even has traditional tea consumers drinking out of its cups.

PART II

OPENING VIGNETTE[1]

When you think of a specialty coffee brand, the name that comes to mind is Starbucks. Starbucks has built its success on selling and serving high-quality coffee, providing uplifting customer service; and creating an inviting atmosphere that makes you want to stay just a little longer.

However, did you know that Starbucks has been introducing many retail and service innovations completely unrelated to coffee? It was one of the first coffee chains to offer free wireless broadband in many of its outlets around the world. Since then, Starbucks has introduced innovative services that its customers may want to use while enjoying their coffee. Starbucks has tied up with Apple's iTunes Wi-Fi Music Store to allow the last 10 songs played at selected Starbucks cafés to be browsed, purchased, and downloaded wirelessly onto customers' iPhones, iPads, or iPods. This music will sync back to consumers' Mac or PC the next time the mobile device is connected. In addition, Starbucks also sells movie DVDs and books from established and new authors. Perhaps, one day, you will no longer see Starbucks as just a place for your favorite vanilla mocha drink or chocolate frappé, but also as a place to relax and explore the latest in music, films, and books.

Another innovation from Starbucks improves on a supplementary service—payment. Through the Starbucks Card Mobile iPhone application, customers can now use their iPhones to pay for their purchases at Starbucks locations inside more than 1,000 Target retail stores across the United States.

Starbucks is a company that has developed service innovations with great success. However, competition continues to be intense and Starbucks has to continue to reinvent itself to maintain its edge.

LO 1

Describe the two components of the *Flower of Service.*

THE FLOWER OF SERVICE[2]

The Flower of Service has two components: the core product and supplementary services. The *core product* is based on the core set of benefits and solutions delivered to customers. The core product is the main component that supplies the desired experience (e.g., a rejuvenating spa treatment or an exhilarating roller coaster ride) or the problem-solving benefit that the customers are looking for (e.g., a management consultant provides advice on how to develop a growth strategy, or a repair service provider restores a piece of equipment to proper working condition).

Surrounding the core product is a variety of service-related activities called *supplementary services*. Supplementary services play two roles. ***Facilitating*** supplementary services are either needed for service delivery (e.g., payment), or help in the use of the main product (e.g., information). ***Enhancing*** supplementary services add extra value and appeal for customers. For example, consultation and information can be very important supplementary services in a health-care context (see Table 4.1). The core product often becomes commoditized, and supplementary services then play an important role in differentiating and positioning the core product against competing services.

Table 4.1 Facilitating and enhancing services provide value to the core product

Facilitating Services	Enhancing Services
o Information o Order taking o Billing o Payment	o Consultation o Hospitality o Safekeeping o Exceptions

In Figure 4.2, the eight clusters are displayed as petals surrounding the center of a flower. The petals are arranged in a clockwise sequence, following how they are likely to be encountered by customers. This sequence may vary. For example, payment may have to be made before service is delivered rather than afterwards. In a well-designed and well-managed service product, the petals and core are fresh and well formed. A badly designed or poorly delivered service is a like a flower with missing, wilted, or discolored petals. Even if the core is perfect, the flower looks unattractive. Think about your own experiences as a customer (or when buying on behalf of an organization). When you were dissatisfied with a particular purchase, was it the core that was at fault, or was it a problem with one or more of the petals?

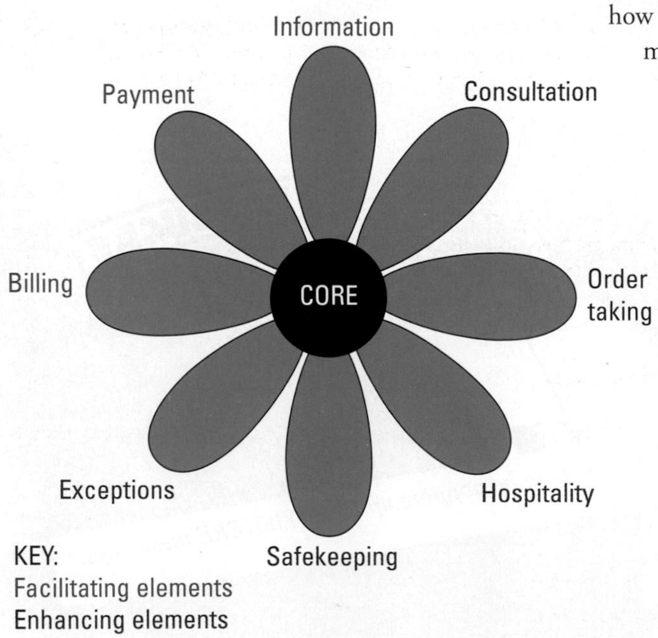

Figure 4.2 The Flower of Service: A core product surrounded by cluster of supplementary services.

FACILITATING SUPPLEMENTARY SERVICES

 **LO 2**

Know how facilitating supplementary services relate to the core product.

Information

To obtain full value from any goods or services, customers need relevant information. This information includes the following:

- Directions to the service site
- Schedules/Service hours
- Price
- Reminders
- Warnings
- Conditions of sale/service (Figure 4.3)
- Notification of changes
- Confirmation of reservations
- Summaries of account activities
- Receipts and tickets

New customers are especially information hungry. Companies should make sure the information they provide is both timely and accurate. If not, it is likely to irritate or cause inconvenience to their customers.

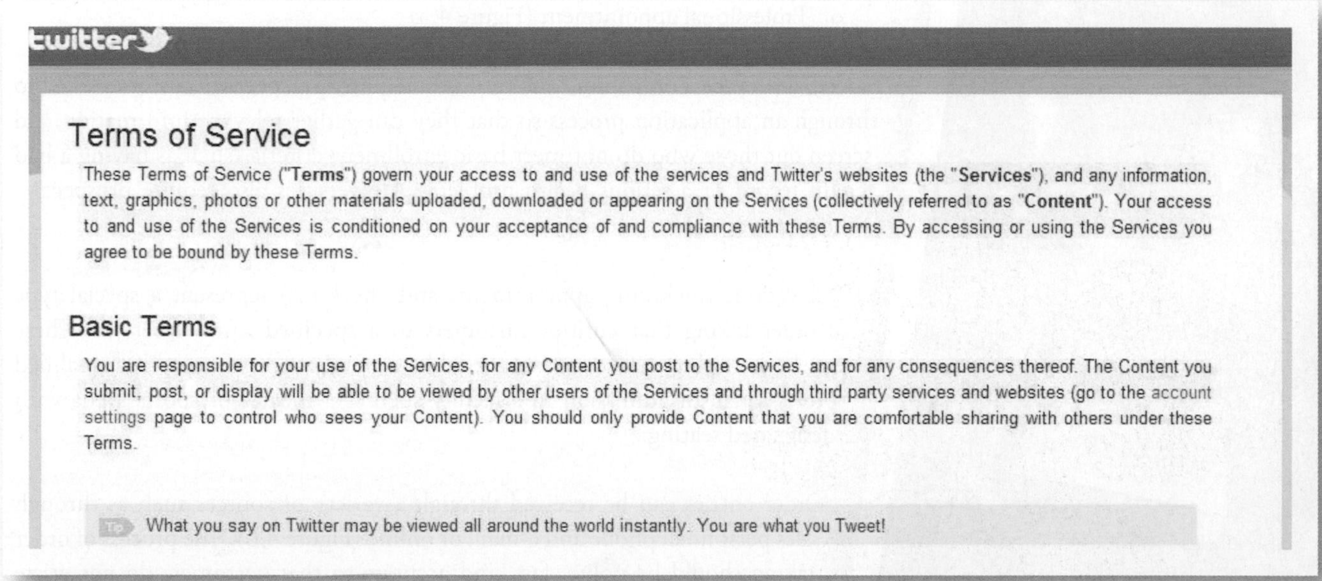

twitter

Terms of Service

These Terms of Service ("**Terms**") govern your access to and use of the services and Twitter's websites (the "**Services**"), and any information, text, graphics, photos or other materials uploaded, downloaded or appearing on the Services (collectively referred to as "**Content**"). Your access to and use of the Services is conditioned on your acceptance of and compliance with these Terms. By accessing or using the Services you agree to be bound by these Terms.

Basic Terms

You are responsible for your use of the Services, for any Content you post to the Services, and for any consequences thereof. The Content you submit, post, or display will be able to be viewed by other users of the Services and through third party services and websites (go to the account settings page to control who sees your Content). You should only provide Content that you are comfortable sharing with others under these Terms.

Tip What you say on Twitter may be viewed all around the world instantly. You are what you Tweet!

Figure 4.3 Twitter.com provides conditions of service to users.

Figure 4.4 Parcels can be tracked around the world with their unique identification number.

Traditional ways of providing information include using frontline employees, printed notices, and brochures. Information can also be provided through videos or software-driven tutorials, touch-screen video displays, or company websites. Many business logistics companies offer shippers the opportunity to track the movements of their packages—each of which has been assigned a unique identification number (Figure 4.4). For example, Amazon.com provides its customers with a reference number that allows tracking of the goods so that customers know when to expect them.

Order Taking

Once customers are ready to buy, a key supplementary element comes into play—order taking. Order taking includes the following:

- Applications
    - Memberships in clubs/programs
    - Subscription services (e.g., utilities)
    - Enrollment-based services (e.g., financial credit, college enrollment)
- Order entry
    - On-site order entry
    - Mail/Telephone/E-mail/Online order
- Reservations or check-ins
    - Seats/Tables/Rooms
    - Vehicles or equipment rental
    - Professional appointment (Figure 4.5)

Figure 4.5 The services of a professional emcee have to be reserved in advance.

Banks, insurance companies, and utilities require prospective customers to go through an application process so that they can gather relevant information and screen out those who do not meet basic enrollment criteria (such as having a bad credit record or a serious health problem). Universities also require prospective students to apply for admission.

Reservations (including appointments and check-ins) represent a special type of order taking that entitles customers to a specified unit of service. These can be an airline seat, a restaurant table, a hotel room, time with a qualified professional, or admission to a facility such as a theater or sports arena with designated seating.

Order entries can be received through a variety of sources such as through sales personnel, phone and e-mail, or online (Figure 4.6). The process of order taking should be polite, fast, and accurate so that customers do not waste time and endure unnecessary mental or physical effort. Technology can be used to make order taking easier and faster for both customers and suppliers. For example, airlines now make use of paperless systems, based on telephone or website reservations. Customers receive a confirmation number when they make the reservation and need only to show identification at the airport to claim their seats and receive boarding passes.

Billing

Billing is common to almost all services (unless the service is provided free of charge). Inaccurate, illegible, or incomplete bills risk disappointing customers who may, up to that point, have been quite satisfied with their experience. If customers are already dissatisfied, the billing mistake may make them even angrier. Billing should also be timely because it encourages people to make payment more promptly. Billing can be:

- Periodic statements of account activity
- Invoices for individual transactions
- Verbal statements of amount due
- Machine displays of amount due for self-payment transactions

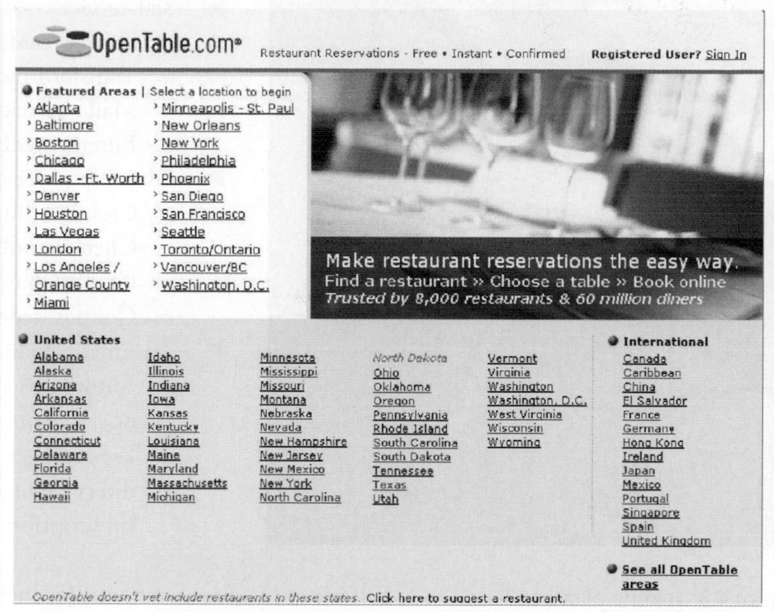

Figure 4.6 Open Table takes dining reservations to a whole new level by allowing diners to bypass the traditional call-and-book experience, with a mere click.

PART II

Perhaps the simplest approach is self-billing. This is when the customer adds up the amount of an order and authorizes a card payment or writes a check. In such instances, billing and payment are combined into a single act, although the seller may still need to check for accuracy.

Busy customers hate to be kept waiting for a bill to be prepared in a hotel, restaurant, or rental car lot. Many hotels and car rental firms have created express checkout options, taking customers' credit card details in advance and documenting charges later by mail. However, accuracy is important. Even though customers use the express checkouts to save time, they certainly don't want to waste time later with corrections and refunds. An alternative express checkout procedure is being used by some car rental companies. An agent meets customers as they return their cars, checks the mileage on the odometer and the fuel gauge readings, and then prints a bill on the spot using a portable wireless terminal (Figure 4.7). Many hotels push bills under guest-room doors on the morning of departure showing charges to date. Others offer customers the option of previewing their bills before checkout on the TV monitor in their room.

Payment

In most cases, a bill requires the customer to take action on payment (and such action may be very slow in coming!). Exceptions include bank statements and other direct debit-paid services, which show charges that will be deducted from a customer's account.

A variety of payment options exist, but all customers expect them to be easy to use and convenient. They include:

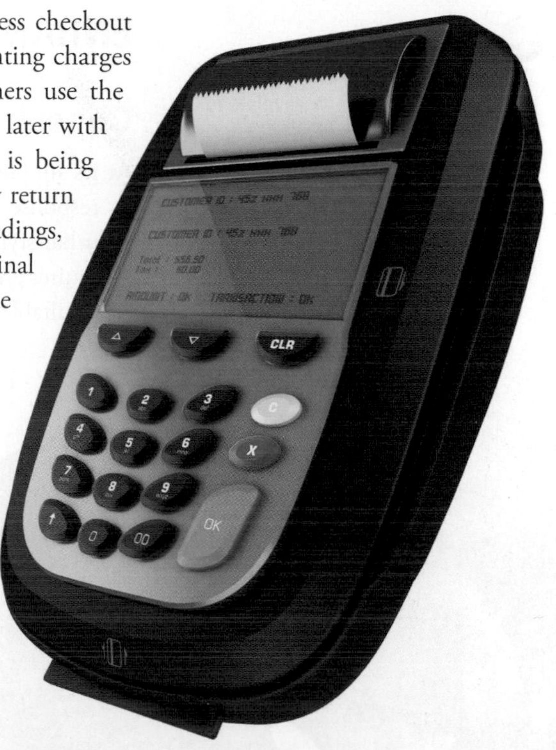

Figure 4.7 A wireless handheld terminal allows bills to be printed on the spot.

- Self-service
  - Insert a card, cash or token into the machine (Figure 4.8)
  - Transfer funds electronically
  - Mail a check
  - Enter a credit card number online
- Direct to payee or intermediary
  - Cash handling or change giving
  - Check handling
  - Credit/Charge/Debit card handling
  - Coupon redemption
- Automatic deduction from financial deposits
  - Automated systems (e.g., machine-readable tickets that operate entry gates)
  - Pre-arranged automatic deduction for bill payment through direct debit (e.g., for bank loans and post-paid cell phone subscription plans)

Figure 4.8 Tokens allow self-service payment.

Self-service payment systems, for instance, require the insertion of coins, banknotes, tokens, or cards in machines. Any equipment breakdown or technical failure will undermine the whole purpose of such a system. Therefore, regular maintenance and prompt repair are important. Most payments still take the form of cash or credit cards. Other alternatives include vouchers, coupons, or pre-paid tickets. Electronic forms of payment like PayPal offer a fuss-free and secure way to make payments when shopping online.

LO 3
Know how enhancing supplementary services relate to the core product.

ENHANCING SUPPLEMENTARY SERVICES

Consultation

At its simplest, consultation consists of advice from a knowledgeable service person in response to the request: "What do you suggest?" For example, you might ask your hairstylist for advice on different hairstyles and products. Effective consultation requires an understanding of each customer's current situation before suggesting a suitable course of action (Figure 4.9).

Examples of consultation include:

- Customized advice
- Personal counseling
- Tutoring/Training in product use
- Management or technical consulting

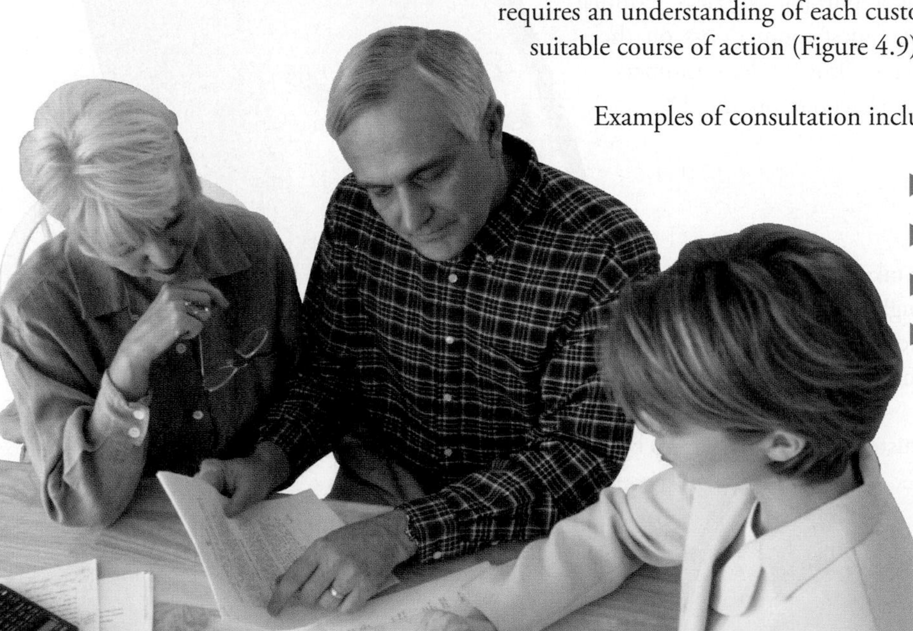

Figure 4.9 An auditor provides a human touch during the process of consultation.

Counseling is a less direct approach to consultation because it involves helping customers understand their situation so that they can come up with their "own" solutions and action programs. This approach can be useful in services like health treatment, in which part of the challenge is to get customers to make significant lifestyle changes and live healthily. For example, diet centers like Weight Watchers use counseling to help customers change behaviors so that weight loss can be sustained after the initial diet is completed (Figure 4.10).

Figure 4.10 Counseling for weight reduction is a form of consultation.

More formalized efforts to provide management and technical consulting for corporate customers include "solution selling" for expensive industrial equipment and services. A sales engineer analyzes a customer's situation and then offers advice about what particular package of equipment and systems will yield the best results. Some consulting services are offered free of charge in the hope of making a sale. Advice can also be offered through tutorials, group training programs, and public demonstrations.

PART II

Hospitality

Hospitality-related services should, ideally, reflect pleasure at meeting new customers and greeting old ones when they return. Well-managed businesses try, at least in small ways, to ensure their employees treat customers as guests. Courtesy and consideration for customers' needs apply to both face-to-face encounters and telephone interactions. Hospitality elements include:

- Greetings
- Food and beverages
- Toilets and washrooms
- Waiting facilities and amenities
  - o Lounges, waiting areas, seating
  - o Weather protection
  - o Magazines, entertainment, newspapers
- Transport

Hospitality is more clearly displayed in face-to-face encounters. In some cases, it starts (and ends) with an offer of transport to and from the service site on courtesy shuttle buses. If customers must wait outdoors before the service can be delivered, then a thoughtful service provider will offer weather protection. If customers have to wait indoors, a waiting area with seating and even entertainment (TV, newspapers, or magazines) may be provided to pass the time. Having customer-contact employees who are naturally warm, welcoming, and considerate helps to create a hospitable atmosphere. Shoppers at Giordano, an international clothing retailer with outlets across Asia Pacific and the Middle East, are greeted with a cheerful "hello" when they enter the store and "thank you" when they leave the store, even if they did not buy anything (Figure 4.11).

The quality of the hospitality services offered by a firm plays an important role in determining customer satisfaction. This is especially true for people-processing services because one cannot easily leave the service facility until delivery of the

Figure 4.11 Giordano provides hospitality with a smile.

Figure 4.12 Some hospitals offers service and rooms similar to that of a five-star hotel.

core service is completed. Private hospitals often seek to enhance their appeal by providing a level of room service that might be expected in a good hotel (Figure 4.12). This includes the provision of quality meals. Some airlines seek to differentiate themselves from their competitors with better meals and a more attentive cabin crew. Singapore Airlines is well-recognized on both counts.[3]

Safekeeping

When customers are visiting a service site, they often want assistance with their personal possessions. In fact, unless certain safekeeping services are provided (such as safe and convenient parking for their cars), some customers may not visit at all. Safekeeping includes:

- Child care, pet care (Figure 4.13)
- Parking for vehicles, valet parking
- Coat rooms
- Baggage handling
- Storage space
- Safe deposit boxes
- Security personnel

Responsible businesses pay close attention to safety and security issues for customers visiting their premises. When Wells Fargo Bank mails bank statements to its customers, it includes a brochure containing information about using its ATM machines safely, educating its customers about how to protect both their ATM cards and themselves from theft and personal injury. The bank also makes sure that its ATM machines are in brightly lit and in highly visible locations.

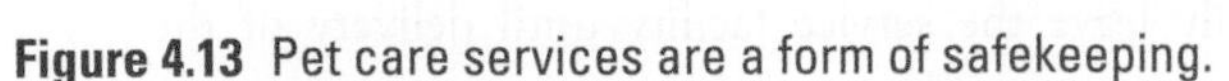

Figure 4.13 Pet care services are a form of safekeeping.

Exceptions

Exceptions involve supplementary services that fall outside the routine of normal service delivery. They include the following:

- Special requests in advance of service delivery
  - Children's needs, dietary requirements
  - Needs arising from medical or physical disability
  - Religious observances
- Handling special communications
  - Complaints
  - Compliments
  - Suggestions
- Problem solving
  - Warranties and guarantees
  - Resolving difficulties that arise from using the product
  - Resolving difficulties caused by service failures or even accidents
  - Assisting customers who have suffered an accident or a medical emergency
- Restitution
  - Refunds and compensation
  - Free repair of defective goods

Companies should anticipate exceptions and develop backup plans and guidelines in advance. That way, employees will not appear helpless and surprised when customers ask for special assistance. Well-defined procedures make it easier for employees to respond promptly and effectively (Figure 4.14).

Managers need to keep an eye on the level of exception requests. Too many requests may indicate that standard procedures need to be changed. For example, if a restaurant often receives requests for special vegetarian meals because there are none on the menu, it may be time to revise the menu to include at least one or two such dishes. A flexible approach to exceptions generally is a good idea because it reflects responsiveness to customer needs. On the other hand, too many exceptions may have a negative impact on other customers, and overburden employees.

Figure 4.14 McDonald's well-established procedures let employees respond promptly and effectively to customers' requests.

Managerial Implications

The eight categories of supplementary services that form the "Flower of Service" collectively provide many options for enhancing core products. Most supplementary services do (or should) represent responses to customer needs. Some are facilitating services such as information and reservations that enable customers to use the core product more effectively. Others are "extras" that enhance the core or even reduce its nonfinancial costs (e.g., meals, magazines, and entertainment are hospitality elements that help pass the time). Some elements, such as billing and payment, are imposed by the service provider. Even if they are not desired by the customer, they still form part of the overall service experience. Any badly handled element may negatively affect customers' perceptions of service quality.

PART II

Not every core product is surrounded by supplementary elements from all eight petals of the Flower of Service. Four categories of processes were introduced in Chapter 1—people, possession, mental stimulus, and information processing. They each have different implications for operational procedures, the degree of customer contact with service personnel and facilities, and requirements for supplementary services. People-processing services tend to be the most demanding in terms of supplementary elements, especially hospitality, because there is close and often extended customer contact. Similarly, high-contact services usually have more customer interaction than low-contact services have. When customers don't visit the service factory, the need for hospitality may be limited to simple courtesies in letters and telecommunications. Possession-processing services sometimes place heavy demands on safekeeping elements, but there may be no need for this particular "petal" when providing information-processing services in which customers and suppliers deal entirely at arm's length. Financial services provided electronically are an exception, however, as these companies must ensure that their customers' intangible financial assets and privacy are carefully safeguarded in transactions that occur via phone or the web (Figure 4.15).

Figure 4.15 Security features ensure that online transactions are safe.

A company's market positioning strategy helps to determine which supplementary services should be included. A strategy of adding benefits to increase customers' perceptions of quality will probably require more supplementary services (and a higher level of performance on all such elements) than a strategy of competing on low prices will. Furthermore, offering progressively higher levels of supplementary services around a common core may allow firms to differentiate their offerings in a product line, similar to the various classes of travel offered by airlines.

The Flower of Service and its petals discussed here can serve as a checklist in the continuing search for new ways to augment existing core products and to design new offerings. Regardless of which supplementary services a firm decides to offer, all of the elements in each petal should receive the care and attention needed to consistently meet defined service standards. That way, the resulting "flower" will always have a fresh and appealing appearance.

LO 4

Examine how service firms use different branding strategies.

BRANDING SERVICE PRODUCTS AND EXPERIENCES

In recent years, more and more service businesses have started talking about their *products*—a term previously largely associated with manufactured goods. What is a product? A *product* is a "bundle of output." A firm can differentiate one bundle of output from another. In a manufacturing context, the concept is easy to understand. Manufacturers simply differentiate their products by using various "models." For example, fast-food restaurants display a menu of their products, and these are the "models" in services. If you like burgers very much, you can easily tell the difference between Burger King's "bundle of output"—a Whopper—and McDonald's "bundle of output"—a Big Mac.

Providers of more intangible services also offer various "models" of products. Buyers of services, especially new buyers, rely on how well known the brand is, as an indicator of quality and reliability of the service, even more so than of goods. Branding also helps to differentiate one bundle of output from another. One example of this is Banyan Tree Hotels & Resorts (featured in Case 4), which carefully crafted specified products for its various target segments and branded them as "Heavenly Honeymoon," "Spa Indulgence," or "Intimate Moments."[4] "Intimate Moments" is a product especially created for couples celebrating their wedding anniversary. It is presented as a surprise to the spouse when guests find their villas decorated with lit candles, incense burning, flower petals spread throughout the room, satin sheets on the decorated bed, chilled champagne or wine, and a private outdoor pool decorated with flowers, candles, and bath oils. The couple is presented with a variety of aromatic massage oils to further inspire those intimate moments. "Packaging" and branding this product allows Banyan Tree to sell it via its website, distributors, and reservations centers and to train staff about it at the individual hotels. Marketing, selling, and delivery of the product would not be as effective if it was not packaged and branded. Let's look next at alternative branding strategies for services.

Branding Strategies for Services

Service firms can choose from among four broad branding alternatives: branded house (i.e., using a single brand to cover all products and services), house of brands (i.e., using a separate standalone brand for each offering), or subbrands and endorsed brands which are both some combination of these two extremes.[5] These alternatives are presented as a spectrum in Figure 4.16 and are discussed in the following sections.

Branded House

The term *branded house* is used to describe a company, such as the Virgin Group, that applies its brand name to multiple offerings in often unrelated fields.[6] The danger of such a branding strategy is that the brand gets overstretched and weakened.

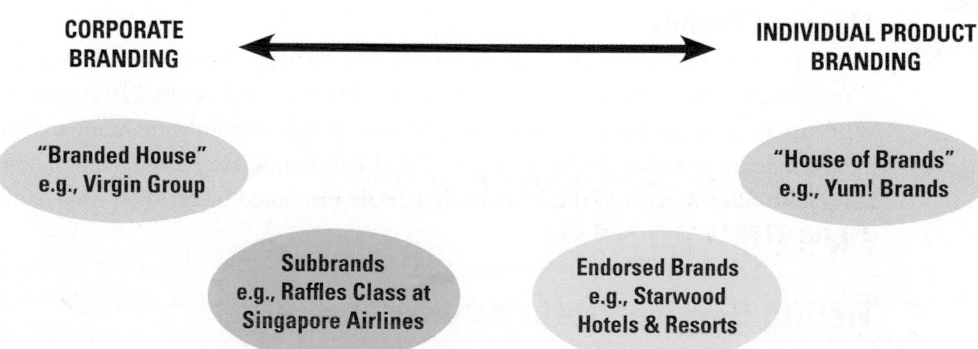

Figure 4.16 The spectrum of branding alternatives.

Subbrands

Next on the spectrum are *subbrands*, for which the corporate or the master brand is the main reference point, but the product itself also has a distinctive name too. FedEx has been successfully using a subbranding strategy. When the company decided to rebrand a ground delivery service it had purchased, it chose the name FedEx Ground and developed an alternative color for the standard logo (purple and green rather than purple and orange). Its other subbrands include FedEx Home Delivery (delivers to US residential addresses), FedEx Freight (regional, less-than-truckload transportation for heavyweight freight), FedEx Custom Critical (nonstop, door-to-door delivery of time-critical shipments), FedEx Trade Networks (customs brokerage, international freight forwarding, and trade facilitation), Fedex Supply Chain Services (a comprehensive suite of solutions that synchronize the movement of goods), and Fedex Kinko's (office and printing services, technology services, shipping supplies, and packing services located in both city and suburban retail stores).[7]

Endorsed Brands

For *endorsed brands*, the product brand dominates, but the corporate name is still featured. Many hotel companies use this approach. They offer a family of endorsed brands. For instance, Intercontinental Hotel Group in itself is well known. However, its product brands are dominant. They are Intercontinental Hotels & Resorts, Crowne Plaza Hotels & Resorts, Hotel Indigo, Holiday Inn Hotels & Resorts, Holiday Inn Express, Staybridge Suites, Candlewood Suites, Forum Hotels & Resorts, Parkroyal Hotels & Resorts, and Centra Hotels & Resorts.[8]

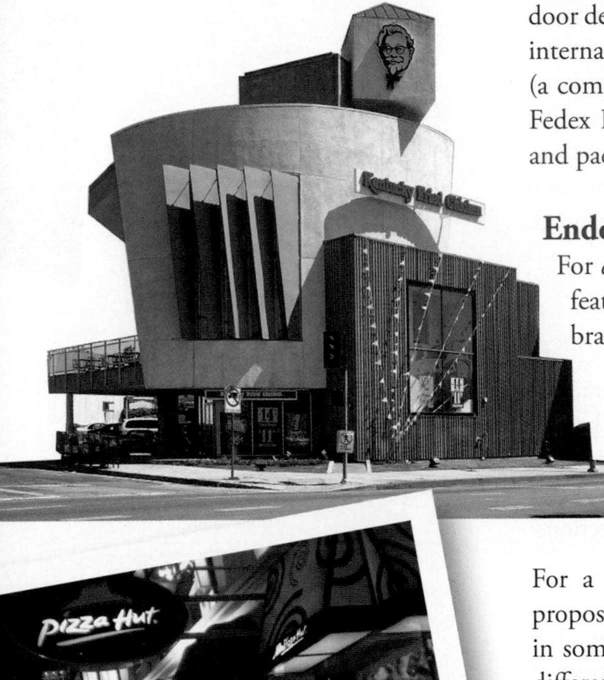

Figure 4.17 KFC and Pizza Hut are just some of the few popular fast food brands under Yum! Brands.

For a multi-brand strategy to succeed, each brand must have a unique value proposition, targeted at a different customer segment. It is important to note that in some instances, segmentation is situation based: The same individual may have different needs (and willingness to pay), such as when vacationing with family or traveling on business. A multi-brand strategy is aimed at encouraging customers to continue buying from within the brand family. Loyalty programs are often used to encourage this.

House of Brands

At the far end of the spectrum is the *house of brands* strategy. A good service example is Yum! Brands Inc., which owns more than 35,000 restaurants across 110 countries. While many may not have heard of Yum! Brands, people certainly are familiar with their restaurant brands—A&W, Kentucky Fried Chicken, Pizza Hut, Taco Bell, and Long John Silver's. Each of these brands is actively promoted under their own name (Figure 4.17).

 **LO 5**

Understand how branding can be used to tier service products.

Tiering Service Products with Branding

In a number of service industries, branding is used not only to differentiate core services but also to clearly differentiate service levels. This is known as *service tiering*. It is common in industries such as hotels, airlines, car rentals, and computer hardware and software support. Table 4.2 shows examples of the key tiers within each of these industries. Other examples of tiering include health-care insurance, cable television, and credit cards.

In the car rental industry, the size and type of cars form the primary basis of tiering. In the airline industry, individual carriers decide what levels of performance should be included with each class of service. Innovative carriers, such as British Airways and Virgin Atlantic, are continually trying to add new service features such as business-class seats that fold flat into beds for overnight travel. In other industries, tiering often reflects an individual firm's strategy of bundling service elements into a limited number of packages, each priced separately. Let's examine two examples next.

Avis Car Rental

Avis focuses on two kinds of customers: consumer customers and business customers. For consumer customers, they tier their service based on different car classes (subcompact, compact, intermediate, standard, full size, specialty, mini-car, premium, luxury, SUV, convertible, and passenger van) and also service. For example, if a customer does not want to drive, then they can opt for Avis Chauffeur Drive. The chauffeur not only drives but also acts as a mobile concierge. Business customers have four programs to choose from that cater to different types of business customers (small and medium-sized businesses, entertainment and production, meeting and group services, and government and military).[9]

Sun Microsystems Hardware and Software Support

Sun Microsystems is an example of branding different tiers in a high-tech, business-to-business product line. The company offers a full range of hardware and software support in a program branded as "SunSpectrum Support" (Figure 4.18).[10] Four different levels of support are made available to customers, with the objective of allowing buyers to choose a level of support that meets the needs of their own organization, as well as their willingness to pay. Support ranges from expensive and mission-critical support at the enterprise level (Platinum Service Plan) to relatively inexpensive assistance with self-service maintenance support (Bronze Service Plan):

Table 4.2 Examples of Service Tiering

Industry	Tiers	Key Service Attributes and Physical Elements Used in Tiering
Lodging	Star or diamond rating (5 to 1)	Architecture; landscaping; room size, furnishings, and décor; restaurant facilities and menus; room service hours; array of services and physical amenities; staffing levels; caliber and attitudes of employees
Airline	Classes (intercontinental): first, business, premium economy, economy[a]	Seat pitch (distance between rows), seat width, and reclining capability; meal and beverage service; staffing ratios; check-in speed; departure and arrival lounges; baggage retrieval speed
Car rental	Class of vehicle[b]	Base on vehicle size (from subcompact to full size), degree of luxury, plus special vehicle types (minivan, SUV, convertible)
Hardware and software support	Support levels[c]	Hours and days of service; speed of response; speed of delivering replacement parts; technician-delivered service versus advice on self-service; availability of additional services

a Only a few airlines offer as many as four classes of intercontinental service; domestic services usually feature one or two classes.
b Avis and Hertz offer seven classes based on size and luxury, plus several special vehicle types.
c Sun Microsystems offers four spport levels.

- Platinum: Mission-critical support with on-site service 24/7 and a two-hour response time.
- Gold: Business-critical support with on-site service from Monday to Friday, from 8 a.m. to 8 p.m., 24/7 telephone service and a four-hour response time.
- Silver: Basic support with on-site service from Monday to Friday, from 8 a.m. to 5 p.m., telephone service from Monday to Friday, from 8 a.m. to 8 p.m., and a four-hour response time.
- Bronze: Self-support with telephone service from 8 a.m. to 5 p.m.

LO 6
Discuss how firms can build brand equity and offer a branded experience.

Building Brand Equity and Developing a Branded Experience

Branding can be used at both the corporate and product levels by almost any service business. In a well-managed firm, the corporate brand not only is easily recognized but also has meaning for customers, standing for a particular way of doing business. Applying distinctive brand names to individual products and service tiers allows the firm to communicate to the target market the distinctive experiences and benefits associated with a specific service concept. In short, it helps marketers to establish a mental picture of the service in customers' minds and clarify the nature of the value proposition.

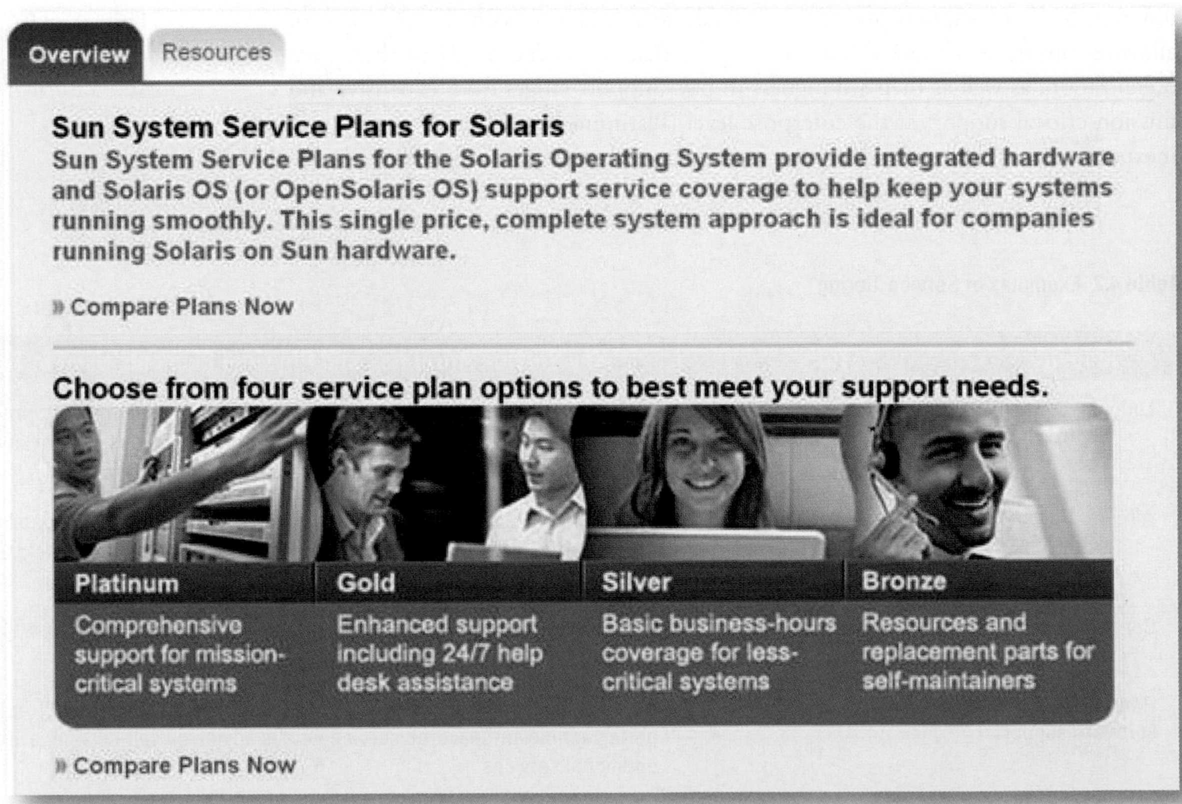

Figure 4.18 Sun Microsystems' service plans for Solaris clearly differentiate service levels.

What are some common characteristics of successful service brands? According to Leonard L. Berry, Distinguished Professor of Marketing at Texas A & M University, there are four key ways in which service companies can build strong brands.[11] They are:

- **Dare to be different.** Companies that are different are able to build their own distinct brand personality. For example, in a world of e-mail, instant messaging, and SMSes, Twitter introduced microblogging and took the world by storm. People could share their thoughts online in short 140-character messages, almost like a cross between Facebook and SMS! In 2010, Twitter had about 190 million visitors monthly, producing about 65 million tweets daily.[12]
- **Determine your own fame.** Companies that become famous over time are the ones that serve a need and provide a service that customers really value, perform service more effectively than competitors do; and have their stories told through customer experience and word-of-mouth. For example, the Boston Consulting Group was ranked eighth on *Fortune*'s list of the "100 Best Companies to Work For" in 2010. It is one of only three companies that have managed to remain in the top 15 positions in the last five years. The Boston Consulting Group is famous for being a leading advisor in business strategy. It helps companies to develop new insights into their businesses, create unique competitive advantages, and achieve better profits.[13]
- **Make an emotional connection.** This involves sparking feelings of closeness, affection, and trust. The Harlem Globetrotters made an emotional connection with people by impressing their audience with excellent ball handling, funny moves, and silliness. Watching them was a fun experience, and they made their audience laugh. The team also worked hard and represented respect, decency, and good values.
- **Internalize the brand.** Service employees are the firm and the brand. They are the ones who help to build brand equity and create experiences for the customers. Therefore, they have to internalize the concepts and values of the service so that they can perform it. The key to helping employees to internalize the brand is through education and communication. Fast-food restaurant Chick-fil-A invests a lot of resources to help their independent store operators to build the brand in their markets. The brand is internalized through a combination of education, market research, customized advice, and tracking each market's performance.

Before we can build a strong brand, we need to understand what contributes to brand equity. What is brand equity? Brand equity is the value premium that comes with a brand. It is what customers are willing to pay for the service, above what they are willing to pay for a similar service that has no brand. Figure 4.19 shows the following six key components:

- *Company's presented brand*—mainly through advertising, service facilities, and personnel.
- *External brand communications*—from word-of-mouth and publicity. These are outside of the firm's control.
- *Customer experience with the company*—what the customer went through when they patronized the company.

PART II

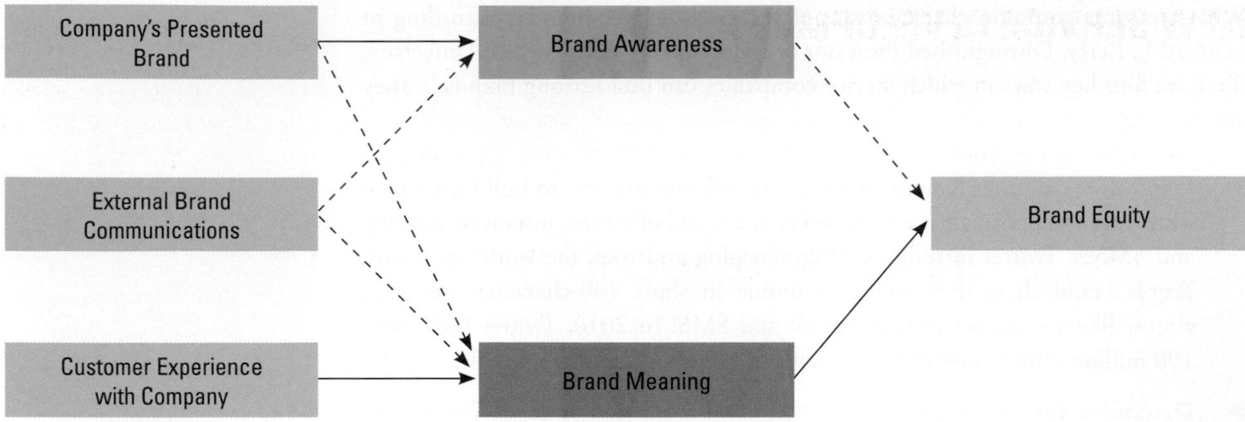

Figure 4.19 A service-branding model.

SOURCE

The bold arrows represent strong relationships and the dotted arrows represent weaker relationships.
Taken from Leonard L. Berry, "Cultivating Service Brand Equity," *Journal of the Academy of Marketing Science* 28, no. 1: 128–137.

- *Brand awareness*—ability to recognize and recall a brand when provided with a cue.
- *Brand meaning*—what comes to the customer's mind when a brand is mentioned
- *Brand equity*—the degree of marketing advantage that a brand has over its competitors.

From Figure 4.19, we can see that a company's marketing and external communications help to build brand awareness. However, it is the customer's actual experience with the brand, or the "moment of truth," that is more powerful in building brand equity. In fact, customer-oriented companies are now moving more toward customer equity rather than brand equity.[14] Firms need to focus on customers, deliver great experiences and create an emotional connection with their customers. How can they do that?

It starts with designing the brand experience, which involves aligning the company's processes, servicescapes, and people alongside its brand proposition. To begin with, we need to have great processes in place (see Chapter 8—Designing and Managing Service Processes). In addition, creating the emotional experience can often be done effectively through the servicescape (which we will learn in Chapter 10—Crafting the Service Environment). The hardest part of crafting the emotional experience is the building of interpersonal relationships where trust is established between the consumers and the firm's employees.[15] In order for this to happen, we need to invest in our employees since they will be the ones who deliver the brand experience that creates customer loyalty (see Chapter 11—Managing People for Service Advantage).

NEW SERVICE DEVELOPMENT

LO 7

List the categories of new service development, ranging from simple style changes to major innovations.

Intense competition and rising consumer expectations have an impact on nearly all service industries. Thus, great brands not only provide existing services well but also continuously improve through innovation and create new approaches to service.

A Hierarchy of New Service Categories

There are many ways for a service provider to innovate. Below, we identify seven categories of new services, ranging from simple style changes to major innovations.

1. *Style changes* are the simplest type of innovation, typically involving no changes in either processes or performance. However, they often are highly visible, create excitement, and may serve to motivate employees. Examples include repainting retail branches and vehicles in new color schemes, designing new uniforms for service employees, introducing a new bank check design, or effecting minor changes in service scripts for employees.
2. *Service improvements* are the most common type of innovation. They involve small changes in the performance of current products, including improvements to either the core product or to existing supplementary services. Often, it is the little things that matter, and customers appreciate it. For example, the elevator in the Lydmar Hotel in Stockholm has a series of buttons where guests can choose their music from a choice of garage, funk, and rhythm and blues. This may be just a simple improvement, but it adds to a customer's experience as it is unique and surprising.[16]
3. *Supplementary service innovations* take the form of adding new facilitating or enhancing service elements to an existing core service or significantly improving an existing supplementary service. FedEx Kinkos now offers customers high-speed Internet access round-the-clock at most of its locations in the US, and in Canada. Low-tech innovations for an existing service can be as simple as adding parking at a retail site or agreeing to accept credit cards for payment. Theme restaurants such as the Rainforest Café enhance the core food service with new experiences (Figure 4.20). The cafés are designed to keep customers entertained with aquariums, live parrots, waterfalls, fiberglass monkeys, talking trees that spout environmentally related information, and regularly timed thunderstorms, complete with lightning.[17]
4. *Process line extensions* often represent distinctive new ways of delivering existing products. The intention is either to offer more convenience and a different experience for existing customers, or to attract new customers who find the traditional approach unappealing. Often, they involve adding a lower-contact distribution channel to an existing high-contact channel, such as having self-service to complement delivery by service employees or creating telephone- or Internet-based service

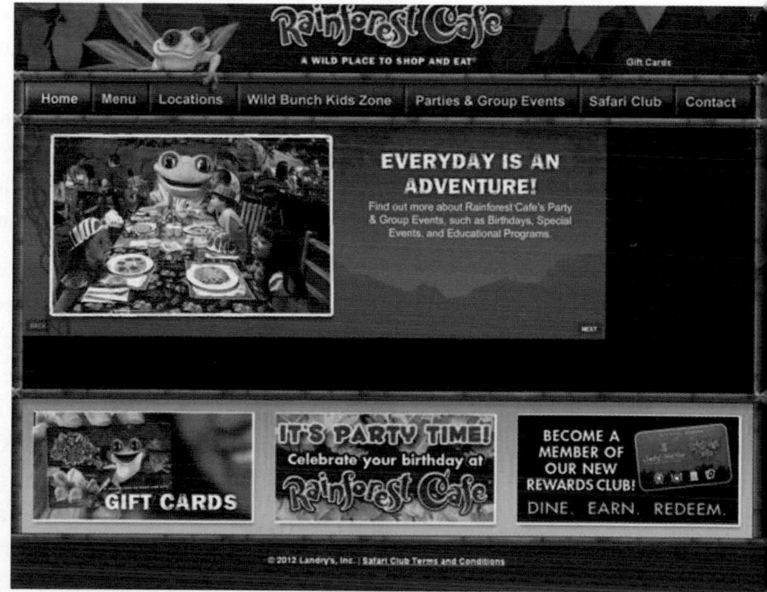

Figure 4.20 Rainforest Café makes a supplementary service innovation by enhancing the core food service with the experience of being in a jungle.

Figure 4.21 E-books can be downloaded and read from the iPhone or iPad.

delivery. For example, websites used to just display an e-mail address or a telephone to contact the service personnel. Therefore, one would still have to call the company to talk to the service personnel. Now, many websites have included chat functions where one can get in touch with an employee "live" and in real time.

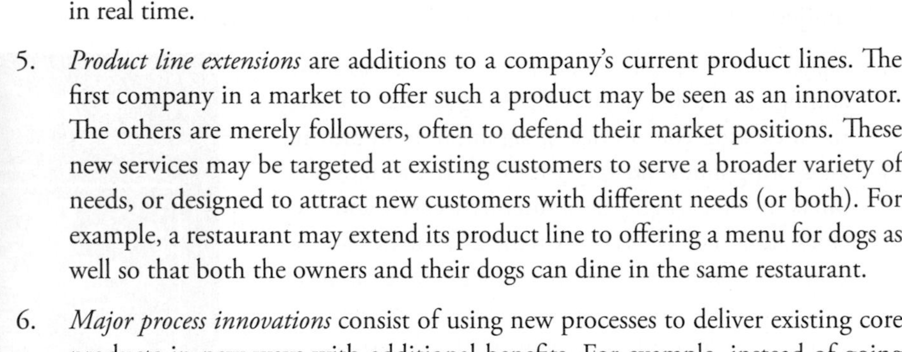

5. *Product line extensions* are additions to a company's current product lines. The first company in a market to offer such a product may be seen as an innovator. The others are merely followers, often to defend their market positions. These new services may be targeted at existing customers to serve a broader variety of needs, or designed to attract new customers with different needs (or both). For example, a restaurant may extend its product line to offering a menu for dogs as well so that both the owners and their dogs can dine in the same restaurant.

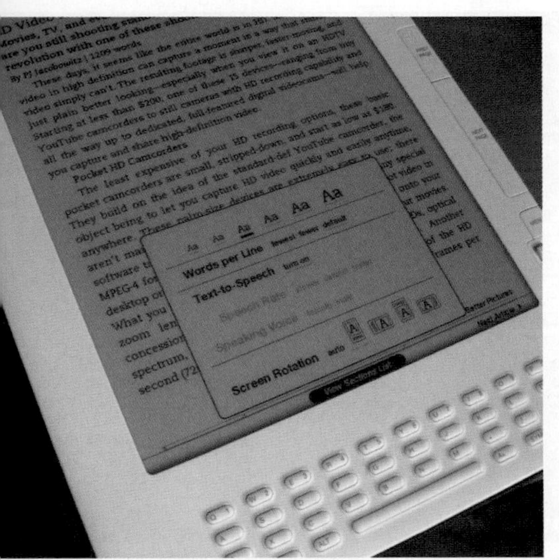

Figure 4.22 The Kindle DX allows one to read newspapers comfortably.

6. *Major process innovations* consist of using new processes to deliver existing core products in new ways with additional benefits. For example, instead of going to a bookstore to buy a physical book from the bookstore, consumers who own an iPhone or iPad can purchase the same book, as an e-book from Apple's iBookstore via its iBook application (Figure 4.21).

   Amazon's Kindle DX Wireless Reading device is another such example. It allows one to read newspapers comfortably with a 9.7-inch display area, and offers free 3G access globally (Figure 4.22). Using the Kindle, *New York Times* subscribers can have their newspaper auto-delivered wirelessly when the physical issue hits the newsstand.[18]

7. *Major service innovations* are new core products for markets that have not been previously defined. They usually include both new service characteristics and radical new processes. Space Adventures, a leading company in the spaceflight industry, flew the first space tourist on the Russian Soyuz spacecraft to the International Space Station in 2001. Today, they provide different space experiences, including lunar missions, orbital space flights, suborbital space

flight, and spacewalk programs (Figure 4.23). These experiences do not come cheap. Suborbital space flights, for example, start from $102,000 and a lunar mission costs $100 million per seat.[19]

Figure 4.23 Space Adventures offers customers a chance to be space tourists.

Major service innovations are relatively rare. More common is the use of new technologies to deliver existing services in new ways, enhancing or creating new supplementary services and greatly improving performance on existing ones through process redesign. Singapore Airlines is such a company. In fact, it pursues service excellence as well as cost effectiveness through smart service innovation.[20]

PART II

Achieving Success in New Service Development

 LO 8

Describe how firms can achieve success in new service development.

Consumer goods have high failure rates, with more than 90% of the 30,000 new products introduced each year ending in failure.[21] Services are not immune to the high failure rates either. For example, Delta Airlines was one of several major carriers attempting to launch a separate low-cost carrier designed to compete with discount airlines such as Jet Blue and Southwest Airlines. However, none of these operations was successful. In banking, many banks have tried to sell insurance products in the hope of increasing the number of profitable relationships with existing customers, but many of these product extensions have also failed.

There are various reasons for failure, including not meeting a consumer need, inability to cover costs from revenues, and poor execution. For example, a study in the restaurant industry found a failure rate of about 26% during the first year, rising to almost 60% within three years. Interestingly, the rate varied widely by the type of food served, ranging from 33% for seafood and burger restaurants to 76% for sandwich shops and bakeries and 86% for restaurants serving Mexican food.[22]

How then can we successfully develop new services? A number of studies have found that the following three factors contribute most to success and can be described as follows[23]:

1. *Market synergy*—The new product fits well with the existing image of the firm, its expertise, and resources. It is better than competing products in terms of meeting customers' needs as the firm has a good understanding of its customers' purchase behavior and receives strong support during and after the launch from the firm and its branches.
2. *Organizational factors*—There is strong interfunctional cooperation and coordination. Development personnel are fully aware of why they are involved and of the importance of new products to the company. Before the launch, the staff understand the new product and its underlying processes, as well as details about direct competitors.
3. *Market research factors*—Detailed and properly designed market research studies are conducted early in the development process. There is a clear idea of the type of information to be obtained. A good definition of the product concept is developed before undertaking field surveys.

CHAPTER SUMMARY

LO 1 ▶ The Flower of Service consists of two components:

- o Core product delivers the main benefits and solutions customers look for.
- o Supplementary services facilitate and enhance the value of the core product.

The core product often becomes commoditized, and supplementary services can then play an important role in differentiating and positioning the core product.

LO 2 ▶ The Flower of Service concept categorizes supplementary services into facilitating and enhancing supplementary services.

- o Facilitating supplementary services are needed for service delivery or help in the use of the core product. They are information, order taking, billing, and payment.

LO 3 ▶ Enhancing supplementary services add value for the customer. They include consultation, hospitality, safekeeping, and dealing with exceptions.

LO 4 ▶ Branding of service products helps firms to differentiate one bundle of output from another. Firms can use a variety of branding strategies, including the following:

- o *Branded house*: applying a brand to multiple, often unrelated services (e.g., Virgin Group).
- o *Subbrands*: using a master brand (often the firm name) together with a specific service brand (e.g., Fedex Ground service) or to identify specific service levels (e.g., Sun Microsystems' Platinum Service Plan).
- o *Endorsed brands*: where the product brand dominates but the corporate brand is still featured (e.g., Starwood Hotels & Resorts).
- o *House of brands*: where individual services are promoted under their own brand names without the corporate brand (e.g., KFC of Yum! Brands).

LO 5 ▶ In many industries, branding is not only used to differentiate core services. It also differentiates service levels, called service tiering. There are some industries where service tiering is common and they include hotels, airlines, car rentals, and credit cards.

LO 6 ▶ Branding is not just about applying distinctive brand names. To build strong brands, there are four key ways:

- o Dare to be different (e.g., in a world of email, instant messaging and SMSes, Twitter introduced microblogging and took the world by storm).
- o Determine your own fame (e.g., the Boston Consulting Group is famous for being a leading advisor in business strategies).
- o Make an emotional connection, (e.g., the Harlem Globetrotters made an emotional connection by impressing their audience with excellent ball handling, funny moves, and silliness).
- o Let employees internalize the brand (e.g., Chick-fil-A invests a lot of resources in its employees in order to internalize the brand).
- o Ultimately, while the firm's external brand communications create brand awareness, it is the customer's service experience that builds brand equity. To build great brands, firms need to align processes, servicescapes, and people with its brand positioning.

LO 7 ▶ Firms need to improve and develop new services to maintain a competitive edge. The seven levels in the hierarchy of new service development are

- o *Style changes*: highly visible, create excitement (e.g., repainting retail branches and vehicles in a new color scheme), but typically do not involve changes in service performance or processes.
- o *Service improvements*: involve modest changes in the performance of current products.
- o *Supplementary service innovations*: significantly improving or adding new facilitating or enhancing service elements.
- o *Process line extensions*: new ways of delivering existing services products, such as creating self-service options.
- o *Product line extensions*: adding new services that typically deliver the same core service but are specified to satisfy different needs.

- *Major process innovations*: using new processes to deliver current products, such as adding online courses to traditional classroom-delivered lectures.
- *Major service innovations*: development of new core products for markets that have not been previously defined.

Major service innovations are relatively rare. More common is the use of new technologies to deliver existing services in new ways, enhancing or creating new supplementary services, and greatly improving performance on existing ones through process redesign.

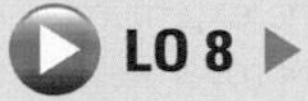

Key factors that enhance the chances of success in new service development can be described as:

- *Market synergy*: The new product fits well with the firm's existing image, expertise and resources; is better at meeting customers' needs over competing services; and receives strong support during and after the launch from the firm and its branches.
- *Organizational factors*: Strong cooperation between the different functional areas in a firm; staff are aware of the importance of the new products in the company, and understand the new products and their underlying processes.
- *Market research*: Detailed and properly designed market research studies are conducted early in the development process. There is a clear idea of the type of information to be obtained. A good definition of the product concept is developed before undertaking field surveys.

UNLOCK YOUR LEARNING

These keywords are found within the sections of each Learning Objective (LO). They are integral to understanding the services marketing concepts taught in each section. Having a firm grasp of these keywords and how they are used is essential to helping you do well on your course, and in the real and very competitive marketing scene out there.

LO 1
1 Core product
2 Enhancing supplementary services
3 Facilitating supplementary services
4 Flower of Service
5 Supplementary services

LO 2
6 Billing
7 Information
8 Order taking
9 Payment
10 Reservations
11 Self-service

LO 3
12 Consultation
13 Counseling
14 Exceptions
15 Hospitality
16 Safekeeping
17 Special requests
18 Supplementary services

LO 4
19 Branded house
20 Branding strategies
21 Bundle of output
22 Endorsed brands
23 House of brands
24 Multi-brand strategy
25 Subbrands

LO 5
26 Service tiering

LO 6
27 "Moments of truth"
28 Brand awareness
29 Brand communications
30 Brand equity
31 Brand meaning
32 Branded experience
33 Branding
34 Building your own fame
35 Dare to be different
36 Emotional connection
37 Internalize the brand
38 Presented brand
39 Service Branding Model

LO 7
40 Major process innovations
41 Major service innovations
42 New service development
43 Process line extensions
44 Product line extensions
45 Service improvements
46 Style changes
47 Supplementary service innovations

LO 8
48 Market research factors
49 Market synergy
50 Organizational factors
51 Success in new service development

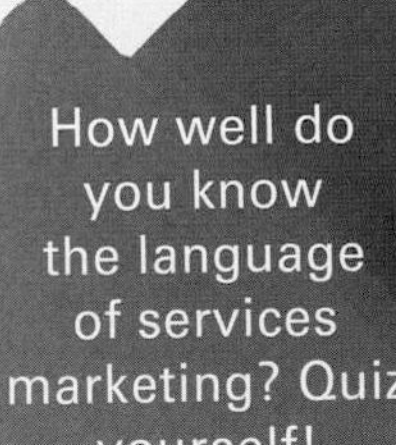

Not for the academically faint-of-heart

For each keyword you are able to recall without referring to earlier pages, give yourself a point (and a pat on the back). Tally your score at the end and see if you earned the right to be called—a *services marketeer*.

SCORE

0 – 10	Services Marketing is done a great disservice.
11 – 20	The midnight oil needs to be lit, pronto.
21 – 30	I know what you *didn't* do all semester.
31 – 40	A close shave with success.
41 – 47	Now, go forth and market.
48 – 51	There should be a marketing concept named after you.

KNOW YOUR ESM

Review Questions

1. Explain what is meant by core product and supplementary services.
2. Explain the *Flower of Service* concept and identify each of its *petals*. What insights does this concept provide for service marketers?
3. What is the difference between enhancing and facilitating supplementary services? Give several examples of each relative to services you have used recently.
4. How is branding used in services marketing? What is the distinction between a corporate brand such as Marriott and the names of its various inn and hotel chains?
5. How can service firms build brand equity?
6. What are the approaches firms can take to create new services?
7. Why do new services often fail? What factors are associated with successful development of new services?

PART II

WORK YOUR ESM

Application Exercises

1. Select a specific service product you are familiar with and identify its core product and supplementary services. Then select a competing service and analyze the differences in terms of core product and supplementary services between the two services.
2. Identify two examples of branding in financial services (e.g., specific types of retail bank accounts or insurance policies), and define their characteristics. How meaningful are these brands likely to be to customers?
3. Using a firm you are familiar with, analyze what opportunities it might have to create product line extensions for its current and/or new markets. What impact might these extensions have on its present services?
4. Select a service firm that you believe is highly successful and has strong brand equity. Conduct a few interviews to find out how consumers experience its service. From the findings, identify the factors that helped that service firm to build strong brand equity.
5. Identify two failed new service developments. Analyze the causes of their failure.
6. Select a service brand you consider to be outstanding. Explain why you think it is outstanding. Also explore any weaknesses of this brand. (You should select an organization you are very familiar with.)

ENDNOTES

1 Bruce Horovitz "Starbucks Aims Beyond Lattes to Extend Brand," *USA Today*, May 18, 2006; Youngme Moon and John Quelch, "Starbucks: Delivering Customer Service," Harvard Business School, Case Series, 2003; Joseph A. Michelli, *The Starbucks Experience: 5 Principles for Turning Ordinary into Extraordinary*. New York: McGraw Hill, 2007. www.starbucks.com and www.hearmusic.com, accessed March 12, 2012.

2 The "Flower of Service" concept was first introduced in Christopher H. Lovelock, "Cultivating the Flower of Service: New Ways of Looking at Core and Supplementary Services," in P. Eiglier and E. Langeard, eds. *Marketing, Operations, and Human Resources: Insights into Services* (Aix-en-Provence, France: IAE, Université d'Aix-Marseille III, 1992, 296–316).

3 Loizos Heracleous and Jochen Wirtz (2010), "Singapore Airlines' Balancing Act—Asia's Premier Carrier Successfully Executes a Dual Strategy: It Offers World-class Service and Is a Cost Leader," *Harvard Business Review* 88, no. 7/8: 145–149.

4 See /www.banyantree.com, accessed March 12, 2012.

5 James Devlin, "Brand Architecture in Services: The Example of Retail Financial Services," *Journal of Marketing Management* 19, (2003): 1043–1065.

6 David Aaker and Erich Joachimsthaler, "The Brand Relationship Spectrum: The Key to the Brand Challenge," *California Management Review* 42, no. 4 (2000): 8–23.

7 http://images.fedex.com/us/services/pdf/Our_Services_Index.pdf, accessed March 12, 2012.

8 http://www.ichotelsgroup.com/, accessed March 12, 2012.

9 http://www.avis.com/car-rental/avisHome/home.ac, accessed March 12, 2012.

10 http://www.sun.com/service/serviceplans/sunspectrum/index.jsp, accessed March 12, 2012.

11 Leonard L. Berry, "Cultivating Service Brand Equity," *Journal of the Academy of Marketing Science* 28, no. 1 (2000): 128–137.

12 Erick Schonfeld, Costolo "Twitter Now Has 190 Million Users Tweeting 65 Million Times a Day", http://techcrunch.com/2010/06/08/twitter-190-million-users/, accessed March 12, 2012.

13 http://www.bcg.com/about_bcg/default.aspx, accessed December 2011.

14 Roland T. Rust, Christine Moorman and Gaurav Bhalia, "Rethinking Marketing", *Harvard Business Review* 88. no. 1 (2010): 94–101.

15 Sharon Morrison and Frederick G. Crane, "Building the Service Brand by Creating and Managing an Emotional Brand Experience," *Brand Management* 14, no. 5 (2007): 410–421.

16 Talk by Rory Sutherland: Sweat the Small Stuff, http://www.ted.com/talks/lang/eng/rory_sutherland_sweat_the_small_stuff.html, accessed March 12, 2012.

17 Chad Rubel, "New Menu for Restaurants: Talking Trees and Blackjack," *Marketing News* 30, (July 29, 1996): 1. www.rainforestcafe.com, accessed March 12, 2012.

18 See Brad Stone, "Looking to Big-Screen E-Readers to Help Save the Daily Press," *The New York Times*, May 3, 2009 and Jane Walls, "Amazon's New Kindle DX Wireless Reading Device," *The First Reporter* (July 8, 2010). http://www.thefirstreporter.com/technology/review-amazons-kindle-dx-wireless/, accessed July 8, 2010.

19 http://www.spaceadventures.com/, accessed, March 12, 2012.

20 Loizos Heracleous and Jochen Wirtz, "Singapore Airlines' Balancing Act," *Harvard Business Review* (July–August 2010): 1–7.

21 Clayton M. Christenson, Scott Cook, and Taddy Hall, "Marketing Malpractice: The Cause and the Cure," *Harvard Business Review* (December 2005): 4–12.

22 H. G. Parsa, John T. Self, David Njite, and Tiffany King, "Why Restaurants Fail," *Cornell Hotel and Restaurant Administration Quarterly* 46, (August 2005): 304–322.

23 Scott Edgett and Steven Parkinson, "The Development of New Financial Services: Identifying Determinants of Success and Failure," *International Journal of Service Industry Management* 5, no. 4 (1994): 24–38; Christopher D. Storey and Christopher J. Easingwood, "The Impact of the New Product Development Project on the Success of Financial Services," *Service Industries Journal* 13, no. 3 (July 1993): 40–54; Michael Ottenbacher, Juergen Gnoth, and Peter Jones, "Identifying Determinants of Success in Development of New High-Contact Services," *International Journal of Service Industry Management* 17, no. 4 (2006): 344–363.

CHAPTER 5

distributing SERVICES through PHYSICAL and ELECTRONIC CHANNELS

LEARNING OBJECTIVES

By the end of this chapter, the reader should be able to:

- **LO 1** Know the four key questions that form the foundation of any service distribution strategy: *What? How? Where?* and *When?*
- **LO 2** Describe the three interrelated flows that show *what* is being distributed.
- **LO 3** Illustrate *how* services can be distributed using the three main options.
- **LO 4** Explain what determines customers' channel preferences.
- **LO 5** Describe the *where* (place) and *when* (time) decisions of physical channels.
- **LO 6** Discuss the factors that have fueled the growth of service delivery via cyberspace.
- **LO 7** Understand the part played by intermediaries in distributing services.
- **LO 8** Explain what determines which market entry strategy a firm should use when it goes global.

OPENING VIGNETTE

Being Global in an Instant? .... Or Does It Take Forever?

Some services spread like wildfire and at incredible speed. For example, Lauren Luke's *panacea81* has become one of the world's most popular YouTube channels in less than 12 months. It has over 88 million views, and Luke has become an Internet celebrity with her short video tutorials showing viewers how to apply make-up for various occasions. She was named the most influential make-up mentor by *Allure* magazine in 2010. Related services, including the British make-up artist's website, have been hugely successful.[1]

Other services, however, may take decades to achieve global distribution. Think of how long it took Starbucks or global supply chain solutions providers such as FedEx or DHL to achieve a global presence! These contrasting examples show both the diversity of the service sector and the importance of differentiating information processing and people- or possession-processing services. Information-processing services can be distributed rapidly. People- or possession-processing services require the building of facilities in every market where they want presence. There is also the need for the growing firm to deal with local labor, building, food hygiene regulations, and more. These require a lot of finances, as well as a lot of management time!

PART II

Figure 5.1 Lauren Luke's make-up videos on YouTube are viewed by hundred millions of audience globally.

Figure 5.2 After the success of her YouTube make-up videos, Lauren Luke launched her cosmetics line, By Lauren Luke, with Sephora.

LO 1

Know the four key questions that form the foundation of any service distribution strategy: *What? How? Where?* and *When?*

DISTRIBUTION IN A SERVICES CONTEXT

What? How? Where? When? Developing responses to these four questions is key to any service distribution strategy. The customer's service experience depends on how the different elements of the Flower of Service are distributed and delivered through physical and electronic channels.

LO 2

Describe the three interrelated flows that show *what* is being distributed.

What Is Distributed?

If you mention distribution, many people are likely to think of moving boxes through physical channels to distributors and retailers for sale to end-users. In services, though, often there is nothing to move. Experiences, performances, and solutions are not physically shipped and stored. How then does distribution work in a services context? Distribution has three interrelated flows, which helps to address the question of *what* is distributed:

- **Information and promotion flow**—distribution of information and promotional materials relating to the service offer. The objective is to get the customer interested in buying the service.
- **Negotiation flow**—reaching an agreement on the service features and configuration, and the terms of the offer so that a purchase contract can be closed. The objective is often to sell the *right* to use a service (e.g., sell a reservation or a ticket).
- **Product flow**—many services, especially those involving people processing or possession processing, require physical facilities for delivery. For information-processing services, such as Internet banking and distance learning, the product flow can be via electronic channels, using one or more centralized sites.

The flow perspective can relate to the core service as well as to the supplementary services of the Flower of Service. Information flow relates to the information and possibly consultation petals. Negotiations flow is present in order taking and potentially billing and payment petals, and product flow relates to the remaining petals and core service.

LO 3

Illustrate *how* services can be distributed using the three main options.

DISTRIBUTION OPTIONS FOR SERVING CUSTOMERS: DETERMINING THE TYPE OF CONTACT

How should services be distributed? Here, a key question is: Does the service or the firm's positioning strategy require customers to be in direct physical contact with its personnel, equipment, and facilities? (As we saw in Chapter 1, this is unavoidable for people-processing services but may not be necessary for other categories.) If so, do customers have to visit the facilities of the service organization, or will the service organization send personnel and equipment to customers' own sites? Alternatively, can transactions between providers and customers be completed at arm's length through the use of either telecommunications or physical channels of distribution? (The three possible options are shown in the first column of Table 5.1.) For each of these three options, should the firm have just a single outlet or offer to serve customers through multiple outlets at different locations?

Table 5.1 Six options for service delivery

Nature of Interaction between Customer and Service Organization	Availability of Service Outlets	
	Single Site	Multiple Sites
Customer goes to service organization	Theater	Café house chain
	Car service workshop	Car rental chain
Service organization comes to customer	House painting	Mail delivery
	Mobile car wash	Auto club road service
Customer and service organization transact remotely (via mail or electronic communication)	Credit card company	Broadcast network
	Local TV station	Telephone company

PART II

Customers Visit the Service Site

When customers have to visit the service site, two key factors need to be considered:

- The convenience of service outlet locations—Elaborate statistical analysis using retail gravity models is sometimes used to help firms make decisions on where to locate supermarkets or similar large stores, relative to the homes and workplaces of future customers.
- Operational hours—Many banks, for instance, are extending their opening hours to meet the needs of busy professionals who do not have time to take care of their banking needs during office hours.

Service Providers Go to Their Customers

For some types of services, the service provider visits the customer. Compass Group, the largest food service organization in the United Kingdom and Ireland, provides catering and support services to over 8,500 locations. They must visit the customer's site because the need is location specific. When should service providers go their customers?

- Going to the customer's site is unavoidable if the object of the service is some immovable physical item, such as a tree to be pruned (Figure 5.3), installed machinery to be repaired, or a house that requires pest control treatment.
- In remote areas like Alaska or Canada's Northwest Territory, service providers often fly to visit their customers because the latter find it so difficult to travel. Australia is famous for its Royal Flying Doctor Service, in which physicians fly to make house calls at farms and sheep stations in the outback.
- In general, service providers are more likely to visit corporate customers at their offices than to visit individuals in their homes, reflecting the larger volume associated with business-to-business (B2B) transactions. However, it may be profitable to serve individuals who are willing to pay a premium for the convenience

Figure 5.3 Tree pruning is a service that has to be provided on-site.

of receiving personal visits. One young veterinary doctor has built her business around house calls to care for sick pets. She has found that customers are willing to pay extra for service that not only saves them time, but is also less stressful for their pets, compared to waiting in a crowded veterinary clinic. Other consumer services of this kind include mobile car washing, office and in-home catering, and made-to-measure tailoring services for business people.

A growing service activity involves the rental at the customer's site of both equipment and labor for special occasions or in response to customers who need to expand their productive capacity during busy periods. Service Insights 5.1 describes the B2B services of Aggreko, an international company that rents generating and cooling equipment around the world.

SERVICE INSIGHTS 5.1

Power and Temperature Control for Rent

You probably think of electricity as coming from a distant power station and of air conditioning and heating as fixed installations. So how would you deal with the following challenges?

- At the 2010 FIFA World Cup in South Africa, they needed temporary power to support the broadcasting of the 64 matches to over three billion people worldwide.
- A tropical cyclone has devastated the small mining town of Pannawonica in Western Australia, destroying everything in its path, including power lines, and electrical power must be restored as soon as possible so that the town and its infrastructure can be rebuilt.
- In Amsterdam, organizers of the World Championship Indoor Windsurfing competition need to power 27 wind turbines that will be installed along the length of a huge indoor pool to create winds of 20–30 mph (32–48 km/h).
- A US Navy submarine needs a shore-based source of power when it is docked at a remote Norwegian port.
- Sri Lanka faces a great shortage of electricity-generating capability after water levels fall dangerously low at major hydroelectric dams due to insufficient monsoon rains two years in a row.
- Hotels in Florida need to be dried out following water damage due to a hurricane.
- A large, power-generating plant in Oklahoma urgently seeks temporary capacity to replace one of its cooling tower destroyed in a tornado the previous day.
- The Caribbean island of Bonaire requires a temporary power station to stabilize its grid after fire damages the main power plant, and resulting in widespread blackouts.

These are all challenges that have been faced and met by a company called Aggreko, which describes

itself as "The World Leader in Temporary Utility Rental Solutions." Aggreko operates from more than 133 locations using more than $1 billion of rental equipment to serve customers in over 100 countries. It rents a "fleet" of mobile electricity generators, oil-free air compressors, and temperature-control devices ranging from water chillers and industrial air conditioners to giant heaters and dehumidifiers.

Aggreko's customer base is dominated by large companies and government agencies. Although much of its business comes from predicted needs, such as backup operations during planned factory maintenance or the filming of a James Bond movie, the firm is ready to resolve problems that arise unexpectedly from emergencies or natural disasters.

Much of the firm's rental equipment is contained in soundproofed, boxlike structures that can be shipped anywhere in the world to create the specific type and level of electrical power output or climate-control capability required by the client. Consultation, installation, and ongoing technical support add value to the core service. Emphasis is placed on solving customer problems rather than just renting equipment. Some customers have a clear idea of their needs in advance. Others require advice on how to develop creative and cost-effective solutions to what may be unique problems. Still others are desperate to restore power that has been lost because of an unexpected disaster. In the last-mentioned instance, speed is essential because downtime can be extremely expensive and lives may depend on the promptness of Aggreko's response.

Delivering service requires Aggreko to ship its equipment to the customer's site. Following the Pannawonica cyclone, Aggreko's West Australian team swung into action, rapidly setting up some 30 generators ranging from 60 to 750 kVA, plus cabling, refueling tankers, and other equipment. The generators were transported by four "road trains," each comprising a giant tractor unit pulling three 40-foot (13-m) trailers. Technicians and additional equipment were flown in on two Hercules aircraft. The Aggreko technicians remained on site for six weeks, providing 24/7 service while the town was rebuilt.

SOURCE

Aggreko's "International Magazine," 1997, www.aggreko.com, accessed March 12, 2012.

PART II

The Service Transaction Is Conducted Remotely

A customer may never see the service facilities or meet service personnel face-to-face when dealing with a service firm through remote transactions. Service encounters with service personnel are more likely via a call center or, even more remotely, by mail or e-mail.

- Repair services for small pieces of equipment sometimes require customers to ship the product to a maintenance facility, where it is serviced and then returned by mail (with the option of paying extra for express shipment). Many service providers offer solutions with the help of logistics firms such as FedEx, and UPS. These solutions range from storage and express delivery of spare parts for aircraft (B2B delivery) to pickup of defective cell phones from customers' homes and return of the repaired phone to the customer (B2C pickup and delivery, also called "reverse logistics").
- Any information-based product can be delivered almost instantly through the Internet to almost any point on the globe (Figure 5.4).

Figure 5.4 Financial advice can be delivered through the Internet.

Figure 5.8 Automated kiosks selling stamps are a form of ministore.

Ministores

An interesting innovation among multi-site service businesses involves creating numerous small service factories to maximize geographic coverage.

- Automated kiosks is one example. ATMs offer many of the functions of a bank branch within a self-service machine that can be located within stores, hospitals, colleges, airports, and office buildings. Automated vending machines for stamps purchase and payment of bills is another example (Figure 5.8).
- Another approach results from separating the front- and back stages of the operation. Taco Bell's innovative K-Minus strategy involves restaurants without kitchens.[6] Food preparation takes place in a central location. The meals are then shipped to restaurants (which can now devote more of their expensive floor area to customer use) and to other "points of access" (such as mobile food carts) where the food can be reheated before serving.

Locating in Multi-purpose Facilities

The most obvious locations for consumer services are close to where customers live or work. Modern buildings often are designed to be multi-purpose, featuring not only office or production space but also such services as a bank (or at least an ATM), a restaurant, a hair salon, several stores, and maybe a health club (Figure 5.9). Some companies even include a children's day-care facility to make life easier for busy working parents.

Interest is growing in locating retail and other services on transportation routes and in bus, rail, and air terminals. Most major oil companies have developed chains of small retail stores to complement the fuel pumps at their service stations, thus offering customers the convenience of one-stop shopping for fuel, vehicle supplies, food, and a selection of basic household products (Figure 5.10). Truck stops on major highways often include laundry centers, restrooms, ATMs, Internet access, restaurants, and inexpensive accommodation in addition to a variety of vehicle maintenance and repair services. Airport terminals—designed as part of the infrastructure for air transportation services—have been transformed into vibrant shopping malls.

Figure 5.9 Many office buildings now include shops.

Locational Constraints

Although customer convenience is important, operational requirements may restrict choice of locations.

- Major hospitals have different health-care services at a single location, requiring a very large facility. Customers who need complex, in-patient treatment must go to the service factory rather than be treated at home. However, an ambulance—or even a helicopter—can be sent to pick them up.
- Airports, for instance, are often inconveniently located relative to travelers' homes, offices, or destinations. Because of noise and environmental factors, finding suitable sites for construction of new airports or expansion of existing ones is a very difficult task. (A governor of Massachusetts was once asked what would be an acceptable location for a second airport to serve Boston; he thought for a moment and then responded, "Nebraska!") One way to make airport access more convenient is to install fast rail links, such as San Francisco's BART service (Figure 5.11) or London's Heathrow Express.

Figure 5.10 A gas station with a supermarket in Beijing.

PART II

Figure 5.11 San Francisco's BART service helps passengers get to the city from the airport more conveniently.

SERVICE INSIGHTS 5.3

Multi-Channel Banking without Branches at First Direct

First Direct, a division of HSBC, has become famous as the originator of the concept of a retail bank without branches. In 2010, First Direct was named best financial service provider at the 2010 Which? Awards. It serves more than 1.2 million customers throughout the United Kingdom (and abroad) through call centers, a website, text messaging on cell phones, and access to HSBC's large network of ATMs.

In January 2000, First Direct—by that time describing itself as "the largest virtual bank in the world"—announced that it would transform itself into an e-bank and set the standard for e-banking. At the heart of the strategy is a multi-channel approach to banking that combines First Direct's telephone banking experience with the strengths of the Internet and the versatility of cell phone technologies to deliver a superior service at fiercely competitive prices. As noted by chief executive Alan Hughes: "We are the first bank in the world to reengineer our entire business for the e-age. The scale of the initiative creates a new category of e-banking and sets a benchmark for the industry around the globe. More than a bank, www.firstdirect.com will be the first Internet banking store."

By 2008, 80% of all customer contact with First Direct and 43% of sales were via e-channels. Some 890,000 customers were using Internet banking, and 370,000 were using SMS (short message service) text messaging. The bank sent out some 2.6 million text messages a month.

A central element in this strategy is to offer Britain's most comprehensive cell phone banking service, recognizing that almost all adults in the United Kingdom either own or use a cell phone. Through SMS text messages, First Direct customers have access to mini-statements for up to three accounts and can be advised when credits or debits enter or leave the account. In addition, they are alerted automatically if their accounts go into the red. First Direct was the first bank to adapt its online banking so that it worked well with the iPhone.

Although person-to-person voice telephone still remains the backbone of the bank's relationship with its customers, in August 2005 the bank launched a new web chat service, enabling customers to "talk" with banking reps through a keyboard and mouse rather than by phone. It promotes this service as offering the immediacy of a phone conversation with the convenience of e-mail.

Is this nontraditional strategy working? The evidence suggests a resounding "yes." An independent global survey of 25,000 customers of financial organizations worldwide found that, among all banks surveyed, First Direct had the greatest proportion of customers prepared to recommend their own bank. For the past 16 years, First Direct has had the highest customer satisfaction rating of banks in the United Kingdom.

SOURCE

Anne-Marie Cagna and Jean-Claude Larréché, "First Direct 2005: The Most Recommended Bank in the World." Fontainebleau, France: INSEAD, 2005; press releases distributed on www.firstdirect.com, accessed March 12, 2012.

E-Commerce: The Move to Cyberspace

Amazon.com pioneered the concept of the virtual store, but now thousands exist all over the world. Among the factors attracting customers into virtual stores are:

- Convenience
- Ease of search (obtaining information and searching for desired items or services)
- A broader selection
- Potential for better prices
- 24/7 service with prompt delivery. This is particularly appealing to customers whose busy lives leave them short of time (see Service Insights 5.4).

Think about the products that you, your family, and friends have purchased lately through the Internet. Why did you select this channel rather than alternative forms of service delivery?

SERVICE INSIGHTS 5.4

Online vs. Brick-and-Mortar: the Great Shopping Race

To compare the results of online shopping versus shopping at retail stores, the *Wall Street Journal* sent two reporters out on an assignment the day after Thanksgiving, which is traditionally one of America's busiest shopping days of the year (retailers call it Black Friday because they make so much profits on that day, it puts them back in the black for the year). Both reporters were given a budget of $2,000 and an identical list of 12 presents to purchase. These gifts ranged from a variety of unbranded items (a cashmere sweater for sister, a sports watch for husband) to a Barbie Magic Pegasus for a four-year-old girl and a Microsoft Xbox 360 video game system for an 11-year-old boy. At that time, this game system was new and, therefore, hard to find. One reporter went to a huge mall at Short Hills in New Jersey. The second reporter stayed home, shopped online, and ordered items to be delivered overnight. The goal was to see how quickly the reporters could complete the assignment and who could get the best gifts for the least amount of money.

In a similar race, a professional shopper and a web expert were given the same assignment. The professional shopper was sent to the same mall as the reporter. The results? The web expert completed the task in just less than three hours and had $800 leftover. However, a few of the items he had purchased were considered poorer quality than those bought at the mall. The professional shopper came in second. He saved $500 but took seven hours and 15 minutes. The two reporters were last. The reporter shopping online spent $1,906 and took seven hours and 40 minutes, but admitted he had become distracted and wasted time surfing the web. The reporter shopping at the mall took eight hours and spent $1,836. However, neither reporter managed to buy the Xbox 360.

SOURCE

Ellen Gamermann and Reed Albergotti, "The Great Holiday Shopping Race," *The Wall Street Journal*, December 3–4, 2005, P6–P7.

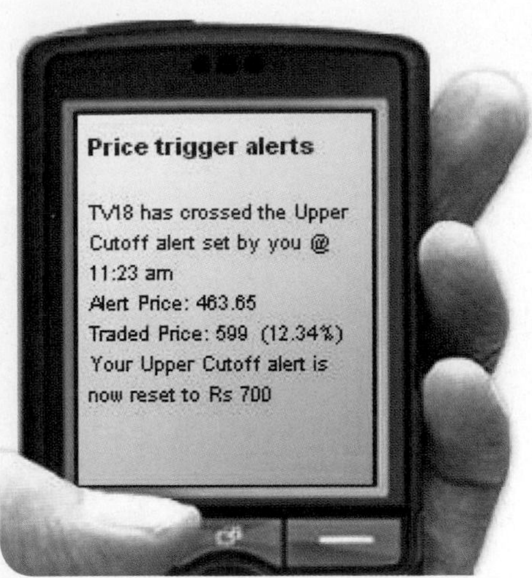

Figure 5.18 SMS price alert when a price level of a stock is reached.

Websites are becoming increasingly sophisticated, but also more user friendly. They often simulate the services of a well-informed sales assistant in steering customers toward items that are likely to be of interest. Some even provide the opportunity for "live" e-mail or chat dialog with helpful customer service personnel. Facilitating searches is another useful service on many sites, ranging from looking at what books are available by a particular author to finding schedules of flights between two cities on a specific date.

Particularly exciting are recent developments that link websites, customer relationship management (CRM) systems, and mobile telephony. Integrating mobile devices into the service delivery infrastructure can be used as a means to (1) *access* services (see Service Insights 5.5), (2) *alert* customers to opportunities or problems by delivering the right information or interaction at the right time, and (3) *update* information in real time to ensure it is continuously accurate and relevant.[9] For example, customers can set stock alerts on their broker's website and get an e-mail or SMS alert when a certain price level is reached (or breached) (Figure 5.18) or when a particular transaction has been conducted, or they can obtain real-time information on stock prices. Customers can respond by accessing the brokerage and trade directly by voice or via an SMS interface, as they prefer.

SERVICE INSIGHTS 5.5

WIZZIT: Reaching Out to the Unbanked in South Africa

Banks are very often associated with physical buildings and branches, as well as ATM networks. WIZZIT Payments (Pty) Ltd (WIZZIT), however, is a bank that does not distribute its services using the normal distribution channels. WIZZIT's tagline is "Live.life.anywhere: With WIZZIT you have your bank in your pocket. Transact from wherever you are, whenever you want to—24/7." It is a "virtual bank," as it has no branches. Instead, WIZZIT uses the cell phone as a distribution platform. In South Africa, there are 16 million people without bank accounts. Opening an account at bank branches is inconvenient as people have to travel a long distance, and it is considered expensive for the rural folks. However, 35% of South Africa's unbanked already own cell phones.

To reach its customers, WIZZIT goes into the rural areas to show the villagers how electronic money works and how they can benefit from it. They also use the "WIZZ Kids," who are young individuals from the lower-income group, to teach potential customers about WIZZIT. These WIZZ Kids earn a commission for each new customer they sign up. To make their services appealing to the low-income consumer, WIZZIT does not have a minimum

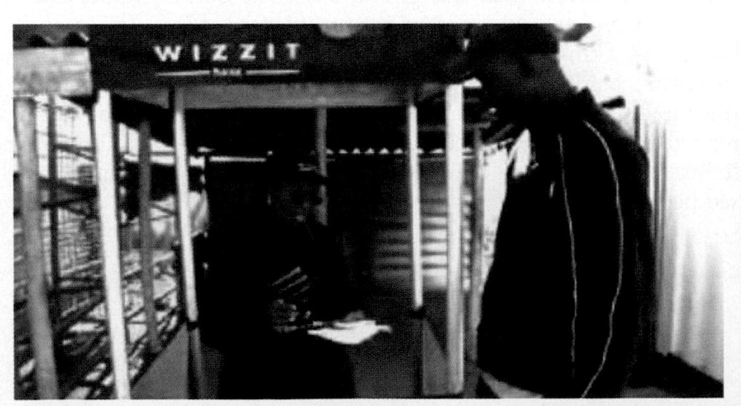

balance requirement, has no monthly fees, and does not charge penalties for nonuse. Payment is by transaction, and the amount depends on the transaction type. Customers can use their cell phones to make person-to-person payments, transfer money, make purchases for pre-paid electricity and pay for their cell phone subscriptions. Customers are also provided with a Maestro brand debit card, which they can use to make purchases and withdraw money at any South African ATM.

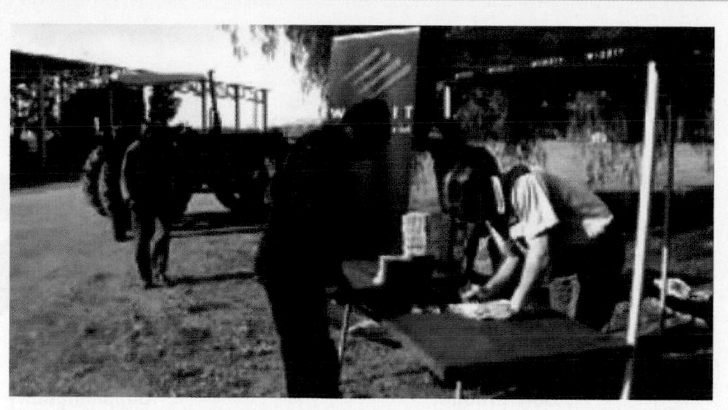

Within its first two years, WIZZIT acquired 50,000 customers. By 2008, it had an estimated customer base of 250,000 customers. People use WIZZIT because they find it convenient, affordable, and secure.

SOURCES

Gautam Ivatury, and Mark Pickens, "Mobile Phone Banking and Low-Income Customers: Evidence from South Africa," white paper, *Consultative Group to Assist the Poor/The World Bank and United Nations Foundation*, 2006; "Cell Phone Banking Reinvented" *SA Computer Magazine*, October 2005; Duncan McLeod "Waving the Wand," *Financial Mail*, 25 November 2005, http://www.wizzit.co.za/, accessed March 12, 2012.

THE ROLE OF INTERMEDIARIES

 **LO 7**

Understand the part played by intermediaries in distributing services.

Many service organizations find it cost-effective to outsource certain tasks. Often, these are supplementary service elements. For instance, despite their increased use of telephone call centers and the Internet, cruise lines and resort hotels still rely on travel agents to handle a large portion of their customer interactions such as giving out information, taking reservations, accepting payment, and ticketing.

How should a service provider work in partnership with one or more intermediaries to deliver a complete service package to customers? In Figure 5.19, we use the Flower of Service framework to show an example in which the core product and certain supplementary elements like information, consultation, and exception are delivered by the original supplier. The delivery of other supplementary services is delegated to an intermediary to complete the offering as experienced by the customer. In other instances, several specialist outsourcers might be involved as intermediaries for specific elements. The challenge for the original supplier is to oversee the overall process. The supplier has to make sure that each element offered by intermediaries fits the overall service concept to create a consistent and seamless branded service experience.

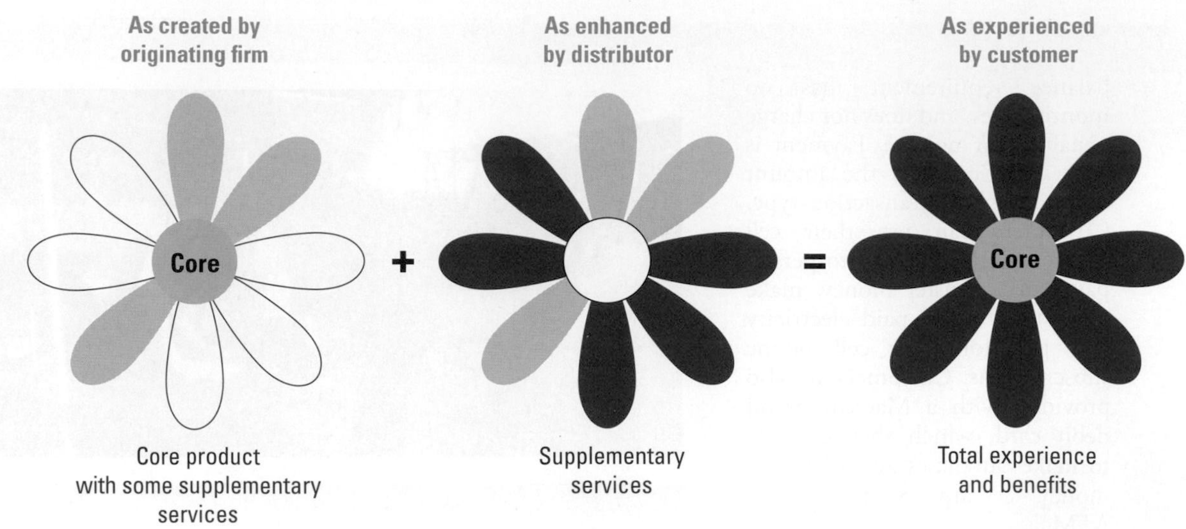

Figure 5.19 Splitting responsibilities for service delivery.

Franchising

Even delivery of the core product can be outsourced to an intermediary. Franchising has become a popular way to expand delivery of an effective service concept, embracing all of the 7 Ps (see Chapter 1) to multiple sites. This is done without the level of monetary investment that would be needed for rapid expansion of company-owned and company-managed sites. A franchisor recruits entrepreneurs who are willing to invest their own time and equity in managing a previously developed service concept. In return, the franchisor provides training on how to operate and market the business, sells necessary supplies, and provides promotional support at a national or regional level to add to local marketing activities. These activities are paid for by the franchisee, but the franchisee must follow the copy and media guidelines of the franchisor.

Figure 5.20 Subway is a popular American fast-food franchise.

Franchising is an attractive strategy for growth-oriented service firms because franchisees are highly motivated to ensure customer service and high-quality service operations.[10] A new franchise business opens every eight minutes of every business day.[11] Although franchising is most commonly associated with fast-food restaurants (for an example, see Figure 5.20), the concept has been applied to a very wide variety of both consumer and B2B services and now spans some 75 different product categories.[12] New concepts are created and commercialized all the time in countries around the world. The fastest-growing categories of concepts are related to health and fitness, publications, security, and consumer services. The franchise industry accounts for approximately 50% of all retail sales and services in the United States. One out of every 12 businesses is a franchised business.[13] In your own role as a consumer, you probably patronize more franchises than you realize.

Nevertheless, there is a high dropout rate among franchisors in the early years of a new franchise system, with one-third of all systems failing within the first four years and no less than three-quarters of all franchisors ceasing to exist after 12 years.[14] Success factors for franchisors include:

- The ability to achieve a larger size with a more recognizable brand name
- Offering franchisees fewer supporting services but longer-term contracts
- Having lower overhead per outlet
- Providing accurate and realistic information about expected characteristics of franchise operations, and support given
- Building a cooperative rather than controlling relationship[15]

Because growth is very important to achieve an efficient scale, some franchisors use "master franchising." Master franchisees often are individuals who have already succeeded as operators of one or several individual franchise outlets. They have the responsibility for recruiting, training, and supporting franchisees within a given geographic area.

While franchising has many success stories, it also has some disadvantages.

- Letting franchisees take over service delivery and other activities will result in some loss of control over the delivery system and, thereby, over how customers experience the actual service.
- Making sure that an intermediary has exactly the same priorities and procedures as laid down by the franchisor is difficult. However, it is necessary for effective quality control. Franchisors usually try to control all aspects of the service performance through a contract. This contract usually has clauses that state that franchisees have to follow the defined service standards, procedures, scripts, and physical presentation strictly. Franchisors may also control the appearance of the servicescape, employee performance, and elements like as service timetables.
- An ongoing problem is that, as franchisees gain experience, they may start to feel that they should not be paying the various fees to the franchisors. They may also believe that they can operate the business better without the restrictions that come about because of the contract. This often leads to legal fights between the two parties.

An alternative to franchising is licensing another supplier to act on the original supplier's behalf to deliver the core product. Trucking companies regularly make use of independent agents (Figure 5.21) instead of locating company-owned branches in each of the different cities they serve. They may also choose to contract with independent "owner-operators" who drive their own trucks.[16]

Figure 5.21 Trucking companies license jobs to local firms in remote areas.

Other service distribution agreements include financial services. Banks seeking to move into investment services often will act as the distributor for mutual fund products created by investment firms that lack extensive distribution channels of their own. Many banks also sell insurance products underwritten by an insurance companies. They collect a commission on the sale but normally are not involved in handling claims.

LO 8

Explain what determines which market entry strategy a firm should use when it goes global.

DISTRIBUTING SERVICES INTERNATIONALLY

Many firms distribute their services internationally, including CNN, Reuters, Google, AMEX, Starbucks, Hertz, Citibank, and McKinsey. When service companies plan to go global, how should they enter new markets?

How to Enter International Markets?

The strategy that is most suitable for entering a new international market depends on (1) how a firm can protect its intellectual property (IP) and control its key sources of value creation, and (2) whether the level of desired interaction with the customer is high or low (see Figure 5.22).

In the case where a firm's IP and value creation sources can be protected through copyright or other legal means, and if only low customer contact is required (i.e., the

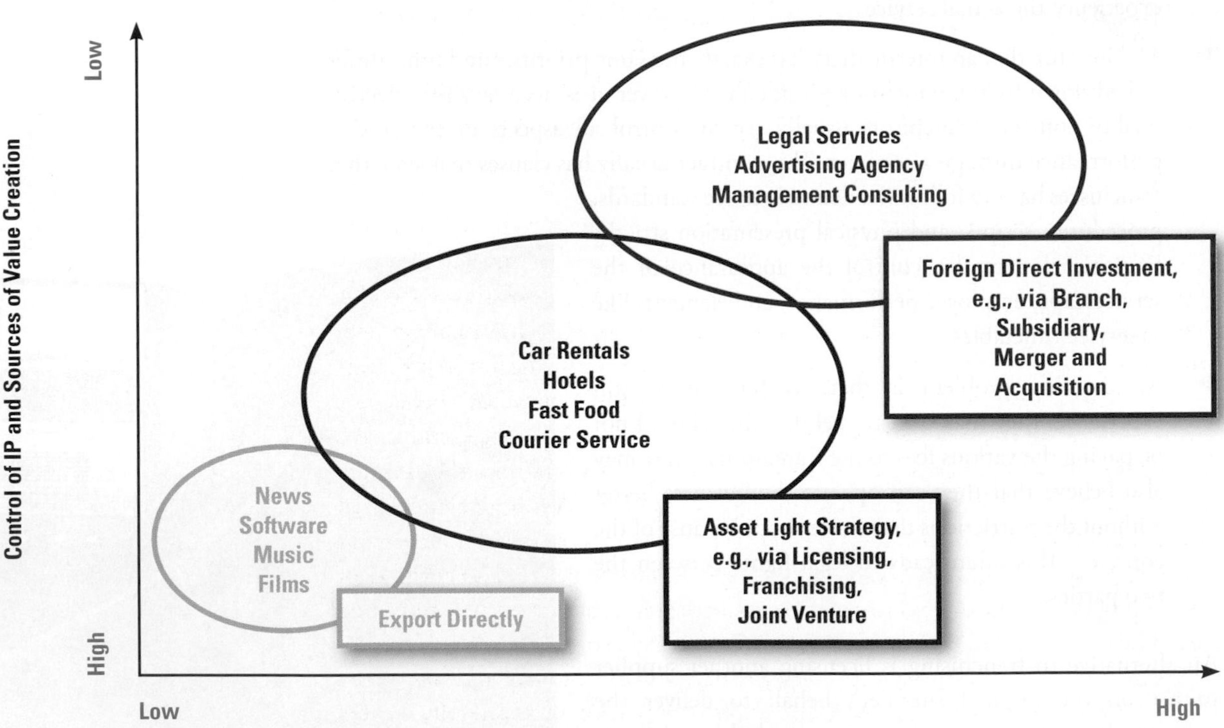

Figure 5.22 How to go international?

service is distributed at arm's length via the Internet or telephone), then a company can simply export the service. In these cases, there is little risk of losing the business to local competitors, distributors, or other local partners. Examples include database services (e.g., Thomson Reuters' Social Sciences Citation Index-related services), online news (e.g., those offered by CNN or the Financial Times), online advertising (e.g., as sold globally by Yahoo or Google), and the downloading of music, films, e-books, and software. If these firms do establish a local presence in international markets, it is usually to organize their local corporate sales and marketing (e.g., Yahoo and Google have sales teams in many countries that sell their advertising services) rather than deliver the service itself.[17]

Some services like fast food, global hotel chains, and courier services allow a firm to control its IP and sources of value creation. This is done through branding, having a global customer base, and global resources, capabilities, and networks. Without these, it would become impossible, or at least very difficult, to deliver the service at a level customers are expecting. Here, customer contact is often at a moderate level. Firms in this category can expand globally through licensing, franchising, or joint ventures without losing control. For example, in terms of branding, brands such as Starbucks and Hard Rock Café add value, and coffee outlets without these brands don't have the same attraction for customers. Large global hotel chains like Starwood Hotels & Resorts or Hilton control customer relationships with millions of customer in their loyalty programs and through global sales offices, which in turn then feed business to locally owned and operated properties. These properties need the customer traffic from the global chain. To cite another example, unlike the global courier service firm that has global resources, capabilities, and network, a local courier service provider is not able to source for inbound shipments from around the world. They also cannot deliver outbound shipments on a global level. Thus, the global courier service firm can safely appoint a local agent without having to fear that that agent will, at some point, become a competitor.

Finally, there are services where the added value comes mainly from the skills and knowledge of the service provider, and where a high degree of customer contact is needed to deliver value. These are often knowledge-based, professional services. Examples include creative design of advertising campaigns and management consulting projects. For such services, value is typically created by the firm's employees through their knowledge and the relationship they have built with their clients. It is difficult to control the sources of value creation for such services. For example, if a firm worked through a licensee or joint-venture partner, it would face the risk that once skill transfer to that partner has happened after a few years of operation, that partner would be able to deliver the service without the support of the firm. When this happens, the partner is likely to show increasing resistance to paying licensing fees or sharing profits. They are then likely to renegotiate the terms of the venture, and could even threaten to go "independent" and cut the original service firm out. Hence, it is necessary for firms in this category to have tight control over its local resources. This usually includes having the local staff on its own payroll, with carefully written contracts that protect the firm's IP and customer base. Here, the most effective ways to enter a new market are typically through foreign direct investment by setting up a branch office, a subsidiary, or through mergers and acquisitions.[18]

CHAPTER SUMMARY

LO 1 ▶ *What? How? Where? When?* Responses to these four questions form the foundation of any service distribution strategy.

LO 2 ▶ *What* is distributed? The flow model of distribution can be mapped onto the Flower of Service concept and includes the following flows of service distribution:

- o Information and promotion flows (includes the information and potentially consultation petals).
- o Negotiation flow (includes the order taking and potentially also billing and payment petals).
- o Product flow (includes the remaining petals of the Flower of Service and the core product).

A service distribution strategy encompasses all three flows.

LO 3 ▶ *How* can services be distributed? Services can be distributed through three main modes:

- o Customers visit the service site (e.g., for people-processing services such as an MRI scan).
- o Service providers go to their customers (e.g., as for high-net-worth private banking services).
- o Service transactions conducted remotely (i.e., at arm's length such as for Skype or buying a travel insurance online).

LO 4 ▶ Customer preferences drive channel choice. Customers often prefer remote channels because of their convenience and when they have high confidence in and knowledge about the product and are technology savvy. However, consumers rely more on personal channels when the perceived risk is high and when there are social motives behind the transaction.

LO 5 ▶ *Where* and *when* should service be delivered? The place and time decisions must reflect customer needs and expectations.

- o Customer convenience and operational requirements are the main factors to consider.
- o Recent location trends include mini-stores, sharing retail space with complementary providers, and locating in multi-purpose facilities (e.g., ATMs in office buildings).
- o There is a move toward extended operating hours, with the ultimate goal of 24/7 service every day of the year, often achieved through the use of self-service technology.

LO 6 ▶ Information-based core and supplementary services can be offered 24/7 on the Internet. Recent technological developments link CRM systems, mobile telephones, websites and smart cards to provide increasingly convenient and sophisticated services.

LO 7 ▶ Service firms frequently use intermediaries to distribute some of the supplementary services (e.g., cruise lines still use travel agencies to provide information, take reservations, collect payment, and often bundle complementary services such as air travel).

- o Service organizations may find it cost-effective to outsource certain tasks.
- o The challenge for the service firm is to ensure that overall service is seamless and experienced as desired.
- o Franchising is frequently used to distribute the core service. There are advantages and disadvantages to franchising:
  - o It allows fast growth, and franchisees are highly motivated to ensure customer orientation, high-quality service operations, and cost-effective operations.
  - o Disadvantages of franchising include the loss of control over the delivery system and the customers' service experience. Hence, franchisors often enforce strict quality controls over all aspects of the operation.

LO 8 ▶ The strategy for entering international markets depend on:

- o How a firm can control its intellectual property (IP) and its sources of value creation.
- o The degree of customer interaction required for the creation of the service.
- o If the value lies in the IP, then the service can simply be exported directly, like for e-books, music, and software.
- o If IP control and customer contact requirements are moderate, then use licensing, franchising, or joint ventures.
- o If there is a high degree of interaction required, and control of IP is low, then have foreign direct investments by setting up a branch, a subsidiary, or going in through mergers and acquisitions.

UNLOCK YOUR LEARNING

These keywords are found within the sections of each Learning Objective (LO). They are integral to understanding the services marketing concepts taught in each section. Having a firm grasp of these keywords and how they are used is essential to helping you do well on your course, and in the real and very competitive marketing scene out there.

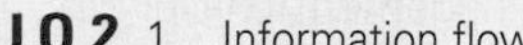

LO 2
1 Information flow
2 Negotiation flow
3 Product flow
4 Promotion flow

LO 3
5 Convenience
6 Customer visits the service site
7 Location specific
8 Operational hours
9 Remote transactions
10 Reverse logistics
11 Service providers visit the customer

LO 4
12 Channel arbitrage
13 Channel choice
14 Channel preferences
15 Impersonal channels
16 Personal channels
17 Self service channels

LO 5
18 24/7
19 Automated kiosks
20 Backstage elements
21 Brick-and-mortar
22 Distribution strategies
23 Locational constraints
24 Mini-stores
25 Multi-purpose facilities
26 Points of access

LO 6
27 Cyberspace
28 E-commerce
29 Electronic channels
30 Mobile telephony
31 Multi-channel
32 Online channel
33 Physical channels
34 "Smart cards"
35 "Smart" cell phones
36 Service delivery innovations
37 Virtual stores
38 Voice recognition technology

LO 7
39 Branded experience
40 Franchisee
41 Franchising
42 Franchisor
43 Independent agents
44 Intermediaries
45 Licensing
46 Master franchising
47 Outsource

LO 8
48 Branch office
49 Control
50 Customer contact
51 Distribute service internationally
52 Foreign direct investment
53 Intellectual property
54 Joint ventures
55 Mergers and acquisitions
56 Subsidiary
57 Value creation

PART II

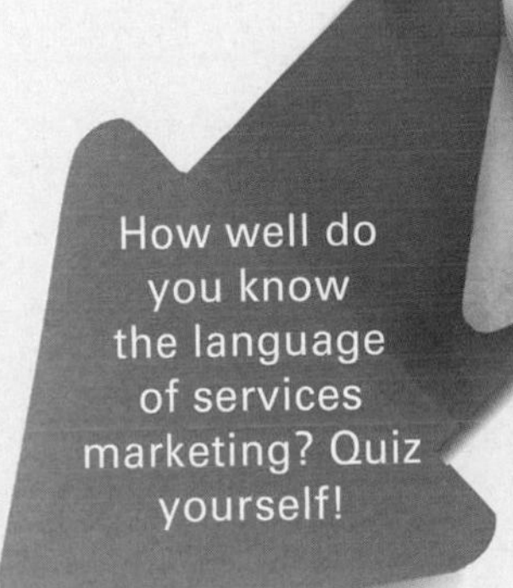

Not for the academically faint-of-heart

For each keyword you are able to recall without referring to earlier pages, give yourself a point (and a pat on the back). Tally your score at the end and see if you earned the right to be called—a *services marketeer.*

SCORE

0 – 11 Services Marketing is done a great disservice.
12 – 20 The midnight oil needs to be lit, pronto.
21 – 30 I know what you *didn't* do all semester.
31 – 40 A close shave with success.
41 – 50 Now, go forth and market.
51 – 57 There should be a marketing concept named after you.

KNOW YOUR ESM

Review Questions

1. What is meant by "distributing services"? How can an experience or something intangible be distributed?
2. What are the different options for service delivery? For each of the options, what factors do service firms need to take into account when using that option?
3. What are the key factors driving place and time decisions of service distribution?
4. What risks and opportunities are entailed for a retail service firm in adding electronic channels of delivery (a) paralleling a channel involving physical stores, or (b) replacing the physical stores with a combined Internet and call center channel? Give examples.
5. Why should service marketers be concerned with new developments in mobile communications?
6. What marketing and management challenges are raised by the use of intermediaries in a service setting?
7. Why is franchising a popular way to expand distribution of an effective service concept? What are some disadvantages of franchising, and how can they be mitigated?
8. What factors do service companies need to understand to choose a strategy for going international that still allows it to control its IP and sources of value creation?

WORK YOUR ESM

Application Exercises

1. An entrepreneur is thinking of setting up a new service business (you can choose any specific business). What advice would you give regarding the distribution strategy for this business? Address the *What? How? Where? When?* of service distribution.
2. Think of three services you buy or use either mostly or exclusively via the Internet. What is the value proposition of this channel over alternative channels (e.g., phone, mail, or branch network)?
3. Which market entry strategy into a new international market should (a) an architectural design firm, (b) an online discount broker, and (c) a satellite TV channel consider and why?

ENDNOTES

1 http://en.wikipedia.org/wiki/Lauren_Luke and ww.bylaurenluke.com, accessed March 12, 2012.

2 Recent research on the adoption of self-service technologies includes: Matthew L. Meuter, Mary Jo Bitner, Amy L. Ostrom, and Stephen W. Brown, "Choosing among Alternative Service Delivery Modes: an Investigation of Customer Trial of Self-Service Technologies," *Journal of Marketing* 69 (April 2005): 61–83; James M. Curran and Matthew L. Meuter, "Self-Service Technology Adoption: Comparing Three Technologies," *Journal of Services Marketing* 19, no. 2 (2005): 103–113.

3 The section was based on the following research: Nancy Jo Black, Andy Lockett, Christine Ennew, Heidi Winklhofer, and Sally McKechnie, "Modelling Consumer Choice of Distribution Channels: an Illustration from Financial Services," *International Journal of Bank Marketing* 20, no. 4 (2002): 161–173; Jinkook Lee, "A Key to Marketing Financial Services: the Right Mix of Products, Services, Channels and Customers," *Journal of Services Marketing* 16, no. 3 (2002): 238–258; and Leonard L. Berry, Kathleen Seiders, and Dhruv Grewal, "Understanding Service Convenience," *Journal of Marketing* 66, no. 3 (July 2002): 1–17. Jiun-Sheng C. Lin and Pei-ling Hsieh, "The Role of Technology Readiness in Customers' Perception and Adoption of Self-Service Technologies," *International Journal of Service Industry Management* 17, no. 5 (2006): 497–517.

4 Paul F. Nunes and Frank V. Cespedes, "The Customer Has Escaped," *Harvard Business Review* 81, no. 11 (2003): 96–105.

5 Michael A. Jones, David L. Mothersbaugh, and Sharon E. Beatty, "The Effects of Locational Convenience on Customer Repurchase Intentions across Service Types," *Journal of Services Marketing* 17, no. 7 (2004): 701–712.

6 James L. Heskett, W. Earl Sasser Jr., and Leonard A. Schlesinger, *The Service Profit Chain*. New York: The Free Press, 1997, 218–220.

7 www.swissotel.com and http://www.eyefortravel.com/node/9187, accessed March 12, 2012.

8 Jochen Wirtz and Jeannette P.T. Ho, "Westin in Asia: Distributing Hotel Rooms Globally," in Jochen Wirtz and Christopher H. Lovelock, eds. *Services Marketing in Asia—A Case Book*. (Singapore: Prentice Hall, 2005, 253–259). www.starwoodhotels.com, accessed March 12, 2012.

9 Katherine N. Lemon, Frederick B. Newell, and Loren J. Lemon, "The Wireless Rules for e-Service," in Roland T. Rust and P. K. Kannan, eds. *New Directions in Theory and Practice*. (New York: Armonk, M.E. Sharpe, 2002, 200–232).

10 James Cross and Bruce J. Walker, "Addressing Service Marketing Challenges through Franchising," in Teresa A. Swartz and Dawn Iacobucci, eds. *Handbook of Services Marketing & Management*. (Thousand Oaks, CA: Sage Publications, 2000, 473–484); Lavent Altinay, "Implementing International Franchising: the Role of Intrapreuneurship," *International Journal of Service Industry Management* 15, no. 5 (2004): 426–443.

11 Quick Franchise Facts, Franchising Industry Statistics, http://www.azfranchises.com/franchisefacts.htm, accessed March 12, 2012.

12 Barry Quinn and Nicholas Alexander, "International Retail Franchising: a Conceptual Framework," *International Journal of Retail & Distribution Management* 30, no. 5 (2002): 264–276.

13 International Franchise Association Educational Foundation Inc., "Franchise Industry Gains 300 Concepts in One Year," November 19, 2007 in http://www.franchise.org/Franchise-News-Detail.aspx?id=36416, accessed March 12, 2012; Quick Franchise Facts, Franchising Industry Statistics, http://www.azfranchises.com/franchisefacts.htm, accessed March 12, 2012; http://www.franchiseek.com/USA/Franchise_USA_Statistics.htm, accessed March 12, 2012.

14 Scott Shane and Chester Spell, "Factors for New Franchise Success," *Sloan Management Review* 39, (Spring 1998): 43–50.

15 Firdaus Abdullah and Mohd Rashidee Alwi, "Measuring and Managing Franchisee Satisfaction: a Study of Academic Franchising," *Journal of Modelling in Management* 3, no. 2 (2008): 182–199; for more articles on factors that affect the success of franchises, see Scott Weaven and Debra Grace "Franchisee Personality: an Examination in the Context of Franchise Unit Density and Service Classification," *European Journal of Marketing* 43, no. 1/2 (2009): 90–109.

16 For a discussion on what to watch for when parts of the service are outsourced, see Lauren Keller Johnson, "Outsourcing Postsale Service: Is Your Brand Protected? Before You Spin Off Repairs, or Parts Distribution, or Customer Call Centers, Consider the Cons as well as the Pros," *Supply Chain Strategy* 1, no. 5 (July 2005): 3–5.

17 For more information on foreign market entry modes, read Shawn M. Carraher and Dianne H. B. Welsh, *Global Entrepreneurship*, Kendall Hunt Publishing Inc., 2009.

18 J. J. Boddewyn, Marsha Baldwin Halbrich and A. C. Perry, "Service Multinationals: Conceptualization, Measurement and Theory," *Journal of International Business Studies* (Fall 1986): 41–58; Sandra Vandermerwe and Michael Chadwick, "The Internationalization of Services," *The Services Industries Journal* 9, no. 1 (January 1989): 79–93.

CHAPTER 6

setting prices and IMPLEMENTING REVENUE MANAGEMENT

LEARNING OBJECTIVES

By the end of this chapter, the reader should be able to:

- **LO 1** Recognize that effective pricing is central to the financial success of service firms.
- **LO 2** Outline the foundations of a pricing strategy as represented by the pricing tripod.
- **LO 3** Define different types of financial costs and explain the limitations of cost-based pricing.
- **LO 4** Understand the concept of net value and how gross value can be enhanced through value-based pricing and reduction of related monetary and nonmonetary costs.
- **LO 5** Describe competition-based pricing and situations where service markets are less price-competitive.
- **LO 6** Define revenue management and describe how it works.
- **LO 7** Discuss the role of rate fences in effective revenue management.
- **LO 8** Be familiar with the issues of ethics and consumer concerns related to service pricing.
- **LO 9** Understand how fairness can be designed into revenue management policies.
- **LO 10** Discuss the seven questions marketers need to answer to design an effective service pricing strategy.

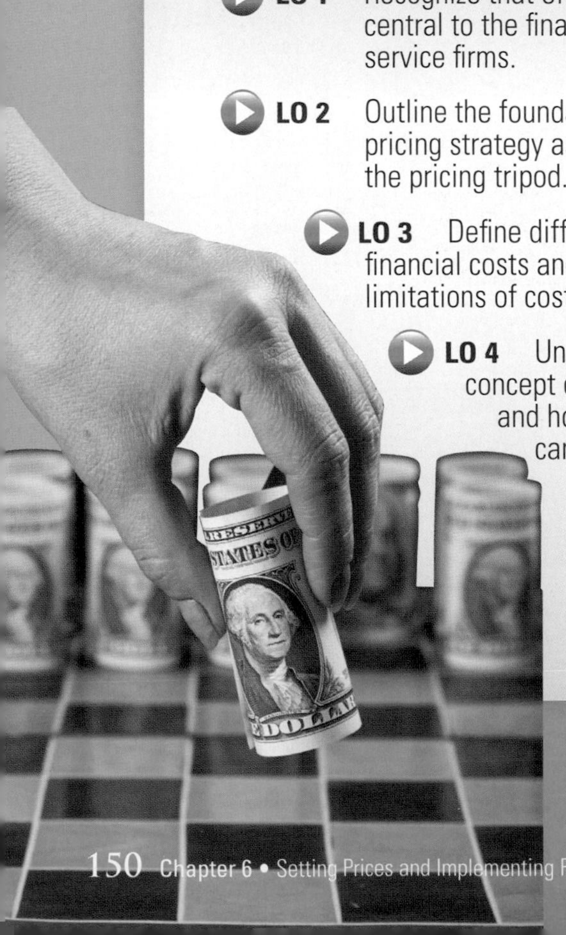

Figure 6.1 Dynamic pricing, a strategy to price the same product differently to different customers at various times, has gained popularity in many industries.

OPENING VIGNETTE

Dynamic Pricing Is Here to Stay[1]

Service firms are often faced with the problem of maximizing revenue and capacity, and one way to do that is through dynamic pricing. But just what is dynamic pricing? Have you had the experience of being on a plane and chatting with your neighbor and discovering that you both paid very different prices for the same air ticket in the same class of seats? That's dynamic pricing at work.

Dynamic pricing is a pricing strategy that varies prices for different customers at different times, based on demand conditions. It is commonly used in the airline industry but has also gained popularity in other industries. For example, the Eagles, the highest-selling American band in United States' history, started a system in early 2010 to increase prices for the best seats and to lower prices of cheaper seats for their show in Sacramento, California. Their highest-priced tickets cost $250, but the cheapest ticket was priced as low as $32. They cooperated with Live Nation Entertainment Inc. to use dynamic pricing for their tickets. Ten categories of ticket prices were set based on anticipated demand. With that, the band hoped to fill more seats and, at the same time, make the tickets more affordable for more fans.

Similarly, in the sporting industry, the San Francisco Giants, a professional baseball team raised their ticket prices when they noticed a jump in demand, and still managed to sell 10,000 tickets in the weekend before their Memorial Day game with the Colorado Rockies. In a previous season, the team had experimented with dynamic pricing and had sold 25,000 extra tickets and earned an extra $500,000 in revenue. Officials from the Major League Basketball and the National Basketball Association expect dynamic pricing to become the norm for the industry.

Dynamic ticket pricing has been so successful in filling seats that it is expected to be a growing trend. Companies like ScoreBig Inc., a new start-up, are hoping to tap on this trend. It has been estimated that about 40–50% of concert tickets are left unsold every year. For sports events, 25–35% of seats are estimated to be unsold every year. ScoreBig Inc. intends to be the Priceline.com of concert and sports tickets by helping to find buyers for these tickets. The tickets are sold at a discount, using demand-based dynamic pricing. ScoreBig Inc. has managed to raise $8.5 million from investors who are convinced that their investment would be worthwhile.

To date, companies in diverse industries like sports, hotels, airlines, and car rental have been able to benefit greatly from using dynamic pricing. With dynamic pricing allowing companies to increase revenues, allocate their resources more effectively, and ultimately help companies focus on improving customer experience, one can certainly expect it to be around for a long while yet.

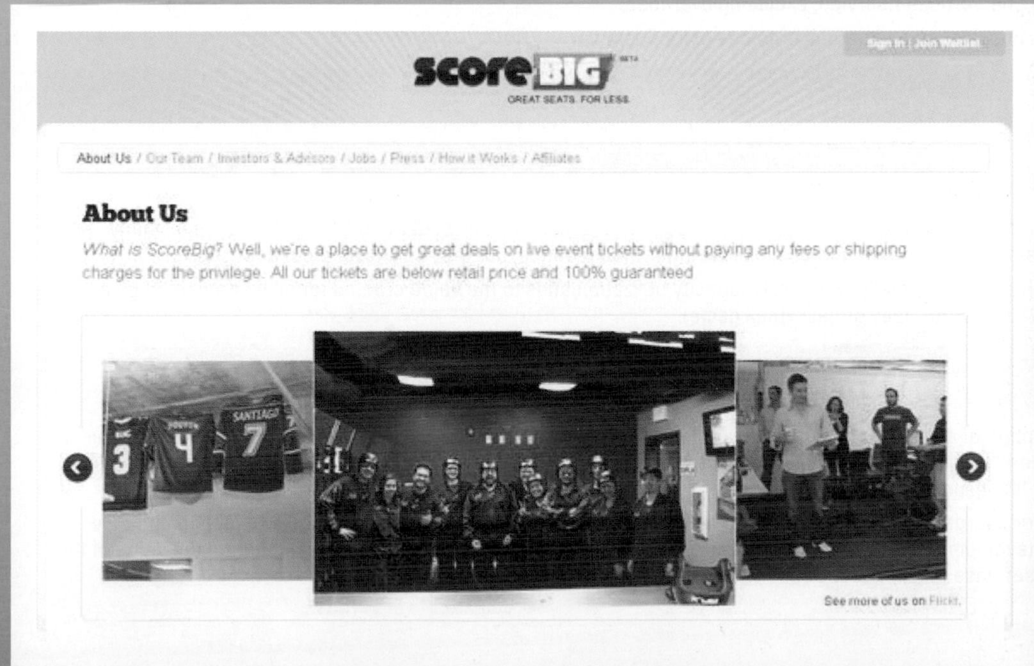

Figure 6.2 Score Big Inc., based in Los Angeles, was founded in 2009.

PART II

 **LO 1**

Recognize that effective pricing is central to the financial success of service firms.

EFFECTIVE PRICING IS CENTRAL TO FINANCIAL SUCCESS

Consumers often find service pricing difficult to understand (e.g., insurance products or hospital bills), risky (when you inquire about an intercontinental flight on three different days, it can happen that you are offered three different prices!), and sometimes even unethical (e.g., many bank customers complain about a variety of fees and charges they consider to be unfair). In this chapter, we will review the role of pricing in services marketing and provide guidelines on how to develop an effective pricing strategy.

Objectives for Establishing Prices

Any pricing strategy must be based on a clear understanding of a company's pricing objectives. The most common pricing objectives are related to revenues and profits as well as building demand and developing a user base (Table 6.1).

Table 6.1 Objectives for pricing of services

Revenue and Profit Objectives
Gain Profit
• Make the largest possible contribution or profit. • Achieve a specific target level, but do not seek to maximize profits. • Maximize revenue from a fixed capacity by varying prices and target segments over time. This is done typically using revenue management systems.
Cover Costs
• Cover fully allocated costs, including corporate overhead. • Cover costs of providing one particular service, excluding overhead. • Cover incremental costs of selling one extra unit or to one extra customer.
Patronage and User Base-Related Objectives
Build Demand
• Maximize demand (when capacity is not a restriction), provided a certain minimum level of revenue is achieved (e.g., many nonprofit organizations are focused on encouraging usage rather than revenue, but they still have to cover costs). • Achieve full capacity utilization, especially when high capacity utilization adds to the value created for all customers (e.g., a "full house" adds excitement to a theater play or basketball game).
Build a User Base
• Encourage trial and adoption of a service. This is especially important for new services with high infrastructure costs and for membership-type services that generate a large amount of revenues from their continued usage after adoption (e.g., cell phone service subscriptions or life insurance plans). • Build market share and/or a large user base, especially if there are a lot of economies of scale that can lead to a competitive cost advantage (e.g., if development or fixed costs are high), or network effects where additional users enhance the value of the service to the existing user base (e.g., Facebook and LinkedIn).

PRICING STRATEGY STANDS ON THREE FOUNDATIONS

LO 2

Outline the foundations of a pricing strategy as represented by the pricing tripod.

In many service industries, pricing used to be viewed from a financial and accounting standpoint. Therefore, cost-plus pricing often was used. Today, however, most services have a good understanding of value-based and competitive pricing. Once the pricing objectives are understood, we can focus on pricing strategy. The foundations of pricing strategy can be described as a tripod. There are three legs, namely, (1) costs to the provider, (2) competitors' pricing, and (3) value to the customer (Figure 6.3). In the pricing tripod, the costs a firm needs to recover usually sets a minimum price, or price floor, for a specific service offering, and the customer's perceived value of the offering sets a maximum price, or price ceiling.

The price charged by competing services typically determines where, within the floor-to-ceiling range, the price can be set. The pricing objectives of the organization then determine where actual prices should be set given the possible range provided by the pricing tripod analysis. Let's look at each leg of the pricing tripod in more detail, starting with cost to the provider.

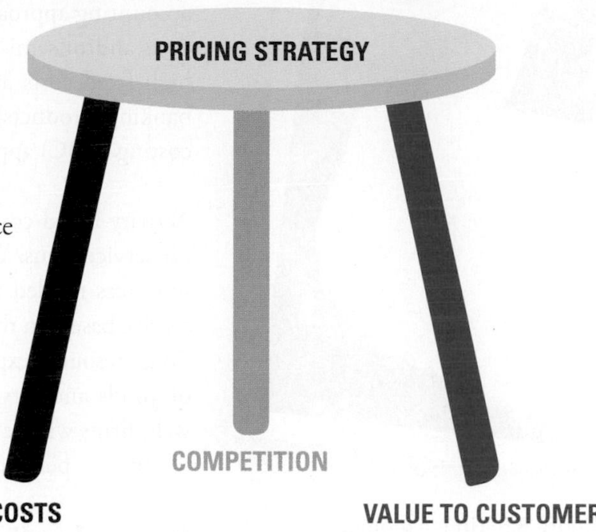

Figure 6.3 The pricing tripod.

Cost-Based Pricing

LO 3

Define different types of financial costs and explain the limitations of cost-based pricing.

It is usually harder to determine the costs involved in producing an intangible performance than it is to trace the costs of producing physical goods. In addition, because of the labor and infrastructure needed to create performances, many service organizations have much higher ratios of fixed costs to variable costs than is typically found in manufacturing firms (Figure 6.4). Service businesses with high fixed costs include those with expensive physical facilities (such as hospitals or colleges) or a fleet of vehicles (such as airlines or trucking companies) or a network (such as railroads or telecommunications and gas pipeline companies).

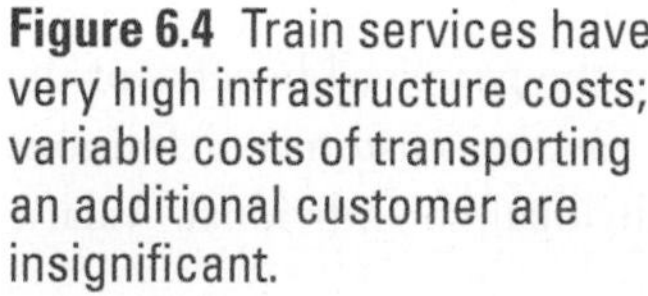

Figure 6.4 Train services have very high infrastructure costs; variable costs of transporting an additional customer are insignificant.

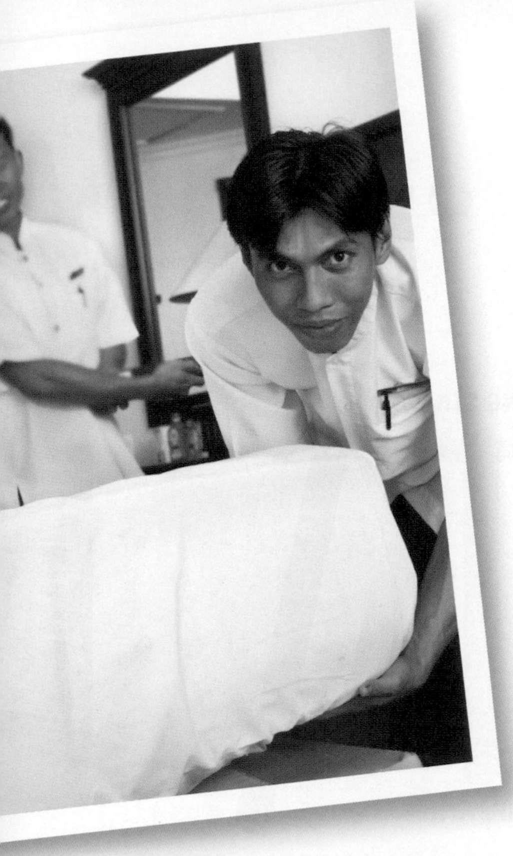

Figure 6.5 Housekeeping services contribute to the cost of hotel rooms.

Establishing the Costs of Providing Service

Even if you have already taken a marketing course, you may find it helpful to review how service costs can be estimated, using fixed, semi-variable, and variable costs. In addition, you can review how the ideas of contribution and breakeven analysis can help in pricing decisions (see Marketing Review on p. 155). These traditional cost-accounting approaches work well for service firms with large proportions of variable costs and/or semi-variable costs (e.g., many professional services). Service firms with high fixed costs and complex product lines with shared infrastructure (e.g., retail banking products) (Figure 6.5) should consider the more complex activity-based costing (ABC) approach.

Activity-based costing is a more accurate way to allocate indirect costs (overheads) for service firms. When determining the indirect cost of a service, a firm looks at the resources needed to perform each activity and then allocates the indirect cost to a service based on the quantities and types of activities required to perform the service. Thus, resource expenses (or indirect costs) are linked to the variety and complexity of goods and services produced and not just on physical volume. If implemented well, firms will be in a better position to estimate the costs of creating specific types of services, performing activities in different locations, or serving specific customers.

Pricing Implications of Cost Analysis

To make a profit, a firm must set its price high enough to cover the full costs of producing and marketing the service. There must also be enough contribution so that there can be a desired profit at the predicted sales volume.

 **LO 4**

Understand the concept of net value and how gross value can be enhanced through value-based pricing and reduction of related monetary and non-monetary costs.

Managers in businesses with high fixed and low variable costs may feel they have a lot of flexibility in pricing and be tempted to set low prices to boost sales (Figure 6.6). However, there will be no profit at the end of the year unless all relevant costs have been recovered. Many service businesses have gone bankrupt because they ignored this fact. Hence, firms that compete on low prices need to have a very good understanding of their cost structures and of the sales volumes needed to break even.

Value-Based Pricing

Another leg of the pricing tripod is value to the customer. No customer will pay more for a service than he or she thinks it is worth. So marketers need to understand how customers perceive service value in order to set an appropriate price.[2]

Figure 6.6 Budget airlines like easyJet, set low prices to encourage higher sales. As a consequence, they need high load factors to break even.

Understanding Net Value

When customers purchase a service, they are weighing the perceived benefits of the service against the perceived costs they will incur. However, customer definitions of value may be highly personal and vary from individual to individual. Valarie Zeithaml proposes four broad expressions of values[3]:

- Value is a low price.
- Value is whatever I want in a product.
- Value is the quality I get for the price I pay.
- Value is what I get for what I give.

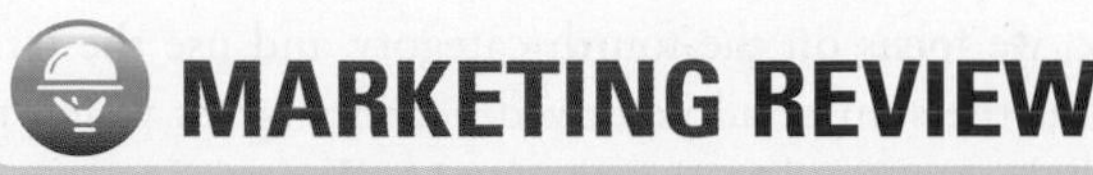

Understanding Costs, Contribution, and Breakeven Analysis

Fixed costs are economic costs that a supplier would continue to incur (at least in the short run) even if no services were sold. These costs are likely to include rent, depreciation, utilities, taxes, insurance, salaries and wages for managers and long-term employees, security, and interest payments.

Variable costs refer to the economic costs associated with serving an additional customer, such as making an additional bank transaction or selling an additional seat on a flight. In many services, such costs are very low. For instance, very little labor or fuel cost is involved in transporting an extra passenger on a flight. In a theater, the cost of seating an extra patron is close to zero. More significant variable costs are associated with such activities as serving food and beverages and installing new parts when undertaking repairs because they often include providing costly physical products in addition to labor. Note that just because a firm has sold a service at a price that exceeds its variable cost doesn't mean the firm is now profitable, since there are still fixed and semi-variable costs to be recouped.

Semi-variable costs fall in between fixed and variable costs. They represent expenses that rise or fall in a stepwise fashion as the volume of business increases or decreases. Examples include adding an extra flight to meet increased demand on a specific air route or hiring a part-time employee to work in a restaurant on busy weekends.

Contribution is the difference between the variable cost of selling an extra unit of service and the money received from the buyer of that service. It goes to cover fixed and semi-variable costs before creating profits.

Determining and allocating economic costs can be a challenging task in some service operations because of the difficulty of deciding how to assign fixed costs in a multi-service facility, such as a hospital. For instance, certain fixed costs are associated with running the emergency department in a hospital. In addition to that, there are also fixed costs of running the hospital. So how much of the hospital's fixed costs should be allocated to the emergency department? A hospital manager might use one of several approaches to calculate the emergency department's share of overhead costs. These could include (1) the percentage of total floor space it occupies, (2) the percentage of employee hours or payroll it accounts for, or (3) the percentage of total patient contact hours involved. Each method is likely to yield a totally different fixed-cost allocation. One method might show the emergency department to be very profitable, while the other might flag it as a loss-making operation.

Breakeven analysis allows managers to know at what sales volume a service will become profitable. This is called the breakeven point. The necessary analysis involves dividing the total fixed and semi-variable costs by the contribution obtained on each unit of service. For example, if a 100-room hotel needs to cover fixed and semi-variable costs of $2 million a year, and the average contribution per room-night is $100, then the hotel will need to sell 20,000 room-nights per year out of a total annual capacity of 36,500. If prices are cut by an average of $20 per room-night (or if variable costs rise by $20), then the contribution will drop to $80, and the hotel's breakeven volume will rise to 25,000 room-nights. The required sales volume is related to:

- *Price sensitivity* (Will customers be willing to pay this much?)
- *Market size* (Is the market large enough to support this level of patronage after taking competition into account?)
- *Maximum capacity* (The hotel in our example has a capacity of 36,500 room-nights per year, assuming no rooms are taken out of service for maintenance or renovation).

PART II

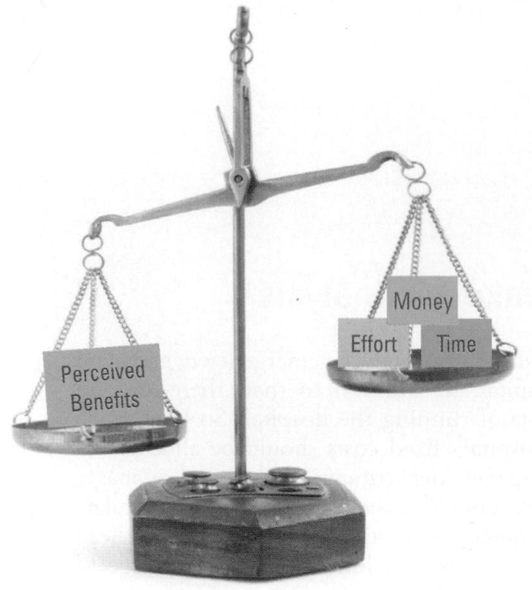

Figure 6.7 Net value equals perceived benefits minus perceived costs.

In this book, we focus on the fourth category and use the term *net value*, which is the sum of all perceived benefits (gross value) minus the sum of all the perceived costs of the service. The greater the positive difference between the two, the greater the net value. If the perceived costs of a service are greater than its perceived benefits, then the service in question will possess negative net value, and the consumer will not buy. The value calculation that customers make in their minds is similar to weighing materials on a pair of old-fashioned scales, with product benefits in one tray and the costs associated with obtaining those benefits in the other tray (Figure 6.7). When customers evaluate competing services, they are basically comparing the relative net values. As discussed in Chapter 4, a marketer can increase the value of a service by adding benefits to the core product and by improving supplementary services (Figure 6.8).

Managing the Perception of Value[4]

Since value is subjective, not all customers have the skills or knowledge to judge the quality and value they receive. This is true especially for credence services (discussed in Chapter 2), for which customers cannot assess the quality of a service even after consumption.[5] Therefore, we have to manage the perception of value.

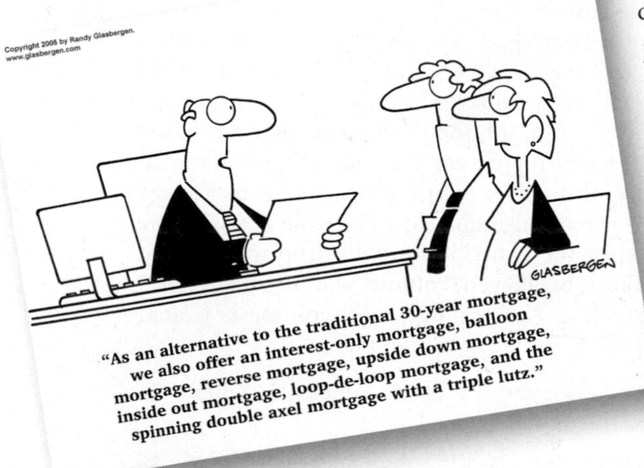

Figure 6.8 Does adding alternatives always create value? Or can it confuse the customer?

Consider a homeowner who calls an electrician to repair a defective circuit. The electrician arrives, carrying a small bag of tools. He disappears into the closet where the circuit board is located, locates the problem, replaces a defective circuit breaker, and everything works! Only 20 minutes have passed. A few days later, the homeowner is horrified to receive a bill for $100, most of it for labor charges. Not surprisingly, customers are often left feeling they have been taken advantage of—take a look at Blondie's reaction to the plumber in Figure 6.9.

To manage the perception of value, effective communications and even personal explanations are needed to help customers understand the value they receive. What customers often fail to recognize are the fixed costs that business owners need to cover. The electrician in our earlier example has to cover the costs for

Figure 6.9 Blondie seeks her money's worth from the plumber.

his office, telephone, insurance, vehicles, tools, fuel, and office support staff. The variable costs of a home visit are also higher than they appear. To the 20 minutes spent at the house, 15 minutes of driving each way might be added, plus 5 minutes each to unload and reload needed tools and supplies from the van, thus effectively tripling the labor time to a total of 60 minutes devoted to this call. The firm still has to add a margin in order to make a profit.

Reducing Related Monetary and Nonmonetary Costs

When we consider customer net value, we need to understand the customer's perceived costs. From a customer's point of view, the price charged by a supplier is only part of the costs involved in buying and using a service. There are other *costs of service*, which are made up of the *related monetary* and *nonmonetary costs.*

PART II

Related Monetary Costs

Customers often spend more in searching for, purchasing, and using the service, above and beyond the purchase price paid to the supplier. For instance, the cost of an evening at the theater for a couple with young children usually far exceeds the price of the two tickets. It can include expenses such as hiring a babysitter, travel, parking, food, and beverages.

Nonmonetary Costs

Nonmonetary costs reflect the time, effort, and discomfort associated with the search, purchase, and use of a service. Like many customers, you may refer to them collectively as "effort" or "hassle." Nonmonetary costs tend to be higher when customers are involved in production (which is particularly important in people-processing services and in self-service) and must travel to the service site. Services high on experience and credence attributes may also create psychological costs such as anxiety. There are four distinct categories of nonmonetary costs: time, physical, psychological, and sensory costs.

- *Time costs* are part of the service delivery. Today's customers often complain that they do not have enough time and therefore are reluctant to waste time on nonenjoyable and nonvalue-adding activities such as traveling to a government office and waiting in a queue.
- *Physical costs* (like fatigue and discomfort) may be part of the costs of obtaining services, especially if customers must go to the service factory, if waiting is involved, if long forms have to be completed, and if delivery is through self-service.
- *Psychological costs* such as mental effort (e.g., filling in account opening forms), perceived risk, cognitive dissonance, feelings of inadequacy, and fear are sometimes attached to buying and using a particular service (Figure 6.10).

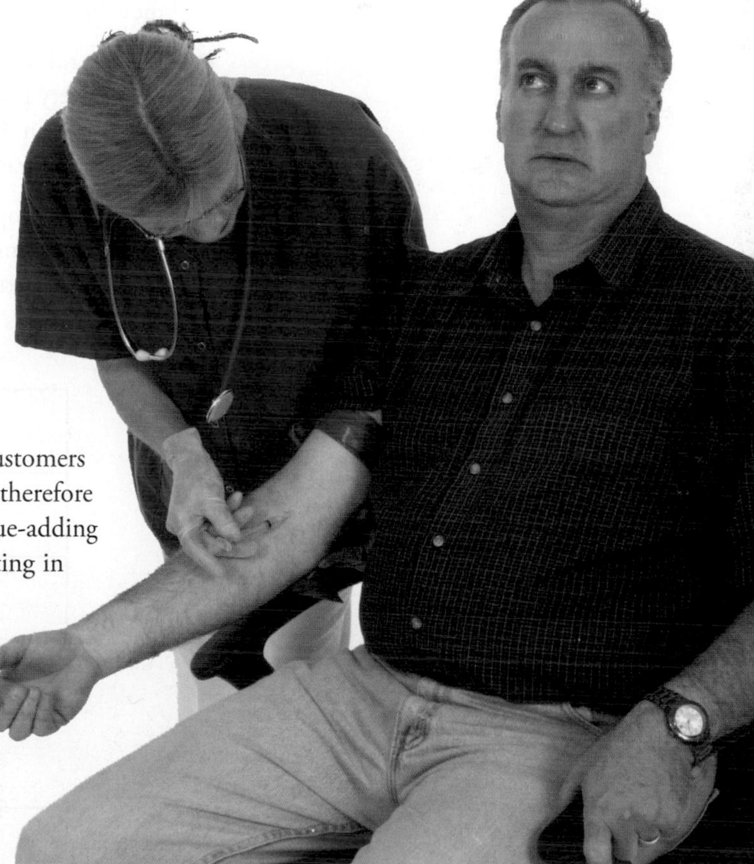

Figure 6.10 Anxiety as an important psychological factor in medical treatment.

- *Sensory costs* relate to unpleasant sensations affecting any of the five senses. In a service environment, these costs may include putting up with crowding, noise, unpleasant smells, drafts, excessive heat or cold, uncomfortable seating, and visually unappealing environments.

As shown in Figure 6.11, service users can incur costs during any of the three stages of the service consumption model as introduced in Chapter 2. As a result, firms have to consider (1) *search costs*, (2) *purchase and service encounter costs*, and (3) *post-purchase* or *after costs*. When you were looking at colleges and universities, how much money, time, and effort did you spend before deciding where to apply? How much time and effort would you put into selecting a new cell phone service provider or a bank, or planning a vacation?

A firm can create competitive advantage by minimizing those nonmonetary and related monetary costs to increase consumer value. Possible approaches include:

- Working with operations experts to reduce the time required to complete service purchase, delivery, and consumption.
- Minimizing unwanted psychological costs of service at each stage. This can be done by getting rid of, or redesigning unpleasant or inconvenient procedures, educating customers on what to expect, and retraining staff to be friendlier and more helpful.
- Getting rid of or minimizing unwanted physical effort, especially during search and delivery processes. Improve signage and "road mapping" in facilities and on webpages can help customers to find their way and prevent them from getting lost and frustrated.
- Decreasing unpleasant sensory costs of service by creating more attractive visual environments, reducing noise, installing more comfortable furniture and equipment, getting rid of offensive smells, and so on.

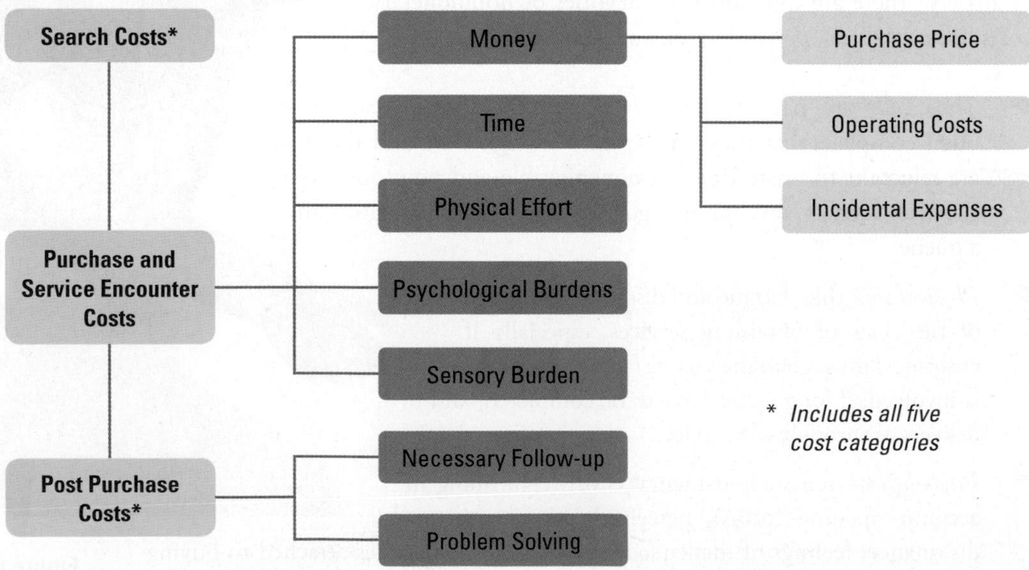

Figure 6.11 Defining total user costs.

- Suggesting ways in which customers can reduce associated monetary costs, including discounts with partner suppliers (e.g., parking) or offering mail or online delivery of activities that previously required a personal visit.

Perceptions of net value may vary widely among customers and from one situation to another for the same customer. Most services have at least two segments: one segment that spends time to save money, and another that spends money to save time. Therefore, many service markets can be segmented by sensitivity to time savings and convenience versus price sensitivity.[6] Consider Figure 6.12, which identifies a choice of three clinics available to an individual who needs to obtain a routine chest x-ray. In addition to varying dollar prices for the service, different time and effort costs are associated with using each service. Depending on the customer's priorities, nonmonetary costs may be as important, or even more important, than the price charged by the service provider.

Competition-Based Pricing

LO 5

Describe competition-based pricing and situations where service markets are less price competitive.

The last leg of the pricing tripod is competition. Firms with relatively similar services need to monitor what their competitors are charging[7] and should to try to price accordingly. When customers see little or no difference between competing offerings, they may just choose what they think is the cheapest. In such a situation, the firm with the lowest cost per unit of service enjoys market advantage and often assumes *price leadership*. Here, one firm acts as the price leader, with others taking their lead from this company. You can sometimes see this happening at the local level when several gas stations compete within a short distance of one another. As soon as one station raises or lowers its prices, the others do the same.

Price competition is greater with (1) an increasing number of competitors, (2) an increasing number of substituting offers, (3) a wider distribution of competitor and/

Which clinic would you patronize if you needed a chest x-ray (assuming that all three clinics offer good technical quality)?

Clinic A	Clinic B	Clinic C
• Price $65 • Located 1 hour away by car or transit • Next available appointment is in 3 weeks • Hours: Monday – Friday, 9 a.m. – 5 p.m. • Estimated wait at clinic is about 2 hours	• Price $125 • Located 15 min away by car or transit • Next available appointment is in 1 week • Hours: Monday – Friday, 8 a.m. – 10 p.m. • Estimated wait at clinic is about 30 to 45 minutes	• Price $185 • Located next to your office building (or college) • Next available appointment is in 1 day • Hours: Monday – Saturday, 8 a.m. – 10 p.m. • By appointment – estimated wait at clinic is about 0–15 minutes

Figure 6.12 Trading off monetary and nonmonetary costs.

or substitution offers, (4) when demand is reduced, and (5) an increasing surplus capacity in the industry. Although some service industries can be fiercely competitive (e.g., airlines or online banking), not all industries are, especially when one or more of the following circumstances reduce price competition:

Figure 6.13 Personalized hairstyling may prevent customers from switching to competing providers.

- **Nonprice-related costs of using competing alternatives are high.** When saving time and effort are of equal or greater importance to customers than price in selecting a supplier, price competition is reduced.
- **Personal relationships matter.** For services that are highly personalized and customized, such as hairstyling (Figure 6.13) or family medical care, relationships with individual providers often are very important to customers, thus discouraging them from responding to competitive offers. Many global banks, for example, prefer to focus on wealthy customers in order to form long-term personal relationships with them.
- **Switching costs are high.** When it takes effort, time, and money to switch providers, customers are less likely to take advantage of competing offers. Cell phone providers often require one- or two-year contracts from their subscribers and charge significant financial penalties for early cancellation of service. Likewise, life insurance firms charge administrative fees or cancellation charges when policy holders want to cancel their policy within a certain time period.
- **Time and location specificity reduces choice.** When people want to use a service at a specific location or at a particular time (or perhaps both), they usually find they have fewer options.[8]

Firms that always react to competitors' price changes run the risk of pricing *lower* than might really be necessary. Managers should be careful not to fall into the trap of comparing competitors' prices dollar for dollar and then seeking to match them. A better strategy is to take into account the entire cost to customers of each competitive offering, including all related monetary and nonmonetary costs, plus potential switching costs. Managers should also examine the impact of distribution, time, and location factors, as well as estimating competitors' available capacity before deciding what response is suitable.

LO 6

Define revenue management and describe how it works.

REVENUE MANAGEMENT: WHAT IT IS AND HOW IT WORKS

Many service businesses now focus on strategies to maximize the revenue (or contribution) that can be obtained from available capacity at any given point in time. Revenue management is important in value creation as it ensures better capacity utilization and reserves capacity for higher-paying segments. It's a sophisticated approach to managing supply and demand under different degrees of constraint.

Airlines,[9] hotels, and car rental firms, in particular, have become skillful at varying their prices in response to the price sensitivity and needs of different market segments at different times of the day, week, or season. More recently, hospitals, restaurants, golf courses (Figure 6.14), on-demand IT services, data processing centers, concert organizers, and even nonprofit organizations increasingly use revenue management.[10] It is most effective when applied to service businesses characterized by:

- High fixed cost structure and relatively fixed capacity, which result in perishable inventory.
- Variable and uncertain demand.
- Varying customer price sensitivity.

It has been suggested that restaurants (which have all the above characteristics) could implement yield management in a manner that makes customers feel they are getting a deal, and yet not have to give permanent discounts. Instead of varying the prices of food, which makes it difficult to increase once it has been lowered, they could vary the minimum spending level at the restaurant. Therefore, if demand is high, the minimum spending is high. If demand is lower, then the minimum spending can be lowered to encourage more demand. This will give restaurants a lot more flexibility in adjusting demand levels.[11]

Figure 6.14 Golf courses have high fixed cost structure so it benefits them to implement revenue management.

Reserving Capacity for High-Yield Customers

In practice, revenue management (also known as yield management) involves setting prices according to predicted demand levels among different market segments. The least price sensitive segment is the first to be provided capacity, paying the highest price. Other segments follow at increasingly lower prices. Because higher-paying segments often book closer to the time of actual consumption, firms need to save capacity for them instead of simply selling on a first-come, first-served basis. For example, business travelers often reserve airline seats, hotel rooms, and rental cars at short notice, but vacationers may book leisure travel months in advance, and convention organizers often block hotel space years in advance of a big event.

A well-designed revenue management system can predict with reasonable accuracy how many customers will use a given service at a specific time at each of several different price levels. This information can be used to increase usage through incentives and schemes, gain market share, or create value. Telecommunication providers are very likely to use these models on historical databases to forecast demand. The objective is to maximize revenues on a day-to-day basis. Service Insights 6.1 shows how revenue management has been implemented at American Airlines, an established industry leader in the field.

How Does Competitors' Pricing Affect Revenue Management?

Because revenue management systems monitor booking pace, they indirectly pick up the effects of competitors' pricing. If a firm prices too low initially, it will experience a higher booking pace, and the cheaper seats fill up quickly. That generally is not desirable, as it means a higher share of late-booking but high-fare-paying customers will not be able to get their seats confirmed. They will therefore fly on competing airlines. If the firm prices too high initially, it will get too low a share of early booking segments (which still tend to offer a reasonable yield) and may later have to offer deeply discounted "last minute" prices to sell excess capacity. Some of the sales of distressed inventory, as it is called in the industry, may take place through reverse auctions, using intermediaries such as Priceline.com.

Price Elasticity

For revenue management to work effectively, there needs to be two or more segments that attach different values to the service and have different price elasticities. To allocate and price capacity effectively, the revenue manager needs to find out how sensitive demand is to price and what net revenues will be generated at different prices for each target segment. The concept of elasticity describes how sensitive demand is to changes in price and is computed as follows:

$$\text{Price elasticity} = \frac{\text{Percentage change in demand}}{\text{Percentage change in price}}$$

When price elasticity is at "unity," sales of a service rise (or fall) by the same percentage that price falls (or rises). If a small change in price has a big impact on sales, demand for that product is said to be *price elastic*. If a change in price has little effect on sales,

SERVICE INSIGHTS 6.1

Pricing Seats on Flight AA333

Revenue management departments use sophisticated yield management software and powerful computers to forecast, track, and manage each flight on a given date separately. Let's look at American Airlines (AA) Flight 333, a popular flight from Chicago to Phoenix, Arizona, which departs daily at 4:50 p.m. on the 1,440-mile (2,317-km) journey.

The 124 seats in coach (economy class) are divided into different fare categories, referred to by yield management specialists as "buckets." There is enormous variation in ticket prices among these seats: round-trip fares range from $298 for a bargain excursion ticket (with various restrictions and a cancellation penalty attached) all the way up to an unrestricted fare of $1,065. Seats are also available at an even higher price in the small first-class section at $1,530. Scott McCartney tells how ongoing analysis by the computer program changes the allocation of seats between each of the seven buckets in economy class.

In the weeks before each Chicago–Phoenix flight, AA's yield management computers constantly adjust the number of seats in each bucket, taking into account tickets sold, historical ridership patterns, and connecting passengers likely to use the route as one leg of a longer trip.

If advance bookings are slim, American adds seats to low-fare buckets. If business customers buy unrestricted fares earlier than expected, the yield management system takes seats out of the discount buckets and preserves them for last-minute bookings that the database predicts will still show up.

With 69 of 124 coach seats already sold four weeks before one recent departure of Flight AA333, AA's computer system began to limit the number of seats in lower-priced buckets. A week later, it totally shut off sales for the bottom three buckets, priced $300 or less. To a Chicago customer looking for a cheap seat, the flight was "sold out"....

One day before departure, with 130 passengers booked for the 124-seat flight, American still offered five seats at full fare because its computer database indicated that 10 passengers were likely not to show up or take other flights. Flight AA333 departed full and no one was bumped.

Although Flight AA333 for that date is now history, it has not been forgotten. The booking experience for this flight was saved in the memory of the yield management program to help the airline do an even better job of forecasting in the future.

SOURCE

Scott McCartney, "Ticket Shock: Business Fares Increase Even as Leisure Travel Keeps Getting Cheaper," *The Wall Street Journal*, November 3, 1997, pp. A1, A10. http://www.aa.com/homePage.do, accessed March 12, 2012.

demand is described as *price inelastic*. The concept is illustrated in the simple chart presented in Figure 6.15, which shows the price elasticity for two segments, one with a highly elastic demand (a small change in price results in a big change in the amount demanded) and the other with a highly inelastic demand (even big changes in price have little impact on the amount demanded).

Designing Rate Fences

LO 7

Discuss the role of rate fences in effective revenue management.

Revenue management is built on the concept of *price customization*—that is, charging different customers different prices for what is actually the same product. As noted by Hermann Simon and Robert Dolan,

PRICE PER UNIT OF SERVICE

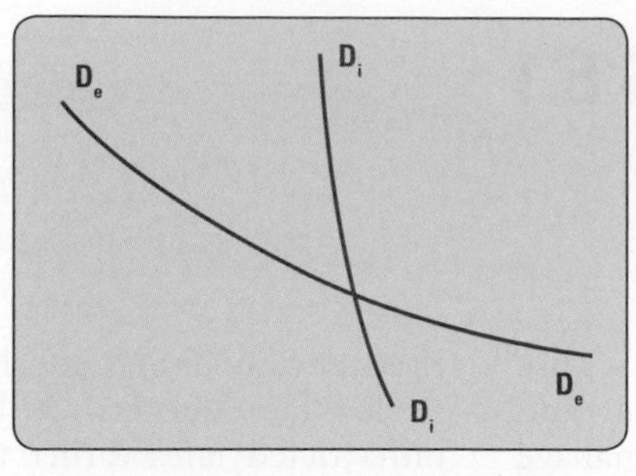

QUANTITY OF UNITS DEMANDED

$$\textbf{Price elasticity} = \frac{\text{Percentage change in demand}}{\text{Percentage change in price}}$$

D_e : Demand is *price elastic*. Small changes in price lead to big changes in demand.

D_i : Demand for service is *price inelastic*. Big changes in price have little impact on demand.

Figure 6.15 Illustration of price elasticity.

> The basic idea of price customization is simple: have people pay prices based on the value they put on the product. Obviously you can't just hang out a sign saying "Pay me what it's worth to you," or "It's $80 if you value it that much but only $40 if you don't." You have to find a way to segment customers by their valuations. In a sense, you have to "build a fence" between high-value customers and low-value customers so the "high" buyers can't take advantage of the low price.[12]

How can a firm make sure that customers who are willing to pay higher prices are unable to take advantage of lower price buckets? Properly designed rate fences allow customers to self-segment on the basis of service characteristics and customers' willingness to pay. Rate fences help companies to restrict lower prices to customers willing to accept certain restrictions on their purchase and consumption experiences.

Figure 6.16 Expect higher prices for seats that have a better view of your favorite musical like Cats.

Fences can be either *physical* or *nonphysical*. *Physical fences* refer to tangible product differences related to the different prices, such as the seat location in a theater (Figure 6.16), the size and furnishing of a hotel room, or the product bundle (e.g., first class is better than economy). *Nonphysical fences* refer to differences in consumption, transaction, or buyer characteristics, but the service is basically the same (e.g., there is no difference in an economy class seat or service whether a person bought a heavily discounted ticket or paid the full fare for it). Examples of nonphysical fences include having to book a certain length of time ahead, not being able to cancel or change a booking (or having to pay cancellation or change penalties), or having to stay over a weekend night. Examples of common rate fences are shown in Table 6.2.

Table 6.2 Key categories of rate fences

Rate Fences	Examples
Physical (product-related) Fences	
• Basic product	• Class of travel (business/economy) • Size of rental car • Size and furnishing of a hotel room • Seat location in a theater or stadium
• Amenities	• Free breakfast at a hotel, airport pickup, etc. • Free golf cart at a golf course • Valet parking
• Service level	• Priority wait-listing, separate check-in counters with no or only short queues • Improved food and beverage selection • Dedicated service hotlines • Personal valet • Dedicated account management team
Nonphysical Fences	
Transaction Characteristics	
• Time of booking or reservation	• Discounts for advance purchase
• Location of booking or reservation	• Passengers booking air tickets for an identical route in different countries are charged different prices. • Customers making reservations online are charged a lower price than those making reservations by phone
• Flexibility of ticket usage	• Fees/Penalties for canceling or changing a reservation (up to loss of entire ticket price) • Nonrefundable reservation fees
Consumption Characteristics	
• Time or duration of use	• Early-bird special in a restaurant before 6:00 p.m. • Must stay over a Saturday night for a hotel booking. • Must stay at least for five nights
• Location of consumption	• Price depends on departure location, especially in international travel. • Prices vary by location (between cities, city center versus edges of the city).
Buyer Characteristics	
• Frequency or volume of consumption	• Members of a certain loyalty tier with the firm (e.g., platinum member) get priority pricing, discounts, or loyalty benefits.
• Group membership	• Child, student, senior citizen discounts • Affiliation with certain groups (e.g., alumni) • Corporate rates
• Size of customer group	• Group discounts based on the size of the group
• Geographic location	• Local customers are charged lower rates than tourists are. • Customers from certain countries are charged higher prices.

In summary, based on a detailed understanding of customer needs, preferences, and willingness to pay, product and revenue managers can design effective products that consist of the core service, physical product features (physical fences), and nonphysical product features (nonphysical fences). In addition, a good understanding of the demand curve is needed so that "buckets" of inventory can be distributed to the various products and price categories. An example from the airline industry is shown in Figure 6.17.

LO 8

Be familiar with the issues of ethics and consumer concerns related to service pricing.

ETHICAL CONCERNS IN SERVICE PRICING

Do you sometimes have difficulty understanding how much it is going to cost you to use a service? Do you believe that many prices are unfair? If so, you're not alone.[13] The fact is, service users can't always be sure in advance what they will receive in return for their money. Many customers assume that a higher-priced service should offer more benefits and greater quality than a lower-priced one. For example, a professional—say, a lawyer—who charges very high fees is assumed to be more skilled than one who is relatively inexpensive. Although price can serve as an indication of quality, it is sometimes hard to be sure if the extra value is really there.

Service Pricing Is Complex

Pricing for services tends to be complex and hard to understand. Comparison across providers may even require complex spreadsheets or even mathematical formulas.

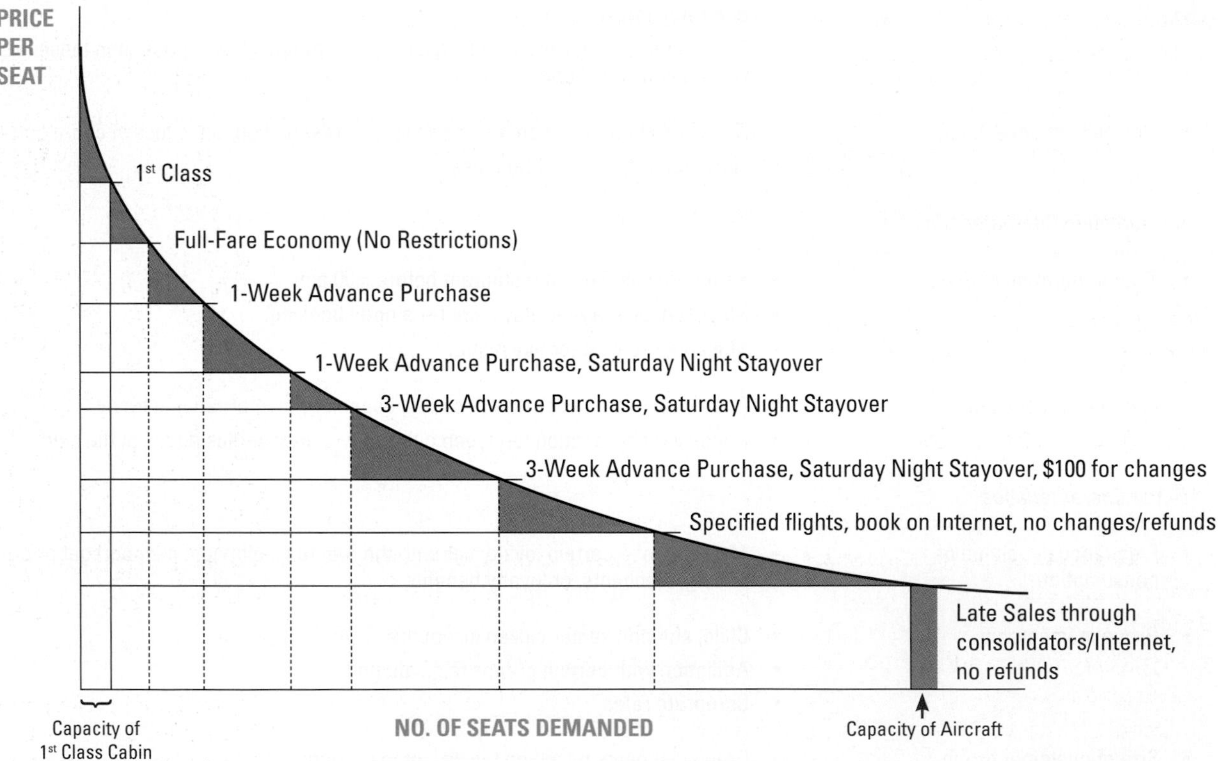

Figure 6.17 Relating price buckets to the demand curve.

In fact, complexity makes it easy (and perhaps more tempting) for firms to engage in unethical behavior. The quoted prices typically used by consumers for price comparisons may be only the first of several charges they can be billed. For example, cell phone companies have a confusing variety of plans to meet the distinct needs and calling patterns of different market segments. Plans can be national, regional, or purely local in scope. Monthly fees vary according to the number of minutes selected in advance. There are usually separate allowances for peak and off-peak minutes. Overtime minutes and "roaming minutes" on other carriers are charged at higher rates. Some plans allow unlimited off-peak calling. Others allow free incoming calls. Some providers charge calls per second, per six-second block, or even per-minute block, resulting in vastly different costs per call. Family plans let parents and children to add their monthly minutes for use on several phones as long as the total for everyone's calling doesn't exceed the monthly limit.

In addition, puzzling new fees have started to appear on bills (Figure 6.18), ranging from "paper bill fee" to pay for the bill itself to obscure sounding fees such as "property tax allotment," "single bill fee," and "carrier cost recovery fee." Bundled plans that include mobile, landline, and Internet services add to the confusion, as the various surcharges can increase the total bill by up to 25%.

Many people find it difficult to forecast their own usage, which makes it hard to compute comparative prices when evaluating competing suppliers whose fees are based on a variety of usage-related factors. It's no coincidence that the humorist Scott Adams (creator of Dilbert) used exclusively service examples when he 'branded' the future of pricing as "confusiology." Noting that firms such as telecommunication companies, banks, insurance firms, and other financial service providers offer nearly identical services, Adams remarks:

> You would think this would create a price war and drive prices down to the cost of providing it (that's what I learned between naps in my economics classes), but it isn't happening. The companies are forming efficient confusopolies so customers can't tell who has the lowest prices. Companies have learned to use the complexities of life as an economic tool.[14]

One of the roles of effective government regulation, says Adams, should be to discourage this tendency for certain service industries to develop into "confusopolies."

Figure 6.18 Puzzling new fees have started to appear on the bills of many service providers.

Piling on the Fees

Not all business models are based on generating income from sales. There is a growing trend today to impose fees that sometimes have little to do with usage. In the United States, the car rental industry advertises bargain rental prices and then tells customers on arrival that other fees like collision and personal insurance are compulsory. Also, staff sometimes fails to clarify certain "small print" contract terms such as, say, a high mileage charge that is added once the car exceeds a very low limit of free miles. The "hidden extras" for car rentals in some Florida resort towns got so bad at one point that people were joking: "The car is free, the keys are extra!"[15]

There has also been a trend of adding (or increasing) fines and penalties. Banks have been heavily criticized for using penalties as an important revenue-generating tool as opposed to using them to educate customers and achieve compliance with payment deadlines (Figure 6.19). Chris Keeley, a New York University student, used his debit card to buy $230 worth of Christmas gifts. His holiday mood soured when he received a notice from his bank that he had overdrawn his checking account. Although his bank authorized each of his seven transactions, it charged him a fee of $31 per payment, totaling $217 for only $230 in purchases. Keeley insisted that he had never requested the so-called overdraft protection on his account and wished his bank had rejected the transactions because he would then simply have paid by credit card. He fumed, "I can't help but think they wanted me to keep spending money so that they could collect these fees."[16]

Figure 6.19 Consumers may be unaware of the high penalty fees imposed on overdrafts.

Some banks don't charge for overdraft protection. Said Dennis DiFlorio, president for retail banking at Commerce Bancorp Inc. in Cherry Hill, NJ: "It's outrageous. It's not about customer convenience. It's just a way for banks to make money off customers." Some banks now offer services that cover overdrafts automatically from savings accounts, other accounts, or even the customer's credit card, and don't charge fees for doing so.[17]

It's possible to design fees and penalties that do not seem unfair to customers. Service Insights 6.2 describes what drives customers' fairness perceptions with service fees and penalties.

LO 9
Understand how fairness can be designed into revenue management policies.

Designing Fairness into Revenue Management

Like pricing plans and fees, revenue management practices can be seen as highly unfair, and customer perceptions have to be carefully managed. Therefore, a well-implemented revenue management strategy should not blindly chase short-term yield maximization. Rather, the following approaches can help firms to reconcile revenue management practices with customer satisfaction, trust, and goodwill[18]:

- **Design Price Schedules and Fences That Are Clear, Logical, and Fair.** Firms should state all fees and expenses (e.g., no-show or cancellation charges) clearly in advance so that there are no surprises (Figure 6.20). A related approach is to develop a simple fee structure so customers can more easily understand how much they have to pay for a particular usage situation. For a rate fence to be seen as fair, customers must understand them easily (i.e., fences have to be transparent and upfront) and see the logic in them.

Figure 6.20 Limousine service providers usually charge for no-shows.

SERVICE INSIGHTS 6.2

Crime and Punishment: How Customers Respond to Fines and Penalties

Various types of penalties are part and parcel of many pricing schedules, ranging from late fees for DVD rentals to cancellation charges for hotel bookings and charges for late credit card payments. Customer responses to penalties can be highly negative and may lead to switching providers and negative word-of-mouth. Young Kim and Amy Smith conducted an online survey using the Critical Incident Technique (CIT) in which 201 respondents were asked to recall a recent penalty incident, describe the situation, and then complete a set of structured questions based on how the respondents felt and how they responded to that incident. Their findings showed that negative consumer responses can be reduced significantly by following three guidelines:

1 **Make Penalties Relative to the Crime Committed.** The survey showed that customers' negative reaction to a penalty increased greatly when they perceived that the penalty was greater than the "crime" committed. Customers' negative feelings were further increased if they were "surprised" by the penalty being suddenly charged to them and they had not been aware of the fee or the size of the fee. These findings suggest that firms can reduce negative customer responses significantly by exploring which amounts are seen as reasonable or fair for a given "customer lapse", and if the fines/fees are explained to customers clearly even before a chargeable incident happens (e.g., in a banking context through a clearly explained fee schedule and through frontline staff that explain at the point of opening an account or selling additional services the potential fines or fees that are associated with various "violations," such as overdrawing beyond the authorized limits, bounced checks, or late payments).

2 **Consider Causal Factors and Customize Penalties.** The study showed that customers' perceptions of fairness were lower and negative responses were higher when they perceived the causes that led to the penalty to be out of their control ("I mailed the check on time—there must have been a delay in the postal system"), rather than when they felt it was within their control and really their fault (e.g., "I forgot to mail the check"). To increase the perception of fairness, firms may want to identify common penalty cases that typically are out of the customer's control and allow the frontline to waive or reduce such fees.

In addition, it was found that customers who generally observe all the rules, and therefore have not paid fines in the past, react particularly negatively if they are fined. One respondent said, "I have always made timely payments and have never been late with a payment—they should have considered this fact and waived the fee." Service firms should take into account customers' penalties history in dealing with penalties, and offer different treatments based on past behavior—perhaps waiving the fine for the first incident while, at the same time, communicating that the fee will be charged for future incidents.

3 **Focus on Fairness and Manage Emotions during Penalty Situations.** Consumers' responses are heavily driven by their perceptions of fairness. Considering customers' perceptions of fairness might mean, for example, that the late fee for keeping a DVD past its due date should not exceed the potentially lost rental fees during that period.

Service companies can also make penalties seem fairer by providing adequate explanations and justifications for the penalty. Ideally, penalties should be imposed for the good of other customers (e.g., "We kept the room for you which we could have given to another guest on our wait list") or community, but not as a way of gaining profit. Finally, frontline employees should be trained in how to handle customers who have become angry or distressed and complain about penalties (see Chapter 13 for some recommendations on how to deal with such situations).

SOURCE

Young "Sally" K. Kim and Amy K. Smith, "Crime and Punishment: Examining Customers' Responses to Service Organizations' Penalties," *Journal of Service Research* 8, no. 2 (2005), 162–180.

Figure 6.21 Cruise packages bundle land tours into their total package price.

- **Use High Published Prices and Frame Fences as Discounts.** Rate fences framed as customer gains (i.e., discounts) generally are seen to be fairer than those framed as customer losses (i.e., surcharges), even if the situations are economically equivalent. For example, a customer who visits her hair salon on Saturdays may think the salon is trying to make a profit if she is faced with a weekend surcharge. However, she is likely to find the higher weekend price more acceptable if the hair salon advertises its peak weekend price as the published price and offers a $5 discount for weekday haircuts. Furthermore, having a high published price helps to increase the reference price and related quality perceptions in addition to the feeling of being rewarded for the weekday patronage.
- **Communicate Consumer Benefits of Revenue Management.** Marketing communications should position revenue management as a win–win practice. Providing different prices and values allows customers to self-segment and enjoy the service. It allows each customer to find the price and benefits (value) that best satisfies his or her needs. For example, charging a higher price for the best seats in the theater recognizes that some people are willing and able to pay more for a better location and makes it possible to sell other seats at lower prices. Furthermore, perceived fairness is affected by what customers perceive as normal. Hence, when communication makes customers more familiar with a particular revenue management practice, unfairness perceptions are likely to decrease over time.[19]
- **Use Bundling to "Hide" Discounts.** Bundling a service into a package hides the discounted price. When a cruise line includes the price of air travel or ground transportation in the cruise package (Figure 6.21), the customer knows only the total price, not the cost of the individual parts. Bundling usually makes price comparisons between the bundles and its individual parts impossible. This reduces unfairness perceptions.[20]
- **Take Care of Loyal Customers.** Firms should try to retain valued customers, even to the extent of not charging the maximum possible amount on a given

transaction. After all, if customers perceive that they are being gouged for price, they will lose trust in the firm. Yield management systems can be programmed to include "loyalty multipliers" for regular customers so that reservations systems can give them special treatment at peak times even when they are not paying premium rates.

- **Use Service Recovery to Compensate for Overbooking.** Many service firms overbook to make allowances for anticipated cancellations and no-shows. Profits increase, but so does the incidence of being unable to honor reservations. Being "bumped" by an airline or "walked" by a hotel can lead to a loss of customer loyalty[21] and affect a firm's reputation negatively. So it's important to back up overbooking programs with well-designed service recovery procedures, such as:

  1) Give customers a choice between keeping their reservation or receiving compensation (e.g., many airlines practice voluntary offloading at check-in against cash compensation and a later flight).
  2) Provide sufficient advance notice so that customers are able to make other arrangements (e.g., offloading and rescheduling to another flight the day before departure, often in combination with cash compensation).
  3) If possible, offer a substitute service that delights customers (e.g., upgrading a passenger to business or first class on the next available flight, often in combination with options 1 and 2 above).

A Westin beach resort found that it can free up capacity by offering guests who are departing the next day the choice of spending their last night in a luxury hotel near the airport or in the city at no cost. Guest feedback on the free room, upgraded service, and a night in the city after a beach holiday has been very positive. From the hotel's perspective, this practice trades the cost of getting a one-night stay in another hotel against that of turning away a multiple-night guest arriving that same day.

PUTTING SERVICE PRICING INTO PRACTICE

LO 10

Discuss the seven questions marketers need to answer to design an effective service pricing strategy.

Although the main decision in pricing usually is seen as how much to charge, there are other important decisions to be made. Table 6.3 summarizes the questions that service marketers need to ask themselves as they prepare to create and implement a well-thought-out pricing strategy. Let's look at each in turn.

How Much to Charge?

For firms to remain in business, they need to make realistic decisions on pricing. The pricing tripod model, discussed earlier (refer to Figure 6.3), provides a useful starting point. First, all the relevant economic costs need to be recovered at different sales volumes, and these set the relevant floor price. Next, the elasticity of demand of the service from both the providers' and customers' perspectives will help to set a ceiling price for any given market segment. Finally, firms need to analyze the intensity of price competition among the providers before they come to a final price.

When a specific figure must be set for the price itself, firms need to think about the pros and cons of setting a rounded price and the ethical issues involved in setting a price that does not include taxes, service charges, and other extras.

Table 6.3 Issues to consider when developing a service pricing schedule

1.	**How much should be charged for this service?** • What costs is the organization attempting to recover? Is the organization trying to achieve a specific profit margin or return of investment by selling this service? • How sensitive are customers to various prices? • What prices are charged by competitors? • What discount(s) should be offered from basic prices? • Are psychological pricing points (e.g., $4.95 versus $5.00) customarily used?
2.	**What should be the basis of pricing?** • Execution of a specific task • Admission to a service facility • Units of time (hour, week, month, year) • Percentage commission on the value of the transaction • Physical resources consumed • Geographic distance covered • Weight or size of the object serviced • Should each service element be billed independently? • Should a single price be charged for a bundled package?
3.	**Who should collect payment?** • The organization that provides the service • A specialist intermediary (travel or ticket agent, bank, retail, etc.) • How should the intermediary be compensated for this work—flat fee or percentage commission?
4.	**Where should payment be made?** • The location at which the service is delivered • A convenient retail outlet or financial intermediary (e.g., bank) • The purchaser's home (by mail or phone)
5.	**When should payment be made?** • Before or after delivery of the service • At which times of the day • On which days of the week
6.	**How should payment be made?** • Cash (exact change or not?) • Token (where can these be purchase?) • Stored value card • Check (how to verify?) • Electronic funds transfer • Charge card (credit or debit) • Credit account with service provider • Vouchers • Third-party payment (e.g., insurance company or government agency?)
7.	**How should prices be communicated to the target market?** • Through what communication medium? (advertising, signage, electronic display, salespeople, customer service personnel) • What is the message content? (how much emphasis should be placed on price?)

More recently, auctions and dynamic pricing have become increasingly popular as a way to price according to demand and customers' value perceptions, as seen in the examples in our opening vignette. See Service Perspective 6.3 for other examples of dynamic pricing in the Internet environment.

SERVICE INSIGHTS 6.3

Dynamic Pricing on the Internet

Dynamic pricing, also known as customized or personalized pricing, also is a new way to achieve price discrimination. It is popular with service suppliers because of its potential to increase profits and at the same time provide customers with what they value. E-tailing, or retailing over the Internet, is suitable for this strategy because changing prices electronically is a simple procedure. Dynamic pricing allows e-tailers to charge different customers different prices for the same product based on information collected about their purchase history, preferences, price sensitivity, and so on. Tickets.com gained up to 45% more revenue per event when pricing of concerts and events was adjusted to meet demand and supply. However, customers may not be happy.

E-tailers often are uncomfortable about admitting to use of dynamic pricing because of the ethical and legal issues associated with price discrimination. Customers of Amazon.com were unhappy when they found out that it was not charging everyone the same price for the same movie DVDs. A study of online consumers by the University of Pennsylvania's Annenberg Public Policy Center found that 87% of respondents did not think dynamic pricing was acceptable.

Reverse Auctions

Travel e-tailers such as Priceline.com, Hotwire.com, and Lowestfare.com follow a customer-driven pricing strategy known as a reverse auction. Each firm acts as an intermediary between potential buyers who ask for quotations for a product or service, and multiple suppliers who quote the best price they're willing to offer. Buyers can then compare the offers and choose the supplier that best meets their needs. For example, if a buyer is looking for a flight and accommodation package, search results often show a variety of combinations of packages one can choose from. All the different airlines and hotels are listed by brand, and the price of each package is listed clearly.

Different business models underlie these services. Although some are provided free to end-users, most e-tailers either receive a commission from the supplier or do not pass on the whole savings to their customers. Others charge customers either a fixed fee or one based on a percentage of the savings.

Traditional Auctions

Other e-tailers, such as eBay, uBid, and Online-Auction, follow the traditional online auction model in which bidders place bids for an item and compete with each other to see who buys it. Marketers of both consumer and industrial products use such auctions to sell outdated or overstocked items, collectibles, rare items, and secondhand merchandise. This form of retailing has become very successful since eBay launched it first in 1995.

Shopbots Help Consumers to Benefit from Dynamic Pricing

Consumers now have tools of their own to prevent themselves from being taken advantage of by practices of dynamic pricing. One approach involves using shopbots to do a comparison of prices and find the cheapest prices available. *Shopbots*, or shopping robots, basically are intelligent agents that automatically collect price and product information from multiple online vendors. A customer has only to visit a shopbot site, such as Dealtime.com, and run a search for the item that they are looking for. The shopbot instantly looks up all the associated retailers to check availability, features, and price, and then presents the results in a comparison table. Different shopbots have links to different retailers. There is even a shopbot site called MegaShopBot.com, which searches for deals within the best shopbots!

There's little doubt that dynamic pricing is here to stay. With further advances in technology and wider applications, its reach will extend to more and more service categories.

SOURCES

Stephan Biller, Lap Mui Ann Chan, David Simchi-Levi, and Julie Swann, "Dynamic Pricing and Direct-to-Customer Model in the Automotive Industry," *Electronic Commerce Research* 5, no. 2 (April 2005), 309–334; Laura Sydell, "New Pricing Plan Soon to Be at Playing for Online Music," July 27, 2009, http://www.npr.org/templates/story/story.php?storyId=111046679&ft=1&f=1006, accessed March 12, 2012; Mikhail 1. Melnik and James Alm, "Seller Reputation, Information Signals, and Prices for Heterogeneous Coins on eBay," *Southern Economic Journal* 72, no. 2 (2005), 305–328; Jean-Michel Sahut, "The Impact of Internet on Pricing Strategies in the Tourism Industry," *Journal of Internet Banking and Finance*, 14, no. 1 (2009), 1–8; "Dynamic Pricing Schemes—Value Led" *Managing Change: Strategic Interactive Marketing*, www.managingchange.com/dynamic/valueled.htm, accessed March 12, 2012; http://www.megashopbot.com/, accessed March 12, 2012.

PART II

What Should Be the Specified Basis for Pricing?

It's not always easy to define a unit of service as the specified basis for pricing. There are many choices. For instance, should price be based on completing a promised service task—such as repairing a piece of equipment or cleaning a jacket? Or should it be based on admission to a service performance, such as an educational program, a concert, or a sports event? Should it be time-based, for instance, using an hour of a lawyer's time? Alternatively, should it be related to a monetary value linked to the service delivery, such as when an insurance company charges different levels of premium to reflect the amount of coverage provided, or a real estate company charges a commission that is a percentage of the selling price of a house?

Some service prices are tied to the consumption of physical resources such as food, drinks, water, or natural gas. Transport firms have traditionally charged by distance, with freight companies using a combination of weight or cubic volume and distance to set their rates (Figure 6.22). For some services, prices may include separate charges for access and for usage. Recent research suggests that access or subscription fees are an important driver of adoption and customer retention, whereas usage fees are much more important drivers of actual usage.[22]

Figure 6.22 Shipment of goods are typically charged by a combination of distance (miles, kilometers, or zones) and weight or size (such as cubic volume).

Price Bundling

An important question for service marketers is whether to charge one price for all elements (referred to as a "bundle") or to price each element separately. If customers prefer to avoid making many small payments, then bundled pricing may be preferable. However, if they dislike being charged for product elements they do not use, itemized pricing may be preferable. Bundled prices offer firms a certain level of guaranteed revenue from each customer while providing customers a clear idea in advance of how much they can expect to pay. Unbundled pricing provides customers with the freedom to choose what to buy and pay for.[23]

Discounting

Selective price discounting targeted at specific market segments can offer important opportunities to attract new customers and fill capacity that would otherwise go unused. However, unless it is used with effective rate fences that allow specific segments to be targeted cleanly, a strategy of discounting should be used carefully. It reduces the average price and contribution received and may attract customers who are only looking for a firm that can offer the lowest price on the next transaction. Volume discounts are sometimes used to encourage large corporate customers to be loyal, instead of spreading their purchases among several different suppliers.

PART II

Who Should Collect Payment?

As discussed in Chapter 4, supplementary services include information, order taking, billing, and payment. Customers appreciate it when a firm makes it easy for them to get price information and make reservations. They also expect bills that are clear, and convenient procedures that make it easier to make payment.

Sometimes, firms use intermediaries such as travel agents who make hotel and transport bookings and collect payment from customers (see Figure 6.23), and ticket agents who sell seats for theaters, concert halls, and sports stadiums. Although the original supplier pays a commission, the intermediary usually is able to offer customers greater convenience in terms of where, when, and how payment can be paid. Using intermediaries may also result in savings in administrative costs. Nowadays, however, many service firms are promoting their websites with best rate or price guarantees as direct channels for customer self-service, thus bypassing traditional intermediaries and avoiding payment of commissions.

Figure 6.23 Travel agencies are intermediaries that help to distribute airline tickets.

Where Should Payment Be Made?

Service delivery sites are not always conveniently located. Airports, theaters, and stadiums, for instance, often are situated some distance from where potential customers may live or work. When consumers have to purchase a service before using it, there are benefits to using intermediaries that are more conveniently located, or allowing payment by mail or bank transfer. A growing number of organizations now accept Internet, telephone, and e-mail bookings with payment by credit card.

When Should Payment Be Made?

Two basic ways are to ask customers to pay in advance (as with an admission charge, airline ticket, or postage stamps) or to bill them once service delivery has been completed (as with restaurant bills and repair charges). Sometimes, a service provider may ask for an initial payment in advance of service delivery, with the balance due later (Figure 6.24). This is quite common for expensive repair and maintenance jobs, when the firm—often a small business with limited working capital—must buy and pay for materials.

"Unless we receive the outstanding balance within ten days, we will have no choice but to destroy your credit rating, ruin your reputation, and make you wish you were never born. If you have already sent the seven cents, please disregard this notice."

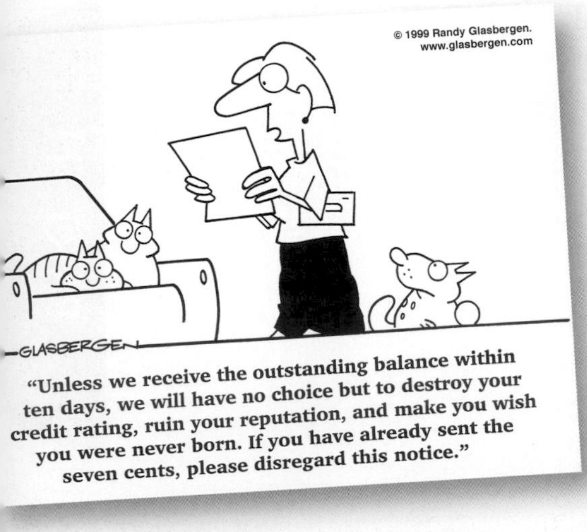

Figure 6.24 Some firms do not leave their customers with much flexibility in dealing with late payment.

Asking customers to pay in advance means the buyer is paying before the benefits are received. However, pre-payments may have benefits for the customer as well as the provider. For example, for public transport, in order to save time and effort, customers may prefer the convenience of buying a monthly travel pass.

Finally, the timing of payment can have an effect on usage patterns. From an analysis of the payment and attendance records of a Colorado-based health club, John Gourville and Dilip Soman found that members' usage patterns were closely related to when they made payment. When members made payments, their use of the club was highest during the months immediately following payment and then slowed down steadily until the next payment. Members with monthly payment plans used the health club much more consistently and were more likely to renew their memberships perhaps because each month's payment encouraged them to use what they were paying for (Figure 6.25).[24]

How Should Payment Be Made?

As shown earlier in Table 6.3, there are many different forms of payment. Cash may appear to be the simplest method, but it raises security problems and is inconvenient

Figure 6.25 Payment schedules can drive health club usage and renewal of membership!

when exact change is required to operate machines. Accepting payment by check for all but the smallest purchases is now fairly common and offers customer benefits, although it may require controls to discourage bad checks, such as a hefty charge for returned checks ($15–$20 on top of any bank charges is not uncommon at retail stores).

Credit and debit cards can be used around the world. As they become more widely used, businesses that refuse to accept them increasingly find themselves at a competitive disadvantage. Many companies also offer customers the convenience of a credit account, which starts a membership relationship between the customer and the firm (see Chapter 12).

Pre-payment systems are also becoming more common. It is based on cards that store value on a magnetic strip or in a microchip embedded within the card. However, service firms that want to accept payment in this form must first install card readers. Service marketers should remember that the simplicity and speed with which payment is made may influence the customer's perception of overall service quality. To save its customers time and effort, Chase Bank has introduced credit cards with what it calls "blink," a technology that can be read by a point-of-sale terminal without physically touching it (Figure 6.26).

Interestingly, a recent study found that the method of payment has an effect on customers' total spending, especially on consumption items such as spending in cafés.[25] Consumers tend to spend more when the method of payment is less tangible or immediate. Consumers are more careful with cash and tend to spend less, followed by credit cards, pre-payment cards, and, finally even less tangible and immediate mechanisms such as payment through one's cell phone service bill.

Figure 6.26 Chase advertises its new fast credit card scanning service, "blink."

How Should Prices Be Communicated to the Target Markets?

People need to know the price they are expected to pay, before purchase. Managers must decide whether or not to include pricing information in advertising for the service. It may be suitable to relate the price to the costs of competing products. Salespeople and customer service representatives should be able to give immediate, accurate responses to customer queries about pricing, payment, and credit. Good signage at retail points of sale will save staff members from having to answer basic questions on prices.

How to communicate prices is important and shapes buying behavior. For example, in a restaurant context, menu psychology looks at how diners respond to pricing information on menu (see Service Insights 6.4).

Finally, when the price is presented in the form of an itemized bill, marketers should make sure that it is both accurate and easy to understand. Hospital bills, which may run to several pages and contain dozens of items, have often been criticized for inaccuracy. Many hotel bills, despite containing fewer entries, are also inaccurate (Figure 6.27). One study estimated that business travelers in the US may be overpaying for their hotel rooms by half a billion dollars a year, with 11.6% of all bills incorrect, resulting in an average overpayment of $11.36.[26]

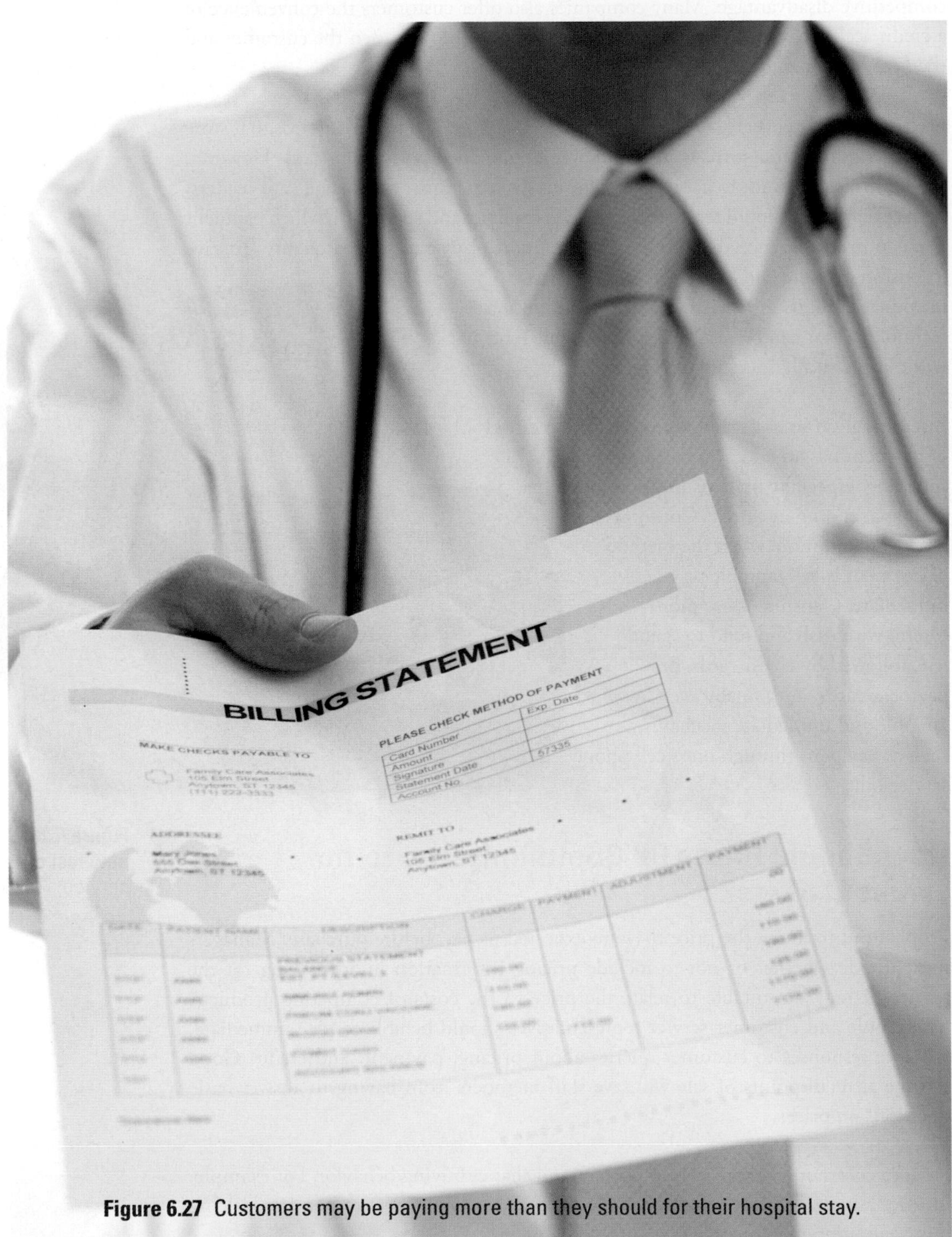

Figure 6.27 Customers may be paying more than they should for their hospital stay.

SERVICE INSIGHTS 6.4

The Psychology of Menu Pricing in Restaurants

Have you ever wondered why you choose certain dishes on the menu and not others? It could be due to the way the dish is displayed. Menu psychology is a growing field of research. Menu engineers and consultants research on the most effective ways to design a menu, including layout and pricing information, in the hope that the diner will spend more money. What can we do to get people to spend more money and to order items with the highest profit margins?

- When showing prices on the menu, avoid using a dollar sign. Prices that come with dollar signs will result in customers spending less, as compared to when there are no dollar signs on the menu.
- Prices that end with "9," like $9.99, make diners feel that they are getting value for money. This is good for a low price, good value positioning, but should not be used by high-end restaurants.
- Where is the best position to place prices? It should be at the end of the description of an item and should not be highlighted in any way.
- In terms of order of items, place the most expensive item at the top of the menu so that the price of the other items looks lower in comparison.
- For layout, the most profitable item on the menu should be placed at the top right hand corner of the page because people tend to look there first.
- A longer description of a dish tends to encourage people to order it. Therefore, menus can be designed to have more detailed and more appetizing descriptions of dishes that are more profitable, and have less description for the less profitable dishes.
- What kind of names should be given to dishes? Using names of mothers, grandmothers, and other relatives (e.g., Aunty May's beef stew) has been shown to encourage people to buy that item.

The next time you have selected a dish from the menu, you may want to stop and see how it is displayed, and whether that potentially have swayed you toward a dish the restaurant want you to order.

CHAPTER SUMMARY

LO 1 ▶ Effective pricing is central to the financial success of service firms. The objectives for establishing prices can be to gain profits, cover costs, build demand, and/or develop a user base. Once a firm sets its pricing objectives, it needs to decide on its pricing strategy.

LO 2 ▶ The foundations of a pricing strategy are the three legs of the pricing tripod:

- The costs the firm needs to recover set the minimum or floor price.
- The customer's perceived value of the offering sets a maximum or ceiling price.
- The price charged for competing services determines where, within the floor-to-ceiling range, the price can be set.

LO 3 ▶ The first leg of the pricing tripod is the cost to the firm.

- Costing services often is complex. Services frequently have high fixed costs, varying capacity utilization, and large shared infrastructures that make it difficult to establish unit costs.
- If services have a large proportion of variable and/or semi-variable costs, then cost-accounting approaches work well (e.g., using contribution and breakeven analysis).
- However, for complex services with shared infrastructure, activity-based costing (ABC) often is more appropriate.

LO 4 ▶ The second leg of the pricing tripod is value to the customer.

- Net value is the sum of all perceived benefits (gross value) minus the sum of all the perceived costs of a service. Customers will only buy if the net value is positive. The net value can be enhanced by either increasing value and/or reducing costs.
- Since value is perceived and subjective, it can be enhanced through communication and education to help customers better understand the value they receive.
- In addition to the price customers pay for the service, costs include related monetary costs (e.g., the taxi fare to the service location) and nonmonetary costs (e.g., time, physical, psychological, and sensory costs) during the search, purchase and service encounter, and post-purchase stages. Firms can enhance net value by reducing these related monetary and non-monetary costs.

LO 5 ▶ The third leg of the pricing tripod is competition.

- Price competition can be fierce in markets with relatively similar services. Here, firms need to closely observe what competitors charge and price accordingly.
- However, services tend to be location- and time-specific, and competitor services have their own set of related monetary and non-monetary costs. Therefore, sometimes the actual prices charged become secondary for competitive comparisons.

LO 6 ▶ Revenue management (RM) increases revenue for the firm through better use of capacity and reservation of capacity for higher-paying segments. Specifically, RM:

- designs products using physical and non-physical rate fences, and prices them for different segments according to their specific reservation prices;
- sets prices according to predicted demand levels of different customer segments; and
- works best in service businesses characterized by (1) high fixed costs and perishable inventory, (2) several customer segments with different price elasticities, and (3) variable and uncertain demand.

LO 7 ▶ Well-designed rate fences are needed to define "products" for each target segment so that customers who are willing to pay higher prices for a service offer are unable to take advantage of lower price buckets. Rate fences can be physical and non-physical:

- Physical fences refer to tangible product differences related to different prices (e.g., seat location in a theater, size of a hotel room, or service level).
- Non-physical fences refer to consumption (e.g., stay must be over a weekend), transactions (e.g., two weeks' advance booking with cancellation and change penalties), or buyer characteristics (e.g., student and group discounts). The service experience is identical across fence conditions although different prices are charged.

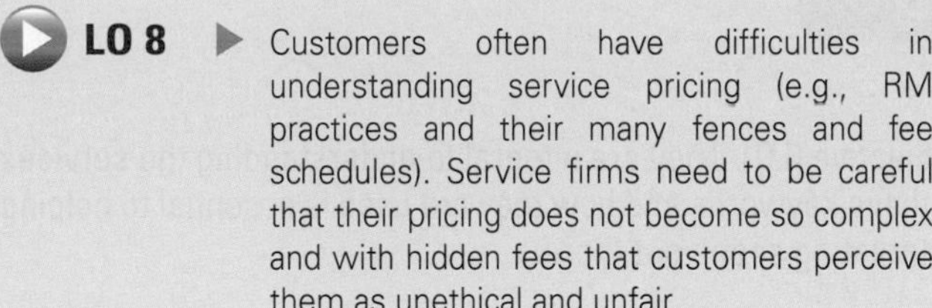

LO 8 ▶ Customers often have difficulties in understanding service pricing (e.g., RM practices and their many fences and fee schedules). Service firms need to be careful that their pricing does not become so complex and with hidden fees that customers perceive them as unethical and unfair.

LO 9 ▶ The following ways help firms to improve customers' fairness perceptions:

- o Design price schedules and fences that are clear, logical, and fair.
- o Use published prices and frame fences as discounts.
- o Communicate consumer benefits of revenue management.
- o Use bundling to "hide" discounts.
- o Take care of loyal customers.
- o Use service recovery or deal with overbooking.

LO 10 ▶ To put service pricing into practice, service marketers need to consider seven questions to have a well-thought-out pricing strategy. The questions are:

- o How much should be charged?
- o What should be the specified basis for pricing?
- o Who should collect payment?
- o Where should payment be made?
- o When should payment be made?
- o How should payment be made?
- o How should prices be communicated to the target markets?

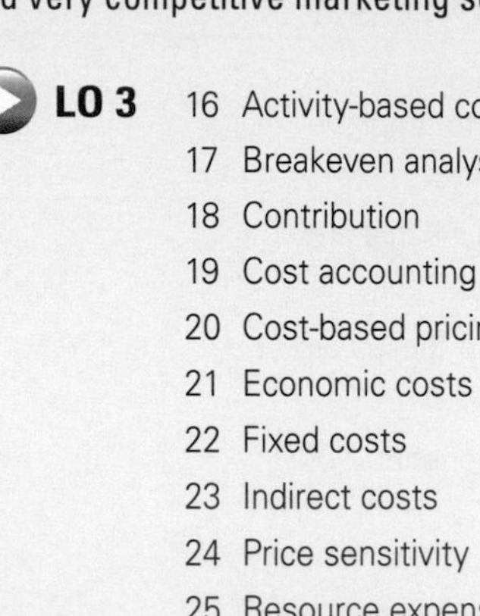

UNLOCK YOUR LEARNING

These keywords are found within the sections of each Learning Objective (LO). They are integral to understanding the services marketing concepts taught in each section. Having a firm grasp of these keywords and how they are used is essential to helping you do well on your course, and in the real and very competitive marketing scene out there.

LO 1

1 Demand
2 Pricing objectives
3 Pricing strategy
4 Profit
5 User base

LO 2

6 Ceiling
7 Competition
8 Competitive pricing
9 Costs
10 Floor
11 Maximum price
12 Minimum price
13 Pricing tripod
14 Value to customer
15 Value-based pricing

LO 3

16 Activity-based costing
17 Breakeven analysis
18 Contribution
19 Cost accounting
20 Cost-based pricing
21 Economic costs
22 Fixed costs
23 Indirect costs
24 Price sensitivity
25 Resource expenses
26 Semi-variable costs
27 Variable costs

LO 4

28 After costs
29 Monetary costs
30 Net value
31 Non-monetary costs
32 Perceived benefits
33 Perceived costs
34 Perception of value
35 Physical costs
36 Post-purchase
37 Psychological costs
38 Purchase costs
39 Search costs
40 Sensory costs
41 Service encounter costs
42 Time costs
43 Value-based pricing

LO 5

44 Competition-based pricing
45 Location specificity
46 Non-price-related costs
47 Price leadership
48 Relationships
49 Switching costs
50 Time specificity

LO 6

51 Distressed inventory
52 Perishable inventory
53 Price elastic
54 Price elasticity
55 Price inelastic
56 Revenue management
57 Reverse auctions
58 Yield management

LO 7

59 "Buckets" of inventory
60 Buyer characteristics
61 Consumption characteristics
62 Non-physical fences
63 Physical fences
64 Price customization
65 Rate fences
66 Transaction characteristics

 **LO 8**

67 "Confusiology"
68 "Confusopolies"
69 Ethical concerns
70 Fairness perception
71 Fees
72 Penalties
73 Unethical behavior

 **LO 9**

74 Bundling
75 Compensate
76 Fences
77 "Loyalty multipliers"
78 Overbooking
79 Price schedules
80 Published prices
81 Service recovery

 **LO 10**

82 Auctions
83 Discounting
84 Dynamic pricing
85 Elasticity of demand
86 Floor price
87 Intermediaries
88 Menu psychology
89 Pre-payment system
90 Price bundling
91 Price competition
92 Pricing strategy
93 Reverse auctions
94 Service pricing into practice
95 Shopbots

PART II

How well do you know the language of services marketing? Quiz yourself!

Not for the academically faint-of-heart

For each keyword you are able to recall without referring to earlier pages, give yourself a point (and a pat on the back). Tally your score at the end and see if you earned the right to be called—a *services marketeer*.

SCORE

0 – 18 Services Marketing is done a great disservice.
19 – 36 The midnight oil needs to be lit, pronto.
37 – 54 I know what you *didn't* do all semester.
55 – 72 A close shave with success.
73 – 90 Now, go forth and market.
91 – 95 There should be a marketing concept named after you.

KNOW YOUR ESM

Review Questions

1. Why is the pricing of services more difficult than the pricing of goods?
2. How can the pricing tripod approach to service pricing be useful in setting a good pricing point for a particular service?
3. How can a service firm compute its unit costs for pricing purposes? How does predicted and actual capacity utilization affect unit costs and profitability?
4. What is the role of non-monetary costs in a business model, and how do they relate to the consumer's value perceptions?
5. Why can't we compare competitor prices dollar-for-dollar in a service context?
6. What is revenue management, how does it work, and what type of service operations benefit most from good revenue management systems and why?
7. Explain the difference between physical and non-physical rate fences using suitable examples.
8. Why are ethical concerns important issues when designing service pricing and revenue management strategies? What are potential consumer responses to service pricing or policies that are perceived as unfair?
9. How can we charge different prices to different segments without customers feeling cheated? How can we even charge the same customer different prices at different times, contexts, and/or occasions, and, at the same time, be seen as fair?
10. What are the seven key decisions managers need to make when designing an effective pricing schedule?

WORK YOUR ESM

Application Exercises

1. Select a service organization of your choice, and find out what its pricing policies and methods are. In what respects are they similar to or different from what has been discussed in this chapter?
2. From the customer perspective, what serves to define value in the following services: (a) a hair salon, (b) a legal firm specializing in business and taxation law, and (c) a nightclub?
3. Review recent bills you have received from service businesses, such as those for telephone, car repair, cable TV, and credit cards. Evaluate each one against the following criteria: (a) general appearance and clarity of presentation, (b) easily understood terms of payment, (c) avoidance of confusing terms and definitions, (d) appropriate level of detail, (e) unanticipated ("hidden") charges, (f) accuracy, and (g) ease of access to customer service in case of problems or disputes.
4. How might revenue management be applied to (a) a professional service firm (e.g., a law firm), (b) a restaurant, and (c) a golf course? What rate fences would you use and why?
5. Collect the pricing schedules of three leading cell phone service providers. Identify all the pricing dimensions (e.g., airtime, subscription fees, free minutes, per second/6 seconds/minute billing, airtime rollover) and pricing levels for each dimension (i.e., the range offered by the players in the market). Determine the usage profile for a particular target segment (e.g., a young executive who uses the phone mostly for personal calls or a full-time student). Based on the usage profile, determine the lowest cost provider. Next, measure the pricing schedule preferences of your target segment (e.g., via conjoint analysis). Finally, advise the smallest of the three providers on how to redesign its pricing schedule to make it more attractive to your target segment.
6. Consider a service of your choice, and develop a comprehensive pricing schedule. Apply the seven questions marketers need to answer for designing an effective pricing schedule.

ENDNOTES

1 Joshua Brustein, "Star Pitchers in a Duel? Tickets Will Cost More," *The New York Times*, June 27, 2010; Adam Satariano, "Eagles Pinch Scalpers with Live Nation Price Hikes (Update 1), *Businessweek*, February 24, 2010; Ethan Smith, "Start-Up Scoops Up Unsold Tickets," *The Wall Street Journal*, December 16, 2010; "Tango Telecom Wins Global Mobile Award 2011 for Dynamic Pricing Deployment," *M2M (Machine to Machine)*, February 21, 2011, http://m2m.tmcnet.com/news/2011/02/21/5326156.htm, accessed March 12, 2012.

2 Gerald E. Smith and Thomas T. Nagle, "How Much Are Customers Willing to Pay?" *Marketing Research* (Winter 2002): 20–25.

3 Valarie A. Zeithaml, "Consumer Perceptions of Price, Quality, and Value: A Means—End Model and Synthesis of Evidence," *Journal of Marketing* 52, (July 1988): 2–21. A recent paper exploring alternative conceptualizations of value is: Chien-Hsin Lin, Peter J. Sher, and Hsin-Yu Shih, "Past Progress and Future Directions in Conceptualizing Customer Perceived Value," *International Journal of Service Industry Management* 16, no. 4 (2005): 318–336.

4 Parts of this section are based on Leonard L. Berry and Manjit S. Yadav, "Capture and Communicate Value in the Pricing of Services," *Sloan Management Review* 37, (Summer 1996): 41–51.

5 Anna S. Mattila and Jochen Wirtz, "The Impact of Knowledge Types on the Consumer Search Process – An Investigation in the Context of Credence Services," *International Journal of Service Industry Management* 13, no. 3 (2002): 214–230.

6 Leonard L. Berry, Kathleen Seiders, and Dhruv Grewal, "Understanding Service Convenience," *Journal of Marketing* 66, (July 2002): 1–17.

7 Laurie Garrow, "Online Travel Data: A Goldmine of New Opportunities," *Journal of Revenue and Pricing Management* 8, no. 2/3, (2009): 247–254.

8 Kristina Heinonen, "Reconceptualizing Customer Perceived Value: The Value of Time and Place," *Managing Service Quality* 14, no. 3 (2004): 205–215.

9 For the latest research in airlines revenue management airline seat inventory control, see: Yoon Sook Song, Seong Tae Hong, Myung Sun Hwang and Moon Gil Yoon, "MILP Model for Network Revenue Management in Airlines," *Journal of Business & Economics Research* 6, no. 2 (2010): 55–62; and for demand for different fare classes, see: Guillermo Gallego, Lin Li, and Richard Ratliff, "Choice-based EMSR Methods for Single-leg Revenue Management with Demand Dependencies," *Journal of Revenue and Pricing Management* 8, no. 2/3 (2009): 207–240.

10 For application of yield management to industries beyond the traditional airline, hotel and car rental contexts, see: Frédéric Jallat and Fabio Ancarani, "Yield Management, Dynamic Pricing and CRM in Telecommunications," *Journal of Services Marketing* 22, no. 6 (2008): 465–478; Sheryl E. Kimes and Jochen Wirtz, "Perceived Fairness of Revenue Management in the US Golf Industry," *Journal of Revenue and Pricing Management* 1, no. 4 (2003): 332–344; Sheryl E. Kimes and Jochen Wirtz, "Has Revenue Management Become Acceptable? Findings from an International Study and the Perceived Fairness of Rate Fences," *Journal of Service Research* 6, (November 2003): 125–135; Richard Metters and Vicente Vargas, "Yield Management for the Nonprofit Sector," *Journal of Service Research* 1, (February 1999): 215–226; Sunmee Choi and Anna S. Mattila, "Hotel Revenue Management and Its Impact on Customers' Perception of Fairness," *Journal of Revenue and Pricing Management* 2, no. 4 (2004): 303–314; Alex M. Susskind, Dennis Reynolds, and Eriko Tsuchiya, "An Evaluation of Guests' Preferred Incentives to Shift Time-Variable Demand in Restaurants," *Cornell Hotel and Restaurant Administration Quarterly* 44, no. 1 (2004): 68–84; Parijat Dube, Yezekael Hayel, and Laura Wynter, "Yield Management for IT Resources on Demand: Analysis and Validation of a New Paradigm for Managing Computing Centres," *Journal of Revenue and Pricing Management* 4, no. 1 (2005): 24–38; and Sheryl E. Kimes and Sonee Singh, "Spa Revenue Management," *Cornell Hospitality Quarterly* 40, no. 1 (2009): 82–95. Ting Li, Eric van Heck, Peter Vervest, "Information Capability and Value Creation

Strategy: Advancing Revenue Management through Mobile Ticketing Technologies," *European Journal of Information Systems* 18 (2009): 38–51.

11 Rafi Mohammed, "A Better Way to Make Deals on Meals," *Harvard Business Review*, January-February 2011, 25.

12 Hermann Simon and Robert J. Dolan, "Price Customization," *Marketing Management* 7, (Fall 1998): 11–17.

13 Lisa E. Bolton, Luk Warlop, and Joseph W. Alba, "Consumer Perceptions of Price (Un)Fairness," *Journal of Consumer Research* 29, no. 4 (2003): 474–491; Lan Xia, Kent B. Monroe, and Jennifer L. Cox, "The Price Is Unfair! A Conceptual Framework of Price Fairness Perceptions," *Journal of Marketing* 68, (October 2004): 1–15. Christian Homburg, Wayne D. Hoyer, and Nicole Koschate, "Customer's Reactions to Price Increases: Do Customer Satisfaction and Perceived Motive Fairness Matter?" *Journal of the Academy of Marketing Science* 33, no. 1 (2005): 36–49.

14 Scott Adams, *The DilbertTM Future—Thriving on Business Stupidities in the 21st Century*. New York: Harper Business, 1997, 160.

15 Ian Ayres and Barry Nalebuff, "In Praise of Honest Pricing," *Sloan Management Review* 45, (Fall 2003): 24–28.

16 Dean Foust, "Protection Racket? As Overdraft and Other Fees Become Huge Profit Sources for Banks, Critics See Abuses," *Business Week* 5, (February 2005): 68–89.

17 The banking examples and data in this section were from Dean Foust, "Protection Racket? As Overdraft and Other Fees Become Huge Profit Sources for Banks, Critics See Abuses," *Business Week* 5, (February 2005): 68–89.

18 Parts of this section are based on Jochen Wirtz, Sheryl E. Kimes, Jeannette P. T. Ho, and Paul Patterson, "Revenue Management: Resolving Potential Customer Conflicts," *Journal of Revenue and Pricing Management* 2, no. 3 (2003): 216–228.

19 Jochen Wirtz and Sheryl E. Kimes, "The Moderating Role of Familiarity in Fairness Perceptions of Revenue Management Pricing," *Journal of Service Research* 9, no. 3 (2007): 229–240.

20 Judy Harris and Edward A. Blair, "Consumer Preference for Product Bundles: The Role of Reduced Search Costs," *Journal of the Academy of Marketing Science* 34, no. 4 (2006): 506–513.

21 Florian v. Wangenheim and Tomas Bayon, "Behavioral Consequences of Overbooking Service Capacity," *Journal of Marketing* 71, no. 4 (October 2007): 36–47.

22 Peter J. Danaher, "Optimal Pricing of New Subscription Services: An Analysis of a Market Experiment," *Marketing Science* 21, Spring 2002, 119–129; Gilia E. Fruchter and Ram C. Rao, "Optimal Membership Fee and Usage Price Over Time for a Network Service," *Journal of Services Research* 4, no. 1 (2001): 3–14.

23 Avery Johnson, "Northwest to Charge Passengers in Coach for Meals," *Wall Street Journal*, February 16, 2005.

24 John Gourville and Dilip Soman, "Pricing and the Psychology of Consumption," *Harvard Business Review* 9, (September 2002): 90–96.

25 Dilip Soman, "The Effect of Payment Transparency on Consumption: Quasi-Experiments from the Field," *Marketing Letters* 14, no. 3 (2003): 173–183.

26 See, for example, Anita Sharpe, "The Operation Was a Success; The Bill Was Quite a Mess," *Wall Street Journal*, September 17, 1997, 1; Gary Stoller, "Hotel Bill Mistakes Mean Many Pay Too Much," *USA Today*, July 12, 2005 (accessed at *www.news.yahoo.com/s/usatoday*)

Figure 7.6 Itau stresses not only its global reach but also its intimate knowledge of Latin America.

Facilitate Customer Involvement in Service Production

When customers are actively involved in service production, they need training to help them perform well, just as employees do. When customers perform well, it benefits the company because it helps to improve productivity.

One way to train customers, as recommended by advertising experts, is to show service delivery in action. Television and videos are effective because of their ability to interest the viewer and to show a sequence of events in visual form. Some dentists show their patients videos of surgical procedures before the surgery takes place so that customers know what to expect. Shouldice Hospital in Toronto, featured in Case 12 (page 576) specializes in hernia repair. It offers potential patients an opportunity to view an online simulation on hernia and explains the hospital experience on its website (see www.shouldice.com). This educational technique helps patients prepare themselves mentally for the experience, and shows them what role they need to play in service delivery to ensure a successful surgery and fast recovery.

Stimulate or Dampen Demand to Match Capacity

Many life service performances, whether a seat at the theater for Friday evening's performance or a haircut at Supercuts on Tuesday morning, are time-specific and cannot be stored for resale at a later date. Advertising and sales promotions can help to change the timing of customer use and thus help to match demand with the available capacity at a given time.

Low demand outside peak periods is a serious problem for service industries with high fixed costs, such as hotels. One strategy is to run promotions that offer extra value, such as room upgrades or free breakfasts to encourage demand without decreasing price. When demand increases, the number of promotions can be reduced or eliminated (see also Chapter 6 on revenue management and Chapter 9 on managing demand and capacity).

LO 2
Understand the challenges of service communications.

CHALLENGES OF SERVICES COMMUNICATIONS

Now that we've discussed the role of market communications, let's examine some of the communication challenges that service firms face. Traditional marketing communication strategies were initially developed for marketing manufactured goods. However, services are often intangible, which affects the way we approach the design of service marketing communications.

Problems of Intangibility

Services are performances rather than objects. Therefore, their benefits can be difficult to communicate to customers, especially when the service in question does not involve tangible actions to customers or their possessions.[3] Intangibility creates four problems for promoting the attributes or benefits of a service. They are: abstractness, generality, nonsearchability, and mental impalpability.[4] Each problem has implications for services communications[5]:

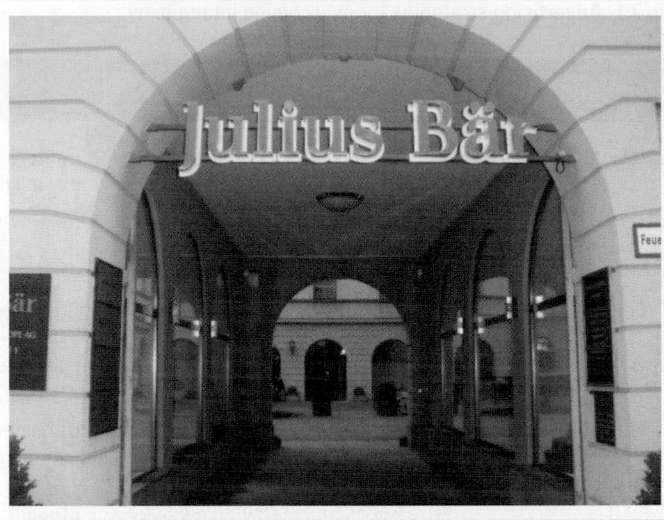

Figure 7.7 Julius Bar, a Swiss private bank is able to portray intangible concepts in its advertisements.

- *Abstractness.* Abstract concepts such as financial security or investment-related matters (Figure 7.7), expert advice, or safe transportation do not correspond directly with physical objects. It can therefore be challenging for marketers to link their services to those intangible concepts.
- *Generality.* This refers to items that comprise a class of objects, persons, or events for instance, airline seats, flight attendants, and cabin service. There may be physical objects that can show these services, so abstractness is not a problem. However, it is not specific enough, so even though most consumers of the service know what they are, it is difficult for marketers to create a unique value proposition to communicate what makes a specific offering distinctly different from, and better than, competing offerings.
- *Nonsearchability.* Many of service attributes cannot be searched or inspected before they are purchased. Physical service attributes, such as the appearance of a health club and the type of equipment installed, can be checked in advance, but the experience of working with the trainers can only be determined through extended personal involvement. As noted in Chapter 2, services usually have more experience and credence attributes than search attributes. Recall that experience attributes are those that need consumers to go through the service to understand it. For services high in credence attributes, one must trust, for example, a surgeon's skill.
- *Mental impalpability.* Many services are sufficiently complex, multi-dimensional, or new. Therefore, one often cannot understand nor interpret a service, what the experience of consuming it will be like, and what benefits will result.

Overcoming the Problems of Intangibility

The intangibility of service presents problems for advertising that need to be overcome. Table 7.1 suggests specific communications strategies marketers can follow to create messages that help to solve each of the four problems created by the intangibility of services.

In addition to using the strategies presented in Table 7.1, using tangible cues and metaphors are two other methods that firms can be used to overcome the four problems of intangibility. Both tangible cues and metaphors help by clearly communicating intangible service attributes and benefits to potential customers.

Tangible Cues. Using tangible cues is one strategy commonly used in advertising. It is helpful to include information that catches the audience's attention and will produce a strong, clear impression on the senses, especially for services that are complex and highly intangible.[6] For example, many business schools feature successful alumni to

PART II

Table 7.1 Advertising strategies for overcoming intangibility

Intangibility Problem	Advertising Strategy	Description
Abstractness	Service consumption episode	Capture and show typical customers benefiting from the service, e.g. by smiling in satisfaction at a staff going out of his way to help.
Generality		
• For objective claim	System documentation	Document facts and statistics about the service delivery system. For example, in the UPS website, they state that they have 216 aircraft in operation.
• For subjective claim	Performance documentation	Document and cite past service performance statistics, such as the number of packages that have been delivered on time.
	Service performance episode	Present actual service delivery being performed by the service personnel. The video mode is best for showing this.
Nonsearchability	Consumption documentation	Obtain and present testimonials from customers who have experienced the service.
	Reputation documentation	If the service is high in credence attributes, then document the awards received or the qualifications of the service provider.
Mental impalpability	Service process episode	Present a clear step-by-step documentation of what exactly will happen during the service experience.
	Case history episode	Present an actual case history of what the firm did for a specific client and how it solved the client's problem.
	Service consumption episode	A story or depiction of a customer's experience with a service

SOURCE

Banwari Mittal and Julie Baker, "Advertising Strategies for Hospitality Services". *Cornell Hotel and Restaurant Administration Quarterly* 43 (April 2002): 53.

Figure 7.8 The Merrill Lynch bull shows a strong commitment to the financial performance of its clients.

make the benefits of its education tangible and communicate what its education could do for potential students in terms of career advancement, salary increases, and lifestyle.

Metaphors. Some companies have created metaphors that are tangible in nature to communicate the benefits of their service offerings and to emphasize key points of differentiation. Insurance companies often use this approach to market their highly intangible products. For example, Allstate advertises that "You're in Good Hands," and Prudential uses the Rock of Gibraltar as a symbol of corporate strength. The Merrill Lynch bull has been a symbol for the wealth manager's business philosophy, which suggests both a bullish market and a strong commitment to its clients' financial performance (Figure 7.8).

Where possible, advertising metaphors should highlight *how* service benefits are actually provided.[7] Consulting firm AT Kearney emphasizes that it includes all management levels in seeking solutions, not just higher-level management. Its clever advertisement, showing bear traps across the office floor, draws attention to the way in which the company differentiates its service through careful work with all levels in its client organizations, thus avoiding the problems left behind by other consulting firms who work mostly with senior management (Figure 7.9).

MARKETING COMMUNICATIONS PLANNING

LO 3
Know the 5 Ws of marketing communications planning.

After discussing the role of marketing communications and how to overcome the challenge of intangibility of service offerings, let's now focus on how to plan and design an effective marketing communication strategy. A useful checklist for marketing communication planning is provided by the "5 Ws" model:

Who is our target audience?

What do we need to communicate and achieve?

How should we communicate this?

Where should we communicate this?

When do the communications need to take place?

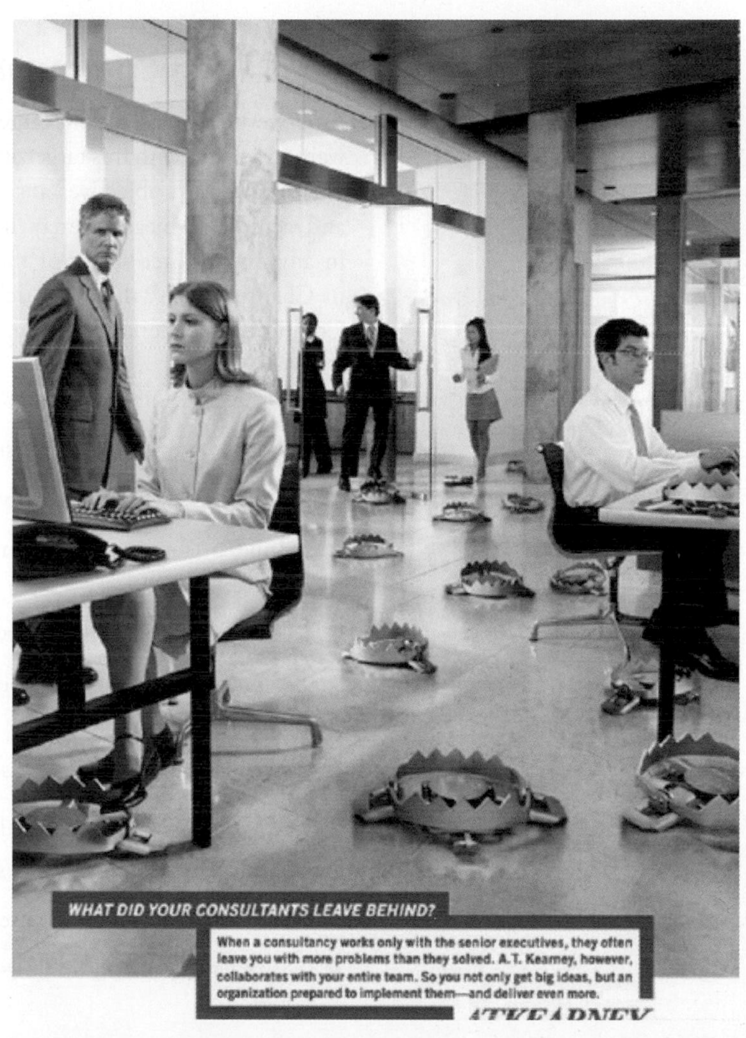

Figure 7.9 AT Kearney uses bear traps as a metaphor for problems.

Let's first consider the issues of defining the target audience (i.e., *who*) and specifying communication objectives (*what*). Then we'll review the wide array of communication tools available to service marketers (*how*). Issues relating to the location (*where*) and scheduling (*when*) of communication activities tend to be highly situation specific, and so we will not address them here.

Defining the Target Audience

Prospects, users, and employees represent the three broad target audiences for any service communication strategy:

- *Prospects*—Marketers of consumer services do not usually know prospects in advance. Therefore, they typically use a traditional communications mix, like media advertising, public relations, and use of purchased lists for e-mail campaigns, direct mail, or telemarketing.
- *Users*—In contrast to prospects, more cost-effective channels can be used to reach existing users. These include cross- or up-selling efforts by frontline employees, point-of-sale promotions, and other information distributed during service encounters. If the firm has a membership relationship with its customers and has a membership database containing contact and profiling information, it

can distribute highly targeted information through e-mail, text messages, direct mail, or telephone.

- *Employees*—Employees serve as a secondary audience for communication campaigns through public media. A well-designed campaign targeted at users, nonusers, or both can also be motivating for employees, especially those in frontline roles. In particular, it may help to shape employees' behavior if the advertising content shows them what is promised to customers. However, there is a risk of demotivating employees if the communication promotes levels of performance that they feel are unrealistic or even impossible to achieve.

Communications directed specifically at staff typically are part of an internal marketing campaign, using company-specific channels, and so are not meant for customers. We will discuss internal communications in Chapter 11.

Specifying Communication Objectives

After we are clear about our target audience, we now need to specify what exactly we want to achieve with this target audience. Marketers need to be clear about their goals. Communication objectives answer the question of what we need to communicate and achieve. Objectives may include shaping and managing customer behavior in any of the three stages of the purchase and consumption process we discussed in Chapter 2 (i.e., the pre-purchase, service encounter, and post-purchase stages). Common educational and promotional objectives for service organizations include:

- Create memorable images of companies and their brands.
- Build awareness and interest in an unfamiliar service or brand.
- Compare a service favorably with competitors' offerings.
- Build preference by communicating the strengths and benefits of a specific brand.
- (Re)position a service relative to competitive offerings.
- Reduce uncertainty and perceived risk by providing useful information and advice.
- Provide reassurance, such as by promoting service guarantees.
- Encourage trial by offering promotional incentives.
- Familiarize customers with service processes in advance of use.
- Teach customers how to use a service to their best advantage.
- Stimulate demand in low-demand periods and shift demand during peak periods.
- Recognize and reward valued customers.

Service Insights 7.1 shows how UPS repositions its service to deliver its promise to customers.

SERVICE INSIGHTS 7.1

UPS Repositions Itself to Deliver

Founded as a messenger company in the United States in 1907, UPS has become one of the world's top service brands, developing new services and expanding into new markets around the globe. In recent years, the company has had to develop communication strategies to change the perceptions of both current and potential customers. Although recognized as a leader in the ground shipping business, the company wanted wider awareness of its other services like supply chain management, multi-modal transportation and financial services. So it started a rebranding and repositioning exercise to make sure that all UPS services were closely identified with the UPS name.

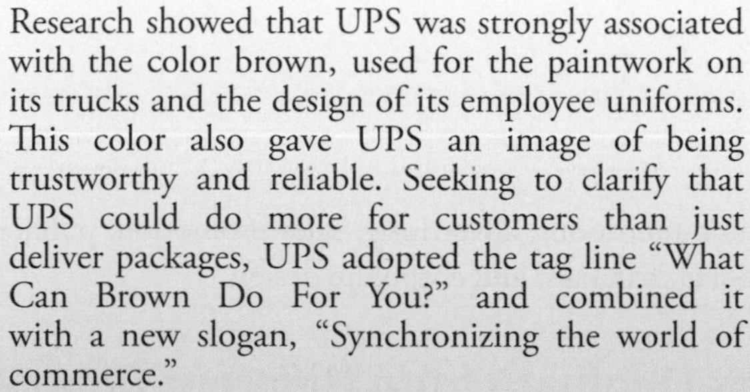

Research showed that UPS was strongly associated with the color brown, used for the paintwork on its trucks and the design of its employee uniforms. This color also gave UPS an image of being trustworthy and reliable. Seeking to clarify that UPS could do more for customers than just deliver packages, UPS adopted the tag line "What Can Brown Do For You?" and combined it with a new slogan, "Synchronizing the world of commerce."

The company understood that changing the perception of a brand had to start with the employees first. Although it can be difficult to change people's mindsets about a company's vision, UPS succeeded. Employees accepted the new brand positioning strategy and learned to work with each other across business units. Working together, they were able to serve customers better.

Today, the company operates in more than 220 countries and territories worldwide and is the world's largest package delivery company. By 2010, it had revenues of close to $50 billion from its four main services, namely Package Operations, Supply Chain and Freight, UPS Supply Chain Solutions, and UPS Freight. UPS has a strong retail presence, with over 4,700 retail stores, 49 mailboxes, 1,000 customer centers, 16,000 authorized outlets and 40,000 drop boxes. Just for its package operations alone, their website has an average of 26.2 million tracking requests daily. The UPS jet fleet has 216 aircraft in operation.

SOURCE

Vivan Manning-Schaffel, "UPS Competes to Deliver," http://www.brandchannel.com/features_effect.asp?pf_id=210, (May 17, 2004) accessed on August 2010; http://www.ups.com/content/us/en/about/facts/worldwide.html, accessed March 12, 2012.

THE MARKETING COMMUNICATIONS MIX

LO 4

Be familiar with the marketing communications mix in a services context.

After understanding our target audience and our specific communications objectives, we now need to select a mix of cost-effective communications channels. Most service marketers have access to numerous forms of communication, referred to collectively as the *marketing communications mix*. Different communication elements have distinctive capabilities relative to the types of messages they can convey and the market segments most likely to be exposed to them. As shown in Figure 7.10a, the

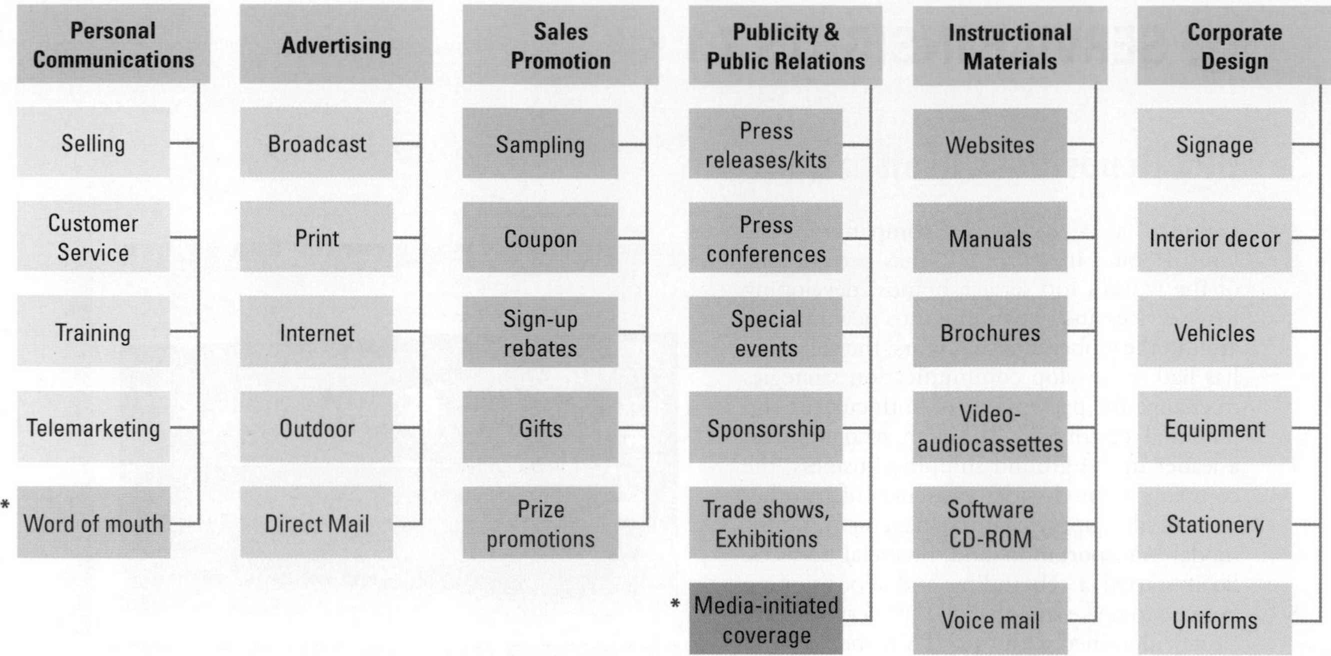

*** Denotes communications originated from outside the organization**

Figure 7.10a The marketing communications mix for services.

mix includes personal communications, advertising, sales promotion, publicity and public relations, instructional materials, and corporate design.

Communications Originate from Different Sources

As shown in Figure 7.10b, the traditional communications mix shown in Figure 7.10a can also be categorized into two main channels: those controlled by the organization and those that are not. Not all communications messages originate from the service provider. Rather, some messages originate from outside the organization. Furthermore, Figure 7.10b shows that messages from an internal source can be further divided into those transmitted through marketing channels (traditional media and the Internet) and those transmitted through the service firm's own service delivery channels. Let's look at the options within each of these three originating sources.

LO 5

Know the communications mix elements of the traditional marketing channels.

Messages Transmitted through Traditional Marketing Channels

As shown in Figure 7.10a, service marketers have a wide array of communication tools at their disposal. Let us briefly review the principal elements.

Advertising

Advertising is the most commonly used form of communication in consumer marketing and is often the first point of contact between service marketers and their customers. Advertising serves to build awareness, inform, persuade, and remind. It plays an important role in providing factual information about services and educating customers about product features and capabilities.

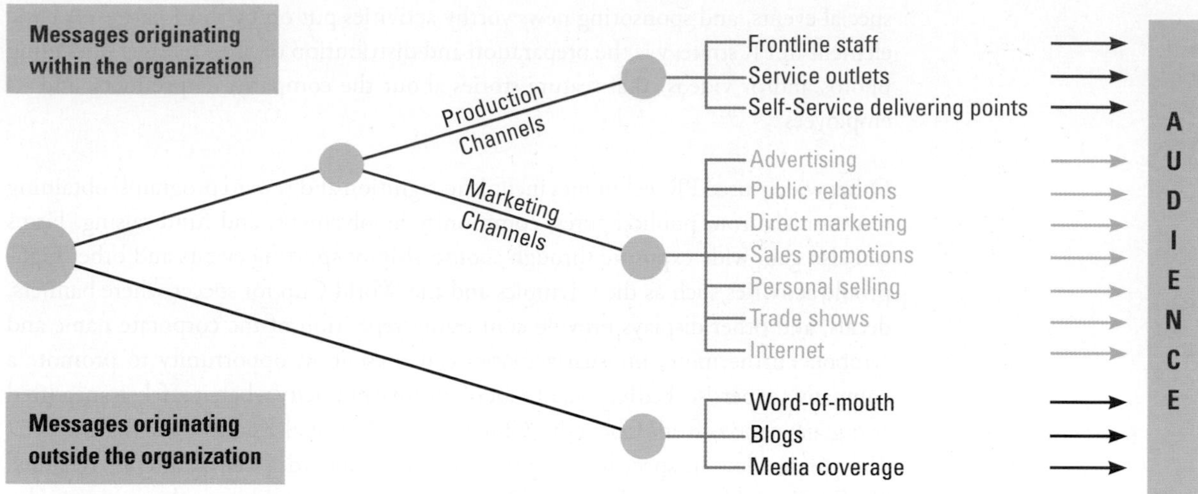

Figure 7.10b Sources of message received by a target audience.

SOURCE

Adapted from Adrian Palmer, *Principles of Services Marketing*, London: McGraw-Hill, 6th edition, 2011, p. 450.

One of the challenges facing advertisers is how to get their messages noticed. In general, people are tiring of ads in all their forms. A study by Yankelovich Partner, a US marketing services consulting firm, found that consumer resistance to advertising has reached an all-time high. The study found that 65% of people feel "constantly bombarded" by ad messages, and 59% feel that ads have very little relevance to them.[8] Robert Shaw of Cranfield School of Management runs a forum in which large companies try to monitor the "marketing payback" from advertising. According to Shaw, the results were "never terribly good," with less than half of the ads generating a positive return on their investment.[9]

How can a firm hope to stand out from the crowd? Longer, louder commercials and larger format ads are not the answer. Marketers are trying to be more creative with their advertising to allow their messages to be more effective. For example, when customers have low involvement with a service, firms should focus on more emotional appeals and the service experience itself.[10] Some advertisers stand out by using striking designs or a distinctively different format. Others, like Comcast, seek to catch the audience's attention through use of humor as they seek to show how slow competing services are compared to their own high-speed Internet cable access. Some firms are now placing advertisements in video games, which can be dynamic advertisements if the games are connected to the Internet (Figure 7.11).[11] Furthermore, Apple iOS apps that function with the iPhone or iPad, and apps for other smartphones and tablets are becoming increasingly important avenues for communication with potential and current customers.

Figure 7.11 Avatars crowd in front of Sony BMG's media island. Virtual video game worlds like *Second Life* lead the wave of in-game advertising.

Public Relations

Public relations (PR) involves efforts to generate positive interest in an organization and its products by sending out news releases, holding press conferences, staging special events, and sponsoring newsworthy activities put on by third parties. A basic element in PR strategy is the preparation and distribution of press releases (including photos and/or videos) that feature stories about the company, its products, and its employees.

Other widely used PR techniques include recognition and reward programs, obtaining testimonials from public figures, community involvement, and fund raising. Firms can also gain wide exposure through sponsorship of sporting events and other high-profile activities such as the Olympics and the World Cup for soccer where banners, decals, and other displays provide continuing repetition of the corporate name and symbol. Furthermore, unusual activities can present an opportunity to promote a company's expertise. FedEx gained a lot of positive publicity when it safely transported two giant pandas from Chengdu, China, to the National Zoo in Washington, DC. The pandas flew in specially designed containers aboard a FedEx aircraft renamed "FedEx PandaOne." (See Figure 7.12.) In addition to press releases, the company also featured information about the unusual shipment on a special page on its website.

Direct Marketing

This category uses tools like mailers, e-mail, and text messaging. These channels allow personalized messages to be sent to highly targeted segments of customers. Direct strategies will most likely succeed when marketers possess a detailed database of information about customers and prospects.

Advances in on-demand technologies such as e-mail spam filters, TiVo, podcasting, and pop-up blockers allow consumers to decide how and when they prefer to be reached and by whom. Because a 30-second television spot interrupts a viewer's favorite program and a telemarketing call interrupts a meal, customers increasingly use such technologies to protect their time. This reduces the effectiveness of mass media and has given rise to *permission marketing*.

In the permission marketing model, the goal is to persuade consumers to volunteer their attention. Permission marketing reaches out only to individuals who have expressed prior interest in receiving certain types of messages. It allows service firms to build stronger relationships with their customers. In particular, e-mail,

Figure 7.12 FedEx transported two giant pandas to National Zoo in Washington, DC.

in combination with websites, can be merged into a one-to-one permission-based medium.[12] For instance, people can be invited to register at the firm's website and state what type of information they would like to receive via e-mail. These e-mails can be designed as the start of a more interactive communication process in which customers can request regular information about topics they are interested in. In addition, if they are particularly excited about a new service or piece of information, they can click through a URL link embedded in the e-mail to view more in-depth information and even video materials. Finally, they can subscribe online for additional services, communicate with other customers, recommend the service to their friends, and the like.

Sales Promotion

A useful way of looking at sales promotions is as a communication with an incentive. Sales promotions usually are specific to a time period, price, or customer group—sometimes all three. Typically, the objective is to get customers to make a purchase decision faster or encourage customers to use a specific service sooner, in greater volume with each purchase, or more frequently.[13] Sales promotions for service firms may take such forms as samples, coupons and other discounts, gifts, and competitions with prizes. Used in these forms, they increase sales during periods when demand would otherwise be weak, speed up the introduction and acceptance of new services, and generally get customers to act faster than they would in the absence of any promotional incentive.[14] Sales promotions need to be used with care because research shows that customers acquired through sales promotions may have lower repurchase rates and lower lifetime values.[15]

Some years ago, SAS International Hotels devised an interesting sales promotion targeted at older customers. If a hotel had vacant rooms, guests over 65 years of age could get a discount equivalent to their years (e.g., a 75-year-old could save 75% of the normal room price). All went well until a Swedish guest checked into one of the SAS chain's hotels in Vienna, announced his age as 102, and asked to be paid 2% of the room rate in return for staying the night. This request was granted, and the energetic centenarian challenged the general manager to a game of tennis—and got that, too. (The results of the game, however, were not disclosed!) Events like these are the stuff of dreams for public relations people. In this case, a clever promotion led to a humorous, widely reported story that placed the hotel chain in a positive light.

Personal Selling

This refers to interpersonal encounters in which efforts are made to educate customers and promote a particular brand or product (Figure 7.13). Many firms, especially those marketing business-to-business services, have a sales team or employ agents and distributors to undertake personal selling efforts on their behalf. For services that are bought less often like property, insurance, and funeral services, the firm's representative may act as a consultant to help buyers make their selections. For industrial and professional firms that sell relatively complex services, each customer may have an account manager they can turn to for advice, education, and consultation.

However, face-to-face selling to new prospects is expensive. A lower-cost alternative is *telemarketing*, involving the use of the telephone to reach potential customers. At the consumer level, people are increasingly frustrated with the intrusive nature of telemarketing, which often is timed to reach them when they are home in the evening

Figure 7.13 To persuade customers of the superiority of one's brand, body language is also important.

More Internet advertisers pay only if a visitor to the host site clicks through on the link to the advertisers' site. This is similar to paying for the delivery of junk mail only to households that read it.[20]

- **Search engine advertising.** Search engines are a form of a reverse broadcast network. Instead of advertisers broadcasting their messages to consumers, search engines let advertisers know exactly what consumers want through their keyword search. Advertisers can then target relevant marketing communications directly at these consumers.[21] One of the greatest success stories of search engine advertising has been Google (see Service Insights 7.2), with firms like Yahoo!, AOL, MSN, and most recently Blink seeking to become major players in this field.

Figure 7.17 Web banners function similarly to traditional banners: Turning consumers' attention to the product or service and selling a pitch though service-provider and consumer interaction is more realize with the "click through" of online advertisement.

SERVICE INSIGHTS 7.2

Google—the Online Marketing Powerhouse

Larry Page and Sergey Brin, who were both fascinated by mathematics, computers, and programming from an early age, founded Google in 1998 while they were Ph.D. students at Stanford University. Seven years later, following Google's successful public offering, they became multi-billionaires, and Google became one of the world's most valuable companies.

The company has the grand vision: "To organize the world's information and make it universally accessible and useful." Its search engine is so useful and user friendly that it has been extremely successful, almost entirely through word-of-mouth from satisfied users. Few company names become verbs, but to "google" has now entered common use in English.

Its popularity has allowed Google to become a new and highly focused advertising medium, allowing advertisers two important ways to reach their customers. They can do so either through sponsored links or through content ads.

Sponsored links appear at the top of search results on Google's website and are identified as "sponsored links." Google prices its sponsored links service as "cost per click," using a sealed-bid auction (i.e., where advertisers submit bids for a search term without knowing other advertisers' bids for the same term). This means prices depend on the popularity of the search terms with which the advertiser wants to be linked. Heavily used terms such as "MBA" are more expensive than less popular terms such as "MSc in Business." Advertisers can easily keep track of their ad performance using the reports in Google's online account control center.

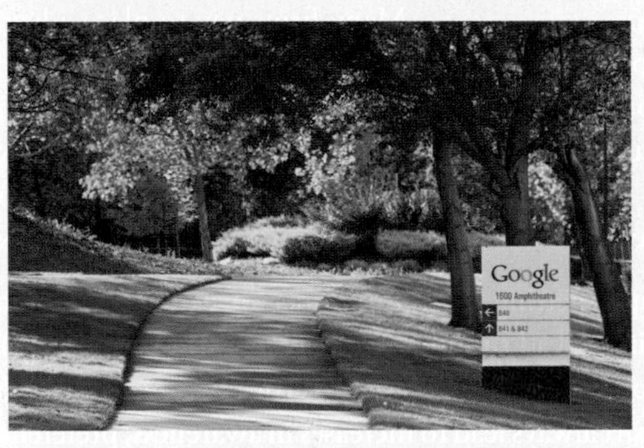

Figure 7.18 Google HQ at Mountain View, California.

Google allows *content ads* to be highly targeted through a number of ways via its Google AdWords service. Ads can be placed next to search results on Google.com (they are, for example, displayed as banner ads). These ads allow businesses to connect with potential customers at the exact moment when they are looking at related topics or even specific product categories. Here, firms buy the opportunity to be linked to certain search categories or terms. To explore this part of Google's advertising business model, just "google" a few words and observe what appears on your screen in addition to the search results.

AdWords also allows advertisers to display their ads at websites that are part of the Google content network rather than only on Google.com. This means these ads are not initiated by a search but are simply displayed when a user browses a website. Such ads are called "placement-targeted ads." Advertisers can specify either individual websites or website content (e.g., about travel or baseball). Placement targeting allows advertisers to handpick their target audiences, which can be very large (e.g., all baseball fans in the United States or even the world), or small and focused (e.g., people interested in fine dining in the Boston area). Google places the ads alongside relevant content of a Google partner's websites. For example, if you read an article on a partner website, you will see an ad block at the foot of the article. These ads have been dynamically targeted to match the content of that article by Google. They can be the same ads that appear on Google.com alongside searches, but here they are distributed in a different way and appear on websites of publishers of all sizes in the Google partner network.

AdWords is complemented by a second service, called AdSense, which represents the other side of Google's advertising model. AdSense is used by website owners who wish to make money by displaying ads on their websites. In return for allowing Google to display relevant ads on their content pages, these website owners receive a share of the advertising revenue generated. An important side effect of AdSense has been that it has created advertising income streams for thousands of small and medium online publishers and blog sites, making those businesses sustainable. Although big media companies like the *New York Times* and CNN also use AdSense, it generates a smaller portion of their total online advertising revenue compared to the typical niche web- or blog site.

Google's ability to deliver an advertising medium that is highly targeted, contextual, and results based has been very attractive to advertisers and led to rapid revenue growth and profits. It's no surprise that Google's success frightens other advertising media.

SOURCES

Roben Farzad and Ben Elgin, "Googling for Gold," *Business Week*, December 5, 2005, 60–70; www.google.com and http://en.wikipedia.org/wiki/Adwords, both accessed March 12, 2012.

A key advantage of online advertising is that it provides a very clear and measurable return on investment, especially when compared to other forms of advertising. Advertisers have several options; they can:

- pay for ads to keyword searches related to their firms;
- sponsor a short text message with a clickthrough link, located next to the search results, and
- buy top rankings in the display of search results through "pay for placement." Since users expect the rankings to reflect the best fit with the keywords used in the search, Google's policy is to shade paid listings that appear at the top of the rankings column and identify them as "sponsored links." Pricing for these ads and placements can be based on either the number of impressions (i.e., eyeballs) or clickthroughs.

SERVICE INSIGHTS 7.3

New Media and Their Implications for Marketing Communications

Technology has created some exciting new communications channels that offer important opportunities for targeting. Among the key developments are TiVo, podcasting, mobile advertising, Web 2.0 technology, YouTube, and social networks and communities.

TiVo

TiVo, also known as Digital Video Recorder (DVR) or personal video, can record many hours of television programs on its hard disk very much like a VCR. However, unlike a VCR, TiVo is "always on" and continuously stores about 30 minutes of the channel that is currently being watched. This means that TiVo users can pause or rewind live TV. In fact, many users begin watching a TV program after the broadcast has started so that they can fast-forward and skip the advertisements. Interestingly, while customers like TiVo because it can be commercial free, TiVo is attracting marketers and advertisers as well with its promise of interactivity, measurability, and long-form advertising.

In June 2004, Charles Schwab & Co. became the first financial services company to use TiVo's new interactive technology, using a 30-second spot featuring golfer Phil Mickelson. The spot allowed viewers to move from the commercial into a four-minute video to watch three segments hosted by Mickelson. Viewers could also order information on Schwab's golf rewards program at the same time. The effectiveness of ads can be immediately measured based on viewer responses.

Podcasting

Podcasting comes from the words "iPod" and "broadcasting." It refers to a group of technologies for distributing audio or video programs over the Internet using a publisher/subscriber model. Podcasting gives broadcast radio or television programs a new distribution method. Once someone has subscribed to a certain feed, they will automatically receive new "episodes" that become available.

Podcasting is so popular that it now has several forms. These include video podcasting for delivery of video clips, mobilecast for downloads onto a cell phone, and blogcast for attachment of an audio or video file to a blog. It is beneficial to include podcasting as part of a firm's marketing communications program because, once a listener has subscribed to a specific show, it means the listener is interested in the topic. Therefore, podcasts can reach a wide audience of listeners who have a narrow focus, more like "narrowcasting" than broadcasting. When the advertising message is more targeted, this leads to a higher return on investment for the advertising dollars spent.

Mobile Advertising

Mobile advertising is a form of advertising through cell phones and other mobile wireless devices. Mobile advertising is quite complex as it can include the Internet, video, text, gaming, music, and much more. For example, advertisements can come in the form of an SMS, MMS, advertisements in mobile games, videos, or even some music before a voicemail recording. Through mobile advertising and the use of a global positioning system, customers can walk into shopping malls and receive advertisements from those malls where they can get coupons or discounts if they visited a particular store within the mall. What will this mean for the consumer? It might be greater convenience, more targeted advertising—or does it mean the invasion of privacy?

Web 2.0

Web 2.0 technology helps the rise of user-generated content and combines it with the power of peer-to-peer communications. It is an umbrella term for various media including Wikipedia, Flickr, YouTube, Twitter, and other social networks. In Web 2.0, content is generated, updated, and revised by multiple users and shared freely. Most importantly, marketers cannot control what is said. Because of this, marketers need to understand Web 2.0 and carefully integrate it into its marketing mix and even participate in conversations.

YouTube

YouTube was founded in February 2005, and the company was bought by Google in late 2006. YouTube is a video-sharing website where registered users can upload videos, and unregistered users can watch most videos and post responses to those videos. By mid-2010, some two billion YouTube video clips were viewed daily. Every minute, 24 hours of video is uploaded to YouTube. Advertisers were quick to see the advantages of using YouTube as a marketing communication channel.

The CEO of Red Hat, Matthew Szulik, used a video called "Truth Happens" to open a keynote address four years ago. That video has been viewed more than 50,000 times on YouTube. Today, the company uses YouTube, blogs, and its own magazines as marketing communication tools.

Figure 7.19 YouTube's headquarters is in this office building at 901 Cherry Avenue, San Bruno, California.

Social Networks and Communities

Social networks such as Facebook and LinkedIn offer communication and learning opportunities for marketers. Second Life has virtual advertising forms and campaigns in different communities, with business functions just like in the real world.

As social networks have gained in popularity, marketers have begun to use applications to analyze the networks within the communities. This allows them to identify those who may be influential in spreading word-of-mouth about specific services. However, marketers who want to take advantage of these rich networks need to remember that they are in a community where people would not welcome marketers. Hence, marketers must come up with creative ways to become part of these networks. For example, virtual gifting in Facebook is becoming very popular and can generate word-of-mouth.

Even the US Army has launched a fan page on Facebook and started using Twitter. Army spokesperson Lindy Kyzer says: "Young people today don't watch the evening news. Their friends are sharing information through Twitter or Facebook. If we have no presence on those spaces, then we're not telling the army's story." However, the Defense Department's computer security restrictions is an obstacle to the social networking campaign, as soldiers are often not allowed to access Facebook or Twitter on military bases, even as some senior commanders write blogs and have a Facebook page. For example, General Ray Odierno, who commands US forces in Iraq, has more than 5,000 friends on his Facebook page, which shows photos from his trips around Iraq but does not have any gossip from the battlefield. According to Kyzer, the security restrictions have not banned soldiers from blogging, but the rules require that blogs are not written without the knowledge of their superiors. She explained: "The commander needs to know what you're up to. If you're blogging in a deployed setting, as a soldier, writing as a soldier, you should let your commander know that."

SOURCES

D. Fichter, "Seven Strategies for Marketing in a Web 2.0 World," *Marketing Library Services* 21, no. 2, March/April 2007 in http://www.infotoday.com/mls/mar07/Fichter.shtml, accessed March 12, 2012; Podcast, http://en.wikipedia.org/wiki/Podcast, accessed March 12, 2012; Mobile Advertising http://en.wikipedia.org/wiki/Mobile_advertising, accessed March 12, 2012; "YouTube Serves Up 1,000 Million Videos a Day Online," *USA Today*, Gannett Co. Inc., July 16, 2006; For YouTube statistics, see http://ksudigg.wetpaint.com/page/YouTube+Statistics?t=anon, accessed August 2, 2010. "US Army Enlists Facebook, Twitter," on http://www.physorg.com/news160077300.html, published on April 27, 2009, accessed March 12, 2012; Thorsten Hennig-Thurau, Edward C. Malthouse, Christian Friege, Sonja Gensler, Lara Lobschat, Arvind Rangaswamy and Bernd Skiera, "The Impact of New Media on Customer Relationships," *Journal of Service Research* 13, no. 3: 311–330, 2010; Michael Zeisser, "Unlocking the Elusisve Potential of Social Networks," *McKinsey Quarterly*, June (2010): 1–3.

Moving from Impersonal to Personal Communications

Communication experts divide impersonal and personal communications. In impersonal communications, messages move in only one direction and generally are targeted at a large group of customers and prospects. In contrast, personal communications is targeted at a single individual. Examples of personal communications are personal selling, telemarketing, and word-of-mouth. Technology, however, has created a gray area between personal and impersonal communications. Think about the e-mail messages you've received. They contain a personal greeting and perhaps some reference to your specific situation or past use of a particular product. Similarly, interactive software can simulate a two-way conversation. A few firms are beginning to experiment with Web-based agents, on-screen simulations that move, speak, and even change expressions.

Furthermore, with advances in on-demand technologies, consumers are increasingly empowered to decide how and when they would like to be reached. This development is transforming marketing communications not only on the Internet but also on TV and radio (see Service Insights 7.3).

LO 7

Know the communications mix elements available via service delivery channels.

Messages Transmitted through Service Delivery Channels

In service firms, service delivery channels offer service firms powerful and cost-effective communications opportunities. Messages can be transmitted through service outlets, frontline employees, and self-service delivery points.

Service Outlets

Both planned and unintended messages reach customers through the service delivery environment. Impersonal messages can be distributed in the form of banners, posters, signage, brochures, video screens, and audio. As we will discuss in Chapter 10, "Crafting the Service Environment," the physical design of the service outlet—what we call the *servicescape*—sends important messages to customers.[22] Interior architects and corporate design consultants can design the servicescape to coordinate the visual elements of both interiors and exteriors in such a way that they communicate and strengthen the positioning of the firm and shape the nature of the customers' service experiences in positive ways (Figure 7.20).

Figure 7.20 The Selentein Winery in Argentina has a very unique servicescape.

Frontline Employees

Employees in frontline positions may serve customers face-to-face, by telephone, or via e-mail. Communication from frontline staff takes the form of the core service and a variety of supplementary services, including providing information, taking reservations, receiving payments, and solving problems. New customers, in particular, often rely on customer service personnel for help in learning to use a service effectively and to solve problems.

The frontline staff have a very important part to play. As discussed in Chapter 4, brand equity is created very much through a customer's personal experience with the service firm. In comparison, mass communications are more suitable for creating awareness and interest.

Self-Service Delivery Points

ATMs, vending machines, and websites are all examples of self-service delivery points. Promoting self-service delivery requires clear signage, step-by-step instructions (perhaps through diagrams or animated videos) on how to operate the equipment, and user-friendly design. Self-service delivery points often can be effectively used in communications with current and potential customers and to cross-sell services and promote new services.

Messages Originating from Outside the Organization

LO 8

Know communications mix elements that originate from outside the firm.

Some of the most powerful messages about a company and its products come from outside the organization and are not controlled by the marketer. They include word-of-mouth, blogs, Twitter, and media coverage.

Word-of-Mouth

Word-of-mouth (WOM) has a powerful influence on people's decisions to use (or avoid using) a service. Recommendations from other customers are generally viewed as more credible than a firm's promotional activities. In fact, the greater the risk customers perceive in purchasing a service, the more actively they will seek and rely on WOM to guide their decision making.[23] In addition, WOM has been found to be an important predictor of top-line growth.[24] There are now ways to measure WOM and these allow firms to test the effect of WOM on sales and market share for brands, individual promotional campaigns, and also for the company as a whole.[25]

Positive WOM is particularly important for service firms, as services tend to have a high proportion of experience and credence attributes and are therefore associated with high perceived risk by potential buyers. In fact, many successful service firms such as Starbucks and Mayo Clinic have built powerful brands largely by relying on WOM from their satisfied customers. As Ron Kaufman, bestselling author, and founder of UP Your Service! College says: "Delighted customers are the only advertisement everyone believes."[26] Because WOM can act as such a powerful and highly credible selling agent, some marketers use a variety of strategies to encourage positive and persuasive comments from existing customers.[27] These include:

- Creating exciting promotions that get people talking about the great service the firm provides. Richard Branson of Virgin Atlantic Airways has repeatedly got people talking about his airline. For example, Branson abseiled off a 407-feet Las Vegas hotel dressed like James Bond in a tuxedo to promote his, then new, Virgin America airline. More and more firms are running creative promotions on social media that can get global attention in a few days.
- Offering promotions that encourage customers to persuade others to join them in using the service (for instance, "bring two friends, and the third eats for free" or "subscribe to two cell phone service plans, and we'll waive the monthly subscription fee for all other immediate family members").
- Developing referral incentive schemes, such as rewarding an existing customer with units of free service, a voucher, or even cash for introducing new customers to the firm (Figure 7.21).

Figure 7.21 Word-of-mouth can be an effective promotional tool.

PART II

- Referencing other purchasers and knowledgeable individuals, for instance: "We have done a great job for ABC Corp., and if you wish, feel free to talk to Mr. Cabral, their MIS manager, who oversaw the implementation of our project."
- Presenting and publicizing testimonials. Advertising and brochures sometimes feature comments from satisfied customers.

In addition to WOM, we also have "word-of-mouse." Viral marketing has spread so fast online that firms cannot ignore it.[28] One of the early success stories of online viral marketing was Microsoft's free e-mail service, Hotmail. It grew from zero to 12 million users in 18 months on a very small advertising budget, thanks mostly to the inclusion of a promotional message with Hotmail's URL in every email sent by its users. Similarly, eBay and other electronic auction firms rely on its users to rate sellers and buyers, and this builds trust in the items offered on their websites.

Besides e-mail, WOM is spread by chat, social media, and online communities that have potential for global reach in a matter of days! Companies are taking advantage of this. Swipely is a company that allows users to conveniently upload their purchases whenever they swipe their credit or debit card, and their friends can then immediately see these transactions and discuss the purchase. [29] It is one way users can update their friends on what they are buying.

In addition to the Web 2.0 and social networks discussed in Service Insights 7.3, blogs and Twitter are two other important channels through which messages are being transmitted on the Internet.

Blogs—A Type of Online WOM[30]

Web logs, usually referred to as blogs, have become common. Blogs are webpages best described as online journals, diaries, or news listings where people can post anything about whatever they like. Their authors, known as bloggers, usually focus on narrow topics, and quite a few have become self-proclaimed experts in certain fields. Blogs can be about anything, ranging from baseball and sex to karate and financial engineering. There are a growing number of travel-oriented sites, ranging from Hotelchatter.com (focused on boutique hotels), CruiseDiva.com (reporting on the cruise industry), and pestiside.hu ("the daily dish of cosmopolitan Budapest"). Some sites, such as the travel-focused tripadvisor.com, allow users to post their own reviews or ask questions that more experienced travelers may be able to answer.[31]

Marketers are interested in the way blogs have developed into a new form of social interaction on the Internet. One can find conversations about any topic, including consumers' experiences with service firms and their recommendations on avoiding or patronizing certain firms. In the exchange of dialog, owners of weblogs create hyperlinks that allow customers to share information with others and influence opinions of a brand or product. Just search for the terms "Citibank and blog" or "Charles Schwab and blog," and you will see an entire list of blogs or blog entries relating to these service firms. Increasingly, service firms monitor blogs and view them as a form of immediate market research and feedback. Some service companies have even started their own blogs, for example, see Google's blog at http://googleblog.blogspot.com (Figure 7.22).

Figure 7.22 Google has its own blog.

Twitter[32]

Twitter is a social networking and microblogging service that allows its users to send updates or read other users' updates. These updates are up to 140 characters in length and can be sent and received through the Twitter website, SMS, or external applications. Created in 2006 by Jack Dorsey, Twitter has become popular worldwide and was the fastest-growing social networking service in 2009. Service firms have started using Twitter in various ways. Comcast, the US cable service provider, has set up @comcastcares to answer customer queries in real time. Zappos's CEO interacts with his customers as if they were friends. Celebrity Ashton Kutcher interacts with his fans while on the move, and airline branding firm SimpliFlying used Twitter to help establish itself as a leader in its niche by holding special trivia quizzes and competitions for its followers around the world.

Media Coverage

Although the online world is rapidly increasing in importance, coverage on traditional media cannot be neglected. Often, newsworthy events are first discussed in the online world but then are picked up and reported in the traditional media that then reach the broad masses. Media coverage of firms and their services is often through a firm's PR activity, but broadcasters and publishers also often initiate their own coverage. In addition to news stories about a company and its services, editorial coverage can take several other forms. For example, journalists responsible for consumer affairs often compare and contrast service offerings from competing organizations, and offer advice on "best buys." In a more specialized context, *Consumer Reports*, the monthly publication of Consumers' Union, sometimes examines services offered on a national basis, including financial services and telecommunications.

SERVICE INSIGHTS 7.4

Consumer Concerns about Online Privacy

Technological advances have made the Internet a serious threat to consumer privacy. Information is secretly collected from people who register and shop or use e-mail, and also those who just surf the Internet, participate in social networks, or contribute to blogs! Individuals are increasingly scared of databases and concerned about their online privacy. Hence, they use several ways to protect themselves, including:

- Providing false information about themselves (e.g., disguising their identity).
- Using technology like anti-spam filters, e-mail shredders, and cookie-busters to hide the identity of their computers from websites.
- Refusing to provide information and avoid websites that require personal information to be disclosed.

Such consumer responses will make information used in CRM systems inaccurate and incomplete, and thereby reduce the effectiveness of a firm's customer relationship marketing and its efforts to provide more customized, personalized, and convenient service. Firms can take several steps to reduce consumer privacy concerns, including:

- Customers' fairness perceptions are key. Marketers need to be careful about how they use the information they collect and whether consumers see their treatment and outcomes as fair. In particular, marketers should continually provide customers with better value such as customization, convenience, and improved offers and promotions to increase fairness perceptions of the information exchange.
- If the information asked for is highly sensitive, all the more it should be seen to be related to the transaction. Therefore, firms should clearly communicate why the information is needed and how sharing the information will benefit the consumer.
- Firms should have a good privacy policy in place. To be effective, it should be readily found on their websites and be in an easy-to-understand language.
- Fair information practices need to be included in the work practices of all service employees to prevent any situation whereby an employee may allow personal customer information to be misused.
- Firms should have high ethical standards of data protection. They can use third-party endorsements like TRUSTe or the Better Business Bureau, and have recognizable privacy seals displayed clearly on their website.

SOURCES

M. Lwin, J. Wirtz, and J. D. Williams, "Consumer Online Privacy Concerns and Responses: A Power-Responsibility Equilibrium Perspective," *Journal of the Academy of Marketing Science* 35, no. 2, (2007), 572–585; Jochen Wirtz and May O. Lwin, "Regulatory Focus Theory, Trust, and Privacy Concern," *Journal of Service Research* 12, no. 2, (2009), 199–207.

Furthermore, investigative reporters may conduct an in-depth study of a company, especially if they believe it is putting customers at risk, cheating them, using deceptive advertising, damaging the environment, or taking advantage of poor workers in developing countries. Some columnists specialize in helping customers who have been unable to get complaints resolved.

Ethical and Consumer Privacy Issues in Communications

 **LO 9**

Appreciate ethical and consumer privacy-related issues in marketing communications.

PART II

We have been focusing on the various communication tools and channels of communication where customers receive information about a firm. However, firms also need to consider the ethical and privacy issues associated with communications. The fact that customers often find it hard to evaluate services makes them more dependent on marketing communication for information and advice. Communication messages frequently include promises about the benefits that customers will receive and the quality of service delivery. When promises are made and then broken, customers are disappointed because their expectations have not been met.[33]

Some unrealistic service promises result from poor internal communications between operations and marketing personnel concerning the level of service performance that customers can reasonably expect. In other instances, unethical advertisers and salespeople purposely overpromise in order to secure sales. Finally, there are promotions that lead people to think that they have a much higher chance of winning prizes or awards than there really is. Fortunately, many consumer watchdog groups are on the lookout for these deceptive marketing practices. They include consumer protection agencies, trade associations within specific industries, and journalists seeking to expose cheating and misrepresentation.

A different type of ethical issue concerns personal privacy. The increase in telemarketing, direct mail, and e-mail is frustrating for those who receive unwanted sales communications. How do you feel when your dinner at home is interrupted by a telephone call from a stranger trying to interest you in buying services in which you have zero interest? Even if you are interested, you may feel, as many do, that your privacy has been violated (see Service Insights 7.4).

To address growing opposition toward these practices, both government agencies and trade associations have acted to protect consumers. In the United States, the Federal Trade Commission's National Do Not Call Registry allows consumers to remove their home and mobile numbers from telemarketing lists for a five-year period. People who continue to receive unauthorized calls from commercial telemarketers can file a complaint, and the telemarketing firm may be subject to heavy fines for such violations.[34] Similarly, the Direct Marketing Association helps consumers remove their names from mailing, telemarketing, and e-mail lists.[35]

THE ROLE OF CORPORATE DESIGN

 **LO 10**

Understand the role of corporate design in communications.

So far, we have focused on communications media and content, but not much on design. Corporate design is key to ensure that a consistent style and message are communicated through all of a firm's communications mix channels. Corporate

Figure 7.23 The Shell brand is one of the most instantly-recognizable global commercial symbols.

design is particularly important for companies operating in competitive markets, where it's necessary to stand out from the crowd and to be instantly recognizable in different locations. Have you noticed how some companies stand out in your mind because of the colors they use, their logos, the uniforms worn by their employees, or the design of their physical facilities?

Many service firms use one distinctive visual appearance for all tangible elements to make it easier to recognize and strengthen a desired brand image. Corporate design strategies usually are created by external consulting firms and include stationery and promotional materials, retail signage, uniforms, and color schemes for painting vehicles, equipment, and building interiors. The following are ways in which companies can stand out from the crowd:

- Many companies use colors in their corporate designs. If we look at gasoline retailing, we see BP's immediately recognizable bright green and yellow service stations; Texaco's red, black and white; and Sunoco's blue, maroon, and yellow.
- Companies in the highly competitive express delivery industry tend to use their names as a central element in their corporate designs. When Federal Express changed its trading name to the more modern "FedEx," it featured the new name in a distinctive, new logo.

- Many companies use a trademarked symbol, rather than a name, as their primary logo. Shell makes a pun of its English name by displaying a yellow scalloped shell on a red background, which has the advantage of making its vehicles and service stations instantly recognizable (Figure 7.23). McDonald's "Golden Arches" (Figure 7.24) is said to be the world's most widely recognized corporate symbol and is featured at all touchpoints, including its restaurants, on employee uniforms and packaging, and in all the company's communications materials.
- Some companies have succeeded in creating tangible, recognizable symbols to associate with their corporate brand names. Animal motifs are common physical symbols for services. Examples include the eagles of the US Postal Service and AeroMexico, the lions of ING Bank and the Royal Bank of Canada, and the ram of investment firm T. Rowe Price.

Figure 7.24 The Golden Arches at the Times Square McDonald's restaurant in New York.

CHAPTER SUMMARY

 **LO 1** ▶ The role of service marketing communication is to:

- o position and differentiate the service.
- o help customers to evaluate the service offering.
- o promote the contribution of service personnel.
- o add value through communication content.
- o facilitate customer involvement in production.
- o stimulate or dampen demand to match capacity.

 **LO 2** ▶ The intangibility of services presents challenges for communications. These challenges are:

- o Abstractness—no one-to-one correspondence with a physical object.
- o Generality—items are part of a class of persons or objects or events.
- o Nonsearchability—cannot be inspected, or searched before purchase.
- o Mental impalpability—difficult to understand and interpret.

There are a number of ways to overcome the communications problems posed by intangibility:

- o Abstractness—use a service consumption episode and show typical customers experiencing the service.
- o Generality—for objective claims, use system documentation showing facts and statistics about the service delivery system, like the number of planes an airline has. For subjective claims, use performance documentation that cites past performance statistics, like number of packages delivered on time. Service performance episodes can also be used, where the actual service delivery being performed by service personnel is shown.
- o Nonsearchability—consumption documentation can be used where testimonials are obtained from customers who have experienced the service. For services high in credence attributes, use reputation documentation, which shows the awards received or the qualifications of the service provider.
- o Impalpability—use a service process episode to present what exactly will happen during the service experience. Alternatively, use a case history episode of what the firm did for a client and how it solved the client's problem, or use service consumption episode showing the customer's experience with a service.

Two additional ways to help overcome the problems of intangibility are:

- o Emphasize tangible cues like employees, facilities, certificates and awards, or its customers.
- o Use metaphors to communicate the value proposition. For example, Prudential uses the Rock of Gibraltar as a symbol of corporate strength.

 **LO 3** ▶ After understanding the challenges of service communications, service marketers need to plan and design an effective communication strategy. They can use the 5 Ws model to guide service communications planning. The 5 Ws are:

- o *Who* is our target audience? Are they prospects, users, and/or employees?
- o *What* do we need to communicate and achieve? Do the objectives relate to consumer behavior in the pre-purchase, service encounter, or post-encounter stage?
- o *How* should we communicate this? Which media mix should we use?
- o *Where* should we communicate this?
- o *When* do the communications need to take place?

 **LO 4** ▶ To achieve the communications objectives, we can use a variety of communications channels, including:

- o Traditional marketing channels (e.g., advertising and telemarketing).
- o Internet (e.g., the firm's website and online advertising) and new media (e.g., Web 2.0, including YouTube and social networks).
- o Service delivery channels (e.g., service outlets and frontline employees).
- o Messages originating from outside the organization (e.g., word-of-mouth and media coverage).

LO 5 ▶ The traditional marketing channels include advertising, public relations, direct marketing (including permission marketing), sales promotions, personal selling, and trade shows. These communication elements typically are used to help companies create a distinctive position in the market and reach prospective customers.

LO 6 ▶ Internet communication channels include the firm's websites and online advertising (e.g., banner advertising, and search engine advertising and optimization).

- o Developments in the Internet technology are driving innovations such as permission marketing and exciting possibilities of highly targeted online advertising.
- o New media communications that blur the line between impersonal and personal communications include TiVo, podcasting, YouTube, mobile advertising, Web 2.0, and social networks and communities.

LO 7 ▶ Service firms usually control service delivery channels and point-of-sale environments that offer them cost-effective ways of reaching their current customers (e.g., through its customer service employees, service outlets, and self-service delivery points).

LO 8 ▶ Some of the most powerful messages about a company and its services originate from outside the organization and are not controlled by the marketer. They include word-of-mouth, blogs, Twitter, social media, and coverage in traditional media.

- o Recommendations from other customers generally are viewed as more credible than firm-initiated communications and are sought by prospects, especially for high-risk purchases.
- o Firms can stimulate word-of-mouth from its customers through a number of means, including creating exciting promotions, referral incentive programs, and referencing customers, all of which are increasingly being shifted to the online environment.

LO 9 ▶ When designing their communication strategies, firms need to bear in mind ethical and privacy issues in terms of promises made, intrusion into people's private lives (e.g., through telemarketing or e-mail campaigns), and protecting the privacy and personal data of customers and prospects.

LO 10 ▶ Besides communication media and content, corporate design is key to achieving a unified image in customers' minds. Good corporate design uses a unified and distinctive visual appearance for tangible elements including all market communications mix elements, stationery, retail signage, uniforms, vehicles, equipment, and building interiors.

UNLOCK YOUR LEARNING

These keywords are found within the sections of each Learning Objective (LO). They are integral to understanding the services marketing concepts taught in each section. Having a firm grasp of these keywords and how they are used is essential to helping you do well on your course, and in the real and very competitive marketing scene out there.

 **LO 1**

1 Add value
2 Capacity
3 Communications
4 Customer involvement
5 Demand
6 Differentiate
7 Position
8 Promotion and education
9 Value proposition

 **LO 2**

10 Abstractness
11 Advertising strategies
12 Case history episode
13 Consumption documentation
14 Generality
15 Intangibility
16 Mental impalpability
17 Metaphors
18 Nonsearchability
19 Performance documentation
20 Reputation documentation
21 Service consumption episode
22 Service performance episode
23 Service process episode
24 System documentation
25 Tangible cues

 **LO 3**

26 5 Ws model
27 Communication objectives
28 Employees
29 Prospects
30 Target audience
31 Users

 **LO 4**

32 Advertising
33 Corporate design
34 Instructional materials
35 Marketing communications mix
36 Personal communications
37 Public relations
38 Publicity
39 Sales promotion
40 Sources of message

 **LO 5**

41 Advertising
42 Direct marketing
43 Do Not Call Registry
44 Permission marketing
45 Personal selling
46 Public relations
47 Sales promotion
48 Second Life
49 Telemarketing
50 Trade shows
51 Traditional marketing channels

 **LO 6**

52 AdWords
53 Banner advertising
54 Clickthroughs
55 Company's website
56 Content ads
57 Eyeballs
58 Google
59 Internet
60 Mobile advertising
61 Online advertising
62 Pinstorm
63 Podcasting
64 Search engine advertising
65 Skyscraper
66 Social networks and communities

67 Sponsored links
68 TiVo
69 Web 2.0
70 YouTube

LO 7
71 ATMs
72 Frontline employees
73 Self-service delivery points
74 Service outlets
75 Servicescape
76 Vending machines

 **LO 8**
77 Blogs
78 Media coverage
79 Online communities
80 Referencing
81 Referral incentive schemes
82 Short messaging service (SMS)
83 Social media
84 Testimonials
85 Twitter
86 Viral marketing
87 Word-of-mouth

 **LO 9**
88 Consumer privacy
89 Ethical
90 Online privacy
91 Overpromise
92 Personal privacy
93 Unethical advertisers

 **LO 10**
94 Colors
95 Corporate design
96 Logo
97 Symbols

PART II

How well do you know the language of services marketing? Quiz yourself!

 **Not for the academically faint-of-heart**

For each keyword you are able to recall without referring to earlier pages, give yourself a point (and a pat on the back). Tally your score at the end and see if you earned the right to be called—a *services marketeer*.

SCORE

0 – 18 Services Marketing is done a great disservice.
19 – 36 The midnight oil needs to be lit, pronto.
37 – 54 I know what you *didn't* do all semester.
55 – 72 A close shave with success.
73 – 90 Now, go forth and market.
91 – 97 There should be a marketing concept named after you.

KNOW YOUR ESM

Review Questions

1. In what ways do the objectives of service communications differ substantially from those of goods marketing? Describe four common educational and promotional objectives in service settings, and provide a specific example for each of the objectives you have listed.
2. What are some challenges in service communications and how can they be overcome?
3. Why is the marketing communications mix larger for service firms than that of firms that market goods?
4. What roles do personal selling, advertising, and public relations play in (a) attracting new customers to visit a service outlet and (b) retaining existing customers?
5. What are the different forms of online marketing? Which do you think would be the most effective online marketing strategies for (a) an online broker and (b) a new nightclub in Los Angeles?
6. Why is permission-based marketing gaining so much focus in service firms' communication strategies?
7. Why is word-of-mouth important for the marketing of services? How can a service firm that is a quality leader in its industry induce and manage word-of-mouth?
8. How can companies use corporate design to differentiate themselves?

WORK YOUR ESM

Application Exercises

1. Which elements of the marketing communications mix would you use for each of the following scenarios? Explain your answers.
   - A newly established hair salon in a suburban shopping center.
   - An established restaurant facing declining patronage because of new competitors.
   - A large, single-office accounting firm in a major city that serves primarily business clients and that wants to aggressively grow its client base.
2. Identify one advertisement (or other means of communications) that aims mainly at managing consumer behavior in the (a) choice, (b) service encounter, and (c) post-consumption stages. Explain how they try to achieve their objectives and discuss how effective they may be.
3. Discuss the significance of search, experience, and credence attributes in the communications strategy of a service provider. Assume that the objective of the communications strategy is to attract new customers.
4. If you were explaining your current university or researching the degree program you are now in, what could you learn from blogs and any other online word-of-mouth you can find? How would that information influence the decision of a prospective applicant to your university? Given that you are an expert about the school and degree you are pursuing, how accurate is the information you found online?
5. Identify an advertisement that runs the risk of attracting mixed segments to a service business. Explain why this may happen, and state any negative consequences that could result.
6. Describe and evaluate recent public relations efforts made by service organizations in connection with three or more of the following: (a) launching a new offering, (b) opening a new facility, (c) promoting an expansion of existing services, (d) announcing an upcoming event, or (e) responding to a negative situation that has arisen. (Pick a different organization for each category.)
7. What tangible cues could a diving school or a dentistry clinic use to position itself as appealing to upscale customers?
8. Explore the websites of a management consulting firm, an Internet retailer, and an insurance company. Assess them for ease of navigation, content, and visual design. What, if anything, would you change about each site?
9. Register at Amazon.com and Hallmark.com and analyze their permission-based communication strategy. What are their marketing objectives? Evaluate their permission-based marketing for a specific customer segment of your choice—what is excellent, what is good, and what could be further improved?
10. Conduct a Google search for (a) MBA programs and (b) vacation (holiday) resorts. Examine two or three contextual ads triggered by your searches. What are they doing right, and what can be improved?

ENDNOTES

1 JD Power's Consumer Center website includes ratings of service providers in finance and insurance, health care, telecommunications, and travel, plus useful information and advice. See http://www.jdpower.com/, accessed March 12, 2012.

2 Starbucks story on how coffee beans are grown and harvested, http://www.starbucks.com/#/coffee-journey, accessed March 12, 2012.

3 For a useful review, see Kathleen Mortimer and Brian P. Mathews, "The Advertising of Services: Consumer Views v. Normative Dimensions," *The Service Industries Journal* 18, (July 1998): 14–19. See also James F. Devlin and Sarwar Azhar, "Life Would Be a Lot Easier If We Were a Kit Kat: Practitioners' Views on the Challenges of Branding Financial Services Successfully," *Brand Management* 12, no. 1 (2004): 12–30.

4 Banwari Mittal, "The Advertising of Services: Meeting the Challenge of Intangibility," *Journal of Service Research* 2, (August 1999): 98–116.

5 Banwari Mittal and Julie Baker, "Advertising Strategies for Hospitality Services," *Cornell Hotel and Restaurant Administration Quarterly* 43, (April 2002): 51–63.

6 Donna Legg and Julie Baker, "Advertising Strategies for Service Firms," in *Add Value to Your Service*, ed., C. Surprenant (Chicago: American Marketing Association, 1987), 163–168. See also Donna J. Hill, Jeff Blodgett, Robert Baer, and Kirk Wakefield, "An Investigation of Visualization and Documentation Strategies in Service Advertising," *Journal of Service Research* 7, (November 2004): 155–166; Debra Grace and Aron O'Cass, "Service Branding: Consumer Verdicts on Service Brands," *Journal of Retailing and Consumer Services* 12, (2005): 125–139.

7 Banwari Mittal, "The Advertising of Services: Meeting the Challenge of Intangibility," *Journal of Service Research* 2, (August 1999): 98–116.

8 "The Future of Advertising–The Harder Hard Sell," *The Economist* (June 24, 2004).

9 "The Future of Advertising–The Harder Hard Sell," *The Economist* (June 24, 2004).

10 Penelope J. Prenshaw, Stacy E. Kovar, and Kimberly Gladden Burke, "The Impact of Involvement on Satisfaction for New, Nontraditional, Credence-Based Service Offerings," *Journal of Services Marketing* 20, no. 7 (2006): 439–452.

11 "Got Game: Inserting Advertisements into Video Games Holds Much Promise," *The Economist* (June 9, 2007): 69.

12 Seth Godin and Don Peppers, *Permission Marketing: Turning Strangers into Friends and Friends into Customers*. New York: Simon & Schuster, 1999; Ray Kent and Hege Brandal, "Improving Email Response in a Permission Marketing Context," *International Journal of Market Research* 45, (Quarter 4, 2003): 489–503.

13 Gila E. Fruchter and Z. John Zhang, "Dynamic Targeted Promotions: A Customer Retention and Acquisition Perspective," *Journal of Service Research* 7, (August 2004): 3–19.

14 Ken Peattie and Sue Peattie, "Sales Promotion—A Missed Opportunity for Service Marketers," *International Journal of Service Industry Management* 5, no. 1 (1995): 6–21.

15 M. Lewis, "Customer Acquisition Promotions and Customer Asset Value," *Journal of Marketing Research* XLIII, (May 2006): 195–203.

16 For instructions on how to register, refer to https://www.donotcall.gov/register/registerinstructions.aspx, accessed on March 12, 2012.

17 Dana James, "Move Cautiously in Trade Show Launch," *Marketing News*, November 20, 2000, 4, 6; Elizabeth Light, "Tradeshows and Expos—Putting Your Business on Show," *Her Business*, March–April 1998, 14–18; and Susan Greco, "Trade Shows versus Face-to-Face Selling," *Inc.*, May 1992, 142.

18 Stefan Lagrosen, "Effects of the Internet on the Marketing Communication of Service Companies," *Journal of Services Marketing* 19, no. 2 (2005): 63–69.

19 Paul Smith and Dave Chaffey, *eMarketing Excellence*. Oxford, UK: Elsevier Butterworth-Heinemann, 2005, 173.

20 "The Future of Advertising–The Harder Hard Sell," *The Economist* (June 24, 2004).

21 Catherine Seda, *Search Engine Advertising: Buying Your Way to the Top to Increase Sales (Voices That Matter)*, Indianapolis, IN: New Riders Press, 2004, 4–5.

22 Mary Jo Bitner, "Servicescapes: The Impact of Physical Surroundings on Customers and Employees," *Journal of Marketing* 56, (April 1992): 57–71.

23 Harvir S. Bansal and Peter A. Voyer, "Word-of-Mouth Processes within a Services Purchase Decision Context," *Journal of Service Research* 3, no. 2 (November 2000): 166–177. Malcom Gladwell explains how different types of epidemics, including word-of-mouth epidemics, develop. Malcom Gladwell, *The Tipping Point*, Little, NY: Brown and Company, 2000, 32.

24 Frederick F. Reichheld, "The One Number You Need to Grow," *Harvard Business Review* 81, no. 12 (2003): 46–55.

25 See Jacques Bughin, Jonathan Doogan and Ole Jorgen Vetvik, "A New Way to Measure Word-of-Mouth Marketing," *McKinsey Quarterly* (April 2010): 1–9.

26 http://www.upyourservice.com/quotes-on-service-by-ron-kaufman?view=quotes&type=2&page=1, accessed March 12, 2012.

27 Jochen Wirtz and Patricia Chew, "The Effects of Incentives, Deal Proneness, Satisfaction and Tie Strength on Word-of-Mouth Behaviour," *International Journal of Service Industry Management* 13, no. 2 (2002): 141–162; Tom J. Brown, Thomas E. Barry, Peter A. Dacin, and Richard F. Gunst, "Spreading the Word: Investigating Antecedents of Consumers' Positive Word-of-Mouth Intentions and Behaviors in a Retailing Context," *Journal of the Academy of Marketing Science* 33, no. 2 (2005): 123–138; John E. Hogan, Katherine N. Lemon, and Barak Libai, "Quantifying the Ripple: Word-of-Mouth and Advertising Effectiveness," *Journal of Advertising Research* (September 2004): 271–280.

28 Joseph E. Phelps, Regina Lewis, Lynne Mobilio, David Perry, and Niranjan Raman, "Viral Marketing or Electronic Word-of-Mouth Advertising: Examining Consumer Responses and Motivations to Pass Along Emails," *Journal of Advertising Research* (December 2004): 333–348; Palto R. Datta, Dababrata N. Chowdhury and Bonya R. Chakraborty, "Viral Marketing: New Form of Word-of-Mouth through Internet," *The Business Review* 3, no. 2 (Summer 2005): 69–75.

29 "Selling Becomes Sociable," *The Economist* (September 11, 2010).

30 This section draws from Lev Grossman, "Meet Joe Blog," *Time*, June 21, 2004, 65; S. C. Horring, L. A. Scheidt, F. Wright, and S. Bonus, "Weblogs as a Bridging Genre," *Information, Technology & People* 18, no. 2 (2005): 142–171.

31 Steven Kurutz, "For Travelers, Blogs Level the Playing Field," *New York Times*, August 7, 2005, TR-3.

32 http://en.wikipedia.org/wiki/Twitter, accessed March 12, 2012.

33 Louis Fabien, "Making Promises: The Power of Engagement," *Journal of Services Marketing* 11, no. 3 (1997): 206–214.

34 www.donotcall.gov/default.aspx, accessed March 12, 2012.

35 https://www.dmachoice.org, accessed March 21, 2011.

PART

THE *ESM* FRAMEWORK

PART I

Understanding Service Products, Consumers, and Markets

- Introduction to Services Marketing
- Consumer Behavior in a Services Context
- Positioning Services in Competitive Markets

PART II

Applying the 4 Ps of Marketing to Services

- Developing Service Products: Core and Supplementary Elements
- Distributing Services through Physical and Electronic Channels
- Setting Prices and Implementing Revenue Management
- Promoting Services and Educating Customers

PART III

Designing and Managing the Customer Interface

The 3 Additional Ps of Services Marketing.

- Designing and Managing Service Processes
- Balancing Demand and Capacity
- Crafting the Service Environment
- Managing People for Service Advantage

PART IV

Developing Customer Relationships

- Managing Relationships and Building Loyalty
- Complaint Handling and Service Recovery

PART V

Striving for Service Excellence

- Improving Service Quality and Productivity
- Organizing for Service Leadership

Designing and Managing the Customer Interface

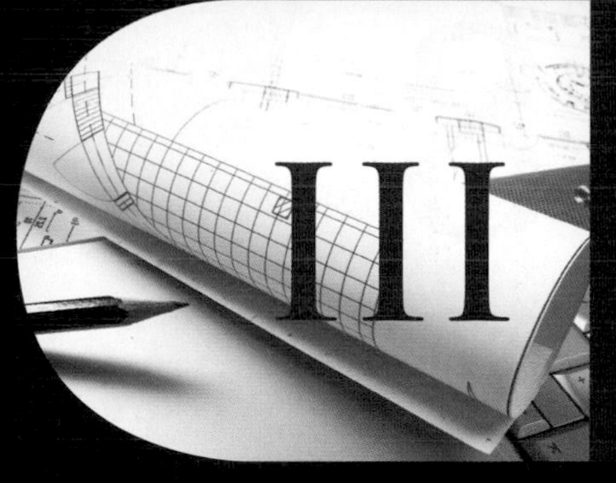

PART

PART III of this book focuses on managing the interface between customers and the service organization. It covers the additional 3 Ps (*P*rocess, *P*hysical environment, and *P*eople) that are unique to services marketing. It consists of the following four chapters:

Chapter 8 Designing and Managing Service Processes

The chapter begins with the design of an effective delivery process. It specifies how operating and delivery systems link together to create the promised value proposition. Very often, customers are actively involved in service creation, especially as co-producers, and the process becomes their service experience.

Chapter 9 Balancing Demand and Capacity

This chapter continues our study of process management and focuses on managing widely fluctuating demand, as well as to balance the level and timing of customer demand against available productive capacity. Well-managed demand and capacity lead to smooth processes with less waiting time for customers. Marketing strategies for managing demand involve smoothing demand fluctuations and inventorying demand through reservation systems and formalized queuing. Understanding customer motivations in different segments is one of the keys to successful demand management.

Chapter 10 Crafting the Service Environment

This chapter focuses on the physical service environment, which is also known as the servicescape. It needs to be engineered to create the right impression and facilitate effective delivery of service processes. The servicescape needs to be managed carefully, because it can have a profound impact on customers' impressions of the firm, guide their behavior throughout the service process, and provide tangible clues of a firm's service quality and positioning.

Chapter 11 Managing People for Service Advantage

This chapter introduces a defining element of many service companies, its people. Many services require direct interaction between customers and contact personnel. The nature of these interactions strongly influences how customers perceive service quality. Hence, service firms devote a significant amount of effort to recruiting, training, and motivating employees. Happy employees who perform well are often a source of competitive advantage for a firm.

CHAPTER 8

designing and managing SERVICE PROCESSES

LEARNING OBJECTIVES

By the end of this chapter, the reader should be able to:

- **LO 1** Explain what we can learn from flowcharting a service.
- **LO 2** Tell the difference between flowcharting and blueprinting.
- **LO 3** Develop a blueprint for a service process with all the typical design elements in place.
- **LO 4** Understand how to use fail-proofing to design fail points out of service processes.
- **LO 5** Know how to set service standards and performance targets for customer service processes.
- **LO 6** Explain the necessity for service redesign.
- **LO 7** Understand how service process redesign can help improve both service quality and productivity.
- **LO 8** Be familiar with the concept of service customers as "co-creators" and the implications of this perspective.
- **LO 9** Understand the factors that lead customers to accept or reject new self-service technologies (SSTs).
- **LO 10** Know how to manage customers' reluctance to change their behaviors in service processes, including adoption of SSTs.

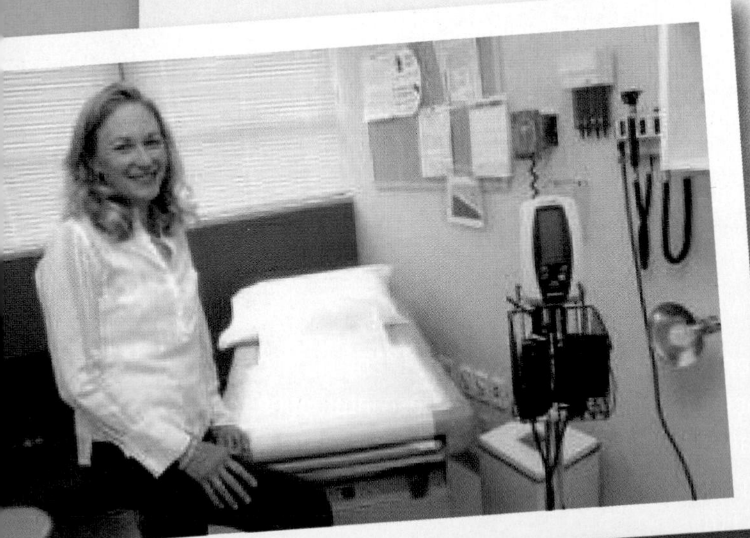

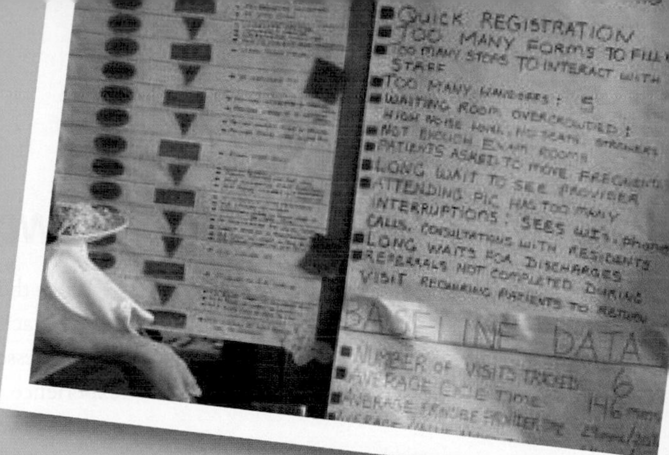

OPENING VIGNETTE

Redesigning Customer Service in a Small Hospital Practice

Things were not going smoothly at Family Medicine Faculty Practice (FMFP), a small practice within a hospital system. Its patients were often placed on hold for very long times when they called; there was a lack of available and convenient appointment slots; the waiting room was frequently crowded with lengthy delays before patients were called back into the clinical area to see their doctors.

Dr. Schwartz, the medical director, and Dr. Bryan, the assistant medical director, decided to change this situation and engaged Coleman Associates, a consulting firm that specializes in Patient Visit Redesign. Over the course of four days, a Coleman Associates team worked closely with the clinic's staff on site, shoulder to shoulder, and radically redesigned work processes. It was an amazing transformation; the redesign started on a Monday afternoon, and by Friday morning the Faculty Practice was operating in a whole new way!

The Redesigned Service Model

FMFP had 12 staff altogether, of which nine were support staff and three were physicians. The clinic was considered lean with only three support staff per physician, which is less than the national average of 4.8 staff per physician. As a central part of the redesign, staff were reorganized into three Patient Care Teams (PCT). Each PCT consisted of a clinician, a medical assistant, and a receptionist who acted like a one-stop shop for all the patients in their care. The PCTs took care of all tasks related to their patients, including walk-ins, collection of payments, filing of medical charts, confirming the next day' appointments, checking insurance eligibility, and any other patient transactions.

The three PCTs shared three "back office" staff: a medical records staffer, a phone attendant, and a flowmaster not assigned specifically to any of the three teams. The *medical records staff* was in charge of getting medical charts 24 hours in advance of clinic sessions and filing lab results in charts on a real-time basis so that no work was left to accumulate. If a patient phoned FMFP for an appointment, the call would be answered by the *phone attendant*. The *flowmaster* was in charge of moving patients from the front waiting room into the exam rooms, and out as smoothly and as fast as possible. The flowmaster communicated with each PCT's medical assistant to get an accurate estimate of the wait time for each patient. Basically, the flowmaster solved any flow problems occurring in the clinic to keep the visit cycle time within 45 minutes for 90% of all visits.

After the redesign, the phone attendant picked up calls and passed it to the relevant PCT receptionist. In future, they had further plans for direct lines to each PCT to eliminate the traffic to the phone attendant. The receptionists would be given wireless phones so that patient calls could still be picked up even as they filed medical charts from visits already completed. PCT receptionists filed charts immediately after visits, thus reducing the incidence of lost charts.

During the booking of appointments, if a patient had a question the receptionist could not answer, she would communicate directly via walkie-talkie with the PCT's medical assistant to get an immediate answer so that work was handled on a real-time basis and not stacked up to be dealt with later.

New tools and equipment helped to stretch FMFP's available resources. Digital floor scales were placed in every exam room to weigh adult patients quickly and privately, so there was no need for an extra stop at a vitals station. In fact, all work was done in the exam room, reflecting the redesign principle: "Organize our work around the patient, not the patient around our work."

PCT members used walkie-talkies to communicate with each other directly. As staff gained more experience working together every day in their PCTs, they also became stronger and more adept in handling variations in patient flow. Stacks of paper seemingly melted during the week when work was being redesigned.

FMFP's staff not only worked harder than ever but were also thrilled with the results and all the compliments they received from delighted patients about the new service processes.

SOURCE

http://www.patientvisitredesign.com/index.html, accessed March 12, 2012.

LO 1

Explain what we can learn from flowcharting a service.

FLOWCHARTING CUSTOMER SERVICE PROCESSES

From the customer's point of view, services are experiences (e.g., calling a customer contact center or visiting a library). From the organization's point of view, services are processes that have to be designed and managed to create the desired customer experience. Processes describe the steps of how service operating systems work and, specify how they link together to create the experience desired by customers. In high-contact services, customers are very much a part of the operation, and the process becomes their experience. Badly designed processes are likely to annoy customers because they often result in slow, frustrating, and poor-quality service delivery. Badly designed processes also make it difficult for frontline employees to do their jobs well, resulting in low productivity and the risk of service failures.

Flowcharting Is a Simple Tool to Document Service Processes

Flowcharting is a technique for displaying the nature and sequence of the different steps involved in delivering service to customers. It is an easy way to understand the total customer service experience. By flowcharting the sequence of encounters that customers have with a service organization, we can gain valuable insights into the nature of an existing service.

Marketers find that creating a flowchart for a specific service is very useful for distinguishing between those steps where customers use the core service and those steps where the service elements supplement the core product (as we discussed in the Flower of Service model in Chapter 4). For example, for restaurants, food and beverages are part of the core product, but supplementary services may include reservations, valet parking, a coat room, being escorted to a table, ordering from the menu, billing, payment, and use of restrooms. If you prepare flowcharts for a variety of services, you will soon notice that, although the core products may differ widely, there are common supplementary elements, such as information, billing, reservations/order taking, and problem resolution.

Flowcharting will help you to understand how customer involvement is different for each of the four categories of services introduced in Chapter 1: people, possession, mental stimulus, and information processing. Let's take one example of each category: staying in a motel, getting a DVD player repaired, obtaining a weather forecast, and purchasing health insurance. Figure 8.1 displays a simple flowchart that demonstrates what is involved in each of the four scenarios. Imagine that you are the customer. Think about the extent and nature of your involvement in the service delivery process and the types of encounters with the organization.

- *Stay at a motel (people processing).* It's late evening. You're driving on a long trip and getting tired. You see a motel with a vacancy sign, and the price displayed seems very reasonable. You park your car, noting that the grounds are clean and the buildings seem freshly painted. When you enter the reception area, you're greeted by a friendly clerk who checks you in and gives you the key to a room. You move your car to the space in front of your assigned unit and let yourself in. After using the bathroom, you go to bed. After a good night's sleep, you rise the next morning, shower, dress, and pack. Then you walk to the reception area.

PEOPLE PROCESSING—STAY AT MOTEL

POSSESSION PROCESSING—REPAIR A DVD PLAYER

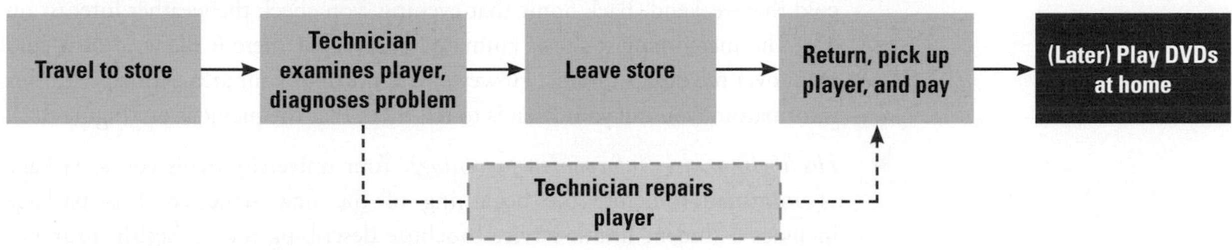

MENTAL STIMULUS PROCESSING—WEATHER FORECAST

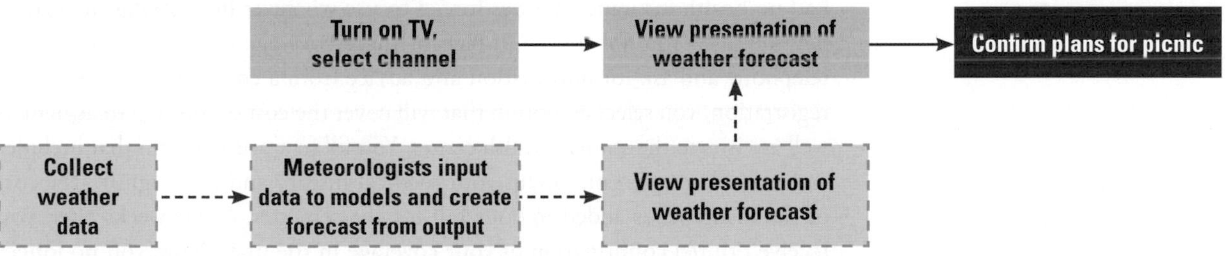

INFORMATION PROCESSING - HEALTH INSURANCE

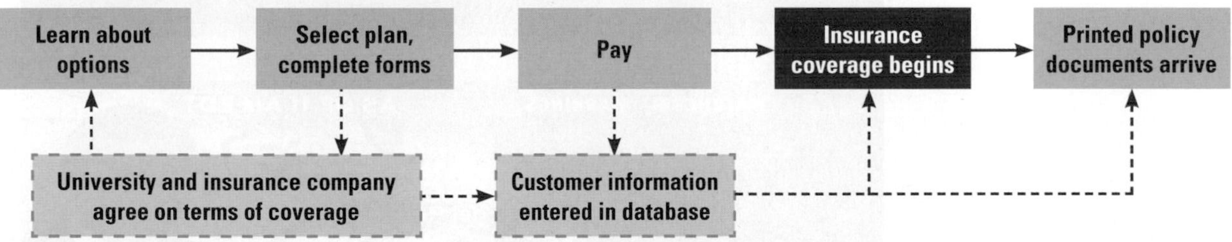

Figure 8.1 Simple flowcharts for delivery of various types of services.

There, you have free coffee, juice, and donuts. After breakfast, you return your key to a different clerk, pay for the room, and then drive away.

- *Repair a DVD player (possession processing)*. When you use your DVD player, the picture quality on the TV screen is poor. Fed up with the situation, you search the online Yellow Pages to find an appliance repair store in your area. At the store, the neatly dressed technician checks your machine carefully yet

PART III

quickly. He tells you that it needs to be adjusted and cleaned. You are impressed by his professional manner. The estimated price seems reasonable. You are also pleased that repairs are guaranteed for three months, so you agree to the work and are told that the player will be ready in three days' time. The technician disappears into the back office with your machine, and you leave the store. On the appointed day, you return to pick up the product, the technician explains the work he did and demonstrates that the machine is now working well. You pay the agreed price and leave the store with your machine. Back home, you plug in the player, insert a DVD, and find that the picture is now much improved.

- *Weather forecast (mental stimulus processing).* You're planning a picnic trip to the lake. However, one of your friends says she has heard that it is going to be really cold this weekend. Back home that evening, you check the weather forecast on TV. The meteorologist shows animated charts that there is likely to be a cold front over the next 72 hours. However, it is north of your area. Armed with this information, you call your friends to tell them that the picnic is on (Figure 8.2).
- *Health insurance (information processing).* Your university mails you a package of information before the beginning of the new semester. This package includes a student health service brochure describing several health insurance options available to students. Although you consider yourself very healthy, you remember the unfortunate experience of a friend. Your friend recently had to pay expensive hospital bills for treatment of a badly fractured ankle. Because he had no health insurance, he was forced to use whatever little savings he had to pay the bills. You don't want to pay for more coverage than you need, so you telephone and ask for information and advice from a counselor. At the time of registration, you select an option that will cover the cost of hospital treatment as well as visits to the student health center. You fill in a printed form that includes some standard questions about your medical history and then sign it. The cost of the insurance is added to your bill for the semester. A few weeks later, you receive printed confirmation of your coverage in the mail. Now, you no longer have to worry about the risk of unexpected medical expenses.

Figure 8.2 The weather forecast is an invaluable guide for an outing.

Insights from Flowcharting

As you can see from these flowcharts, your role as a customer for each of these service products varies sharply from one category to another. The first two examples involve physical processes, and the last two are information based. At the motel, you made advance judgments about service quality based on the physical appearance of the building and grounds. You rent a bedroom, bathroom, and other physical facilities for the night. Parking is included, too. The management has added value by offering a simple breakfast as part of the package.

Your role at the appliance repair store, however, is limited to briefly explaining what is wrong with the machine, leaving the machine, and returning several days later to pick it up. You have to trust the technician to do a good job in your absence. However, the three months' repair guarantee lowers the risk. You enjoy the benefits later when you use the repaired machine.

The weather forecasting and health insurance are related to intangible actions and your role is less active. The TV station you watch competes with other stations (and with radio stations, newspapers, and the Internet) for an audience, so it must appeal to people based on its graphic design, the personality and presentation skills of its meteorologist, the convenience of its schedule, and the reputation for accuracy. You did not need to pay to obtain the forecast. However, you may incur some time costs in that you had to watch some advertisements first. After all, advertising revenues help to fund the station's operations. Delivery of the information you need takes only a couple of minutes, and you can act on it immediately.

Obtaining health insurance is also an intangible action, but it takes more time and mental effort. You have to evaluate several options and complete a detailed application. Then you may have to wait for the policy to be issued and coverage to begin. Your choice of health plans will reflect the cost relative to the benefits offered. How clearly these benefits are explained may influence your decision. If their brand names mean anything to you, you may also be influenced by the reputation of the companies providing the insurance.

USE BLUEPRINTING TO DOCUMENT AND MANAGE SERVICE PROCESSES

LO 2

Tell the difference between flowcharting and blueprinting.

A key tool we use to document existing services processes, redesign them, and even to design new service processes is known as *blueprinting*. Blueprinting is a more complex form of *flowcharting*. A flowchart describes an existing process, often in a fairly simple form to get a clearer picture of the steps a customer goes through to receive and experience a service. In contrast, a blueprint specifies in detail how a service process is constructed, including what is visible to the customer and all that goes on in the back office. [1]

Perhaps you're wondering where the term blueprinting comes from and why we're using it here. The design for a new building or a ship is usually done on architectural drawings called blueprints. The term "*blueprints*" is used because the drawings used to be printed on special paper on which all the drawings and notes appear in blue.

These blueprints show what the product should look like and what specifications it should follow. Unlike the physical architecture of a building or piece of equipment, service processes have a largely intangible structure. That makes them all the more difficult to visualize. The same is also true of processes such as logistics and supply chains, industrial engineering, decision theory, and computer systems analysis, each of which uses blueprint-like techniques to describe processes involving flows, sequences, relationships, and dependencies.

LO 3

Develop a blueprint for a service process with all the typical design elements in place.

Developing a Blueprint

Service blueprints map customer, employee, and service system interactions. In particular, they show key customer actions, how customers and employees interact (called the line of interaction), the front-stage actions by service employees, and how these are supported by backstage activities and systems. By showing interrelationships among employee roles, operational processes, supplies, information technology, and customer interactions, blueprints can help bring together marketing, operations, and human resource management within a firm. Together, they can then develop better service processes, including defining service scripts and roles to guide interactions between staff members and customers (as discussed in Chapter 2); designing fail points and excessive customer waits out of processes; and finally, setting service standards and targets for service delivery teams.

Typical service blueprints have the following design characteristics that help to see how a blueprint should be developed:

- **Front-stage activities** map the overall customer experience, the desired inputs and outputs, and the sequence in which delivery of that output should take place.
- **Physical evidence of front-stage activities** is what the customer can see and uses to assess service quality.
- **Line of visibility.** A key characteristic of service blueprinting is that it clearly separates what customers experience front-stage from the activities of employees and support processes backstage, where customers can't see them. Between the two lies what is called the *line of visibility*. When a firm clearly understands the line of visibility, it is better able to manage physical and other evidence for front-stage activities to give customers the desired experience and quality signals. Some firms are too focused on operations and neglect the customer's purely front-stage perspective. Accounting firms, for instance, often have detailed documented procedures and standards for how to conduct an audit, but may lack clear standards for hosting a meeting with clients or for how staff members should answer the telephone.
- **Backstage activities** must be performed to support a particular front-stage step.
- **Support processes and supplies.** Many support processes involve a lot of information. The information needed at each step in the blueprint is usually provided by information systems. For example, without the right information at the front-line staff's fingertips, processes such as banking, online broking, and even borrowing a book from your university library could not be completed and the service process would break down completely. Supplies are also necessary for many services. The required supplies need to be made available for both

front- and backstage steps. For example, restaurants need to have the supplies of the right fresh produce and wines, and car rental firms of vehicles. Supplies are essential to deliver high-quality core services.

- **Potential fail points.** Blueprinting gives managers the chance to identify potential *fail points* in the process. Fail points are where there is a risk of things going wrong and affecting service quality. When managers are aware of these fail points, they are better able to design them out of a process (e.g., use poka-yokes as discussed later in this chapter) and have backup plans for failures that are not preventable (e.g., departure delays due to bad weather).
- **Identifying customer waits.** Blueprints can also identify stages in the process at which customers commonly have to wait (Figure 8.3) and where there are points of potentially excessive waits. These can then either be designed out of the process, or if that is not always possible, firms can implement strategies to make waits less unpleasant for customers (see the strategies discussed on the Managing Demand and Capacity section in Chapter 9).
- **Service standards and targets** should be established for each activity, reflecting customer expectations. They include specific times set for the completion of each task and the acceptable wait between each customer activity. Developing service blueprints gives marketing and operational personnel detailed process knowledge that can then be used to develop standards. The final service blueprint should contain key service standards for each front-stage activity, including times for completion of a task and maximum customer wait times in between tasks. Standards should then be used to set targets for service delivery teams to ensure that service processes perform well against customer expectations.

Figure 8.3 Long waiting lines indicate operational problems that need to be addressed.

How should you get started on developing a service blueprint?

- Identify all the key activities involved in creating and delivering the service in question and then show the links between these activities.[2]
- Keep activities at the "big picture" level first. You can later "drill down" on any activity to get a higher level of detail. In an airline context, for instance, the passenger activity of "boarding aircraft" is actually made up of a series of actions. Some of the steps include waiting for seat rows to be announced, giving an agent a boarding pass for verification, walking down the jetway, entering the aircraft, letting flight attendants verify the boarding pass, finding a seat, stowing the carry-on bag, and sitting down (Figure 8.4).

Figure 8.4 Baggage collection is one of the last steps in an air travel service process.

Blueprinting the Restaurant Experience: A Three-Act Performance

To show how blueprinting of a high-contact, people-processing service can be done, we examine the experience of dinner for two at Chez Jean. It is an upscale restaurant that enhances its core food service with a variety of other supplementary services (Figure 8.5). In full-service restaurants, the cost of buying the food ingredients is about 20–30% of the price of the meal. The balance can be seen as the fees that customers are willing to pay for "renting" a table and chairs in a pleasant setting, hiring the services of food preparation experts and their kitchen equipment, and having serving staff to wait on them in the dining room.

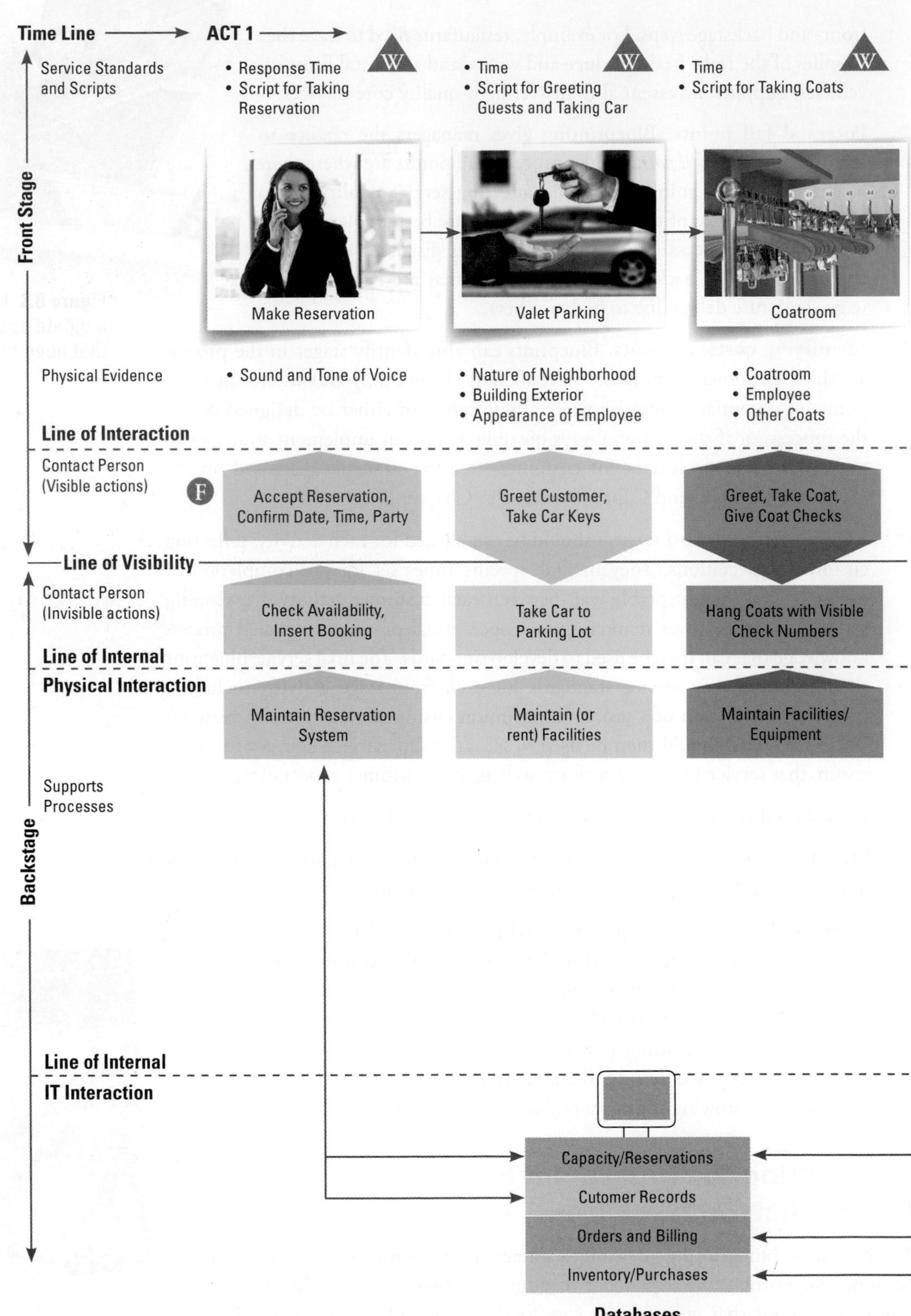

Figure 8.5 Blueprinting a full-service restaurant experience.

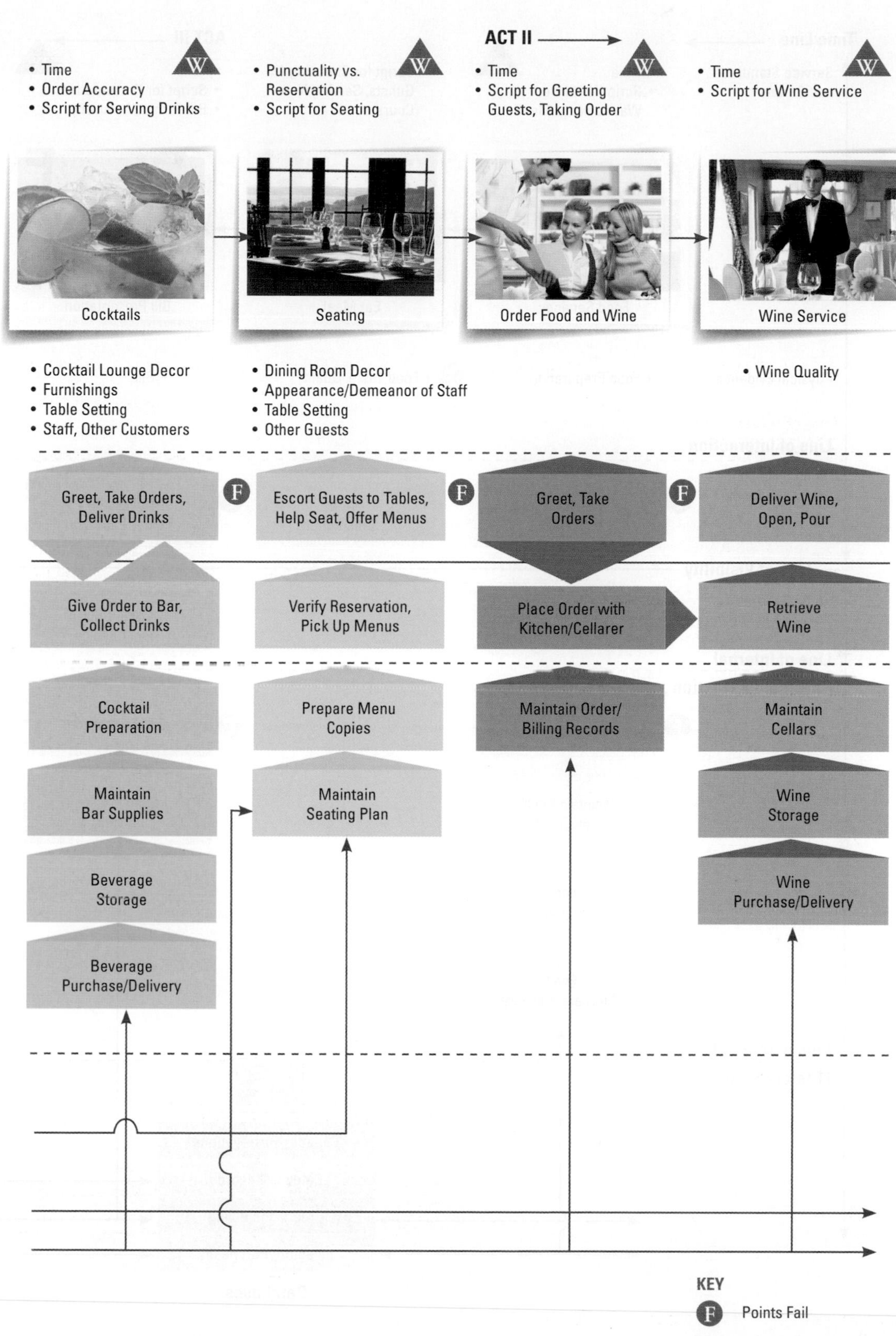

ACT II
• Time
• Order Accuracy
• Script for Serving Drinks
• Punctuality vs. Reservation
• Script for Seating
• Time
• Script for Greeting Guests, Taking Order
• Time
• Script for Wine Service
Cocktails
Seating
Order Food and Wine
Wine Service
• Cocktail Lounge Decor
• Furnishings
• Table Setting
• Staff, Other Customers
• Dining Room Decor
• Appearance/Demeanor of Staff
• Table Setting
• Other Guests
• Wine Quality
Greet, Take Orders, Deliver Drinks
Escort Guests to Tables, Help Seat, Offer Menus
Greet, Take Orders
Deliver Wine, Open, Pour
Give Order to Bar, Collect Drinks
Verify Reservation, Pick Up Menus
Place Order with Kitchen/Cellarer
Retrieve Wine
Cocktail Preparation
Prepare Menu Copies
Maintain Order/ Billing Records
Maintain Cellars
Maintain Bar Supplies
Maintain Seating Plan
Wine Storage
Beverage Storage
Wine Purchase/Delivery
Beverage Purchase/Delivery
KEY
Points Fail
Risk of Excessive Wait (Standard times should specify limits.)

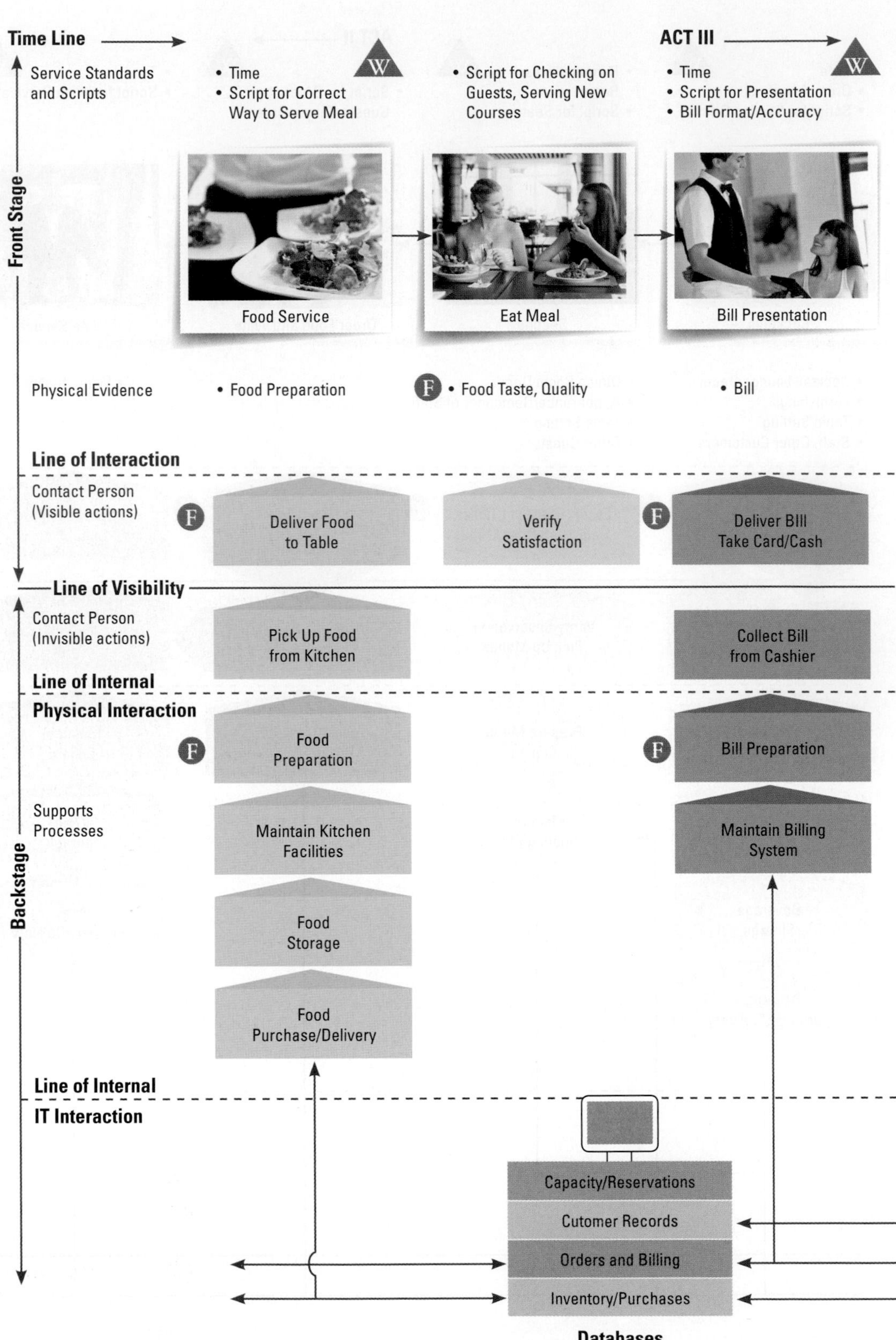

Figure 8.5 (Continued)

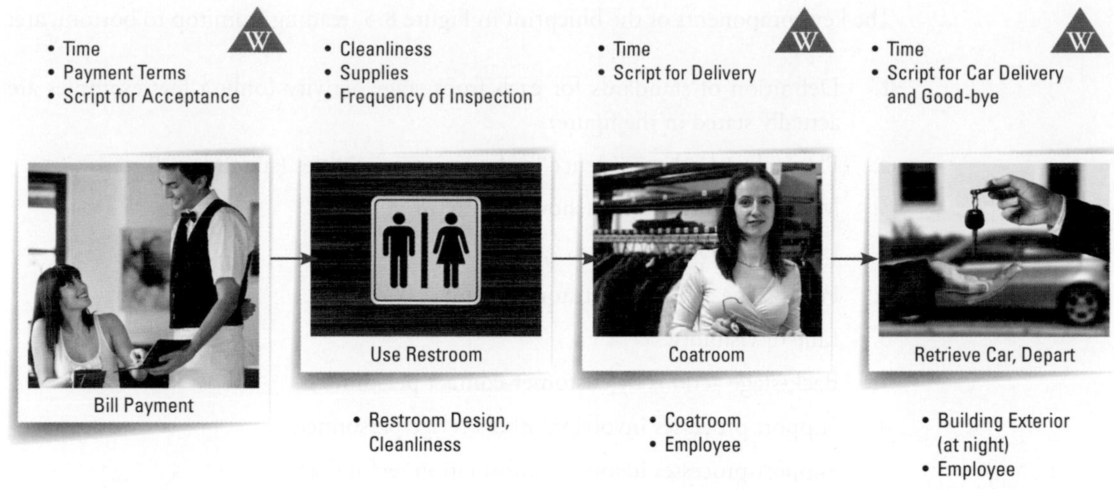
• Time
• Payment Terms
• Script for Acceptance
W
• Cleanliness
• Supplies
• Frequency of Inspection
• Time
• Script for Delivery
W
• Time
• Script for Car Delivery and Good-bye
W
Bill Payment
Use Restroom
Coatroom
Retrieve Car, Depart
• Restroom Design, Cleanliness
• Coatroom
• Employee
• Building Exterior (at night)
• Employee

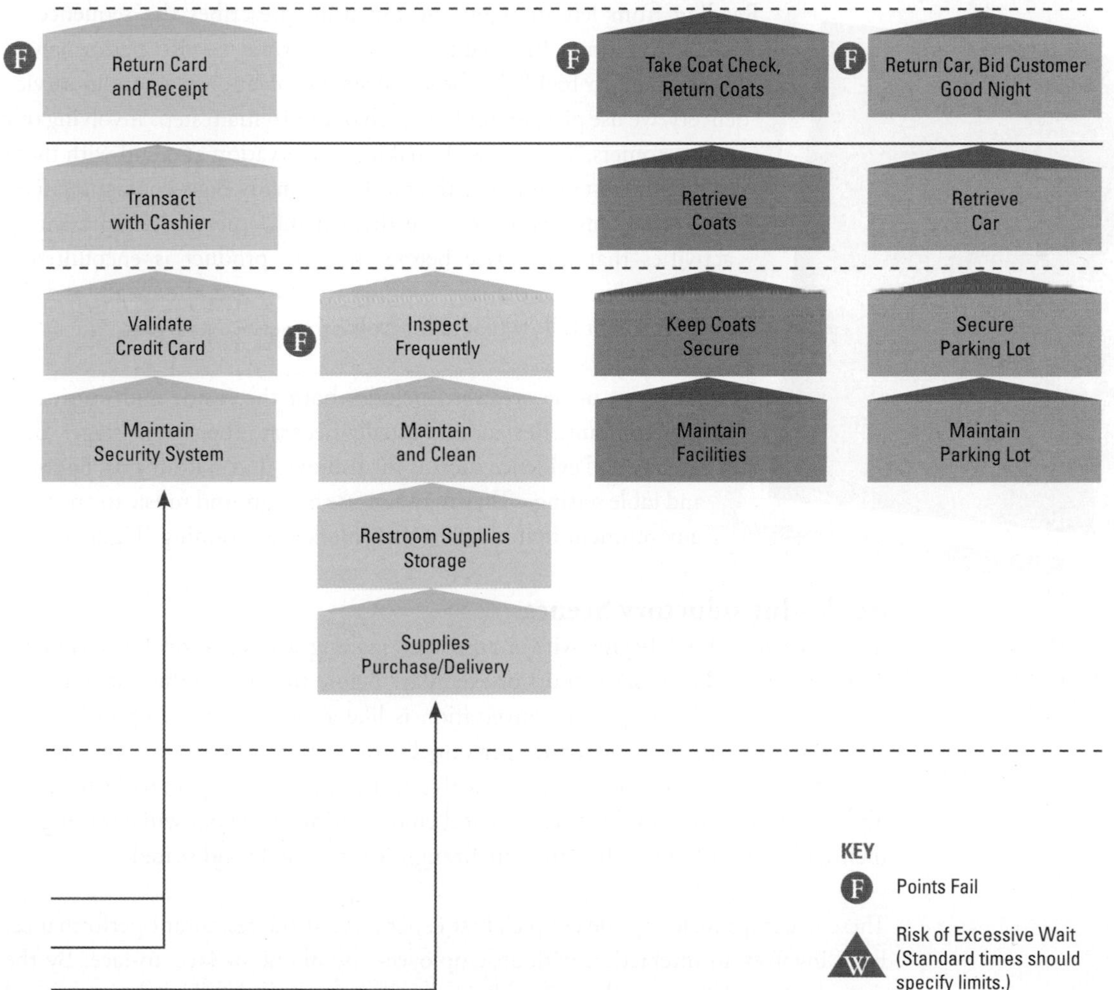
F
Return Card and Receipt
F
Take Coat Check, Return Coats
F
Return Car, Bid Customer Good Night
Transact with Cashier
Retrieve Coats
Retrieve Car
Validate Credit Card
F
Inspect Frequently
Keep Coats Secure
Secure Parking Lot
Maintain Security System
Maintain and Clean
Maintain Facilities
Maintain Parking Lot
Restroom Supplies Storage
Supplies Purchase/Delivery
KEY
F Points Fail
W Risk of Excessive Wait (Standard times should specify limits.)

PART III

The key components of the blueprint in Figure 8.5, reading from top to bottom, are:

1. Definition of standards for each front-stage activity (only a few examples are actually stated in the figure).
2. Physical and other evidence for front-stage activities (stated for all steps).
3. Main customer actions (shown by pictures).
4. Line of interaction.
5. Front-stage actions by customer-contact personnel.
6. Line of visibility.
7. Back-stage actions by customer-contact personnel.
8. Support processes involving other service personnel.
9. Support processes involving information technology.

Figure 8.6 Two hosts welcome diners in a servicescape that clearly communicates the restaurant's positioning.

Reading from left to right, the blueprint prescribes the sequence of actions over time. In Chapter 2, we compared service performances to a theater. To highlight the involvement of human actors in service delivery, we use pictures to show each of the 14 main steps involving our two customers. We start with making a reservation and end with them leaving the restaurant after the meal. Like many high-contact services, the "restaurant drama" can be divided into three acts representing activities that take place before the core product is encountered, during delivery of the core product (in this case, the meal), and the activities that follow that still involve the service provider.

The stage, or *servicescape*, includes both the inside and outside of the restaurant. Restaurants usually decorate their front stage. They use physical evidence such as furnishings, décor, uniforms, lighting, and table settings. They may also use background music to create an environment that matches their market positioning (Figure 8.6).

Act I—Introductory Scenes

In this drama, Act I begins with a customer making a reservation by telephone. This action could take place hours or even days before the visit to the restaurant. In theatrical terms, the telephone conversation is like a radio drama. Impressions are created by the nature of the service personnel's voice, speed of response, and style of the conversation. When our customers arrive at the restaurant, a valet parks their car. They leave their coats in the coatroom and enjoy a drink at the bar while waiting for their table. The act ends when they are brought to their table and seated.

These five steps make up the couple's first experience of the restaurant performance. Each involves an interaction with an employee—by phone or face–to-face. By the time the two of them reach their table in the dining room, they have been exposed to several supplementary services. They have also come into contact with quite a number of cast characters. This includes five or more contact personnel, as well as many other customers.

Standards can be set for each service activity, but these should be based on a good understanding of guest expectations (remember our discussion in Chapter 2 of how expectations are formed). Below the line of visibility, the blueprint identifies key actions to make sure that each front-stage step is performed in a way that meets or exceeds customer expectations. These actions include recording reservations, handling customers' coats, delivery and preparation of food, maintenance of facilities and equipment, training and assignment of staff for each task, and use of information technology to access, input, store, and transfer relevant data.

Act II—Delivery of the Core Product

As the curtain rises on Act II, our customers are finally about to experience the core service they came for. To keep it simple, we have divided the meal into just four scenes. If all goes well, the two guests will have an excellent meal, nicely served in a pleasant atmosphere, and perhaps a fine wine to enhance it. But, if the restaurant fails to satisfy their expectations (and those of its many other guests) during Act II, it is going to be in serious trouble. There are a number of potential fail points. Is the menu information complete? Is everything listed on the menu actually available this evening? Will explanations and advice be given in a friendly manner for guests who have questions about specific menu items or are unsure about which wine to order?

After our customers decide on their meals, they place their orders with the server, who must then pass on the details to personnel in the kitchen, bar, and billing desk. Mistakes in the transfer of information are often the cause of quality failures in many organizations. Bad handwriting or unclear verbal requests can lead to incorrect preparation or delivery of the wrong items.

In the other scenes of Act II, our customers may assess not only the quality of the food and drink—the most important dimension of all—but also how quickly it is served (not too quickly, for guests do not want to feel rushed!) and the style of service. Even if the server can perform the job correctly, the experience of the customer can still be spoiled if the server is disinterested, unfriendly, or even overly friendly.

Act III—The Drama Concludes

The meal may be over, but much is still taking place both front-stage and backstage as the drama moves to its close. The core service has now been delivered, and we will assume that our customers are happily digesting it. Act III should be short. The action in each of the remaining scenes should move smoothly, quickly, and pleasantly, with no shocking surprises at the end. Most customers' expectations would probably include the following:

- An accurate bill that is easy to understand is presented quickly when the customer asks for it (Figure 8.7).
- Payment that is handled politely and quickly (with all major credit cards accepted).
- The guests are thanked for their patronage and invited to come again.
- Customers visiting the restrooms find them clean and properly supplied.
- The right coats are retrieved from the coatroom.
- The customer's car is brought to the door without much of a wait, in the same condition as when it was left. The attendant thanks them again and wishes them a good evening.

Figure 8.7 The billing process should be quick and painless to ensure customer convenience.

Identifying Fail Points

Running a good restaurant is not easy business, and many things can go wrong. A good blueprint should draw attention to points in service delivery where things are particularly at risk of going wrong. From a customer's perspective, the most serious fail points, marked in our blueprint by F, are those that will result in failure to access or enjoy the core product. They involve the reservation (Could the customer get through by phone? Was a table available at the desired time and date? Was the reservation recorded accurately?) and seating (Was a table available when promised?).

Since service delivery takes place over time, there is also the possibility of delays between specific actions, requiring the customers to wait. Common locations for such waits are identified on the blueprint by W. Excessive waits will annoy customers. In practice, every step in the process—both front-stage and backstage—has some potential for failures and delays. In fact, failures often lead directly to delays (reflecting orders that were never passed on) or time spent correcting mistakes.

LO 4

Understand how to use fail-proofing to design fail points out of service processes.

David Maister coined the acronym OTSU ("opportunity to screw up") to stress the importance of thinking about all the things that might go wrong in delivering a particular type of service.[3] It's only by identifying all the possible OTSUs associated with a particular process that service managers can put together a delivery system that is designed to avoid such problems.

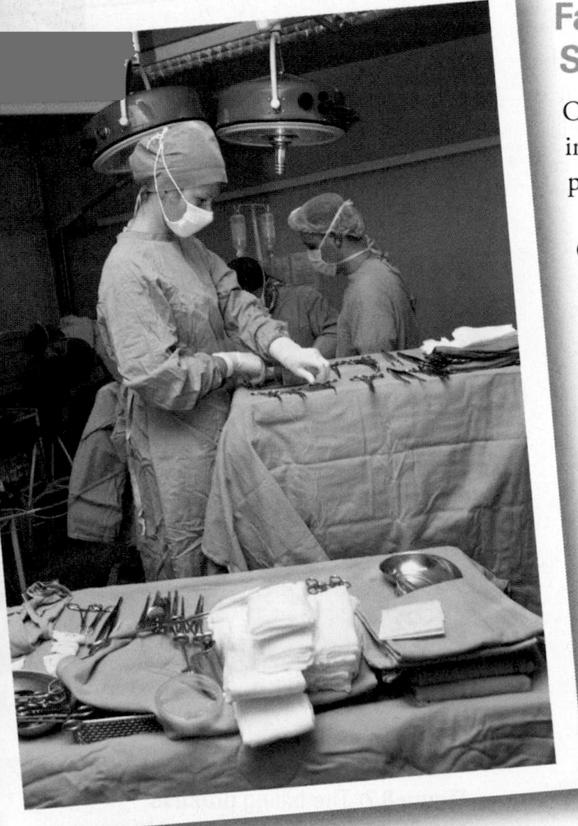

Figure 8.8 The practice of poka-yoke is observed in the operating room.

Fail-Proofing to Design Fail Points out of Service Processes

Once fail points have been identified, careful analysis of the reasons for failure in service processes is necessary. This analysis often reveals opportunities for fail-proofing certain activities in order to reduce or even get rid of the risk of errors.[4]

One of the most useful Total Quality Management (TQM) methods in manufacturing is the application of *poka-yoke*, or fail-safe methods, to prevent errors in the manufacturing processes. Richard Chase and Douglas Steward introduced this concept to fail-safe service processes.[5]

Server poka-yokes ensure that service employees do things correctly, as asked, in the right order, and at the right speed. Examples include surgeons whose surgical instrument trays have individual indentations for each instrument. For a given operation, all of the instruments are nested in the tray, so it is clear if the surgeon has not removed all instruments from the patient before closing the incision (Figure 8.8).

Some service firms use poka-yokes to ensure that certain steps or standards in the customer–staff interaction are followed. A bank ensures eye contact by requiring tellers to record the customer's eye color on a checklist at the start of a transaction. Some firms place mirrors at the exits of staff areas to ensure a neat appearance. Frontline staff can then automatically check their appearance before greeting a customer. At one restaurant, servers place round coasters in front of those diners who have ordered a decaffeinated coffee and square coasters in front of the others.

Designing poka-yokes is part art and part science. It can be used to design frequently occurring service failures out of service processes and to ensure that certain service standards or service steps are followed. A three-step approach for effectively using poka-yokes includes systematically collecting data on problem occurrence, analyzing the root causes, and establishing preventive solutions. Service Insights 8.1 demonstrates how these three steps can be applied to prevent service failures caused by customers.

SERVICE INSIGHTS 8.1

A Framework to Prevent Customer Failures

Companies can use service redesign to improve reliability and quality. If the service fails, they can have good service recovery procedures in place. However, it can be hard to fix failures caused by customers themselves. A good way is to employ the following three-step approach to prevent customer-generated failures.

1. Systematically collect information on the most common failure points.

2. Identify their root causes. It's important to note that an employee's explanation may not be the true cause. Instead, the cause must be investigated from the customer's point of view. Human causes of customer failure include the lack of needed skills, a failure to understand his/her role, and insufficient preparation. Shortcomings in processes may often involve slowness, excessive complexity, and lack of clarity. Other causes may include weaknesses in design of the servicescape and poorly designed technology, such as self-service machines that are not user friendly.

3. Create strategies to prevent the failures identified. The five strategies listed below may need to be combined for maximum effectiveness.

   (a) Redesign processes (e.g., redesign customers' role as well as processes). For example, customers may now have the option of borrowing library books through self-service machines, which is very different from borrowing a book from the library itself.

   (b) Use technology (e.g., use information systems to help customers make choices from a large set). For example, financial service firms may use technology to help customers self-diagnose their financial needs and select a suitable portfolio of investments for retirement.

   (c) Manage customer behavior (e.g., remind customers when payment is due, reward them for avoiding failure).

   (d) Encourage "customer citizenship" (e.g., customers help one another to prevent failure, e.g., in weight-loss programs).

   (e) Improve the servicescape (e.g., impacts customer experiences and contributes to failures). Many firms forget that customers need user friendly, directional signs to help them find their way around, failing which, they might become very frustrated.

Helping customers to avoid failure can become a source of competitive advantage, especially when companies increasingly deploy self-service technologies.

SOURCE

Adapted from Stephen S. Tax, Mark Colgate, and David E. Bowen, "How to Prevent Your Customers from Failing," *Sloan Management Review* (Spring 2006): 30–38.

PART III

LO 5

Know how to set service standards and performance targets for customer service processes.

Setting Service Standards and Targets

The service blueprint, combined with discussions with customers and frontline employees, helps firms to see which service and process attributes are important to customers at each touchpoint. Those aspects that require the attention of management (i.e., attributes most important to customers and most difficult to manage) should be the basis for setting standards. The standards set for each step in the process should be high enough to satisfy and even delight customers.

Our restaurant blueprint shows key standards for each touchpoint. As the saying goes, "What is not measured is not managed." Therefore, especially for larger service firms, process performance needs to be measured and compared against standards, and performance targets need to be set. To be effective, standards must be measureable. This means that even soft and intangible, but important, service attributes need to be made measurable. This is often achieved by using service process indicators that try to capture the essence or at least approximate these important attributes. For example, in a retail banking context, the attribute "responsiveness" can be operationalized as "processing time to approve a loan application." Service standards are then ideally based on customer expectations, and policy decisions based on how to meet these expectations cost-effectively. In cases where standards do not meet customer needs, expectations need to be managed (e.g., application approval times can be communicated in brochures, application forms, and the firm's website, or by service employees verbally when dealing with exceptional cases).

Finally, performance targets define specific process and/or team performance targets (e.g., 80% of all applications within 24 hours) for which team leaders or department heads will be held accountable. Figure 8.9 shows the relationship between indicators, standards, and targets.[6]

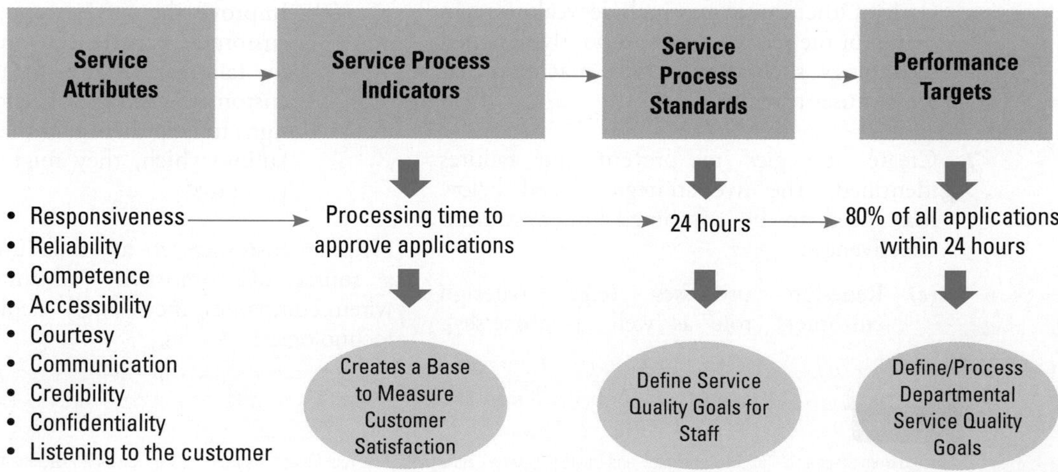

Figure 8.9 Setting standards and targets for customer service processes.

Figure 8.10 A doctor rejoices together with an expectant mother.

Consumer Perceptions and Emotions in Service Processes

Start and finish strongly

While firms should try to achieve high standards at each step of the service delivery process, this may not be always possible to do so. However, it is always important to start and finish strongly. Perceptions of their service experiences tend to be accumulated over time.[7] If things go badly wrong at the start, customers may simply walk out. Even if they stay, they may now be looking for other things that aren't quite right. On the other hand, if the first steps go really well, customers' zones of tolerance may increase so that they are more willing to overlook minor mistakes later in the service performance. However, performance standards should not be allowed to fall off toward the end of service delivery. A strong finish is important for overall satisfaction and leaves a lasting impression.[8]

Emotionprints

In order to manage the customer experience well, firms can also look at the expected associated emotions at each stage of the service processes. Flowcharts that describe how customers feel are called "emotionprints." For example, it can be anticipated that expectant mothers will feel happy and excited when they first see the ultrasound photo of their fetus (Figure 8.10). On the other hand, expectant mothers may also be anxious at a test for abnormalities in a fetus. Hence, hospitals can anticipate common customer emotions at each step in a process and train their staff to react accordingly. An attitude of celebration would include cheering and applauding. However, faced with an emotionally negative situation in the service process, staff could show compassion by listening attentively and speaking softly.[9]

PART III

LO 6

Explain the necessity for service redesign.

SERVICE PROCESS REDESIGN

Service processes become outdated over time as changes in technology, customer needs, added service features, new service offerings, and even changes in legislation make existing processes inefficient or irrelevant.[10] When this happens, service processes should be redesigned. Mitchell T. Rabkin MD, the former president of Boston's Beth Israel Hospital (now Beth Israel-Deaconess Medical Center), characterized the problem as "institutional rust" and declared: "Institutions are like steel beams—they tend to rust. What was once smooth, shiny, and nice tends to become rusty."[11] He suggested two main reasons for this situation. The first involves changes in the external environment. As a result, some practices may no longer be needed. Therefore, there may be a need to redesign the underlying processes or even create brand new processes so that the organization can remain relevant and responsive. In health care, such changes may reflect new forms of competition, legislation, technology, health insurance policies, and changing customer needs (Figure 8.11).

Figure 8.11 Health care can be redesigned to better meet customers' needs.

The second reason for institutional rusting occurs internally. Often, it reflects a natural weakening of internal processes, rules, and regulations, or the development of unofficial standards (see Service Insights 8.2). There are many symptoms that indicate that the processes are not working well and need to be redesigned. They include:

- A lot of information exchange.
- Data that is not useful.
- A high ratio of checking or control activities to value-adding activities.
- Increased processing of exceptions.
- Growing numbers of customer complaints about inconvenient and unnecessary procedures.

SERVICE INSIGHTS 8.2

Rooting Out Unofficial Standards in a Hospital

One of the special characteristics of Mitchell T. Rabkin's 30-year appointment as President of Boston's Beth Israel Hospital was his policy of regularly visiting all areas of the hospital. He usually did so unannounced and in a low-key fashion. No one working at the hospital was surprised to see Dr. Rabkin drop by at almost any time of the day or night. His natural curiosity gave him a lot of insights into how effectively service procedures were working and the hardly noticeable ways in which things could go wrong. As the following story reveals, he discovered that messages often get distorted over time.

> One day, I was in the EU [emergency unit], chatting with a house officer [physician] who was treating a patient with asthma. He was giving her medication through an intravenous drip. I looked at the formula for the medication and asked him, "Why are you using this particular cocktail?" "Oh," he replied, "that's hospital policy." Since I was certain that there was no such policy, I decided to investigate.

What had happened went something like this. A few months earlier, Resident [physician] A says to Intern B, who is observing her treat a patient: "This is what I use for asthma." On the next month's rotation, Intern B says to new Resident C: "This is what Dr. A uses for asthma." The following month, Resident C says to Intern D, "This is what we use for asthma." And finally, within another month, Intern D is telling Resident E, "It's hospital policy to use this medication."

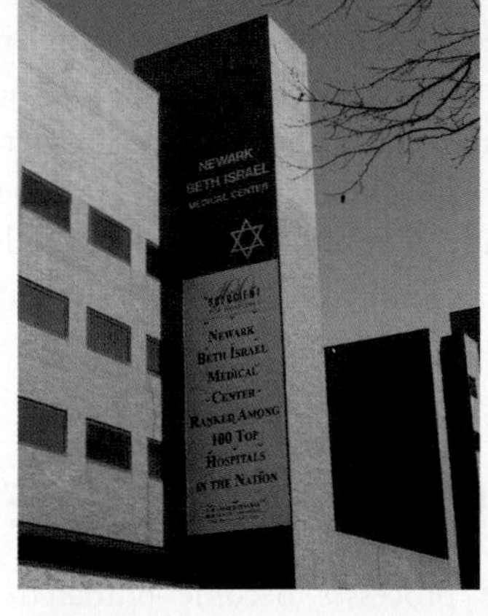

As a result of conversations like these, well-intentioned but unofficial standards keep cropping up. It is a particular problem in a place like this, as there isn't a policy manual where you must look up the policy for everything you do. We prefer to rely on people's intelligence and judgment and limit written policies to overall, more general issues. One always has to be aware of the growth of institutional rust and to be clear about what is being done and why it is being done.

SOURCE

Christopher Lovelock, *Product Plus*. (New York: McGraw-Hill, 1994), 355.

Service Process Redesign to Improve Both Quality and Productivity

LO 7

Understand how service process redesign can help improve both service quality and productivity.

Managers in charge of service process redesign projects should look for opportunities to achieve a quantum leap in both productivity and service quality at the same time. Service Insights 8.3 shows how Singapore's National Library Board did just that.

SERVICE INSIGHTS 8.3

Process Redesign in Singapore's Libraries[12]

In this digital age, libraries have suffered from reduced usage. The National Library Board of Singapore (NLB) has had to work hard to change people's view that the library was a place with rows of shelves full of old books and unfriendly staff. NLB managed to transform its library services through clever use of the latest technologies to expand its services, go virtual, encourage use of the libraries, and promote lifelong learning of its members, all while dramatically increasing productivity. At the core of that transformation was the radical redesign of its service processes.

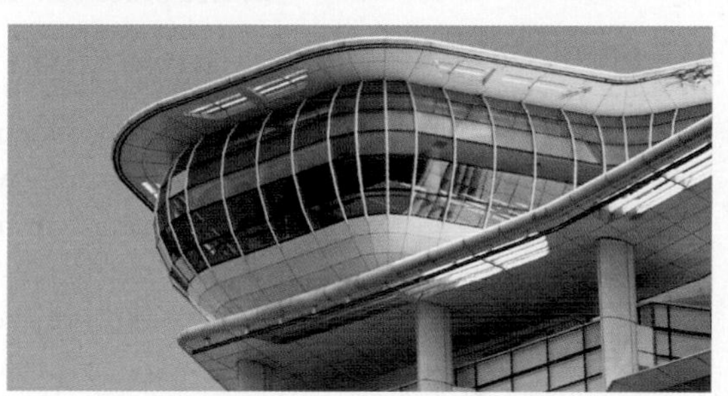

One of the many examples how NLB used advanced technology to redesign processes is its electronic library management system (ELiMS) based on radio frequency identification (RFID). In fact, NLB was the first public library in the world to prototype RFID, an electronic system for automatically identifying items. It uses RFID tags, or transponders, that are contained in smart labels consisting of a silicon chip and coiled antenna. They receive and respond to radio frequency queries from an RFID transceiver, which enables remote automatic storage, retrieval, and sharing of information. Unlike barcodes, which need to be manually scanned, RFID simply broadcasts its presence and automatically sends data about the item to electronic readers. This technology is already in use in mass transit cashless ticketing systems, ski resort lift passes, and security badges for controlled access to buildings.

NLB installed RFID tags in its over 10 million books, making it one of the largest users of RFID tags in the world. After redesigning the processes with RFID, customers don't have to spend time waiting anymore; they can check out the book themselves using the self-service kiosks, and books can be returned simply at any book drop at any library in its system. From the outside, the book drop looks like an ATM, but with a large hole covered by a flap. A user simply places the book in the box below the flap, the book is scanned using RFID, and a message on the screen instantly confirms that the book has been recorded as "returned" in the user's account.

To go one step further, NLB pioneered "smart bookshelves." When a book was either removed or placed on a bookshelf, the RFID technology took note of it. Therefore, if a book was put in the wrong place, the bookshelf 'knew' and alerted library staff. With a handheld device, the librarian could then locate the book within moments. This allowed books to be traced easily, and both staff and customers saved time in not having to search for specific books. To further enhance convenience and productivity, NLB has been moving toward completely side-stepping the handling of physical books—library members can now download some 800,000 e-books and 600 e-magazines for free from its website. Another recent innovation was a dispensing machine for some of its most popular books.

And the result of NLB's rigorous redesigning of service processes? A world-class library, winner of Singapore Quality Award, highly regarded by librarians around the world, and featured in teaching case studies at top business schools such as Harvard Business School and INSEAD.

Examining service blueprints is an important step in identifying such opportunities and then redesigning the ways in which tasks are performed.[13] Redesign efforts typically focus on achieving the following four key objectives, and, ideally, redesign efforts should achieve all four at the same time:

1) Reduced number of service failures.
2) Reduced cycle time from customer initiation of a service process to its completion.
3) Enhanced productivity.
4) Increased customer satisfaction.

Service process redesign includes reconstruction, rearrangement, and substitution of service processes. These efforts typically include:

- **Examining the service blueprint with key stakeholders.** By closely examining a service blueprint, service managers can identify problems in a service process and discover ways to improve it. Each of the stakeholders in a process (i.e., the customer, frontline employees, support staff, and IT teams) should be invited to review the blueprint with the purpose of brainstorming for ideas on how to improve the process. This involves identification of missing or unnecessary steps and changes in sequence. Stakeholders also highlight ways in which developments in information technology, equipment, and new methods offer advantages. For example, Avis does research each year on what factors car renters care about the most. The company breaks down the car rental process into more than 100 steps, including making reservations, finding the pickup counter, getting to the car, driving it, returning it, paying the bill, and so on. Because Avis knows customers' key concerns, it claims it can quickly identify ways to improve their satisfaction while also driving the firm's productivity.
- **Eliminating nonvalue-adding steps.** Often, activities at the front-end and backend processes of services can be simplified with the goal of focusing on the benefit-producing part of the service encounter. For example, a customer wanting to rent a car is not interested in filling out forms, or processing payment, or waiting for the returned car to be checked. Service redesign tries to get rid of these steps. Now, some car rental companies allow customers to rent a car online and pick it up from a designated car park (a large electronic board lists the name of the customer, the car, and the parking lot number). The key is in the car, and the only interaction with a car rental employee is at the exit when driving the car out of the car lot. At the exit, the customer's driver's license is checked and the contract signed (including the customer confirming the condition of the car). When returning the car, it is simply parked at an allocated area at the rental company's car lot. After that, the key is returned to a safe deposit box, the final bill is mailed to the billing address, and payment is deducted from the customer's credit card. The customer does not have to come into contact with service personnel. The outcomes of such process redesigns typically include increased productivity and customer satisfaction at the same time.
- **Shifting to self-service.** There can be great gains in productivity and sometimes even service quality when there is increased self-service (Figure 8.12). For example, FedEx succeeded in shifting more than 50% of its transactions from

its call centers to its website, thus reducing the number of employees in its call centers by some 20,000 persons.[14] Businesses are also taking advantage of smartphones and tablets to shift to self-service. For example, Fish & Co., an innovative seafood restaurant chain in Southeast Asia and the Middle East, replaced its menu with an iPad so that customers can perform self-service ordering. An app shows all the delicious food available with lots of drill-down information if desired, and allows diners to send their orders directly to the kitchen. At the back end, the app links to the restaurant's point-of-sale system to complete the order. Customers can have fun by connecting to social media websites like Facebook and sharing their meal orders with their friends. The app also has features that up-sell menu items and combine dishes with recommended side orders.[15]

Figure 8.12 When firms shift to self-service, they may require the services of shipping firms like Cosco to help in delivering the core product to the customer.

THE CUSTOMER AS CO-CREATORS

 **LO 8**

Be familiar with the concept of service customers as "co-creators" and the implications of this perspective.

Service process redesign for productivity and efficiency calls for customers to be more involved in the delivery of the service. Blueprinting helps to specify the role of customers and to identify the extent of contact between them and service providers.

Levels of Customer Participation

Customer participation refers to the actions and resources supplied by customers during service production and/or delivery, including mental, physical, and even emotional inputs.[16] Some degree of customer participation in service delivery is unavoidable in people-processing services and in many other services involving real-time contact between customers and providers. However, as Mary Jo Bitner and her colleagues show, the extent of such participation varies widely and can be divided into three broad levels.[17]

Low Participation Level

With a low participation level, employees and systems do all the work. Service products tend to be standardized. Payment may be the only thing the customer needs to be involved in. In situations where customers come to the service factory, all that is needed is the customers' physical presence. Examples include visiting a movie theater

Figure 8.13 Possession-processing services have little customer involvement.

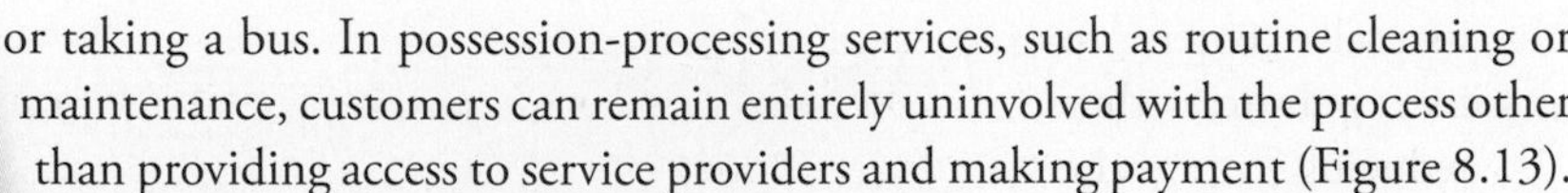

or taking a bus. In possession-processing services, such as routine cleaning or maintenance, customers can remain entirely uninvolved with the process other than providing access to service providers and making payment (Figure 8.13).

Moderate Participation Level

With a moderate participation level, customers need to help the firm in creating and delivering service. For example, they may need to provide information, put in personal effort, or provide physical possessions. When getting their hair washed and cut, customers must let the stylist know what they want and cooperate during the different steps in the process. If a client wants an accountant to prepare a tax return, she must first pull together information and documents that the accountant can use to prepare the return correctly. The client must also be prepared to respond to any questions the accountant may have.

High Participation Level

With a high participation level, customers work actively with the provider to co-produce the service. Service cannot be created without the customer's active participation (Figure 8.14). In fact, if customers fail to play their part properly and do not perform certain necessary tasks, they will affect the quality of the service outcome (Figure 8.15). Marriage counseling and educational services fall into this category. In weight loss or rehabilitation, the goal is to improve the patient's physical condition. However, the patient has to play an active part to help, perhaps by closely following a dietary and exercise plan provided by the doctor. Successful delivery of many B2B services requires customers and providers to work closely together as members of a team, such as for management consulting and supply chain management services.

Figure 8.14 Yoga classes are services that require high participation from the customer.

Customers as Service Co-Creators

Customers are involved in service processes and can be thought of as service co-creators. Value is created when the customer and service providers interact during production, consumption, and delivery of service. This means that they are participating actively in the process. Hence, it is not a process that only the company takes responsibility for. The performance of the customer also affects the quality and productivity of the output. Therefore, service firms need to educate and train customers so that they have the skills and motivation needed to perform their tasks well. More than that, firms also need to look at how they can contribute to value that the customer wants to obtain from the service. [18]

Reducing Service Failures Caused by Customers

Stephen Tax, Mark Colgate, and David Bowen found that customers cause about one-third of all service problems.[19] They argue that recovering from instances of customer failure is difficult. This is because customers and the company may have different views of what caused the problem. Therefore, firms should focus on preventing customer failures as is described in Service Insights 8.4.

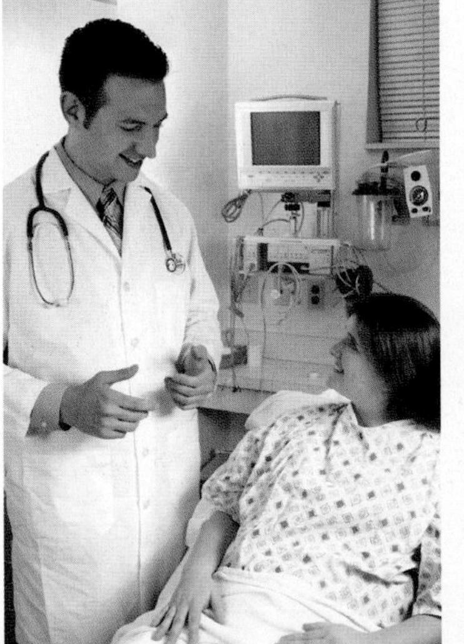

Figure 8.15 Doctor–patient relationships must be mutally cooperative for effective treatment.

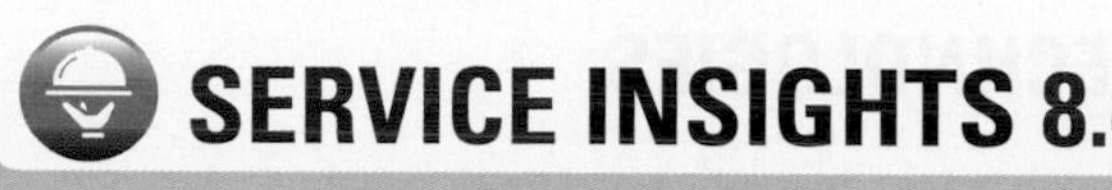

A Three-Step Approach to Preventing Customer Failures

Fail-safe methods (or poka-yokes) need to be designed not only for employees but also for customers, especially when customers participate actively in the creation and delivery processes. Customer poka-yokes focus on preparing the customer for the encounter (including getting them to bring the right materials for the transaction and to arrive on time, if applicable), understanding and anticipating their role in the service transaction, and selecting the correct service or transaction. A good way is to use the following three-step approach to prevent customer-generated failures through the application of poka-yokes.

1 Systematically collect information on the most common failure points.

2 Identify their root causes. It is important to note that an employee's explanation may not be the true cause. Instead, the cause must be investigated from the customer's point of view. Human causes of customer failure include lack of needed skills, failure to understand their role, and insufficient preparation. Some processes are complex and unclear. Other causes may include weaknesses in design of the servicescape or self-service technology (e.g., "unfriendly" user machines and websites).

3 Create strategies to prevent the failures that have been identified. The five strategies listed below may need to be combined for maximum effectiveness.

(a) Redesign processes (e.g., redesign customers' role as well as processes). For example, aircraft lavatory doors must be locked in order for the lights to be switched on. ATMs use beepers so that customers do not forget to retrieve their cards at the end of their transaction. In future, biometric identification (e.g., fingerprint reading combined with voice recognition) could replace cards and PINs at ATMs. This way, problems of lost cards or forgotten PINs are designed out of the process and customer convenience is increased.

(b) Use technology. For example, hospitals can use automated systems that send SMSes or e-mails to patients to confirm and remind them of their appointments and tell them how to reschedule an appointment if required.

(c) Manage customer behavior. For example, one may print dress code requests on invitations, send reminders of dental appointments, or print user guidelines on customer cards (e.g., "Please have your account and pin number ready before calling our service reps").

(d) Encourage "customer citizenship" (e.g., customers help one another to prevent failure, like in weight-loss programs).

(e) Improve the servicescape. Many firms forget that customers need user-friendly directional signs to help them find their way around, failing which they might become very frustrated.

Helping customers to avoid failure can become a source of competitive advantage, especially when companies increasingly use self-service technologies.

PART III

SOURCE

Stephen S. Tax, Mark Colgate, and David E. Bowen, "How to Prevent Customers from Failing," *MIT Sloan Management Review* 47, (Spring 2006): 30–38.

LO 9

Understand the factors that lead customers to accept or reject new self-service technologies (SSTs).

SELF-SERVICE TECHNOLOGIES

The ultimate form of involvement in service production is for customers to take on the whole activity themselves. This means they use the facilities or system provided by the service firm. The customer's time and effort replace those of a service employee. In the case of telephone, smartphone, and Internet-based services, customers even provide their own terminals (Figure 8.16).

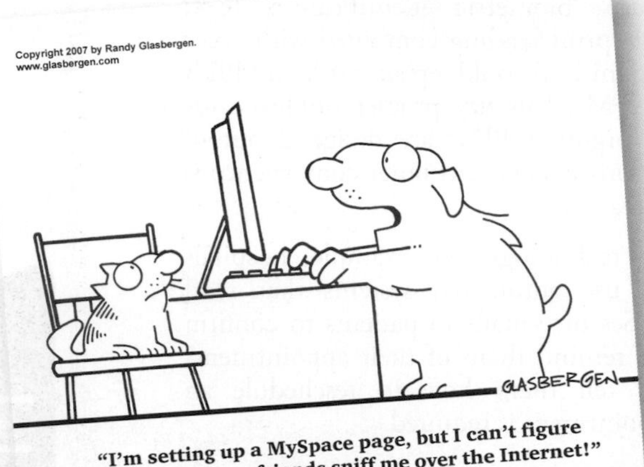

Figure 8.16 Many Internet-based services require customers to serve themselves.

Consumers are faced with a variety of self-service technologies (SSTs) that allow them to produce a service without direct service employee involvement.[20] SSTs include automated banking terminals, self-service scanning at supermarket checkouts, self-service gasoline pumps, automated telephone systems such as phone banking, automated hotel checkout, self-service train ticketing machines (Figure 8.17), and numerous Internet-based services.

Information-based services can easily be offered using SSTs. These services include not only supplementary services such as getting information, placing orders, and reservations and making payment but also delivery of core products in fields such as banking, research, entertainment, and self-paced education. Even consultation and sales processes, traditionally carried out face-to-face, have been transformed into self-service with the use of electronic recommendation agents.[21] Recent academic research suggests ways to make them more effective (see Service Insights 8.5). Many companies have developed strategies designed to encourage customers to serve themselves through the Internet. They hope that this will result in customers reducing the use of more expensive alternatives such as direct contact with employees, and the use of intermediaries like brokers and travel agents.

Nevertheless, not all customers take advantage of SSTs. Matthew Meuter and his colleagues observe: "For many firms, often, the challenge is not managing the technology but rather getting consumers to try the technology."[22]

Figure 8.17 Tourists appreciate easy-to-understand instructions when traveling abroad and making payment for train tickets.

SERVICE INSIGHTS 8.5

Making Electronic Recommendation Agents More Effective

Consumers often face a confusing variety of choices when purchasing goods and services from online vendors. One way in which these "e-tailers" try to assist consumers is to offer electronic recommendation agents as part of their service. Recommendation agents are low-cost "virtual salespeople" designed to help customers make their selections from among large numbers of competing offerings. These recommendation agents list offerings that are ranked according to consumer preferences. However, research by Lerzan Aksoy shows that many existing recommendation agents rank choices differently from the customers they are designed to help. First, they emphasize product attributes differently from customers. Second, they may use decision strategies that do not match the simple rules of thumb used by customers.

The research simulated the selection of a cell phone from among 32 alternatives. Each of these was described on a website as having different features relating to price, weight, talk time, and standby time.

The study results showed that it helps consumers to use a recommendation agent that thinks like them, either in terms of attribute weights or decision strategies. When the ways in which agents work are completely different from theirs, consumers are not better off and may actually be worse off than if they had simply used a randomly ordered list of options. Even though the subjects in this research tended to listen to the agent's recommendations, those who felt it had a dissimilar decision strategy and dissimilar attribute weights from their own were less likely to come back to the website, recommend it to friends, or believe that the site had met their expectations well.

In conclusion, to make recommendation agents add value to the customer and enhance sales and repeat business, firms need to closely understand their customers' decision-making strategies, attributes, and attribute weightings (refer to Chapter 2 on consumer decision making, and Chapter 3 on determinant attributes).

SOURCE

Lerzan Aksoy, Paul N. Bloom, Nicholas H. Lurie, and Bruce Cooil, "Should Recommendation Agents Think Like People?" *Journal of Service Research* 8, (May 2006): 297–315.

PART III

Psychological Factors in Customer Self-Service

Given the large amount of time and money needed for firms to design, implement, and manage SSTs, it is important for service marketers to understand how consumers decide between using an SST option and relying on a human provider. From a customer's point-of-view, there are both advantages and disadvantages to using SSTs. The advantages of using SSTs are:

- Greater convenience, including time savings, faster service, flexibility of timing (e.g., through 24/7 availability) and flexibility of location (e.g., many ATMs).
- Cost savings.
- Greater control over service delivery and higher perceived level of customization.

Customers may even derive fun, enjoyment, and even spontaneous delight from SST usage. For example, children take a lot of delight in doing self-scanning at supermarket checkouts as they find this activity very fun. It has been found that if SST is perceived to deliver service quality, it can have a positive impact on the intention to return to a retail store.[23] James Curran, Matthew Meuter, and Carol Surprenant found in their research that multiple attitudes drive customer intentions to use a specific SST. These include overall attitudes toward related service technologies, global attitudes toward the specific service firm, and attitudes toward its employees.[24] However, there are always some consumers who feel uncomfortable with SSTs, feel anxious and stressed, or may view service encounters as social experiences and prefer to deal with people.

What Aspects of SSTs Please or Annoy Customers?

Research suggests that customers both love and hate SSTs.[25] They love SSTs when:

- They help them to get out of difficult situations. This is often because SST machines are conveniently located and accessible 24/7. A website is as close as the nearest computer. Therefore, this is easier to get to than the company's physical sites. If you need cash urgently and the bank is closed, wouldn't you be glad that you can obtain cash at an ATM near your house?
- Customers also love SSTs when they perform better than the service employee. For example, SSTs allow users to get detailed information and complete transactions faster than they could get through face-to-face or telephone contact. Experienced travelers rely on SSTs to save time and effort at airports, rental car facilities, and hotels. Sometimes, a well-designed SST can deliver better service than a human being can. Said one customer about the experience of buying convenience-store items from a new model of automated vending machine, "A guy in the store can make a mistake or give you a hard time, but not the machine. I definitely prefer the machine."[26] As a *Wall Street Journal* article summarized the trend, "Have a Pleasant Trip: Eliminate Human Contact."[27] In short, many customers like SSTs when they work well.

However, customers hate SSTs when they fail. Users get angry when they find that self-service machines are out of service, their PIN numbers are rejected, websites are down, or tracking numbers do not work. Even when SSTs do work, customers dislike poorly designed technologies that make service processes difficult to understand and use. It is common to hear complaints about the difficulty in finding one's way around a poorly designed website.

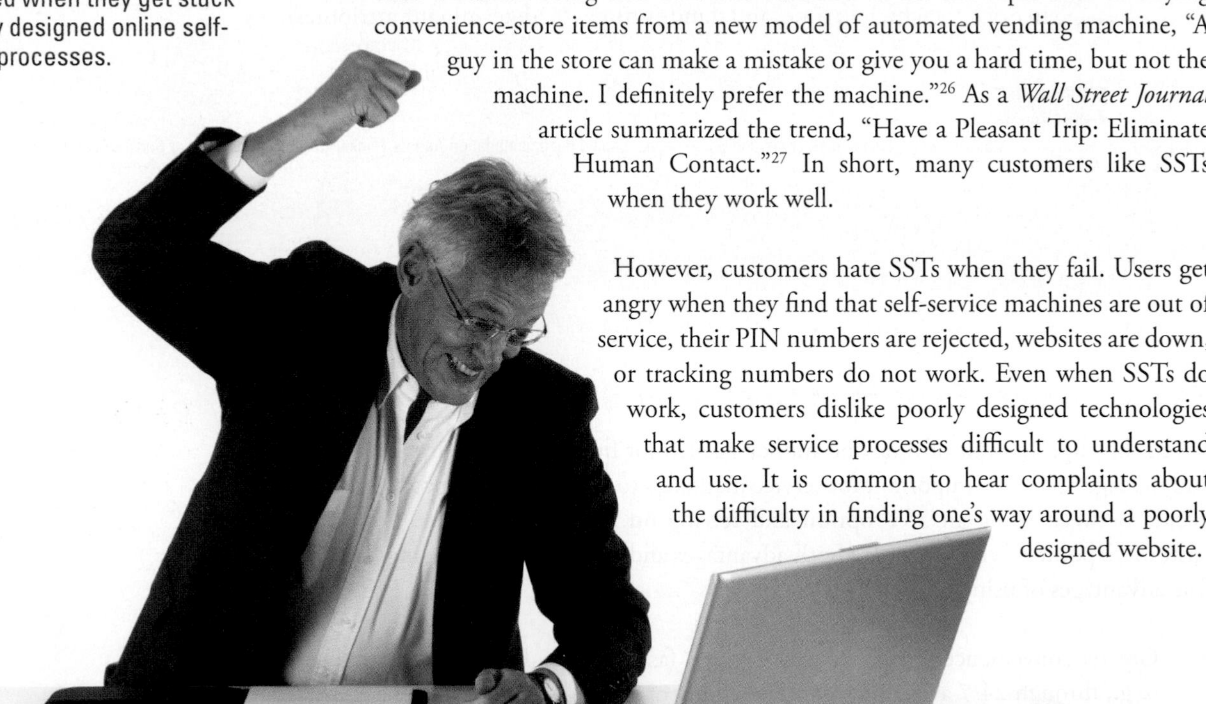

Figure 8.18 Customers feel frustrated when they get stuck in poorly designed online self-service processes.

Users also get frustrated when they themselves mess up due to mistakes such as forgetting their passwords, failing to provide information as requested, or simply hitting the wrong button (Figure 8.18). Self-service logically implies that customers can cause their own dissatisfaction. But even when it is the customers' own fault, they may still blame the service provider for not providing a simpler and more user-friendly system.[28]

A key problem with SSTs is that so few of them include effective service recovery systems. Very often, when the process fails, there is no simple way to solve the problem on the spot. Usually, customers are forced to telephone or make a personal visit to the service company to solve the problem. This may be exactly what they were trying to avoid in the first place! Mary Jo Bitner suggests that managers should put their firms' SSTs to the test by asking the following basic questions:[29]

- **Does the SST work reliably?** Firms must make sure that SSTs work as promised and that the design is user friendly for customers. Southwest Airlines' online ticketing system has set a high standard for simplicity and reliability. It boasts the highest percentage of online ticket sales of any airline—clear evidence of customer acceptance.
- **Is the SST better than the interpersonal alternative?** If it doesn't save time or provide ease of access, cost savings, or some other benefit, then customers will continue to use the familiar interpersonal choice. Amazon.com's success reflects its efforts to create a highly personalized yet efficient alternative to visiting a retail store.
- **If it fails, what systems are in place to recover?** It is very important for firms to provide systems, structures, and recovery technologies that will allow timely service recovery when things go wrong (Figure 8.19). Some banks have a phone located beside each ATM. This links customers to a 24-hour customer service center if they have questions or run into difficulties. Supermarkets that have installed self-service checkout lanes usually have one employee to keep watch on the lanes. This practice combines security with customer assistance. In telephone-based service systems, well-designed voicemail menus include an option for customers to reach a customer service representative.

Managing Customers' Reluctance to Change

LO 10

Know how to manage customers' reluctance to change their behaviors in service processes, including adoption of SSTs.

Increasing the customers' participation level in a service process or shifting the process entirely to self-service using SSTs requires the firm to change customer behavior. This is often a difficult task, as customers do not like being forced to use SST.[30] Service Insights 8.6 identifies ways of dealing with customer resistance to change, particularly when the innovation is one that is very different and unique. Once the kind of changes has been decided, marketing communications can help prepare customers for the change, explain the rationale, the benefits, and what customers will need to do differently in the future.

Figure 8.19 As a fail-sure measure, department stores normally have employees on standby near self-checkout lanes to assist if there are problems.

SERVICE INSIGHTS 8.6

Managing Customers' Reluctance to Change

Customer resistance to changes in familiar processes and set patterns of behavior can make it difficult to improve productivity and even quality. The following six steps can help smooth the path of change.

1. **Develop customer trust.** It is more difficult to introduce productivity-related changes when people do not trust the firms that made those changes. Customers' willingness to accept change may be closely related to the degree of goodwill they bear toward the firm.

2. **Understand customers' habits and expectations.** People often get used to using a service, with certain steps taken in a fixed sequence. They have their own individual service script or flowchart in mind. Innovations that change these deeply rooted routines are likely to face resistance unless changes to be expected are carefully explained to customers.

3. **Pretest new procedures and equipment.** To see how customers may respond to new procedures and equipment, marketing researchers can use concept and laboratory testing and/or field testing. If service personnel are going to be replaced by automatic equipment, it is important to create designs that customers of almost all types and backgrounds will find easy to use. Even the phrasing of instructions needs careful thought. Unclear and complex instructions may discourage customers with poor reading skills. If instructions are written in a way that seems as if customers are being given orders, then it will turn off those who are used to personal courtesies from the service personnel whom the machine replaces.

4. **Publicize the benefits.** Introduction of self-service equipment or procedures requires consumers to perform part of the task themselves. Although this additional "work" may be have benefits such as extended service hours, time savings, and, in some instances, monetary savings, these benefits may not be obvious. They have to be promoted. Useful strategies may include use of mass media advertising, on-site posters and signage, and personal communications to inform people of the innovation, arouse their interest in it, and clarify the specific benefits to customers of changing their behavior and using new delivery systems.

5. **Teach customers to use innovations and promote trial.** Service personnel should be on hand to demonstrate new equipment and answer questions. Providing reassurance as well as educational assistance is important for gaining acceptance of new procedures and technologies. For web-based innovations, it is important to provide access to e-mail, chat, or even telephone-based assistance. Promotional incentives such as price discounts, loyalty points, and lucky draws may also serve to stimulate trial. Once customers have tried a self-service option (particularly an electronically based one) and find that it works well, they will be more likely to use it regularly in the future.

6. **Monitor performance and continue to seek improvements.** Introducing quality and productivity improvements is an ongoing process, especially for SSTs. If customers are displeased with new procedures, they may revert to their previous behavior. Therefore, it is important to monitor utilization, frequency of transaction failures (and their fail points), and customer complaints over time. Service managers must work hard to continuously improve SSTs so that there will be continued usage.

CHAPTER SUMMARY

LO 1 ▶ Flowcharting is a technique for displaying the nature and sequence of the different steps in delivering a service to the customer. It is a simple way to visualize the total customer service experience.

LO 2 ▶ Blueprinting is a more complex form of flowcharting, specifying in detail how service processes are constructed, including what is visible to the customer and all that goes on in the back office. Blueprints facilitate the detailed design and redesign of customer service processes.

LO 3 ▶ A blueprint typically has the following design elements:

- The ***front-stage activities*** that map the overall customer experience, the desired inputs and outputs, and the sequence in which delivery of that output should take place.
- The ***physical evidence*** the customer can see and use to assess service quality.
- The ***line of visibility*** that clearly separates what customers experience and can see at the frontstage and the backstage processes that customers can't see.
- The ***backstage activities*** that must be performed to support a particular front-stage step.
- The ***support processes and supplies*** where support processes are typically provided by information systems and where supplies are needed for both front- and backstage steps.
- ***Fail points*** are where there is a risk of things going wrong and affecting service quality. Fail points should be designed out of a process (e.g., via the use of poka-yokes) and firms should have backup plans for failures that are not preventable.
- Common ***customer waits*** in the process and points of potentially excessive waits. These should then either be designed out of the process, or if that is not possible, firms can implement strategies to make waits less unpleasant.
- ***Service standards and targets*** should be established for each activity, reflecting customer expectations. These include specific times to be set for the completion of each task and the acceptable wait between each customer activity.

LO 4 ▶ A good blueprint identifies fail points where things can go wrong. Fail-safe methods, also called poka-yokes, can then be designed to prevent and/or recover such failures for both employees and customers. A three-step approach can be used to develop poka-yokes:

1. Collect information on the most common fail points.
2. Identify the root causes of those failures.
3. Create strategies to prevent the failures that have been identified.

LO 5 ▶ Service blueprints help to set service standards that should be high enough to satisfy customers. As standards need to be measurable, important but subjective or intangible service attributes need to be operationalized. This can often be achieved through service process indicators that capture the essence or at least approximate these attributes. Once standards are decided, performance targets can be set.

Firms should put emphasis on creating a strong start in its service process to set the tone, and have a strong finish to leave a good, lasting impression. A tool that helps to manage customer emotions is "emotionprints," which document likely customer emotions at each stage of the service process. The objective is to manage the customer experience well.

LO 6 ▶ Changes in technology, customer needs, and service offerings require customer service processes to be redesigned periodically. Symptoms indicating that a process is not working well include:

- A lot of information exchange is required.
- A lot of data available that is not useful.
- A high ratio of checking or control activities to value-adding activities.
- Increased processing of exceptions.
- Growing numbers of customer complaints about inconvenient and unnecessary procedures.

 **LO 7** ▶ Service process redesign efforts aim to:

1. reduce number of service failures.
2. reduce cycle time.
3. improve productivity.
4. increase customer satisfaction.

Service process redesign includes reconstruction, rearrangement, or substitution of service processes. These efforts typically include:

- o Examining the service blueprint with key stakeholders. Customers frontline employees, support staff and IT teams are invited to review the blueprint and to brainstorm for ideas on how to improve the process.
- o Elimination of nonvalue-adding steps
- o Shifting to self-service.

LO 8 ▶ Customers often are involved in service processes as co-producers and, therefore, can be thought of as "service co-creators." Their performance affects the quality and productivity of output. Therefore, service firms need to educate and train customers so that they have the skills and motivation needed to perform their tasks well.

LO 9 ▶ The ultimate form of customer involvement is self-service. Most people welcome SSTs that offer more convenience (i.e., time savings, faster service, 24/7 availability, and more locations), cost savings, better control, information, and customization. However, poorly designed technology and inadequate education on how to use SSTs can cause customers to reject SSTs.

Three basic questions can be used to assess the potential for success of an SST:

- o Does the SST work reliably?
- o Is the SST better for customers than to other service delivery alternatives?
- o If the SST fails, are there systems in place to recover the service?

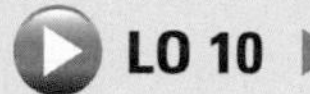 **LO 10** ▶ Increasing the customers' participation level in a service process or shifting the process entirely to self-service requires the firm to change customer behavior. There are six steps to guide this process and reduce customer reluctance to change:

- o Develop customer trust.
- o Understand customers' habits and expectations.
- o Pretest new procedures and equipment.
- o Publicize the benefits of changes.
- o Teach customers to use innovations and promote trial.
- o Monitor performance and continue to seek improvements.

UNLOCK YOUR LEARNING

These keywords are found within the sections of each Learning Objective (LO). They are integral to understanding the services marketing concepts taught in each section. Having a firm grasp of these keywords and how they are used is essential to helping you do well on your course, and in the real and very competitive marketing scene out there.

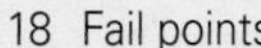

LO 1

1 Customer involvement
2 Flowcharting
3 Information processing
4 Intangible actions
5 Mental stimulus processing
6 People processing
7 Physical processes
8 Possession processing
9 Sequence of encounters
10 Service processes

LO 2

11 Architectural drawings
12 Blueprinting

LO 3

13 Backstage activities
14 Core product
15 Customer waits
16 Drama
17 Excessive waits
18 Fail points
19 Front-stage activities
20 Interactions
21 Interrelationships
22 Line of interaction
23 Line of visibility
24 Performance
25 Service blueprints
26 Service standards
27 Servicescape
28 Supplementary services
29 Supplies
30 Support processes
31 Targets

LO 4

32 Customer failures
33 Fail-proofing
34 Poka-yoke
35 Redesign processes
36 Service processes
37 Total Quality Management

LO 5

38 Customer perceptions
39 Emotionprints
40 Indicators
41 Performance standards
42 Service standards
43 Targets
44 Touchpoints

LO 6

45 Institutional rusting
46 Processes
47 Service process redesign

LO 7

48 Cycle time
49 Gains in productivity
50 Nonvalue-adding steps
51 Productivity
52 Self-service
53 Service blueprints
54 Service processes
55 Service quality
56 Stakeholders

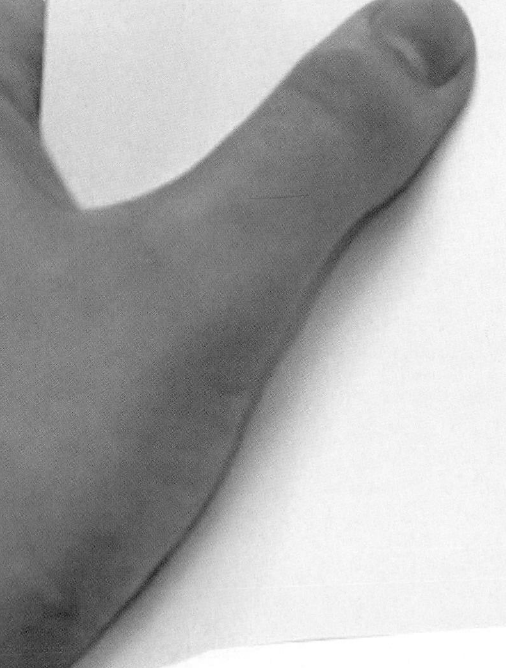

LO 8

57 Co-creators
58 Customer failures
59 Customer participation
60 Fail-safe methods
61 High participation
62 Low participation
63 Moderate participation
64 People-processing services
65 Poka-yokes
66 Possession-processing services
67 Redesign processes
68 Root causes
69 Service co-creators
70 Service failures
71 Technology
72 Value

LO 9

73 Attitudes
73 Convenience
75 Customer self-service
76 Effective service recovery
77 Frustrated
78 Information-based services
79 Internet-based services
80 Psychological factors
81 Self-service technologies

LO 10

82 Customer resistance to change
83 Customer trust
84 Procedures
85 Reluctance to change

How well do you know the language of services marketing? Quiz yourself!

PART III

Not for the academically faint-of-heart

For each keyword you are able to recall without referring to earlier pages, give yourself a point (and a pat on the back). Tally your score at the end and see if you earned the right to be called—a *services marketeer.*

SCORE

0 – 16 Services Marketing is done a great disservice.
17 – 32 The midnight oil needs to be lit, pronto.
33 – 48 I know what you *didn't* do all semester.
49 – 64 A close shave with success.
65 – 80 Now, go forth and market.
81 – 85 There should be a marketing concept named after you.

KNOW YOUR ESM

Review Questions

1. How does flowcharting help us to understand the difference between people-, possession-, mental-, and information-processing services?
2. What are the typical design elements of a service blueprint?
3. How can fail-safe methods be used to reduce service failures?
4. Why is it important to develop service standards and targets?
5. Why is periodic process redesign necessary for service firms, and what are the typical symptoms that a service process is not working well?
6. What are the four key objectives of service process redesign?
7. What efforts are typically involved in service process redesign?
8. Why does the customer's role as a co-creator need to be designed into service processes?
9. Explain what factors make customers like and dislike self-service technologies (SSTs).
10. How can you test whether an SST has the potential to be successful, and what can a firm do to increase its chances of customer adoption?

WORK YOUR ESM

Application Exercises

1. Review the blueprint of the restaurant visit in Figure 8.5. Identify several possible "OTSUs" ("opportunity to screw up") for each step in the front-stage process. Consider possible causes underlying each potential failure and suggest ways to eliminate or minimize these problems.
2. Prepare a blueprint for a service with which you are familiar. Upon completion, consider (a) the tangible cues or indicators of quality from the customer's perspective, considering the line of visibility; (b) whether all steps in the process are necessary; (c) the extent to which standardization is possible and advisable throughout the process; (d) the location of potential fail points and how they could be designed out of the process and what service recovery procedures could be introduced; and (e) the potential measures of process performance.
3. Think about what happens in a doctor's office when a patient comes for a physical examination. How much participation is needed from the patient in order for the process to work smoothly? If a patient refuses to cooperate, how can that affect the process? What can the doctor do in advance to ensure that the patient cooperates in the delivery of the process?
4. Observe supermarket shoppers who use self-service checkout lanes, and compare them to those who use the services of a checker. What differences do you observe? How many of those conducting self-service scanning appear to run into difficulties, and how do they resolve their problems?
5. Identify three situations in which you use self-service delivery. For each situation, what is your motivation for using self-service delivery rather than having service personnel do it for you?
6. What actions could a bank take to encourage more customers to bank by phone, mail, Internet, or through ATMs rather than visit a branch?
7. Identify one website that is exceptionally user friendly and another that is not. What are the factors that make for a satisfying user experience in the first instance and a frustrating one in the second? Specify recommendations for improvements in the second website.

ENDNOTES

1 See how service blueprinting is used to improve service processes. Sameer Kumar, Angelena Phillips, and Julia Rupp, "Using Six Sigma DMAIC to Design a High-Quality Summer Lodge Operation," *Journal of Retail & Leisure Property* 8, no. 3 (2009): 173–191.

2 G. Lynn Shostack, "Designing Services That Deliver," *Harvard Business Review* 62, (January–February 1984): 133–139.

3 David Maister, now president of Maister Associates, coined the term OTSU while teaching at Harvard Business School.

4 See how poka-yokes can be used to improve business operations. Sameer Kumar, Brett Hudson, and Josie Lowry, "Consumer Purchase Process Improvements in E-tailing Operations," *International Journal of Productivity and Performance Management* 59, no. 4 (2010): 388–403; Sameer Kumar, Angelena Phillips, and Julia Rupp, "Using Six Sigma DMAIC to Design a High-Quality Summer Lodge Operation," *Journal of Retail & Leisure Property* 8, no. 3 (2009): 173–191.

5 This section is based in part on Richard B. Chase and Douglas M. Stewart, "Make Your Service Fail-Safe," *Sloan Management Review* 35, (Spring 1994): 35–44.

6 This section was adapted from Jochen Wirtz and Monica Tomlin, "Institutionalizing Customer-driven Learning through Fully Integrated Customer Feedback Systems," *Managing Service Quality* 10, no. 4 (2000): 205–215.

7 See, for example, Eric J. Arnould and Linda L. Price, "River Magic: Extraordinary Experience and the Extended Service Encounter," *Journal of Consumer Research* 20, (June 1993): 24–25; Eric J. Arnould and Linda L. Price, "Collaring the Cheshire Cat: Studying Customers' Services Experience through Metaphors," *The Service Industries Journal* 16, (October 1996): 421–442; and Nick Johns and Phil Tyas, "Customer Perceptions of Service Operations: Gestalt, Incident or Mythology?" *The Service Industries Journal* 17, (July 1997): 474–488.

8 David E. Hansen and Peter J. Danaher, "Inconsistent Performance during the Service Encounter: What's a Good Start Worth?" *Journal of Service Research* 1, (February 1999): 227–235; Richard B. Chase and Sriram Dasu, "Want to Perfect Your Company's Service? Use Behavioral Science," *Harvard Business Review* 79, (June 2001): 79–84; Richard B. Chase, "It's Time to Get to First Principles in Service Design," *Managing Service Quality* 14, no. 2/3 (2004): 126–128.

9 Sriram Dasu and Richard B. Chase, "Designing the Soft Side of Customer Service," *MIT Sloan Management Review* 52, no. 1 (2010): 33–39.

10 Jochen Wirtz and Monica Tomlin, "Institutionalizing Customer-Driven Learning through Fully Integrated Customer Feedback Systems," *Managing Service Quality* 10, no. 4 (2000): 205–215.

11 Mitchell T. Rabkin, MD, cited in Christopher H. Lovelock, *Product Plus*. (New York: McGraw-Hill, 1994), 354–355.

12 Kah Hin Chai, Jochen Wirtz, and Robert Johnston, "Using Technology to Revolutionize the Library Experience of Singaporean Readers," in *Essentials of Services Marketing*, eds. Christopher Lovelock, Jochen Wirtz, and Patricia Chew. (Singapore: Prentice Hall, 2009), 534–536, http://www.nlb.gov.sg, accessed March 12, 2012.

13 See, for example, Michael Hammer and James Champy, *Reengineering the Corporation: A Manifesto for Business Revolution*. New York: HarperCollins Publishers Inc, 2003.

14 Leonard L. Berry and Sandra K. Lampo, "Teaching an Old Service New Tricks – The Promise of Service Redesign," *Journal of Service Research* 2, no. 3 (February 2000): 265–275.

15 Victoria Ho, "Businesses Swallow the Tablet and Smile," *The Business Times*, March 14, 2011.

16 Amy Risch Rodie and Susan Schultz Klein, "Customer Participation in Services Production and Delivery," in *Handbook of Service Marketing and Management*, eds. T. A. Schwartz and D. Iacobucci. (Thousand Oaks, CA: Sage Publications, 2000), 111–125.

17 Mary Jo Bitner, William T. Faranda, Amy R. Hubbert, and Valarie A. Zeithaml, "Customer Contributions and Roles in Service Delivery," *International Journal of Service Industry Management* 8, no. 3 (1997): 193–205.

18 Atefeh Yazdanparast, Ila Manuj, and Stephen M. Swartz, "Co-creating Logistics Value: A Service-Dominant Logic Perspective," *The International Journal of Logistics Management* 21, no. 3 (2010): 375–403; Evert Gummesson, Robert F. Lusch, and Stephen L. Vargo, "Transitioning from Service Management to Service-Dominant Logic," *International Journal of Quality and Service Sciences* 2, no. 1 (2010): 8–22; Kristina Heinonen, Tore Strandvik, and Karl-Jacob Mickelsson, "A Customer-Dominant Logic of Service," *Journal of Service Management* 21, no. 4 (2010): 531–548; Robert F. Lusch, Stephen L. Vargo, and Matthew O'Brien, "Competing through Service: Insights from Service Dominant Logic," *Journal of Retailing* 83, no. 1 (2007): 5–18; Stephen L. Vargo and Robert F. Lusch, "Service-Dominant Logic: Continuing the Evolution," *Journal of the Academy of Marketing Science* 36, no. 1 (2008): 1–10. Loic Ple and Ruben Chumpitaz Caceres, "Not Always Co-Creation: Introducing Interactional Co-Destruction of Value in Service-Dominant Logic" *Journal of Services Marketing* 24, no. 6 (2010): 430–437.

19 Stephen S. Tax, Mark Colgate, and David E. Bowen, "How to Prevent Customers from Failing," *MIT Sloan Management Review* 47, (Spring 2006): 30–38.

20 Matthew L. Meuter, Amy L. Ostrom, Robert I. Roundtree, and Mary Jo Bitner, "Self-Service Technologies: Understanding Customer Satisfaction with Technology-Based Service Encounters," *Journal of Marketing* 64, (July 2000): 50–64.

21 Gerard Haübl and Kyle B. Murray, "Preference Construction and Persistence in Digital Marketplaces: The Role of Electronic Recommendation Agents," *Journal of Consumer Psychology* 13, no. 1 (2003): 75–91; Lerzan Aksoy, Paul N. Bloom, Nicholas H. Lurie, and Bruce Cooil, "Should Recommendation Agents Think Like People?" *Journal of Service Research* 8, (May 2006): 297–315.

22 Matthew L. Meuter, Mary Jo Bitner, Amy L. Ostrom, and Stephen W. Brown, "Choosing among Alternative Service Delivery Modes: An Investigation of Customer Trial of Self-Service Technologies," *Journal of Marketing* 69, (April 2005): 61–83.

23 Hyun-Joo Lee, Ann E. Fairhurst and Min-Young Lee, "The Importance of Self-Service Kiosks in Developing Consumers' Retail Patronage Intentions," *Managing Service Quality* 19, no. 6 (2009): 687–701.

24 James M. Curran, Matthew L. Meuter, and Carol G. Surprenant, "Intentions to Use Self-Service Technologies: A Confluence of Multiple Attitudes," *Journal of Service Research* 5, (February 2003): 209–224.

25 Meuter *et al.*, 2000; Mary Jo Bitner, "Self-Service Technologies: What Do Customers Expect?" *Marketing Management* (Spring 2001): 10–11.

26 Jeffrey F. Rayport and Bernard J. Jaworski, "Best Face Forward," *Harvard Business Review* 82, (December 2004).

27 Kortney Stringer, "Have a Pleasant Trip: Eliminate All Human Contact," *Wall Street Journal* (October 31, 2002).

28 Neeli Bendapudi and Robert P. Leone, "Psychological Implications of Customer Participation in Co-Production," *Journal of Marketing* 67, (January 2003): 14–28.

29 Bitner, 2001, op. cit.

30 Machiel J. Reinders, Pratibha A. Dabholkar, and Ruud T. Frambach, "Consequences of Forcing Consumers to Use Technology-Based Self-Service," *Journal of Service Research* 11, no. 2 (2008): 107–123.

PART III

CHAPTER 9

balancing DEMAND and CAPACITY

LEARNING OBJECTIVES

By the end of this chapter, the reader should be able to:

- **LO 1** Know the different demand—supply situations that fixed capacity firms may face.
- **LO 2** Describe the building blocks of dealing with the problem of fluctuating demand.
- **LO 3** Understand what is meant by *productive capacity* in a service context.
- **LO 4** Be familiar with basic ways to *manage capacity*.
- **LO 5** Understand demand patterns and recognize that demand varies by segment, so examine how to predict segment-specific variations in demand.
- **LO 6** Be familiar with the five basic ways to *manage demand*.
- **LO 7** Understand how to use the marketing mix elements of price, product, place, and promotion to smooth out fluctuations in demand.
- **LO 8** Know how to use waiting lines and queuing systems to inventory demand.
- **LO 9** Understand how customers perceive waits and how to make waiting less burdensome for them.
- **LO 10** Know how to use reservation systems to inventory demand.

Figure 9.1 The beauty and splendor of Tungudalur, a ski resort in Westfjords, Iceland, is now enjoyed all year long.

OPENING VIGNETTE

Summer on the Ski Slopes

It used to be that ski resorts shut down once the snow melted and no skiing could be done on the slopes. The chairlifts stopped operating, the restaurants closed, and the lodges were locked until the next winter. Over time, however, some ski operators recognized that a mountain offers summer pleasures, too. They kept lodging and restaurants open for hikers and picnickers. Some even built alpine slides, curving tracks in which wheeled toboggans could run from the top of the mountain to the base. This created demand for tickets on the ski lifts.

The arrival of the mountain biking craze created opportunities for equipment rentals as well as chairlift rides. Killington Resort in Vermont has long encouraged summer visitors to ride to the top, see the view, and eat at the mountaintop restaurant. Now, however, it also enjoys a brisk business in renting mountain bikes and related equipment (such as helmets). Beside the base lodge, where racks of skis are available for rental in winter, the summer visitor can now choose from rows of mountain bikes. Usually, bikers use the specially equipped chairlifts to carry their bikes up to the top of the mountain, and then ride them down marked trails, but, once in a while, a biker will actually choose to ride up the mountain. Serious hikers do the same; they climb to the top through trails, get refreshments at the restaurant, and then take the chairlift back down to the base.

Most large ski resorts look for a variety of additional ways to attract guests to their hotels and rental homes during the summer. Mont Tremblant in Québec, for instance, is located beside an attractive lake. In addition to swimming and other water sports on the lake, the resort offers visitors activities like a championship golf course, tennis, rollerblading, and specially designed activities for children. Hikers and mountain bikers ride the lifts up the mountain. This is a wonderful example of how service development and marketing generated demand for otherwise idle service capacity!

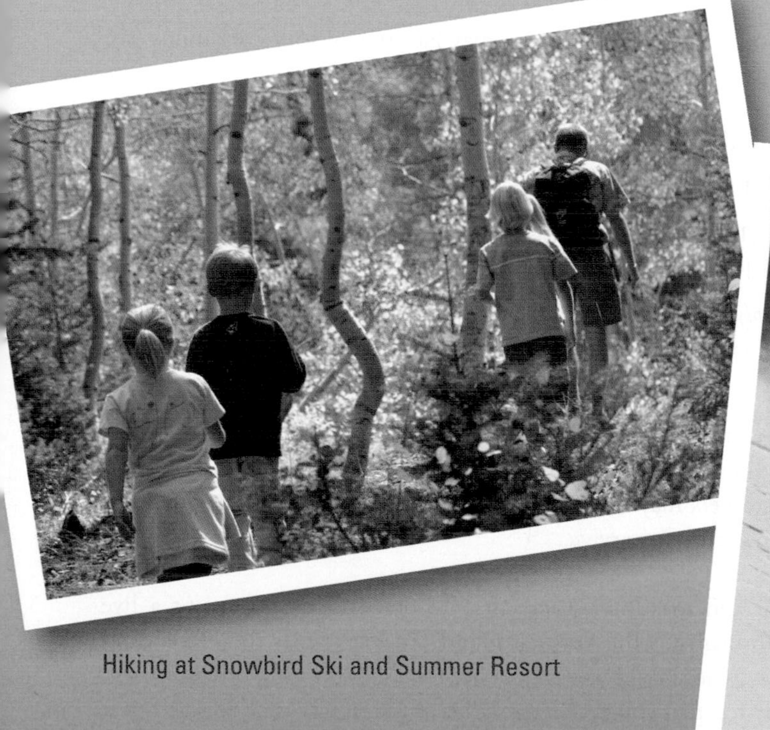

Hiking at Snowbird Ski and Summer Resort

Skiing at Snowbird Ski and Summer Resort

FLUCTUATIONS IN DEMAND THREATEN PROFITABILITY

Many services with limited capacity face wide swings in demand. In the Opening Vignette, this wide swing in demand is caused by the change of seasons. This is a problem because service capacity usually cannot be kept aside for sale at a later date. The effective use of expensive productive capacity is one of the secrets of success in such businesses. The goal should be to utilize staff, labor, equipment, and facilities as *productively* as possible. By working with managers in operations and human resources, service marketers may be able to develop strategies to bring demand and capacity into balance in ways that create benefits for customers as well as to improve profitability for the business. For ski resort operators, the effective use of capacity postwinter requires changing the nature of the activities so that the slopes and facilities can still be utilized.

Figure 9.2 Keeping a balance between demand and capacity is a win-win for business owners and customers.

LO 1

Know the different demand—supply situations that fixed capacity firms may face.

From Excess Demand to Excess Capacity

For fixed capacity firms, the problem is a familiar one. "It's either feast or famine for us!" sighs the manager. "In peak periods, we're disappointing prospective customers by turning them away. In low periods, our facilities are idle, our employees are standing around looking bored, and we're losing money." In other words, demand and supply are not in balance.

At any given moment, a fixed-capacity service may face one of four conditions (see Figure 9.3):

- *Excess demand*—The level of demand exceeds maximum available capacity. As a result, some customers are denied service and business is lost.
- *Demand exceeds optimum capacity*—No one is turned away, but conditions are crowded, service quality seems worse, and customers may feel dissatisfied.
- *Demand and supply are well balanced* at the level of optimum capacity. Staff and facilities are busy without being overworked, and customers receive good service without delays.
- *Excess capacity*—Demand is below optimum capacity, and productive resources are not fully used, resulting in low productivity. When there is low usage, there is a risk that customers may find the experience disappointing or have doubts about whether the firm can survive.

Sometimes, optimum and maximum capacities are one and the same. At a live theater or sports performance, a full house is grand, since it excites the players and the audience. It creates a more satisfying experience for all. With most other services, however, you probably feel that you get better service if the facility is not operating at full capacity. The quality of restaurant service, for instance, often becomes worse when every table is occupied because the staff is rushed and there is a greater likelihood of errors or delays. If you are traveling alone in an aircraft with high-density seating, you tend to feel more comfortable if the seat next to you is empty.

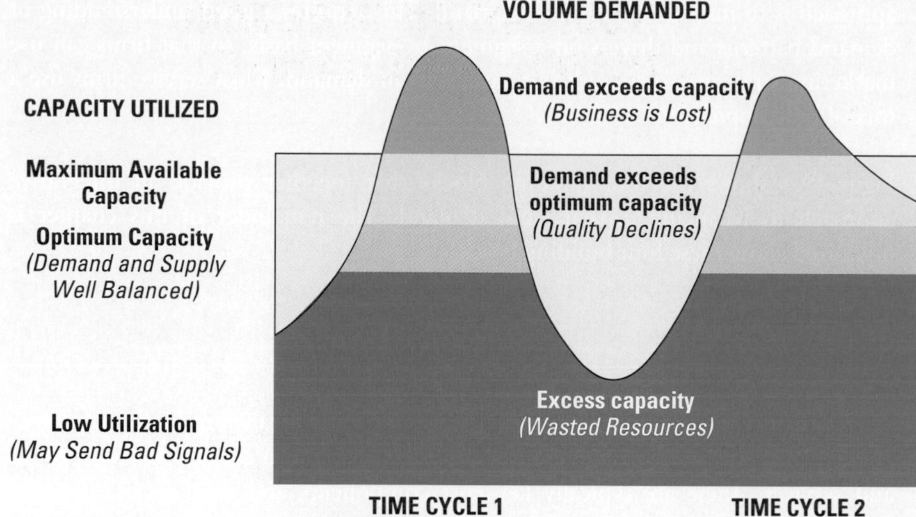

Figure 9.3 Implications of variations in demand relative to capacity.

Building Blocks of Managing Capacity and Demand

LO 2

Describe the building blocks of dealing with the problem of fluctuating demand.

There are two basic approaches to the problem of fluctuating demand. One is to adjust the level of capacity to meet variations in demand. This requires an understanding of what productive capacity means and how it may be increased or decreased. The second

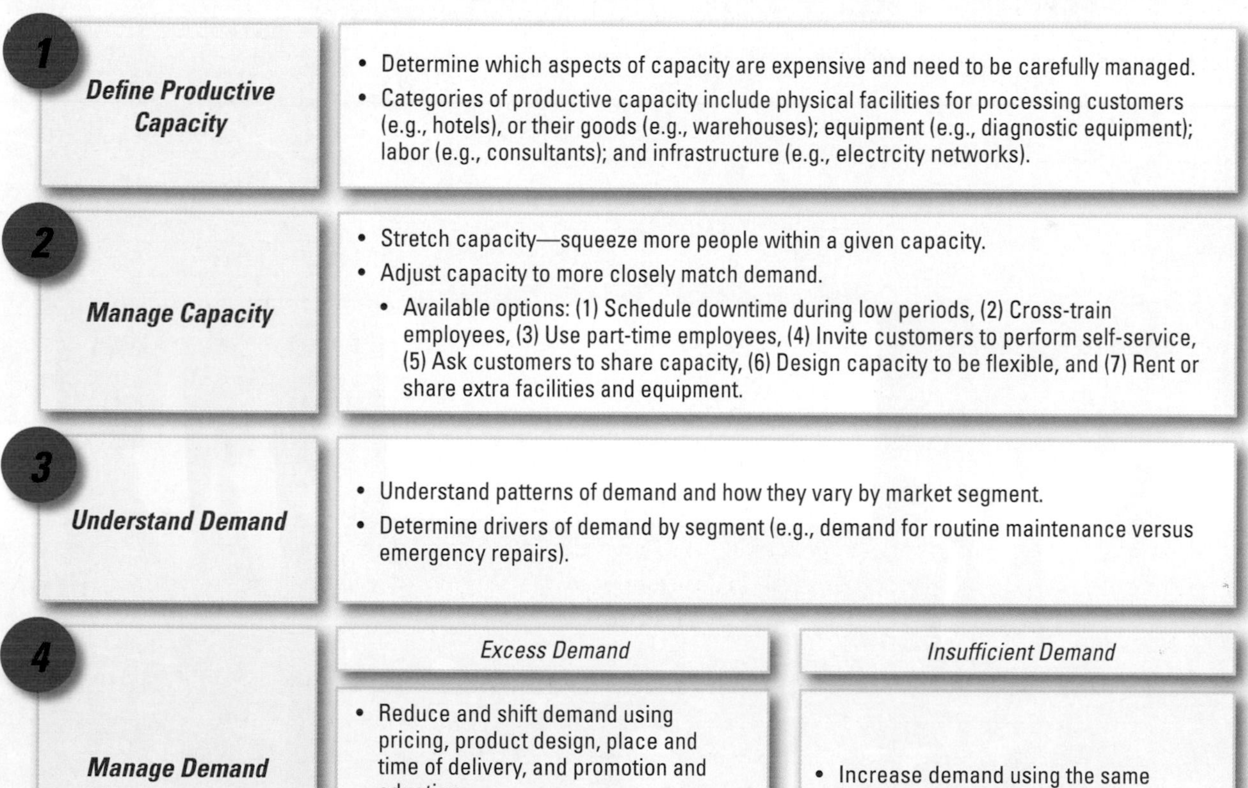

Figure 9.4 Building blocks of managing capacity and demand.

approach is to manage the level of demand. This requires a good understanding of demand patterns and drivers on a segment-by-segment basis, so that firms can use marketing strategies to smooth out variations in demand. Most service firms use a mix of both approaches.[1]

Figure 9.4 shows the four building blocks that together provide an integrative approach to balancing capacity and demand. The remainder of this chapter is organized along these four building blocks.

DEFINING PRODUCTIVE SERVICE CAPACITY

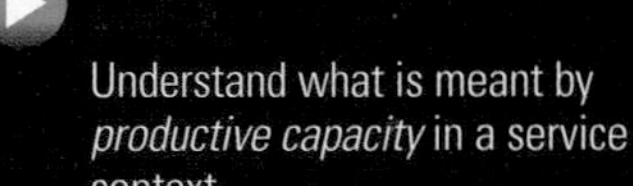

Understand what is meant by *productive capacity* in a service context.

When we refer to managing capacity, we implicitly mean "productive capacity." This term refers to the resources or assets that a firm can use to create goods and services. These are typically key cost components and need to be managed carefully. In a service context, productive capacity can take several forms:

1. *Physical facilities designed to contain customers* and used for *people-processing services or mental stimulus-processing services*. Examples include medical clinics, hotels, passenger aircrafts, and college classrooms. The main form of capacity limitation is likely to be in terms of furnishings such as beds, rooms, or seats. In some cases, local laws may limit the number of people allowed in a physical facility for health or safety reasons (Figure 9.5).

Figure 9.5 Cinemas have to follow strict safety regulations on seating capacity in case of fire emergencies.

2. *Physical facilities designed for storing or processing goods* that either belong to customers or are being offered to them for sale. Examples include pipelines, warehouses, parking lots (Figure 9.6), and railroad freight wagons.
3. *Physical equipment used to process people, possessions, or information* may include a huge range of items and may be very situation-specific. Examples include diagnostic equipment (Figure 9.7), airport security detectors, toll gates, and bank ATMs. If there is not enough equipment capacity for a given level of demand, it can bring service to a crawl (or even a complete stop).
4. *Labor* is a key element of productive capacity in all high-contact services and many low-contact ones (Figure 9.8). If not enough staff are on duty, customers might be kept waiting or service becomes rushed. Professional services are especially dependent on highly skilled staff to create high value-added, information-based output. Abraham Lincoln captured it well when he said that "a lawyer's time and expertise are his stock in trade."

Figure 9.6 Car parks 'store' customers' cars temporarily when they are out shopping.

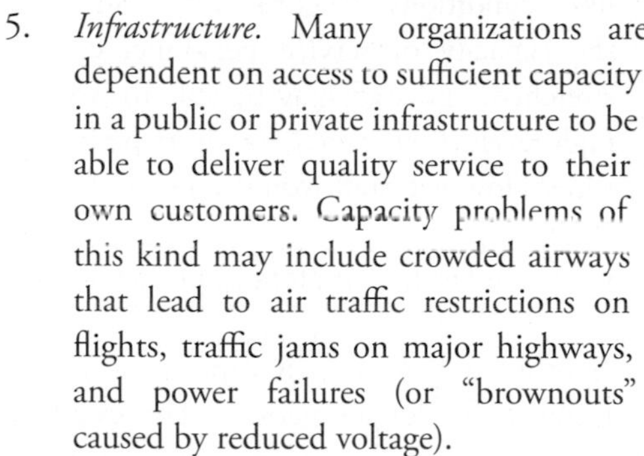

5. *Infrastructure.* Many organizations are dependent on access to sufficient capacity in a public or private infrastructure to be able to deliver quality service to their own customers. Capacity problems of this kind may include crowded airways that lead to air traffic restrictions on flights, traffic jams on major highways, and power failures (or "brownouts" caused by reduced voltage).

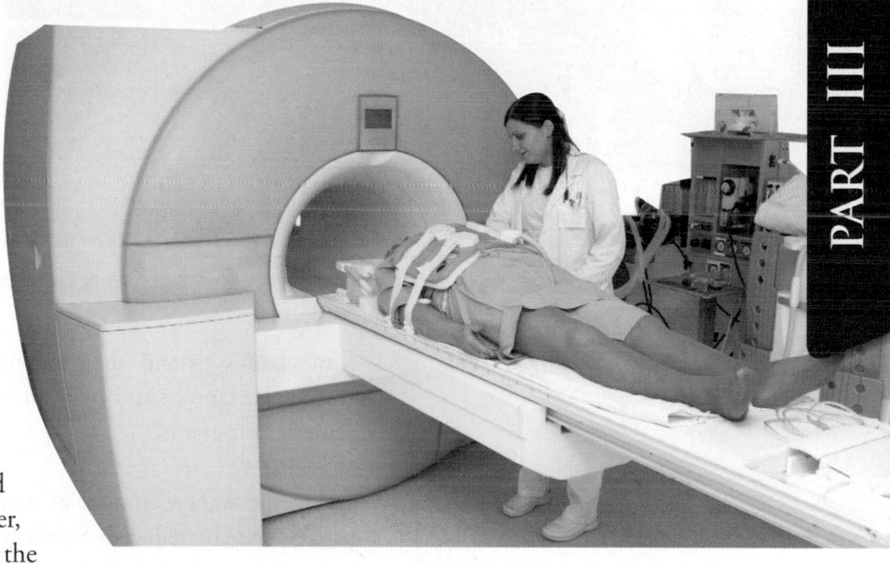

Financial success in businesses that are limited in capacity depends largely on how their capacity is used. If capacity is always used efficiently and profitably, that would be ideal. In practice, however, it is difficult to achieve this. Demand levels are not the only factors that change over time. The time and effort required to process each person or thing may also vary widely at any point in the process. In both professional services and repair jobs, diagnosis and treatment times vary according to the nature of the customers' problems.

Figure 9.7 Productive capacity is expressed in terms of available hours for MRI scanning equipment.

Figure 9.8 Restaurants need to ensure sufficient manpower to meet customer demands.

 **LO 4**

Be familiar with basic ways to *manage capacity.*

MANAGING CAPACITY

Although service firms may encounter capacity limitations because of varying demand, there are a number of ways in which capacity can be adjusted to reduce the problem. Capacity can be stretched or shrunk, and the overall capacity can be adjusted to match demand.

Figure 9.9 Rush hour crowd stretches the capacity of train services.

Stretching Capacity Levels

Here, the actual level of capacity remains unchanged. More people are being served with the same level of capacity. For example, the normal capacity for a subway car may offer 40 seats and allow standing room for another 60 passengers with enough handrail and floor space for all. Yet, at rush hour, perhaps up to 200 people can squeeze into a subway car, although under sardine-like conditions (Figure 9.9). Similarly, the capacity of service personnel can be stretched, and staff may be able to work at high levels of efficiency for short periods of time. However, staff would quickly tire and begin to provide poor service if they had to work that fast for a prolonged period of time.

Another way to stretch capacity is to use facilities for longer periods. For example, some banks extend their opening hours during weekdays and even open on weekends. Universities may offer evening and weekend classes as well as summer semester programs.

Lastly, the average amount of time that customers (or their possessions) spend in the process may be reduced. Sometimes, this is achieved by minimizing slack time. For example, a restaurant can buzz tables, seat arriving diners, and present menus quickly, and the bill can be presented promptly to a group of diners relaxing at the table after a meal.[2] In other instances, it may be achieved by cutting back the level of service, say, offering a simpler menu at busy times of the day.

Adjusting Capacity to Match Demand

Unlike the previous option, this option involves changing the overall level of capacity to match variations in demand. This strategy is also known as *chasing demand.* There are several actions that managers can take to adjust capacity as needed.[3] These actions start from the easiest to implement, to the more difficult.

- *Schedule downtime during periods of low demand.* To make sure that 100% of capacity is available during peak periods, maintenance, repair, and renovations should be carried out when demand is expected to be low. Employees should take their holidays during such periods.

Figure 9.10 Supermarket employees are cross-trained as cashiers and stockers.

- *Cross-train employees.* Even when the service delivery system appears to be operating at full capacity, certain employees may not be busy. If employees can be cross-trained to perform a variety of tasks, they can be shifted to where help is needed most, thereby increasing total capacity. In supermarkets, for instance, the manager may call on stockers to operate cash registers when lines become too long. Likewise, during slow periods, the cashiers may be asked to help stock shelves (Figure 9.10).
- *Use part-time employees.* Many organizations hire. extra workers during their busiest periods. Examples include postal workers and retail store associates during the Christmas season, extra staff for tax preparation service firms at the end of the financial year, and additional hotel employees during holiday periods and for major conferences.
- *Invite customers to perform self-service.* If the number of employees is limited, capacity can be increased by involving customers in co-production of certain tasks. One way to do this is by adding self-service technologies such as electronic kiosks at the airport for airline ticketing and check-in, or automated check-out stations at supermarkets.
- *Ask customers to share.* Capacity can be stretched by asking customers to share a unit of capacity normally meant for one individual. For instance, at busy airports and train stations, if the supply of taxis is not enough to meet demand, travelers going in the same direction may sometimes be given the choice of sharing a ride at a lower rate.
- *Create flexible capacity.* Sometimes, the problem does not lie in overall capacity but in the mix available to serve the needs of different market segments. One solution is to design physical facilities to be flexible. For example, the tables in a restaurant can be all two-seaters. When necessary, two tables can be combined to seat four people, or three tables combined to seat six. In an airline context, an airline may have too few seats in economy even though there are empty seats in the business class cabin on a given flight. When designing its 777 airliner, Boeing faced stiff competition from Airbus and what were described as "outrageous demands" from potential customers. The airlines wanted an aircraft in which galleys and lavatories could be relocated, plumbing and all, to almost anywhere in the cabin within a matter of hours. Boeing managed to solve this challenging problem. Airlines can rearrange the passenger cabin of the 777 within hours, varying the number of seats among different classes.
- *Rent or share extra facilities and equipment.* To reduce spending on fixed assets, a service business may be able to rent extra space or machines at peak times. Two firms with complementary demand patterns, where when one is high and the other is low, may enter into formal sharing agreements. For example, some universities rent out student accommodation to visitors during the peak holiday season when their own students have their summer break and the first-year students have not moved onto campus yet.

LO 5

Understand demand patterns and recognize that demand varies by segment, so examine how to predict segment-specific variations in demand.

UNDERSTANDING PATTERNS OF DEMAND

Now let's look at the other side of the equation. In order to effectively manage demand for a particular service, managers need to understand that demand often differs by market segment. For instance, a repair and maintenance shop that services industrial electrical equipment may already know that a certain proportion of its work consists of regularly scheduled jobs (Figure 9.11). The rest may come from walk-in business and emergency repairs. Although it might seem hard to predict or control the timing and volume of such work, further analysis might show that there is more walk-in business on some days of the week than others. For example, emergency repairs are often requested following damage due to thunderstorms (which tend to be seasonal in nature and can often be predicted a day or two in advance). If a firm understands its service demand patterns, it is able to schedule less preventive maintenance work on days where a high level of demand is expected so that it can take on more profitable emergency repairs.

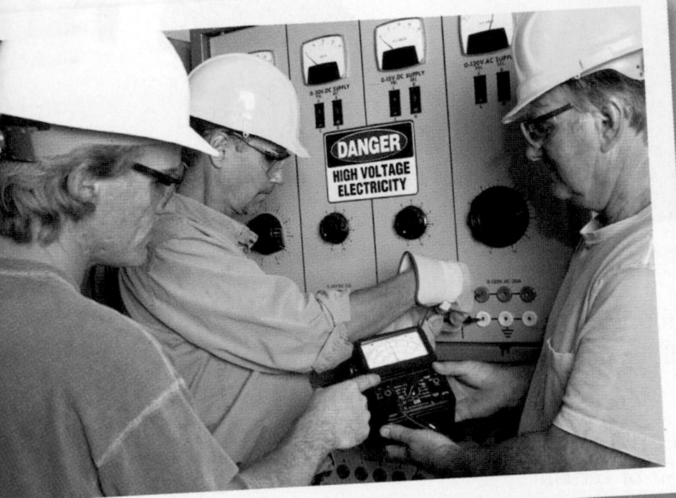

Figure 9.11 Scheduled maintenance checks at a power plant.

To understand the patterns of demand by segment, we should begin by getting some answers to a series of important questions about the patterns of demand and their underlying causes (Table 9.1).

Most cycles influencing demand for a particular service vary in length from one day to 12 months. In many instances, multiple cycles may operate at the same time.

Table 9.1 Questions about demand patterns and their underlying causes

1. **Do demand levels follow a predictable cycle?**
   If so, is the duration of the *demand cycle*
   - One *day* (varies by hour)
   - One *week* (varies by day)
   - One *month* (varies by day or by week)
   - One *year* (varies by month or by season or reflects annual public holidays)
   - Another period
2. **What are the underlying causes of these cyclical variations?**
   - Employment schedules
   - Billing and tax payment/refund cycles
   - Wage and salary payment dates
   - School hours and vacation
   - Seasonal changes in climate
   - Occurrence of public or religious holidays
   - Natural cycles, such as coastal tides
3. **Do demand levels seem to change randomly?**
   If so, could the underlying causes be
   - Day-to-day changes in the weather
   - Health events whose occurrence cannot be pinpointed exactly
   - Accidents, fires, and certain criminal activities
   - Natural disasters (e.g., earthquakes, storms, mudslides, and volcanic eruptions)
4. **Can demand for a particular service over time be disaggregated by market segment to reflect such components as follows?**
   - Use patterns by a particular type of customer or for a particular purpose
   - Variations in the net profitability of each completed transaction

For example, demand levels for public transport may vary by time of day (highest during commute hours), day of week (less travel to work on weekends but more leisure travel), and season of year (more travel by tourists in summer) (Figure 9.12). The demand for service during the peak period on a Monday in summer is likely to be very different from the demand during the peak period on a Saturday in winter. This shows day-of-week and seasonal variations at the same time. No strategy for smoothing demand is likely to succeed unless the firm understands why customers from a market segment choose to use the service when they do. For example, if you try to get commuters to shift their travel to off-peak periods, it is likely to fail. This is because travel is determined by people's employment hours.

Keeping good records of each transaction helps a lot when it comes to analyzing demand patterns based on past experience. Queuing systems supported by sophisticated software can automatically track customer consumption patterns by type of customer, service requested, and date and time of day. Where it is relevant, it is also useful to record weather conditions and other special factors (a strike, an accident, a big convention in town, a price change, the launch of a competing service, etc.) that might have influenced demand.

Figure 9.12 In summer, many tourists flock to Cologne, Germany, to take in its rich heritage.

LO 6

Be familiar with the five basic ways to *manage demand.*

MANAGING DEMAND

Once we have understood the demand patterns of the different market segments, we can manage demand. There are five basic approaches to managing demand:

- *Take no action and leave demand to find its own levels.*
- *Reduce demand in peak periods.*
- *Increase demand in low periods.*
- *Inventory demand using a queuing system.*
- *Inventory demand using a reservation system.*

Table 9.2 links these five approaches to the two problems of excess demand and excess capacity. Many service businesses face both situations at different points in the cycle of demand and should consider use of the strategies described. Next in this section, we will discuss how marketing mix elements can help to shape demand levels. This is followed by two sections on how to inventory demand through waiting lines and queuing systems, and then through reservation systems.

LO 7

Understand how to use the marketing mix elements of price, product, place, and promotion to smooth out fluctuations in demand.

Marketing Mix Elements Can Be Used to Shape Demand Patterns

Several marketing mix variables can be used to encourage demand during periods of excess capacity and to decrease or shift demand during periods when there is a lack of capacity. Price often is the first variable to be proposed for bringing demand and supply into balance (Figure 9.13). However, changes in product, distribution strategy, and communication efforts can also be used to reshape demand patterns. Although we discuss each element separately here, effective demand management efforts often require changes in two or more elements at the same time.

Use Price and Nonmonetary Costs to Manage Demand

One of the most direct ways to balance supply and demand is through the use of pricing. Nonmonetary costs, too, may have a similar effect. For instance, if customers learn they are likely to face increased time and effort costs during peak periods, those who dislike spending time waiting in crowded and unpleasant conditions will try to come during less busy times. Similarly, cheaper prices may encourage at least some people to change the timing of their behavior, whether it is for shopping, travel, or sending in equipment for repair.

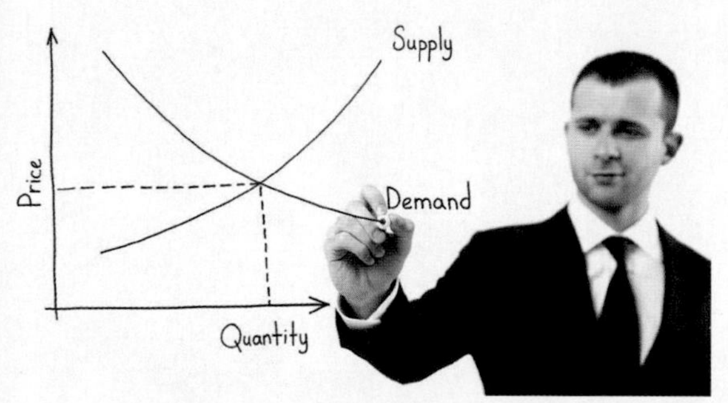

Figure 9.13 Managers are instrumental in pricing a product or service.

For the monetary price of a service to be effective as a demand management tool, managers must have some sense of the shape and slope of a product's demand curve. They must understand how the quantity of service demanded responds to changes in the price per unit at a particular point in time. It's also important to determine whether the demand curve for a specific service varies sharply from one time period to another. For instance, will the same person be willing to pay more for a weekend stay in a hotel on Cape Cod in summer than in winter (when the weather can be freezing)? The answer is probably "yes." If so, very different pricing schemes may be needed to fill capacity in each time period.

Table 9.2 Alternate demand management strategies for different capacity situations

	CAPACITY SITUATION	
Approaches to Manage Demand	**Insufficient Capacity (Excess Demand)**	**Excess Capacity (Insufficient Demand)**
Take no action	• Unorganized queuing results (may irritate customers and discourage future use)	• Capacity is wasted (customers may have a disappointing experience for services such as theater)
Reduce demand	• Higher prices will increase profits • Change product elements (e.g., don't offer time-consuming services during peak times) • Modify time and place of delivery (e.g., extend opening hours) • Communication can encourage use in other time slots (can this effort be focused on less profitable and less desirable segments?)	• Take no action (but see preceding)
Increase demand	• Take no action unless opportunities exist to stimulate (and give priority to) more profitable segments	• Lower prices selectively (try to avoid cannibalizing existing business; ensure that all relevant costs are covered) • Change product elements (find alternative value propositions for service during low seasons) • Use communications and variation in products and distribution (but recognize extra costs, if any, and make sure that appropriate trade-offs are made between profitability and use levels)
Inventory demand by a formalized queuing system	• Match the appropriate queue configuration to the service process • Consider a priority system for most desirable segments and make other customers shift to off-peak periods • Consider separate queues based on urgency, duration, and premium pricing of service • Shorten customers' perceptions of waiting time and make their waits more comfortable	• Not applicable
Inventory demand by reservation system	• Focus on yield and reserve capacity for less price-sensitive customers • Consider a priority system for important segments • Make other customers shift to off-peak periods	• Clarify that capacity is available and let customers make reservations at their preferred time slots.

PART III

Figure 9.14 Bed and breakfast inns are dependent on the seasonal tide of tourists.

When capacity is limited, however, the goal in a profit-seeking business should be to make as much use of the capacity as possible for the most profitable segments at any given time. Capacity availability will be prioritized for the firm's most valuable segments. Airlines, for instance, hold a certain number of seats for business passengers paying full fare and place many conditions on fares for tourists (using non-physical rate fences such as requiring advance purchase and a Saturday night's stay). This is to prevent business travelers from taking advantage of cheap fares designed to attract tourists who can help fill the aircraft. Pricing strategies of this nature are known as *revenue management* and are discussed in Chapter 6.

Change Product Elements

Sometimes, pricing alone will be ineffective in managing demand. The Opening Vignette is a good case in point. If there is no snow for skiing opportunities, no skiers would buy lift tickets for use on a midsummer day at any price. It is the same for a variety of other seasonal businesses (Figure 9.14). Thus, educational institutions offer weekend and summer programs for adults and senior citizens. Small pleasure boats offer cruises in the summer and a dockside venue for private functions in winter months. These firms recognize that no amount of price discounting is likely to bring in business out of season. Therefore, a new service product targeted at different segments is needed to encourage demand.

During the course of a 24-hour period, there can be product variations. Some restaurants provide a good example of this. They change menus and levels of service at different times of the day, vary lighting and decor, and open or close the bar. The goal is to appeal to different needs within the same group of customers, to reach out to different customer segments, or to do both, according to the time of day. Product elements can also be changed to increase capacity during peak periods. For example, the lunch menu is designed to contain only dishes that are fast to prepare during the busy lunch period.

Modify the Place and Time of Delivery

Rather than trying to change demand for a service that continues to be offered at the same time in the same place, firms can also change the time and place of delivery. The following basic options are available:

- *Vary the times when the service is available.* This strategy shows changing customer preference by day of week, by season, and so on. For example, people usually have more time to watch movies on weekends. Therefore, there are more time slots for shows on weekends than on weekdays. Similarly, retailers also tend to stay open till later on Fridays and Saturdays as there are more shoppers on those days. Shops may also extend their hours in the days leading up to Christmas or during school holiday periods.
- *Offer the service to customers at a new location.* One approach is to operate mobile units that take the service to customers, rather than requiring them to visit fixed-site service locations. Traveling libraries, mobile car wash services, in-office tailoring services, home-delivered meals and catering services, and vans equipped with primary-care medical facilities are examples of this. A cleaning and repair firm that wishes to generate business during low-demand periods might offer free pickup and delivery of movable items that need servicing.

Promotion and Education

Even if the other variables of the marketing mix remain unchanged, communication efforts alone may be able to help smooth demand. Signage, advertising, publicity, and sales messages can be used to educate customers about the timing of peak periods and encourage them to make use of the service at off-peak times when there will be fewer delays.[4] Examples include US Postal Service requests to "Mail Early for Christmas," and communications from sales reps to industrial maintenance firms advising customers of periods when preventive maintenance work can be done quickly. In addition, management can ask service personnel (or intermediaries such as travel agents) to encourage customers with flexible schedules to favor off-peak periods.

Changes in pricing, product characteristics, and distribution must be communicated clearly. If a firm wants to obtain a particular response to variations in marketing mix elements, it must, of course, inform customers fully about their choices. As discussed in Chapter 7, short-term promotions that combine both pricing and communication elements, as well as other incentives, may provide customers with attractive incentives to shift the timing of service usage.

Not all demand is desirable. Some demands are unrelated to a firm's service or take up more of the firm's service capacity than is desired. Such undesirable demand can be discouraged through education and communication. Discouraging undesirable demand may help to keep peak demand levels within the service capacity of the organization. For example, Service Insights 9.1 shows how a marketing campaign was used to reduce undesirable demand for emergency services and free up capacity. Many calls to 911 numbers are not really problems that fire, police, or ambulance services should be solving. Such calls make it difficult for the organization to respond to the real needs of its target customers.

PART III

SERVICE INSIGHTS 9.1

Discouraging Demand for Non-emergency Calls

Have you ever wondered what it's like to be the person who sends out the emergency vehicles for an emergency telephone service such as 911? People differ widely in what they consider to be an emergency.

Imagine yourself in the huge communications room at Police Headquarters in New York. A gray-haired sergeant is talking patiently by phone to a woman who has dialed 911 because her cat has run up a tree and she's afraid it's stuck there. "Ma'am, have you ever seen a cat skeleton in a tree?" the sergeant asks her. "All those cats get down somehow, don't they?" After the woman has hung up, the sergeant turns to a visitor and shrugs. "These kinds of calls keep pouring in," he says. "What can you do?" The trouble is, when people call the emergency number with complaints about noisy parties next door, pleas to rescue cats, or requests to turn off leaking fire hydrants, they may be slowing response times to fires, heart attacks, or violent crimes.

At one point, the situation in New York City got so bad that officials were forced to develop a marketing campaign to discourage people from making inappropriate requests for emergency assistance through the 911 number. The problem was that, what might seem like an emergency to the caller—a beloved cat stuck up a tree, a noisy party that was preventing a tired person from getting needed sleep—was not a life- (or property-) threatening situation of the type that the city's emergency services should be called on to solve. So a communications campaign, using a variety of media, was developed to urge people not to call 911 unless they were reporting a *dangerous emergency*. For help in resolving other problems, they were asked to call their local police station or other city agencies.

 **LO 8**

Know how to use waiting lines and queuing systems to inventory demand.

INVENTORY DEMAND THROUGH WAITING LINES AND QUEUING SYSTEMS

One of the challenges of services is that they cannot normally be stored for later use. A hairstylist cannot pre-package a haircut for the following day; it must be done in real time. In an ideal world, nobody would ever have to wait to conduct a service transaction. However, firms cannot afford to provide a lot of extra capacity that would not be used most of the time.

In businesses where demand regularly exceeds supply, managers often can take steps to inventory demand. This task can be achieved in one of two ways: (1) by asking customers to wait in line—usually on a first-come, first-served basis, or (2) by offering customers the opportunity to reserve or book space in advance. However, it should be noted that if the queuing and reservation systems are in place at the same time, customers waiting in a queue might feel that it is unfair that they have to queue, and the others just jump queue because they had made a reservation earlier. Hence, it may not be advisable to use both systems at the same time, unless the perceptions of unfairness are carefully managed. We will discuss wait line and queuing systems in this section, and reservation systems in the next.

Waiting Occurs Everywhere

Waiting is something that occurs everywhere. Nobody likes to wait or to be kept waiting (Figure 9.15). It's boring, time wasting, and sometimes physically uncomfortable, especially if there is nowhere to sit or if you are outdoors. Almost every organization faces the problem of waiting lines somewhere in its operation. People are kept waiting on the phone, listening to recorded messages like "your call is important to us." They line up with their supermarket carts to check out their grocery purchases, and they wait for their bills after a restaurant meal. They sit in their cars waiting to enter drive-in car washes and to pay at toll booths.

Physical objects wait for processing, too. Customers' e-mails sit in customer service staff's inboxes, appliances wait to be repaired, and checks wait to be cleared at a bank.

Figure 9.15 Hertz helps its customers to avoid the time and hassle of waiting in line.

In each instance, a customer may be waiting for the outcome of that work—an answer to an e-mail, an appliance that is working again, and a check credited to a customer's balance.

Managing Waiting Lines

The problem of reducing customer waiting time often requires a variety of approaches. Increasing capacity by adding more space or more staff is not always the best solution in situations where customer satisfaction must be balanced against cost considerations. Managers should consider a variety of ways, including:

1. Rethinking the design of the queuing system.
2. Installing a reservations system.
3. Tailoring the queuing system to different market segments.
4. Managing customers' behavior and their perceptions of the wait.
5. Redesigning processes to shorten the time of each transaction.

Points 1 to 4 are discussed in the next few sections of this chapter. Point 5 is discussed in Chapter 8 on customer service process redesign. Disneyland, called "The Happiest Place on Earth," has taken the business of managing wait lines very seriously (see Service Insights 9.2).

SERVICE INSIGHTS 9.2

Disney Turns Queue Management into a Science

Have you ever been in a queue at Disneyland? Very often, we may not realize how long we have been waiting, as there are many sights to see while we queue. We may be watching a video, looking at other customers enjoying themselves, or reading the various posters on the wall. As our waiting time is occupied, we may not realize that a long time has passed.

Disney has taken the management of waiting lines to another level. At Walt Disney World, there is a Disney Operational Command Center, where the technicians are monitoring queues throughout the theme park to make sure that they are not too long and people are moving along. To them, patience is not a virtue in the theme park business. Inside the Command Center, computer programs, video cameras, digital maps of the park, and other tools help technicians to spot where there might be queues that are too long. Once there is a wait problem, they will send a staff to fix the problem immediately.

A wait problem may be dealt with in several ways. For example, they may send a Disney character to entertain the waiting customers. Alternatively, they can deploy more capacity. If there is a long queue for a boat ride, then they will deploy more boats so that the queue moves faster. Since Disney World is divided into different "lands," if there is less crowd in one land compared to another, they may reroute a mini-parade toward that area, so that the crowds will follow and the crowd distribution becomes more even. They have also added video games to wait areas.

With the Command Center in place, they have managed to increase the average number of rides that a visitor to Magic Kingdom normally takes, from nine rides to ten rides. Disney continues to experiment with different types of technology to help them manage customer waiting time. They are experimenting with smartphone technology at the moment to see how it can be used to help them to manage waiting lines. Disney does all this in the hope that customers will not be frustrated by the waits, and will return more often.

SOURCE

Brooks Barnes, "Disney Tackles Major Theme Park Problem: Lines," *The New York Times*, December 27, 2010, http://www.nytimes.com/2010/12/28/business/media/28disney.html, accessed March 12, 2012.

Different Queue Configurations

There are different types of queues, and the challenge for managers is to select the most suitable type. Figure 9.16 shows diagrams of several types you have probably experienced yourself.

- In *single line, sequential stages,* customers proceed through several serving operations, as in a cafeteria. Some stages, however, may take longer to process than previous stages. Many cafeterias have lines at the cash register because the cashier takes longer to calculate how much you owe and to return change than the servers take to place food on your plate.
- *Parallel lines to multiple servers* offer more than one serving station. This allows customers to select one of several lines in which to wait. Banks and ticket windows are common examples. The disadvantage of this design is that lines may not move at equal speed. Have you ever chosen what looked like the shortest queue, only to watch in frustration as other queues moved at twice the speed of yours, just because someone in your line has a complicated transaction?

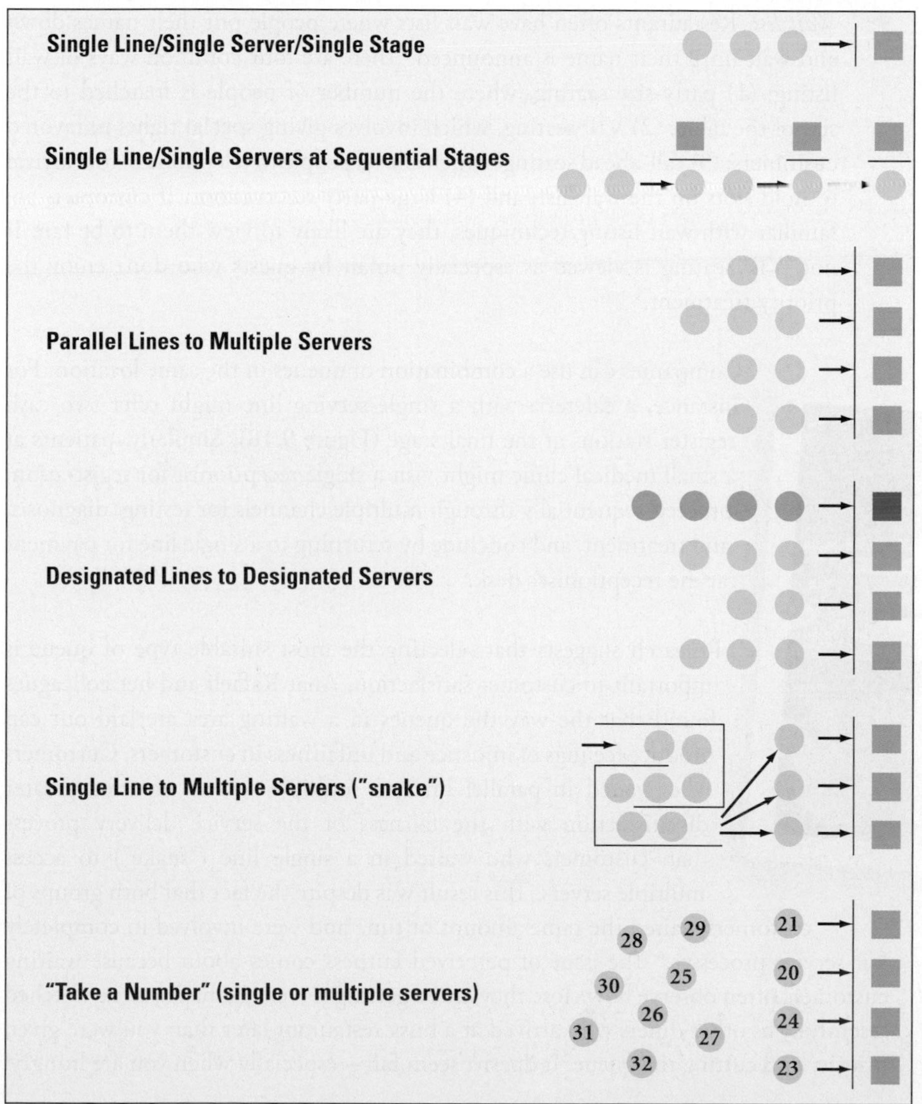

Figure 9.16 Alternative queue configurations.

PART III

Figure 9.17 Post offices use the single line to multiple servers approach to control human traffic.

- A *single line to multiple servers*, commonly known as a "snake," This type of waiting line solves the problem of the parallel lines to multiple servers moving at different speeds. This method is commonly used at post offices and airport check-ins (Figure 9.17).
- *Designated lines* involve assigning different lines to categories of customers. Examples include express lines (for instance, for 12 items or less) and regular lines at supermarket check-outs, and different check-in stations for first-class, business-class, and economy-class airline passengers.
- *Take a number* saves customers the need to stand in a queue. This procedure allows them to sit down and relax (if seating is available) or to guess how long the wait will be and do something else in the meantime. Of course, customers then risk losing their place if earlier customers are served faster than expected. Users of this method include large travel agents, government offices, and outpatient clinics in hospitals.
- *Wait list.* Restaurants often have wait lists where people put their names down and wait until their name is announced. There are four common ways of wait listing: (1) party-size seating, where the number of people is matched to the size of the table; (2) VIP seating, which involves giving special rights to favored customers; (3) call-ahead seating, which allows people to telephone before arrival to hold slots on the wait list; and (4) large-party reservations. If customers are familiar with wait listing techniques, they are likely to view them to be fair. If not, VIP seating is viewed as especially unfair by guests who don't enjoy the priority treatment.[5]

Figure 9.18 Single queuing systems in cafés usually have more than one cash register stations.

Companies can use a combination of queues in the same location. For instance, a cafeteria with a single serving line might offer two cash register stations at the final stage (Figure 9.18). Similarly, patients at a small medical clinic might visit a single receptionist for registration, proceed sequentially through multiple channels for testing, diagnosis, and treatment, and conclude by returning to a single line for payment at the receptionist's desk.

Research suggests that selecting the most suitable type of queue is important to customer satisfaction. Anat Rafaeli and her colleagues found that the way the queues in a waiting area are laid out can produce feelings of injustice and unfairness in customers. Customers who waited in parallel lines to multiple servers reported greater dissatisfaction with the fairness of the service delivery process than customers who waited in a single line ("snake") to access multiple servers. This result was despite the fact that both groups of customers waited the same amount of time and were involved in completely fair service processes.[6] The issue of perceived fairness comes about because waiting customers often observe how close they are to getting served. Perhaps you've watched resentfully as other diners who arrived at a busy restaurant later than you were given priority and cutting the queue. It doesn't seem fair—especially when you are hungry!

Virtual Waits

One of the problems of waiting in line is the waste of customers' time. The "virtual queue" strategy is a creative way of taking the physical waiting out of the wait altogether. Instead, customers register their place in line on a computer, which estimates the time at which they will reach the front of the virtual line and should return to claim their place.[7] Service Insights 9.3 describes the virtual queuing systems used in two very different industries: a theme park and a call center.

SERVICE INSIGHTS 9.3

Waiting in a Virtual Queue

Disney is well-known for its efforts to give visitors to its theme parks information on how long they may have to wait to ride a particular attraction and for entertaining guests while they are waiting in line. However, the company found that the long waits at its most popular attractions were still a major source of dissatisfaction, and so created an innovative solution.

The virtual queue concept was first tested at Disney World. At the most popular attractions, guests were able to register their place in line with a computer and were then free to use the wait time visiting other places in the park. Surveys showed that guests who used the new system spent more money, saw more attractions, and had significantly higher satisfaction. After further refinement, the system—now named Fastpass—was introduced at the five most popular attractions at Disney World and subsequently extended to all Disney theme parks worldwide. It is now used by more than 50 million guests a year.

Fastpass is easy to use. When guests approach a Fastpass attraction, they are given two clear choices: obtain a Fastpass ticket there and return at the appointed time, or wait in a standby line. Signs indicate how long the wait is in each instance. To use the Fastpass option, guests insert their park admission tickets into a special turnstile and receive Fastpass tickets stating return times. Guests have some flexibility because the system allows them a 60-minute window beyond the printed return time.

Just like the Fastpass system, call centers also use virtual queues. There are different types of virtual queuing systems for call centers. The first-in, first-out queuing system is very common. When callers call in, they will hear a message that informs them of the estimated wait time for the call to be taken by an agent. The caller can (1) wait in the queue and get connected to an agent when his turn arrives, or (2) choose to receive a callback. When the caller chooses this option, he has to enter his telephone number and tell his name. He then hangs up the phone. However, his virtual place in the queue is kept. When he is nearly at the head of the queue, the system calls the customer back and puts him at the head of the queue where an agent will attend to him next. In both situations, the customer is unlikely to complain. In the first situation, it is their choice to wait in the queue, and the person can still do something else as he already knows the estimated wait time. In the second situation, the person does not have to wait for very long before reaching an agent. The call center also benefits because there are fewer frustrated customers that may take up the valuable time of the agents by complaining about how long they have to wait. In addition, firms also reduce aborted or missed calls from customers.

SOURCE

Duncan Dickson, Robert C. Ford, and Bruce Laval, "Managing Real and Virtual Waits in Hospitality and Service Organizations," *Cornell Hotel and Restaurant Administration Quarterly* 46, February 2005, 52–68; "Virtual Queue," Wikipedia, www.en.wikipeidao.org/wiki/virtual_queuing, accessed March 12, 2012.

PART III

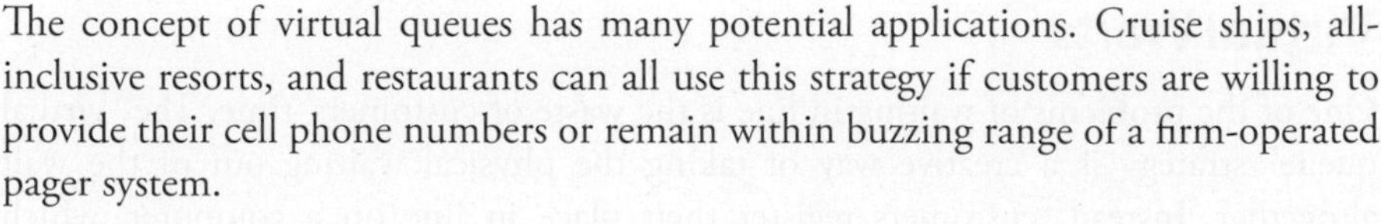

The concept of virtual queues has many potential applications. Cruise ships, all-inclusive resorts, and restaurants can all use this strategy if customers are willing to provide their cell phone numbers or remain within buzzing range of a firm-operated pager system.

Queuing Systems Can Be Tailored to Market Segments

Although the basic rule in most queuing systems is "first come, first served," not all queuing systems are organized in that way. Market segmentation is sometimes used to design queuing strategies for different types of customers. Allocation to separate queuing areas may be based on any of the following:

- ***Urgency of the job.*** At many hospital emergency units, a nurse is assigned to greet incoming patient and decide which patients require priority medical treatment and which patients can safely be asked to register and then sit down while they wait for their turn.
- ***Duration of service transaction.*** Banks, supermarkets, and other retail services often have "express lanes" for shorter, less complicated tasks.
- ***Payment of a premium price.*** Airlines usually offer separate check-in lines for first-class and economy-class passengers. There are also more staff attending to passengers in the first-class line, resulting in reduced waits for those who have paid more for their tickets. At some airports, premium passengers may also enjoy faster lanes for the security check.
- ***Importance of the customer.*** Members of frequent flyer clubs frequently get priority wait-listing. For example, the next seat that becomes available is given to a platinum card holder of the airline's loyalty program. These members can also jump the queue with priority access to call centers. Even when traveling economy class, members of frequent flyer clubs can use the shorter business-class check-in lines.

LO 9

Understand how customers perceive waits and how to make waiting less burdensome for them.

CUSTOMER PERCEPTIONS OF WAITING TIME

People don't like wasting their time on unproductive activities any more than they like wasting money. Customer dissatisfaction with delays in receiving service often can stimulate strong emotions, even anger.[8] In fact, it has been found that if customers are dissatisfied with the wait, they must be more satisfied with the service to have the same level of loyalty as customers who were satisfied with the wait.[9]

Figure 9.19 While waiting, time can seem to pass very slowly.

The Psychology of Waiting Time

Service marketers recognize that customers experience waiting time in different ways, depending on the circumstances. Why are some people willing to wait for 50% of their time at an amusement park, but complain if they have to wait for 20 minutes for a taxi? David Maister and other researchers have the following suggestions on how to use the psychology of waiting to make waits less stressful and unpleasant for customers (Figure 9.19).[10]

- ***Unoccupied time feels longer than occupied time.*** When you are sitting around with nothing to do, time seems to crawl. Service firms should give customers something to do or to distract them while waiting so they are less bored (Figure 9.20). For example, BMW car owners can wait in comfort in BMW service centers where waiting areas are furnished with designer furniture, plasma TVs, Wi-Fi hotspots, magazines, and freshly brewed cappuccinos. Many customers even bring their own entertainment in the form of a cell phone with messaging and games, or an iPad.

Figure 9.20 Keeping occupied by reading magazines will make the wait for the spa treatment feel shorter.

- ***Solo waits feel longer than group waits.*** It is nice to wait with people whom you know. Talking to friends is one way of helping to pass the time while waiting.
- ***Physically uncomfortable waits feel longer than comfortable waits.*** "My feet are killing me!" is one of the most often heard comments when people are forced to stand in line for a long time. Whether they are seated or standing, waiting is unpleasant if the temperature is too hot or too cold, or if there's no protection from rain or snow.
- ***Pre- and post-process waits feel longer than in-process waits.*** Waiting to buy a ticket to enter a theme park is different from waiting to ride on a roller coaster once you're in the park.
- ***Unfair waits are longer than equitable waits.*** Perceptions about what is fair or unfair sometimes vary from one culture or country to another. In the United States, Canada, or Britain, for example, people expect everybody to wait their turn in line and are likely to get irritated if they see others jumping ahead or being given priority for what seems to be no good reason. When people perceive that waiting is fair, it reduces the negative effect of waiting.
- ***Unfamiliar waits seem longer than familiar ones.*** People who use a service often know what to expect and are less likely to worry while waiting. New or occasional users will often wonder not only about the length of the wait but also about what will happen next.
- ***Uncertain waits are longer than known, finite waits.*** Although any wait may be frustrating, we usually can adjust if they know how long they are expected to wait. Imagine waiting for a delayed flight and not being told how long the delay is going to be (Figure 9.21). You don't know whether you have the time to get up and walk about in the terminal or whether to stay at the gate in case the flight is called any minute.
- ***Unexplained waits are longer than explained waits.*** Have you ever been in a subway or an elevator that has stopped for no apparent reason, without anyone telling you why? In addition to uncertainty about the length of the wait, there's added worry about what is going to happen. Has there been an accident on the line? Will you be stuck for hours with strangers?
- ***Anxiety makes waits seem longer.*** Can you remember waiting for someone to show up at the arranged meeting time, and worrying about whether you had gotten the time or location correct? While waiting in unfamiliar locations, especially outdoors and at night, people often worry about their personal safety.
- ***The more valuable or important the service, the longer people will wait.*** People will often queue up overnight under uncomfortable conditions to get good seats to a major concert or sports event that is expected to sell out fast.

Figure 9.21 Uncertain wait for a delayed flight can cause frustration.

PART III

 LO 10

Know how to use reservation systems to inventory demand.

INVENTORY DEMAND THROUGH RESERVATION SYSTEMS

As an alternative, or in addition, to waiting lines, reservation systems can be used to inventory demand (Figure 9.22). Ask someone what services come to mind when you talk about reservations and, most likely, they will cite airlines, hotels, restaurants, car rentals, and theaters. Suggest terms with similar meanings as "bookings" or "appointments" and they may add haircuts, visits to professionals such as doctors and consultants, vacation rentals, and service calls to fix anything from a broken refrigerator to a neurotic laptop. There are many benefits in having a reservation system:

Figure 9.22 Most libraries have a reservation system for books, magazines and audio-visual materials.

- Customer dissatisfaction due to excessive waits can be avoided. One aim of reservations is to guarantee that service will be available when customers want it. Customers who hold reservations should be able to avoid queues because they have been guaranteed service at a specific time.
- Reservations allow demand to be controlled and smoothed out in a more manageable way. A well-organized reservation system allows the organization to change demand for service from a first-choice time to earlier or later times, from one class of service to another ("upgrades" and "downgrades"), and even from first-choice locations to alternative ones. In this way, there can be higher capacity utilization.
- Reservation systems allow the implementation of revenue management and preselling of a service to different customer segments (see Chapter 6 on revenue management). For example, requiring reservations for normal repair and maintenance allows management to make sure that some time will be kept free for handling emergency jobs. Since these are unpredictable, higher prices can be charged and these bring with them higher margins.
- Data from reservation systems also help organizations to prepare operational and financial projections for future periods. Systems vary from a simple appointment book using handwritten entries for a doctor's office, to a central, computerized data bank for an airline's global operations.

The challenge in designing reservation systems is to make them fast and user friendly for both staff and customers. Many firms now allow customers to make their own reservations on a self-service basis via their websites. Whether talking with a reservation agent or making their own bookings, customers want quick answers about whether a service is available at a preferred time and at what price. They also appreciate it if the system can provide further information about the type of service they are reserving. For instance, can a hotel assign a specific room on request? Or can it at least assign a room with a view of the lake rather than one with a view of the parking lot? Some businesses now, in fact, charge a fee for making a reservation (see Service Insights 9.4). Northwest Airlines charges $15 to reserve some of the most desirable economy class seats, and Air Canada charges $12 for advanced seat reservations on certain flights.[11]

Of course, problems arise when customers fail to show or when service firms overbook. Marketing strategies for dealing with these operational problems include

SERVICE INSIGHTS 9.4

Pay to Get That Hard-to-Get Table Reservation!

PrimeTimeTables is an exclusive online company that helps customers to get table reservations. What is so special about that? Well, PrimeTimeTables is able to get reservations at the most popular dining spots, where only people who are somebody or have the right connections can secure a table. Many of those reservations are not open to the ordinary diner. The company is able to get a table on a specific day—and on short notice. Currently, the company focuses on areas where it is difficult to get reservations, namely New York City, Philadelphia, and the Hamptons. Individuals pay a membership fee of $500 to join and $45 for each reservation made.

Pascal Riffaud, the entrepreneur behind this idea, is the president of Personal Concierge International, a leading company providing exclusive concierge services in the United States. During his work experience as President of Personal Concierge, Riffaud built a large network of contacts with exclusive restaurants, allowing him to obtain those hard-to-get reservations.

His clients were delighted with his service and kept flooding him with requests for reservations. However, there have been protests from restaurant owners who feel he is upsetting their reservations management systems and selling their tables. Even though Riffaud does cancel unsold reservations, restaurant owners feel these could have been sold to other customers who really wanted a table. Restaurants may have to rethink the way they handle reservations!

SOURCE

K. Severson, "Now, for $45, an Insider's Access to Hot Tables," *The New York Times*, 31, January 2007, available: http://www.primetimetables.com, accessed March 12, 2012.

requiring a deposit, canceling non-paid reservations after a certain time, and providing compensation to victims of overbooking (see Chapter 6 on revenue management).

Reservation Strategies Should Focus on Yield

Increasingly, service firms are looking at their "yield"—that is, the average revenue received per unit of capacity. The aim is to increase this yield in order to improve profitability. As noted in Chapter 6, revenue management strategies that achieve this goal are widely used in such industries with relatively fixed capacity like passenger airlines, hotels, and car rentals. Revenue management systems based on mathematical modeling are of greatest value for service firms that find it expensive to modify their capacity but incur relatively low costs when they sell another unit of available capacity.[12]

Yield analysis forces managers to recognize the opportunity cost of selling capacity for a given date to a customer from one market segment when another might subsequently yield a higher rate. Think about the following problems facing sales managers for different types of service organizations with capacity limitations:

- Should a hotel accept an advance booking from a tour group of 200 room nights at $140 each when some of these same room nights might possibly be sold later at short notice to business travelers at the full posted rate of $300?
- Should a railroad with 30 empty freight cars accept an immediate request for a shipment worth $1,400 per car, or hold the cars for a few more days in the hope of getting priority shipment that would be twice as valuable?
- Should a print shop process all jobs on a first-come, first-served basis, with a guaranteed delivery time for each job, or should it charge a premium rate for "rush" work, and tell customers with "standard" jobs to expect some variability in completion dates?

Decisions on such problems need to be handled with information. Good information, based on detailed recordkeeping of past usage and supported by current market intelligence, is the key to allocating the inventory of capacity among different segments. The decision to accept or reject business should be based on realistic estimates of the probabilities of obtaining higher-rated business and awareness of the need to maintain current customer relationships. Information may have to be collected through special studies, such as customer surveys or reviews of similar situations. It may also be necessary to collect information on competitive performance because changes in the capacity or strategy of competitors may require corrective action.

When new strategies are under consideration, operations researchers often can contribute useful insights by developing simulation models of the effect of changes in different variables. Such an approach is particularly useful in service "network" environments, such as theme parks and ski resorts, where customers can choose between multiple activities at the same site. Madeleine Pullman and Gary Thompson modeled customer behavior at a ski resort, where skiers can choose between different lifts and ski runs of varying lengths and levels of difficulty. Through analysis, they were able to find out the potential future effect of lift capacity upgrades (bigger or faster chairlifts), capacity expansion in the form of more land for skiing, industry growth, day-to-day price variations, customer response to information about wait times at different lifts, and changes in the customer mix.[13]

Figure 9.23 shows capacity allocation in a hotel setting. Demand from different types of customers varies not only by day of the week but also by season. These allocation decisions by segment are captured in reservation databases that are available worldwide. They tell reservation personnel when to stop accepting reservations at certain prices, even though many rooms may still remain unbooked. Loyalty program members, who are mainly business travelers, are obviously a very desirable segment (Figure 9.24).

Similar charts can be drawn for most businesses with capacity limitations. In some instances, capacity is measured in terms of seats for a given performance, seat miles, or room nights. In other instances, it may be in terms of machine time, labor time, billable professional hours, vehicle miles, or storage volume.

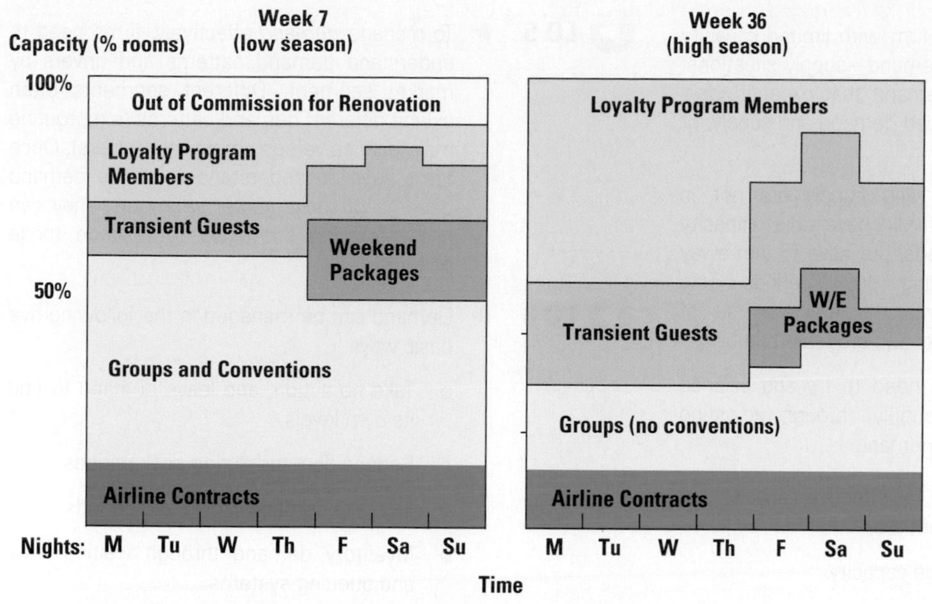

Figure 9.23 Setting capacity allocation targets by segment for a hotel.

Figure 9.24 Some banks will work with airlines to offer air mails loyalty credit card to business travelers.

PART III

CHAPTER SUMMARY

LO 1 ▶ At any one time, a firm with limited capacity can face different demand—supply situations: excess demand, demand that exceeds ideal capacity, well-balanced demand and supply, or excess capacity.

- o When demand and supply are not in balance, firms will have idle capacity during low periods, but have to turn away customers during peak periods. This situation prevents the efficient use of productive assets and erodes profitability.
- o Firms therefore need to try and balance demand and supply through adjusting capacity and/or demand.

LO 2 ▶ The building blocks for effective capacity and demand management are:

- o Define productive capacity.
- o Use capacity management tools.
- o Understand demand patterns and drivers by a customer segment.
- o Use demand management tools.

LO 3 ▶ When we refer to managing capacity, we implicitly mean *productive capacity*.

- o There are several different forms of productive capacity in services: physical facilities for processing customers; physical facilities for processing goods; physical equipment for processing people, possessions or information; and labor and infrastructure.

LO 4 ▶ *Capacity* can be managed in a number of ways, including:

- o Stretching capacity—some capacity are elastic and more people can be served with the same capacity through crowding (e.g., in a subway car), extending operating hours, or speeding up customer processing times.
- o Adjusting capacity to more closely match demand by (1) scheduling downtime during low periods, (2) cross-training employees, (3) using part-time employees, (4) inviting customers to perform self-service, (5) asking customers to share capacity, (6) designing capacity to be flexible, and (7) renting or sharing extra facilities and equipment.

LO 5 ▶ To manage *demand* effectively, firms need to understand demand patterns and drivers by market segment. Different segments often exhibit different demand patterns (e.g., routine maintenance versus emergency repairs). Once firms have an understanding of the demand patterns of their market segments, they can use marketing strategies to reshape those patterns.

LO 6 ▶ Demand can be managed in the following five basic ways:

- o Take no action, and leave demand to find its own levels.
- o Reduce demand during peak periods.
- o Increase demand during low periods.
- o Inventory demand through waiting lines and queuing systems.
- o Inventory demand through reservation systems.

LO 7 ▶ The following marketing mix elements can be used to help smooth out fluctuations in demand:

- o Use price and non-monetary customer costs to manage demand.
- o Change product elements to attract different segments at different times.
- o Modify the place and time of delivery (e.g., through extended opening hours).
- o Promotion and education (e.g., "mail early for Christmas").

LO 8 ▶ *Waiting line and queuing systems* help firms inventory demand over short periods of time. There are different types of queues with their respective advantages and applications. Queuing systems include single line with sequential stages, parallel lines to multiple servers, single line to multiple servers, designated lines, taking a number, and wait list.

Not all queuing systems are organized on a "first come, first served" basis. Rather, good systems often segment waiting customers by:

- o Urgency of the job (e.g., hospital emergency units).
- o Duration of the service transaction (e.g., express lanes).

- o Premium service based on a premium price (e.g., first-class check-in counters).
- o Importance of the customer (e.g., frequent travelers get priority wait-listing).

LO 9 ▶ Customers don't like wasting their time waiting. Firms need to understand the *psychology of waiting* and take active steps to make waiting less frustrating. We discussed 10 possible steps, including keeping customers occupied or entertained while waiting, informing customers how long the wait is likely to be, providing them with an explanation of why they have to wait, and avoiding perceptions of unfair waits.

LO 10 ▶ Effective *reservation systems* inventory demand over a longer period of time and offer several benefits. They:

- o Help to reduce or even avoid customers waiting in queues and thereby avoid dissatisfaction due to excessive waits.
- o Allow the firm to control demand and smooth it out.
- o Enable the use of revenue management to focus on increasing yield by reserving scarce capacity for higher-paying segments, rather than just selling off capacity on a first come first serve basis.

PART III

UNLOCK YOUR LEARNING

These keywords are found within the sections of each Learning Objective (LO). They are integral to understanding the services marketing concepts taught in each section. Having a firm grasp of these keywords and how they are used is essential to helping you do well on your course, and in the real and very competitive marketing scene out there.

LO 1
1 Excess capacity
2 Excess demand
3 Fixed-capacity service
4 Maximum capacity
5 Optimum capacity

LO 2
6 Building blocks
7 Manage capacity
8 Manage demand
9 Productive capacity
10 Understand demand

LO 3
11 Equipment
12 Infrastructure
13 Labor
14 Physical facilities

LO 4
15 Adjusting capacity
16 Capacity limitations
17 Chasing demand
18 Cross-train employees
19 Downtime
20 Flexible capacity
21 Part-time employees
22 Self-service
23 Stretching capacity

LO 5
24 Demand by segment
25 Demand patterns
26 Manage demand
27 Patterns of demand
28 Queuing systems
29 Seasonal

LO 6
30 Five basic approaches
31 Increase demand
32 Inventory demand
33 Managing demand
34 Queuing system
35 Reduce demand
36 Reservation system
37 Take no action
38 Waiting lines

LO 7
39 Demand management tool
40 Non-monetary costs
41 Place of delivery
42 Price
43 Product elements
44 Promotion and education
45 Time of delivery
46 Undesirable demand

LO 8
47 "Snake"
48 "Take a number"
49 Designated lines
50 Managing waiting lines
51 Multiple servers
52 Parallel lines
53 Queue configurations
54 Sequential stages
55 Single line
56 Virtual queue
57 Virtual waits
58 Wait-list

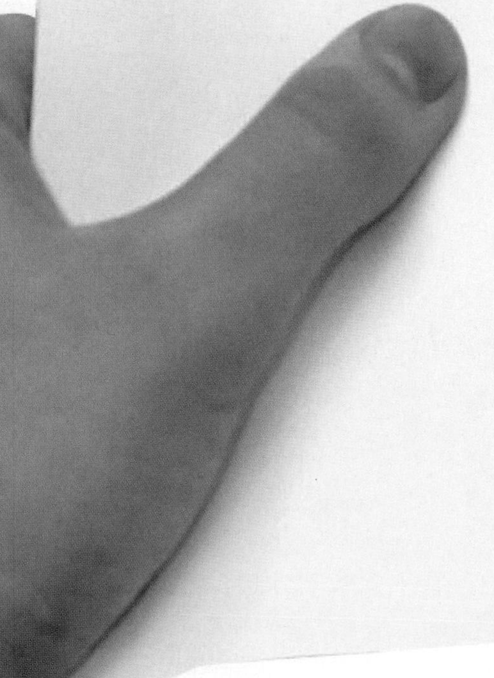

LO 9

59 Equitable waits
60 Explained waits
61 Finite waits
62 In-process waits
63 Occupied time
64 Perceptions of waiting time
65 Post-process waits
66 Pre-process waits
67 Psychology of waiting time
68 Solo waits
69 Uncertain waits
70 Unexplained waits
71 Unfair waits
72 Unfamiliar waits
73 Unoccupied time

LO 10

74 Inventory demand
75 Reservation strategies
76 Reservation systems
77 Revenue management systems
78 Yield analysis

How well do you know the language of services marketing? Quiz yourself!

PART III

Not for the academically faint-of-heart

For each keyword you are able to recall without referring to earlier pages, give yourself a point (and a pat on the back). Tally your score at the end and see if you earned the right to be called—a *services marketeer.*

SCORE

0 – 15	Services Marketing is done a great disservice.
16 – 30	The midnight oil needs to be lit, pronto.
31 – 45	I know what you *didn't* do all semester.
46 – 60	A close shave with success.
61 – 75	Now, go forth and market.
76 – 78	There should be a marketing concept named after you.

KNOW YOUR ESM

Review Questions

1. What is the difference between ideal capacity and maximum capacity? Provide examples of a situation where (a) the two might be the same and (b) the two are different.
2. Describe the building blocks for managing capacity and demand.
3. What is meant by productive capacity in services?
4. Why is capacity management particularly important for service firms?
5. What actions can firms take to adjust capacity to more closely match demand?
6. How can firms identify the factors that affect demand for their services?
7. What actions can firms take to adjust demand to more closely match capacity?
8. How can marketing mix elements be used to reshape demand patterns?
9. What are the advantages and disadvantages of the different types of queues for an organization serving large numbers of customers? For which type of service might each of the queuing types be more suitable?
10. How can firms make waiting more pleasant for their customers?
11. What are the benefits of having an effective reservation system?

WORK YOUR ESM

Application Exercises

1. Explain how flexible capacity can be created in each of the following situations: (a) a local library, (b) an office-cleaning service, (c) a technical support helpdesk, (d) an Interflora franchise.
2. Identify some specific examples of firms in your community (or region) that significantly change their product and/or marketing mix in order to increase patronage during low-demand periods.
3. Select a service organization of your choice, and identify its particular patterns of demand with reference to the checklist provided in Table 9.1 and answer: (a) What is the nature of this service organization's approach to capacity and demand management? (b) What changes would you recommend in relation to its management of capacity and demand and why?
4. Review the 10 suggestions on the psychology of waiting. Which are the most relevant in (a) a supermarket; (b) a city bus stop on a rainy, dark evening; (c) a doctor's office; and (d) a ticket line for a football game expected to be a sell-out?
5. Give examples, based on your own experience, of a reservation system that worked really well and of one that worked really badly. Identify and examine the reasons for the success and failure of these two systems. What recommendations would you make to both firms to improve (or further improve in the case of the good example) their reservation systems?

ENDNOTES

1 Kenneth J. Klassen and Thomas R. Rohleder, "Combining Operations and Marketing to Manage Capacity and Demand in Services," *The Service Industries Journal* 21, (April 2001): 1–30.

2 Breffni M. Noone, Sheryl E. Kimes, Anna S. Mattila, and Jochen Wirtz, "The Effect of Meal Pace on Customer Satisfaction," *Cornell Hospitality Quarterly* 48, no. 3 (2007): 231–245.

3 Based on material in James A. Fitzsimmons and M. J. Fitzsimmons, *Service Management: Operations, Strategy, and Information Technology*, 6th ed. New York: Irwin McGraw-Hill, 2008; W. Earl Sasser, Jr., "Match Supply and Demand in Service Industries," *Harvard Business Review* 54, (November–December 1976): 133–140

4 Kenneth J. Klassen and Thomas R. Rohleder, "Using Customer Motivations to Reduce Peak Demand: Does It Work?" *The Service Industries Journal* 24, (September 2004): 53–70.

5 Kelly A. McGuire and Sheryl E. Kimes, "The Perceived Fairness of Waitlist-Management Techniques for Restaurants," *Cornell Hotel and Restaurant Administration Quarterly* 47, (May 2006): 121–134.

6 Anat Rafaeli, G. Barron, and K. Haber, "The Effects of Queue Structure on Attitudes," *Journal of Service Research* 5, (November 2002): 125–139.

7 Duncan Dickson, Robert C. Ford, and Bruce Laval, "Managing Real and Virtual Waits in Hospitality and Service Organizations," *Cornell Hotel and Restaurant Administration Quarterly* 46, (February 2005): 52–68.

8 Ana B. Casado Diaz and Francisco J. Más Ruiz, "The Consumer's Reaction to Delays in Service," *International Journal of Service Industry Management* 13, no. 2 (2002): 118–140.

9 Frederic Bielen and Nathalie Demoulin, "Waiting Time Influence on the Satisfaction—Loyalty Relationship in Services," *Managing Service Quality* 17, no. 2 (2007): 174–193.

10 This section is based on David H. Maister, "The Psychology of Waiting Lines," in J. A. Czepiel, M. R. Solomon, and C. F. Surprenant, eds. *The Service Encounter*. Lexington (MA: Lexington Books/D.C. Heath, 1986, 113–123). Peter Jones and Emma Peppiat, "Managing Perceptions of Waiting Times in Service Queues," *International Journal of Service Industry Management* 7, no. 5 (1996): 47–61. Clay M. Voorhees, Julie Baker, Brian L. Bourdeau, E. Deanne Brocato, and J. Joseph Cronin, Jr. "Moderating the Relationships among Perceived Waiting Time, Anger and Regret," *Journal of Service Research* 12, no. 2, (November 2009): 138–155. Kelly A. McGuire, Sheryl E. Kimes, Michael Lynn, Madeline E. Pullman and Russell C. Lloyd, "A Framework for Evaluating the Customer Wait Experience," *Journal of Service Management* 21, no. 3 (2010): 269–290. Also, see the findings for wait situations in stressful service encounters such as dental appointments by Elizabeth Gelfand Miller, Barbarah E. Kahn, and Mary Frances Luce, "Consumer Wait Management Strategies for Negative Service Events: A Coping Approach," *Journal of Consumer Research* 34, no. 5 (2008): 635–648.

11 Susan Carey, "Northwest Airlines to Charge Extra for Aisle Seats," *The Wall Street Journal* March 14, 2006.

12 Sheryl E. Kimes and Richard B. Chase, "The Strategic Levers of Yield Management," *Journal of Service Research* 1, (November 1998): 156–166; Anthony Ingold, Una McMahon-Beattie, and Ian Yeoman, eds., *Yield Management Strategies for the Service Industries*, 2nd edn. London: Continuum, 2000.

13 Madeleine E. Pullman and Gary M. Thompson, "Evaluating Capacity- and Demand-Management Decisions at a Ski Resort," *Cornell Hotel and Restaurant Administration Quarterly* 43, (December 2002): 25–36; Madeleine E. Pullman and Gary Thompson, "Strategies for Integrating Capacity with Demand in Service Networks," *Journal of Service Research* 5, (February 2003): 169–183.

- ***Develop user-friendly "wayfinding" systems.*** Hospitals are complex buildings, and it is very frustrating for visitors, especially first-timers, when they cannot find their way, especially when rushing to see a loved one who has been hospitalized.
- ***Design the layout*** of patient care units and the location of nurse stations to reduce unnecessary walking within the building. This can reduce tiredness and the waste of time. In this way, the quality of patient care can be improved. Well-designed layouts also enhance staff communication and activities.

SOURCE

Ulrich, R., Quan, X., Zimring, C., Joseph, A., & Choudhary, R. (2004). The role of the physical environment in the hospital of the 21st century: A once-in-a-lifetime opportunity. Report to the center for health design for the Designing the 21st Century Hospital Project funded by the Robert Wood Johnson Foundation, (September).

 **LO 2**

Explain how environmental psychology helps us to understand customer as well as employee responses to service environments.

THE THEORY BEHIND CONSUMER RESPONSES TO SERVICE ENVIRONMENTS

We now understand why service firms take so much effort to design the service environment. But why does the service environment have such important effects on people and their behaviors? The field of environmental psychology studies how people respond to particular environments. We can apply the theories from this field to better understand and manage how customers behave in different service settings.

Feelings Are a Key Driver of Customer Responses to Service Environments

Two important models help us better understand consumer responses to service environments. The first, the Mehrabian—Russell Stimulus—Response Model shows that our feelings are central to how we respond to different elements in the environment. The second, Russell's Model of Affect, focuses on how we can better understand those feelings and their effects on response behaviors.

The Mehrabian—Russell Stimulus—Response Model

Figure 10.7 displays a simple and basic model of how people respond to environments. The environment and how people view and interpret it, whether consciously or unconsciously, influence how people feel in that setting.[7] People's feelings are the central and most important element in the model, and these drives their responses to that environment. Similar environments can lead to very different feelings and subsequent responses. For example, when we are in a rush, we may dislike being in a crowded department store with lots of other customers, find ourselves unable to get what we want as fast as we wish, and thus seek to avoid that environment. However, if we are not in a rush and feel excited about being part of the crowd during seasonal festivities in the very same environment, then we may have feelings of pleasure and excitement that would make us want to stay and enjoy the experience.

In environmental psychology, the typical outcome variable is "approach" or "avoidance" of an environment; that is, people may choose to visit or stay away from

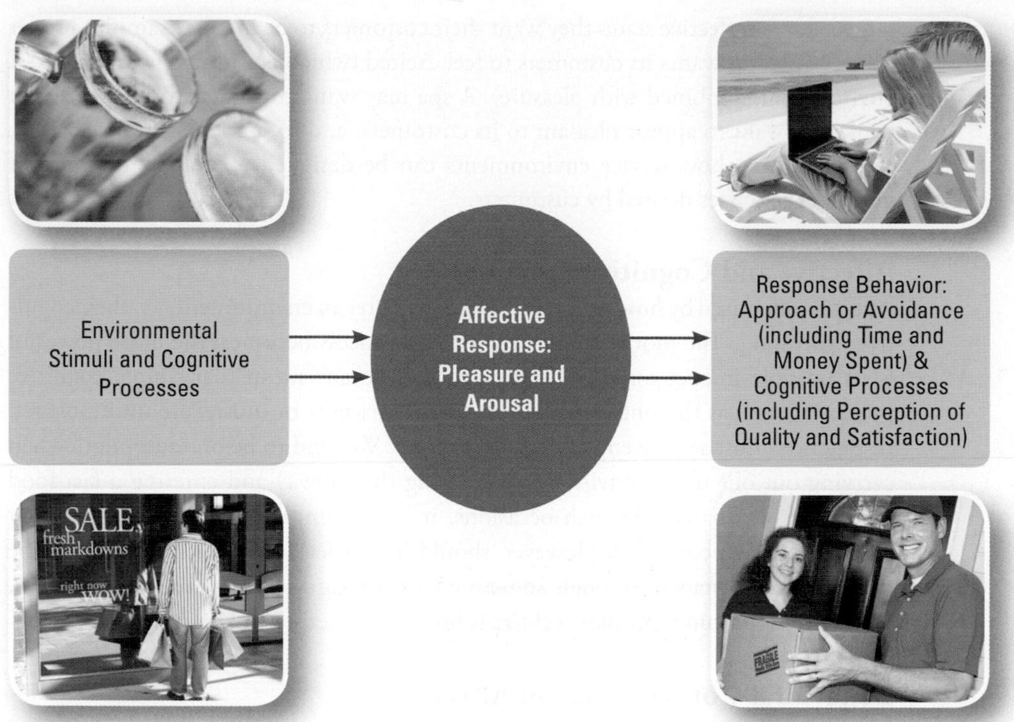

Figure 10.7 Model of environmental responses.

the servicescape. Of course, in services marketing, we can add a long list of more detailed, additional outcomes that a firm might want to manage, including how much time and money people spend, and how satisfied they are with the service experience after they have left.

Russell's Model of Affect

Since affect or feelings are central to how people respond to an environment, we need to understand those feelings better. For this, Russell's model of affect in Figure 10.8 is widely used. The model proposes that emotional responses to environments can be described along the two main dimensions of pleasure and arousal.[8] Pleasure is a direct response to the environment, depending on how much an individual likes or dislikes the environment. Arousal refers to how stimulated the individual feels, ranging from deep sleep (lowest level of internal activity) to highest level of stimulation such as when bungee jumping. Arousal depends largely on the information rate or load of an environment. For example, environments are considered to be stimulating (i.e., have a high information rate) when they are complex, have movement or change in it, and have novel and surprising elements.

Arousing
Distressing
Exciting
Unpleasant
Pleasant
Boring
Relaxing
Sleepy

Figure 10.8 The Russell model of affect.

The strength of Russell's model is its simplicity. It allows direct judgment of how customers feel while they are in a service environment. Therefore, firms can set targets for the affective states they want their customers to be in. For example, a roller coaster operator wants its customers to feel excited (which is a relatively high arousal environment combined with pleasure). A spa may want customers to feel relaxed, a bank may want to appear pleasant to its customers, and so on. Later in this chapter, we will discuss how service environments can be designed to deliver the types of service experiences desired by customers.

Affective and Cognitive Processes

Affect is influenced by how people sense and interpret an environment, i.e. their cognitive processing. The more complex a cognitive process becomes, the more powerful is its possible impact on affect. However, this doesn't mean that simple cognitive processes, such as the unconscious perception of scents or music, are unimportant. In practice, most service encounters are routine. We tend to be on "autopilot" when carrying out our usual activities such as using the subway and entering a fast-food restaurant or a bank. On such occasions, it is the simple cognitive processes that determine how people feel. However, should higher levels of cognitive processes be triggered, for instance, through something surprising in the service environment, then what determines people's feelings is how they interpret this surprise.

Behavioral Consequences of Affect

At the most basic level, pleasant environments result in approach behaviors and unpleasant ones in avoidance. Arousal increases the basic effect of pleasure on behavior. If the environment is pleasant, increasing arousal can create excitement, leading to a stronger positive response. On the other hand, if a service environment is unpleasant, increasing arousal levels would move customers into the 'distressed' region. For example, loud, fast-paced music would increase the stress levels of shoppers trying to make their way through crowded aisles on a pre-Christmas Friday evening. In such situations, retailers should try to lower the information load of the environment.

Finally, customers have strong affective expectations of some services. Think of an experience such as a romantic candlelit dinner in a restaurant, a relaxing spa visit, or an exciting time at the stadium or the dance club. When customers have strong affective expectations, it is important that the environment be designed to match those expectations.[9]

 **LO 3**

Be familiar with the integrative servicescape model.

The Servicescape Model—An Integrative Framework

Building on the basic models in environmental psychology, Mary Jo Bitner developed a comprehensive model that she named the "servicescape."[10] Figure 10.9 shows the main dimensions she identified in service environments: ambient conditions, space/functionality, and signs, symbols, and artifacts Because individuals tend to perceive these dimensions holistically, the key to effective design is how well each individual dimension fits together with everything else.

Bitner's model shows that there are customer- and employee-response moderators. This means that the same service environment can have different effects on different customers, depending on who that customer is and what she or he likes. For example, rap music may be sheer pleasure to some customer segments, and sheer torture to others.

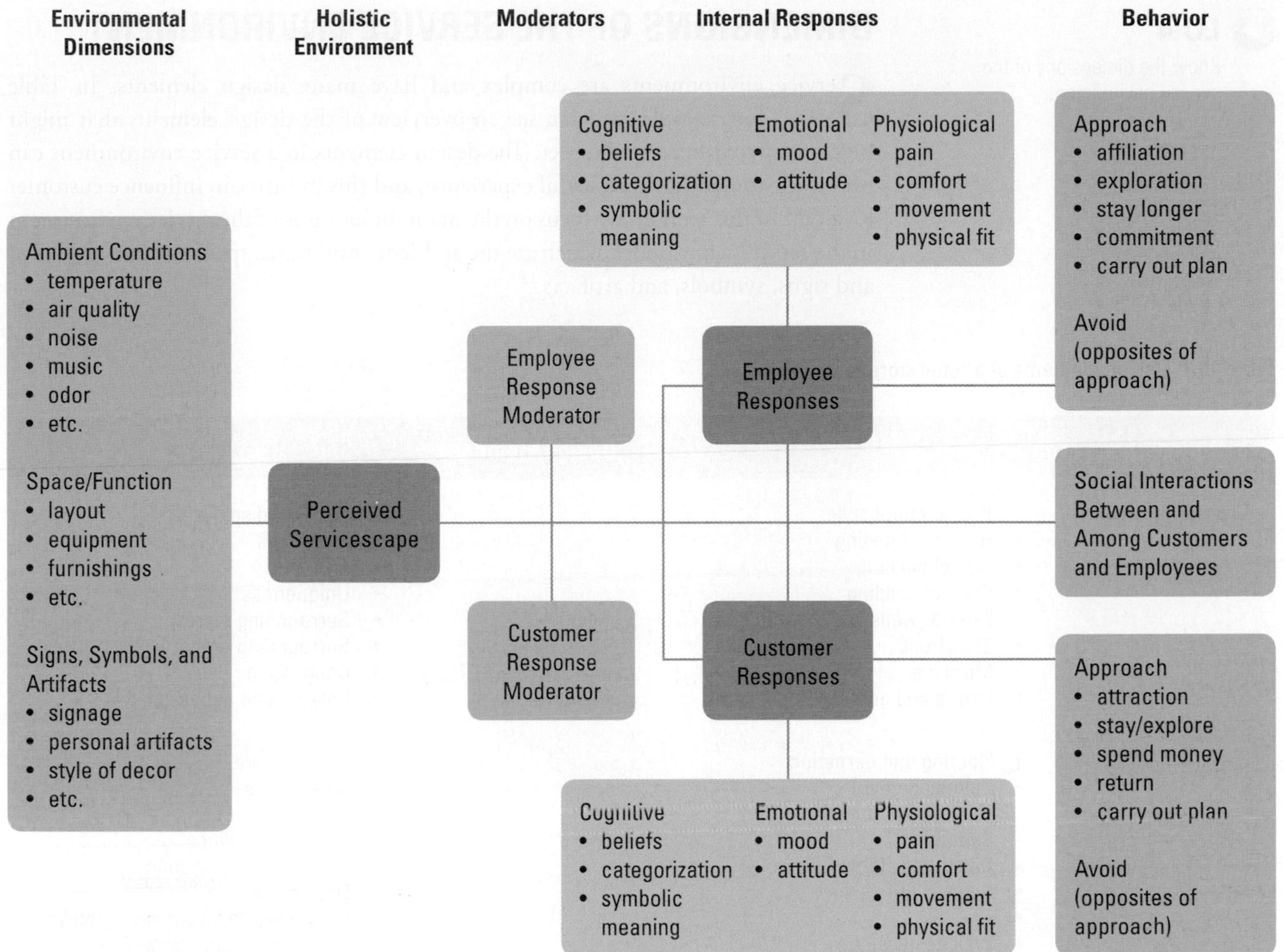

Figure 10.9 The servicescape model.

SOURCE

Bitner, M. J. (1992) "Servicescapes: The impact of physical surroundings on customers and employees," *Journal of Marketing* 56 (April): 57–71.

An important contribution of Bitner's model is the inclusion of employee responses to the service environment. After all, employees spend much more time there than customers. It is therefore important that designers become aware of how a particular environment enhances (or at least does not reduce) the productivity of frontline personnel and the quality of service that they deliver.

Internal customer and employee responses can be grouped into (1) cognitive responses (e.g., quality perceptions and beliefs), (2) emotional responses (e.g., feelings and moods), and (3) physiological responses (e.g., pain and comfort). These internal responses lead to observable behavioral responses such as avoiding a crowded supermarket, or responding positively to a relaxing environment by remaining there longer and spending extra money on impulse purchases. It's important to understand that the behavioral responses of customers and employees must be shaped in ways that aid production and purchase of high-quality services. Consider how the outcomes of service transactions may differ in situations where both customers and frontline staff feel stressed rather than relaxed and happy.

PART III

LO 4

Know the dimensions of the service environment.

DIMENSIONS OF THE SERVICE ENVIRONMENT

Service environments are complex and have many design elements. In Table 10.1, for example, you can see an overview of the design elements that might be encountered in a retail outlet. The design elements in a service environment can lead to customers having a joyful experience, and this in turn can influence customer loyalty.[11] In this section, we focus on the main dimensions of the service environment in the servicescape model, which are the ambient conditions, space and functionality, and signs, symbols, and artifacts.[12]

Table 10.1 Design elements of a retail store environment

Dimensions	Design Elements	
Exterior facilities	• Architectural style • Height of building • Size of building • Color of building • Exterior walls and exterior signs • Storefront • Marquee • Lawns and gardens	• Window displays • Entrances • Visibility • Uniqueness • Surrounding stores • Surrounding areas • Congestion • Parking and accessibility
General interior	• Flooring and carpeting • Color schemes • Lighting • Scents • Odors (e.g., tobacco smoke) • Sounds and music • Fixtures • Wall composition • Wall textures (paint, wallpaper) • Ceiling composition	• Temperature • Cleanliness • Width of aisles • Dressing facilities • Vertical transportation • Dead areas • Merchandise layout and displays • Price levels and displays • Cash register placement • Technology, modernization
Store layout	• Allocation of floor space for selling, merchandise, personnel, and customers • Placement of merchandise • Grouping of merchandise • Workstation placement • Placement of equipment • Placement of cash register	• Waiting areas • Traffic flow • Waiting queues • Furniture • Dead areas • Department locations • Arrangements within departments
Interior displays	• Point-of-purchase displays • Posters, signs, and cards • Pictures and artwork • Wall decorations • Theme setting • Ensemble	• Racks and cases • Product display • Price display • Cut cases and dump bins • Mobiles
Social dimensions	• Personnel characteristics • Employee uniforms • Crowding	• Customer characteristics • Privacy • Self-service

SOURCES

Barry Berman and Joel R. Evans, *Retail management—A Strategic Approach*, 8th ed. Upper Saddle River, NJ: Prentice Hall, 2001, 604; L. W. Turley and Ronald E. Milliman, "Atmospheric Effects on Shopping Behavior: A Review of the Experimental Literature," *Journal of Business Research* 49 (2000): 193–211.

The Effect of Ambient Conditions

LO 5

Discuss the key ambient conditions and their effects on customers.

Ambient conditions refer to the characteristics of the environment that relate to the five senses. Even when they're not consciously noticed, they may still affect a person's emotional well-being, perceptions, and even attitudes and behaviors. They are made up of hundreds of design elements and details that must work together if they are to create the desired service environment.[13] The resulting atmosphere creates a mood that is perceived and interpreted by the customer.[14] Ambient conditions are perceived both separately and holistically. They include lighting and color schemes, size and shape perceptions, sounds such as noise and music, temperature, and scents or smells (Figure 10.10). Clever design of these conditions can bring out the desired behavioral responses from consumers. Servicescapes can, in fact, be an important part of brand building for a firm.[15] Consider the new trend to transform dental clinics into relaxing dental spas, as described in Service Insights 10.2.

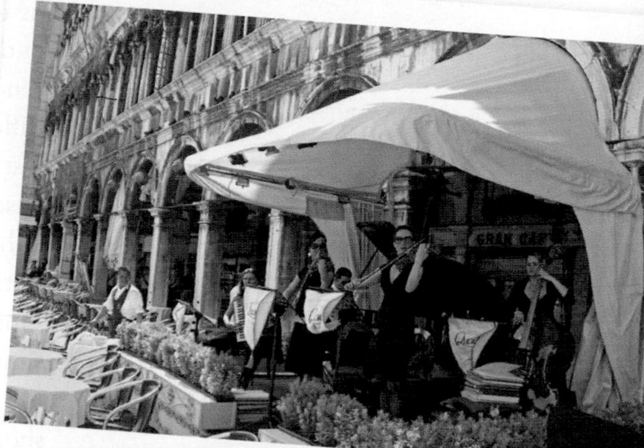

Figure 10.10 Classical live music may enhance the diners' experience.

SERVICE INSIGHTS 10.2

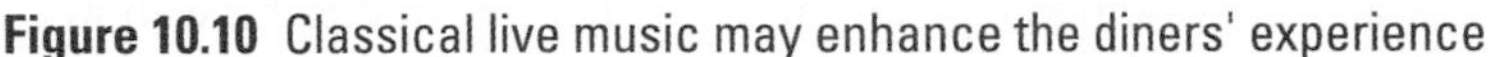

Cutting the Fear Factor at the Dentist

Dentistry is not a service that most people look forward to. Some patients simply find it uncomfortable, especially if they have to remain in a dental chair for a long period of time. Many are afraid of the pain associated with certain procedures. Others risk their health by not going to the dentist at all. Now, however, some dentists are turning to the concept of "spa dentistry." In spa dentistry, juice bars, neck rubs, foot massages, and even scented candles and the sound of wind chimes are used to pamper patients and distract them from the treatments inside their mouths.

"It's not about gimmicks," says Timothy Dotson, owner of the Perfect Teeth Dental Spa in Chicago, as a patient breathed strawberry-scented nitrous oxide. "It's treating people the way they want to be treated. It helps a lot of people overcome fear." His patients seem to agree. "Nobody likes coming to the dentist, but this makes it so much easier," remarked one woman as she waited for a crown while a heated massage pad was kneading her back.

Hot towels, massages, aromatherapy, coffee, fresh cranberry-orange bread, and white wine spritzers reflect dentists' efforts to meet changing consumer expectations, especially at a time when there is growing consumer demand for aesthetic care to whiten and reshape teeth to create a perfect smile. The goal is to attract patients who might otherwise find visiting the dentist a stressful situation. Many dentists who offer spa services do not charge extra for them. They argue that the costs are more than covered by repeat business and patient referrals.

In Houston, Max Greenfield has decorated his Image Max Dental Spa with fountains and modern art. Patients can change into a robe, try eight different aromas of oxygen, and meditate in a relaxation room decorated like a Japanese garden. The actual dental area has lambskin leather chairs, hot aromatherapy towels, and a procedure known as "bubble gum jet massage" that uses air and water to clean teeth.

Although dental offices from Los Angeles to New York are adopting spa techniques, some question whether this approach is good dentistry or just a passing fad. "I just can't see mingling the two businesses together," remarked the dean of one university dental school.

SOURCE

Adapted from "Dentists Offer New Services to Cut the Fear Factor," *Chicago Tribune* syndicated article, February 2003.

Let us next discuss a number of important ambient dimensions, starting with music.

Music

Music can have powerful effects on perceptions and behaviors in service settings, even if played at volumes one can hardly hear. The various elements of music such as tempo, volume, and harmony are perceived holistically. Their effect on internal and behavioral responses depends on the individual. For example, younger people tend to have different tastes in music than older people and therefore respond differently to the same piece of music.[16] Numerous research studies have found that fast-tempo music and high-volume music increase arousal levels. This can then lead customers increasing the pace of various behaviors. People tend to adjust their pace, either voluntarily or involuntarily, to match the tempo of music. This means that restaurants can speed up table turnover by increasing the tempo and volume of the music and serve more diners during the course of an evening. Alternatively, they can slow diners down with slow-beat music and softer volume to keep them longer in the restaurant and increase beverage revenues.[17] Likewise, studies have shown that shoppers walk less rapidly and increase their level of impulse purchases when slow music is played. Playing familiar music in a store was shown to stimulate shoppers and reduce their browsing time, whereas playing unfamiliar music induced shoppers to spend more time there.[18] In situations that require waiting for service, effective use of music may shorten the perceived waiting time and increase customer satisfaction. Relaxing music proved effective in lowering stress levels in a hospital's surgery waiting room. And pleasant music has even been shown to enhance customers' perceptions of service personnel.[19]

Providing the right mix of music to restaurants, retail stores, and even call centers has become an industry in its own right. For example, Texas-based company DMX provides music to over 300 corporate clients through creating signature mixes of between 200 and 800 licensed songs and pipes the music into their clients' outlets. These music mixes are updated remotely about once a month.[20]

Figure 10.11 Classical music can be used to deter vandals and loiterers.

Would it surprise you to learn that music can also be used to deter the wrong type of customers? Many service environments, including subway systems, supermarkets, and other public locations, attract individuals who do not have the intention to buy. Some are jaycustomers whose behavior causes problems for management and customers alike (see Chapter 13). In the United Kingdom, an increasingly popular strategy for driving such individuals away is playing classical music (Figure 10.11). People who like to loiter around or destroy public property find it very painful to listen to classical music. Co-op, a

UK grocery chain, has been experimenting with playing classical music outside its stores to stop teenagers from hanging around and intimidating customers. Its staff are equipped with a remote control and, as reported by Steve Broughton of Co-op, "can turn the music on if there's a situation developing and they need to disperse people."[21]

Scent

After music, let us focus on scent as the next important ambient dimension. Ambient scent or smell, which spreads throughout an environment, may or may not be consciously perceived by customers and is not related to any particular product. The presence of scent can have a strong impact on mood, feelings, and evaluations, and even purchase intentions and in-store behaviors.[22] We experience the power of smell when we are hungry and we smell freshly baked croissants long before we pass a local bakery. This smell makes us aware of our hunger and points us to the solution (i.e., walk into the bakery and get some food).

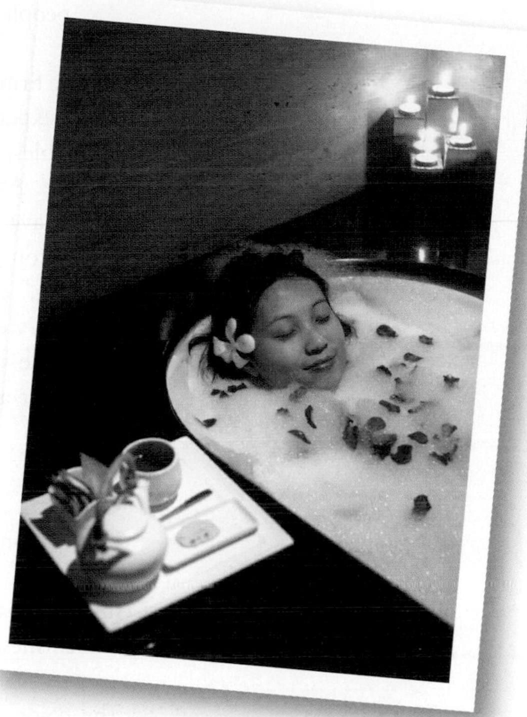

Figure 10.12 Aromatherapy can induce a state of relaxation and rejuvenation.

Service marketers are interested in how to make you hungry and thirsty in the restaurant, relax you in a dentist's waiting room, and energize you to work out harder in a gym. In aromatherapy, it is generally accepted that scents have special characteristics and can be used to obtain certain emotional, physiological, and behavioral responses (Figure 10.12). Table 10.2 shows the generally assumed effects of some aromatherapy scents on people. In service settings, research has shown that scents can have significant impact on customer perceptions, attitudes, and behaviors. For example:

PART III

Table 10.2 Aromatherapy—the effects of selected fragrances on people

Fragrance	Aroma Type	Aromatherapy Class	Traditional Use	Potential Psychological Effect on People
Eucalyptus	Camphoraceous	Toning, stimulating	Deodorant, antiseptic, soothing agent	Stimulating and energizing
Lavender	Herbaceous	Calming, balancing, soothing	Muscle relaxant, soothing agent, astringent	Relaxing and calming
Lemon	Citrus	Energizing, uplifting	Antiseptic, soothing agent	Soothing energy levels
Black pepper	Spicy	Balancing, soothing	Muscle relaxant, aphrodisiac	Balancing people's emotions

SOURCES

http://www.aromatherapy.com/, accessed March 12, 2012; Dana Butcher, "Aromatherapy—Its Past & Future." *Drug and Cosmetic Industry* 16, no. 3 (1998): 22–24; Shirley Price and Len Price (2007), *Aromatherapy for Health Professionals*, 3rd ed. Mattila, A. S., & Wirtz, J. (2001). Congruency of scent and music as a driver of in-store evaluations and behavior. *Journal of Retailing* 77, 273–289.

- Gamblers plunked 45% more quarters into slot machines when a Las Vegas casino was scented with a pleasant artificial smell. When the intensity of the scent was increased, spending jumped by 53%.[23]
- People were more willing to buy Nike sneakers and pay more for them—an average of US$10.33 more per pair—when they tried on the shoes in a floral-scented room. The same effect was found even when the scent was so faint that people could not detect it, i.e., the scent was perceived unconsciously.[24]

Service firms have recognized the power of scent and increasingly make it part of their brand experience. For example, Westin Hotels uses a white tea fragrance throughout its lobbies, and Sheraton scents its lobbies with a combination of fig, clove, and jasmine. As a response to the trend of scenting servicescapes, professional service firms have entered the scent marketing space. For example, Ambius, a Rentokil Initial company, offers scent-related services such as "sensory branding," "ambient scenting," and "odor remediation" for retail, hospitality, health-care, financial, and other services. Firms can outsource their servicescape scenting to Ambius, which offers one-stop solutions ranging from consulting, and designing exclusive signature scents for a service firm, to managing the ongoing scenting of all the outlets of a chain.[25]

Color

In addition to music and scent, researchers have found that colors have a strong impact on people's feelings. Color "is stimulating, calming, expressive, disturbing, impressional, cultural, exuberant, symbolic. It pervades every aspect of our lives, embellishes the ordinary, and gives beauty and drama to everyday objects."[26]

The color system normally used in psychological research is the Munsell system, which defines colors in the three dimensions of hue, value, and chroma.[27] *Hue* is the pigment of the color (i.e., the name of the color: red, orange, yellow, green, blue, or violet). *Value* is the degree of lightness or darkness of the color, relative to a scale that extends from pure black to pure white. *Chroma* refers to hue intensity, saturation, or brilliance. High-chroma colors are seen as rich and vivid, whereas low-chroma colors are seen as dull.

Figure 10.13 Bright and warm colors are usually used in environments with children to provide an attractive and cheery effect.

Hues are classified into warm colors (red, orange, and yellow hues) and cold colors (blue and green). Orange (a mix of red and yellow) is the warmest of the colors, and blue is the coldest. These colors can be used to manage the perceived warmth of an environment. For example, if a violet is too warm, you can cool it off by reducing the amount of red. Or if a red is too cold, warm it up by giving it a shot of orange.[28] Table 10.3 summarizes common associations and responses to colors.

Research in a service environment context has shown that, despite differing color preferences, people are generally drawn to warm-color environments (Figure 10.13). Warm colors encourage fast decision making and in service situations are best suited for low-involvement decisions or impulse purchases. Cool colors are favored when consumers need time to make high-involvement purchase decisions.[29]

Table 10.3 Common associations and human responses to colors

Color	Degree of Warmth	Nature Symbol	Common Association and Human Responses to Color
Red	Warm	Earth	High energy and passion; can excite and stimulate emotions, expressions, and warmth
Orange	Warmest	Sunset	Emotions, expressions, and warmth
Yellow	Warm	Sun	Optimism, clarity, intellect, and mood enchancing
Green	Cool	Growth, grass and trees	Nurturing, healing, and unconditional love
Blue	Coolest	Sky and ocean	Relaxation, serenity, and loyalty
Indigo	Cool	Sunset	Meditation and spirituality
Violet	Cool	Violet flower	Spirituality, reduces stress, can create an inner feeling of calm

SOURCES

Sara O. Marberry and Laurie Zagon, *The Power of Color—Creating Healthy Interior Spaces.* New York: John Wiley, 1995, 18; Sarah Lynch, *Bold Colors for Modern Rooms: Bright Ideas for People Who Love Color.* Gloucester, MA: Rockport Publishers, 2001, 24–29.

Although we have an understanding of the general effects of colors, we need to bear in mind that colors may have different meanings in different cultures. For example, a transportation company in Israel decided to paint its buses green as part of an environmentalism public relations campaign. This seemingly simple act resulted in unexpectedly negative reactions from different groups of people. Some customers found the green buses blended in with the environment and were more difficult to see. Others felt it did not look pleasant. Some people felt that it represented undesirable notions such as terrorism or opposing sports teams.[30]

Spatial Layout and Functionality

LO 6

Determine the roles of spatial layout and functionality.

In addition to ambient conditions, spatial layout and functionality are other key dimensions of the service environment. A service environment generally has to fulfill specific purposes and customer needs, so its spatial layout and functionality are particularly important.

Spatial layout refers to the floor plan, size and shape of furnishings, counters, and potential machinery and equipment, and the ways in which they are arranged. *Functionality* refers to the ability of those items to help in the performance of service transactions. Both dimensions affect the user-friendliness and the ability of the facility to service customers well. Tables that are too close together in a café, counters in a bank that lack privacy, uncomfortable chairs in a lecture theater (Figure 10.14), and lack of car parking space can all leave negative impressions on customers as well as affect service experience and buying behavior and, consequently, the business performance of the service facility.

Figure 10.14 Uncomfortable chairs in a lecture theater makes it harder for students to concentrate.

LO 7

Understand the roles of signs, symbols and artifacts.

Signs, Symbols, and Artifacts

Many things in the service environment act as signals to communicate the firm's image. They also help customers find their way (e.g., to certain service counters, departments, or the exit) and to let them know the service script (e.g., for a queuing system). First-time customers will automatically try to draw meaning from the signs, symbols, and artifacts to guide them through the service environment and service processes.

Figure 10.15 Confusing signs can lead people nowhere.

Signs are signals that can be used (1) as labels (e.g., to indicate the name of the department or counter), (2) for giving directions (e.g., entrance, exit, way to lifts and toilets), (3) for communicating the service script (e.g., take a queue number and watch for your number to be called, or clear the tray after your meal), and (4) for reminders about behavioral rules (e.g., switch off or turn your mobile devices to silent mode during the performance, or smoking/no-smoking areas). Signs are often used to teach behavioral rules in service settings. Some signs are quite interesting and may be quite obvious, but other signs need the person to think a little before understanding the meaning (Figure 10.15).

One challenge for designers is to use signs, symbols, and artifacts to guide customers clearly through the process of service delivery. This task is especially important when there are many new customers or many who seldom visit a service facility. It is also important in self-service situations, especially when there are few service employees available to help customers through the process.

Customers become confused when they cannot make out clear signals from a servicescape. They may become angry and frustrated as a result. Think about the last time you were in a hurry and tried to find your way through an unfamiliar hospital, shopping center, or airport where the signs were not clear. At many service facilities, customers' first point of contact is likely to be the car park. As emphasized in Service Insights 10.3, the principles of effective environment design apply even in this environment.

LO 8

Know how service employees and other customers are part of the servicescape.

People Are Part of the Service Environment, Too

The appearance and behavior of both service personnel and customers can strengthen, or weaken, the impression created by a service environment. Dennis Nickson and his colleagues use the term "aesthetic labor" to capture the importance of the physical image of service personnel who serve customers directly.[32] Employees at Disney theme parks are called cast members. Whether the staff are acting as Cinderella, one of Snow White's seven dwarfs, or as a park cleaner or the person managing Buzz Lightyear's Tomorrowland booth, these cast members must dress up and look the part. Once dressed up, they must "perform" for the guests.

For customers, marketing communications may seek to attract those who will not only appreciate the ambience created by the service provider but also actively enhance it by their appearance and behavior. In hospitality and retail settings, newcomers often look at the existing customers before deciding whether to patronize the service firm. Figure 10.16 shows the interior of two restaurants. Imagine that you have just entered each of these two dining rooms. How is each restaurant positioning itself within the restaurant industry? What sort of meal experience can you expect from

SERVICE INSIGHTS 10.3

Guidelines for Parking Design

Car parks play an important role at many service facilities. Effective use of signs, symbols, and artifacts in a parking lot helps customers find their way. It also displays a positive image for the service firm.

- *Friendly warnings*—All warning signs should communicate a customer benefit. For instance, "Fire lane—for everyone's safety, we ask you not to park in the fire lane."
- *Safety lighting*—Good lighting in all areas makes life easier for customers and improves safety. Firms may want to draw attention to this with notices stating that "parking lots have been specially lit for your safety."
- *Help customers remember where they left their vehicle*—Forgetting where one left the family car in a large parking structure can be a nightmare. Many car parks have used color-coded floors to help customers remember which level they parked on. In addition, many car parks also mark sections with special symbols such as different kinds of animals. This helps customers to remember both the level and the section where the car is parked. At Boston's Logan Airport, each level has been assigned a theme connected with Massachusetts. Examples include Paul Revere's Ride, Cape Cod, or the Boston Marathon. An image is attached to each theme—a male figure on horseback, a lighthouse, or a woman runner. While waiting for the elevator, travelers hear a few bars of music that are tied to the theme for that level. For the Boston Marathon floor, it is the theme music from *Chariots of Fire*, an Oscar-winning movie about an Olympic runner.

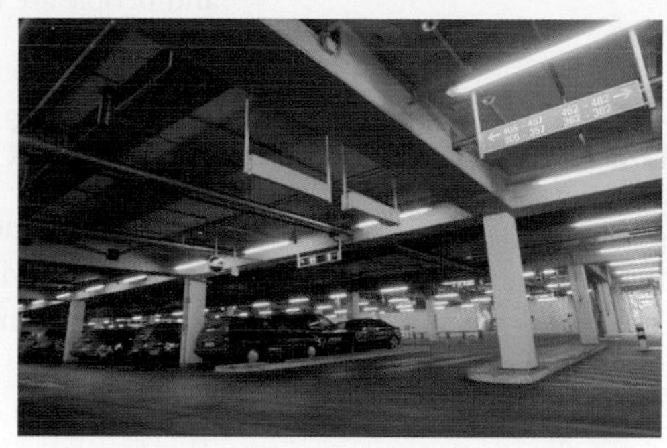

- *Maternity parking*—Handicapped spaces in a car park are often required by law, but parking in these spaces requires special stickers on the vehicle. A few thoughtful organizations have extended this idea to create special expectant mother parking spaces, painted with a blue/pink stork. This strategy shows a sense of caring and understanding of customer needs.
- *Fresh paint*—Curbs, cross walks, and lot lines should be repainted regularly before any cracking, peeling, or disrepair becomes obvious. Repainting often gives positive cleanliness signals and sends out a positive image.[31]

PART III

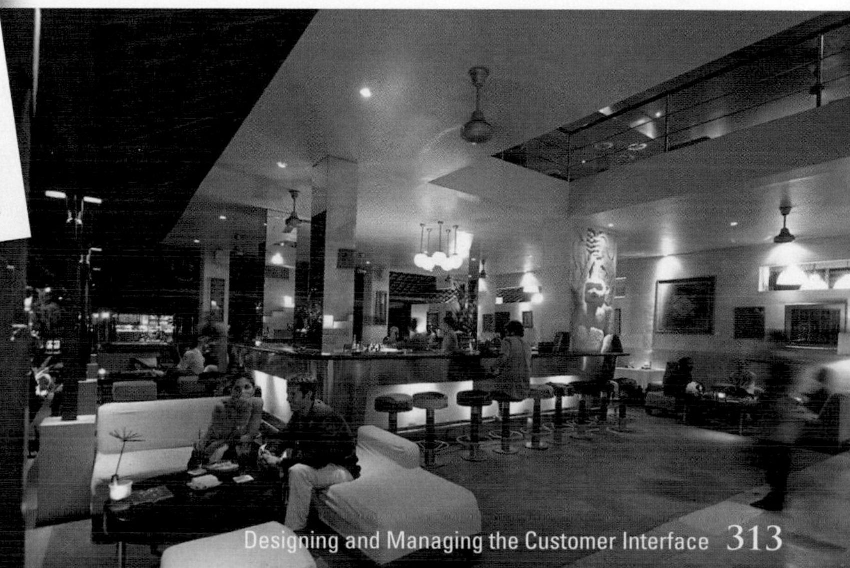

Figure 10.16 Distinctive servicescapes—from table settings to furniture and room design—create different customer expectations of these two restaurants.

each restaurant? And what are the clues that you use to make your judgments? In particular, what assumptions do you make from looking at the customers who are already seated in each restaurant? In summary, both employees and customers are part of the servicescape. The physical appearance is the hardware to create the atmosphere, and people are the software to shape the experience.

LO 9

Discuss the key ambient conditions and their effects on customers.

PUTTING IT ALL TOGETHER

Although individuals often perceive particular aspects or individual design features of an environment, it is the total configuration of all those design features that determines consumer responses. That is, consumers perceive service environments holistically.[33]

Design with a Holistic View

Whether a dark, glossy, wooden floor is the perfect flooring depends on everything else in that service environment. These include the type, color scheme, and materials of the furniture, the lighting, the promotional materials, and the overall brand perception and positioning of the firm (Figure 10.17). Servicescapes have to be designed as a whole, which means no dimension of the design can be planned without considering other aspects because everything depends on everything else. In this way, servicescape design is more like an art. Therefore, professional designers tend to specialize in specific types of servicescapes. For example, a handful of famous interior designers do nothing but create hotel lobbies around the world. Similarly, there are design experts, who focus exclusively on restaurants, bars, clubs, cafes and bistros, or retail outlets, or health-care facilities, and so forth.[34]

Figure 10.17 Arne Jacobson's enduring egg chair instantly brightens up any servicescape.

Design from a Customer's Perspective

Many service environments are built with a focus on physical appearance. Designers sometimes forget that the most important design factor should be the customers who will be using the environment. Ron Kaufman, the founder of UP Your Service! College, experienced the following design weaknesses in two new service environments:

- "A new Sheraton Hotel just had opened in Jordan without clear signage that would guide guests from the ballrooms to the restrooms. The signs that did exist were etched in muted gold on dark marble pillars. More "obvious" signs were apparently inappropriate amid such elegant décor. Very swish, very chic, but who were they designing it for?"
- "At a new airport lounge in a major Asian city, a partition of colorful glass hung from the ceiling. My luggage lightly brushed against it as I walked inside. The entire partition shook and several panels came undone. A staff member hurried over and began carefully reassembling the panels. (Thank goodness nothing broke.) I apologized profusely. 'Don't worry,' she replied, 'This happens all the time.'" An airport lounge is a heavy traffic area. People are always moving in and out. Kaufman keeps asking: "What were the interior designers thinking? Who were they designing it for?"

"I am regularly amazed," declared Kaufman, "by brand new facilities that are obviously user 'unfriendly'! Huge investments of time and money… but who are they designing it for? What were the architects thinking about? Size? Grandeur? Physical exercise?" He draws the following key learning point: "It's easy to get caught up in designing new things that are 'cool' or 'elegant' or 'hot.' But if you don't keep your customer in mind throughout, you could end up with an investment that's not."[35]

Alain d'Astous explored environmental aspects that irritate shoppers. His findings highlighted the following problems:

- *Ambient conditions* (ordered by level of irritation):
  - The store is not clean.
  - It is too hot inside the store or the shopping centre.
  - The music inside the store is too loud.
  - There is a bad smell in the store.
- *Environmental design variables*:
  - There is no mirror in the dressing room.
  - A customer is unable to find what he or she needs.
  - Directions within the store are inadequate.
  - The arrangement of store items has been changed.
  - The store is too small.
  - It is easy to lose one's way in a large shopping center.[36] (Figure 10.18)

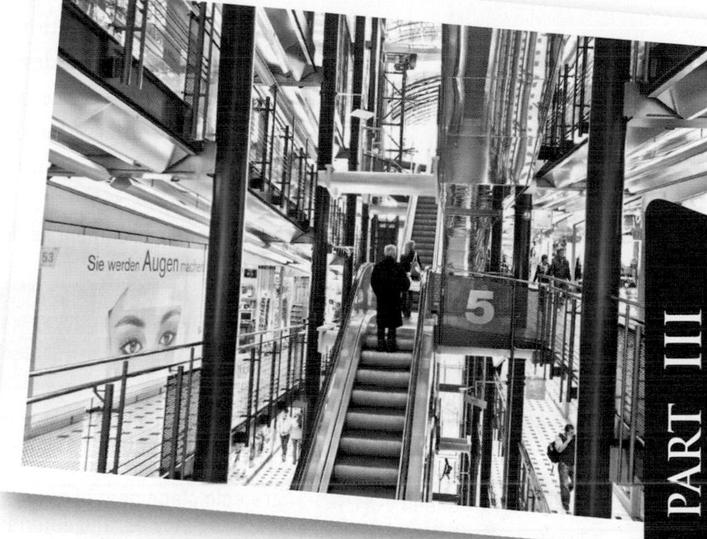

Figure 10.18 Badly designed shopping centers affect the shopping experience.

Tools to Guide Servicescape Design

As a manager, how would you find out which aspects of the servicescape irritate customers and which aspects they like? Some of the tools that you can use are:

- ***Keen observation*** of customers' behavior and responses to the service environment by management, supervisors, branch managers, and frontline staff.
- ***Feedback and ideas from frontline staff and customers*** using a variety of research tools ranging from suggestion boxes to focus groups and surveys. (This type of survey is called environmental surveys if they focus on the design of the service environment.)
- ***Photo audit*** is a method of asking customers (or mystery shoppers) to take photographs of their service experience. These photographs can be used later as a basis for further interviews of their experience or included as part of a survey about the service experience.[37]
- ***Field experiments*** can be used to control specific dimensions in an environment and observe its effects. For instance, researchers can experiment with various types of music and scents and then measure the time and money customers spend in the environment. Laboratory experiments, using slides or videos, or other ways to create real-world service environments (such as virtual tours via computer) can be used to examine the impact of changes in design elements.

These methods are used when the real environment cannot really be controlled. Examples include testing of different color schemes, spatial layouts, and styles of furnishing.

- ***Blueprinting*** or flowcharting (described in Chapter 8) can be extended to include the physical evidence in the environment. Design elements and tangible cues can be documented as the customer moves through each step of the service delivery process. Photos and videos can supplement the map to make it clearer.

Table 10.4 shows an examination of a customer's visit to a movie theater. It identifies how different environmental elements at each step are better than expected or fails to meet expectations. The service process was broken up into steps, decisions, duties, and activities, all designed to take the customer through the entire service encounter. The more a service company can see, understand, and experience the same things as its customers, the more it will be able to realize mistakes in the design of its environment and further improve on what is already working well.

Table 10.4 A visit to the movies: The service environment as perceived by the customer

Steps in the Service Encounter	Design of the Service Environment	
	Exceeds Expectations	**Fails Expectations**
Locate a parking lot	Ample room in a bright place near the entrance, with a security officer protecting your valuables	Insufficient parking spaces, so patrons have to park in another lot
Queue up to obtain tickets	Strategic placement of mirrors, posters of upcoming movies, and entertainment news to ease perception of long wait, if any; movies and time slots easily seen; ticket availability clearly communicated	A long queue and having to wait for a long while; difficult to see quickly what movies are being shown at what time slots and whether tickets are still available
Check tickets to enter the theater	A very well-maintained lobby with clear directions to the theater and posters of the movie to enhance patrons' experience	A dirty lobby with rubbish strewn and unclear or misleading directions to the movie theater
Go to the restroom before the movie starts	Sparkling clean, spacious, brightly lit, dry floors, well stocked, nice décor, clear mirrors wiped regularly	Dirty, with an unbearable odor; broken toilets; no hand towels, soap, or toilet paper; overcrowded; dusty and dirty mirrors
Enter the theater and locate your seat	Spotless theater; well designed with no bad seats; sufficient lighting to locate your seat; spacious, comfortable chairs, with drink and popcorn holders on each seat; and a suitable temperature	Rubbish on the floor, broken seats, sticky floor, gloomy and insufficient lighting, burned-out exit signs
Watch the movie	Excellent sound system and film quality, nice audience, an enjoyable and memorable entertainment experience overall	Substandard sound and movie equipment, uncooperative audience that talks and smokes because of lack of "No Smoking" and other signs; a disturbing and unenjoyable entertainment experience overall
Leave the theater and return to the car	Friendly service staff greet patrons as they leave; an easy exit through a brightly lit and safe parking area, back to the car with the help of clear lot signs	A difficult trip, as patrons squeeze through a narrow exit, unable to find the car because of no or insufficient lighting

SOURCE

Adapted from Albrecht, S. (1996). See things from the customer's point of view —how to use The 'Cycles of Service' to understand what the customer goes through to do business with you. *World's Executive Digest.* (December) 53–58.

CHAPTER SUMMARY

LO 1 ▶ Service environments fulfill four core purposes. Specifically, they:

- o Shape customers' experiences and their behaviors.
- o Play an important role in determining customer perceptions of the firm, and its image and positioning. Customers often use the service environment as an important quality signal.
- o Can be a core part of the value proposition (e.g., as for theme parks and resort hotels).
- o Facilitate the service encounter and enhance productivity.

LO 2 ▶ Environmental psychology helps us to understand the effects service environments have on customers and service employees. There are two key models:

- o The Mehrabian—Russell Stimulus—Response model holds that environments influence peoples' affective state (or emotions and feelings), which in turn drives their behavior.
- o Russell's model of affect holds that affect can be modeled with the two interacting dimensions of pleasure and arousal, which, together, determine whether people approach, spend time and money in an environment, or avoid it.

LO 3 ▶ The servicescape model, which builds on the above theories, represents an integrative framework that explains how customers and service staff respond to key environmental dimensions.

LO 4 ▶ The servicescape model emphasizes three dimensions of the service environment:

- o Ambient conditions (including music, scents, and colors).
- o Spatial layout and functionality.
- o Signs, symbols, and artifacts.

LO 5 ▶ Ambient conditions refer to those characteristics of the environment that relate to our five senses. Even when not consciously perceived, they still can affect people's internal and behavioral re-sponses. Important ambient dimensions include:

- o Music—its tempo, volume, harmony, and the familiarity shape behavior by affecting emotions and moods. People tend to adjust their pace to match the tempo of the music.
- o Scent—ambient scent can stir powerful emotions and relax or simulate customers.
- o Color—colors can have strong effects on people's feelings, with warm (e.g., a mix of red and orange) and cool colors (e.g., blue) having different impact. Warm colors are associated with elated mood states, while cool colors are linked to peacefulness and happiness.

LO 6 ▶ Effective spatial layout and functionality are important for efficiency of the service operation and enhancement of its user-friendliness.

- o Spatial layout refers to the floor plan, size and shape of furnishing, counters, potential machinery and equipment, and the ways in which they are arranged.
- o Functionality refers to the ability of those items to facilitate service operations.

LO 7 ▶ Signs, symbols, and artifacts help customers to draw meaning from the environment and guide them through the service process. They can be used to:

- o Label facilities, counters, or departments.
- o Show directions (e.g., to entrance, exit, elevator, toilet).
- o Communicate the service script (e.g., take a number and watch it to be called).
- o Reinforce behavioral rules (e.g., "please turn your cell phones to silent").

LO 8 ▶ The appearance and behavior service employees and other customers in a servicescape can be part of the value proposition and can strengthen (or weaken) the positioning of the firm.

LO 9 ▶ Service environments are perceived holistically. Therefore, no individual aspect can be optimized without considering everything else, making designing service environments an art rather than a science.

- o Because of this challenge, professional designers tend to specialize in specific types of environments, such as hotel lobbies, clubs, health-care facilities, and so on.
- o The best service environments should be designed with the customer's perspective in mind, guiding them smoothly through the service process.
- o Tools that can be used to design and improve servicescapes include careful observation, feedback from employees and customers, photo audits, field experiments, and blueprinting.

UNLOCK YOUR LEARNING

These keywords are found within the sections of each Learning Objective (LO). They are integral to understanding the services marketing concepts taught in each section. Having a firm grasp of these keywords and how they are used is essential to helping you do well on your course, and in the real and very competitive marketing scene out there.

LO 1
1 Attention-creating medium
2 Differentiation
3 Effect-creating medium
4 Enhance productivity
5 Image
6 Message-creating medium
7 Positioning
8 Service environments
9 Servicescapes
10 Shape customers' experiences
11 Value proposition

LO 2
12 Affective expectations
13 Affective processes
14 Approach
15 Arousal
16 Avoidance
17 Behavioral consequences
18 Cognitive processes
19 Environmental psychology
20 Mehrabian—Russell Stimulus—Response model

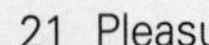

21 Pleasure
22 Russell's model of affect

LO 3
23 Bitner
24 Cognitive responses
25 Emotional responses
26 Internal responses
27 Physiological responses
28 Servicescape model

LO 4
29 Dimensions of service environment

LO 5
30 Ambient conditions
31 Ambient scenting
32 Aromatherapy
33 Brilliance
34 Chroma
35 Color
36 Hue
37 Music
38 Odor remediation
39 Saturation
40 Scent
41 Sensory branding
42 Value

LO 6
43 Functionality
44 Spatial layout

LO 7
45 Artifacts
46 Parking design
47 Signs
48 Symbols

LO 8
49 Aesthetic labor
50 People

LO 9
51 Ambient conditions
52 Blueprinting
53 Customer's perspective
54 Environmental design
55 Field experiments
56 Flowcharting
57 Holistic view
58 Observation
69 Photo audit
60 Servicescape design

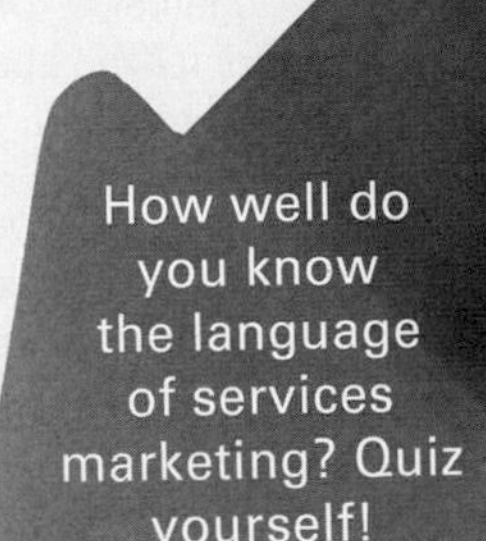

Not for the academically faint-of-heart

For each keyword you are able to recall without referring to earlier pages, give yourself a point (and a pat on the back). Tally your score at the end and see if you earned the right to be called—a *services marketeer.*

SCORE

0 – 11 Services Marketing is done a great disservice.
12 – 22 The midnight oil needs to be lit, pronto.
23 – 33 I know what you *didn't* do all semester.
34 – 44 A close shave with success.
45 – 55 Now, go forth and market.
56 – 60 There should be a marketing concept named after you.

KNOW YOUR ESM

Review Questions

1. What are the four main purposes service environments fulfill?
2. Describe how the Mehrabian—Russell Stimulus—Response model and Russell's model of affect explain consumer responses to a service environment.
3. What is the relationship or link between Russell's model of affect and the servicescape model?
4. Explain why different customers and service staff respond very differently to the same service environment.
5. Explain the dimensions of ambient conditions and how each can influence customer responses to the service environment.
6. What are the roles of signs, symbols, and artifacts?
7. What are the implications of the fact that environments are perceived holistically?
8. What tools are available for aiding our understanding of customer responses and for guiding the design and improvement of service environments?

WORK YOUR ESM

Application Exercises

1. Identify firms from three different service industries where the service environment is a crucial part of the overall value proposition. Analyze and explain in detail the value that is delivered by the service environment in each of the three industries.
2. Visit a service environment, and have a detailed look around. Experience the environment and try and feel how the various design elements shape what you feel and how you behave in that setting.
3. Select a bad and a good waiting experience and contrast the two situations with respect to the service environment and other people waiting.
4. Visit a self-service environment and analyze how the design dimensions guide you through the service process. What do you find most effective for you, and what seems least effective? How could that environment be improved to further ease the "way-finding" for self-service customers?
5. Take a digital camera and conduct a photo audit of a specific servicescape. Photograph examples of excellent and very poor design features. Develop concrete suggestions on how this environment could be improved.

ENDNOTES

1 Beatriz Plaza, "The Bilbao Effect," *Museum News*, (September/October 2007): 13–15, 68; Denny Lee, "Bilbao, 10 Years Later," *The New York Times*, September 23, 2007 in http://travel.nytimes.com/2007/09/23/travel/23bilbao.html, accessed March 12, 2012. http://en.wikipedia.org/wiki/Guggenheim_Museum_Bilbao, accessed March 12, 2012.

2 The term *servicescape* was coined by Mary Jo Bitner in her paper "Servicescapes: The Impact of Physical Surroundings on Customers and Employees," *Journal of Marketing* 56, (1992): 57–71.

3 Madeleine E. Pullman and Michael A. Gross, "Ability of Experience Design Elements to Elicit Emotions and Loyalty Behaviors," *Decision Sciences* 35, no. 1 (2004): 551–578.

4 Anja Reimer and Richard Kuehn, "The Impact of Servicescape on Quality Perception," *European Journal of Marketing* 39, 7/8(2005): 785–808.

5 Lisa Takeuchi Cullen, "Is Luxury the Ticket?" *Time*, August 22, 2005, 38–39.

6 For a review of the literature on hospital design effects on patients, see: Karin Dijkstra, Marcel Pieterse, and Ad Pruyn, "Physical Environmental Stimuli That Turn Healthcare Facilities into Healing Environments through Psychologically Mediated Effects: Systematic Review," *Journal of Advanced Nursing* 56, no. 2 (2006): 166–181. See also the painstaking effort the Mayo Clinic extends to lowering noise levels in their hospitals: Leonard L. Berry and Kent D. Seltman, *Management Lessons from Mayo Clinic: Inside One of the World's Most Admired Service Organizations*. McGraw-Hill, 2008, 171–172. For a study on the effects of servicescape design in a hospital setting on service workers' job stress and job satisfaction, and subsequently, their commitment to the firm, see: Janet Turner Parish, Leonard L. Berry, and Shun Yin Lam, "The Effect of the Servicescape on Service Workers," *Journal of Service Research* 10, no. 3 (2008): 220–238.

7 Robert J. Donovan and John R. Rossiter, "Store Atmosphere: An Environmental Psychology Approach," *Journal of Retailing* 58, no. 1 (1982): 34–57.

8 James A. Russell, "A Circumplex Model of Affect," *Journal of Personality and Social Psychology* 39, no. 6 (1980): 1161–1178.

9 Jochen Wirtz, Anna S. Mattila, and Rachel L. P. Tan, "The Moderating Role of Target-Arousal on the Impact of Affect on Satisfaction – An Examination in the Context of Service Experiences," *Journal of Retailing* 76, no. 3 (2000): 347–365. Jochen Wirtz, Anna S. Mattila and Rachel L. P. Tan, "The Role of Desired Arousal in Influencing Consumers' Satisfaction Evaluations and In-Store Behaviours," *International Journal of Service Industry Management* 18, no. 2 (2007): 6–24.

10 Mary Jo Bitner, "Servicescapes: The Impact of Physical Surroundings on Customers and Employees," *Journal of Marketing* 56, (April 1992): 57–71.

11 Terje Slatten, Mehmet Mehmetoglu, Goran Svensson and Sander Svaeri, "Atmospheric Experiences That Emotional Touch Customers: A Case Study from a Winter Park," *Managing Service Quality* 19, no. 6 (2009): 721–746.

12 For a comprehensive review of experimental studies on the atmospheric effects refer to: L. W. Turley and Ronald E. Milliman, "Atmospheric Effects on Shopping Behavior: A Review of the Experimental Literature," *Journal of Business Research* 49, (2000): 193–211.

13 Patrick M. Dunne, Robert F. Lusch and David A. Griffith, *Retailing*, 4th ed., Orlando, FL: Hartcourt, 2002, 518.

14 Barry Davies and Philippa Ward, *Managing Retail Consumption*, West Sussex, UK: John Wiley & Sons, (2002), 179.

15 Saminan Gheorghe and Silvia Hodges, "Branding Services through Servicescapes: Understanding the Role of Servicescapes as an Identity-building Tool for Services and Perception-Shaping Tool for Customers". Paper presented at 2009 Frontiers in Service Conference, Honolulu, Hawaii, October 31.

16 Steve Oakes, "The Influence of the Musicscape within Service Environments," *Journal of Services Marketing* 14 no. 7 (2000): 539–556.

17 Laurette Dubé and Sylvie Morin, "Background Music Pleasure and Store Evaluation Intensity Effects and Psychological Mechanisms," *Journal of Business Research* 54, (2001): 107–113

18 Clare Caldwell and Sally A. Hibbert, "The Influence of Music Tempo and Musical Preference on Restaurant Patrons' Behavior," *Psychology and Marketing* 19, no. 11 (2002): 895–917.

19 For a review of the effects of music on various aspects of consumer responses and evaluations see: Steve Oakes and Adrian C. North, "Reviewing Congruity Effects in the Service Environment Musicscape," *International Journal of Service Industry Management* 19, no. 1 (2008): 63–82.

20 See www.dmx.com for in-store music solutions provided by DMX; see also Leah Goodman, "Shoppers Dance to Retailers' Tune," *Financial Times*, August 21, 2008, 10.

21 This section is based on: *The Economist*, "Classical Music and Social Control: Twilight of the Yobs," January 8th, 2005, 48.

22 Eric R. Spangenberg, Ayn E. Crowley, and Pamela W. Henderson, "Improving the Store Environment: Do Olfactory Cues Affect Evaluations and Behaviors?" *Journal of Marketing* 60, (April 1996): 67–80; Paula Fitzerald Bone and Pam Scholder Ellen, "Scents in the Marketplace: Explaining a Fraction of Olfaction," *Journal of Retailing* 75, no. 2 (1999): 243–262; Jeremy Caplan, "Sense and Sensibility," *Time* 168, no. 16 (2006): 66–67.

23 Alan R. Hirsch, "Effects of Ambient Odors on Slot Machine Usage in a Las Vegas Casino," *Psychology and Marketing* 12, no. 7 (1995): 585–594.

24 Alan R. Hirsch and S.E. Gay, "Effect on Ambient Olfactory Stimuli on the Evaluation of a Common Consumer Product," *Chemical Senses* 16, (1991): 535.

25 See Ambius' website for details of its scent marketing, ambient scenting, and sensory branding services at: http://www.ambius.com/services/microfresh.aspx; accessed on March 12, 2012.

26 Linda Holtzschuhe, *Understanding Color—An Introduction for Designers*, 3rd edn. New Jersey: John Wiley, 2006, 51.

27 Albert Henry Munsell, *A Munsell Color Product*. New York: Kollmorgen Corporation, 1996.

28 Linda Holtzschuhe, *Understanding Color—An Introduction for Designers*, 3rd edn. New Jersey: John Wiley, 2006.

29 Joseph A. Bellizzi, Ayn E. Crowley, and Ronald W. Hasty, "The Effects of Color in Store Design," *Journal of Retailing* 59, no. 1 (1983): 21–45.

30 Anat Rafaeli and Iris Vilnai-Yavetz, "Discerning Organizational Boundaries through Physical Artifacts," in N. Paulsen and T. Hernes, eds. *Managing boundaries in organizations: Multiple perspectives* (UK: Basingstoke, Hampshire, Macmillan, 2003); Anat Rafaeli and Iris Vilnai-Yavetz, "Emotion as a Connection of Physical Artifacts and Organizations," *Organization Science* 15, no 6 (2004): 671–686; and Anat Rafaeli and Iris Vilnai-Yavetz, "Managing Organizational Artifacts to Avoid Artifact Myopia," in A. Rafaeli and M. Pratt, eds. *Artifacts and Organization: Beyond Mere Symbolism*, (Mahwah, NJ: Lawrence Erlbaum Associates Inc., 2005, 9–21).

31 Lewis P. Carbone and Stephen H. Haeckel, "Engineering Customer Experiences," *Marketing Management* 3, no. 3 (Winter 1994): 9–18; Lewis P. Carbone, Stephen H. Haeckel and Leonard L. Berry, "How to Lead the Customer Experience," *Marketing Management* 12, no. 1 (Jan/Feb 2003): 18; Leonard L. Berry and Lewis P. Carbone, "Build Loyalty through Experience Management," *Quality Progress* 40, no. 9 (September 2007): 26–32.

32 Dennis Nickson, Chris Warhurst, and Eli Dutton, "The Importance of Attitude and Appearance in the Service Encounter in Retail and Hospitality," *Managing Service Quality* 2, (2005): 195–208.

33 Anna S. Mattila and Jochen Wirtz, "Congruency of Scent and Music as a Driver of In-store Evaluations and Behavior," *Journal of Retailing* 77, (2001): 273–289.

34 Christine M. Piotrowski, *Designing Commercial Interiors*. New York: John Wiley & Sons, Inc., 2007; Martin M. Pegler, *Cafes & Bistros*. New York: Retail Reporting Corporation, 1998; Paco Asensio, *Bars & Restaurants*. New York: HarperCollins International, 2002; Bethan Ryder, *Bar and Club Design*. London: Laurence King Publishing, 2002.

35 Ron Kaufman, "Service Power: Who Were They Designing It For?" Newsletter. May 2001, http://Ron Kaufman.com.

36 Alan d'Astous, "Irritating Aspects of the Shopping Environment," *Journal of Business Research* 49, (2000): 149–156. See also: K. Douglas Hoffman, Scott W. Kelly, and Beth C. Chung, "A CIT Investigation of Servicscape Failures and Associated Recovery Strategies," *Journal of Services Marketing* 17, no. 4 (2003): 322–40.

37 Madeleine E. Pullman and Stephani K. A. Robson, "Visual Methods: Using Photographs to Capture Customers' Experience with Design," *Cornell Hotel and Restaurant Administration Quarterly* 48, no. 2 (2007): 121–144.

PART III

CHAPTER 11

managing people for SERVICE ADVANTAGE

LEARNING OBJECTIVES

By the end of this chapter, the reader should be able to:

- **LO 1** Explain why service employees are so important to the success of a firm.
- **LO 2** Understand the factors that make the work of frontline staff so demanding and often difficult.
- **LO 3** Describe the cycles of failure, mediocrity, and success in HR for service firms.
- **LO 4** Understand the key elements of the Service Talent Cycle and know how to get HR right in service firms.
- **LO 5** Know how to attract, select and hire the right people for service jobs.
- **LO 6** Explain the key areas in which service employees need training.
- **LO 7** Understand why empowerment is so important in many frontline jobs.
- **LO 8** Explain how to build high-performance service delivery teams.
- **LO 9** Know how to motivate and energize service employees so that they will deliver service excellence and productivity.
- **LO 10** Understand the role of service leadership and culture in developing people for service advantage.

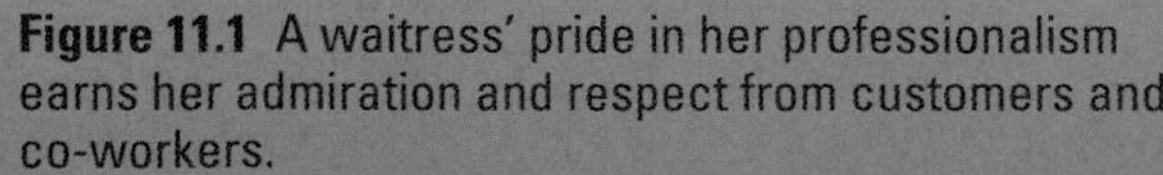

Figure 11.1 A waitress' pride in her professionalism earns her admiration and respect from customers and co-workers.

OPENING VIGNETTE

Cora Griffith—The Outstanding Waitress[1]

Cora Griffith is a waitress for the Orchard Café at the Paper Valley Hotel in Appleton, Wisconsin. She is excellent in her role, appreciated by first-time customers, famous with her regular customers, and admired and respected by her co-workers. Cora loves her work and it shows. She implements the following nine rules of success:

1. **Treat Customers Like Family.** First-time customers are not allowed to feel like strangers. Cora smiles, chats, and includes everyone at the table in the conversation. She is as respectful to children as she is to adults and makes it a point to learn and use everyone's name. "I want people to feel like they're sitting down to dinner right at my house. I want them to feel they're welcome, that they can get comfortable, that they can relax. I don't just serve people, I pamper them."
2. **Listen First.** Cora has developed her listening skills to the point that she rarely writes down customers' orders. She listens carefully and provides a customized service: "Are they in a hurry? Or do they have a special diet or like their selection cooked in a certain way?"
3. **Anticipate Customers' Wants.** She refills beverages and brings extra bread and butter in a timely manner. One regular customer, for example, who likes honey with her coffee gets it without having to ask. "I don't want my customers to have to ask for anything, so I always try to anticipate what they might need."
4. **Simple Things Make the Difference.** She manages the details of her service, keeps track of the cleanliness of the utensils and their correct placement. The fold for napkins must be just right. She inspects each plate in the kitchen before taking it to the table. She provides crayons for small children to draw pictures while waiting for the meal. "It's the little things that please the customer."
5. **Work Smart.** Cora scans all her tables at once, looking for opportunities to combine tasks. "Never do just one thing at a time. And never go from the kitchen to the dining room empty-handed. Take coffee or iced tea or water with you." When she refills one water glass, she refills others. When clearing one plate, she clears others. "You have to be organized, and you have to keep in touch with the big picture."
6. **Keep Learning.** Cora makes it an ongoing effort to improve existing skills and learn new ones.
7. **Success Is Where You Find It.** Cora is satisfied with her work. She finds satisfaction in pleasing her customers, and she enjoys helping other people enjoy. Her positive attitude is a positive force in the restaurant. "If customers come to the restaurant in a bad mood, I'll try to cheer them up before they leave." Her definition of success: "To be happy in life."
8. **All for One, One for All.** She has been working with many of the same co-workers for more than eight years. The team supports one another on the crazy days when 300 conventioneers come to the restaurant for breakfast at the same time. Everyone helps out. The wait staff cover for one another, the managers bus the tables, and the chefs garnish the plates. "We are like a little family. We know each other very well and we help each other out. If we have a crazy day, I'll go in the kitchen towards the end of the shift and say, 'Man, I'm just proud of us. We really worked hard today.'"
9. **Take Pride in Your Work.** Cora believes in the importance of her work and in the need to do it well. "I don't think of myself as 'just a waitress'… I've chosen to be a waitress. I'm doing this to my full potential, and I give it my best. I tell anyone who's starting out: take pride in what you do. You're never just an anything, no matter what you do. You give it your all … and you do it with pride."

Cora Griffith is a success story. She is loyal to her employer and dedicated to her customers and co-workers. She is proud of being a waitress, proud of "touching lives." Says Cora, "I have always wanted to do my best. However, the owners really are the ones who taught me how important it is to take care of the customer and who gave me the freedom to do it. The company always has listened to my concerns and followed up. Had I not worked for the Orchard Café, I would have been a good waitress, but I would not have been the same waitress."

PART III

 LO 1

Explain why service employees are so important to the success of a firm.

SERVICE EMPLOYEES ARE EXTREMELY IMPORTANT

Highly capable and motivated people are at the center of service excellence and productivity. Cora Griffin in our Opening Vignette is a powerful demonstration of a frontline employee delivering service excellence and productivity and, at the same time, having high job satisfaction. Many of the topics in Cora Griffin's nine rules of success are the result of good HR strategies for service firms. After reading this chapter, you will know how to get HR right in service firms, and how to get satisfied, loyal, motivated, and productive service employees.

From a customer's perspective, the encounter with service staff is probably the most important aspect of a service. From the firm's perspective, the service levels, and the way service is delivered by frontline personnel can be an important source of differentiation as well as competitive advantage. But why are service employees so important to customers and the firm's competitive positioning? This is because the frontline:

- **Is a core part of the product.** Often, service employees are the most visible element of the service. They deliver the service and affect service quality greatly.
- **Is the service firm.** Frontline employees represent the service firm, and, from a customer's perspective, they are the firm.
- **Is the brand.** Frontline employees and the service they provide are often a core part of the brand. It is the employees who determine whether the brand promise is delivered.
- **Affects sales.** Service personnel are often extremely important for generating sales, cross-sales, and up-sales.
- **Determines productivity.** Frontline employees have heavy influence on the productivity of frontline operations.

Figure 11.2 Service personnel represent the firm and often build personal relationships with their customers.

Furthermore, frontline employees play a key role in anticipating customers' needs, customizing the service delivery (Figure 11.2), and building personalized relationships with customers.[2] When these activities are performed effectively, it should lead to customer loyalty. The story of Cora Griffith and many other success stories of how employees putting in the extra effort have made a difference and strengthen the belief that highly motivated people are at the core of service excellence.[3] Increasingly, they are a key factor in creating and maintaining competitive positioning and advantage.

The Frontline in Low-Contact Services

Much research in service management relates to high-contact services. However, many services are moving toward using low-contact delivery channels such as call centers, where contact is voice-to-voice rather than face-to-face. A growing number of transactions no longer even involve frontline staff. As a result, a large and increasing number of customer-contact employees work by telephone or e-mail, never meeting customers face-to-face. So, are frontline employees really that important for such services?

Most people do not call the service hotline or visit the service center of their mobile operator or credit card company more than once or twice a year. However these occasional service encounters are the "moments of truth" that drive a customer's perceptions of the service firm (see Figure 11.3). Also, it is likely that these interactions are about service problems and special requests. These very few instances of contact determine whether a customer thinks, "Your customer service is excellent! When I need help, I can call you, and this is one important reason why I bank with you," or "Your service stinks. I don't like interacting with you, and I am going to switch away from your bank at the next opportune moment!"

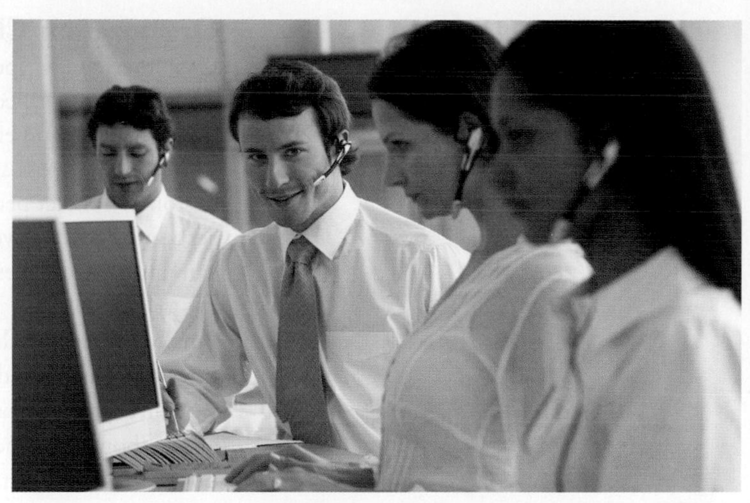

Figure 11.3 The pleasant personality of call center staff can result in a positive "moment of truth," where a firm's service quality will be viewed positively.

Therefore, the service delivered by the frontline, whether it is face-to-face, "ear to ear," or via e-mail, Twitter, or chat, is highly visible and important to customers, and is a critical component of a service firm's marketing strategy.

FRONTLINE WORK IS DIFFICULT AND STRESSFUL

LO 2

Understand the factors that make the work of frontline staff so demanding and often difficult.

The service profit chain needs high-performing, satisfied employees to achieve service excellence and customer loyalty (see Chapter 15 for a detailed discussion). However, these customer-facing employees work in some of the most demanding jobs in service firms. Perhaps you have worked in one or more of such jobs, which are common in the health-care, hospitality, retailing, and travel industries. There is a story that has been virally passed from one person to another, about a JetBlue flight attendant who abruptly quit his job after 28 years as a flight attendant. Apparently, he was fed up with a difficult passenger with a bag problem, who had sworn at him. He scolded the passenger publicly over the airplane intercom, announced that he had had enough, and opened the emergency slide to get off the plane.[4] This is an example of how stress can affect a person at work. Let's discuss the main reasons why these jobs are so demanding. You can relate these to your own experiences, while recognizing that there may be differences between working part time for short periods and full time as a career.

Boundary Spanning

The organizational behavior literature refers to service employees as *boundary spanners*. They link the inside of an organization to the outside world. Because of the position they occupy, their role frequently pulls them in opposite directions, so they often experience role conflict, and as a result, role stress. Let us look at the sources of role conflict in more detail.

Sources of Role Conflict

There are three main causes of role stress in frontline positions: (1) organization/client, (2) person/role, and (3) inter-client conflicts.

Organization/Client Conflict

Customer contact personnel are required to meet both operational and marketing goals. They are expected to delight customers (which takes time), and yet they also have to be fast and efficient at operational tasks. In addition, they are often expected to do selling, cross-selling, and up-selling, too. For instance, it is common to hear customer contact personnel suggest: "Now would be a good time to open a separate account to save for your children's education," or "For only $25 more per night, you can upgrade to the executive floor."

Finally, sometimes they must make sure that the company's pricing is followed, even if that might be in direct conflict with customer satisfaction (e.g., "I am sorry, but we don't serve ice water in this restaurant, but we have an excellent selection of still and carbonated mineral waters," or "I am sorry, but we cannot waive the fee for the bounced check for the third time this quarter.") This type of conflict is also called the "two-bosses dilemma," where service employees have the unpleasant choice of whether to stick to the company's rules or to satisfy customer demands. The problem is especially bad in organizations that are not customer oriented.

Person/Role Conflict

Service staff may have conflicts between what their job requires and their own personalities, self-perception, and beliefs. For example, the job may require staff to smile and be friendly even to rude customers (see also the section on jaycustomers in Chapter 12). V. S. Mahesh and Anand Kasturi note from their consulting work with service organizations around the world that thousands of frontline staff, when asked, usually describe customers who cause problems as "overdemanding," "unreasonable," "refuse to listen," "always want everything their way, immediately," and also "arrogant."[5]

Providing quality service requires an independent, warm, and friendly personality. These traits are more likely to be found in people with higher self-esteem. However, many frontline jobs are seen as low-level jobs, which require little education, offer low pay, and very little career advancement. If a firm cannot move away from this image, frontline jobs may not be similar to staff's self-perception and lead to person/role conflicts.

Inter-client Conflict

Conflicts between customers are not uncommon (e.g., smoking in nonsmoking sections, jumping queues, talking on a cell phone in a movie theater, or being excessively noisy in a restaurant). It is usually the service staff who are asked to tell the customer to behave. This is a stressful and unpleasant task, as it is difficult and often impossible to satisfy both sides.

Although employees may experience conflict and stress, they are still expected to smile and be friendly toward customers. We call this emotional labor, which, in itself, is an important cause of stress. Let us look at emotional labor in more detail in the next section.

Emotional Labor

The term *emotional labor* was first used by Arlie Hochschild in her book *The Managed Heart.*[6] Emotional labor occurs when there is a gap between the way frontline staff feel inside and the emotions that management requires them to display to their customers. Frontline staff are expected to be cheerful, friendly, compassionate, sincere, or even humble. Although some service firms make an effort to recruit employees with such characteristics, there will definitely be situations when employees do not feel such positive emotions, yet are required to hide their true feelings in order to meet customer expectations (Figure 11.4).

Figure 11.4 Emotional labor and forced smiles can be difficult for service employees.

The stress of emotional labor is nicely shown in the following story: A flight attendant was approached by a passenger with "Let's have a smile." She replied with "Okay. I'll tell you what, first you smile and then I'll smile, okay?" He smiled. "Good," she said. "Now hold that for eight hours," and walked away. Figure 11.5 captures emotional labor in airline industry.

Firms need to be aware of ongoing emotional stress among their employees[7] and make sure that their employees are trained to deal with emotional stress and cope with pressure from customers. If not, employees will use a variety of ways to resist the stress of emotional labor.[8] For example, because of Singapore Airlines' reputation for service excellence, its customers tend to have very high expectations and can be very demanding. This puts a lot of pressure on its frontline employees. The commercial training manager of Singapore Airlines (SIA) explained,

> We have recently undertaken an external survey and it appears that more of the "demanding customers" choose to fly with SIA. So the staff are really under a lot of pressure. We have a motto: "If SIA can't do it for you, no other airline can." So we encourage staff to try to sort things out and to do as much as they can for the customer. Although they are very proud and indeed protective of the company, we need to help them deal with the emotional turmoil of having to handle their customers well and, at the same time, feel they're not being taken advantage of. The challenge is to help our staff deal with difficult situations and take the brickbats. This will be the next thrust of our training programs.[9]

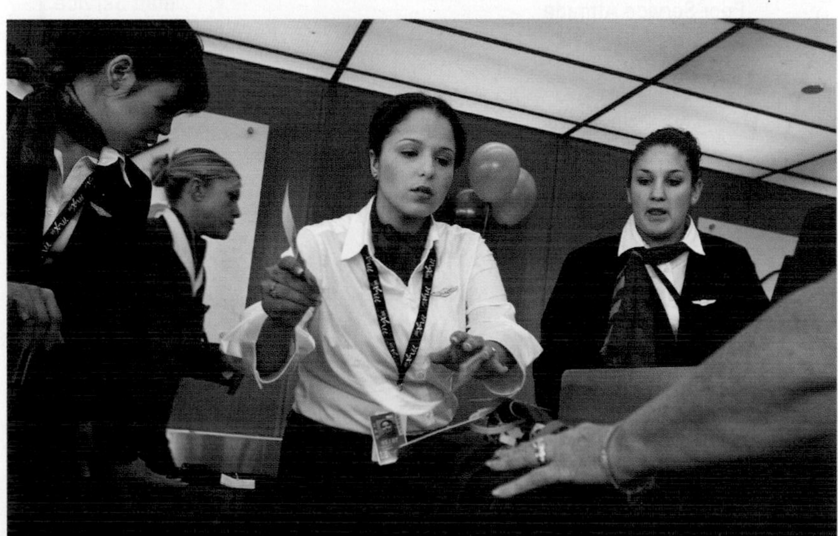

Figure 11.5 Airline staff face stress of emotional labor due to high expectation of the customers.

PART III

LO 3

Describe the cycles of failure, mediocrity, and success in HR for service firms.

CYCLES OF FAILURE, MEDIOCRITY, AND SUCCESS

After having discussed the importance of frontline employees and how difficult their work is, let's look at the big picture of how poor, mediocre, and excellent firms set up their frontline employees for failure, mediocrity, or success. All too often, bad working environments are connected to terrible service, with employees treating customers the way their managers treat them. Businesses with high employee turnover are often stuck in what has been termed the "*Cycle of Failure*." Others, which offer job security but are heavily rule- and procedure-based, may suffer from an equally undesirable "*Cycle of Mediocrity*." However, if managed well, there is potential for a virtuous cycle in service employment, called the "*Cycle of Success*."[10]

The Cycle of Failure

In many service industries, the search for productivity leads to simplifying work processes and paying the lowest possible wages. Such employees perform repetitive tasks that need little or no training. Among consumer services, gas stations, fast-food restaurants, and call center operations are often examples of this mindset (although there are exceptions). The Cycle of Failure captures the effect of such a strategy. There are two separate cycles, but they affect each other. One involves failures with employees, and the second, with customers (Figure 11.6).

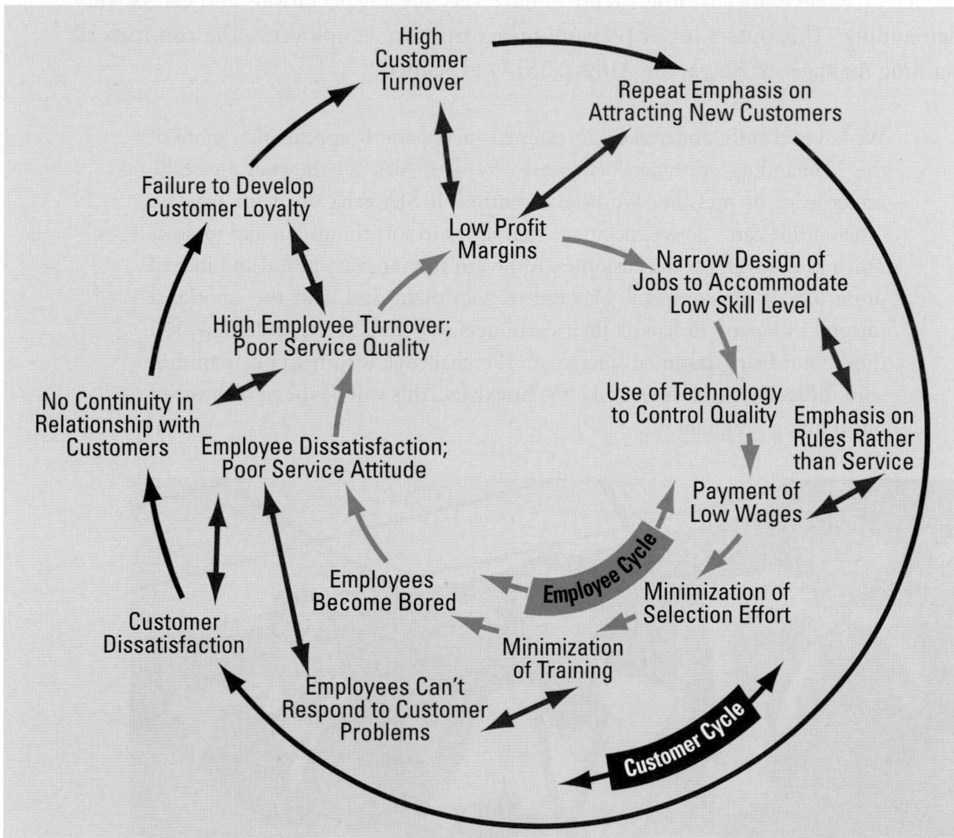

Figure 11.6 The Cycle of Failure.

SOURCE

From MIT *Sloan Management Review*. Copyright 1991 by Massachusettes Institute of Technology. All rights reserved. Distributed by Tribune Media Services.

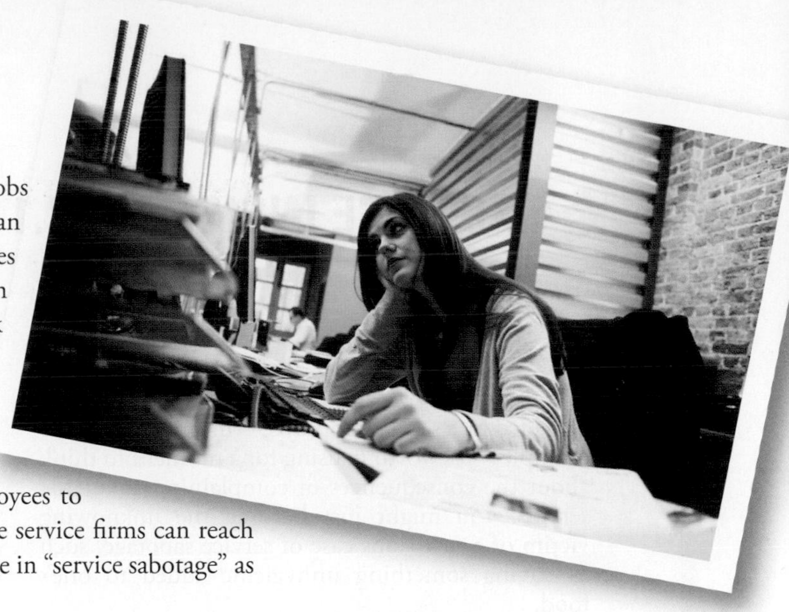

Figure 11.7 Employees in the cycle of failure are bored and dissatisfied.

The *employee cycle of failure* begins with a narrow design of jobs for low skill levels. There is an emphasis on rules rather than service, and technology is used to control quality. Low wages are paid, and there is little investment in employee selection and training. As a result, there are bored employees who lack the ability to respond to customer problems. They then become dissatisfied and develop a poor service attitude. The results for the firm are low service quality and high employee turnover. Because of low profit margins, the cycle repeats itself with the hiring of more low-paid employees to work in the same unrewarding manner (Figure 11.7). Some service firms can reach such low levels of employee morale that frontline staff engage in "service sabotage" as described in Service Insights 11.1.[11]

The *customer cycle of failure* begins with repeated emphasis on attracting new customers. Since the employees are dissatisfied, the customers become dissatisfied with employee performance. High staff turnover means that customers are always served by new faces, so there is no continuity. Because these customers fail to become loyal to the supplier, they turn over as quickly as the staff, requiring an ongoing search for new customers to maintain sales volume.

Managers make many excuses for allowing the cycle of failure to continue. Most are focused on employees:

- "You just can't get good people nowadays."
- "People today just don't want to work."
- "To get good people would cost too much and you can't pass on these cost increases to customers."
- "It's not worth training our frontline people when they leave you so quickly."
- "High turnover is simply an inevitable part of our business. You've got to learn to live with it."[12]

Many managers ignore the long-term financial effects of low-pay/high-turnover human resource strategies. They often fail to measure three key cost variables: (1) the cost of constantly recruiting, hiring, and training; (2) the lower productivity of inexperienced new workers; and (3) the costs of having to always attract new customers (which requires extensive advertising and promotional discounts). It also ignores two revenue variables: future revenue if the customer had stayed loyal to the brand; and income from potential customers who are turned off by negative word-of-mouth.

The Cycle of Mediocrity

The Cycle of Mediocrity is most likely to be found in large organizations that operate on lots of rules and procedures (Figure 11.9).

In such environments, service delivery standards tend to be rule based. Service is standardized, and the emphasis is on achieving operational efficiencies. Job responsibilities are narrowly defined, and categorized by grade and scope of

SERVICE INSIGHTS 11.1

Service Sabotage by the Frontline

The next time you are dissatisfied with the service provided by a service employee—in a restaurant, for example—it's worth pausing for a moment to think about the consequences of complaining about the service. You might just become the unknowing victim of a malicious case of service sabotage, such as having something unhygienic added to one's food.

There is actually a fairly high incidence of service sabotage by frontline employees. Lloyd Harris and Emmanuel Ogbonna found that 90% of them accepted that frontline behavior with malicious intent to reduce or spoil the service—service sabotage—is an everyday occurrence in their organizations.

Harris and Ogbonna classify service sabotage along two dimensions: covert—overt, and routinized—intermittent behaviors. Covert behaviors are concealed from customers, whereas overt actions are purposefully displayed often to co-workers and also to customers. Routinized behaviors are ingrained into the culture, whereas intermittent actions are sporadic and less common. Some true examples of service sabotage classified along these two dimensions appear in Figure 11.8.

Openness of Service Sabotage Behaviors

Covert ← → *Overt*

"Normality" of Service Sabotage Behaviors: *Routinized* ↑ ↓ *Intermittent*

Customary-Private Service Sabotage	**Customer-Public Service Sabotage**
Many customers are rude or difficult, not even polite like you or I. Getting your own back evens the score. There are lots of things that you do that no one but you will ever know – smaller portions, doggy wine, a bad beer – all that and you serve with a smile! Sweet revenge! — Waiter It's perfectly normal to file against some of the s**t that happens. Managers have always asked for more than fair and customers have always wanted something for nothing. Getting back at them is natural – it's always happened, nothing new in that. — Front of House Operative	You can put on a real old show. You know – if the guest is in a hurry, you slow it right down and drag it right out and if they want to chat, you can do the monosyllabic stuff. And all the time, you know that your mates are round the corner laughing their heads off! — Front of House Operative The trick is to do it in a way that they can't complain about. I mean, you can't push it too far but some of them are so stupid that you can talk to them like a four-year-old and they would not notice. I mean, really putting them down is really patronizing. It's great fun to watch! — Waiter
Sporadic-Private Service Sabotage	**Sporadic-Public Service Sabotage**
I don't often work with them but the night shift here really gets to me. They are always complaining. So, to get back at them, just occasionally, I put a spanner in the works – accidentally-on-purpose misread their food orders, slow the service down, stop the glass washer so that they run out – nothing heavy. — Senior Chef I don't know why I do it. Sometimes it's simply a bad day, a lousy week, I dunno – but kicking someone's bags down the back stairs is not that unusual – not every day – I guess a couple of times a month. — Front of House Supervisor	The trick is to get them and then straight away launch into the apologies. I've seen it done thousands of times – burning hot plates into someone's hands, gravy dripped on sleeves, drink spilt on backs, wigs knocked off – that was funny, soups split in laps, you get the idea! — Long Serving General Attendant Listen, there's this rule that we are supposed to greet all customers and smile at them if they pass within 5 meters. Well, this ain't done 'cos we think it's silly but this guy we decided to do it to. It started off with the waiters – we'd all go up to him and grin at him and say "hello." But it spread. Before you know it, managers and all have cottoned on and this poor chap is being met and greeted every two steps! He doesn't know what the hell is going on! It was so funny – the guy spent the last three nights in his room – he didn't dare go in the restaurant. — Housekeeping Supervisor

Figure 11.8 Examples of service sabotage.

SOURCE

Lloyd C. Harris and Emmanuel Ogbonna, "Exploring Service Sabotage: The Antecedents, Types, and Consequences of Frontline, Deviant, Antiservice Behaviors," *Journal of Service Research* 4, no. 3 (2002): 163–183.

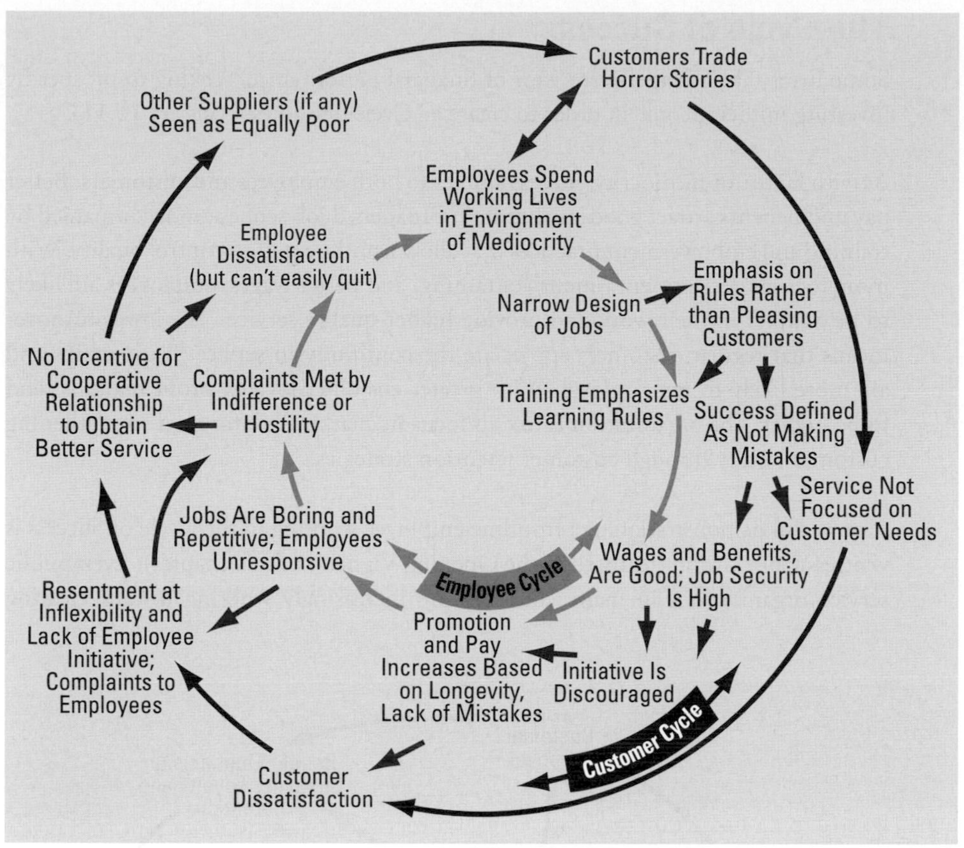

Figure 11.9 The Cycle of Mediocrity.

SOURCE

Christopher Lovelock, "Managing services: The human factor." In W. J. Glynn and J. G. Barnes, *Understanding Service Management* 228, Chichester, (UK) John Wiley & Sons.

responsibilities. The unions also have work rules. Salary increases and promotions are largely based on how long the person has been working in the company. Successful performance in a job is often measured by lack of mistakes rather than by high productivity or outstanding customer service. Training focuses on learning the rules and the technical aspects of the job, not on improving relationships with customers and co-workers. Since employees are given very little freedom to do their work in the way they think is necessary or suitable, jobs tend to be boring and repetitive (Figure 11.10). However, unlike the Cycle of Failure, most positions provide adequate pay and often good benefits, combined with high security. Thus, employees are reluctant to leave.

Figure 11.10 Employees in the cycle of mediocrity are not very productive and motivated.

Customers find such organizations frustrating to deal with. There are many rules, there is a lack of service flexibility, and employees are generally unwilling to make an effort to serve customers well. There is little incentive for customers to cooperate with the organization to achieve better service. When they complain to employees who are already unhappy, the poor service attitude becomes worse. However, customers often remain with the organization, as there is nowhere else for them to go. This could either be because the service provider holds a monopoly, or because all other available players are seen as being equally bad or worse.

The Cycle of Success

Some firms take a longer-term view of financial performance, seeking to prosper by investing in their people in order to create a "Cycle of Success" (Figure 11.11).

As with failure or mediocrity, success applies to both employees and customers. Better pay and benefits attract good-quality staff. Broadened job scopes are accompanied by training and empowerment practices that allow frontline staff to control quality. With more focused recruitment, intensive training, and better wages, employees are likely to be happier in their work and provide higher-quality service. The lower turnover means that regular customers appreciate the continuity in service relationships and are more likely to remain loyal. With greater customer loyalty, profit margins tend to be higher. The organization is free to focus its marketing efforts on strengthening customer loyalty through customer retention strategies.

A powerful demonstration of a frontline employee working in the Cycle of Success is waitress Cora Griffin (featured in the Opening Vignette of this chapter). Even public service organizations in many countries are increasingly working toward creating

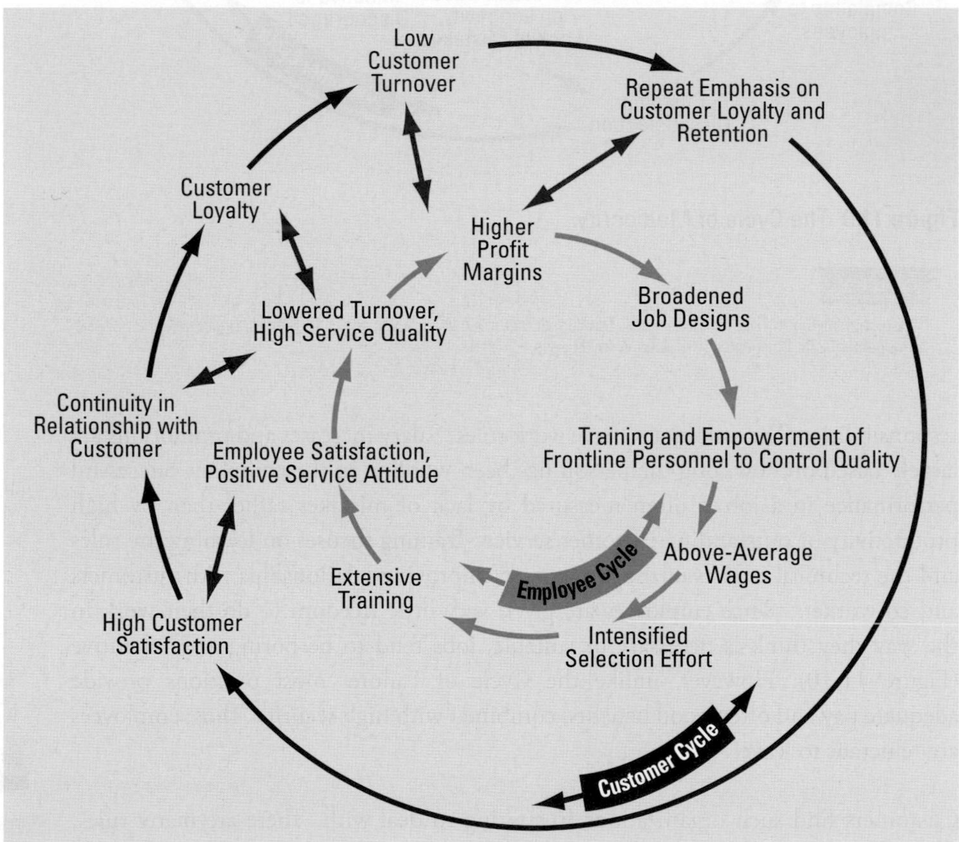

Figure 11.11 The Cycle of Success.

SOURCE

their own cycles of success, and offering their users good-quality service at a lower cost to the public.[13]

When we look at the three cycles, it is, of course, ideal for firms to be operating under the conditions in the Cycle of Success. However, firms operating under the other two cycles can still survive if some element of their offering meets customer expectations. For example, in a restaurant context, customers may be dissatisfied with the service provided by the staff, but if they are willing to accept it because they like the restaurant's quality of food, then that element has met their expectations. Nevertheless, for long-run profitability and success, firms should ideally move toward the Cycle of Success.

HUMAN RESOURCE MANAGEMENT—HOW TO GET IT RIGHT?

LO 4
Understand the key elements of the Service Talent Cycle and know how to get HR right in service firms.

Any manager who thinks logically would like to operate in the Cycle of Success. But what strategies will help service firms to move in that direction? Figure 11.12 shows the Service Talent Cycle, which is our guiding framework for successful HR practices in service firms. We will discuss the recommended practices one by one in this section.

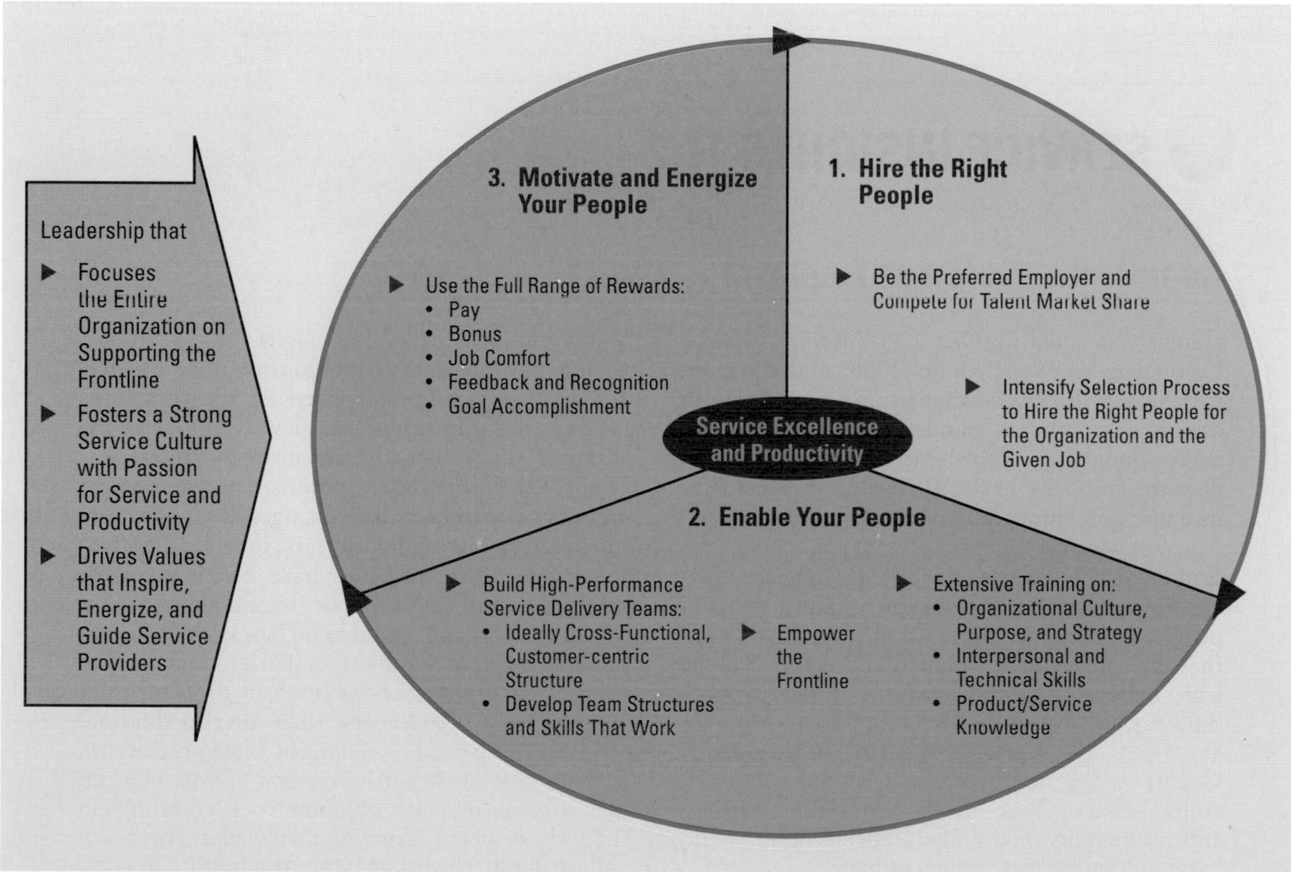

Figure 11.12 The Service Talent Cycle.

LO 5

Know how to attract, select, and hire the right people for service jobs.

Figure 11.13 A firm does not need to pay top dollars to attract top performers.

Hire the Right People

Employee effort is a strong driver of customer satisfaction over and above employee satisfaction.[14] Therefore, it is important to hire the right employees. As Jim Collins said, "The old adage 'People are the most important asset' is wrong. The *right* people are your most important asset.'" We would like to add: "... and the wrong people are a liability that is often difficult to get rid of." Hiring the right people includes competing for applications from the best employees in the labor market, then selecting the best candidates for the specific jobs to be filled from this pool.

Be the Preferred Employer

To be able to select and hire the best people, they first have to apply for a job with you and then accept your job offer in preference to offers. That means a firm has to first compete for talent market share, or as global consulting firm McKinsey & Company calls it, "the war for talent."[15] In order to effectively compete in the labor market, a firm has to be attractive for potential employees. This includes having a good image in the community as a place to work, and delivering high quality products and services that make employees feel proud to be part of the team. Top people expect above-average packages. In our experience, it takes a salary in the range of the 60th to 80th percentile of the market to attract top performers to top companies (Figure 11.13). See Service Insights 11.2 on how Google has managed, for the last few years, to remain one of the best companies in the world to work for.

SERVICE INSIGHTS 11.2

Google, the Preferred Employer

Google was voted number 1 in *Fortune's* 100 Best Companies to Work for in 2008, and continues to rank very highly on that list. So the immediate question on people's minds will be: Why? What makes Google one of the best? What kind of culture does the company have? What kind of benefits do its employees enjoy? What are its employees like?

Employees of Google are called Googlers. They are widely perceived as fun-loving and interesting people. At the same time, when it comes to work, they are achievement oriented and driven. Google has a culture of being innovative, unconventional, different, and fun, and in line with this, its employees are given the freedom to work independently. Google's experience thus far suggests that pampering employees actually results in increased productivity and profitability. Certainly, Googlers seem willing to work long hours for the company.

What kind of benefits do Googlers enjoy? The list is long, but top on the list is gourmet food for free, and food is just the appetizer! At the company's headquarters in Mountain View, California, the "campus" offers many free amenities, including Wi-Fi enabled shuttle buses, motorized scooters to get around, car washes, and oil changes. If Googlers are interested in buying hybrid cars, they get a $5,000 subsidy for that. Googlers have five free on-site doctors, unlimited sick days, free flu shots, a gym to work out at, and a pool to do laps with lifeguards on duty. For more domestic activities, there are free on-site laundry services or one can drop off their laundry at the dry cleaners. There are also childcare services, and pets are welcome at the workplace on a temporary basis. For leisure and sports, one can play a game of pool, do some rock climbing on the wall, or play a game of volleyball at the beach volleyball pit. The list goes on. As a result, Googlers can spend long and productive hours at work. However, it must be noted that the benefits offered to employees working at other Google offices tend to be less significant.

Google has a new engineering headquarters in Zurich, Switzerland. This building was partly designed by the engineers who work there. Life there is just as fun. There are meeting places that are designed to look like Swiss chalets and igloos. People can get from one floor to another using fireman poles, and there is a slide that allows them to reach the cafeteria very quickly. There are other areas like a games room, a library with architecture in the style of an English country house, and an aquarium where staff can lie in a bath of red foam and gaze at fish if they feel stressed out.

The Google Campus, Mountain View, California

Because the firm is seen as such a desirable place to work in, it can be extremely selective in its recruiting, hiring only the best and the brightest. This may work particularly well for its engineers, who tend to get the most kudos. However, despite the company's stellar reputation as an employer, some observers question whether this very positive environment can be maintained as the company grows and its workforce matures.

"The slide gets people to the cafeteria quickly"

PART III

SOURCES

Adam Lashinsky "Google Is No. 1: Search and Enjoy"; "100 Best Companies to Work For: Life Inside Google"; "The Perks of Being a Googler," *Fortune*, January 10, 2007; "Inside the Googleplex," *The Economist*, September 1, 2007; Robert Levering and Milton Moskowitz "100 Best Companies to Work for 2008: Top 50 Employers," January 22, 2008, http://money.cnn.com/galleries/2008/fortune/0801/gallery.bestcos_top50.fortune/index.html, accessed March 12, 2012; http://money.cnn.com/magazines/fortune/bestcompanies/2011/, accessed March 12, 2012; Jane Wakefield, "Google Your Way to a Wacky Office," *BBC News Website*, March 13, 2008, http://news.bbc.co.uk/1/hi/technology/7290322.stm, accessed March 12, 2012.

Select the Right People

There's no such thing as the perfect employee (Figure 11.14). Different positions are often best filled by people with different skill sets, styles, and personalities. For example, The Walt Disney Company assesses prospective employees in terms of their potential for on-stage or backstage work. On-stage workers, known as cast members, are given to those people with the appearance, personalities, and skills to match the job.

What makes outstanding service performers so special? Often, it is things that *cannot* be taught. It is the people's natural qualities, which they would bring with them to

Figure 11.14 There's no such thing as a perfect employee.

any employer. The logical conclusion is that service firms should devote great care to attracting and hiring the right candidates. Increasingly, the top companies are using employee analytics to improve their ability to attract and retain the best talent. Employee analytics are similar to customer analytics. For example, it is used to predict who would be a better performer. Service firms can also use employee analytics to place the right employees in the right job.[16] Apart from the purpose of data analysis, let's next review some tools that can help you identify the right candidates for a given firm and job, and perhaps even more importantly, reject those candidates who do not fit.

Tools to Identify the Best Candidates

Excellent service firms use a number of methods to identify the best candidates in their applicant pool. These approaches include interviewing applicants, observing behavior, conducting personality tests, and providing applicants with a realistic job preview.[17]

Use Multiple, Structured Interviews

To improve hiring decisions, successful recruiters like to use structured interviews built around job requirements and to use more than one interviewer. People tend to be more careful in their judgments when they know that another individual is also judging the same applicant. Another advantage of using two or more interviewers is that it reduces the risk of "similar to me" bias—that we all like people who are similar to ourselves (Figure 11.15).

Figure 11.15 Is the "similar to me" bias coming into play?

Observe Candidate Behavior

The hiring decision should be based on the behavior that recruiters observe, not just the words they hear. As John Wooden said, "Show me what you can do. Don't tell me what you can do. Too often, the big talkers are the little doers."[18] Behavior can be directly or indirectly observed by using behavioral simulations or assessment center tests. Also, past behavior is the best predictor of future behavior. Hire the person who has won service excellence awards, received many complimentary letters, and has great references from past employers (Figure 11.16).

Figure 11.16 References are a good way to assess past behavior.

Conduct Personality Tests

Many managers hire employees based on personality.[19] Personality tests help to identify measurable traits that are related to a particular job, such as a willingness to treat customers and colleagues with courtesy, consideration, and tact; sensitivity to customer needs; and the ability to communicate accurately and pleasantly. Research has also shown that certain traits like being hardworking and the belief in one's capabilities to manage situations tend to result in strong employee performance and service quality.[20] Hiring decisions based on such tests tend to be accurate, especially in identifying and rejecting unsuitable candidates.

For example, the Ritz-Carlton Hotels Group uses personality profiles on all job applicants. Employees are selected based on whether they have a personality suited to working in a service context. Traits such as a ready smile, a willingness to help others, and the ability to multi-task allow employees to go beyond learned skills. An applicant to Ritz-Carlton shared her experience of going through the personality test for a job as a junior-level concierge at the Ritz-Carlton Millenia Singapore. Her best advice: "Tell the truth. These are experts; they will know if you are lying," and then she added:

> On the big day, they asked if I liked helping people, if I was an organized person, and if I liked to smile a lot. "Yes, yes, and yes," I said. But I had to support it with real-life examples. This, at times, felt rather intrusive. To answer the first question for instance, I had to say a bit about the person I had helped—why she needed help, for example. The test forced me to recall even insignificant things I had done, like learning how to say hello in different languages, which helped to get a fix on my character."[21]

Give Applicants a Realistic Preview of the Job

During the recruitment process, service companies should inform candidates about the reality of the job, thereby giving them a chance to "try on the job" and see whether it's a good fit or not. At the same time, recruiters can observe how candidates respond to the job's realities. Some candidates may withdraw if they realize the job is not a good match for them. Au Bon Pain, a chain of French bakery cafés, lets applicants work for two paid days in a café prior to the final selection interview. Managers can observe candidates in action, and candidates can assess whether they like the job and the work environment (Figure 11.17). In the ultimate recruitment and interview process, Donald Trump worked with the NBC network to produce the reality TV series, *The Apprentice*, where the winner received the chance to join the Trump organization and manage a project selected by Trump himself.

Train Service Employees Actively

LO 6

Explain the key areas in which service employees need training.

If a firm has good people, investments in training can yield outstanding results. Having a good career development program for employees can help them to feel that

Figure 11.17 Au Bon Pain allows candidates to get a taste of the real job before the final selection interview.

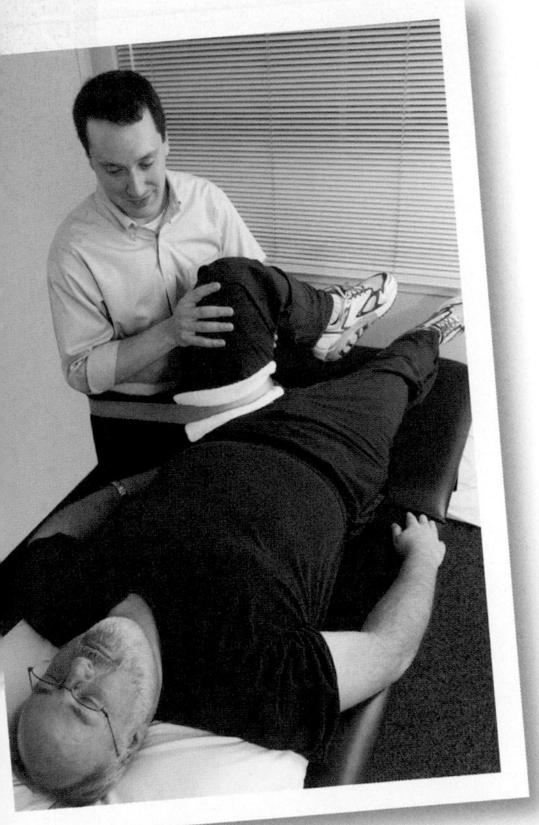

Figure 11.18 A physiotherapist displaying technical competence, as well as a warm and friendly smile.

they are valued and taken care of. In turn, employees will work to meet customers' needs, resulting in customer satisfaction, loyalty, and, ultimately, profitability for the firm.[22] Service champions show a strong commitment to training in words, dollars, and action. Employees of Apple retail stores, for example, are given intensive training on how to interact with customers, how to phrase words in a positive rather than negative way, and what to say when customers react emotionally. Employees are supposed to help customers solve problems rather than to sell.[23]

There are many aspects in a firm that service employees need to be trained on. They need to learn:

- **Organizational culture, purpose, and strategy.** Start strong with new hires. Focus on getting emotional commitment to the firm's core strategy, and promote core values such as commitment to service excellence, responsiveness, team spirit, mutual respect, honesty, and integrity. Use managers to teach, and focus on "what," "why," and "how" rather than the specifics of the job.[24] For example, new recruits at Disneyland attend the "Disney University Orientation." It consists of a detailed discussion of the company's history and philosophy, the service standards expected of cast members, and a comprehensive tour of Disneyland's operations.[25]
- **Interpersonal and technical skills.** Interpersonal skills tend to be generic across service jobs. These include visual communications skills such as making eye contact, attentive listening, understanding body language, and even facial expressions. Technical skills include all the required knowledge related to processes (e.g., how to handle a merchandise return), machines (e.g., how to operate the terminal, or cash machine), and rules and regulations related to customer service processes. Both technical and interpersonal skills are *necessary together*. Neither skill alone is enough to perform a job well (Figure 11.18).[26]

- **Product/Service knowledge.** Knowledgeable staff are a key aspect of service quality. They must be able to explain product features effectively and also position the product correctly. At an Apple retail store, for example, all the products are openly displayed for customers to try them out. Staff members need to be able to answer questions about any of the product features, usage, and any other aspects of service like maintenance, service bundles, etc.

Of course, training has to result in observable changes in behavior. If employees do not apply what they have learned, then the investment is wasted. Learning is not only about becoming smarter but also about changing behaviors and improving decision making. To achieve this, repeated practice is needed.

Figure 11.19 A Formula One technician being briefed by his foreman.

Training and learning professionalizes the frontline. Well-trained employees feel and act like professionals (Figure 11.19). A waiter who knows about food, cooking, wines, dining etiquette, and how to effectively interact with customers (even complaining ones), feels professional, has a higher self-esteem, and is respected by his customers. Training is therefore extremely effective in reducing person/role stress. Service Insights 11.3 is a great example of how UP Your Service! College enables and energizes front line employees.

Empower the Front Line

 **LO 7**

Understand why empowerment is so important in many frontline jobs.

After being the preferred employer, selecting the right candidates, and training them well, the next step is empowering the frontline. Nearly all excellent service firms have stories of employees who recovered failed service transactions, or went the extra mile to make a customer's day or avoid some kind of disaster for that client (as an example, see Service Insights 11.4—Empowerment at Nordstrom).[27] To allow this to happen, employees have to be empowered. For example, Nordstrom trains and trusts its employees to do the right thing, and empowers them to do so. Its employee handbook has only one rule: "Use good judgment in all situations." Employee self-direction has become increasingly important, especially in service firms. This is because frontline staff are often on their own when they face their customers. Therefore, it is difficult for managers to closely monitor their behavior.[28] Research has also linked high empowerment to higher customer satisfaction.[29]

Research has shown that empowerment is most important when the following factors are present within the organization and its environment:

- The firm offers personalized, customized service and is based on competitive differentiation.
- The firm has extended relationships with customers rather than short-term transactions.
- The organization uses technologies that are complex and nonroutine in nature.
- Service failures often are nonroutine and cannot be designed out of the system. Frontline employees have to respond quickly to recover the service.
- The business environment is unpredictable and surprises are to be expected.
- Existing managers are comfortable with letting employees work on their own for the benefit of both the organization and its customers.[30]

SERVICE INSIGHTS 11.3

UP Your Service! College Builds Cultures That Inspire People to Excel in Service

Having a service-oriented attitude is not something that comes naturally to everyone, especially if the culture within the organization does not support a "customer first" mentality. This is where UP Your Service! College (UYSC) comes in.

"All organizations can create a sustainable competitive advantage by building a Superior Service Culture," notes Ron Kaufman, author of the bestselling book series *UP Your Service!* and founder of UYSC. He adds, "A powerful service reputation attracts the best customers, the most loyal employees, and the highest industry margins."

UYSC combines customer service training courses with culture building activities that uplift the spirit of service throughout an organization. This creates an atmosphere where staff are inspired to excel in service delivery to customers and to one another.

The comprehensive UYSC course curriculum includes:

- **Course 100: Achieving Superior Service™** teaches fundamental service principles to raise service levels and improve the customer experience at every point of contact.
- **Course 200: Building Service Partnerships™** demonstrates the importance of building powerful service partnerships with partners and colleagues.
- **Course 300: Increasing Customer Loyalty™** teaches how to increase customer loyalty, manage customer expectations and handle situations professionally when things go wrong.

"An uplifting course for employees at Microsoft with College founder Ron Kaufman at the center"

These courses are closely integrated with Service Leadership Workshops, Service Momentum Events, and Service Culture Building Activities. Unlike many other training programs, UYSC builds a common service language throughout all levels of the organization, resulting in everyone applying the same service principles in their work every day. The courses are facilitated by certified course leaders and feature video-based instructions by Ron Kaufman to ensure consistent high-quality training.

To date, organizations using the UYSC-proven curriculum include major multi-nationals, large domestic companies, and government entities such as Dubai Bank, Dubai Properties, ManuLife, Nokia, Riyadh Care Hospital, Singapore Central Provident Fund, Singapore General Hospital, Tatweer, TECOM, Wipro, and Xerox Emirates.

SOURCE

http://www.upyourservice.com/ and http://www.ronkaufman.com/, accessed March 12, 2012.

SERVICE INSIGHTS 11.4

Empowerment at Nordstrom

Van Mensah, a men's clothes sales associate at Nordstrom, received a disturbing letter from one of his loyal customers. The gentleman had purchased some $2,000 worth of shirts and ties from Mensah, and mistakenly washed the shirts in hot water. They all shrank. He was writing to ask Mensah's professional advice on how he should deal with his situation (the gentleman did not complain and readily conceded the mistake was his).

Mensah immediately called the customer and offered to replace those shirts with new ones at no charge. He asked the customer to mail the other shirts back to Nordstrom—at Nordstrom's expense. "I didn't have to ask for anyone's permission to do what I did for that customer," said Mensah. "Nordstrom would rather leave it up to me to decide what's best."

Middlemas, a employee who has been with Nordstrom for a long time, says to other employees, "You will never be criticized for doing too much for a customer, you will only be criticized for doing too little. If you're ever in doubt as to what to do in a situation, always make a decision that favors the customer before the company." Nordtrom's Employee Handbook confirms this. It reads:

Welcome to Nordstrom

We're glad to have you with our Company.
Our number one goal is to provide outstanding customer service.
Set both your personal and professional goals high.
We have great confidence in your ability to achieve them.

Nordstrom Rules:

Rule#1: Use your good judgment in all situations.
There will be no additional rules.
Please feel free to ask your department manager, store manager, or division general manager any question at any time.

SOURCE

Robert Spector and Patrick D. McCarthy, *The Nordstrom Way*. New York: John Wiley & Sons, Inc., 2000, 15–16, 95.

Levels of Employee Involvement

Empowerment can take place at several levels:

- *Suggestion involvement* empowers employees to make recommendations through formalized programs. McDonald's, for example, listens closely to its frontline. Did you know that innovations ranging from the Egg McMuffin, to methods of wrapping burgers without leaving a thumbprint on the bun, were invented by employees?
- *Job involvement* represents opening up of job content. Jobs are redesigned to allow employees to use a wider variety of skills. To cope with the added demands accompanying this form of empowerment, employees require training. Supervisors need to be reoriented from directing the group to supporting its performance.

- *High involvement* gives even the lowest-level employees a sense of involvement in the company's overall performance. Information is shared. Employees develop skills in teamwork, problem solving, and business operations, and they participate in work-unit management decisions. There is profit sharing, often in the form of bonuses.

Southwest Airlines is an example of a high-involvement company. It trusts its employees and gives them the freedom and authority to do their jobs. Southwest's mechanics and pilots feel free to help ramp agents' load bags. When a flight is running late, it is not uncommon to see pilots helping passengers in wheelchairs to board the aircraft, assisting operations agents by taking boarding passes, or helping flight attendants clean the cabin between flights. In addition, Southwest employees use common sense, not rules, when it is in the best interests of the customer.

LO 8

Explain how to build high performance service delivery teams.

Build High-Performance Service-Delivery Teams

A team has been defined as "a small number of people with complementary skills who are committed to a common purpose, set of performance goals, and approach for which they hold themselves mutually accountable."[31] Many services require people to work in teams, often across functions for well-coordinated delivery, especially when different individuals each play specialist roles. For example, health-care services depend heavily on effective teamwork (see Figure 11.20).

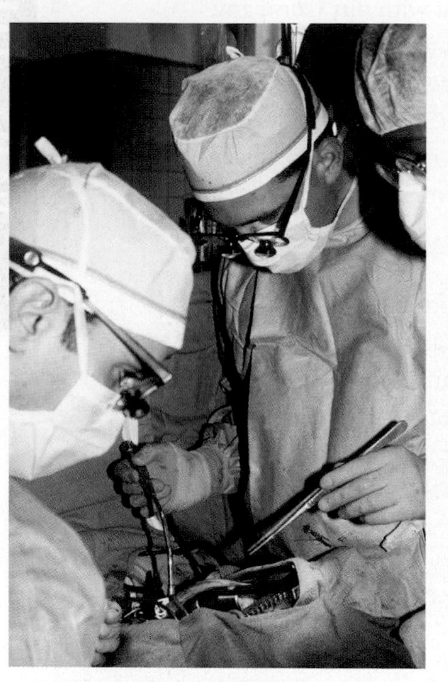

Figure 11.20 Surgical teams work under particularly demanding conditions.

Research confirms that frontline staff feel the lack of interdepartmental support prevents them from satisfying their customers (Figure 11.21).[32] In many industries, firms need to create cross-functional teams and give them the authority and responsibility to serve customers from end-to-end. Such teams are also called self-managed teams.[33]

Teams, training, and empowerment go hand in hand. Singapore Airlines uses teams to provide emotional support and to mentor its cabin crew, and the company effectively assesses, rewards, and promotes staff (see Service Insights 11.5).

Figure 11.21 Lack of cooperation within a team will lead to problems in the company.

SERVICE INSIGHTS 11.5

Singapore Airline's Team Concept

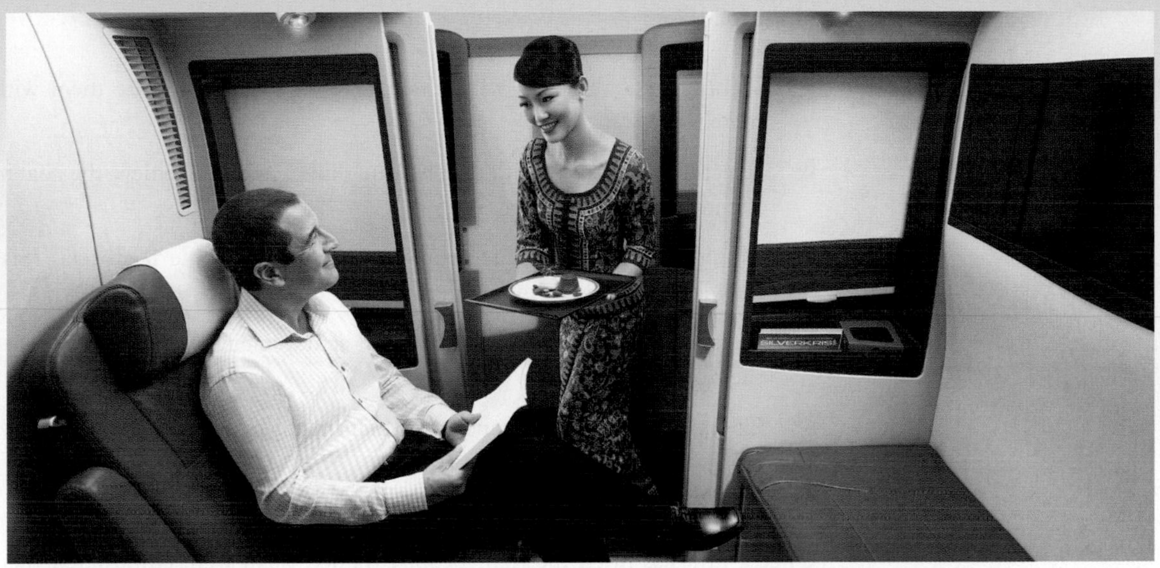

Figure 11.22 Cabin crew serving in the A380 first class cabin.

SIA understands the importance of teamwork in the delivery of service excellence. This is difficult because many crew members are scattered around the world. SIA's answer is the "team concept."

Poh Leong Choo, Senior Manager for Crew Services, explained: "In order to effectively manage our 6,600 crew, we divide them into teams, small units, with a team leader in charge of about 13 people. We will roster them to fly together as much as we can. Flying together, as a unit, allows them to build up camaraderie, and crew members feel like they are part of a team, not just a member. The team leader will get to know them well, their strengths and weaknesses, and will become their mentor and their counsel, and someone to whom they can turn to if they need help or advice. The 'check trainers' oversee 12 or 13 teams and fly with them whenever possible, not only to inspect their performance but also to help their team develop."

"The interaction within each of the teams is very strong. As a result, when a team leader does a staff appraisal, they really know the staff. You would be amazed how meticulous and detailed each staff record is. So, in this way, we have good control, and through the control, we can ensure that the crew delivers the promise. They know that they're being constantly monitored and so they deliver. If there are problems, we will know about them and we can send them for retraining. Those who are good will be selected for promotion."

According to Giam Ming Toh, Senior Manager for Crew Performance, "What is good about the team concept is that, despite the huge number of crew, people can relate to a team and have a sense of belonging. 'This is my team.' And they are put together for one to two years and they are rostered together for about 60–70% of the time, so they do fly together quite a fair bit".

SOURCE

Jochen Wirtz and Robert Johnston, "Singapore Airlines: What It Takes to Sustain Service Excellence - A Senior Management Perspective," *Managing Service Quality* 13, no. 1 (2003), 10–19; and Loizos Heracleous, Jochen Wirtz, and Nitin Pangarkar, *Flying High in Competitive Industry: Secrets of the World's Leading Airline*. Singapore: McGraw-Hill, 2009. Photo courtesy of Singapore Airlines. Disclaimer: The information above was obtained in 2009.

Creating Successful Service Delivery Teams

It's not easy to make teams work well. Skills like cooperation, listening to others, coaching, and encouraging one another are needed. Team members must learn how to voice differences, tell one another hard truths, and ask tough questions. All these require training. Management also needs to set up a structure that will move the teams toward success. To succeed in the global economy, managers need to do each of the following:

- Identify what the team will achieve. Define goals and share them with team members.
- Select team members with care. All the skills needed to achieve the goal must be found within the team.
- Monitor the team and its team members and provide feedback. This aligns individual goals with those of the organization.
- Keep team members informed of goal achievement, update them, and reward them for their efforts.
- Coordinate with other managers to achieve the overall company objectives. [34]

LO 9

Know how to motivate and energize service employees so that they will deliver service excellence and productivity.

Motivate and Energize People

Once a firm has hired the right people, trained them well, empowered them, and organized them into effective service delivery teams, how can it ensure that they will deliver? Staff performance is a function of ability and motivation.[35] Motivating and rewarding strong service performers are some of the most effective ways of retaining them. Employees learn quickly that those who get promoted are the truly outstanding service providers and that those who get fired are those that do not deliver at the customer level (Figure 11.23).

Figure 11.23 Rewarding employees according to their performances is essential to the success of a business.

A major reason why service businesses fail is that they do not use the full range of available rewards effectively. Many firms think in terms of money as reward, but they does not pass the test of an effective reward. Paying more than what is seen as fair only has short-term motivating effects, and wears off quickly. On the other hand, bonuses that depend on performance have to be earned again and again. Therefore, they tend to be more lasting in their effectiveness. Other, more lasting rewards are the job content itself, recognition and feedback, and goal accomplishment.

Job Content

People are motivated and satisfied simply by knowing that they are doing a good job. This is true especially if the job:

- Has a variety of different activities.
- Needs the completion of "whole" pieces of work.
- Has an impact on the lives of others.
- Comes with freedom and flexibility.
- Is a source of direct and clear feedback about how well employees did their work (e.g., grateful customers and sales).

Figure 11.24 When people are focused on goal achievement, it will motivate and energize them.

Feedback and Recognition

Humans are social beings, and they like to feel a sense of belonging. This is possible if there is recognition and feedback from the people around them, i.e., their colleagues and bosses. If employees receive recognition and are thanked for service excellence, they will want to continue achieving it. If carried out well, star employee of the month-type of awards can recognize high performances and be highly motivating. Feedback can also come from customers. Employees are highly satisfied and motivated when they work in jobs where they can make a positive impact on others. Hence, putting employees in touch with end-users and letting them hear positive feedback from customers can be very motivating. [36]

Goal Achievement

Goals focus people's energy. Achieving important goals is a reward in itself. Goals that are specific, difficult but achievable, and accepted by the staff are strong motivators (Figure 11.24). They result in higher performance than without goals, or having unclear goals (e.g., "do your best"), or having goals that are impossible to achieve. In short, well-communicated and mutually accepted goals are effective motivators.

SERVICE LEADERSHIP AND CULTURE

 **LO 10**

Understand the role of service leadership and culture in developing people for service advantage.

So far, we have discussed the key strategies that help to move an organization toward service excellence. However, to truly get there, we need a strong service culture that is continuously reinforced and developed by management that is in line with the firm's strategy.[37] *Charismatic leadership*, also called *transformational leadership*, changes the values, goals, and aspirations of the frontline to be in line with those of the firms. Under this kind of leadership, staff are more likely to do their best and go "above and beyond the call of duty," because it is similar to their own values, beliefs, and attitudes.[38]

Leonard Berry found that some of the core values in excellent service firms included excellence, innovation, joy, teamwork, respect, integrity, and social profit.[39] These values are part of the firm's culture. A *service culture* can be defined as:

- Shared perceptions of *what* is important in an organization.
- Shared values and beliefs of *why* those things are important.[40]

In order for values and beliefs to be shared by all employees, they may have to be instilled in them. Employees also have to be continually reminded of this. For example, Ritz-Carlton translated the key product and service requirements of its customers into the Ritz-Carlton Gold Standards, which include a credo, motto, three steps of service, and 12 service values (see Service Insights 11.6).

Ritz-Carlton's service values are split into different levels. Service values 10, 11, and 12 are functional values such as safety, security, and cleanliness. The next level

SERVICE INSIGHTS 11.6

Ritz-Carlton's Gold Standards

Gold Standards

Our Gold Standards are the foundation of The Ritz-Carlton Hotel Company, LLC. They encompass the values and philosophy by which we operate and include:

The Credo

The Ritz-Carlton Hotel is a place where the genuine care and comfort of our guests are our highest mission.

We pledge to provide the finest personal service and facilities for our guests who will always enjoy a warm, relaxed, yet refined ambience.

The Ritz-Carlton experience enlivens the senses, instills well-being, and fulfills even the unexpressed wishes and needs of our guests.

Motto

At The Ritz-Carlton Hotel Company, LLC, "We are Ladies and Gentlemen serving Ladies and Gentlemen." This motto exemplifies the anticipatory service provided by all staff members.

Three Steps of Service

1. A warm and sincere greeting. Use the guest's name.
2. Anticipation and fulfillment of each guest's needs.
3. Fond farewell. Give a warm good-bye and use the guest's name.

http://corporate.ritzcarlton.com/en/about/goldstandards.htm - top

Service Values: I Am Proud to Be Ritz-Carlton

1. I build strong relationships and create Ritz-Carlton guests for life.
2. I am always responsive to the expressed and unexpressed wishes and needs of our guests.
3. I am empowered to create unique, memorable and personal experiences for our guests.
4. I understand my role in achieving the Key Success Factors, embracing Community Footprints and creating The Ritz-Carlton Mystique.
5. I continuously seek opportunities to innovate and improve The Ritz-Carlton experience.
6. I own and immediately resolve guest problems.
7. I create a work environment of teamwork and lateral service so that the needs of our guests and each other are met.
8. I have the opportunity to continuously learn and grow.
9. I am involved in the planning of the work that affects me.
10. I am proud of my professional appearance, language, and behavior.
11. I protect the privacy and security of our guests, my fellow employees and the company's confidential information, and assets.
12. I am responsible for uncompromising levels of cleanliness and creating a safe and accident-free environment.

The 6th Diamond

Mystique
Emotional Engagement
Functional

The Employee Promise

At The Ritz-Carlton, our Ladies and Gentlemen are the most important resource in our service commitment to our guests.

By applying the principles of trust, honesty, respect, integrity, and commitment, we nurture and maximize talent to the benefit of each individual and the company.

The Ritz-Carlton fosters a work environment where diversity is valued, quality of life is enhanced, individual aspirations are fulfilled, and The Ritz-Carlton Mystique is strengthened.

THREE STEPS OF SERVICE

1
A warm and sincere greeting. Use the guest name, if and when possible.
2
Anticipation and compliance with guest needs.
3
Fond farewell. Give them a warm good-bye and use their names, if and when possible.

"We Are Ladies and Gentlemen Serving Ladies and Gentlemen"

THE EMPLOYEE PROMISE

At The Ritz-Carlton, our Ladies and Gentlemen are the most important resource in our service commitment to our guests.

By applying the principles of trust, honesty, respect, integrity and commitment, we nurture and maximize talent to the benefit of each individual and the company.

The Ritz-Carlton fosters a work environment where diversity is valued, quality of life is enhanced, individual aspirations are fulfilled, and The Ritz-Carlton mystique is strengthened.

THE RITZ-CARLTON®

CREDO

The Ritz-Carlton Hotel is a place where the genuine care and comfort of our guests is our highest mission.

We pledge to provide the finest personal service and facilities for our guests who will always enjoy a warm, relaxed yet refined ambience.

The Ritz-Carlton experience enlivens the senses, instills well-being, and fulfills even the unexpressed wishes and needs of our guests.

SOURCE

of excellence is emotional engagement, which covers values 4 to 9. They relate to learning and professional growth of its employees, teamwork, service, problem solving, service recovery, innovation, and continuous improvement. Beyond the guests' functional needs and emotional engagement is the third level, which relates to values 1, 2, and 3 and is called "the Ritz-Carlton Mystique." This level aims to create unique, memorable, and personal guest experiences, which Ritz-Carlton believes can only occur when employees deliver on the guests' expressed and unexpressed wishes and needs, and when they strive to build lifetime relationships between Ritz-Carlton and its guests.[41]

Tim Kirkpatrick, Director of Training and Development of Ritz-Carlton's Boston Common Hotel said, "The Gold Standards are part of our uniform, just like your name tag. But remember, it's just a laminated card until you put it into action."[42] To reinforce these standards, every morning briefing includes a discussion directly related to the standards. The aim of these discussions is to keep the Ritz-Carlton philosophy at the centre of its employees' minds.

A strong service culture is one where the entire organization understands that the frontline is the lifeline of the business and focuses on it. When firms have a passion for service, top management is informed of and actively involved in what happens at the frontline. This shows that what happens at the frontline is crucially important to them. They achieve this by regularly talking to and working with frontline staff and customers. Many spend a lot of time at the frontline serving customers themselves. For example, Disney World's management spends two weeks every year in frontline staff jobs such as sweeping streets, selling ice cream, or working as ride attendants, to better appreciate and understand what really happens on the ground.[43]

Figure 11.25 shows the inverted pyramid, which highlights the importance of the frontline. It shows that the role of top management and middle management is to support the frontline in their task of delivering service excellence to their customers.

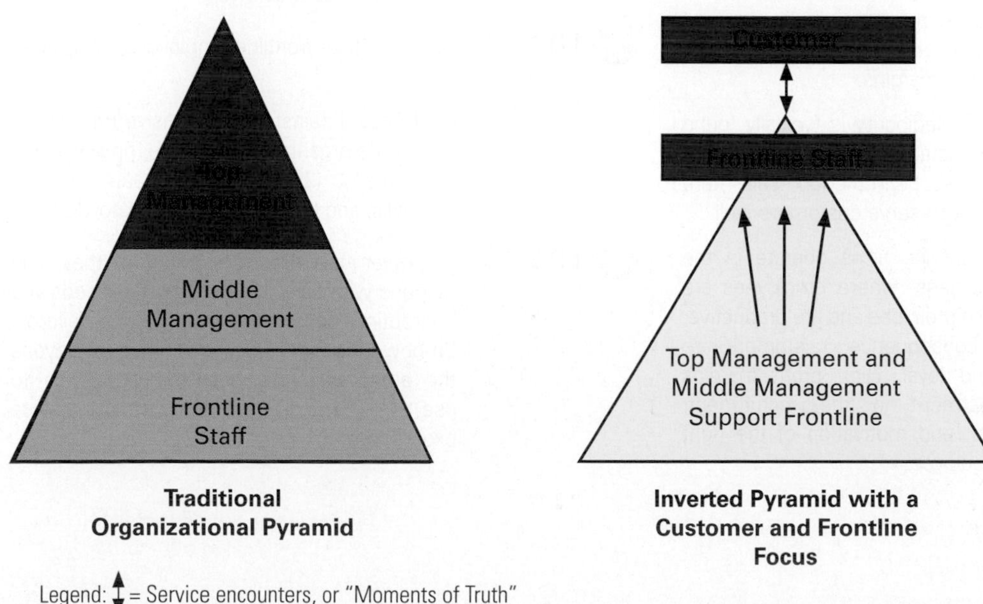

Figure 11.25 The inverted organizational pyramid.

CHAPTER SUMMARY

LO 1 ▶ Service employees are extremely important to the success of a service firm because they:

- o Are a core part of the service product.
- o Represent the service firm in the eyes of the customer.
- o Are a core part of the brand as they deliver the brand promise.
- o Generate sales, cross-sales and up-sales.
- o Are a key driver of the productivity of the frontline operations.
- o Are a source of customer loyalty.
- o Are the ones who leave an impression on the customer in those few but critical 'moments of truth' encounters, even in low-contact services.

LO 2 ▶ The work of frontline employees is difficult and stressful because they are in boundary spanning positions which often have:

- o Organization/client conflicts.
- o Person/role conflict.
- o Inter-client conflicts.
- o Emotional labor and emotional stress.

LO 3 ▶ We used three types of cycles involving frontline employees and customers to describe how firms can be set up for failure, mediocrity, and success:

- o The Cycle of Failure involves a low pay and high employee turnover strategy, and as a consequence results in high customer dissatisfaction and defections, which decrease profit margins.
- o The Cycle of Mediocrity is typically found in large bureaucracies, offering job security but not much scope in the job itself. There is no incentive to serve customers well.
- o Successful service firms operate in the Cycle of Success, where employees are satisfied with their jobs and are productive, and as a consequence, customers are satisfied and loyal. High profit margins allow investment in the recruitment, development and motivation of the right frontline employees.

LO 4 ▶ The Service Talent Cycle is a guiding framework for successful HR strategies in service firms, helping them to move their firms into the cycle of success. Implementing the service talent cycle correctly will give firms highly motivated employees who are willing and able to deliver service excellence and go the extra mile for their customers, and are highly productive at the same time. It has four key prescriptions:

- o Hire the right people.
- o Enable frontline employees.
- o Motivate and energize them.
- o Have a leadership team that emphasizes and supports the frontline.

LO 5 ▶ To hire the right people, firms need to attract, select, and hire the right people for their firm and any given service job. Best-practice HR strategies start with recognition that, in many industries, the labor market is highly competitive. Competing for talent by being the preferred employer requires:

- o That the company be seen as a preferred employer, and as a result, receive a large number of applications from the best potential candidates in the labor market.
- o That careful selection ensures new employees fit both job requirements and the organization's culture. Select the best suited candidates using screening methods such as observation, personality tests, structured interviews, and providing realistic job previews.

LO 6 ▶ To enable their frontline employees, firms need to:

- o Conduct painstaking extensive training on: (1) the organizational culture, purpose, and strategy, (2) interpersonal and technical skills, and (3) product/service knowledge.

LO 7 ▶ Empower the frontline so that they can respond with flexibility to customer needs and nonroutine encounters and service failures. Empowerment and training will give employees the authority, skills, and self-confidence to use their own initiative in delivering service excellence.

LO 8 ▶ Organize frontline employees into effective service delivery teams (often cross-functional) that can serve their customers from end to end.

LO 9 ▶ Finally, energize and motivate employees with a full set of rewards, ranging from pay, satisfying job content, recognition and feedback, to goal accomplishment.

LO 10 ▶ Top and middle managers, including frontline supervisors, need to continuously reinforce a strong culture that emphasizes service excellence. Effective service leadership involves:

- Focusing the entire organization on supporting the front line.
- Having a strong communications effort to shape the culture and get the message to everyone in the company.

PART III

UNLOCK YOUR LEARNING

These keywords are found within the sections of each Learning Objective (LO). They are integral to understanding the services marketing concepts taught in each section. Having a firm grasp of these keywords and how they are used is essential to helping you do well on your course, and in the real and very competitive marketing scene out there.

 **LO 1**
1 Brand
2 Low-contact services
3 "Moments of truth"
4 Personalized relationships
5 Productivity
6 Service employees
7 Service firm

 **LO 2**
8 Boundary spanning
9 Emotional labor
10 Inter-client conflict
11 Organization/Client conflict
12 Person/Role conflict
13 Role conflict

LO 3
14 Customer cycle of failure
15 Cycle of Failure
16 Cycle of Mediocrity
17 Cycle of Success
18 Employee cycle of failure
19 Service sabotage

 **LO 4**
20 Human resource management
21 Service Talent Cycle

 **LO 5**
22 Hire
23 Multiple, structured interviews
24 Observe behavior
25 Personality tests
26 Preferred employer
27 Preview of the job
28 Select

 **LO 6**
29 Interpersonal skills
30 Organizational culture
31 Product knowledge
32 Service knowledge
33 Technical skills
34 Training

 **LO 7**
35 Employee involvement
36 Employee self-direction
37 Empowerment
38 High involvement
39 Job involvement
40 Suggestion involvement

 **LO 8**
41 Cross-functional teams
42 Effective teamwork
43 Self-managed teams
44 Service-delivery team

 **LO 9**
45 Energize
46 Feedback
47 Goal achievement
48 Job content
49 Motivate
50 Recognition

 **LO 10**
51 Charismatic leadership
52 Culture
53 Inverted organizational pyramid
54 Ritz-Carlton's Gold Standards
55 Service culture
56 Service leadership
57 Transformational leadership

 **Not for the academically faint-of-heart**

For each keyword you are able to recall without referring to earlier pages, give yourself a point (and a pat on the back). Tally your score at the end and see if you earned the right to be called—a *services marketeer.*

SCORE

0 – 12 Services Marketing is done a great disservice.
13 – 23 The midnight oil needs to be lit, pronto.
24 – 33 I know what you *didn't* do all semester.
34 – 43 By George! You're getting there.
44 – 53 Now, go forth and market.
54 – 57 There should be a marketing concept named after you.

KNOW YOUR ESM

Review Questions

1. Why are service personnel so important for service firms?
2. There is a trend of service delivery moving from high contact to low contact. Are service employees still important in low-contact services? Explain your answer.
3. What is emotional labor? Explain the ways in which it may cause stress for employees in specific jobs. Illustrate your answer with suitable examples.
4. What are the key barriers for firms to break the Cycle of Failure and move into the Cycle of Success? And how should an organization trapped in the Cycle of Mediocrity proceed?
5. List five ways in which investment in hiring and selection, training, and ongoing motivation of employees will have a positive impact on customer satisfaction for organizations like (a) a restaurant, (b) an airline, (c) a hospital, and (d) a consulting firm.
6. Describe the key components of the Service Talent Cycle.
7. What can a service firm do to become a preferred employer, and as a result, receive a large number of applications from the best potential candidates in the labor market?
8. How can a firm select the best-suited candidates from a large number of applicants?
9. What are the key types of training service firms should conduct?
10. What are the factors that favor a strategy of employee empowerment?
11. How can frontline employees be effectively motivated to deliver service excellence?
12. How can a service firm build a strong service culture that emphasizes service excellence?

PART III

WORK YOUR ESM

Application Exercises

1. An airline runs a recruiting advertisement for cabin crew that shows a picture of a small boy sitting in an airline seat and clutching a teddy bear. The headline reads: "His mom told him not to talk to strangers. So what's he having for lunch?" Describe the types of personalities that you think would be (a) attracted to apply for the job by that ad, and (b) discouraged from applying.
2. Consider the following jobs: emergency department nurse, bill collector, computer repair technician, supermarket cashier, dentist, kindergarten teacher, prosecuting attorney, server in a family restaurant, server in an expensive French restaurant, stockbroker, and undertaker. What type of emotions would you expect each of them to display to customers in the course of doing their job? What drives your expectations?
3. Use the Service Talent Cycle as a diagnostic tool on a successful and an unsuccessful service firm you are familiar with. What recommendations would you prescribe to each of these two firms?
4. Think of two organizations you are familiar with, one that has a very good service culture, and one that has a very poor service culture. Describe the factors that contributed to shaping those organizational cultures. What factors do you think contributed most? Why?
5. Which issues do you see as most likely to create boundary spanning problems for employees in a customer contact center at a major Internet service provider? Select four issues and indicate how you would mediate between operations and marketing to create a satisfactory outcome for all three groups.
6. Identify the factors needed to make service teams successful in (a) an airline, (b) a restaurant, and (c) a customer contact centre.

ENDNOTES

1 Adapted from Leonard L. Berry, Discovering the Soul of Service—The Nine Drivers of Sustainable Business Success. New York: Free Press, 1999, 156–159.

2 Liliana L. Bove, and Lester W. Johnson, "Customer Relationships with Service Personnel: Do We Measure Closeness, Quality or Strength?" *Journal of Business Research* 54 (2001): 189–197; Magnus Söderlund and Sara Rosengren, "Revisiting the Smiling Service Worker and Customer Satisfaction," *International Journal of Service Industry Management* 19, no. 5 (2008): 552–574; Anat Rafaeli, Lital Ziklik, and Lorna Doucet, "The Impact of Call Center Employees' Customer Orientation Behaviors and Service Quality," *Journal of Service Research* 10, no. 3 (2008): 239–255.

3 Recent research established the link between extra-role effort and customer satisfaction; e.g., Carmen Barroso Castro, Enrique Martín Armario, and David Martín Ruiz, "The Influence of Employee Organizational Citizenship Behavior on Customer Loyalty," *International Journal of Service Industry Management* 15, no. 1 (2004): 27–53.

4 http://www.fiveguysproductions.com/2010/08/just-little-excitement-on-my-flight.html, accessed March 12, 2012, "Just a Little Excitement on my Flight Today," posted on August 9, 2010 by Phil.

5 Vaikakalathur Shankar Mashesh and Anand Kasturi, "Improving Call Centre Agent Performance: A UK—India Study Based on the Agents' Point of View." *International Journal of Service Industry Management* 17, no. 2 (2006): 136–157. On potentially conflicting goals, see also: Detelina Marinova, Jun Ye, and Jagdip Singh, "Do Frontline Mechanisms Matter? Impact of Quality and Productivity Orientations on Unit Revenue, Efficiency, and Customer Satisfaction," *Journal of Marketing* 72, no. 2 (2008): 28–25.

6 Arlie R. Hochschild, *The Managed Heart: Commercialization of Human Feeling* (Berkeley: University of California Press, 1983).

7 See also Michel Rod and Nicholas J. Ashill, "Symptoms of Burnout and Service Recovery Performance," *Managing Service Quality* 19, no. 1 (2009): 60–84; Jody L. Crosno, Shannon B. Rinaldo, Hulda G. Black, and Scott W. Kelley, "Half Full or Half Empty: The Role of Optimism in Boundary-Spanning Positions," *Journal of Service Research* 11, no. 3 (2009): 295–309.

8 For how frontline staff resist emotional labor, see: Jocelyn A. Hollander and Rachel L. Einwohner, "Conceptualizing Resistance," *Sociological Forum* 19, no. 4 (2004): 533–554; Diane Seymour, "Emotional Labour: A Comparison Between Fast Food and Traditional Service Work," *International Journal of Hospitality Management* 19, no. 2, (2000): 159–171; Peter John Sandiford and Diane Seymour, "Reacting to the Demands of Service Work: Emotional Resistance in the Coach Inn Company," *The Service Industries Journal* 31, nos. 7–8 (May 2011): 1195–1217.

9 Jochen Wirtz and Robert Johnston, "Singapore Airlines: What It Takes to Sustain Service Excellence—A Senior Management Perspective," *Managing Service Quality* 13, no.1 (2003): 10–19; and Loizos Heracleous, Jochen Wirtz, and Nitin Pangarkar, *Flying High in a Competitive Industry: Secrets of the World's Leading Airline.* (Singapore: McGraw-Hill, 2009).

10 The terms "Cycle of Failure" and "Cycle of Success" were coined by Leonard L. Schlesinger and James L. Heskett, "Breaking the Cycle of Failure in Services," *Sloan Management Review* (Spring 1991): 17–28. The term "Cycle of Mediocrity" comes from Christopher H. Lovelock, "Managing Services: The Human Factor," in W. J. Glynn and J.G. Barnes eds. *Understanding Services Management.* (Chichester, UK: John Wiley & Sons, 1995), 228

11 Lloyd C. Harris and Emmanuel Ogbonna, "Exploring Service Sabotage: The Antecedents, Types, and Consequences of Frontline, Deviant, Antiservice Behaviors," *Journal of Service Research* 4, no. 3 (2002): 163–183.

12 Leonard Schlesinger and James L. Heskett, "Breaking the Cycle of Failure," *Sloan Management Review* (Spring 1991): 17–28.

13 Reg Price and Roderick J. Brodie, "Transforming a Public Service Organization from Inside Out to Outside In," *Journal of Service Research* 4, no. 1 (2001): 50–59.

14 Mahn Hee Yoon, "The Effect of Work Climate on Critical Employee and Customer Outcomes," *International Journal of Service Industry Management* 12, no. 5 (2001): 500–521.

15 Charles A. O'Reilly III and Jeffrey Pfeffer, *Hidden Value—How Great Companies Achieve Extraordinary Results with Ordinary People* (Boston, Massachusetts: Harvard Business School Press, 2000), 1.

16 Thomas H. Davenport, Jeanne Harris and Jeremy Shapiro, "Competing on Talent Analytics" *Harvard Business Review* (October 2010): 52–58.

17 This section was adapted from: Benjamin Schneider and David E. Bowen, *Winning the Service Game* (Boston: Harvard Business School Press, 1995), 115–126.

18 John Wooden, *A Lifetime of Observations and Reflections On and Off the* Court (Chicago: Lincolnwood, 1997), 66.

19 Michael J. Tews, Kathryn Stafford, and J. Bruce Tracey, "What Matters Most? The Perceived Importance of Ability and Personality for Hiring Decisions," *Cornell Hospitality Quarterly* 52, no. 2 (2011): 94–101.

20 See Tom J. Brown, John C. Mowen, D. Todd Donovan, and Jane W. Licata, "The Customer Orientation of Service Workers: Personality Trait Effects on Self- and Supervisor Performance Ratings," *Journal of Marketing Research* 39, no. 1 (2002): 110–119; Salih Kusluvan, Zeynep Kusluvan, Ibrahim Ilhan and Lutfi Buyruk, "The Human Dimension: A Review of Human Resources Management Issues in the Tourism and Hospitality Industry," *Cornell Hospitality Quarterly* 51, no. 2 (May 2010): 171–214; Hui Liao and Aichia Chuang, "A Multilevel Investigation of Factors Influencing Employee Service Performance and Customer Outcomes," *Academy of Management Journal* 47, no. 1 (2004): 41–58; Androniki Papadopoulou-Bayliss, Elizabeth M. Ineson and Derek Wilkie, "Control and Role Conflict in Food Service Providers," *International Journal of Hospitality Management* 20, no. 2 (2001): 187–199.

21 Serene Goh, "All the Right Staff," and Arlina Arshad, "Putting Your Personality to the Test," *The Straits Times* September 5, 2001, H1.

22 Donald W. Jackson Jr. and Nancy J. Sirianni, "Building the Bottomline by Developing the Frontline: Career Development for Service Employees," *Business Horizons* 52 (2009): 279–287; Timothy R. Hinkin and J. Bruce Tracey, "What Makes It So Great? An Analysis of Human Resources Practices among Fortune's Best Companies to Work For," *Cornell Hospitality Quarterly* 51, no. 2 (May 2010): 158–170; Rick Garlick, "Do Happy Employees Really Mean Happy Customers? Or Is There More to the Equation? *Cornell Hospitality Quarterly* 51, no. 3 (August 2010): 304–307.

23 Yukari Iwatani Kane and Ian Sherr, "Secrets from Apple's Genius Bar: Full Loyalty, No Negativity," *The Wall Street Journal*, June 15, 2011, http://online.wsj.com/article/SB10001424052702304563104576364071955678908.html, accessed March 12, 2012.

24 Leonard L. Berry, *Discovering the Soul of Service—The Nine Drivers of Sustainable Business Success* (New York: The Free Press, 1999), 161.

25 Disney Institute, *Be Our Guest: Perfecting the Art of Customer Service.* Disney Enterprises (2001).

26 David A. Tansik, "Managing Human Resource Issues for High Contact Service Personnel," in D. E. Bowen, R. B. Chase, T. G. Cummings, and Associates eds. *Service Management Effectiveness* (San Francisco: Jossey-Bass, 1990), 152–176.

27 Parts of this section are based on David E. Bowen and Edward E. Lawler, III, "The Empowerment of Service Workers: What, Why, How and When," *Sloan Management Review* (Spring 1992): 32–39.

28 Dana Yagil, "The Relationship of Customer Satisfaction and Service Workers' Perceived Control—Examination of Three Models," *International Journal of Service Industry Management* 13, no. 4 (2002): 382–398.

29 Graham L. Bradley and Beverley A. Sparks, "Customer Reactions to Staff Empowerment: Mediators and Moderators," *Journal of Applied Social Psychology* 30, no. 5 (2000): 991–1012.

30 David E. Bowen and Edward E. Lawler, III, "The Empowerment of Service Workers: What, Why, How and When," *Sloan Management Review* (Spring 1992): 32–39.

31 Jon R. Katzenbach and Douglas K. Smith, "The Discipline of Teams," *Harvard Business Review* (March–April, 1993): 112.

32 Andrew Sergeant and Stephen Frenkel, "When Do Customer Contact Employees Satisfy Customers?" *Journal of Service Research* 3, no. 1 (August 2000): 18–34.

33 Ad de Jong, Ko de Ruyter, and Jos Lemmink, "Antecedents and Consequences of the Service Climate in Boundary-Spanning Self-Managing Service Teams," *Journal of Marketing* 68 (April 2004): 18–35.

34 Mike Osheroff, "Teamwork in the Global Economy," *Strategic Finance* 88, no. 8 (Feb 2007): 25, 61

35 This section is based on Schneider and Bowen, *Winning the Service Game*, 145–173.

36 Adam M. Grant, "How Customers Can Rally Your Troops," *Harvard Business Review* (June 2011): 96–103.

37 The authors of the following paper emphasize the role of alignment between tradition, culture and strategy that together form the basis for the firms HR practices: Benjamin Schneider, Seth C Hayes, Beng-Chong Lim, Jana L. Raver, Ellen G. Godfrey, Mina Huang, Lisa H. Nishii, and Jonathan C. Ziegert, "The Human Side of Strategy: Employee Experiences of a Strategic Alignment in a Service Organization," *Organizational Dynamics* 32, no. 2 (2003): 122–141.

38 Scott B. MacKenzie, Philip M. Podsakoff, and Gregory A. Rich, "Transformational and Transactional Leadership and Salesperson Performance," *Journal of the Academy of Marketing Science* 29, no. 2 (2001): 115–134.

39 Leonard L. Berry, *On Great Service—A Framework for Action*, 236–237; Leonard L. Berry and Kent D. Seltman, *Management Lessons from Mayo Clinic: Inside One of the World's Most Admired Service Organization.* McGraw Hill (2008). The following study emphasized the importance of the perceived ethical climate in driving service commitment of service employees: Charles H. Schwepker Jr. and Michael D. Hartline, "Managing the Ethical Climate of Customer-Contact Service Employees," *Journal of Service Research* 7, no. 4 (2005): 377–397.

40 Schneider and Bowen, *Winning the Service Game*, 240.

41 Joseph A. Mitchelli, *The New Gold Standard: 5 Leadership Principles for Creating a Legendary Customer Experience Courtesy of The Ritz-Carton Hotel Company*. McGraw-Hill, 2008: 61–66, and 191–197.

42 Paul Hemp, "My Week as a Room-Service Waiter at the Ritz," *Harvard Business Review 80*, (June 2002): 8–11.

43 Catherine DeVrye, *Good Service Is Good Business*, (Upper Saddle River, NJ:Prentice Hall, 2000), 11.

THE *ESM* FRAMEWORK

PART I

Understanding Service Products, Consumers, and Markets

- Introduction to Services Marketing
- Consumer Behavior in a Services Context
- Positioning Services in Competitive Markets

PART II

Applying the 4 Ps of Marketing to Services

- Developing Service Products: Core and Supplementary Elements
- Distributing Services through Physical and Electronic Channels
- Setting Prices and Implementing Revenue Management
- Promoting Services and Educating Customers

PART III

Designing and Managing the Customer Interface

The 3 Additional Ps of Services Marketing.

- Designing and Managing Service Processes
- Balancing Demand and Capacity
- Crafting the Service Environment
- Managing People for Service Advantage

PART IV

Developing Customer Relationships

- Managing Relationships and Building Loyalty
- Complaint Handling and Service Recovery

PART V

Striving for Service Excellence

- Improving Service Quality and Productivity
- Organizing for Service Leadership

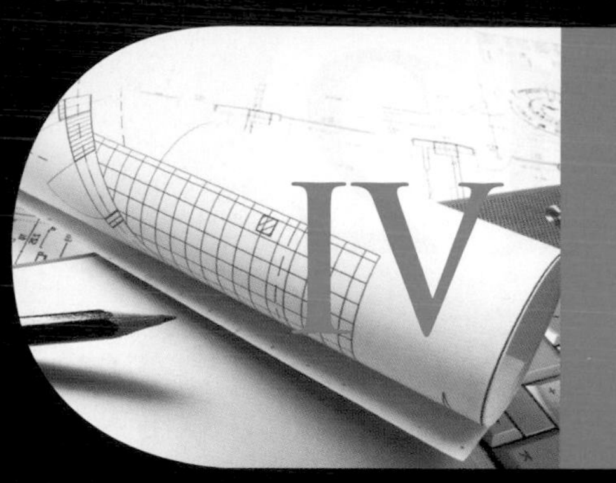

Developing Customer Relationships

PART IV of this book focuses on developing customer relationships through building loyalty, and also managing customer dissatisfaction for long-term profitability. It consists of the following two chapters:

Chapter 12 Managing Relationships and Building Loyalty

This chapter focuses on achieving profitability by creating relationships with customers from the right segments, and then finding ways to build and reinforce their loyalty using the Wheel of Loyalty as an organizing framework. This chapter closes with a discussion of customer relationship management (CRM) systems.

Chapter 13 Complaint Handling and Service Recovery

This chapter examines how effective complaint handling and professional service recovery can be implemented. It starts with a review of consumer complaining behavior and the principles of effective service recovery systems. We also discuss service guarantees as a powerful way of institutionalizing effective service recovery and as an effective marketing tool signaling high-quality service. The chapter also discusses how to deal with jaycustomers who take advantage of service recovery policies and abuse the service in other ways.

CHAPTER 12

managing RELATIONSHIPS and BUILDING LOYALTY

LEARNING OBJECTIVES

By the end of this chapter, the reader should be able to:

- **LO 1** Recognize the important role customer loyalty plays in driving a service firm's profitability.
- **LO 2** Calculate the lifetime value (LTV) of a loyal customer.
- **LO 3** Understand why customers are loyal to a particular service firm.
- **LO 4** Know the core strategies of the Wheel of Loyalty that explain how to develop a loyal customer base.
- **LO 5** Appreciate why it is so important for service firms to target the "right" customers.
- **LO 6** Use service tiering to manage the customer base and build loyalty.
- **LO 7** Understand the relationship between customer satisfaction and loyalty.
- **LO 8** Know how to deepen the relationship through cross-selling and bundling.
- **LO 9** Understand the role of financial and non-financial loyalty rewards in enhancing customer loyalty.
- **LO 10** Appreciate the power of social, customization, and structural bonds in enhancing loyalty.
- **LO 11** Understand what factors cause customers to switch to a competitor, and how to reduce such switching.
- **LO 12** Understand the part played by Customer Relationship Management (CRM) systems in delivering customized services and building loyalty.

Figure 12.1 From high-rollers to casual gamblers, the glittering lights of Harrah's promise customer satisfaction.

OPENING VIGNETTE

Harrah's Entertainment's Customer Relationship Management[1]

Harrah's Entertainment is the world's largest gaming company with its four main brands Harrah's, Caesar's, Horseshoe, and the London Clubs family of casinos. It is a leader in the use of highly sophisticated loyalty programs. Harrah's was first to launch a tiered customer loyalty program in the gaming industry. Today, it has four tiers in its loyalty program—Gold, Platinum, Diamond, and Seven Stars (by invitation only). The program is integrated across all its properties and services. Customers identify themselves (and earn points) at every touchpoint throughout the company, ranging from its gaming tables, restaurants, and hotels, to the gift shops and shows. The points collected can be used to obtain cash, merchandise, lodging, show tickets, vacations, and events.

What is special about Harrah's is not its loyalty program, but what it does with the information gleaned about its customers when they use their cards to earn points. At the back end, Harrah's has linked all its databases from casino management, hotel reservations, and events to allow it to have a holistic view of each of its customers. Harrah's now has detailed data on over 42 million customers and knows each customer's preferences and behaviors. These range from how much they spend on each type of game and their likes in food and drinks, to entertainment and lodging preferences. All this information about the customer is captured in real time.

Harrah's uses this data to drive its marketing and on-site customer service. For example, if a Diamond card holder on slot machine 278 signals for service, a Harrah's associate is able to ask, "The usual, Mr. Jones?" and then track the time it takes for a server to fill the guest's request. In another example, when a customer wins a jackpot, Harrah's can tailor a customer-specific reward to celebrate that win. Harrah's also knows when a customer is approaching his maximum gaming limit on a particular evening and when the customer is likely to stop playing. Just before the limit is reached, Harrah's can offer him a heavily discounted ticket in real time via text message for a show with available seats. This keeps the customer on the premises (and spending) and makes him feel valued as he gets a very special deal just when he wanted to stop playing. At the same time, it uses otherwise wasted capacity in Harrah's shows and restaurants.

Figure 12.2 Harrah's hits the jackpot with its technological innovation in developing customer relationships.

Likewise, when a customer makes a call to its call center, the staff will have detailed real-time information about a customer's preferences and spending habits, and can then tailor promotions that cross-sell or up-sell its services. Harrah's does not do blanket promotions that target all its customers at the same time, which is, according to Harrah's Chairman, President, and CEO Gary Loveman, "a margin eroding nightmare". Rather, it uses highly targeted promotions that create the right incentives for each of its different customers. It also uses control groups to measure the success of a promotion in dollars and cents and to further fine-tune its campaigns.

With its data-driven customer relationship management (CRM), Harrah's is able to transform customer interactions into personal and differentiated ones. As a result, Harrah's increased the share-of-wallet of its Harrah's Total Rewards card holders to an impressive 50% plus, up from 34% before its CRM program was implemented.

THE SEARCH FOR CUSTOMER LOYALTY

Targeting, acquiring, and retaining the "right" customers is at the core of many successful service firms. In Chapter 3, we discussed segmentation and positioning. In this chapter, we emphasize the importance of focusing on desirable, loyal customers within the chosen segments and then building and maintaining their loyalty through carefully planned relationship marketing strategies. The objectives are to build relationships and to develop loyal customers who will do a growing volume of business with the firm in the future.

Loyalty in a business context describes a customer's willingness to continue buying from a firm over the long term and recommending the firm's products to friends and associates. Customer loyalty does not just refer to customer behavior. It also includes preference, liking, and future intentions.

"Few companies think of customers as annuities," says Frederick Reichheld, author of *The Loyalty Effect*, and a major researcher in this field.[2] However, that is what a loyal customer can mean to a firm—a regular source of revenue over a period of many years. The active management of the customer base and customer loyalty is also referred to as *customer asset management*.[3]

In a marketing context, the term defection is used to describe customers who stop buying and transfer their brand loyalty to another supplier. Reichheld and Sasser made the term *zero defections* popular. Zero defections means keeping every customer the company can serve profitably.[4] Not only does a rising defection rate show that something is wrong with quality (or that competitors offer better value), it may also be showing a fall in profits. Big customers do not disappear overnight. They often may show their increasing dissatisfaction by steadily reducing their purchases and shifting part of their business elsewhere.

LO 1

Recognize the important role customer loyalty plays in driving a service firm's profitability.

Why Is Customer Loyalty so Important to a Firm's Profitability?

How much is a loyal customer worth in terms of profits? Reichheld and Sasser analyzed the profit per customer in different service businesses. It was grouped by the number of years that a customer had been with the firm.[5] They found that the longer customers remained with a firm in each of these industries, the more profitable they became. Annual profit increases per customer as shown in Figure 12.3 for a few sample industries. The industries studied (with average profits from a first-year customer shown in parentheses) were credit cards ($30), industrial laundry ($144), industrial distribution ($45), and automobile servicing ($25). The same loyalty effect was found in the Internet context. It usually took more than a year to recover customer acquisition costs, and profits then increased as customers stayed longer with the firm.[6]

Reichheld and Sasser state that there are four factors that cause this growth. These factors are:

1. **Profit derived from increased purchases (or, in a credit card and banking environment, higher account balances).** Over time, business customers often

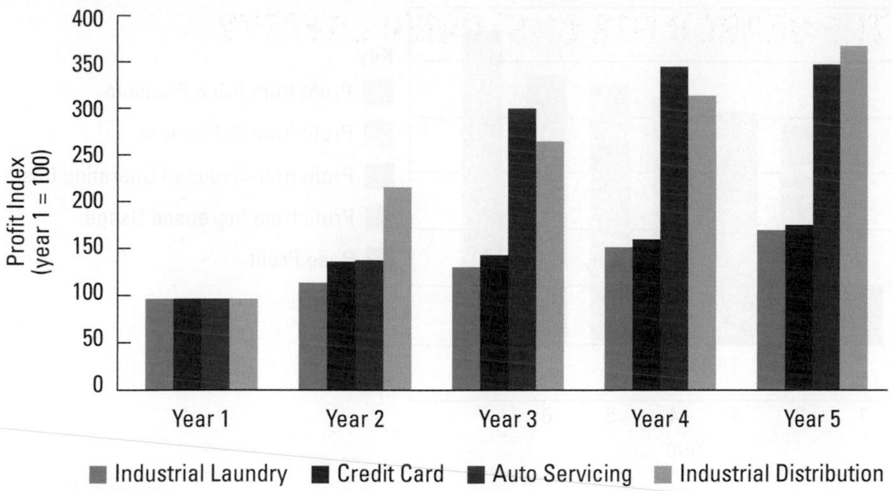

Figure 12.3 How much profit a customer generates over time.

SOURCE

Reprinted by permission of *Harvard Business Review* from Frederick J. Reichheld and W. Earl Sasser Jr., "Zero Defections: Quality Comes to Services" Harvard Business Review 73 (Sept–Oct 1990), 108.

grow larger and so need to purchase in greater quantities. Individuals may also purchase more as their families grow or as they become more affluent. Both types of customers may be willing to combine their purchases with a single supplier who provides high quality service.

2. **Profit from reduced operating costs.** As customers become more experienced, they make fewer demands on the supplier (for instance, they have less need for information and assistance, and make more use of self-service options). They may also make fewer mistakes when involved in operational processes. This contributes to greater productivity.
3. **Profit from referrals to other customers.** Positive word-of-mouth recommendations are like free sales and advertising, saving the firm from having to invest as much money in these activities.
4. **Profit from price premium.** New customers often benefit from introductory promotional discounts. Long-term customers, however, are more likely to pay regular prices, and when they are highly satisfied they tend to be less price-sensitive.[7] Moreover, customers who trust a supplier may be more willing to pay higher prices at peak periods or for express work.

Figure 12.4 shows the relative contribution of each of these different factors over a seven-year period, based on an analysis of 19 different product categories (both goods and services). Reichheld argues that the economic benefits of customer loyalty noted above often explain why one firm is more profitable than a competitor.

Assessing the Value of a Loyal Customer

It's a mistake to assume that loyal customers are always more profitable than those who make one-time transactions.[8] Loyal customers may not spend more than one-

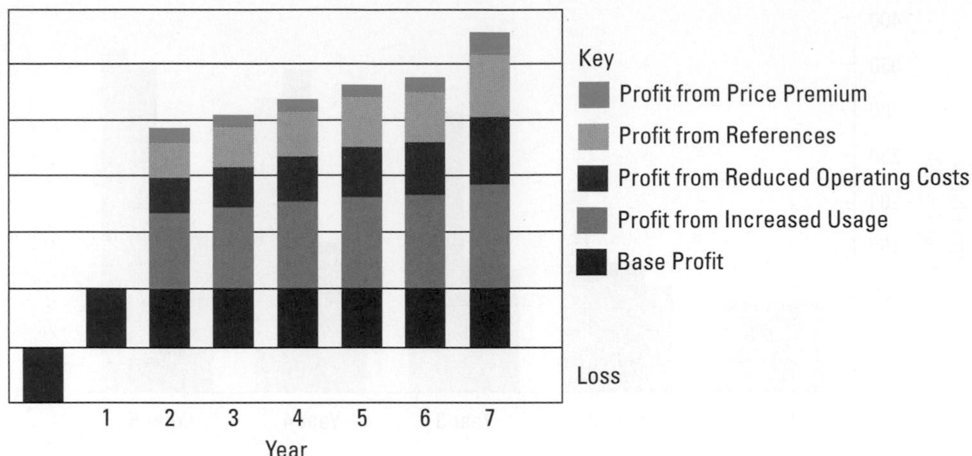

Figure 12.4 Why customers are more profitable over time.

SOURCE

Why Customers Are More Profitable Over Time from Frederick J. Reichheld and W. Earl Sasser Jr. "Zero Defections: Quality Comes to Services," Harvard Business Review 73 (Sept–Oct 1990), 108. Reprinted by permission of Harvard Business School.

time buyers, and in some instances, they may even expect price discounts. Also, profits do not necessarily increase with time for all types of customers.[9] In most mass market business-to-customer (B2C) services—such as banking, mobile phone services, and hospitality—customers cannot negotiate prices. However, in many B2B contexts, large customers have a lot of bargaining power and therefore will nearly always try to negotiate lower prices when contracts come up for renewal. This forces suppliers to share the cost savings resulting from doing business with large, loyal customers. DHL has found that although each of its major accounts generates significant business, they yield below average margins. In contrast, DHL's smaller, less powerful accounts provide significantly higher profitability (Figure 12.5).[10]

Figure 12.5 DHL prices differently for different market segments.

Recent studies have also shown that the profit impact of a customer may vary a lot depending on the stage of the service product lifecycle. For instance, referrals by satisfied customers and negative word-of-mouth from "defected" customers have a much greater effect on profit in the early stages of the service product's lifecycle than in later stages, where the focus is much more on generating cash flow from the existing customer base instead of new customers.[11]

Some of the challenges that you will probably face in your work are to determine the costs and revenues associated with serving customers to different market segments at different points in their customer lifecycles, and to predict future profitability. For insights on how to calculate customer value, see the box, "Worksheet for Calculating Customer Lifetime Value."[12]

Worksheet for Calculating Customer Lifetime Value[13]

Calculate the lifetime value (LTV) of a loyal customer.

Calculating customer value is an inexact science that is subject to a variety of assumptions. You may want to try varying these assumptions to see how it affects the final figures. Generally speaking, revenues per customer are easier to track on an individualized basis than are the associated costs of serving a customer, unless (1) no individual records are kept and/or (2) the accounts served are very large and all account-related costs are individually documented and assigned.

Acquisition Revenues Less Costs

If individual account records are kept, the initial application fee paid and initial purchase (if relevant) should be found in these records. Costs, by contrast, may have to be based on average data. For instance, the marketing cost of acquiring a new client can be calculated by dividing the total marketing costs (advertising, promotions, selling, etc.) devoted toward acquiring new customers by the total number of new customers acquired during the same period. If each acquisition takes place over an extended period of time, you may want to build in a lagged effect between when marketing expenditures are incurred and when new customers come on board. The cost of credit checks—where relevant—must be divided by the number of new customers, not the total number of applicants, because some applicants will probably fail this hurdle. Account set-up costs will also be an average figure in most organizations.

Annual Revenues and Costs

If annual sales, account fees, and service fees are documented on an individual-account basis, account revenue streams (except referrals) can be easily identified. The first priority is to segment your customer base by the length of its relationship with your firm. Depending on the sophistication and precision of your firm's records, annual costs in each category may be directly assigned to an individual account holder or averaged for all account holders in that age category.

Value of Referrals

Computing the value of referrals requires a variety of assumptions. To get started, you may need to conduct surveys to determine (1) what percentage of new customers claim that they were influenced by a recommendation from another customer and (2) what other marketing activities also drew the firm to that individual's attention. From these two items, estimates can be made of what percentage of the credit for all new customers should be assigned to referrals. Additional research may be needed to clarify whether "older" customers are more likely to be effective recommenders than "younger" ones.

Net Present Value

Calculating net present value (NPV) from a future profit stream will require choice of an appropriate annual discount figure. (This could reflect estimates of future inflation rates.) It also requires assessment of how long the average relationship lasts. The NPV of a customer, then, is the sum of the anticipated annual profit on each customer for the projected relationship lifetime, suitably discounted each year into the future.

ACQUISITION			YEAR 1	YEAR 2	YEAR 3	YEAR n
Initial Revenue		*Annual Revenues*				
Application fee[a]	______	Annual account fee[a]	______	______	______	______
Initial purchase[a]	______	Sales	______	______	______	______
		Service fees[a]	______	______	______	______
		Value of referrals[b]	______	______	______	______
Total Revenues	══════		══════	══════	══════	══════
Initial Costs	______	*Annual Costs*				
Marketing	______	Account management	______	______	______	______
Credit check[a]	______	Cost of sales	______	______	______	______
Account setup[a]	______	Write-offs (e.g., bad debts)	______	______	______	______
Less total costs	______		______	______	______	______
Net Profit (Loss)	══════		══════	══════	══════	══════

[a] If applicable.

[b] Anticipated profits from each new customer referred (could be limited to the first year or expressed as the net present value of the estimated future stream of profits through year *n*); this value could be negative if an unhappy customer starts to spread negative word-of-mouth that causes existing customers to defect.

PART IV

LO 3

Understand why customers are loyal to a particular service firm.

Why Are Customers Loyal?

After understanding how important loyal customers can be for the bottom line of a service firm, let's explore what it is that makes a customer loyal. Customers are not automatically loyal to any one firm. Rather, we need to give our customers a reason to combine their buying with only us and then staying with us. We need to create value for them to become and remain loyal. Just ask yourself: What service companies are you loyal to? And why are you loyal to these firms? Research has shown that relationships can create value for individual consumers through such factors as inspiring greater confidence, offering social benefits, and providing special treatment (see Service Insights 12.1). We will next discuss how we can systematically think about creating value for our loyal customers using the Wheel of Loyalty.

SERVICE INSIGHTS 12.1

How Customers See Relational Benefits in Service Industries

What benefits do customers see themselves receiving from an extended relationship with a service firm? Researchers seeking answers to this question conducted two studies. The first consisted of in-depth interviews with 21 respondents from a broad cross-section of backgrounds. Respondents were asked to identify service providers that they used on a regular basis and invited to identify and discuss any benefits they received as a result of being a regular customer. Among the comments were:

- "I like him [hairstylist] ... He's really funny and always has lots of good jokes. He's kind of like a friend now."
- "I know what I'm getting—I know that if I go to a restaurant that I regularly go to, rather than take a chance on all of the new restaurants, the food will be good."
- "I often get price breaks. The little bakery that I go to in the morning, every once in a while, they'll give me a free muffin and say, 'You're a good customer, it's on us today.'"
- "You can get better service than drop-in customers ... We continue to go to the same automobile repair shop because we have gotten to know the owner on a kind of personal basis, and he ... can always work us in."
- "Once people feel comfortable, they don't want to switch to another dentist. They don't want to train or break a new dentist in."

After evaluating and grouping the comments, the researchers designed a second study in which they collected 299 survey questionnaires. Results showed that most of the benefits that customers derived from relationships could be grouped into three categories. The first, and most important, group involved what the researchers labeled confidence benefits, followed by social benefits, and special treatment.

- *Confidence benefits* included feelings by customers that in an established relationship, there was less risk of something going wrong, greater confidence in correct performance, and the ability to trust the provider. Customers experienced lowered anxiety when purchasing because they knew what to expect, and they typically received the firm's highest level of service.
- *Social benefits* included mutual recognition between customers and employees, being known by name, friendship with the service provider, and enjoyment of certain social aspects of the relationship.
- *Special treatment benefits* included better prices, discounts on special deals that were unavailable to most customers, extra services, higher priority when there was a wait, and faster service than most customers.

SOURCE

Kevin P. Gwinner, Dwayne D. Gremler, and Mary Jo Bitner, "Relational Benefits in Services Industries: The Customer's Perspective," *Journal of the Academy of Marketing Science* 26, no. 2 (1998): 101–114.

THE WHEEL OF LOYALTY

LO 4

Know the core strategies of the Wheel of Loyalty that explain how to develop a loyal customer base.

Building customer loyalty is difficult. Just try and think of all the service firms you yourself are loyal to. You are likely to only come up with very few examples. This shows that, although firms spend huge amounts of money and effort on building loyalty, they often are not successful in building true customer loyalty. We use the Wheel of Loyalty shown in Figure 12.6 as an organizing framework for thinking of how to build customer loyalty. It is made up of three sequential strategies.

- First, the firm needs a solid foundation for creating customer loyalty that includes targeting the right portfolio of customer segments, attracting the right customers, tiering the service, and delivering high levels of satisfaction.
- Second, to truly build loyalty, a firm needs to develop close bonds with its customers. It can either deepen the relationship through cross-selling and bundling, or add value to the customer through loyalty rewards and higher-level bonds.
- Third, the firm needs to identify and reduce the factors that result in "churn", the loss of existing customers and the need to replace them with new ones.

We discuss each of the components of the Wheel of Loyalty in the sections that follow.

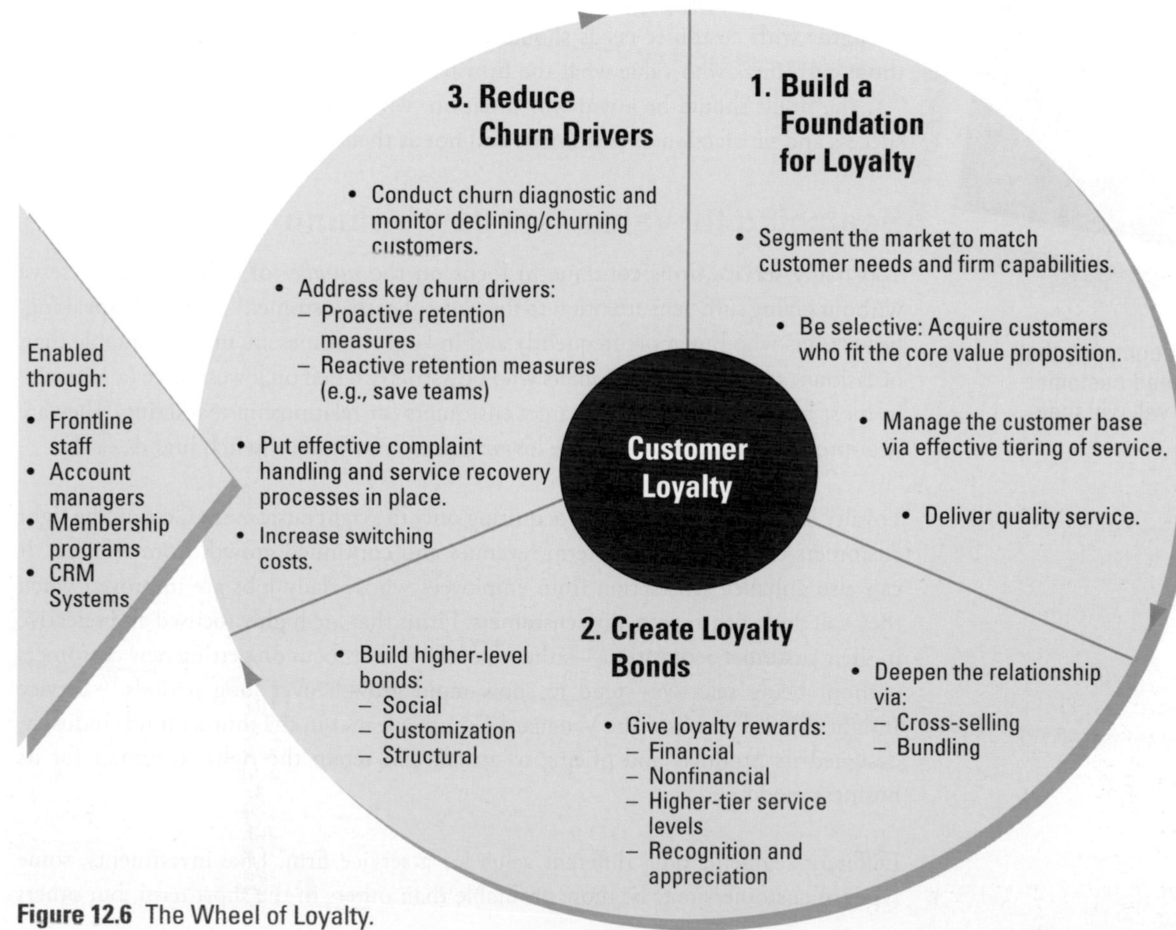

Figure 12.6 The Wheel of Loyalty.

PART IV

BUILDING A FOUNDATION FOR LOYALTY

Many elements are involved in creating long-term customer relationships and loyalty. In Chapter 3 we discussed segmentation and positioning. In this section, we emphasize the importance of focusing on serving several desirable customer segments and then building and maintaining their loyalty through carefully thought-out relationship marketing strategies.

LO 5

Appreciate why it is so important for service firms to target the "right" customers.

Targeting the Right Customers

Loyalty management starts with segmenting the market to match customer needs and firm capabilities; in short, identify and target the right customers. "Who should we be serving?" is a question that every service business needs to ask regularly. Companies need to choose their target segments carefully and match them to what the firm can deliver. Managers must think carefully about how customer needs relate to such operational elements as speed and quality, the times when service is available, the firm's capacity to serve many customers all at once, and the physical features and appearance of service facilities. They also need to consider how well their service personnel can meet the expectations of specific types of customers, in terms of both personal style and technical ability.[14] Finally, they need to ask themselves whether their company can match or exceed competing services that are directed at the same types of customers (Figure 12.7).

Figure 12.7 A company that is able to exceed customer expectations will win their loyalty.

The result of carefully targeting customers by matching the company capabilities and strengths with customer needs should be a superior service offering in the eyes of those customers who value what the firm has to offer. As Frederick Reichheld said, "... the result should be a win-win situation, where profits are earned through the success and satisfaction of customers, and not at their expense."[15]

Searching for Value, Not Just Volume

Too many service firms continue to focus on the *number* of customers they serve without giving sufficient attention to the *value* of each customer.[16] Generally speaking, heavy users who buy more frequently and in larger volumes are more profitable than occasional users. Service customers who buy strictly based on lowest price (a minority in most markets) are not good target customers for relationship marketing. They are deal-prone, continuously seek the lowest price on offer, and switch brands easily.

Loyalty leaders are choosy about acquiring only the right customers. Getting the right customers can bring in long-term revenues and continued growth from referrals. It can also enhance satisfaction from employees whose daily jobs are improved when they can deal with appreciative customers. Firms that are highly focused and selective in their customer acquisition—rather than those that focus on getting new customers without being selective—tend to show rapid growth over long periods.[17] Service Insights 12.2 shows how the Vanguard Group, a leader in the mutual funds industry, designed its products and pricing to attract and retain the right customers for its business model.

Different segments offer different value for a service firm. Like investments, some types of customers may be more profitable than others in the short term, but others

SERVICE INSIGHTS 12.2

Vanguard Discourages the Acquisition of "Wrong" Customers

The Vanguard Group is a growth leader in the mutual fund industry that built its $1.6 trillion in managed assets by 2011 through carefully targeting the right customers for its business model. Its share of new sales, which was around 25%, reflected its share of assets or market share. However, it had a far lower share of redemptions (customer defections in the fund context), which gave it a market share of net cash flows of 55% (new sales minus redemptions), and made it the fastest-growing mutual fund in its industry.

How did Vanguard achieve such low redemption rates? The secret was in its careful customer acquisition, and its product and pricing strategies, which encouraged the acquisition of the "right" customers.

John Bogle, Vanguard's founder, believed that the quality of index funds and their lower management fees would lead to higher returns over the long run. He offered Vanguard's clients the lowest management fees through a policy of not trading (its index funds hold the market they are designed to track), not having a sales force, and spending only a small portion of what its competitors did on advertising. Another important part of keeping its costs low was its aim to discourage the acquisition of customers who were not long-term index holders.

Bogle attributes the high customer loyalty Vanguard has achieved to a great deal of focus on customer defections or low redemption rates. Low redemption rates meant that the firm was attracting the right kind of loyal, long-term investors. The stability of its loyal customer base has been key to Vanguard's cost advantage. When an institutional investor redeemed $25 million from an index fund bought only nine months earlier, he regarded the acquisition of this customer a failure of the system. He explained, "We don't want short-term investors. They muck up the game at the expense of the long-term investor." At the end of his chairman's letter to the Vanguard Index Trust, Bogle repeated: "We urge them [short-term investors] to look elsewhere for their investment opportunities."

This care and attention to acquiring the right customers is famous. For example, Vanguard once turned away an institutional investor who wanted to invest $40 million because the firm suspected that the customer would churn the investment within the next few weeks, creating extra costs for existing customers. The potential customer complained to Vanguard's CEO, who not only supported the decision, but also used it as an opportunity to remind his teams why they needed to be selective about the customers they accept.

Furthermore, Vanguard introduced a number of changes to industry practices that discouraged active traders from buying its funds. For example, Vanguard did not allow telephone transfers for index funds, redemption fees were added to some funds, and the standard practice subsidizing new accounts at the expense of existing customers was rejected because the practice was considered as disloyal to its core investor base. These product and pricing policies in effect turned away heavy traders, but made the fund extremely attractive for long-term investors.

Finally, Vanguard's pricing was set up to reward loyal customers. For many of its funds, investors pay a one-time fee upfront, which goes into the funds themselves to make up for all current investors for the administrative costs of selling new shares. This fee subsidizes long-term investors, and penalizes short-term investors.

SOURCE

Adapted from Frederick F. Reichheld, *Loyalty Rules! How Today's Leaders Build Lasting Relationships*. Boston: MA, Harvard Business School Press, 2001, 24–29, 84–87, 144–145; www.vanguard.com, accessed on March 12, 2012.

PART IV

may have greater potential for long-term growth. Similarly, the spending patterns of some customers may be stable over time, while others may be varied, e.g. spending heavily in boom times but cutting back sharply in recessions. A wise marketer seeks a mix of segments in order to reduce the risks associated with variations in demand.[18]

Finally, managers shouldn't assume that the "right customers" are always big spenders. Depending on the service business model, the right customers may come from a large group of people that no other supplier is doing a good job of serving. Many firms have built successful strategies on serving customer segments that had been neglected by established players, which didn't see them as being "valuable" enough. Examples include Enterprise Rent-A-Car, which targets customers who need a temporary replacement car. It avoided the more traditional segment of business travelers targeted by its principal competitors. Similarly, Charles Schwab focused on retail stock buyers, and Paychex provides small businesses with payroll and human resource services.[19]

LO 6

Use service tiering to manage the customer base and build loyalty.

Managing the Customer Base through Effective Tiering of Service

Marketers should adopt a strategic approach to retaining, upgrading, and even ending relationships with customers. Customer retention involves developing long-term, cost-effective links with customers for the mutual benefit of both parties. However, these efforts need not necessarily target all the customers in a firm with the same level of intensity. Research has confirmed that customer profitability and return on sales can be increased by focusing a firm's resources on top-tier customers.[20] Furthermore, different customer tiers often have quite different service expectations and needs. According to Valarie Zeithaml, Roland Rust, and Katharine Lemon, it is important for service firms to understand the needs of customers within different profitability tiers and adjust their service levels accordingly.[21] Zeithaml, Rust, and Lemon illustrate this principle through a four-level pyramid (Figure 12.8).

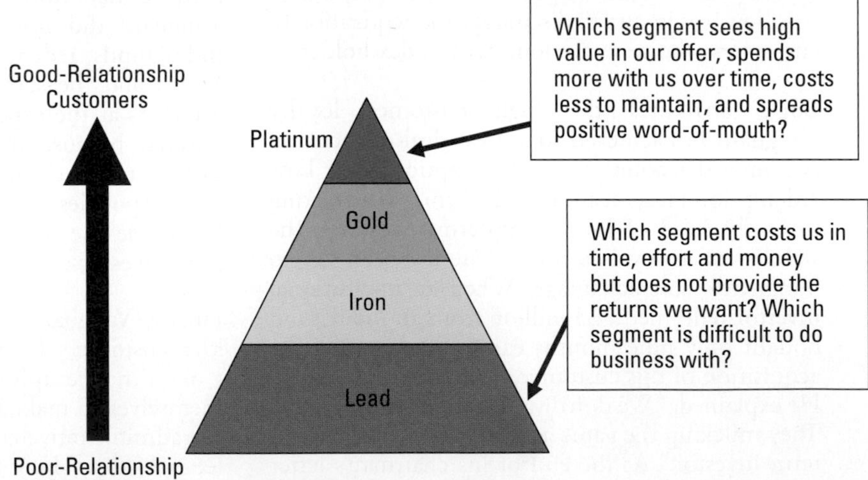

Figure 12.8 The customer pyramid.

SOURCE

Valerie A. Zeithaml, Roland T. Rust, and Katherine N. Lemon "The Customer Pyramid: Creating and Serving Profitable Customers", *California Management Review* 43, no. 4, Summer 2001, Figure 1, pp. 118–142 Copyright © 2001 by the Regents of the University of California. Reprinted by permission of The Regents for electronic posting add"

- *Platinum.* These customers form a very small percentage of a firm's customer base. They are heavy users and contribute a large share of the profits. This segment is usually less price sensitive, but expects highest service levels in return. They are likely to be willing to invest in and try new services.
- *Gold.* The gold tier includes a larger percentage of customers than the platinum. However, individual customers contribute less profit than platinum customers do. They tend to be slightly more price sensitive and less committed to the firm.
- *Iron.* These customers provide the bulk of the customer base. Their numbers give the firm economies of scale. Hence, they are important so that a firm can build and maintain a certain capacity level and infrastructure, which are often needed for serving gold and platinum customers well. However, iron customers in themselves may only be marginally profitable. Their level of business is not enough to justify special treatment.
- *Lead.* Customers in this tier tend to generate low revenues for a firm. However, they often still require the same level of service as iron customers do. Therefore, from the firm's perspective, they are frequently a loss-making segment.

Figure 12.9 ING Direct offers high interest rates that keep customers happy.

Tiering the service means that the firm delivers different services and service levels to different customer groups. The benefit features for platinum and gold customers should be designed to encourage them to remain loyal because these customers are the very ones competitors would like most to steal. Among loyal segments, the focus should be on developing and growing the relationship, perhaps via loyalty programs.[22]

By contrast, among lead-tier customers at the bottom of the pyramid, the options are to either to move them to the iron segment (e.g., through increasing sales, increasing prices, and/or cutting servicing costs) or to end the relationship with them. Imposing a minimum balance or fee that is waived when a certain level of revenue is generated may encourage customers who use several suppliers to consolidate their buying with a single firm instead. Another way to move customers from the lead tier to iron is to encourage them to use low-cost service delivery channels. For instance, lead-tier customers may be charged a fee for face-to-face interactions but the fee is waived when such customers use electronic channels. In the cellular telephone industry, for example, low-use mobile users can be encouraged to use prepaid packages that do not require the firm to send out bills and collect payment. This also reduces the risk of bad debts on such accounts.

Divesting or terminating customers comes when the firm realizes that not all existing customer relationships are worth keeping.[23] Some relationships may no longer be profitable for the firm because they cost more to maintain than the contributions they generate. Some customers no longer fit the firm's strategy either because that strategy has changed or because the customers' behavior and needs have changed.

Occasionally, customers are "fired" outright. ING Direct is one such company that does so. It sells a no-frills type of consumer banking; it only has a handful of basic products, and it lures low-maintenance customers with no minimum balance nor fees and slightly higher interest rates (its Orange savings account paid 1.5% in August 2010) (Figure 12.9). To offset that generosity, its business model pushes its customers toward online transactions, and the bank routinely fires customers who don't fit its business model. When a customer calls too often (the average customer phone call costs the bank $5.25 to handle) or wants too many exceptions to the rule, the bank's sales associates basically say: "Look, this doesn't fit you. You need to go back to your community bank and get the kind of contact you're comfortable with." As a result, ING Direct's cost per account is only one-third of the industry average.[24]

Each service firm needs to regularly examine its customer portfolio and consider ending unsuccessful relationships. Legal and ethical considerations, of course, will determine and how to take such actions. For example, a bank may introduce a minimum monthly fee for accounts with a low balance (e.g., below $1,000), but, for social responsibility considerations, waive this fee for customers on social security.

LO 7

Understand the relationship between customer satisfaction and loyalty.

Customer Satisfaction and Service Quality Are Prerequisites for Loyalty

The foundation for building true loyalty lies in customer satisfaction. Highly satisfied or even delighted customers are more likely to consolidate their purchases, spread positive word-of-mouth, and become loyal advocates of a firm.[25] On the other hand, dissatisfaction drives customers away and is a key factor in switching behavior. Recent research even showed that increases in customer satisfaction lead to increases in stock prices. See Service Insights 12.3.

The satisfaction—loyalty relationship can be divided into three main zones: defection, indifference, and affection (Figure 12.10). The *zone of defection* occurs at low satisfaction levels. Customers will switch unless switching costs are high or there are no other choices. Extremely dissatisfied customers can turn into 'terrorists'

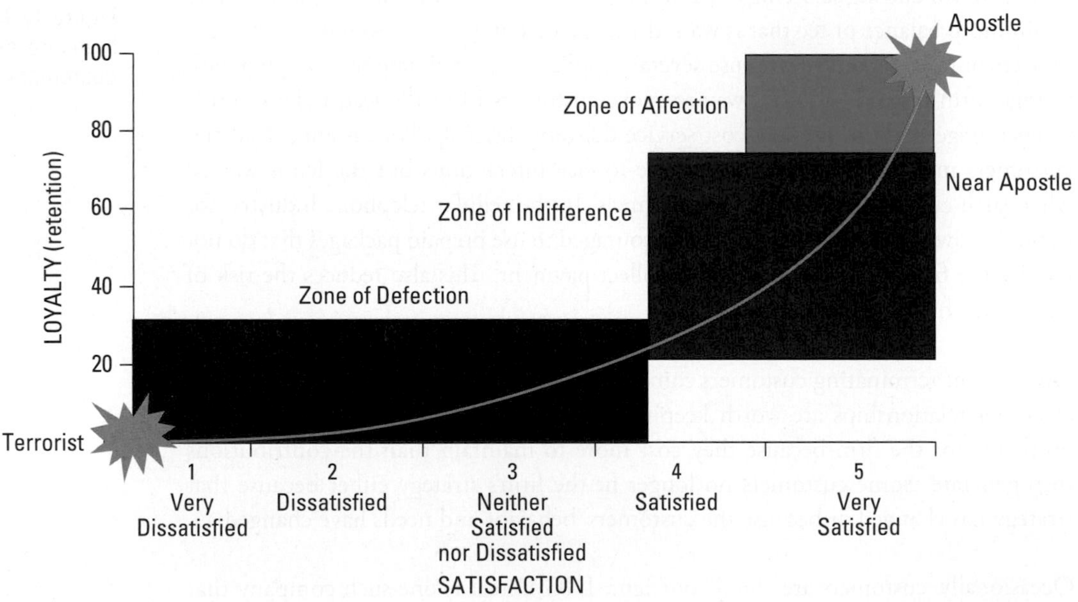

Figure 12.10 The customer satisfaction-loyalty relationship.

SOURCE

Adapted from Thomas O. Jones and W. Earl Sasser, Jr., "Why Satisfied Customers Defect," *Harvard Business Review*, November-December 1995, p. 91.

SERVICE INSIGHTS 12.3

Customer Satisfaction and Wall Street—High Returns and Low Risk!

Does a firm's customer satisfaction levels have anything to do with its stock price? This was the interesting research question Claes Fornell and his colleagues wanted to answer. More specifically, they examined whether investments in customer satisfaction led to excess stock returns. If so, were these returns associated with higher risks as would be predicted by finance theory?

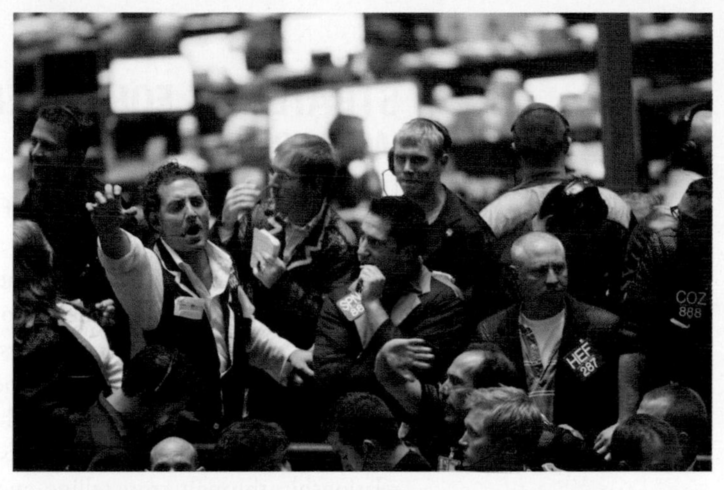

Can customer satisfaction data help to outperform the market?

The researchers built two stock portfolios, one hypothetical back-dated portfolio and a real-world portfolio. Both portfolios consisted only of firms that did well in terms of their customer satisfaction ratings, as measured by the American Customer Satisfaction Index (ACSI). Their findings are striking for managers and investors alike! Fornell and his colleagues discovered that ACSI was significantly related to stock prices of the individual firms and outperformed the market. However, simply publishing the latest data on the ACSI index did not immediately move share prices. Instead, share prices seemed to adjust slowly over time, as firms published other results (perhaps earnings data or other "hard" facts that may lag customer satisfaction). Therefore, acting faster than the market to changes in the ACSI index generated excess stock returns. The results are in line with research in marketing, which holds that satisfied customers improve the level and the stability of cash flow.

For marketing managers, this study's findings confirm that investments (or "expenses" if you talk to accountants) in managing customer relationships and the cash flows they produce increase a firm's value. Although the results are convincing, be careful if you want to invest in firms that show high increases in customer satisfaction in future ACSI releases. Your finance friends will tell you that efficient markets learn fast! You know this has happened when you see stock prices move as a response to future ACSI releases. You can learn more about the ACSI at www.theacsi.org.

SOURCES

Claes Fornell, Sunil Mithas, Forrest V. Morgeson III, and M.S. Krishnan, "Customer Satisfaction and Stock Prices: High Returns, Low Risk," *Journal of Marketing* 70 (January 2006): 3–14. Lerzan Aksoy, Bruce Cooil, Christopher Groening, Timothy L. Keiningham, and Atakan Yalçin, "The Long-Term Stock Market Valuation of Customer Satisfaction," *Journal of Marketing* 72, no. 4 (2008): 105–122.

providing a lot of negative word-of-mouth for the service provider.[26] The *zone of indifference* is found at moderate satisfaction levels. Here, customers are willing to switch if they find a better choice. Finally, the *zone of affection* is located at very high satisfaction levels, where customers may have such high attitudinal loyalty that they do not look for alternative service providers. Customers who praise the firm in public and refer others to the firm are described as "apostles." High satisfaction levels lead to improved future business performance.[27]

STRATEGIES FOR DEVELOPING LOYALTY BONDS WITH CUSTOMERS

Having the right portfolio of customer segments, attracting the right customers, tiering the service, and delivering high levels of satisfaction are a solid foundation for creating customer loyalty as shown in the wheel of loyalty in Figure 12.6. However, firms can do more to "bond" more closely with their customers. Research shows that, when customers are loyal to a company, they are attracted to visit the company. However, once there, it is the loyalty program that will attract them to spend money.[28] Therefore, there is a need to have a variety of strategies to develop loyalty bonds with customers. Specific strategies include (1) deepening the relationship through cross-selling and bundling, (2) creating loyalty rewards, and (3) building higher-level bonds such as social, customization, and structural bonds.[29] We will discuss each of these three strategies next.

LO 8

Know how to deepen the relationship through cross-selling and bundling.

Deepening the Relationship

To build closer ties with its customers, firms can deepen the relationship through bundling and/or cross-selling services. For example, banks like to sell as many financial products to an account or household as possible. Once a family has its current account, credit card, savings account, safe deposit box, car loan, mortgage, etc. with the same bank, the relationship is so deep that switching becomes a major hassle. Therefore, customers are not likely to switch unless they are very dissatisfied with the bank.

In addition to higher switching costs, there is often also value for the customer too when buying all particular services from a single provider. One-stop shopping typically is more convenient and less hassle than buying individual services from different providers. When having many services with the same firm, the customer may achieve a higher service tier and receive better services, and sometimes service bundles do come with price discounts.

LO 9

Understand the role of financial and nonfinancial loyalty rewards in enhancing customer loyalty.

Encouraging Loyalty through Financial and Nonfinancial Rewards

Few customers buy only from only one supplier. This is especially true in situations where service delivery involves separate transactions (such as a car rental) instead of being continuous in nature (as with insurance coverage). In many instances, consumers are loyal to several brands (sometimes described as "polygamous loyalty") but avoid others. In such instances, the marketing goal is to strengthen the customer's preference for one brand over others and to gain a greater share of the customer's

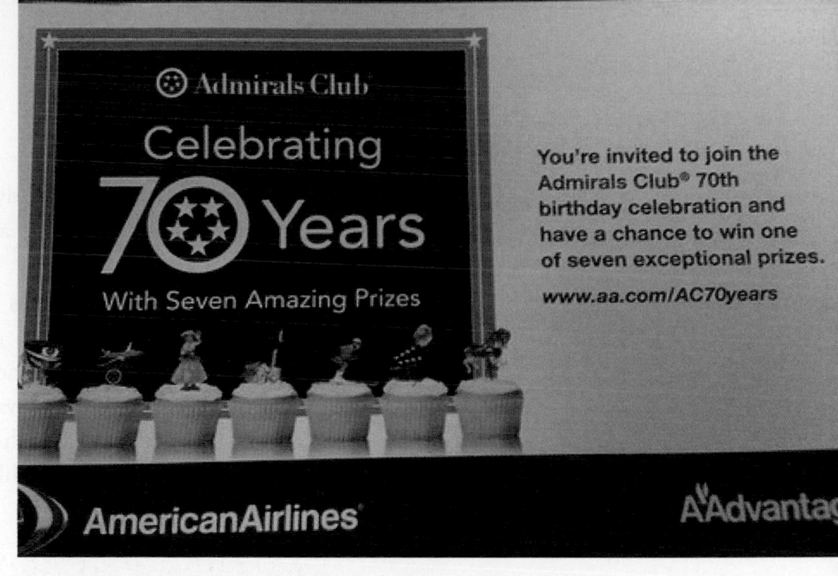

Figure 12.11 American Airlines tries to make its loyalty program enticing.

spending on that service category (also referred to as increasing "share-of-wallet"). Well-designed loyalty programs can achieve increased share-of-wallet reward-based bonds.[30] Incentives that offer rewards based on the frequency of purchase, value of purchase, or a combination of both, represent a basic level of customer bonding. These rewards can be *financial* or *nonfinancial* in nature.

Financial Rewards

Financial rewards are customer incentives that have a financial value (also called "hard benefits"). These include discounts on purchases, loyalty program rewards such as frequent flier miles (Figure 12.11), and the cash-back programs provided by some credit card issuers.

Besides airlines and hotels, an increasing number of service firms ranging from retailers (such as department stores, supermarkets,[31] book shops, and petrol stations), telecommunications providers, and café chains to courier services and cinema chains have or are launching similar reward programs in response to the increasing competitiveness of their markets. Many firms denominate their awards in miles that can be credited to a selected frequent flyer program. In short, air miles have become a form of promotional currency in the service sector.[32]

Recent research in the credit card industry suggests that financial rewards-based loyalty programs strengthen the customers' perception of the value proposition and lead to increased revenues due to fewer defections and higher usage levels.[33]

Interestingly, if a firm has loyalty program partners, (e.g., an airline may partner credit card companies, hotels, car rental firms, where loyalty program points can also be earned with these companies), satisfaction with the core service can have a positive impact on buying from program partners. In the same way, satisfaction with the service of program partners can have a positive impact on the buying of the core service. [34]

Even well-designed rewards programs by themselves are not enough to keep a firm's most desirable customers. If you are dissatisfied with the quality of service, or believe that you can get better value from a less expensive service, you may quickly become disloyal. No service business that has a rewards program for frequent users can ever afford to lose sight of its broader goals of offering high service quality and good value relative to the price and other costs incurred by customers.[35] Sometimes, what the customer wants is just for the firm to deliver the basic service well, meet their needs, and solve their problems quickly and easily, and they will be loyal.[36]

Finally, customers can be frustrated with financial rewards-based programs so that instead of creating loyalty and goodwill, they breed dissatisfaction. This can happen when customers feel they are excluded from a reward program because of low balances or volume of business, if the rewards are seen as having little or no value, if they cannot redeem their loyalty points because of black-out dates during high-demand periods, and if redemption processes are too troublesome and time consuming.[37]

And some customers already have so many loyalty cards in their wallet that they simply are not interested in adding more cards to that pile.

Nonfinancial Rewards

Nonfinancial rewards (also called "soft benefits") provide benefits that cannot be translated directly into monetary terms. Examples include giving priority to loyalty program members on reservation wait lists and virtual queues in call centers. Some airlines provide benefits such as higher baggage allowances, priority upgrading, access to airport lounges and the like to its frequent flyers, even when they are only flying in economy class.

Important intangible rewards include special recognition and appreciation. Customers tend to value the extra attention given to their needs and appreciate the implicit service guarantee offered by high-tier loyalty program memberships. This includes efforts to meet their occasional special requests. Many loyalty programs also provide important status benefits to customers in the top tiers who feel part of an elite group (e.g., the Seven Stars card holders with Harrah's Entertainment in our opening vignette) and enjoy their special treatment.[38]

Nonfinancial rewards, especially if linked to higher-tier service levels, are typically more powerful than financial ones. Higher-tier service can create a lot of value for customers. Unlike financial rewards, nonfinancial rewards directly relate to the firm's core service and improve the customers' experience and value perception. In the hotel context, for example, redeeming loyalty points for free gifts does nothing for the guest experience. However, getting priority for reservations, early check-in, late check-out, upgrades, and receiving special attention and appreciation make your stay more pleasant and makes you want to come back.

Service Insights 12.4 describes how British Airways has designed its Executive Club, effectively combining financial and nonfinancial loyalty rewards.

SERVICE INSIGHTS 12.4

Rewarding Value of Use, Not Just Frequency, at British Airways

Unlike some frequent flyer programs, in which customer usage is measured simply in miles, British Airways' (BA) Executive Club members receive both *air miles* toward redemption of air travel awards and *points* toward silver or gold tier status for travel on BA. With the creation of the OneWorld alliance with American Airlines, Qantas, Cathay Pacific, and other airlines, Executive Club members have been able to earn miles (and sometimes points) by flying these partner airlines, too.

As shown in Table 12.1, silver and gold card holders are entitled to special benefits, such as priority reservations and a superior level of on-the-ground service. For instance, even if a gold card holder is only traveling in economy class, he or she will be entitled to first-class standards of treatment at check-in and in the airport lounges. Miles can be accumulated for up to three years (after which they expire), but tier status is valid for only 12 months beyond the membership year in which it was earned.

This means that the right to special privileges must be re-earned each year. The objective of awarding tier status is to encourage passengers who have a choice of airlines to concentrate their travel on British Airways. Few passengers travel so often that they will be able to obtain the benefits of gold tier status (or its equivalent) on more than one airline.

Points given also vary according to the class of service. Longer trips earn more points than shorter ones. However, tickets at deeply discounted prices may earn fewer miles and no points at all. To reward purchase of higher-priced tickets, passengers earn points at double the economy rate if they travel in club (business class), and at triple the rate in first class.

Although the airline makes no promises about complimentary upgrades, members of BA's Executive Club are more likely to receive such invitations than other passengers. Tier status is an important consideration. Unlike many airlines, BA tends to limit upgrades to situations in which a lower class of cabin is overbooked. They do not want frequent travelers to believe that they can plan on buying a less expensive ticket and then automatically receive an upgraded seat.

Table 12.1 Benefits offered by British Airways to its most valued passengers

Benefit	Silver-tier Members	Gold-tier Members
Reservations	Dedicated silver phone line	Dedicated gold phone line
Reservation assurance	If flight is full, guaranteed seat in economy when booking full fare ticket at least 24 hours in advance and checking in at least one hour in advance	If flight is full, guaranteed seat in economy when booking full fare ticket at least 24 hours in advance and checking in at least one hour in advance
Priority wait list and standby	Higher priority	Highest priority
Check-in desk	Club (regardless of travel class)	First (regardless of travel class)
Lounge access	Club departure lounges for passenger and one guest regardless of class of travel	First-class departure lounge for passenger and one guest, regardless of travel class; use of arrivals lounges; lounge access anytime, allowing use of lounges even when not flying BA intercontinental flights
Preferred boarding	Board aircraft at leisure	Board aircraft at leisure
Special services assistance		Problem solving beyond that accorded to other BA travelers
Bonus air miles	+100%	+100%
Upgrade for two		Free upgrade to next cabin for member and companion after earning 2,500 tier points in one year; another upgrade for two after 3,500 points in same year. Award someone else with a Silver Partner card on reaching 4,500 points within membership year.
Special privilege		Concorde Room access at Heathrow Terminal 5 for those who earn 5,000 points

SOURCE

British Airways Executive Club, www.britishairways.com/travel/ecbenftgold/public/en_us, accessed July 2011.

PART IV

LO 10

Appreciate the power of social, customization, and structural bonds in enhancing loyalty.

Building Higher-Level Bonds

One objective of loyalty rewards is to motivate customers to combine their purchases with one provider or at least make it the preferred provider. However, reward-based loyalty programs are quite easy for other suppliers to copy and seldom provide a sustained competitive advantage. In contrast, higher-level bonds tend to offer a longer-term competitive advantage. We discuss next the three main types of higher-level bonds, which are (1) social, (2) customization, and (3) structural bonds.

Figure 12.12 A knowledgeable and charismatic lecturer helps build social bonds with students.

Social Bonds

Have you ever noticed how your favorite hairdresser calls you by your name when you go for a haircut or how she asks why she hasn't seen you for a long time? Social bonds are usually based on personal relationships between providers and customers. There is an element of trust, which is important for loyalty.[39] Social bonds are more difficult to build than financial bonds and may take longer to achieve, but they are also harder for other suppliers to imitate. A firm that has created social bonds with its customers has a better chance of keeping them for the long term because of the trust the customers place in the staff.[40] When social bonds include shared relationships (Figure 12.12) or experiences between customers, such as in country clubs or educational settings, they can be a major loyalty driver for the organization.[41]

Figure 12.13 Starbucks' employees are encouraged to learn their customers' preferences.

Customization Bonds

These bonds are built when the service provider succeeds in providing customized service to its loyal customers. For example, Starbucks' employees are encouraged to learn their regular customers' preferences and customize their service accordingly (Figure 12.13). Many large hotel chains capture the preferences of their customers through their loyalty program databases. Firms offering customized service are likely to have more loyalty customers.[42] For example, when customers arrive at their hotel, they find that their individual needs have already been met. These range from preferred drinks and snacks in the mini bar, to the kind of pillow they like, and the newspaper they want to receive in the morning. When a customer becomes used to this special service, he or she may find it difficult to adjust to another service provider who is not able to customize the service (at least immediately as it takes time for the new provider to learn about someone's needs and preferences).[43]

Structural Bonds

Structural bonds are commonly seen in B2B settings. They are created by getting customers to align their way of doing things with the supplier's own processes, thus linking the customer to the firm. This situation makes it more difficult for competitors to draw them away. Examples include joint investments in projects and sharing of information, processes, and equipment. Structural bonds can be created in a B2C environment, too. For instance, some car rental companies offer travelers the opportunity to create customized pages on the firm's website where they can get details of past trips including the types of cars, insurance coverage, and so forth. This simplifies and speeds up the task of making new bookings.

Have you noticed that, while all these bonds tie a customer closer to the firm, they also deliver the confidence, social, and special treatment benefits that customers desire (refer to Service Insights 12.1)? In general, bonds will not work well unless they also generate value for the customer!

STRATEGIES FOR REDUCING CUSTOMER DEFECTIONS

LO 11
Understand what factors cause customers to switch to a competitor, and how to reduce such switching.

So far, we have discussed drivers of loyalty and how to tie customers more closely to the firm. A complementary approach is to understand the drivers for customer defections, also called customer churn, and work on eliminating or at least reducing those drivers.

Analyze Customer Defections and Monitor Declining Accounts

The first step is to understand the reasons for customer switching. Susan Keveaney conducted a large-scale study across a range of services and found several key reasons why customers switch to another provider (Figure 12.14).[44] These were:

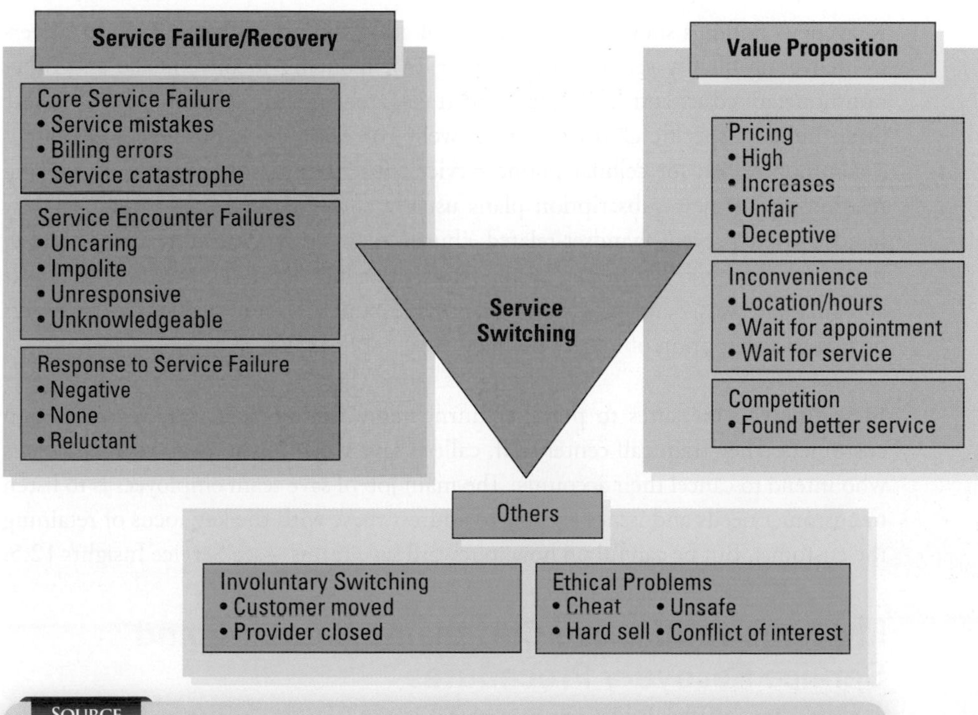

SOURCE
Adapted from Susan M. Keaveney, "Customer Switching Behavior in Service Industries: An Exploratory Study," *Journal of Marketing* 59 (April 1995), 71–82.

Figure 12.14 What drives customers to switch away from a service firm?

- Core service failures (44% of respondents).
- Dissatisfactory service encounters (34%).
- High, deceptive, or unfair pricing (30%).
- Inconvenience in terms of time, location, or delays (21%).
- Poor response to service failure (17%).

Many respondents decided to switch after a series of related incidents, such as a service failure followed by an unsatisfactory service recovery.

Many service firms regularly conduct what is called *churn diagnostics*. This includes the analysis of data from churned and declining customers, exit interviews (call center staff often have a short set of questions they ask when a customer cancels an account to gain a better understanding of why customers defect), and in-depth interviews of former customers by a third-party research agency, which typically yield a more detailed understanding of churn drivers.[45]

Some firms even try to predict churn of individual accounts. For example, cell phone service providers use *churn alert systems*. These systems keep track of the activity in individual customer accounts. The objective is to predict when a customer might switch. Important accounts at risk are flagged and efforts are made to keep the customer, such as sending a voucher and/or having a customer service representative call the customer to check on the health of the customer relationship and start corrective action if needed.

Address Key Churn Drivers

Keaveney's findings show the importance of addressing some general churn drivers by delivering quality service (see Chapter 14), reducing inconvenience and other nonmonetary costs, and having fair and transparent pricing (Chapter 6). There are often industry-specific churn drivers as well. For example, handset replacement is a common reason for cellular phone service subscribers to discontinue an existing relationship, as new subscription plans usually come with heavily subsidized new handsets. To prevent handset-related churn, many providers now offer handset replacement programs, offering current subscribers heavily discounted new handsets at regular intervals. Some providers even provide handsets free to high-value customers or against redemption of loyalty points.

In addition to measures to prevent churn, many firms take active steps to retain customers. They train call center staff, called "save teams," who deal with customers who intend to cancel their accounts. The main job of save team employees is to listen to customer needs and issues and try to address these with the key focus of retaining the customer. But be careful on how to reward save teams—see Service Insights 12.5.

Implement Effective Complaint Handling and Service Recovery Procedures

Effective complaint handling and excellent service recovery are important to keep unhappy customers from switching providers. Well-managed firms make it easy for customers to voice their problems and respond with suitable service recovery strategies.

SERVICE INSIGHTS 12.5

Churn Management Gone Wrong

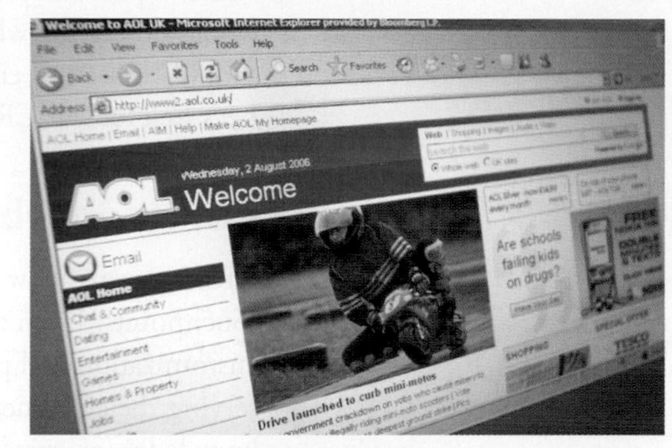

America Online (AOL) found itself on the wrong end of churn management when about 300 of its subscribers filed complaints with the New York state attorney general's office, saying that AOL had ignored their demands to cancel the service and stop billing them. After an investigation by the State of New York, AOL eventually agreed to pay $1.25 million in penalties and costs and to change some of its customer service practices to settle the case.

What went wrong? AOL had been rewarding its call center employees for "saving" customers who called in to cancel their service. Employees could earn high bonuses if they were able to persuade half or more of such customers to stay with the firm. As claimed by the attorney general's office, this may have led AOL's employees to make it difficult to cancel service. As a response, AOL agreed in a settlement to have service cancellations requests recorded and verified by a third-party monitor, and to provide up to four months' worth of refunds to all New York subscribers who claim that their cancellations had been ignored (AOL did not admit to any wrongdoing in that settlement). Eliot Spitzer, New York's Attorney General at the time, said, "This agreement helps to ensure that AOL will strive to keep its customers through quality service, not stealth retention programs."

SOURCE

The Associated Press, "AOL to Pay $1,25M to Settle Spitzer Probe," *USA Today*, 25.08.2005, p. 5B.

In that way, customers will remain satisfied, and this will reduce the intention to switch.[46] We will discuss in depth on how to do that effectively in Chapter 13.

Increase Switching Costs

Another way to reduce churn is to increase switching barriers.[47] Many services have natural switching costs. For example, it is a lot of work for customers to change their primary banking account, especially when many direct debits, credits, and other related banking services are tied to that account. Also, many customers are reluctant to learn about the products and processes of a new provider.[48]

Switching costs can also be created by having contractual penalties for switching, such as the transfer fees payable to some brokerage firms for moving shares and bonds to another financial institution. However, firms need to be careful so that they are not seen as holding their customers hostage. A firm with high switching barriers and poor service quality is likely to generate negative attitudes and bad word-of-mouth. At some point, a previously inert customer may have enough and switch the service provider.[49]

 **LO 12**

Understand the part played by Customer Relationship Management (CRM) systems in delivering customized services and building loyalty.

CRM: CUSTOMER RELATIONSHIP MANAGEMENT

Service marketers have understood for some time the power of relationship management, and certain industries have applied it for years. Examples include the corner grocery store, the neighborhood car repair shop, and providers of banking services to high-net-worth clients. However, mention CRM, and immediately costly and complex IT systems and infrastructure come to mind. But CRM is actually the whole process by which relations with the customers are built and maintained.[50] It should be seen as enabling the successful implementation of the Wheel of Loyalty. Let's first look at CRM systems before we move to a more strategic perspective.

Common Objectives of CRM Systems

CRM systems allow customer information to be captured and deliver it to the various touchpoints. From a customer perspective, well-implemented CRM systems deliver customization and personalization. This means that, at each transaction, the person serving the customer will have easy access to the customer's relevant account details, knowledge of customer preferences and past transactions, or history of a service problem. This can result in a vast service improvement and increased customer value. Personalization and improved communication will result in more loyalty.[51]

From a company's perspective, CRM systems allow the company to better understand, segment, and tier its customer base, better target promotions and cross-selling, and even implement churn alert systems that signal if a customer is in danger of defecting.[52] Service Insights 12.6 highlights some common CRM applications.

SERVICE INSIGHTS 12.6

Common CRM Applications

- **Data collection.** The system captures customer data such as contact details, demographics, purchasing history, service preferences, and the like.
- **Data analysis.** The data captured is analyzed and grouped by the system according to criteria set by the firm. This is used to tier the customer base and tailor service delivery accordingly.
- **Sales force automation.** Sales leads, cross-sell, and up-sell opportunities can be effectively identified and processed. The entire sales cycle from lead generation to close of sales and after-sales service can be tracked through the CRM system.
- **Marketing automation.** Mining of customer data allows the firm to target its market. A good CRM system allows the firm to achieve one-to-one marketing and cost savings, often through loyalty and retention programs. This results in increasing the return on investment (ROI) on its marketing expenditure. CRM systems also allow firms to judge the effectiveness of marketing campaigns through the analysis of responses.
- **Call center automation.** Call center staff have customer information at their fingertips and can improve their service levels to all customers. Furthermore, caller ID and account numbers allow call centers to identify the customer tier the caller belongs to, and to tailor the service accordingly. For example, platinum callers get priority in waiting loops.

WHAT DOES A COMPREHENSIVE CRM STRATEGY INCLUDE?[53]

Rather than viewing CRM as a technology, we should view it as a system that focuses on the profitable development and management of customer relationships. Figure 12.15 provides five key processes involved in a CRM strategy:

1. ***Strategy development*** involves looking at business strategy, including the company's vision, industry trends, and competition. It is usually the responsibility of top management. For customer relationship management to have a positive impact on a firm's performance, the firm's strategy is key.[54] Therefore, business strategy should guide the development of customer strategy, including the choice of target segments, customer base tiering, the design of loyalty bonds, and churn management (as discussed in the Wheel of Loyalty, Figure 12.6).

2. ***Value creation*** translates business and customer strategies into value propositions for customers and the firm. The value created for customers includes all the benefits that are delivered through priority tiered services, loyalty rewards, and

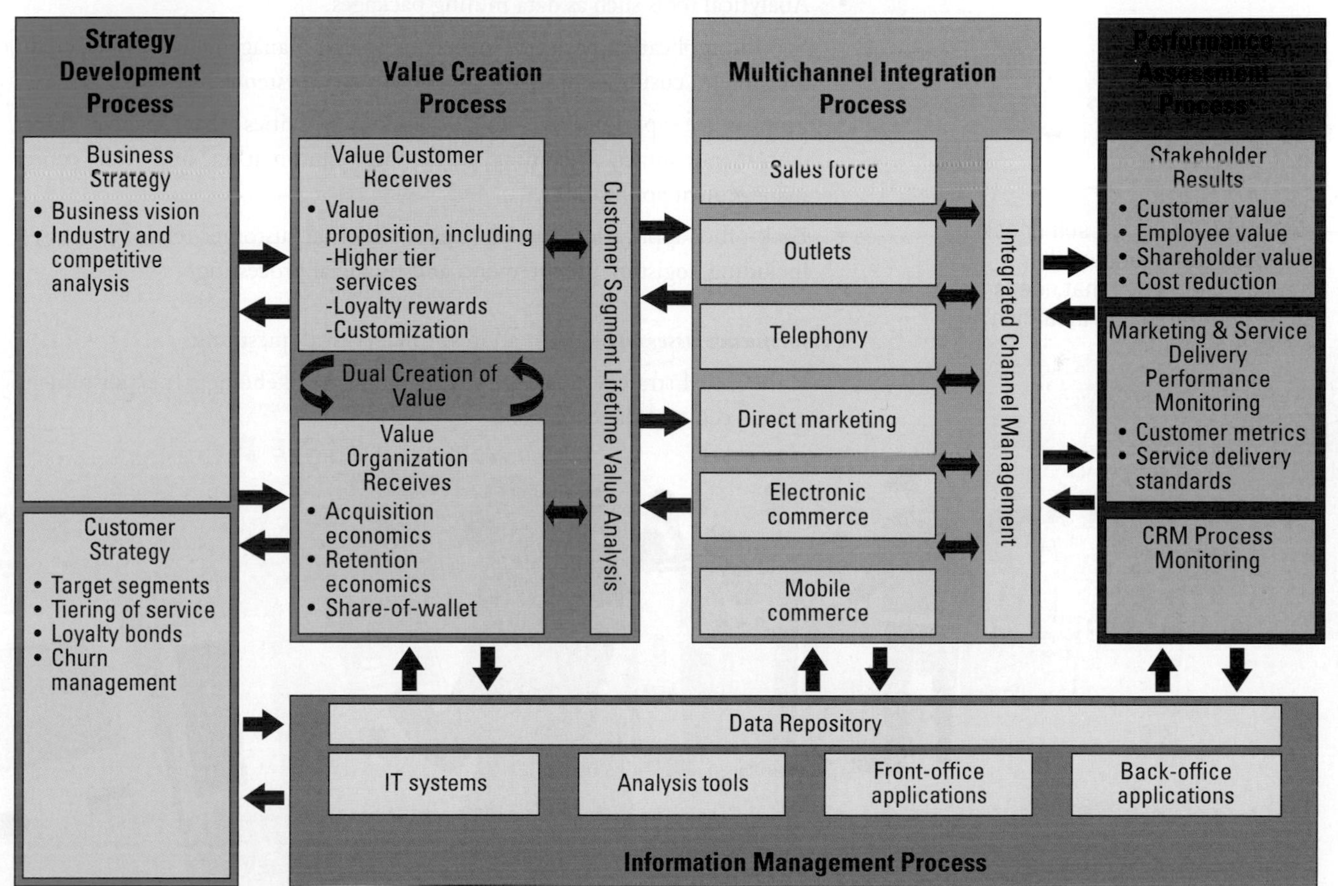

Figure 12.15 An integrated framework for CRM strategy.

SOURCE

Adapted from: Adrian Payne and Pennie Frow, "A Strategic Framework for Customer Relationship Management," *Journal of Marketing* 69 (October 2005): 167–176.

PART IV

customization and personalization. The values created for the firm include reduced customer acquisition and retention costs, increased share-of-wallet, and reduced customer serving costs. Customers need to participate in CRM (e.g., through volunteering information) so that they benefit from the firm's CRM strategy. CRM seems most successful when there is a win-win situation for the firm and its customers.[55]

3. ***Multi-channel integration.*** Most service firms interact with their customers through a multitude of channels, and it has become a challenge to serve customers well across these many potential interfaces, and offer a unified customer interface that delivers customization and personalization. CRM's channel integration addresses this challenge.

4. ***Information management.*** Service delivery across many channels depends on the firm's ability to collect customer information from all channels at the various touchpoints (Figure 12.16). The information management process includes:
   - The data repository that contains all the customer data.
   - IT systems including IT hardware and software.
   - Analytical tools such as data mining packages.
   - Specific application packages such as campaign management analysis, credit assessment, customer profiling, and churn alert systems.
   - Front-office applications, which support activities that involve direct customer contact, including sales force automation and call center management applications.
   - Back-office applications, which support internal customer-related processes, including, logistics, procurement, and financial processing.

5. ***Performance assessment*** must address three critical questions:
   - Is the CRM strategy creating value for its key stakeholders (i.e., customers, employees, and shareholders)?

Figure 12.16 Airport self check-in kiosks represent another service touchpoint that needs to be integrated into an airline's CRM system.

- Are the marketing objectives (ranging from customer acquisition, share-of-wallet, and retention to customer satisfaction) and service delivery performance objectives (e.g., call center service standards such as call waiting) being achieved?
- Is the CRM process itself performing up to expectations? (e.g., Are the relevant strategies being set? Is customer and firm value being created? Is the information management process working effectively? Is integration across customer service channels being achieved effectively?)

Common Failures in CRM Implementation

Unfortunately, the majority of CRM implementations have failed in the past. According to the Gartner Group, the CRM implementation failure rate is 55%, and Accenture claims it to be as high as around 60%. A key reason for this high failure rate is that firms often think just installing CRM systems is having a customer relationship strategy. They forget that the system is just a tool to enhance the firm's customer servicing capabilities, and is not the strategy itself.

Furthermore, CRM cuts across many departments and functions (e.g., from customer contact centers, online services and distributions, to branch operations, employee training, and IT departments), programs (ranging from sales and loyalty programs to launching of new services, and cross-selling initiatives), and processes (e.g., from credit line authorization all the way to complaint handling and service recovery). The wide-ranging scope of CRM makes it challenging to implement and to get it right. Common reasons for CRM failures include:[56]

- **Viewing CRM as a technology initiative.** It's easy to let the focus shift toward technology and its features, with the result that the IT department rather than top management or marketing taking the lead in coming up with the CRM strategy. This often results in a lack of direction from management and a lack of understanding of customers and markets during implementation.
- **Lack of customer focus.** Many firms implement CRM without the goal of allowing for improving service delivery for valued customers across all delivery channels.
- **Insufficient appreciation of customer lifetime value (LTV).** Marketing does not take into account the different profitabilities of different customers. Furthermore, the servicing costs for different customers are often not well captured (e.g., by using activity-based costing as discussed in Chapter 6).
- **Inadequate support from top management.** Without ownership and active involvement from top management, the CRM implementation will not be successful.
- **Failing to re-engineer business processes.** It is nearly impossible to implement CRM successfully without redesigning customer service and back-office processes. Many implementations fail because CRM is being fitted into existing processes, rather than redesigning the processes to fit a customer-centric CRM implementation. Redesigning also requires change management and employee involvement and support, which are often lacking.

PART IV

- **Underestimating the challenges in data integration.** Firms frequently fail to integrate customer data that usually are scattered across the organization. However, one way to take advantage of the full potential of CRM is to make customer knowledge available in real time to all employees who need it.

In the long run, firms can put their CRM strategies at risk if customers believe that CRM is being used in a way that is harmful to them.[57] Examples include feeling that they are not being treated fairly (including not being offered attractive pricing or promotions that are offered, for example, to new accounts, but not to existing customers) and potential privacy concerns (see Service Insights 12.7). Being aware and actively avoiding these weaknesses is a first step toward a successful CRM implementation.

How to Get CRM Implementation Right

Despite the horror stories of millions of dollars sinking into unsuccessful CRM projects, more and more firms are getting it right. "No longer a black hole, CRM is becoming a basic building block of corporate success," argue Darrell Rigby and Dianne Ledingham.[58] Even CRM systems that have been implemented but have not yet shown results can be well positioned for future success. Experienced McKinsey consultants believe that even CRM systems that have yet to show results can still be turned around. They recommend taking a step back and focusing on how to build customer loyalty, rather than focusing on the technology itself.[59] Rather than using CRM to transform entire businesses through the implementation of the CRM model shown in Figure 12.15, service firms should focus on clearly defined problems within their customer relationship cycle. These narrow CRM strategies often reveal additional opportunities for further improvements, which, taken together, can develop into broad CRM implementation extending across the entire company.[60]

Among the key questions managers should ask when defining their customer relationship strategy are:

1. How should our value proposition change to increase customer loyalty?
2. How much customization or one-to-one marketing and service delivery is appropriate and profitable?
3. What is the incremental profit potential of increasing the share-of-wallet with our current customers? How much does this vary by customer tier and/or segment?
4. How much time and resources can we allocate to CRM right now?
5. If we believe in customer relationship management, why haven't we taken more steps in that direction in the past? What can we do today to develop customer relationships without spending a lot on technology?[61]

Answering these questions can even lead to the conclusion that a CRM system may not be the best investment or highest priority at the moment. In any case, we emphasize that the system is merely a tool to drive the strategy and must thus be customized to deliver that strategy (Figure 12.17).

Figure 12.17 CRM can help companies create two-way channels with customers.

SERVICE INSIGHTS 12.7

CRM Extreme—A Glimpse into Ordering Pizza in 2018?

Operator: "Thank you for calling Pizza Delight. Linda speaking, how may I help you?"

Customer: "Good evening, can I order …"

Operator: "Sir, before taking your order, could I please have the number of your multi-purpose smart card?"

Customer: "Hold on …. it's …. um … CA-4555 9831."

Operator: "Thank you! Can I please confirm you're Mr Thompson calling from 10940 Wilford Boulevard? You are calling from your home number 432-3876, your cell phone number is 992-4566, and your office number is 432-9377."

Customer: "How in the world did you get my address and all my numbers?"

Operator: "Sir, we are connected to the Integrated Customer Intimacy System."

Customer: "I would like to order a large seafood pizza …"

Operator: "Sir, that's not a good idea."

Customer: "Why?!?"

Operator: "According to your medical records, you have very high blood pressure and a far too high cholesterol level, Sir."

Customer: "What? … What do you recommend then?"

Operator: "Try our Low Fat Soybean Yoghurt Pizza. You'll like it."

Customer: "How do you know?"

Operator: "You borrowed the book 'Popular Soybean Dishes' from the City Library last week, Sir."

Customer: "OK, I give up … Get me three large ones then. How much will that be?"

Operator: "That should be enough for your family of eight, Sir. The total is $54.90."

Customer: "Can I pay by credit card?"

Operator: "I'm afraid you'll have to pay us cash, Sir. Your credit card is over the limit and your checking account has an overdue balance of $2,435.88. That's excluding the late payment charges on your home equity loan, Sir."

Customer: "I guess I'll have to run to the ATM and withdraw some cash before your guy arrives."

Operator: "You can't do that, Sir. Based on the records, you've reached your daily machine withdrawals limit for today."

Customer: "Never mind. Just send the pizzas, I'll have the cash ready. How long is it gonna take?"

Operator: "About 45 minutes Sir, but if you don't want to wait you can always come and collect it on your Harley, registration number L.A.6468 …"

Customer: "#@$#@%^%%@"

Operator: "Sir, please watch your language. Remember, on 28th April 2017 you were convicted of using abusive language at a traffic warden …"

Customer: (Speechless)

Operator: "Is there anything else, Sir?"

SOURCE

This story was adapted from various sources, including www.lawdebt.com/gazette/nov2004/nov2004.pdf (accessed in January 2006) and a video created by the American Civil Liberties Union (ACLU) available at www.aclu.org/pizza. This video aims to communicate the privacy threats that CRM poses to consumers. ACLU is a nonprofit organization that campaigns against government's and corporations' aggressive collection of information on people's personal life and habits.

CHAPTER SUMMARY

LO 1 ▶ Customer loyalty is an important driver of a service firm's profitability. The profits derived from loyal customers come from (1) increased purchases, (2) reduced operation costs, (3) referral of new customers, and (4) price premiums. Also, customer acquisition costs can be amortized over a longer period of time.

LO 2 ▶ However, it is not true that loyal customers are always more profitable. They may expect price discounts for staying loyal. To truly understand the profit impact of the customers, firms need to learn how to calculate the *LTV* of their customers. LTV calculations need to include (1) acquisition costs, (2) revenue streams, (3) account-specific servicing costs, (4) expected number of years the customer will stay with the firm, and (5) discount rate for future cash flows.

LO 3 ▶ Customers are only loyal if there is a benefit for them to be so. Common benefits customers see in being loyal include:

- *Confidence benefits*, including feeling that there is less risk of something going wrong, ability to trust the provider, and receipt of the firm's highest level of service.
- *Social benefits*, including being known by name, friendship with the service provider, and enjoyment of certain social aspects of the relationship.
- *Special treatment benefits*, including better prices, extra services, and higher priority.

LO 4 ▶ It is not easy to build customer loyalty. The *Wheel of Loyalty* offers a systematic framework that guides firms on how to do so. The framework has three components that follow a sequence.

- First, firms need to build a *foundation for loyalty* without which loyalty cannot be achieved. The foundation delivers confidence benefits to its loyal customers.
- Once the foundation is laid, firms can then create *loyalty bonds* to strengthen the relationship. Loyalty benefits deliver social and special treatment benefits.
- Finally, besides focusing on loyalty, firms also have to work on reducing *customer churn*.

To build the foundation for loyalty, firms need to:

LO 5 ▶ Segment the market and *target the "right" customers*. Firms need to choose their target segments carefully and match them to what the firm can do best. Firms need to focus on customer value, instead of just going for customer volume.

LO 6 ▶ Manage the customer base via *service tiering*, which divides the customer base into different value tiers (e.g., platinum, gold, iron, and lead). It helps to tailor strategies to the different service tiers. The higher tiers offer higher value for the firm but also expect higher service levels. For the lower tiers, the focus should be on increasing profitability through building volume, increasing prices, cutting servicing costs, and as a last resort even ending unprofitable relationships.

LO 7 ▶ Understand that the foundation for loyalty lies in *customer satisfaction*. The satisfaction loyalty relationship can be divided into three main zones: defection, indifference, and affection. Only highly satisfied or delighted customers who are in the zone of affection will be truly loyal.

Loyalty bonds are used to build relationships with customers. There are three different types of customer bonds:

LO 8 ▶ Cross-selling and bundling *deepen relationships* that make switching more difficult and often increase convenience through one-stop shopping.

LO 9 ▶ Loyalty programs aim at building share of-wallet through *financial rewards* (e.g., loyalty points) and *nonfinancial rewards* (e.g., higher-tier service levels, and recognition and appreciation).

LO 10 ▶ Higher-level bonds include *social, customization*, and *structural bonds*. These bonds tend to be more difficult to be copied by competition than reward-based bonds.

LO 11 ▶ The final step in the Wheel of Loyalty is to understand what causes customers to leave and then systematically reduce these *churn drivers*.

- Common causes for customers to switch include core service failures and dissatisfaction, perceptions that pricing is deceptive and unfair, inconvenience, and poor response to service failures.

- To prevent customers from switching, firms should analyze and address key reasons why their customers leave them, have good complaint handling and service recovery processes in place, and potentially increase customers' switching costs.

LO 12 ▶ Finally, *CRM systems* should be seen as enabling the successful implementation of the Wheel of Loyalty. CRM systems are particularly useful when firms have to serve large numbers of customers across many service delivery channels. An effective CRM strategy includes five key processes:

- *Strategy development*, including choice of target segments, tiering of service, and design of loyalty rewards.
- *Value creation*, including delivering benefits to customers through tiered services and loyalty programs (e.g., priority wait-listing and upgrades).
- *Multi-channel integration* to provide a unified customer interface across many different service delivery channels (e.g., from the website to the branch office)
- *Information management*, which includes the data repository, analytical tools (e.g., campaign management analysis and churn alert systems), and front- and back-office applications.
- *Performance assessment*, which has to address the three questions of:
  - (1) Is the CRM creating value for customers and the firm?
  - (2) Are its marketing objectives being achieved?
  - (3) Is the CRM system itself performing according to expectations?

Performance assessment should lead to continuous improvement of the CRM strategy and system.

PART IV

UNLOCK YOUR LEARNING

These keywords are found within the sections of each Learning Objective (LO). They are integral to understanding the services marketing concepts taught in each section. Having a firm grasp of these keywords and how they are used is essential to helping you do well on your course, and in the real and very competitive marketing scene out there.

LO 1
1 Customer loyalty
2 Loyalty effect
3 Price premium
4 Profitability
5 Referrals
6 Value of loyal customers

LO 2
7 Acquisition costs
8 Acquisition revenues
9 Customer lifetime value
10 Net present value
11 Value of referrals

LO 3
12 Confidence benefits
13 Relational benefits
14 Social benefits
15 Special treatment benefits

LO 4
16 Build foundation for loyalty
17 Create loyalty bonds
18 Reduce churn drivers
19 Wheel of Loyalty

LO 5
20 Loyalty leaders
21 Searching for value
22 Targeting

LO 6
23 Customer base
24 Customer pyramid
25 Customer retention
26 Gold
27 Iron
28 Lead
29 Loyalty programs
30 Platinum
31 Tiering of service

LO 7
32 Customer satisfaction
33 Satisfaction—loyalty relationship
34 Service quality
35 Zone of affection
36 Zone of defection
37 Zone of indifference

LO 8
38 Deepening the relationship

LO 9
39 Financial rewards
40 "Polygamous loyalty"
41 "Share-of-wallet"
42 Nonfinancial rewards

LO 10
43 Customization bonds
44 Higher-level bonds
45 Social bonds
46 Structural bonds

LO 11
47 Churn diagnostics
48 Churn drivers
49 Churn management
50 Complaint handling
51 Customer churn
52 Customer defections
53 Declining accounts
54 Service recovery
55 Switching costs

LO 12
56 CRM applications
57 CRM implementation
58 CRM strategy
59 CRM systems
60 Customer lifetime value
61 Customer relationship management
62 Data integration
63 Failures in CRM
64 Information management
65 Multichannel integration
66 Performance assessment
67 Strategy development
68 Value creation

How well do you know the language of services marketing? Quiz yourself!

Not for the academically faint-of-heart

For each keyword you are able to recall without referring to earlier pages, give yourself a point (and a pat on the back). Tally your score at the end and see if you earned the right to be called—a *services marketeer.*

SCORE

0 – 13 Services Marketing is done a great disservice.
14 – 25 The midnight oil needs to be lit, pronto.
26 – 40 I know what you *didn't* do all semester.
41 – 52 By George! You're getting there.
53 – 64 Now, go forth and market.
65 – 68 There should be a marketing concept named after you.

KNOW YOUR ESM

Review Questions

1. Why is customer loyalty an important driver of profitability for service firms?
2. Why is targeting the "right customers" so important for successful customer relationship management?
3. How can you estimate a customer's lifetime value (LTV)?
4. How do the various strategies described in the Wheel of Loyalty relate to one another?
5. How can a firm build a foundation for loyalty?
6. What is tiering of services? Explain why it is used and what are its implications for firms and their customers.
7. Identify some key measures that can be used to create customer bonds and encourage long-term relationships with customers.
8. What are the arguments for spending money to keep existing customers loyal?
9. What is the role of CRM in delivering a customer relationship strategy?

WORK YOUR ESM

Application Exercises

1. Identify three service businesses that you buy from on a regular basis. Now, for each business, complete the following sentence: "I am loyal to this business because ..."
2. What conclusions do you draw about (a) yourself as a consumer, and (b) the performance of each of the businesses in Exercise 1? Assess whether any of these businesses managed to develop a sustainable competitive advantage through the way it won your loyalty.
3. Identify two service businesses that you used several times but have now stopped to buying from (or plan to stop soon) because you were dissatisfied. Complete the sentence: "I stopped using (or will soon stop using) this organization as a customer because ..."
4. Again, what conclusions do you draw about yourself and the firms in Exercise 3? How would each of these firms avoid your defection? What could each of these firms do to avoid defections in the future of customers with a profile similar to yours?
5. Evaluate the strengths and weaknesses of two frequent user programs, each one from a different service industry. Assess how each program could be improved further.
6. Design a questionnaire and conduct a survey asking about two loyalty programs. The first is about membership/loyalty programs your classmates or their families like best and keep them loyal to that firm. The second should be about a loyalty program that is not well perceived and does not seem to add value to the customer. Use open-ended questions, such as "What motivated you to sign up in the first place?", "Why are you using this program?", "Has participating in the program changed your purchasing/usage behavior in any way?", "Has it made you less likely to use competing suppliers?", "What do you think of the rewards available?", "Did membership in the program lead to any immediate benefits in the use of the service?", "What are the three things you like best about this loyalty membership program?", "What did you like least?" and "What are some suggested improvements?" Analyze what features make loyalty/membership programs successful, and what features do not achieve the desired results. Use frameworks such as the Wheel of Loyalty to guide your analysis and presentation.
7. Approach service employees in two or three firms with implemented CRM systems. Ask the employees about their experience interfacing with these systems, and whether or not the CRM systems (a) help them understand their customers better and/or (b) lead to improved service experiences for their customers. Ask them about potential concerns and improvement suggestions they may have about their organizations' CRM systems.

ENDNOTES

1 Stanley, T. (2006), "High stakes analytics. Optimize: Business Strategy & Execution for CIOs," (February). www.cognos.com/company/success/harrahs.html, accessed March 12, 2012; Voight, J. (2007), "Total rewards pays off for Harrah's," Brandweek.com, 17, (September). www.brandweek.com/bw/news/recent_display.jsp?vnu_content_id=1003641351, accessed March 12, 2012; J. N. Hoover, "2007 Chief Of The Year: Tim Stanley," InformationWeek, 8. (December 2007) www.informationweek.com/story/showArticle.jhtml?articleID=204702770, accessed March 12, 2012; James L. Heskett, W. Earl Sasser, and Joe Wheeler, *The Ownership Quotient*. Boston: Harvard Business Press, 2008: 9–13; www.harrahs.com, accessed March 12, 2012.

2 Frederick F. Reichheld and Thomas Teal, *The Loyalty Effect*, Boston: Harvard Business School Press, 1996.

3 Ruth Bolton, Katherine N. Lemon, and Peter C. Verhoef, "The Theoretical Underpinnings of Customer Asset Management: A Framework and Propositions for Future Research," *Journal of the Academy of Marketing Science* 32, no. 3 (2004): 271–292.

4 Frederick F. Reichheld and W. Earl Sasser, Jr., "Zero Defections: Quality Comes to Services," *Harvard Business Review* (October 1990): 105–111.

5 Reichheld and Sasser, *op. cit.*

6 Frederick F. Reichheld and Phil Schefter, "E-Loyalty—Your Secret Weapon on the Web," *Harvard Business Review* (July–August, 2002): 105–113.

7 Christian Homburg, Nicole Koschate, and Wayne D. Hoyer, "Do Satisfied Customers Really Pay More? A Study of the Relationship Between Customer Satisfaction and Willingness to Pay," *Journal of Marketing* 69 (April 2005): 84–96.

8 Grahame R. Dowling and Mark Uncles, "Do Customer Loyalty Programs Really Work?' *Sloan Management Review* (Summer 1997): 71–81; Werner Reinartz and V. Kumar, "The Mismanagement of Customer Loyalty," *Harvard Business Review* (July 2002): 86–94.

9 Werner J. Reinartz and V. Kumar, "On the Profitability of Long-Life Customers in a Non-contractual Setting: An Empirical Investigation and Implications for Marketing," *Journal of Marketing* 64 (October 2000): 17–35.

10 Jochen Wirtz, Indranil Sen, and Sanjay Singh, "Customer Asset Management at DHL in Asia," in *Services Marketing in Asia—A Case Book*, by Jochen Wirtz and Christopher Lovelock eds., (Singapore: Prentice Hall, 2005, 379–396).

11 John E. Hogan, Katherine N. Lemon, and Barak Libai, "What is the True Cost of a Lost Customer?" *Journal of Services Research* 5, no. 3 (2003): 196–208.

12 For a discussion on how to evaluate the customer base of a firm, see Sunil Gupta, Donald R. Lehmann, and Jennifer Ames Stuart, "Valuing Customers," *Journal of Marketing Research* 41, no. 1 (2004): 7–18.

13 To use a customer lifetime value calculator and see a worked problem, see http://hbsp.harvard.edu/multimedia/flashtools/cltv/index.html, accessed March 12, 2012.

14 It has even been suggested to let "chronically dissatisfied customer go to allow front-line staff focus on satisfying the 'right' customers," see Ka-shing Woo and Henry K.Y. Fock, "Retaining and Divesting Customers: An Exploratory Study of Right Customers, 'At-Risk' Right Customers, and Wrong Customers," *Journal of Services Marketing* 18, no. 3 (2004): 187–197.

15 Frederick F. Reichheld, *Loyalty Rules—How Today's Leaders Build Lasting Relationships*, Boston: MA, Harvard Business School Press, 2001, 45.

16 Yuping Liu, "The Long-Term Impact of Loyalty Programs on Consumer Purchase Behavior and Loyalty," *Journal of Marketing* 71, no. 4 (October 2007): 19–35.

17 Frederick F. Reichheld, *Loyalty Rules—How Today's Leaders Build Lasting Relationships*, Boston: MA, Harvard Business School Press, 2001, 43, 84–85.

18 Ravi Dhar and Rashi Glazer, "Hedging Customers," *Harvard Business Review* 81, (May 2003): 86–92

19 David Rosenblum, Doug Tomlinson, and Larry Scott, "Bottom-Feeding for Blockbuster Business," *Harvard Business Review* (March 2003): 52–59.

20 Christian Homburg, Mathias Droll, and Dirk Totzek, "Customer Prioritization: Does It Pay Off, and How Should It Be Implemented?" *Journal of Marketing* 72, no. 5 (2008): 110–130.

21 Valarie A. Zeithaml, Roland T. Rust, and Katharine N. Lemon, "The Customer Pyramid: Creating and Serving Profitable Customers," *California Management Review* 43, no. 4 (Summer 2001): 118–142

22 Werner J. Reinartz and V. Kumar, "The Impact of Customer Relationship Characteristics on Profitable Lifetime Duration," *Journal of Marketing* 67, no. 1 (2003): 77–99.

23 Vikras Mittal, Matthew Sarkees, and Feisal Murshed, "The Right Way to Manage Unprofitable Customers," *Harvard Business Review* (April 2008): 95–102.

24 Elizabeth Esfahani, "How to Get Tough with Bad Customers," *ING Direct*, October 2004, and https://home.ingdirect.com/index.html, accessed March 12, 2012.

25 Not only is there a positive relationship between satisfaction and share of wallet, but the greatest positive impact is seen at the upper extreme levels of satisfaction. For details, refer to Timothy L. Keiningham, Tiffany Perkins-Munn, and Heather Evans, "The Impact of Customer Satisfaction on Share of Wallet in a Business-to-Business Environment," *Journal of Service Research* 6, no. 1 (2003): 37–50; See also: Beth Davis-Sramek, Cornelia Droge, John T. Mentzer, and Matthew B. Myers, "Creating Commitment and Loyalty Behavior among Retailers" What Are the Roles of Service Quality and Satisfaction?" *Journal of the Academy of Marketing Science* 37, no. 4 (2009): 440–454; Ina Garnefeld, Sabrina Helm, and Andreas Eggert, "Walk Your Talk: An Experimental Investigation of the Relationship between Word of Mouth and Communicators' Loyalty," *Journal of Service Research* 14, no. 1 (2011): 93–107.

26 Florian V. Wangenheim, "Postswitching Negative Word of Mouth," *Journal of Service Research* 8, no. 1 (2005): 67–78.

27 Neil A. Morgan and Lopo Leotte Rego, "The Value of Different Customer Satisfaction and Loyalty Metrics in Predicting Business Performance," *Marketing Science* 25, no. 5 (September–October 2006): 426–439.

28 Heiner Evanschitzky, B. Ramaseshan, David M. Woisetschlager, Verena Richelsen, Markus Blut, and Christof Backhaus, "Consequences of Customer Loyalty to the Loyalty Program and to the Company," *Journal of the Academy of Marketing Science* 26 (July 2011) (published online).

29 Leonard L. Berry and A. Parasuraman, "Three Levels of Relationship Marketing," in *Marketing Services—Competing through Quality* (New York, NY: The Free Press, 1991, 136–142); and Valarie A. Zeithaml, Mary Jo Bitner, and Dwayne D. Gremler, *Services Marketing*. 5th ed., (New York, NY: McGraw-Hill, 2008), Chapter 7.

30 Michael Lewis, "The Influence of Loyalty Programs and Short-Term Promotions on Customer Retention,"*Journal of Marketing Research* 41 (August 2004): 281–292; Jochen Wirtz, Anna S. Mattila, and May Oo Lwin, "How Effective Are Loyalty Reward Programs in Driving Share of Wallet?" *Journal of Service Research* 9, no. 4 (2007): 327–334.

31 Richard Ho, Leo Huang, Stanley Huang, Tina Lee, Alexander Rosten, and Christopher S. Tang, "An Approach to Develop Effective Customer Loyalty Programs: The VIP Program AT T & T Supermarkets Inc.," *Managing Service Quality* 19, no. 6 (2009): 702–720.

32 Katherine N. Lemon and Florian V. Wangenheim, "The Reinforcing Effects of Loyalty Program Partnerships and Core Service Usage," *Journal of Service Research* 11, no. 4 (2009): 357–370; Frederick DeKay, Rex S. Toh and Peter Raven, "Loyalty Programs: Airlines Outdo Hotels," *Cornell Hospitality Quarterly* 50, no. 3 (2009): 371–382.

33 Ruth N. Bolton, P. K. Kannan, and Matthew D. Bramlett, "Implications of Loyalty Program Membership and Service Experience for Customer Retention and Value," *Journal of the Academy of Marketing Science* 28, no. 1 (2000): 95–108; Michael Lewis, "The Influence of Loyalty Programs and Short-Term Promotions on Customer Retention," *Journal of Marketing Research* 41, no. 3 (2004): 281–292.

34 Katherine N. Lemon and Florian V. Wangenheim, "The Reinforcing Effects of Loyalty Program Partnerships and Core Service Usage," *Journal of Service Research* 11, no. 4 (2009): 357–370.

35 See, for example: Iselin Skogland and Judy Siguaw, "Are Your Satisfied Customers Loyal?" *Cornell Hotel and Restaurant Administration Quarterly* 45, no. 3 (2004): 221–234.

36 Matthew Dixon, Karen Freeman, and Nicholas Toman, "Stop Trying to Delight Your Customers," *Harvard Business Review* July–August (2010): 116–122.

37 Bernd Stauss, Maxie Schmidt, and Adreas Schoeler, "Customer Frustration in Loyalty Programs," *International Journal of Service Industry Management* 16, no. 3 (2005): 229–252.

38 On the perception of design of loyalty tiers, see: Xavier Drèze and Joseph C. Nunes, "Feeling Superior: The Impact of Loyalty Program Structure on Consumers' Perceptions of Status," *Journal of Consumer Research* 35, no. 6 (2009): 890–905.

39 Nelson Oly Ndubisi, "Relationship Marketing and Customer Loyalty," *Marketing Intelligence & Planning* 25, no. 1 (2007): 98–106.

40 Paolo Guenzi, Michael D. Johnson, and Sandro Castaldo, "A Comprehensive Model of Customer Trust in Two Retail Store," *Journal of Service Management* 20, no. 3 (2009): 290–316; Alessandro Arbore, Paolo Guenzi, and Andrea Ordanini, "Loyalty Building, Relational Trade-offs and Key Service Employees: The Case of Radio DJs," *Journal of Service Management* 20, no. 3 (2009): 317–341.

41 Mark S. Rosenbaum, Amy L. Ostrom, and Ronald Kuntze, "Loyalty Programs and a Sense of Community," *Journal of Services Marketing* 19, no. 4 (2005): 222–233; Isabelle Szmigin, Louise Canning, and Alexander E. Reppel, "Online Community: Enhancing the Relationship Marketing Concept through Customer Bonding," *International Journal of Service Industry Management* 16, no. 5 (2005): 480–496; Inger Roos, Anders Gustafsson, and Bo Edvardsson, "The Role of Customer Clubs in Recent Telecom Relationships," *International Journal of Service Industry Management* 16, no. 5 (2005): 436–454; Dennis Pitta, Frank Franzak, Danielle Fowler, "A Strategic Approach to Building Online Customer Loyalty: Integrating Customer Profitability Tiers," *Journal of Consumer Marketing* 23, no. 7 (2006): 421–429.

42 Rick Ferguson and Kelly Hlavinka, "The Long Tail of Loyalty: How Personalized Dialogue and Customized Rewards Will Change Marketing Forever," *Journal of Consumer Marketing* 23, no. 6 (2006): 357–361.

43 Rick Ferguson and Kelly Hlavinka, "The Long Tail of Loyalty: How Personalized Dialogue and Customized Rewards Will Change Marketing Forever," *Journal of Consumer Marketing* 23, no. 6 (2006): 357–361.

44 Susan M. Keaveney, "Customer Switching Behavior in Service Industries: An Exploratory Study," *Journal of Marketing* 59 (April 1995): 71–82.

45 For a more detailed discussion of situation-specific switching behavior, refer to Inger Roos, Bo Edvardsson, and Anders Gustafsson, "Customer Switching Patterns in Competitive and Noncompetitive Service Industries," *Journal of Service Research* 6, no. 3 (2004): 256–271.

46 Gianfranco Walsh, Keith Dinnie, and Klaus-Peter Wiedmann, "How Do Corporate Reputation and Customer Satisfaction Impact Customer Defection? A Study of Private Energy Customers in Germany," *Journal of Services Marketing* 20, no. 6 (2006): 412–420.

47 Jonathan Lee, Janghyuk Lee, and Lawrence Feick, "The Impact of Switching Costs on the Consumer Satisfaction—Loyalty Link: Mobile Phone Service in France," *Journal of Services Marketing* 15, no. 1 (2001): 35–48; Shun Yin Lam, Venkatesh Shankar, M. Krishna Erramilli, and Bvsan Murthy, "Customer Value, Satisfaction, Loyalty, and Switching Costs: An Illustration from a Business-to-Business Service Context," *Journal of the Academy of Marketing Science* 32, no. 3 (2004): 293–311; Michael A. Jones, Kristy E. Reynolds, David L. Mothersbaugh, and Sharon Beatty, "The Positive and Negative Effects of Switching Costs on Relational Outcomes," *Journal of Service Research* 9, no. 4 (2007): 335–355.

48 Moonkyu Lee and Lawrence F. Cunningham, "A Cost/Benefit Approach to Understanding Loyalty," *Journal of Services Marketing* 15, no. 2 (2001): 113–130; Simon J. Bell, Seigyoung Auh, and Karen Smalley, "Customer Relationship Dynamics: Service Quality and Customer Loyalty in the Context of Varying Levels of Customer Expertise and Switching Costs," *Journal of the Academy of Marketing Science* 33, no. 2 (2005): 169–183.

49 Lesley White and Venkat Yanamandram, "Why Customers Stay: Reasons and Consequences of Inertia in Financial Services," *International Journal of Service Industry Management* 14, no. 3 (2004): 183–194.

50 For an overview on CRM, see: V. Kumar and Werner J. Reinartz, *Customer Relationship Management: A Database Approach.* Hoboken, NJ: John Wiley & Sons, 2006; B. Ramaseshan, David Bejou, Subhash C. Jain, Charlotte Mason, and Joseph Pancras, "Issues and Perspective in Global Customer Relationship Management," *Journal of Service Research* 9, no. 2 (2006): 195–207; V. Kumar, Sarang Sunder, and B. Ramaseshan, "Analyzing the Diffusion of Global Customer Relationship Management: A Cross-Regional Modeling Framework," *Journal of International Marketing* 19, no. 1 (2011): 23–39.

51 Dwayne Ball, Pedro S. Coelho, and Manuel J. Vilares, "Service Personalization and Loyalty," *Journal of Services Marketing* 20, no. 6 (2006): 391–403.

52 Kevin N. Quiring and Nancy K. Mullen, "More Than Data Warehousing: An Integrated View of the Customer," in *The Ultimate CRM Handbook—Strategies & Concepts for Building Enduring Customer Loyalty & Profitability*, John G. Freeland, ed., (New York: McGraw-Hill, 2002, 102–108).

53 This section is adapted from: Adrian Payne and Pennie Frow, "A Strategic Framework for Customer Relationship Management," *Journal of Marketing* 69 (October 2005): 167–176.

54 Martin Reimann, Oliver Schilke, and Jacquelyn S. Thomas, "Customer Relationship Management and Firm Performance: The Mediating Role of Business Strategy," *Journal of the Academy of Marketing Science* 38, no. 3 (2010): 326–346.

55 William Boulding, Richard Staelin, Michael Ehret, and Wesley J. Johnston, "A Customer Relationship Management Roadmap: What Is Known, Potential Pitfalls, and Where to Go," *Journal of Marketing* 69, no. 4 (2005): 155–166.

56 This section is largely based on: Sudhir H. Kale, "CRM Failure and the Seven Deadly Sins," *Marketing Management* (September/October 2004): 42–46.

57 William Boulding, Richard Staelin, Michael Ehret, and Wesley J. Johnston, "A Customer Relationship Management Roadmap: What Is Known, Potential Pitfalls, and Where to Go," *Journal of Marketing* 69, no. 4 (2005): 155–166.

58 Darrell K. Rigby and Dianne Ledingham, "CRM Done Right," *Harvard Business Review*, (November 2004): 118–129.

59 Manuel Ebner, Arthur Hu, Daniel Levitt, and Jim McCrory, "How to Rescue CRM?" *The McKinsey Quarterly* 4, (Technology, 2002).

60 Darrell K. Rigby and Dianne Ledingham, "CRM Done Right," *Harvard Business Review*, (November 2004): 118–129.

61 Darrell K. Rigby, Frederick F. Reichheld, and Phil Schefter, "Avoid the Four Perils of CRM," *Harvard Business Review* (February 2002): 108.

CHAPTER 13

complaint handling and SERVICE RECOVERY

LEARNING OBJECTIVES

By the end of this chapter, the reader should be able to:

- **LO 1** Recognize the actions that customers may take in response to service failures.
- **LO 2** Understand why customers complain.
- **LO 3** Know what customers expect from the firm when they complain.
- **LO 4** Understand how customers respond to effective service recovery.
- **LO 5** Explain the service recovery paradox.
- **LO 6** Know the principles of effective service recovery systems.
- **LO 7** Be familiar with the guidelines for frontline employees on how to handle complaining customers and recover from a service failure.
- **LO 8** Recognize the power of service guarantees.
- **LO 9** Understand how to design effective service guarantees.
- **LO 10** Know when firms should not offer service guarantees.
- **LO 11** Be familiar with the seven groups of jaycustomers and understand how to manage them effectively.

Figure 13.1 JetBlue's reputation for customer service excellence was temporarily grounded.

OPENING VIGNETTE

Too Little, Too Late—JetBlue's Service Recovery[1]

It was a terrible ice storm in the East Coast of the United States. Hundreds of passengers were trapped for 11 hours inside JetBlue planes at the John F. Kennedy International Airport in New York. These passengers were furious. No one in JetBlue did anything to get the passengers off the planes. On top of that, JetBlue cancelled more than 1,000 flights over six days, leaving even more passengers stranded. This incident cancelled out much that JetBlue had done right to become one of the strongest customer service brands in the United States. JetBlue was going to be ranked number four by *Business Week* in a list of top 25 customer service leaders, but because of this incident it was pulled from the rankings. What happened?

Figure 13.2 JetBlue's new Customer Bill of Rights and publicity campaigns involving the Simpsons were measures taken to win customers back.

There was no service recovery plan. No one—not the pilot, flight attendants, or station manager—had the authority to get the passengers off the plane. JetBlue's offer of refunds and travel vouchers did not seem to reduce the anger of the passengers, who had been stranded for so many hours. David Neeleman, JetBlue's CEO, sent a personal e-mail to all customers in the company's database to explain what caused the problem, apologized profusely, and detailed its service recovery efforts. He even appeared on late-night television to apologize and admitted that the airline should have had better contingency planning. However, the airline still had a long way to go to repair the damage done to its reputation.

Slowly, the airline rebuilt its reputation, starting with its new Customer Bill of Rights. The bill required the airline to provide vouchers or refunds in certain situations when flights were delayed. Neeleman also changed JetBlue's information systems to keep track of the locations of its crew, upgraded the website to allow online rebooking, and trained staff at the headquarters to help out at the airport when needed. All these activities were aimed at climbing its way back up to the heights it fell from. In June 2011, JetBlue Airways was on the list of J. D. Power Customer Service Champions for the seventh consecutive year. (J. D. Power and Associates conducts customer satisfaction research based on survey responses from millions of customers worldwide.) This shows that JetBlue's customers have finally forgiven its service failure and support its efforts to deliver continued service excellence.

CUSTOMER COMPLAINING BEHAVIOR

The first law of service quality and productivity might be: Do it right the first time. But we can't ignore the fact that failures continue to occur, sometimes for reasons outside the organization's control such as the ice storm that caused the JetBlue incident in our opening vignette.[2] How well a firm handles complaints and resolves problems will decide whether it builds customer loyalty or watches its customers take their business elsewhere.

LO 1

Recognize the actions that customers may take in response to service failures.

Customer Response Options to Service Failure

Chances are, you're not always satisfied with at least some of the services you receive. How do you respond to your dissatisfaction with these services? Do you complain to an employee, ask to speak to the manager, or file a formal complaint? Or perhaps do you just grumble to your friends and family, and choose another supplier the next time you need a similar type of service?

If you are among those who do not complain to the firm about poor service, you are not alone. Research around the globe has shown that most people will choose not to complain, especially if they think it will do no good. Figure 13.3 shows the courses of action a customer may take in response to a service failure. This model suggests at least three major courses of action:

1. Take some form of public action (including complaining to the firm or to a third party, such as a consumer affairs body or one that controls the industry, or even civil or criminal court).

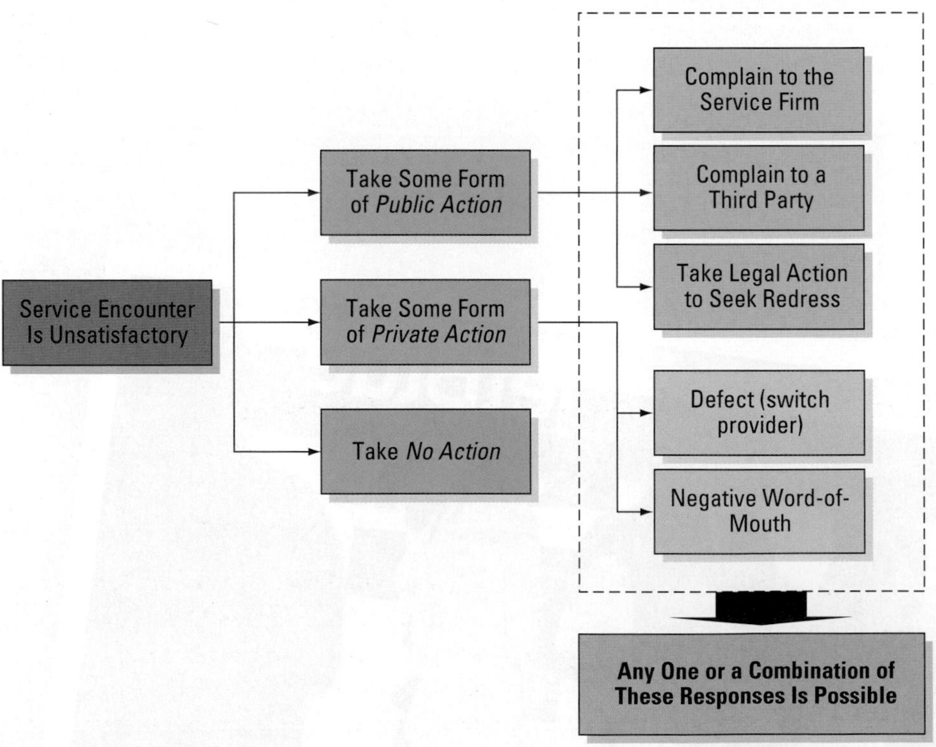

Figure 13.3 Customer response categories to service failures.

2. Take some form of private action (including abandoning the supplier).

3. Take no action (Figure 13.4).

It's important to remember that a customer can take any one or a combination of actions. Managers need to be aware that the impact of a defection can go far beyond the loss of that customer's future revenue stream. Angry customers often tell many other people about their problems.[3] The Internet allows unhappy customers to reach thousands of people by posting complaints on bulletin boards, blogs and even setting up their own websites to talk about their bad experiences with specific organizations.

Understanding Customer Complaining Behavior

LO 2
Understand why customers complain.

To be able to deal effectively with dissatisfied and complaining customers, managers need to understand key aspects of complaining behavior, starting with the questions posed below.

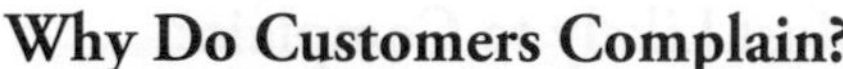

Why Do Customers Complain?

In general, studies of consumer complaining behavior have identified four main purposes for complaining:

1. *Obtain restitution or compensation.* Consumers often complain to recover some economic loss by seeking a refund, compensation, and/or have the service performed again.[4]
2. *Release their anger.* Some customers complain to rebuild self-esteem and/or to release their anger and frustration. When service processes are too focused on rules and unreasonable, or when employees are rude, customers' self-esteem, self-worth, or sense of fairness can be negatively affected. They may become angry and emotional.
3. *Help to improve the service.* When customers are highly involved with a service (e.g., at a college, an alumni association, or their main banking connection), they give feedback to try and contribute toward service improvements.
4. *Out of concern for others.* Finally, some customers are motivated by concern for others. They want to spare other customers from experiencing the same problems and may feel good raising a problem to improve a service.

Figure 13.4 Some customers may just be frustrated but do not take any action to complain, as seen here in an interaction with an online service.

PART IV

What Proportion of Unhappy Customers Complain?

Research shows that, on average, only 5–10% of customers who have been unhappy with a service actually complain.[5] Sometimes the percentage is far lower. A review of the records of a public bus company showed that formal complaints occurred at the rate of about three complaints for every million passenger trips. Assuming two trips a day, a person would need 1,370 years (roughly 27 lifetimes) to make a million trips. In other words, the rate of complaints was incredibly low, especially since public bus companies are rarely known for service excellence. However, although usually only a small number of dissatisfied customers complain, there's evidence that consumers across the world are becoming better informed, more self-confident, and more firm about seeking satisfactory outcomes for their complaints.

Figure 13.5 Customers often view complaining as difficult and unpleasant.

Why Don't Unhappy Customers Complain?

A number of studies, including findings by TARP, a customer satisfaction and measurement firm, have identified a number of reasons why customers don't complain. Customers may not want to take the time to write a letter, send an e-mail, fill in a form, or make a phone call, particularly if they don't see the service as being important enough to be worth the effort. Many customers believe that no one would be concerned about their problem or would be willing to deal with it, and that complaining is simply not worth their while. In some situations, people simply don't know where to go or what to do. Also, many people feel that complaining is unpleasant and would like to avoid the stress of a confrontation (Figure 13.5).[6]

Who Is Most Likely to Complain?

Research findings show that people in higher socio-economic levels are more likely to complain than those in lower levels. Their better education, higher income, and greater social involvement give them the confidence, knowledge, and motivation to speak up when they encounter problems. Furthermore, those who complain also tend to be more knowledgeable about the product in question.

Where Do Customers Complain?

Studies show that the majority of complaints are made at the place where the service was received. One of the authors of this book completed a consulting project developing and implementing a customer feedback system. He found that an amazing 99% of customer feedback was given face-to-face or over the phone to customer service representatives. Less than 1% of all complaints were submitted via e-mail, letters, customer feedback cards, or the firm's website. A survey of airline passengers found that only 3% of respondents who were unhappy with their meal actually complained about it, and they all complained to the flight attendant. None complained to the company's headquarters or to a consumer affairs office.[7] Also, customers tend to use interactive channels such as face-to-face or the telephone when they want a problem to be fixed, but use noninteractive channels to complain (e.g., e-mail or letters) when they mainly want to release their anger and frustration.[8]

In practice, even when customers do complain, managers often don't hear about the complaints made to frontline employees. Without a formal customer feedback system, only a tiny proportion of the complaints may reach corporate headquarters.[9] If unhappy customers have already used other channels of complaint, but their problem is not solved, then they are more likely to turn to online public complaining. This is due to "double deviation". The service performance already caused dissatisfaction in the first instance, and the resolution of the problem also failed.[10]

What Do Customers Expect Once They Have Made a Complaint?

LO 3

Know what customers expect from the firm when they complain.

Whenever a service failure occurs, people expect to be treated fairly. However, recent studies have shown that many customers feel that they have not been treated fairly nor received good enough compensation. When this happens, their reactions tend to be immediate, emotional, and enduring. In contrast, outcomes that are perceived as fair have a positive impact on customer satisfaction.[11]

Stephen Tax and Stephen Brown found that as much as 85% of the variation in the satisfaction with a service recovery was due to three dimensions of fairness (see Figure 13.6):[12]

- ***Procedural justice*** refers to the policies and rules that any customer has to go through to seek fairness. Customers expect the firm to take responsibility, followed by a convenient and responsive recovery process. That includes flexibility of the system and consideration of customer inputs into the recovery process.
- ***Interactional justice*** involves the employees of the firm who provide the service recovery and their behavior toward the customer. It is important to give an explanation for the failure and to make an effort to resolve the problem. Furthermore, the recovery effort must be seen as genuine, honest, and polite.
- ***Outcome justice*** concerns the compensation that a customer receives as a result of the losses and inconveniences caused by the service failure. This includes compensation for not only the failure but also time, effort, and energy spent during the process of service recovery.

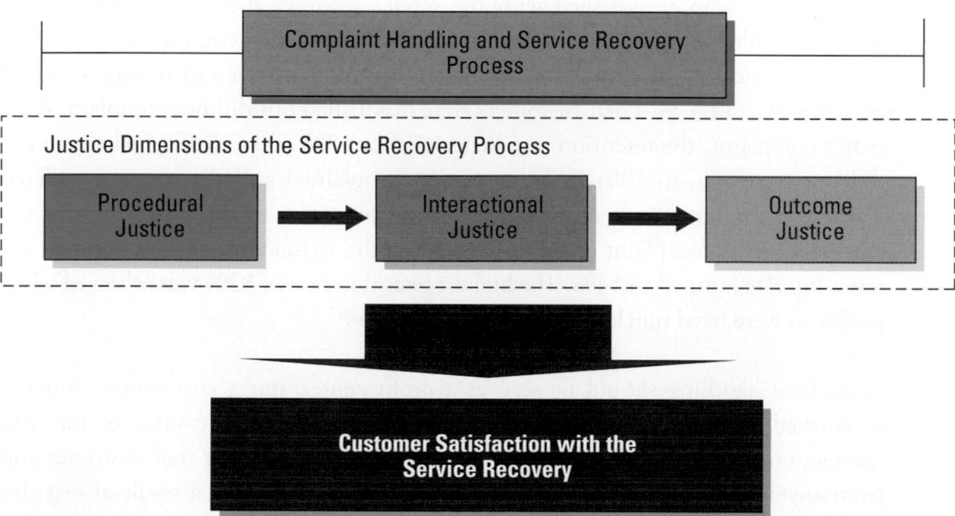

Figure 13.6 Three dimensions of perceived fairness in service recovery processes.

SOURCE

Adapted from Stephen S. Tax and Stephen W. Brown, "Recovering and Learning from Service Failure," *Sloan Management Review* 49, no. 1 (Fall 1998): 75–88.

PART IV

LO 4

Understand how customers respond to effective service recovery.

CUSTOMER RESPONSES TO EFFECTIVE SERVICE RECOVERY

"Thank Heavens for Complainers" was the provocative title of an article about customer complaining behavior, which also featured a successful manager exclaiming, "Thank goodness I've got a dissatisfied customer on the phone! The ones I worry about are the ones I never hear from."[13] Customers who do complain give a firm the chance to correct problems (including some the firm may not even know it has), restore relationships with the complainer, and improve future satisfaction for all.

Service recovery is a term for the systematic efforts by a firm to correct a problem following a service failure and to retain a customer's goodwill. Service recovery efforts play an important role in achieving (or restoring) customer satisfaction and loyalty.[14] In every organization, things may occur that have a negative impact on relationships with customers. The true test of a firm's commitment to satisfaction and service quality isn't in the advertising promises, but in the way it responds when things go wrong for the customer. Although complaints tend to have a negative effect on service personnel's commitment to customer service, employees with a positive attitude toward service and their own jobs are more likely to explore additional ways in which they can help customers, and view complaints as a potential source of improvement.[15]

Impact of Effective Service Recovery on Customer Loyalty

When complaints are satisfactorily resolved, there is a much higher chance that the customers involved will remain loyal. In fact, recent research has shown that complainants who are satisfied with the service recovery they experienced are 15 times more likely to recommend a company than dissatisfied complainants.[16] TARP research found that intentions to repurchase for different types of products ranged between 9% and 37% when customers were dissatisfied but did not complain. For a major complaint, the retention rate increased from 9% when dissatisfied customers did not complain, to 19% if the customer complained and the company offered a listening ear but was unable to resolve the complaint to the satisfaction of the customer. If the complaint could be resolved to the satisfaction of the customer, the retention rate jumped to 54%. The highest retention rate of 82% was achieved when problems were fixed quickly—typically on the spot![17]

Complaint handling should be seen as a profit center, not a cost center. When a dissatisfied customer defects, the firm loses more than just the value of the next transaction. It may also lose a long-term stream of profits from that customer and from anyone else who is deterred from patronizing that firm as a result of negative comments from an unhappy friend.[18]

LO 5

Explain the service recovery paradox.

The Service Recovery Paradox

The *service recovery paradox* describes the phenomenon where customers who experience an excellent service recovery after a failure feel even more satisfied than customers who had no problem in the first place.[19] For example, a passenger may arrive at the check-in counter and find that there are no seats due to overbooking, even though he has a confirmed seat. To recover the service, the passenger is upgraded to a business class seat at no additional charge. The customer ends up being delighted and even more satisfied than before the problem had occurred.

The service recovery paradox may lead to the thinking that it may be good for customers to experience service failure so that they can be delighted as a result of an excellent service recovery. However, this approach would be too expensive for the firm. It is also important to note that the service recovery paradox does not always apply. For example, a study of repeated service failures in a retail banking context showed that the service recovery paradox held for the first service failure that was recovered to customers' full satisfaction.[20] However, if a second service failure occurred, the paradox disappeared. It seems that customers may forgive a firm once but become disappointed if failures happen again. Furthermore, the study also showed that customers' expectations were raised after they experienced a very good recovery. Thus, excellent recovery becomes the standard they expect for dealing with future failures.

Whether a customer comes out delighted from a service recovery probably may also depend on how serious the failure was. No one can replace spoiled wedding photos, a ruined holiday, or an injury caused by service equipment. In such situations, it's hard to imagine anyone being truly delighted even when a most professional service recovery is conducted. In conclusion, the best strategy, of course, is to do it right the first time.

PRINCIPLES OF EFFECTIVE SERVICE RECOVERY SYSTEMS

LO 6
Know the principles of effective service recovery systems.

Managers need to recognize that current customers are a valuable asset base and develop effective procedures for service recovery following unsatisfactory experiences. We discuss three guiding principles for how to get it right: (1) make it easy for customers to give feedback, (2) enable effective service recovery, and (3) establish appropriate compensation levels. A fourth principle, learning from customer feedback and driving service improvements, will be discussed in Chapter 14 in the context of customer feedback systems. The components of an effective service recovery system are shown in Figure 13.7.

Make It Easy for Customers to Give Feedback

How can managers overcome unhappy customers' reluctance to complain about service failures? The best way is to address the reasons for their reluctance directly. Table 13.1 gives an overview of what can be done to overcome those reasons we identified earlier in this chapter. Many companies have improved their complaint-collection procedures by adding special toll-free phone lines, links on their websites, and clearly displayed customer comment cards in their branches (see Figure 13.8). In their customer newsletters, some companies feature service improvements that were the direct result of customer feedback under the motto "You told us, and we responded."

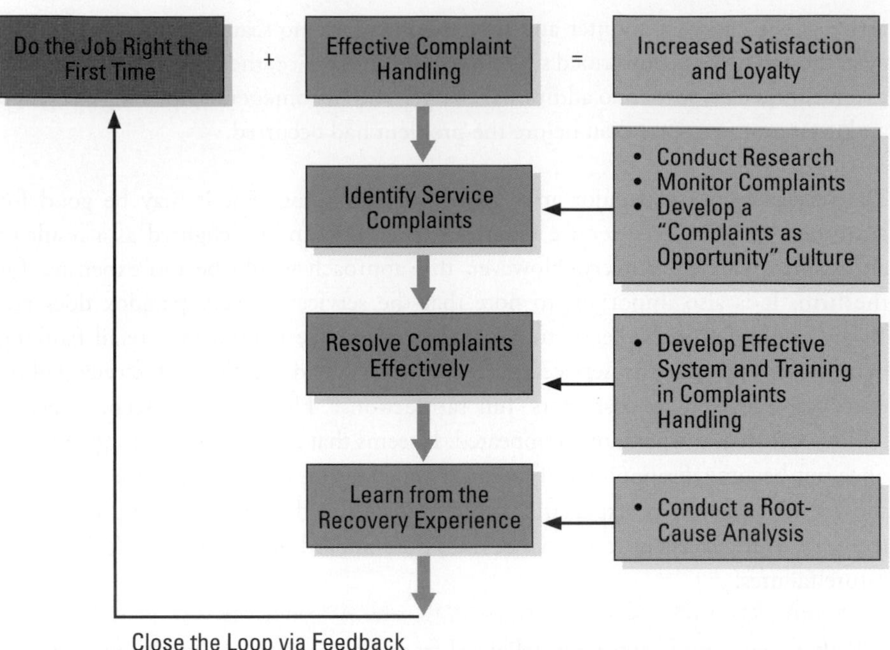

Figure 13.7 Components of an effective service recovery system.

SOURCE

Christopher H. Lovelock, Paul G. Patterson, and Jochen Wirtz, *Services Marketing: An Asia-Pacific and Australian Perspective*, 5th edition, (Sydney: Pearson Australia, 2011, 413.

Table 13.1 Strategies to reduce customer complaint barriers

Complaint Barriers for Dissatisfied Customers	Strategies to Reduce These Barriers
Inconvenience • Difficult to find the right complaint procedure • Effort, e.g., writing and mailing a letter	Make feedback easy and convenient: • Put customer service hotline numbers, e-mail the website and/ or postal addresses on all customer communications materials (letters, bills, brochures, website, phone book, yellow pages listings, etc.)
Doubtful payoff • Uncertain whether any or what action will be taken by the firm to address the issue the customer is unhappy with	Reassure customers that their feedback will be taken seriously and will pay off: • Have service recovery procedures in place and communicate this to customers, e.g., in customer newsletter and website. • Feature service improvements that resulted from customer feedback.
Unpleasantness • Fear of being treated rudely • Fear of being hassled • Feeling embarrassed	Make providing feedback a positive experience: • Thank customers for their feedback (can be done publicly and in general by addressing the entire customer base). • Train service employees not to hassle and to make customers feel comfortable. • Allow for anonymous feedback.

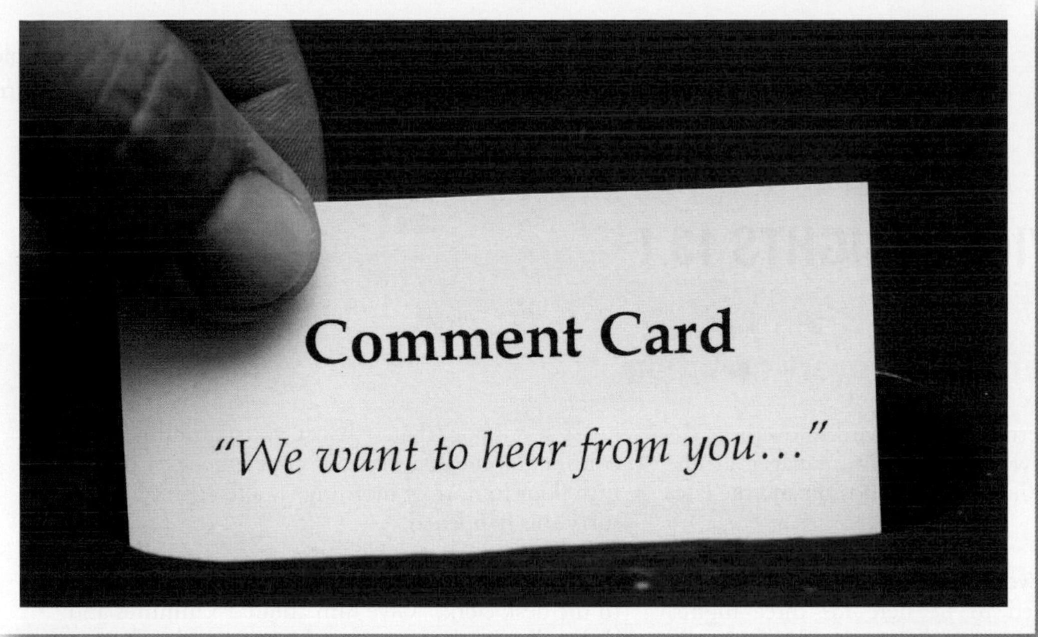

Figure 13.8 Comment cards are commonly found in restaurants and hotels to gather customers' feedback.

Enable Effective Service Recovery

Recovering from service failures requires commitment, planning, and clear guidelines. Specifically, effective service recovery should be (1) proactive, (2) planned, (3) trained, and (4) empowered.

Service Recovery Should Be Proactive

Service recovery ideally is done on the spot, preferably before customers have a chance to complain (see Service Insights 13.1). Service personnel should be sensitive to signs of dissatisfaction and ask whether customers might be experiencing a problem. For example, the waiter may ask a guest who has only eaten half of his dinner: "Is everything all right, Sir?" The guest may say, "Yes, thank you. I am not very hungry," or "The steak is well done but I had asked for medium-rare." The second response then gives the waiter a chance to recover the service, rather than have an unhappy diner leave the restaurant who might not return.

Recovery Procedures Need to Be Planned

Backup plans have to be developed for service failures, especially for those that occur regularly and cannot be designed out of the system.[21] For example, revenue management practices in the travel and hospitality industries often result in overbooking. Therefore, travelers are denied boarding or hotel guests do not have rooms even though they had confirmed seats or reservations. Firms should identify the most common service problems such as overbooking and then develop solution sets for employees to follow. In contact centers, the customer service representatives have prepared scripts to guide them in a service recovery situation.

Recovery Skills Must Be Taught

Customers and employees easily feel insecure at the point of service failure because things are not turning out as they had expected. With effective training of how to handle recovery solution sets for routine service failure (e.g., as in our hotel example in Service Insights 13.1) and for nonroutine service failures, frontline staff can turn distress into delight with confidence and skill.[22]

SERVICE INSIGHTS 13.1

Effective Service Recovery in Action

The lobby is deserted. It's not hard to overhear the conversation between the night manager at the Marriott Long Wharf Hotel in Boston and the late-arriving guest.

"Yes, Dr. Jones, we've been expecting you. I know you are scheduled to be here for three nights. I'm sorry to tell you, Sir, but we are booked solid tonight. A large number of guests we assumed were checking out did not. Where is your meeting tomorrow, Sir?"

The doctor told the clerk where it was.

"That's near the Omni Parker House! That's not very far from here. Let me call them and get you a room for the evening. I'll be right back."

A few minutes later, the desk clerk returned with the good news.

"They're holding a room for you at the Omni Parker House, Sir. And, of course, we'll pick up the tab. I'll forward any phone calls that come here for you. Here's a letter that will explain the situation and expedite your check-in, along with my business card so you can call me directly here at the front desk if you have any problems."

The doctor's mood was moving from exasperation toward calm. But the desk clerk was not finished with the encounter. He reached into the cash drawer. "Here are two $10 bills. That should more than cover your cab fare from here to the Parker House and back again in the morning. We don't have a problem tomorrow night, just tonight. And here's a coupon that will get you complimentary continental breakfast on our concierge level on the fifth floor tomorrow morning ... and again, I am so sorry this happened."

As the doctor walks away, the night manager turns to the desk clerk, "Give him about 15 minutes and then call to make sure everything went okay."

A week later, when it was still a peak period for hotels in that city, the same guest who had overheard the exchange is in a taxi, en route to the same hotel. Along the way, he tells about the great service recovery episode he had witnessed the week before. The two travelers arrive at the hotel and make their way to the front desk, ready to check in.

They are greeted with unexpected news: "I am so sorry, gentlemen. I know you were scheduled here for two nights. But we are booked solid tonight. Where is your meeting scheduled tomorrow?"

The would-be guests exchange a rueful glance as they give the desk clerk their future plans. "That's near the Méridien. Let me call over there and see if I can get you a room. It won't but take a minute." As the desk clerk walks away, the tale teller says, "I'll bet he comes back with a letter and a business card."

Sure enough, the desk clerk returns to deliver the solution; it's not a robotic script but all the elements from the previous week's show are on display. What the tale teller thought was pure desk-clerk initiative the previous week, he now realizes was a planned, seemingly spontaneous yet predetermined response to a specific category of service problem.

SOURCE

Ron Zemke and Chip R. Bell, *Knock Your Socks Off Service Recovery.* New York: AMACOM, 2000, 59–60.

Recovery Requires Empowered Employees

Employees should be given the freedom to use their judgment and communication skills to develop solutions that will satisfy complaining customers. This is especially true for out-of-the-ordinary failures for which a firm may not have developed and trained solution sets. Employees need to be able to make decisions and spend money in order to resolve service problems promptly and recover customer goodwill. At the Ritz-Carlton and Sheraton hotels, employees are given the freedom to be proactive, rather than reactive. They take ownership of the situation and help resolve customers' problems to the best of their ability. In this day and age, where online public complaining is gaining popularity, employees may even be empowered to respond online, for example, to complaints in the form of tweets, by tweeting back with a solution to resolve the problem.[23]

How Generous Should Compensation Be?

How much compensation should a firm offer when there has been a service failure? Or would an apology be sufficient instead? The following rules of thumb can help managers to answer these questions:

- **What is the positioning of your firm?** If a firm is known for service excellence and charges a premium price for quality, then customers will expect service failures to be rare, so the firm should make a major effort to recover the few failures that do occur and be prepared to offer something of greater value. However, in a mass market business, customers are likely to accept an apology and rework of the service.
- **How severe was the service failure?** The general guideline is "let the punishment fit the crime." Customers expect less for minor inconveniences (here, often a sincere apology will do), but much more if there was major damage in terms of time, effort, annoyance, or anxiety.
- **Who is the affected customer?** Long-term customers and those who spend heavily at a service provider expect more, and it is worth making an effort to save their business. One-time customers tend to demand less and also contribute less to a firm's profit. Hence, compensation can be less, but should still be fair. There is always the possibility that a first-time user will become a repeat customer if he or she is treated well.

The overall rule of thumb for compensation at service failures should be "well-dosed generosity." Overly generous compensation is expensive, and it also may lead customers to become suspicious about the underlying motives. Also, overgenerosity does not seem to result in higher repeat purchase rates than simply offering a fair compensation.[24] There is a risk, too, that a reputation for overgenerosity may encourage dishonest customers to actively "seek" service failures.[25]

Dealing with Complaining Customers

 **LO 7**

Be familiar with the guidelines for front line employees on how to handle complaining customers and recover from a service failure.

Both managers and frontline employees must be prepared to deal with upset customers who can become confrontational and sometimes behave in unacceptable ways toward service personnel who aren't at fault in any way. Service Insights 13.2 provides specific guidelines for effective problem resolution, designed to help calm upset customers and to deliver a solution that they will see as fair and satisfying.

PART IV

Copyright 2006 by Randy Glasbergen. www.glasbergen.com

CUSTOMER SERVICE DEPT.

"Who picked 'I Can't Get No Satisfaction' to be our on-hold music?"

SERVICE INSIGHTS 13.2

Guidelines for the Front-Line: How to Handle Complaining Customers and Recover from a Service Failure

1. ***Act fast.*** If the complaint is made during service delivery, then time is very important to achieve a full recovery. When complaints are made after the fact, many companies try to respond within 24 hours or sooner.

2. ***Acknowledge the customer's feelings.*** This helps to build an emotional connection, the first step in rebuilding a relationship that has some problems.

3. ***Don't argue with customers.*** The goal should be to gather facts to reach a solution that is accepted by the firm and the customer. It is not to argue and prove that the customer is wrong. Arguing gets in the way of listening and seldom reduces anger.

4. ***Show that you understand the problem from each customer's point of view.*** Seeing situations through the customers' eyes is the only way to understand what they think has gone wrong and why they're upset. Service personnel should avoid jumping to conclusions with their own interpretations.

5. ***Clarify the truth and sort out the cause.*** A failure may result from inefficiency of service, misunderstanding by customers, or the misbehavior of a third party. If you've done something wrong, apologize immediately in order to win the understanding and trust of the customer. The more the customer can forgive you, the less he expects to be compensated. Don't act as if you are trying to defend yourself. Acting that way may suggest that the organization has something to hide or is not willing to fully look into the situation.

6. ***Give customers the benefit of doubt.*** Not all customers are truthful and not all complaints are genuine. However, customers should be treated as though they have a valid complaint until clear evidence proves that it is not true. If a lot of money is involved (as in insurance claims or potential lawsuits), careful investigation needs to be carried out. If the amount involved is small, it may not be worth arguing about a refund or other compensation. However, it's still a good idea to check records to see if there is a past history of doubtful complaints by the same customer.

7. ***Propose the steps needed to solve the problem.*** When solutions are not immediately available, tell the customers how the firm intends to take action to deal with the problem. This also sets expectations about the time involved, so firms should be careful not to overpromise!.

8. ***Keep customers informed of progress.*** Nobody likes being left in the dark. Uncertainty causes people to be anxious and stressed. Therefore, customers should be kept informed about what is going on regularly.

9. ***Consider compensation.*** When customers do not receive the service outcomes that they have paid for, or have suffered serious inconvenience and/or loss of time and money because the service failed, there should either be a monetary payment or some other compensation (e.g., an upgrade on a flight or a free dessert in a restaurant). This type of recovery may also reduce the risk of legal action by angry customers.

10. ***Continue trying to regain customer goodwill.*** When customers have been disappointed, one of the hardest things to do is to restore their confidence and keep the relationship going. Firms must try to calm the customers and convince them that actions are being taken to avoid the same problem in the future. Truly exceptional recovery efforts can be extremely effective in building loyalty and referrals.

11. ***Self-check the system and improve it.*** After the customer has left, you should check to see whether the service failure was caused by an accidental mistake or system problems. Use every complaint to perfect the whole service system. Even if the complaint is found to be a misunderstanding by customers, it also means that a part of your communications may not be effective.

SERVICE GUARANTEES

One way for customer-focused firms to have professional complaint handling and effective service recovery is through offering service guarantees. In fact, a growing number of companies offer customers a service guarantee, promising that if service delivery fails to meet pre-defined standards, the customer can have one or more forms of compensation, such as an easy-to-claim replacement, refund, or credit.[26]

The Power of Service Guarantees

 **LO 8**

Recognize the power of service guarantees.

Service guarantees are powerful tools for both promoting and achieving service quality for the following reasons:[27]

1. Guarantees force firms to focus on what their customers want and expect in each element of the service.
2. Guarantees set clear standards. These tell customers and employees what the company stands for. Payouts to compensate customers for poor service cause managers to take guarantees seriously because they highlight the financial costs of quality failures.
3. Guarantees require the development of systems for generating meaningful customer feedback and acting on it.
4. Guarantees force service organizations to understand why they fail and encourage them to identify and overcome potential fail points.
5. Guarantees build "marketing muscle" by reducing the risk of the purchase decision and building long-term loyalty.

From the customer's perspective, the primary function of service guarantees is to lower the perceived risks associated with purchase.[28] Sara Bjőrlin Lidén and Per Skålén found that, even when dissatisfied customers were unaware that a service guarantee existed before making their complaint, they were positively impressed to learn that the company has a pre-planned procedure for handling failures and to find that their complaints were taken seriously.[29]

The benefits of service guarantees can be seen clearly in the case of Hampton Inn's "100% Hampton Guarantee" ("If you're not 100% satisfied, you don't pay"—see Figure 13.9). As a business-building program, Hampton's strategy of offering to refund the cost of the room to a guest who expresses dissatisfaction has attracted new customers and also served as a powerful retention device. People choose to stay at a Hampton Inn because they are confident they will be satisfied. At least as important, the guarantee has become a vital tool to help managers identify new opportunities for quality improvement.

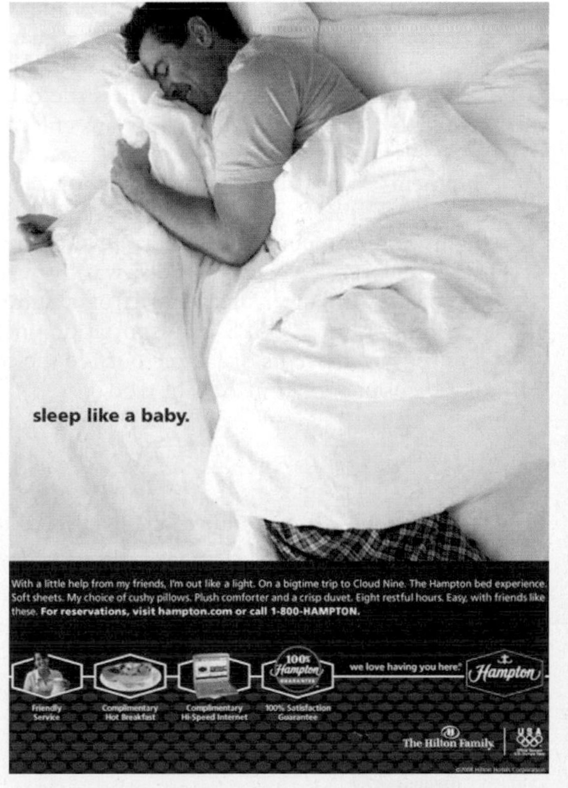

Figure 13.9 Hampton Inn includes its "100% satisfaction guaranteed" in its advertising.

PART IV

LO 9

Understand how to design effective service guarantees.

How to Design Service Guarantees

Some guarantees are simple and unconditional. Others appear to have been written by lawyers and contain many restrictions. Compare the examples in Service Insights 13.3 and ask yourself which guarantees you trust and are confident about, and whether you would like to do business with that firm.

SERVICE INSIGHTS 13.3

Examples of Service Guarantees

United States Postal Service Express Mail Guarantee

Service Guarantee: Express Mail international mailings are not covered by this service agreement. Military shipments delayed due to customs inspections are also excluded. If the shipment is mailed at a designated USPS Express Mail facility on or before the specified deposit time for overnight delivery to the addressee, delivery to the addressee or agent will be attempted before the applicable guaranteed time. Signature of the addressee's agent, or delivery employee is required upon delivery. If a delivery attempt is not made by the guaranteed time and the mailer files a claim for a refund, the USPS will refund the postage unless the delay was caused by: proper retention for law enforcement purposes; strike or work stoppage; late deposit of shipment; forwarding, return, incorrect address or incorrect ZIP code; delay or cancellation of flights; governmental action beyond the control of the Postal Service or air carriers; war, insurrection or civil disturbance; breakdowns of a substantial portion of the USPS transportation network resulting from events or factors outside the control of the Postal Service or Acts of God.

L. L. Bean's Guarantee

Our Guarantee. Our products are guaranteed to give 100% satisfaction in every way. Return anything purchased from us at any time if it proves otherwise. We do not want you to have anything from L. L. Bean that is not completely satisfactory.

Excerpt from the "Quality Standard Guarantees" from an Office Services Company

- We guarantee six-hour turnaround on documents of two pages or less ... (does not include client subsequent changes or equipment failures).
- We guarantee that there will be a receptionist to greet you and your visitors during normal business hours... (short breaks of less than five minutes are not subject to this guarantee).
- You will not be obligated to pay rent for any day on which there is not a manager on site to assist you (lunch and reasonable breaks are expected and not subject to this guarantee).

The Bugs Burger Bug Killer Guarantee (a Pest Control Company)

- You don't owe us a penny until all the pests on your premises have been eradicated.
- If you're ever dissatisfied with the BBBK's service, you will receive a refund for as much as 12 months of service—plus fees for another exterminator of your choice for the next year.
- If a guest spots a pest on your premises, the exterminator will pay for the guest's meal or room, send a letter of apology, and pay for a future meal or stay.
- If your premises are closed down because of the presence of roaches or rodents, BBBK will pay any fines, as well as all lost profit, plus $5,000.

SOURCE

Printed on back of Express Mail receipt, January 2006.
Printed in all L. L. Bean catalogs and on the company's website, *www.llbean.com/customerService/aboutLLBean/guarantee.html*, accessed March 12, 2012.
Reproduced in Eileen C. Shapiro, *Fad Surfing in the Boardroom.* Reading, MA: Addison-Wesley, 1995: 18.
Reproduced in Christopher W. Hart, "The Power of Unconditional Service Guarantees." *Harvard Business Review* (July–August 1990).

The two service guarantees from L. L. Bean and BBBK are powerful, unconditional, and earn trust. The other two are weakened by the many conditions attached to the guarantee. The United States Postal Service has added six new conditions in recent years! Hart argues that service guarantees should be designed to meet the following criteria[30]:

1. **Unconditional**—Whatever is promised in the guarantee must be totally unconditional and there should not be any element of surprise for the customer.
2. **Easy to understand and communicate** to the customer so that he is clearly aware of the benefits that can be gained from the guarantee.
3. **Meaningful to the customer** in that the guarantee is on something important to the customer and the compensation should be more than enough to cover the service failure.[31]
4. **Easy to invoke**—It should be easy for the customer to invoke the guarantee.
5. **Easy to collect on**—If a service failure occurs, the customer should be able to easily collect on the guarantee without any problems.
6. **Credible**—The guarantee should be believable (Figure 13.10).

Is Full Satisfaction the Best You Can Guarantee?

Full satisfaction guarantees have generally been considered the best possible design. However, customers may raise questions such as "What does full satisfaction mean?" or "Can I invoke a guarantee when I am dissatisfied, although the fault does not lie with the service firm?"[32] A new type of guarantee, called the "combined guarantee," addresses this issue. It combines the wide scope of a full satisfaction guarantee with the low uncertainty of attribute-specific performance standards. The combined guarantee tends to be more effective than either a full satisfaction or an attribute-specific guarantee design.[33] Table 13.2 shows examples of the various types of guarantees.

Figure 13.10 To leave a clear stamp of service quality on customers, the guarantee must be unconditional, meaningful, credible, easily understood, invoked, and collected.

Table 13.2 Types of service guarantees

Term	Guarantee Scope	Example
Single attribute-specific guarantee	One key attribute of the service is covered by the guarantee.	"Any of three specified popular pizzas is guaranteed to be served within 10 minutes of ordering on working days between 12 a.m. and 2 p.m. If the pizza is late, the customer's next order is free."
Multiattribute-specific guarantee	A few important attributes of the service are covered by the guarantee.	Minneapolis Marriott's guarantee: "Our quality commitment to you is to provide: • a friendly, efficient check-in; • a clean, comfortable room, where everything works; • a friendly efficient check-out. If we, in your opinion, do not deliver on this commitment, we will give you $20 in cash. No questions asked. It is your interpretation."
Full-satisfaction guarantee	All aspects of the service are covered by the guarantee. There are no exceptions.	Lands' End's guarantee: "If you are not completely satisfied with any item you buy from us, at any time during your use of it, return it and we will refund your full purchase price. We mean every word of it. Whatever. Whenever. Always. But to make sure this is perfectly clear, we've decided to simplify it further. GUARANTEED. Period."
Combined guarantee	All aspects of the service are covered by the full-satisfaction promise of the guarantee. Explicit minimum performance standards on important attributes are included in the guarantee to reduce uncertainty.	Datapro Information Services guarantees "to deliver the report on time, to high quality standards, and to the contents outlined in this proposal. Should we fail to deliver according to this guarantee, or should you be dissatisfied with any aspect of our work, you can deduct any amount from the final payment which is deemed as fair."

SOURCE

Wirtz, J. and Kum, D. "Designing Service Guarantees—Is Full Satisfaction the Best You Can Guarantee?" *Journal of Services Marketing* 15, no. 14 (2002): 282–299.

LO 10

Know when firms should not offer service guarantees.

Is It Always Beneficial to Introduce a Service Guarantee?

Managers should think carefully about their firm's strengths and weaknesses when deciding whether or not to introduce a service guarantee. Amy Ostrom and Christopher Hart identified a number of situations in which a guarantee may be inappropriate:[34]

- Companies that already have a strong reputation for service excellence may not need a guarantee. In fact, it might not fit their image to offer one. Rather, best practice service firms will be expected to do what's right without offering a service guarantee.
- A firm whose service is currently poor must first work to improve quality to a level above what is guaranteed. Otherwise, too many customers will invoke the guarantee with serious cost implications.

- Service firms whose quality is truly uncontrollable because of external forces like the weather should not offer a guarantee.
- When consumers see little financial, personal, or physiological risk associated with purchasing and using a service, a guarantee adds little value but still costs money to design, implement, and manage.

In markets where there is little perceived difference in service quality among competing firms, the first firm to institute a guarantee may be able to obtain a first-mover advantage and create value differentiation for its services. If more than one competitor already has a guarantee in place, then the only real way to make an impact is to launch a highly distinctive guarantee beyond what is already offered by competitors.[35]

DISCOURAGING ABUSE AND OPPORTUNISTIC CUSTOMER BEHAVIOR

Throughout this chapter, we have discussed the importance of professional complaint handling and service recovery. However, we have to recognize that not all complaints are honest. When firms have generous service recovery policies or offer guarantees, there is always the fear that some customers may take advantage of that. Also, not all complaining customers are right or reasonable in their behavior, and some customers may actually be the cause of complaints by other customers.[36] We refer to such people as *jaycustomers.*

A jaycustomer is someone who acts in a thoughtless or abusive way, causing problems for the firm, its employees, and other customers. Every service has its share of jaycustomers. Jaycustomers are undesirable. At best, a firm should avoid attracting them in the first place, and at worst, a firm needs to control or prevent their abusive behavior. Let's first describe the main types of jaycustomers before we discuss how to deal with them.

Seven Types of Jaycustomers[37]

LO 11

Be familiar with the seven groups of jaycustomers and understand how to manage them effectively.

We have identified seven broad categories and given them general names, but many customer contact personnel have come up with their own special terms.

The Cheat

There are many ways in which customers can cheat service firms. Cheating ranges from writing compensation letters with the sole purpose of exploiting service recovery policies and cheating on service guarantees, to inflating or faking insurance claims and "wardrobing" (e.g., using an evening dress or tuxedo for an evening and then returning it back to the retailer).[38] Fake returns have become more common and socially accepted.[39] The following quotes describe the thinking of these customers nicely:

> On checking in to a hotel, I noticed that they had a "100% satisfaction or your money back" guarantee, I just couldn't resist the opportunity to take advantage of it, so on checking out, I told the receptionist that I wanted a

PART IV

refund as the sound of the traffic kept me awake all night. They gave me a refund, no questions asked. These companies can be so stupid they need to be more alert.[40]

I've complained that service was too slow, too quick, too hot, too cold, too bright, too dark, too friendly, too impersonal, too public, too private … it doesn't matter really, as long as you enclose a receipt with your letter, you just get back a standard letter and gift coupon.[41]

Firms cannot easily check whether a customer is faking dissatisfaction or truly is unhappy. At the end of this section, we will discuss how to deal with this type of consumer fraud.

The Thief

The thief jaycustomer has no intention of paying and sets out to steal goods and services (or to pay less than full price by switching price tickets). Shoplifting is a major problem in retail stores. For those with technical skills, it's sometimes possible to bypass electricity meters, access telephone lines free of charge, or bypass normal cable TV feeds. Riding free on public transportation, sneaking into movie theaters, or not paying for restaurant meals are also popular. Finding out how people steal a service is the first step in preventing theft or catching thieves and, charging them in court where necessary. However, firms must take into account that there are some honest but absentminded customers who forget to pay.

The Rulebreaker

Many service businesses need rules of behavior for employees and customers to guide them safely through the various steps of the service encounter. Some of these rules are set down by government agencies for health and safety reasons. Air travel provides one of the best of examples of rules designed to ensure safety.

Rules set by service providers are meant to help smooth operations, avoid unreasonable demands on employees, prevent misuse of products and facilities, protect themselves

Figure 13.11 Dangerous skiers are rule breakers who pose a danger to others and need to be policed.

legally, and discourage individual customers from misbehaving. Ski resorts, for instance, are getting tough on careless skiers. Skiers can be seriously injured or even killed if they crash into each other. Therefore, ski patrol members must sometimes take on a policing role. Just as dangerous drivers can lose their licenses, dangerous skiers can lose their lift tickets (Figure 13.11).

There are risks attached to making lots of rules. The firm may become too inflexible. Instead of being customer-oriented, employees become like police officers, making sure that customers follow all the rules. However, the fewer the rules, the clearer the important ones can be.

The Belligerent

You've probably seen him (or her) in a store, at the airport, in a hotel or restaurant. The person is shouting angrily, or may be mouthing insults, threats, and curses. Service personnel are often abused, even when they are not to blame. If an employee lacks the power to resolve the problem, the belligerent may become even more angry, even to the point of physical attack. Unfortunately, when angry customers yell at service personnel, the latter sometimes respond in the same way. This can lead to arguments and reduce the likelihood of solving the problem (Figure 13.12).

What should an employee do when an aggressive customer does not listen? In a public place, the main aim should be to move the person away from other customers. Sometimes, supervisors may have to settle disagreements between customers and staff members. At other times, they need to support the employee's actions. If a customer has physically attacked an employee, then it may be necessary to get security officers or the police.

Figure 13.12 Confrontations between customers and service employees can easily escalate.

Telephone rudeness poses a different problem. One way to handle customers who continue to shout at a telephone-based employee is for the latter to say firmly, "This conversation isn't getting us anywhere. Why don't I call you back in a few minutes when you've had time to digest the information?" In many cases, a break to think (and cool down) is exactly what's needed.

PART IV

The Family Feuders

People who get into arguments with members of their own family—or worse, with other customers—make up a subcategory of belligerents we call "family feuders." Employee intervention may calm the situation or actually make it worse. Some situations require detailed analysis and a carefully thought-out response. Others, such as customers starting a food fight in a nice restaurant (yes, such things do happen!), require an almost immediate response. Service managers in these situations need to be prepared to think on their feet and act fast.

The Vandal

The level of physical abuse to service facilities and equipment is truly surprising. Soft drinks are poured into bank cash machines; there are burn holes from cigarettes on carpets, tablecloths, and bedcovers; hotel furniture is broken; telephone handsets are torn off; glass is smashed and fabrics are torn. The list is endless. Customers don't cause all of the damage, of course. Bored or drunk young people are the source of much exterior vandalism. However, much of the problem does come from paying customers who choose to misbehave.

The best cure for vandalism is prevention. Improved security discourages some vandals (Figure 13.13). Good lighting helps, as well as open design of public areas. Companies can choose vandal-resistant surfaces and protective coverings for equipment. Educating customers to use equipment properly can reduce the likelihood of abuse or careless handling. Finally, customers can be made to provide security deposits or signed agreements in which they agree to pay for any damage that they cause.

The Deadbeat

They are the ones who delay payment. Once again, preventive action is better than a cure. A growing number of firms insist on pre-payment. Any form of ticket sale is a good example of this. Direct marketing organizations ask for your credit card number as they take your order. The next best thing is to present the customer with a bill immediately on completion of service. If the bill is to be sent by mail, the firm should send it promptly, while the service is still fresh in the customer's mind.

Customers may have good reason for the delay and acceptable payment arrangements can be worked out. There may be other aspects to think about as well. If the client's problems are only temporary ones, what is the long-term value of maintaining the relationship? Will it create positive goodwill and word-of-mouth to help the customer work things out? If creating and maintaining long-term relationships are the firm's goals, they need to explore working with the customer toward a solution.

Figure 13.13 Installing surveillance cameras in public car parks can discourage vandalism.

Dealing with Consumer Fraud

Dishonest customers may steal from the firm, refuse to pay for the service, pretend to be dissatisfied, or cause service failures to occur on purpose. What steps can a firm take to protect itself against such behavior?

The working assumptions should be, "If in doubt, believe the customer." However, as Service Insights 13.4 shows, it is very important to keep track of customers who repeatedly invoke service guarantees or ask for compensation. For example, one Asian airline found that the same customer lost his suitcase on three flights in a row. The chances of this truly happening are probably lower than winning in the national lottery, so frontline staff were made aware of this individual. The next time he checked in his suitcase, the check-in staff videotaped the suitcase almost from check-in to pickup in the baggage claim at the traveler's destination. It turned out that a companion collected the suitcase and took it away while the traveler again made his way to the lost baggage counter to report his missing suitcase. This time, the police were waiting for him and his friend. In another example, Continental Airlines consolidated some 45 separate customer databases into a single data warehouse to improve service but also to detect customer fraud. The airline found one customer who received 20 bereavement fares in 12 months off the same dead grandfather!

To be able to effectively detect consumer fraud, maintaining a central data warehouse of all compensation payments, service recoveries, returned goods, and any other benefits given to customers based on special circumstances is needed (i.e., such transactions cannot be kept only at the local or branch level, but must be captured in a centralized system). It is important to merge customer data across departments and channels for detecting unusual transactions and the systems that allow them.[42]

Research has shown that customers who think they were treated unfairly in any way (see our earlier discussion regarding fairness) are much more likely to take advantage of a firm's service recovery effort. In addition, consumers tend to take advantage of large firms more often than small ones—customers think that large firms can easily afford the recovery costs. Also, one-time customers are much more likely to cheat than loyal customers, and customers who do not have a personal relationship with service employees are more likely to take advantage of service recovery policies.

Service guarantees are often used as payouts in service recovery, and it has been shown that the amount of a guarantee payout (e.g., whether it is a 10% or 100% money-back guarantee) had no effect on consumer cheating. A further finding was that customers were also reluctant to cheat if the service quality provided was truly high compared to when it was just satisfactory.[43]

These findings suggest a number of important managerial implications:

1. Firms should ensure that their service recovery procedures are fair.
2. Large firms should recognize that consumers are more likely to cheat on them and have robust fraud detection systems in place.
3. Firms can implement and thus reap the bigger marketing benefits of 100% money-back guarantees without worrying that the large payouts would increase cheating.

4. Guarantees can be offered to regular customers or as part of a membership program because repeat customers are unlikely to cheat on service guarantees.
5. Truly excellent services firms have less to worry about cheating than the average service provider.

SERVICE INSIGHTS 13.4

Tracking Down Guests Who Cheat

As part of its guarantee tracking system, Hampton Inn has developed ways to identify guests who appeared to be cheating. Guests showing high invocation trends receive personalized attention and follow-up from the company's Guest Assistance Team. Wherever possible, senior managers telephone these guests to ask about their recent stays. The conversation might go as follows: "Hello, Mr. Jones. I'm the director of guest assistance at Hampton Inn, and I see that you've had some difficulty with the last four properties you've visited. Since we take our guarantee very seriously, I thought I'd give you a call and find out what the problems were."

The typical response is dead silence! Sometimes the silence is followed with questions of how headquarters could possibly know about their problems. These calls have their humorous moments as well. One individual, who had invoked the guarantee 17 times in what appeared to be a trip that took him across the US and back, was asked, "Where do you like to stay when you travel?" "Hampton Inn," came the enthusiastic response. "But," said the executive making the call, "our records show that the last 17 times you have stayed at a Hampton Inn, you have invoked the 100% Satisfaction Guarantee." "That's why I like them!" proclaimed the guest (who turned out to be a long-distance truckdriver on a per diem for his accommodation expenses).

SOURCE

Christopher W. Hart and Elizabeth Long, *Extraordinary Guarantees* (New York: AMACOM, 1997).

CHAPTER SUMMARY

LO 1 ▶ When customers are dissatisfied, they have several alternatives. They can take some forms of:

- o Public action (e.g., complain to the firm, a third party or even take legal action).
- o Private action (e.g., switch to another provider and/or spread negative word-of-mouth).
- o Take no action.

LO 2 ▶ To effectively recover from a service failure, firms need to understand customer complaining behavior and motivations, and also what customers expect in response.

- o Customers typically complain for any combination of the following four reasons. They want (1) restitution or compensation, (2) vent their anger, (3) help to improve the service, and (4) spare other customers from experiencing the same problems (i.e., they complain for altruistic reasons).
- o In practice, most dissatisfied customers do not complain as they may not know where to complain, and find it requires too much effort and is unpleasant, and perceive the payoffs of their effort uncertain.
- o The people who are most likely to complain tend to be better educated, have higher income, are more socially involved, and have more product knowledge.

LO 3 ▶ Once customers make a complaint, they expect firms to deal with them in a fair manner along three dimensions of fairness:

- o Procedural fairness—Customers expect the firm to have a convenient, responsive, and flexible service recovery process.
- o Interactional justice—Here, customers expect an honest explanation, a genuine effort to solve the problem, and polite treatment.
- o Outcome justice—Customers expect compensation that reflects the loss and inconvenience suffered as a result of the service failure.

LO 4 ▶ Effective service recovery can, in many cases, avoid customer switching and restore confidence in the firm. When customers complain, they give the firm a chance to correct problems, restore the relationship with the complainer, and improve future satisfaction. Service recovery is, therefore, an important opportunity to retain a valued customer.

LO 5 ▶ The *service recovery paradox* describes the phenomenon where customers who experience an excellent service recovery after a failure feel even more satisfied than customers who had no problem in the first place. However, it is important to note that this paradox does not always apply. It is still best to get it right the first time rather than provide expensive service recovery.

LO 6 ▶ Effective service recovery systems should:

- o make it easy for customers to give feedback (e.g., provide hotline numbers and e-mail addresses on all communications materials) and encourage them to provide feedback.
- o enable effective service recovery by making it (1) proactive, (2) pre-planned, (3) trained, and (4) empowered.
- o establish appropriate compensation levels. Compensation should be higher if (1) a firm is known for service excellence, (2) the service failure is serious, and (3) the customer is important to the firm.

LO 7 ▶ The guidelines for frontline employees to effectively handle customer complaints and service recovery include (1) act fast; (2) acknowledge the customer's feelings; (3) don't argue with the customer; (4) show that you understand the problem from the customer's point of view; (5) clarify the truth and sort out the cause; (6) give customers the benefit of doubt; (7) propose the steps needed to solve the problem; (8) keep customers informed of progress; (9) consider compensation; (10) persevere to regain customer goodwill; and (11) check the service delivery system and improve it.

LO 8 ▶ Service guarantees are a powerful way to institutionalize professional complaint handling and service recovery. Service guarantees set clear standards for the firm, and they also reduce customers' risk perceptions and can build long-term loyalty.

LO 9 ▶ Service guarantees should be designed to be (1) unconditional, (2) easy to understand and communicate, (3) meaningful to the customer, (4) easy to invoke, (5) easy to collect on, and (6) credible.

LO 10 ▶ Not all firms stand to gain from service guarantees. Specifically, firms should be careful offering service guarantees when (1) they already have a reputation for service excellence, (2) service quality is too low and has to be improved first; (3) aspects of service quality are uncontrollable because of external factors (e.g., weather); and (4) customers perceive low risk when buying the service.

LO 11 ▶ Not all customers are honest, polite, and reasonable. Some may want to take advantage of service recovery situations and others may inconvenience and stress frontline employees and other customers alike. Such customers are called jaycustomers.

- There are seven groups of jaycustomers: (1) the Cheat, (2) the Thief, (3) the Rule Breaker, (4) the Belligerent, (5) the Family Feuders, (6) the Vandal, and (7) the Deadbeat.
- Different types of jaycustomers cause different problems for firms and may spoil the service experience of other customers. Hence, firms need to manage their behavior, even if that means, for example, keeping track of how often a customer invokes a service guarantee, or as a last resort, blacklisting them from using the firm's facilities.

UNLOCK YOUR LEARNING

These keywords are found within the sections of each Learning Objective (LO). They are integral to understanding the services marketing concepts taught in each section. Having a firm grasp of these keywords and how they are used is essential to helping you do well on your course, and in the real and very competitive marketing scene out there.

LO 1
1 Complain
2 Defection
3 No action
4 Private action
5 Public action
6 Service failure

LO 2
7 Anger
8 Compensation
9 Concern for others
10 Customer complaining behavior
11 Customer feedback system
12 Dissatisfied customers
13 "Double deviation"
14 Interactive channels
15 Noninteractive channels
16 Online public complaining
17 Restitution
18 Socio-economic levels
19 Unpleasant

LO 3
20 Interactional justice
21 Outcome justice
22 Perceived fairness
23 Procedural justice
24 Service recovery processes

LO 4
25 Complaint handling
26 Customer satisfaction
27 Loyalty
28 Service failure
29 Service recovery

LO 5
30 Full satisfaction
31 Repeated service failure
32 Service recovery paradox

LO 6
33 Affected customer
34 Appropriate compensation
35 Complaint collection procedures
36 Customer complaint barriers
37 Empowered
38 Fair compensation
39 Feedback
40 Online public complaining
41 Overly generous compensation
42 Planned
43 Positioning
44 Proactive
44 Revenue management practices
45 Service recovery system
46 Severe service failure
47 Trained

LO 7
48 Complaining customers
49 Confrontational
50 Effective problem resolution

LO 8
51 "Marketing muscle"
52 Customer feedback
53 Perceived risks
54 Service guarantees
55 Standards

LO 9
56 "Combined guarantee"
57 Attribute-specific guarantee
58 Believable
59 Credible
60 Easy to invoke
61 Easy to understand
62 Full satisfaction
63 Meaningful
64 Simple
65 Unconditional

 **LO 10**
66 Distinctive guarantee
67 Guarantee inappropriate
68 Service excellence
69 Service quality

 **LO 11**
70 100% money-back guarantees
71 Abuse
72 Customer fraud
73 Delay payment
74 Employee intervention
75 Fake returns
76 Faking dissatisfaction
77 Jaycustomer
78 Misuse
79 Physical abuse
80 Rudeness
81 Shoplifting
82 The Belligerent
83 The Cheat
84 The Deadbeat
85 The Family Feuders
86 The Rulebreaker
87 The Thief
88 The Vandal
89 Vandalism

How well do you know the language of services marketing? Quiz yourself!

 **Not for the academically faint-of-heart**

For each keyword you are able to recall without referring to earlier pages, give yourself a point (and a pat on the back). Tally your score at the end and see if you earned the right to be called—a *services marketeer.*

SCORE

0 – 17 Services Marketing is done a great disservice.
18 – 33 The midnight oil needs to be lit, pronto.
34 – 50 I know what you *didn't* do all semester.
51 – 67 By George! You're getting there.
68 – 84 Now, go forth and market.
85 – 89 There should be a marketing concept named after you.

KNOW YOUR ESM

Review Questions

1. How do customers typically respond to service failures?
2. Why don't many more unhappy customers complain? And what do customers expect the firm to do once they have filed a complaint?
3. Why would a firm prefer its unhappy customers to come forward and complain?
4. What is the service recovery paradox? Under what conditions is this paradox most likely to hold? Why is it best to deliver the service as planned, even though the paradox does hold in a specific context?
5. What can a firm do make it easy for dissatisfied customers to complain?
6. Why should a service recovery strategy be proactive, planned, trained, and empowered?
7. How generous should compensations related to service recovery be?
8. How should service guarantees be designed? What are the benefits of service guarantees over and above a good complaint handling and service recovery system?
9. Under what conditions is it not suitable to introduce a service guarantee?
10. What are the different types of jaycustomers and how can a service firm deal with such customers?

WORK YOUR ESM

Application Exercises

1. Think about the last time you experienced a less-than-satisfactory service experience. Did you complain? Why? If you did not complain, explain why not.
2. When was the last time you were truly satisfied with an organization's response to your complaint. Describe in detail what happened and what made you satisfied.
3. What would be an appropriate service recovery policy for a wrongly bounced check for (a) your local savings bank, (b) a major national bank, (c) a private bank for high-net-worth individuals. Please explain your rationale, and also compute the economic costs of the alternative service recovery policies.
4. Design an effective service guarantee for a service with high perceived risk. Explain (a) why and how your guarantee would reduce perceived risk of potential customers, and (b) why current customers would appreciate being offered this guarantee although they are already a customer of that firm and, therefore, are likely to perceive lower levels of risk.
5. How generous should compensation be? Review the following incident and comment. Then evaluate the available options, comment on each, select the one you recommend, and defend your decision.

   "The shrimp cocktail was half frozen. The waitress apologized and didn't charge me for any of my dinner," was the response of a very satisfied customer about the service recovery he received. Consider the following range of service recovery policies a restaurant chain could set and try to establish the costs for each policy:

   Option 1: Smile and apologize, defrost the prawn cocktail, return it, smile, and apologize again.

   Option 2: Smile and apologize, replace the prawn cocktail with a new one, and smile and apologize again.

   Option 3: Smile, apologize, replace the prawn cocktail, and offer a free coffee or dessert

   Option 4: Smile, apologize, replace the prawn cocktail, and waive the bill of $80 for the entire meal.

   Option 5: Smile, apologize, replace the prawn cocktail, waive the bill for the entire dinner, and offer a free bottle of champagne.

   Option 6: Smile, apologize, replace the prawn cocktail, waive the bill for the entire dinner, offer a free bottle of champagne, and give a voucher valid for another dinner, to be redeemed within three months.
6. Identify the possible behavior of jaycustomers for a service of your choice. How can the service process be designed to minimize or control the behavior of jaycustomers?

ENDNOTES

1 "An Extraordinary Stumble at JetBlue," Business Week, March 5, 2007, http://www.businessweek.com/magazine/content/07_10/b4024004.htm, accessed March 12, 2012; Tschohl, J. "Too Little, Too Late: Service Recovery Must Occur Immediately—as JetBlue discovered." Service Quality Institute, (May 2007), http://www.customer-service.com, accessed March 12, 2012. http://investor.jetblue.com/phoenix.zhtml?c=131045&p=irol-newsArticle_print&ID=1571778&highlight=, accessed March 12, 2012.

2 Even failures by other customers also have an impact on how a firm's customers feel about the firm. See Wen-Hsien Huang, "Other-Customer Failure: Effects of Perceived Employee Effort and Compensation on Complainer and Non-Complainer Service Evaluations," *Journal of Service Management* 21, no. 2 (2010): 191–211.

3 Roger Bougie, Rik Pieters, and Marcel Zeelenberg, "Angry Customers Don't Come Back, They Get Back: The Experience and Behavioral Implications of Anger and Dissatisfaction in Service," *Journal of the Academy of Marketing* Science 31, no. 4 (2003): 377–393; and Florian V. Wangenheim, "Postswitching Negative Word of Mouth," *Journal of Service Research* 8, no. 1 (2005): 67–78.

4 For research on cognitive and affective drivers of complaining behavior, see: Jean-Charles Chebat, Moshe Davidow, and Isabelle Codjovi, "Silent Voices: Why Some Dissatisfied Consumers Fail to Complain," *Journal of Service Research* 7, no. 4 (2005): 328–342.

5 Stephen S. Tax and Stephen W. Brown "Recovering and Learning from Service Failure", *Sloan Management Review* 49, no. 1 (Fall 1998): 75–88.

6 Kelli Bodey and Debra Grace, "Segmenting Service "Complainers" and "Non-Complainers" on the Basis of Consumer Characters," *Journal of Services Marketing* 20, no. 3 (2006): 178–187; Jean-Charles Chebat, Moshe Davidow, and Isabelle Codjovi, "Silent Voices: Why Some Dissatisfied Consumers Fail to Complain," *Journal of Service Research* 7, no. 4 (2005): 328–342; Nancy Stephens and Kevin P. Gwinner, "Why Don't Some People Complain? A Cognitive-Emotive Process Model of Consumer Complaining Behavior," *Journal of the Academy of Marketing Science* 26, no. 3 (1998): 172–189; Technical Assistance Research Programs Institute (TARP), *Consumer Complaint Handling in America; An Update Study, Part II*, Washington, DC: TARP and US Office of Consumer Affairs, April 1986; "A Penny for Your Thoughts: When Customers Don't Complain" in Knowledge@W.P. Carey, September 27, 2006, http://knowledge.wpcarey.asu.edu/article.cfm?articleid=1303#, accessed March 12, 2012; Customer Care Measurement & Consulting (CCMC), *2007 National Customer Rage Study*, Customer Care Alliance, 2007.

7 John Goodman, "Basic Facts on Customer Complaint Behavior and the Impact of Service on the Bottom Line," *Competitive Advantage*, (June 1999): 1–5.

8 Anna Mattila and Jochen Wirtz, "Consumer Complaining to Firms: The Determinants of Channel Choice," *Journal of Services Marketing* 18, no. 2 (2004): 147–155; Kaisa Snellman and Tiina Vihtkari, "Customer Complaining Behavior in Technology-Based Service Encounters," *International Journal of Service Industry Management* 14, no. 2 (2003): 217–231; Terri Shapiro and Jennifer Nieman-Gonder, "Effect of Communication Mode in Justice-Based Service Recovery." *Managing Service Quality* 16, no. 2 (2006): 124–144.

9 Technical Assistance Research Programs Institute (TARP), *Consumer Complaint Handling in America: An Update Study, Part II*, Washington, DC: TARP and US Office of Consumer Affairs, April 1986.

10 Thomas M. Tripp and Yany Gregoire, "When Unhappy Customers Strike Back on the Internet," *MIT Sloan Management Review* 52, no. 3 (Spring 2011): 37–44; Sven Tuzovic, "Frequent (Flier) Frustration and the Dark Side of Word-of-Web: Exploring Online Dysfunctional Behavior in Online Feedback Forums," *Journal of Services Marketing* 24, no. 6 (2010): 446–457.

11 For review on complaint handling and customer satisfaction, see Katja Gelbrich and Holger Roschk, "A Meta-Analysis of Organisational Complaint Handling and Customer Responses,"

PART IV

Journal of Service Research 14, no. 1 (2011): 24–43. See also Klaus Schoefer and Adamantios Diamantopoulos, "The Role of Emotions in Transating Perceptions of (In)Justice into Postcomplaint Behavioral Responses," *Journal of Service Research* 11, no. 1 (2008): 91–103; Yany Grégoire and Robert J. Fisher, "Customer Betrayal and Retaliation: When Your Best Customers Become Your Worst Enemies," *Journal of the Academy of Marketing Science* 36, no. 2 (2008): 247–261.

12 Stephen S. Tax and Stephen W. Brown, "Recovering and Learning from Service Failure", *Sloan Management Review* 49, no. 1 (Fall 1998): 75–88; See also Tor Wallin Andreassen, "Antecedents of Service Recovery," *European Journal of Marketing* 34, no. 1 and 2 (2000): 156–175; Ko de Ruyter and Martin Wetzel, "Customer Equity Considerations in Service Recovery," *International Journal of Service Industry Management* 13, no. 1 (2002): 91–108; Janet R. McColl-Kennedy and Beverley A. Sparks, "Application of Fairness Theory to Service Failures and Service Recovery," *Journal of Service Research* 5, no. 3 (2003): 251–266; and Jochen Wirtz and Anna Mattila, "Consumer Responses to Compensation, Speed of Recovery and Apology after a Service Failure," *International Journal of Service Industry Management* 15, no. 2 (2004): 150–166

13 Oren Harari, "Thank Heavens for Complainers," *Management Review* (March 1997): 25–29.

14 Tom DeWitt, Doan T. Nguyen, and Roger Marshall, "Exploring Customer Loyalty Following Service Recovery," *Journal of Service Research* 10, no. 3 (2008): 269–281.

15 Simon J. Bell and James A. Luddington, "Coping with Customer Complaints." *Journal of Service Research* 8, no. 3 (February 2006): 221–233.

16 Customer Care Measurement & Consulting (CCMC), *2007 National Customer Rage Study*, Customer Care Alliance, 2007.

17 Technical Assistance Research Programs Institute (TARP), *Consumer Complaint Handling in America: An Update Study, Part II*, Washington, DC: TARP and US Office of Consumer Affairs, April 1986.

18 For a discussion on how to quantify complaint management profitability, see: Bernd Stauss and Andreas Schoeler, "Complaint Management Profitability: What Do Complaint Managers Know?" *Managing Service Quality* 14, no. 2/3 (2004): 147–156, and for a comprehensive treatment of all aspects of effective complaint management, see Bernd Stauss and Wolfgang Seidel, *Complaint Management: The Heart of CRM*, Mason, Ohio: Thomson, 2004; and Janelle Barlow and Claus Mø'ller, *A Complaint Is a Gift*. 2nd ed., San Francisco, CA: Berrett-Koehler Publishers, 2008.

19 Celso Augusto de Matos, Jorge Luiz Henrique, and Carlos Alberto Vargas Rossi, "Service Recovery Paradox: A Meta-Analysis," *Journal of Service Research* 10, no. 1 (2007): 60–77; Chihyung Ok, Ki-Joon Back, and Carol W. Shankin, "Mixed Findings on the Service Recovery Paradox," *The Service Industries Journal* 27, no. 5 (2007): 671–686; Stefan Michel and Matthew L. Meuter, "The Service Recovery Paradox: True but Overrated?" *International Journal of Service Industry Management* 19, no. 4 (2008): 441–457; Randi Priluck and Vishal Lala, "The Impact of the Recovery Paradox on Retailer—Customer Relationships," *Managing Service Quality* 19, no. 1 (2009): 42–59; Tor Wallin Andreassen, "From Disgust to Delight: Do Customers Hold a Grudge?" *Journal of Service Research* 4, no. 1 (2001): 39–49;

20 James G. Maxham III and Richard G. Netemeyer, "A Longitudinal Study of Complaining Customers' Evaluations of Multiple Service Failures and Recovery Efforts," *Journal of Marketing* 66, no. 4 (2002): 57–72.

21 Christian Homburg and Andreas Fürst, "How Organizatonal Complaint Handling Drives Customer Loyalty: An Analysis of the Mechanistic and the Organic Approach," *Journal of Marketing* 69, (July 2005): 95–114.

22 Ron Zemke and Chip R. Bell, *Knock Your Socks Off Service Recovery*, New York: AMACOM, 2000, 60.

23 Josh Bernoff and Ted Schadler, "Empowered," *Harvard Business Review*, July–August 2010, 95–101.

24 Rhonda Mack, Rene Mueller, John Crotts, and Amanda Broderick, "Perceptions, Corrections and Defections: Implications for Service Recovery in the Restaurant Industry," *Managing Service Quality* 10, no. 6 (2000): 339–46.

25 Jochen Wirtz and Janet R. McColl-Kennedy, "Opportunistic Customer Claiming During Service Recovery," *Journal of the Academy of Marketing Science* 38, no. 5 (2010): 654–675.

26 For an excellent review of extant academic literature on service guarantees, see: Jens Hogreve and Dwayne D. Gremler, "Twenty Years of Service Guarantee Research," *Journal of Service Research* 11, no. 4 (2009): 322–343.

27 Christopher W. L. Hart, "The Power of Unconditional Service Guarantees," *Harvard Business Review* (July–August 1988): 54–62.

28 L. A. Tucci and J. Talaga, "Service Guarantees and Consumers' Evaluation of Services." *Journal of Services Marketing* 11, no. 1 (1997): 10–18; Amy Ostrom and Dawn Iacobucci, "The Effect of Guarantees on Consumers' Evaluation of Services," *Journal of Services Marketing* 12, no. 5 (1998), 362–78.

29 Sara Björlin Lidén and Per Skålén, "The Effect of Service Guarantees on Service Recovery," *International Journal of Service Industry Management* 14, no. 1 (2003): 36–58.

30 Christopher W. Hart, "The Power of Unconditional Service Guarantees."

31 For a scientific discussion on the optimal guarantee payout amount, see: Tim Baker and David A. Collier, "The Economic Payout Model for Service Guarantees," *Decision Sciences* 36, no. 2 (2005): 197–220).

32 McDougall, H. Gordon, Terence Levesque, and Peter VanderPlaat, "Designing the Service Guarantee: Unconditional or Specific?" *Journal of Services Marketing* 12, no. 4 (1998): 278-293; Jochen Wirtz, "Development of a Service Guarantee Model," *Asia Pacific Journal of Management* 15, no. 1 (1998): 51–75.

33 Jochen Wirtz and Doreen Kum, "Designing Service Guarantees—Is Full Satisfaction the Best You Can Guarantee?" *Journal of Services Marketing* 15, no. 4 (2001): 282–299.

34 Amy L. Ostrom and Christopher Hart, "Service Guarantee: Research and Practice," in *Handbook of Services Marketing and Management*, T. Schwartz and D. Iacobucci, eds., (California: Thousand Oaks, Sage Publications, 2000, 299–316).

35 For a decision support model and whether to have a service guarantee, and if yes, on how to design and implement it, see: Louis Fabien, "Design and Implementation of a Service Guarantee," *Journal of Services Marketing* 19, no. 1 (2005): 33–38.

36 Ray Fisk, Stephen Grove, Lloyd C. Harris, Kate L. Daunt, Dominique Keeffe, Rebekah Russell-Bennett, and Jochen Wirtz, "Customers Behaving Badly: A State of the Art Review, Research Agenda and Implications for Practitioners", *Journal of Services Marketing* 24, no. 6 (2010): 417–429; Lloyd C. Harris and Kate L. Reynolds, "Jaycustomer Behavior: An Exploration of Types and Motives in the Hospitality Industry," *Journal of Services Marketing* 18, no. 5 (2004): 339–357; Kate L. Reynolds and Lloyd C. Harris, "Dysfunctional Customer Behavior Severity: An Empirical Examination," *Journal of Retailing* 85, no. 3 (2009): 321–335; Kate L. Daunt and Harris C. Lloyd, "Customers Acting Badly: Evidence from the Hospitality Industry," *Journal of Business Research* 64, no. 10 (2011): 1034–1042.

37 This section is adapted and updated from Christopher Lovelock, *Product Plus*. New York: McGraw-Hill, 1994, Chapter 15.

38 Lloyd C. Harris, and Kate L. Reynolds, "The Consequences of Dysfunctional Customer Behavior", *Journal of Service Research* 6 no. 2 (2003): 144–161; Wirtz, Jochen and Doreen Kum, "Consumer Cheating on Service Guarantees," *Journal of the Academy of Marketing Science* 32, no. 2 (2004): 159–175; Chu Wujin, Eitan Gerstner, and James D. Hess, "Managing Dissatisfaction: How to Decrease Customer Opportunism by Partial Refunds," *Journal of Service Research* 1, no. 2 (1998): 140–55.

39 Lloyd C. Harris, "Fraudulent Return Proclivity: An Empirical Analysis," *Journal of Retailing* 84, no. 4 (2008): 461–476.

40 Kate L. Reynolds and Lloyd C. Harris, "When Service Failure is Not Service Failure: An Exploration of the Forms and Motives of "Illegitimate" Customer Complaining," *Journal of Services Marketing* 19, no. 5 (2005): 326

41 Lloyd C. Harris, and Kate L. Reynolds, "Jaycustomer Behavior: An Exploration of Types and Motives in the Hospitality Industry", *Journal of Services Marketing* 18, no. 5 (2004): 339

42 Jill Griffin, "What Your Worst Customers Teach You about Loyalty," January 24, 2006, http://www.marketingprofs.com/6/griffin5.asp, accessed March 12, 2012.

43 Jochen Wirtz and Doreen Kum, "Consumer Cheating on Service Guarantees," *Journal of the Academy of Marketing Science* 32, no. 2 (2004): 159–175; Jochen Wirtz and Janet R. McColl-Kennedy, "Opportunistic Customer Claiming during Service Recovery," *Journal of the Academy of Marketing Science* 38, no. 5 (2010): 654–675; Heejung Ro and June Wong, "Customer Opportunistic Complaints Management: A Critical Incident Approach," *International Journal of Hospitality Management*, forthcoming (2012).

THE *ESM* FRAMEWORK

PART I

Understanding Service Products, Consumers, and Markets

- Introduction to Services Marketing
- Consumer Behavior in a Services Context
- Positioning Services in Competitive Markets

PART II

Applying the 4 Ps of Marketing to Services

- Developing Service Products: Core and Supplementary Elements
- Distributing Services through Physical and Electronic Channels
- Setting Prices and Implementing Revenue Management
- Promoting Services and Educating Customers

PART III

Designing and Managing the Customer Interface

The 3 Additional Ps of Services Marketing.

- Designing and Managing Service Processes
- Balancing Demand and Capacity
- Crafting the Service Environment
- Managing People for Service Advantage

PART IV

Developing Customer Relationships

- Managing Relationships and Building Loyalty
- Complaint Handling and Service Recovery

PART V

Striving for Service Excellence

- Improving Service Quality and Productivity
- Organizing for Service Leadership

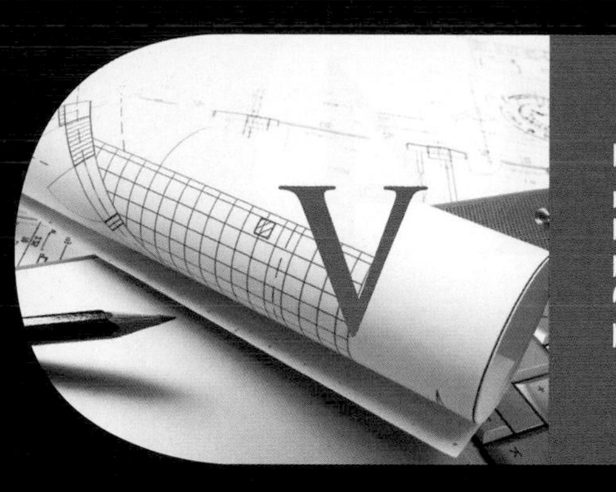

Striving for Service Excellence

PART V of this book focuses on service quality and productivity, and how firms can achieve service leadership. It consists of the following two chapters:

Chapter 14 Improving Service Quality and Productivity

This chapter deals with productivity and quality. Both productivity and quality are necessary and related to financial success in services. Chapter 14 covers service quality, diagnosing quality shortfalls using the gaps model, and reviewing strategies to close quality gaps. Customer feedback systems are introduced as an effective tool for systematically listening to and learning from customers. Productivity is concerned with bringing down costs, and key approaches for increasing productivity are discussed.

Chapter 15 Organizing for Service Leadership

This chapter uses the service profit chain as an integrative model to demonstrate the strategic links involved in running a successful service organization. Implementing the service profit chain requires integration of the three key functions of business: marketing, operations, and human resources. We discuss how to move a service organization to higher levels of performance in each functional area. The chapter closes with the role of leaders in nurturing an effective service culture, and the qualities needed for leaders of the future.

CHAPTER 14

improving SERVICE QUALITY and PRODUCTIVITY

LEARNING OBJECTIVES

By the end of this chapter, the reader should be able to:

- **LO 1** Explain how quality and productivity relate to each other in a service context.
- **LO 2** Describe the dimensions of service quality.
- **LO 3** Demonstrate how to use the gaps model for diagnosing and addressing service quality problems.
- **LO 4** Differentiate between hard and soft measures of service quality.
- **LO 5** Explain the common objectives of effective customer feedback systems.
- **LO 6** Describe key customer feedback collection tools.
- **LO 7** Be familiar with hard measures of service quality and control charts.
- **LO 8** Select suitable tools to analyze service problems.
- **LO 9** Appreciate the financial implications of quality improvements.
- **LO 10** Define and measure service productivity.
- **LO 11** Understand the differences between productivity, efficiency, and effectiveness.
- **LO 12** Recommend the key methods to improve service productivity.
- **LO 13** Know how productivity improvements impact quality and value.
- **LO 14** Explain how TQM, ISO 9000, the Malcolm-Baldrige Approach, and Six Sigma relate to managing and improving service quality and productivity.

OPENING VIGNETTE

Improving Service Quality in a Ferry Company[1]

Sealink British Ferries, whose routes linked Britain to Ireland and several European countries, was a poor service quality provider. Its top-down, military-style structure focused on the operational aspects of ship movements, not the quality of customers' experiences. In 1991, Sealink was acquired by the Swedish company Stena Line, which is one of the world's largest car-ferry operators today. In contrast to Sealink, Stena had a whole department devoted to improving its service quality.

Before the takeover, Sealink did not focus on punctual or reliable operations, and ferries were often late. Customer complaints were ignored, and there was little pressure from customer service managers to improve the situation. After the takeover, things started to change. The ferry operator solved the problem of late departures and arrivals by concentrating on individual problem areas. On one route, for instance, the port manager involved all operational staff and gave each person responsibility over a particular aspect of the improvement process, thus creating employee "ownership." They kept detailed records of each sailing, together with reasons for late departures. They also kept track of competitors' performance. In this way, staff members in different job positions had close links with each other. Customer service staff also learned from experience. Within two years, the Stena ferries on this route were operating at close to 100% punctuality.

On-board service was another area chosen for improvement. Historically, customer service managers did what was convenient for staff rather than customers. This meant that staff could be having meal breaks at times when customer demand for service was greatest. As one observer noted, "Customers were ignored during the first and last half hour on board, when facilities were closed. Customers were left to find their own way around [the ship]... Staff only responded to customers when [they] initiated a direct request and made some effort to attract their attention."

Personnel from each on-board functional area had to choose a particular area for service quality and productivity improvements, and work in small groups to achieve this. Initially, some teams were more successful than others, resulting in differing levels of service from one ship to another. After that, managers shared ideas and experiences, learning from each others' successes and failures, and made further changes on their individual ships. Together, the employees have come up with almost 1,500 improvement ideas since 2006.

By 2011, Stena Line had 35 ships sailing on 19 routes, carrying about 16 million passengers and three million vehicles each year. They included three of the world's largest fast ferries. Stena was a leader in all its markets. The company's focus was on constant service and product improvement. Says the company's website:

> "Making Good Time" sums up the essence of Stena Line's activities—fast, convenient, and efficient sea travel. Travelling with Stena Line is about more than just getting from one place to another; it is also about escaping from everyday life, relaxing, spending time together, and eating well. A travel alternative that cannot be beaten.

PART V

LO 1

Explain how quality and productivity relate to each other in a services context.

INTEGRATING SERVICE QUALITY AND PRODUCTIVITY STRATEGIES

The Stena Line success story in the opening vignette is an excellent example that shows how improving service quality and productivity can turn a failing business around. We will learn in this chapter that quality and productivity are twin paths to creating value for both customers and companies.

In broad terms, quality focuses on the benefits created for the customer's side of the equation, and productivity addresses the financial costs incurred by the firm. If not properly integrated, these two aspects can be in conflict. For example, making service processes more efficient may not result in a better-quality experience for customers. In addition, getting service employees to work faster may sometimes be welcomed by customers but may make them feel rushed and unwanted at other times. Likewise, marketing strategies designed to improve customer satisfaction can prove costly and disruptive if the implications for operations and human resources have not been carefully thought through. The bottom line is that quality and productivity improvement strategies must be considered together rather than separately. Marketing, operations, and human resource managers need to work together to ensure they can deliver quality experiences more efficiently to improve the long-term profitability of the firm.

Figure 14.1 Service quality can be difficult to manage for the fussy diner.

WHAT IS SERVICE QUALITY?

What do we mean when we speak of service quality? Since services are intangible, it is hard to evaluate the quality of a service compared to goods. In addition, customers are often involved in service production, so a distinction needs to be drawn between the process of service delivery and the actual output (or outcome) of the service.

We define service quality as a high standard of performance that consistently meets or exceeds customer expectations. As suggested humorously by the restaurant illustration in Figure 14.1, service quality can be difficult to manage, even when failures are tangible in nature.

LO 2

Describe the dimensions of service quality.

Dimensions of Service Quality

Valarie Zeithaml, Leonard Berry, and A. Parasuraman have conducted intensive research on service quality and identified 10 dimensions used by consumers in evaluating service quality (Table 14.1). In subsequent research, they found a high degree of correlation between several of these variables and so consolidated them into five broad dimensions:

- *Tangibles* (appearance of physical elements).
- *Reliability* (dependable and accurate performance).
- *Responsiveness* (promptness and helpfulness).

- *Assurance* (credibility, security, competence, and courtesy) (Figure 14.2).
- *Empathy* (easy access, good communications, and customer understanding).[2]

Table 14.1 Generic dimensions used by customer to evaluate service quality

Dimensions of Service Quality	Definition	Sample Illustrations
Tangibles	Appearance of physical facilities, equipment, personnel, and communication materials	Are the hotel's facilities attractive? Is my accountant dressed appropriately? Is my bank statement easy to understand?
Reliability	Ability to perform the promised service dependably and accurately	Does my lawyer call me back when promised? Is my telephone bill free of errors? Is my TV repaired right the first time?
Responsiveness	Willingness to help customers and provide prompt service	When there is a problem, does the firm resolve it quickly? Is my stockbroker willing to answer my questions? Is the cable TV company willing to give me a specific time when the installer will show up?
Assurance		
• Credibility	Trustworthiness, believability, honesty of the service provider	Does the hospital have a good reputation? Does my stockbroker not pressure me to buy? Does the repair firm guarantee its work?
• Security	Freedom from danger, risk, or doubt	Is it safe for me to use the bank's ATMs at night? Is my credit card protected against unauthorized use? Can I be sure that my insurance policy provides complete coverage?
• Competence	Possession of the skills and knowledge required to perform the service	Can the bank teller process my transaction without fumbling around? Is my travel agent able to obtain the information I need when I call? Does the dentist appear to be competent?
• Courtesy	Politeness, respect, consideration, and friendliness of contact personnel	Does the flight attendant have a pleasant demeanor? Are the telephone operators consistently polite when answering my calls? Does the plumber take off muddy shoes before stepping on my carpet?
Empathy		
• Access	Approachability and ease of contact	How easy is it for me to talk to a supervisor when I have a problem? Does the airline have a 24-hour, toll-free phone number? Is the hotel conveniently located?
• Communication	Listening to customers and keeping them informed in the language they can understand	When I have a complaint, is the manager willing to listen to me? Does my doctor avoid using technical jargon? Does the electrician call when he or she is unable to keep a scheduled appointment?
• Understanding the customer	Making the effort to know customers and their needs	Does someone in the hotel recognize me as a regular customer? Does my stockbroker try to determine my specific financial objectives? Is the moving company willing to accommodate my schedule?

LO 3

Demonstrate how to use the gaps model for diagnosing and addressing service quality problems.

IDENTIFYING AND CORRECTING SERVICE QUALITY PROBLEMS

After understanding what service quality is, let us explore a model that allows us to identify and correct service quality problems.

Figure 14.2 Julius Bär, a provider of private banking services, emphasizes its dedication to service excellence.

The Gaps Model in Service Design and Delivery

Valarie Zeithaml, A. Parasuraman, and Leonard Berry identified four potential gaps within the service organization that may lead to a fifth and most serious final gap—the difference between what customers expected and what they perceived was delivered.[3] Figure 14.3 extends and refines their framework to identify a total of six types of gaps that can occur at different points during the design and delivery of a service performance.

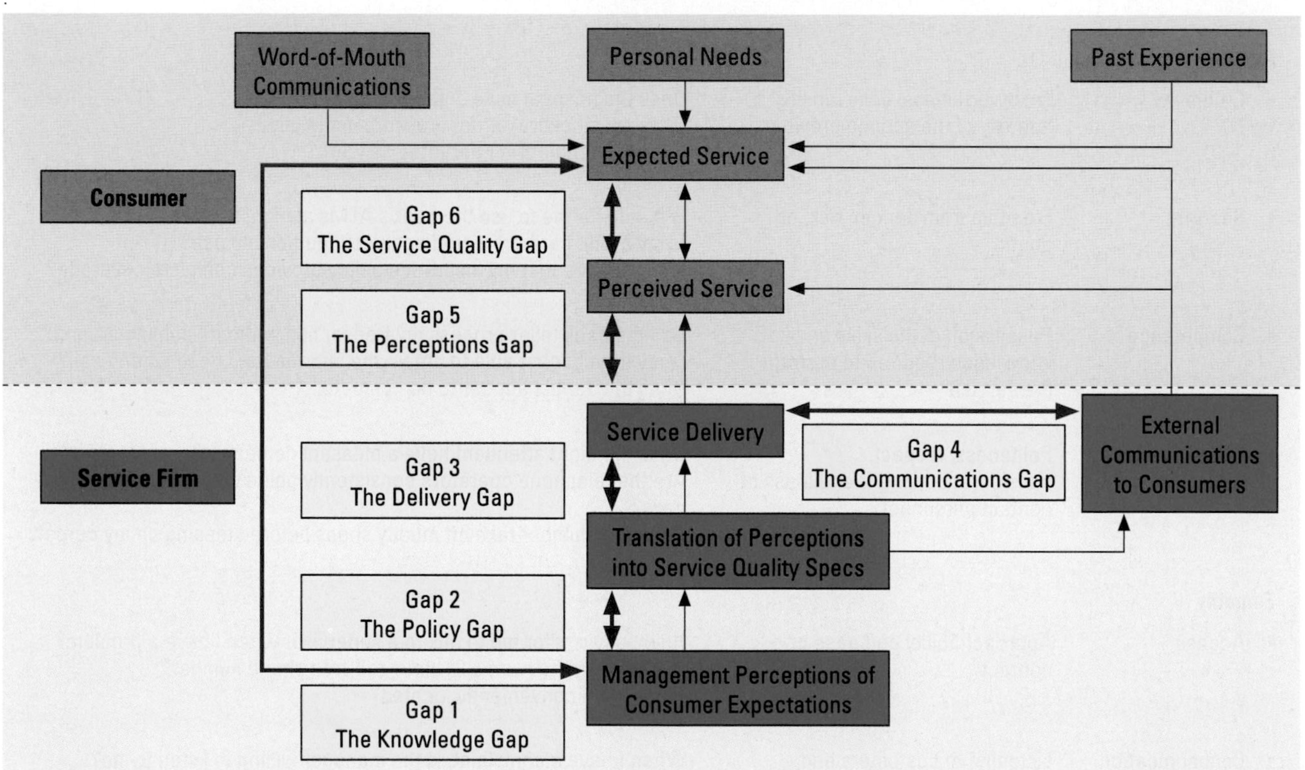

Figure 14.3 The Gaps Model.

SOURCE

Adapted from the original five-gaps model developed by Parasuraman, A., Zeithaml, V. A., & Berry, L. L. "A conceptual model of service quality and its implications for future research". *Journal of Marketing* 49, Fall 1985 41–50; Zeithaml, V. A., Bitner, M. J., & Gremler, D. *Services Marketing: Integrating Customer Focus Across the Firm* (p. 46.). NY: McGraw Hill/Irwin, 2006. A further gap (Gap 5) was added by Christoper Lovelock (1994), *Product Plus* (p. 112). NY: McGraw Hill.

Let's explore the six gaps in more detail:

- **Gap 1:** The **knowledge gap** is the difference between what senior management believes customers expect and what customers actually need and expect.
- **Gap 2:** The **policy gap** is the difference between management's understanding of customers' expectations and the service standards they set for service delivery. We call it the policy gap because the management has made a policy decision not to deliver what they think customers expect. Reasons for setting standards below customer expectations are typically cost and feasibility considerations.
- **Gap 3:** The **delivery gap** is the difference between service standards and the service delivery teams' actual performance on these standards.
- **Gap 4:** The **communications gap** is the difference between what the company communicates, and what the customer understands and subsequently experiences. This gap is caused by two subgaps.[4] First, the *internal* communications gap is the difference between what the company's advertising and sales personnel think are the product's features, performance, and service quality level and what the company is actually able to deliver. Second, the *external* communications gap (also referred to as the overpromise gap) can be caused by advertising and sales personnel being assessed by the sales they generate. This can lead them to overpromise in order to capture sales.
- **Gap 5:** The **perceptions gap** is the difference between what is actually delivered and what customers feel they have received because they are unable to accurately judge service quality accurately.
- **Gap 6:** The **service gap** is the difference between what customers expect to receive and their perception of the service that is actually delivered.

In this model, Gaps 1, 5, and 6 represent external gaps between the customer and the organization. Gaps 2, 3, and 4 are internal gaps occurring between various functions and departments within the organization.

Key Ways to Close the Gaps in Service Quality

Gaps at any point in service design and delivery can damage relationships with customers. The service quality gap (Gap 6) is the most important. Hence, the main goal in improving service quality is to close or narrow this gap as much as possible. However, to achieve this, service organizations usually need to work on closing the other five gaps depicted in Figure 14.3. Improving service quality requires identifying the specific causes of each gap and then developing strategies to close them.

We summarize a series of generic prescriptions for closing the six quality gaps in Table 14.2. These prescriptions are a good starting point to think about how to close specific gaps in an organization. However, each firm must develop its own customized approach to ensure that service quality becomes and remains a key objective.

PART V

Table 14.2 Suggestions for closing service quality gaps

Types of Quality Gap	Proposed Solutions
Gap 1: The Knowledge Gap	*Suggestion: Educate management about what customers expect* • Increase interactions between customers and management. • Facilitate and encourage communication between frontline employees and management. • Implement an effective customer feedback system that includes satisfaction research, complaint content analysis and customer panels. • Sharpen market research procedures, including questionnaire and interview design, sampling, and field implementation, and repeat research studies once in a while.
Gap 2: The Policy Gap	*Suggestion: Establish the right service processes and specify standards* • Get the customer service processes right: o Use a rigorous, systematic, and customer-centric process for designing and redesigning customer service processes. o Standardize repetitive work tasks to ensure consistency and reliability by substituting hard technology for human contact and improving work methods (soft technology). • Develop tiered service products that meet customer expectations: o Consider premium, standard, and economy-level products to allow customers to self-segment according to their needs, or o Offer customers different levels of service at different prices. • Set, communicate, and reinforce measurable customer-oriented service standards for all work units: o Establish for each step in service delivery a set of clear service quality goals that are challenging, realistic, and explicitly designed to meet customer expectations. o Ensure that employees understand and accept goals, standards, and priorities.
Gap 3: The Delivery Gap	*Suggestion: Ensure that performance meets standards that are based on customer needs and expectations* • Ensure that customer service teams are motivated and able to meet service standards: o Improve recruitment with a focus on employee—job fit; select employees for the abilities and skill needed to perform their job well. o Train employees on the technical and soft skills needed to perform their assigned tasks effectively, including interpersonal skills, especially for dealing with customers under stressful conditions. o Clarify employee roles and ensure that employees understand how their jobs contribute to customer satisfaction; teach them about customer expectations, perceptions, and problems. o Build cross-functional service teams that can offer customer-centric service delivery and problem resolution. o Empower managers and employees in the field by pushing decision-making power down the organization. o Measure performance, provide regular feedback, and reward customer service team performance as well as individual employees and managers or attaining quality goals. • Install the right technology, equipment, support processes, and capacity: o Select the most appropriate technologies and equipment for enhanced performance. o Ensure that employees working on internal support jobs provide good service to their own internal customer, the frontline personnel. o Balance demand against productive capacity. • Manage customers for service quality: o Educate customers so that they can perform their roles and responsibilities in service delivery effectively.

Types of Quality Gap	Proposed Solutions
Gap 4: The Communications Gap	*Suggestion: Close the internal and external communications gaps by ensuring that communications promises are realistic and correctly understood by customers* • Educate managers responsible for sales and marketing communications about operational capabilities: o Seek inputs from frontline employees and operations personnel when new communications programs are being developed. o Let service providers preview advertisements and other communications before customers are exposed to them. o Get sales staff to involve operations staff in face-to-face meetings with customers. o Develop internal educational and motivational advertising campaigns to strengthen understanding and integration among the marketing, operations, and human resource functions, and to standardize service delivery across different locations. • Align incentives for sales teams with those of service delivery teams. This will avoid the problem where the sale teams focus exclusively on generating sales (e.g., through overpromising) and neglect customer satisfaction (e.g., through disappointed expectations). • Ensure that communications content sets realistic customer expectations. • Be specific with promises and mange customers' understanding of communication content: o Pre-test all advertising, brochures, telephone scripts, and website content prior to external release to see if target audience interprets them as the firm intends (if not, revise and retest). Make sure that the advertising content reflects those service characteristics that are most important to customers. Let them know what is and is not possible, and why. o Identify and explain, in real time, the reasons for shortcomings in service performance, highlighting those that cannot be controlled by the firm. o Document beforehand what tasks and performance guarantees are included in an agreement or contract. After the completion of the work, explain what work was performed in relation to a specific billing statement.
Gap 5: The Perception Gap	*Suggestion: Tangibilize and communicate the service quality delivered* • Make service quality tangible and communicate the service quality delivered: o Develop service environments and physical evidence cues that are consistent with the level of service provided. o For complex and credence services, keep customers informed during service delivery on what is being done, and give debriefings after the delivery so that customers can appreciate the quality of service they received. o Provide physical evidence (e.g., for repairs, show customers the damaged components that were removed).
Gap 6: The Service Gap	*Suggestion: Close gaps 1 to 5 to consistently meet customer expectations* • Gap 6 is the accumulated outcome of all the preceding gaps. It will be closed when Gaps 1 to 5 have been addressed.

SOURCE

Adapted and extended from Valarie A. Zeithaml, A. Parasuraman, and Leonard L. Berry, *Delivering Service Quality: Balancing Customer Perceptions and Expectations.* New York: The Free Press, 1990, chapters 4–7; and Valarie A. Zeithaml, Mary Jo Bitner and Dwayne Gremler, *Services Marketing: Integrating Customer Focus Across the Firm,* 4th ed. New York: McGraw-Hill, 2006, Chapter 2. The remaining prescriptions were developed by the authors.

MEASURING AND IMPROVING SERVICE QUALITY

We now understand the gaps model and the general prescriptions on how to close the six quality gaps. Let us next discuss how to use measurement to guide our service quality improvement efforts. It is commonly said that "what is not measured is not managed." Without measurement, managers cannot be sure whether service quality gaps exist, let alone what types of gaps, where they exist, and what potential corrective actions should be taken. Measurement is also needed to find out whether goals for improvement are met after changes have been carried out.

LO 4

Differentiate between hard and soft measures of service quality.

Soft and Hard Service Quality Measures

Customer-defined standards and measures of service quality can be grouped into two broad categories: "soft" and "hard." Soft standards and their measures are those that cannot easily be observed and must be collected by talking to customers, employees, or others. As noted by Valarie Zeithaml and Mary Jo Bitner, soft standards "provide direction, guidance, and feedback to employees on ways to achieve customer satisfaction and can be quantified by measuring customer perceptions and beliefs."[5] SERVQUAL (see Appendix 14.1) is an example of a complex soft measurement system, and we will discuss a variety of customer feedback tools later in this chapter.

Figure 14.4 Social media such as Facebook and Twitter have been deployed by organizations to gather valuable feedback from customers in recent years.

Hard standards and measures are characteristics and activities that can be counted, timed, or measured through audits. Such measures may include how many telephone calls were dropped while customers were on hold, the temperature of a particular food item, how many trains arrived late, how many bags were lost, or how many patients made a complete recovery following a specific type of surgery. Organizations that are known for excellent service make use of both soft and hard measures. These organizations are good at listening to both their customers and their customer-contact employees (Figure 14.4).

We will next give you a comprehensive overview of soft measures in the section on customer feedback, followed later by a section on hard measures.

LEARNING FROM CUSTOMER FEEDBACK[6]

How can companies measure their performance against soft standards of service quality? According to Leonard Berry and A. Parasuraman:

> [C]ompanies need to establish ongoing listening systems using multiple methods among different customer groups. A single service quality study is a snapshot taken at a point in time and from a particular angle. Deeper insight and more informed decision making come from a continuing series of snapshots taken from various angles and through different lenses, which form the essence of systematic listening.[7]

In this section, we discuss how customer feedback can be systematically collected, analyzed, and passed on to relevant departments through a customer feedback system (CFS) to achieve customer-driven learning and service improvements.[8]

Key Objectives of Effective Customer Feedback Systems

 **LO 5**

Explain the common objectives of effective customer feedback systems.

"It is not the strongest species that survive, nor the most intelligent, but the ones most responsive to change," wrote Charles Darwin. Similarly, many planners have concluded that, in increasingly competitive markets, the best competitive advantage for a firm is to learn and change faster than the competition.[9] Effective customer feedback systems facilitate fast learning. Their objectives usually fall into the following three main categories:

1. Assessment and Benchmarking of Service Quality and Performance

The objective is to answer the question "How satisfied are our customers?" This objective includes learning about how well a firm performed in comparison to its main competitor(s), in comparison to the previous year (or quarter, or month), and where the firm wants to be the following year. Benchmarking does not only have to be with companies from the same industry. For example, Southwest Airlines benchmarks Formula One pit-stops for speedy turnaround of aircraft; Pizza Hut benchmarks Federal Express for on-time package delivery; and Ikea examines the military for excellence in coordination and logistics management.

2. Customer-Driven Learning and Improvements

Here, the objective is to answer the questions, "What makes our customers happy or unhappy?" and "What are the strengths we want to cement, and what are the weaknesses we need to improve?" For this, more specific or detailed information on processes and products is required to guide a firm's service improvement efforts and to see which areas have possible high returns for quality investment.

3. Creating a Customer-Oriented Service Culture

This objective is concerned with focusing the organization on customer needs and customer satisfaction, and moving the entire organization toward a service quality culture.

Of the three objectives just discussed, firms seem to do well on the first but miss great opportunities in the other two. Neil Morgan, Eugene Anderson, and Vikas Mittal concluded in their research on customer satisfaction information usage (CSIU) the following:

> Many of the firms in our sample do not appear to gain significant customer-focused learning benefits from their CS [customer satisfaction] systems, because they are designed to act primarily as a control mechanism [i.e., our assessment or benchmarking]. … [Firms] may be well served to reevaluate how they deploy their existing CSIU resources. The majority of CSIU resources … are consumed in CS data collection. This often leads to too few resources being allocated to the analysis, dissemination, and utilization of this information to realize fully the potential payback from the investment in data collection.[10]

Describe key customer feedback collection tools.

Use a Mix of Customer Feedback Collection Tools[11]

Renee Fleming, soprano and America's beautiful voice, once said, "We singers are unfortunately not able to hear ourselves sing. You sound entirely different to yourself. We need the ears of others—from outside." Likewise, firms need to listen to the voice of the customer. Table 14.3 gives an overview of typically used feedback tools and their ability to meet various requirements. Recognizing that different tools have different strengths and weaknesses, service marketers should select a mix of customer feedback collection tools that jointly deliver the needed information. As Leonard Berry and A. Parasuraman observed, "Combining approaches enables a firm to tap the strengths of each and compensate for weaknesses."[12]

Table 14.3 Strengths and weaknesses of key customer feedback collection tools

	Level of Measurement					Potential for		
Collection Tools	**Firm**	**Process**	**Transaction Specific**	**Actionable**	**Representative, Reliable**	**Service Recovery**	**Firsthand Learning**	**Cost-effectiveness**
Total market survey (including competitors)	●	○	○	○	●	○	○	○
Annual survey on overall satisfaction	●	◐	○	○	●	○	○	○
Transactional survey	●	●	◐	◐	●	○	○	○
Service feedback cards	◐	●	●	◐	◐	●	◐	●
Mystery shopping	○	◐	●	●	○	○	◐	○
Unsolicited feedback (e.g., complaints)	○	◐	●	●	○	●	◐	●
Focus group discussions	○	◐	●	●	○	◐	●	◐
Service reviews	○	◐	●	●	○	●	●	◐

Legend: ● meets requirements fully; ◐ moderately; ○ hardly at all

SOURCE

Adapted from Jochen Wirtz and Monica Tomlin, "Institutionalizing Customer-driven Learning through Fully Integrated Customer Feedback Systems," *Managing Service Quality* 10, no. 4 (2000): 210.

Total Market, Annual, and Transactional Surveys

Total market surveys and *annual surveys* typically measure satisfaction with all major customer service processes and products.[13] The level of measurement usually is high, with the objective of obtaining a global index or indicator of overall service satisfaction for the entire firm.

Overall indices such as these tell us how satisfied customers are, but not why they are happy or unhappy. There are limits to the number of questions that can be asked about each individual process or product. For example, a typical retail bank may have 30–50 key customer service processes (e.g., from car loan applications to cash deposits at the teller). Many surveys have room for only one or two questions per process (e.g., how satisfied are you with our ATM services?) and cannot address issues in greater detail.

In contrast, *transactional surveys*, also called intercept surveys, typically are conducted after customers have completed a specific transaction (Figure 14.5). At this point, if time allows, they may be asked about the process in some depth. Such feedback can tell the firm why customers are happy or unhappy with the process, and usually shows how customer satisfaction can be improved.

All three survey types are representative and reliable when designed properly. Representativeness and reliability are required for:

1) Accurate assessments of where the company, a process, branch, team, or individual stands relative to quality goals. It is important to have a representative and reliable sample, so as to ensure that observed changes in quality scores are not the result of sample biases and/or random errors.

2) Evaluations of individual service employees, service delivery teams, branches, and/or processes, especially when incentive schemes are linked to such measures. The methodology has to be water-tight if staff are to trust and buy into the results, especially when surveys deliver bad news.

Figure 14.5 Transactional surveys are typically conducted following service delivery.

The potential for service recovery is important and should, if possible, be incorporated into feedback collection tools. However, many surveys promise that the respondents would remain anonymous, which then makes it impossible to identify and respond to dissatisfied respondents. In personal encounters or telephone surveys, interviewers can be instructed to ask customers whether they would like the firm to get back to them on dissatisfying issues.

Service Feedback Cards

This powerful and inexpensive tool involves giving customers a feedback card (or an online pop-up form, e-mail, or SMS) following completion of a major service process and inviting them to return it by mail or other means to a central customer feedback unit (Figure 14.6). For example, a feedback card can be attached to each housing loan approval letter or to each hospital invoice. These cards are a good indicator of process quality and yield specific feedback on what works well and what doesn't. However, customers who are delighted or very dissatisfied are likely to be overrepresented among the respondents. This affects the reliability and representativeness of this tool.

PART V

Figure 14.6 The widespread use of SMS text messaging allows for convenient mobile feedback.

Mystery Shopping

Service businesses often use "mystery shoppers" to determine whether frontline staff are displaying desired behaviors (see Service Insights 14.1). Banks, retailers, car rental firms, and hotels are among the industries making active use of mystery shoppers. For example, the central reservation offices of a global hotel chain may appoint a company to conduct a large-scale monthly mystery caller survey to assess the skills of individual associates in relation to the phone sales process. Such actions as correctly positioning of the various products, up-selling and cross-selling, and closing the deal are measured. The survey also examines the quality of the phone conversation on such dimensions as "a warm and friendly greeting" and "establishing rapport with the caller." Mystery shopping gives in-depth insights for coaching, training, and performance evaluation.

Unsolicited Customer Feedback

Customer complaints, compliments, and suggestions can be transformed into a stream of information that can be used to help monitor quality and highlight improvements needed to the service design and delivery. Complaints and compliments are rich sources of detailed feedback on what makes customers unhappy and what delights them.[14] Therefore, similar to feedback cards, unsolicited feedback is not a reliable measure of overall customer satisfaction, but it is a good source of improvement ideas.

Detailed customer complaint and compliment letters, recorded telephone conversations, and direct feedback from employees serve as an excellent tool for communicating internally what customers want, and allow employees and managers at all levels to "listen" to customers firsthand. For example, Singapore Airlines prints complaint and compliment letters in its monthly employee magazine, *Outlook*. Southwest Airlines shows staff videotapes of customers providing feedback. Seeing actual customers giving comments about their service leaves a much deeper and lasting impression on staff and encourages them to improve further.

For complaints, suggestions, and inquiries to be useful as research input, they have to be channeled into a central collection point, logged, grouped, and analyzed.[15] That requires a system for capturing customer feedback where it is made, and then reporting it to a central unit.

Focus Group Discussions and Service Reviews

Both tools give great specific insights on potential service improvements and ideas. Usually, focus groups are organized by key customer segments or user groups to focus on the needs of these users. Service reviews are in-depth, one-on-one interviews that are usually conducted once a year with a firm's most valuable customers (Figure 14.7). Usually, a senior executive of the firm visits the customer and discusses issues such as how well the firm performed the previous year and what should be maintained or changed. The senior executive then goes back to the organization and discusses the feedback with his or her account managers. Both then write a letter back to the client detailing how the firm will respond to that customers' service needs and how the account will be managed the following year.

SERVICE INSIGHTS 14.1

Customers as Quality Control Inspectors?

Mystery shopping is a good method for checking whether frontline employees display the desired and trained behaviors and follow the specified service procedures, but don't use customer surveys for this. Ron Kaufman, founder of Up Your Service! College, describes a recent service experience:

"We had a wonderful ride in the hotel car from the airport. The driver was so friendly. He gave us a cold towel and a cool drink. He offered a choice of music, talked about the weather, and made sure we were comfortable with the air conditioning. His smile and good feelings washed over us, and I liked it!"

"At the hotel, I signed the guest registration and gave my credit card. Then the counter staff asked me to complete another form." It read:

Limousine Survey

To consistently ensure the proper application of our quality standards, we value your feedback on our limousine service:

1. Were you greeted by our airport representative?	YES/NO
2. Were you offered a cold towel?	YES/NO
3. Were you offered cold water?	YES/NO
4. Was a selection of music available?	YES/NO
5. Did the driver ask you about the air conditioning?	YES/NO
6. Was the driver driving at safe speed?	YES/NO

Room Number: ______________

Limo Number: ______________

Date: ______________

Kaufman continued: "As I read the form, all the good feelings fell away. The driver's enthusiasm suddenly seemed a charade. His concern for our well-being became just a checklist of actions to follow. His good mood was merely an act to meet the standard, not a connection with his guests. I felt like the hotel's quality control inspector, and I did not like it. If the hotel wants my opinion, make me an advisor, not an inspector. Ask me: What did you enjoy most about your ride from the airport? (I'd told them about their wonderful driver). What else could we do to make your ride even more enjoyable? (I'd have recommended offering the use of a cell phone)."

SOURCE

Apart from providing an excellent learning opportunity (especially when the reviews across all customers are compiled and analyzed), service reviews focus on retention of the most valuable customers and get high marks for service recovery potential.

Figure 14.7 Service reviews being conducted with an important B2B customer.

Analysis, Reporting, and Dissemination of Customer Feedback

Choosing the relevant feedback tools and collecting customer feedback are meaningless if the company is unable to pass the information to the relevant parties to take action. To drive continuous improvement and learning, a reporting system needs to deliver feedback and its analysis to frontline staff, process owners, branch or department managers, and top management.

The feedback loop to the frontline should be immediate for complaints and compliments. In addition, we recommend three types of service performance reports to provide the information necessary for service management and team learning:

1) A monthly *Service Performance Update* provides process owners with timely feedback on customer comments and operational process performance. Here, the verbatim feedback should be included to the process manager who can, in turn, discuss them with his or her service delivery teams.
2) A quarterly *Service Performance Review* provides process owners and branch or department managers with trends in process performance and service quality.
3) An annual *Service Performance Report* gives top management a representative assessment of the status and long-term trends relating to customer satisfaction with the firm's services.

These reports should be short and reader friendly, focusing on key indicators and providing an easily understood commentary for the people in charge to act on.

HARD MEASURES OF SERVICE QUALITY

LO 7

Be familiar with hard measures of service quality and control charts.

Having learned about the various tools for collecting soft service quality measures, let's explore hard measures in more detail. Hard measures typically refer to operational processes or outcomes and include such data as uptime, service response times, failure rates, and delivery costs. In a complex service operation, multiple measures of service quality will be recorded at many different points. In low-contact services in which customers are not deeply involved in the service delivery process, many operational measures apply to backstage activities.

FedEx was one of the first service companies to understand the need for a firm-wide index of service quality that embraced all the key activities that affect customers. By publishing a single, composite index on a frequent basis, senior managers hoped that all FedEx employees would work toward improving quality. The firm recognized the danger of using percentages as targets, because they might lead to self-satisfaction. In an organization as large as FedEx, which ships millions of packages a day, even delivering 99.9% of packages on time (which would mean one in 1,000 packages is delivered late) or having 99.999% of flights arrive safely would lead to horrendous problems. Instead, the company decided to approach quality measurement from the baseline of zero failures (see Service Insights 14.2).

How can we show performance on hard measures? For this, *control charts* are a simple method of displaying performance on hard measures over time against specific quality standards. The charts can be used to monitor and communicate individual variables or an overall index. Since they are visual, trends are easily identified. Figure 14.8 shows an airline's performance on the important hard standard of on-time departures. The trends displayed suggest that this issue needs to be addressed by management, as performance is not consistent and not very satisfactory. Of course, control charts are only as good as the data on which they are based.

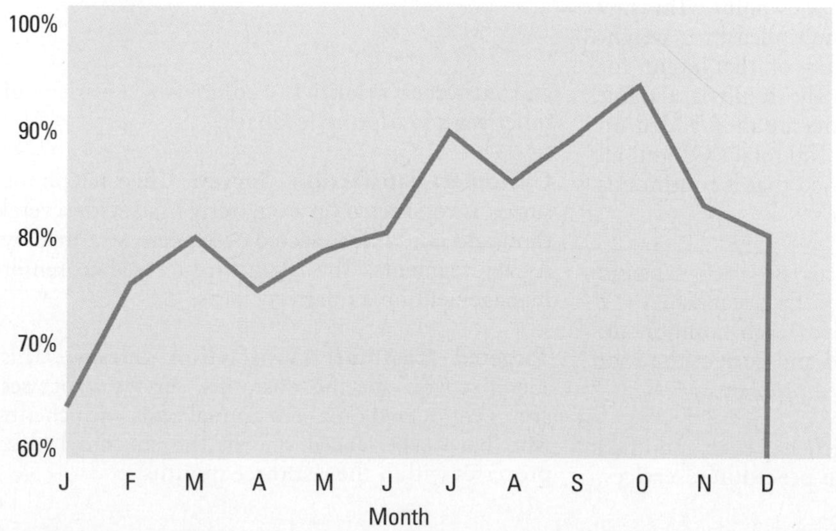

Figure 14.8 A control chart for departure delays showing percentage of flights departing within 15 minutes of schedule.

PART V

SERVICE INSIGHTS 14.2

FedEx's Approach to Listening to the Voice of the Customer

"We believe that service quality must be mathematically measured," declared Frederick W. Smith, Chairman, President, and CEO of FedEx Corporation. The company has a commitment to clear quality goals, followed up with continuous measurement of progress against those goals. This practice forms the foundation for its approach to quality. As noted by one senior executive:

> It's only when you examine the types of failures, the number that occurs of each type, and the reasons why, that you begin to improve the quality of your service. For us, the trick was to express quality failures in absolute numbers. That led us to develop the Service Quality Index or SQI [pronounced "sky"].[16]

Since FedEx had systematically cataloged customer complaints, it was able to develop what CEO Smith calls the "Hierarchy of Horrors," which referred to the eight most common complaints by customers: (1) wrong day delivery, (2) right day, late delivery, (3) pick-up not made (4) lost package, (5) customer misinformed, (6) billing and paperwork mistakes, (7) employee performance failures, and (8) damaged packages. This list was the foundation on which FedEx build its customer feedback system.

FedEx refined the list of "horrors" and developed its SQI, a 12-item measure of satisfaction and service quality from the customers' viewpoint. The raw numbers of each event are multiplied by a weight that highlights the seriousness of that event for customers (see Table 14.4). The result is a point score for each item. The points are then added up to generate that day's index. The total SQI and all its 12 items are tracked daily so that a continuous index can be computed.

To ensure a continuing focus on each separate component of the SQI, FedEx established 12 Quality Action Teams, one for each component. The teams had to understand and correct the root causes underlying the observed problems.

In addition to the SQI, which has been modified over time to reflect changes in procedures, services, and customer priorities, FedEx uses a variety of other ways to capture feedback.

Table 14.4 Composition of FedEx's Service Quality Index (SQI)

Failure Type	Weighting Factor x No. of Incidents = Daily Points
Late delivery—right day	1
Late delivery—wrong day	5
Tracing requests unanswered	1
Complaints reopened	5
Missing proofs of delivery	1
Invoice adjustments	1
Missed pickups	10
Lost packages	10
Damaged packages	10
Aircraft delays (minutes)	5
Overgoods (packages missing labels)	5
Abandoned calls	1
Total failure points (SQI)	XXX,XXX

Customer Satisfaction Survey. This telephone survey is conducted on a quarterly basis with several thousand randomly selected customers, stratified by its key segments. The results are relayed to senior management on a quarterly basis.

Targeted Customer Satisfaction Survey. This survey covers specific customer service processes and is conducted on a semiannual basis with clients who have experienced one of the specific FedEx processes within the last three months.

FedEx Center Comment Cards. Comment cards are collected from each FedEx storefront business center. The results are tabulated twice a year and relayed to managers in charge of the centers.

Online Customer Feedback Surveys. FedEx has commissioned regular studies to get feedback for its online services, such package tracking, as well as ad hoc studies on new products.

The information from these various customer feedback measures has helped FedEx to maintain a leadership role in its industry and played an important role in enabling it to receive the prestigious Malcolm Baldrige National Quality Award.

SOURCES

"Blueprints for Service Quality: The Federal Express Approach," *AMA Management Briefing*, New York: American Management Association, 1991, 51–64; Linda Rosencrance, "BetaSphere delivers FedEx some customer feedback," *Computerworld* 14, no. 14 (2000): 36; Madan Birla, *Fedex Delivers: How the World's Leading Shipping Company Keeps Innovating and Outperforming the Competition*, John Wiley, 2005, 91–92.

TOOLS TO ANALYZE AND ADDRESS SERVICE QUALITY PROBLEMS

LO 8

Select suitable tools to analyze service problems.

After having assessed service quality using soft and hard measures, how can we now drill deeper to identify common causes of quality shortfalls and take corrective actions? When a problem is caused by controllable, internal forces, there's no excuse for allowing it to recur. After all, maintaining customers' goodwill after a service failure depends on keeping promises made to the effect that "we're taking steps to ensure that it doesn't happen again!" With prevention as a goal, let's look briefly at some tools for determining the root causes of specific service quality problems.

Root Cause Analysis: The Fishbone Diagram

Cause-and-effect analysis uses a technique first developed by the Japanese quality expert, Kaoru Ishikawa. Groups of managers and staff brainstorm all the possible reasons that might cause a specific problem. The reasons are then grouped into one of five groupings—Equipment, Manpower (or People), Material, Procedures, and Other—on a cause-and-effect chart, popularly known as a fishbone diagram because of its shape. This technique has been used for many years in manufacturing and, more recently, also in services.

To apply this tool better to service organizations, we show an extended framework that has eight rather than five groupings (see Figure 14.9).[17] "People" has been further broken down into "Front-Stage Personnel" and "Backstage Personnel." This highlights the fact that front-stage service problems are often experienced directly by customers, whereas backstage failures tend to show up more indirectly through a ripple effect.

In addition, "Information" has been separated from "Procedures." This recognizes the fact that many service problems result from information failures. For example, these

PART V

failures are often because front-stage personnel do not have the required information at their fingertips or do not tell customers what to do and when to do it.

"Customers" were added as a further source of root causes. In manufacturing, customers do not really affect the day-to-day operational processes. However, in a high-contact service, they are involved in front-stage operations. If they don't play their own parts correctly, they may reduce service productivity and cause quality problems for themselves and other customers. For instance, an aircraft can be delayed if a passenger tries to board at the last minute with an oversized suitcase which then has to be loaded into the cargo hold. Figure 14.9, displays 27 possible reasons for late departures of passenger aircraft.[18]

Once all the main possible causes for flight delays have been identified, it is necessary to see how much impact each cause has on actual delays. This can be established using frequency counts in combination with Pareto analysis, which is discussed next.

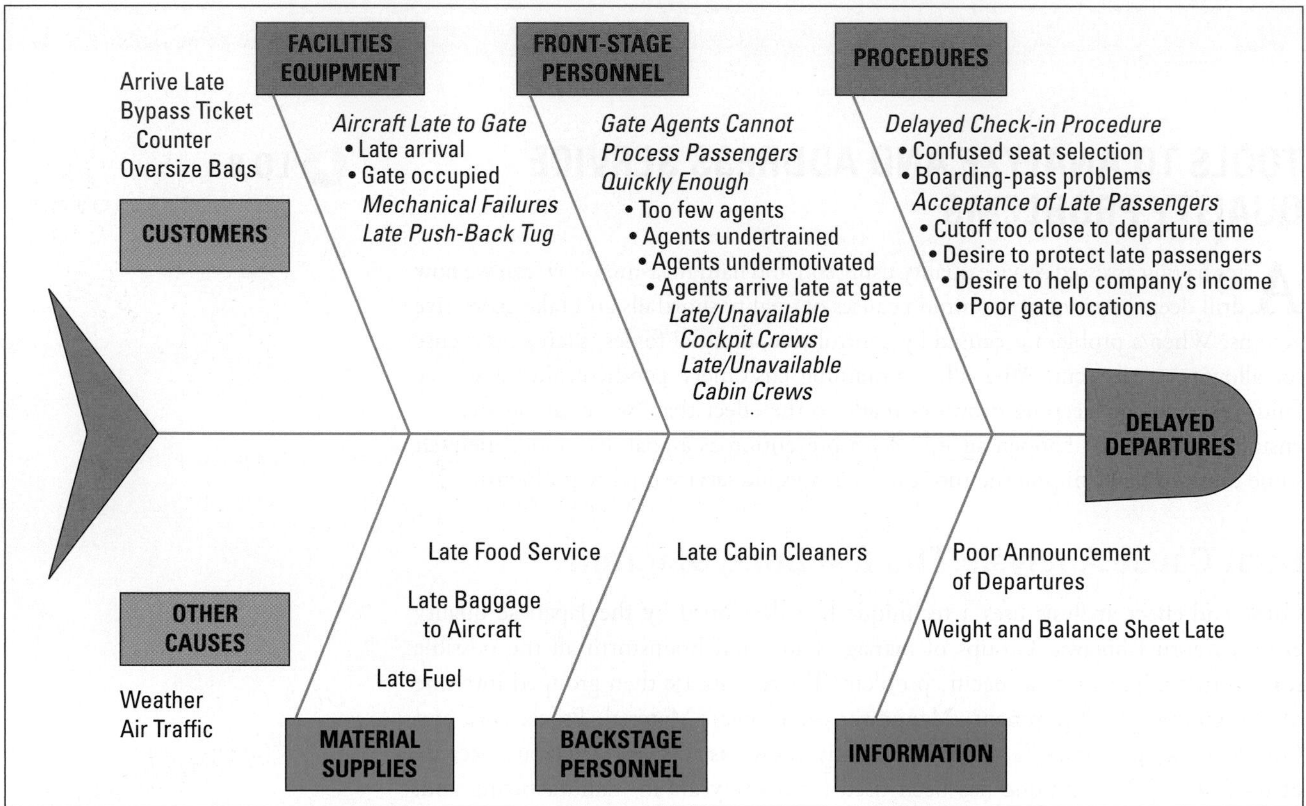

Figure 14.9 A cause-and-effect chart for flight departure delays.

Pareto Analysis

Pareto Analysis (so named after the Italian economist who first developed it) identifies the main causes of observed outcomes. This type of analysis often reveals that around 80% of the value of one variable (in this instance, number of service failures) is caused by only 20% of the causal variables (i.e., number of possible causes as identified by the fishbone diagram).

In the airline example, findings showed that 88% of the company's late departing flights from the airports it served were caused by only four (15%) of all the possible factors. In fact, more than half the delays were caused by a single factor: acceptance of late passengers (i.e., situations when the staff held a flight for one more passenger who was checking in after the official cutoff time).

On such occasions, the airline made a friend of the passenger who was late, but risked frustrating all the other passengers who were already onboard, waiting for the aircraft to depart. Other major delays included waiting for pushback (a vehicle must arrive to pull the aircraft away from the gate), waiting for fueling, and delays in signing the weight and balance sheet (a safety requirement relating to the distribution of the aircraft's load that the captain must follow on each flight). Further analysis, however, showed that the reasons are slightly different from one airport to another (see Figure 14.10).

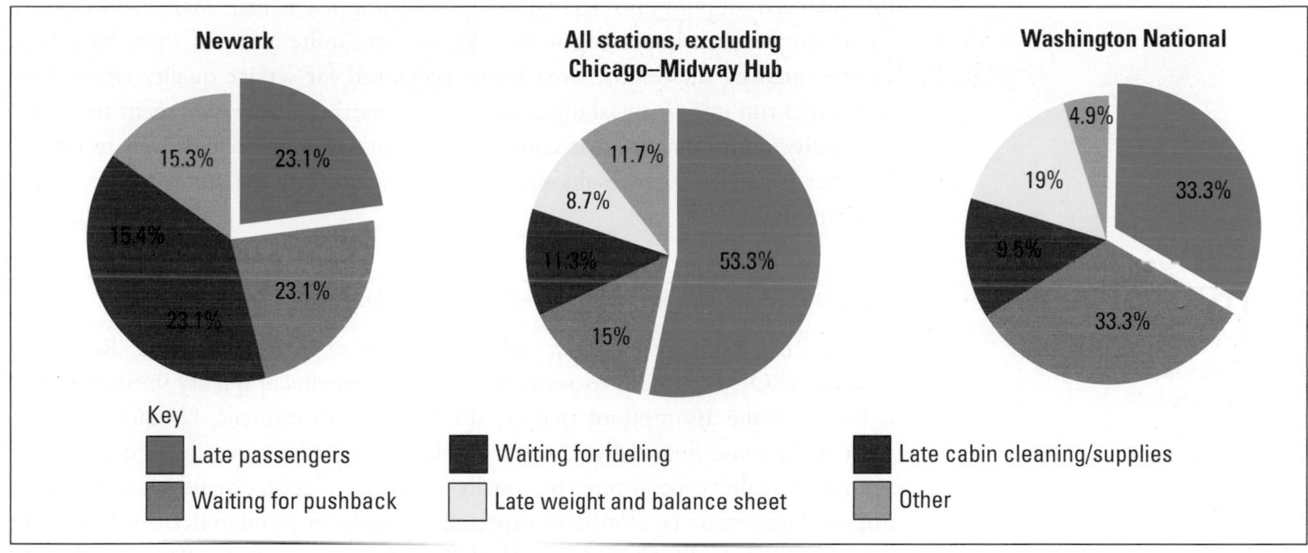

Figure 14.10 Analysis of causes of flight departure delays.

By combining the fishbone diagram and Pareto analysis, we can identify the main causes of service failure.

Blueprinting—A Powerful Tool for Identifying Fail Points

Fishbone diagrams and Pareto analyses tell us the causes and importance of quality problems. Blueprints allow us to drill down further to identify where exactly in a service process the problem was caused. As described in Chapter 8, a well-constructed blueprint enables us to see the process of service delivery by showing the sequence of front-stage interactions that customers experience as they encounter service providers, facilities, and equipment, together with supporting backstage activities, which are hidden from the customers and are not part of their service experience.

Blueprints can be used to identify the potential fail points where failures are most likely to occur, and they help us to understand how failures at one point (such as incorrect entry of an appointment date) may affect the later stages of the process (the customer arrives at the doctor's office and is told the doctor is unavailable). By adding frequency counts to the fail points in a blueprint, managers can identify the specific types of failures that occur most frequently and thus need urgent attention. Knowing what can go wrong and where, is an important first step in preventing service quality problems. (See Chapter 8 for a more detailed discussion of blueprints and how they can be used to design and redesign customer service processes.)

RETURN ON QUALITY

We now understand how to drill down to specific quality problems, and we can use what we have learned from Chapter 8 on how to design and redesign improved service processes. However, the picture is incomplete without understanding the financial implications related to quality improvements. Many firms pay a lot of attention on improving service quality; and quite a few of them have been disappointed by the results. Even firms recognized for service quality efforts have sometimes run into financial difficulties. This is partly because they spent too much on quality improvements that customers do not value or do not even recognize. In other instances, such results show poor or incomplete execution of the quality program itself.

LO 9

Appreciate the financial implications of quality improvements.

Assess Costs and Benefits of Quality Initiatives

Roland Rust, Anthony Zahonik, and Timothy Keiningham argue for a "Return on Quality" (ROQ) approach to assess the costs and benefits of quality initiatives. This is based on the assumptions that (1) quality is an investment, (2) quality efforts must make sense financially, (3) it is possible to spend too much on quality, and (4) not all quality expenditures are equally justified.[19] Hence, expenditures on quality improvement must be related to expected increases in profitability. An important implication of the ROQ perspective is that quality improvement efforts may benefit from being coordinated with productivity improvement programs.

To see if new quality improvement efforts make sense, its costs must be worked out beforehand. Firms also have to predict how customers will respond to the improvement efforts. Will the program allow the firm to attract more customers (e.g., through word-of-mouth of current customers), increase share-of-wallet, and/or to reduce defections? If so, how much additional net income will be generated?

With good documentation, it is sometimes possible for a firm that operates in a number of locations to examine past experience and judge the strength of a relationship between specific service quality improvements and revenues (see Service Insights 14.3).

Determine the Optimal Level of Reliability

How far should we go in improving service reliability? A company with poor service quality can often achieve big jumps in reliability with relatively modest investments

SERVICE INSIGHTS 14.3

Quality of Facilities and Room Revenues at Holiday Inn

To find out the relationship between product quality and financial performance in a hotel context, Sheryl Kimes analyzed three years of quality and operational performance data from 1,135 franchised Holiday Inn hotels in the United States and Canada.

Indicators of product quality came from the franchisor's quality assurance reports. These reports were based on unannounced, semi-annual inspections by trained quality auditors who were rotated among different regions and who inspected and rated different quality dimensions of each hotel. Sheryl Kimes used 12 of these quality dimensions in her study: two relating to the guest rooms (bedroom and bathroom) and 10 relating to commercial areas (e.g., exterior, lobby, public restrooms, dining facilities, lounge facilities, corridors, meeting area, recreation area, kitchen, back of house). Each quality dimensions usually included 10–12 individual items that could be passed or failed. The inspector noted the number of defects for each dimension and the total number for the entire hotel.

Holiday Inn Worldwide also provided data on revenue per available room (RevPAR) at each hotel. To adjust for differences in local conditions, Kimes analyzed sales and revenue statistics obtained from thousands of US and Canadian hotels and reported in the monthly Smith Travel Accommodation Reports (a widely used service in the travel industry). This data enabled Kimes to calculate the RevPAR for the immediate midscale competitors of each Holiday Inn hotel. The results were then used to make the RevPARs comparable across all Holiday Inns in the sample. The average daily room rate at the time was about $50.

For the purposes of the research, if a hotel had failed at least one item in an area, it was considered "defective" in that area. The findings showed that as the number of defects in a hotel increased, the RevPAR decreased. Quality dimensions that showed quite a strong impact on RevPAR were the exterior, the guest room, and the guest bathroom. Even a single defect resulted in a statistically significant reduction in RevPAR. However, the combination of defects in all three areas showed an even larger effect on RevPAR over time. Kimes calculated that the average annual revenue impact on a defective hotel was a revenue loss of $204,400 compared to a non-defective hotel.

Using a Return on Quality perspective, the results showed that the main focus of increased expenditures on housekeeping and preventive maintenance should be the hotel exterior, the guest rooms, and bathrooms.

SOURCE

Sheryl E. Kimes, "The relationship between product quality and Revenue per Available Room at Holiday Inn," *Journal of Service Research* 2, (November 1999): 138–144.

in improvements. As illustrated in Figure 14.11, initial investments in reducing service failure often bring dramatic results. However, at some point, diminishing returns set in as further improvements require increasing levels of investment, even becoming prohibitively expensive. What level of reliability should we target?

Typically, the cost of service recovery is lower than the cost of an unhappy customer. This suggests that service firms should increase reliability up to the point that the incremental improvement equals the cost of service recovery or the cost of failure. Although this strategy results in a service that is less than 100% failure-free, the firm can still aim to satisfy 100% of its target customers by ensuring that either they

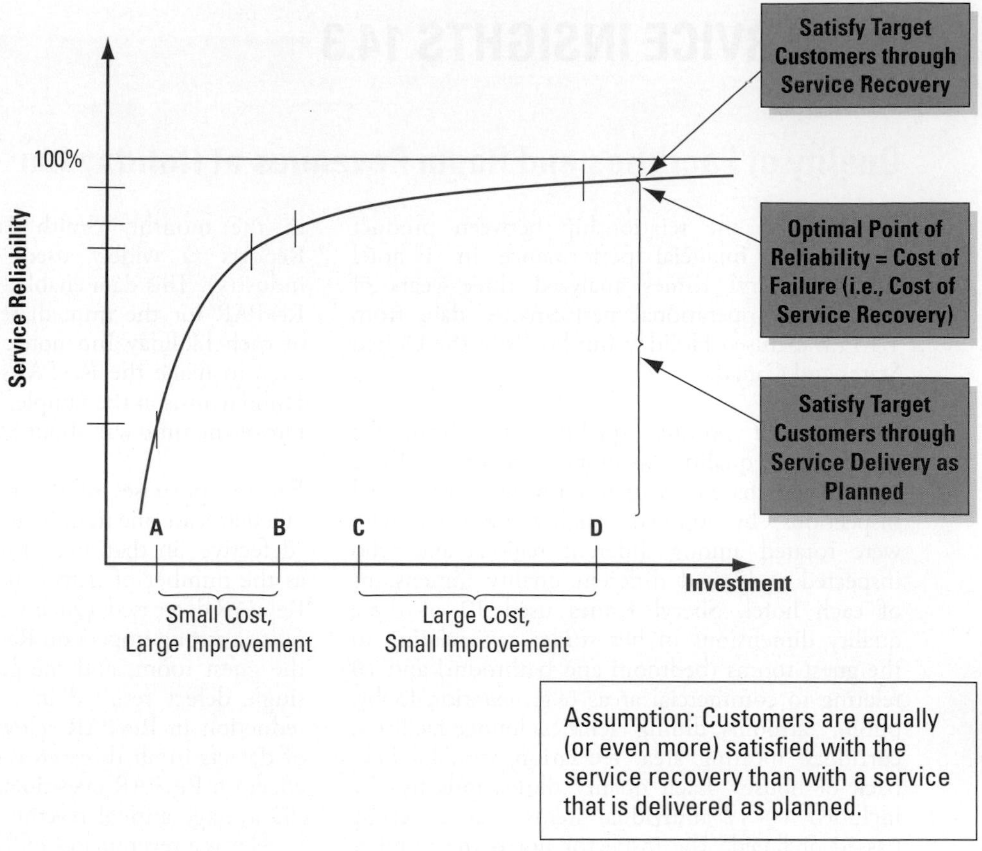

Figure 14.11 When does improving service reliability become uneconomical?

receive the service as planned or, if a failure occurs, they obtain a satisfying service recovery (see Chapter 13).

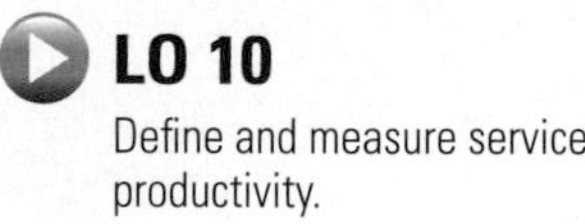

LO 10

Define and measure service productivity.

DEFINING AND MEASURING PRODUCTIVITY

We have highlighted in the introduction of this chapter that we need to look at quality and productivity improvement strategies together rather than in isolation. A firm needs to ensure that it can deliver quality experiences more efficiently to improve its long-term profitability. Let us first discuss what productivity is and how it can be measured.

Defining Productivity in a Service Context

Simply defined, productivity measures the amount of output produced relative to the amount of inputs used. Hence, improvements in productivity are reflected by an increase in the ratio of outputs to inputs. An improvement in this ratio might be achieved by cutting the resources required to create a given volume of output or by increasing the output obtained from a given level of inputs.

What do we mean by "input" in a service context? Input varies according to the nature of the business. It may include labor (both physical and intellectual), materials, energy, and capital (consisting of land, buildings, equipment, information systems, and financial assets) (Figure 14.12).

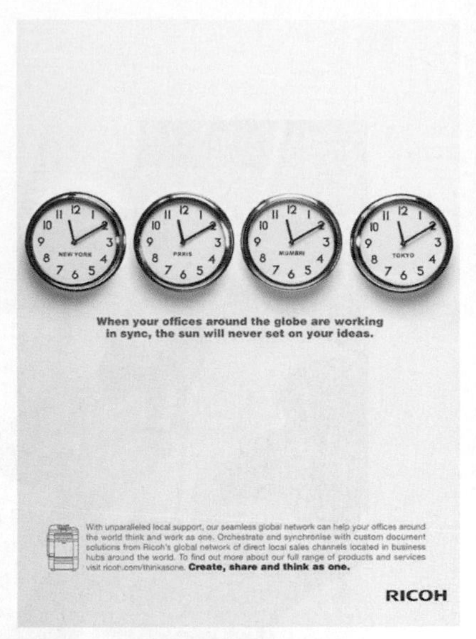

Figure 14.12 Companies like Ricoh supply equipment and services to increase their customers' productivity.

Measuring Productivity

Measuring productivity is difficult in services when the output is difficult to define. In a people-processing service, such as a hospital, we can look at the number of patients treated over a year and the hospital's average bed occupancy. However, how do we take into account the different types of medical activities performed, such as removal of cancerous tumors, treatment of diabetes, or setting of broken bones? What about differences between patients? How do we judge the difference in outcomes? Some patients get better, some develop complications, and, sadly, some even die.

The measurement task is perhaps simpler in possession-processing services, since many are like manufacturing organizations and perform routine tasks with easily measurable inputs and outputs. Examples include garages that change a car's oil and rotate its tires, or fast-food restaurants that offer limited and simple menus. However, the task gets more complicated when the garage mechanic has to find and repair a water leak, or when we are dealing with a French restaurant known for its varied and exceptional cuisine. What about information-based services? How should we define the output of an investment bank or a consulting firm?

LO 11

Understand the difference between productivity, efficiency, and effectiveness.

Service Productivity, Efficiency, and Effectiveness

When we look at the issue of productivity, we need to differentiate productivity, efficiency, and effectiveness.[20] *Productivity* refers to the output that one can get from a certain amount of inputs. The more output one can get from the given amount of inputs, the higher the productivity. *Efficiency* involves comparison to a standard that is usually time based. For example, how long does it take for an employee to perform a particular task compared to a set standard? The faster the task can be completed, the higher the efficiency. *Effectiveness* can be defined as the degree to which an organization is meeting its goals and desired outcomes, which would typically include customer satisfaction (Figure 4.13).

Figure 14.13 Productivity for the firm may result in customer frustration when they cannot talk to service personnel.

Classical techniques of productivity measurement focus on outputs and benchmarking, rather than outcomes. This means that productivity and efficiency are stressed, but effectiveness is neglected. In freight transport, for instance, a ton-mile of output for freight that is delivered late is treated the same for productivity purposes as a similar shipment delivered on time. Similarly, suppose a hairdresser usually serves three customers per hour. However, she can increase her output to one every 15 minutes by reducing conversation with the customer and by rushing her customers. Even if the haircut itself is just as good, the delivery process may be perceived as functionally inferior, leading customers to rate the overall service experience less positively (Figure 14.14). In this example, productivity and efficiency have been achieved, but not effectiveness.

Figure 14.14 A counselor needs to take his time in a session so that patients can gain greater satisfaction from their group therapy.

In the long run, organizations that are more effective in consistently delivering outcomes desired by customers should be able to command higher prices for their output. Therefore, there is a need to stress effectiveness and outcomes (including quality and value generated for customers) in addition to productivity and efficiency.

IMPROVING SERVICE PRODUCTIVITY

Intensive competition in many service sectors pushes firms to continually seek ways to improve their productivity.[21] This section discusses various possible approaches to and sources of productivity gains.

 **LO 12**

Recommend the key methods to improve service productivity.

Generic Productivity Improvement Strategies

Traditionally, operations managers have been in charge of improving service productivity. They usually take the following actions:

- Carefully controlling costs at every step in the process.
- Reducing waste of materials and labor.
- Training employees to work more productively (faster is not necessarily better if it leads to mistakes or unsatisfactory work that has to be redone).
- Providing employees with equipment and databases that enable them to work faster and/or to a higher level of quality.
- Broadening the variety of tasks that a service worker can perform (which may require revised labor agreements) so as to get rid of bottlenecks and wasteful downtime by allowing managers to deploy workers wherever they are needed most.
- Installing expert systems that allow paraprofessionals to take on work previously performed by more experienced individuals earning higher salaries.

Although improving productivity can be approached in small steps, major gains often require redesigning customer service processes. For example, it's time for service process redesign when customers face unbearably long wait times, as happens often in health care (Figure 14.15). We discussed service process redesign in depth in Chapter 8.

Customer-Driven Approaches to Improve Productivity

Figure 14.15 Long waiting times often indicate a need for service process redesign.

In situations where customers are deeply involved in the service production process, operations managers should also be examining how customer inputs can be made more productive. Marketing managers should be thinking about what marketing strategies should be used to influence customers to behave in more productive ways. Some of these strategies include:

- **Change the timing of customer demand.** By encouraging customers to use a service outside peak periods and offering them incentives to do so, managers can make better use of their productive assets and provide better service. The issues that relate to managing demand in capacity-constrained service businesses are discussed in detail in Chapter 9; revenue management strategies are explored in Chapter 6.
- **Encourage use of lower cost service delivery channels and self-service.** Shifting delivery to more cost-effective service delivery channels, such as the Internet or self-service machines, improves productivity. It also helps in demand management by reducing the pressure on employees and certain types of physical facilities at peak hours. Many technological innovations are designed to get customers to perform tasks previously undertaken by service employees (Figure 14.16). The issues related to customers playing a more active role as co-producers of the service are discussed in detail in the context of service process design in Chapter 8.
- **Ask customers to use third parties.** In some instances, managers may be able to improve service productivity by using third parties. Specialist intermediaries may enjoy economies of scale, allowing them to perform the task more cheaply than the core service provider. This allows the service provider to focus on quality and productivity in its own area of expertise. An example of an intermediary is a travel agency. We discussed the use of intermediaries in detail in Chapter 5 in the context of distribution.

Figure 14.16 Self-service pumps with credit card readers have increased gas station productivity.

PART V

Know how productivity improvements impact quality and value.

How Productivity Improvements Impact Quality and Value

Managers should see productivity improvements as business processes used to transform resource inputs into the outcomes desired by customers. This is especially so for processes that not only cross departmental and sometimes geographic boundaries, but also those that link the backstage and front-stage areas of the service operation. Hence, as firms make productivity improvements, they need to examine the impact on the customer experience.

Front-Stage Efforts to Improve Productivity

In high-contact services, many productivity improvements are quite visible. Some changes simply require acceptance by customers, while others require customers to have new patterns of behavior in their dealings with the organization. If a lot of changes are suggested, then it makes sense to conduct market research first to determine how customers may respond. Failure to consider the effects on customers may result in a loss of business and cancel out anticipated productivity gains. (Refer back to Chapter 8 on how to manage and overcome customers' reluctance to change in service processes.)

How Backstage Changes May Impact Customers

The marketing implications of backstage changes depend on whether they affect or are noticed by customers. If airline mechanics develop a procedure for servicing jet engines more quickly without incurring increased wage rates or material costs, the airline has obtained a productivity improvement that has no impact on the customer's service experience.

Other backstage changes, however, may extend front-stage and affect customers. Marketers should be updated on proposed backstage changes to prepare customers for them. At a bank, for instance, the decision to install new computers and printers may be due to plans to improve internal quality controls and reduce the cost of preparing monthly statements. However, this new equipment may change the appearance of bank statements and the time of the month when they are posted. If customers are likely to notice such changes, an explanation may be needed. If the new statements are easier to read and understand, the change may be worth promoting as a service improvement.

A Caution on Cost-Reduction Strategies

Service productivity improvements usually focus on getting rid of waste and reducing labor costs if it does not involve new technology. Reducing front-stage staffing either means that the remaining employees have to work harder and faster or that there are not enough personnel to serve customers fast at busy times. Although employees may be able to work faster for a short period of time, few can do that for long periods. They become tired, make mistakes, and treat customers in a cold manner. Workers who are trying to do two or three things at the same time may do a poor job of each task. Too much stress leads to dissatisfaction and frustration. A better way is to search for service process redesign opportunities that lead to great improvements in productivity and at the same time increase service quality. Biometrics is set to become a new technology that may allow both (see Service Insights 14.4).

SERVICE INSIGHTS 14.4

Biometrics—The Next Frontier in Driving Productivity and Service Quality?

Intense competitive pressures and extremely low margins in service industries do not allow firms to increase costs to improve quality. Rather, the trick is to always look for ways to achieve great improvements in service quality and efficiency at the same time. This is something Wirtz and Heracleous termed *cost-effective service excellence*. The Internet has, in the past, allowed many firms to do just that. It has changed industries including financial services, book and music retailing, and travel agencies. Biometrics may be the next major technology driving further service and productivity improvements in the service sector.

Biometrics is the identification of individuals based on a physical characteristic or trait. Physical characteristics include fingerprints, facial recognition, hand geometry, and the structure of the iris. Traits include signature formation, keystroke patterns and voice recognition. Biometrics, as something you are, is both more convenient and safer than something you know (passwords or pieces of personal information) or something you have (card keys, smart cards, or tokens). There is no risk of forgetting, losing, copying, loaning, or getting your biometrics stolen (Figure 14.17).

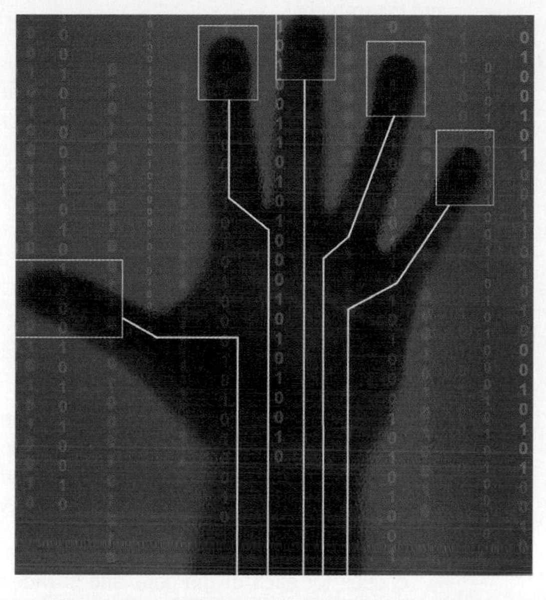

Figure 14.17 Customers cannot forget or lose their biometrics!

Applications of biometrics range from controlling access to service facilities (used by Disney World to provide access to season pass holders), voice recognition at call centers (used by the Home Shopping Network and Charles Schwab to enable fast and hassle-free client authentication), self-service access to safe deposit vaults at banks (used by the Bank of Hawaii and First Tennessee Bank), and cashing checks in supermarkets (used by Kroger, Food 4 Less, and BI-LO).

Biometrics are currently in use in various industries. In the healthcare industry, they are used to protect the medical records of patients. In the finance industry, biometrics are used for authentication for transactions. Schools use it for library book issue, or for debit of catering accounts based on the child's finger scan. The use of biometrics will become increasing more prevalent.

SOURCES

Jochen Wirtz and Loizos Heracleous, "Biometrics Meets Services," *Harvard Business Review*, February 2005, 48–49; Loizos Heracleous and Jochen Wirtz, "Biometrics—The Next Frontier in Service Excellence, Productivity and Security in the Service Sector," *Managing Service Quality* 16, no. 1 (2006): Catherine J Tilton, "The Role of Biometrics in Enterprise Security, " *Dell Power Solutions*, 2006, www.dell.com/powersolutions; http://en.wikipedia.org/wiki/Biometrics_in_schools, accessed March 12, 2012.

CHAPTER SUMMARY

LO 1 ▶ Quality and productivity are twin paths for creating value for customers and the firm. Quality focuses on the benefits created for customers, and productivity affects the financial costs to the firm.

LO 2 ▶ Customers' perceived service quality consists of five main dimensions: (1) tangibles, (2) reliability, (3) responsiveness, (4) assurance, and (5) empathy.

LO3 ▶ The gaps model is an important tool to diagnose and address service quality problems. We identified six gaps that can be the cause of quality shortfalls:

- Gap 1—the knowledge gap.
- Gap 2—the policy gap.
- Gap 3—the delivery gap.
- Gap 4—the communications gap.
- Gap 5—the perceptions gap.
- Gap 6—the service quality gap. It is the most important gap. In order to close Gap 6, the other five gaps have to be closed first.
- We summarized a series of potential causes for each of the gaps and provided generic prescriptions for addressing the causes and thereby closing the gaps.

LO 4 ▶ There are both soft and hard measures of service quality. *Soft measures* are usually based on perceptions of and feedback from customers and employees. *Hard measures* relate to processes and their outcomes.

LO 5 ▶ Feedback from customers (i.e., mostly soft measures) should be systematically collected via a *customer feedback system* (CFS). The key objectives of a CFS are:

- Assessment and benchmarking of service quality and performance.
- Customer-driven learning and improvement.
- Creating a customer-oriented service culture.

LO 6 ▶ Firms can use a variety of tools to collect customer feedback, including (1) total market surveys, (2) annual surveys on overall satisfaction, (3) transactional surveys, (4) service feedback cards, (5) mystery shopping, (6) unsolicited customer feedback (e.g., compliments and complaints), (7) focus group discussions, and (8) service reviews.

▶ A reporting system is needed to channel feedback and its analysis to the relevant parties to take action.

LO 7 ▶ *Hard measures* relate to operational processes and outcomes and can be counted, timed, or observed. *Control charts* are a simple method of displaying performance on hard measures over time against specific quality standards.

LO 8 ▶ Key tools to analyze and address important service quality problems are:

- *Fishbone diagrams* to identify the causes of quality problems.
- *Pareto analysis* to assess the frequency of quality problems and identify the most common causes.
- *Blueprinting* to exactly determine the location of fail points in a customer service process and then help to redesign the process.

LO 9 ▶ There are financial implications of service quality improvements. A *return on quality* (*ROQ*) approach assesses the costs and benefits of specific quality initiatives.

LO10 ▶ Besides quality, productivity is another important path to increase value.

LO 11 ▶ It is important to differentiate these three concepts:

- *Productivity* involves the amount of outputs based on a given level of inputs (e.g. input/output ratio).
- *Efficiency* involves is usually time based and compared to a standard such as industry average (e.g. speed of delivery).
- *Effectiveness* refers to the degree a goal, such as customer satisfaction, is met.

Productivity and efficiency cannot be separated from effectiveness. Firms that strive to be more productive, efficient, and effective in consistently delivering customer satisfaction will be more successful.

LO 12 ▶ Generic methods to improve productivity include (1) cost control; (2) reduction of waste of materials and labor; (3) training employees to work more productively; (4) providing employees with equipment and information that will enable them to work faster and better; (5) broadening the job scope of employees to reduce bottlenecks and downtime; (6) using expert systems so that paraprofessionals can do the work previously done by higher-paid experts.

▶ Customer-driven methods to improve productivity include (1) changing the timing of customer demand to better match capacity to demand; (2) encouraging the use of lower-cost service delivery channels and replacing labor with machines and SSTs; and (3) getting customers to use third parties for parts of the service delivery.

LO 13 ▶ When improvements are made to productivity, firms need to bear in mind that both front-stage and backstage improvements can have an impact on service quality and the customer experience.

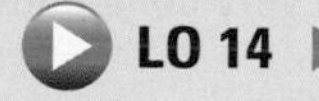

LO 14 ▶ TQM, ISO 9000, Malcolm-Baldrige Approach, and Six Sigma are systematic and often complementary approaches to managing and improving service quality and productivity.

PART V

UNLOCK YOUR LEARNING

These keywords are found within the sections of each Learning Objective (LO). They are integral to understanding the services marketing concepts taught in each section. Having a firm grasp of these keywords and how they are used is essential to helping you do well on your course, and in the real and very competitive marketing scene out there.

LO 1
1 Intangible
2 Productivity
3 Service quality

LO 2
4 Access
5 Assurance
6 Communication
7 Competence
8 Courtesy
9 Credibility
10 Empathy
11 Reliability
12 Responsiveness
13 Security
14 Tangibles

LO 3
15 Close the gaps
16 Communications gap
17 Delivery gap
18 Knowledge gap
19 Perceptions gap
20 Policy gap
21 Service gap

LO 4
22 Hard measures
23 Hard standards
24 Soft measures
25 Soft standards

LO 5
26 Assessment
27 Benchmarking
28 Customer feedback systems
29 Customer-driven improvements
30 Customer-driven learning
31 Customer-oriented service culture

LO 6
32 Annual surveys
33 Customer feedback collection tools
34 Feedback loop
35 Focus group discussion
36 Mystery shopping
37 Service feedback cards
38 Service performance report
39 Service performance review
40 Service performance update
41 Service reviews
42 Total market surveys
43 Transactional surveys
44 Unsolicited customer feedback

LO 7
45 Hard measures
46 Operational processes
47 Service quality
48 Service quality index (SQI)

LO 8
49 Blueprinting
50 Cause-and-effect analysis
51 Fishbone diagram
52 Pareto analysis
53 Return on quality
54 Root cause analysis
55 Service quality problems

LO 9
56 Assess benefits
57 Assess costs
58 Quality improvement
59 Quality initiatives
60 Return on quality
61 Service reliability

LO 10
62 Defining productivity
63 Input
64 Measuring productivity
65 People-processing services
66 Possession-processing services

 **LO 11**

67 Effectiveness
68 Efficiency
69 Financial value
70 Productivity
71 Time-based

 **LO 12**

72 Customer demand
73 Customer-driven approaches
74 Productivity improvement strategies
75 Self-service
76 Service delivery channels
77 Service process redesign

 **LO 13**

78 Backstage
79 Biometrics
80 Cost-reduction strategies
81 Front-stage
82 Service productivity improvements

 **APPENDICES**

83 SERVQUAL
84 DMAIC
85 ISO 9000
86 Malcolm-Baldrige Model
87 Six Sigma
88 Total Quality Management

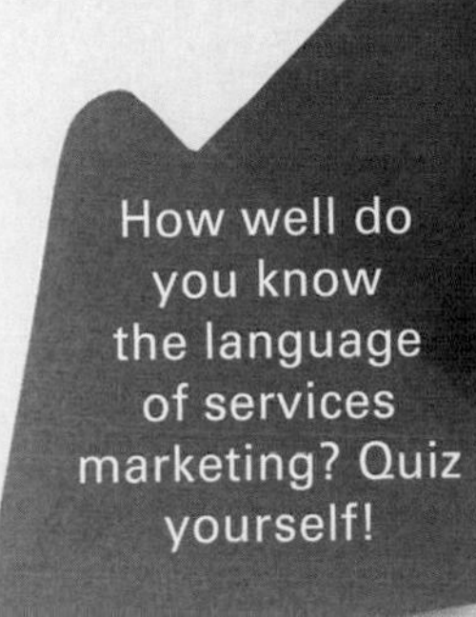

 **Not for the academically faint-of-heart**

For each keyword you are able to recall without referring to earlier pages, give yourself a point (and a pat on the back). Tally your score at the end and see if you earned the right to be called—a *services marketeer.*

SCORE

0 – 18 Services Marketing is done a great disservice.
19 – 34 The midnight oil needs to be lit, pronto.
35 – 50 I know what you *didn't* do all semester.
51 – 66 By George! You're getting there.
67 – 83 Now, go forth and market.
84 – 88 There should be a marketing concept named after you.

PART V

KNOW YOUR ESM

Review Questions

1. Explain the relationships between service quality, productivity, and profitability.
2. Identify the gaps that can occur in service quality, and the steps that service marketers can take to prevent them.
3. Why are both soft and hard measures of service quality needed?
4. What are the main objectives of an effective customer feedback system?
5. What are the key customer feedback collection tools? What are the strengths and weaknesses of each of these tools?
6. What are the main tools service firms can use to analyze and address service quality problems?
7. Why is productivity more difficult to measure in service than in manufacturing firms?
8. What are the key tools for improving service productivity?
9. How do concepts such as TQM, ISO 9000, Malcolm-Baldrige Approach, and Six Sigma relate to managing and improving service quality and productivity? (Refer to Appendix 14.3.)

WORK YOUR ESM

Application Exercises

1. Review the five dimensions of service quality. What do they mean in the context of (a) an industrial repair shop, (b) a retail bank, (c) a Big 4 accounting firm?
2. How would you define "excellent service quality" for an inquiry/information service provided by your cable or electricity company? Call a service organization, go through a service experience, and evaluate it against your definition of "excellence."
3. Collect a few customer feedback forms and tools (customer feedback cards, questionnaires, and online forms), and explain how the information gathered with those tools can be used to achieve the main objectives of effective customer feedback systems.
4. Consider your own recent experiences as a service consumer. On which dimensions of service quality have you most often experienced a large gap between your expectations and your perceptions of the service performance? What do you think the underlying causes might be? What steps should management take to improve quality?
5. In what ways can you, as a consumer, help to improve productivity for at least three service organizations that you patronize? What distinctive characteristics of each service make some of these actions possible?
6. Do a literature search, and identify the critical factors for a successful implementation of ISO 9000, the Malcolm-Baldrige Model, and Six Sigma in service firms. (Refer to Appendix 14.3).

APPENDIX 14.1

MEASURING SERVICE QUALITY USING SERVQUAL

To measure customer satisfaction with various aspects of service quality, Valarie Zeithaml and her colleagues developed a survey instrument called SERVQUAL.[22] It's based on the premise that customers can evaluate a firm's service quality by comparing their perceptions of its service with their own expectations. SERVQUAL is seen as a generic measurement tool that can be applied across a broad spectrum of service industries.

In its basic form, the scale contains 21 perception items and a series of expectation items, reflecting the five dimensions of service quality described in Table 14.5. Respondents complete a series of scales that measure their expectations of companies in a particular industry on a wide array of specific service characteristics. Subsequently, they are asked to record their perceptions of a specific company whose services they have used. When perceived performance ratings are lower than expectations, this is a sign of poor quality. The reverse indicates good quality.

Limitations of SERVQUAL

SERVQUAL is widely used, but there are a number of limitations of this measure.[23] Therefore, the majority of researchers using SERVQUAL omits from, adds to, or changes the list of statements purporting to measure service quality. Other research suggests that SERVQUAL mainly measures two factors: intrinsic service quality (resembling what Grönroos termed "functional quality") and extrinsic service quality (which refers to the tangible aspects of service delivery and resembles to what Grönroos referred to as technical quality").[24]

These different findings don't undermine the value of Zeithaml, Berry, and Parasuraman's achievement in identifying some of the key underlying constructs in service quality. Rather, they highlight the difficulty of measuring customer perceptions of quality and the need to customize dimensions and measures to the research context.

Table 14.5 The SERVQUAL scale

The SERVQUAL scale includes five dimensions: tangibles, reliability, responsiveness, assurance, and empathy. Within each dimension, several items are measured on a seven-point scale, from strongly agree to strongly disagree, for a total of 21 items.

SERVQUAL Questions

Note: For actual survey respondents, instructions are also included, and each statement is accompanied by a seven-point scale ranging from "strongly agree = 7" to "strongly disagree = 1." Only the end points of the scale are labeled. There are no words above the numbers 2 through 6.

Tangibles

- Excellent banks (refer to cable TV companies, hospitals, or the appropriate service business throughout the questionnaire) will have modern-looking equipment.
- The physical facilities at excellent banks will be visually appealing.
- Employees at excellent banks will be neat in appearance.
- Materials (e.g. brochures or statements) associated with the service will be visually appealing in an excellent bank.

Reliability

- When excellent banks promise to do something by a certain time, they will do so.
- When customers have a problem, excellent banks will show a sincere interest in solving it.
- Excellent banks will perform the service right the first time.
- Excellent banks will provide their services at the time they promise to do so.
- Excellent banks will insist on error-free records.

Responsiveness

- Employees of excellent banks will tell customers exactly when service will be performed.
- Employees of excellent banks will give prompt service to customers.
- Employees of excellent banks will always be willing to help customers.
- Employees of excellent banks will never be too busy to respond to customer requests.

Assurance

- The behavior of employees of excellent banks will instill confidence in customers.
- Customers of excellent banks will feel safe in their transactions.
- Employees of excellent banks will be consistently courteous with customers.
- Employees of excellent banks will have the knowledge to answer customer questions.

Empathy

- Excellent banks will give customers individual attention.
- Excellent banks will have operating hours convenient to all their customers.
- Excellent banks will have employees who give customers personal attention.
- The employees of excellent banks will understand the specific needs of their customers.

SOURCE

Adapted from Parasuraman, A., Zeithaml, V. A., and Berry, L. "SERVQUAL: A Multiple Item Scale for Measuring Consumer Perceptions of Service Quality," *Journal of Retailing* 64, (1988): 12–40.

APPENDIX 14.2

MEASURING SERVICE QUALITY IN ONLINE ENVIRONMENTS

SERVQUAL was developed to measure service quality mostly in a face-to-face service encounter context. However, in today's online environment, different service quality dimensions with new measurement items become relevant (Figure 14.18).

To measure electronic service quality on websites, Parasuraman, Zeithaml, and Malhotra created a 22-item scale called E-S-QUAL, reflecting the four key dimensions of *efficiency* (Is navigation easy? Can transactions be completed quickly? Does the website load quickly?), *system availability* (i.e., Is the site always available? Does it launch right away? Is it stable and does not crash?), *fulfillment* (i.e., are orders delivered as promised? And offerings are described truthfully?), and *privacy* (i.e., Is information privacy is protected and personal information not shared with other sites?).[25] Service Insights 14.5 offers the latest perspectives on this topic and addresses the challenge of integrating service quality measures across both virtual and physical channels.

Figure 14.18 When commitment and constant improvement meet head-on the challenge of changing markets, technologies and environments, success becomes a clearer picture.

SERVICE INSIGHTS 14.5

New Thinking on Defining and Measuring E-Service Quality

"To managers of companies with a Web presence," say Joel Collier and Carol Bienstock, "an awareness of how customers perceive service quality is essential to understanding what [they] value in an online service transaction." E-service quality involves more than just interactions with a website (described as process quality). It extends to include outcome quality and recovery quality, and each must be measured. The separation of customers from providers during online transactions highlights the importance of evaluating how well a firm handles customers' questions, concerns, and frustrations when problems arise.

- **Process quality.** Customers initially evaluate their experiences with an e-retailing website against five process quality dimensions: *privacy*, *design*, *information*, *ease of use*, and *functionality*. This last construct refers to quick page loads, links that don't lead to dead ends, a variety of payment options, accurate execution of customer commands, and ability to appeal to a universal audience (including the disabled and those who speak other languages).
- **Outcome quality.** Customers' evaluations of process quality have a significant effect on their evaluation of outcome quality, made up of *order timeliness*, *order accuracy*, and *order condition*.
- **Recovery quality.** In the event of a problem, customers evaluate the recovery process against *interactive fairness* (ability to locate and interact with technology support for a website, including telephone-based assistance), *procedural fairness* (policies, procedures, and responsiveness in the complaint process), and *outcome fairness*. How the company responds has a significant effect on the customer's satisfaction level and future intentions.

Multi-channel Issues

Going one step further, Rui Sousa and Christopher Voss note that many services offer customers a choice of both virtual and physical delivery channels. Customers' evaluations of service quality are formed across all points of contact they have with the firm. In a multi-channel setting, researchers must measure *physical quality*, *virtual quality*, and *integration quality*—the ability to provide customers with a seamless service experience across multiple channels. Achieving consistency across such interactions is particularly relevant when a firm adds new virtual channels, accompanied by specialist support systems that often are poorly integrated with existing systems. To avoid such fragmentation and achieve consistent service quality, Sousa and Voss call for explicit links between the firm's marketing and operations functions.

SOURCES

Joel E. Collier and Carol C. Bienstock, "Measuring Service Quality in E-Retailing," *Journal of Service Research* 8, (February 2006): 260–275; Rui Sousa and Christopher A. Voss, "Service Quality in Multichannel Services Employing Virtual Channels," *Journal of Service Research* 8, (May 2006): 356–371.

APPENDIX 14.3

SYSTEMATIC APPROACHES TO QUALITY AND PRODUCTIVITY IMPROVEMENT AND PROCESS STANDARDIZATION

LO 14

Explain how TQM, ISO 9000, the Malcolm-Baldrige Approach, and Six Sigma relate to managing and improving service quality and productivity.

Many of the thinking, tools, and concepts introduced in Chapter 14 originate from Total Quality Management (TQM), ISO 9000, Six Sigma, and the Malcolm-Baldrige Model. We discuss each of these approaches and relate them back to the service quality and productivity context in the following sections.

Total Quality Management

Total Quality Management (TQM) concepts were originally developed in Japan. They are widely used in manufacturing and more recently in service firms, including educational institutions (see Service Insights 14.6). TQM can help organizations to attain service excellence, increase the productivity of service delivery processes, and be a continued source of value creation through the feeding of innovative processes for the firm.[26]

Some concepts and tools of TQM can be directly applied to services. As discussed in this chapter, TQM tools such as control charts, flow charts, and fishbone diagrams are being used by service firms with great results for monitoring service quality and determining the root causes of specific problems.

Sureshchander *et al.* identified 12 critical dimensions for successful implementation of TQM in a service context: (1) top management commitment and visionary leadership; (2) human resource management; (3) technical system, including service process design and process management; (4) information and analysis system; (5) benchmarking; (6) continuous improvement; (7) customer focus; (8) employee satisfaction; (9) union intervention and employee relations; (10) social responsibility; (11) servicescapes; and (12) service culture.[27]

ISO 9000 Certification

There are 162 countries that are members of the International Organization for Standardization (ISO) based in Geneva, Switzerland, that promotes standardization and quality to facilitate international trade. ISO 9000 comprises requirements, definitions, guidelines, and related standards to provide an independent assessment and certification of a firm's quality management system. The official ISO 9000 definition of quality is: "The totality of features and characteristics of a product or service that bear on its ability to satisfy a stated or implied need. Simply stated, quality is about meeting or exceeding your customer's needs and requirements." To ensure quality, ISO 9000 uses many TQM tools and internalizes their use in participating firms.

SERVICE INSIGHTS 14.6

TQM in Educational Institutions

Higher educational institutions are increasingly competing for talented students and have started to accept that they have to be more customer centric in their approach to increase student satisfaction. What is the meaning of service quality in a higher educational institution? Sakthivel, Rajendran, and Raju proposed a TQM model with five variables that measure different dimensions of service quality in an institution of higher learning, and they suggest that these variables will increase student satisfaction.

- **Commitment of top management.** Top management has to "walk the talk" and make sure that what is preached in terms of educational excellence and service quality is really being practiced.
- **Course delivery.** While institutions of higher learning hire people with expert knowledge, there is a need for such expert knowledge to be transmitted expertly, with passion.
- **Campus facilities.** Attention needs to be focused on having excellent infrastructure and facilities for student learning as well as for their extracurricular activities. These facilities also have to be properly maintained.
- **Courtesy.** This is a positive attitude toward students that will create a friendly learning environment.
- **Customer feedback and improvement.** Continuous feedback from students can lead to improvements.

The researchers studied engineering students from a mix of ISO-certified and non-ISO certified institutions, and found that ISO 9001:2000 certified institutions were adopting TQM faster and offered a better quality education than non-ISO certified institutions.

Furthermore, their findings showed that while all five variables together did predict student satisfaction, two variables in particular were more important in affecting student satisfaction. The variables were commitment of top management and campus facilities. Top management needs to be committed to quality assurance in making sure the other variables are in place to improve the student experience.

Figure 14.19 Higher learning increasingly focus on service quality and TQM.

SOURCE

P. B. Sakthivel, G. Rajendran, and R. Raju, "TQM Implementation and Students' Satisfaction of Academic Performance," *The TQM Magazine* 17, no. 6 (2005): 573–589.

Service firms generally adopted ISO 9000 standards later than manufacturing firms did. Major service sectors that have adopted ISO 9000 certification include wholesale and retail firms, IT service providers, health-care providers, consultancy firms, and educational institutions. By adopting ISO 9000 standards, service firms, especially small ones, can not only ensure that their services conform to customer expectations but also achieve improvements in productivity.

Malcolm—Baldrige Model

The Malcolm—Baldrige National Quality Award (MBNQA) was developed by the National Institute of Standards and Technology (NIST) with the goal of promoting best practices in quality management and recognizing and publicizing quality achievements among US firms. Countries other than the United States have similar quality awards that follow the MBNQA model.

The framework is generic and does not distinguish between manufacturing and service organizations, but the award has a specific service category, and the model can be used to create a culture of ongoing service improvements. Major services firms that have won the award include Ritz-Carlton, FedEx, the University of Wisconsin, Xerox Business Services, Boeing Aerospace Support, Caterpillar Financial Services Corp., and AT&T. Research has confirmed that employing this framework can improve organizational performance.[28]

The Malcolm—Baldrige Model assesses firms on seven areas:

1) Leadership commitment to a service quality culture.
2) Planning priorities for improvement, including service standards, performance targets, and measurement of customer satisfaction, defects, cycle time, and productivity.
3) Information and analysis that will aid the organization to collect, measure, analyze, and report strategic and operational indicators.
4) Human resources management that enables the firm to deliver service excellence, ranging from hiring the right people, to development, involvement, empowerment, and motivation.
5) Process management, including monitoring, continuous improvement, and process redesign.
6) Customer and market focus that allows the firm to determine customer requirements and expectations.
7) Business results.[29]

Six Sigma

The Six Sigma approach was originally developed by Motorola to improve product quality and reduce warranty claims, and was soon adopted by other manufacturing firms to reduce defects in a variety of areas.

Subsequently, service firms embraced various Six Sigma strategies to reduce defects, reduce cycle times, and improve productivity.[30] As early as 1990, GE Capital applied

PART V

Six Sigma methodology to reduce the backroom costs of selling consumer loans, credit card insurance, and payment protection. Its president and CEO Denis Nayden said,

> Although Six Sigma was originally designed for manufacturing, it can be applied to transactional services. One obvious example is in making sure the millions of credit card and other bills GE sends to customer are correct, which drives down our costs of making adjustments. One of our biggest costs in the financial business is winning new customers. If we treat them well, they will stay with us, reducing our customer-origination costs.[31]

Statistically, Six Sigma means achieving a quality level of only 3.4 defects per million opportunities (DPMO). To understand how stringent this target is, consider mail deliveries. If a mail service delivers with 99% accuracy, it misses 3,000 items out of 300,000 deliveries. But if it achieves a Six Sigma performance level, only one item out of this total will go astray.

Over time, Six Sigma has evolved from a defect reduction approach to an overall business improvement approach. As defined by Pande, Neuman, and Cavanagh:

> Six Sigma is a comprehensive and flexible system for achieving, sustaining and maximizing business success. Six Sigma is uniquely driven by close understanding of customer needs, disciplined use of facts, data, and statistical analysis, and diligent attention to managing, improving, and reinventing business processes.[32]

Process improvement and process design/redesign are two strategies that form the cornerstone of the Six Sigma approach. Process improvement strategies aim to identify and eliminate the root causes of the service delivery problems, thereby improving service quality. Process design/redesign strategies act as a supplementary strategy to improvement strategy. If a root cause can't be identified or effectively eliminated within the existing processes, either new processes are *designed* or existing process are *redesigned* to fully or partially address the problem.

The most popular Six Sigma improvement model for analyzing and improving business processes is the DMAIC model, shown in Table 14.6. DMAIC stands for:

- **D**efine the opportunities.
- **M**easure key steps/inputs.
- **A**nalyze to identify root causes.
- **I**mprove performance.
- **C**ontrol to maintain performance.

Which Approach Should a Firm Adopt?

As there are various approaches to systematically improving a service firm's service quality and productivity, the question arises as to which approach should be adopted—TQM, ISO 9000, the Malcolm-Baldrige model, or Six Sigma. TQM can be applied at differing levels of complexity, and basic tools such as flowcharting,

Table 14.6 Applying the DMAIC model to process improvement and redesign

	Process Improvement	Process Design/Redesign
Define	• Identify the problem • Define requirements • Set goals	• Identify specific or broad problems • Define goal/change vision • Clarify scope and customer requirements
Measure	• Validate problem/process • Refine problem/ goal • Measure key steps/inputs	• Measure performance to requirements • Gather process efficiency data
Analyze	• Develop causal hypothesis • Identify root causes • Validate hypothesis	• Identify best practices • Assess process design • Refine requirements
Improve	• Develop ideas to measure root causes • Test solutions • Measure results	• Design new process • Implements new process, structures and systems
Control	• Establish measures to maintain performance • Correct problems as needed	• Establish measures and reviews to maintain performance • Correct problems as needed

SOURCE

Reproduced from Pande, P., Neuman, R. P., and Cavanagh, R. R. (2000). *The Six Sigma Way*. New York: McGraw-Hill.

frequency charts, and fishbone diagrams probably should be adopted by any type of service firm. ISO 9000 seems to suit the next level of commitment and complexity, followed by the Malcolm—Baldrige Model, and finally Six Sigma. While these are the traditional approaches, there are also other approaches that are not traditionally used, including Japanese-quality systems such as *Kansei* engineering and Quality Function Deployment that can help to incorporate the voice of the customer into a firm's service design to improve service quality.[33]

Any one of the approaches can be a useful framework for understanding customer needs, analyzing processes, and improving service quality and productivity. Firms can choose a particular program, depending on their own needs and desired level of sophistication. Each program has its own strengths, and firms can use more than one program to add on to the other. For example, the ISO 9000 program can be used for standardizing the procedures and process documentation, and then the Six Sigma and Malcolm—Baldrige programs can be used to improve processes and to focus on performance improvement across the organization.

A key success factor of any of these programs depends on how well the particular quality improvement program is part of the overall business strategy. Firms that implement one of these programs due to peer pressure or just as a marketing tool will be less likely to succeed than firms that view these programs as important development tools.[34] Service champions make best practices in service quality management a core part of their organizational culture.[35]

The National Institute of Standards and Technology (NIST), which organizes the Malcolm-Baldrige Award program, has an index called the "Baldrige Index" of Malcolm-Baldrige Award winners. It was observed that winners always outperformed the S&P 500 index.[36] Sadly, Motorola, a two-time winner of the award, has been suffering financially and losing market share partly due to the firm's failure to keep up with new technology. Clearly, success cannot be taken for granted. Commitment and constant improvement that follow changing markets, technologies, and environments are keys for sustained success.

ENDNOTES

1 Adapted from Audrey Gilmore, "Service Marketing Management Competencies: A Ferry Company Example," *International Journal of Service Industry Management* 9, no. 1 (1998): 74–92, www.stenaline.com, accessed March 12, 2012.

2 Valarie A. Zeithaml, A. Parasuraman, and Leonard L. Berry, *Delivering Quality Service*. New York: The Free Press, 1990.

3 A. Parasuraman, Valarie A. Zeithaml, and Leonard L. Berry, "A Conceptual Model of Service Quality and Its Implications for Future Research," *Journal of Marketing* 49, (Fall 1985): 41–50; Valarie A. Zeithaml, Leonard L. Berry, and A. Parasuraman, "Communication and Control Processes in the Delivery of Services," *Journal of Marketing* 52, (April 1988): 36–58.

4 The subgaps in this model are based on the seven-gap model by Christopher Lovelock, Product Plus, New York: McGraw-Hill, 1994: 112.

5 Valarie A. Zeithaml, Mary Jo Bitner, and Dwayne D. Gremler, *Services Marketing: Integrating Customer Focus across the Firm 5/E*, New York: McGraw-Hill, 2009, 297.

6 This section is based partially on Jochen Wirtz and Monica Tomlin, "Institutionalizing Customer-driven Learning through Fully Integrated Customer Feedback Systems," *Managing Service Quality* 10, no. 4 (2000): 205–215. Additional reading on service quality measurement can be found in Ching-Chow Yang, "Establishment and Applications of the Integrated Model of Service Quality Measurement," *Managing Service Quality* 13, no. 4 (2003): 310–324.

7 Leonard L. Berry and A. Parasuraman, "Listening to the Customer—The Concept of a Service Quality Information System," *Sloan Management Review* 38, (Spring 1997): 65–76.

8 Customer listening practices have been shown to affect service performance, growth, and profitability. See William J. Glynn, Sean de Búrca, Teresa Brannick, Brian Fynes, and Sean Ennis, "Listening Practices and Performance in Service Organizations," *International Journal of Service Industry Management* 14, no. 3 (2003): 310–330.

9 Baker W. E. and Sinkula J. M., "The Synergistic Effect of Market Orientation and Learning Orientation on Organizational Performance," *Journal of the Academy of Marketing Science* 27, no. 4 (1999): 411–427.

10 Neil A. Morgan, Eugene W. Anderson, and Vikas Mittal, "Understanding Firms' Customer Satisfaction Information Usage," *Journal of Marketing* 69, (July 2005): 131–151.

11 For reading on customer feedback online tools, refer to Robert A. Opoku, "Gathering Customer Feedback Online and Swedish SMEs," *Management Research News* 29, no. 3 (2006): 106–127.

12 Leonard L. Berry and A. Parasuraman provide an excellent overview of all key research approaches discussed in this section plus a number of other tools in their paper, "Listening to the Customer – The Concept of a Service Quality Information System," *Sloan Management Review* 38, (Spring 1997): 65–76.

13 For a discussion on suitable satisfaction measures, see Jochen Wirtz and Lee Meng Chung, "An Examination of the Quality and Context-Specific Applicability of Commonly Used Customer Satisfaction Measures," *Journal of Service Research* 5, (May 2003): 345–355.

14 Note that feedback provided to the firm is very different to that posted publicly. For example, one business owner had the opportunity to meet members of an online community who had given his restaurant only mediocre ratings. To his surprise, he found that the reviewers were not in the same segment as his customer base, and even though they liked his food, they downgraded his restaurant as they felt the price was too high. It turned out that price was the issue as the reviewers were less affluent then their normal customers. See: Duncan Simester, "When You Shouldn't Listen to Your Critics," *Harvard Business Review*, June 2011: 42. Hence, this shows that online reviews are not reliable because we do not know if the people who are rating the restaurant are even the same as the target customer, and using the same yardsticks. In fact, we are not even sure whether the person was hired by the company to provide the feedback. Hence, it is

sometimes difficult to find out whether publicly posted feedback and ratings are legitimate. Yet, customers in the market do look at the feedback in online reviews to make their purchasing decisions. See: Raymond R. Liu and Wei Zhang, "Informational Influence of Online Customer Feedback: An Empirical Study," *Database Marketing and Customer Strategy Management* 17, no. 2 (2010): 120–131.

15 Robert Johnston and Sandy Mehra, "Best-practice Complaint Management," *Academy of Management Executive* 16, no. 4 (2002): 145–154.

16 Comments by Thomas R. Oliver, then senior vice president, sales and customer service, Federal Express; reported in Christopher H. Lovelock, *Federal Express: Quality Improvement Program*. Lausanne: International Institute for Management Development, 1990.

17 Christopher Lovelock, *Product Plus: How Product + Service = Competitive Advantage*. New York: McGraw-Hill, 1994, 218.

18 These categories and the research data that follow have been adapted from information in D. Daryl Wyckoff, "New Tools for Achieving Service Quality," *Cornell Hotel and Restaurant Administration Quarterly* (August-September 2001), 25–38.

19 Roland T. Rust, Anthony J. Zahonik, and Timothy L. Keiningham, "Return on Quality (ROQ): Making Service Quality Financially Accountable," *Journal of Marketing* 59 (April 1995): 58-70; and Roland T. Rust, Christine Moorman, and Peter R. Dickson, "Getting Return on Quality: Revenue Expansion, Cost Reduction, or Both?" *Journal of Marketing* 66 (October 2002): 7–24.

20 Kenneth J. Klassen, Randolph M. Russell, and James J. Chrisman, "Efficiency and Productivity Measures for High Contact Services," *The Service Industries Journal* 18 (October 1998): 1–18; James L. Heskett, *Managing in the Service Economy*. New York: The Free Press, 1986.

21 For a more in-depth discussion on service productivity, refer to Cynthia Karen Swank, "The Lean Service Machine," *Harvard Business Review* 81, no. 10 (2003): 123–129.

22 A. Parasuraman, Valarie A. Zeithaml, and Leonard Berry, "SERVQUAL: A Multiple Item Scale for Measuring Consumer Perceptions of Service Quality," *Journal of Retailing* 64, (1988): 12–40.

23 See, for instance, Francis Buttle, "SERVQUAL: Review, Critique, Research Agenda," *European Journal of Marketing* 30, no. 1 (1996): 8–32; Simon S. K. Lam and Ka Shing Woo, "Measuring Service Quality: A Test-Retest Reliability Investigation of SERVQUAL," *Journal of the Market Research Society* 39, (April 1997): 381–393; Terrence H. Witkowski and Mary F. Wolfinbarger, "Comparative Service Quality: German and American Ratings Across Service Settings," *Journal of Business Research* 55, (2002): 875–881; Lisa J. Morrison Coulthard, "Measuring Service Quality: A Review and Critique of Research Using SERVQUAL," *International Journal of Market Research* 46, Quarter 4, (2004): 479–497.

24 Gerhard Mels, Christo Boshoff, and Denon Nel, "The Dimensions of Service Quality: The Original European Perspective Revisited," *The Service Industries Journal* 17, (January 1997): 173–189.

25 A. Parasuraman, Valarie A. Zeithaml, and Arvind Malhotra, "E-S-QUAL: A Multiple-Item Scale for Assessing Electronic Service Quality," *Journal of Service Research* 7, no. 3 (2005): 213–233.

26 C. Mele and M. Colurcio, "The Evolving Path of TQM: Towards Business Excellence and Stakeholder Value," *International Journal of Quality and Reliability Management* 23, no. 5 (2006): 464–489; C. Mele, "The Synergic Relationship Between TQM and Marketing in Creating Customer Value," *Managing Service Quality* 17, no. 3 (2007): 240–258.

27 G. S. Sureshchandar, Chandrasekharan Rajendran, and R. N. Anantharaman, "A Holistic Model for Total Service Quality," *International Journal of Service Industry Management* 12, no. 4 (2001): 378–412.

28 Susan Meyer Goldstein and Sharon B. Schweikhart, "Empirical Support for the Baldrige Award Framework in US Hospitals," *Health Care Management Review* 27, no. 1 (2002): 62–75.

29 Allan Shirks, William B. Weeks, and Annie Stein, "Baldrige-Based Quality Awards: Veterans Health Administration's 3-Year Experience," *Quality Management in Health Care* 10, no. 3 (2002): 47–54; National Institute of Standards and Technology, "Baldrige FAQs," http://www.nist.gov/baldrige/about/baldrige_faqs.cfm, accessed March 12, 2012.

30 Jim Biolos, "Six Sigma Meets the Service Economy," *Harvard Business Review* 80, (November 2002): 3–5.

31 Mikel Harry and Richard Schroeder, *Six Sigma—The Breakthrough Management Strategy Revolutionizing the World's Top Corporations.* New York: Currency, 2000, 232.

32 Peter S. Pande, Robert P. Neuman, and Ronald R. Cavanagh, *The Six Sigma Way: How GE, Motorola, and Other Top Companies Are Honing their Performance.* New York: McGraw-Hill, 2000.

33 Marvin E. Gonzalez, Rene Dentiste Mueller, and Rhonda W. Mack, "An Alternative Approach in Service Quality: An e-banking Case Study," *The Quality Management Journal* 15, no. 1 (2008): 41–59.

34 Gavin Dick, Kevin Gallimore and Jane C. Brown, "ISO 9000 and Quality Emphasis: An Empirical study of Front-Room and Back Room Dominated Service Industries," *International Journal of Service Industry Management* 12, no. 2 (2001): 114–136; and Adrian Hughes and David N. Halsall, "Comparison of the 14 Deadly Diseases and the Business Excellence Model," *Total Quality Management* 13, no. 2 (2002): 255–263.

35 Cathy A. Enz and Judy A. Siguaw, "Best Practices in Service Quality," *Cornell Hotel and Restaurant Administration Quarterly* (October 2000): 20–29.

36 Eight NIST Stock Investment Study", (USA: Gaithersburg, National Institute of Standards and Technology, March 2002).

CHAPTER 15

organizing for SERVICE LEADERSHIP

LEARNING OBJECTIVES

By the end of this chapter, the reader should be able to:

- **LO 1** Understand the implications of the Service Profit Chain for service management.
- **LO 2** Appreciate that marketing, operations, and human resource management functions need to be closely integrated in service businesses, and understand how this can be achieved.
- **LO 3** Be familiar with the four levels of service performance.
- **LO 4** Understand what actions are required to move a service firm from being a service loser to rising as a service leader.
- **LO 5** Discuss the role of leaders in nurturing an effective service culture.
- **LO 6** Describe the qualities of leaders of the future.

OPENING VIGNETTE

Reinvention and Leadership at American Express

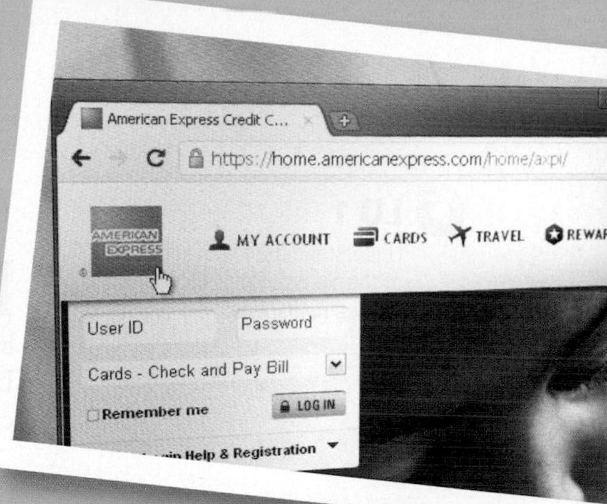

Figure 15.1 American Express offers travel and expense management solutions to customers.

"Frankly, you can't be a jerk in the service business and be successful for a long period of time," says Kenneth Chenault, CEO of American Express. "When you're in the service business, reputation is everything." However, he also cautions: "Sometimes when you are very successful, you become arrogant, and what I've tried to instill [here] is a very strong sense of customer needs [and] respect for your colleagues."

American Express, best known today as an icon in travel and financial services, has evolved through what it describes as "150 years of reinvention and customer service." Established in 1850 in New York, it was among the first and most successful express delivery firms created during the westward expansion of the United States. Its largest clients were banks. Delivering their small parcels—stock certificates, notes, currency, and other financial instruments—was much more profitable than transporting larger freight. As the railroads grew, the company focused less on its delivery business in favor of creating and selling its own financial products. It launched money orders in 1882 and the world's first traveler's checks in 1891. The American Express name became increasingly visible overseas, and offices were opened in Europe.

From the 1920s onward, the company focused on travel services, supported by selling traveler's checks and money orders (and profited from investing the substantial float on these products). The first American Express charge card was issued in 1958. This business grew rapidly and included both individual and corporate cardholders. Gold and platinum cards followed, offering extra features and privileges in return for a higher annual fee.

In an effort to diversify, American Express sought to create a "financial supermarket" through buying up other financial service firms. However, these acquisitions did not provide the anticipated returns and the company stumbled in the early 1990s. Meanwhile, its card business faced intense competition from Visa and MasterCard, on which merchants paid lower commission rates.

In 1991, a group of Boston restaurateurs, upset about high rates, staged a revolt nicknamed the Boston Fee Party, and refused to accept American Express cards. Other merchants joined them, both at home and abroad. Chenault, then a rising young executive, headed the successful effort to help achieve a peaceful solution and to reduce rates. Promoted to president and COO, he broadened the cards' appeal by offering new features and loyalty programs, creating new types of cards, and signing up mass market retailers, including Wal-Mart.

Soon after being named CEO in 2001, Chenault faced the challenge of helping the company recover from both the human trauma of seeing the World Trade Center destroyed across the street from the firm's headquarters and the sharp decline in travel that followed 9/11. Widely praised for his leadership, Chenault offered a road map designed to make the company leaner and able to respond faster to opportunities as the economy recovered. By 2005, he had completed the dismantling of the "financial supermarket" and refocused the business on its core activities of card services and travel, with operations in 130 countries. As a result, American Express fared comparatively well during the global financial crisis in 2009 through to 2012.

Chenault looks back at 2001 as "critical and fundamental to our company's success. It tested our management in incredible ways." Asked by a reporter to describe his leadership philosophy, he responded, "The role of a leader is to define reality and give hope."

SOURCE

Nelson D. Schwartz, "What's in the Cards for Amex?" *Fortune*, January 22, 2001, 58–70; Greg Farrell, "A CEO and a Gentleman," *USA Today*, April 25, 2005, 1B, 3B; "Our History. Becoming American Express: 150+ Years of Reinvention and Customer Service," home.americanexpress.com and http://home3.americanexpress.com/corp/os/history/circle.aspm, accessed March 12, 2012.

LO 1

Understand the implications of the Service Profit Chain for service management.

THE SERVICE PROFIT CHAIN

In our opening vignette, we see how a service leader like American Express reinvents itself with a focus on the changing customer needs. "Businesses succeed by getting, keeping, and growing customers," say respected consultants and authors Don Peppers and Martha Rogers.[1] Arguing that Wall Street's ongoing obsession with current-period revenue and earnings can actually destroy value, they declare:

> Investors today want executives to demonstrate that their companies can make money and grow, the old-fashioned way—by earning it from the value proposition they offer customers. They want a firm's customers to buy more, to buy more often, and to stay loyal longer. They want a firm to show that it can go out and get more customers....

Both employees and customers are equally important, and success in one area rubs off on the other. This is clearly shown in the Service Profit Chain model we will discuss next, where we pull in key lessons from earlier chapters, particularly those on managing employees, building customer loyalty, and improving service quality and productivity. We use these lessons to examine the challenging task of leading a service business that seeks to be customer focused and market oriented.

Important Links in the Service Profit Chain

James Heskett and his colleagues at Harvard argue that when service companies put employees and customers first, there is a big change in the way they manage and measure success. They relate profitability, customer loyalty, and customer satisfaction to the value created by satisfied, loyal, and productive employees:

> Top-level executives of outstanding service organizations spend little time setting profit goals or focusing on market share ... Instead, they understand that, in the new economics of service, frontline workers and customers need to be the center of management concern. Successful service managers pay attention to the factors that drive profitability ... investment in people, technology that supports frontline workers, revamped recruiting and training practices, and compensation linked to performance for employees at every level.
>
> The service-profit chain, developed from analyses of successful service organizations, puts "hard" values on "soft" measures. It helps managers target new investments to develop service and satisfaction levels for maximum competitive impact, widening the gap between service leaders and their merely good competitors.[2]

The Service Profit Chain, shown in Figure 15.2, shows the links in a managerial process that are proposed to lead to success in service businesses.

Table 15.1 provides a useful summary, highlighting the behaviors required of service leaders in order to manage their organizations effectively. Working backward from the desired end results of revenue growth and profitability, Links 1 and 2 focus on customers. The links include an emphasis on identifying and understanding customer needs, making investments to ensure customer retention, and having a commitment to adopt new performance measures that track such variables as satisfaction and

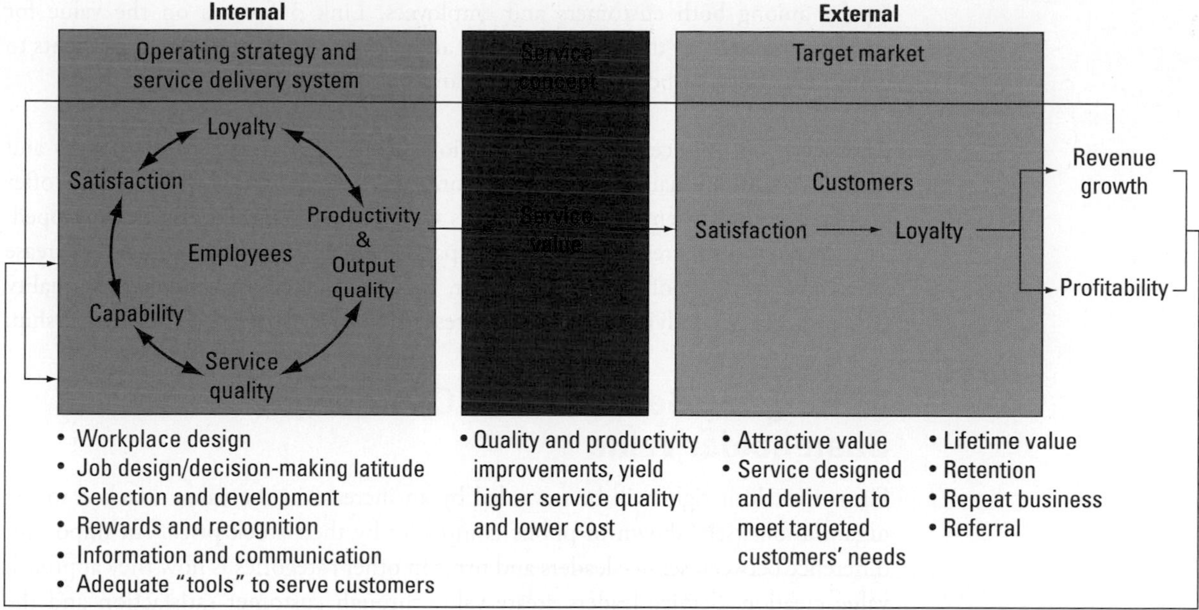

Figure 15.2 The service profit chain.

SOURCE

Reprinted by permission of *Harvard Business Review*. From Putting the service-profit chain to work. By J. L. Heskett, T. O. Jones, G. W. Loveman, W. E. Sasser Jr., and L. A. Schlesinger, (March–April), 166.

Table 15.1 Links in the service profit chain

Links in the Service Profit Chain
1. Customer loyalty drives profitability and growth.
2. Customer satisfaction drives customer loyalty.
3. Value drives customer satisfaction.
4. Quality and productivity drive value.
5. Employee loyalty drives service quality and productivity.
6. Employee satisfaction drives employee loyalty.
7. Internal quality drives employee satisfaction.
8. Top management leadership underlies the chain's success.

SOURCE

James L. Heskett *et al.*, "Putting the Service Profit Chain to Work," *Harvard Business Review*, March–April 1994; James L. Heskett, W. Earl Sasser, and Leonard L. Schlesinger, *The Service Profit Chain*, Boston: Harvard Business School Press, 1997.

loyalty among both customers and employees. Link 3 focuses on the value for customers created by the service concept, and highlights the need for investments to continually improve both service quality and productivity.

Another set of service leadership behaviors (Links 4–7) relate to employees and include organizational focus on the frontline. The design of jobs should offer greater freedom for employees. Managers with potential should also be developed. This category also stresses the idea that paying higher wages can actually decrease labor costs because of reduced turnover, higher productivity, and higher quality (Chapter 11). Underlying the chain's success (Link 8) is top management leadership.

Getting the Service Profit Chain Right Creates Shareholder Value

Firms that do it right will be rewarded by an increase in the value attached to the organization itself, shown in public companies by their stock price. An important difference between service leaders and firms in other categories is how they approach value creation. Service leaders create value through customer satisfaction and the relationships in the earlier parts of the Service Profit Chain. Nonleaders often aim to increase shareholder value through tactical measures to increase sales, short-term cost cutting, selected sell-offs, and taking advantage of financial market dynamics.

LO 2

Appreciate that marketing, operations, and human resource management functions need to be closely integrated in service businesses, and understand how this can be achieved.

INTEGRATING MARKETING, OPERATIONS, AND HUMAN RESOURCES

The relationships in the Service Profit Chain show that, in service firms, three management functions play very important and interrelated roles in meeting the needs of their customers: marketing, operations, and human resources (HR). Figure 15.3 shows how these departments depend on each other.

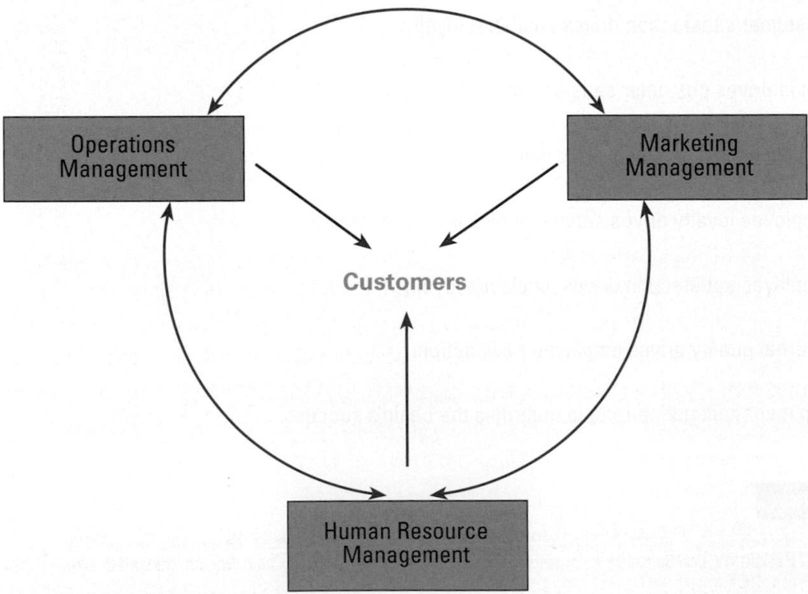

Figure 15.3 Marketing, operations, and human resources functions must collaborate to serve the customer.

How Are Marketing, Operations, and Human Resources Linked?

In what ways do the departments depend on each other? As we've seen, many service firms, especially those involving people-processing services, are actually "factories in the field." Customers enter when they need the service. When customers are actively involved in production and the service output is consumed as it is produced, the services marketing function depends on the procedures, personnel, and facilities managed by operations. In a high-contact service, the quality and commitment of the frontline have become a major source of competitive advantage. Service organizations cannot afford to have HR specialists who do not understand customers. When employees understand and support the goals of their organization, have the skills and training needed to succeed in their jobs, and recognize the importance of creating and maintaining customer satisfaction, both marketing and operations activities should be easier to manage.

Each of the three functions should have requirements and goals that relate to customers and contribute to the mission of the firm. They can be expressed generally as follows:

- **The marketing function.** To target the types of customers whom the firm is able to serve well and create ongoing relationships with. This can be achieved by delivering a carefully defined service product package in return for a price that offers value to customers and profits to the firm. Customers will recognize that this package is one of the qualities that deliver solutions to their needs and is better than that offered by other competing firms (Figure 15.4).
- **The operations function.** To create and deliver the service package to targeted customers. This is done by selecting those operational techniques that allow the firm to continuously meet customer-driven price, schedule, and quality goals. The techniques should also allow the business to reduce its costs through continuing improvements in productivity. The chosen operational methods will match skills that employees and intermediaries currently have or can be trained to develop. The firm will have the resources to support these operations with the necessary facilities, equipment, and technology (Figure 15.5). At the same time, the firm will avoid negative impacts on employees and the broader community.
- **The human resource function.** To recruit, train, and motivate frontline employees, service delivery team leaders, and managers who can work well together for a satisfactory pay package. These employees have to balance the twin goals of customer satisfaction and operational effectiveness. Employees will want to stay with the firm and to improve their own skills because they value the working environment, appreciate the challenges they face, and take pride in the services they help to create and deliver.

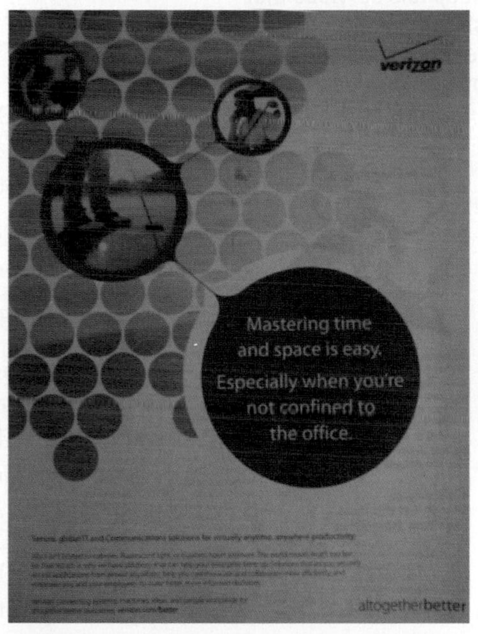

Figure 15.4 Verizon delivers solutions to companies that need to be productive virtually anytime, anywhere.

As service firms place more emphasis on developing a strong market orientation and serving customers well, there is increased potential for conflict among the three functions, especially between marketing and operations. How comfortably can the

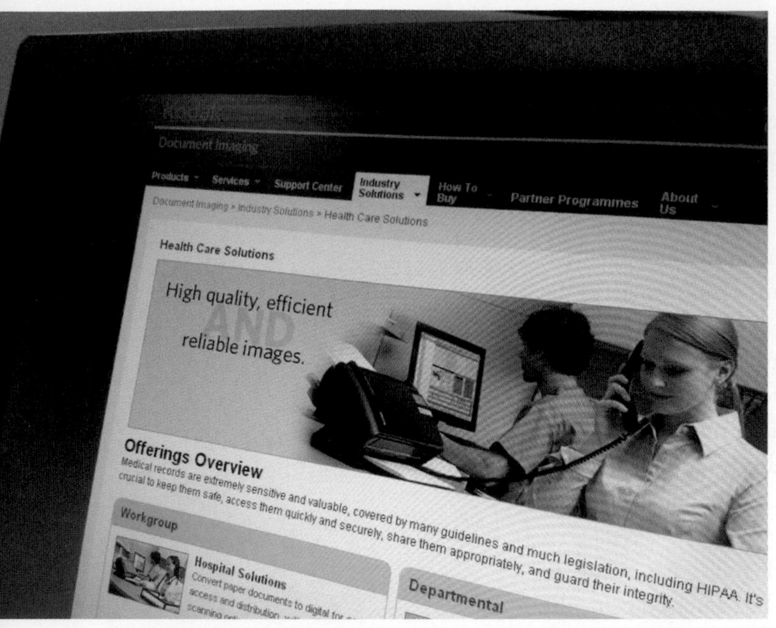

Figure 15.5 Kodak offers hospitals services that streamline processes, integrate technologies and improve overall productivity.

three functions coexist in a service business, and how are their relative roles perceived? Sandra Vandermerwe makes the point that high-value creating enterprises should be thinking in term of *activities*, not functions.[3]

Yet, in many firms, we still find individuals from marketing and operations having conflicts with each other. Marketers may see their role as one of continually adding value to the product offering, enhancing its appeal to customers, and stimulating sales. Operations managers, however, may see their job as cutting down on "extras" to reflect the reality of service constraints—such as staff and equipment—and the need to control cost. After all, they may argue, no value will be created if we operate at a loss. Conflicts may also occur between human resources and the other two functions, especially where employees are in boundary spanning roles that require them to balance customer satisfaction against operational efficiency.

Part of the challenge of service management is to ensure that each of these three functions cooperate with the other. Potential ways to reduce interfunctional conflict and break down the barriers between departments include:

1. Transferring individuals internally to other functions and allowing them to develop a more holistic perspective and be able to view issues from the different perspectives of the various departments.
2. Establishing cross-functional project teams (e.g., for new service development or customer service process redesign).
3. Having cross-functional service delivery teams.
4. Appointing individuals whose job is to integrate specific objectives, activities, and processes between departments. For example, Robert Kwortnik and Gary Thompson suggest forming a department in charge of "service experience management" that integrates marketing and operations.[4]
5. Carrying out internal marketing and training (see Chapter 11).
6. Having top management's commitment to ensure that the overarching objectives of all departments are integrated.

Do We Need Additional Skill Sets besides Marketing, Operations, and Human Resources?

Services systems are becoming increasingly complex. Many services are crucially dependent on information technology and communications infrastructures (e.g., in global financial service firms), large and complex facilities (e.g., in integrated airport infrastructures), complex process engineering (e.g., globally integrated supply chains in B2B contexts), and so on. At a higher level, service systems are evolving into a science in which it is necessary to have experts who have knowledge that cuts across the different disciplines such as information technology, engineering, and service management (see Service Insights 15.1).

SERVICE INSIGHTS 15.1

IBM's Service Science Initiative

Organizations have many functional departments such as marketing, logistics, and research that work independently, rather than jointly together. Even business schools train their graduates in specific disciplines such as accounting, finance, marketing, and operations management. The result is that employees often lack the knowledge about how to integrate across functions. Furthermore, they tend to know even less about other important disciplines, such as information technology or process engineering, that are also necessary for designing and managing complex service systems well.

IBM recognized this problem and has been leading the world in its initiative on service science, which IBM termed Service Science, Management and Engineering (SSME). SSME combines knowledge in computer science, operations research, engineering, business strategy, management science, social and cognitive science, and legal science so that the necessary skills are developed for the service economy. IBM has been mobilizing universities and research centers to collaborate with them.

Today, service science has become a part of the curriculum in many universities around the world. These universities focus on interdisciplinary research and teaching so that they are able to produce "T" graduates—those who have in-depth knowledge in one specialized area, as well as knowledge that cuts across several disciplines so that experts from these various disciplines can work together well.

Service science is an approach to enable us to study, design, and manage effective service systems that create value for our customers. Companies that recognize this will hire graduates with the necessary knowledge and skills in service science so that they can have an edge in the competitive service economy. By studying services marketing, you have made a first step toward becoming familiar with service science, but you need to be aware that all these other disciplines are also important and you should work on picking up key concepts in those fields, too.

SOURCES

"Are We Ready for 'SERVICE'?" ThinkTank, October 10, 2005, www.research.ibm.com/ssme/20051010_services.shtml, accessed March 12, 2012; M. M. Davis and I. Berdrow, "Service Science: Catalyst for Change in Business School Curricula," *IBM Systems Journal* 47, no. 1 (2008): 29–39; R. C. Larson, "Service Science: At the Intersection of Management, Social, and Engineering Sciences," *IBM Systems Journal* 47, no. 1 (2008): 41–51; Paul P. Maglio and Jim Spohrer, "Fundamentals of Service Science," *Journal of the Academy of Marketing Science* 36, no. 1 (2008): 18–20.

CREATING A LEADING SERVICE ORGANIZATION

So far, we have discussed the service profit chain that prescribes best-practice management thinking about how to run a service firm, and the need for integration across functions and discipline to be able to create and effective service profit chain for a service business. Let us next explore what it takes to move a firm from being a service loser to becoming a service leader.

From Losers to Leaders: Four Levels of Service Performance

LO 3

Be familiar with the four levels of service performance.

Service leadership is based on excellent performance across multiple areas. To capture this performance spectrum, we need to judge the firm within each of the three functional areas described earlier: marketing, operations, and human resources. Table 15.2 changes and extends an operations-oriented framework proposed by Richard Chase and Robert Hayes.[5] Service performers are grouped into four levels: loser, nonentity, professional, and leader. At each level, there is a short description of a typical firm across 12 dimensions.

Table 15.2 Four levels of service performance

Level	1. Loser	2. Nonentity
Marketing Function		
Role of marketing	Tactical role only; advertising and promotions lack focus; no involvement in product or pricing decision	Uses mix of selling and mass communication, using simple segmentation strategy; makes selective use of price discounts and promotions; conducts and tabulates basic satisfaction surveys
Competitive appeal	Customers patronize a firm for reasons other than performance	Customers neither seek nor avoid the firm
Customer profile	Unspecified; a mass market to be served at a minimum cost	One or more segments whose basic needs are understood
Service quality	Highly variable, usually unsatisfactory. Subservient to operations priorities	Meets some customer expectations; consistent on one or two key dimensions, but not all
Operations Function		
Role of operations	Reactive; cost oriented	The principal line management function creates and delivers product, focuses on standardization as key to productivity, and defines quality from internal perspective
Service delivery (frontstage)	A necessary evil. Locations and schedules are unrelated to preferences of customers, who are routinely ignored	Sticklers for tradition; "If it ain't broke, don't fix it"; tight rules for customers; each step in delivery run independently
Backstage operations	Divorced from front-stage operations; cogs in a machine	Contributes to individual front-stage delivery steps but organized separately; unfamiliar with customers
Productivity	Undefined; managers are punished for failing to stick within budget	Based on standardization; rewarded for keeping costs below budget
Introduction of new technology	Late adopter, under duress, when necessary for survival	Follows the crowd when justified by cost savings
Human Resources Function		
Role of human resources	Supplies low-cost employees who meet minimum skill requirements for the job	Recruits and trains employees who can perform competently
Workforce	Negative constraint: poor performers, do not care, disloyal	Adequate resource, follows procedures but uninspired; turnover often high
Frontline management	Controls workers	Controls the process
Note: This framework was inspired by, and expands upon, work in service operations management by Richard Chase and Robert Hayes.		

3. Professional	4. Leader
Marketing Function	
Has clear positioning strategy against competition; uses focused communications with distinctive appeals to clarify promises and educate customers; pricing is based on value; monitors customer usage and operates loyalty programs; uses a variety of research techniques to measure customer satisfaction and obtain ideas for service enhancements; works with operations to introduce new delivery systems	Innovative leader in chosen segments, known for marketing skills; brands at product/process level; conducts sophisticated analysis of relational databases as inputs to one-to-one marketing and proactive account management; uses state-of-the-art research techniques; uses concept testing, observation, and lead customers as inputs to new-product development; close to operations/HR
Customers seek out the firm based on its sustained reputation for meeting customer expectations	Company's name is synonymous with service excellence; its ability to delight customers raises expectations to levels that competitors can't meet
Groups of individuals whose variation in needs and value to the firm are clearly understood	Individuals are selected and retained based on their future value to the firm, including their potential for new service opportunities and their ability to stimulate innovation.
Consistently meets or exceeds customer expectations across multiple dimensions	Raises customer expectations to new levels; improves continuously
Operations Function	
Plays a strategic role in competitive strategy; recognizes a trade-off between productivity and customer-defined quality; willing to outsource; monitors competing operations for ideas, threats	Recognized for innovation, focus, and excellence; an equal partner with marketing and HR management; has in-house research capability and academic contacts; continually experimenting
Driven by customer satisfaction, not tradition; willing to customize, embrace new approaches; emphasis on speed, convenience, and comfort	Delivery is a seamless process organized around the customer; employees know whom they are serving; focuses on continuous improvement
Process is explicitly linked to front-stage activities; sees role as serving "internal customers," who, in turn, serve external customers	Closely integrated with front-stage delivery, even when geographically far apart; understands how own role relates to the overall process of serving external customers; continuing dialog
Focuses on reengineering backstage processes; avoids productivity improvements that will degrade customers' service experience; continually refining processes for efficiency	Understands the concept of return on quality; actively seeks customer involvement in productivity improvement; ongoing testing of new processes and technologies
An early adopter when IT promises to enhance service for customers and provide a competitive edge	Works with technology leaders to develop new applications that create first-mover advantage; seeks to perform at levels competitors cannot match
Human Resources Function	
Invests in selective recruiting, ongoing training; keeps close to employees, promotes upward mobility; strives to enhance the quality of working life	Sees the quality of employees as a strategic advantage; the firm is recognized as outstanding place to work; HR helps top management to nurture culture
Motivated, hard-working, allowed some discretion in choice of procedures, offers suggestions	Innovative and empowered; very loyal, committed to the firm's values and goals; creates procedures
Listens to customers; coaches and facilitates workers	Source of new ideas for top management; mentors, workers to enhance career growth, value to firm

Under the marketing function, we look at the role of marketing, competitive appeal, customer profile, and service quality. Under the operations function, we look at the part of operations, service delivery (front-stage), backstage operations, productivity, and introduction of new technology. Finally, under the human resources function, we examine the role of HRM, the workforce, and frontline management. Obviously, there are overlaps between these dimensions and across functions. There may also be differences in the relative importance of some dimensions in different industries and across different delivery systems. The goal is to get some idea of what needs to be changed in firms that are not performing as well as they might.

Service Losers

These firms are at the bottom. They fail in marketing, operations, and human resource management alike. Customers buy from them because there is usually no other choice. This is a reason why losers continue to survive. New technology is only introduced under pressure, and the uncaring workforce has a negative impact on performance. The Cycle of Failure presented earlier in (Figure 11.6, p. 328) describes how such organizations behave in relation to employees and what the consequences are for customers.

Service Nonentities

Although there is still a lot of room for improvement, nonentities have gotten rid of the worst features of losers. As shown in Table 15.2, nonentities have a traditional operations mind-set where cost savings can be obtained through standardization. Their marketing strategies are simple. The roles of human resources and operations can be summarized, respectively, by the ideals "adequate is good enough" and "if it ain't broke, why fix it." Consumers do not seek out nor do they avoid such organizations. Managers may talk about improving quality and other goals but are unable to set clear priorities, to have a clear direction, nor gain the respect and commitment of their employees (Figure 15.6). A few firms may compete in this way and you will find it difficult to tell one from the other. They may use price discounts to try to attract new customers. The Cycle of Mediocrity (Figure 11.9, p. 331) shows the human resources environment of many such firms and its consequences for customers.

Figure 15.6 Employees will be confused if the managers do not have a clear direction.

Service Professionals

Service professionals are in a different league from non-entities and have a clear market positioning strategy. Customers within the target segments seek out these firms based on their sustained reputation for meeting expectations. Marketing is more sophisticated, using targeted communications and pricing based on value to the customer. Research is used to measure customer satisfaction and obtain ideas for service enhancement. Operations and marketing work together to introduce new delivery systems and recognize the trade-off between productivity and customer-defined quality. There are explicit links between backstage and front-stage activities and the firm has a much more proactive, investment-oriented approach to HRM. The Cycle of Success (Figure 11.11, p. 332) highlights the HR strategies that lead to a high level of performance by most employees of organizations in the service professionals category (and by all who work for service leaders), together with its positive impact on customer satisfaction and loyalty.

Service Leaders

These organizations are the best in their respective industries. Service professionals are good, but service leaders are outstanding. When we think of service leaders, we think of Starbucks, Ritz-Carlton, Southwest Airlines, and IBM. Their company names are linked to service excellence and an ability to delight customers. Service leaders are innovative in each functional area of management and also have excellent internal communications and coordination among the three functions. This is made possible through a relatively flat organizational structure and the use of teams to a great extent.

Figure 15.7 The Bank of America offers excellent services to its customers and is also one of the best companies to work for.

Marketing efforts by service leaders make use of CRM systems that offer insights about customers on a one-to-one basis. They use concept testing, observation, and contacts with lead customers to develop new breakthrough services that respond to previously unrecognized needs. Operations specialists work with technology leaders around the world to develop new applications that will create a first-mover advantage. As a result, the firm can perform at levels that competitors cannot hope to reach for a long period of time. Internally, there are clear standards and standardized processes that employees can follow, and this facilitates the work of employees.[6] Senior executives see quality of their employees as an important competitive advantage. HRM works with them to develop and maintain a service-oriented culture and to create an outstanding working environment that attracts and retains the best people (Figure 15.7). The employees themselves are committed to the firm's values and goals. Because they are involved, empowered, and quick to take on change, they are a continuous source of new ideas (Figure 15.8).

LO 4

Understand what actions are required to move a service firm from being a service loser to rising as a service leader.

Moving to a Higher Level of Performance

Firms can move up or down the performance ladder. Organizations that focus on satisfying their current customers may miss important changes in the marketplace and find themselves turning into has-beens. These businesses may continue to serve a loyal but decreasing group of customers, but are unable to attract new consumers with different expectations. Companies whose original success was based on a specific technological process may find that competitors have managed to find higher-performing alternatives. Organizations whose management has worked for years to build up a loyal workforce with a strong service ethic may find that such a culture can be quickly destroyed as a result of a merger or acquisition that brings in new leaders with different focus or who emphasize short-term profits. Unfortunately, senior managers sometimes deceive themselves into thinking that their companies have achieved a superior level of performance when, in fact, the foundations of that success are crumbling.

Figure 15.8 Good HRM produces engaged and encouraged employees who serve the company cause better.

In most markets, we find companies that are moving up the performance ladder. They put in effort to coordinate their marketing, operations, and human resource management functions in order to gain better competitive positions and better satisfy their customers. For example, Microsoft has recognized that the customer and partner experience is increasingly important to earn high levels of satisfaction and loyalty. Microsoft has been shifting the organization from developer-centric to a more customer-focused culture using a companywide initiative called Customer and Partner Experience (CPE). CPE's objective is to monitor, manage, and improve every perception point customers and partners encounter as they try, buy, download, use, integrate, and upgrade Microsoft's software.

Leading Change toward a Higher Performance Level

It requires human leaders to take a service firm in the right direction, set the right strategic priorities, and ensure that the relevant strategies are implemented throughout the organization. A transformation of an organization and moving it up the performance ladder can take place in two different ways: evolution or turnaround.

Evolution in a business context involves continual changes. Here, top management must work actively to change the focus and strategy of the firm to take advantage of changing conditions and new technologies. Without a continuing series of changes, it's unlikely that a firm can remain successful in a dynamic marketplace.

A different type of transformation occurs in *turnaround* situations in which leaders (usually new ones) seek to bring organizations back from the brink of failure and set them on a healthier course. Chan Kim and Renée Mauborgne, both professors at INSEAD, have identified four hurdles leaders face in reorienting and formulating a strategy in turnaround situations.[7]

- *Cognitive hurdles* are present when people cannot agree on the causes of current problems and the need for change.
- *Resource hurdles* exist when the organization has limited funds.
- *Motivational hurdles* exist when employees are reluctant to make needed changes.
- *Political hurdles* take the form of organized resistance from parties that are interested in protecting their positions.

Turning around an organization that has limited resources requires concentrating those resources where the need and the likely payoffs are greatest. John Kotter, perhaps the best-known authority on leadership, argues that, in most successful change management processes, those in leadership roles must go through eight complicated and often time-consuming stages[8]:

1) Creating a sense of urgency to develop the incentive to change.
2) Putting together a team strong enough to direct the process.
3) Creating an appropriate vision of where the organization needs to go.
4) Communicating that new vision broadly.
5) Empowering employees to act on that vision.

6) Producing sufficient short-term results to create credibility and counter cynicism.

7) Building momentum and using that to tackle the tougher change problems.

8) Anchoring the new behaviors in the organizational culture.

Noted author Rosabeth Moss Kanter suggests it can be advantageous in turnaround situations to bring in new CEOs from outside the organization.[9] Such individuals would not have been involved in the previous management's dynamics and are, therefore, able to identify problems and change habits. New CEOs may also have more credibility in representing and respecting customers. Exemplary turnaround leaders, Kanter says, understand the powerful, unifying effect of focusing on customers. This focus can help in the difficult task of obtaining cooperation across departments and divisions. In addition to breaking down barriers between marketing, operations, and human resources or between various product or geographic divisions, turnaround CEOs may also need to relook at financial priorities to enable collaborative groups to tackle new business opportunities (Figure 15.9).

LO 5

Discuss the role of leaders in nurturing an effective service culture.

LEADERSHIP, ORGANIZATIONAL CULTURE, AND CLIMATE

So far, we have discussed how we can move a firm from a service loser to a service leader. To close this chapter, we take a brief look at a theme that runs throughout the book: the leader's role in nurturing an effective culture within the firm.[10] *Organizational culture* can be defined as including:

- Shared perceptions or themes regarding what is important in the organization.
- Shared values about what is right and wrong.
- Shared understanding about what works and what doesn't work.
- Shared beliefs and assumptions about *why* these beliefs are important.
- Shared styles of working and relating to others.

Figure 15.9 A company culture can be dynamic when leadership and management skills work in hand-in-glove.

A service-oriented culture includes having clear marketing goals and a strong drive to be the best in delivering superior value or service quality.[11] Once the values of the organization are part of the hearts and minds of its employees, they can work independently and yet be collaborative, as they are all thinking with the mission and goals in their minds when making decisions.[12]

Transforming an organization to develop and nurture a new culture along each of these five dimensions is no easy task for even the most gifted leader. It is even more difficult when the organization is part of an industry that prides itself on deeply rooted traditions, including many different departments run by independent-minded professionals in different fields who are very sensitive to how they are perceived by fellow professionals in the same field at other institutions. This situation often is found in such pillars of the nonprofit world as colleges and universities, major hospitals, and large museums. Service Insights 15.2 describes the challenges faced by a new director in transforming Boston's Museum of Fine Arts at a low point in its history.

SERVICE INSIGHTS 15.2

Reversing Course at the Museum of Fine Arts, Boston

Boston's highly respected Museum of Fine Arts, founded in 1870, had been going downhill for several years when the board recruited a new director in June 1994. Their choice was Art Historian Malcolm Rogers, then Deputy Director of the National Portrait Gallery in London. Arriving in Boston, Rogers found an institution facing financial difficulties and low staff morale from recent staff cutbacks. Corporate memberships had slumped, and attendance had declined.

One of the new director's first acts was to host a breakfast for the entire staff and introduce what would become a central theme:

> We are one museum, not a collection of departments. The museum consists of security guards, curators, technicians, benefactors, volunteers, public relations personnel. We all have our individual professional expertise. By working cooperatively with colleagues, we all have areas that can be improved.

Rogers' "one museum" theme, repeated regularly, sent the message that operating as one museum is more important than having traditionally independent curators who operated the museum's many different art departments and set priorities for acquisitions and exhibitions. One curator quickly resigned. While he was recognized for his good humor and friendly, outgoing manner, the new director showed that he could be blunt and decisive. He was very tough with expenditures and began a program to cut staff size by 20%. However, his cutbacks did not extend to services for museum visitors. Instead, he set about creating a more welcoming environment. Said Rogers:

> I'm firmly committed to the idea that museums are here to serve the community, and that's going to be one of the keynotes of my work here in Boston—to encourage the MFA to turn out toward its public and to satisfy as broad a constituency as possible.

He soon reopened the main entrance on Huntington Avenue, which had been closed to save money, and reversed the trend of shortening opening hours, another of his predecessor's cost-cutting initiatives. Daily schedules were extended and seven-day operations started. Three nights a week, the museum remained open until 10 p.m. On "Community Days," three Sundays a year, the MFA was open to the public free of charge.

Each successive year, Rogers launched activities to improve the museum's facilities and image, including new exterior lighting to better display the MFA's imposing facade at night, expanding the main restaurant, and opening a new rooftop terrace. Making the MFA an evening destination, especially for people living in or close to the city, was another objective. The broader variety of exhibitions (to encourage multiple visits per year), upgraded restaurants, and improved museum atmosphere all played a role. An ambitious $500-million capital campaign was launched, part of which would fund construction of a major building expansion.

Externally, Rogers enjoyed a much higher public profile than his predecessors. Said Pat Jacoby, then the deputy director of marketing and development: "Malcolm personifies marketing: He's accessible, he's an advocate of PR, he cares about the visitors, and he believes the MFA can set the standard for other museums." Rogers declared:

> Marketing is central to the life of a great museum that's trying to get its message out. It's part of our educational outreach, our social outreach. Unfortunately, certain people don't like the word "marketing." What I see out there—and also to a certain extent inside the museum—is a very conservative culture that cannot accept that institutions previously considered "elite" should actually be trying to attract a broader public and also listening to what the public is saying. But it's all to do with fulfilling your mission.
>
> Clearly part of a museum's mission is guardianship of precious objects, but unless we're communicating those objects to people effectively and our visitors are enjoying them—and the ambience of the setting in which they are displayed and interpreted—then we're only operating at

PART V

50% effectiveness or less. Having said this, I want to stress that the mission comes first and that marketing is absolutely the servant of our mission. We're not just in the business of finding out what people want and then giving it to them.

Rogers sought to pick a mix of exhibitions that combined high scholarly content with popular appeal. His view, shared by the senior staff and supported by the board, was that one show in five should be of a "blockbuster" nature, which meant hosting such an exhibition at least once every two years. He also sought to display art from the MFA's permanent collection to best advantage, including small revolving shows. Paintings in the 15 European galleries were rehung in innovative ways designed to stimulate the audience and engage them more actively. However, there was much criticism among the art community when 27 Impressionist paintings from the MFA's celebrated Monet collection were loaned (for a reported $1-million fee) to a gallery at the Bellagio casino in Las Vegas, where they were seen by 450,000 visitors.

In 2002, the MFA board adopted a long-term strategic plan, titled *One Museum—Great Museum—Your Museum*. It was organized around 10 strategic goals (Table 15.3), each supported by a set of initiatives and over 200 detailed action plans.

By mid-2006, many of these initiatives were well underway. The fundraising drive for the new extension had passed $335 million mark. Attendance had begun to grow again, after slumping nationwide following 9/11. The MFA continued its strategy of periodically exhibiting nontraditional art forms and art collections, including *Speed, Style and Beauty: Cars from the Ralph Lauren Collection*, featuring 16 classic European cars owned by the fashion designer. Rogers argued that these vehicles were as much works of art as furniture, long an accepted component of many art museums' collections. Despite such criticisms as the *New York Times* review headlined "Art with Lousy Mileage but Shiny Celebrity Gloss," attendance exceeded its goals and met an important objective of attracting a much higher proportion of male visitors than usually came to the museum.

Table 15.3 Ten strategic goals for the MFA

Collections	1. Continue to improve the quality of the collection 2. Improve management, care, and knowledge of the collection 3. Provide and promote worldwide electronic access to the collection
Experiencing	4. Engage, educate, and delight visitors 5. Retain and expand audiences by understanding their needs 6. Schedule an exhibition program that meets a variety of objectives
Facilities	7. Enlarge and improve the physical plant
Financial	8. Pursue fund-raising required by the Master Site plan and other strategic goals 9. Ensure fiscal stability
Organization	10. Adopt an audience-aware, results-oriented experimental attitude and realign the organization to support these activities

SOURCES

Christopher Lovelock, "Museum of Fine Arts, Boston," *Services Marketing*, 4th ed. Upper Saddle River, NJ: Prentice Hall, 2001, 625–638; V. Kasturi Rangan and Marie Bell, "Museum of Fine Arts Boston," Harvard Business School Case 9-506-027; Museum of Fine Arts website, www.mfa.org, accessed March 12, 2012.

While culture is more overarching and less measurable, *organizational climate* is the part of the organization's culture that can be felt and seen. It is culture translated into more concrete aspects that can be experienced by the employees. Six key factors that influence an organization's working climate are:

- Its *flexibility* (how free employees feel to innovate).
- Employees' sense of *responsibility* to the organization.
- The level of *standards* that people set.
- The perceived suitability of *rewards*.
- The *clarity* people have about mission and values.
- The level of *commitment* to a common purpose.[13]

From an employee's perspective, this climate is directly related to managerial policies and procedures, especially those linked to human resource management. In short, climate represents the shared views of employees about the practices, procedures, and types of behaviors that get rewarded and supported in a particular setting.

Many climates often exist at the same time within a single organization. A climate must relate to something specific, for instance, service, support, innovation, or safety. A climate for service refers to employee views of the practices, procedures, and behaviors related to customer service and service quality that are expected and that get rewarded when performed well.

Leaders are responsible for creating cultures and the service climates that go along with them. Why are some leaders more effective than others in bringing about a desired change in climate? As presented in Service Insights 15.3, research suggests that it may be a matter of leadership style.

Creating a new climate for service, based on an understanding of what is needed for market success, may require a complete rethink of human resource management activities, operational procedures, and the firm's reward and recognition policies.

LEADERSHIP IN THE FUTURE[14]

LO 6

Describe the qualities of leaders of the future.

What are some aspects of leadership that will be different from what we are used to today? There are two main interlinked aspects of leadership that are likely to become more important. They are collective genius and leadership from behind. Many of the people working in teams, which form collective genius, are stars in their own right. In order to lead them effectively, their leader needs to take a backseat and let different members lead at different points (Figure 15.10).

Figure 15.10 When leaders can effectively communicate a clear and exciting vision for the future, people listen and follow attentively.

SERVICE INSIGHTS 15.3

The Impact of Leadership Styles on Climate

Daniel Goleman, an applied psychologist at Rutgers University, identified six styles of leadership. He investigated how successful each style has proven to be in affecting climate or working atmosphere. This was based on a major study of the behavior and impact on their organizations on thousands of executives.

Coercive leaders demand immediate obedience ("Do what I tell you"). They were found to have a negative impact on climate. Goleman comments that this controlling style is useful only in a crisis or in dealing with problem employees. *Pacesetting leaders* set high standards for performance. They are very energetic. This style can be summarized as "Do as I do, now." This style, too, was found to have a negative impact on climate. In practice, the pacesetting leader may destroy morale by assuming too much, too soon, of subordinates—expecting them to know already what to do and how to do it. When others turn out to be less capable than expected, the leader may start focusing on details and micromanaging. This style is likely to work only when seeking to get quick results from a highly motivated, skilful and experienced team.

The research found that the most effective style for achieving a positive change in climate came from *authoritative leaders* who have the skills and personality to move people toward a vision. These leaders build confidence using a "Come with me" approach. The research also found that three other styles had quite positive impacts on climate: *affiliative leaders* who believe that "People come first," seeking to create harmony and build emotional bonds; *democratic leaders* who looked for agreement through participation ("What do you think?"); and *coaching leaders* who work to develop people for the future and whose style might be summarized as "Try this."

SOURCE

Daniel Goleman, "Leadership that Gets Results," *Harvard Business Review* 78, March–April 2000, 78–93.

Collective Genius

Traditionally, leaders set a course and inspire people to follow. In the future, because of business diversity and interdependence between various parties, the leadership style needs to be more collaborative and use a team approach to problem solving. In fact, there are many knowledgeable and talented people who will not follow if leaders lead from the position of authority. Instead, we have a process of collective genius.

Increasingly, leaders will come from emerging countries with very different styles because they come from different cultures. For example, in Africa, leadership is often based on the principle of "I am because we are." HCL Technologies, an Indian information technology company that is often said to have the world's most modern management, emphasizes that the employee is first, and the customer is second. The company uses a model of distributed leadership, where leaders of various groups share leadership with the CEO. Again, this emphasizes the notion of leadership using collective genius, which is team based in nature.

Leadership from Behind

Leadership from behind is one where the leader is not afraid of sharing power with others. These leaders create an environment where their employees are willing to step forward and lead, and different people can be leading at different points of time depending on their expertise and skill sets. Leadership then becomes a collective activity (Figure 15.11). If necessary, the leader who generally leads from behind can also step forward and lead from the front, if needed, such as in moments of crises.

In the future, innovation will remain key for organizations to succeed and become more important as competitive intensity increases. Innovation calls for leading from behind, as it is a creative process that requires taking full advantage of the talents of a diverse group of people. This group of people will see that their collective efforts can yield results that are far superior to their individual efforts.

Figure 15.11 In the global commercial melting pot, innovative leadership can inspire a diverse team of talent into achieving far more than individual effort.

CHAPTER SUMMARY

LO 1 ▶ The Service Profit Chain shows that service leadership in an industry requires high performance in several related areas:

- o Customer relationships must be managed effectively and there must be strategies to build and sustain loyalty.
- o Value must be created and delivered to the target customers in ways that lead them to see the firm's offering as superior to competing offerings.
- o Service quality and productivity must be continuously improved.
- o Service employees must be enabled and motivated.
- o Top management's leadership needs to drive and support all the components of the Service Profit Chain.

LO 2 ▶ To be successful, the marketing, operations, and human resource management functions need to be tightly integrated and work closely together in well-coordinated ways.

- o Integration means that the key deliverables and objectives of the various functions are not only compatible but also mutually reinforcing.
- o Ways to improve integration include (1) internal transfers across functional areas, (2) cross-functional project teams, (3) cross-functional service delivery teams, (4) appointing individuals to integrate objectives, activities, and processes between departments, (5) internal marketing and training, and (6) management commitment that ensures the overarching objectives of all functions are integrated.

LO 3 ▶ There are four levels of service performance, and only the last two follow the Service Profit Chain's principles:

- o *Service losers.* They follow the cycle of failure and are poor performers in marketing, operations, and HRM. Service losers survive because monopoly situations give customers little choice but to buy from them.
- o *Service nonentities.* Their performance still leaves much to be desired, but they have eliminated the worst features of losers. They typically function in the cycle of mediocrity.
- o *Service professionals.* They have a clear market position, and customers in target segments seek them out based on their sustained reputation for meeting expectations. They typically function in the cycle of success.
- o *Service leaders.* They are the crème de la crème of their respective industries. They typically perfect and internalize the cycle of success for their service business.

We contrasted the description and actions of a service leader against professionals, nonentities, and losers along the three functional areas in Table 15.2 (pp. 482–483).

LO 4 ▶ Companies that are able to move up the performance ladder typically put in effort to coordinate their marketing, operations, and human resource management functions in order to gain better competitive positions and to better satisfy their customers.

▶ No organization can hope to move up the performance ladder and achieve enduring success without change, which can be in the form of evolutionary change or turnaround change. Evolutionary change involves making a series of changes as the firm faces a dynamic marketplace. Turnaround changes often involve bringing a new leader to bring the organization back from the brink of failure.

▶ To overcome *barriers for change*, leadership must navigate through eight stages for successful change management.

- o Creating a sense of urgency to develop the incentive to change.
- o Putting together a team strong enough to direct the process.
- o Creating an appropriate vision of where the organization needs to go.
- o Communicating that new vision broadly.
- o Empowering employees to act on that vision.
- o Producing sufficient short-term results to create credibility and counter cynicism.
- o Building momentum and using that to tackle tougher change problems.
- o Anchoring the new behaviors in the organizational culture.

 **LO 5** ▶ Exemplary leaders understand the powerful, unifying effect of focusing on customers and creating a *culture for service*. It is, therefore, an important role of leaders to develop a strong organizational culture so that its employees have shared:

- Perceptions of what is important to the company and why it is important.
- Values about what is right and wrong.
- Understanding of what works and what does not.
- Beliefs and assumptions about why these beliefs are important.
- Shared styles of working and relating to others.

▶ Organizational climate is the aspect of organizational culture that is experienced by employees, and measurable. Many climates often exist at the same time within a single organization. Among six key factors that influence an organization's working climate are:

- Its *flexibility* (how free employees feel to innovate).
- Their sense of *responsibility* to the organization.
- The level of *standards* that people set.
- The perceived *suitability of rewards*.
- The *clarity people have about mission and values*.
- The level of *commitment to a common purpose*.

 **LO 6** ▶ Collective genius and leadership from behind are two main trends that will become important in leadership of tomorrow. Many of the people who work in teams that form collective genius, are stars in their own right. In order to lead them effectively, the leader needs to lead from behind and let different members lead at different points. Leadership from behind takes advantage of the talents of a diverse group of people, yielding far superior results than individual efforts.

PART V

UNLOCK YOUR LEARNING

These keywords are found within the sections of each Learning Objective (LO). They are integral to understanding the services marketing concepts taught in each section. Having a firm grasp of these keywords and how they are used is essential to helping you do well on your course, and in the real and very competitive marketing scene out there.

 **LO 1**
1 Customer loyalty
2 Customer satisfaction
3 Productive employees
4 Profitability
5 Service Profit Chain
6 Shareholder value
7 Top management leadership

 **LO 2**
8 Cross-functional project teams
9 Human resource function
10 Interfunctional conflict
11 Internal transfers
12 Marketing function
13 Operations function

 **LO 3**
14 Service leaders
15 Service losers
16 Service nonentities
17 Service performance
18 Service professionals

 **LO 4**
19 Cognitive hurdles
20 Evolution
21 Leadership roles
22 Motivational hurdles
23 Performance ladder
24 Performance level
25 Political hurdles
26 Resource hurdles
27 Turnaround

 **LO 5**
28 Affiliative leaders
29 Authoritative leaders
30 Coercive leaders
31 Organizational climate
32 Organizational culture
33 Pacesetting leaders
34 Service-oriented culture

How well do you know the language of services marketing? Quiz yourself!

 **Not for the academically faint-of-heart**

For each keyword you are able to recall without referring to earlier pages, give yourself a point (and a pat on the back). Tally your score at the end and see if you earned the right to be called—a *services marketeer*.

SCORE

0 – 6	Services Marketing is done a great disservice.
7 – 13	The midnight oil needs to be lit, pronto.
14 – 19	I know what you *didn't* do all semester.
20 – 25	By George! You're getting there.
26 – 31	Now, go forth and market.
32 – 34	There should be a marketing concept named after you.

KNOW YOUR ESM

Review Questions

1. What are the implications of the Service Profit Chain for service management?
2. Supporters of the Service Profit Chain argue that strong links connect employee satisfaction and loyalty, service quality and productivity, value, and customer satisfaction and loyalty. Do you think these same relationships would prevail in low-contact environments in which customers use self-service technology? Why or why not?
3. Why do the marketing, operations, and human resource management functions need to be closely coordinated in service organizations?
4. What are the causes of tension among the marketing, operations, and human resource functions? Provide specific examples of how these tensions might vary from one service industry to another.
5. How are the four levels of service performance defined? Based on your own service experiences, provide an example of a company for each category.
6. "Exemplary turnaround leaders understand the powerful, unifying effect of focusing on customers." Comment on this statement. Is focusing on customers more likely to have a unifying effect within a company under turnaround conditions than at other times?
7. What is the relationship among leadership, climate, and culture?
8. What kind of qualities will be more common in leaders of the future? Explain why these qualities are necessary.

WORK YOUR ESM

Application Exercises

1. Analyze a service firm along the key aspects of the Service Profit Chain. Assess how well the firm is performing at the various components of the Service Profit Chain, and make specific suggestions for improvements.
2. Contrast the roles of marketing, operations, and human resources in (1) a gas station chain, (2) a web-based brokerage firm, and (3) an insurance company.
3. Select a company you know well, and obtain additional information from a literature review, website, company publication, blog, and so on. Evaluate the company on as many dimensions of service performance as you can, identifying where you believe it fits on the service performance spectrum shown in Table 15.2.
4. What is the role of senior management in moving a firm toward consistently delivering service excellence?
5. Based on all you've learned working throughout this book, what do you believe are the key drivers of success for service organizations? Try and develop an integrative causal model that explains the important drivers of success for a service organization.

ENDNOTES

1 Don Peppers and Martha Rogers, *Return on Customer*. New York: Currency Doubleday, 2005, 1.

2 James L. Heskett, Thomas O. Jones, Gary W. Loveman, W. Earl Sasser Jr., and Leonard A. Schlesinger, "Putting the Service Profit Chain to Work," *Harvard Business Review* 72, March/April 1994; James L. Heskett, W. Earl Sasser, Jr., and Leonard A. Schlesinger, *The Service Profit Chain*. New York: The Free Press, 1997.

3 Sandra Vandermerwe, *From Tin Soldiers to Russian Dolls*. Oxford: Butterworth-Heinemann, 1993, 82.

4 Robert J. Kwortnik Jr. and Gary M. Thompson, "Unifying Service Marketing and Operations With Service Experience Management," *Journal of Service Research* 11, no. 4 (2009): 389–406.

5 Richard B. Chase and Robert H. Hayes, "Beefing Up Operations in Service Firms," *Sloan Management Review*, (Fall 1991): 15–26.

6 Rosabeth Moss Kanter, "Transforming Giants," *Harvard Business Review*, (January 2008): 43–52.

7 W. Chan Kim and Renée Mauborgne, "Tipping Point Leadership," *Harvard Business Review* 81, (April 2003): 61–69.

8 John P. Kotter, *What Leaders Really Do*. Boston: Harvard Business School Press, 1999, 10–11.

9 Rosabeth Moss Kanter, "Leadership and the Psychology of Turnaround," *Harvard Business Review* 81, (June 2003): 58–67.

10 This section is based, in part, on Benjamin Schneider and David E. Bowen, *Winning the Service Game*. Boston: Harvard Business School Press, 1995; David E. Bowen, Benjamin Schneider, and Sandra S. Kim, "Shaping Service Cultures through Strategic Human Resource Management," in T. Schwartz and D. Iacobucci, eds., *Handbook of Services Marketing and Management*. Thousand Oaks, (CA: Sage Publications, 2000, 439–454.)

11 Hans Kasper, "Culture and Leadership in Market-Oriented Service Organisations," *European Journal of Marketing* 36, no. 9/10 (2002): 1047–1057.

12 Rosabeth Moss Kanter, "Transforming Giants," *Harvard Business Review* (January 2008): 43–52

13 Daniel Goleman, "Leadership That Gets Results," *Harvard Business Review 78*, (March–April, 2000): 78–93.

14 Linda A. Hill, "Where Will We Find Tomorrow's Leaders?" *Harvard Business Review*, (January 2008): 123–129.

CASE STUDY

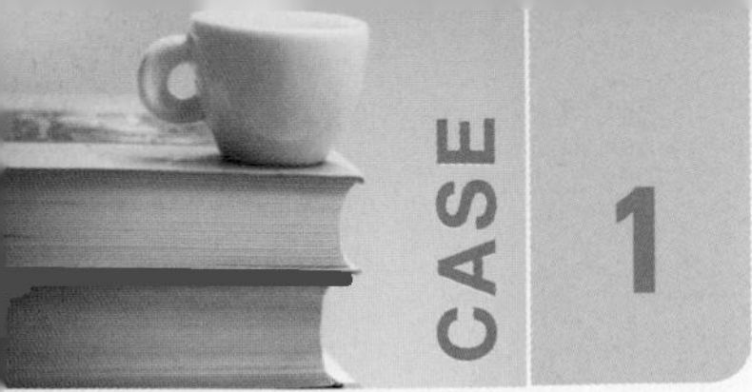

Sullivan Ford Auto World

Christopher H. Lovelock

A young health-care manager unexpectedly finds herself running a family-owned car dealership that is in financial trouble. She is very concerned about the poor performance of the service department and wonders whether a turnaround is possible.

Viewed from Wilson Avenue, the Sullivan Ford Auto World dealership presented a festive sight. Flags waved, and strings of triangular pennants in red, white, and blue fluttered gaily in the late afternoon breeze. Rows of new model cars and trucks gleamed and winked in the sunlight. Geraniums graced the flowerbeds outside the showroom entrance. A huge rotating sign at the corner of Wilson Avenue and Route 78 sported the Ford logo and identified the business as Sullivan Ford Auto World. Banners below urged "Let's Make a Deal!"

Inside the handsome, high-ceilinged showroom, four of the new model Fords were on display—a dark-green Explorer SUV, a red Mustang convertible, a white Focus sedan, and a red Ranger pickup truck. Each vehicle was polished to a high sheen. Two groups of customers were chatting with salespeople, and a middle-aged man sat in the driver's seat of the Mustang, studying the controls.

Upstairs in the comfortably furnished general manager's office, Carol Sullivan-Diaz finished running another spreadsheet analysis on her laptop. She felt tired and depressed. Her father, Walter Sullivan, had died of a sudden heart attack four weeks earlier at the age of 56. As executor of his estate, the bank had asked her to temporarily assume the position of general manager of the dealership. The only visible change that she had made to her father's office was installing an all-in-one laser printer, scanner, copier, and fax, but she had been very busy analyzing the current position of the business.

Sullivan-Diaz did not like the look of the numbers on the printout. Auto World's financial situation had been deteriorating for 18 months and had been running in the red for the first half of the current year. New car sales had declined, dampened in part by rising interest rates. Margins had been squeezed by promotions and other efforts to move new cars off the lot. Reflecting rising fuel prices, industry forecasts of future sales were discouraging, and so were her own financial projections for Auto World's sales department. Service revenues, which were below average for a dealership of this size, had also declined, although the service department still made a small surplus.

Had she had made a mistake last week, Carol wondered, in turning down Bill Froelich's offer to buy the business? Admittedly, the amount was substantially below the offer from Froelich that her father had rejected two years earlier, but the business had been more profitable then.

THE SULLIVAN FAMILY

Walter Sullivan purchased a small Ford dealership in 1983, renaming it Sullivan's Auto World, and had built it up to become one of the best known in the metropolitan area. In 1999, he borrowed heavily to purchase the current site at a major suburban highway intersection, in an area of the city with many new housing developments.

There had been a dealership on the site, but the buildings were 30 years old. Sullivan had retained the service and repair bays but torn down the showroom in front of them and replaced it with an attractive modern facility. On moving to the new location, which was substantially larger than the old one, he renamed his business Sullivan Ford Auto World.

Everybody seemed to know Walt Sullivan. He was a consummate showman and entrepreneur, appearing in his own radio and television commercials, and was active in community affairs. His approach to car sales emphasized promotions, discounts, and deals in order to maintain volume. He was never happier than when making a sale.

Carol Sullivan-Diaz, aged 28, was the eldest of Walter and Carmen Sullivan's three daughters. After obtaining a bachelor's degree in economics, she went on to take an MBA degree and then embarked on a career in health-care management. She was married to Dr. Roberto Diaz, a surgeon at St. Luke's Hospital. Her 20-year-old twin sisters, Gail and Joanne, who were students at the state university, lived with their mother.

In her own student days, Sullivan-Diaz had worked part time in her father's business on secretarial and bookkeeping tasks and as a service writer in the service department, so she was quite familiar with the operations of the dealership. At business school, she decided on a career in health-care management. After graduation, she worked as an executive assistant to the president of St. Luke's, a large teaching hospital. Two years later, she joined Heritage Hospitals, a large multi-hospital facility that also provided long-term care, as the assistant director of marketing, a position she had held for almost three years. Her responsibilities included designing new services, complaint handling, market research, and introducing an innovative day-care program for hospital employees and neighborhood residents.

Carol's employer had given her a six-week leave of absence to put her father's affairs in order. She doubted that she could extend that leave much beyond the two weeks still remaining. Neither she nor other family members were interested in making a career of running the dealership. However, she was prepared to take time out from her health-care career to work on a turnaround if that seemed a viable proposition. She had been successful in her present job and believed it would not be difficult to find another health management position in the future.

THE DEALERSHIP

Like other car dealerships, Sullivan Ford Auto World operated both sales and service departments, often referred to in the trade as "front end" and "back end," respectively. Both new and used vehicles were sold, since a high proportion of new car and van purchases involved trading in the purchaser's existing vehicle. Auto World would also buy well-maintained used cars at auctions for resale. Purchasers who decided that they could not afford a new car would often buy a "preowned" vehicle instead, while shoppers who came in looking for used cars could sometimes be persuaded to buy new ones. Before being put on sale, used vehicles were carefully serviced, with parts being replaced as needed. They were then thoroughly cleaned by a detailer whose services were hired as required. Dents and other blemishes were removed at a nearby body shop, and, occasionally, the vehicle's paintwork was resprayed, too.

The front end of the dealership employed a sales manager, seven salespeople, an office manager, and a secretary. One of the salespeople had given notice and would be leaving at the end of the following week. The service department, when fully staffed, consisted of a service manager, a parts supervisor, nine mechanics, and two service writers. The Sullivan twins often worked part-time as service writers, filling in at busy periods, when one of the other writers was sick or on vacation, or when—as currently—there was an unfilled vacancy. The job entailed scheduling appointments for repairs and maintenance, writing up each work order, calling customers with repair estimates, and assisting customers when they returned to pick up their cars and pay for the work that had been done.

Sullivan-Diaz knew from her own experience as a service writer that it could be a stressful job. Few people liked to be without their car, even for a day. When a car broke down or was having problems, the owner was often nervous about how long it would take to get it fixed and, if the warranty had expired, how much the labor and parts would cost. Customers were quite unforgiving when a problem was not fixed completely on the first attempt and they had to return their vehicle for further work.

Major mechanical failures were not usually difficult to repair, although parts replacement costs might be expensive. It was often the "little" things, like water leaks and wiring problems, that were the hardest to diagnose and correct, and it might be necessary for the customer to return two or three times before such a problem was resolved. In these situations, parts and material costs were relatively low, but labor costs mounted up quickly, being charged out at US$75 an hour. Customers could sometimes be quite abusive, yelling at service writers over the phone or arguing with service writers, mechanics, and the service manager in person.

Turnover in the service writer job was high, which was one reason why Carol—and more recently her sisters—had often been pressed into service by their father to "hold the fort," as he described it. More than once, she had seen an exasperated service writer respond sharply to a complaining customer or hang up on one who was being abusive over the telephone. Gail and Joanne were currently taking turns to cover the vacant position, but there were times when both of them had classes and the dealership had only one service writer on duty.

By national standards, Sullivan Ford Auto World stood toward the lower end of medium-sized dealerships, selling around 1,100 cars a year, equally divided between new and used vehicles. In the most recent year, its revenues totaled US$26.6 million from new and used car sales and US$2.9 million from service and parts—down from US$30.5 million and US$3.6 million, respectively, in the previous year. Although the unit value of car sales was high, the margins were quite low, with margins for new cars being substantially lower than those for used ones. Industry guidelines suggested that the contribution margin (known as the departmental selling gross) from car sales should be about 5.5 percent of sales revenues, and from service, around 25 percent of revenues. In a typical dealership, 60 percent of the selling gross would traditionally come from sales and 40 percent from service, but the balance was shifting from sales to service. The selling gross was then applied to fixed expenses, such as administrative salaries, rent or mortgage payments, and utilities.

For the most recent 12 months at Auto World, Sullivan-Diaz had determined that the selling gross figures were 4.6 percent and 24 percent, respectively, both of them lower than those in the previous year and insufficient to cover the dealership's fixed expenses. Her father had made no mention of financial difficulties, and she had been shocked to learn from the bank after his death that Auto World had been two months behind in mortgage payments on the property. Further analysis also showed that accounts payable had also risen sharply in the previous six months. Fortunately, the dealership held a large insurance policy on Sullivan's life, and the proceeds from this was more than sufficient to bring mortgage payments up to date, pay down all overdue accounts, and leave some funds for future contingencies.

OUTLOOK

The opportunities for expanding new car sales did not appear promising, given declining consumer confidence and recent layoffs at several local plants, which were expected to hurt the local economy. However, promotional incentives had reduced the inventory to manageable levels. From discussions with Larry Winters, Auto World's sales manager, Sullivan-Diaz had concluded that costs could be cut by not replacing the departing sales representative, maintaining inventory at its current reduced level, and trying to make more efficient use of advertising and promotion. Although Winters did not have Walter's exuberant personality, he had been Auto World's leading sales representative before being promoted, and had shown strong managerial capabilities in his current position.

As she reviewed the figures for the service department, Sullivan-Diaz wondered what potential might exist for improving its sales volume and selling gross. Her father had never been very interested in the parts and service business, seeing it simply as a necessary adjunct of the dealership. "Customers always seem to be miserable back there," he had once remarked to her. "But here in the front end, everybody's happy when someone buys a new car." The service facility was not easily visible from the main highway, being hidden behind the showroom. Although the building looked old and greasy, the equipment itself was modern and well maintained. There was sufficient capacity to handle more repair work, but a higher volume would require hiring one or more new mechanics.

Customers were required to bring cars in for servicing before 8:30 a.m. After parking their cars, customers entered the service building by a side door and waited their turn to see the service writers, who occupied a cramped room with peeling paint and an interior window overlooking the service bays. Customers stood while work orders for their cars were prepared. Ringing telephones frequently interrupted the process. Filing cabinets containing customer records and other documents lined the far wall of the room.

If the work were of a routine nature, such as an oil change or tune-up, the customer was given an estimate immediately. For more complex jobs, they would be called with an estimate later in the morning once the car had been examined. Customers were required to pick up their cars by 6:00 p.m. on the day the work was completed. On several occasions, Carol had urged her father to computerize the service work order process, but he had never acted on her suggestions, so all orders continued to be handwritten on large yellow sheets, with carbon copies.

The service manager, Rick Obert, who was in his late forties, had held the position since Auto World opened at its current location. The Sullivan family considered him to be technically skilled, and he managed the mechanics effectively. However, his manner with customers could be gruff and argumentative.

CUSTOMER SURVEY RESULTS

Another set of data that Sullivan-Diaz had studied carefully was the results of the customer satisfaction surveys that were mailed to the dealership monthly by a research firm retained by Ford USA.

Purchasers of all new Ford cars were sent a questionnaire by mail within 30 days of making the purchase and asked to use a five-point scale to rate their satisfaction with the dealership sales department, vehicle preparation, and the characteristics of the vehicle itself.

The questionnaire asked how likely the purchaser would recommend the dealership, the salesperson, and the manufacturer to someone else. Other questions asked if the customers had been introduced to the dealer's service department and been given explanations on what to do if their cars needed service. Finally, there were some classification questions relating to customer demographics.

A second survey was sent to new car purchasers nine months after they bought their cars. This questionnaire began by asking about satisfaction with the vehicle and then asked customers if they had taken their vehicles to the selling dealer for service of any kind. If so, respondents were then asked to rate the service department on 14 different attributes—ranging from the attitudes of service personnel to the quality of the work performed—and then to rate their overall satisfaction with service from the dealer.

Customers were also asked about where they would go in the future for maintenance service, minor mechanical and electrical repairs, major repairs in those same categories, and bodywork. The options listed for service were the selling dealer, another Ford dealer, "some other place," or "do it yourself." Finally, there were questions about overall satisfaction with the dealer sales department and the dealership in general, as well as the likelihood of their purchasing another Ford product and buying it from the same dealership.

Dealers received monthly reports summarizing customer ratings of their dealership for the most recent month and for several previous months. To provide a comparison of how other Ford dealerships performed, the reports also included regional and national rating averages. After analysis, completed questionnaires were returned to the dealership. Since these included each customer's name, a dealer could see which customers were satisfied and which were not.

In the 30-day survey of new purchasers, Auto World achieved better than average ratings on most dimensions. One finding that puzzled Carol was that almost 90 percent of respondents answered "yes" when asked if someone from Auto World had explained what to do if they needed service, but less than a third said that they had been introduced to someone in the service department. She resolved to ask Larry Winters about this discrepancy.

The nine-month survey findings disturbed her. Although vehicle ratings were in line with national averages, the overall level of satisfaction with service at Auto World was consistently low, placing it in the bottom 25 percent of all Ford dealerships. The worst ratings for service concerned promptness of writing up orders, convenience of scheduling the work, convenience of service hours, and appearance of the service department. On length of time to complete the work, availability of needed parts, and quality of work done ("Was it fixed right?"), Auto World's rating was close to the average. For interpersonal variables such as attitude of service department personnel, politeness, understanding of customer problems, and explanation of work performed, its ratings were relatively poor.

When Sullivan-Diaz reviewed the individual questionnaires, she found that there was a wide degree of variation between customers' responses on these interpersonal variables, ranging all the way across a five-point scale from "completely satisfied" to "very dissatisfied." Curious, she went to the service files and examined the records for several dozen customers who had recently completed the nine-month surveys. At least part of the ratings could be explained by which service writers the customer had dealt with. Those who had been served two or more times by her sisters, for instance, gave much better ratings than those who had dealt primarily with Jim Fiskell, the service writer who had recently quit.

Perhaps the most worrying responses were those relating to customers' likely use of Auto World's service department in the future. More than half indicated that they would use another Ford dealer or "some other place" for maintenance service (such as oil change, lubrication, or tune-up) or for minor mechanical and electrical repairs. About 30 percent would use another source for major repairs. The rating for overall satisfaction with the selling dealer after nine months was below average and the customer's likelihood of purchasing from the same dealership again was a full point below that of buying another Ford product.

OPTIONS

Sullivan-Diaz pushed aside the spreadsheets she had printed out and shut down her laptop. It was time to go home for dinner. She saw the options for the dealership as basically twofold: either prepare the business for an early sale at what would amount to a distress price, or take a year or two to try to turn it around financially. In the latter instance, if the turnaround succeeded, the business could subsequently be sold at a higher price than it presently commanded, or the family could install a general manager to run the dealership for them.

Bill Froelich, owner of another nearby dealership plus three more in nearby cities, had offered to buy Auto World for a price that represented a fair valuation of the net assets, according to Auto World's accountants, plus $250,000 in goodwill. However, the rule of thumb when the auto industry was enjoying good times was that goodwill should be valued at $1,200 per vehicle sold each year. Carol knew that Froelich was eager to develop a network of dealerships in order to achieve economies of scale. His prices on new cars were very competitive and his nearest dealership clustered several franchises—Ford, Lincoln-Mercury, Volvo, and Jaguar—on a single large property.

AN UNWELCOME DISTURBANCE

As Carol left her office, she spotted the sales manager coming up the stairs leading from the showroom floor. "Larry," she said, "I've got a question for you."

"Fire away!" replied the sales manager.

"I've been looking at the customer satisfaction surveys. Why aren't our sales reps introducing new customers to the folks in the Service Department? It's supposedly part of our sales protocol, but it only seems to be happening about one-third of the time!"

Larry Winters shuffled his feet. "Well, Carol, basically I leave it to their discretion. We tell them about service, of course, but some of the guys on the floor feel a bit uncomfortable taking folks over to the service bays after they've been in here. It's quite a contrast, if you know what I mean."

Suddenly, the sound of shouting arose from the floor below. A man of about 40, wearing a windbreaker and jeans, was standing in the doorway yelling at one of the salespeople. The two managers could catch snatches of what he was saying, in between various obscenities:

"... three visits ... still not fixed right ... service stinks ... who's in charge here?" Everybody else in the showroom stopped what they were doing and turned to look at the newcomer.

Winters looked at his young employer and rolled his eyes. "If there was something your dad couldn't stand, it was guys like that, yelling and screaming in the showroom and asking for the boss. Walt would go hide out in his office! Don't worry, Tom'll take care of that fellow and get him out of here. What a jerk!"

"No," said Sullivan-Diaz, "I'll deal with him! One thing I learned when I worked at St. Luke's was that you don't let people yell about their problems in front of everybody else. You take them off somewhere, calm them down, and find out what's bugging them."

Exhibit 1: Marketing cars is a different proposition to marketing services for the same vehicles.

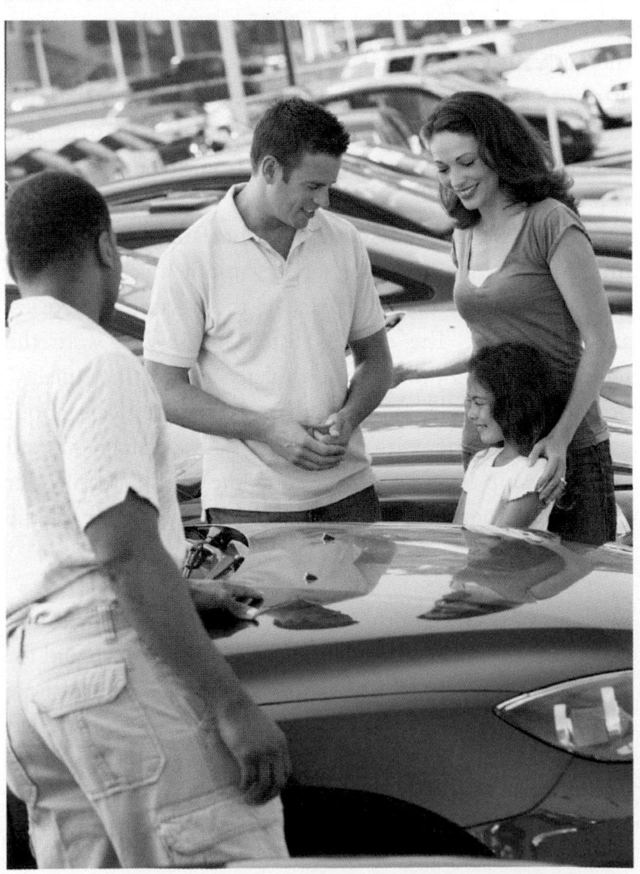

She stepped quickly down the stairs, wondering to herself, "What else have I learned in health care that I can apply to this business?"

STUDY QUESTIONS

1. How does marketing cars differ from marketing service for those same vehicles?
2. Compare and contrast the sales and service departments at Auto World.
3. From a consumer is perspective, what useful parallels do you see between operating a car sales and service dealership and operating health services?
4. What advice would you give to Carol Sullivan-Diaz?

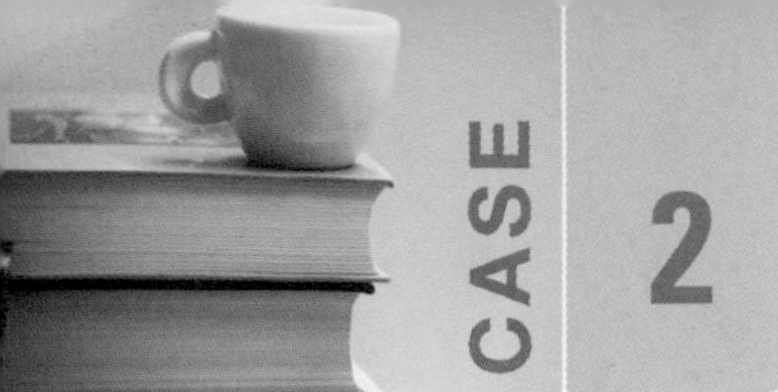

CASE 2

Dr. Beckett's Dental Office

Lauren K. Wright

A dentist seeks to differentiate her practice on the basis of quality. She constructs a new office and redesigns the practice to deliver high-quality service to her patients and to improve productivity through increased efficiency. However, it's not always easy to convince patients that her superior service justifies higher fees that are not always covered by insurance.

MANAGEMENT COMES TO DENTISTRY

"I just hope the quality differences are visible to our patients," mused Dr. Barbro Beckett as she surveyed the new office that housed her well-established dental practice. She had recently moved to her current location from an office she felt was too cramped to allow her staff to work efficiently—a factor that was becoming increasingly important as the costs of providing dental care continued to rise. While Dr. Beckett realized that productivity gains were necessary, she did not want to compromise the quality of service her patients received.

The classes Dr. Beckett took in dental school taught her a lot about the technical side of dentistry but nothing about the business side. She received no formal training in the mechanics of running a business or understanding customer needs. In fact, professional guidelines discouraged marketing or advertising of any kind. That had not been a major problem 22 years earlier, when Dr. Beckett started her practice, since profit margins had been good then. But the dental care industry had changed dramatically. Costs rose as a result of labor laws, malpractice insurance, and the constant need to invest in updating equipment and staff training as new technologies were introduced. Dr. Beckett's overhead was now between 70% and 80% of revenues before accounting for her wages or office rental costs.

At the same time, there was also a movement in the United States to reduce health-care costs to insurance companies, employers, and patients by offering "managed health care" through large health maintenance organizations (HMOs). The HMOs set the prices for various services by putting an upper limit on the amount that their doctors and dentists could charge for various procedures. The advantage to patients was that their health insurance covered virtually all costs. But the price limitations meant that HMO doctors and dentists would not be able to offer certain services that might provide better quality care but were too expensive. Dr. Beckett had decided not to become an HMO provider because the reimbursement rates were only 80–85% of what she normally charged for treatment. At these rates, she felt that she could not provide high-quality care to patients.

These changes presented some significant challenges to Dr. Beckett, who wanted to offer the highest level of dental care rather than being a low-cost provider. With the help of a consultant, she decided that her top priority was differentiating the practice on the basis of quality. She and her staff developed an internal mission statement that reflected this goal. The mission statement (prominently displayed in the back office) read, in part: *"It is our goal to provide superior dentistry in an efficient, profitable manner within the confines of a caring, quality environment."*

Since higher-quality care was more costly, Dr. Beckett's patients often had to pay fees for costs that were not covered by their insurance policies. Therefore, if the quality differences were not substantial, these patients might decide to switch to an HMO dentist or another lower-cost provider.

REDESIGNING THE SERVICE DELIVERY SYSTEM

The move to a new office gave Dr. Beckett a unique opportunity to rethink almost every aspect of her service. She wanted the work environment to reflect her own personality and values as well as provide a pleasant place for her staff to work.

Facilities and Equipment

Dr. Beckett first looked into the office spaces that were available in the Northern California town, where she practiced. She didn't find anything she liked, so she hired an architect from San Francisco to design a contemporary office building with lots of light and space. This increased the building costs by $100,000, but Dr. Beckett felt that it would be a critical factor in differentiating her service.

Dr. Beckett's new office was Scandinavian in design (reflecting her Swedish heritage and attention to detail). The waiting room and reception area were filled with modern furniture in muted shades of brown, grey, green, and purple. Live plants and flowers were abundant, and the walls were covered with art. Classical music played softly in the background. Patients could enjoy a cup of coffee or tea and browse through the large selection of current magazines and newspapers while waiting for their appointments.

The treatment areas were both functional and appealing. There was a small, sound-proof conference room at the front of the office where children could watch movies or play with toys while their parents were being treated. Educational videos and readings were available here to demonstrate different dental procedures and to explain what patients needed to do to maximize their treatment outcomes.

The chairs in the examining rooms were covered in leather and were very comfortable. Each room had a large window that allowed patients to watch birds eating at the feeders that were filled each day. There were also attractive mobiles hanging from the ceiling to distract patients from the unfamiliar sounds and sensations they might be experiencing. Headphones were available with a wide selection of music.

The entire back office staff (including Dr. Beckett) wore uniforms in cheerful shades of pink, purple, and blue that matched the office décor. Dr. Beckett's dental degrees were prominently displayed, along with certificates from various programs that she and her staff had attended to update their technical skills (Exhibit 1). All the equipment in the treatment rooms was very modern and spotlessly clean. Each room had a chairside computer monitor where both patients and staff could view digital x-rays and photos while discussing treatment options. The digital x-rays provided many benefits, including reduced radiation emissions (80% less than traditional x-rays), high-quality images that could be viewed immediately, and digital storage and transmission capabilities. The hygienists used a tool called a DIAGNOdent during teeth cleaning procedures. The DIAGNOdent was a non-invasive laser that scanned teeth for decay and detected cavities that were first starting to develop so that they could be treated at a very early stage.

Exhibit 1: A modern, state-of-the-art treatment room projects a professional image to visiting patients.

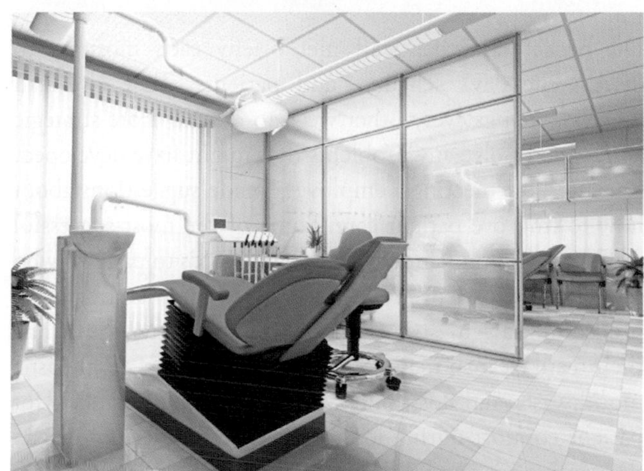

Service Personnel

There were eight employees in the dental practice, including Dr. Beckett (who was the only dentist.) The seven staff members were separated by job function into "front office" and "back office" workers. Front-office duties (covered by two employees) included receptionist and secretarial tasks and financial/budgeting work. The back office was divided into hygienists and chairside assistants.

The three chairside assistants helped the hygienists and Dr. Beckett with treatment procedures. They had specialized training for their jobs but did not need a college degree. The two hygienists handled routine exams and teeth cleaning, plus some treatment procedures. In many dental offices, hygienists tend to act like "prima donnas" because of their education (a bachelor's degree plus specialized training) and experience. According to Dr. Beckett, such an attitude could destroy any possibility of team work among the office staff. She felt very fortunate that her hygienists viewed themselves as part of a larger team that worked together to provide quality care to patients.

Dr. Beckett valued her friendships with staff members and also understood that they were a vital part of the service delivery. "Ninety percent of patients' perceptions of quality comes from their interactions with the front desk and the other employees—not from the staff's technical skills," she stated. When Dr. Beckett began to redesign her practice, she discussed her goals with the staff and involved them in the decision-making process. The changes meant new expectations and routines for most employees, and some were not willing to adapt. There was some staff turnover (mostly voluntary), as the new office procedures were implemented. The current group worked very well as a team.

Dr. Beckett and her staff met briefly each morning to discuss the day's schedule and patients. They also had longer meetings every other week to discuss more strategic issues and resolve any problems that might have developed. During these meetings, employees made suggestions about how to improve patient care. Some of the most successful staff suggestions included "thank you" cards to patients who referred other patients; follow-up calls to patients after major procedures; a "gift" bag to give to patients after they'd had their teeth cleaned that contained a toothbrush, toothpaste, mouthwash, and floss; buckwheat pillows and blankets for patient comfort during long procedures; coffee and tea in the waiting area; and a photo album in the waiting area with pictures of staff and their families (Exhibit 2).

Exhibit 2: Service delivery is enhanced through customized interaction with patients both young and old.

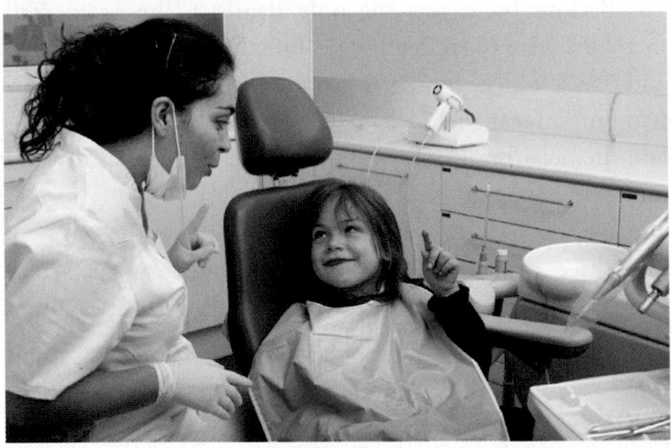

The expectations for staff performance (in terms of both technical competence and patient interactions) were very high. However, Dr. Beckett provided her employees with many opportunities to update their skills by attending classes and workshops. She also rewarded their hard work by giving monthly bonuses if business had been good. Since she shared the financial data with her staff, they could see the difference in revenues if the schedule was slow or patients were dissatisfied. This provided an extra incentive to improve service delivery. The entire office also went on trips together once a year (paid for by Dr. Beckett); spouses were welcome to participate but had to cover their own trip expenses. Past destinations for these excursions included Hawaii and Washington, DC.

Procedures and Patients

With the help of a consultant, all the office systems (including billing, ordering, lab work, and patient treatment) were redesigned. One of the main goals was to standardize some of the routine procedures so that error was reduced and all patients would receive the same level of care. Specific times were allotted for each procedure, and the staff worked very hard to see that these times were met. Office policy specified that patients should be kept waiting no longer than 20 minutes without being given the option to reschedule, and employees often called patients in advance if they knew there would be a delay. They also attempted to fill in cancellations to make sure office capacity was maximized. Staff members substituted for each other when necessary or helped with tasks that were not specifically in their job descriptions in order to make things run more smoothly.

Dr. Beckett's practice included about 2,000 "active" patients (and many more who came infrequently). They were mostly white-collar workers with professional jobs (university employees, health-care workers, and managers/ owners of local establishments). She did no advertising; all of her new business came from positive word-of-mouth by current patients. Dr. Beckett's practice was so busy that patients often had to wait three to four months for a routine cleaning and exam (if they didn't have their appointments automatically scheduled every six months), but they didn't seem to mind the delay.

The dentist believed that referrals were a real advantage because new patients didn't come in "cold." She did not have to sell herself because they had already been told about her service by friends or family. All new patients were required to have an initial exam so that Dr. Beckett could do a needs assessment and educate them about her service. She believed this was the first indication to patients that her practice was different from others they had experienced.

THE BIGGEST CHALLENGE

"Redesigning the business was the easy part," Dr. Beckett sighed. "Demonstrating the high level of quality to patients is the hard job." She said it was especially difficult since most people disliked going to the dentist or felt that it was an inconvenience and came in with a negative attitude. Dr. Beckett tried to reinforce the idea that quality dental care depended on a positive long-term relationship between patients and the dental team. The website for the practice (*chicogentledental.com*) was designed to emphasize this concept. This philosophy was also reflected in a section of the patient mission statement hanging in the waiting area: *"We are a caring, professional dental team serving motivated, quality-oriented patients interested in keeping healthy smiles for a lifetime. Our goal is to offer a progressive and educational environment. Your concerns are our focus."*

Exhibit 3: A team of closely knit professionals working under the guidance of a clear, common mission statement can help overcome the most negative pre-conceived notions about visiting the dentist.

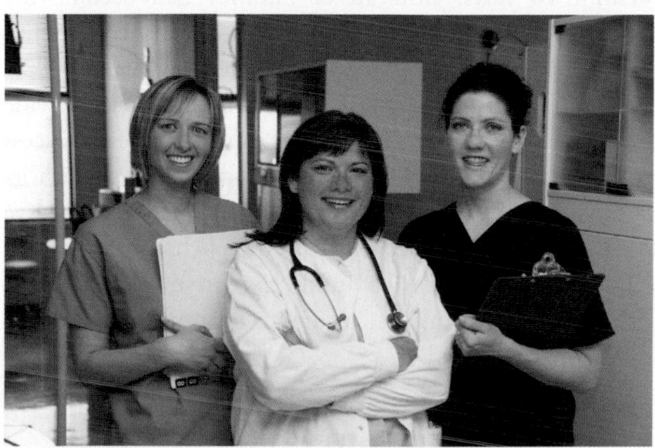

Although Dr. Beckett enjoyed her work, she admitted it could be difficult to maintain a positive attitude. The job required precision and attention to detail, and the procedures were often painful for patients. She often felt as though she was "walking on eggshells" because she knew patients were anxious and uncomfortable, which made them more critical of her service delivery. It was not uncommon for patients to say negative things to Dr. Beckett even before treatment began (such as, "I really hate going to the dentist—it's not you, but I just don't want to be here!"). When this happened, she reminded herself that she was providing quality service whether patients appreciated it or not. "The person will usually have to have the dental work done anyway," she remarked, "So I just do the best job I can and make them as comfortable as possible." Even though patients seldom expressed appreciation for her services, she hoped that she made a positive difference in their health or appearance that would benefit them in the long run.

STUDY QUESTIONS

1. Which of the seven elements of the services marketing mix are addressed in this case? Give examples of each "P" you identify.
2. Why do people dislike going to the dentist? Do you feel Dr. Beckett has addressed this problem effectively?
3. How do Dr. Beckett and her staff educate patients about the service they are receiving? What else could they do?
4. What supplementary services are offered? How do they enhance service delivery?
5. Contrast your own dental care experiences with those offered by Dr. Beckett's practice. What differences do you see? Based on your review of this case, what advice would you give to (a) your current or former dentist, and (b) Dr. Beckett?
6. Evaluate Dr. Beckett's web site (*chicogentledental.com*). What strengths do you think the web site has? What improvements would you suggest?

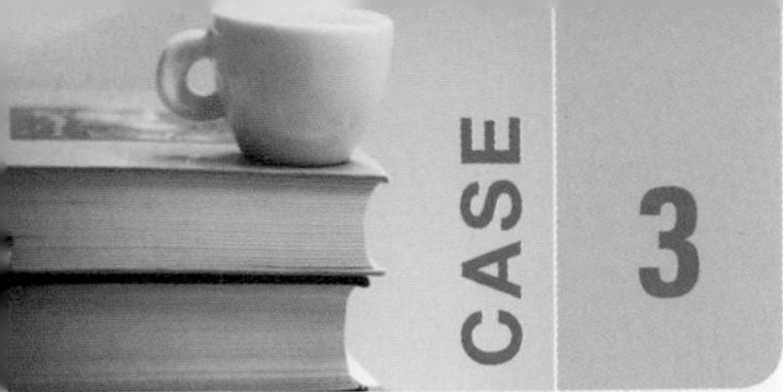

Bouleau & Huntley: Cross-Selling Professional Services

Jochen Wirtz and Suzanne Lowe

A professional firm specializing in pension fund audits sought to extend the firm's relationships with existing clients in the Philippines by offering consulting services. But the first attempt at cross-selling was a flop. What went wrong and why?

Juan Miguel Duavit, a new partner and co-director in the Manila office of Bouleau & Huntley, pondered over what had gone wrong earlier in the day at his meeting with the National Metals Corporation, a Philippines-based major metals manufacturer, where his carefully prepared consulting presentation had been greeted by a bewildered silence.

THE FIRM

Duavit, 42, joined Bouleau & Huntley three months earlier, in March 2012. Bouleau & Huntley is a multinational corporation with headquarters in New York that specialised in pension funds auditing and human resource management. Its Manila office has been serving clients in the Philippines for the past 14 years.

The firm was founded in 1923 by Robert Bouleau, a New York actuary, and William Huntley, an insurance executive, who had noted that American corporations were rapidly creating new pension funds for their executives. The two men recognized that this trend would create vast new opportunities for a professional firm that could advise firms properly and audit their plans every year, as required by US laws at the time.

Within 10 years, Bouleau & Huntley had become the leader of a new profession, with a well-established presence in the United States. Subsequently, it began opening offices overseas. By 2012, Bouleau & Huntley was a worldwide firm with 42 offices, 325 partners, and revenues in excess of US$1.2 billion. The firm continued to flourish with its combination of high-quality professionalism and aggressive marketing. New divisions had been launched in four areas closely related to pension funds: executive compensation, personnel management, insurance consulting, and re-insurance consulting.

Expansion into the Philippines

The Philippines has a Retirement Act, the Republic Act No. 7641, which requires that an employee facing compulsory retirement at age 65 must receive from his employer a retirement benefit based on his final monthly salary and the number of years worked with the firm. Most companies turn to the private insurance industry for pension schemes.

Having repeatedly been sought out by various prestigious clients in the Philippines, Bouleau & Huntley opened its Manila office in 1998. By 2012, the office had 11 partners and 120 employees in the Philippines, operating from its headquarters in Metro Manila, with small satellite offices in Cebu and Luzon. The firm's total revenues in the Philippines were 545 million pesos (approximately US$13 million).[1]

The firm's mission for its Philippines office, as stated by its geographic director, Jose Arellano, was "to serve large international companies active in the Philippines and to develop a national clientele among leading Filipino

 Jochen Wirtz is Professor of Marketing, NUS Business School, and Director of the UCLA – NUS Executive MBA Program. Suzanne Lowe is President, Expertise Marketing LLC.

The authors gratefully acknowledge Professor Christopher Lovelock for his contribution to earlier versions of this case. Furthermore, the authors thank Professor Leonardo R. Perez Jr., Chairman, Marketing Management Department, College of Business & Economics, De La Salle University; Tom Sablak, FSA, MAAA, EA, FCA, Partner at October Three; LLC; Debbie Smith, Partner, National Professional Standards; Anna Dourdourekas, Senior Manager, Independence and Ethics, Grant Thornton LLP; and Pressy Santos-Rowe (a former fellow student at the London Business School of the first author) for their feedback and assistance with the writing of this case.

1 Peso is the Philippine currency. The exchange rate in January 2012 was ₱100 = US$2.26.

companies." In keeping with Bouleau & Huntley's firm-wide growth goals for selected lines of business in its total portfolio of services, the Manila office had been assigned the task of experimenting with expansion into other types of professional activities that could be adopted worldwide throughout Bouleau & Huntley.

Duavit Changes Jobs

Duavit graduated from the prestigious University of the Philippines (UP). After a two-year stint with Oracle Corporation as a brand manager, he spent two years in the United States, obtaining an MBA from the Wharton School. Upon returning to the Philippines, he joined the glass division of Glasscore, holding several jobs in marketing and strategic planning over a four-year period. Through a UP classmate, he was recruited by the Manila office of Ascent Strategic Consultants (ASC), where he enjoyed a very successful career for 12 years, spending the last seven as a partner in ASC. However, over time, he began to feel restless. His personal interest in the "soft" side of consulting problems, dealing with people rather than profits and efficiency alone, was not shared by the leader in ASC.

It was through Jose Arellano, one of his neighbors in the plush Sangun district, that Duavit first became familiar with Bouleau & Huntley. Both men served on the board of the private school attended by their children and had come to know each other socially. Over dinner one evening, Arellano suggested that his friend think seriously about joining Bouleau & Huntley. "I've been working with our strategy committee in New York to develop new lines of professional activity," he told Duavit. "We believe strategy consulting is a natural added service line that our current clients would find valuable. What you have done with ASC is of real interest to us, and I am sure you would enjoy working with our personnel management and compensation partners." Warming to his theme, Arellano continued:

> We've been hugely successful in our major activity of pension fund auditing. Worldwide, we have 350 Fortune 500 companies as our steady clients. Historically, it's been a very profitable business, enjoying steady growth as the pension funds themselves grow in size. However, this has attracted new competition, and the business is becoming more price sensitive than in the past. In addition, it is heavily influenced either positively or negatively by regulatory and national political decisions totally beyond our control.
>
> In the Philippines, we have decided to explore entering new professional areas, such as the strategy and general management consulting that you know so well. We think the synergies of cross-selling your strategy consulting services with our main line of pension fund auditing services are obvious. There are two international trends that have informed our thinking about this idea.
>
> One is that large strategy consulting firms like the Boston Consulting Group and McKinsey & Company are beginning to sell strategy work in what they call emerging markets like the Philippines. Also, as I'm sure you are aware, the Big Four accounting firms are forbidden from selling strategy work to their audit clients in the United States. But they recognize that, in Europe and many Asian countries, the rules are looser, and they are working hard to offer "one-stop shopping" to their clients.
>
> It won't surprise you that we are keen to capture our share of the strategy consulting market and to consolidate our hold on our pension audit clients before the strategy consultancies or Big Four accounting firms can take away our market share. With someone like you on board and with the team we will help you build up, it should be possible to bring new value to our pension fund audit clients, generate additional cash flow from them, gain new clients for the firm, and protect our competitive advantage.

Duavit and Arellano had discussed these opportunities further in conversations during the subsequent months and confirmed their mutual interest. Both men agreed that a vast potential existed in the Philippines among leading Filipino companies, as well as with the Asian affiliates of multi-national groups headquartered in Manila. Arellano made several calls and exchanged confidential e-mails with the managing director and several senior partners of the firm about hiring Duavit on a quasi-equal basis to himself, in recognition of his extensive experience and in anticipation of expected cross-selling results.

Finally, over lunch at Manila Hotel one day, Arellano answered Duavit's discerning questions about the cross-selling environment at Bouleau & Huntley. Arellano provided Duavit with several examples that the firm, although new at cross-selling in the Philippines, had successfully supported cross-selling in other countries and regions. Arellano offered Duavit immediate directorship, a new departure for Bouleau & Huntley, plus a compensation package so generous that it was "impossible to refuse." Not only would Duavit receive a fixed compensation package equal to his current total remuneration, but there was a provision for a large bonus (up to 30% of his salary) on incremental business from existing clients and up to 50% for the successful acquisition of new clients.

Working at Bouleau & Huntley

Duavit joined the Manila office of Bouleau & Huntley in March 2012. His new colleagues welcomed him warmly, but he was surprised to find them somewhat reticent about discussing their own clients. Duavit ascribed this to professional respect for confidentiality. He set to work, following up several leads of his own. Within three months, he brought in two new consulting clients. He was also involved in arranging for Bouleau & Huntley to audit a supplementary pension fund that one of his former employers was creating for its senior executives. He had started building up a team of four younger consultants, including one bright young man who, after spending two years in Bouleau & Huntley's compensation practice, had decided to move on to strategic work.

Duavit was already looking forward to the day when he could propose that this enthusiastic consultant should become the first junior partner of the new Manila practice. Despite these early successes, he remained concerned about the reserved attitude of his colleagues. One day, when he was lunching with three of them, he answered their questions about his work at ASC. Describing a project that he had directed the previous year to reorganize a major oil company, he encountered a mixture of disbelief and incomprehension.

"Do you mean that you and your colleagues actually restructured this enormous company last year?" one of them asked.

"Yes," Duavit replied. "We helped them simplify their structure, reduce the number of levels from 11 to 6, and even helped them relocate 482 people, saving about 644 million pesos (US$14.9 million) in overhead costs. Then we streamlined their management information and planning systems. Total fees amounted to 81 million pesos (US$1.9 million) for 15 months of continued work by a team that ranged in size from four to seven consultants."

"Hey, what happened to their pension funds?" interjected another of his colleagues.

"Nothing, I believe," responded Duavit, slightly surprised. "Do you want an introduction to their CEO to sell him a pension fund audit?"

"No, we were just curious about the name of the guy who set up their last pension fund," another replied.

Despite his successful selling and high-quality client work in his first three months at the firm, Duavit was surprised to see that his kind of work did not interest them at all. He made a mental note to work harder to better understand the obscure workings of his actuarial colleagues' assignments. He marveled at the enormous fees the firm charged for what seemed to him was tedious, arcane, and repetitive work. He was also deeply impressed by two things: their extensive use of standardized software systems that seemed to be doing all the work, and the ease with which they obtained repeat business year after year without any need for the costly and time-consuming "developmental" work required in his own type of consulting. All his pension auditing colleagues did was send a letter of renewal at the end of each year, with a prepared space for the company to sign. It seemed so easy! One Friday afternoon, just before 5 p.m., Duavit was beginning to check a 50-page report due at the client's the following Monday and he still had to write a proposal before going home for the weekend. Two of his partner colleagues poked their heads in at his open doorway. They were carrying their briefcases and were evidently leaving for home. Quickly sizing up the situation, one of them, Victor Vasquez, remarked cheerily, "My dear *pare* (the Filipino equivalent of "pal" or "chap"), you're obviously in the wrong business! You should have gotten an actuarial degree like us, instead of wasting your time at Wharton! See you on Monday! Cheers!"

Duavit immediately sent Arellano an e-mail outlining his concerns that his new colleagues didn't seem very enthusiastic to help him build the firm's Philippines strategy-consulting revenues. Isn't cross-selling a strategic mandate, he asked Arellano? Arellano replied promptly, and promised to encourage Vasquez (and other Bouleau & Huntley actuaries) to introduce Duavit to their pension fund audit clients.

A PRESENTATION AT THE NATIONAL METALS CORPORATION

Two weeks later, Duavit felt Arellano's support was finally coming to fruition. Vasquez had agreed to introduce him to his largest client, the National Metals Corporation, a company involved in refining and marketing copper, chromium, and nickel. Since Duavit had led an ASC consulting team for Amix, a large mill for primary and semi-finished iron and steel in Indonesia, several years earlier, he knew the metal business and was certain that he could do something beneficial for Vasquez's client.

Vasquez and Duavit briefly communicated about an upcoming meeting that Vasquez had arranged. Duavit generally described his plan to present a brief overview of his work to the client. Although he didn't say so directly, he felt certain Vasquez understood his real goals, which were to impress Vasquez's client and seek an introduction to one of his colleagues.

At the National Metals Corporation's main administrative office in Makati City, Vasquez led Duavit along a series of tortuous corridors to the office of Carlos Aseniero. Duavit was a bit surprised to find that his colleague's principal contact was a harassed-looking little man in a cluttered office. Aseniero greeted them politely and cleared several files off the chairs so the two visitors could sit down.

After the introductions were made and Vasquez confirmed that the audit report would be ready on the promised date, Duavit launched into his presentation. He delivered a thorough but succinct analysis of five years of published figures, complete with diagrams he had prepared that very morning. He compared overall profitability, days of inventory, and asset rotation for the National Metals Corporation against three of its main Asian competitors. Duavit concluded what he considered to be a stimulating 15-minute presentation by inviting Aseniero to introduce him to the appropriate National Metals colleague who could make use of Bouleau & Huntley's strategic consulting services to help the company increase market share and improve profitability.

Expecting an interested response, Duavit was amazed to be greeted by complete silence in the room. Not only Aseniero but also Vasquez appeared somewhat bewildered by what they had just heard.

Seeking to regain the initiative, Duavit asked Aseniero, "Do you think that your boss would be interested in pursuing these issues further?"

Looking slightly ill at ease, Aseniero replied, "You have to understand that my office reports to the assistant finance director, reflecting the immense amounts of money the company is investing in this pension fund. The fund is also used as collateral for some of the company's borrowings. I don't believe that my boss, Mr. Perez, participates in strategy discussions with our board. Of course, I could ask him to arrange an appointment with our director general (CEO), but I'm told he's a very busy man."

"Thank you, Mr. Aseniero," Vasquez said, rising to his feet and holding out his hand. "My colleague and I really appreciate your willingness to take time out of your busy schedule."

Duavit also shook hands with Aseniero and thanked him but found it difficult to hide his disappointment. The two partners left the office and retraced their way back to the reception area.

"What happened?" Duavit asked, as the two of them climbed back into Vasquez's new top-of-the range Audi. "I thought that I gave him a very convincing line. Wasn't he interested? Or did he simply not understand?"

Vasquez eased the Audi out of the parking lot and frowned. "Duavit, I owe you an apology. I didn't really understand what you wanted to present to Aseniero, nor did I have a good grasp of your expertise. I didn't support you very well in that meeting. I think your presentation overwhelmed him rather than impressed him. And it made us look like we hadn't done our homework about what our client needs. I'll never be that unprepared again!"

Duavit remained silent for a time. It was becoming clear to him that, despite Arellano's individual encouragement to Vasquez, the actuarial partners in general appeared to be more interested in using him and his work to bring in new clients for their own practice, rather than the other way around. Duavit also realized that he and Vasquez didn't really understand each other's perspectives at all. Yet he liked what Jose Arellano had told him about Bouleau & Huntley's combination of professionalism and aggressive marketing. Obviously, a lot still needed to be done before the synergies he and Arellano had dreamed about could be achieved.

"Well, let's use this situation to help us improve," Duavit said eventually, as Vasquez accelerated onto Ayala Avenue. "Victor, let's think this experience through and decide, together with our other partners, what we should do differently to implement our firm's cross-selling strategies. I know we want to succeed as a team. Our clients depend on us to bring them value, and today we acted pretty tactically. What do you think?"

"I agree, Juan," Vasquez answered. "In fact, Jose has given me the task of setting up the agenda for our yearly Manila Partners meeting in Makati City next month. I still have nothing for the morning of the third day. Let's work together to present our ideas on cross-selling key strategies and propose cross-selling processes that could be used by all the partners to improve their results. How much time do you think we'll need?"

APPENDIX: THE AUDITING AND CONSULTING WORLD IN 2012

Until the 1970s, auditing firms had focused mostly on auditing activities. However, with the rise of information technology (IT), many firms, including the Big Six (now Big Four) accounting firms, branched into IT and management consulting. Soon, revenues from consulting activities far exceeded their auditing revenues.

Things came to a head after the collapse and bankruptcy of the energy giant, Enron, in December 2001 and the document-destruction scandal and subsequent indictment of its auditor Arthur Andersen by the US Justice Department. Arthur Andersen's dual role of auditor and consultant for Enron put it in the spotlight, raising concern about the issue of conflict of interest from serving corporate managers and auditing (i.e., protecting public interest).

Critics argued that the provision of non-audit services by audit firms could interfere with the independence of auditors and compromise the quality of their audits. In fact, a few academic studies found that there was more "creative accounting" among companies that also engaged their auditors in large consulting projects than in firms that made little use of their auditors for non-auditing-related services. As a result, Ernst & Young's decision to sell off its consulting arm to Gemini Consulting two years before the Enron collapse was hailed as a stroke of genius. After the Enron incident, PricewaterhouseCoopers sold its PwC Consulting unit to IBM Corporation, while Andersen Worldwide sold its IT consulting practices on a piecemeal basis.

Over the next decade, the world's economies shifted, making more "mundane" work like operations management and auditing attractive again for big accounting and management consultancies. The trend was globally noticeable by mid-2011.

Moreover, also by mid-2011, cross-selling of pension fund auditing and consultancy services appeared to present much less conflict of interest, especially in emerging markets. Pension funds were generally managed separately from other financial aspects of a business. Thus, unlike auditing of accounts, pension fund auditing was not concerned with the operations of a firm. Hence, it would be easier for pension fund auditors to maintain independence, even if their firm provided consultancy services to their audit clients. Nevertheless, Bouleau & Huntley would have to be sensitive to potential conflict of interests and how its activities were perceived in the market.

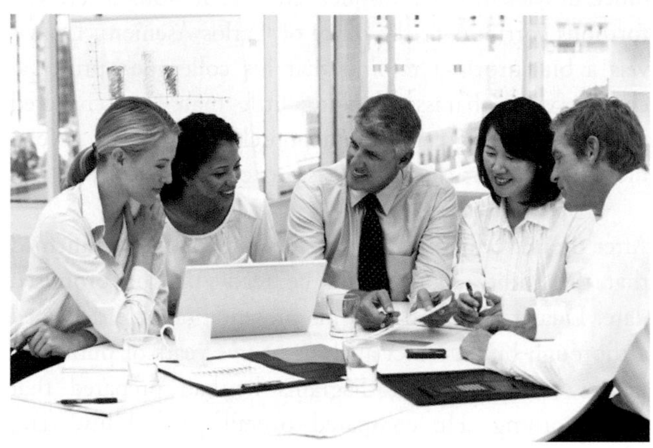

STUDY QUESTIONS

1. What do you see as the key differences between pension fund auditing and management consulting? How good is the fit between the two?
2. Evaluate the visit to the National Metals Corporation. What happened?
3. What are the lessons of this experience?
4. What actions should Bouleau & Huntley take now?

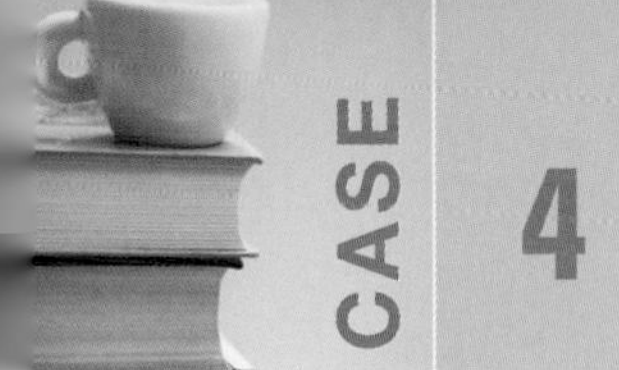

CASE 4

CASE STUDY

Banyan Tree: Branding the Intangible

Jochen Wirtz

Banyan Tree Hotels and Resorts had become a leading player in the luxury resort and spa market in Asia. As part of its growth strategy, Banyan Tree had launched new brands and brand extensions that included resorts, spas, residences, destination club memberships, retail outlets, and even museum shops. Now, the company is preparing to aggressively grow its global footprint in the Americas, Caribbean, Europe and the Middle East while preserving its distinctive Asian identity and strong brand image of Banyan Tree.

A brand synonymous with private villas, tropical garden spas, and retail galleries promoting traditional craft, Banyan Tree Hotels and Resorts received its first guest in 1994 in Phuket, Thailand. Since then, it had grown into a leading manager and developer of niche and premium resorts, hotels, and spas in Asia Pacific.

Despite having minimal advertising, Banyan Tree achieved a global exposure and a high level of brand awareness through the company's public relations and global marketing programs. Much interest was also generated by the company's socially responsible business values and practices caring for the social and natural environments. With a firm foothold in the medium-sized luxury resorts market, the company introduced a new and contemporary brand, Angsana, in 2000 to gain a wider customer base.

As the resorts market became increasingly crowded with similar competitive offerings, lured by the success of Banyan Tree, the company had to contemplate about expanding its business and preserving its distinct identity. Banyan Tree and Angsana resorts were expanding geographically outside of Asia and also into the urban hotel market in major cities throughout the world. With around 34 hotels and resorts scheduled to open over the next three years, Banyan Tree faced the challenge of translating and maintaining the success of a niche Asian hospitality brand into various market segments on a global scale.

COMPANY BACKGROUND

By early 2009, Banyan Tree Holdings Ltd (BTHR) managed and/or had ownership interests in 25 resorts and hotels, 68 spas, 65 retail galleries, and two golf courses in more than 55 locations in 23 countries. Since its establishment in 1994, the company's flagship brand, Banyan Tree, had won some 400 international tourism, hospitality, design, and marketing awards, some of which included "Best Resort Hotel in Asia Pacific" (Phuket) for four consecutive years from Business Traveller Awards since 2002, "Seychelles' Best Resort" and "Seychelles' Best Spa" from World Travel Awards (2003), "Best Hotels for Rooms" (Bangkok) from UK Conde Nast Traveller (2006), "Best Hotel (Luxury)" (Lijiang) from Hospitality Design Awards (2007), and "PATA Gold Award—Ecotourism Project Category" (Bintan) from Pacific Asia Travel Association Gold Awards (2008).[1]

BTHR was founded by Ho Kwon Ping, a travel enthusiast and former journalist, and his wife Claire Chiang, a strong advocate of corporate social responsibility. Prior to entering the hotel and resort business, Ho spent some 15 years managing the family business, which was into everything imaginable, such as commodities, food products, consumer electronics, and property development. It competed mainly on cost and was not dominant in any particular either country or industry. Meanwhile, Chiang was deeply involved in sociology and social issues.

The closing of a factory in Thailand one year after its opening—because it lost out to other low-cost producers

Jochen Wirtz is Professor of Marketing and Academic Director of the UCLA—NUS Executive MBA Program at the National University of Singapore.

The support and feedback of the management of Banyan Tree Hotels & Resorts in the writing of this case are gratefully acknowledged.

1 The complete list of awards won by Banyan Tree can be found on the company's website at *www.banyantree.com*.

in Indonesia—was the last straw for Ho, who then realized that a low-cost strategy was not only difficult to follow but would also lead nowhere. Determined to craft out something proprietary that would allow the company to become a price maker rather than a price taker, Ho decided that building a strong brand was the only way for him to maintain a sustainable competitive advantage.

The idea of entering the luxury resorts market was inspired by the gap in the hotel industry that giant chains such as the Hilton and Shangri-La could not fill. There was a market segment that wanted private and intimate accommodation but without the expectation of glitzy chain hotels. This was fueled by the sharp price gap between the luxurious Aman Resorts and other resorts in the luxury resorts market. For example, in 2004 the Amanpuri in Thailand, one of Aman's resorts, charged a rack rate for its villas ranging from US$650 to over US$7,000 a night, whereas the prices of other luxury resorts, such as the Shangri-La Hotel and Phuket Arcadia Beach Resort by Hilton in Thailand were priced below US$350.

Noticing the big difference in prices between Aman Resorts and the other resorts in the luxury resorts market, Ho saw potential for offering an innovative niche product that could also bridge the price gap in this market. Ho and Chiang had backpacked throughout the world in their youth, and were seasoned travelers themselves. Their extensive travel experience is evident in their non-conforming beliefs that resorts should provide more than just accommodation. Ho and Chiang hit upon the idea of building a resort comprising individual villas, with locally inspired architectural design and positioned as a romantic and intimate escapade for guests. Banyan Tree moved its positioning into the higher end of the luxury market, and by 2008, its rack rates were typically between US$1,200 and $7,000 for the resort in Phuket, and between €1,500 and €4,200 for the resort in the Seychelles.

Operations at Banyan Tree began with only one resort in Phuket, situated on a former mining site once deemed too severely ravaged to sustain any form of development by a United Nations Development Program planning unit and the Tourism Authority of Thailand. It was a bold decision, but the company, together with Ho, Chiang, and Ho's brother Ho Kwon Cjan, restored it after extensive rehabilitation works costing a total of $250 million. The Banyan Tree Phuket was so successful when it was finally launched that the company worked quickly to build two other resorts, one at Bintan Island in Indonesia and the other at Vabbinfaru Island in the Maldives. The company never looked back since. Even though Asia's travel industry experienced periodic meltdowns such as the Asian economic crisis in 1997/8, the September 11 attacks on the World Trade Center in 2001, the dot.com crisis in 2001/2, severe acute respiratory syndrome (SARS) in 2003, and the Indian Ocean tsunami on December 26, 2004, no employee was retrenched and room rates at Banyan Tree rose steadily.

BRAND ORIGINS

Known as *Yung Shue Wan* in the local dialect, Banyan Tree Bay was a fishing village on Lamma Island in Hong Kong where Ho and his wife Chiang lived for three idyllic years before he joined the family business. Despite the village's modest and rustic setting, they remember it to be a sanctuary of romance and intimacy. The large canopies of the Banyan Tree also showed semblance of the shelter afforded by Asia's tropical rainforests. Ho and Chiang thus decided to name their resort Banyan Tree, and position it as a sanctuary for the senses.

THE SERVICE OFFERING

Unlike most other resorts then, Banyan Tree resorts comprised individual villas that came with a private pool, Jacuzzi, or spa treatment room, each designed to offer guests exclusivity and utmost privacy. For example, a guest could skinny-dip in the private pool within his villa without being seen by other guests, putting him in a world of his own (see Exhibit 1).

Exhibit 1: A world of privacy in a double pool villa at Banyan Tree Phuket.

All Banyan Tree hotels and resorts were designed around the concept of providing "a sense of place" to reflect and enhance the culture and heritage of the destination. This is reflected in the architecture, furnishings, landscape, vegetation and the service offers. To create a sense of exotic sensuality and ensure the privacy of its guests, the resorts are designed to blend into the natural landscape of the surrounding environment and use the natural foliage and boulders as the privacy screen (see Exhibit 2 showing Banyan Tree Seychelles). The furnishings of Banyan Tree villas were deliberately native to convey the exoticism of the destination with its rich local flavor and luxurious feel. The spa pavilions in Seychelles were constructed around the large granite boulders and lush foliage to offer an outdoor spa experience in complete privacy. The resorts' local flavor was also reflected in the services offered, some of which were unique to certain resorts. Employees were allowed to vary the service delivery process according to local culture and practices, as long as these were consistent with the brand promise of romance and intimacy. Thus, in Phuket, for instance, a couple could enjoy dinner on a traditional Thai long tail boat accompanied by private Thai musicians while cruising instead of dining in a restaurant. Banyan Tree Phuket also offered wedding packages in which couples were blessed by Buddhist monks. In the Maldives, wedding ceremonies could be conducted underwater among the corals. Guests could also choose to dine in a castaway sandbank with only their private chefs and the stars for company, and watch the sunset toasting champagne on a Turkish gullet returning from a trip watching a school of spinner dolphins.

Exhibit 2: Banyan Tree Seychelles blends well into its natural environment.

Products and services were conceived with the desired customer experience in mind. One such product was the "Intimate Moments" package, specially created for couples. This was presented as a surprise when guests returned to find their villas decorated with lit candles, incense oil lamps burning, flower petals spread throughout the room, satin sheets on the decorated bed, a chilled bottle of champagne or wine and tidbits placed next to the outdoor bath which itself is decorated with flowers and candles and bath oils. The couple was presented with a variety of aromatic massage oils to further inspire those intimate moments.

Another draw of the resorts was the Banyan Tree Spa, found at every Banyan Tree property. The pioneer of the tropical garden spas concept, Banyan Tree Spas offered a variety of aromatic oil massages, and face and body beauty treatments using traditional Asian therapies, with a choice of indoor or outdoor treatment. The spa products used were natural, indigenous products made from local herbs and spices. Non-clinical in concept, Banyan Tree Spas relied mainly on the "human touch" instead of energy-consuming, high-tech equipment. The spa experience was promoted as a sensorial, intimate experience that would rejuvenate the "body, mind, and soul" and was mainly targeted at couples who would enjoy their treatments together.

Exhibit 3: The Banyan Tree Spa Pavilion with a view.

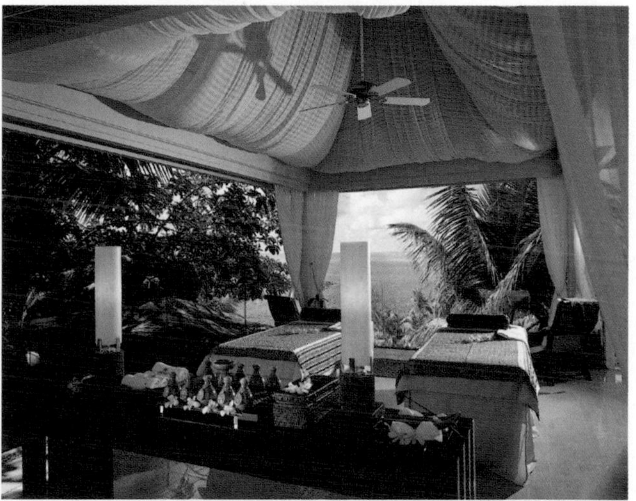

In line with Banyan Tree's ethos of conserving local culture and heritage and promoting cottage crafts, Chiang founded the Banyan Tree Gallery, a retail outlet showcasing indigenous crafts. Banyan Tree Gallery outlets were set up in each resort. Items sold were made by local artisans and included traditionally woven handmade fabrics, garments, jewelry, handicrafts, tribal art, and spa accessories, such as incense candles and massage oils, which guests could use at home to recreate the Banyan Tree experience.

Exhibit 4: A contemporary Asian shopping experience with a strong sense of corporate responsibility at Banyan Tree Gallery.

Banyan Tree Gallery embarked on projects to support the various communities in the locations Banyan Tree resorts are situated, and worked closely with village cooperatives and not-for-profit craft marketing agents to provide gainful employment to the artisans. While acting as a marketing channel for Asian crafts like basket weaving, hill tribe cross-stitching and lacquer ware, Banyan Tree Gallery also educated its customers about the crafts with an accompanying write-up. In the course of Banyan Tree Gallery's operations, the community outreach extended from across Thailand to Laos, Cambodia, India, Nepal, Sri Lanka, Indonesia, Malaysia, and Singapore.

The result of Banyan Tree's efforts was "a very exclusive, private holiday feeling", as described by one guest. Another guest commented, "It's a treat for all the special occasions like honeymoons and wedding anniversaries. It's the architecture, the sense of place and the promise of romance."

MARKETING BANYAN TREE

In the first two years after Banyan Tree was launched, the company's marketing communications was managed by an international advertising agency. The agency also designed the Banyan Tree logo shown in Exhibit 5 and, together with the management, came up with the marketing tagline "Sanctuary for the Senses."

Exhibit 5: The Banyan Tree logo.

BANYAN TREE

HOTELS

AND RESORTS

Though furnished luxuriously, Banyan Tree resorts were promoted as providing romantic and intimate "smallish" hotel experiences, rather than luxurious accommodation as touted by most competitors then. "Banyan Tree Experiences" was marketed as intimate private moments. The resorts saw themselves as setting the stage for guests to create those unforgettable memories.

When Banyan Tree was first launched, extensive advertising was carried out for a short period of time to gain recognition in the industry. Subsequently, the company scaled down on advertising and kept it minimal, mainly in high-end travel magazines in key markets. The advertisements were visual in nature with succinct copy or showcase the awards and accolades won. Exhibit 6 shows a Banyan Tree advertisement highlighting award-winning Banyan Tree Spa.

Exhibit 6: An advertisement showcasing "Spa of the Year" award from Conde Nast Traveller.

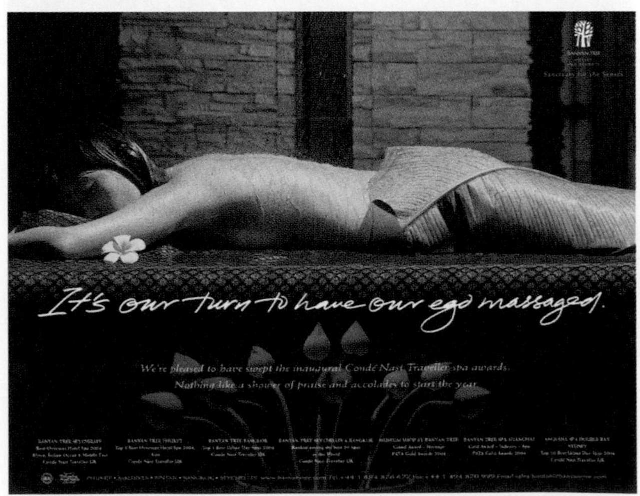

Brand awareness for Banyan Tree was generated largely through public relations and global marketing programs. For example, relationships with travel editors and writers were cultivated to encourage visits to the resorts. This helped to increase editorial coverage on Banyan Tree, which management felt was more effective in conveying the "Banyan Tree Experience" from an impartial third-party perspective. Its website, www.banyantree.com, increasingly drove online bookings and provided vivid information about the latest offerings of Banyan Tree's fast-growing portfolio.

The management of marketing activities was centralized at its headquarters in Singapore in order to maintain consistency in brand building. BTHR appointed a few key wholesalers in each targeted market and worked closely with them to promote sales. Rather than selling through wholesale and retail agents that catered to the general market, BTHR chose to work only with agents specializing in exclusive luxury holidays targeted at wealthy customers. Global exposure was also achieved through Banyan Tree's membership in the Small Luxury Hotels and Leading Hotels of the World. Targeting high-end consumers, they represent various independent exclusive hotels and have sales offices in major cities around the world.

The end of 2007 marked a new stage of Banyan Tree's global expansion, with the launch of its own GDS code "BY." GDS is a Global Distribution System that is used by travel providers to process airline, hotel, car rental reservations across 640,000 terminals of travel agents and other distribution partners around the world. Prior to BY, Banyan Tree was represented by its marketing partners, Leading Hotels of the World (LW) and Small Luxury Hotels (LX). Now, Banyan Tree had its unique identity on the GDS code, further strengthening its brand presence and customer ownership. Banyan Tree now had enough critical mass to ensure the economic feasibility of a GDS private label. The acquisition of its own GDS code meant that Banyan Tree was transitioning from a relatively small regional player to a global brand in the eyes of the travel industry.

BRAND VALUES

Banyan Tree embraced certain values, such as actively caring for the natural and human environment, revitalizing local communities, which in turn created pride and respect among staff. The company hoped to build the brand on values that employees and customers could identify with and support as part of their own life values. A dedicated corporate social responsibility committee, headed by Chiang and featuring general managers and valued associates from each resort, was formed to focus on these issues with both a regional overview and simultaneously local perspectives. Thus, the company worked actively to preserve, protect, and promote the natural and human environments in which Banyan Tree resorts were located.

PRESERVING THE ENVIRONMENT

Resorts were built using local materials as far as possible and, at the same time, minimizing the impact on the environment. At Banyan Tree Bintan, for example, the 70 villas located in a rainforest were constructed around existing trees, cutting down as few trees as possible, to minimize the impact the resort had on the natural environment. The villas were built on stilts and platforms to avoid cutting trees and possible soil erosion. At Banyan Tree Maldives Vabbinfaru and Banyan Tree Seychelles, fresh water supply was obtained by the more expensive method of desalination, instead of extracting water from the underground water table, which risked long-term disruption of the ecological system. Toiletries, such as shampoo, hair conditioner, bath foam, and body lotion, provided in the resorts were non-toxic and biodegradable, and filled in reusable containers made from celadon or ceramic. Refuse was recycled where possible and treated through an in-house incinerator system otherwise. Waste water was also treated and recycled in the irrigation of resort landscapes.

Through the retail arm Banyan Tree Gallery, the human environment efforts were evident in the active sourcing of traditional crafts from indigenous tribes to provide gainful employment. These employment opportunities provided a source of income for the tribes and, at the same time, preserve their unique heritage.

In line with the Banyan Tree Group's Green Imperative initiative, Banyan Tree Gallery constantly used eco-friendly and recycled materials in the development of its merchandise. Examples included photo frames made using discarded telephone directories, elephant dung paper stationary, and lead-free celadon and ceramic spa amenities. Unique collections like the black resin turtles stationery range and leaf-inspired merchandise were created to promote environmental awareness, and were accompanied by a write-up to educate the consumer on the targeted conservation campaign. In support of animal rights, the galleries did not carry products made from shell or ivory.

Besides trying to conduct business in an environmentally responsible manner, BTHR actively pursued a number of key initiatives, including its Greening Communities program. Greening Communities was launched as a challenge to seven participating resorts. It planted 28,321 trees in the first two years of the program. Banyan Tree Lijiang, for example, planted some 20,000 fruit trees to create additional income for families of the supporting community. While trees will absorb carbon and improve the quality of the environment, the main goal of this program was to engage local communities, associates, and guests to share the causes of climate change and actions that can reduce our collective carbon footprint.

CREATING BRAND OWNERSHIP AMONG EMPLOYEES

All Banyan Tree employees were trained to the basic standards of five-star service establishments, which included greeting guests, remembering their first names, and anticipating their needs. In addition, some employees got a taste of the "Banyan Tree Experience" as part of their training. The management believed that the stay would help employees understand better what guests will experience and, in return, enhance their delivery of special experiences for the guests.

Although management imposed strict rules in the administration of the resorts, employees were empowered to exercise creativity and sensitivity. For example, the housekeeping teams were not restricted by a standard bed decoration. Rather, they were given room for creativity although they had general guidelines for turning the bed to keep in line with the standards of a premium resort. Banyan Tree invested liberally in staff welfare: Employees were taken to and from work in air-conditioned buses, and had access to various amenities, including good-quality canteens, medical services, and childcare facilities. Staff dormitories had televisions, telephones, refrigerators, and attached bathrooms.

The company's generous staff welfare policies apparently paid off. Ho said, "The most gratifying response is the sense of ownership that our staff began to have. It's not a sense of financial ownership, but they actually care about the property. In our business, service and service standards do not always mean the same thing as in a developed country, where standards are measured by efficiency and productivity, by people who are already quite well versed in a service culture. We operate in places that, sometimes, have not seen hotels. People come from villages. What we need—more than exact standards—is for them to have a sense of hospitality, a sense that the guest is an honored person who, by virtue of being there, is able to give a decent livelihood to the people who work. This creates a culture in which everybody is friendly and helpful."

INVOLVING GUESTS IN ENVIRONMENTAL CONSERVATION

Part of the company's corporate social responsibility initiatives was designed to encourage environmental conservation and help ecological restoration. To create greater environmental awareness, Banyan Tree organized activities that involved interested guests in their research and environmental preservation work. In the Maldives, for instance, guests were invited to take part in the coral transplantation program (see Exhibit 7 for a picture of guest involvement in the long-running coral planting program). Guests who participated in the program were then encouraged to return several years later to see the progress of their efforts. Guests were also offered free marine biology sessions allowing them to learn more about the fascinating marine life and its conservation. Guests also had an opportunity to take part in the Green Sea Turtle Headstarting Projects. The response from guests was tremendously positive.

In 2002, Banyan Tree established The Green Imperative Fund (GIF) to further support community-based and environmental initiatives in the regions where it has a presence. Guests were billed US$2 per room night at Banyan Tree properties and US$1 at Angsana properties (of which they could opt out if they wished) and the company matched dollar for dollar. Details of the program were communicated to guests through various methods, including sand-filled turtles and in-villa turndown gifts.

Guests were generally happy to know that their patronage contributed to meaningful causes, like the construction of new schools for the local community, the restoration of coral reefs, and ensuring the longevity of local village crafts.

Exhibit 7: A guest participates in planting corals at the Banyan Tree Maldives and Angsana Ihuru.

INVOLVING THE LOCAL COMMUNITY

In addition to engaging local craftsmen to produce indigenous art and handicrafts for sale at its galleries, Banyan Tree also involved the local community in all aspects of its business, even as the resorts were being built. Villas were constructed with as much indigenous material as possible, most of which was supplied by local traders. Traditional arts and handicrafts that complemented the villas' aesthetics were also purchased from local artisans.

The company believed in building profitable resorts that would benefit the surrounding environment and contribute to local economies through the creation of employment and community development projects. Thus, besides providing employment for the local community, the company brought business to the local farmers and traders by making it a point to purchase fresh produce from them. Whenever possible, the company supported other regional tourism ventures that would benefit the wider local community and enhance the visitor's experience. The Banyan Tree Maldives Marine Laboratory is a prime example, being the first fully equipped private research facility to be fully funded and operated by a resort. The Lab seeks to lead conservation efforts in the Maldives to protect and regenerate coral and marine life for the future of the tourism industry as well as to promote awareness and education of this field to the local community.

Recognizing that the disparity in lifestyles and living standards between guests and the local community might create a sense of alienation within the local community, a Community Relations Department was set up to develop and manage community outreach programs. After consultations with community stakeholders, a number of funding scholarships for needy children were given, a school and childcare centre were built, lunches and parties for the elderly were hosted, and local cultural and religious activities were supported.

One of BTHR's formalized programs was Seedlings, which aimed to help young adults from local communities and motivate them and provide the means for completing their education to successfully enter the labor force as adults. This program benefited the community at large, as it provided the next generation with educational opportunities to break the poverty cycle.[2]

GROWING BANYAN TREE

In 2002, BTHR took over the management of a city hotel in the heart of Bangkok from Westin Hotel Company. The hotel was rebranded as Banyan Tree Bangkok after extensive renovation works were completed to upgrade the hotel's facilities and build new additional spa amenities and a Banyan Tree Gallery. This was the first Banyan Tree hotel to be located in the city area, unlike the other beachfront Banyan Tree properties. Banyan Tree planned to open city hotels in Seoul, Beijing, Shanghai, and Hangzhou, and Angsana expanded into Dubai and London.

As the Banyan Tree brand became established, the company began expanding its network of spas and retail outlets. Standalone Banyan Tree Spas and Banyan Tree Galleries were set up as separate ventures, independent of Banyan Tree hotels and resorts, in various cities such as Singapore, Shanghai, Sydney, India, and Dubai, operating either in other hotels or as standalone outlets. Its most recent spa was The World Spa by Banyan Tree, located on board of the ResidenSea, a residential cruise ship, offering Banyan Tree signature spa treatments to the world's only resort community travelling the globe.

In addition to the Spa Academy in Phuket, which opened in 2001, and to support its fast-growing spa business, Banyan Tree opened two new spa academies in Lijiang, China, and Bangkok, Thailand, in 2007.

2 Detailed information on BTHR's CSR activities can be found at http://www.banyantree.com/csr.

After establishing a foothold in the luxury resort market, BTHR introduced the Angsana brand in response to the demand from hotel operators in Asia that were keen to introduce spa services in their hotels. As the positioning of these hotels did not fit that of Banyan Tree, the company decided to launch a new brand, Angsana, a more contemporary and affordable brand than Banyan Tree, to run as standalone spa businesses in other hotels.

The first Angsana Spa was opened in 1999 at Dusit Laguna, one of several hotels at Laguna Phuket, an integrated resort development with shared facilities located at Bang Tao Bay in Thailand. The Angsana Spa was so well received that the company quickly set up five other such spas in various hotels in Thailand. In 2000, BTHR opened its first Angsana Resort & Spa, complete with an Angsana Gallery, located less than one kilometer away from Banyan Tree Bintan in Indonesia.

In 2003, Banyan Tree launched The Museum Shop by Banyan Tree, a joint partnership with Singapore's National Heritage Board to showcase Asia's rich and diverse cultural heritage through unique museum-inspired merchandise. Designed to inspire and educate shoppers, The Museum Shop by Banyan Tree makes history more accessible and approachable to the layperson. By 2008, Banyan Tree had 65 retail outlets, ranging from Banyan Tree Galleries, Banyan Tree Spa Galleries, The Museum Shop by Banyan Tree, Elements Jewelry by Banyan Tree, and Angsana Galleries to Angsana Spa Galleries.

Exhibit 8: Extending the Banyan Tree Maldives experience on board the Banyan Velaa.

Banyan Tree Galleries are the retail outlets supporting the hotels, while Banyan Tree Spa Galleries support the spa outlets, selling more spa-focused merchandise such as signature aromatherapy amenities, essential oils, candles, and body care products. The Museum Shop by Banyan Tree is located in various museums in Singapore, and the merchandise sold will be inspired by the artifacts exhibited in the respective museums. The Elements Jewelry by Banyan Tree sells specialized merchandise such as jewelry and fashion items.

Exhibit 9: Angsana Maldives Ihuru.

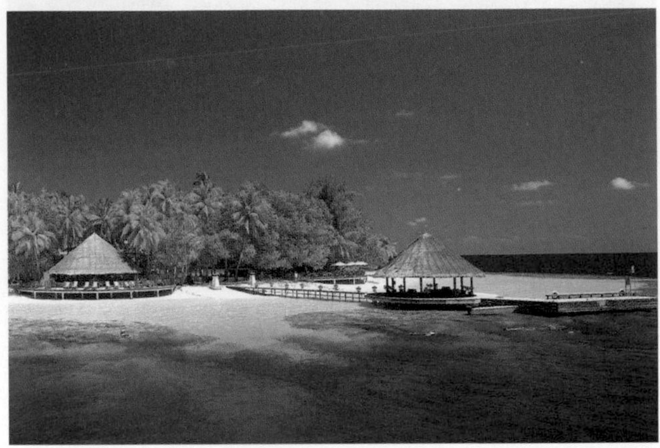

THE ROAD AHEAD

To diversify its geographic spread, Ho had started to venture into locations in South America (the first resort in Mexico opened in 2009), Southern Europe, and the Middle East, where he hoped to replicate Banyan Tree's rapid success. However, given the higher costs of doing business in the Americas and Europe, would the same strategy that had brought fame and success to Banyan Tree in Asia be workable in the rest of the world? Ho's ultimate vision was "to string a necklace of Banyan Tree Resorts around the world; not quantity, but a number of jewels that form a chain around the world." In 2008 alone, Banyan Tree signed management contracts that would expand its operations to at least an additional 50 Banyan Tree and Angsana properties by 2011. Of the properties under development, the majority were resorts and/or integrated resorts, and approximately 10 were city hotels.

While expanding the company's network of hotels and resorts, spas, and retail outlets, Ho had to be mindful of the brands' focus and be careful not to dilute the brands. He also had to consider the strategic fit of the company's portfolio of brands, which comprised Banyan Tree and Angsana.

Banyan Tree certainly stood out among its competitors in the resorts industry when it was first launched. Since then, its success had attracted various competitors that offer similar products and services. Thus, it was imperative that Banyan Tree retained its competitive advantage to prevent losing its distinctive position in the market.

STUDY QUESTIONS

1. What are the main factors that contributed to Banyan Tree's success?
2. Evaluate Banyan Tree's brand positioning and communication strategies. Can Banyan Tree maintain its unique positioning in an increasingly overcrowded resorts market?
3. Discuss whether the brand portfolio of Banyan Tree, Angsana, and Colours of Angsana, as well as the product portfolio of beach resorts and city hotels, spas, galleries, and museum shops fit as a family. What are your recommendations to Banyan Tree for managing these brands and products in the future?
4. What effect does the practice of corporate social responsibility have on brand equity?
5 What potential problems do you foresee bringing Banyan Tree to the Americas, Europe and the Middle East? How could Banyan Tree address those issues?

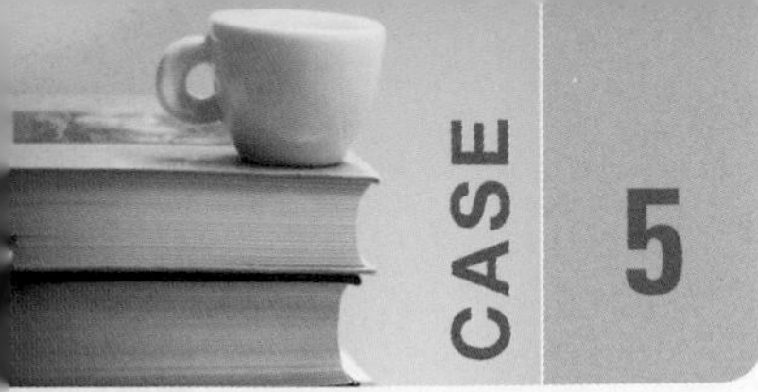

Giordano: Positioning for International Expansion

Jochen Wirtz

As it looks to the future, a successful Asian retailer of casual apparel must decide whether to maintain its existing positioning strategy. Management wonders what factors will be critical to success and whether the firm's competitive strengths in merchandise selection and service are readily transferable to new international markets.

To make people "feel good" and "look great."

Giordano's Corporate Mission

In mid-2009, Giordano, a Hong Kong-based retailer of casual clothes targeted at men, women, and children through its five company brands—Giordano, Giordano Concepts, Giordano Ladies, Giordano Junior, and Blue Star Exchange—was operating more than 1,800 retail stores and counters in some 30 markets worldwide. Its main markets were Mainland China, Hong Kong, Japan, Korea, Singapore, and Taiwan. Other regions in which it had a presence were Australia, Indonesia, Malaysia, Middle East, and North America. In September 2008, there were 1,757 Giordano and Giordano Junior stores, 46 Giordano Ladies stores, 29 Giordano Concept stores, and 111 Blue Star Exchange stores. Sales had grown to HK$4,950 million (US$561 million) by 2007 (see Exhibit 1). Giordano stores were located in retail shopping districts with good foot traffic. Views of a typical storefront and store interior are shown in Exhibit 2. In most geographic markets serviced by Giordano, the retail clothing business was deemed to be extremely competitive.

The board and top management team were eager to maintain Giordano's success in existing markets and to enter new markets, especially in mainland China. Several issues were under discussion. First, in what ways, if at all, should Giordano change its current positioning in the marketplace? Second, would the factors that had contributed to Giordano's success in the past remain equally critical over the coming years or were new key success factors emerging? Finally, as Giordano sought to enter new markets around the world, were its competitive strengths readily transferable to other markets?

COMPANY BACKGROUND

Giordano was founded in Hong Kong by Jimmy Lai in 1980. In 1981, it opened its first retail store in Hong Kong and also began to expand its market by distributing Giordano merchandise in Taiwan through a joint venture. In 1985, it opened its first retail outlet in Singapore.

Responding to slow sales, Giordano changed its positioning strategy in 1987. Until 1987, it had sold exclusively men's casual apparel. When Lai and his colleagues realized that an increasing number of female customers were attracted to their stores, he repositioned the chain as a retailer of value-for-money merchandise, selling discounted casual unisex apparel, with the goal of maximizing unit sales instead of margins. This shift in strategy was successful, leading to a substantial increase in turnover. In 1994, Peter Lau Kwok Kuen succeeded Lai and became chairman of the company.

Management Values and Human Resource Policies

A willingness to try new and unconventional ways of doing business and to learn from past errors was part of Lai's management philosophy and soon became an integral part of Giordano's culture. Lai saw the occasional failure as a current limitation that indirectly pointed management to the right decision in the future. To demonstrate his commitment to this philosophy, Lai took the lead by being a role model for his employees, adding:

This case is based on published information and quotes from a wide array of sources. The generous help and feedback provided by Alison Law, former Assistant to Chairman, Giordano International Ltd, to earlier versions of this case are gratefully acknowledged. The author thanks Zhaohui Chen for his excellent research assistance.

Exhibit 1: Giordano's financial highlights (1998–2008).

	2008 (6 Months ended 30 June)	2007	2006	2005	2004	2003	2002	2001	2000	1999	1998
Turnover (million HK$)	2,342	4,950	4,372	4,413	4,003	3,389	3,588	3,479	3,431	3,092	2,609
Turnover increase (percent)	11.6	13.2	(0.01)	0.10	18.1	(5.5)	3.1	1.4	11.0	18.5	(13.4)
Profit after tax and minority interests (million HK$)	206	304	218	431	393	266	328	377	416	360	76
Profit after tax and minority interests increase over previous year (percent)	32.9	39.4	(49.4)	9.6	47.7	(18.9)	(13.0)	(9.4)	15.3	373.7	11.8
Shareholders' fund (million HK$)	1928	1927	1,987	2,122	1,954	1,799	1,794	1,695	1,558	1,449	1,135
Working capital (million HK$)	716	736	862	1,029	1,004	961	861	798	1,014	960	725
Total debt to equity ratio	0.45	0.47	0.45	0.36	0.35	0.4	0.3	0.4	0.3	0.3	0.3
Inventory turnover on sales (days)	28	33	35	31	30	24	26	30	32	28	44
Return on total assets (percent)	7	10.3	7.3	15.2	14.9	10.7	13.7	16.8	20.7	21.5	5.3
Return on average equity (percent)	10.8	15.1	10.0	19.9	20.9	14.8	18.8	23.2	27.7	27.9	6.9
Return on sales (percent)	8	6	4.7	9.2	9.8	7.8	9.1	10.8	12.1	11.6	2.9
Earning per share (cents)	13.9	19.8	13.8	27.5	27.20	18.50	22.80	26.30	29.30	25.65	5.40
Cash dividend per share (cents)	6.5	21.5	26.5	26.5	23.00	21.00	19.00	14.00	15.25	17.25	2.25

Source: *Annual Reports 1998 through 2008*, Giordano International.

> … Like in a meeting, I say, look, I have made this mistake. I'm sorry for that. I hope everybody learns from this. If I can make mistakes, who … do you think you are that you can't make mistakes?

He also believed strongly that empowerment would minimize mistakes—that if everyone was allowed to contribute and participate, mistakes could be minimized.

Another factor that contributed to the firm's success was its dedicated, ever-smiling sales staff of over 11,000. Giordano considered frontline workers to be its customer service heroes. Charles Fung, executive director and general manager (Taiwan), remarked:

Exhibit 2: The typical Giordano storefront.

Even the most sophisticated training program won't guarantee the best customer service. People are the key. They make exceptional service possible. Training is merely a skeleton of a customer service program. It's the people who deliver that give it form and meaning.

Giordano had stringent selection procedures to make sure that the candidates selected matched the desired employee profile. Selection continued into its training workshops, which tested the service orientation and character of a new employee.

Giordano's philosophy of quality service could be observed not only in Hong Kong but also in its overseas outlets. The company had been honored by numerous service awards over the years (see Exhibit 3). Fung described its obsession with providing excellent customer service in the following terms:

> The only way to keep abreast with stiff competition in the retail market is to know the customers' needs and serve them well. Customers pay our pay checks; they are our bosses ... Giordano considers service to be a very important element [in trying to draw customers] ... service is in the blood of every member of our staff.

Giordano believed and invested heavily in employee training and has been recognized for its commitment to training and developing its staff by such awards as the Hong Kong Management Association Certificate of Merit

Exhibit 3: Selected awards Giordano received

Award	Awarding Organization	Category	Year(s)
Mystery Shoppers Award	Singapore Retailers Association (SRA)	–	2006
Top Service Award	Next Magazine Taiwan	Chain Stores of Fashion & Accessories	2006
Service and Courtesy—Supervisory Level	Hong Kong Retail Management	Fashion & Accessories	2006
Best Service Performance Brand; Best Service Performance	Department of Economic Development of Dubai	Large Business; Service Performance	2006
The Wall Street Journal Asia 2007 Survey	The Wall Street Journal Asia	Most admired publicly traded companies in Asia	2007
Dubai Service Excellence Performance Award	Dubai Department of Economic Development	Customer Service	2007
4th Premier Asian Licensing Award	Hong Kong Trade Development Council and the International Licensing Industry Merchandiser's Association	Best Licensee	2007
Top Service Award 2008	Next Magazine	Chain Store of Fashion & Accessories	2008
Hong Kong Brands Awards 2008	American Chamber of Commerce Hong Kong	Fashion and Apparel	2008
2008 Service and Courtesy Award	Hong Kong Retail Management Association (HKRMA)	Junior Frontline Level and the Supervisor Level	2008
Caring Company 2008/2009	Hong Kong Council of Society Service (HKCSS)	Corporate Social Responsibility	2009

for Excellence in Training and the People Developer Award from Singapore, among others. Fung explained:

> Training is important. However, what is more important is the transfer of learning to the store. When there is a transfer of learning, each dollar invested in training yields a high return. We try to encourage this [transfer of learning] by cultivating a culture and by providing positive reinforcement, rewarding those who practice what they learned.

Giordano offered what Fung claimed was "an attractive package in an industry where employee turnover is high." Giordano motivated its people through a base salary that probably was below market average, but added attractive performance-related bonuses. These initiatives and Giordano's emphasis on training had resulted in a lower staff turnover rate.

Giordano was only too aware that managing its human resources (HR) became a major challenge when it decided to expand into global markets. To replicate its high-service quality positioning, Giordano knew it needed to consider the HR issues involved in setting up retail outlets in unfamiliar territory. For example, the recruitment, selection, and training of local employees required modifications to its formula for success in its current markets, owing to differences in the culture, education, and technology of the new countries. Labor regulations also affected HR policies such as compensation and welfare benefits.

Focusing Giordano's Organizational Structure on Simplicity and Speed

Giordano maintained a flat organizational structure. The company's decentralized management style empowered line managers and, at the same time, encouraged fast and close communication and coordination. For example, top management and staff had desks located next to each other, separated only by shoulder panels. This closeness allowed easy communication, efficient project management, and speedy decision making, which were all seen as critical ingredients to success amid fast-changing consumer tastes and fashion trends. This kept Giordano's product development cycle short. The firm made similar demands on its suppliers.

In addition, the company kept its operations lean to focus on what it considered its competitive advantage: service. One of their main strategic objectives was to disengage from manufacturing to focus on retailing. This was implemented by reducing its interest in their joint ventures with key manufacturers. This allowed the group to channel its resources from the Garment Trading & Manufacturing Division to the more profitable Retail & Distribution Division.[1]

Service

Giordano's commitment to service began with its major Customer Service Campaign in 1989. In that campaign, yellow badges bearing the words "Giordano Means Service" was worn by every Giordano employee, and its service philosophy had three tenets: "We welcome unlimited try-ons; we exchange—no questions asked; and we serve with a smile." As a result, the firm started receiving its numerous service-related awards over the years. It had also been ranked number one for eight consecutive years by the *Far Eastern Economic Review* for being innovative in responding to customers' needs. Furthermore, proving its expansion success in the Middle East, in 2006, Giordano received double awards for exceptional service and customer-centricity from the Government of Dubai.

Giordano's management had launched several creative, customer-focused campaigns and promotions to extend its service orientation. For instance, in Singapore, Giordano asked its customers what they thought would be the fairest price to charge for a pair of jeans and charged each customer the price that they were willing to pay. This one-month campaign was immensely successful, with some 3,000 pairs of jeans sold every day during the promotion. In another service-related campaign, over 10,000 free T-shirts were given to customers for giving feedback and criticizing Giordano's services.

To ensure customer service excellence, performance evaluations were conducted frequently at the store level, as well as for individual employees. Internal competitions were designed to motivate employees and store teams to do their best in serving customers. Every month, Giordano awarded the "Service Star" to individual employees, based on nominations provided by shoppers. In addition, every Giordano store was evaluated every month by

1 Management Discussion and Analysis, p. 30, *Interim Financial Report 2008*, Giordano International.

Giordano to dispose of their interest in garment manufacturing subsidiary (accessed via http://www.giordano.com.hk/web/HK/investors/news/2008-06-30_Placita%20Disposal_E.pdf, on March 9, 2009).

mystery shoppers. Based on the combined results of these evaluations, the "Best Service Shop" award was given to the top store. Customer feedback cards were available at all stores and were collected and posted at the office for further action. Increasingly, customers were providing feedback via the firm's corporate website.

In late 2006, Giordano opened Giordano University, located at Dongguan in China. At its initial stage, the University trained staff located in Hong Kong and Mainland China. There are plans to offer training to its other markets and even franchisees and authorized dealers. Giordano's efforts on staff training and development reaped results as was shown by the many service awards it clinched.

Value for Money

Lai explained the rationale for Giordano's value-for-money policy:

> Consumers are learning a lot better about what value is. So we always ask ourselves how can we sell it cheaper, make it more convenient for the consumer to buy and deliver faster today than [we did] yesterday. That is all value, because convenience is value for the consumer. Time is value for the customer.

Giordano was able to sell value-for-money merchandise consistently through careful selection of suppliers, strict cost control, and by resisting the temptation to increase retail prices unnecessarily. For instance, in 2003, to provide greater shopping convenience to customers, Giordano started to open kiosks in subway and train stations aimed at providing their customers with a "grab and go" service.

Inventory Control

In order to maximize use of store space for sales opportunities, a central distribution center replaced the function of a back storeroom in its outlets. Information technology (IT) was used to facilitate inventory management and demand forecasting. When an item was sold, the barcode information—identifying size, color, style, and price—was recorded by the point-of-sale cash register and transmitted to the company's main computer. At the end of each day, the information was compiled at the store level and sent to the sales department and distribution center. The compiled sales information became the store's order for the following day. Orders were filled during the night and were ready for delivery by early morning, ensuring that new inventory was already on the shelves before a Giordano store opened for business.

Another advantage of its IT system was that information was disseminated to production facilities in real time. Such information allowed customers' purchase patterns to be studied, and this provided valuable input to its manufacturing operations, resulting in fewer problems and costs related to slow-moving inventory. The use of IT also allowed more efficient inventory holding. Giordano's inventory turnover on sales was reduced from 58 days in 1996 to merely 28 days in 2008. Its excellent inventory management reduced costs and allowed reasonable margins, while still allowing Giordano to reinforce its value-for-money philosophy. All in all, despite the relatively lower margins than those of its peers, Giordano was still able to post healthy profits. Such efficiency became a crucial factor when periodic price wars occurred.

PRODUCT POSITIONING

Fung recognized the importance of limiting the firm's expansion and focusing on one specific area. Simplicity and focus were reflected in the way Giordano merchandised its goods. Its stores featured no more than 100 variants of 17 core items, whereas competing retailers might feature 200–300 items. He believed that merchandising a wide range of products made it difficult to react quickly to market changes.

Giordano was also willing to experiment with new ideas and its perseverance despite past failures. It ventured into mid-priced women's fashion by introducing new product lines, such as the label "Giordano Ladies." This featured a line of smart blouses, dress pants, and skirts targeted at executive women. Reflecting retailer practices for such clothing, Giordano enjoyed higher margins on upscale women's clothing—typically 50–60% of selling price compared to 40% for casual wear.

Here, however, Giordano ran into some difficulties, as it found itself competing with more than a dozen seasoned players in the retail clothing business, including Esprit. Initially, the firm failed to differentiate its new Giordano Ladies line from its mainstream product line and even sold both through the same outlets. In 1999, however, Giordano took advantage of the boom that followed the Asian currency crisis in many parts of Asia, to aggressively relaunch its "Giordano Ladies" line, which subsequently met with great success.

As of September 2008, the reinforced "Giordano Ladies" focused on a select segment—the "office ladies, but dressier" market, with 46 "Giordano Ladies" shops in Hong Kong, Taiwan, Singapore, Malaysia, Indonesia, and China, offering personalized and exceptional service as one of its core offerings. Among other things, the employees were trained to memorize names of regular customers and recall their past purchases.

During the late 1990s, Giordano had begun to reposition its brand by emphasizing differentiated, functionally value-added products and broadening its appeal by improving on visual merchandising and apparel. In 1999, the firm launched Blue Star Exchange (BSE), a new line of casual clothing for the price-conscious customer. Giordano's relatively mid-priced positioning worked well—inexpensive, yet contemporary-looking outfits appealed to Asia's frugal customers, especially during a period of economic slowdown. However, over time, this positioning became inconsistent with the brand image that Giordano had tried hard to build over the years. As one senior executive remarked, "The feeling went from 'this is nice and good value' to 'this is cheap.'" As such, Giordano started to focus on establishing clear brand images and creating distinct identities between its brands. In September 2006, Giordano announced that it would rebrand Bluestar Exchange. As explained by Peter Lau:

> The apparel retail market is getting increasingly competitive, regardless of whether you are talking about the high end or the mass market. In order to succeed, you must achieve meaningful differentiation from your competitors or else you risk becoming lost in the crowd. We believe it is time to give Bluestar Exchange a makeover to sharpen its image, and decided to go outside the company to get a fresh perspective.[2]

The newly revamped brand, now known as Blue Star Exchange (BSX) (see Exhibit 4), was unveiled at the launch of its first flagship store in Hong Kong in April 2007. The shift saw BSX evolve from price to "fun sell," targeting the key youth demographic.[3] Expansion plans to bring BSX to other countries were made, following careful review and tweaking after its Hong Kong debut.

Exhibit 4: Giordano's first BSX store in Hong Kong.[8]

Additionally, having achieved success in its value-for-money lines, Giordano now wanted to penetrate the "upper premium" segment. This was done via the introduction of Giordano Concepts and its existing Giordano Ladies range. The lines focused on quality lifestyle and targeted the fashion-conscious consumer in the affluent market segment. In contrast to its unisex Giordano stores that carried a majority of items for women, Giordano Concept stores carry 60% of items catering to males.

To create alignment between the new up-market positioning and brand image, Giordano Concepts and Giordano Ladies stores were distinctly different from its mainstream stores. This included revamping store interiors and staff image to exude exclusivity, induce curiosity, and, more importantly, appeal to an affluent target group. For instance, to enhance its white-themed summer collection of 2006, flagship Concept stores in Hong Kong and Taiwan were dressed in abstract wall patterns and modern images.

Giordano gradually remarketed its core brand in ways that sought to create the image of a trendier label. To continue connecting with customers, Giordano launched several promotions. Among its successes was the "World Without Strangers" slogan. First launched in South Asia as a means to raise funds for the 2004 Indian Ocean tsunami victims in Phuket, it gained popularity with its other markets and was launched across the region in 2005. The slogan extended to a range of T-shirts and rubber wristbands that promoted international friendship. The products came in a variety of colors and brought across the message through words like

2 Giordano Re-brand Blue Star Exchange article (accessed via http://www.giordano.com.hk/web/HK/investors/news/Blue Star%20 Rebranding.html in January 2008).

3 Blue Star shifts from price to "fun" sell, James Murphy, Asia's Media & Marketing Newspaper; November 3, 2006, p. 11.

"Strength, Explore, Listen, Believe, Imagine, and Accept."[4] Ishwar Chugani, Executive Director for Giordano Middle East, explained:

> The words are designed to be personal watchwords, such as "have strength in your convictions," or "explore the world around you," almost reminders to live outside the box and experience the variety of life .... The shirts are a sign of solidarity for fellow humans, spreading a message of peace, acceptance and open-mindedness, which is something we can all use from time to time.[5]

In light of international crises and fragile cross-border friendships, "World Without Strangers" served as a mediator and avenue through which customers could express themselves. The company has been able to act as a mouthpiece for society, championing various themes from environmentalism to community work, and even the economy. An example would be the "Cheer U Up" collection, produced in collaboration with Mr. Jim Chim Sui-man. This collection aimed to lift the spirits of the people in the financial turmoil during the 2009 global economic crisis. The firm's skills in executing innovative and effective promotional strategies helped the retailer to gain public favor and approval.

Exhibit 5: Giordano's first Concepts store in Hong Kong.[9]

Giordano's Competitors

To beat the intense competition prevalent in Asia—especially in Hong Kong—founder Jimmy Lai believed that Giordano had to develop a distinctive competitive advantage. So he benchmarked Giordano against best-practice organizations in four key areas: (1) computerization (from The Limited), (2) a tightly controlled menu (from McDonald's), (3) frugality (from Wal-Mart), and (4) value pricing (as implemented at the British retail chain Marks & Spencer). The emphasis on service and the value-for-money concept had proven to be successful.

Giordano's main competitors in the value-for-money segment had been Hang Ten, Bossini, Baleno, and, at the higher end, Esprit. Exhibit 5 shows the relative positioning of Giordano and its competitors: The Gap, Bossini, Hang Ten, Baleno, and Esprit.

Hang Ten and Bossini were generally positioned as low-price retailers offering reasonable quality and service. The clothes emphasized versatility and simplicity. But while Hang Ten and Baleno were more popular among teenagers and young adults, Bossini had broader appeal. Their distribution strategies were somewhat similar, but they focused on different markets. For instance, while Hang Ten was mainly strong in Taiwan, Baleno increasingly penetrated Mainland China and Taiwan. However, Bossini was very strong in Hong Kong and relatively strong in China. The company planned to make its business in China into the group's largest turnover and profit contributor. The geographic areas in which Giordano, The Gap, Espirit, Bossini, Baleno, and Hang Ten operate are shown in Exhibit 6.

Esprit is an international fashion lifestyle brand. It promoted a "lifestyle" image, and its products are strategically positioned as good quality and value for money—a position that Giordano was occupying. By 2008, Esprit had a distribution network of over 12,000 stores and outlets in more than 40 countries in Europe, Asia, America, Middle East, and Australia. Its main markets were in Europe, which

4 Al-Bawaba News_Giordano world without strangers spreading goodwill October 11, 2005 (accessed via Factiva in December 2007).

5 Al-Bawaba News_Giordano world without strangers spreading goodwill October 11, 2005 (accessed via Factiva in December 2007).

Exhibit 6: Giordano Ladies.[10]

accounted for approximately 86.7% of sales. The Esprit brand products were principally sold via directly managed retail outlets, wholesale customers (including department stores, specialty stores and franchisees), and by licensees for products manufactured under license, principally through the licensees' own distribution networks.

Although each of these firms had slightly different positioning strategies, they competed in a number of areas. For example, all firms emphasized advertising and sales promotion heavily, selling fashionable clothes at attractive prices. Almost all stores were also located primarily in good ground-floor areas, drawing high-volume traffic, and facilitating shopping, browsing, and impulse buying. However, none had been able to match the great customer value offered by Giordano.

A threat from US-based The Gap was also looming, which had already entered the Japanese market. After 2005, when garment quotas had been largely abolished, imports into the region became more cost-effective for this US competitor. Through franchise partners such as FJ Benjamin Holdings Ltd. The Gap expanded its international presence with franchises in Bahrain, Greece, Indonesia, Korea, Kuwait, Oman, Qatar, Malaysia, Russia, Saudi Arabia, Philippines, Singapore, Turkey, and the United Arab Emirates. Financial data for Giordano, Esprit, The Gap, and Bossini are shown in Exhibit 7.

Giordano's Growth Strategy

Early in its existence, Giordano's management had realized that regional expansion was required to achieve substantial growth and economies of scale. By 2007, Giordano had

Exhibit 7: Market positioning of Giordano and principal competitors.

Firms	Positioning	Target market
Giordano (www.giordano.com.hk)	Value for money Mid-priced but trendy fashion	Unisex casual wear for all ages (under different brands)
The Gap (www.gap.com)	Value for money Mid-priced but trendy fashion	Unisex casual wear for all ages (under different brands)
Esprit (www.esprit-intl.com)	More up-market than Giordano Stylish, trendy	Ladies' casual, but also other specialized lines for children and men
Bossini (www.bossini.com)	Value for money (comparable to Giordano)	Unisex, casual wear, both young and old
Baleno (www.baleno.com.hk)	Value for money Trendy, young-age casual wear	Unisex appeal, young adults
Hang Ten (www.hangten.com)	Value for money Sporty lifestyle	Casual wear and sports wear, teens and young adults

over 1,800 stores in more than 30 markets. Exhibit 8 shows the growth achieved across a number of dimensions from 1998 to 2007. Despite a drop in profits in 2006 due to the unforeseen warm winter as well as the astounding rise in rental expenses in Hong Kong, Giordano showed relatively consistent growth over the years as profits rebounded in 2007 with a 39.4% increase.

Driven in part by its desire for growth and in part by the need to reduce its dependence on Asia in the wake of the 1998 economic meltdown, Giordano set its sights on markets outside Asia. Australia was an early target, and the number of retail outlets increased from four outlets in 1999 to 56 outlets in 2008. Although the Asian financial crisis had caused Giordano to rethink its regional strategy, the company was still determined to enter and further penetrate new Asian markets. This determination led to its successful

Exhibit 8: Geographic presence of Giordano and its principal competitors.

Country	Giordano	The Gap	Esprit	Bossini	Baleno	Hang Ten
Asia						
Hong Kong/ Macau	X	–	X	X	X	X
Singapore	X	X	X	X	X	X
South Korea	X	X	X	X	–	X
Taiwan	X	–	X	X	X	X
China	X	X	X	X	X	X
Malaysia	X	X	X	X	X	X
Indonesia	X	X	X	X	X	–
Philippines	X	–	X	X	–	X
Thailand	X	–	X	X	X	–
Japan	X	X	–	–	–	X
Middle East	X	X	X	X	X	X
World						
USA and Canada	X	X	X	X	–	X
Europe	–	X	X	X	–	–
Australia	X	–	X	–	–	–
Total	**1,585**	**3,117**	**9,751**	**827**	**1,160**	**NA**

Note: "X" indicates presence in the country/ region; "-" indicates no presence.

Sources: *Giordano International Limited*, retrieved March 9, 2009 from http://www.giordano.com.hk/web/HK/ourCompany.html; Annual Report 2007, *Gap Inc.*, retrieved March 9, 2009 from http://media.corporate-ir.net/media_files/IROL/11/111302/AR07.pdf; *Esprit*, Retrieved March 9, 2009 from http://www.esprit.com/index.php?command=Display&navi_id=104; *Bossini International Holdings Limited*, retrieved March 9, 2009 from http://www.bossini.com/bossini/html/eng/common/global.jsp ; *Baleno*, retrieved March 9, 2009 from http://www.baleno.com.hk/EN/stores_list_map.asp; *Hang Ten*, retrieved March 9, 2009, 2005 from *http://www.hangten.com.hk/countryLink.do.*

expansion in Mainland China (see Exhibit 9), where the number of retail outlets grew from 253 in 1999 to 881 in 2008. Giordano's management foresaw both challenges and opportunities arising from the People's Republic of China's accession to the World Trade Organization.

Exhibit 9: Competitive financial data for Giordano, The Gap, Esprit, and Bossini.

	Giordano	The Gap	Esprit	Bossini
Turnover (US$ million)	639	15, 736	4,403	298
Profit after tax and minority interests (US$ million)	39.2	833	832	8.2
Return on total assets (percentage)	7.0	10.6	33.1	6.97
Return on average equity (percentage)	10.8	19.5	46.0	9.71
Return on sales (percentage)	8.0	5.3	20.7	
Number of employees	11,000 12, 100	154,000	10,541	4,300
Sales per employee (US$ '000)	52.81	102.18	457.43	69.02

Note: The Gap reports its earnings in US$. All reported figures have been converted into US$ at the following exchange rate (as of March 2009): US$1 = HK$7.75.

Sources: *Annual Report 2007*, Giordano International; *Annual Report 2007*; The Gap; *2007 Annual Report*, Esprit International; *Financial Report 2007/8*, Bossini International Holdings Limited; *Annual Report 2007/08.*

Giordano opened more stores in Indonesia, bringing its total in that country to 100 stores. In Malaysia, Giordano planned to refurnish its outlets and intensify its local promotional campaigns to consolidate its leadership position in the Malaysian market. To improve store profitability, Giordano had already converted some of its franchised Malaysian stores into company-owned stores.

Having gained a foothold in the Far East, Giordano began expansion into India in 2006, and into North American and the Middle East in 2007. In June 2007, Giordano unveiled its first franchised store in Cairo, Egypt. Since the launch of its first store in Chennai, Giordano has increased its presence in India to nine stores in five cities.[6]

The senior management team knew that Giordano's future success in such markets would depend on a detailed

6 Giordano opens three new stores in India, November 20, 2008 (http://www.giordano.com.hk/web/HK/investors/IR2008/2008-11-20%20Pune%20+%20Mumbai.pdf); accessed March 9, 2009.

understanding of consumer tastes and preferences for fabrics, colors, and advertising. In the past, the firm had relied on maintaining a consistent strategy across different countries, including such elements as positioning, service levels, information systems, logistics, and HR policies. However, implementation of such tactical elements as promotional campaigns was usually left mostly to local managers. A country's overall performance in terms of sales, contribution, service levels, and customer feedback was monitored by regional headquarters (for instance, Singapore for Southeast Asia) and the head office in Hong Kong. Weekly performance reports were distributed to all managers.

As the organization expanded beyond Asia, it was becoming clear that different strategies had to be developed for different regions or countries. For instance, to enhance profitability in Mainland China, the company recognized that better sourcing was needed to enhance price competitiveness. Turning around the Taiwan operation required refocusing on basic designs, streamlining product portfolio, and implementing their micromarketing strategy more aggressively. In Europe, Giordano was investigating a variety of market entry opportunities.

Decisions Facing the Senior Management Team

Although Giordano had been extremely successful, it faced a number of challenges. A key issue was how the Giordano brand should be positioned against the competition in both new and existing markets. Was repositioning required in existing markets, and would it be necessary to follow different positioning strategies for different markets (e.g., Hong Kong versus Southeast Asia)?

A second issue was the sustainability of Giordano's key success factors. Giordano had to carefully explore how its core competencies and the pillars of its success were likely to develop over the coming years. Which of its competitive advantages were likely to be sustainable and which ones were likely to be eroded?

A third issue was Giordano's growth strategy in Asia as well as across continents. Would Giordano's competitive strengths be readily transferable to other markets? Would strategic adaptations to its strategy and marketing mix be required, or would tactical moves suffice?

STUDY QUESTIONS

1. Describe and evaluate Giordano's product, business, and corporate strategies.
2. Describe and evaluate Giordano's current positioning strategy. Should Giordano reposition itself against its competitors in its current and new markets? Should it have different positioning strategies for different geographic markets?
3. What are Giordano's key success factors and sources of competitive advantage? Are its competitive advantages sustainable, and how would they develop in the future?
4. Could Giordano transfer its key success factors to new markets as it expanded both in Asia and the other parts of the world?
5. How do you think Giordano adapted/would have adapted its marketing and operations strategies and tactics when entering and penetrating your country?
6. What general lessons can be learned from Giordano for other major clothing retailers in your country?

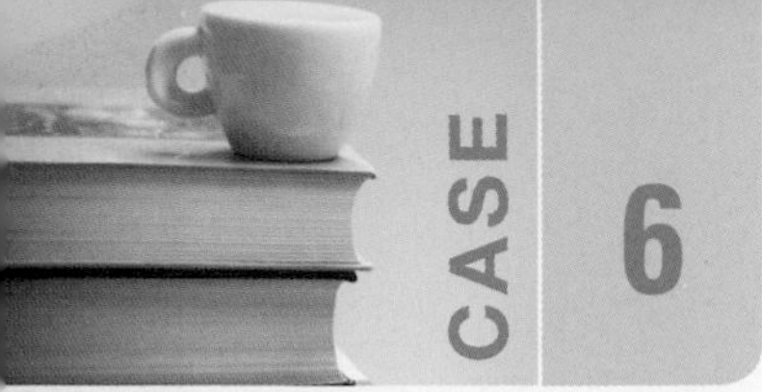

Kiwi Experience

Mark Colgate

How do you manage a business where customers are unlikely to buy again? Answer: the Kiwi Experience Way! This case explores how to truly get inside the heads of your target market, how to build a culture of service excellence, and how other customers can add as much to the experience as the employees—but only if you encourage them to do so.

"Are you ready for a most excellent adventure?" shouted Rob, the driver of the Kiwi Experience bus, as it climbed to the top of an extinct volcano on a beautiful sunny morning in Auckland. It was the start of another trip around New Zealand, for the driver and the bus, but the first for the 40 like-minded travelers who were unprepared for the burst of enthusiasm as the panoramic view unveiled itself.

Virtually all of the travelers were unaware and unsure of what to expect from this trip. They had never traveled on Kiwi Experience before, although all had heard of the company through various mediums before they bought their tickets. This knowledge had reduced their uncertainty somewhat.

One of the passengers, Rory Gillies, a 23-year-old Scotsman, had heard much about Kiwi Experience while traveling around Australia. He was curious to find out what made this bus service so successful and so different from others that were offered in New Zealand. As they boarded the bus, after taking in the sights of Auckland, Rory approached Rob the driver.

"Have you been busy this summer?" Rory asked. "I haven't stopped," replied Rob, "and what's more, I can only remember once or twice when my bus has not been full!" "So what does Kiwi Experience do that makes it so successful then?" continued Rory. "If I told you, it would ruin the trip for you," Rob suggested, "but jump on and maybe I'll give you a few ideas along the way."

Mark Colgate is Associate Professor of Service Excellence at the Gustavson School of Business, University of Victoria. The support and feedback of the management of Kiwi Experience in the writing of this case are gratefully acknowledged. All statistics on Zealand's tourism industry were taken from http://www.stats.govt.nz/tourism.

COMPANY BACKGROUND

Kiwi Experience (KE) is an adventure transport network formed in December 1988 by three partners. The fundamental concept behind the venture was to create a coach transport network that was neither an express point-to-point service nor an inflexible coach tour. Instead, they set out to create a transport tour experience that had the advantages of both. This meant that KE was going to offer the flexibility of the traditional express service in that customers could get on or off the bus where they wanted, in addition to the guidance, information, and access to excitement-oriented places that a good adventure tour would offer, without the inherent drawbacks of either.

This was an innovation in the marketplace and the first of its kind in the world. In fact, the concept was so original that, in the beginning, staff at KE had to spend much of their time explaining the concept to potential customers. Clarifying that KE passengers can get on and off the coach wherever they like (on a pass that lasts for six months), yet they are still part of an adventure trip that takes them to places off the beaten track. Since their inception, more than 90% of customers have broken their journey at some point, which proves this concept has been popular with travelers. Today, many copies of the KE concept can be seen all over the world.

Neil Geddes, one of the founders of the company, outlines the KE concept:

> I have always thought that a coach was a great way to get around, as meeting people is one of the fun things about traveling. But I could never understand the fact that everyone is stuck on one coach and you all had to do the same things. I don't believe you can create the ideal holiday for more than just the one person—this is why KE was invented.

The company's service offering is specifically designed for backpackers, adventurers, and other like-minded travelers. This means that KE is developed around the high-volume, low-margin business where minimizing costs is key.

Although KE has no specific target market in terms of age (they believe a backpacker tends to be defined in terms of lifestyle rather than age), it is the 18–30 age group that travels on KE the most, with 18–22 being the most common age range. Similarly, many nationalities travel on KE with backpackers from the UK, Germany, USA, Canada, Denmark, Switzerland, and Nordic countries, making up the bulk of customers. Less than 1% of all customers actually come from New Zealand itself.

NEW ZEALAND AS A TOURIST DESTINATION

In 2011, New Zealand hosted a total of 2.5 million international visitors aged 15 years and over (compared to 1.6 million in 1999). This is expected to grow to 3.1 million by 2016. Total visitor expenditure in 2011 reached NZ$5.8 billion. This was down from $6.6 billion in 2006 just before the financial crisis hit New Zealand's tourism industry hard. The average expenditure for tourists on holiday is around NZ$3,014 per person (down about 10% from 2006). New Zealand's current share of international tourism is small at only 1–2%, but given the size of the country, they do incredibly well.

New Zealand is marketed abroad as a "clean, green" adventure playground, with beautifully natural destinations such as Milford Sound, Abel Tasman National Park, or the Tongariro Alpine Crossing. Activities such as bungee jumping or whale watching exemplify typical tourist attractions, marketed primarily to individual and small-group travelers.

As a labor-intensive industry, tourism generates an increasingly wide range of jobs for New Zealanders. The number of equivalent full-time jobs supported directly by tourism in NZ was approximately 180,000 in 2010, about 10% of the workforce. Tourism's direct and indirect value-added contribution to the economy was $15.7 billion in 2011, which was a very significant 9% of the total New Zealand GDP.

GROWTH OF KIWI EXPERIENCE

KE has grown rapidly since its creation. Although some of the increase in passengers is undoubtedly due to the growth in visitors to New Zealand, the percentage increase of passengers traveling on KE is well above the percentage increase in overseas visitors. In fact, the number of KE passengers has increased faster than the growth of international visitors. KE is clearly taking a larger slice of a growing market.

In fact, KE has grown to a size that the original owners never thought possible; they now have 30 buses and over 40 drivers. They thought they had reached market saturation a few years ago. However, the idea of a backpacking holiday and the types of people undertaking backpacking holidays has grown immensely over the last few years. The KE directors' limited definition of backpacking has had to be broadened to encompass the types of people who now travel on KE. For instance, professionals who only have three weeks' of holiday are now opting for a backpacker-style holiday around New Zealand.

Exhibit 1: The iconic KE bus.

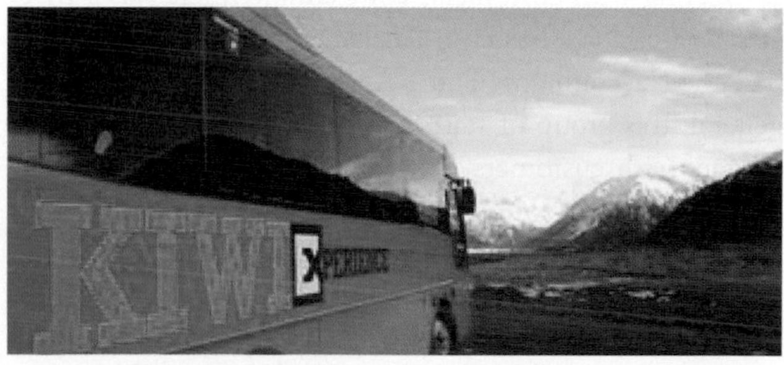

The success of KE is due to many other factors besides the growth in the backpacking market itself.

THE "EXPERIENCE"

"How did you enjoy Waitomo Caves?" Rob asked Rory at a stop en route to Rotorua. "Amazing," he replied. "I saw the caves while blackwater rafting, and I really enjoyed the candlelight walk you took us all on through the Ruakuri Scenic Reserve to see the glow worms. It didn't stop there though; later on a group of us from the coach went down to the Waitomo Tavern for a few drinks—I feel a bit rough today!" Rob laughed. Rory, he thought, was slowly coming to grips with what the KE was all about.

The Kiwi Experience concept is based on being the best in the market for those people who want to see the real New Zealand. Backpacking is all about traveling, meeting other people, getting value for money, and getting involved in the local environment and culture. The service KE offers allows them to do that. It allows backpackers to choose where and on what they want to spend their money on, at a price they can afford.

When Neil Geddes was asked what makes the KE so good, he had a simple reply:

> We ensure we give the customers what they want better than anyone else. Our service is not designed around what is good for the drivers; it is designed around what is good for the customer. We are close to our market, we are proud to be close to our market. When we [the directors of KE] travel, we stay in backpackers' hostels, so as to learn and understand what the market wants. That is how we ensure that we always offer the best possible service for our clients. That is our core strength.

KE tries to get all people working within the business interacting with customers. For example, there was a BBQ at a backpackers' hostel in Auckland recently at which KE had their accountants and other staff meet the guests. In general, this group of staff does not usually come in direct contact with customers, but this event gave them a better understanding of who KE's customers are and where they come from.

Being first in the marketplace has also helped, as it has meant that KE has gained a lead in understanding what their target market wants and how to service these needs effectively. This understanding has led KE staff to comprehend that it is both the driver of the coach and the interaction between backpackers that help create the "KE Experience."

The Drivers

"The drivers are the single most important people in our company, we know that," states Neil Geddes. Their market research has shown the driver makes or breaks a KE trip. This is why KE undertakes a very comprehensive and strict selection process for its drivers, along with a very thorough training program.

The first thing the directors look for when selecting drivers is a certain type of person—they must be fun, young, and adventurous. They must have an outgoing personality and be proud to show off New Zealand. While this means that most drivers are from New Zealand, it is not necessarily always the case. Secondly, they must have extensive driving experience as it is critical that they are a safe driver.

KE receives hundreds of applications for their driver jobs; one of the reasons is the pay. The drivers are rewarded nicely for doing their job well, particularly through bonuses and commission they may receive at the end of each trip. However, only very few drivers fit the strict selection criteria that KE have. The drivers must undergo a series of driving tests and interviews before they are selected. Even then, they may not necessarily get the job.

All prospective drivers are then taken on a "dummy" trip around New Zealand. The drivers are asked to take notes of the various activities that are on offer and record any other information that may assist them in doing their job effectively. After this initial training, drivers are taken on a proper KE trip, where they observe how an experienced driver operates. The prospective driver could be asked to take over the driving or the commentary at any moment in time. Only when the drivers perform satisfactorily in these two tests will they then be taken on as a KE staff member.

Driving a KE bus is a highly rewarding job, but a stressful one, too. There are many responsibilities placed on a driver apart from having to safely drive 40 people around the whole of New Zealand. These include the following:

- Providing informative and knowledgeable commentary
- Booking all accommodation every night
- Ensuring people on the bus interact as much as possible
- Socializing as much as possible with the passengers
- Organizing group meals and other group activities (see Exhibit 2)
- Organizing paid excursions
- Undertaking regular checks and maintenance (e.g. cleaning) of the bus
- Listening and responding to customer complaints

Because of the above factors, drivers of KE buses rarely last three years within the company. Not all leave because of the intensive nature of the job; many leave because they obtain other jobs elsewhere.

Exhibit 2: A KE costume party organized by one of its drivers.

Each driver is debriefed by an operations manager after each trip. This enables the operations manager to understand how tired the driver is and whether he or she should be taken off the duty roster for a couple of weeks. An exhausted driver cannot provide the best service for the customers on the bus, and this will only harm the reputation of both the driver and KE in the long run. An experienced operations manager can easily spot when a certain driver needs a rest. The drivers are also required to fill out a survey at the end of each trip that asks them how the trip has gone and about the problems they have encountered. The survey also includes a section that enables the driver to make recommendations to improve the overall quality of the KE.

It is clear, therefore, that the drivers are the single most important asset that KE possesses. Their enthusiasm, knowledge, and personality will have a huge impact on customers' perception of the overall quality of the trip, and of KE as a whole.

Customer Interaction

Market research has shown that the interaction between the customers on the bus is the second most important part of a KE trip. Backpackers generally enjoy meeting other like-minded people, which is the nature of their trip. In fact many backpackers travel for the specific purpose of meeting new friends and acquaintances. Therefore, it is important that KE manages this interaction well to ensure this occurs.

KE does several things to ensure that they achieve the correct customer mix on the buses and that the customers interact well together (beyond the normal interaction that would occur). First, KE ensures, as best as they can, that they and their booking agents do not book people who are not suited to this kind of experience on the bus. For example, older travelers may not be interested in some of the things that KE does. This strategy is important, as it prevents potential customers from having a negative experience on the trip. These customers' negative experience could also influence the experience the other customers on the bus are having. Ultimately, it may well lead to negative word-of-mouth for KE.

One way the company ensures this occurs is by sending representatives from their booking agents on tour to help them understand the types of people who would enjoy traveling with KE. Second, the drivers are trained to notice any passengers on the bus who are affecting the quality of the service other passengers are receiving. The driver will then take appropriate action. For example, in extreme cases, the driver may ask certain passengers to leave the bus, with a full refund being offered to encourage them to do so. In this case, KE has realized that it is important to remove people from the bus who may be influencing the enjoyment of a significant proportion of other customers.

Finally, the driver encourages social interaction between the customers on the bus. This enables different customers to meet each other, and forms bonds and friendships at an early stage within the trip. This may increase the positive experiences that customers have on their bus, which should positively impact the impression that customers have about the overall trip. The drivers usually encourage interaction through group meals and social activities in the evening, for example, fancy dress competitions (Exhibit 2).

ADVERTISING AND WORD-OF-MOUTH

"Why did you choose Kiwi Experience anyway?" Rob asked Rory, as the inter-Islander ferry pulled away from the Wellington Harbour on its three-and-a-half hour trip to Picton in the South Island. "I never really planned to; before I left Scotland, I'd always planned to hire a Campervan," replied Rory.

"So what made you change your mind then?" quizzed Rob. "I kept hearing of KE when I was traveling around Australia," said Rory. "Every time I stopped at a backpackers, I'd meet at least one person who would have a Kiwi Experience story to tell. Then when I came to New Zealand, KE did a slide show in the Backpackers I was staying at, and that really swung it for me!"

Many service organizations can rely on repeat purchases to maintain and enhance their profitability. For example, airlines often have passengers who have flown with them many times before. For KE, however, this is not the case. It is very unusual for passengers to travel with KE for a second time. KE relies heavily on new and referral customers for virtually all of their sales. Promoting and stimulating word-of-mouth is vitally important.

KE has realized this and promotes heavily in its target market and, wherever possible, attempts to stimulate word-of-mouth. One thing KE has realized is that it is important to advertise overseas. Backpackers often start searching for information well before they have left their own country to come to New Zealand, a fact that Neil Geddes acknowledges:

> A significant number of our customers look for travel options well before they come near New Zealand. Most people mistakenly believe that backpackers turn up and make up their mind when they get into New Zealand. In fact, around 25% of customers buy their KE ticket overseas. For us, therefore, it is important to advertise overseas.

Other research that KE has undertaken shows that 75% of customers have heard of KE before they enter New Zealand. This assists in sales since customers are familiar with the service before they purchase it. Word-of-mouth accounts for some of the people who have heard of KE before they enter the country, but a large percentage of customers hear of KE through other advertising. For example, KE places leaflets in backpackers' and youth hostels along commonly visited destinations that backpackers visit before they come to New Zealand, such as Hawaii, Sydney, Bangkok, and Fiji.

Once the backpackers are in New Zealand, then the advertising really starts. KE uses people called "street fighters," backpackers who hand out brochures at railway terminals, bus stations, and others, throughout the gateway cities of Auckland and Christchurch. They also spread the word through backpacker hostels. KE prefers recruiting backpackers who have had the "Experience" as they are informed, motivated, and credible communicators who can sell the KE service better than anyone else. KE, it seems, really does fight for every customer they get.

The distinctive branding that KE uses on their leaflets and brochures certainly helps get their advertisements noticed. Exhibits 3 and 4 show their new brand logo and ad execution which was launched in 2006. Their brand research revealed a profile of their target market that helped to shape their new brand:

> 18- to 35-year-old men and women. They have a sense of anticipation; they crave the unknown and are seeking total adventure. The thought of meeting new people is an essential criteria in their choice of holiday ... They spend time wondering what the dynamics of the group might be, and the 'unknown' is a thrill for them. They are free of the day-to-day rat race and they yearn to be their hedonistic selves. Each day is a new feeling, a new experience ... There is little time for thinking on this holiday, only time for doing! These men and women love a laugh—they love the sensation of not taking anything too seriously (there will be other times in their life when they will have to be grown-up) ... Right now, life is about living—to the max.

KE also holds slide shows in backpackers' hostels in Auckland and Christchurch to persuade consumers who are still unsure about which mode of transport to use around New Zealand. These slide shows are an attempt to make the service that KE offers more tangible and to reduce the perceived risk customers may have about taking the trip.

KE also creates their own propaganda letters, called "Bullsheets," which they send to their major booking agents in New Zealand. This enables agents to be better informed about the service KE offers. Finally, KE tries to ensure their service is mentioned in popular travel guides such as *Lonely Planet*, which is widely read by backpackers (although the most recent write-up of KE was less than complimentary).

KE ensures that word-of-mouth will be positive by monitoring the performance of their service at all times. KE does this by surveying customers on every single bus. One of the directors and the operations manager will read these surveys so as to monitor what is happening. They then use these surveys to improve their service to the marketplace.

Exhibit 3: The KE logo.

Exhibit 4: An advertisement from KE.

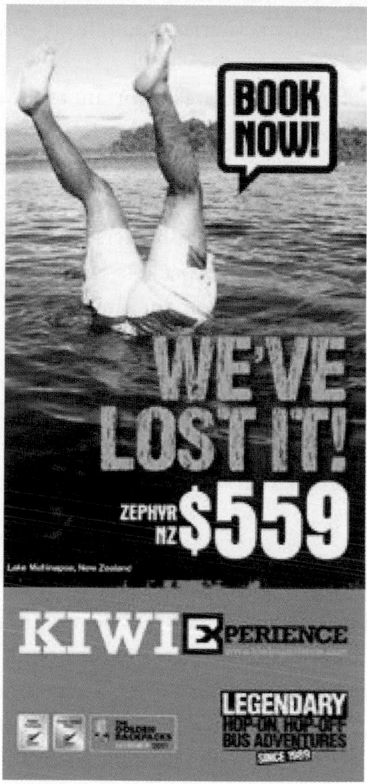

Although their core experience has basically remained the same, they continually try and add value to their service.

This strategy has worked, says Neil Geddes:

> We have always had a strong and loyal customer following that is proud to have traveled with us, and proud to tell other people about KE. That is the one good thing about the backpacker market. They enjoy giving good information to other travelers. We rely on a huge rate of first-time users and we achieve that by having good word-of-mouth.

In essence, therefore, KE attempts to create positive word-of-mouth by always ensuring that they offer a consistently high quality of service.

COMPETITION

"There goes our rivals," screamed Rob, as another bus whisked past the KE bus as they approached Franz Joseph Glacier. A huge "Boooo" was released from the passengers, and various faces were pulled as the competition disappeared in the distance. "They weren't hanging about," stated Rory. "They have got to get back to Auckland as soon as possible, no time to look at the scenery!" replied Rob. "Yeah, right, it is not as if it's important or anything," laughed Rory.

The competition KE faces comes from many places. Direct competition comes from another national backpacker coach services, several "regional" backpacker buses, and other tour buses and coach services that travel around New Zealand. By far, KE's single biggest competition is the alternative national backpacking bus, Magic Bus. This bus service was created by the national coach company whose market had been diminished by the introduction of KE. The routes and prices offered by the two companies are now fairly similar. KE takes a minimum of 26 days to travel around New Zealand, while the Magic Bus takes 25 days (KE also travels to other locations that Magic Bus does not, for example, the southeast of the South Island). Exhibit 5 below shows a comparison of some of the similar trips and prices the two companies offer. In recent years, KE has priced itself away from Magic Bus so that now there is a 10–30% premium (depending on the route), whereas the difference before was just 2–3%. There is also another new bus company called Stray, which portrays itself as more "independent" than Magic Bus and KE, but has older buses. The debate about which bus company to take, even how to travel around New Zealand, is a heated one among travelers. See http://backpackercompare.com/nz-backpacker-bus/ for updated discussion!

Exhibit 5: KE and Magic Bus: Comparison of trips and prices for 2012.

Company	Pass	Length of Trip	Price in NZ$
KE	All of New Zealand	26	1730
Magic Bus	All of New Zealand	25	1328
KE	Auckland to Christchurch	16	879
Magic Bus	Auckland to Christchurch	13	782

The other backpacking bus services that exist operate in other very specific regions of New Zealand; there are currently four of these in operation. Most of these bus services had been in existence before KE was created. Since the introduction of KE, and the competition that followed, these buses have been hit badly, as passengers have favored a national bus pass over a regional one.

The third type of competition comes from other national bus companies that either offer express services to different points in New Zealand, or specific tours around New Zealand that do not allow the passenger to get on and off the bus wherever they desire. These buses pose a threat to KE, but a smaller one than the backpacking buses, as they tend to attract different market segments.

The fourth type of competition comes from other modes of transport that can be taken around New Zealand. The main sources of this type of competition are rental campervans and cars, especially in the winter when a large number of unused cars and campervans are "dumped" into the market. However, customers with different psychographic, behavioral, and demographic (particularly in terms of income) variables are likely to use rental cars or campervans compared to those types of people who would use backpacker buses.

The domestic airlines in New Zealand are not a large threat to KE, as it is a relatively small country; they really only pose a threat over larger distances. In fact, KE has attempted to overcome any possible threat from the airlines by creating strategic alliances with them. For example, one of the national passes KE offers includes an Air New Zealand flight from Christchurch to Auckland. There are other similar passes KE offers. The railway network in New Zealand offers little competition as it is limited in its coverage.

The final form of competition to KE is from other countries. Most travelers have a limited time to spend on holiday and must, therefore, make decisions about where to spend their time. New Zealand competes for this time with countries like Australia, USA, Fiji, Thailand, and, most recently, South Africa, which has become a larger threat. Staff at KE are aware that they must promote New Zealand as well as KE itself.

ADVENTURE ACTIVITIES

Rory's face was white as he approached the bus. "Are you ready to go?" asked Rob. "Just about, the skydiving was incredible, but I feel a bit dizzy," replied Rory. "Wait until you do the bungee in Queenstown, then you'll know what dizzy means," Rob stated. "No thanks," said Rory, "I think I've had enough excitement to last me a lifetime."

One of KE's major appeals is the enormous amount of paid excursions and activities that are on offer. From swimming with dolphins to aerobatic flights, the list is almost endless. By purchasing a KE bus ticket, a passenger is also entitled to discounts on many activities throughout New Zealand.

The activities offered on KE are important to the organization for a variety of reasons. First, it helps KE differentiate itself from other competitors, since some activities and discounts are exclusive to KE. This is one way that KE attempts to exceed the expectations that customers may have, before the start of the trip. Second, backpackers are usually adventurers who are looking for excitement and activities that will challenge them. By offering these activities, KE is fulfilling these customer needs. Finally, these activities also provide an additional source of revenue, since KE is paid a commission for bringing passengers to these activities by the service operator. This enables KE to earn incremental income from their passengers.

One risk for KE is that these activities do not always match or offer the same quality of service that KE offers. If an activity that is offered turns out to be of low quality, it will reflect poorly on KE since it recommended it. It is important, therefore, that KE ensures that a constant (excellent) standard of quality is maintained so as to protect their brand image. Neil Geddes states how KE attempts to achieve this:

> We assess every single activity that we offer, and we monitor their performance continuously. We ask questions on a customer questionnaire regarding the paid excursions they undertook. We also ensure every activity is up to adequate safety standards, beyond those of legal requirements, and we get feedback from our drivers on the quality of these activities.

MEMORABILIA

"Okay, everyone, squeeze in together!" shouted the photographer along the Queenstown waterfront. All the passengers on the KE bus shuffled together to ensure they all appeared in the photo. "Rob, jump in at the front!" shouted Rory, "We can't have a group photograph without you!" Rob was reluctantly pushed into the photograph, and the picture was taken. Queues quickly formed to order a copy of the photo (see Exhibit 6 for an example).

Souvenirs and memories of the KE trip are a small but important part of KE. Not only do they provide additional revenue for the organization, but they are also positive

Exhibit 6: A KE group photo from August 2011 in Queenstown.

reminders of the KE trip, which hopefully will generate loyalty and positive word-of-mouth for a long time. Memorabilia can take the form of many things, such as T-shirts, sweatshirts, baseball caps, and group photographs.

FLEXIBILITY AND VALUE FOR MONEY

"I'm going to leave the bus here in Queenstown," stated Rory to Rob. "A group of us are going to hang around here for a few weeks, and take in the amazing scenery." "Great idea," said Rob. "Make sure you book yourself on the bus; one comes through here every day in the summer." "Thanks for a great time," added Rory, "Maybe you'll be driving the next bus we catch!"

If there is one thing that the management of KE constantly strives for, it is greater frequency of its bus services. This is because they have realized that the more often the buses operate, the more flexible their service becomes. This increases its attractiveness to potential customers.

KE offers daily departures for about four months of the year (January–April) and four to five times a week throughout the rest of the year (although some of the more off-beat routes run less frequently). However, KE has learned to stay flexible and change their departure dates quickly. As they are in a high-volume, low-margin business, they must always be very fluid in the way they operate. This has sometimes led to customers being stuck in various places for longer times than they had planned. Magic Bus has picked up on this and now offers guaranteed seats (and guaranteed hostel beds) anytime of the year if you give them 24 hours' or more notice—a guarantee that KE does not yet extend to its clients.

One way that this flexibility is created is through the reservation system, which can tell KE where their customers are, where they got off the bus and for how long. This enables customer flows to be managed effectively and ensures that the buses are as full as possible. This is important to KE, as it only makes any significant amount of profit on the last 15% of their business. This is due to the fact that they work on very fine breakevens, which are significantly higher than for traditional package tours. The reservation system is not faultless, though, and every now and then, overbooking and underbooking occur (where they tell a backpacker the bus is full when it is in fact not).

Market research has shown that value for money is the third most important aspect of the KE trip. The price of the tickets, along with the activities offered, and the flexibility and the quality of the service mean that many backpackers feel they are often obtaining value from KE. To date, KE has managed to maintain this perception, and it is one of the fundamental reasons for KE's success.

However, KE does not intend to stand still. Neil Geddes knows that, in order to stay ahead of the competition, they must always improve their service offering:

> We are our own biggest threat, being seen as mainstream, or not leading edge, or by becoming a service that is perceived as not being for independent travelers. We must continually move with the market to ensure we offer the best possible experience for our customers.

The challenges for KE are clear and present. They need to be seen as leading edge but not mainstream. They also need to ensure they avoid being labeled a "booze bus," which its competitor Contiki suffers from. Finding high-quality bus drivers is always a constant source of worry, as is the reservation system.

"Hey, Rory!" shouted Rob, as Rory walked toward his backpackers. "Did you ever work out the answer to your question?" Rory turned around and looked puzzled. "What question?" he said. "Oh you mean the one about why Kiwi Experience is so successful?"

"That's it! Did you ever work it out?" asked Rob. "Yeah, I think I did … no, I know I did," Rory said forcefully. "It's just difficult to express it all. Maybe one day I'll put it down on paper," he stated.

"Well, don't forget to mention me if you ever do," laughed Rob.

STUDY QUESTIONS

1. How does KE maintain a continual customer focus?
2. What role do culture and leadership play in the success of KE?
3. Brainstorm on how other service companies might get customers to pay a more active role (rather than passive) in the service experience.

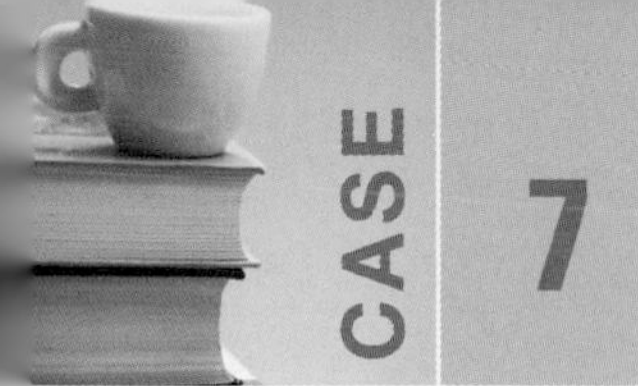

CASE 7

CASE STUDY

Distribution at American Airlines

Benjamin Edelman

American Airlines sought to reduce the fees it had paid to global distribution services (GDSs) to distribute its air travel services to travel agents. But GDSs held significant tactical advantages. For example, GDSs had signed long-term exclusive contracts with the corporate customers who were American's best customers. Furthermore, travel agents tended to favor whichever GDS offered the highest commissions—impeding price competition among GDSs. Against this backdrop, American considered how best to cut its GDS costs.

The GDS Negotiation Team at American Airlines faced the formidable task of reducing American's ticket distribution costs. Ticket distribution was increasingly electronic—with more than 95 percent of tickets existing only in a database, never printed on paper or "distributed" in the physical sense. Yet American continued to pay hundreds of millions of dollars per year to Global Distribution System's (GDS's) intermediaries that let travel agents book and confirm flights on American. If American simply refused to pay these costs, it would disappear from GDS listings—disrupting relationships with the travel agents whose corporate accounts were American's most profitable customers. But paying top dollar for database services was equally untenable, particularly as American struggled with rising fuel prices and increased competition from new entrants.

American had a proposed response to high GDS fees: a Source Premium Policy that would force travel agents to pay the extra cost incurred by American as a result of the agency's choice of GDS. This policy would reduce American's GDS expense, but travel agents were up in arms. If American pushed forward with the Source Premium Policy, travel agents might steer passengers elsewhere—leaving American even worse off than under GDS's high fees.

Professor Benjamin Edelman prepared this case. HBS cases are developed solely as the basis for class discussion. Cases are not intended to serve as endorsements, sources of primary data, or illustrations of effective or ineffective management.

*American did not disclose specific fees, but publicly available sources provide some information. See, for example, note 18.

THE STRUCTURE AND HISTORY OF AIRLINE TICKET DISTRIBUTION

American Airlines' operations grew rapidly after World War II. In 1921, American's corporate predecessor had just five small airplanes for transporting airmail. But expansion was brisk: in 1946, American ordered 220 new planes.

Early logistics proved challenging, and even taking reservations could be complex. Initially, passenger listings were stored on paper records in reservations offices at each point of departure. To request a reservation, a passenger would call American or visit a "city ticket office" retail location. American staff would use telephone or teletype to check with the departure city to assure that space was available on the specified flight on the specified day. A 1967 HBS teaching case described American's Chicago reservations office:

> A large cross-hatched board dominates one wall, its spaces filled with cryptic notes. At rows of desks sit busy men and women who continually glance from thick reference books to the wall display while continuously talking on the telephone and filling out cards. One man sitting in the back of the room is using field glasses to examine a change that has just been made on the display board. The chatter of teletype and sound of card sorting equipment fills the air.[1]

As American's network grew and passenger volume increased, paper passenger lists and telephone confirmations proved inadequate. American in 1952 introduced the Magnetronic Reservisor to help automate inventory control. Using a mechanical console installed on each desk, an agent pushed buttons to indicate the desired date and flight. If space was available, a light on the console would be illuminated. When a flight sold out, a member of staff removed a wire from the master control board, breaking the circuit and disabling the agent's light on any future requests for that flight. The Reservisor offered major productivity improvements: a trial in the Boston reservations office served an additional 200 passengers daily, with 20 fewer reservations staff. Yet reservations remained complex: processing a typical round-trip ticket required the efforts of 12 different people, taking up to three hours from start to finish. With so many steps, errors were widespread, and reservation agent productivity was decreasing as itineraries became more complex.[2]

An improved alternative came from a chance meeting between American Airlines then-president C. R. Smith and IBM then-president Thomas Watson, Jr. on an American Airlines flight in 1956. Aviation historian Robert Serling recounts their conversation:

> "What line of business are you in?" CR asked.
>
> "Business machines, computers. How about you?"
>
> "Airlines. This one, as a matter of fact."
>
> "You must be having all sorts of problems these days. What's your biggest one?"
>
> "Answering the goddamned telephone."[3]

American and IBM collaborated on the design of an improved inventory management system, ultimately called the Semi-Automated Business Reservations Environment (SABRE). IBM provided the hardware, while AA and IBM jointly built the software. The initial investment was comparable to half a dozen Boeing 707 jet airplanes.[4]

Despite SABRE's cost, American viewed the program as a success. Customers would still call or visit American staff to book flights, but SABRE eliminated time-consuming checks with departure city reservation lists. American reported that SABRE allowed for a 30 percent reduction in reservation staff.

In a 1976 innovation, American's marketing department began providing SABRE terminals to interested travel agencies. American anticipated strategic advantages from travel agents' use of the terminals: SABRE would make it particularly easy for agents to browse and confirm American flights. SABRE was installed at 130 travel agents locations within the first year, and hundreds more in the next.[5] American reported that the first 200 travel agent installations of SABRE yielded $20.1 million of annual incremental passenger revenue, a 500 percent return on investment.[6] Seeing American's success, competing airlines scrambled to implement similar systems of their own: United offered travel agents Apollo, while TWA offered PARS, DELTA offered DATAS II, and Eastern offered System One.

The Rise of Competing Global Distribution Systems

Most travel agencies chose computer terminals from a single provider. Each terminal used different commands to perform the same tasks, and installing multiple providers added complexity, particularly in duplication of accounting records. Travel agencies therefore sought systems that could book flights on multiple airlines. In response, airlines upgraded their offerings to allow bookings on competing carriers. For example, a travel agent with American Airlines' SABRE could use SABRE to book flights on United, while an agent with United's Apollo could equally book flights on American. This multicarrier approach was initially called a Customer Reservation System (CRS), later a Global Distribution System (GDS).

The rise of the GDS created the prospect of opportunistic behavior. For example, if an airline owned a GDS, it could configure the GDS to show the airline's own flights first—even if others offered a lower fare or a more direct routing. Furthermore, airlines that owned GDS's could charge other airlines for preferred placement in GDS listings. From 1983 to 1987, a series of cases challenged these "display bias" tactics, and, in 1984, the Department of Transportation established a set of regulations to standardize GDS operations. In particular, regulations forbade GDS's from using ranking flights based on carrier identity, (e.g., ranking some flights higher merely because they were operated by a preferred carrier. Additional rules prohibited GDS's from charging discriminatory booking fees or from unreasonably limiting travel agents' ability to switch GDS's) or use multiple GDS's. Finally, GDS's owned by airlines had to provide non-owner airlines with information and capabilities as accurate and reliable as those provided to the owner. Conversely, in a rule often referred to as "mandatory participation," an airline that owned GDS's had to offer service in all other GDS's also. Exhibit 1 presents excerpts of these rules.

Exhibit 1: Regulation of GDS Relationships (as of 2002) (excerpted).

§255.7—System owner participation in other systems.

(a) Each system owner shall participate in each other's system (to the extent that such owner participates in such an enhancement in its own system) if the other system offers commercially reasonable terms for such participation. Fees shall be presumed commercially reasonable if:

(1) they do not exceed the fees charged by the system of such system owner in the United States; or

(2) they do not exceed the fees being paid by such system owner to another system in the United States.

(b) Each system owner shall provide complete, timely, and accurate information on its airline schedules, fares, and seat availability to each other's system in which it participates on the same basis and at the same time that it provides such information to the system that it owns, controls, markets, or is affiliated with. If a system owner offers a fare or service that is commonly available to subscribers to its own system, it must make that fare or service equally available for sale through other systems in which it participates.

§255.8—Contracts with subscribers.

(a) No subscriber contract may have a term in excess of five years. No system may offer subscribers or potential subscribers a subscriber contract with a term in excess of three years unless the system simultaneously offers such subscribers or potential subscribers a subscriber contract with a no longer than three years. No contract may contain any provision that automatically extends contract beyond its stated date of termination, whether because of the addition or deletion of equipment or because of some other event.

§255.9—Use of third-party hardware, software, and databases.

(a) No system may prohibit or restrict, directly or indirectly, the use of:

(1) third-party computer hardware or software in conjunction with CRS services, except necessary to protect the integrity of the system; or

(2) a CRS terminal to access directly any other system or database providing information about airline services, unless the terminal is owned by the system.

(b) This section prohibits, among other things, a system's:

(1) imposition of fees in excess of commercially reasonable levels to certify third-party equipment;

(2) undue delays or redundant or unnecessary testing before certifying such equipment ...

§255.10—Marketing and booking information.

(a) Each system shall make available to all U.S. participating carriers on nondiscriminatory terms all marketing, booking, and sales data relating to carriers that it elects to generate from its system. The data made available shall be as complete and accurate as the data provided a system owner.

Source: 14 CFR Ch. 11

Initially, travel agents were of limited importance, for travelers directly contacted whatever airline they wished to fly. But the 1978 deregulation of US air travel brought major changes: airlines could set their own schedules, fares, and routes without government oversight. Suddenly, travel agents played a key role in helping travelers find the best choices in an increasingly competitive marketplace. By 1989, more than 80 percent of tickets were booked through travel agents.[7]

Payments and Competition under Global Distribution Systems

Initially, an airline had paid all the costs of the GDSs it created. But as the airline and GDSs began to keep each other at arms length, they formalized the fee structure charged to airline participants. In particular, when a GDS issued a ticket on an airline, the GDS would charge the airline a fee for each flight segment in the passenger's itinerary. In 2002, on average, an airline paid a GDS of $4.25 per flight segment. The average ticket included more than one segment, and the average booking fee per ticket was $11. At United Airlines, GDS fees totaled 3.3 percent of revenue for tickets sold through the GDSs.[8]

GDSs, in turn, spent a portion of this fee on payments to travel agents: The more a GDS offered a travel agent, the more likely that travel agent was to choose that GDS rather than a competitor. By 2002, fewer than half of travel agencies paid monthly fees for GDS services, and 60 percent of travel agents received a signing bonus for joining a GDS. In addition, GDSs paid travel agents "incentive payments" of $1 to $1.70 per segment.[9]

A European Commission diagram[10] summarized the resulting payment flow:

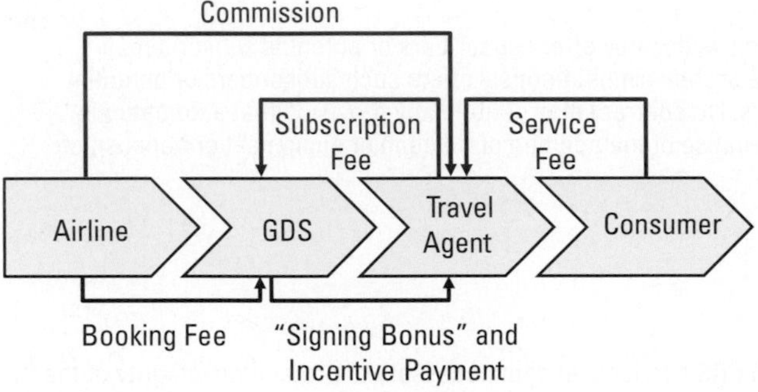

Because travel agents did not pay booking fees, they had no direct incentive to use the system that charged airlines the lowest fees. Instead, a travel agent would typically choose whichever GDS offered the travel agent the largest incentive payment.

Most travel agents still used only one GDS. Accessing more than one GDS required more training, more equipment, and considerable accounting complexity.

In general, airlines participated in all four GDSs. Airlines recognized that each travel agent could access only one GDS, and no airline wanted to turn away travel agents that might book its tickets.

US GDS DEREGULATION

By 2000, a comprehensive GDS regulation was increasingly viewed as unnecessary. Although major airlines still obtained 58 percent of their bookings from "brick-and-mortar" travel agencies, 10 percent of bookings came from airlines' own websites, and these bookings did not need to pass through a GDS. Furthermore, 15 percent of bookings came from new online travel agencies such as Expedia and Travelocity. These bookings did use GDSs (e.g., Travelocity used SABRE, and Expedia and Orbitz used Worldspan.) But a new set of "direct connect" systems was expected to let online travel agencies bypass GDSs to work directly with airlines.[11]

Meanwhile, by 2002, American had sold SABRE and United had sold Apollo. Airlines' divestitures of their GDSs reduced concerns about a GDS favoring its parent airline.

After a series of consultations, the Department of Transportation in 2002 decided to remove most regulation of GDSs. After a brief transition period, the regulations shown in Exhibit 1 would no longer apply. Instead, airlines and GDSs could negotiate privately to establish the parameters of their relationship. These changes went into effect in January 2004.[12]

In 2003, on the eve of full deregulation, airlines and GDSs entered their first round of comprehensive negotiations. Thanks to revised regulations, airlines were no longer required to submit all their fares to all GDSs. Thus, some airlines introduced "web fares," lower prices available only to customers who booked tickets directly with an airline, typically on the airline's website. However, GDSs wanted to provide airlines' lowest prices to their travel agents and to their travel agents' passengers. If an airline guaranteed to provide a GDS with access to all of its fares, as of 2003, a GDS typically offered the airline discounts (averaging 12 percent) on the GDS's fees.[13] The Department of Transportation applauded this result: "As we predicted, the airlines' control over access to their webfares has led some of the [GDS] systems to offer airlines discounted booking fees in return for the ability to sell those fares."[14]

Exhibit 2 presents GDS market shares as of 2003.

BOOKING TRAVEL AFTER GDS DEREGULATION

Despite lowered prices from GDSs, not all airlines used GDSs. As of 2004, Southwest participated only in SABRE. Furthermore, Southwest offered limited functions (e.g., no immediate booking confirmations), and SABRE could sell only Southwest's highest fares. JetBlue also limited its use of GDSs. For example, in 2004, it withdrew from SABRE, reporting that most of its customers did not require GDS services.[15] In lieu of GDSs, these airlines encouraged passengers to book directly, for example, by telephone or online.[16]

Exhibit 2: GDS Market Shares (as of 2003).

	USA/ Canada	Central/ South America	Europe/ Middle East	Asia/ Pacific	World-wide
Amadeus	9%	38%	49%	15%	26%
Galileo	21%	6%	31%	15%	22%
SABRE	42%	50%	13%	4%	24%
Worldspan	28%	6%	8%	4%	24%
Abacus				19%	4%
Topas				4%	1%
Infini				4%	1%
TravelSky				36%	8%

Source: Adapted from MetaGroup estimates based on interviews with GDS's and airlines.

Exhibit 3: Distribution Channel Prevalence.

	1999	2002	2005
Airline web sites	3%	13%	38%
Airline call centers	26%	24%	
Online travel agents	4%	17%	
Traditional travel agents	67%	46%	

Source: Adapted from "Airline Ticketing: Impact of Changes in the Airline Ticket Distribution Industry." General Accounting Office. July 2003. "Consultation Paper on the Possible Revision of Regulation 2299/89 on a Code of Conduct for Computerised Reservation Systems." European Commission Directorate-General for Energy and Transport. February 23, 2007.

In contrast, other airlines still obtained most of their bookings through GDSs. For example, as of 2004, 70 percent of American's tickets were booked through travel agents.[17] See Exhibit 3, tabulating distribution channel prevalence by year. American's 2001 operations included 112,400,000 flight segments booked through GDSs. For these bookings, American paid more than $424 million of GDS fees.[18] GDSs in turn, earned high profits compared with airlines. See Exhibit 4, comparing profits at SABRE and Amadeus with profits at American and United.

For leisure customers, direct web-based bookings were increasingly common. But business customers continued to favor bookings through travel agencies. Many companies required that their employees use travel agents in order to assure compliance with corporate travel policies, facilitate streamlined payment and accounting, and receive personalized assistance with complicated or changing trips.

THE 2006 GDS NEGOTIATIONS

In 2006, American Airlines faced the impending expiration of its 2003 three-year contracts with the four then-existing GDSs. American had achieved some cost reductions in 2003, but it still considered GDS's fees excessive. American sought to reduce fees considerably through 2006 contracts.

By July, American had reached agreements with Worldspan and Galileo. Under these agreements, Worldspan and Galileo would offer additional services to travel agents: "Worldspan Super Access" and "Galileo Content Continuity." If a travel agent chose one of these new services, it would be able to view and book all of American's fares. However, by entering

Exhibit 4: Profits at airlines and GDS's—net profit before special items.

Year	American Airlines	United Airlines	US Airlines Collectively	SABRE	Amadeus
1999	$985	$1,235	$5,400	$331	$117
2000	$813	$50.0	$2,500	$144	$129
2001	($1,800)	($2,145)	($8,300)	$31.1	$110
2002	($3,500)	($3,212)	($11,300)	$214	$156
2003	($1,200)	($2,808)	($3,600)	$83.3	$200
2004	($751)	($1,721)	($9,100)	$190	$294
2005	($857)		($1,143)	$172	

Source: SEC 10-K filings of American Airlines, United Airlines, and SABRE. IATA Economics Briefing, December 7, 2005. Amadeus financial statements. Note: Amounts in millions of dollars of profit and (loss). Amadeus values converted from Euros to Dollars as of corresponding years.

one of these agreements, the agent would accept a reduction or elimination of its incentive payment from the GDS. For example, a Galileo Content Continuity travel agent would give up $0.80 of its GDS incentive payment.[19] At the same time, for tickets booked through these new services, American's GDS payment would be approximately $0.60 per segment. In contrast, SABRE and Amadeus held firm in charging American GDS fees of more than $4 per segment.*

On July 12, 2006, American announced its Source Premium Policy. Effective September 1, American would charge travel agents a $3.50 "source premium" fee per segment for all segments booked through GDSs other than those AA designated as "competitive booking sources." Worldspan Super Access and Galileo Content Continuity were designated as competitive, hence, not subject to the fee. Any travel agent that chose one of these services would not pay the source premium fee. However, the source premium would apply to all SABRE and Amadeus bookings and to all Worldspan and Galileo bookings other than through the Super Access and Content Continuity programs. Exhibit 5 gives excerpts of the Source Premium Policy.

Travel Agents' Response

Some travel agents reacted negatively to American's proposed policy. Just one day after American's announcement, the American Society of Travel Agents issued a press release condemning American's approach. ASTA CEO Kathryn Sudeikis complained, "American's announcement tells every travel agency in America: if you want to sell us, run your business the way we tell you or you'll be forced to pay us for the privilege of booking our services. This policy of shifting still more costs off of American's financial statements onto the backs of travel agents and their customers is unconscionable. American is trying to use its market power to impose its costs on other market players, as a condition to providing what travel agents clearly require to do business efficiently."[20]

Travel agents objected to the Source Premium Policy in part because GDS incentive payments were the major remaining form by which airlines paid most travel agents. By 2002, airlines had largely eliminated ordinary travel agent commissions. Without GDS payments, most travel agents would receive no payments from the airlines whose tickets they sold, making it increasingly difficult for travel agents to offer services to customers without a separately itemized charge. (However, most travel agents had already begun to charge customers for each ticket issued.)

Exhibit 5: Source Premium Policy (as of August 31, 2006).

American Airlines wishes to provide all agencies access to full schedule, fare, and inventory content through the distribution source of their choice, on terms that allow American to compete with its low-cost rivals.

To achieve this end, American has negotiated full content access deals with many distribution providers that offer new, cost-effective products. These products are referred to as "Competitive Booking Sources." Travel agencies that use Competitive Booking Sources to create bookings will have access to full American content.

American recognizes that some travel agencies or corporate travel departments may value the use of certain GDS providers that do not qualify as Competitive Booking Sources. Accordingly, American currently intends to preserve flexibility for these agencies and corporations by providing full content access through other presently available providers, referred to as "Other Booking Sources," although these sources are more expensive to American. In exchange for the flexibility to choose Other Booking Sources, agencies that use these sources will be required to bear a portion of the cost of content distribution via these sources. Also, American, consistent with any applicable contractual obligations, may eventually withhold content from Other Booking Sources, particularly if an Other Booking Source fails to display American content on neutral terms as compared with other airlines.

		Source Premium per Net Booked Segment
Competitive Booking Sources	Worldspan Super Access Product Galileo Content Continuity Program All G2 Switchworks GDS Products All Farelogix GDS Products	NONE
Other Booking Sources	Any Amadeus GDS Product Any SABRE Product Any Other Worldspan Product Any Other Galileo/Apollo Program	$3.50

The Source Premium will be applied to all Other Booking Source net bookings originated or changed on or after September 1, 2006.

Source: American Airlines—http://www.aa.com/agency.

Travel agents also suggested that American's move was improper, unjustified, or even unfair. Airlines had always paid GDS's to distribute airlines' tickets, and most travel agents saw little reason for change. American's surcharges on SABRE-issued tickets were particularly hard for travel agents to understand because American had created SABRE and because American had previously encouraged travel agents to install and rely on SABRE terminals.

Travel agents that specialized in expensive corporate tickets thought they were not getting appropriate credit for the high revenues they provided. "Whether the fare is $1,800 or $180, a roundtrip of non-stops booked through one of AA's non-preferred channels still would generate a $7 fee," commented travel industry newsletter *The Beat*, citing industry sources.[21]

Additional complications came from travel agents' long-term contracts with GDSs. American's July announcement offered just seven weeks until implementation. But most travel agents had long-term contracts with GDSs; the average such contract lasted three years.[22] So, even if a travel agent wanted to move to a different GDS at American's suggestion, the travel agent would need some time to do so. Travel agents faced further complications from their relationships with many airlines: if each airline came to favor a different GDS, a travel agent might be forced to pay extra fees no matter which GDS it chose.

Those critical of American's Source Premium Policy often cited Northwest's August 2004 Shared GDS Fee. Northwest had proposed to charge travel agencies $7.50 for each round-trip ticket and $3.75 for each one-way ticket issued via a GDS.[23] Northwest's fee prompted an uproar from travel agents and GDS's, and Northwest dropped the fee just two weeks later.[24]

Travelers' Perspective

The Business Travel Coalition (BTC), an association of companies buying air travel, weighed in largely against GDS fees. The BTC's key concern was obtaining access to all fares without exclusion of airlines' lowest fares.

The BTC also expressed concern about the overall secrecy of airlines' dealings with travel agents. The BTC claimed that corporate travel managers "have been somewhat in the dark about the depth of the financial arrangements between the GDSs and TMCs," adding that "never has there been a process involving industry structural change that has been so cloaked in secrecy."[25]

American's Approach

Despite these challenges, American staff insisted that the Source Premium Policy was the right way forward. "We need to help travel agents understand how expensive some channels can be," explained Cory Garner, Manager of Distribution Strategy. "Right now, an agency chooses a GDS and the airline pays the bill. If an agency is protected from the financial consequences of its choice of GDS, how can it be expected to make the most economical decision on behalf of the customer?"

Seeing the struggle between American, GDSs, and travel agents, one source called the negotiation a "poker game."[26] Another industry insider pondered the competitive implications, particularly at American hub cities: "What if the other carriers say nothing until after September. [L]ook for market share swings, especially in O'Hare and Dallas/Fort Worth, not to mention other big AA markets?"[27]

By mid-August, American had largely reached agreement on key pricing terms with remaining GDSs SABRE and Amadeus. But American's Charlie Sultan, Managing Director of Sales, Planning and Analysis, explained that other issues remained unresolved. Particularly controversial were potential future agreements in which American might seek to communicate directly with travel agents or large customers, without routing bookings through a GDS. Sultan told *The Beat*: "We were not willing to sign up for [an agreement] that said, 'We cannot sit down with our travel agency partners or corporate partners and figure out how the two of us can do business if it involves potentially not booking through SABRE.' That is not pro-consumer, or pro-agency or pro-supplier. That is only pro-SABRE."[28]

As September 1 neared, Charlie Sultan and co-lead negotiator Chris Degroot had a choice to make. American could follow through in implementing the Source Premium Policy—reducing GDS expenses, but risking losing business as travel agents encouraged customers to choose other carriers. Or American could cancel the Source Premium Policy—preserving travel agent relationships, but making little headway on distribution costs.

STUDY QUESTIONS

1. American Airlines could distribute directly via the Internet and its own call centers in a highly cost-effective manner. Why then should American Airlines sell via travel agents at all?

2. American Airlines spends hundreds of millions of dollars on GDS fees. In the end, who is paying for these costs? How are the economic costs paid for in this channel?

3. From a GDS perspective, what techniques can it use to retain and protect is current business model?

4. Should American Airlines implement the Source Premium Policy?

---

1 R.F. Meyer. "American Airlines SABRE (A)." Harvard Business School Case No. EA-C 768 (1967).

2 Copeland, Duncan, Richard Mason, and James McKenney. "SABRE: The Development of Information-Based Competence and Execution of Information-Based Competition." *IEEE Annals of the History of Computing* 17, no. 3 (1995).

3 Serling, Robert. "Eagle: The Story of American Airlines." New York: St. Martin's Press, 1985

4 Copeland, et al. Id.

5 Copeland, et al. Id.

6 US District Court, Central District of California. "Memorandum from T.G. Plaskett to A.V. Casey." American Airlines Documents AA080713-AA080714, January 17, 1977.

7 Labich, Kenneth. "Should Airlines Be Reregulated?" *Fortune*. June 19, 1989.

8 CRS Regulations, Final Rule, RIN 2105-AC65, January 7, 2004. Citing United Reply Comments.

9 CRS Regulations, Final Rule, RIN 2105-AC65, January 7, 2004. Citing SABRE Comments. See also, Promedia.travel. "The Evolving Managed Travel Distribution Chain in 2006." http://www.thebeat.travel/blog/ downloads/promedia-GDS-guide.pdf.

10 "Consultation Paper on the Possible Revision of Regulation 2299/89 on a Code of Conduct for Computerised Reservation Systems." European Commission Directorate-General for Energy and Transport. February 23, 2007.

11 CRS Regulations, Final Rule, RIN 2105-AC65, January 7, 2004. Citing Galileo Comments and Guerin-Calvert, Jernigan & Hurdle Declaration.

12 CRS Regulations, Final Rule, RIN 2105-AC65, January 7, 2004.

13 Alamardi, Fariba, 2006. "The Future of Airline Distribution." *Journal of Air Transport Management* 12 (2006): 122–134.

14 67 FR 69381.

15 Kontzer, Tony. "JetBlue Pulls Out of SABRE, As Web Sales Rise." *Information Week*. December 20, 2004.

16 CRS Regulations, Final Rule, RIN 2105-AC65, January 7, 2004. Citing SABRE comments.

17 CRS Regulations, Final Rule, RIN 2105-AC65, January 7, 2004. Citing American comments.

18 See e.g. George Nicoud III, American Airlines, "Follow-Up to July 12, 2002 Testimony," available at http://govinfo.library.unt.edu/ncecic/other_testimony/american_letter.pdf.

19 "Interview: Travelport SVP Kurt Ekert." *The Beat*. July 31, 2006.

20 "American Airlines Announcement Threatens to Throw Industry into Chaos, Says ASTA." American Society of Travel Agents. July 13, 2006.

21 "Galileo Reveals Incentive Cut Amid AAngst." *The Beat*. July 13, 2006.

22 CRS Regulations, Final Rule, RIN 2105-AC65, January 7, 2004.

23 "Northwest Airlines to Charge for GDS Bookings." *M-Travel Travel Distribution News*. August 24, 2004.

24 Karantzavelou, Vicky. "ACTA Welcomes Northwest Decision to Drop Shared GDS Fees." *Travel Daily News*. September 6, 2004.

25 "BTC Attacks Airlines, Cites AA-SABRE PNR Issue." *The Beat*. August 9, 2006.

26 "80 Cent: Galileo Matches SABRE Number in Fee, Not Cut." *The Beat*. July 14, 2006.

27 "Galileo Reveals Incentive Cut Amid AAngst." *The Beat*. July 13, 2006.

28 "Interview: AA Exec Details SABRE Impasse." *The Beat*. August 10, 2006.

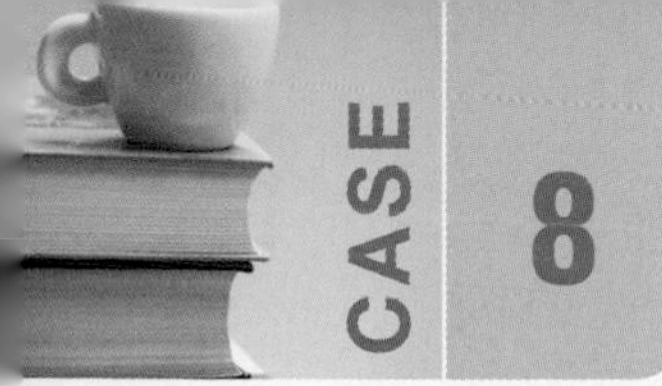

CASE 8

CASE STUDY

Managing Word-of-Mouth: The Referral Incentive Program That Backfired

Patricia Chew and Jochen Wirtz

A referral incentive program was introduced, but resulted in fewer referrals than expected, especially from the desired target segments!

INTRODUCTION

Nguyen Trung Hung stared in dismay at the field-test reports on his desk. He was the sales and promotions manager at AHL Insurance Corporation, the fifth-largest insurance company in Vietnam, and he had been the main driving force behind the company's new initiative to expand its customer base through the implementation of a "recommend-a-friend" incentive program, the first of its kind in the industry in Vietnam. He felt it would be a good tool to meet their objective of customer base expansion, in the light of increasingly intense competition within the insurance industry. Before the actual implementation of the program, the company had conducted a three-month field test and offered the incentive program to a small number of customers in each of the four segments it had identified in its database.

Based on the success of similar programs in the banking and mobile phone industries, he had thought that the initiative would be a runaway success. Results, however, were far below expectations, although the program was not a complete failure. There were referrals generated, but it was mainly from the low-yield segments of its customer base. Moreover, its higher-revenue customers, who had traditionally generated the highest number of referrals, seemed to have generated fewer rather than more referrals during the referral-program trial period.

 This case is based on in-depth qualitative interviews on referral programs in general, and the observations from those interviews were translated into the insurance context for the purpose of illustrating people's responses to referral programs.

BACKGROUND INFORMATION ON AHL

AHL Insurance Corporation had its humble beginnings as an automobile insurer in Huế, the capital city of Thua Thien-Hue province in 1985. The founder, Nguyen Anh Dung, was an insurance salesman who decided to start his own business in Huế, believing that it was a niche market with a lot of untapped potential. Since then, the company has grown tremendously. Over the years, it has expanded its markets and product lines to meet the changing needs of its customers. Today, it has 13 offices in different cities in Vietnam, such as Hanoi, Ho Chi Minh City, Ha Phong, Da Nang, Can Tho, and Huế. There are currently more than 30,000 independent agents serving the needs of its customers.

The mission of AHL is to provide quality service and to build relationships with its customers through mutual trust and integrity. AHL aims to be the customers' first and best choice and maintain its position of leadership as a comprehensive provider of insurance products, so it has a variety of insurance products to meet both the personal and business needs of its customers.

The main strengths of AHL lie not only in the diversity of its products, but also in the excellent customer service provided by its agents. On top of that, in an industry where some firms have gained a bad reputation by making it difficult for its customers to make insurance claims, AHL actually trains dedicated agents to explain the little details of claims to its customers and these agents also help customers to expedite the claims process. As a result, it has earned the trust and loyalty of its customers over the years.

CUSTOMER SEGMENTS

When the idea for the "recommend-a-friend" program was first brought up, the company used its sophisticated customer relationship management (CRM) system to segment its customers into four groups. The "Apostles" were customers who had been with the company for over 10 years, and they had basically consolidated most of their insurance purchases with AHL. Besides themselves, their family members had also purchased various kinds of insurance products from AHL, ranging from life insurance, investment-linked plans, retirement plans, and children's education plans to property liabilities, automobile insurance, etc. Those Apostles running their own businesses would also buy products like group insurance packages, commercial property liabilities, and disability packages from AHL. They were not price sensitive and were willing to pay a premium for a customized insurance plan to meet their individual needs. One distinguishing feature of the Apostles was the fact that they really helped to promote and recommend AHL to their family members, friends, and associates. This was the group of customers who had traditionally generated the most referrals for AHL to date. As is typical of most companies, this group of customers generated about 80% of the company's revenue.

The "Loyals" were customers who had been with AHL for more than seven years on average. Compared to the Apostles, they bought fewer kinds of products and generated fewer referrals. They generally consolidated their insurance purchases with a few companies and were reluctant to pay a premium for customized plans, preferring to buy the standardized ones. The "Leads" were termed such because of their seeming inertia. They usually bought only personal insurance products and might have one or two insurance policies that are long term in nature, such as the life, health, endowment, and retirement insurance plans. When agents tried to sell them other kinds of plans, they were not open to the idea. Like the Loyals, they also tended to use several insurance companies to meet their insurance needs based on price and coverage but were not as price sensitive as the "Butterflies." In terms of referrals, this group would provide the occasional referral. Lastly, the Butterflies were customers who bought the occasional short-term insurance policies such as travel-related products and might hold long-term policies from other insurance companies. This group of customers was highly price sensitive. They would flock to wherever there were any deals or promotional incentives on insurance plans.

THE "RECOMMEND-A-FRIEND" INCENTIVE PROGRAM

The program was based on a point system. Points were awarded on the basis of profitability and term of the insurance products sold. The higher the sum assured, and the longer the insurance coverage, the more points the referrer could collect. The points system was transparent as the referrer could check beforehand how many points they would get if their friends bought a certain kind of product or plan from AHL. Points could be accumulated and exchanged for a variety of gifts featured in a glossy and attractive catalog.

For example, with 50,000 points, which is the highest number of points one could accumulate for a single referral, one could exchange for a branded watch costing US$800. Other products of lesser value in the catalog included Seiko watches; Samsonite travel luggage; Parker pens; iPhones; electrical goods like shavers, blenders, juicers, vacuum cleaners, microwave ovens, toasters, and television sets; DVD and CD players; and restaurant vouchers. In all, there were about 300 items in the catalog. The lowest number of points awarded was 50 points, for short-term travel insurance plans.

REFERRALS

Thus far, the Butterflies and Leads had generated the most referrals since the launch of the "recommend-a-friend" referral incentive program. However, since they themselves usually did not purchase the high-sum assured policies, or long-term policies, their friends were also people who bought similar kinds of policies. As a result, short-term policies such as travel policies that cover a few days, or up to one year, and childcare policies that are typically no longer than two years had been very popular. These policies typically did not produce high profit margins for the company, and the insured values tended to be lower.

What was alarming was the fact that the number of referrals from the Apostles had fallen since the start of the program. Nguyen Trung Hung had expected that this group would be motivated to refer even more friends to AHL. Their recommendations usually resulted in individuals buying policies that were long term and of high sums assured, thus generating higher profits for the company. Exhibit 1 details the results of the referrals in the three months of the field test. Five hundred customers from each of the four segments were selected to participate in the field test. For each segment, a control group consisting also of 500 customers was selected and monitored during the market testing.

INITIAL INTERVIEW RESULTS

Three months after the launch of the program, Nguyen Trung Hung had asked his marketing managers to conduct some interviews with customers from various segments, to get their views about the program. As a result, about 30 in-depth individual interviews were conducted with customers from each of the four segments, in their homes. Exhibit 2 shows some verbatim comments by the respondents.

FUTURE DIRECTION

Nguyen Trung Hung knew that, before the next meeting with the marketing director, he had to come up with a report about the results of the field test and also provide possible solutions to the problem. He was up for a promotion and did not want this project to affect his chances. What should he do next? Why were the results the way they were? Should he abandon the program even though about US$50,000 had been invested in it? Alternatively, should he change certain features of the program before relaunching it so that it is more targeted, because the different segments of customers seemed to react quite differently to the program? Was there a need for more market research to see what each group of customers would prefer in a referral incentive program?

Exhibit 1: Referral frequency and value index by customer segment.

	Apostles	Control Group	Loyals	Control Group	Leads	Control Group	Butterflies	Control Group
Number of referrals over three months before the test	22	21	17	15	3	4	1	1
Number of referrals during the three test months	15	19	11	14	8	3	16	1
Conversion rate (i.e., customers who actually took up a policy)	32%	33%	27%	28%	18%	22%	12%	18%
Average policy value sold (US$'000)	173	185	143	148	59	65	33	41

Note: The index refers to the number of referrals received per 1,000 customers per year. The average policy value closed by the referred customer is shown in thousand U.S. dollars ('000).

Exhibit 2: Verbatim comments about the incentive program.

Apostles	Loyals	Leads	Butterflies
"… I would only recommend if I thought it was good for the person. I would not do anything in a self-serving way …" 39, marketing manager	"… the gifts they offer. I have enough junk in my house already, I don't need anymore of it.." 29, unemployed	"… the kind of thing, I leave it to the individual, I don't push …" 26, administrative assistant	"… I will definitely be motivated to get in those customers because the incentive is very relevant to me … I'll definitely do it fast–speak to anyone close to me and not so close to me …" 22, student
"… It's almost like a forced recommendation because, ultimately, you think there is something to benefit yourself. I do the recommendation out of helping somebody …." 64, businesswoman	"… I will not go out of my way to recommend just to obtain the incentive. That would be a waste of my time. I do have better things to do with my time." 32, home maker	"… the reward that I have makes me want to tell others …" 18, student	"… When they started the program, I email everyone on my mailing list. I'm aiming to get the Tag Heuer. It would indeed be a dream for me!" 20, waitress
"… I'm not the kind who looks at incentives. I look at ties. If the person is close to me …and he needs an insurance, then I will want to help him out by giving him advice on what to buy …" 35, banquet manager	"… if the company was good, they wouldn't need an incentive program. When they do that, I start to have doubts about them, and am worried about my investment …" 35, IT executive	I'm excited by incentives. I love the incentives in the catalog. I would definitely recommend it to anyone who is interested …" 22, clerical assistant	"… I'm saving a lot. I like the feeling of exchanging points for something that I don't have to pay money for." 35, home maker
"… being a businessman who is time scarce, I never bother with it …" 56, businessman	"… I recommend my friends because the agents and customer service officers provide good service. I don't care if I get the incentive or not …" 27, professional sportsman	"… I've already gotten my friends and family to buy some insurance, and I got a Swatch watch in return. Isn't that wonderful?" 26, sales executive	"… since it's free, why don't I take advantage of it right? It would be stupid not to." 25, security guard
"… it's the service that the company has been providing that I like. It's not what they are offering …" 41, management consultant	"… the incentives that they are offering are just not worthwhile in the time that I would have to spend getting what they offer." 46, director	"… if it wasn't for the rewards, I would not have told others about the company." 40, home maker	"… whichever company is giving away freebies, I always try to take advantage of that … it saves me a lot of money. I'll queue up overnight if I have to." 19, student
"… I can buy those things with my own money. Why should I then be motivated to recommend based on the gifts?" 44, pilot	"… I think the incentive is immaterial … I will take it as an extra bonus. In the first place, we're doing word of mouth already all the time for people unknowingly …" 32, teacher		

The Accra Beach Hotel: Block Booking of Capacity during a Peak Period

Sheryl E. Kimes, Jochen Wirtz and Christopher H. Lovelock

Cherita Howard, Sales Manager for the Accra Beach Hotel, a 141-room hotel on the Caribbean island of Barbados, was debating what to do about a request from the West Indies Cricket Board. The Board wanted to book a large block of rooms more than six months ahead during several of the hotel's busiest times and was asking for a discount. In return, it promised to promote the Accra Beach in all advertising materials and television broadcasts as the host hotel for the upcoming West Indies Cricket Series, an important international sporting event.

THE HOTEL

The Accra Beach Hotel and Resort had a prime beachfront location on the south coast of Barbados, just a short distance from the airport and the capital city of Bridgetown. Located on three and a half acres of tropical landscape and fronting one of the best beaches on Barbados, the hotel featured rooms offering panoramic views of the ocean, pool, or island.

The centerpiece of its lush gardens was the large swimming pool, which had a shallow bank for lounging plus a swim-up bar. In addition there was a squash court and a fully equipped gym. Guests could also play golf at the Barbados Golf Club, which was only 15 minutes away and with which the hotel was affiliated.

The Accra Beach had two restaurants and two bars, as well as extensive banquet and conference facilities. It offered state-of-the-art conference facilities to local, regional, and international corporate clientele and had hosted a number of large summits in recent years. It had three conference rooms, which could be configured in a number of ways to be used for large corporate meetings, training seminars, product displays, dinners, and wedding receptions. A business center provided guests with Internet access, faxing capabilities, and photocopying services.

The hotel's 188 standard rooms were categorized into three groups—Island View, Pool View, and Ocean View—and

Exhibit 1: Beach view of the Accra Beach Hotel.

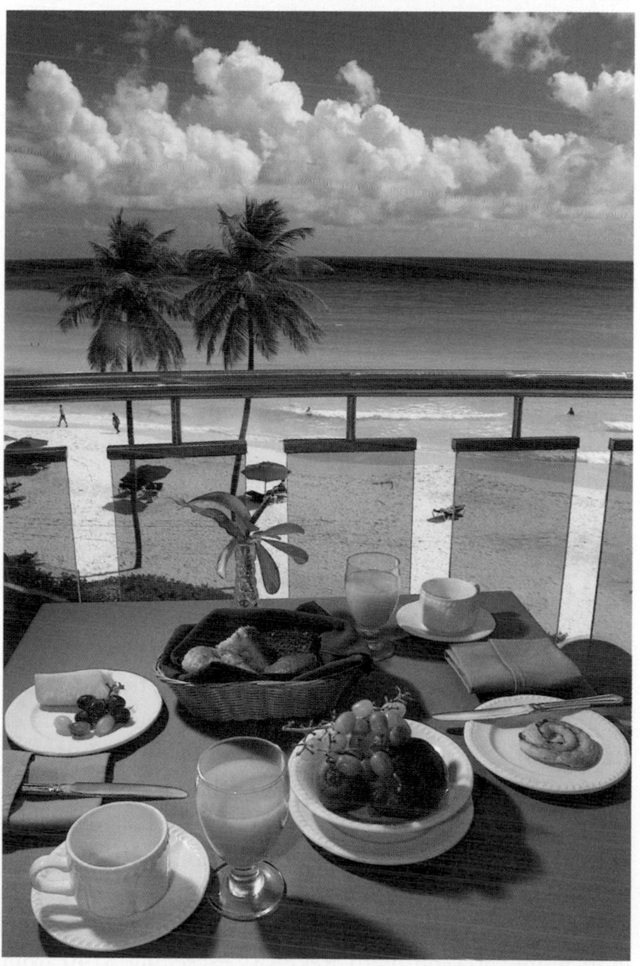

there were also 24 Ocean View Junior Suites, four two-bedroom, and six Penthouse Suites, each decorated in tropical pastel prints and handcrafted furniture. All rooms were equipped with cable/satellite TV, air-conditioning,

Note: Certain data have been disguised for confidentiality reasons.

Exhibit 2: Pool view of the Accra Beach Hotel.

ceiling fans, hairdryer, coffee percolator, direct-dial telephone, bathtub/shower, and a balcony.

Standard rooms were configured with either a king-size bed or two twin beds in the Island and Ocean View categories, while the Pool View rooms had two double beds. The eight Penthouse Suites and four two-bedroom Suites all offered ocean views and contained all the features listed for the standard rooms plus added comforts. They were built on two levels, featuring a living room with a bar area on the third floor of the hotel, and a bedroom accessed by an internal stairway on the fourth floor. These suites also had a bathroom containing a Jacuzzi, shower stall, double vanity basin, and a skylight. The 24 Junior Suites were fitted with a double bed or two twin beds, plus a living room area with a sofa that can be converted into another bed.

HOTEL PERFORMANCE

The Accra Beach enjoyed a relatively high occupancy rate, with the highest occupancy rates achieved from January through March and the lowest generally during the summer (Exhibit 3). Their average room rate followed a similar pattern, with the highest room rates (US$150–170) being achieved from December through March but relatively low rates (US$120) during the summer months (Exhibit 4). The hotel's revenue per available room (RevPAR), a product of the occupancy rate times the average room rate, showed even more variation, with RevPARs exceeding $140 from January to March but falling to less than $100 from June to October (Exhibit 5). The rates on the Penthouse Suites ranged from $310 to $395, while those on the Junior Suites ranged from $195 to $235. Guests had to pay Barbados' Value-Added Tax (VAT) of 8.75% on room charges and 15% on meals.

Cherita Howard, the hotel's sales manager, worked extensively with tour operators and corporate travel

Exhibit 3: Accra Beach Hotel.

Monthly Occupancy Rate		
Year	**Month**	**Occupancy**
2 Years Ago	January	87.7%
2 Years Ago	February	94.1%
2 Years Ago	March	91.9%
2 Years Ago	April	78.7%
2 Years Ago	May	76.7%
2 Years Ago	June	70.7%
2 Years Ago	July	82.0%
2 Years Ago	August	84.9%
2 Years Ago	September	64.7%
2 Years Ago	October	82.0%
2 Years Ago	November	83.8%
2 Years Ago	December	66.1%
Last Year	January	87.6%
Last Year	February	88.8%
Last Year	March	90.3%
Last Year	April	82.0%
Last Year	May	74.7%
Last Year	June	69.1%
Last Year	July	76.7%
Last Year	August	70.5%
Last Year	September	64.7%
Last Year	October	71.3%
Last Year	November	81.7%
Last Year	December	72.1%

Exhibit 4: Accra Beach Hotel.

Average Daily Room Rate		
Year	Month	Average Room Rate (in US$)
2 Years Ago	January	$159.05
2 Years Ago	February	$153.73
2 Years Ago	March	$157.00
2 Years Ago	April	$153.70
2 Years Ago	May	$144.00
2 Years Ago	June	$136.69
2 Years Ago	July	$122.13
2 Years Ago	August	$121.03
2 Years Ago	September	$123.45
2 Years Ago	October	$129.03
2 Years Ago	November	$141.03
2 Years Ago	December	$152.87
Last Year	January	$162.04
Last Year	February	$167.50
Last Year	March	$158.44
Last Year	April	$150.15
Last Year	May	$141.79
Last Year	June	$136.46
Last Year	July	$128.49
Last Year	August	$128.49
Last Year	September	$127.11
Last Year	October	$132.76
Last Year	November	$141.86
Last Year	December	$151.59

Note: Average room rate is inclusive of VAT.

Exhibit 5: Accra Beach Hotel.

Revenue per Available Room (RevPAR)		
Year	Month	Revenue per Available Room (in US$)
2 Years Ago	January	$139.49
2 Years Ago	February	$144.66
2 Years Ago	March	$144.28
2 Years Ago	April	$120.96
2 Years Ago	May	$110.45
2 Years Ago	June	$96.64
2 Years Ago	July	$100.15
2 Years Ago	August	$102.75
2 Years Ago	September	$79.87
2 Years Ago	October	$105.80
2 Years Ago	November	$118.18
2 Years Ago	December	$101.05
Last Year	January	$141.90
Last Year	February	$148.67
Last Year	March	$143.02
Last Year	April	$123.12
Last Year	May	$105.87
Last Year	June	$94.23
Last Year	July	$98.55
Last Year	August	$90.59
Last Year	September	$82.24
Last Year	October	$94.62
Last Year	November	$115.89
Last Year	December	$109.24

Note: RevPAR refers to revenue per available room and is computed by multiplying the room occupancy rate (see Exhibit 3) with the average room rate (Exhibit 4). RevPAR is inclusive of VAT.

managers to promote the hotel. The hotel had traditionally promoted itself as a resort destination, but, in the last few years, it had shifted its focus to promoting its convenient location and attracted many business customers. The Accra Beach Hotel was named Hotel of the Year by the Barbados Hotel Association in 2002 and 2005.

The composition of hotel guests had changed drastically over the past few years. Traditionally, the hotel's clientele had been dominated by tourists from the UK and Canada, but recently, the percentage of corporate customers had increased dramatically. Now, the majority of hotel guests were corporate clients from companies such as Barbados Cable & Wireless and the Caribbean International Banking Corporation (Exhibit 6) who came for business meetings with local companies.

Sometimes, guests who were on vacation (particularly during the winter months) felt uncomfortable finding themselves surrounded by business people. As one vacationer put it, "There's just something weird about being on vacation and going to the beach and then seeing suit-clad business people chatting on their cell phones." However, the hotel achieved a higher average room rate from business guests than vacationers and had found the volume of corporate business to be much more stable than that of tour operators and individual guests.

Exhibit 6: Accra Beach Hotel: Market segments.

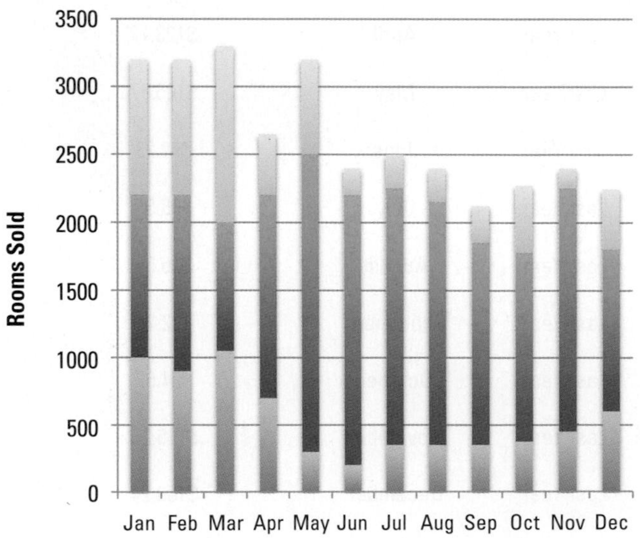

THE WEST INDIES CRICKET BOARD

Cherita had been approached by the West Indies Cricket Board (WICB) about the possibility of the Accra Beach Hotel serving as the host hotel for next spring's West Indies Cricket Home Series, an important international sporting event among cricket-loving nations. The location of this event rotated among several different Caribbean nations, and Barbados would be hosting the next one, which would feature visiting teams from India and New Zealand.

Cherita and Jon Martineau, General Manager of the hotel, both thought that the marketing exposure associated with hosting the teams would be very beneficial for the hotel. However, they were concerned about accepting the business because they knew from past experience that many of the desired dates were usually very busy days for the hotel. They were sure that the rate that the WICB was willing to pay would be lower than the average rate of US$140–150 they normally achieved during these times. And in contrast to regular guests, who could usually be counted on to have a number of meals at the hotel, team members and officials would probably be less likely to dine at the hotel because they would be on a per diem. On average, both corporate customers and vacationers spend about $8 per person for breakfast and about $25 per person for dinner (per person including VAT). The contribution margin on food and beverage is approximately 30%. About 80% of all guests have breakfast at the hotel and approximately 30% of all guests would dine at the hotel (there are many other attractive restaurant options nearby). Mr. Martineau thought that only about 25% of the cricket group would have breakfast at the hotel and maybe only about 10% would dine at the hotel. Also, they worried about how the hotel's other guests might react to the presence of the cricket teams. Still, the marketing potential for the hotel was substantial. The WICB had promised to list the Accra Beach as the host hotel in all promotional materials and during the televised matches.

The West Indies Home Series was divided into three parts, and each would require bookings at the Accra Beach Hotel. The first part pitted the West Indies team against the Indian team and would run from April 24 to May 7. The second part featured the same two teams and would run from May 27 to 30. The final part showcased the West Indies team against the New Zealand team and would run from June 17 to 26.

The WICB wanted 50 rooms (including two suites at no additional cost) for the duration of each part and was willing to pay US$130 per night per room. Both breakfast and VAT were to be included, and each team had to be housed on a single floor of the hotel. In addition, the WICB insisted that laundry service for team uniforms (cricket teams typically wear all-white clothing) and practice gear be provided at no additional charge for all team members. Cherita estimated that it would cost the hotel about $20 per day if they can do the laundry in-house, but about $200 per day if they had to send it to an outside source.

Cherita called Ferne Armstrong, the hotel's reservations manager, and asked her what she thought. Like Cherita, Ferne was concerned about the possible displacement of higher-paying customers but offered to do further investigation into the expected room sales and associated room rates for the desired dates. Since the dates were over six months in the future, Ferne had not yet developed forecasts. But she was able to provide data on room sales and average room rates from the same periods during the previous year (Exhibit 7).

Soon after Cherita returned to her office to analyze Ferne's data, she was interrupted by a phone call from the head of the WICB wanting to know the status of his request. She promised to have an answer for him before the end of the day. As soon as she hung up, Jon Martineau called and chatted about the huge marketing potential of being the host hotel.

Cherita shook her head and wondered, "What should I do?"

STUDY QUESTIONS

1. What factors lead to variations in demand for rooms at a hotel such as the Accra Beach?
2. Identify the various market segments currently served by the hotel. What are the pros and cons of seeking to serve customers from several segments?
3. What are the key considerations facing the hotel as it reviews the booking requests from the West Indies Cricket Board?[1]
4. What action should Cherita take and why?

Exhibit 7: Room sales and average daily room rates for same periods in previous year.

Date of WICB Home Series	Rooms Sold Last Year during the Same Period	Average Daily Room Rate (ADR) in US$
Part 1		
April 24	141	$129
April 25	138	$120
April 26	135	$128
April 27	134	$135
April 28	123	$133
April 29	128	$124
April 30	141	$119
May 1	141	$124
May 2	141	$121
May 3	139	$122
May 4	112	$118
May 5	78	$126
May 6	95	$130
May 7	113	$130
Part II		
May 27	99	$131
May 28	114	$132
May 29	114	$136
May 30	125	$136
Part III		
June 17	124	$125
June 18	119	$122
June 19	112	$126
June 20	119	$111
June 21	125	$110
June 22	116	$105
June 23	130	$106
June 24	141	$101
June 25	141	$110
June 26	125	$115

Note: ADR excludes VAT.

1 For simplification of calculations, assume that each room will hold only one occupant, that is, 50 rooms equate to 50 cricket players.

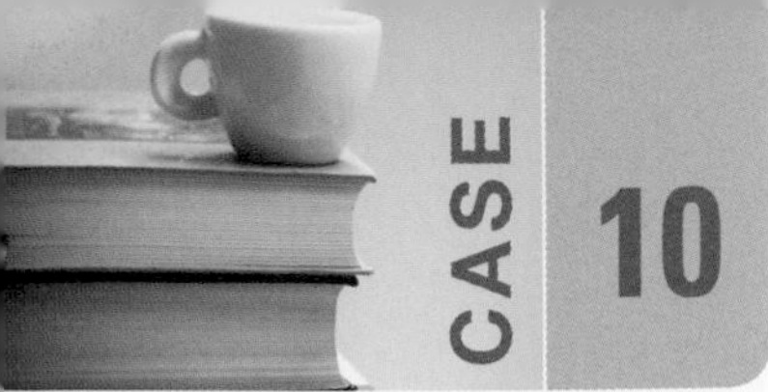

CASE 10

Revenue Management of Gondolas: Maintaining the Balance between Tradition and Revenue

Sheryl E. Kimes

A ride on a gondola, one of the historical black boats of Venice, is considered by many to be part of the quintessential Venice experience. However, while demand for gondolas is extremely high, the number of boats has dropped from several thousand gondolas in the 18th century to about 400 today. In addition, there is pressure to maintain some of the tradition associated with the gondolas, so increasing revenue is tricky. The question now is how can a balance between tradition and revenue be maintained?

Although Venice is considered to be one of the most beautiful and romantic cities in the world, modern Venice has faced many challenges, including a loss of population to other parts of Italy and physical damage from flooding, pollution, and age. The Venetian economy depends heavily on tourism; the beauty of the architecture and canals and the many art and cultural attractions draw 20 million visitors per year from around the world.

Venice is set on over 100 islands interconnected by about 150 canals. All transportation within the city is either by boat or on foot. A ride on a gondola, one of the historical black boats of Venice, is considered by many to be part of the quintessential Venice experience. Although the demand for gondola rides is extremely high, the number of boats has dropped from several thousand gondolas in the 18th century to about 400 today. Gondolas are regulated by the City of Venice, and there is a strong desire to maintain their tradition. But, at the same time, the economic impact on the city and its population is considerable. The question is how to best balance the maintenance of tradition with the economic impact on the gondolier and the city.

Exhibit 1: Gondola traffic at the Grand Canal in Venice.

TOURISM IN VENICE

In 2010, Venice received an average of 60,000 tourists per day, of which less than half spend the night. About 75% of the tourists come from outside of Italy. Venice has one of the highest ratios of tourists to local residents (89 visitors for every 100 Venetians—the highest in Europe). During busy periods (the summer, over Christmas, and during Carnival), even more people enter the city. Since 2004, there has been a 30% increase in the number of overnight stays. Germans represent the largest proportion of overnight tourists followed by Americans, Austrians, and French.

THE GONDOLA

The first mention of the gondola was recorded in 1094, but gondolas became popular during the 15th century and helped people better maneuver around the canals of Venice. Gondolas are designed to navigate the shallow, narrow canals of Venice and are strictly bound by tradition. The gondolas are 11 meters long, 1.4 meters wide, and weigh about 500 kilograms. The left side is higher than the right side by 24 centimeters and the bottoms are flat so that they can function in the very shallow water (sometimes much less than a meter deep). The gondolas are constructed of 280 pieces of eight different types of wood and only have metal in the head and stem of the boat. Gondolas are traditionally

Exhibit 2: Gondolas moored at San Marco, Venice.

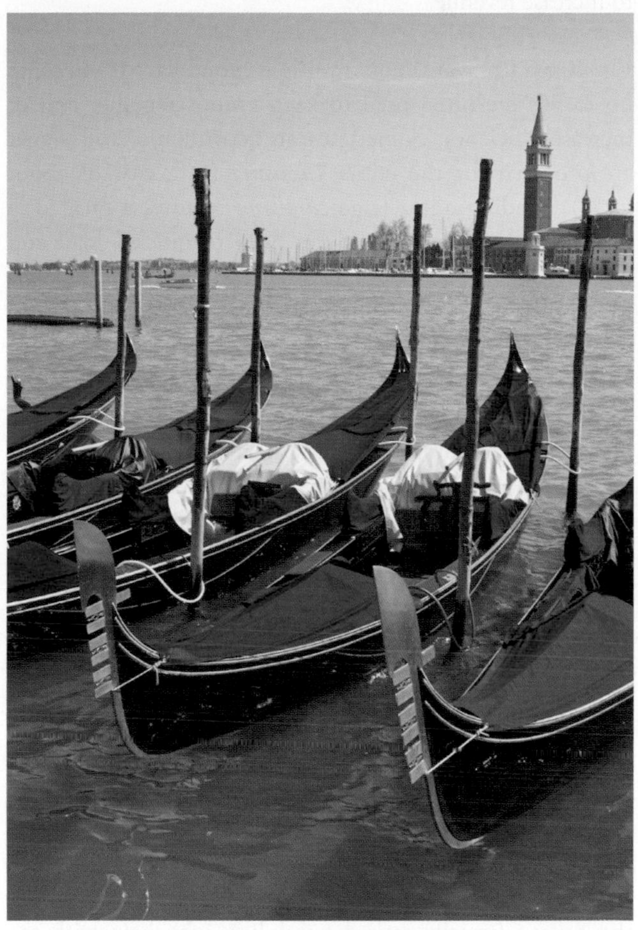

black and take about three to six months to build at a cost of approximately €20,000–30,000.

Gondoliers

Gondolas are owned and steered by gondoliers. Their numbers have dropped from several thousands in the 18th century to only 425 today. Gondoliers are usually male and must have been born in Venice. Traditionally, being a gondolier was passed from one generation to the next, but in recent years, this has changed because many young people have decided to take more lucrative and less physically demanding jobs. To become a gondolier, potential applicants take a test that measures their boat-handling skills, their language ability, their knowledge of the city, and their ability to work with tourists.

Exhibit 3: Venetian gondolier dressed in a traditional outfit.

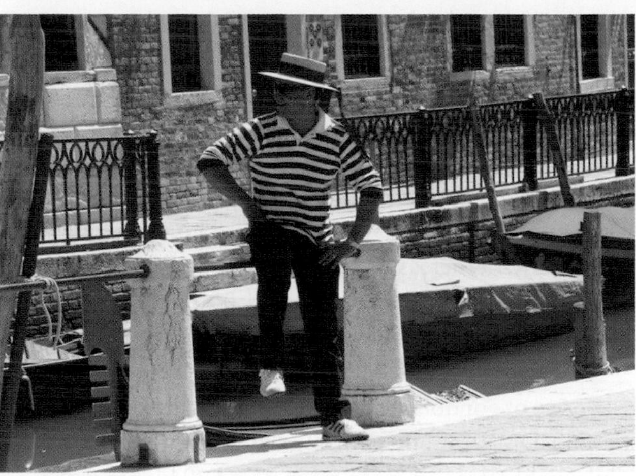

Gondoliers are divided into 10 *traghetti* (or ferry stations). Each *traghetto* elects representatives (called *barcali*) who will represent the *traghetto* to the government. Gondola rides are available at about eight *stazi* (ferry stations) throughout the city.

THE ROLE OF GONDOLAS IN TOURISM

Gondolas were once the primary source of transportation in Venice, but with the advent of faster and less expensive motorboats and *vaporetti* (a form of water-based bus), gondolas have become more of a tourist activity than a source of transportation.[1] During the 1920s, it was thought that gondolas would disappear, and a lively debate ensued with even Mussolini chiming in that the gondola tradition needed to be preserved. Even by the late 19th century, Mark Twain had commented that gondolas were little more than an anachronism.

As mass tourism increased, the design and operation of gondolas were altered in order to be able to accommodate more tourists and generate additional revenue. The boats were lengthened and narrowed, and a more elaborate oar link was developed so that the gondola could be steered by one oarsman. These modifications, along with a few other design changes, provided more space for passengers. In addition, as the amount of motorized boat traffic has increased, it has become more difficult to safely maneuver the gondolas through the narrow canals.

1 Much of the discussion on the next two pages is taken from Robert C. Davis and Garry R. Marvin, *Venice: The Tourist Maze.* Berkeley, California: University of California Press, 2004.

Pricing and Distribution

By 1930, tour guides such as Baedeker's listed gondola prices by the hour and by the trip, and by 1945, the gondola trips were based more on the experience rather than actual transportation to a destination.

Since World War II, the tourist demand for gondola rides has been extremely high and the posted rates have increased accordingly. Whereas the posted rate was $0.42 for 50 minutes in 1930, it had reached $1.00 by 1945, $5.00 by 1965, and had climbed to $70 by 1999.

The price of gondola rides is regulated by the city. Day rates are €80 for 40 minutes for a maximum of six passengers, while night rates (7 p.m. to 8 a.m.) are €20 higher. Although the rates are regulated, they are not always followed, and many prices are set through negotiation. Due to the popularity of gondola rides, it is quite possible to share the gondola with strangers.

Gondolas are typically booked in one of three ways: either directly with the gondolier, through a hotel, or through a third-party travel agency. Hotels and travel agencies often package the gondola ride with other services such as a dinner or live music and take a sizable commission.

About 80% of gondola business comes from tour operators. Typically, tour operators either package the gondola ride with other travel options such as hotel rooms, bus tours, and transfers, or sell them separately. In the former case, customers do not even know the cost of the gondola ride because it is included in the package price.

Even when customers can see the price, it is generally on a per person basis, so the price does not seem exorbitant. That being said, the rates are based on six people per gondola. Given that tour operator rates range from €35 to over €70 per person, the revenue associated with one 50-minute gondola ride is substantial. The tour operator passes along some of this revenue to the *stazi*, who in turn distribute it to the gondoliers, but still is able to maintain a very good profit margin even after covering costs.

The gondoliers seem to like working with the tour operators because of the guaranteed business and steady stream of business. In addition, much of the tour operator business arrives en masse, which makes it easier and more efficient to fill and dispatch gondolas. Still, the tour operator profit margin is high and there may be opportunities for the *stazi* to increase revenue.

Carovane (caravans) of multiple gondolas (sometimes up to 30) are often used to keep groups together and to increase efficiency. Sometimes an accordionist and singer are provided for the entire *carovana* (at a cost of about €150). Sending out a large *carovana* requires a great deal of coordination because of the need to quickly load and unload customers. Gondolas are not the most stable of boats for customers to board, and retired gondoliers are assigned to assist with loading and unloading.

The *carovana* follow a set route and can easily return to the dock within 50 minutes for the next group of passengers. Each of the *stazi* has different routes, which are designed to ensure a smooth flow and to avoid traffic tie-ups with *vaparettos* and other commercial boats.

Demand and Revenue

Firm statistics on the number of gondola rides do not exist, but it is estimated that about one quarter of all tourists take a gondola ride. In 2004, it was estimated that there were at least three million gondola rides. Even with a rate of $20 per person, this is a sizable business.

Gondolas generate income for not only the gondoliers, the *ganzeri* (usually retired gondoliers who help with the boats), and the group leaders of the *stazi*, but also for the boat construction trade (including the boatyard, the oar markers, the smiths, and the gilders). It also provides jobs and revenue for hat makers and tailors (who supply the traditional gondolier uniform) and generate a sizable amount of souvenir sales.

The Dilemma

Although the demand for gondola rides is extremely high, capacity issues seem to be constraining the number of rides that can be offered. This, combined with the pressure to maintain some of the tradition associated with the gondolas, makes increasing revenue tricky. Still, the revenue provided by the gondola industry is substantial and plays an important role in the Venice economy. How should they proceed?

Interesting Websites on Gondolas

- http://www.gondolaonline.org/03.html
- http://findarticles.com/p/articles/mi_qn4159/is_20040829/ai_n12760617
- http://www.news.com.au/story/0,23599,21067634-27984,00.html
- http://www.gondolavenezia.it/history_tariffe.asp?Pag=43
- http://www.venicewelcome.com/servizi/tour-ing/venicewalktours.htm
- http://researchnews.osu.edu/archive/venice.htm

STUDY QUESTIONS

1. What can be done to increase the capacity of gondolas? What revenue impact would this have?
2. How can you balance revenue maximization with the maintenance of cultural heritage? Is it possible? If so, what would you recommend?
3. Consider the pricing structure of gondolas. What sort of changes would you recommend? How would customers react? What revenue impact would your recommendations have?

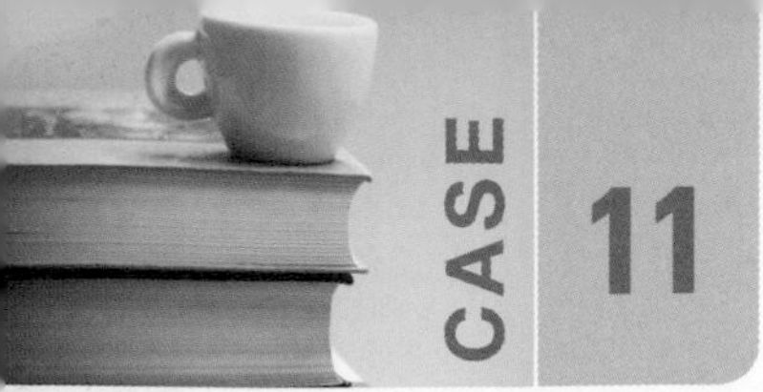

Aussie Pooch Mobile: Expansion by Franchising

Lorelle Frazer

After creating a mobile service that washes dogs outside their owners' homes, a young entrepreneur has successfully franchised the concept. Her firm now has more than 150 franchises in many parts of Australia, as well as up to 50 in other countries. She and her management team are debating how best to plan future expansion.

Elaine and Paul Beal drew up in their four-wheel drive outside 22 Ferndale Avenue, towing a bright blue trailer with red and white lettering. As Aussie Pooch Mobile franchisees whose territory covered four suburbs of Brisbane, Australia, they were having a busy day. It was only 1 p.m., and they had already washed and groomed 16 dogs at 12 different houses. Now they were at their last appointment—a "pooch party" of 10 dogs at Number 22, where five other residents of the street had arranged to have their dogs washed on a biweekly basis.

Prior to their arrival outside the house, there had been ferocious growling and snarling from a fierce-looking Rottweiler. But when the animal caught sight of the brightly colored trailer, he and two other dogs in the yard bounded forward eagerly to the chain link fence, in a flurry of barking and wagging tails.

Throughout the residential areas of Brisbane and in a number of other Australian cities, dogs of all shapes and sizes were being washed and groomed by Aussie Pooch Mobile franchisees. By late 2011, the company had grown to over 150 franchisees and claimed to be "Australia's largest mobile dog wash and care company." A key issue facing its managing director, Christine Taylor, and members of the management team was how to plan and shape future expansion (see Exhibit 1).

Exhibit 1: Chris Taylor with dogs.

FOUNDING AND EXPANSION

Located in Burpengary, Queensland, just north of Brisbane, Aussie Pooch Mobile Pty. Ltd. (APM) was founded in 1991 by Christine Taylor, then aged 22. Taylor had learned customer service early, working in her parents' bait and tackle shop from the age of eight. Growing up in an environment with dogs and horses as pets, she knew she wanted to work with animals and learned dog grooming skills from working in a local salon. At 16, Taylor left school and began her own grooming business on a part-time basis, using a bathtub in the family garage. Since she was still too young to drive, her parents would take her to pick up the dogs from their owners. She washed and groomed animals at home and then returned them.

Once Taylor had learned to drive and bought her own car, she decided to take her service to the customers. So she went mobile, creating a trailer in which the dogs could be washed outside their owners' homes and naming the fledging venture "The Aussie Pooch Mobile." Soon, it became a full-time job. Eventually, she found she had more business than she could handle alone, so she hired assistants. The next step was to add a second trailer. Newly married, she and her husband David McNamara ploughed their profits into the purchase of additional trailers and gradually expanded until they had six mobile units.

The idea of franchising came to Taylor when she found herself physically constrained by a difficult pregnancy:

> David would go bike riding or head to the coast and have fun with the jet ski and I was stuck at home and felt like I was going nuts, because I'm a really active person. I was hungry for information on how to expand the business, so I started researching other companies and reading heaps of books and came up with franchising as the best way to go, since it would provide capital and also allow a dedicated group of small business people to help expand the business further.

As existing units were converted from employees to franchisee operations, Taylor noticed that they quickly became about 20% more profitable. Initially, APM focused on Brisbane and the surrounding region of southeast Queensland. Subsequently, it expanded into New South Wales and South Australia in 1995, Canberra, Australian Capital Territory (ACT) in 1999, and Victoria in 2000 (Exhibit 2). Expansion into Western Australia came in mid-2004.

In 1996, a New Zealand division of the firm was launched in Tauranga, a small city 200 km southeast of Auckland, under the name Kiwi Pooch Mobile. In 2000, Taylor expanded operations into New Caledonia through a master franchise agreement, launching "La Pooch Mobile." In 2001, Aussie Pooch Mobile launched into the United Kingdom, beginning with a town in northern England. Soon, there were four operators under a master franchisee. The following year saw the official launch of The Pooch Mobile Malaysia, also under a master franchisee. When setting up the company's presence in the United States in 2006, Taylor offered the master franchise to a top performing Australian master franchisee to provide them with further opportunities to grow.

Exhibit 2: Map image.

By late 2011, the company had 150 mobile units in Australia, with 49 located in Queensland, 43 in New South Wales, 10 in South Australia, 18 in Victoria, and the remainder spread across the remaining states and territories. The company bathed more than 30,000 dogs each month and had an annual turnover of approximately $6.5 million.

APM was a member of the Franchise Council of Australia and complied with the Franchising Code of Conduct. The management team consisted of Christine Taylor as managing director and David McNamara as director responsible for overseeing trailer design and systems support. Each state had its own manager and training team. The central support office also housed staff who provided further assistance to managers and franchisees.

APM's expansion benefited from the leverage provided by several master franchisees, who had obtained the rights to work a large territory and sell franchises within it. Said Taylor:

> I look at the business as if it's my first child. I see it now starting to come of age where it wants to go alone, but still needs me to hold its hand a little bit, whereas initially it needed me there the whole time. With the support staff we have in place, the business is now gaining the support structure it needs to work without me. This is what I am aiming towards. I appreciate that a team of people can achieve much more than one person alone.

THE SERVICE CONCEPT

Aussie Pooch Mobile specialized in bringing its dog washing services to customers' homes. Dogs were washed in a hydrobath installed in a specially designed trailer, which was parked in the street. The trailer had partially open sides and a roof to provide protection from sun and rain (Exhibit 3). Apart from flea control products and a few grooming aids, APM did not attempt to sell dog food and other pet supplies. The company had resisted the temptation to diversify into other fields. "Our niche is in the dog bathing industry," declared Taylor. "I don't want us

Exhibit 3: Dog trailer image.

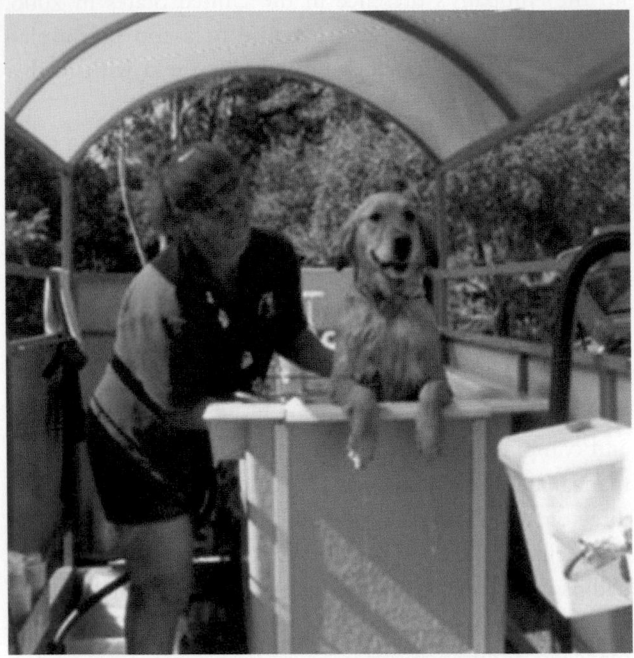

to be a jack of all trades because you'll never be good at anything. We now have an exclusive range of products that customer demand has driven us to providing, but we still work closely with vets and pet shops and are by no means a pet shop on wheels."

In contrast to retail pet service stores, where customers brought their animals to the store or kennel, APM brought the service to customers' homes, with the trailer parked outside on the street. The use of hydrobath equipment, in which warm, pressurized water was pumped through a shower head, enabled operators to clean dogs more thoroughly than would be possible with a garden hose. The bath was designed to rid the dog of fleas and ticks, and improve its skin condition as well as clean its coat and eliminate smells. Customers supplied water and electrical power.

The fee paid by customers varied from $22–$70 per dog, depending on breed and size, condition of coat and skin, behavior, and geographic location, with discounts for multiple animals at the same address. On average, regular customers paid a fee of $25 for one dog, $45 for two, and $65 for three. At "pooch parties," a concept developed at APM, the homeowner acting as host typically received one complimentary dog wash at the discretion of the operator. Additional services, for which an extra fee was charged, included the recently introduced aromatherapy bath ($2.50) and blow drying of the animal's coat for $5–$10 (on average, $8). Blow drying was especially recommended in cool weather to prevent the animal from getting cold. Operators also offered free advice to customers about their dogs' diet and health care, including such issues as ticks and skin problems. They encouraged customers to have their dogs bathed on a regular basis. Most customers made appointments once every two or four weeks.

A SATISFIED CUSTOMER

The process of bathing a dog involved a sequence of carefully coordinated actions, as exemplified by Elaine Beal's treatment of Zak the Rottweiler. "Hello, my darling. Who's a good boy?" crooned Elaine as she patted the enthusiastic dog, placed him on a leash, and led him out through the gate to the footpath on this warm, sunny day. Paul busied himself connecting hoses and electrical cords to the house, while Elaine began back-combing Zak's coat in order to set it up for the water to get underneath. She then led the now placid dog to the hydrobath inside the trailer, where he sat patiently while she removed his leash and clipped him to a special collar in the bath for security. Meanwhile the water had been heating to the desired temperature.

Over the next few minutes, Elaine bathed the dog, applied a medicated herbal shampoo to his coat, and rinsed him thoroughly with the pressure-driven hose. After releasing Zak from the special collar and reattaching his leash, she led him out of the hydrobath and onto the footpath, where she wrapped him in a chamois cloth and dried him. Next, she cleaned the dog's ears and eyes with disposable baby wipes, all the time continuing to talk soothingly to him. She checked his coat and skin to ensure there were no ticks or skin problems, gave his nails a quick clip, and sprayed a herbal conditioner and deodorizer onto Zak's now gleaming coat and brushed it in. Returning Zak to the yard and removing the leash, Elaine patted him and gave him a large biscuit, specially formulated to protect the animal's teeth.

THE AUSTRALIAN MARKET

Australia's population of 22.7 million in 2011 was small in relation to the country's vast land area of 7.7 million km^2. A federal nation, Australia was divided into six states—New South Wales (NSW), Victoria, Queensland, South Australia, Western Australia, and the island of Tasmania—plus two territories: the large but thinly populated Northern

Territory, and the small Australian Capital Territory (ACT), which contained the federal capital, Canberra, and its suburbs. The average annual earning for employed persons was $66,000.

With much of the interior of the continent uninhabitable and many other areas inhospitable to permanent settlement, most of the Australian population was concentrated in a narrow coastal band running clockwise from Brisbane on the southeast coast through Sydney and Melbourne, to Adelaide, the capital of South Australia. Some 2,700 km (1,600 miles) to the west lay Perth, known as the most isolated city in the world. A breakdown of the population by state and territory is shown in Exhibit 4. The northern half of the country was in the tropics, Brisbane and Perth enjoyed a sub-tropical climate, and the remaining major cities had a temperate climate. Melbourne was known for its sharp fluctuations in temperature.

Exhibit 4: Population of Australia by state and territory, March 2011.

State/Territory	Population (000)
New South Wales	7,267.2
Victoria	5,605.6
Queensland	4,561.7
South Australia	1,654.2
Western Australia	2,331.5
Tasmania	510.2
Australian Capital Territory	363.8
Northern Territory	229.2
Australia Total	**2,2546.3**

Source: Australian Bureau of Statistics 2011.

There were about 3.4 million domestic dogs in the country in 2009, and approximately 36% of the nation's eight million households owned at least one. Western Australia had the lowest proportion of dogs per population, while Tasmania had the highest. In 2011, it was estimated that Australians spent an estimated $3.6 billion on dog-related goods and services, of which 30% went to dog food, 37% to veterinary services, 15% to dog products and equipment, and 17% to other services, including washing and grooming (Exhibit 5).

Exhibit 5: Distribution of consumer expenditures on dog-related goods and services 2010.

Product/Service	Allocation
Dog Food	31%
Vet Charges	44%
Dog Services	21%
Pet Purchases	4%
Total dog-related expenditure	**$3.6 billion**

Source: Australian Companion Animal Council, '*The Pet Care Industry to the Australian Economy: 7th Edition 2010*' Report.

FRANCHISING IN AUSTRALIA

Australia was home to a number of internationally known franchise operators, including Hertz Rent-a-Car, Avis, McDonald's, KFC, Pizza Hut, Subway, Kwik Kopy, and Snap-on Tools. By contrast, most Burger King outlets operated under the name Hungry Jack's, an acquired Australian chain with significant brand equity.

By the beginning of the 21st century, the Australian franchising sector had reached a stage of early maturity. McDonald's, KFC, and Pizza Hut opened their first outlets in Australia in the 1970s. These imported systems were followed by many home-grown business format franchises such as Just Cuts (hairdressing), Snap Printing, Eagle Boys Pizza, and VIP Home Services, all of which grew into large domestic systems and then expanded internationally, principally to New Zealand and Southeast Asia.

In 2010, Australia boasted more than 1,000 business-format franchise systems holding 70,000 outlets. Although the United States had many more systems and outlets, Australia had more franchisors per capita, reflecting the relative ease of entry into franchising in this country.

Most of the growth in franchising occurred in business-format franchising as opposed to product franchising. Business-format franchises provided franchisees with a full business system and the rights to operate under the franchisor's brand name, whereas product franchises merely allowed independent operators to supply a manufacturer's product, such as car dealerships or soft-drink bottlers.

Typically, franchisees were required to pay an upfront franchise fee (averaging $30,000 in service industries and

$40,000 in retailing) for the right to operate under the franchise system within a defined geographic area. This initial fee was included in the total start-up cost of the business (ranging from around $89,000 in the service sector to more than $275,000 in the retail industry). In addition, franchisees paid a royalty on all sales and an ongoing contribution toward advertising and promotional activities designed to build brand awareness and preference. Would-be franchisees who lacked sufficient capital might be able to obtain bank financing against personal assets such as property or an acceptable guarantor.

FRANCHISING TRENDS

The rapid growth of franchising globally had been stimulated in part by demographic trends, including the increase in dual-income families, which had led to greater demand for outsourcing of household services such as lawn mowing, house cleaning, and pet grooming. Some franchise systems offered multiple concepts under a single corporate brand name. For instance, VIP Home Services had separate franchises available in lawn mowing, cleaning, car washing, and rubbish removal. Additional growth came from conversion of existing individual businesses to a franchise format. For instance, Eagle Boys Pizza had often approached local pizza operators and offered them the opportunity to join this franchise. Almost half the franchise systems in Australia were in retail trade (26% non-food and 17% food). Another large and growing industry was the property and business service sector (22%), as shown in Exhibit 6. Most franchisees were former white-collar workers or blue-collar supervisors who craved independence and a lifecycle change.

Over the years, Australia's franchising sector had experienced a myriad of regulatory regimes. Finally in 1998, in response to perceived problems in many franchising systems, the federal government introduced a mandatory Franchising Code of Conduct, administered under what is now the *Competition and Consumer Act 2011* (formerly the *Trade Practices Act*). Among other things, the Code required that potential franchisees be given full disclosure about the franchisor's background and operations prior to signing a franchise agreement. In contrast, the franchising sector in the United States faced an inconsistent set of regulations that varied from one state to another. In the United Kingdom, there were no specific franchising regulations beyond those applying to all corporations operating in designated industries.

Exhibit 6: Distribution of franchise systems in Australia by industry 2010.

Industry	Percentage
Retail trade – non-food	25.6%
Retail food	17%
Administration and support services	15.4%
Other services	11.2%
Rental, hire, and real estate services	7.1%
Education and training	6%
Financial and insurance services	4.6%
Professional, scientific, and technical	3.6%
Arts and recreational services	3.1%
Construction	1.6%
Information media and telecommunications	1.5%
Transport, postal, and warehousing	1.4%
Manufacturing	0.7%
Health care and social assistance	0.7%
Electricity, gas, water, and waste services	0.3%
Wholesale trade	0.2%
Unclassified	0%
Total – All industries	**100%**

Source: Franchising Australia 2010, Asia-Pacific Centre for Franchising Excellence, Griffith University.

Master franchising arrangements had become common in Australian franchise systems. Under master franchising, a local entrepreneur was awarded the rights to sub-franchise the system within a specific geographic area, such as an entire state. Because of Australia's vast geographic size, it was difficult for a franchisor to monitor franchisees who were located far from the head office. The solution was to delegate many of the tasks normally handled by the franchisor itself to master franchisees instead. This made them responsible for recruiting, selecting, training, and monitoring franchisees in their territories as well as overseeing marketing and operations.

Not all franchisees proved successful, and individual outlets periodically failed. The main reasons for failure appeared to be poor choice of location or territory and the franchisee's own shortcomings. In addition to the technical skills required in a given field, success often hinged on the franchisee's sales and communication abilities. Disputes in franchising were not uncommon but could usually be resolved internally without recourse to legal action. The causes of conflict most frequently cited by franchisees related to franchise fees and alleged misrepresentations made by the franchisor. By contract, franchisors cited conflicts based on lack of adherence to the system by franchisees.

FRANCHISING STRATEGY AT AUSSIE POOCH MOBILE

New APM franchisees were recruited through newspaper advertisements and "advertorials" as well as by word-of-mouth. The concept appealed to individuals who sought to become self-employed Interested individuals were invited to meet with a representative of the company to learn more. If they wished to proceed further, they had to complete an application form and submit a refundable deposit of $250 to hold a particular area for a maximum of four weeks, during which the applicant could further investigate the characteristics and prospects of the designated territory. This fee was credited to the purchase cost of the franchise if the applicant decided to proceed or returned if the applicant withdrew the application. A new franchise cost $34,700 excluding the federal goods and services tax (GST) (up from $24,000 in 2002, and $19,500 in 1999). Exhibit 7 identifies how APM costed out the different elements.

Exhibit 7: Aussie Pooch Mobile: Breakdown of franchise purchase cost.

Item	Cost (2011)	
Initial training		$2,500
Initial franchise fee and documents		500
Guaranteed income		4,800
Exclusive territory plus trailer registration		10,900
Fixtures, fittings, stock, insurance, etc.:		
Aussie Pooch Mobile trailer and hydrobath	11,000	
Consumables (shampoo, conditioner, etc.)	2,000	
Retail products	350	
Insurance	300	13,650
Initial advertising		2,000
Bookkeeping services		250
Communications levy		100
Total franchise cost (excluding GST)		**$34,700**

SELECTION REQUIREMENTS FOR PROSPECTIVE FRANCHISEES

APM had set a minimum educational requirement of passing Year 10 of high school (or equivalent) for prospective franchisees. Taylor noted that successful applicants tended to be outdoors people who shared four characteristics:

> They are motivated and outgoing. They love dogs, and they want to work for themselves. Obviously, being great with dogs is one part of the business—our franchisees understand that the dog's even an extended member of the customer's family—but it really important that they can handle the bookwork side of the business as well, because that's basically where your bread and butter is made.

Other desirable characteristics included people skills and patience, plus a good telephone manner. Would-be franchisees are also required a valid driver's license, access to a vehicle that was capable of towing a trailer, and the ability to do this type of driving in an urban setting. Originally, Taylor had expected that most franchisees would be relatively young, with parents willing to buy their children a franchise and set them up with a job, but, in fact, only about half of all franchisees were aged 21–30, 40% were aged 31–40, and 10% were in their forties or fifties. About 60% were female.

Potential franchisees were offered a trial work period with an operator to see if they liked the job and were suited to the business, including skills with animals and people as well as sufficient physical fitness.

HOW THE FRANCHISE WORKED

In return for the franchise fee, successful applicants received the rights to a geographically defined franchise, typically comprising about 12,000 homes. Franchisees also obtained an APM trailer with all necessary products and solutions to service the first 100 dogs, plus red uniform shirts and cap, advertising materials, and stationery. The trailer was built to industrial-grade standards. Its design included many refinements developed by APM in consultation with franchisees to simplify the process of dog washing and enhance the experience for the animal. Operators were required to travel with a mobile phone, which they had to pay for themselves.

In addition to franchised territories, APM had 19 company-owned outlets. These were operated by representatives who leased the territory and equipment and in return paid APM 25% of the gross weekly revenues (including GST). Taylor had no plans to increase the number of representatives. The reps generally were individuals who either could not currently afford the start-up cost or who were evaluated by the company for their suitability as franchisees. Typically, reps either became franchisees within about six months or left the company.

ASSISTING FRANCHISEES, OLD AND NEW

The franchisor provided two weeks' pre-opening training for all new franchisees, and representatives also spent about 10 hours with each one to help them open their new territories. Training topics included operational and business procedures, effective use of the telephone, hydrobathing techniques, dog grooming techniques, and information on dog health and behavior. Franchisees were given a detailed operations manual containing 104 pages of instructions on running the business in accordance with company standards.

To help new franchisees get started, APM placed advertisements in local newspapers for a period of 10 weeks. It also prepared human interest stories for distribution to these newspapers. Other promotional activities at the time of launch included distributing pamphlets in the territory and writing to local vets and pet shops to inform them of the business. APM guaranteed new franchisees a weekly income of $600 for the first eight weeks and paid for a package of insurance policies for six months, after which the franchisee became responsible for the coverage.

Ongoing support by the franchisor included marketing efforts, monthly newsletters, a telephone hotline service for advice, an insurance package, regular (but brief) field visits, and additional training. If a franchisee fell sick or wished to take a vacation, APM would offer advice on how to best deal with this situation, in many cases organizing a trained person to help out. It also organized periodic meetings for franchisees in the major metropolitan areas at which guest presenters spoke on topics relating to franchise operations. Previous guest speakers included veterinarians, natural therapists, pharmacists, and accountants. More recently, APM had offered one-day seminars, providing more team support and generating greater motivation than the traditional meeting style.

To further support individual franchisees, APM had formed a Franchise Advisory Council, composed of a group of experienced franchisees who had volunteered their time to help other franchisees and the system as a whole. Each franchisee was assigned to a team leader, who was a member of the FAC. The Council facilitated communications between franchisees and the support office, meeting with the managers every three months to discuss different issues within the company.

FEES

In return for these services and support from the franchisors, franchisees paid a royalty fee of 10% of their gross weekly income, plus an advertising levy of an additional 2.5%. Income was reported on a weekly basis, and fees had to be paid weekly. In addition to these fees, operating costs for a franchisee included car-related expenses and purchase of consumable products such as shampoo, insurance, telephone, and stationery. Exhibit 8 shows the average weekly costs that a typical franchisee might expect to incur.

Franchisees included several couples, like the Beals, but Taylor believed that having two operators work together was not really efficient, although it could be companionable. Paul Beal, a retired advertising executive, had other interests and did not always accompany Elaine. Some couples split the work, with one operating three days a week and the

Exhibit 8: Average annual operating expenses for an Aussie Pooch Mobile franchisee.

Expense	Cost (2011)
Consumable products	$2,880
Car registration	430
Car insurance	500
Fuel	3,360
Insurances	1,151
Repairs and maintenance	1,104
Phones, stationery, etc.	1,920
Communications levy	624
Franchise royalties	5,583
Advertising levy	1,395
Total	**$18,947**

other three or even four days. All franchisees were required to be substantially involved in the hands-on running of the business; some had more than one territory and employed additional operators to help them.

ADVERTISING AND MARKETING

The company advertised Aussie Pooch Mobile services in the Yellow Pages as well as paying for listings in the White Pages of local phone directories. Aussie Pooch Mobile also had a national website and Facebook page and paid for Google Adwords to promote the national website. It promoted a single telephone number nationwide in Australia, staffed by an answering service 24 hours a day, seven days a week. Customers paid only a local call charge of 25 cents to access this number. They could leave their name and telephone number, which would then be electronically sorted and forwarded via alphanumeric pagers to the appropriate franchisee, who would then return the call to arrange a convenient appointment time.

APM offered its franchisees expert advice on local advertising and promotions, and also made promotional products and advertising templates available to franchisees who were also encouraged to set-up their own Facebook pages. Other corporate communication activities included maintaining the website, www.aussiepm.com.au; distributing public relations releases to the media; and controlling all aspects of corporate identity such as trailer design, business cards, and uniforms.

"I try to hold the reins pretty tightly on advertising matters," said Taylor. APM's franchise agreement required individual franchisees to submit their plans for promotional activity for corporate approval. She shook her head as she remembered an early disaster, involving an unauthorized campaign by a franchisee who had placed an offer of a free dog wash in a widely distributed coupon book. Unfortunately, this promotion had set no expiration date or geographic restriction, with the result that customers were still presenting the coupon more than a year later across several different franchise territories.

With APM's approval, some franchisees had developed additional promotional ideas. For example, Elaine and Paul Beal wrote informative articles and human interest stories about dogs for their local newspaper. When a client's dog died, Elaine sent a sympathy card and presented the owner with a small tree to plant in memory of the pet.

DEVELOPING A TERRITORY

Obtaining new customers and retaining existing ones were important aspects of each franchisee's work. The brightly colored trailer often attracted questions from passersby and presented a useful opportunity to promote the service. Operators could ask satisfied customers to recommend the service to their friends and neighbors. Encouraging owners to increase the frequency of washing their dogs was another way to build business. Knowing that a dog might become lonely when its owner was absent and was liable to develop behavioral problems, Elaine Beal sometimes recommended the acquisition of a "companion pet." As Paul remarked, "Having two dogs is not twice the trouble, it halves the problem!"

However, to maximize profitability, franchisees also had to operate as efficiently as possible, minimizing time spent in non-revenue producing activities such as travel, set-up, and socializing. As business grew, some franchisees employed additional operators to handle the excess workload so that the trailer might be in service for extended hours, seven days a week. Eventually, a busy territory might be split, with a portion sold off to a new franchisee.

APM encouraged this practice. The company had found that franchisees reached a comfort zone at about 80 dogs a week and then their business stopped growing because they could not physically wash any more dogs. Franchisees could set their own price when selling all or part of a territory, and APM helped them to coordinate the sale. When a territory was split, a franchisee usually was motivated to rebuild the remaining half to its maximum potential.

COMPETITION

Although many dog owners had traditionally washed their animals themselves (or had not even bothered), there was a growing trend toward paying a third party to handle this task. Dog washing services fell into two broad groups. One consisted of fixed-site operations to which dog owners brought their animals for bathing. The locations for these businesses included retail sites in suburban shopping areas, kennels, and service providers' own homes or garages. The second type of competition, which had grown in popularity in recent years, consisted of mobile operations that traveled to customers' homes.

With few barriers to entry, there were numerous dog washing services in most major metropolitan areas. The majority of dog washing services in Australia were believed to be standalone operations, but there were other franchisors in addition to Aussie Pooch Mobile. Of these, the most significant appeared to be Jim's Dogwash and HydroDog.

JIM'S DOGWASH

One of Australia's best-known, locally developed franchisors was Melbourne-based Jim's Group, which described itself as one of the world's largest home service franchise organisations. The company had originated with a mowing service started by Jim Penman in Melbourne in 1982 when he abandoned ideas of an academic career after his PhD thesis was rejected. In 1989, Penman began franchising the service, known as Jim's Mowing, as a way to facilitate expansion. The business grew rapidly, using master franchisees in different regions to recruit and manage individual franchisees. Over the following years, an array of other home-related services were launched under the Jim's brand, including Jim's Trees, Jim's Paving, Jim's Cleaning, Jim's Appliance Repair, and Jim's Floors.

Jim's Dogwash made its debut in 1996, employing a bright red, fully enclosed trailer emblazoned with a logo that showed Jim with a dog. It had nine master franchisees and 52 franchises in Australia, and four masters and nine franchisees in New Zealand. Jim's expansion through strategy had been achieved in part by creating smaller territories than APM and pricing them relatively inexpensively in order to stimulate recruitment of new franchisees.

A territory, typically encompassing about 2,000 homes, currently sold from $26,000 up to $42,000, which included GST and the cost of the trailer. Ongoing franchise fees included a flat monthly royalty (rather than royalties being calculated on a percentage of sales) of $408.12 including GST; a monthly advertising levy, also set as a flat monthly fee of $156.97 including GST; and a $6.28 per lead fee including GST. Jim's fee for washing a dog including blow drying ranged from $28–$68, with an average $50 per dog. In recent years, Jim's Dogwash started offering aromatherapy and also sold pet food and accessories.

HYDRODOG

Another franchised dog washing operation was HydroDog, based on the Gold Coast in Queensland. HydroDog commenced operations in 1994 and sold its first franchise in 1996. In 2002, HydroDog had 49 units in Queensland, nine in New South Wales, eight in Western Australia, and one each in Victoria, South Australia, and the Northern Territory. By 2011, HydroDog had five master franchisees and more than 200 franchisees across Australia. However, it had no international operations. The distribution of franchise units across Australia was broken down as follows:

- Queensland: 57 units
- Victoria: 35 units
- Western Australia: 14 units
- South Australia: 22 units
- Northern Territory: 3 units
- Tasmania: 3 units
- The remainder, in New South Wales

A new franchise unit cost $24,950 (including GST) in 2002, of which $10,800 was accounted for by the initial franchise fee for a 10,000-home territory. By 2011, the franchise fee had increased to $41,950 plus GST; this included the trailer, equipment, launch promotions and everything a franchisee needed to start their business. The territory size had also changed, with a minimum of 5,000 homes, although most territories included more than that number and were based on a designated suburb. On average, the company washed about 30,000 dogs per month.

HydroDog's dog grooming services, which included blow drying, ranged in price from $20 to $40. In addition to their dog grooming services, franchisees sold dog food products, including dry biscuits and cooked or raw meats (chicken, beef, or kangaroo), as well as dog toys and other accessories. They did not offer aromatherapy.

DEVELOPING A STRATEGY OF GROWTH FOR THE FUTURE

For the directors of Aussie Pooch Mobile, managing continued expansion presented an ongoing challenge. However, as Chris Taylor pointed out, "You can be the largest but you may not be the best. Our focus is on doing a good job and making our franchisees successful."

To facilitate expansion outside its original base of southeast Queensland, APM appointed a franchise sales manager in Sydney for the New South Wales market and another in Melbourne for both Victoria and South Australia. One question was whether to adopt a formal strategy of appointing master franchisees. Currently, there were master franchisees on the Gold Coast, in the ACT, the regional cities of Toowoomba and Bundaberg in Queensland, and in Newcastle and Port Macquarie in New South Wales.

Also, Taylor had long been attracted by the idea of expanding internationally. In 1996, the company licensed a franchisee in New Zealand to operate a subsidiary named Kiwi Pooch Mobile. However, there was only one unit operating by early 2002 and she wondered how best to increase this number. Another subsidiary had been established as a master franchise in the French province of New Caledonia, a large island northeast of Australia. Launched in late 2000 under the name of La Pooch Mobile, it had one unit. Another master franchise territory was established in Malaysia in late 2001, and there were two units operating by 2002.

In 2001, APM granted exclusive rights for operation in the United Kingdom to a British entrepreneur who operated under the name The Pooch Mobile. Thus far, four units were operating in the English county of Lincolnshire, 200 km (125 miles) north of London. This individual noted that English people traditionally washed their dogs very infrequently, often as little as once every two to three years, but once they had tried The Pooch Mobile, they quickly converted to becoming monthly clients, primarily for the hygiene benefits.

As the company grew, the directors knew it was likely to face increased competition from other providers of dog washing services. But as one successful franchisee remarked: "Competition keeps us on our toes. It's hard being in the lead and maintaining the lead if you haven't got anybody on your tail."

STUDY QUESTIONS

1. How did Christine Taylor succeed in evolving the local dog washing service she developed as a teenager into an international franchise business?
2. Compare and contrast the tasks involved in recruiting new customers and recruiting new franchisees.
3. From a franchisee's perspective, what is the advantage offered by belonging to the APM franchise rather than going it alone?
4. In planning for future expansion, how should Christine Taylor evaluate the market potential of Australia versus that of overseas? What strategies do you recommend and why?

CASE 12

Shouldice Hospital Limited (Abridged)

James Heskett and Roger Hallowell

Two shadowy figures, enrobed and in slippers, walked slowly down the semi-darkened hall of the Shouldice Hospital. They did not notice Alan O'Dell, the hospital's Managing Director, and his guest. Once they were out of earshot, O'Dell remarked good naturedly, "By the way they act, you'd think our patients own this place. And while they're here, in a way they do." Following a visit to the five operating rooms, O'Dell and his visitor once again encountered the same pair of patients still engrossed in discussing their hernia operations, which had been performed the previous morning.

HISTORY

An attractive brochure that was recently printed, although neither dated nor distributed to prospective patients, described Dr. Earle Shouldice, the founder of the hospital:

> Dr. Shouldice's interest in early ambulation stemmed, in part, from an operation he performed in 1932 to remove the appendix from a seven-year-old girl and the girl's subsequent refusal to stay quietly in bed. In spite of her activity, no harm was done, and the experience recalled to the doctor the postoperative actions of animals upon which he had performed surgery. They had all moved about freely with no ill effects.

By 1940, Shouldice had given extensive thought to several factors that contributed to early ambulation following surgery. Among them were the use of a local anesthetic, the nature of the surgical procedure itself, the design of a facility to encourage movement without unnecessarily causing discomfort, and the post-operative regimen. With these things in mind, he began to develop a surgical technique for repairing hernias[1] that was superior to others; word of his early success generated demand.

Dr. Shouldice's medical license permitted him to operate anywhere, even on a kitchen table. However, as more and more patients requested operations, Dr. Shouldice created new facilities by buying a rambling 130-acre estate with a 17,000-square-foot main house in the Toronto suburb of Thornhill. After some years of planning, a large wing was added to provide a total capacity of 89 beds.

Dr. Shouldice died in 1965. At that time, Shouldice Hospital Limited was formed to operate both the hospital and clinical facilities under the surgical direction of Dr. Nicholas Obney. In 1999, Dr. Casim Degani, an internationally recognized authority, became surgeon-in-chief. By 2004, 7,600 operations were performed per year.

THE SHOULDICE METHOD

Only external (vs. internal) abdominal hernias were repaired at Shouldice Hospital. Thus most first-time repairs, "primaries," were straightforward operations requiring about 45 minutes. The remaining procedures involved patients suffering recurrences of hernias previously repaired

---

Professor James Heskett prepared the original version of this case, "Shouldice Hospital Limited," HBS No. 683-068. This version was prepared jointly by Professor James Heskett and Roger Hallowell (MBA 1989, DBA 1997). HBS cases are developed solely as the basis for class discussion. Cases are not intended to serve as endorsements, sources of primary data, or illustrations of effective or ineffective management.

1 Most hernias, known as external abdominal hernias, are protrusions of some part of the abdominal contents through a hole or slit in the muscular layers of the abdominal wall, which is supposed to contain them. Well over 90% of these hernias occur in the groin area. Of these, by far the most common are inguinal hernias, many of which are caused by a slight weakness in the muscle layers brought about by the passage of the testicles in male babies through the groin area shortly before birth. Aging also contributes to the development of inguinal hernias. Because of the cause of the affliction, 85% of all hernias occur in males.

elsewhere.[2] Many of the recurrences and very difficult hernia repairs required 90 minutes or more.

In the Shouldice method, the muscles of the abdominal wall were arranged in three distinct layers, and the opening was repaired, each layer in turn, by overlapping its margins as the edges of a coat might be overlapped when buttoned. The end result reinforced the muscular wall of the abdomen with six rows of sutures (stitches) under the skin cover, which was then closed with clamps that were later removed. (Other methods might not separate muscle layers, often involved fewer rows of sutures, and sometimes involved the insertion of screens or meshes under the skin.)

A typical first-time repair could be completed with the use of pre-operative sedation (sleeping pill) and analgesic (pain killer) plus a local anesthetic, an injection of Novocain in the region of the incision. This allowed immediate postoperative patient ambulation and facilitated rapid recovery.

The Patients' Experience

Most potential Shouldice patients learned about the hospital from previous Shouldice patients. Although thousands of doctors had referred patients, doctors were less likely to recommend Shouldice because of the generally regarded simplicity of the surgery, often considered a "bread and butter" operation. Typically, many patients had their problem diagnosed by a personal physician, and then contacted Shouldice directly. Many more made this diagnosis themselves.

The process experienced by Shouldice patients depended on whether or not they lived close enough to the hospital to visit the facility to obtain a diagnosis. Approximately 10 percent of Shouldice patients came from outside the province of Ontario, most of them from the United States. Another 60 percent of patients lived beyond the Toronto area. These out-of-town patients often were diagnosed by mail using the Medical Information Questionnaire shown in Exhibit 1 on pages 579 and 580. Based on information in the questionnaire, a Shouldice surgeon would determine the type of hernia the respondent had and whether there were signs that some risk might be associated with surgery (for example, an overweight or heart condition, or a patient who had suffered a heart attack or a stroke in the past six months to a year, or whether a general or local anesthetic was required). At this point, a patient was given an operating date and sent a brochure describing the hospital and the Shouldice method. If necessary, a sheet outlining a weight-loss program prior to surgery was also sent. A small proportion was refused treatment, either because they were overweight, represented an undue medical risk, or because it was determined that they did not have a hernia.

Arriving at the clinic between 1:00 p.m. and 3:00 p.m. the day before the operation, a patient joined other patients in the waiting room. He or she was soon examined in one of the six examination rooms staffed by surgeons who had completed their operating schedules for the day. This examination required no more than 20 minutes, unless the patient needed reassurance. (Patients typically exhibited a moderate level of anxiety until their operation was completed.) At this point, it occasionally was discovered that a patient had not corrected his or her weight problem; others might be found not to have a hernia at all. In either case, the patient was sent home.

After checking administrative details, about an hour after arriving at the hospital, the patient was directed to the room number shown on his or her wrist band. Throughout the process, patients were asked to keep their luggage (usually light) with them.

All patient rooms at the hospital were semiprivate, containing two beds. Patients with similar jobs, backgrounds, or interests were assigned to the same room to the extent possible. Upon reaching their rooms, patients busied themselves unpacking, getting acquainted with roommates, shaving themselves in the area of the operation, and changing into pajamas.

At 4:30 p.m., a nurse's orientation provided the group of incoming patients with information about what to expect, including the need for exercise after the operation and the daily routine. According to Alan O'Dell, "Half are so nervous they don't remember much." Dinner was then served, followed by further recreation, and tea and cookies at 9:00 p.m. Nurses emphasized the importance of attendance at that time because it provided an opportunity for pre-operative patients to talk with those whose operations had been completed earlier that same day.

Patients to be operated on early were awakened at 5:30 a.m. to be given pre-op sedation. An attempt was made

2 Based on tracking of patients over more than 30 years, the gross recurrence rate for all operations performed at Shouldice was 0.8%. Recurrence rates reported in the literature for these types of hernia varied greatly. However, one text stated, "In the United States, the gross rate of recurrence for groin hernias approaches 10%."

to schedule operations for roommates at approximately the same time. Patients were taken to the preoperation room where the circulating nurse administered Demerol, an analgesic, 45 minutes before surgery. A few minutes prior to the first operation at 7:30 a.m., the surgeon assigned to each patient administered Novocain, a local anesthetic, in the operating room. This was in contrast to the typical hospital procedure in which patients were sedated in their rooms prior to being taken to the operating rooms.

Upon completion of their operation, during which a few patients were "chatty" and fully aware of what was going on, patients were invited to get off the operating table and walk to the postoperation room with the help of their surgeons. According to the Director of Nursing:

> "Ninety-nine percent accept the surgeon's invitation. While we use wheelchairs to return them to their rooms, the walk from the operating table is for psychological as well as physiological [blood pressure, respiratory] reasons. Patients prove to themselves that they can do it, and they start their all-important exercise immediately."

Throughout the day after their operation, patients were encouraged by nurses and housekeepers alike to exercise. By 9:00 p.m. on the day of their operations, all patients were ready and able to walk down to the dining room for tea and cookies, even if it meant climbing stairs, to help indoctrinate the new "class" admitted that day. On the fourth morning, patients were ready for discharge.

During their stay, patients were encouraged to take advantage of the opportunity to explore the premises and make new friends. Some members of the staff felt that the patients and their attitudes were the most important element of the Shouldice program. According to Dr. Byrnes Shouldice, son of the founder, a surgeon on the staff, and a 50 percent owner of the hospital:

> Patients sometimes ask to stay an extra day. Why? Well, think about it. They are basically well to begin with. But they arrive with a problem and a certain amount of nervousness, tension, and anxiety about their surgery. Their first morning here, they're operated on and experience a sense of relief from something that's been bothering them for a long time. They are immediately able to get around, and they've got a three-day holiday ahead of them with a perfectly good reason to be away from work with no sense of guilt. They share experiences with other patients, make friends easily, and have the run of the hospital. In summer, the most common after-effect of the surgery is sunburn.

The Nurses' Experience

Thirty-four full-time-equivalent nurses staffed Shouldice each 24-hour period. However, during non-operating hours, only six full-time-equivalent nurses were on the premises at any given time. While the Canadian acute-care hospital average ratio of nurses to patients was 1:4, at Shouldice, the ratio was 1:15. Shouldice nurses spent an unusually large proportion of their time in counseling activities. As one supervisor commented, "We don't use bedpans." According to a manager, "Shouldice has a waiting list of nurses wanting to be hired, while other hospitals in Toronto are short-staffed and perpetually recruiting."

The Doctors' Experience

The hospital employed 10 full-time surgeons and eight part-time assistant surgeons. Two anesthetists were also on site. The anesthetists floated among cases except when general anesthesia was in use. Each operating team required a surgeon, an assistant surgeon, a scrub nurse, and a circulating nurse. The operating load varied from 30 to 36 operations per day. As a result, each surgeon typically performed three or four operations each day.

A typical surgeon's day started with a scrubbing shortly before the first scheduled operation at 7:30 a.m. If the first operation was routine, it usually was completed by 8:15 a.m. At its conclusion, the surgical team helped the patient walk from the room and summoned the next patient. After scrubbing, the surgeon could be ready to operate again at 8:30 a.m. Surgeons were advised to take a coffee break after their second or third operation. Even so, a surgeon could complete three routine operations and a fourth involving a recurrence and still be finished in time for a 12:30 p.m. lunch in the staff dining room.

Upon finishing lunch, surgeons not scheduled to operate in the afternoon examined incoming patients. A surgeon's day ended by 4:00 p.m. In addition, a surgeon could expect to be on call one weekday night in 10 and one weekend in 10. Alan O'Dell commented that the position appealed to doctors who "want to watch their children grow up. A doctor on call is rarely called to the hospital and has regular hours." According to Dr. Obney:

Exhibit 1: Medical information questionnaire.

FAMILY NAME (Last Name) | FIRST NAME | MIDDLE NAME

STREET & NUMBER (or Rural Route or P.O. Box) | Town/City | Province/State

County | Township | Zip or Postal Code | Birthdate: Month Day Year

Telephone Home .... Work .... if none, give neighbour's number .... | Married or Single | Religion

NEXT OF KIN: Name | Address | Telephone #

INSURANCE INFORMATION: Please give name of Insurance Company and Numbers. | Date form completed

HOSPITAL INSURANCE: (Please bring hospital certificates)
O.H.I.P. Number ______ BLUE CROSS Number ______

OTHER HOSPITAL INSURANCE
Company Name ______
Policy Number ______

SURGICAL INSURANCE: (Please bring insurance certificates)
O.H.I.P. Number ______ BLUE SHIELD Number ______

OTHER SURGICAL INSURANCE
Company Name ______
Policy Number ______

WORKMEN'S COMPENSATION BOARD
Claim No. | Approved Yes No | Social Insurance (Security) Number

Occupation | Name of Business | Are you the owner? Yes No | If Retired – Former Occupation

How did you hear about Shouldice Hospital? (If referred by a doctor, give name & address)

Are you a former patient of Shouldice Hospital? Yes No Do you smoke? Yes No

Have you ever written to Shouldice Hospital in the past? Yes No

What is your preferred admission date? (Please give as much advance notice as possible)
No admissions Friday, Saturday or Sunday.

FOR OFFICE USE ONLY

Date Received | Type of Hernia | Weight Loss lbs.

Consent to Operate ☐
Heart Report ☐
Special Instructions | Approved

Referring Doctor Notified | Operation Date

SHOULDICE HOSPITAL

7750 Bayview Avenue
Box 379, Thornhill, Ontario L3T 4A3 Canada
Phone (418) 889-1125

(Thornhill - One Mile North Metro Toronto)

MEDICAL

INFORMATION

Patients who live at a distance often prefer their examination, admission and operation to be arranged all on a single visit — to save making two lengthy journeys. The whole purpose of this questionnaire is to make such arrangements possible, although, of course, it cannot replace the examination in any way. Its completion and return will not put you under any obligation.

Please be sure to fill in both sides.

This information will be treated as confidential.

(continued on next page)

Exhibit 1: (Continued)

THIS CHART IS FOR EXPLANATION ONLY

Ordinary hernias are mostly either at the navel ("belly-button") - or just above it

or down in the groin area on either side

An "Incisional hernia" is one that bulges through the scar of any other surgical operation that has failed to hold - wherever it may be.

Right Groin Left Groin

THIS IS YOUR CHART – PLEASE MARK IT!

(MARK THE POSITION OF EACH HERNIA YOU WANT REPAIRED WITH AN "X")

Right Groin Left Groin

APPROXIMATE SIZE...
Walnut (or less) ☐ ☐
Hen's Egg or Lemon ☐ ☐
Grapefruit (or more) ☐ ☐

ESSENTIAL EXTRA INFORMATION

Use only the sections that apply to your hernias and put a ✓ in each box that seems appropriate.

NAVEL AREA (AND JUST ABOVE NAVEL) ONLY

	Yes	No
Is this navel (bellybutton) hernia your FIRST one?	☐	☐
If it's NOT your first, how many repair attempts so far?	☐	

GROIN HERNIAS ONLY

	RIGHT GROIN Yes	RIGHT GROIN No	LEFT GROIN Yes	LEFT GROIN No
Is this your FIRST GROIN HERNIA ON THIS SIDE?	☐	☐	☐	☐

How many hernia operations in this groin already? Right ☐ Left ☐

DATE OF LAST OPERATION ☐

INCISIONAL HERNIAS ONLY (the ones bulging through previous operation scars)
Was the original operation for your Appendix? ☐, or Gallbladder? ☐
or Stomach? ☐, or Prostate? ☐, or Hysterectomy? ☐, or Other?..............................
....

How many attempts to repair the hernias have been made so far? ☐

PLEASE BE ACCURATE!: Misleading figures, when checked on a admission day, could mean postponement of your operation till your weight is suitable.

HEIGHT.............ft..............ins. WEIGHT...........lbs. Nude or just pyjamas Recent gain?............lbs. Recent loss?.............lbs.

Waist (muscles relaxed)........................ins. Chest (not expanded).......................ins.

GENERAL HEALTH

Age.............years is your health now GOOD ☐, FAIR ☐, or POOR ☐

Please mention briefly any severe past illness – such as a "heart attack" or a "stroke", for example, from which you have now recovered (and its approximate date).....................
....

We need to know about other present conditions, even though your admission is NOT likely to be refused because of them.

Please tick ☑ any condition for which you are having regular treatment:

- Blood Pressure ☐
- Excess body fluids ☐
- Chest pain ("angina") ☐
- Irregular Heartbeat ☐
- Diabetes ☐
- Asthma & Bronchitis ☐
- Ulcers ☐
- Anticoagulants (to delay blood-clotting or to "thin the blood") ☐

Other...

Name of any prescribed pills, tablets or capsules you take regularly -

Did you remember to MARK AN "X" on your body chart to show us where each of your hernias is located?

> When I interview prospective surgeons, I look for experience and a good education. I try to gain some insight into their domestic situation and personal interests and habits. I also try to find out why a surgeon wants to switch positions. And I try to determine if he's willing to perform the repair exactly as he's told. This is no place for prima donnas.

Dr. Shouldice added:

> Traditionally, a hernia is often the first operation that a junior resident in surgery performs. Hernia repair is regarded as a relatively simple operation compared to other major operations. This is quite wrong, as is borne out by the resulting high recurrence rate. It is a tricky anatomical area and occasionally very complicated, especially to the novice or those doing very few hernia repairs each year. But, at Shouldice Hospital, a surgeon learns the Shouldice technique over a period of several months. He learns when he can go fast and when he must slow down. He develops a pace and a touch. If he encounters something unusual, he is encouraged to consult immediately with other surgeons. We teach each other and try to encourage a group effort. And he learns not to take risks to achieve absolute perfection. Excellence is the enemy of good.

Chief Surgeon Degani assigned surgeons to an operating room on a daily basis by noon of the preceding day. This allowed surgeons to examine the specific patients whom they were to operate on. Surgeons and assistants were rotated every few days. Cases were assigned to give doctors a non-routine operation (often involving a recurrence) several times a week. More complex procedures were assigned to more senior and experienced members of the staff. Dr. Obney commented:

> If something goes wrong, we want to make sure that we have an experienced surgeon in charge. Experience is most important. The typical general surgeon may perform 25 to 50 hernia operations per year. Ours perform 750 or more.

The 10 full-time surgeons were paid a straight salary, typically $144,000.[3] In addition, bonuses to doctors were distributed monthly. These depended on profit, individual productivity, and performance. The total bonus pool paid to the surgeons in a recent year was approximately $400,000. Total surgeon compensation (including benefits) was approximately 15 percent more than the average income for a surgeon in Ontario.

Training in the Shouldice technique was important because the procedure could not be varied. It was accomplished through direct supervision by one or more of the senior surgeons. The rotation of teams and frequent consultations allowed for an ongoing opportunity to appraise performance and take corrective action. Wherever possible, former Shouldice patients suffering recurrences were assigned to the doctor who performed the first operation "to allow the doctor to learn from his mistake." Dr. Obney commented on being a Shouldice surgeon:

> A doctor must decide after several years whether he wants to do this for the rest of his life because, just as in other specialties—for example, radiology—he loses touch with other medical disciplines. If he stays for five years, he doesn't leave. Even among younger doctors, few elect to leave.

THE FACILITY

The Shouldice Hospital contained two facilities in one building—the hospital and the clinic. On its first-level, the hospital contained the kitchen and dining rooms. The second level contained a large, open lounge area, the admission offices, patient rooms, and a spacious glass-covered Florida room. The third level had additional patient rooms and recreational areas. Patients could be seen visiting each others' rooms, walking up and down hallways, lounging in the sunroom, and making use of light recreational facilities ranging from a pool table to an exercycle. Alan O'Dell pointed out some of the features of the hospital:

> The rooms contain no telephone or television sets. If a patient needs to make a call or wants to watch television, he or she has to take a walk. The steps are designed specially with a small rise to allow patients recently operated on to negotiate the stairs without undue discomfort. Every square foot of the hospital is carpeted to reduce the hospital feeling and the possibility of a fall. Carpeting also gives the place a smell other than that of disinfectant.

3 All monetary references in the case are to Canadian dollar. US$1 equaled C$1.33 on February 23, 2004.

This facility was designed by an architect with input from Dr. Byrnes Shouldice and Mrs. W. H. Urquhart (the daughter of the founder). The facility was discussed for years, and many changes in the plans were made before the first concrete was poured.

> A number of unique policies were also instituted. For example, parents accompanying children here for an operation stay free. You may wonder why we can do it, but we learned that we save more in nursing costs than we spend for the parent's room and board.

Patients and staff were served food prepared in the same kitchen, and staff members picked up food from a cafeteria line placed in the very center of the kitchen. This provided an opportunity for everyone to chat with the kitchen staff several times a day, and the hospital staff to eat together. According to O'Dell, "We use all fresh ingredients and prepare the food from scratch in the kitchen."

The Director of Housekeeping pointed out:

> I have only three on my housekeeping staff for the entire facility. One of the reasons for so few housekeepers is that we don't need to change linens during a patient's four-day stay. Also, the medical staff doesn't want the patients in bed all day. They want the nurses to encourage the patients to be up socializing, comparing notes [for confidence], encouraging each other, and walking around, getting exercise. Of course, we're in the rooms straightening up throughout the day. This gives the housekeepers a chance to josh with the patients and to encourage them to exercise.

The clinic housed five operating rooms, a laboratory, and the patient-recovery room. In total, the estimated cost to furnish an operating room was $30,000. This was considerably less than for other hospitals, which require a bank of equipment with which to administer anesthetics for each room. At Shouldice, two mobile units were used by the anesthetists when needed. In addition, the complex had one "crash cart" per floor for use if a patient should suffer a heart attack or stroke.

ADMINISTRATION

Alan O'Dell described his job:

> We try to meet people's needs and make this as good a place to work as possible. There is a strong concern for employees here. Nobody is fired. [This was later reinforced by Dr. Shouldice, who described a situation involving two employees who confessed to theft in the hospital. They agreed to seek psychiatric help and were allowed to remain on the job.] As a result, turnover is low.
>
> Our administrative and support staff are non-union, but we try to maintain a pay scale higher than the union scale for comparable jobs in the area. We have a profit-sharing plan that is separate from the doctors'. Last year, the administrative and support staff divided up $60,000.
>
> If work needs to be done, people pitch in to help each other. A unique aspect of our administration is that I insist that each secretary is trained to do another's work and in an emergency is able to switch to another function immediately. We don't have an organization chart. A chart tends to make people think they're boxed in jobs.[4] I try to stay one night a week, having dinner and listening to the patients, to find out how things are really going around here.

Operating Costs

The 2004 budgets for the hospital and clinic were close to $8.5 million[5] and $3.5 million, respectively.[6]

THE MARKET

Hernia operations were among the most commonly performed operations on males. In 2000, an estimated 1,000,000 such operations were performed in the United States alone. According to Dr. Shouldice:

> When our backlog of scheduled operations gets too large, we wonder how many people decide instead to have their local doctor perform the operation. Every time we've expanded our capacity, the backlog has declined briefly, only to climb once again. Right now, at 2,400, it is larger than it has ever been and is growing by 100 every six months.

4 The chart in Exhibit 2 was prepared by the case writer, based on conversations with hospital personnel.

5 This figure included a provincially mandated return on investment.

6 The latter figure included the bonus pool for doctors.

Exhibit 2: The organization chart.

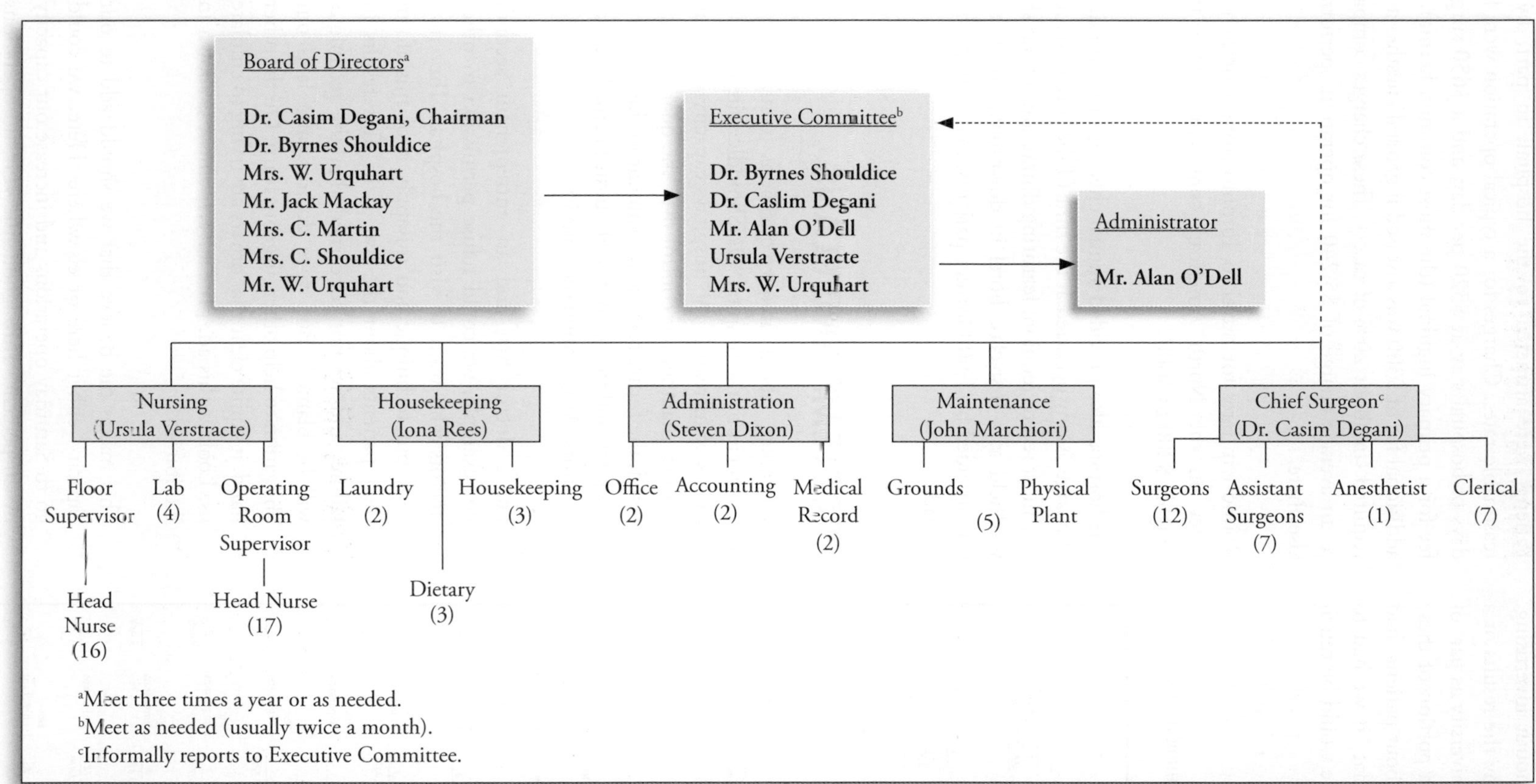

The hospital relied entirely on word-of-mouth advertising, the importance of which was suggested by the results of a poll carried out by students of DePaul University as part of a project (Exhibit 3 on page 586 shows a portion of these results). Although little systematic data about patients had been collected, Alan O'Dell remarked that "if we had to rely on wealthy patients only, our practice would be much smaller."

Exhibit 3: Shouldice Hospital annual patient reunion data.

Direction: For each question, please place a check mark as it applies to you.

1. Sex
   - Male 41 95.34%
   - Female 2 4.65%

2. Age
   - 20 or less ___
   - 21–40 4 9.30%
   - 41–60 17 39.54%
   - 61 or more 22 51.16%

3. Nationality

   Directions: Please place a check mark in nation you represent and please write in your province, state or country where it applies.

   - Canada 38 Province 88.37%
   - America 5 State 11.63%
   - Europe ___ Country ___
   - Other ___ ___

4. Education level
   - Elementary 5 11.63%
   - High School 18 41.86%
   - College 1980 30.23%
   - Graduate work 7 16.28%

5. Occupation ___

6. Have you been overnight in a hospital other than Shouldice before your operation? Yes 31 No 12

7. What brought Shouldice Hospital to your attention?

   Friend 23 (53.49%) Doctor 9 (20.93%) Relative 7 (16.28%) Article ___ Other 4 (Please explain) 9.30%

8. Did you have a single 25 (58.14%) or double 18 (41.86%) hernia operation?

9. Is this your first Annual Reunion? Yes 20 (46.51%) No 23 (53.49%)

   If no, how many reunions have you attended? ___

   - 2-5 reunions - 11 47.63%
   - 6-10 reunions - 5 21.73%
   - 11-20 reunions - 4 12.39%
   - 21-36 reunions - 3 13.05%

10. Do you feel that Shouldice Hospital cared for you as a person?

    Most definitely 37 (86.05%) Definitely 6 (13.95%) Very little ___ Not at all ___

11. What impressed you the most about your stay at Shouldice? Please check one answer for each of the following.

		Very Important	Important	Somewhat Important	Not Important
A.	Fees charged for operation and hospital stay	10	3	6	24
B.	Operation Procedure	33 (76.74%)	9 (20.93%)	1 (2.33%)	___
C.	Physician's Care	31 (72.10%)	12 (27.90%)	-	-
D.	Nursing Care	28 (65.12%)	14 (32.56%)	1 (2.32%)	___
E.	Food Service	23 (53.48%)	11 (25.59%)	7 (16.28%)	2 (4.65%)
F.	Shortness of Hospital Stay	17 (39.53%)	15 (34.88%)	8 (18.60%)	3 (6.98%)
G.	Exercise; Recreational Activities	17 (39.53%)	14 (32.56%)	12 (27.91%)	-
H.	Friendships with Patients	25 (58.15%)	10 (23.25%)	5 (11.63%)	3 (6.98%)
I.	"Shouldice Hospital hardly seemed like a hospital at all."	25 (58.14%)	13 (30.23%)	5 (11.63%)	___

12. In a few words, give the MAIN REASON why you returned for this annual reunion.

Patients were attracted to the hospital, in part, by its reasonable rates. Charges for a typical operation were four days of hospital stay at $320 per day, and a $650 surgical fee for a primary inguinal (the most common hernia). An additional fee of $300 was assessed if general anesthesia was required (in about 20% of cases). These charges compared to an average charge of $5,240 for operations performed elsewhere.

Round-trip fares for travel to Toronto from various major cities on the North American continent ranged from roughly $200 to $600.

The hospital also provided annual checkups to alumni, free of charge. Many occurred at the time of the patient reunion. The most recent reunion, featuring dinner and a floor show, was held at a first-class hotel in downtown Toronto and was attended by 1,000 former patients, many from outside Canada.

PROBLEMS AND PLANS

When asked about major questions confronting the management of the hospital, Dr. Shouldice cited a desire to seek ways of increasing the hospital's capacity while, at the same time, maintaining control over the quality of service delivered, the future role of government in the operation of the hospital, and the use of the Shouldice name by potential competitors. As Dr. Shouldice put it:

> I'm a doctor first and an entrepreneur second. For example, we could refuse permission to other doctors who want to visit the hospital. They may copy our technique and misapply it or misinform their patients about the use of it. This results in failure, and we are concerned that the technique will be blamed. But we're doctors, and it is our obligation to help other surgeons learn. On the other hand, it's quite clear that others are trying to emulate us. Look at this ad. [The advertisement is shown in Exhibit 4.]
>
> This makes me believe that we should add to our capacity, either here or elsewhere. Here, we could go to Saturday operations and increase our capacity by 20 percent. Throughout the year, no operations are scheduled for Saturdays or Sundays, although patients whose operations are scheduled late in the week remain in the hospital over the weekend. Or,

Exhibit 4: Advertisement by a Shouldice competitor.

with an investment of perhaps $4 million in new space, we could expand our number of beds by 50 percent and schedule the operating rooms more heavily.

However, given government regulations, do we want to invest more in Toronto? Or should we establish another hospital with similar design, perhaps in the United States? There is also the possibility that we could diversify into other specialties offering similar opportunities such as eye surgery, varicose veins, or diagnostic services (e.g., colonoscopies).

For now, we're also beginning the process of grooming someone to succeed Dr. Degani when he retires. He's in his early 60s, but, at some point, we'll have to address this issue. And for good reason, he's resisted changing certain successful procedures that I think we could improve on. We had quite a time changing the schedule for the administration of Demerol to patients to increase their comfort level during the operation. Dr. Degani has opposed a Saturday operating program on the premise that he won't be here and won't be able to maintain proper control.

Alan O'Dell added his own concerns:

How should we be marketing our services? Right now, we don't advertise directly to patients. We're

Exhibit 5: The Shouldice Hospital grounds a haven for rest and recuperation.

even afraid to send out this new brochure we've put together, unless a potential patient specifically requests it, for fear it will generate too much demand. Our records show that just under 1 percent of our patients are medical doctors, a significantly high percentage. How should we capitalize on that? I'm also concerned about this talk of Saturday operations. We are already getting good utilization of this facility. And if we expand further, it will be very difficult to maintain the same kind of working relationships and attitudes. Already there are rumors floating around among the staff about it. And the staff is not pleased.

The matter of Saturday operations had been a topic of conversation among the doctors as well. Four of the older doctors were opposed to it. While most of the younger doctors were indifferent or supportive, at least two who had been at the hospital for some time were particularly concerned about the possibility that the issue would drive a wedge between the two groups. As one put it, "I'd hate to see the practice split over the issue."

STUDY QUESTIONS

1. What is the market for this service? How successful is Shouldice Hospital?
2. Define the service model for Shouldice. How does each of its elements contribute to the hospital's success?
3. As Dr. Shouldice, what actions, if any, would you like to take to expand the hospital's capacity and how would you implement such changes?

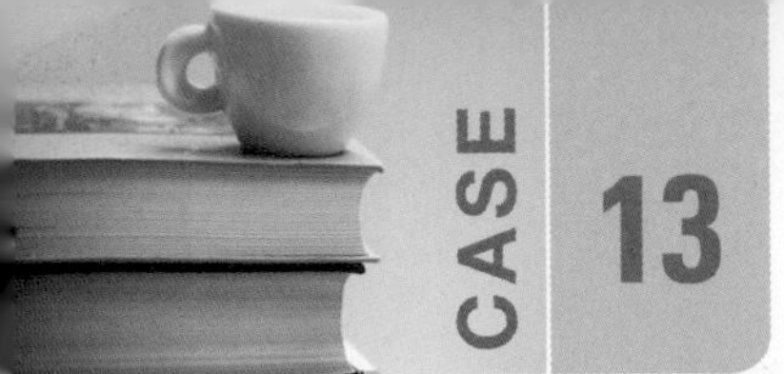

Red Lobster

Christopher H. Lovelock

A peer review panel of managers and service workers from a restaurant chain must decide whether or not a waitress has been unfairly fired from her job.

"It felt like a knife was going through me!" declared Mary Campbell, 53, after she was fired from her waitressing job at a restaurant in the Red Lobster chain. Instead of suing for what she considered unfair dismissal after 19 years of service, Campbell called for a peer review, seeking to recover her job and three weeks of lost wages.

Three weeks after the firing, a panel of employees from different Red Lobster restaurants was reviewing the evidence and trying to determine whether the server had, in fact, been unjustly fired for allegedly stealing a guest comment card completed by a couple of customers whom she had served.

PEER REVIEW AT DARDEN INDUSTRIES

Red Lobster is owned by Darden Industries, which also owns other restaurant chains like Olive Garden, Longhorn Steakhouse, The Capital Grill, Bahama Breeze, and Seasons 52. The company has about 1,900 restaurants serving 400 million meals a year. Red Lobster, which has more than 180,000 employees, adopted a policy of encouraging peer review of disputed employee firings and disciplinary actions several years earlier. The company's key objectives are to limit worker lawsuits and ease workplace tensions.

Advocates of the peer review approach, which has been adopted at several other companies, believe it is a very effective way of channeling constructively the pain and anger that employees feel after being fired or disciplined by their managers. By reducing the incidence of lawsuits, a company could also save on legal expenses.

A Darden spokesperson stated that the peer review program has been "tremendously successful" in keeping valuable employees from unfair dismissal. Each year, about 100 disputes end up in peer review, with only 10 subsequently resulting in lawsuits. Red Lobster managers and many employees also credite peer review with reducing racial tensions. Ms. Campbell, who said she had received dozens of calls of support, chooses peer review over a lawsuit not only because it is much cheaper, but "I also liked the idea of being judged by people who know how things work in a little restaurant."

THE EVIDENCE

The review panel included a general manager, an assistant manager, a server, a hostess, and a bartender, who had all volunteered to review the circumstances of Mary Campbell's firing. Each panelist had received peer review training and was receiving regular wages plus travel expenses. The instruction to panelists was simply to do what they felt was fair.

Campbell was fired by Jean Larimer, the general manager of the Red Lobster in Marston, where Campbell had worked as a restaurant server. The reason given for the firing was that Campbell had asked the restaurant's hostess, Eve Taunton, for the key to the guest comment box and stole a card from it. The card was completed by a couple of guests whom Campbell had served and who seemed dissatisfied with their experience at the restaurant. Subsequently, the guests learned that their comment card, which complained that their prime rib of beef was too rare and their waitress was "uncooperative," had been removed from the box.

Jean Larimer's Testimony

Larimer, who supervised 100 full- and part-time employees, testified that she dismissed Campbell after one of the two customers had complained angrily to her and her supervisor. "She [the guest] felt violated," declared the manager, "because her card was taken from the box and her complaint about the food was ignored." Larimer drew the

This case is based on information in a story by Margaret A. Jacobs in the *Wall Street Journal.* Real names have been changed.

panel's attention to the company rule book, pointing out that Campbell had violated the policy that forbade removal of company property.

Mary Campbell's Testimony

Campbell testified that the female customer had requested that her prime rib be cooked "well done" and then subsequently complained that it was fatty and undercooked. The waitress told the panel that she had politely suggested that "prime rib always has fat on it," but arranged to have the meat cooked some more. However, the woman still seemed unhappy. She poured some steak sauce over the meat, but then pushed away her plate without eating all the food. When the customer remained displeased, Campbell offered her a free dessert. But the guests decided to leave, paid the bill, filled out the guest comment card, and dropped it in the guest comment box.

Exhibit 1: The restaurant scene becomes the testing ground for the validity of peer review.

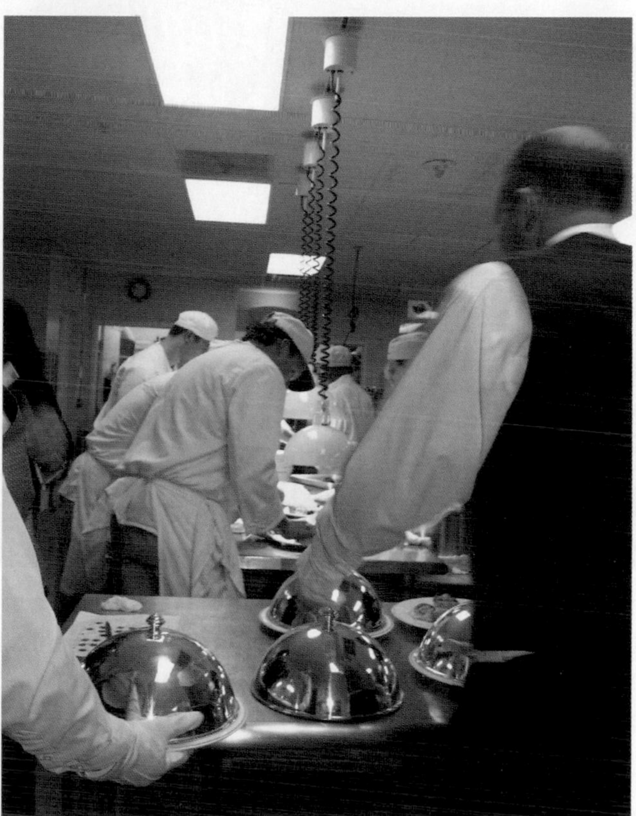

Admitting she was consumed by curiosity, Campbell asked Eve Taunton, the restaurant's hostess, for the key to the box. After removing and reading the card, she pocketed it. Her intent, she declared, was to show the card to Ms. Larimer, who had been concerned earlier that the prime rib served at the restaurant was overcooked, not undercooked. However, she forgot about the card and later, accidentally, threw it out.

Eve Taunton's testimony

At the time of the firing, Taunton, a 17-year-old student, was working at Red Lobster for the summer. "I didn't think it was a big deal to give her [Campbell] the key," she said. "A lot of people would come up to me to get it."

THE PANEL DELIBERATES

Having heard the testimony, the members of the review panel had to decide whether Ms. Larimer had been justified in firing Ms. Campbell. The panelists' initial reactions to the situation were split by rank, with the hourly workers supporting Campbell and the managers supporting Larimer. But then the debate began in earnest in an effort to reach consensus.

STUDY QUESTIONS

1. What are the marketing implications of this situation?
2. Evaluate the concept of peer review. What are its strengths and weaknesses? What type of environment is required to make it work well?
3. Review the evidence. Do you believe the testimony presented?
4. What decision would you make and why?

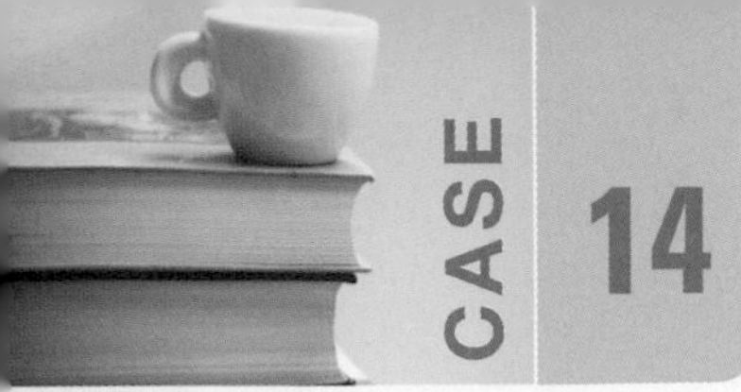

CASE 14

Singapore Airlines: Managing Human Resources for Cost-effective Service Excellence

Jochen Wirtz and Loizos Heracleous

Singapore Airlines (SIA) has managed and organized its human resources (HR) to achieve sustainable competitive advantage and outperform other airlines in its peer group for decades. The case describes the role of HR in SIA's pursuit of the apparent conflicting objectives of service excellence and cost-effectiveness, at the same time, through its approach to recruitment, selection, training, motivation, and retention of its employees.

"At the end of the day, it's the software, people like us, who make the real difference."

Patrick Seow, Senior Rank Trainer,
Singapore Airlines Training School, and Senior Flight Steward

This case is based on the following earlier publications: Loizos Heracleous and Jochen Wirtz (2010), "Singapore Airlines' Balancing Act—Asia's Premier Carrier Successfully Executes a Dual Strategy: It Offers World-Class Service and Is a Cost Leader", *Harvard Business Review*, 88, no. 7/8, July–August, 145–149. Loizos Heracleous, Jochen Wirtz, and Nitin Pangarkar, *Flying High in a Competitive Industry: Cost-Effective Service Excellence at Singapore Airlines*. McGraw-Hill Education (Asia) 2009. Jochen Wirtz, Loizos Heracleous, and Nitin Pangarkar (2008), "Managing Human Resources for Service Excellence and Cost-Effectiveness at Singapore Airlines", *Managing Service Quality* 18, no. 1 (2008) 4–19.

"In Singapore, we always want to be the best in a lot of things. SIA is no different. ... a lot of things that we have been taught from young, from our Asian heritage ... filial piety, the care and concern, hospitality, and, of course, the most important part is trying, if we can, to do whatever we can to please the customer. And how do we do it? Sometimes, people just wonder, 'How do you guys manage to do it with limited time and resources on a flight?' yet we manage to do it somehow. Call us magicians."

Lim Suet Kwee, Senior Rank Trainer,
Singapore Airlines Training School, and Senior Flight Stewardess

A cookbook based on recipes from SIA's International Culinary Panel.

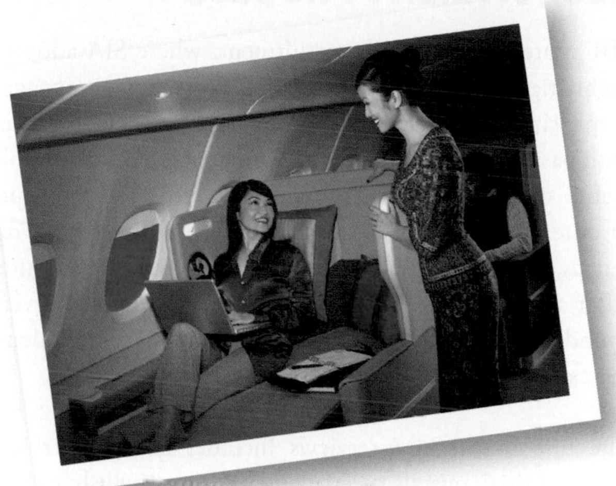

SIA's new business class has the widest seats in the industry.

HR AND COST-EFFECTIVE SERVICE EXCELLENCE AT SINGAPORE AIRLINES

Over the past four decades, SIA has earned a stellar reputation in the fiercely competitive commercial aviation business by providing customers with high-quality service and dominating the business-travel segments. SIA has been the most awarded airline in the world for many years. For example, it won the World's Best Airline award 21 out of the 22 times it has been awarded from the prestigious UK travel magazine *Condé Nast Traveler*, and it won the Skytrax's Airline of the Year award three times over the past decade.

One key element of SIA's competitive success is that it manages to navigate skillfully between poles that most companies think of as distinct: delivering service excellence in a cost-effective way. SIA's costs are below all other full-service airlines, and, in fact, its cost levels are so low that they are comparable to those of budget airlines. From 2001 to 2009, SIA costs per available seat kilometer were just 4.6 cents. According to a 2007 International Air Transport Association study, the costs for full-service European airlines were 8–16 cents, for US airlines 7–8 cents, and for Asian airlines 5–7 cents per available seat kilometer. SIA had even lower costs than most low-cost carriers in Europe had and the US had, which ranged from 4–8 cents and 5–6 cents, respectively.

A key challenge of implementing business-level strategies, such as effective differentiation at SIA (through service excellence and innovation) combined with superior levels of operational efficiency, is the effective alignment of functional strategies such as HR, marketing, or operations with the business-level strategy. The focus of this case is on how human resource (HR) practices, a crucial aspect of any service business, contribute to SIA's success through creating capabilities that support the company strategy.

Five interrelated and mutually supportive elements inherent in SIA's HR strategy (see Figure 1), along with leadership and role modeling by top management, play a key role in SIA's ability to deliver its business strategy of service excellence in a cost-effective way. Let us next take a closer look at how the five elements work and complement each other at SIA.

STRINGENT SELECTION AND RECRUITMENT PROCESS

HR strategy begins with recruitment, where SIA adopts a highly rigorous and strict selection process. Senior managers emphasize that SIA looks for cabin crew who can empathize with passengers and who are cheerful, friendly, and humble. Cabin crew applicants are required to meet a multitude of criteria starting with an initial screening looking at age ranges, academic qualifications, and physical attributes. After these baseline requirements, they undertake several rounds of interviews, uniform checks, a water confidence test, a psychometric test, and even attend a tea party.

The first round of interviews includes group interviews for an initial overall assessment and an English passage reading test to assess language competency. The next round involves a one-on-one, in-depth interview aiming to evaluate whether the applicant possesses SIA's required core values and competencies, and then a psychometric test is administered to further confirm the earlier results.

Figure 1: The five core elements of SIA's HR strategy.

Source: This model was derived from the authors' interviews with SIA's senior management and service personnel.

The uniform test after this allows the interviewer to assess the look of the applicant in SIA's *sarong kebaya*. This evaluation includes the posture, gait, and general appearance of the applicant in the uniform. Selected candidates from this round will also have to undertake a water confidence test in SIA's training pool in its flight safety wing, where applicants jump from a height of three meters. This tests the applicant's confidence with water in case they have to aid passengers for an emergency evacuation on water.

The next interview is the management round where the senior vice president and senior cabin crew staff interview those shortlisted. In the final stage, the applicants attend an apparently informal tea party that gives management a further opportunity to observe applicants' interaction style and demeanor.

From the 18,000 applications received annually, only some 600–900 new cabin crew are hired to cover turnover rates of 10%, including both voluntary and directed attrition, and company growth. After the initial training, new crew are carefully monitored for the first six months of flying through monthly reports from the inflight supervisor during this probationary period. Usually, around 75% are confirmed for an initial five-year contract, some 20% have their probation extended, and the rest leave the company.

This meticulous selection process ensures with reasonable certainty that SIA hires applicants with the desired attributes with a selection rate of 3–4% of its applicant pool. Despite the stringent procedures and strict rules about appearance and behavior, many educated young people around the region apply to join SIA due to the perceived social status and glamour associated with SIA's cabin crew. SIA's reputation as a service leader in the airline industry and an extensive and holistic developer of talent enables it to have its pick of applicants. Many school leavers and graduates view SIA as a desirable company to work for and as an opportunity to move to more lucrative jobs in other companies after having worked with SIA typically for two five-year contracts or more.

EXTENSIVE INVESTMENT IN TRAINING AND RETRAINING

SIA places considerable emphasis on training, which is one of its focal points in its HR strategy. According to Ms. Lam Seet Mui, Senior Manager for Human Resource

Development, "SIA invests huge amounts of money in infrastructure and technology, but, ultimately, you need people to drive it. At SIA, we believe that people actually do make a difference, so the company has in place a very comprehensive and holistic approach to developing our human resources. Essentially, we do two types of training, namely, functional training and general management-type training." Almost half of SIA spending is on functional training and retraining.

Even though training is often emphasized as a key element of success in service industries, SIA remains the airline with the highest emphasis on this aspect. Newly recruited cabin crew are required to undertake intensive four-month training courses—the longest and most comprehensive in the industry. SIA's training aims to enable cabin crew to provide gracious service reflecting warmth and friendliness while maintaining an image of authority and confidence in the passengers' minds. SIA's holistic training includes not only safety and functional issues but also beauty care, gourmet food, and wine appreciation, as well as the art of conversation.

As SIA's reputation for service excellence grows stronger, its customers tend to have even higher expectations, which increase the pressure on its frontline staff. According to Ms. Lim Suu Kuan, Commercial Training Manager, the motto of SIA is this: "If SIA can't do it for you, no other airline can. The challenge is to help the staff deal with difficult situations and take the brickbats. The company helps its staff deal with the emotional turmoil of having to satisfy and even please very demanding customers without feeling that they are being taken advantage of." Former CEO Dr. Cheong Choong Kong also commented that "to the company, training is forever and no one is too young to be trained, nor too old."

Continuous training and retraining has been vital to SIA in sustaining service excellence by equipping staff with an open mind-set to accept change and development and to deliver the new services SIA introduces regularly. SIA group has seven training schools for the seven core functional areas of cabin crew, flight operations, commercial training, information technology, security, airport services training and engineering. SIA Management Development Centre (MDC) also offers general management training under the purview of its HR division. MDC provides executive and leadership programs for all staff with the objective of generating effective managers and visionary leaders.

SIA's training programs (about 70% of which are in-house) develop 9,000 people a year. Often, training is aimed to support internal initiatives such as the Transforming Customer Service (TCS) program involving staff in five key operational areas: cabin crew, engineering, ground services, flight operations, and sales support. According to Ms. Lam Seet Mui, Senior Manager for HR Development, "To ensure that the TCS culture is promoted company-wide, it is also embedded into all management training. The program aims at building team spirit among our staff in key operational areas so that together we will make the whole journey as pleasant and seamless as possible for our passengers. One has to realize that it is not just the ticketing or reservations people and the cabin crew who come into contact with our passengers. The pilots, station managers, and station engineers have a role in customer service as well, because from time to time they do come into contact with passengers." She also added, "But TCS is not just about people. In TCS, there is the 40-30-30 rule, which is a holistic approach to people, processes (or procedures) and products. SIA focuses 40% of the resources on training and invigorating our people, 30% on reviewing processes and procedures, and 30% on creating new product and service ideas."

SIA's leadership and relationship management with staff play a key role in the success of its training initiatives. As Mr. Timothy Chua, Project Manager (New Service Development) put it, "I see myself first as a coach and second as a team player." SIA managers often assume the role of mentors and coaches to guide new employees, rather than just being managers and superiors.

SIA also adopts a job rotation approach to allow management to obtain a more holistic picture of the organization. Rotating to other departments every two to three years enables managers to develop a deeper understanding of operations at other areas of the organization, which promotes a corporate outlook, reduces the likelihood of inter-department conflicts, and facilitates change and innovation, as people bring fresh perspectives and approaches to their new roles. Constant job rotation is a core part of employee learning and development.

BUILDING HIGH-PERFORMANCE SERVICE DELIVERY TEAMS

Effective teams are often a prerequisite to service excellence. In view of this, SIA aims to create "esprit de corps" among its cabin crew. The 6,600 crew members are formed into teams of 13 individuals where team members are rostered to fly together as much as possible, allowing them to build camaraderie and better understand each other's personalities and capabilities. The team leader learns about individuals' strengths and weaknesses and acts as a counselor to whom they can turn to for help or advice. There are also "check trainers" who oversee 12 to 13 teams and often fly with them to inspect performance and generate feedback that aids the team's development. According to Ms. Gladys Chia (Assistant Manager of Training), "Team leaders are able to monitor and point out what can be improved in the crew; team leaders are the ones to evaluate the crew, monitor staff development, staff performance, supervise them. They see the feedback and monitor back the performance."

According to Mr. Sim Kay Wee, Senior Vice President (Cabin Crew), "The interaction within each of the teams is very strong. As a result, when team leaders do staff appraisal, they really know the staff. You would be amazed how meticulous and detailed each staff record is, even though there are 6,600 of them. We can pinpoint any staff's strengths and weaknesses easily. So, in this way, we have good control; and through this, we can ensure that the crew delivers the promise. If there are problems, we will know about them and we can send them for retraining. Those who are good will be selected for promotion."

Further, Mr. Toh Giam Ming, Senior Manager (Crew Performance), suggested that "What is good about the team concept is that despite the huge number of crew members, people can relate to a team and have a sense of belonging: 'This is my team.' They are put together for one to two years and are rostered together for about 60% to 70% of the time, so they do fly together quite a fair bit. So, especially for the new people, I think they find that they have less problem adjusting to the flying career. Because once you get familiar with the team, there is support and guidance on how to do things." Mr. Choo added, "The individual, you see, is not a digit or a staff number. If you don't have team flying, with 7,000-odd people, it can be difficult for you to really know a particular person."

SIA's cabin crew engages in some seemingly unrelated activities; for example, the performing arts circle for talented employees, where during the biennial cabin crew gala dinner, they raised over half a million dollars for charity. There are also gourmet, language, and sports circles. The company believes that such activities encourage empathy for others, an appreciation of the finer things in life, camaraderie and teamwork.

EMPOWERMENT OF FRONTLINE TO DELIVER SERVICE QUALITY

Over time, the soft skills of flight crew and other service personnel get honed, leading to service excellence that is difficult to replicate, not only in terms of how the service is delivered but also in terms of the mindset that supports this delivery. Virtually all outstanding service firms have legendary stories of employees who recovered failed service transactions, walked the extra mile to make a customer's day, or averted some kind of disaster for a customer. Mr. Toh shared such a story:

"This particular passenger was a wheelchair-bound lady in her eighties, was very ill, suffering from arthritis. She was traveling from Singapore to Brisbane. What happened was that a stewardess found her gasping for air owing to crippling pain. The stewardess used her personal hot-water bottle as a warm compress to relieve the passenger's pain and knelt to massage the lady's legs and feet for 45 minutes. By that time, the lady's feet were actually swollen. The stewardess offered her a new pair of flight support stockings without asking her to pay for them. She basically took care of the old lady throughout the trip, seven to eight hours. When the old lady got back to Brisbane, her son called the hotel in which the crew were staying to try and trace this stewardess to thank her personally. He then followed up with a letter to us. I don't know if training contributes to it, or if it is personal. I mean, you don't find people who'd do this purely as a result of training, I think. We find the right people, give them the right support, give them the right training, and with the right support people will do this kind of thing." Such thoughtful actions are part of the culture at SIA. According to Mr. Choo, the crew members "are very proud to be part of the SIA team, very proud of the tradition and very proud that SIA is held up as a company that gives excellent care to customers. So they want to live up to that."

Employees need to feel empowered in order to expend discretionary effort. It is pertinent that employees are able to make decisions independently as frontline staff frequently have to handle customers on their own since it is not feasible or even desirable for managers to constantly monitor employees' actions. At SIA, senior management emphasizes that staff must have a clear concept of the boundaries of their authority and that it is the responsibility of management to communicate and explain the empowerment limits. Empowerment of the front line is especially important during service recovery processes and in situations where customer have special needs. For example, the usual baggage allowance is 20 kg but frontline staff at SIA are empowered to raise it to 25 or 50 kg if they feel that it is right and justifiable. "If you are a clerk, you should know what your officer and your senior officer can do. If these two officers are not around, you can make decisions up to the limits of their authority," said Mr. Yap.

MOTIVATING STAFF THROUGH REWARDS AND RECOGNITION

Rewards and recognition is one of the key levers that any organization can use to encourage appropriate behavior, emphasize both positive as well as undesirable practices, and recognize excellence. SIA employs various forms of reward and recognition including interesting and varied job content, symbolic actions, performance-based share options, and a significant percentage of variable pay components linked to individual staff contributions and company's financial performance. SIA keeps base salaries low by offering employees bonuses of up to 50% of their annual base salary, a formula that is hardwired and depends on SIA's profitability. The numerous international accolades received by the airline over the years, including "best airline," "best cabin crew service," and "Asia's most admired company," serve as further sources of motivation.

The company also holds companywide meetings to keep staff updated about latest developments and circulates newsletters. As Ms. Lim noted, "It's about communication. For example, if we add a new service at check-in, we will talk to the people involved before, during, and after implementation. We will discuss the importance and the value of it, and make sure everyone is aware of what we are doing and why. It helps to give staff pride in what they do."

Communication also aids in recognizing service excellence. Staff going the extra mile receive recognition through such honors as the annual Deputy Chairman's Award. Mr. Sim stresses the importance of recognition: "We know that a pat on the back, a good ceremony, photographs and write-ups in the newsletters can be more motivating than mere financial rewards. Hence, we put in a lot of effort to ensure that heroes and heroines are recognized for their commitment and dedication."

Finding the right people and creating a service-oriented culture are key. Mr. Choo said, "Here, there are some intangibles. I think what makes it special is a combination of many things. First, you've got to ensure that you find the right people for the job, and after that, training matters a great deal: the way you nurture them, the way you monitor them, and the way you reward them. The recognition you give need not necessarily be money. I think another very important ingredient is the overall culture of cabin crew, the fact that you have people who really are very proud of the tradition. And I think a lot of our senior people—and it rubs off on the junior crew—take pride in the fact that they helped build up the airline; they are very proud of it and they want to ensure that it remains that way." Mr. Toh added, "Among other contributing factors is a deeply ingrained service culture not just among the cabin crew but also in the whole company. I think it goes back to 35 years ago when the airline was set up. A very, very strong service culture throughout the whole organization, very strong commitment from top management. We take every complaint seriously. We respond to every compliment and complaint. We try to learn from the feedback; it's a never-ending process."

SIA's reward and evaluation system is highly aligned with the desired behaviors. The key element is "onboard assessment," which encompasses image (grooming and uniform turnout), service orientation (crew's interaction and passenger handling capabilities), product knowledge and job skills, safety and security knowledge, adherence to procedures, work relationship (teamworking spirit), and, for the crew member in charge, additional factors such as people management skills and preflight briefing session. The Appendix shows the evaluation form for cabin crew.

SIA offers about average pay by Singaporean standards, which is low by global standards. Occasionally, there have been disputes between SIA group management and the labor unions. In 2007, the airline was in the spotlight again when the Air Line Pilots' Association Singapore (ALPA-S) disagreed with the management's proposed salary rate for pilots flying the Airbus A380, and the case had to be settled by the Industrial Arbitration Court.

BEYOND HUMAN RESOURCES

For three and a half decades, SIA has managed to achieve what many others in the aviation industry can only dream of, cost-effective service excellence and sustained superior performance. Understanding the underpinnings of SIA's competitive success has important implications for organizations more broadly. One of the key implications concerns strategic alignment, in particular aligning human resource practices to a company's competitive strategy.

At SIA, the human resource management practices outlined above enable the development of service excellence, customer orientation, adaptability, and cost consciousness *capabilities*, that in turn support its *dual strategy* of differentiation through service excellence and low cost.

The SIA experience highlights how training and development should be employed in order to achieve a holistically developed workforce that can effectively support the company's strategy. Key questions for leaders therefore are: What sort of behaviors and attitudes do our reward and evaluation systems encourage? Are these aligned with what is needed to support our strategy? Do we train and develop our people in a way that develops the right capabilities to support our strategy? Do we go beyond technical training to address attitudes and ways of thinking?

No organization can stand still. The recent socioeconomic crises at the macro-level and the emergence of high-quality full-service airlines in the Middle East (e.g., Emirates) and Asian budget carriers (e.g., AirAsia) at the industry level, mean that SIA not only needs to sustain its focus on achieving cost-effective service excellence but also reexamine and reinvent some ingredients of its recipe for success.

STUDY QUESTIONS

1. Describe what is so special about SIA's five elements of its successful HR practices?
2. Evaluate the effectiveness of each element's contribution toward SIA's leadership in service excellence and cost-effectiveness.
3. Despite evidence that such practices help service firms achieve higher company performance, many organizations have not managed to execute them as effectively. Why do you think that is the case?
4. Why do you think are US full-service airlines largely undifferentiated low-quality providers? What are the reasons that none of the full-service airlines positioned itself and delivers as a high service quality provider?
5. Some of SIA's HR practices would be illegal in the United States and Europe (e.g., making renewal of contracts dependent on employees maintaining their body weight; or having all its cabin crew on time-based contracts that are renewable every five years). Is this fair competition (i.e., desired competition between regulatory frameworks, as was favored by Margaret Thatcher, former prime minister of the United Kingdom), or is it arbitration of regulatory environments that encourage a "race to the bottom" in terms of employee rights?
6. How do people feel if they are working in a culture that focuses so intensely on customers, but cuts costs to the bone internally?
7. View http://youtu.be/fNEJrd6GkSY (Across the World with the Singapore Girl) and http://youtu.be/P5sGKR6NJBw (Singapore Airlines SQ Girl), and discuss how these videos are perceived by SIA cabin crew.

APPENDIX: CABIN CREW PERFORMANCE MANAGEMENT (PM) QUESTIONS

1. How is the cabin crew area structured and how does this influence the PM system?

Our crew are formed into 36 groups known as wards, each headed by a ward leader who monitors the performance of the crew. The ward leader, in turn, reports to a Cabin Crew Executive (CCE). Each CCE has six ward leaders under his or her charge and also oversees other aspects of crew administration/management such as communication and welfare.

2. Describe the performance management tool/process that you use to monitor your cabin crew.

The performance of a crew member is measured through "onboard assessments" (OBA) carried out by a more senior crew member on the same flight. Elements assessed in OBA are:

a) Image—on grooming and uniform turnout

b) Service Orientation—crew's interaction and passenger handling capabilities

c) Product Knowledge and Job Skills—crew's performance with the various bar and meal services and crew's familiarity with procedures/job and product knowledge

d) Safety and Security—knowledge of and adherence to safety and security procedures

e) Work Relationship—to assess crew's general attitude and teamwork/team spirit

f) People Management Skills—supervisory and man-management skills, development of junior crew, ability to plan and coordinate the various services

g) Preflight Session—effectiveness of the preflight briefing

***Sections f & g are only applicable to the crew-in-charge.*

In addition, there is also a "closed assessment," which is carried out in conjunction with the OBA. In the closed assessment, we look at crew's attitude, interest toward the jobs, and biases/apprehension toward certain passengers

3. How frequently do the assessments occur?

It varies from rank to rank and is tracked over a Financial Year (FY).

a) New Crew on Probation—six OBAs during the six-month probation period

b) Flight Steward/Stewardess—minimum four per FY

c) Supervisory Crew—three to four times per FY

d) Crew-in-Charge—twice per FY

4. What level of feedback is given to the individual—at the time of checks and cumulatively, that is, during the quarterly review, annual review, etc.? How do you manage a good quality of interaction rather than just making sure the meeting happens?

The OBA is an open appraisal and the appraiser discusses the strengths and weaknesses with the appraisee. The appraisee views and endorses the OBA. All returned OBAs are scanned and flagged out for the ward leader's monitoring if the scores fall outside our predetermined thresholds. If necessary, the ward leader will go on the appraisees' flight to check out the crew personally. The ward leader can (and often does) call in the crew for a discussion at any time if deemed necessary.

Concerted effort is made for the ward leader to fly with each crew member in his ward at least once a year. The ward leader will take this opportunity to review/discuss the records of the crew. In addition, the ward leader is required to carry out an annual assessment of all crew in his ward before finalising the annual appraisal score.

The annual appraisal is weighted as follows:

Elements	Weightage %
OBA	60
Discipline	15
Attendance Record	10
Passenger Feedback	10
Ward Leader Assessments	5

5. **What degree of alignment is there between the company values and the areas assessed?**

The company's core values are embedded in the elements assessed in the OBAs, such as service orientation and product knowledge (pursuit of excellence), safety and security (safety), and work relationship and people management (teamwork).

6. **How do you train assessors and what level of on-going training occurs to ensure rater consistency?**

All crew promoted to supervisory rank have to attend a one-day appraisal workshop where they are taught the basics of assessment and coached on the use of the OBA form. There's also an ongoing process to review all OBAs that have been improperly done and pick out appraisers who habitually give extreme ratings for follow-up by the ward leaders.

CASE 15

CASE STUDY

Customer Asset Management at DHL in Asia

Jochen Wirtz, Indranil Sen, and Sanjay Singh

DHL serves a wide range of customers, from global enterprises to the occasional customer who ships the odd one or two documents a year. To be able to effectively manage such a diverse customer base, DHL implemented a sophisticated customer segmentation cum loyalty management system. The focus of this system is to assess the profitability from its customers, reduce customer churn, and increase DHL's share of shipments.

COMPANY BACKGROUND AND MARKET ENVIRONMENT

DHL, the international air express and logistics company, serves a wide range of customers, from global enterprises with sophisticated and high-volume supply-chain solutions shipping anything from spare parts to documents, to the occasional customer who ships the odd one or two documents a year. Exhibits 1 and 2 show some of DHL's logistics operations. To be able to effectively manage such a diverse customer base, DHL implemented a sophisticated customer segmentation cum loyalty management system. The focus of this system is to assess the profitability from its customers, reduce customer churn, and increase DHL's share of shipments.

Exhibit 1: DHL logistics hub in Singapore.

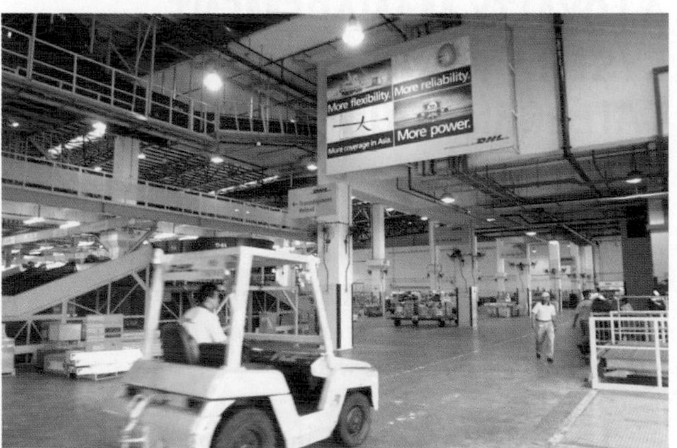

Jochen Wirtz is Professor of Marketing at the NUS Business School, National University of Singapore; Indranil Sen, Research & Planning Manager Asia Pacific who was in charge of designing and implementing DHL's loyalty marketing across Asia, and Sanjay Singh, who was studying for his MBA at the NUS Business School while this case was written.

Exhibit 2: DHL logistics.

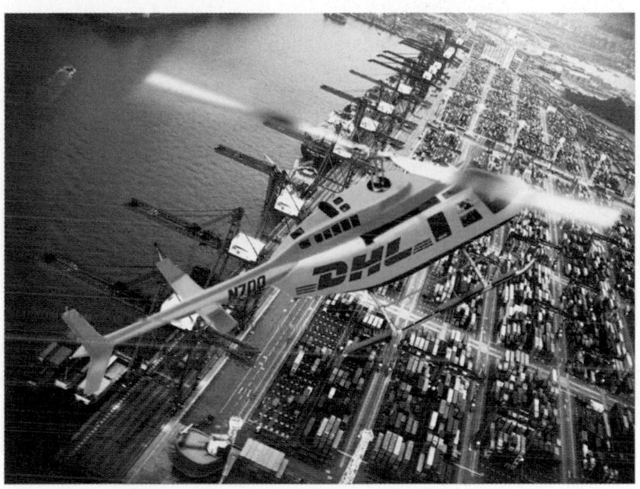

CUSTOMER SEGMENTATION

To achieve this, the first task was to segment its customers into actionable segments with distinct needs. DHL defined three main segments. First, "strategic customers" are extremely high-volume shippers with a full range of logistics solutions and express shipment needs. This segment consists of approximately of DHL's top 250 customers worldwide, which are mostly large multi-nationals. Second, the "relationship customers" segment consists of customers who use DHL to ship their products and documents regularly, but with a lower volume than that of the strategic customers segment and also not as sophisticated supply-chain needs. Finally, the "direct customers" segment ships infrequently with DHL. The customer segmentation can be represented in the form of the familiar customer pyramid in Exhibit 3.

These segments are further divided into subsegments based on the kind of service required (Exhibit 4). The needs of

Exhibit 3: The customer pyramid.

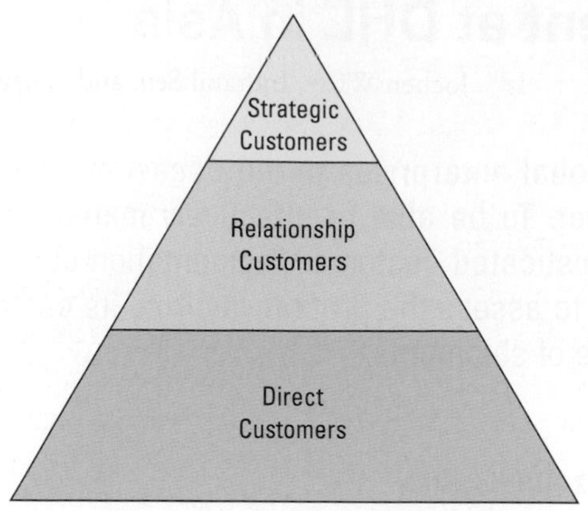

Exhibit 4: Customer subsegmentation.

	Strategic Customers	Relationship Customers	Direct Customers
Basic Products			
Special Programs			
Customized Solutions			

direct customers and many of the relationship customers often are fully met by DHL's *basic products*. For relationship customers with special needs, DHL also offers some *special programs* like direct distribution to its partners, test services, and parts distribution to fulfill these needs. Strategic customers almost always use *customized solutions*, such as providing bulk-breaking facilities and planned production support for precision delivery schedules, and DHL aims to meet their entire express delivery needs.

Customers using DHL's basic products find it easier to switch because switching costs are low and all its key competitors also offer similar products. In contrast, switching costs are significantly higher for customers with special programs, and highest for clients using customized solutions.

Exhibit 5 shows some output of DHL's segmentation analysis for one of its country markets. The majority of revenue and profits were derived from only 18% of the customers, its relationship customers. The direct customer segment consisted of 75% of the total customer base and

Exhibit 5: Segment Analysis.

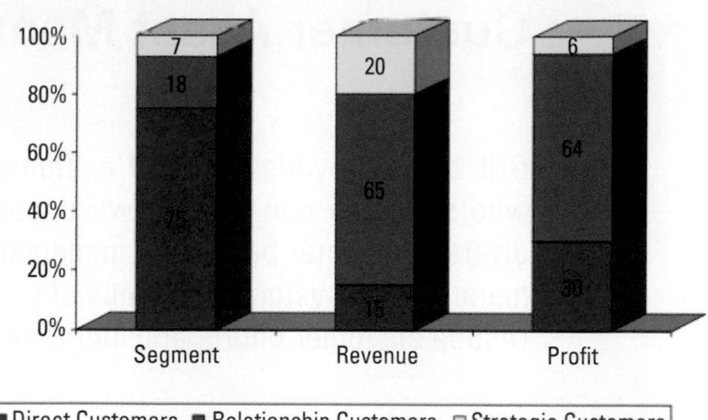

contributed only 15% of revenues and 30% of profits. The strategic customer segment contributed only 6% to profits. Similar patterns are observed for all countries where this analysis was conducted.

The verdict seems clear: focus on the relationship customers segment for maximum profitability. However, this does not mean that DHL should neglect the other segments. DHL should deploy cutting-edge technology and best-practice infrastructure to maintain the loyalty of the strategic customer segment because there is high future business potential for this group. Extra effort is put into upgrading the direct customers who have high volume potential and latent needs for special program products.

A LOYALTY MANAGEMENT SYSTEM: FURTHER CATEGORIZATION OF SEGMENTS

To focus service and sales staff on customer retention and development, it is necessary to get more information about DHL's customers. Each of these three segments is further classified into six categories, and the data is used to take corrective and proactive measures to enhance customer loyalty. These six categories were:

1) **Lost.** The customer in this category has stopped shipping with DHL. This could be for external reasons such as a customer gone into liquidation, or for internal reasons such as service performance failure or an increase in prices. Once the reason has been identified, it is easier for DHL to control internal reasons and reduce customer churn. Sales and service staff can then focus on regaining potentially profitable accounts.

2) **Decreased performer.** This category refers to customers who have shipped considerably less over a given period compared to a similar period in the past. Again, the reasons for lower shipments may be external or internal to DHL. The decreased performer in each segment triggers an alarm bell to warn sales staff of any potential impending customer churn.

3) **Maintained.** This category is for customers who continue to trade with DHL within a given bandwidth of shipment volume.

4) **Increased performer.** The customer in this category has shipped considerably more over a given period. Again, the reasons for increased performance may be external or internal. Sales staff follow up with the customer to identify the causes for increase in volumes and, particularly, to find out whether the increase in trading is a result of a DHL initiative. If so, the successful initiatives are further improved to gain better results.

5) **New.** This category is for any customer who has shipped for the first time with DHL. Special efforts are made by the sales staff to make them permanent customers.

6) **Regained.** This customer was previously "lost" but has recommenced shipping with DHL recently. The reasons for this renewed activity may be external (e.g., renewed business activity of a lapsed customer) or internal (e.g., the shipment was made as a result of reactive measures by DHL to regain the customer).

The data collected is graphically represented for each segment, as given in Exhibit 6, and is reported to sales, marketing, and customer service departments and senior management. This makes it easy to understand the impact of the change in the customer base. Any increased percentage of decreased performers immediately prompts DHL's sales and customer service staff to take corrective action.

Exhibit 6: Segment analysis.

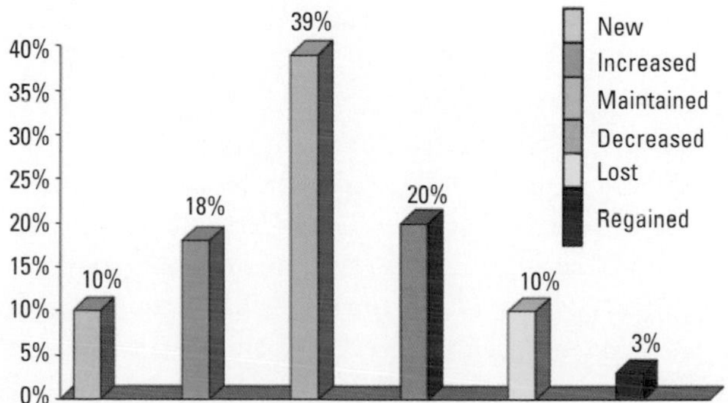

By classifying each customer and collecting data, the sales force is forewarned about potential customer defections. This means that DHL can take corrective action and identify any shortcomings in service performance as well as customer dissatisfaction, leading to more proactive measures in the future. The data also makes it possible to calculate the defection rate of customers for each tier of the customer pyramid and to calculate the lifetime value of each segment. The change in the lifetime value of all customers gives management an idea of the revenue and profit implications of its marketing and service initiatives.

The expected increase or decrease in revenue for the month is also calculated and represented graphically, as shown in Exhibit 7, illustrating the impact of the change in the customer segment portfolio on DHL's revenues.

Exhibit 7: Relationship customers—estimated revenue—impact of changes in account activity.

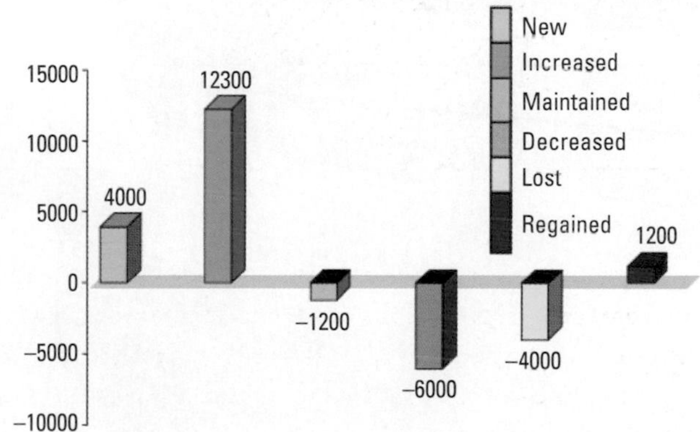

Similarly, sales staff can study the reasons for up-trading for each customer and tap the remaining potential for further up-trading. This program also helps DHL to send targeted communications to the customers based on market segments instead of general communications to all customers, thereby making communication cost-effective.

After a short period after implementation, this initiative had already been yielding impressive results, and further modules were being developed and pilot-tested for potential rollout (Exhibit 8).

Exhibit 8: DHL Delivery Man.

STUDY QUESTIONS

1. What are the main challenges in implementing this segmentation in DHL's customer database?
2. How would you recommend DHL to address those challenges?
3. What are the various possible practical applications of this segmentation methodology by other functional departments (e.g., sales, customer service)?

Dr. Mahalee Goes to London: Global Client Management

Christopher H. Lovelock

A senior account officer at an international bank is about to meet a wealthy Asian businessman who seeks funding for a buyout of his company. The prospective client has already visited a competing bank.

It was a Friday in mid-February and Dr. Kadir Mahalee, a wealthy businessman from the Southeast Asian nation of Tailesia, was visiting London on a trip that combined business and pleasure. Mahalee held a doctorate from the London School of Economics and had earlier been a professor of international trade and a government trade negotiator. He was the founder of Eximsa, a major export company in Tailesia. Business brought him to London every two to three months. These trips provided him with the opportunity to visit his daughter Leona, the eldest of his four children, who lived in London. Several of his 10 grandchildren were attending college in Britain. He was especially proud of his grandson, Anson, who was a student at the Royal Academy of Music. In fact, he had scheduled this trip to coincide with a violin recital by Anson at 2 p.m. on this particular Friday.

The primary purpose of Mahalee's visit was to resolve a delicate matter regarding his company. He had decided to retire and wished to make arrangements for the company's future. His son, Victor, was involved in the business and ran Eximsa's trading office in Europe. However, Victor was in poor health and unable to take over the firm. Mahalee believed that a group of loyal employees were interested in buying his company, if the necessary credit could be arranged.

Before leaving Tailesia, Mahalee discussed the possibility of a buyout with his trusted financial adviser, Lee Siew Meng, who recommended that he talk to several banks in London because of the potential complexity of the business deal:

> The London banks are experienced in buyouts. Also, you need a bank that can handle the credit for the interested buyers in New York and London, as well as Asia. Once the buyout takes place, you'll have significant cash to invest. This would be a good time to review your estate plans as well.

Referring Mahalee to two competing firms, The Trust Company and Global Private Bank, Lee added:

> I've met an account officer from Global who called on me several times. Here's his business card; his name is Miguel Kim. I've never done any business with him, but he did seem quite competent. Unfortunately, I don't know anyone at the Trust Company, but here's their address in London.

After checking into the Savoy Hotel in London the following Wednesday, Mahalee telephoned Kim's office. Since Kim was out, Mahalee spoke to the account officer's secretary, described himself briefly, and arranged to stop by Global's Lombard Street office around mid-morning on Friday.

On Thursday, Mahalee visited The Trust Company. The two people he met were extremely pleasant and had spent some time in Tailesia. They seemed very knowledgeable about managing estates and gave him some good recommendations on handling his complex family affairs. However, they were clearly less experienced in handling business credit, his most urgent need.

The next morning, Mahalee had breakfast with Leona. As they parted, she said, "I'll meet you at 1:30 p.m. in the lobby of the Savoy, and we'll go to the recital together. We mustn't be late if we want to get front-row seats."

On his way to Global Private Bank, Mahalee stopped at Mappin & Webb's jewelry store to buy his wife a present for their anniversary. His shopping was pleasant and leisurely. He purchased a beautiful emerald necklace that he knew his wife would like. When he emerged from the jewelry store, he was caught in an unexpected snow flurry. He had difficulty finding a taxi and his arthritis started acting up, making walking to the nearest Tube station out of the question. At last, he caught a taxi and arrived at the Lombard Street location of Global Bancorp about noon. After going into the street-level branch of Global Retail Bank, he was redirected by a security guard to the Private Bank offices on the second floor.

He arrived at the Private Bank's nicely appointed reception area at 12:15 p.m. The receptionist greeted him and contacted Miguel Kim's secretary, who came out promptly to see Mahalee, and declared:

Exhibit 1: Receiving a client on short notice would require a bank's vice president to rely on all her expertise and experience to clinch the deal.

> Mr. Kim was disappointed that he couldn't be here to welcome you, Dr. Mahalee, but he had a lunch appointment with one of his clients that was scheduled over a month ago. He expects to return at about 1:30. In the meantime, he has asked another senior account officer, Sophia Costa, to assist you.

Sophia Costa, 41, was the vice president of the bank and had worked for Global Bancorp for 14 years (two years longer than Miguel Kim). She had visited Tailesia once, but had not met Mahalee's financial adviser nor any member of the Mahalee family. An experienced relationship manager, Costa was knowledgeable about offshore investment management and fiduciary services. Miguel Kim had looked into her office at 11:45 a.m. and asked her if she would cover for him in case a prospective client, a Dr. Mahalee, whom he had expected to see earlier, should happen to arrive. He told Costa that Mahalee was a successful Tailesian businessman planning for his retirement but that he had never met the prospect personally, then rushed off to lunch.

The phone rang in Costa's office, and she reached across the desk to pick it up. It was Kim's secretary. "Dr. Mahalee is in reception, Ms. Costa."

STUDY QUESTIONS

1. Prepare a flowchart of Dr. Mahalee's service encounters.
2. Putting yourself in Mahalee's shoes, how do you feel (both physically and mentally) after speaking with the receptionist at Global? What are your priorities right now?
3. As Sophia Costa, what action would you take in your first five minutes with Mahalee?
4. What would be a good outcome of the meeting for both the client and the bank? How should Costa try to bring about such an outcome?

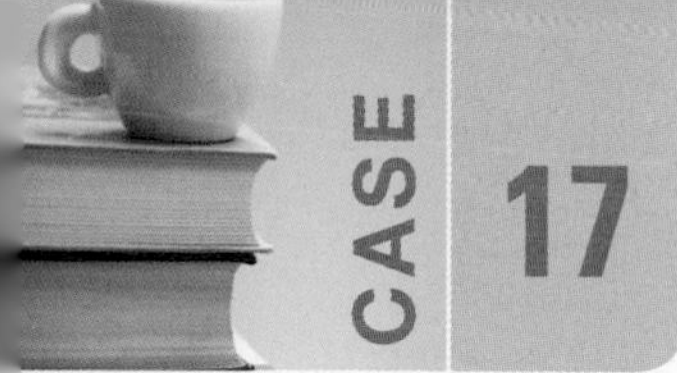

CASE 17

Hilton HHonors Worldwide: Loyalty Wars

John Deighton and Stowe Shoemaker

Hilton Hotels regards frequent guest programs as the lodging industry's most important marketing tool, serving to direct promotional and customer service efforts at the heavy user. How should management of Hilton's international guest rewards program respond when Starwood, a competing hotel group operating several brands, ups the ante in the loyalty stakes?

Jeff Diskin, head of Hilton HHonors® (Hilton's guest reward program), opened *The Wall Street Journal* on February 2, 1999, and read the headline, "Hotels Raise the Ante in Business-Travel Game." The story read, "Starwood Hotels and Resorts Worldwide Inc. is expected to unveil tomorrow an aggressive frequent-guest program that it hopes will help lure more business travelers to its Sheraton, Westin, and other hotels. Accompanied by a $50-million ad campaign, the program ratchets up the stakes in the loyalty-program game that big corporate hotel companies, including Starwood and its rivals at Marriott, Hilton, and Hyatt are playing."[1]

Diskin did not hide his concern: "These guys are raising their costs, and they're probably raising mine, too. They are reducing the cost-effectiveness of the industry's most important marketing tool by deficit spending against their program. Loyalty programs have been at the core of how we attract and retain our best customers for over a decade. But they are only as cost-effective as our competitors let them be."

Professor John Deighton of Harvard Business School and Professor Stowe Shoemaker of the William F. Harrah College of Hotel Administration, University of Nevada, Las Vegas, prepared this case. HBS cases are developed solely as the basis for class discussion. Cases are not intended to serve as endorsements, sources of primary data, or illustrations of effective or ineffective management. The case reflects the status of Hilton Hotels Corporation and Hilton HHonors Worldwide as of January 1999. Hilton has made numerous changes since that time, including Hilton Hotels Corporation's acquisition of Promus Hotel Corporation.

1 *The Wall Street Journal*, February 2, 1999, p. B1.

LOYALTY MARKETING PROGRAMS

The idea of rewarding loyalty had its origins in coupons and trading stamps. First in the 1900s and again in the 1950s, America experienced episodes of trading-stamp frenzy that became so intense that congressional investigations were mounted. Retailers would give customers small adhesive stamps in proportion to the amount of their purchases, to be pasted into books and eventually redeemed for merchandise. The best-known operator had been the S&H Green Stamp Company. Both episodes had lasted about 20 years, declining as the consumer passion for collecting abated, and vendors came to the conclusion that any advantage they might once have held had been competed away by emulators.

Loyalty marketing in its modern form was born in 1981 when American Airlines introduced the AAdvantage frequent-flyer program, giving "miles" in proportion to miles traveled, redeemable for free travel. It did so in response to the competitive pressure that followed airline deregulation. The American Airlines program had no need for stamps because it took advantage of the data warehousing capabilities of computers. Soon, program administrators realized that they had a tool that did not merely reward loyalty but identified by name and address the people who accounted for most of aviation's revenues and made a one-to-one relationship possible.

Competing airlines had launched their own programs, but, unlike stamp programs, frequent-flyer programs seemed to survive emulation. By 1990, almost all airlines were offering them. In the late 1990s, Delta Airlines and United Airlines linked their programs together, as did American and US Airways in the United States. Internationally, United Airlines and Lufthansa combined with 11 other airlines to form Star Alliance, and American, British Airways, and four others formed an alliance called Oneworld. In these alliances, qualifying flights on any of the member airlines could be credited to the frequent-flyer club of the flyer's choice.

As the decade ended, computer-based frequency programs were common in many service industries, including car rentals, department stores, video and book retailing, credit cards, movie theaters, and the hotel industry.

THE HOTEL INDUSTRY

Chain brands were a major factor in the global hotel market of 13.6 million rooms.[2] The chains supplied reservation services, field sales operations, loyalty program administration, and the management of hotel properties under well-recognized names such as Hilton and Marriott. (See Exhibit 1 for details of the seven largest US hotel chains competing in the business-class hotel segment.)

While the brands stood for quality, there was less standardization of operations in hotel chains than in many other services. The reason was that behind a consumer's experience of a hotel brand might lie any of many methods of control. A branded hotel might be owned and managed by the chain, but it might be owned by a third party and managed by the chain, or owned by the chain and managed by a franchisee, or, in some cases, owned and managed by the franchisee. Occasionally, chains managed one another's

2 World Trade Organization.

Exhibit 1: The US lodging industry.

	Countries	Properties	Rooms	Owned Properties	Franchised Properties	Management Contracts
Marriott International[a]	53	1,764	339,200	49	936	776
Bass Hotels and Resorts[b]	90	2,700	447,967	76	2,439	185
Hilton Hotels Corp.[c]	11	272	91,060	39	207	16
Starwood Hotels and Resorts Worldwide, Inc.[d]	72	695	212,950	171	291	233
Hyatt[e]	45	246	93,729	NA	NA	NA
Carlson[f]	50	581	112,089	1	542	38
Hilton International[g]	50	224	62,941	154	0	70
Promus[h]	11	1,398	198,526	160	1,059	179

a Includes Marriott Hotels, Resorts and Suites; Courtyard, Residence Inn, TownePlace Suites, Fairfield Inn, SpringHill Suites, Marriott Vacation Club International; Conference Centers, Marriott Executive Residences, Ritz-Carlton, Renaissance, and Ramada International.

b Includes InterContinental, Forum, Crowne Plaza, Holiday Inn, Holiday Inn Express, and Staybridge.

c Includes Hilton Hotels, Hilton Garden Inns, Hilton Suites, Hilton Grand Vacation Clubs, and Conrad International.

d Includes St. Regis, Westin Hotels and Resorts, Sheraton Hotels and Resorts, Four Points, Sheraton Inns, and The W Hotels. Does not include other Starwood-owned hotels, flagged under other brands (93 properties for 29,322 rooms).

e Includes Hyatt Hotels, Hyatt International, and Southern Pacific Hotel Corporation (SPHC). Because it is a privately held corporation, it will not divulge the breakdown of rooms between ownership, franchise, and management contract.

f Includes Radisson Hotels Worldwide, Regent International Hotels, and Country Inns and Suites.

g A wholly owned subsidiary of what was once known as the Ladbroke Group. In spring 1999, Ladbroke changed its name to Hilton Group PLC to reflect the emphasis on hotels.

h Includes such brands as Doubletree, Red Lion, Hampton Inn, Hampton Inn & Suites, Embassy Suites, and Homewood Suites.

Source: World Trade Organization and company information.

brands because one chain could be another's franchisee. Starwood, for example, ran hotels under the Hilton brand as Hilton's franchisee. Information about competitors' operating procedures therefore circulated quite freely in the industry.

Consumers

For most Americans, a stay in a hotel was a relatively rare event. Of the 74 percent of Americans who traveled overnight in a year, only 41 percent used a hotel, motel, or resort. The market in which Hilton competed was smaller still, defined by price point and trip purpose, and divided among business, convention, and leisure segments.

The **business** segment accounted for one-third of all room nights in the market that Hilton served. About two-thirds of these stays were at rates negotiated between the guest's employer and the chain, but since most corporations negotiated rates with two and sometimes three hotel chains, business travelers had some discretion to choose where they would stay. About one-third of business travelers did not have access to negotiated corporate rates and had full discretion to choose their hotel.

The **convention** segment, comprising convention, conference, and other meeting-related travel, accounted for another third of room nights in Hilton's competitive set. The choice of hotel in this instance was in the hands of a small number of professional conference organizers, typically employees of professional associations and major corporations.

The **leisure** segment accounted for the final third. Leisure guests were price sensitive, often making their selections from among packages of airlines, cars, tours, and hotels assembled by a small group of wholesalers and tour organizers at rates discounted below business rates.

Although the chains as a whole experienced demand from all segments, individual properties tended to draw disproportionately from one segment or another. Resort hotels served leisure travelers and some conventioneers, convention hotels depended on group and business travel, and hotels near airports were patronized by guests on business, for example. These segmentation schemes, however, obscured the fact that the individuals in segments differentiated by trip purpose and price point were often the same people. Frequent travelers patronized hotels of various kinds and price segments, depending, for example, on whether a stay was a reimbursable business expense, a vacation, or a personal expense.

Competition

Four large global brands dominated the business-class hotel market (Table A). Each competed at more than one price point. (Exhibit 2 shows the price points in the industry, and Exhibit 3 shows the distribution of brands across price points.)

STARWOOD. Beginning in 1991, Barry Sternlicht built Starwood Hotels and Resorts Worldwide from a base in a real estate investment trust. In January 1998, Starwood bought Westin Hotels and Resorts, and, a month later, it bought ITT Corporation, which included Sheraton Hotels and Resorts, after a well-publicized battle with Hilton Hotels Corporation. By year end, Starwood had under unified management the Westin, Sheraton, St. Regis, Four Points, and Caesar 's Palace brands. Starwood had recently announced plans to create a new brand, W, aimed at younger professionals.

MARRIOTT. Marriott International operates and franchises hotels under the Marriott, Ritz-Carlton, Renaissance, Residence Inn, Courtyard, TownePlace Suites, Fairfield Inn, SpringHill Suites, and Ramada International brands. It also operates conference centers and provides furnished corporate housing. A real estate investment trust, Host Marriott owned some of the properties operated by Marriott International, as well as some Hyatt, Four Season, and Swissotel properties.

HYATT. The Pritzker family of Chicago owns Hyatt Corporation, the only privately owned major hotel chain. Hyatt comprises Hyatt Hotels, operating hotels and

Table A

Marriott International	339,200 rooms
Starwood Hotels and Resorts	212,900 rooms
Hyatt Hotels	93,700 rooms
Hilton Hotels	91,100 rooms
Hilton International	62,900 rooms

Source: Company records.

Exhibit 2: Price segments in the lodging industry.

- Luxury: Average rack rate over $125, full-service hotels with deluxe amenities for leisure travelers and special amenities for business and meeting markets. Chains in this segment include Four Seasons, Hilton, Hyatt, InterContinental (a Bass Hotels and Resorts brand), Marriott Hotels and Resorts, Renaissance (a Marriott International brand), Ritz-Carlton (also a Marriott International brand), Sheraton (a Starwood Hotels and Resorts brand), and Westin (also a Starwood Hotels and Resorts brand).
- Upscale: Average rack rate between $100 and $125, full-service hotels with standard amenities. Includes most all-suite, non-extended-stay brands. Crowne Plaza (a Bass Hotels and Resorts brand), Doubletree Guest Suites (a Promus Hotel Corp. brand), Embassy Suites (also a Promus Hotel Corp. brand), Radisson (a Carlson Worldwide Hospitality brand), Hilton Inn, and Clarion (a Choice Hotels brand) are all examples of chains in this segment.
- Midmarket with food and beverage (F&B): Average rack rate between $60 and $90, full-service hotels with lower service levels and amenities than the upscale segment. Examples include Best Western, Courtyard (a Marriott International brand), Garden Inn (a Hilton brand), Holiday Inn (a Bass Hotels and Resorts brand), and Howard Johnson (a Cendant brand).
- Midmarket without F&B: Average rack rate between $45 and $70, with limited-service and comparable amenities to the midmarket with F&B segment. Examples of chains in this segment include Hampton Inns (a Promus brand), Holiday Inn Express (a Bass Hotels and Resorts brand), and Comfort Inn (a Choice Hotels brand).
- Economy: Average rack rate between $40 and $65, with limited service and few amenities. Fairfield Inn (a Marriott International brand), Red Roof Inn, Travelodge, and Days Inn of America (a Cendant brand) are examples of economy chains.
- Budget: Average rack rate between $30 and $60, with limited service and basic amenities. Motel 6, Super 8, and Econo Lodge are the best-known chains in this segment.
- Extended stay: Average rack rate between $60 and $90, targeted to extended-stay market and designed for extended length of stay. Marriott International has the following two brands in this market: Residence Inn by Marriott and TownePlace Suites. Other chains include Homewood Suites (a Bass Hotels and Resorts brand), Summerfield Suites, and Extended Stay America.

Source: US lodging chains segmented by RealTime Hotel Reports Inc., authors of the 1998 Lodging Survey.

Exhibit 3: Segments served by the major chains.

	Luxury	Upscale	Midmarket with Food and Beverage	Midmarket without Food and Beverage	Economy	Budget	Extended Stay
Hilton	X	X	X	X			
Hyatt	X						
Marriott	X	X	X		X		X
Starwood	X	X	X				X

Source: Company records.

resorts in the United States, Canada, and the Caribbean; and Hyatt International, operating overseas. Hyatt also owns Southern Pacific Hotel Group, a three- and four-star hotel chain based primarily in Australia. Although the companies operates independently, they run joint marketing programs.

The 1990s had been a time of consolidation and rationalization in the lodging industry, partly due to application of information technologies to reservation systems and control of operations. Diskin reflected on the trend: "Historically, bigger has been better because it has led to economies of scale and bigger and better brands to leverage. Historically, big players could win even if they did not do a particularly good job on service, performance, or programs. Now [after the Starwood deal] there's another big player. It would have been nice if it had been Hilton that was the largest hotel chain in the world, but biggest is not the only way to be the best."

MARKETING THE HILTON BRAND

The Hilton brand was controlled by two entirely unrelated corporations, Hilton Hotels Corporation (HHC), based in Beverley Hills, California, and Hilton International (HIC), headquartered near London, England. In 1997, however, HHC and HIC agreed to reunify the Hilton brand worldwide. They agreed to cooperate on sales and marketing, standardize operations, and run the Hilton HHonors loyalty program across all HHC and HIC hotels. At the end of 1998, HHC divested itself of casino interests and announced "a new era as a dedicated hotel company."

The exit from gaming, the reunification of Hilton's worldwide marketing, and the extension of the brand into the middle market under the Hilton Garden Inns name were initiatives that followed the appointment in 1997 of Stephen F. Bollenbach as President and Chief Executive Officer of Hilton. Bollenbach had served as Chief Financial Officer of Marriott and most recently as Chief Financial Officer of Disney, and he brought to Hilton a passion for branding. To some members of the Hilton management team, the focus on brand development was a welcome one. "Hilton's advantage has been a well-recognized name, but a potentially limiting factor has been a widely varying product and the challenge of managing customer expectation with such a variety of product offerings. Since Hilton includes everything from world-renowned properties like The Waldorf-Astoria and Hilton Hawaiian Village to the smaller middle-market Hilton Garden Inns, it's important to give consumers a clear sense of what to expect from the various types of hotels," observed one manager.

In mid-1999, the properties branded as Hilton hotels comprised:

1. 39 owned or partly owned by HHC in the United States
2. 207 franchised by HHC to third-party managers in the United States
3. 16 managed by HHC in the United States on behalf of third-party owners
4. 10 managed internationally under HHC's Conrad International brand
5. 220 managed by HIC in over 50 countries excluding the US.

The executives at Hilton HHonors worked for these 492 hotels and their 154,000 rooms. The previous year had been successful. Revenues had been in the region of $158 per night per guest, and occupancy had exceeded break-even. Hotels like Hilton's tended to cover fixed costs at about 68 percent occupancy, and 80 percent of all revenue at higher occupancy levels flowed to the bottom line. Advertising, selling, and other marketing costs (a component of fixed costs) for this group of hotels were not published, but industry norms ran at about $750 per room per year.[3]

Hilton HHonors Program

Hilton HHonors was the name Hilton gave to its program designed to build loyalty to the Hilton brand worldwide. Hilton HHonors Worldwide (HHW) operated the program, not as a profit center but as a service to its two parents, HHC and HIC. It was required to break even each year and to measure its effectiveness through a complex set of program metrics. Diskin ran the limited liability corporation with a staff of 30, with one vice president overseeing the program's marketing efforts and one with operational and customer service oversight. (Exhibit 4 shows the income statement for HHW.)

3 For the purpose of consistency in calculation among class members, assume an occupancy of 70 percent. The information in this paragraph has been masked. No data of this kind are publicly available, and these data are not to be interpreted as indicative of information private to either HHC or HIC.

Exhibit 4: Hilton HHonors Worldwide: 1998 Income Statement.

(While these data are broadly reflective of the economic situation, certain competitively sensitive information has been masked.)		
	$ (Thousands)	
Revenues		
Contributions from hotels		
Domestic	$39,755	
International	$10,100	
Strategic partner contributions	$18,841	
Membership fees[a]	$1,141	
Total		**$69,837**
Expenses		
Redemptions		
Cash payments to hotels	$12,654	
Deferred liability[b]	$9,436	
Airline miles purchases	$17,851	
Member acquisition expenses	$7,273	
Member communication expenses	$4,236	
Program administration expenses	$17,988	
Total		**$69,438**
Net Income		**$399**

a From members of the Hilton Senior HHonors program only. The Senior HHonors program invited people over 60 to receive discounted stays in exchange for a membership fee. Regular HHonors members do not pay a membership fee.

b More points were issued than redeemed. From the outstanding balance, a deferred liability was charged to HHW's income statement, based on estimating the proportion of points that would ultimately be redeemed.

Source: Company records (masked). For purposes of consistency in calculation among class members, assume an average nightly revenue of $158 per room. Assume that airline miles are purchased from the airline by Hilton at 1 cent per mile.

Membership in the Hilton HHonors program was open to anyone who applied, at no charge. Members earned points toward their Hilton HHonors account whenever they stayed at HHC or HIC hotels. When Hilton HHonors members accumulated enough points in the program, they could redeem them for stays at HHonors hotels, use them to buy products and services from partner companies, or convert them to miles in airline frequent-flyer programs. (Exhibit 5 shows how points in the program flowed among participants in the program, as detailed in the text that follows.)

Exhibit 5: How the Hilton HHonors Program Works.

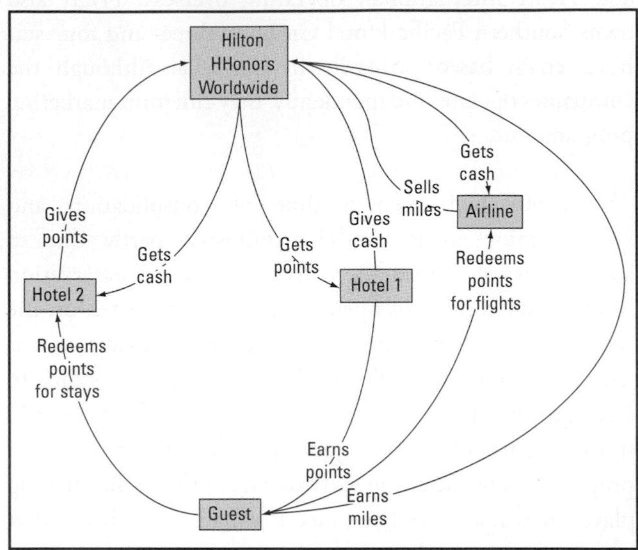

Source: Company.

There were four tiers of membership—Blue, Silver, Gold, and Diamond. The program worked as follows at the Blue level in 1998.

- When a member stayed at a Hilton hotel and paid a so-called business rate,[4] the hotel typically paid HHW 4.5 cents per dollar of the guest's folio (folio is the total charge by the guest before taxes). HHW credited the guest's Hilton HHonors account with 10 points per eligible dollar of folio.
- Hilton guests could earn mileage in partner airline frequent-flyer programs for the same stay that earned them HHonors points, a practice known as Double Dipping. (Hilton was the only hotel chain to offer double dipping; other chains with frequency programs required guests to choose between points in the hotel program or miles in the airline program.) If the member chose to double dip, HHW bought miles from the relevant airline and credited the guest's airline frequent-flyer account at 500 miles per stay.

4 Hilton distinguished three kinds of rates. "Business rates" were higher than "leisure rates," which in turn were higher than "ineligible rates," which referred to group tour wholesale rates, airline crew rates, and other deeply discounted rates.

- If the guest used points to pay for a stay, HHW reimbursed the hosting hotel at more than the costs incremental to the cost of leaving the room empty but less than the revenue from a paying guest. The points needed to earn a stay depended on the class of hotel and fell when occupancy was low. As illustration, redemption rates ranged from 5,000 points to get 50 percent off the $128 cost of a weekend at the Hilton Albuquerque, to 25,000 points for a free weekend night at the $239 per night Hilton Boston Back Bay. A number of exotic rewards were offered, such as a two-person, seven-night diving adventure in the Red Sea for 350,000 points, including hotel and airfare.
- Members earned points by renting a car, flying with a partner airline, using the Hilton Credit Card from American Express, or buying products promoted in mailings by partners such as FTD Florists and Mrs. Field's Cookies. Members could buy points at $10 per thousand for up to 20% of the points needed for a reward.
- Members had other benefits besides free stays. They had a priority-reservation telephone number. Check-in went faster because information on preferences was on file. Members were favored over nonmembers when they asked for late checkout. If members were dissatisfied, they were guaranteed a room upgrade certificate in exchange for a letter explaining their dissatisfaction. Points could be exchanged for airline miles and vice versa and to buy partner products such as airline tickets, flowers, Mrs. Field's Cookies products, Cannondale bicycles, AAA membership, Princess Cruises trips, and car rentals.

Members were awarded Silver VIP status if they stayed at HHonors hotels four times in a year. They earned a 15 percent bonus on base points, received a 5,000-point bonus after seven stays in a quarter, and received a 10,000-point discount when they claimed a reward costing 100,000 points. They were given a certificate for an upgrade to the best room in the hotel after every fifth stay.

Members were awarded Gold VIP status if they stayed at HHonors hotels 16 times or for 36 nights in a year. They earned a 25 percent bonus on base points, received a 5,000-point bonus after seven stays in a quarter, and received a 20,000-point discount when they claimed a reward costing 100,000 points. They were given a certificate for an upgrade to the best room in the hotel after every fifth stay and were upgraded to best available room at time of check-in.

The top 1 percent of members were given Diamond VIP status. This level was not mentioned in promotional material, and no benefits were promised. Diskin explained, "Our goal at the time was to underpromise and overdeliver. If you stay a lot, we say thank you, and as a reward we want to give you Diamond VIP status. We get a lot more bang, more affinity, and more vesting from the customer if we do something unexpected. As an industry, we should never overpromise. It leads the public to decide that this is all smoke and mirrors, and it makes it harder for us to deliver genuine value." Table B shows HHW's member activity in 1998.

A further 712,000 stays averaging 2.4 nights were recorded in 1998 for which no Hilton HHonors membership card was presented but instead airline miles were claimed and airline membership numbers were captured so that the guest could be given a unique identifier in the Hilton database. Spendings on these stays totaled $327 million.

Guests identified by their HHonors or airline membership numbers occupied 22.5 percent of all the rooms occupied in the Hilton Hotels and Hilton International network in a year. They were a much smaller proportion of all the guests who stayed with Hilton in a year because they tended to be frequent travelers. Hilton's research found that Hilton HHonors members spent about $4.6 billion on accommodation per year, not all of which was with Hilton. The industry estimated that members of the frequent-stayer programs of all the major hotel chains represented a market worth $11.1 billion and that the average member belonged to 3.5 programs.

Rationales for the Program

1. Revenue and Yield Management

Hotel profitability was acutely sensitive to revenue. A trend in the industry was to appoint a "revenue manager" to each property to oversee the day-to-day decisions that affected hotel revenue. Yield management models were probabilistic algorithms that helped this manager set a reservations policy. He or she used past history and other statistical data to make continuously updated recommendations regarding hotel booking patterns and what price to offer a particular guest. Simulation studies had shown that, when booking was guided by a good-yield management model, a company's revenue increased by 20 percent over a simple "first come, first served, fixed price" policy.

Table B: Members' Paid Activity in 1998

	Members (000)	Members Active in 1998 (000)	Stays for Which Members Paid (000)	Nights for Which They Paid (000)	Spending on Which They Earned Points ($000)	Stays per Active Member in 1998	Nights per Active Member in 1998	Reward Claimed by Members
Diamond	24	20	310	521	$62,000	15.5	26.1	27,000
Gold	220	84	1,110	1,916	$266,000	13.2	22.8	34,200
Silver	694	324	1,023	1,999	$341,000	3.2	6.2	70,200
Blue	1,712	992	1,121	2,579	$439,000	1.1	2.6	48,600
Total	2,650	1,420	3,564	7,015	$1,108,000	2.5	4.9	180,000

Source: Company records (certain competitively sensitive information has been masked).

In the hotel industry, effectively managing yield means utilizing a model to predict that a room is highly likely to come available due to cancellation or no-show, as well as driving business to higher-paying or longer-staying guests. Variable pricing means that the rate charged for a room depends not only on its size and fittings but also on the day of booking, the day of occupation, the length of stay, and customer characteristics. Of these factors, customer characteristics are the most problematic.

Customer characteristics were needed by the model to estimate "walking cost," the cost of turning a customer away. That cost, in turn, depended on the customer 's future lifetime value to the chain, a function of their willingness to pay, and past loyalty to the chain. These were considered "soft" variables, notoriously difficult to estimate. The better the historical information on a customer, however, the better the estimate. As Adam Burke, HHonors' senior director of marketing for North America, put it, "Who gets the room—the person paying $20 more that you may never see again, or the guy spending thousands of dollars in the system? If we have the right data, the model can be smart enough to know the difference." Some in the hotel industry argued that a benefit of a frequent-guest program was to let the reservations system make those distinctions.

2. Collaborating with Partners

HHW partnered with 25 airlines, three car rental firms, and a number of other firms. Burke explained, "Why is Mrs. Field's Cookies in the program? We have several objectives—regional relevance to consumers, access to partners' customers, making it easier for members to attain rewards. A franchisee may say, 'Why are we doing something with FTD Florists?' We point out that their investment keeps costs down and gives a broader range of rewards to our members."

Burke explained why Hilton offered double dipping: "We have 2.5 million members. The airline frequent-flyer programs have 20, 30, 40 million members who aren't HHonors members and do travel a lot. Airlines don't mind us talking to their members because—through double dipping—we don't compete with their programs. In fact, we complement them by allowing our joint customers to earn both currencies."

3. Working with Franchisees

The Hilton HHonors program was a strong factor in persuading hotel owners to become Hilton franchisees or give Hilton a management contract to run their property. Franchisees tended to be smaller hotels, more dependent on "road warrior" business than many of Hilton's convention hotels, resort hotels, and flagship properties. They saw value in a frequent-guest program to attract business, and HHW's program cost was comparable with or lower than its competitors'. The program's ability to drive business, however, remained its biggest selling point. Diskin elaborated, "Seven or eight years ago, some operators were concerned about the cost of the program. We took a bunch of the most vocal, critical guys and we put them in a room for two days with us to discuss the importance of building long-term customer loyalty, and they came out saying, 'We need to spend more money on the program!'"

4. Relations with Guests

The program let the most valuable guests be recognized on-property. Diskin explained:

> In a sense, the loyalty program is a safe haven for the guest. If there is a problem and it is not taken care of at the property level, the guest can contact our customer service team. It's a mechanism to make sure we hear about those problems. We also do outbound after-visit calling, and we call HHonors members because they're the best database and the most critical guests we have. They have the most experience and the highest expectations. We do feedback groups with members in addition to focus groups and quantitative research. We invite a bunch of members in the hotel down for dinner, and we say we want to talk about a subject. I get calls from people that are lifelong loyalists, not because of any changes we've made, but because once we invited them and asked them their opinion. People care about organizations that care about them.

Hilton customized guests' hotel experience. Diskin explained, "We build guest profiles that keep track of preferences, enabling the hotel to provide customized services. For instance, consider the guest that always wants a room that is for nonsmokers and has a double bed. This information can be stored as part of the member 's record so that when she or he makes a reservation, the guest will receive this type of room without having to ask, no matter where the guest is staying."

HHW used direct mail to cultivate the relationship between members and the Hilton brand. Diskin explained, "Certainly you want to focus much of your effort on your highest-revenue guests, but there are also opportunities to reach out and try to target other customer segments. For example, we worked with a nontravel partner to overlay data from their customer files onto our total membership base and identified segments that might like vacation ownership, others who would be great for the casinos, and some that might like the business and teleconferencing services we offer."

Diskin was concerned that some travelers spread their hotel patronage among several chains and did not receive the service to which their total expenditure entitled them. He noted, "Our research suggests that a quarter of the frequent travelers are members of loyalty programs but don't have true loyalty to any one brand. They never get to enjoy the benefits of elite-program status because they don't consolidate their business with one chain. They typically don't see the value in any of the loyalty schemes because they haven't changed their stay behavior to see the benefits."

5. Helping Travel Managers Gain Compliance

A significant proportion of Hilton's business came from contracts with large corporate clients. Hilton offered discounted rates if the corporation delivered enough stays. Burke explained:

> If you are a corporate travel manager, you want employees to comply with the corporate travel policy. You negotiated a rate by promising a volume of stays. While some travel managers can tell employees that they have to follow the company policy if they want to get reimbursed, many others can only recommend. What if someone is a very loyal Marriott customer, yet Marriott is not one of that company's preferred vendors? A travel office is going to have a real hard time getting that guy to stay at Hilton if they can't mandate it.

We respond with a roster of offerings to give that Marriott traveler a personal incentive to use us, the preferred vendor. Our overall objective is to use the program as a tool that can help the travel manager with compliance to their overall travel policy.

Member Attitudes

HHW made extensive use of conjoint analysis to measure what members wanted from the Hilton HHonors program. Burke explained:

> Members come in for an hour-and-a-half interview. They're asked to trade off program elements, including services and amenities in the hotel, based on the value they place on those attributes relative to their cost. The results help us determine the appropriate priorities for modifying the program. We find that different people have different needs. Some people are service oriented. No amount of miles or points is ever going to replace a warm welcome and being recognized by the hotel as a loyal customer. Other people are games players. They go after free stays, and they know the rules as well as we do. We've been in feedback groups where these people will educate us on how our program works! And, of course, many people are a combination of both.

Using a sample that was broadly representative of the program's upper-tier membership categories, program research found that Hilton HHonors members had an average of over 30 stays in all hotel chains per year, staying 4.2 nights per stay. Between 1997 and 1998, Hilton experienced a 17.5 percent increase in member utilization of HHonors hotels globally. Despite this improvement, more than half of HHonors member stays went to competing chains annually—this was primarily attributable to Hilton's relatively limited network size and distribution. The conjoint analysis suggested that roughly one in five HHonors member stays was solely attributable to their membership in the program—making these stays purely incremental.

The study found that the most important features of a hotel program were room upgrades and airline miles, followed by free hotel stays and a variety of on-property benefits and services. Members wanted a streamlined reward-redemption process and points that did not expire. These findings led to refinements in the terms of membership for 1999, but Diskin was exploring more innovative approaches to the rewards program.

Diskin recognized that, in their market research studies, consumers tended to describe an ideal program that was simply a version of the programs with which they were familiar. He was looking for more radical innovation:

> Hilton and Marriott tend to attract "games players." We want not only to compete effectively on the reward elements but also to introduce them to the more high-touch, high-feel kind of guest experience. The customer base that we have accumulated comprises games players primarily. So we've got to deliver that benefit but still go further.
>
> We've been on a mission to dramatically improve the stay experience for members of the upper-tier ranks of the program. That is the key to competitive distinctiveness. That's not something that anybody can imitate. We want our best customers to feel that when they go to Hilton, they know Hilton knows they're the best customer and they're treated special. We want them to think, "I'm going to have the kind of room I want, I'm going to have the kind of stay I like, and if I have a problem, they're going to take care of it." We want the staff to know who's coming in each day and make sure that these guests get a personal welcome. Our new customer reservation system will get more information down to the hotel. We'll know a lot more about our incoming guests. We will have a guest manager in the hotel whose job it is to make you feel special and to address any concerns you may have.

THE STARWOOD ANNOUNCEMENT

The Wall Street Journal of February 2, 1999, announced the birth of the Starwood Preferred Guest Program, covering Westin Hotels Resorts, Sheraton Hotels Resorts, The Luxury Collection, Four Points, Caesar's, and Starwood's new W brand hotels, representing more than 550 participating properties worldwide. It became clear that Starwood was adding program features that might be expensive to match. Four features in particular were of concern.

No blackout dates

All frequent guest and airline programs until now had ruled that members could not claim free travel during the very height of seasonal demand and when local events guaranteed a hotel full occupancy. Starwood was saying that, if there was a room to rent, points were as good as money.

No capacity control

Programs until now had let hotel properties limit the number of rooms for free stays. Starwood was telling hotels that all unreserved rooms should be available to guests paying with points.

Paperless rewards

Guests had had previously to exchange points for a certificate and then use the certificate to pay for an authorized stay. Under Starwood's system, individual properties would be able to accept points to pay for a stay.

Hotel reimbursement

Now that blackout dates were abolished, a property, particularly an attractive vacation destination, might have to contend with many more points-paying guests than before. Starwood therefore raised the rate at which it reimbursed hotels for these stays. To meet the cost, it charged participating hotels 20 percent to 100 percent more than its competitors on paid stays.

Starwood was pledging to invest $50 million in advertising to publicize the program—significantly more than HHW had historically spent on program communications. (Exhibit 6 compares the loyalty programs of the four major business-class hotel chains after the Starwood announcement.)

DISKIN'S DILEMMA

Without any doubt, Starwood had raised the ante in the competition for customer loyalty. Diskin had to decide whether to match or pass. He mused:

> Do we have to compete point for point? Or do we want to take a different positioning and hold on to our loyal members and differentiate HHonors from Starwood and other competitors? We're in a cycle where, for 10 years, the cost to our hotels of our frequent-guest program as a percent of the folio has been cycling down. Yet activation, retention, and member spend per visit all have improved. If we can deliver the same amount of business to the Hilton brand and it costs less, Hilton makes more margin. That attracts investors, franchise ownership, new builders. That's another reason why they buy the Hilton flag.

As Diskin saw it, Starwood's Preferred Guest announcement was a solution to a problem Hilton did not have, arising from its recent purchases of the Sheraton and Westin chains:

> They are trying to develop the Starwood brand with the Starwood Preferred Guest Program. They are targeting the most lucrative part of the business, the individual business traveler, where Sheraton and Westin independently have never been as effective as Marriott, Hyatt, and Hilton. Sheraton's frequent-guest program wasn't very effective. They changed it every few years; they used to have members pay for it. Westin never had enough critical mass of properties for it to be important for enough people.

Exhibit 6: Membership offerings of the four major business-class hotel chains in 1998.

Chain	Membership Restrictions*	Point Value	Eligible Charges	New Member Bonus	Airline Mileage Accrual
Starwood	One stay per year to remain active—basic; 10 stays or 25 room nights per year—medium; 25 stays or 50 room nights	2 Starpoints = $1 basic; 3 Starpoints = $1 medium or premium	Room rate, F&B, laundry/valet, phone, in-room movies	Periodically	Starpoints earned can be converted to miles 1:1; cannot earn both points and miles for the same stay
Hilton	One stay per year to remain active—Blue; 4 stays per year or 10 nights—medium; 16 stays per year or 36 nights—premium; 28 stays or 60 nights—top	10 pts. = $1—Blue; +15% bonus on points earned—medium; +25% bonus on point earned—premium; +50% bonus on points earned—top	Room rate, F&B, laundry, phone	Periodically	500 miles per qualifying stay in addition to point earnings
Hyatt	One stay per year to remain active—basic; 5 stays or 15 nights per year—medium; 25 stays or 50 nights per year—premium	5 pts. = $1; +15% bonus on points earned—medium; +30% bonus on points earned—premium	Room rate, F&B, laundry, phone	Periodically	500 miles per stay; not available if earning points
Marriott	No requirements for basic; 15 nights per year—medium; 50 nights per year—premium	10 pts. = $1; +20% bonus on points earned—medium; +25% bonus on points earned—premium	Room rate, F&B, laundry, phone	Double points for the first 120 days	3 miles per dollar spent at full-service hotels; 1 mile per dollar spent at other hotels; not available if earning points

* Most programs run three tiers. For ease of comparison, the three levels are named basic, medium, and premium. HHonors has four tiers.

Exhibit 6: *(Continued)*

Chain	Affinity Credit Card Point Accrual	Point Purchase	Bonus Threshold Rewards	Exchange Hotel Points for Airline Miles	Hotel Rewards
Starwood	1,000 hotel pts. first card use; 1 hotel pt. = $1 spent; 4 hotel points = $1 spent at Starwood hotels	NA	NA	1:1 conversion except JAL, KLM, Ansett, Qantas, Air New Zealand; 5,000 bonus miles when you convert 20,000 hotel points; minimum 2,000 Starpoints—basic; minimum 15,000—medium; no minimum for premium	5 categories; 1 free night category 1 is 3,000 Starpoints; 1 free night category 5 is 12,000 Starpoints
Hilton	5,000 hotel pts. for application; 2,500 hotel points first card use; 2 hotel pts. = $1 spent; 3 hotel pts. = $1 spent at HHonors Hotels	$10 = 1,000 pts. up to 20% of the total points of the reward	2,000 pts. = 4 stays per quarter	10,000 pts. = 1,500 miles; 20,000 pts. = 3,500 miles; 50,000 pts. = 10,000 miles; minimum 10,000 hotel points exchange, can also exchange airline miles for hotel points	5 categories: free weekend night 10,000 lowest; 35,000 highest
Hyatt	None	$10 = 500 pts. up to 10% of the total points of the reward	None basic	3 pts. = 1 mile; minimum 9,000 points exchange	Weekend night no category: 8,000 pts.; if premium time, there is an additional 5,000 pts.; come with partner awards
Marriott	5,000 hotel pts. first card use; 1 hotel pt. = $1 spent; 3 hotel points = $1 spent at Marriott Rewards hotels	$10 =1,000 pts. up to 10% of the total points of the reward	None basic	10,000 pts. = 2,000 miles; 20,000 pts. = 5,000 miles; 30,000 pts. = 10,000 miles; minimum = 10,000 hotel points exchange	2 categories: 20,000 free weekend low category, and 30,000 high category

Source: Assembled by the case writers from the promotional materials of each hotel chain in 1999.

> So now, together, they can address Westin's critical-mass problem and Sheraton's relevance.

But if frequent-guest programs were a good idea, perhaps bigger programs were an even better idea. Diskin reflected: "Hotel properties routinely pay 10 percent commission to a travel agent to bring them a guest. Yet they continually scrutinize the cost of these programs. Of course, they're justified in doing so, but the return on investment clearly justifies the expenditure. And our competitors certainly seem to see a value in increasing their investment in their programs."

Diskin tried to predict Hyatt's and Marriott's response to the Starwood announcement. The industry was quite competitive enough. He thought back to his early years at United Airlines and recalled the damage that price wars had done to that industry.

STUDY QUESTIONS

1. What are the strengths and weaknesses of the Hilton HHonors program from the standpoints of:
   a. Hilton Hotels Corp. and Hilton International?
   b. member properties (franchised hotels)?
   c. guests?
   d. corporate travel departments?
2. How does the value generated to Hilton by the program compare to its cost?
3. What is Starwood attempting to do and how should Jeff Diskin respond?

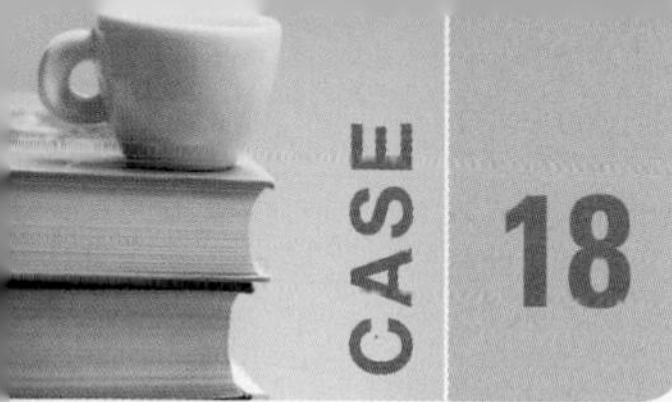

CASE 18

The Royal Dining Membership Program Dilemma

Sheryl E. Kimes, Rohit Verma, Christopher W. Hart, and Jochen Wirtz

The Royal Dining membership program is highly popular with diners and generates significant revenues. However, it might be displacing regular, full-price paying customers and could have a negative effect on the painstakingly built and maintained high-end luxury image of the Hong Kong Grand Hotel. In addition, quite a few managers and waiting staff have expressed unhappiness with the program, the conflicts it creates with diners, and the type of customers it attracts.

Erica Liu, Program Manager for the Royal Dining (RD) Membership Program at the Hong Kong Grand Hotel, hung up the phone after a call from a disgruntled customer. Just then, Jerome Tan, VP of Hotel Operations, walked into her office. "I tell you, Jerome," sighed Erica. "I've been getting calls from customers complaining about all the rules we have for the RD program. It's driving me nuts." "Tell me about it," Jerome replied. "These RD members really annoy our staff. All they're looking for is free stuff. I heard the ultimate one yesterday. Some guy walked into the Cantonese Café with 10 little kids and wanted them all to eat for free! Yes, we have a rule that kids under five can eat for free, but not the whole city! It turned out it was his son's birthday party. Can you believe that?" Erica sighed again. "I guess that means we're going to have to create another rule for members to complain about. I mean, I think it's a great program, and all and it definitely brings in a lot of business, but how are we going to deal with all these problems?"

THE HONG KONG GRAND LAUNCHES A DINING MEMBERSHIP PROGRAM

The Hong Kong Grand, a 140-room landmark hotel on Hong Kong Island, opened in the late 1800s and is considered a national monument. It is one of the world's well-known grand hotels and has received numerous awards including Best Luxury Hotel and Best Hotel in Asia. Its guest list has included such luminaries as Queen Elizabeth II, Bill Gates, and James Michener, and it is one of the most photographed sites in Hong Kong. The hotel has four restaurants, ranging from the 56-seat Hollywood Road Deli to the fine-dining 112-seat Kabuki. All the restaurants take reservations and are open for lunch and dinner. The adjoining convention center, the second-largest meeting space in Hong Kong, provides an ideal setting for upscale conferences, and the

Exhibit 1: The Hong Kong Grand's restaurants.

Restaurant Name	Cuisine	Restaurant Type	Average Check (HK$)	Number of Seats	A la Carte or Buffet	Average Lunch Duration (hours)	Average Dinner Duration (hours)	Hours of Operation for each Meal
Cantonese Café	Local/Buffet	Local/Buffet	$76	106	Both	1.0	1.0	5
Kabuki	Japanese	Fine Dining	$250	112	a la carte	1.0	1.5	5
Hollywood Road Deli	American Style	Casual	$104	56	a la carte	0.5	0.5	5
Dragon Boat	International	Smart casual	$109	72	Both	1.0	1.0	5

 Sheryl E. Kimes, and Rohit Verma are with the Cornell University School of Hotel Administration. Christopher Hart is formerly with Harvard Business School and the Cornell University School of Hotel Administration, and Jochen Wirtz is with the National University of Singapore.

The names of the hotel, restaurants, and membership program have been disguised.

adjoining shopping mall offers a multitude of shopping and dining options. For more information on Hong Kong Grand restaurants, see Exhibit 1.

The ownership of the Hong Kong Grand changed recently. Previously, the company that owned the shopping center had also owned the hotel and had restricted the number of restaurants that operated in the mall. Once they sold the hotel, that restriction was lifted and the hotel restaurants had to contend with much more vigorous competition and its restaurants were often empty. As a response, the Hong Kong Grand launched the Royal Dining (RD) membership program.

The RD program was designed to encourage Hong Kong residents to dine in the restaurants at a discounted rate. With a food cost as a percentage of sales that averaged 32 percent of gross revenue, even a 50 percent discount yielded a reasonable gross margin. In addition, the RD program required the purchase of annual memberships, which provided a substantial revenue stream with practically no variable cost.

THE ROYAL DINING MEMBERSHIP PROGRAM

The RD membership program offered members the opportunity to receive discounted meals and rooms at the restaurants and bars located in the Hong Kong Grand. The program was an immediate hit. Within the first year, over 1,000 memberships were sold. Local residents welcomed the opportunity to dine at the four hotel restaurants at major discounts. The hotel's restaurant revenue increased sharply from the added sales. By 2012, the program had a total of 4,200 members.

The RD membership card gave customers a 50% discount when two adults dined at one table and ordered at least one dish per person (starter, main course, or set menu). Typically, members dined for free; their dining companions paid for the meal. If members dined alone, they received only a 10% discount. The discount was calculated on the total food bill and did not include beverages, taxes, or service charges. It also was not available for take-away orders or private dining events. Children dining with members also received the discount. Children under five ate for free in the buffet restaurant. In addition, special children's menus were available in the a la carte restaurants. See Exhibit 2 for the complete program rules.

Exhibit 2: Royal Dining Membership Rules.

Royal Dining annual membership fee: HK$1,588 (ca. US$210)

PRICE REDUCTION SCHEDULE:	
Member plus 1 guest (2 adults)	50%*
Member plus 2 guests (3 adults)	33%
Member plus 3 guests (4 adults)	25%
Member plus 4 guests or more (up to a total of 10 adults)	20%
Member dining alone	10%

* 50% discount is applicable only when there are two adult dining parties at a table and when a minimum of two food items are ordered (e.g., one set menu and one starter, or one main course and one starter). Two dining parties may not necessarily order a main course but at least two starter orders are required. In the event that only one food item is ordered for sharing and there are two parties dining, a 10% discount is applicable instead of the 50% discount. Members and their guests have to order a dish per person in order to enjoy the varying discounts. Side dishes are excluded from this discount benefit.

Conditions:

- The price-reduction structure is calculated on the total food bill only, excluding beverages, government taxes, and service charge. Reduction does not apply to private dining and take-away.
- One card per table, per party, per occasion. Not valid with any other discounts or promotions.
- A 10% reduction will also be applied to bar snacks, where applicable.

OTHER BENEFITS

- A flat 20% discount will be given to members during Chinese New Year blackout dates when dining with a minimum of five or more people at one table at all restaurants except Kabuki.
- 1 Special Occasion voucher for 50% discount on total food bill in any one of the hotel's restaurants, when dining in a party of 6–12 people. Not available during Chinese New Year period—the eve to the 15th day of Chinese New Year.
- Discounted room rates at the Hong Kong Grand (subject to availability).
- Birthday and wedding vouchers, and discounts at several stores in the hotel.

The card came with other benefits, including discounted room rates at the Hong Kong Grand (subject to availability), birthday and wedding vouchers, and discounts at several stores. Members could not use the card on Valentine's Day, Mother's Day, Christmas Eve, Christmas Day, and the first few days of the Chinese New Year. Although RD program

Exhibit 3: Royal Dining membership.

Membership Type	Number of Members	% Active Cards	Average Visits p.a.	Average Party Size	Average % Discount
RD—Traditional	78	71%	6.7	2.4	35
RD—Epicure	641	76%	6.5	2.7	38
Credit Card—Traditional	3,214	28%	3.5	2.5	35
Credit Card—Epicure	310	20%	2.5	2.6	32
Totals	**4,243**	**49%**	**4.8**	**2.5**	**35**

rules stated that restaurants could restrict seating availability during busy periods, this was rarely done.

Types of Memberships

Two types of memberships were available: Royal Dining Traditional (HK$1,588 per year) and Royal Dining Epicure (HK$2,588 per year). The majority of members opted for the Epicure membership because it included a free room night at the hotel.

In addition, RD cards were given for free to all premium members of a well-known credit card company. The credit card company paid the Hong Kong Grand a discounted rate (HK$275 per year) for each member in the Traditional program and HK$400 per year for Epicure memberships, which were given only to their most valued customers. Both the Hong Kong Grand and the credit card company saw a mutually beneficial partnership evolving from the alliance of the two highly regarded brands. About 85% of all members were premium customers of the credit card company and thus did not pay for their RD cards. Of the credit card members, 3,214 were Traditional members; and 310 were Epicure members (see Exhibit 3).

Not surprisingly, the purchased RD cards had a higher likelihood of being used—about 75 percent—and were used more frequently—about once every month and a half—than those given to credit card holders. The 25 percent of credit card members who used their memberships used it an average of once every four months. The average party size was comparable (about 2.5 customers); as was the average net revenue—HK$225—except for the credit card Epicure members, whose average revenue was HK$325. The average discount for all RD transactions was 35 percent (see Exhibit 3).[1]

The percentage of restaurant revenue derived from the RD program ranged from under 3 percent at the Hollywood Road Deli to over 60 percent at Kabuki. (See Exhibit 4.)

Competing Programs

Food and dining out were important parts of Hong Kong's national identity. Along with shopping, eating out was often seen as a national pastime. Indeed, Hong Kong has frequently been referred to as a "gourmet paradise" and "the World's Fair of food."[2] In response to RD, several other hotels had developed dining programs in an attempt

Exhibit 4: Royal Dining program share of restaurant revenue.

Restaurant	Last Financial Year Revenue (Million HK$)	% of Revenue from:	
		RD Members	Credit Card Members
Hollywood Road Deli	23.3	3.4	2.4
Dragon Boat	20.1	4.0	5.9
Kabuki	53.5	42.8	19.6
Cantonese Café	15.4	1.3	1.4

1 For a list of commonly used restaurant terminology, see Appendix A.

2 http://en.wikipedia.org/wiki/Hong Kong cuisine.

to emulate the Hong Kong Grand and tie into the local passion for eating out.

THE PROGRAM DILEMMA

After finishing a meeting, Susan Li, VP of Finance, decided to stop by Erica Liu's office to say hello. Jerome Tan was there and the two were in a heated conversation that abruptly stopped when she knocked. "Let me guess. The two of you are arguing about the RD program again!" Their looks confirmed her suspicion. "I don't see why you have so many problems with it. It's produced a lot of incremental revenue that has boosted our bottom line." (See Exhibits 5 to 7.)

"But, Susan," Jerome exclaimed, "the RD members are displacing lots of our regular customers, especially during busy periods, and we're practically giving meals away. I feel that we should develop other programs to fill the restaurants and increase revenue—without all these cheapskates." Erica jumped in. "Jerome, I keep telling you this, but you're forgetting about all the money these people spend to become members. That is pure profit—hardly any cost involved. And the members deserve to get value for their money—or they won't renew their annual memberships. What do we give them, though? More rules that make them feel like anything *but* members. I tell you, I can understand why they complain."

"Erica, you just don't know what it's like to be working in the restaurants," Jerome replied. "These RD members are so pushy and always ask for more, more, more—and they try to game the system. For example, remember that rule about how only one discount card per table can be presented, even if there are two parties and each of them is a member? Well, since we have so many members, it's pretty common for several people at the table to have membership cards. And,

Exhibit 5: Table configuration of Hong Kong Grand restaurants.

Table Size	Cantonese Café	Kabuki	Hollywood Road Deli	Dragon Boat
	Tables			
2	5	2	16	8
4	20	15	3	12
5	0	0	0	0
6	0	0	2	0
8	2	2	0	1
10	0	0	0	0
Bar		10		
Tempura		Table for 10		
Teppanyaki		Table for 12		

Exhibit 6: Number of customers for each restaurant by meal period and day of week.

	Cantonese Café	Kabuki	Hollywood Road Deli	Dragon Boat
	Average Number of Lunch Customers			
Monday	195	298	250	203
Tuesday	190	336	291	228
Wednesday	228	327	333	254
Thursday	228	344	333	269
Friday	244	370	375	277
Saturday	325	242	375	306
Sunday	244	225	354	337
	Average Number of Dinner Customers			
Monday	325	190	260	170
Tuesday	358	249	286	198
Wednesday	293	257	286	161
Thursday	341	272	286	246
Friday	317	372	312	359
Saturday	317	327	312	320
Sunday	325	301	234	218

Exhibit 7: Average revenue for each restaurant by meal period and day of week.

	Cantonese Café	Kabuki	Hollywood Road Deli	Dragon Boat
	Average Lunch Revenue			
Monday	$17,937	$39,107	$26,692	$25,563
Tuesday	$17,199	$42,576	$27,485	$30,170
Wednesday	$16,166	$38,231	$30,791	$29,003
Thursday	$16,751	$44,450	$32,208	$27,484
Friday	$18,052	$46,411	$35,783	$30,596
Saturday	$15,404	$40,234	$38,381	$28,890
Sunday	$19,227	$39,324	$41,110	$27,629
	Average Dinner Revenue			
Monday	$20,754	$100,088	$21,437	$21,581
Tuesday	$25,671	$81,638	$25,738	$22,238
Wednesday	$24,438	$96,045	$20,451	$29,778
Thursday	$25,664	$109,375	$32,395	$28,136
Friday	$31,273	$113,909	$47,283	$31,160
Saturday	$28,678	$126,059	$40,559	$29,790
Sunday	$18,986	$112,027	$28,715	$24,368

then they all want to use their cards so they can save more money. When we tell them that it's against the rules, they say it's unfair because it penalizes people for dining together, that if they had come as couples and sat at separate tables, each table would have received a 50 percent discount. To get around the rule, guess what they're doing?" Pausing for effect, he said, "I'll tell you what they do. They show up separately and then ask to be seated at adjacent tables. Once seated, they push the tables together and try to get double the discount! How do you handle that situation if you're the server? Doesn't exactly fit with the ambience we're trying so hard to create, does it? And it does a number on the servers' attitudes." (See Exhibit 8 for sample comments.)

Exhibit 8: Sample server comments about the Royal Dining program.

- "My RD customers love the program. For many of them, this is the only reason they come out to The Dragon Boat." – *Dragon Boat*
- "I am sick of this program! I hate having to explain the rules to people trying to use multiple cards per table" – *Cantonese Café*
- "While it's sometimes tough to have to explain rules to customers, I have to admit that the program benefits the restaurant and helps make my job more secure and earn more service fees and tips."– *Kabuki*
- "I think it's embarrassing! I'm working at the Hong Kong Grand and I have to deal with tacky discounts?!" – *Kabuki*
- "I'm sure it makes sense to management but dealing with customers who don't understand how the program works is the worst. The rules should be more clear to the customers" – *Hollywood Road Deli*
- "The RD discount ruins the tip. I work for half as much!" – *Dragon Boat*

Jerome was getting visibly upset. The more upset he got, the more flustered Erica became. Her program was adversely affecting people whose attitudes and behavior were vital to creating the dining experience. As Susan tried to calm him down, Carmen Teo, VP of Marketing walked in. "I heard you from my office around the corner! I thought I'd better come down before someone had to call security!" she said with a laugh. Erica quickly said, "What do you think of the RD program, Carmen?" Carmen though for a long moment and then said, "I certainly can see the point of the program, but I just don't know. We spend so much money trying to build and maintain our luxury image—and then we offer a discount program that is very much at odds with it. I know it generates profits that we otherwise would never see, but what are the costs? Our guests pay a lot to be here and expect a wonderful experience. I don't know if we can provide this experience when we have coupon-wavers in there with them."

Jerome chimed in. "Especially when our customers have become so much more creative in getting around the rules." Erica agreed, saying, "Yes, and that's why we have so many rules now—and that's why I get so many calls complaining about them! Again, these people are spending a lot of money for their memberships and we're making it very difficult for them! I can see why they're annoyed."

Carmen said, "The question we need to think about is how to provide good value to our RD members that keeps the revenue flowing, while protecting the hotel from possible abuses of the program and negative impact on the guest experience. The answers are anything but obvious."

Susan jumped in, "Let me give you an alternative view. We have owners who are very much focused on the bottom line. Imagine their reaction if we suddenly dumped the program. I'm thinking that maybe we should extend the discount to beverages since our cost of sales is so much lower. Right now our food cost percentage is 32 percent, but the beverage cost percentage is only 24 percent. I think it would be a strong contributor to financial performance." Jerome groaned. "But, Susan, one of the only things that I can possibly see as a good thing for this program is that while we're basically giving the food away, we at least get a decent profit from the beverages. That would cost us more money!"

Erica checked her watch and noticed that she and Jerome were due at another meeting. "Well, it's nice that we're all in agreement. Anyone want to take over my job?"

Erica shook her head as she walked out the door and thought about the meeting she had with the hotel executive committee in two days. Jerome, Carmen, and Susan all were members, and high on the meeting's agenda was the future of the RD program. She thought to herself, "I need to present a comprehensive analysis of the program's costs and benefits and recommendations about where to go from here. How will I resolve all the differing views?"

"Better get to work," Erica thought, as she reached for a bottle of aspirin.

STUDY QUESTIONS

1. In Erica Liu's shoes, what would you present to the executive committee?
2. As Erica Liu, what analyses would you run to assess the financial performance of the RD membership program?
3. What effect does the RD membership program have on the brand and value perception of its local customers in Hong Kong and its full-paying hotel guests and diners? How could the hotel address these issues?
4. Review the rules set for the RD program. How would you go about setting rules for the program that protect the hotel against abuse, but does not make RD members feel that the program is unnecessarily restrictive and difficult to use?
5. How could negative server attitudes toward RD customers be handled?

APPENDIX A—RESTAURANT TERMINOLOGY

- Cover: A customer
- Average check: The average amount paid per customer
- Party: The number of customers at a particular table
- Total check: The total check amount from a party
- Server: A waiter or waitress
- Seat occupancy: The percentage of seats occupied during a given period.
- Table occupancy: The percentage of tables occupied during a given period.
- Revenue per available seat hour (RevPASH): Total revenue divided by the number of seat-hours available.
- Meal duration: The length of a meal. Varies based on the type of restaurant and the meal period (e.g., lunch, dinner). Dinners average 150 percent the time spent at lunch.
- Meal period: The length of time that the restaurant is open for a given meal. Depending upon the part of the world, most restaurants offer lunch from 11 a.m. to 2:30 or 3 p.m., while dinner is typically offered from 5:30 or 6 p.m. until 10 p.m.
- Restaurant types (in the context of The Hong Kong Grand):
    - Fine dining: Full-service, sit-down restaurant with a comprehensive menu and served in a fairly luxurious setting. High average check per person. The type of restaurant that most people visit a few times per year.
    - Upscale casual: Full-service, sit-down restaurant with a comprehensive menu and served in a casual setting. High average check per person. The type of restaurant that people might visit once a month.
    - Casual: Full-service, sit-down restaurant with a somewhat limited menu and served in a casual setting. Moderate average check per person. The sort of restaurants that people might visit once a month.
    - Fast Casual: Limited-service restaurant with a fairly limited menu. Customers can either take their food with them or eat it in the restaurant. These restaurants are fairly casual with a low to moderate average check. The type of restaurant that most people might visit a few times per month.
    - Quick Service (Fast Food): Limited service restaurant with a limited menu. Customers can either take their food with them or eat it in the restaurant. These restaurants are very casual with a low average check. The type of restaurant that most people might visit on a weekly basis.

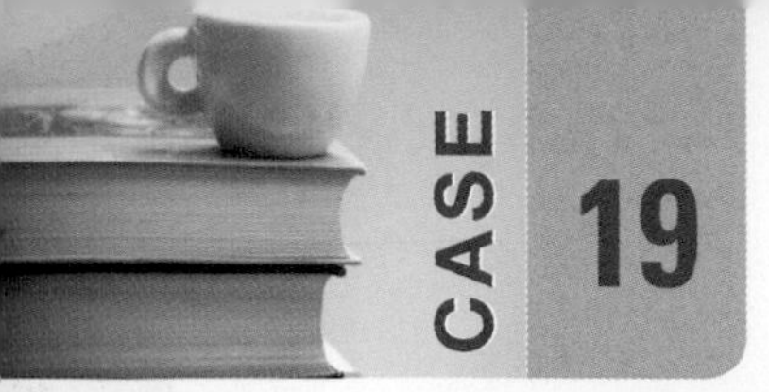

CASE 19

LAURIER
Business & Economics

The Complaint Letter

T. F. Cawsey and Gordon H. G. McDougall

The General Manager of a UK hotel[1] needs to decide how to respond to a complaint letter received from a Canadian visitor. He also needs to decide on what actions to take internally to ensure the problem does not recur, and what implications this might have for the hotel staff.

As Andres Metz, General Manager of the Heathrow ATMI Hotel, finished a second reading of the complaint letter (Exhibit 1), he was very concerned. The series of events described in the letter indicated that the hotel employees had failed to perform the basic services for this guest. There were as well, potential systems problems that needed examination. While Andres knew it was only one letter, it suggested significant issues that needed attention.

The Heathrow ATMI Hotel, a 578-guest-room hotel, targeted business travelers. Extensive renovations had been completed recently, and a marketing campaign announcing the new improvements had been launched. The hotel itself was billed as a "contemporary upscale hotel" offering two restaurants, three lounges or bars and a conference and training center. The hotel staff spoke Afrikaans, Arabic, Chinese, Dutch, English, French, German, Greek, Hindi, Italian, Japanese, Maltese, Portuguese, Punjabi, Russian, Spanish, and Swahili and were well trained to serve the needs of international travelers.

ATMI Hotels was a subsidiary of a global hotel company that owned or leased over 2,500 hotels worldwide. The ATMI Division, headed by Christopher Britton, was operated as an independent business unit. Recently, the operating profit for the unit was up over 50 percent, driven by market share gains in the United Kingdom. ATMI took third place in an industry rating of business hotel chains in the UK.

The strategy of ATMI's parent was to:

- Strengthen our portfolio of strongly differentiated brands through increased room night delivery to franchisees, enhanced hotel management skills and brand innovation.
- Grow our management and franchised fee income by exploiting significant potential in the *upscale* segment worldwide and building large-scale, strong *mid-scale* positions in major world markets.
- Focus the organization by containing or reducing operating costs through simplification, reduction of asset ownership, infrastructure improvements, and investing in the skills of our people.
- Continue to reduce capital by selling the real estate assets of the majority of our hotel portfolio while retaining management or franchise agreements in most cases. Ownership of assets will continue only if assets present strategic brand value for the group.
- Return excess funds to shareholders or reinvest in growth opportunities, while maintaining appropriate efficient debt levels.

As Andres reviewed the letter, he remembered the "hospitality promise"—"If any part of your stay is not satisfactory, we promise to make it right or you won't pay for that part of your stay." He wondered how to respond and what action he should take with hotel staff.

STUDY QUESTIONS

1. What are the issues that Mr. Metz should note and be concerned with?
2. How credible is the evidence provided by the letter? That is, does it form the basis for action or is it part of the background noise of running a complex service operation such as the hotel in this case?
3. What services marketing concepts can help us to understand the situation faced by the Hotel Manager?

1 The hotel name is disguised.

Exhibit 1: The complaint letter.

September 8, 2004

Mr. Christopher Britton
Chief Operating Officer
ATMI Hotels
368 Bridgeport Avenue
Rummidge, England

Dear Sir;

As a customer of yours, I want to provide you with our experiences at ATMI Hotels Heathrow on August 24, of this year. Initially, I had not planned to do anything but since then I have reflected on my experience and finally decided I needed to provide you with feedback - particularly given the "hospitality promise" on your website.

My wife and I arrived at the hotel around 10 p.m. after a flight from Canada and the usual tiring immigration procedures, baggage check, and struggle to find your hotel. Opon arrival, we hoped to check in and proceed to our room quickly as we had been up since 5 a.m. our time.

As I entered the hotel, I was somewhat apprehensive because a busload of tourists had arrived just ahead of us. However, they gathered to one side of the hotel lobby and I was able to line up at one of the three open check-in lines. The initial greeting was courteous and appropriate. We were checked in and the desk person asked if we wanted a room upgrade. After I clarified that this would cost money, I declined the offer.

We then went to our room on the third floor, I believe, and discovered the room was a disaster, totally not made up. I phoned the switchboard and was put through to reception immediately. There were profuse apologies and we were told that someone would be up immediutely with another key.

Within 5 minutes, someone did meet us with a key to a room on the fifth floor, a quick, fast response.

However, when we got to the new room, it was not made up! If anything, it was worse. Frankly, I did not want to touch anything in that room but did go to the phone.

I phoned the switchboard. The operator said, "This shouldn't have happened. I will put you through to the night manager." I said that was not necessary. I just wanted a room.

However, the operator insisted and I was put through to the night manager. Again, there were profuse apologies and the manager said, "This shouldn't have happened. I will fix this and get right back to you." I indicated that I just wanted a room - I didn't want the organization fixed, just a room. The manager repeated, "I will get right back to you."

We waited 5, 10, 15 minutes. Inexplicably, the manager did not return the call even though he said he would.

Finally around 20 minutes later, I phoned switchboard again. I said we were waiting for a room and that the night manager had promised to call me back. The operator said, "This is probably my fault as I was doing work for the assistant manager." I did not and do not understand this part of the conversation but again, I was told that they would call right back. Again, I repeated that "I just need a room."

I waited another 5 minutes - it was now 11 p.m. at night and we were quite tired - there was no return phone call.

My wife and I went down to reception and again lined up. After a brief time, we were motioned forward by the person who initially registered us. I explained that we needed a room. He said "You were taken care of. You got a room." I replied: "No, I did not have a room, I just had two rooms that were not made up and we needed a clean one for the night."

Again there were profuse apologies. The reception person then said "Excuse me, just for a moment so I can fix this." I said "Really, I just would like a room." The person at the reception desk went around the corner and began to yell at someone working there. This went on for a several minutes. He then returned to his station, called me forward again, apologized again and located a third room for us. As well, he gave us coupons for a complimentary breakfast.

The third room was made up. We had hoped for an upgrade but this was clearly not the case. The room looked clean but was "more tired" than the previous rooms. The carpets were a bit worn and the wallpaper was faded. However, it was clean and we were delighted to find a place to sleep.

In the middle of the night, I woke up and went to the washroom. I noticed that the invoice for the room had been delivered to our room. To my absolute shock, a 72 £[2] "room change" charge was added to the price of our room.

I woke early the next morning (because we had to catch an early plane to Paris) to discuss this charge with someone at reception. One person was serving a hotel guest and I waited for a few minutes until the same reception person from the previous night came to the desk. He motioned me forward and then immediately left to open up the five or six other computer stations in the reception area. He had a tendency to not make eye contact. This may have been a cultural phenomenon or it may have been his dismay at having to deal with me again. I cannot say.

I showed him the invoice. He said, "Oh, there will be no charge for that room." I said that I was concerned as the invoice did show the charge. He said, "It is taken care of". I said "Regardless, I would like something to prove that there would not be another charge to my credit card." After one further exchange and insistence on my part, he removed the charge from my invoice.

My wife and I had breakfast and appreciated it being complimentary. We were able to get to the airport in time for our flight.

We thought that you would want to know of our experience. Customer service is a critical part of the hospitality industry and I am certain that ATMI Hotels would wish feedback on experiences such as these.

I look forward to your reply.

Yours truly,

Dr. Mark Hankins
666 Newberry Dr.
Kitchener, Ontario
Canada

cc. General Manager
ATMI Hotel
London Heathrow
22 Uphill Road
Heathrow, England

Guest Relations Department
ATMI Hotels
17 Cedar Road
Birmingham, England

2 £1 = C$2.35006 Canadian dollars.

CASE 20

CASE STUDY

The Broadstripe Service Guarantee

Jochen Wirtz and Sven Tuzovic

Cable companies traditionally focused on discounts for bundles of TV, Internet, and phone plans to win new customers instead of delivering great customer service. Broadstripe, a small cable company, launched a service guarantee with the aim of becoming the best-in-class service provider. Twenty months after the launch, Broadstripe's management was reviewing the performance of the guarantee and had to decide what changes should be made, if any.

Broadstripe, a small provider of cable, Internet, and phone services in four States (Michigan, Oregon, Maryland, and Washington) faced a difficult situation. Tony Lent, Chief Commercial Officer at Broadstripe, was convinced that the company had to dramatically improve its customer service.

However, how does a small cable company differentiate itself from better-known industry giants and establish a best-in-class customer experience? Should a company at the edge of bankruptcy invest in customer service altogether?

THE CABLE INDUSTRY

Traditionally, cable companies tried to appeal to customers with discounts for bundles of TV, Internet, and phone plans. Customer service, however, had mostly been disregarded. As a consequence, customer satisfaction ratings in the cable industry had been the lowest of any industry. Results of the American Customer Satisfaction Index (ACSI) showed that the largest providers (Comcast, Timer Warner Cable, and Charter Communications) only had an ACSI score average of 59 on a scale from 1 to 100 over the past seven years, compared to an average of 82 for Internet retailers, 75 for banks, and 65 for airlines. Importantly, the cable industry was also lagging behind their satellite TV or telecommunication competitors with DIRECT TV and DISH Network scoring an average of 68.

As competition from satellite TV and phone companies intensified, an increasing number of consumers disconnected their subscription TV services in favor of online video services such as Netflix and Hulu. Responding to these competitive pressures, cable companies turned to customer service to try and improve their negative reputation. Several cable companies began to develop customer-oriented policies. For example, Time Warner Cable offered an on-time guarantee that promised that a service representative showed up on time for installations and service appointments. The company claimed that it was the first company in the industry to introduce the on-time guarantee. Comcast, the nation's largest cable TV provider, had begun to offer a 30-day money-back guarantee and a $20 credit if a technician was late.

Exhibit 1: Broadstripe's logo displayed at its headquarters.

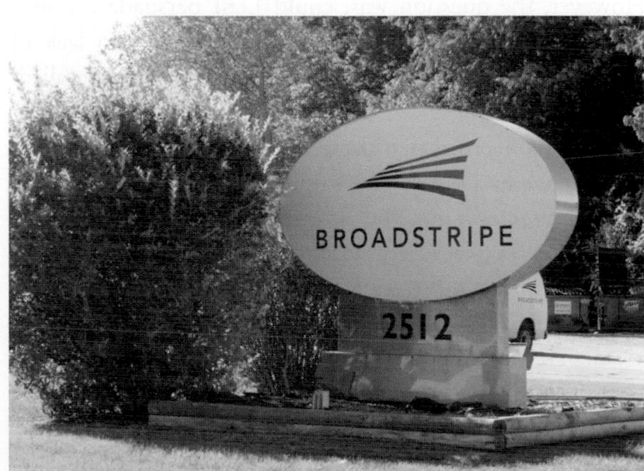

Jochen Wirtz is Professor of Marketing and Academic Director of the UCLA – NUS Executive MBA Program at the National University of Singapore. For his other publications and free downloads of sample chapters from his books, see wwww.jochenwirtz.com. Sven Tuzovic is Assistant Professor of Marketing at Pacific Lutheran University in Tacoma, WA.

The support and feedback of Tony Lent, Chief Commercial Officer at Broadstripe, in the writing of this case are gratefully acknowledged.

This case was prepared as a basis for class discussion rather than to illustrate effective or ineffective handling of an administrative situation.

THE IDEA OF A SERVICE GUARANTEE FACED INTERNAL RESISTANCE

In early 2009, Broadstripe filed for Chapter 11 bankruptcy protection due to competitive pressures, shrinking subscriber numbers, and a high debt burden due to acquisitions that had been made before the financial crisis. The subsequent restructuring cut operational costs, and the firm divested a number of its holdings.

At the same time, Lent saw the necessity to dramatically improve the customer service experience, and he was convinced that a powerful service guarantee would be effective in driving service level improvements internally and in communicating its commitment to service excellence externally. Lent explained:

> As a relatively small cable company, I knew we would have to do something to break through the noise. There are over 900 cables companies in the USA. Of the top 25 cable companies, two-thirds had money-back guarantees. Most of these guarantees were for 30 days. All of these guarantees were only for new customers. Many of these guarantees were soft guarantees—they were in place but nobody told prospective customers about them.
>
> My "ah ha" moment was when I saw GM's "May the Best Car Win" campaign. I saw a lot of parallels between GM and Broadstripe. For example, we were both bankrupt, both had perceived quality issues, and both needed to change customers' perceptions in a hurry."

However, the question was, could Lent persuade the new management to approve his ideas? There was no lack of resistance to investing into a service guarantee. Lent recalled:

> I was concerned that there was a lag effect from the time we had put service improvements in place and getting credit for the improvements we made in the marketplace. For example, we invested heaps into adding more staff, improving the technology in our call centers which included a workforce management system, recording calls for training purposes, instituting post install surveys, and adding a call-back service, but it took time for customers and prospects to realize that we had become a much better company. I also wanted to institute a 60-day money-back guarantee [MBG] to instill pride, a sense of leadership, and as a forcing function for all employees to drive customer orientation.
>
> In December of 2009, I got into a heated argument with a member of our executive leadership team over the 60-day MBG. He took the position that the timing was not good. I disagreed. My exact words were, "If not now—when?" Ultimately, we agreed to disagree and I took my case to the senior leadership team of Broadstripe and ultimately prevailed.

BROADSTRIPE'S SERVICE IMPROVEMENT EFFORTS

Broadstripe started a grass-root approach to improve its customer experience. For example, the Northwest region traditionally had been a problematic area. The company invested significantly into upgrading its network, overhauling customer service, and implementing a number of customer-focused initiatives. Key consumer concerns addressed issues such as rate increases and call center responsiveness. Tamara Shelman, Senior Vice President of Customer Care, and her team decided to dramatically increase staffing levels, extend call center hours, and require all service representatives to undergo extensive training.

THE BROADSTRIPE SERVICE GUARANTEE

To support its service initiative, Broadstripe launched several service guarantees over the past years. Initially, the company introduced *Broadstripe Forever VIP*, the first lifetime price guarantee in the industry (see Exhibit 2), which offered new and existing customers the opportunity to lock in one price for life for (V)ideo, (I)nternet, and (P)hone service.

In February 2010, the company launched a 60-day MBG (see Exhibit 3) offering both new and existing Broadstripe residential customers 60 days to test the cable provider's services. This was followed by the *Broadstripe Challenge* in May 2010, which was a total satisfaction service guarantee that invited customers to take advantage of the existing 60-day MBG and test the service. If customers were not totally satisfied, Broadstripe paid for the subscriber to restore the service with their previous cable provider.

Exhibit 2: Tony Lent, MBA from the University of Michigan, stands in front of a poster of the newly launched Forever Pricing Guarantee.

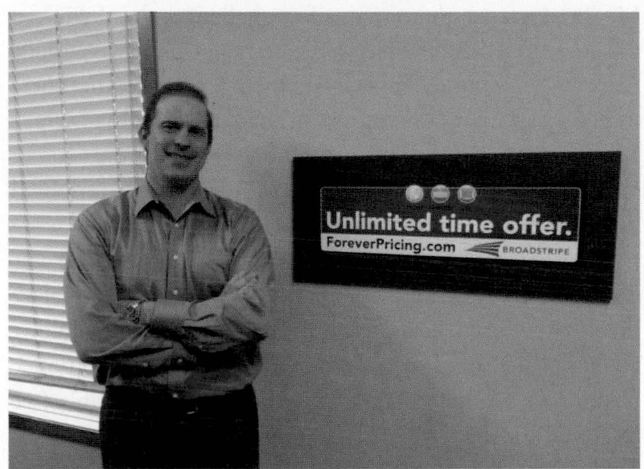

According to Lent, Broadstripe's 60-day MBG went beyond any money-back guarantee program in the industry: "We took the industry's best satisfaction guarantee and made it better."

From a service operations perspective, implementing the service guarantee enabled Broadstripe to identify and focus on closing service quality gaps. For example, the company noticed an increase in refund requests in the Pacific Northwest.

As it turned out, problems were traced back to "nodes" of the network infrastructure affecting high-speed data services. Once the company identified the cause, it decided to improve the infrastructure by adding new CMTS[1] while temporarily stopping its direct mail campaign in this area. Lent argued: "We did not want to make a difficult situation worse." Since then, the situation improved, which led to the company's decision to continue again with its direct mail campaign. Overall, service failures were lower since the introduction of the service guarantee. According to Lent, the number of "trouble tickets"[2] was down approximately 30 percent from when the company first instituted the

Exhibit 3: Broadstripe's 60-day MBG.

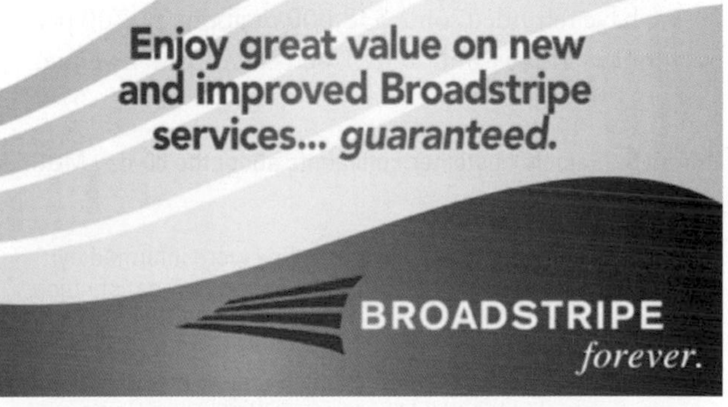

60-day MBG. In addition, customer churn had experienced a step-function decrease since the first launch in January 2010. In fact, by the end of 2010, Broadstripe actually started to grow its subscriber base for the first time in over five years.

The service guarantee and the service improvements it had driven helped to change the public's perception about Broadstripe. In July 2010, Broadstripe was recognized by *St. Louis Small Business Monthly* as one of 14 "Best Telecommunications Companies in the Business."[3] Yet, probably the most significant indicator of Broadstripe's

1 CMTS (cable modem termination system) refers to equipment that is located in a cable company's "headend" (an unstaffed facility). It is used to provide high-speed data services (e.g., cable Internet).

2 Trouble tickets are a measure that refers to customer complaints and any problems with the Internet or TV channels.

3 The magazine *Small Business Monthly* (SBMON.com) publishes a list every year of "Best in Business" based on nominations from its readers of top businesses in various industries for the St. Louis metro area.

successful service improvements was the company's recent announcement that its rating from the Better Business Bureau (BBB) was changed from an "F" rating to an "A+" rating.[4] According to the BBB, Broadstripe met the accreditation standards, which included a commitment to ethical business practices and to resolving any consumer complaint.

From a marketing perspective, Broadstripe saw increasing response rates to its direct mail campaigns. Response rates of nonsubscribers improved to 0.7 percent compared to an industry average of 0.5 percent, and response rates of current subscribers to cross-selling offers reached 0.7 percent compared to an industry average of 0.3 percent. In addition, Broadstripe's customer service representatives reported good success in utilizing the guarantee as a tool to close deals with prospective clients (see Exhibit 5 for sample customer responses). As a result, sales from technicians have doubled over the last two years, now accounting for 4–5 percent of total sales compared to an industry average of 1–2 percent.

The improvements in service operations, public perception, and marketing effectiveness were reflected in an improving bottom line. Lent noted:

> Since January of 2010 we have recorded approximately $162 million in revenue, since then we have refunded some $38,000 or about $1,700 per month. This is only 0.023 percent of our revenue.

Exhibit 5: Sample customer comments about the 60-day MBG.

Typical customers comments when they were informed by sales staff that Broadstripe offered a 60-day, full-satisfaction money-back guarantee:

- "I used to have your service and the telephone service was not reliable but I'd like to try everything again to see if we are happy since you offer a 60-day money back guarantee."
- "You have a 60-day Money Back? Ok then. I guess if it doesn't work I will just call back."
- "You're right, I've got nothing to lose since Broadstripe offers a 60-day Money Back."
- "Ok, I guess I'll go ahead and set it up"

4 The BBB is a national organization that evaluates and monitors ethical business practices. Based on file information about a business, the BBB assigns letter grades from A+ (highest) to F (lowest) based on the rating of 16 different factors (for details about the factors see www.BBB.org).

> Our operating margin runs at 26.7 percent, much higher than 2009.

Moving forward, there were a few challenges that Lent had to address. He had just received an e-mail from his colleague Ancy Vue, Customer Service Supervisor, who felt that there were issues with customers taking advantage of Broadstripe's MBG. She had prepared a list of a few recent customer claims (see Exhibit 6) and wanted to discuss her proposed handling of those claims.

This e-mail was timely as Lent had already planned to analyze the MBG in more detail. He wanted to spend time thinking about how he could redesign the MBG and develop a policy on how to deal with potentially opportunistic claims (see Exhibit 7 for the terms and conditions of the guarantee).

Then he thought how the policy could be better communicated on Broadstripe's website. Currently, the MBG was only promoted on Broadstripe's product category pages, for example, Digital TV (see Exhibit 8). However, there was no specific link in the "Help Desk" tab that allowed customers to access the terms and conditions quickly or to invoke the MBG online. He wondered if making the MBG more "visible" and allow easy invocation of the guarantee online would potentially increase customer claims.

Finally and most critically, his senior management committee wanted an update from him about the performance of the guarantee. Lent was asked to present on (a) the financial performance of the MBG program, (b) how competitors had been reacting since its launch, (c) how the MBG program had affected Broadstripe's service culture, in particular among employees in the call centers, and (d) the extent subscribers were taking undue advantage of the service guarantee. Lent was thinking through these questions while starting to look through some key data in his spreadsheet (see Exhibit 9).

Exhibit 6: Sample customer claims when invoking the guarantee.

- "Services are not up to snuff so how do I go about getting my money back?"
- "I haven't made a payment on any of my services but heard that I can get my money back after 60 days."
- "I want the 60 Day Money Back because I don't need the services anymore."
- "The program I want [NFL Sunday] is not available so I want my money back."

Exhibit 7: Terms and conditions of Broadstripe's 60-day MBG.

Broadstripe's 60-day guarantee is for a limited time and is only available in Broadstripe serviceable areas. To be eligible for a money-back guarantee refund, customers must timely pay for all services, taxes and fees and comply with applicable service agreement(s) and terminate service by calling to request a refund within 60 days of service activation.

Broadstripe will refund customers up to $75 (installation charge) to switch customers back to their previous provider within 60 days of initiating new service if they are not satisfied with their new Broadstripe services. The "Switch Back Refund" applies only to digital cable, Internet, and/or home phone service. Customers requesting a "Switch Back Refund" need to provide Broadstripe with written documentation (bill, work order, invoice, etc.) that details installation charges incurred "switching back" to their previous provider. Customers wishing to obtain a "Switch Back Refund" will need to call Broadstripe to make arrangements for sending to Broadstripe acceptable written documentation of installation charges.

To request a refund in:

- Maryland, please call 877-882-7623.
- Michigan, please call 800-444-6997.
- Oregon, please call 800-829-2225.
- Washington, please call 800-829-2225.

Broadstripe services covered by our 60-Day, money-back guarantee are:

- Digital Cable
- Internet
- In-home networking
- In-home wire maintenance
- Home Phone
- DVR
- HBO
- cinemax
- starz
- SHOWTIME
- Hispanic Tier (Maryland Customers Only)
- Digital Sports and Adventure Tier
- HD Tier
- Pay-Per-View movies, events and adult content are excluded from the money-back guarantee.

The refund will not apply if refunded service is reestablished with Broadstripe by customer within 90 days of disconnection. Broadstripe's money-back guarantee policies are subject to change. Broadstripe 2011.

Exhibit 8: Broadstripe's website featuring the MBG.

HOME | BILL PAY | NEWS | HELP | BUSINESS CLASS

Google Custom Search | Search

BROADSTRIPE

Why Broadstripe Digital TV?

Broadstripe Digital TV features:

- Tons of the most popular channels, including all your local channels - watch thousands of programs!
- Access to Pay-Per-View shows and movies
- Commercial-free music channels
- HD channels with programming ranging from live sports to prime-time dramas (HD equipment required)
- Parental controls so you can decide what your kids watch

With Digital you can access Pay-Per-View shows and movies, watch thousands of programs, enjoy the benefits of a DVR, commercial-free music channels and use parental controls to decide what your kids do and don't watch.

Enjoy HD channels that range from live sports to prime time dramas & nature documentaries:

- Access premium movie channels such as HBO, Showtime and Starz.
- All your local channels including NBC, CBS, ABC, Fox and PBS...yes you can still "Dance with the Stars..." and you don't have to have a set top box!

Lock in a low price for LIFE when you bundle with the Broadstripe Forever VIP!

Order Now! or Our Sales Team Will Call You!

View Packages

Broadstripe's new 60-day, money-back guarantee is the BEST in the industry! Now, new and existing customers get a 60-day, money-back guarantee on any new video, internet, or phone service! Broadstripe has recently invested millions of dollars on a major upgrade to our network so customers can enjoy more reliable products, faster internet speeds and better customer care. You can count on Broadstripe to deliver the best overall value on in-home communications and entertainment...it's guaranteed!

Broadstripe's sixtyday guarantee is a limited time only guarantee and is only available in Broadstripe serviceable areas. To be eligible for a money-back guarantee refund, customers must timely pay for all services, taxes and fees and comply with applicable service agreement(s) and terminate service and request a refund in writing within 60 days of service activation. The refund will not apply if service is reestablished by customer within 90 days of disconnection. Broadstripe's money-back guarantee policies are subject to change. Call Broadstripe for restrictions and complete details.

Exhibit 9: Service guarantee operating data.

Key Performance Indicators	Cumulative after 12 Months	Monthly Average of 12 Months	Cumulative after 20 Months	Monthly Average of 20 Months
Number of new RGUs[1]	94,624	7,885	162,474	8,124
Number of unique customers who invoked the MBG	209	17.42	420	21.00
Number of disconnected unique customers	209		420	
Number of disconnected RGUs	470	39.17	928	46.40
% of customers disconnected using 60-day MBG	0.50%		0.60%	
Refund		$91.56		$86.00
Service credits issued[2]	$19,594.37	1,632.86	$36,119.35	1,805.97

1 RGU (revenue-generating units) refers to digital cable, Internet, and home phone services.
2 Service credits refer to total refunds paid out to customers.

STUDY QUESTIONS

1. Explain the impact of a well-designed service guarantee on a firm's service employees, service operations, current and potential customers, and on marketing and sales.
2. Evaluate the design and communication of Broadstripe's service guarantee. Would you recommend any changes?
3. Can the guarantee be successful in creating a culture for service excellence within Broadstripe? What else may be needed for achieving such a culture?
4. Do you think customers might take undue advantage of this guarantee and "stage" service failures to invoke the guarantee? If yes, how could Broadstripe minimize potential cheating on its guarantee?
5. Imagine you are in Lent's position. How would you conduct the analysis and what would you present to the management committee?

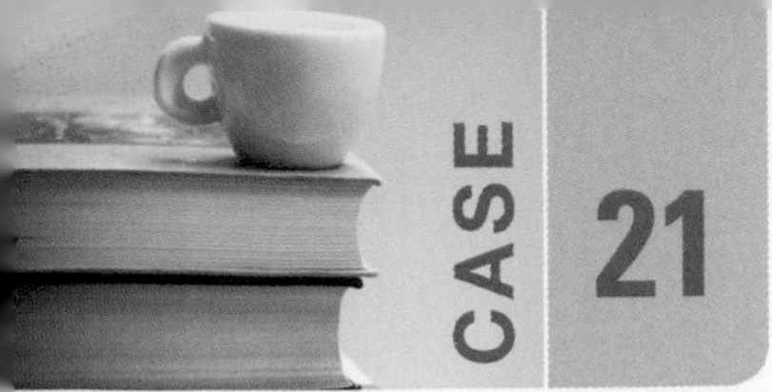

Starbucks: Delivering Customer Service

Youngme Moon and John Quelch

Starbucks, the dominant specialty-coffee brand in North America, must respond to recent market research indicating that the company is not meeting customer expectations in terms of service. To increase customer satisfaction, the company is debating a plan that would increase the amount of labor in its stores and theoretically increase speed of service. However, the impact of the plan (which would cost $40 million annually) on the company's bottom line is unclear.

In mid-2002, Christine Day, Starbucks' senior vice president of administration in North America, sat in the seventh-floor conference room of Starbucks' Seattle headquarters and reached for her second cup of *toffee nut latte*. The handcrafted beverage—a buttery, toffee-nut-flavored espresso concoction topped with whipped cream and toffee sprinkles—had become a regular afternoon indulgence for Day ever since its introduction earlier that year.

As she waited for her colleagues to join her, Day reflected on the company's recent performance. While other retailers were still reeling from the post-9/11 recession, Starbucks was enjoying its 11th consecutive year of 5 percent, or higher, comparable store sales growth, prompting its founder and chairman, Howard Schultz, to declare: "I think we've demonstrated that we are close to a recession-proof product."[1]

Day, however, was not feeling nearly as sanguine, in part because Starbucks' most recent market research had revealed some unexpected findings. "We've always taken great pride in our retail service," said Day, "but according to the data, we're not always meeting our customers' expectations in the area of customer satisfaction."

As a result of these concerns, Day and her associates had come up with a plan to invest an additional $40 million annually in the company's 4,500 stores, which would allow each store to add the equivalent of 20 hours of labor a week. "The idea is to improve speed of service and thereby increase customer satisfaction," said Day.

In two days, Day was due to make a final recommendation to both Schultz and Orin Smith, Starbucks' CEO, about whether the company should move forward with the plan. "The investment is the EPS [earnings per share] equivalent of almost seven cents a share," said Day. In preparation for her meeting with Schultz and Smith, Day had asked one of her associates to help her think through the implications of the plan. Day noted, "The real question is, do we believe what our customers are telling us about what constitutes 'excellent' customer service? And if we deliver it, what will the impact be on our sales and profitability?"

COMPANY BACKGROUND

The story of how Howard Schultz managed to transform a commodity into an upscale cultural phenomenon had become the stuff of legends. In 1971, three coffee fanatics—Gerald Baldwin, Gordon Bowker, and Ziev Siegl—opened a small coffee shop in Seattle's Pike Place Market. The shop specialized in selling whole arabica beans to a niche market of coffee purists.

In 1982, Schultz joined the Starbucks marketing team. Shortly thereafter, he traveled to Italy, where he became fascinated with Milan's coffee culture, in particular, the role the neighborhood espresso bars played in Italians' everyday

1 Jake Batsell, "A Grande Decade for Starbucks," The Seattle Times, June 26, 2002.

social lives. Upon his return, the inspired Schultz convinced the company to set up an espresso bar in the corner of its only downtown Seattle shop. As Schultz explained, the bar became the prototype for his long-term vision:

> The idea was to create a chain of coffeehouses that would become America's "third place." At the time, most Americans had two places in their lives—home and work. But I believed that people needed another place, a place where they could go to relax and enjoy others, or just be by themselves. I envisioned a place that would be separate from home or work, a place that would mean different things to different people.

A few years later, Schultz got his chance when Starbucks' founders agreed to sell him the company. As soon as Schultz took over, he immediately began opening new stores. The stores sold whole beans and premium-priced coffee beverages by the cup and catered primarily to affluent, well-educated, white-collar patrons (skewed female) between the ages of 25 and 44. By 1992, the company had 140 such stores in the Northwest and Chicago and was successfully competing against other small-scale coffee chains such as Gloria Jean's Coffee Bean and Barnie's Coffee & Tea.

That same year, Schultz decided to take the company public. As he recalled, many Wall Street types were dubious about the idea: "They'd say, 'You mean, you're going to sell coffee for a dollar in a paper cup, with Italian names that no one in America can say? At a time in America when no one's drinking coffee? And I can get coffee at the local coffee shop or doughnut shop for 50 cents? Are you kidding me?'"[2]

Ignoring the skeptics, Schultz forged ahead with the public offering, raising $25 million in the process. The proceeds allowed Starbucks to open more stores across the nation.

By mid-2002, Schultz had unequivocally established Starbucks as the dominant specialty-coffee brand in North America. Sales had climbed at a compound annual growth rate (CAGR) of 40 percent since the company had gone public, and net earnings had risen at a CAGR of 50 percent. The company was now serving 20 million unique customers in well over 5,000 stores around the globe and was opening on average three new stores a day. (See Exhibits 1–3 for company financials and store growth over time.)

What made Starbucks' success even more impressive was that the company had spent almost nothing on advertising to achieve it. North American marketing primarily consisted of point-of-sale materials and local-store marketing and was far less than the industry average. (Most fast-food chains had marketing budgets in the 3–6 percent range.)

For his part, Schultz remained as Chairman and Chief Global Strategist in control of the company, handing over day-to-day operations in 2002 to CEO Orin Smith, a Harvard MBA (1967) who joined the company in 1990.

THE STARBUCKS VALUE PROPOSITION

Starbucks' brand strategy was best captured by its "live coffee" mantra, a phrase that reflected the importance the company attached to keeping the national coffee culture alive. From a retail perspective, this meant creating an "experience" around the consumption of coffee, an experience that people could weave into the fabric of their everyday lives.

There were three components to this experiential branding strategy. The first component was the coffee itself. Starbucks prided itself on offering what it believed to be the highest-quality coffee in the world, sourced from the Africa, Central and South America, and Asia-Pacific regions. To enforce its exacting coffee standards, Starbucks controlled as much of the supply chain as possible: It worked directly with growers in various countries of origin to purchase green coffee beans. It oversaw the custom-roasting process for the company's various blends and single-origin coffees. It controlled distribution to retail stores around the world.

The second brand component was service, or what the company sometimes referred to as "customer intimacy." "Our goal is to create an uplifting experience every time you walk through our door," explained Jim Alling, Starbucks' Senior Vice President of North American retail. "Our most loyal customers visit us as often as 18 times a month, so it could be something as simple as recognizing you and knowing your drink or customizing your drink just the way you like it."

The third brand component was atmosphere. "People come for the coffee," explained Day, "but the ambience is what makes them want to stay." For that reason, most Starbucks had seating areas to encourage lounging, and layouts that

2 Batsell.

Exhibit 1: Starbucks' financials, FY 1998 to FY 2002 (in million $).

	FY 1998	FY 1999	FY 2000	FY 2001	FY 2002
Revenue					
Co-owned North American	1,076.8	1,375.0	1,734.9	2,086.4	2,583.8
Co-owned Int'l (UK, Thailand, Australia)	25.8	48.4	88.7	143.2	209.1
Total company-operated retail	1,102.6	1,423.4	1,823.6	2,229.6	2,792.9
Specialty operations	206.1	263.4	354.0	419.4	496.0
Net revenues	**1,308.7**	**1,686.8**	**2,177.6**	**2,649.0**	**3,288.9**
Cost of goods sold	578.5	747.6	961.9	1,112.8	1,350.0
Gross profit	**730.2**	**939.2**	**1,215.7**	**1,536.2**	**1,938.9**
Joint-venture income[a]	1.0	3.2	20.3	28.6	35.8
Expenses:					
Store operating expense	418.5	543.6	704.9	875.5	1,121.1
Other operating expense	44.5	54.6	78.4	93.3	127.2
Depreciation & amortization expense	72.5	97.8	130.2	163.5	205.6
General & admin expense	77.6	89.7	110.2	151.4	202.1
Operating expenses	**613.1**	**785.7**	**1,023.8**	**1,283.7**	**1,656.0**
Operating profit	**109.2**	**156.7**	**212.3**	**281.1**	**310.0**
Net income	**68.4**	**101.7**	**94.5**	**181.2**	**215.1**
% Change in monthly comparable store sales[b]					
North America	5%	6%	9%	5%	7%
Consolidated	5%	6%	9%	5%	6%

Source: Adapted from company reports and Lehman Brothers, November 5, 2002.

a Includes income from various joint ventures, including Starbucks' partnership with the Pepsi-Cola Company to develop and distribute Frappuccino and with Dreyer 's Grand Ice Cream to develop and distribute premium ice creams.

b Includes only company-operated stores open 13 months or longer.

Exhibit 2: Starbucks' store growth.

	FY 1998	FY 1999	FY 2000	FY 2001	FY 2002
Total North America	**1,755**	**2,217**	**2,976**	**3,780**	**4,574**
Company-operated	1,622	2,038	2,446	2,971	3,496
Licensed stores[a]	133	179	530	809	1,078
Total international	**131**	**281**	**525**	**929**	**1,312**
Company-operated	66	97	173	295	384
Licensed stores	65	184	352	634	928
Total stores	**1,886**	**2,498**	**3,501**	**4,709**	**5,886**

Source: Company reports.

a Includes kiosks located in grocery stores, bookstores, hotels, airports, and so on.

Exhibit 3: Additional data, North American company-operated stores (FY2002).

	Average
Average hourly rate with shift supervisors and hourly partners	$9.00
Total labor hours per week, average store	360
Average weekly store volume	$15,400.00
Average ticket	$3.85
Average daily customer count, per store	570

Source: Company reports.

were designed to provide an upscale yet inviting environment for those who wanted to linger. "What we have built has [a] universal appeal," remarked Schultz. "It's based on the human spirit, it's based on a sense of community, the need for people to come together."[3]

Channels of Distribution

Almost all of Starbucks' locations in North America were company-operated stores located in high-traffic, high-visibility settings, such as retail centers, office buildings, and university campuses.[4] In addition to selling whole-bean coffees, these stores sold rich-brewed coffees, Italian-style espresso drinks, cold-blended beverages, and premium teas. Product mixes tended to vary depending on a store's size and location, but most stores offered a variety of pastries, sodas, and juices, along with coffee-related accessories and equipment, music CDs, games, and seasonal novelty items. (About 500 stores even carried a selection of sandwiches and salads.)

Beverages accounted for the largest percentage of sales in these stores (77 percent); this represented a change from 10 years earlier, when about half of store revenues had come from sales of whole-bean coffees. (See Exhibit 4 for retail sales mix by product type; see Exhibit 5 for a typical menu board and price list.)

Starbucks also sold coffee products through noncompany-operated retail channels; these so-called "specialty operations" accounted for 15 percent of net revenues. About 27 percent of these revenues came from North American food-service accounts, that is, sales of whole-bean and ground coffees to hotels, airlines, restaurants, and the like. Another 18 percent came from domestic retail store licenses

3 Batsell.

4 Starbucks had recently begun experimenting with drive-throughs. Less than 10 percent of its stores had drive-throughs, but in these stores, the drive-throughs accounted for 50 percent of all business.

Exhibit 4: Product mix, North American company-operated stores (FY2002).

	Percent of Sales
Retail Product Mix	
Coffee beverages	77%
Food items	13%
Whole-bean coffees	6%
Equipment & accessories	4%

Source: Company reports.

that, in North America, were only granted when there was no other way to achieve access to desirable retail space (e.g., in airports).

The remaining 55 percent of specialty revenues came from a variety of sources, including international licensed stores, grocery stores and warehouse clubs (Kraft Foods handled marketing and distribution for Starbucks in this channel), and online and mail-order sales. Starbucks also had a joint venture with Pepsi-Cola to distribute bottled Frappuccino beverages in North America, as well as a partnership with Dreyer 's Grand Ice Cream to develop and distribute a line of premium ice creams.

Day explained the company's broad distribution strategy:

> Our philosophy is pretty straightforward—we want to reach customers where they work, travel, shop, and dine. In order to do this, we sometimes have to establish relationships with third parties that share our values and commitment to quality. This is a particularly effective way to reach newcomers with our brand. It's a lot less intimidating to buy Starbucks at a grocery store than it is to walk into one of our coffeehouses for the first time. In fact, about 40 percent of our new coffeehouse customers have already tried the Starbucks brand before they walk through our doors. Even something like ice cream has become an important trial vehicle for us.

Starbucks Partners

All Starbucks employees were called "partners." The company employed 60,000 partners worldwide, about 50,000 in North America. Most were hourly-wage employees (called *baristas*), who worked in Starbucks retail stores. Alling remarked, "From day one, Howard has made clear his belief that partner satisfaction leads to customer satisfaction. This belief is part of Howard's DNA, and because it's been pounded into each and every one of us, it's become part of our DNA, too."

The company had a generous policy of giving health insurance and stock options to even the most entry-level partners, most of whom were between the ages of 17 and 23. Partly as a result of this, Starbucks' partner satisfaction rate consistently hovered in the 80–90 percent range, well above the industry norm,[5] and the company had recently been ranked 47th in the *Fortune* magazine list of best places to work, quite an accomplishment for a company with so many hourly-wage workers.

In addition, Starbucks had one of the lowest employee turnover rates in the industry—just 70 percent, compared with fast-food industry averages as high as 300 percent. The rate was even lower for managers, and as Alling noted, the company was always looking for ways to bring turnover down further: "Whenever we have a problem store, we almost always find either an inexperienced store manager or inexperienced baristas. Manager stability is key. It not only decreases partner turnover but also enables the store to do a much better job of recognizing regular customers and providing personalized service. So our goal is to make the position a lifetime job."

To this end, the company encouraged promotion from within its own ranks. About 70 percent of the company's store managers were ex-baristas, and about 60 percent of its district managers were ex-store managers. In fact, upon being hired, all senior executives had to train and succeed as baristas before being allowed to assume their positions in corporate headquarters.

DELIVERING ON SERVICE

When a partner was hired to work in one of Starbucks' North American retail stores, he or she had to undergo two types of training. The first type focused on "hard skills," such as learning how to use the cash register and learning how to

5 Industrywide, employee satisfaction rates tended to be in the 50–60 percent range. Source: Starbucks, 2000.

Exhibit 5: Typical menu board and price list for a North American company-owned store.

Espresso Traditions Classic Favorites	Tall	Grande	Venti
Toffee Nut Latte	2.95	3.50	3.80
Vanilla Latte	2.85	3.40	3.70
Caffe Latte	2.55	3.10	3.40
Cappuccino	2.55	3.10	3.40
Caramel Macchiato	2.80	3.40	3.65
White Chocolate Mocha	3.20	3.75	4.00
Caffe Mocha	2.75	3.30	3.55
Caffe Americano	1.75	2.05	2.40
Espresso	**Solo**	**Doppio**	
Espresso	1.45	1.75	
Extras			
Additional Espresso Shot	.55		
Add flavored syrup	.30		
Organic milk & soy available upon request			
Frappuccino Ice Blended Beverages	**Tall**	**Grande**	**Venti**
Coffee	2.65	3.15	3.65
Mocha	2.90	3.40	3.90
Caramel Frappuccino	3.15	3.65	4.15
Mocha Coconut (limited offering)	3.15	3.65	4.15
Crème Frappuccino Ice Blended Crème	**Tall**	**Grande**	**Venti**
Toffee Nut Crème	3.15	3.65	4.15
Vanilla Crème	2.65	3.15	3.65
Coconut Crème	3.15	3.65	4.15
Tazo Tea Frappuccino Ice Blended Teas	**Tall**	**Grande**	**Venti**
Tazo Citrus	2.90	3.40	3.90
Tazoberry	2.90	3.40	3.90
Tazo Chai Crème	3.15	3.65	4.15
Brewed Coffee	**Tall**	**Grande**	**Venti**
Coffee of the Day	1.40	1.60	1.70
Decaf of the Day	1.40	1.60	1.70

Cold Beverages	Tall	Grande	Venti
Iced Caffe Latte	2.55	3.10	3.50
Iced Caramel Macchiato	2.80	3.40	3.80
Iced Caffe Americano	1.75	2.05	3.40
Coffee Alternatives	**Tall**	**Grande**	**Venti**
Toffee Nut Crème	2.45	2.70	2.95
Vanilla Crème	2.20	2.45	2.70
Caramel Apple Cider	2.45	2.70	2.95
Hot Chocolate	2.20	2.45	2.70
Tazo Hot Tea	1.15	1.65	1.65
Tazo Chai	2.70	3.10	3.35
Whole Beans: Bold Our most intriguing and exotic coffees		**1/2 lb**	**1 lb**
Gold Coast Blend		5.70	10.95
French Roast		5.20	9.95
Sumatra		5.30	10.15
Decaf Sumatra		5.60	10.65
Ethiopia Sidame		5.20	9.95
Arabian Mocha Sanani		8.30	15.95
Kenya		5.30	10.15
Italian Roast		5.20	9.95
Sulawesi		6.10	11.65
Whole Beans: Smooth richer, more flavorful coffees		**1/2 lb**	**1 lb**
Espresso Roast		5.20	9.95
Decaf Espresso Roast		5.60	10.65
Yukon Blend		5.20	9.95
Café Verona		5.20	9.95
Guatemala Antigua		5.30	10.15
Arabian Mocha Java		6.30	11.95
Decaf Mocha Java/SWP		6.50	12.45
Whole Beans: Mild The perfect introduction to Starbucks coffees		**1/2 lb**	**1 lb**
Breakfast Blend		5.20	9.95
Lightnote Blend		5.20	9.95
Decaf Lightnote Blend		5.60	10.65
Colombia Narino		5.50	10.45
House Blend		5.20	9.95
Decaf House Blend		5.60	10.65
Fair Trade Coffee		5.95	11.45

Source: Starbucks location: Harvard Square, Cambridge, Massachusetts, February 2003.

mix drinks. Most Starbucks beverages were handcrafted, and to ensure product quality, there was a prespecified process associated with each drink. Making an espresso beverage, for example, required seven specific steps.

The other type of training focused on "soft skills." Alling explained:

> In our training manual, we explicitly teach partners to connect with customers—to enthusiastically welcome them to the store, to establish eye contact, to smile, and to try to remember their names and orders if they're regulars. We also encourage partners to create conversations with customers using questions that require more than a yes or no answer. So for example, "I noticed you were looking at the menu board—what types of beverages do you typically enjoy?" is a good question for a partner to ask.

Starbucks' "Just Say Yes" policy empowered partners to provide the best service possible, even if it required going beyond company rules. "This means that if a customer spills a drink and asks for a refill, we'll give it to him," said Day. "Or if a customer doesn't have cash and wants to pay with a check (which we aren't supposed to accept), then we'll give her a sample drink for free. The last thing we want to do is win the argument and lose the customer."

Most barista turnover occurred within the first 90 days of employment; if a barista lasted beyond that, there was a high probability that he or she would stay for three years or more. "Our training ends up being a self-selection process," Alling said. Indeed, the ability to balance hard and soft skills required a particular type of person, and Alling believed the challenges had only grown over time:

> Back in the days when we sold mostly beans, every customer who walked in the door was a coffee connoisseur, and it was easy for baristas to engage in chitchat while ringing up a bag. Those days are long gone. Today, almost every customer orders a handcrafted beverage. If the line is stretching out the door and everyone's clamoring for their coffee fix, it's not that easy to strike up a conversation with a customer.

The complexity of the barista's job had also increased over time; making a *venti tazoberry and crème*, for instance, required 10 different steps. "It used to be that a barista could make every variation of drink we offered in half a day," Day observed. "Nowadays, given our product proliferation, it would take 16 days of eight-hour shifts. There are literally hundreds of combinations of drinks in our portfolio."

This job complexity was compounded by the fact that almost half of Starbucks' customers customized their drinks. According to Day, this created a tension between product quality and customer focus for Starbucks:

> On the one hand, we train baristas to make beverages to our preestablished quality standards—this means enforcing a consistent process that baristas can master. On the other hand, if a customer comes in and wants it their way—extra vanilla, for instance—what should we do? Our heaviest users are always the most demanding. Of course, every time we customize, we slow down the service for everyone else. We also put a lot of strain on our baristas, who are already dealing with an extraordinary number of sophisticated drinks.

One obvious solution to the problem was to hire more baristas to share the workload. However, the company had been extremely reluctant to do this in recent years, particularly given the economic downturn. Labor was already the company's largest expense item in North America (see Exhibit 3), and Starbucks stores tended to be located in urban areas with high wage rates. Instead, the company had focused on increasing barista efficiency by removing all non-value-added tasks, simplifying the beverage production process, and tinkering with the facility design to eliminate bottlenecks.

In addition, the company had recently begun installing automated espresso machines in its North American cafés. The verismo machines, which decreased the number of steps required to make an espresso beverage, reduced waste, improved consistency, and generated an overwhelmingly positive customer and barista response.

Measuring Service Performance

Starbucks tracked service performance using a variety of metrics, including monthly status reports and self-reported checklists. The company's most prominent measurement tool was a mystery shopper program called the "Customer Snapshot." Under this program, every store was visited by an anonymous mystery shopper three times a quarter. Upon completing the visit, the shopper would rate the store on four "Basic Service" criteria:

- ***Service***—Did the register partner verbally greet the customer?

  Did the barista and register partner make eye contact with the customer? Say "thank you"?

- ***Cleanliness***—Was the store clean? The counters?

  The tables?

  The restrooms?

- ***Product quality***—Was the order filled accurately? Was the temperature of the drink within range? Was the beverage properly presented?

- ***Speed of service***—How long did the customer have to wait?

  The company's goal was to serve a customer within three minutes, from back-of-the-line to drink-in-hand. This benchmark was based on market research which indicated that the three-minute standard was a key component in how current Starbucks customers defined "excellent service."

In addition to Basic Service, stores were also rated on "Legendary Service," which was defined as "behavior that created a memorable experience for a customer, that inspired a customer to return often and tell a friend." Legendary Service scores were based on secret shopper observations of service attributes such as partners initiating conversations with customers, partners recognizing customers by name or drink order, and partners being responsive to service problems.

During 2002, the company's Customer Snapshot scores had increased across all stores (see Exhibit 6), leading Day to comment, "The Snapshot is not a perfect measurement tool, but we believe it does a good job of measuring trends over the course of a quarter. In order for a store to do well on the Snapshot, it needs to have sustainable processes in place that create a well-established pattern of doing things right so that it gets 'caught' doing things right."

COMPETITION

In the United States, Starbucks competed against a variety of small-scale specialty-coffee chains, most of which were regionally concentrated. Each tried to differentiate itself from Starbucks in a different way. For example, Minneapolis-based Caribou Coffee, which operated more than 200 stores in nine states, differentiated itself on store environment. Rather than offer an upscale, pseudo-European atmosphere, its strategy was to simulate the look and feel of an Alaskan lodge, with knotty-pine cabinetry, fireplaces, and soft seating. Another example was California-based Peet's Coffee & Tea, which operated about 70 stores in five states. More than 60 percent of Peet's revenues came from the sale of whole beans. Peet's strategy was to build a super-premium brand by offering the freshest coffee on the market. One of the ways it delivered on this promise was by "roasting to order," that is, by hand-roasting small batches of coffee at its California plant and making sure that all of its coffee shipped within 24 hours of roasting.

Starbucks also competed against thousands of independent specialty-coffee shops. Some of these independent coffee shops offered a wide range of food and beverages, including beer, wine, and liquor; others offered satellite televisions or Internet-connected computers. Still others differentiated themselves by delivering highly personalized service to an eclectic clientele.

Finally, Starbucks competed against donut and bagel chains such as Dunkin Donuts, which operated over 3,700 stores in 38 states. Dunkin Donuts attributed half of its sales to coffee and, in recent years, had begun offering flavored coffee and non-coffee alternatives, such as Dunkaccino (a coffee and chocolate combination available with various toppings) and Vanilla Chai (a combination of tea, vanilla, honey, and spices).

CAFFEINATING THE WORLD

The company's overall objective was to establish Starbucks as the "most recognized and respected brand in the world."[6] This ambitious goal required an aggressive growth strategy, and, in 2002, the two biggest drivers of company growth were retail expansion and product innovation.

Retail Expansion

Starbucks already owned close to one-third of America's coffee bars, more than its next five biggest competitors combined. (By comparison, the US's second-largest player, Diedrich Coffee, operated fewer than 400 stores.) However, the company had plans to open 525 company-operated and

6 Starbucks 2002 Annual Report.

Exhibit 6: Customer Snapshot scores (North American stores) Source: Company information.

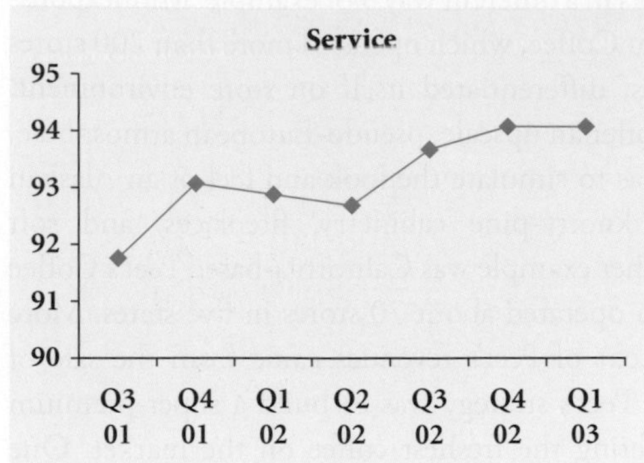

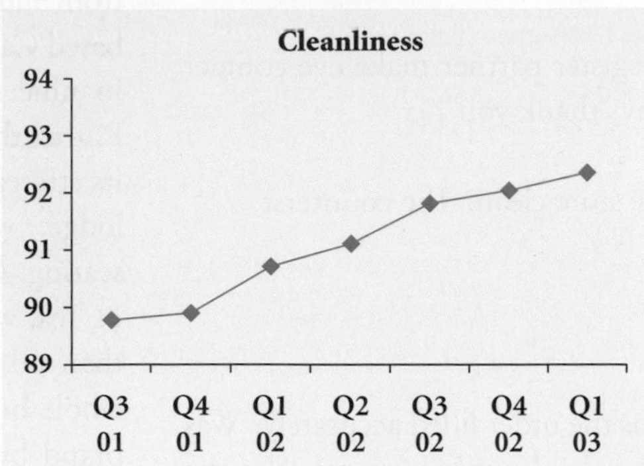

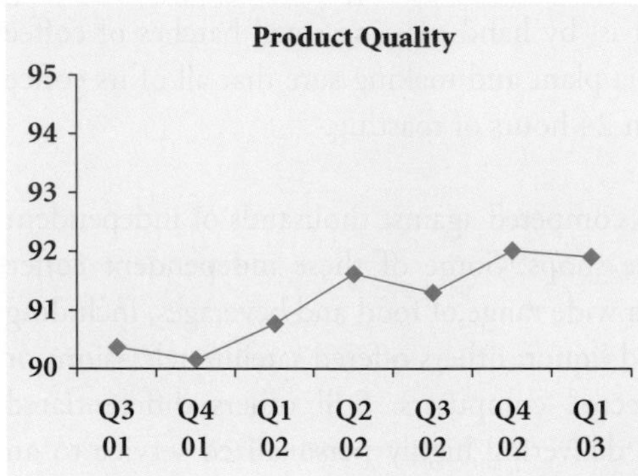

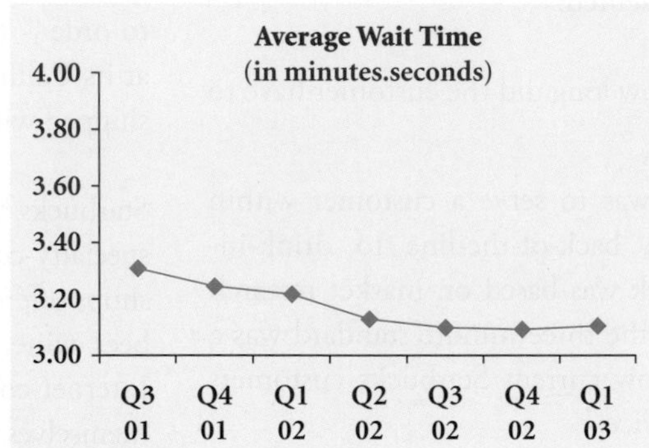

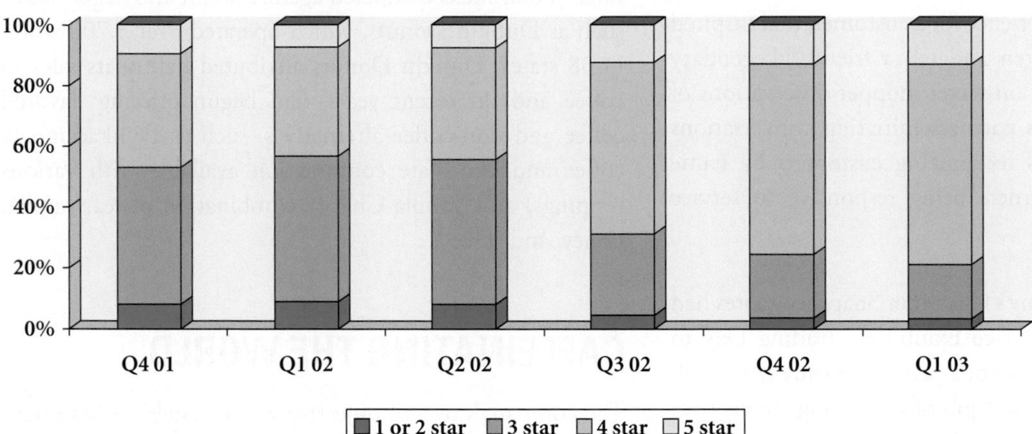

225 licensed North American stores in 2003, and Schultz believed that there was no reason North America could not eventually expand to at least 10,000 stores. As he put it, "These are still the early days of the company's growth."[7]

The company's optimistic growth plans were based on a number of considerations:

- First, coffee consumption was on the rise in the United States, following years of decline. More than 109 million people (about half of the US population) now drank coffee every day, and an additional 52 million drank it on occasion. The market's biggest growth appeared to be among drinkers of specialty coffee,[8] and it was estimated that about one-third of all US

7 Dina ElBoghdady, "Pouring It On: The Starbucks Strategy? Locations, Locations, Locations," The Washington Post, August 25, 2002.

8 National Coffee Association.

Exhibit 7: Total US Retail coffee market (includes both in-home and out-of-home consumption).

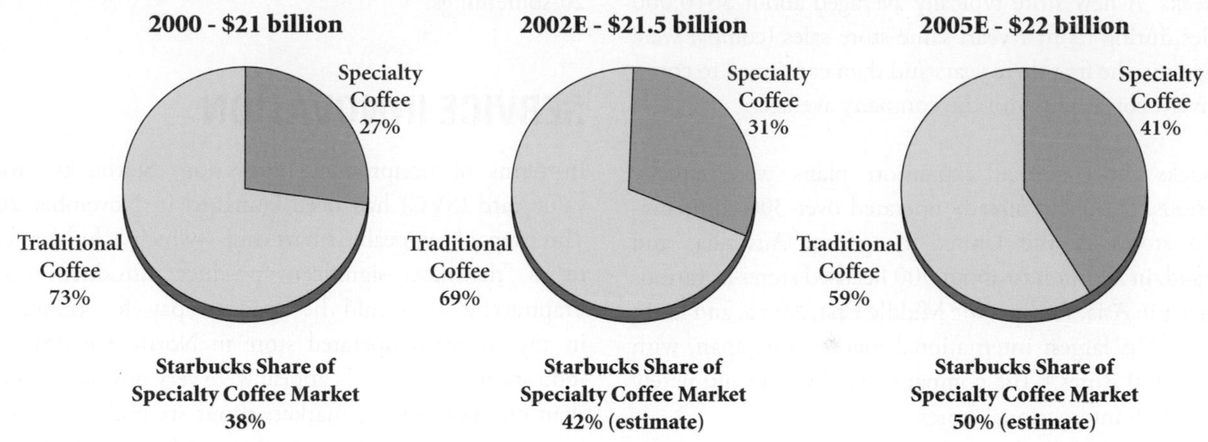

Other estimates[a] for the US retail coffee market in 2002:

- In the home, specialty coffee[b] was estimated to be a $3.2-billion business, of which Starbucks was estimated to have a 4% share.
- In the food-service channel, specialty coffee was estimated to be a $5-billion business, of which Starbucks was estimated to have a 5% share.
- In grocery stores, Starbucks was estimated to have a 7.3% share in the ground-coffee category and a 21.7% share in the whole-beans category.
- It was estimated that, over the next several years, the overall retail market would grow less than 1% per annum, but growth in the specialty-coffee category would be strong, with compound annual growth rate (CAGR) of 9–10%.
- Starbucks' US business was projected to grow at a CAGR of approximately 20% top-line revenue growth.

Source: Adapted from company reports and Lehman Brothers, November 5, 2002.

a The value of the retail coffee market was difficult to estimate, given the highly fragmented and loosely monitored nature of the market (i.e., specialty coffeehouses, restaurants, delis, kiosks, street carts, grocery and convenience stores, and vending machines).

b Specialty coffee includes espresso, cappuccino, latte, café mocha, iced/ice-blended coffee, gourmet coffee (premium whole bean or ground), and blended coffee.

coffee consumption took place outside of the home, in places such as offices, restaurants, and coffee shops. (See Exhibit 7.)

- Second, there were still eight states in the United States without a single company-operated Starbucks. In fact, the company was only in 150 of the roughly 300 metropolitan statistical areas in the nation.
- Third, the company believed it was far from reaching saturation levels in many existing markets. In the Southeast, for example, there was only one store for every 110,000 people (compared with one store for every 20,000 people in the Pacific Northwest). More generally, only seven states had more than 100 Starbucks locations.

Starbucks' strategy for expanding its retail business was to open stores in new markets while geographically clustering stores in existing markets. Although the latter often resulted in significant cannibalization, the company believed that this was more than offset by the total incremental sales associated with the increased store concentration. As Schultz readily conceded, "We self-cannibalize at least a third of our stores every day."[9]

When it came to selecting new retail sites, the company considered a number of criteria, including the extent to which the demographics of the area matched the profile of the typical Starbucks drinker, the level of coffee consumption in the area, the nature and intensity of competition in the local market, and the availability of attractive real estate. Once a decision was made to move forward with a site, the company was capable of designing,

9 ElBoghdady.

permitting, constructing, and opening a new store within 16 weeks. A new store typically averaged about $610,000 in sales during its first year; same-store sales (comps) were strongest in the first three years and then continued to comp positively, consistent with the company average.

Starbucks' international expansion plans were equally ambitious. Starbucks already operated over 300 company-owned stores in the United Kingdom, Australia, and Thailand, in addition to about 900 licensed stores in various countries in Asia, Europe, the Middle East, Africa, and Latin America. (Its largest international market was Japan, with close to 400 stores.) The company's goal was to ultimately have 15,000 international stores.

Product Innovation

The second big driver of company growth was product innovation. Internally, this was considered one of the most significant factors in comparable store sales growth, particularly since Starbucks' prices had remained relatively stable in recent years. New products were launched on a regular basis; for example, Starbucks introduced at least one new hot beverage every holiday season.

The new-product development process generally operated on a 12- to 18-month cycle, during which the internal research and development (R&D) team tinkered with product formulations, ran focus groups, and conducted in-store experiments and market tests. Aside from consumer acceptance, whether a product made it to market depended on a number of factors, including the extent to which the drink fit into the "ergonomic flow" of operations and the speed with which the beverage could be hand-crafted. Most importantly, the success of a new beverage depended on partner acceptance. "We've learned that no matter how great a drink it is, if our partners aren't excited about it, it won't sell," said Alling.

In recent years, the company's most successful innovation had been the 1995 introduction of a coffee and noncoffee-based line of Frappuccino beverages, which had driven same-store sales primarily by boosting traffic during nonpeak hours. The bottled version of the beverage (distributed by PepsiCo) had become a $400-million[10] franchise; it had managed to capture 90 percent of the ready-to-drink coffee category due in large part to its appeal to noncoffee-drinking 20-somethings.

10 Refers to sales at retail. Actual revenue contribution was much lower due to the joint-venture structure.

11 Stanley Holmes, "Starbucks' Card Smarts," BusinessWeek, March 18, 2002.

SERVICE INNOVATION

In terms of nonproduct innovation, Starbucks' stored-value card (SVC) had been launched in November 2001. This prepaid, swipeable smart card—which Schultz referred to as "the most significant product introduction since Frappuccino"[11]—could be used to pay for transactions in any company-operated store in North America. Early indications of the SVC's appeal were very positive: After less than one year on the market, about six million cards had been issued, and initial activations and reloads had already reached $160 million in sales. In surveys, the company had learned that cardholders tended to visit Starbucks twice as often as cash customers did and tended to experience reduced transaction times.

Day remarked, "We've found that a lot of the cards are being given away as gifts, and many of those gift recipients are being introduced to our brand for the first time. Not to mention the fact that the cards allow us to collect all kinds of customer-transaction data, data that we haven't even begun to do anything with yet."

The company's latest service innovation was its T-Mobile HotSpot wireless Internet service, which it planned to introduce in August 2002. The service would offer high-speed access to the Internet in 2,000 Starbucks stores in the United States and Europe, starting at $49.99 a month.

STARBUCKS' MARKET RESEARCH: TROUBLE BREWING?

Interestingly, although Starbucks was considered one of the world's most effective marketing organizations, it lacked a strategic marketing group. In fact, the company had no chief marketing officer, and its marketing department functioned as three separate groups—a market research group that gathered and analyzed market data requested by the various business units, a category group that developed new products and managed the menu and margins, and a marketing group that developed the quarterly promotional plans.

This organizational structure forced all of Starbucks' senior executives to assume marketing-related responsibilities. As

Day pointed out, "Marketing is everywhere at Starbucks—it just doesn't necessarily show up in a line item called 'marketing.' Everyone has to get involved in a collaborative marketing effort." However, the organizational structure also meant that market- and customer-related trends could sometimes be overlooked. "We tend to be great at measuring things, at collecting market data," Day noted, "but we are not very disciplined when it comes to using this data to drive decision making." She continued:

> This is exactly what started to happen a few years ago. We had evidence coming in from market research that contradicted some of the fundamental assumptions we had about our brand and our customers. The problem was that this evidence was all over the place—no one was really looking at the "big picture." As a result, it took a while before we started to take notice.

Starbucks' Brand Meaning

Once the team did take notice, it discovered several things. First, despite Starbucks' overwhelming presence and convenience, there was very little image or product differentiation between Starbucks and the smaller coffee chains (other than Starbucks' ubiquity) in the minds of specialty coffeehouse customers. There *was* significant differentiation, however, between Starbucks and the independent specialty coffeehouses (see Table A).

Table A: Qualitative brand meaning: Independents vs. Starbucks.

Independents:

- Social and inclusive
- Diverse and intellectual
- Artsy and funky
- Liberal and free-spirited
- Lingering encouraged
- Particularly appealing to younger coffeehouse customers
- Somewhat intimidating to older, more mainstream coffeehouse customers

Starbucks:

- Everywhere—the trend
- Good coffee on the run
- Place to meet and move on
- Convenience oriented; on the way to work
- Accessible and consistent

Source: Starbucks, based on qualitative interviews with specialty coffeehouse customers.

More generally, the market research team discovered that Starbucks' brand image had some rough edges. The number of respondents who strongly agreed with the statement "Starbucks cares primarily about making money" was up from 53 percent in 2000 to 61 percent in 2001, while the number of respondents who strongly agreed with the statement "Starbucks cares primarily about building more stores" was up from 48 percent to 55 percent. Day noted, "It's become apparent that we need to ask ourselves, 'Are we focusing on the right things? Are we clearly communicating our value and values to our customers, instead of just our growth plans?'" (see Table B)

Table B: The top five attributes consumers associate with the Starbucks brand.

- Known for specialty/gourmet coffee (54% strongly agree)
- Widely available (43% strongly agree)
- Corporate (42% strongly agree)
- Trendy (41% strongly agree)
- Always feel welcome at Starbucks (39% strongly agree)

Source: Starbucks, based on 2002 survey.

The Changing Customer

The market research team also discovered that Starbucks' customer base was evolving. Starbucks' newer customers tended to be younger, less well-educated, and in a lower income bracket than Starbucks' more established customers. In addition, they visited the stores less frequently and had very different perceptions of the Starbucks brand compared to more established customers (see Exhibit 8).

Furthermore, the team learned that Starbucks' historical customer profile—the affluent, well-educated, white-collar female between the ages of 24 and 44—had expanded. For example, about half of the stores in southern California had large numbers of Hispanic customers. In Florida, the company had stores that catered primarily to Cuban-Americans.

Customer Behavior

With respect to customer behavior, the market research team discovered that, regardless of the market—urban versus rural, new versus established—customers tended to use the stores the same way. The team also learned that, although the company's most frequent customers averaged

Exhibit 8: Starbucks' customer retention information.

% OF STARBUCKS' CUSTOMERS WHO FIRST STARTED VISITING STARBUCKS …	
In the past year	27
1–2 years ago	20
2–5 years ago	30
5 or more years ago	23

Source: Starbucks, 2002. Based on a sample of Starbucks' 2002 customer base.

	New Customers (First Visited in the Past Year)	Established Customers (First Visited 5+ Years Ago)
Percent female	45	49%
Average age	36	40
Percent with college degree +	37	63
Average income	$65,000	$81,000
Average # cups of coffee/ week (includes at home and away from home)	15	19
Attitudes toward Starbucks:		
High-quality brand	34%	51%
Brand I trust	30%	50%
For someone like me	15%	40%
Worth paying more for	8%	32%
Known for specialty coffee	44%	60%
Known as the coffee expert	31%	45%
Best-tasting coffee	20%	31%
Highest-quality coffee	26%	41%
Overall opinion of Starbucks	**25%**	**44%**

Source: Starbucks, 2002. "Attitudes toward Starbucks" measured according to the percent of customers who agreed with the above statements.

18 visits a month, the typical customer visited just five times a month (see Figure A).

Measuring and Driving Customer Satisfaction

Finally, the team discovered that, despite its high Customer Snapshot scores, Starbucks was not meeting expectations in terms of customer satisfaction. The satisfaction scores were considered critical because the team also had evidence of a direct link between satisfaction level and customer loyalty (see Exhibit 9 for customer satisfaction data).

While customer satisfaction was driven by a number of different factors (see Exhibit 10), Day believed that the customer satisfaction gap could primarily be attributed to a *service gap* between Starbucks scores on key attributes and customer expectations. When Starbucks had polled its customers to determine what it could do to make them feel more like valued customers, "improvements to service"—in particular, speed-of-service—had been mentioned most frequently (see Exhibit 11 for more information).

REDISCOVERING THE STARBUCKS CUSTOMER

Responding to the market research findings posed a difficult management challenge. The most controversial proposal was the one on the table before Day—it involved relaxing the labor-hour controls in the stores to add additional 20 hours

Exhibit 9: Starbucks' customer behavior, by satisfaction level.

	Unsatisfied Customer	Satisfied Customer	Highly Satisfied Customer
Number of Starbucks Visits/Month	3.9	4.3	7.2
Average Ticket Size/Visit	$3.88	$4.06	$4.42
Average Customer Life (Years)	1.1	4.4	8.3

Source: Self-reported customer activity from Starbucks survey, 2002.

Figure A: Customer visit.

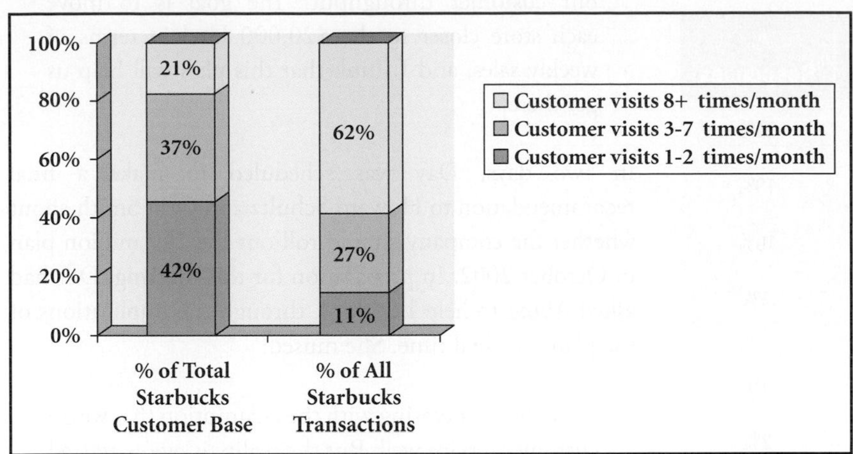

Exhibit 10: Importance rankings of key attributes in creating customer satisfaction.

To be read: 83% of Starbucks' customers rate a clean store as being highly important (90+ on a 100-point scale) in creating customer satisfaction.

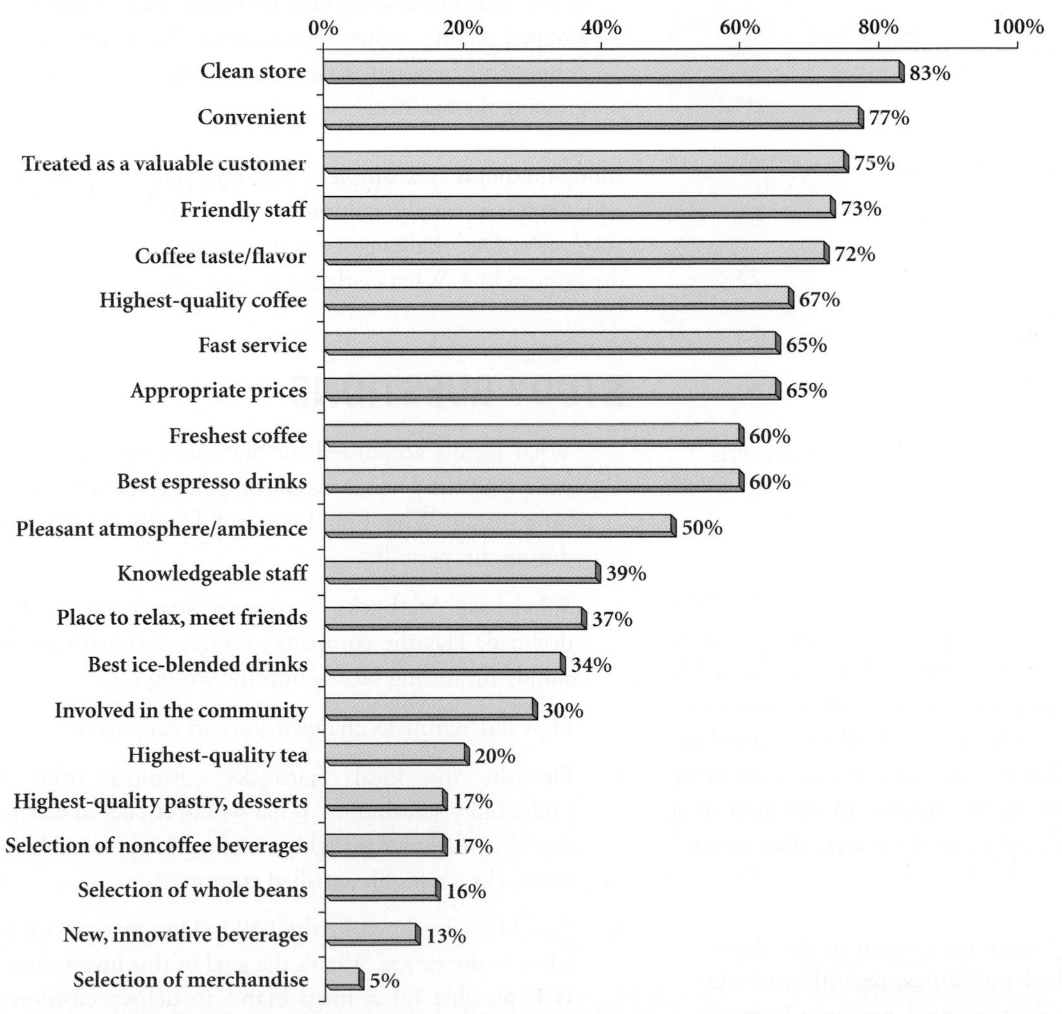

Source: Self-reported customer activity from Starbucks survey, 2002.

Exhibit 11: Factors driving "valued customer" perceptions.

How could Starbucks make you feel more like a valued customer?	% Responses
Improvements to Service (total)	**34%**
Friendlier, more attentive staff	19%
Faster, more efficient service	10%
Personal treatment (remember my name, remember my order)	4%
More knowledgeable staff	4%
Better service	2%
Offer Better Prices/Incentive Programs (total)	**31%**
Free cup after X number of visits	19%
Reduce prices	11%
Offer promotions, specials	3%
Other (total)	**21%**
Better quality/variety of products	9%
Improve atmosphere	8%
Community outreach/charity	2%
More stores/more convenient locations	2%
Don't Know/Already Satisfied	**28%**

Source: Starbucks, 2002. Based on a survey of Starbucks' 2002 customer base, including highly satisfied, satisfied, and unsatisfied customers.

of labor per week per store, at a cost of an extra $40 million per year. Not surprisingly, the plan was being met with significant internal resistance. "Our CFO is understandably concerned about the potential impact on our bottom line," said Day. "Each $6 million in profit contribution translates into a penny a share. But my argument is that if we move away from seeing labor as an expense to seeing it as a customer-oriented investment, we'll see a positive return." She continued:

> We need to bring service time down to the three-minute level in all of our stores, regardless of the time of day. If we do this, we'll not only increase customer satisfaction and build stronger long-term relationships with our customers, we'll also improve our customer throughput. The goal is to move each store closer to the $20,000 level in terms of weekly sales, and I think that this plan will help us get there.

In two days, Day was scheduled to make a final recommendation to Howard Schultz and Orin Smith about whether the company should roll out the $40 million plan in October 2002. In preparation for this meeting, Day had asked Alling to help her think through the implications of the plan one final time. She mused:

> We've been operating with the assumption that we do customer service well. But the reality is, we've started to lose sight of the consumer. It's amazing that this could happen to a company like us—after all, we've become one of the most prominent consumer brands in the world. For all of our focus on building the brand and introducing new products, we've simply stopped talking about the customer. We've lost the connection between satisfying our customers and growing the business.

Alling's response was simple: "We know that both Howard and Orin are totally committed to satisfying our retail customers. Our challenge is to tie customer satisfaction to the bottom line. What evidence do we have?"

STUDY QUESTIONS

1. What factors accounted for Starbucks' success in the early 1990s and what was so compelling about its value proposition? What brand image did Starbucks develop during this period?
2. Why have Starbucks' customer satisfaction scores declined? Has the company's service declined or is it simply measuring satisfaction the wrong way?
3. How has Starbucks changed since its early days?
4. Describe the ideal Starbucks customer from a profitability standpoint. What would it take to ensure that this customer is highly satisfied? How valuable to Starbucks is a highly satisfied customer?
5. Should Starbucks make the $40 million investment in labor in the stores? What's the goal of this investment? Is it possible for a mega-brand to deliver customer intimacy?

Glossary

A

activity-based costing (ABC): an approach to costing based on identifying the activities being performed and then determining the resources that each consumes.

adequate service: the minimum level of service that a customer will accept without being dissatisfied.

advertising: any paid form of nonpersonal communication by a marketer to inform, educate, or persuade members of target audiences.

arm's-length transactions: interactions between customers and service suppliers in which mail or telecommunications minimizes the need to meet face-to-face.

attitude: a person's consistently favorable or unfavorable evaluations, feelings, and action tendencies toward an object or idea.

auction: a selling procedure managed by a specialist intermediary in which the price is set by allowing prospective purchasers to bid against each other for a product offered by a seller.

augmented product: core product (a good or a service) plus supplementary elements that add value for customers (*see also* **flower of service**).

B

backstage (or technical core): those aspects of service operations that are hidden from customers.

banner ads: small, rectangular boxes on web sites that contain text and perhaps a picture to support a brand.

benchmarking: comparing an organization's products and processes to those of competitors or leading firms in the same or other industries to find ways to improve performance, quality, and cost-effectiveness.

benefit: an advantage or gain that customers obtain from the performance of a service or use of a physical good.

blog: a publicly accessible "web log" containing frequently updated pages in the form of journals, diaries, news listings, etc.; authors, known as bloggers, typically focus on specific topics.

blueprint: a visual map of the sequence of activities required for service delivery that specifies front-stage and backstage elements and the linkages between them.

boundary-spanning positions: jobs that straddle the boundary between the external environment, where customers are encountered, and the internal operations of the organization.

brand: a name, phrase, design, symbol, or some combination of these elements that identifies a company's services and differentiates it from competitors.

business model: the means by which an organization generates income from sales and other sources through choice of pricing mechanisms and payors (e.g, user, advertiser or sponsor, other third parties), ideally sufficient to cover costs and create value for its owners. (*Note:* For nonprofits and public agencies, donations and designated tax revenues may be an integral part of the model.)

C

chain stores: two or more outlets under common ownership and control, and selling similar goods and services.

chase demand strategy: adjusting the level of capacity to meet the level of demand at any given time.

churn: loss of existing customer accounts and the need to replace them with new ones.

clicks and mortar: a strategy for offering service through both physical stores and virtual storefronts via web sites on the Internet.

competition-based pricing: setting prices relative to those charged by competitors.

competitive advantage: a firm's ability to perform in ways that competitors cannot or will not match.

complaint: a formal expression of dissatisfaction with any aspect of a service experience.

complaint log: a detailed record of all customer complaints received by a service provider.

conjoint analysis: a research method for determining the utility values that consumers attach to varying levels of a product's attributes.

consumption: purchase and use of a service or good.

control chart: a chart that graphs quantitative changes in service performance on a specific variable relative to a predefined standard.

control model of management: an approach based on clearly defined roles, top-down control systems, a hierarchical organizational structure, and the assumption that management knows best.

core competency: a capability that is a source of competitive advantage.

corporate culture: shared beliefs, norms, experiences, and stories that characterize an organization.

corporate design: consistent application of distinctive colors, symbols, and lettering to give a firm an easily recognizable identity.

cost leader: a firm that bases its pricing strategy on achieving the lowest costs in its industry.

cost-based pricing: relating the price to be charged for a product to the costs associated with producing, delivering, and marketing it.

credence attributes: product characteristics that customers zmay not be able to evaluate even after purchase and consumption.

critical incident: a specific encounter between customer and service provider in which the outcome has proved especially satisfying or dissatisfying for one or both parties.

critical incident technique (CIT): a methodology for collecting, categorizing, and analyzing critical incidents that have occurred between customers and service providers.

CRM system: information technology (IT) systems and infrastructure that support the implementation and delivery of a customer-relationship management strategy.

customer contact personnel: service employees who interact directly with individual customers, either in person or through mail and telecommunications.

customer equity: the total combined customer lifetime value (*see definition*) of the company's entire customer base.

customer interface: all points at which customers interact with a service organization.

customer lifetime value (CLV): the net present value of the stream of future contributions or profits expected over each customer's purchases during his or her anticipated lifetime as a customer of a specific organization.

customer relationship management (CRM): the overall process of building and maintaining profitable customer relationships by delivering superior customer value and satisfaction.

customer satisfaction: a short-term emotional reaction to a specific service performance.

customer training: training programs offered by service firms to teach customers about complex service products.

customization: tailoring service characteristics to meet each customer's specific needs and preferences.

cyberspace: a virtual reality without physical existence, in which electronic transactions or communications occur.

D

data mining: extracting useful information about individuals, trends, and segments from often massive amounts of customer data.

data warehouse: a comprehensive database containing customer information and transaction data.

database marketing: building, maintaining, and using customer databases and other databases for contacting, selling, cross-selling, up-selling, and building customer relationships.

defection: a customer's decision to transfer brand loyalty from a current service provider to a competitor.

delivery channels: physical and electronic means by which a service firm (sometimes assisted by intermediaries) delivers one or more product elements to its customers.

demand curve: A curve that shows the number of units the market will buy at different prices.

demand cycle: a period of time during which the level of demand for a sendee will increase and decrease in a somewhat predictable way before repeating itself.

demographic segmentation: dividing the market into groups based on demographic variables such as age, gender, family life cycle, family size, income, occupation, education, religion, or ethnic group.

desired service: the "wished for" level of service quality that a customer believes can and should be delivered.

discounting: a strategy of reducing the price of an item below the normal level.

dynamic pricing: a technique, employed primarily by e-tailers to charge different customers different prices for the same products, based on information collected about their purchase history, preferences, and price sensitivity.

E

e-commerce: buying, selling, and other marketing processes supported by the Internet (*see also* **e-tailing**).

emotional labor: expressing socially appropriate (but sometimes false) emotions toward customers during service transactions.

empowerment: authorizing employees to find solutions to service problems and make appropriate decisions about responding to customer concerns without having to obtain a supervisor's approval.

enablement: providing employees with the skills, tools, and resources they need to use their own discretion confidently and effectively.

enhancing supplementary services: supplementary services that may add extra value for customers.

e-tailing: retailing through the Internet instead of through physical stores.

excess capacity: an organization's capacity to create service output that is not fully utilized.

excess demand: demand for a service at a given time that exceeds the organization's ability to meet customer needs.

expectations: internal standards that customers use to judge the quality of a service experience.

experience attributes: product performance features that customers can evaluate only during service delivery.

expert systems: interactive computer programs that mimic a human expert's reasoning to draw conclusions from data, solve problems, and give customized advice.

F

facilitating supplementary services: supplementary services that aid in the use of the core product or are required for service delivery.

fail point: a point in a process at which there is a significant risk of problems that can damage service quality (sometimes referred to humorously as an OTSU, short for "opportunity to screw up").

financial outlays: all monetary expenditures incurred by customers in purchasing and consuming a service.

fishbone diagram: a chart-based technique that relates specific service problems to different categories of underlying causes (also known as a cause-and-effect chart).

fixed costs: costs that do not vary with production or sales revenue.

flat-rate pricing: quoting a fixed price for a service in advance of delivery.

flowchart: a visual representation of the steps involved in delivering service to customers (*see also* **blueprint**).

flower of service: a visual framework for understanding the supplementary service elements that surround and add value to the product core (*see also* **augmented product**).

focus group: a group, typically consisting of six to eight people and carefully preselected on certain characteristics (e.g., demographics, psychographics, or product ownership), who are convened by researchers for in-depth, moderator-led discussion of specific topics.

franchise: a contractual association between a franchiser (typically a manufacturer, wholesaler, or service organization) and independent businesspeople (franchisees) who buy the right to own and operate one or more units in the franchise system.

frequency program (FPs): a program designed to reward customers who buy frequently and in substantial amounts.

front stage: those aspects of service operations and delivery that are visible or otherwise apparent to customers.

G

geographic segmentation: dividing a market into geographic units such as countries, regions, or cities.

goods: physical objects or devices that provide benefits for customers through ownership or use.

H

high-contact services: services that involve significant interaction among customers, service personnel, and equipment and facilities.

human resource management (HRM): coordination of tasks related to job design, employee recruitment, selection, training, and motivation; also includes planning and administering other employee-related activities.

I

image: a set of beliefs, ideas, and impressions held regarding an object.

impersonal communications: one-way communications directed at target audiences who are not in personal contact with the message source (including advertising, promotions, and public relations).

information processing: intangible actions directed at customers' assets.

information-based services: all services in which the principal value comes from the transmission of data to customers; also includes mental stimulus processing and information processing (*see definitions*).

in-process wait: a wait that occurs during service delivery.

inputs: all resources (labor, materials, energy, and capital) required to create service offerings.

intangibility: (*see* **mental intangibility** *and* **physical intangibility**).

intangible: something that is experienced and that cannot be touched or preserved.

integrated marketing communications (IMC): a concept under which an organization carefully integrates and coordinates its many communication channels to deliver a clear, consistent, and compelling message about the organization and its products.

internal communications: all forms of communication from management to employees within an organization.

internal customers: employees who receive services from an internal supplier (another employee or department) as a necessary input to performing their own jobs.

internal marketing: marketing activities directed internally to employees to train and motivate them and instill a customer focus.

internal services: service elements within any type of business that facilitate creation of, or add value to, its final output.

Internet: a large public web of computer networks that connects users from around the world to each other and to a vast information repository.

inventory: for *manufacturing*, the physical output stockpiled after production for sale at a later date; for *services*, future output that has not yet been reserved in advance, such as the number of hotel rooms still available for sale on a given day.

involvement model of management: an approach based on the assumption that employees are capable of self-direction and, if properly trained, motivated, and informed, can make good decisions concerning service operations and delivery.

iTV: (interactive television) procedures that allow viewers to alter the viewing experience by controlling TV program delivery (e.g., TiVo, video on demand) and/or content.

J

jaycustomer: a customer who acts in a thoughtless or abusive way, causing problems for the firm, its employees, and other customers.

L

levels of customer contact: the extent to which customers interact physically with the service organization.

low-contact services: services that require minimal or no direct contact between customers and the service organization.

loyalty: a customer's commitment to continue patronizing a specific firm over an extended period of time.

M

market focus: the extent to which a firm serves few or many markets.

market segmentation: the process of dividing a market into distinct groups within each of which all customers share relevant characteristics that distinguish them from customers in other segments, and respond in similar ways; to a given set of marketing efforts.

marketing communications mix: a full set of communication tools (both paid and unpaid) available to marketers, including advertising, sales promotion, events, public relations and publicity, direct marketing, and personal selling.

marketing implementation: a process that turns marketing plans into projects and ensures that such projects are executed in a way that accomplishes the plan's stated objectives.

marketing research: the systematic design, collection, analysis, and reporting of customer and competitor data and findings relevant to a specific marketing situation facing an organization.

marketplace: a location in physical space or cyberspace (*see definition*) where suppliers and customers meet to do business.

mass customization: offering a service with some individualized product elements to a large number of customers at a relatively low price.

maximum capacity: the upper limit to a firm's ability to meet customer demand at a particular time.

medium-contact services: services that involve only a limited amount of contact between customers and elements of the service organization.

membership relationship: a formalized relationship between the firm and a specified customer that may offer special benefits to both parties.

mental intangibility: difficulty for customers in visualizing an experience in advance of purchase and understanding the process and even the nature of the outcome (*see also* **physical intangibility**).

mental stimulus processing: intangible actions directed at people's minds.

mission statement: a succinct description of what the organization does, its standards and values, whom it serves, and what it intends to accomplish.

molecular model: a framework that uses a chemical analogy to describe the structure of a service offering.

moment of truth: a point in service delivery at which customers interact with service employees or self-service equipment and the outcome may affect perceptions of service quality.

mystery shopping: a research technique that employs individuals posing as ordinary customers to obtain feedback on the service environment and customer–employee interactions.

N

needs: subconscious, deeply felt desires that often concern long-term existence and identity issues.

net value: the sum of all perceived benefits (gross value) minus the sum of all perceived outlays.

nonfinancial outlays: time expenditures, physical and mental effort, and unwanted sensory experiences associated with searching for, buying, and using a service.

nonmonetary costs: (*see* **nonfinancial outlays**).

O

opportunity cost: the potential value of income or other benefits foregone as a result of choosing one course of action instead of other alternatives.

optimum capacity: a point beyond which a firm's efforts to serve additional customers will lead to a perceived decline in service quality.

organizational climate: employees' shared perceptions of the practices, procedures, and types of behaviors that are rewarded and supported in a particular setting.

organizational culture: shared values, beliefs, and work styles that are based on an understanding of what is important to the organization and why.

OTSU ("opportunity to screw up"): (*see* **fail point**).

outputs: the final outcome of the service delivery process as perceived and valued by customers.

P

Pareto analysis: an analytical procedure to identify what proportion of problem events is caused by each of several different factors.

people: customers and employees who are involved in service production.

people processing: services that involve tangible actions to people's bodies.

perception: a process by which individuals select, organize, and interpret information to form a meaningful picture of the world.

perceptual map: a visual illustration of how customers perceive competing services.

permission marketing: a marketing communication strategy that encourages customers to volunteer permission to a company to communicate with them through specified channels so they may learn more about its products and continue to receive useful information or something else of value to them.

personal communications: direct communications between marketers and individual customers that involve two-way dialog (including face-to-face conversations, phone calls, and email).

personal selling: two-way communications between service employees and customers designed to influence the purchase process directly.

physical effort: undesired consequences to a customer's body resulting from involvement in the service delivery process.

physical evidence: visual or other tangible clues that provide evidence of service quality.

physical intangibility: service elements that are not accessible to examination by any of the five senses; (*more narrowly*) elements that cannot be touched or preserved by customers.

place and time: management decisions about when, where, and how to deliver services to customers.

positioning: establishing a distinctive place in the minds of customers relative to the attributes possessed by or absent from competing products.

possession processing: tangible actions to goods and other physical possessions belonging to customers.

post-process wait: a wait that occurs after service delivery has been completed.

post-encounter stage: the final stage in the service purchase process, in which customers evaluate the service experienced, form their satisfaction/dissatisfaction judgment with the service outcome, and establish future intentions.

predicted service: the level of service quality a customer believes a firm will actually deliver.

pre-process wait: a wait before service delivery begins.

pre-purchase stage: the first stage in the service purchase process, in which customers identify alternatives, weigh benefits and risks, and make a purchase decision.

price and other user outlays: expenditures of money, time, and effort that customers incur in purchasing and consuming services.

price bucket: an allocation of service capacity (e.g., seats) for sale at a particular price.

price bundling: charging a base price for a core service plus additional fees for optional supplementary elements.

price elasticity: the extent to which a change in price leads to a corresponding change in demand in the opposite direction. (Demand is described as *price inelastic* when changes in price have little or no effect on demand.)

price leader: a firm that takes the initiative on price changes in its market area and is copied by others.

process: a particular method of operations or series of actions, typically involving steps that need to occur in a defined sequence.

product: the core output (either a service or a manufactured good) produced by a firm.

product attributes: all features (both tangible and intangible) of a good or service that can be evaluated by customers.

product elements: all components of the service performance that create value for customers.

productive capacity: the amount of facilities, equipment, labor, infrastructure, and other assets available to a firm to create output for its customers.

productivity: how efficiently service inputs are transformed into outputs that add value for customers.

promotion and education: all communication activities and incentives designed to build customer preference for a specific service or service provider.

psychographic segmentation: dividing a market into different groups based on personality characteristics, social class, or lifestyle.

psychological burdens: undesired mental or emotional states experienced by customers as a result of the service delivery process.

public relations: efforts to stimulate positive interest in a company and its products by sending out news releases, holding press conferences, staging special events, and sponsoring newsworthy activities put on by third parties.

purchase process: the stages a customer goes through in choosing, consuming, and evaluating a service.

Q

quality: the degree to which a service satisfies customers by consistently meeting their needs, wants, and expectations.

queue: a line of people, vehicles, other physical objects, or intangible items waiting their turn to be served or processed.

queue configuration: the way in which a waiting line is organized.

R

rate fences: techniques for separating customers so that segments for whom the service offers high value are unable to take advantage of lower-priced offers.

reengineering: analysis and redesign of business processes to create dramatic performance improvements in such areas as cost, quality, speed, and customers' service experiences.

relationship marketing: activities aimed at developing long-term, cost-effective links between an organization and its customers for the mutual benefit of both parties.

repositioning: changing the position a firm holds in a consumer's mind relative to competing services.

retail displays: presentations of merchandise, service experiences, and benefits in store windows and other locations.

retail gravity model: a mathematical approach to retail site selection that involves calculating the geographic center of gravity for the target population and then locating a facility to optimize customers' ease of access.

return on quality: financial return obtained from investing in service quality improvements.

revenue management: a pricing and product design strategy based on charging different prices to different segments at different times to maximize the revenue that can be derived from a firm's available capacity during a specific time frame (also known as *yield management*).

role: a combination of social cues that guides behavior in a specific setting or context.

role congruence: the extent to which both customers and employees act out their prescribed roles during a service encounter.

S

sales promotion: a short-term incentive offered to customers and intermediaries to stimulate faster or larger purchase.

satisfaction: a person's feelings of pleasure or disappointment resulting from a consumption experience when comparing a product's perceived performance or outcome in relation to his or her expectations.

script: a learned sequence of behaviors obtained through personal experience or communication with others.

search attributes: product characteristics that consumers can readily evaluate prior to purchase.

segment: a group of current or prospective customers who share common characteristics, needs, purchasing behavior, or consumption patterns.

sensory burdens: negative sensations experienced through a customer's five senses during the service delivery process.

service: an economic activity offered by one party to another, typically without transfer of ownership, creating value from rental of, or access to, goods, labor, professional skills, facilities, networks, or systems, singly or in combination.

service blueprint: (*see* **blueprint, flowchart**).

service concept: what the firm offers, to whom, and through what processes.

service delivery system: the part of the total service system during which final "assembly" of the elements takes place and the product is delivered to the customer; it includes the visible elements of the service operation.

service encounter: a period of time during which customers interact directly with a service.

service encounter stage: the second stage in the service purchase process in which the required service is delivered through interactions between customers and the service provider.

service factory: a physical site where service operations take place.

service failure: a perception by customers that one or more specific aspects of service delivery have not met their expectations.

service focus: extent to which a firm offers few or many services.

service guarantee: a promise that if service delivery fails to meet predefined standards, the customer is entitled to one or more forms of compensation.

service marketing system: the part of the total service system in which the firm has any form of contact with its customers, from advertising to billing; it includes contacts made at the point of delivery.

service model: an integrative statement that specifies the nature of the service concept (what the firm offers, to whom, and through what processes), the service blueprint (how the concept is delivered to target customers), and the accompanying business model (how revenues will be generated sufficient to cover costs and ensure financial viability).

service operations system: the part of the total service system in which inputs are processed and the elements of the service product are created.

service preview: a demonstration of how a service works, to educate customers about the roles they are expected to perform in service delivery.

service quality: customers' long-term, cognitive evaluations of a firm's service delivery.

service quality information system: an ongoing service research process that provides timely, useful data to managers about customer satisfaction, expectations, and perceptions of quality.

service recovery: systematic efforts by a firm after a service failure to correct a problem and retain a customer's goodwill.

service sector: the portion of a nation's economy represented by services of all kinds, including those offered by public and nonprofit organizations.

service profit chain: a strategic framework that links employee satisfaction to performance on service attributes to customer satisfaction, then to customer retention, and finally to profits.

services marketing mix: (*see* seven (7) Ps).

servicescape: the design of any physical location where customers come to place orders and obtain service delivery.

SERVQUAL: a pair of standardized 22-item scales that measure customers' expectations and perceptions concerning five dimensions of service quality.

seven (7) Ps: seven strategic elements, each beginning with P, in the services marketing mix, representing the key ingredients required to create viable strategies for meeting customer needs profitably in a competitive marketplace.

standardization: reducing variation in service operations and delivery.

stickiness: a web site's ability to encourage repeat visits and purchases by providing users with easy navigation, problem-free execution of tasks, and keeping its audience engaged with interactive communication presented in an appealing fashion.

sustainable competitive advantage: a position in the marketplace that can't be taken away or minimized by competitors in the short run.

T

tangible: capable of being touched, held, or preserved in a physical form over time.

target market: a part of the qualified available market with common needs or characteristics that a company decides to serve.

target segments: segments selected because their needs and other characteristics fit well with a specific firm's goals and capabilities.

time expenditures: the time spent by customers during all aspects of the service delivery process.

three-stage model of service consumption: a framework depicting how consumers move from a pre-purchase stage (in which they recognize their needs, search for and evaluate alternative solutions, and make a decision), to a service encounter search (in which they obtain service delivery), and then a post-encounter stage (in which they evaluate service performance against expectations).

third-party payments: payments to cover all or part of the cost of a service or good made by a party other than the user (who may or may not have made the actual purchase decision).

total costs: the sum of the fixed and variable costs for any given level of production.

transaction: an event during which an exchange of value takes place between two parties.

transactional survey: a technique to measure customer satisfaction and perceptions of service quality while a specific service experience is still fresh in the customer's mind.

U

undesirable demand: a request for service that conflicts with the organization's mission, priorities, or capabilities.

V

value chain: the series of departments within a firm or external partners and subcontractors that carry out value-creating activities to design, produce, market, deliver, and support a product or service offering.

value exchange: the transfer of benefits and solutions offered by a seller in return for financial and other value offered by a purchaser.

value proposition: a specified package of benefits and solutions that a company intends to offer and how it proposes to deliver them to customers, emphasizing key points of difference relative to competing alternatives.

value-based pricing: the practice of setting prices based on what customers are willing to pay for the value they believe they will receive.

variability: a lack of consistency in inputs and outputs during the service production process.

variable costs: costs that depend directly on the volume of production or service transactions.

viral marketing: using the Internet to create word-of-mouth effects to support marketing efforts.

W

wheel of loyalty: a systematic and integrated approach to targeting, acquiring, developing, and retaining a valuable customer base.

word-of-mouth: positive or negative comments about a service made by one individual (usually a current or former customer) to another.

Y

yield: the average revenue received per unit of capacity offered for sale.

yield management: (*see* revenue management).

Z

zone of tolerance: the range within which customers are willing to accept variations in service delivery.

Credits

Chapter 1 — p. 4: © Andres Rodriguez/123RF.COM; p. 5: Royal Caribbean International; p. 7: © Kobby Dagan/123RF.COM; p. 8: Rolls-Royce plc; p. 13: Used with permission by Randy Glasbergen; p. 14: © Chiramanas Jutidharabongse/123RF.COM; p. 16: Flickr/Hans van de Bruggen; p. 16: © Phil Date/123RF.COM; p. 17: © Pavel Losevsky/Dreamstime.com; p. 18: © Lisa Young/123RF.COM; p. 21: © Leloft1911/Dreamstime.com, p. 22: © Kirill Zdorov/Dreamstime.com; p. 22: Flickr/michaeljung; p. 23: © Steve Cukrov/123RF.COM; p. 23: © iStockphoto.com/Erwin Ps.

Chapter 2 — p. 34: David Shankbone/Wikipedia; p. 35: © Piotr Marcinski/Dreamstime.com; p. 37: © Hertz System Inc. 2012; p. 38: © iStockphoto.com/Ben Blankenburg; p. 40: © iStockphoto.com/mathieukor; p. 41: "Award Recipients at the HSMAI Adrian Awards in New York". Used with permission from HSMAI; p. 43: International Exchange Programs Pty Ltd; p. 43: ChinaBridal.com; p. 44: © Zurich Insurance Company Ltd; p.44: © kurhan/123RF.COM; p. 45: © Patryk Kosmider/Dreamstime.com; p. 46: Flickr/dave weatherall; p. 48: © Courtesy of Singapore Airlines; p. 49: © iStockPhoto.com/Edward ONeil Photography Inc.; p. 50: Used with permission by JuanJ; p. 50: © Stephen Coburn /Dreamstime.com; p. 51: Used with permission by Randy Glasbergen; p. 53: © iStockphoto.com/ugur bariskan; p. 53: © Qi Feng/123RF.COM; p. 54: © Ron Chapple/Dreamstime.com; p. 55: © HongQi Zhang/123RF.COM; p. 55: © Tyler Olson/123RF.COM; p. 58: © Progressive Casualty Insurance Company.

Chapter 3 — p. 66: © Anatoliy Samara/123RF.COM; p. 67: © Anatoliy Samara/123RF.COM; p. 70: © Jan Miks/123RF.COM; p. 73: Photo by Contiki Holidays; p. 74: Lcro77/Dreamstime.com; p. 75: © 123RF.COM; p. 77: Air Charter Team; p. 77: © iStockphoto.com/Remus Eserblom; p. 78: © Rentokil Initial plc; p. 80: Flickr/Alex Kwong; p. 80: Used with permission by Randy Glasbergen; p. 81: © Thomas Becker/123RF.COM; p. 82: © auremar/123RF.COM; p. 82: © iStockphoto.com/kutay tanir; p. 83: © Rene Drouyer/Dreamstime.com; p. 86: Flickr/http2007, p. 88: © Free Stock Photography.

Chapter 4 — p. 96: © Norman Kin Hang Chan/123RF.COM; p. 97: © iStockphoto.com/korhan hasim isik; p. 97: © CartoonStock; p. 97: © CartoonStock; p. 99: © Twitter; p. 100: © iStockphoto.com/Oxford; p. 100: Reprinted by permission of Dr. R. L. Bramble, All rights reserved; p. 101: OpenTable, Inc.; p. 101: © iStockphoto.com/Baris Simsek; p. 102: © Rramirez125/Dreamstime.com; p. 102: © iStockphoto.com/Edward Bock; p. 103: © CartoonStock; p. 104: © naiyyer/123RF.COM; p. 104: © Sabri Hakim/Dreamstime.com; p. 104: © Tatjana Strelkova/Dreamstime.com; p. 105: © Yoshikatsu Tsuno/Getty Image; p. 106: © iStockphoto.com/dra_schwartz; p. 108: Courtesy of Carol M Highsmith/Wikipedia; p. 108: Courtesy of BrokenSphere/Wikipedia; p. 110: Sun Microsystems, Inc.; p. 113: Landry's, Inc.; p. 114: © iStockphoto.com/Emrah Turudu; p. 114: Flickr/texqas; p. 115: © iStockphoto.com/Dieter Spears.

Chapter 5 — p. 122: © iStockphoto.com/Martin McCarthy; p. 123: Used with permission by Lauren Luke; p. 125: Prince's Landscape & Construction Pte Ltd (Singapore); p. 126: © Aggreko Plc; p. 127: Used with permission by Randy Glasbergen; p. 128: Courtesy of Emirates airline; p. 129: © iStockphoto.com; p. 129: © tito/123RF.COM; p. 130: stampsjoann.net; p. 130: © Paul Hakimata/123RF.COM; p. 131: © Hse0193/Dreamstime.com; p. 131: © Bay Area Rapid Transit District; p. 132: Flickr/B'Rob; p. 133: © Swissôtel Hotels & Resorts; p. 134: Used with permission by Randy Glasbergen; p. 135: © iStockPhoto.com; p. 135: Flickr/CiscoANZ; p. 136: © first direct; p. 138: © moneycontrol.com; p. 138: © The World Bank Group; p. 139: © The World Bank Group; p. 140: © iStockphoto.com/Tupungato; p. 141: © iStockphoto.com.

Chapter 6 — p. 150: © Lightkeeper/Dreamstime.com; p. 151: ScoreBig, Inc.; p. 153: © Yali Shi/Dreamstime.com; p. 154: © Erwin Purnomo Sidi/Dreamstime.com; p. 154: © tupungato/123RF.COM; p. 156: Used with permission by Randy Glasbergen; p. 156: © King Features. All rights reserved; p. 157: © Ken Hurst/Dreamstime.com; p. 160: © iStockphoto.com/Ilka-Erika Szasz-Fabian; p. 161: © iStockphoto.com/iShootPhotos, LLC; p. 164: Associated Press/Yomiuri Shimbun; p. 167: © iStockphoto.com/WendellandCarolyn; p. 168: © Dana Rothstein/Dreamstime.com; p. 168: © iStockphoto.com/Hermann Danzmayr; p. 170: © iStockphoto.com/Joel Carillet; p. 174: © iStockphoto.com/Mayumi Terao; p. 176: Used with permission by Randy Glasbergen; p. 176: © Andres Rodriguez/Dreamstime.com; p. 177: © JPMorgan Chase & Co.; p. 178: © Andre Blais/Dreamstime.com.

Chapter 7 — p. 188: © Tupungato/Dreamstime.com; p. 189: Flickr/John Pannell; p. 190: © iStockphoto.com; p. 190: eBay Inc.; p. 190: Mutual of Wausau Insurance Corporation; p. 191: © iStockphoto.com/Shaun Lowe; p. 192: Adrian Michael/Wikimedia; p. 193: Flickr/sporst; p. 194: Joerg Hackemann/123RF.COM; p. 195: AT Kearney; p. 197: © iStockphoto.com/Kerstin Waurick; p. 199: © Linden Research, Inc.; p. 200. Associated Press/Ng Han Guan; p. 201: Used with permission by Randy Glasbergen; p. 202: Used with permission by Randy Glasbergen; p. 202: Jon Helgason/123RF.COM; p. 203: © iStockphoto.com/adrian beesley; p. 204: Flickr/Håkan Dahlström; p. 207: Flickr/sjsharktank; p. 208: Flickr/longhorndave; p. 209: Konrad Bak/123RF.COM; p. 211: © Google; p. 214: Wikimedia/Seo75; p. 215: Getty Image/McKroes.

Chapter 8 — p. 226: Melissa Stratman/Coleman Associates; p. 227: Melissa Stratman/Coleman Associates; p. 230: © Ilene MacDonald/Alamy; p. 233: gemenacom/123RF.COM; p. 233: Ping Han/123RF.COM; p. 234: Wavebreak Media Ltd/123RF.COM; p. 234: Rui Santos/123RF.COM; p. 234: Alena Brozova/123RF.COM; p. 235: Heinz Leitner/123RF.COM; p. 235: Christos Meimaroglou/123RF.COM; p. 235: Denis Raev/123RF.COM; p. 235: bowie15/123RF.COM; p. 236: 36clicks/123RF.COM; p. 236: 123RF Limited/123RF.COM; p.236: Phil Date/123RF.COM; p. 237: Phil Date/123RF.COM; p. 237: pixbox/123RF.COM; p. 237: © iStockphoto.com/Arpad Benedek; p. 238: Buena Vista Images/Getty Images; p. 239: © Dwphotos/Dreamstime.com; p. 240: © Millan/Dreamstime.com; p. 243: © iStockphoto.com/kristian sekulic; p. 243: Wavebreak Media Ltd/123RF.COM; p. 244: Courtesy of J. Bennett; p. 245: © Jordan Tan/Dreamstime.com; p. 247: © iStockphoto.com/Holger Mette; p. 248: © Erwin Purnomo Sidi/Dreamstime.com; p. 248: Dzmitry Halavach/123RF.COM; p. 248: © iStockphoto.com/Jeffrey Smith; p. 250: Used with permission by Randy Glasbergen; p. 250: Kristina Afanasyeva/123RF.COM; p. 252: © Ivonne Wierink/Dreamstime.com; p. 253: Max Melchior.

Chapter 9 — p. 264: Flickr/arnitr; p. 265: Snowbird Ski and Summer Resort; p. 266: © Gualtiero Boffi/Dreamstime.com; p. 268: © iStockphoto.com; p. 269: © iStockphoto.com/Vladimir Piskunov; p. 269: © iStockphoto.com; p. 270: Chuck Peterson; p. 271: © iStockphoto.com/Sean Locke; p. 272: © iStockphoto.com/Lisa F. Young; p. 273: Erick Gustafson; p. 274: © iStockphoto.com/sorendls; p. 276: © Karin Hildebrand Lau/Dreamstime.com; p. 278: © Sean Pavone/Dreamstime.com; p. 279: © Hertz; p. 282: © Roman Milert/Dreamstime.com; p. 282: © iStockphoto.com/Britta Kasholm-Tengve; p. 284: Used with permission by Randy Glasbergen; p. 285L © iStockphoto.com; p. 285: Cathy Yeulet/123RF.COM; p. 286: © iStockphoto.com/Chris Schmidt; p. 289: © iStockphoto.com/Nadya Lukic.

Chapter 10 — p. 296: © FMGB Guggenheim Bilbao Museoa, Photo: Erika Ede, 2008. All rights reserved; p. 297: aneb/123RF.COM; p. 299: Flickr/Brian Sayler; p. 299: Used with permission from Fairmont Hotels & Resorts; p. 300: Flickr/Karen Roe; p. 300: © iStockphoto.com/4FR; p. 301: Marlins69/Wikimedia; p. 303: Suprijono Suharjoto/123RF.COM; p. 303: Ivan Mikhaylov/123RF.COM; p. 303: Lisa Young/123RF.COM; p. 303: Yuri Arcurs/123RF.COM; p. 303: maridav/123RF.COM; p. 303: © iStockphoto.com/DeborahMaxemow; p. 307: © Thomas Smith/Dreamstime.com; p. 308: © Djk/Dreamstime.com; p. 309: Paulus Rusyanto/123RF.COM; p. 310: © Monika Adamczyk/Dreamstime.com; p. 311: Malgorzata Biernikiewicz/123RF.COM; p. 312: Flickr/NNECAPA; p. 313: jeanbellon design co.; p. 313: Flickr/s.rejeki; p. 313: © iStockPhoto; p. 314: Dmitry Koksharov/123RF.COM; p. 315: Joerg Hackemann/123RF.COM.

Chapter 11 — p. 322: © iStockphoto.com/quavondo; p. 323: © iStockphoto.com/quavondo; p. 324: © iStockphoto.com/iofoto; p. 325: © iStockphoto.com/claudiobaba; p. 327: © iStockphoto.com/PeskyMonkey; p. 327: © iStockphoto.com/GYI NSEA p. 329: © iStockphoto.com/Chris Schmidt; p. 331: © iStockphoto.com/coloroftime; p. 334: Used with permission by Randy Glasbergen; p. 335: Sean Ren (seanren.com); p. 335: Flickr/Robert Nyman; p. 336: Used with permission by Randy Glasbergen; p. 336: © iStockphoto.com/Radu Razvan; p. 337: Used with permission by Randy Glasbergen; p. 338: Flickr/one2c900d; p. 339: Simon Jones; p. 340: Photo Courtesy of Ron Kaufman; p. 342: Wikipedia; p. 342: Used with permission by Randy Glasbergen; p. 343: Courtesy of Singapore Airlines; p. 344: © iStockphoto.com/Ng Choon Boon.

Chapter 12 — p. 358: © iStockphoto.com/Valerie Loiseleux; p. 359: kzenon/123RF.COM; p. 359: © iStockphoto.com/Jacob Wackerhausen; p. 362: © iStockphoto.com/sharrocks; p. 366: © Lisa F. Young/Dreamstime.com; p. 367: ©The Vanguard Group, Inc., used with permission.; p. 369: Associated Press/Newscast Limited; p. 371: © iStockphoto.com/GYI NSEA; p. 373: Flickr/Rachel from Cupcakes Take the Cake; p. 376: stylephotographs/123RF.COM; p. 376: Associated Press; p. 379: Getty Image/Bloomberg; p. 382: © iStockphoto.com/GYI NSEA; p. 384: kurhan/123RF.COM; p. 385: nobilior/123RF.COM.

Chapter 13 — p. 394: © iStockphoto.com/Ivan Cholakov; p. 395: Associated Press/TMRRY ARROYO; p. 395: © iStockphoto.com/GYI NSEA; p. 397: Used with permission by Randy Glasbergen; p. 398: CartoonStock; p. 403: Brad Calkins/123RF.COM; p. 407: © Hilton Hotels Corporation; p. 409: © Tomasz Tulik/Dreamstime.com; p. 412: © iStockphoto.com/Ben Blankenburg; p. 413: Richard Hutchings/PhotoEdit Inc.; p. 414: © iStockphoto.com/David H. Lewis.

Chapter 14 — p. 431: Flickr/Martin Pettitt; p. 430: Betsie Van der Meer/Getty Images; p. 434: Associated Press/KEYSTONE; p. 438: © iStockphoto.com/Andrea Zanchi; p. 441: © iStockphoto.com/Thomas Dickson; p. 442: © iStockphoto.com/Ravi Tahilramani; p. 444: © iStockphoto.com/endopack; p. 453: Lowe New York; p. 453: Used with permission by Randy Glasbergen; p. 454: © iStockphoto.com/clearstockconcepts; p. 455: © iStockphoto.com/airportrait; p. 455: © iStockphoto.com / WendellandCarolyn p. 457: © Samc3352/Dreamstime.com; p. 465: iofoto/123RF.COM; p. 468: © iStockphoto.com/Andrew Rich.

Chapter 15 — p. 476: Shawn Hempel/123RF.COM; p. 477: © iStockphoto.com/Günay Mutlu; p. 481: Flickr/PopCultureGeek.com; p. 482: Kodak; p. 486: dny3d/123RF.COM; p. 487© Gerry Boughan/Dreamstime.com; p. 488: miszaqq/123RF.COM; p. 490: © Dreamstime.com; p. 493: © iStockphoto.com/kali9; p. 495: © iStockPhoto.com.

Case Studies — p. 519–527 – Used with permission by Banyan Tree Hotels & Resorts. All rights reserved; p. 528–537: Used with permission by Giordano International Ltd.; p. 538–546: Used with permission by Kiwi Experience; p. 559-560: Used with permission by Accra Beach Hotel and Resort; p. 565: iStockphoto.com/fotoVoyager; p. 589: iStockphoto.com/Sergey Kashkin; p. 590–597: Used with permission by Singapore Airlines; p. 598: iStockphoto.com/GYI NSEA; p. 599–602: Used with permission by DHL; p. 604: Cosmonaut Creative Media LLC.; p. 622: © Sebcz/Dreamstime.com; p. 623: iStockphoto.com/webphotographeer.

Name Index

A

B

C

D

E

F

G

H

I

J

K

S

Z

Subject Index

A

B

C

D

E

F

G

H

I

J

Q

R

T

U

V

W

Y

Z